1997

19682

To Chip
From. Dexter Armstrong

THE

𝕸𝖊𝖙𝖗𝖔𝖕𝖔𝖑𝖎𝖙𝖆𝖓 𝕿𝖆𝖇𝖊𝖗𝖓𝖆𝖈𝖑𝖊 𝕻𝖚𝖑𝖕𝖎𝖙.

SERMONS PREACHED AND REVISED

BY

C. H. SPURGEON,

DURING THE YEAR 1883.

VOL. XXIX.

Pilgrim PUBLICATIONS
Pasadena, Texas 77501
1973

TO

THE ONE GOD OF HEAVEN AND EARTH

IN

THE TRINITY OF HIS SACRED PERSONS

BE ALL HONOUR AND GLORY,

WORLD WITHOUT END,

AMEN.

TO THE GLORIOUS FATHER, AS THE COVENANT GOD

OF ISRAEL;

TO THE GRACIOUS SON, THE REDEEMER OF HIS PEOPLE;

TO THE HOLY GHOST, THE AUTHOR OF

SANCTIFICATION;

BE EVERLASTING PRAISE FOR THAT GOSPEL OF THE

FREE GRACE OF GOD

HEREIN PROCLAIMED UNTO MEN.

A painting of Charles Haddon Spurgeon which hung with portraits of his distinguished predecessors in the Pastor's Vestry at the Tabernacle.

CONTENTS.

vi

INDEX OF SCRIPTURE TEXTS.

VOLUME XXIX.

THE STAR AND THE WISE MEN.

A Sermon

DELIVERED ON LORD'S-DAY MORNING, DECEMBER 24TH, 1882, BY

C. H. SPURGEON,

AT THE METROPOLITAN TABERNACLE, NEWINGTON.

"Now when Jesus was born in Bethlehem of Judea in the days of Herod the king, behold, there came wise men from the east to Jerusalem, saying, Where is he that is born King of the Jews? for we have seen his star in the east, and are come to worship him.

When they had heard the king, they departed; and, lo, the star, which they saw in the east, went before them, till it came and stood over where the young child was. When they saw the star, they rejoiced with exceeding great joy."—Matthew ii. 1, 2, 9, 10.

SEE, dear friends, the glory of our Lord Jesus Christ even in his state of humiliation! He is born of lowly parents, laid in a manger, and wrapped in swaddling bands; but, lo! the principalities and powers in the heavenly places are in commotion. First, one angel descends to proclaim the advent of the new-born King, and suddenly there is with him a multitude of the heavenly host singing glory unto God. Nor was the commotion confined to the spirits above; for in the heavens which over-hang this earth there is a stir. A star is deputed on behalf of all the stars, as if he were the envoy and plenipotentiary of all worlds to represent them before their King. This star is put in commission to wait upon the Lord, to be his herald to men afar off, his usher to conduct them to his presence, and his body-guard to sentinel his cradle. Earth, too, is stirred. Shepherds have come to pay the homage of simple-minded ones: with all love and joy they bow before the mysterious child; and after them from afar come the choice and flower of their generation, the most studious minds of the age. Making a long and difficult journey, they too at last arrive, the representatives of the Gentiles. Lo! the kings of Seba and Sheba offer gifts—gold, frankincense, and myrrh. Wise men, the leaders of their peoples, bow down before him, and pay homage to the Son of God. Wherever Christ is he is honourable. "Unto you that believe he is honour." In the day of small things, when the cause of God is denied entertainment, and is hidden away with things which are despised, it is still most glorious. Christ, though a child, is still King of kings; though among the oxen, he is still distin-guished by his star.

Beloved friends, if wise men of old came to Jesus and worshipped, should not we come also? My intense desire this morning is that we all may pay homage to him of whom we sing, "Unto us a child is born; unto us a son is given." Let those of us who have long worshipped

No. 1,698.

worship anew with yet lowlier reverence and intenser love. And God grant—oh, that he would grant it!—that some who are far off from him spiritually, as the Magi were far off locally, may come to-day and ask, "Where is he that is born King of the Jews? for we have come to worship him." May feet that have been accustomed to broad roads, but unaccustomed to the narrow path, this day pursue that way till they see Jesus, and bow before him with all their hearts, finding salvation in him. These wise men came naturally, traversing the desert; let us come spiritually, leaving our sins. These were guided by the sight of a star; let us be guided by faith in the divine Spirit, by the teaching of his word and all those blessed lights which the Lord uses to conduct men to himself. Only let us come to Jesus. It was well to come unto the babe Jesus, led by the feeble beams of a star; you shall find it still more blessed to come to him now that he is exalted in the highest heavens, and by his own light reveals his own perfect glory. Delay not, for this day he cries, "Come unto me, all ye that labour and are heavy laden, and I will give you rest."

This morning let us try to do three things. First, let us *gather light from this star;* secondly, let us *gather wisdom from these wise men;* and thirdly, *let us act as wise men helped by our own particular star.*

I. First, then, LET US GATHER LIGHT FROM THIS STAR. May the Spirit of the Lord enable us so to do.

I suppose you have each one his own imagination as to what this star was. It would seem to have been altogether supernatural, and not a star, or a comet of the ordinary kind. It was not a constellation, nor a singular conjunction of planets: there is nothing in the Scriptures to support such a conjecture. In all probability it was not a star in the sense in which we now speak of stars: for we find that it moved before the wise men, then suddenly disappeared, and again shone forth to move before them. It could not have been a star in the upper spheres like others, for such movements would not have been possible. Some have supposed that the wise men went in the direction in which the star shone forth in the heavens, and followed the changes of its position: but it could not in that case have been said that it stood over the place where the young child was. If the star was at its zenith over Bethlehem, it would have been in its zenith over Jerusalem too; for the distance is so small that it would not have been possible to observe any difference in the position of the star in the two places. It must have been a star occupying quite another sphere from that in which the planets revolve. We believe it to have been a luminous appearance in mid-air; probably akin to that which led the children of Israel through the wilderness, which was a cloud by day and a pillar of fire by night. Whether it was seen in the daylight or not we cannot tell. Chrysostom and the early fathers are wonderfully positive about many things which Scripture leaves in doubt, but as these eminent divines drew upon their imagination for their facts, we are not under bonds to follow them. They aver that this star was so bright as to be visible all day long. If so, we can imagine the wise men travelling day and night; but if it could be seen only by night, the picture before us grows far more singular and weird-like as we see these easterns quietly pursuing their star-lit way, resting *perforce* when the ~~sun~~ was up, but noiselessly hurrying at night through slumbering lands. These questions are not of much importance to us, and therefore we will not dwell long upon them.

Only here is a first lesson : *if it should ever be that men should fail to preach the gospel, God can conduct souls to his Son by a star.* Ah ! say not only by a star, but by a stone, a bird, a blade of grass, a drop of dew.

> " Remember that Omnipotence
> Has servants everywhere."

Therefore, despond not when you hear that one minister has ceased to preach the gospel, or that another is fighting against the vital truth of God. Their apostasy shall be to their own loss rather than to the hurt of Jesus and his church; and, sad though it be to see the lamps of the sanctuary put out, yet God is not dependent upon human lights, he is the Shekinah light of his own holy place. Mortal tongues, if they refuse to preach his word, shall have their places supplied by books in the running brooks and sermons in stones. The beam shall cry out of the wall, and the timber shall answer it. When chief priests and scribes have all gone out of the way, the Lord puts stars into commission, and once more in very deed the heavens are telling the glory of God, and the firmament is showing his handiwork. Sooner than lack speakers for the incarnate God, mountains and hills shall learn eloquence and break forth into testimony. Jehovah's message shall be made known to the utmost ends of the earth. God shall save his own elect ; he shall give to Christ to see of the travail of his soul and to be satisfied. His counsel shall stand, and he will do all his pleasure. Hallelujah !

Now, when the Lord does use a star to be his minister, what is the order of his ministry? We may learn by this enquiry what kind of ministry God would have ours to be if we are stars in his right hand. We also shine as lights in the world : let us see how to do it.

We notice, first, that star-preaching is *all about Christ.* We do not know what the colour of the star was, nor the shape of the star, nor to what magnitude it had attained ; these items are not recorded, but what is recorded is of much more importance : the wise men said—" We have seen *his* star." Then the star which the Lord will use to lead men to Jesus must be Christ's own star. The faithful minister, like this star, belongs to Christ; he is Christ's own man in the most emphatic sense. Before we can expect to be made a blessing, dear friends, we must ourselves be blessed of the Lord. If we would cause others to belong to Jesus, we must belong wholly to Jesus ourselves. Every beam in that star shone forth for Jesus. It was *his* star, always, and only, and altogether. It shone not for itself, but only as *his* star: as such it was known and spoken of—" we have seen his star." As I have already said, there is no note taken of any peculiarity that it had except this one, that it was the star of the King. I wish that you and I, whatever our eccentricities or personalities may be, may never make so much of them as to attract men's attention to them. May people never dwell upon our attainments or our deficiencies, but may they always observe this one thing, that we are men of God, that we are ambassadors of Christ, that we are Christ's servants, and do not attempt to shine for ourselves, or to make ourselves conspicuous : but that we labour to shine for him, that his way may be known upon earth, his saving health among all people. Brother, it is well for us to forget ourselves in our message, to sink ourselves in our Master. We know the names of several of the stars, yet they may each one envy that star which remains anonymous, but can never be forgotten because men who sought the King of Israel knew it as "*his* star." Though you be but a very little star, twinkling for Jesus ; however feeble your light may be, be it plain that you are *his* star, so that if men wonder *what* you are, they may never wonder whose you are, for on your very forefront it shall be written, " Whose I am and whom I serve." God will not lead men to Christ by us unless we are Christ's heartily, wholly, unreservedly. In his temple our Lord uses no borrowed vessels ; every bowl before the altar must be his own. It is not consistent with the glory of God for him to use borrowed vessels. He is not so poor as that comes to. This lesson is worthy of all acceptation. Are you in a hurry to preach, young man? Are you sure you are Christ's ? Do you think it must be a fine thing to hold a company of people listening to your words? Have you looked at it in another light? Have you weighed the responsibility of having to speak as Christ would have you speak, and of yielding yourself in your entire personality to the utterance of the mind of God? You must be consecrated and concentrated if you hope to be used of the Lord. If you have one ray, or ten thousand rays, all must shine with the one design of guiding men to Jesus. You have nothing now to do with any object, subject, design, or endeavour, but Jesus only : in him, and for him, and to him must you live henceforth, or you will never be chosen of the Lord to conduct either wise men or babes to Jesus. See ye well to it that perfect consecration be yours.

Note next that true star-preaching *leads to Christ*. The star was Christ's star itself, but it also led others to Christ. It did this very much because it moved in that direction. It is a sad thing when a preacher is like a sign-post pointing the way but never following it on his own account. Such were those chief priests at Jerusalem: they could tell where Christ was born, but they never went to worship him ; they were indifferent altogether to him and to his birth. The star that leads to Christ must always be going to Christ. Men are far better drawn by example than driven by exhortation. Personal piety alone can be owned of God to the production of piety in others. " Go," say you : but they will not go. Say " come," and lead the way : then they will come. Do not the sheep follow the shepherd? He who would lead others to Christ should go before them himself, having his face towards his Master, his eyes towards his Master, his steps toward his Master, his heart towards his Master. We are so to live that we may without boasting exhort those around us to have us for an example. Oh, that all who think themselves to be stars would themselves diligently move towards the Lord Jesus. The star in the east led wise men to Christ because it went that way itself : there is a wisdom in example which truly wise men are quick to perceive. This star had such an influence upon the chosen men that they could not but follow it : it charmed them across the desert. Such a charm may reside in you and in me, and we may exercise a powerful ministry over many'hearts, being to them as loadstones, drawing them to the Lord

Jesus. Happy privilege! We would not merely show the road, but induce our neighbours to enter upon it. We read of one of old, not that they told him of Jesus, but that "they brought him to Jesus." We are not only to tell the story of the cross, but we are to persuade men to fly to the Crucified One for salvation. Did not the king in the parable say to his servants, "Compel them to come in." Assuredly he girds his own messengers with such a compelling power that men cannot hold out any longer, but must follow their lead and bow at the King's feet. The star did not draw, "as it were with a cart rope," nor by any force, material and physical; yet it drew these wise men from the remote east right to the manger of the new-born child. And so, though we have no arm of the law to help us, nor patronage, nor pomp of eloquence, nor parade of learning, yet we have a spiritual power by which we draw to Jesus thousands who are our joy and crown. The man sent of God comes forth from the divine presence permeated with a power which makes men turn to the Saviour and live. Oh! that such power might go forth from all God's ministers, yea, from all God's servants engaged in street-preaching, in Sunday-schools, in tract-visitation, and in every form of holy service. God uses those whose aim and intent it is to draw men to Christ. He puts his Spirit into them, by which Spirit they are helped to set forth the Lord Jesus as so lovely and desirable that men run to him and accept his glorious salvation. It is a small thing to shine, but it is a great thing to draw. Any cast-away may be brilliant; but only the real saint will be attractive for Jesus. I would not pray to be an orator, but I do pray to be a soul-winner. Do not aim, beloved brethren, at anything short of leading men to Jesus. Do not be satisfied to lead them to orthodox doctrine, or merely to bring them to a belief in those views which you hold to be Scriptural, valuable as that may be. It is to the person of the incarnate God that we must bring them; to his feet we must conduct them that they may worship him: our mission is not accomplished, it is a total failure, unless we conduct our hearers to the house where Jesus dwells, and then stand over them, keeping watch over their souls for Jesu's sake.

Once more, the star which God used in this case was a star that *stopped at Jesus:* it went before the wise men till it brought them to Jesus, and then it stood still over the place where the young child was. I admire the manner of this star. There are remarkable stars in the theological sky at the present time: they have led men to Jesus, so they say, and now they lead them into regions beyond, of yet undeveloped thought. The gospel of the Puritans is "old-fashioned"; these men have discovered that it is unsuitable for the enlarged intellects of the times; and so these stars would guide us further still. To this order of wandering stars I do not belong myself, and I trust I never shall. Progress beyond the gospel I have no desire for. "God forbid that I should glory save in the cross of our Lord Jesus Christ." When the star had come to the place where the young child was, it stood still: and so should the gracious mind become settled, fixed, immovable. The wise men knew where to find that star, and where to find the young child by it: so be it with us. Oh, you that have hitherto been diligent in leading souls to Christ, never indulge for a single moment the notion that you need a broader philosophy or a deeper spirituality than are to be found in Jesus. Abide in him. Cry, " Oh God, my heart is fixed. My heart is fixed." There is nothing beyond Christ which is worth a moment's thought. Do not lose your paradise in Christ for another taste of that tree of knowledge-of-good-and-evil which ruined our first parents. Stick you to the old points: your one subject Christ, your one object to bring men to Christ, your one glory the glory of Christ. Standing by your Lord, and there alone, from this day to the last day, you will secure a happy, honoured, and holy life. They said of Greece after her fall that it had become so ruined that you might search for Greece in Greece and fail to find it: I fear I must say that some professed preachers of the gospel have roamed so far away from it that you cannot find the gospel in their gospel, nor Christ himself in the Christ they preach. So far have some diverged from the grand essential soul-saving truth beyond which no man ought to dare to think of going, that they retain nothing of Christianity but the name. All that is beyond truth is a lie; anything beyond revelation is at best a minor matter, and most probably is an old wives' fable, even though he may be of the masculine gender who invented it. Stand you to your colours you who hope to be used of the Lord. Abide so that men shall find you in twenty years' time shining for Jesus and pointing to the place where the Saviour is to be found, even as you are doing now. Let Jesus Christ be your ultimatum. Your work is done when you bring souls to Jesus, and help to keep them there, by being yourself " steadfast, unmovable." Be not carried away from the hope of your calling; but hold fast even the form of sound words, for it may be that in letting go the form you may lose the substance also.

II. Now that we have somewhat rejoiced in the light of the star, let us see if we can GATHER WISDOM FROM THE WISE MEN. Perhaps you have heard the "much speaking" of tradition as to who they were, whence they came, and how they travelled. In the Greek church, I believe, they know their number, their names, the character of their retinue, and what kind of ornaments were on their dromedaries' necks. Details which are not found in the word of God you may believe or not, at your pleasure, and you will be wise if your pleasure is not to believe too much. We only know that they were Magi, wise men from the East, possibly of the old Parsee religion—watchers if not worshippers of the stars. We will not speculate about them, but learn from them.

They did not content themselves with admiring the star and comparing it with other stars, and taking notes as to the exact date of its appearance, and how many times it twinkled, and when it moved, and all that; but *they practically used the teaching of the star.* Many are hearers and admirers of God's servants, but they are not wise enough to make fit and proper use of the preaching. They notice the peculiarity of the preacher's language, how much he is like one divine, how much he is unlike another; whether he coughs too often, or speaks too much in his throat; whether he is too loud or too low; whether he has not a provincial tone, whether there may not be about him a commonness of speech approaching to vulgarity; or, on the other hand, whether he may not be too florid in his diction. Such fooleries as these are the constant observations of men for whose souls we labour. They are perishing, and yet toying with such small matters.

With many it is all they go to the house of God for: to criticise in this paltry fashion. I have even seen them come to this place with opera glasses, as if they came hither to inspect an actor who lived and laboured to amuse their leisure hours. Such is the sport of fools; but these were wise men, and therefore practical men. They did not become star-gazers, and stop at the point of admiring the re- markable star; but they said, "Where is he that is born King of the Jews? for we have seen his star in the, east, and are come to worship him." They set out at once to find the new-born King, of whose coming the star was the signal. Oh, my dear hearers, how I wish that you were all wise in this same manner! I would sooner preach the dullest sermon that was ever preached than preach the most bril- liant that was ever spoken if I could by that poor sermon lead you quite away from myself to seek the Lord Jesus Christ. That is the one thing I care about. Will you never gratify me by enquiring after my Lord and Master? I long to hear you say, "What is the man talking about? He speaks about a Saviour; we will have that Saviour for ourselves. He talks about pardon through the blood of Christ; he speaks about God coming down among men to save them; we will find out if there is any reality in this pardon, any truth in this salvation. We will seek Jesus, and find for ourselves the blessings which are reported to be laid up in him." If I heard you all saying this I should be ready to die of joy.

Is not this a good day on which to set out to find your Saviour? Some of you that have postponed it long, would it not be well to set out at once ere this expiring year has seen its last day? These wise men appear to have set out as soon as they discovered the star: they were not among those who have time to waste in needless delays. "There is the star," said they; "away we go beneath its guidance. We are not satisfied with a star, we go to find the King whose star it is!" And so they set out to find Christ immediately and resolutely.

Being wise men, *they persevered in their search after him.* We cannot tell how far they journeyed. Travelling was extremely difficult in those times. There were hostile tribes to avoid, the broad rivers of the Tigris and the Euphrates to cross, and trackless deserts to penetrate; but they made nothing of difficulty or danger. They set out for Jerusalem, and to Jerusalem they came, seeking the King of the Jews. If it be true that God has taken upon himself our nature, we ought to resolve to find him, let it cost what it may. If we must circumnavigate the globe to find a Saviour, the distance and the expense ought to be nothing so long as we may but reach him. Were the Christ in the bowels of the earth, or in the heights of heaven we ought not to rest till we come at him. Everything that was necessary for their expedition the wise men soon gathered together, regardless of expense; and off they went follow- ing the star that they might discover the Prince of the kings of the earth.

At length they came to Jerusalem, and here new trials awaited them. It must have been a great trouble to them when they asked, "Where is he that is born King of the Jews?" and the people shook their heads as if they thought the question an idle one. Neither rich nor poor in the metropolitan city knew anything of Israel's King. The ribald multitude replied, "Herod is king of the Jews. Mind how you speak of another king, or your head may have to answer for it. The tyrant brooks no rival." The wise men must have been more astonished still when they found that Herod was troubled. They were glad to think that he was born who was to usher in the age of gold ; but Herod's face grew blacker than ever at the bare mention of a king of the Jews His eyes flashed, and a thunder-cloud was upon his brow ; a dark deed of murder will come of it, though for the moment he conceals his malice. There is tumult all through the streets of Jerusalem, for no man knows what grim Herod may do now that he has been roused by the question, "Where is he that is born King of the Jews?" Thus there was a ferment in Jerusalem, beginning at the palace; but this did not deter the wise men from their search for the promised Prince. They did not pack up their bales and go back and say, " It is useless to try to discover this questionable personage who is unknown even in the country of which he is King, and who appears to be terribly un-welcome to those who are to be his subjects. We must leave to another day the solution of the question : ' Where is he that is born King of the Jews ?'"

These earnest-minded seekers were not dispirited by the clergy and the learned men when they came together. To the chief priests and scribes the question was put, and they answered the enquiry as to where Christ would be born, but not a mother's son among them would go with the wise men to find this new-born King. Strange apathy! Alas, how common! Those who should have been leaders were no leaders ; they would not even be followers of that which is good, for they had no heart towards Christ. The wise men rose superior to this serious discouragement. If the clergy would not help them they would go to Jesus by themselves. Oh, dear friend, if you are wise you will say, "I will find Christ alone if none will join me : if I dig to the centre, I will find him; if I fly to the sun, I will find him ; if all men put me off, I will find him ; if the ministers of the gospel appear indifferent to me, I will find him : the kingdom of heaven of old suffered violence, and the violent took it by force, and so will I." The first Christians had to leave all the authorized teachers of the day behind, and to come out by themselves : it will be no strange thing if you should have to do the same. Happy will it be if you are deter-mined to go through floods and flames to find Christ; for he will be found of you. Thus these men were wise because, having started on the search, they persevered in it till they found the Lord and wor-shipped him.

Notice that they were wise because, when they again saw the star, " *they rejoiced with exceeding great joy.*" While enquiring among the priests at Jerusalem they were perplexed, but when the star shone out again, they were at ease and full of joy : this joy they expressed, so that the evangelist recorded it. In these days very wise people think it necessary to repress all emotion, and appear like men of stone or ice. No matter what happens, they are stoical, and raised far above the enthusiasm of the vulgar. It is wonderful how fashions change, and folly stands for philosophy. But these wise men were children enough to be glad when their perplexity was over, and the clear light shone forth. It is a good sign when a man is not ashamed to be happy because he hears a plain, unmistakable testimony for the Lord Jesus. It is good to see the great man come down from his pedestal, and, like a little child, rejoice to hear the simple story of the cross. Give me the hearer who looks not for fineries, but cries out, " Lead me to Jesus. I want a guide to Jesus, and nothing else will suit me." Why, truly, if men did but know the value of things they would rejoice more to see a preacher of the gospel than a king. If the feet of the heralds of salvation be blessed, how much more their tongues when they tell out the tidings of a Saviour. These wise men, with all their mystic learning, were not ashamed to rejoice because a little star lent them its beams to conduct them to Jesus. We unite with them in rejoicing over a clear gospel ministry. For us all else is darkness, sorrow, and vexation of spirit; but that which leads us to our own glorious Lord is spirit, and light, and life. Better the sun should not shine than that a clear gospel should not be preached. We reckon that a country flourishes or decays according as gospel light is revealed or withdrawn.

Now follow these wise men a little further. They have come to the house where the young child is. What will they do? Will they stand looking at the star? No: *they enter in.* The star stands still, but they are not afraid to lose its radiance, and behold the Sun of righteousness. They did not cry, " We see the star, and that is enough for us ; we have followed the star, and it is all we need to do." Not at all. They lift the latch, and enter the lowly residence of the babe. They see the star no longer, and they have no need to see it, for there is he that is born King of the Jews. Now the true Light has shone upon them from the face of the child ; they behold the incarnate God. Oh, friends ! how wise you will be if, when you have been led to Christ by any man, you do not rest in his leadership, but must see Christ for yourselves. How much I long that you may enter into the fellowship of the mystery, pass through the door, and come and behold the young child, and bow before him. Our woe is that so many are so unwise. We are only their guides, but they are apt to make us their end. We point the way, but they do not follow the road ; they stand gazing upon us. The star is gone; it did its work, and passed away: Jesus remains, and the wise men live in him. Will any of you be so foolish as to think only of the dying preacher, and forget the ever-living Saviour? Come, be wise, and hasten to your Lord at once.

These men were wise, last of all—and I commend their example to you—because when they saw the child *they worshipped.* Theirs was not curiosity gratified, but devotion exercised. We, too, must worship the Saviour, or we shall never be saved by him. He has not come to put away our sins, and yet to leave us ungodly and self-willed. Oh you that have never worshipped the Christ of God, may you be led to do so at once ! He is God over all, blessed for ever, adore him ! Was God ever seen in such a worshipful form before ? Behold he bows the heavens ; he rides upon the wings of the wind ; he scatters flames of fire ; he speaks, and his dread artillery shakes the hills : you worship in terror. Who would not adore the great and terrible Jehovah? But is it not much better to behold him here, allied to your nature, wrapped like other children in swaddling clothes, tender, feeble, next akin to your own

self ? Will you not worship God when he thus comes down to you and
becomes your brother, born for your salvation ? Here nature itself
suggests worship: O may grace produce it ! Let us hasten to worship
where shepherds and wise men and angels have led the way.

Here let my sermon come to a pause even as the star did. Enter
the house and worship ! Forget the preacher. Let the starlight shine
for other eyes. Jesus was born that you might be born again. He lived
that you might live. He died that you might die to sin. He is risen,
and to-day he maketh intercession for transgressors that they may be
reconciled to God through him. Come, then ; believe, trust, rejoice,
adore ! If you have neither gold, frankincense, nor myrrh, bring your
faith, your love, your repentance, and falling down before the Son of God
pay him the reverence of your hearts.

III. And now I turn to my third and last point, which is this : LET
US ACT AS WISE MEN UNDER THE LIGHT OF OUR STAR. We too have
received light to lead us to the Saviour : I might say that for us many
stars have shone to that blessed end. I will, however, on this point
content myself with asking questions.

*Do you not think that there is some light for you in your particular
vocation,* some call from God in your calling ? Listen to me, and then
listen to God. These men were watchers of the stars ; therefore a star
was used to call them. Certain other men soon after were fishermen,'
and by means of an amazing take of fish the Lord Jesus made them
aware of his superior power, and then he called them to become fishers
of men. For a star-gazer a star ; for a fisherman a fish. The Master-
Fisher hath a bait for each one of his elect, and oftentimes he selects a
point in their own calling to be the barb of the hook. Were you busy
yesterday at your counter ? Did you hear no voice saying " Buy the
truth and sell it not" ? When you closed the shop last night did you
not bethink yourself that soon you must close it for the last time ? Do you
make bread ? and do you never ask yourself, " Has my soul eaten the bread
of heaven ?" Are you a farmer ? do you till the soil ? Has God never spoken
to you by those furrowed fields and these changing seasons, and made
you wish that your heart might be tilled and sown ? Listen ! God is
speaking ! Hear, ye deaf ; for there are voices everywhere calling you to
heaven. You need not go miles about to find a link between you and
everlasting mercy : the telegraphic wires are on either side of the
road, God and human souls are near each other. How I wish that your
common vocation would be viewed by you as concealing within itself
the door to your high vocation. Oh that the Holy Spirit would turn
your favourite pursuits into opportunities for his gracious work upon
you. If not among the stars, yet among the flowers of the garden, or
the cattle of the hills, or the waves of the sea may he find a net in which
to enclose you for Christ. I wish that those of you who conclude that
your calling could never draw you to Christ would make a point of
seeing whether it might not be so. We are to learn from ants, and
swallows, and cranes, and conies ; surely we need never be short of
tutors. It did seem that a star was an unlikely thing to head a
procession of eastern sages, and yet it was the best guide that could be
found ; and so it may seem that your trade is an unlikely thing to bring
you to Jesus, and yet the Lord may so use it. There may be a

message from the Lord to thee in many a left-handed providence; a voice for wisdom may come to thee from the mouth of an ass; a call to a holy life may startle thee from a bush, a warning may flash upon thee from a wall, or a vision may impress thee in the silence of night when deep sleep falleth upon men. Only be thou ready to hear and God will find a way of speaking to thee. Answer the question as the wise men would have answered it, and say, " Yes, in our calling there is a call to Christ."

Then, again, *what should you and I do better in this life than seek after Christ!* The wise men thought all other pursuits of small account compared with this. " Who is going to attend to that observatory and watch the rest of the stars ? " They shake their heads, and say they do not know : these things must wait ; they have seen *his* star, and they are going to worship him. But who will attend to their wives and families, and all besides, while they make this long journey? They reply that every lesser thing must be subordinate to the highest thing. Matters must be taken in proportion, and the search after the King of the Jews, who is the desire of all nations, is so out of all proportion great that all the rest must go. Are not you, also, wise enough to judge in this sensible fashion? Do you not think, dear friends, it would be well to use all to-morrow in seeking Jesus? It will be a leisure day, could you spend it better than in seeking your Redeemer? If you were to take a week, and give it wholly to your own soul, and to seeking Christ, would it not be well spent? How can you live with your soul in jeopardy? Oh that you would say, " I must get this matter right ; it is an all-important business, and I must see it secure." This would be no more than common-sense. If you are driving, and a trace is broken, do you not stop the horse, and set the harness right? How, then, can you go on with the chariot of life when all its harness is out of order, and a fall means eternal ruin? If you will stop driving to arrange a buckle for fear of accident, I would beg of you to stop anything and everything to see to the safety of your soul. See how the engineer looks to the safety-valve : are you content to run more desperate risks? If your house were not insured, and you carried on a hazardous trade, the probability is you would feel extremely anxious until you had arranged that matter : but your soul is uninsured, and it may burn for ever,—will you not give heed to it? I beseech you be just to yourself, —kind to yourself. Oh! see to your eternal well-being. You are not certain that you will get home to dinner to-day. Life is frail as a cobweb. You may be in hell before yon clock strikes one! Remember that. There is not a step between you and everlasting destruction from the presence of God if you are as yet unregenerate ; and your only hope is to find the Saviour, trust the Saviour, obey the Saviour. Wherefore, like these wise men, put everything on one side, and set out now upon an earnest, resolute, persevering endeavour to find Jesus. I was about to say—resolve to find Jesus, or to die; but I will change the words, and say—resolve to find him, and live.

When we do come near to Jesus, let us ask ourselves this question, " *Do we see more in Jesus than other people do ?*" for if we do, we are God's elect, taught of God, illuminated by his Spirit. We read in the Scriptures that when these wise men saw the young child they fell down and worshipped him. Other people might have come in and seen the child, and said, " Many children are as interesting as this poor woman's babe." Ay, but as these men looked, they *saw*: all eyes are not so blessed. Eyes that see are gifts from the All-seeing One. Carnal eyes are blind; but these men saw the Infinite in the infant; the Godhead gleaming through the manhood; the glory hiding beneath the swaddling bands. Undoubtedly there was a spiritual splendour about this matchless child! We read that Moses' father and mother saw that he was a "goodly child"; they saw he was "fair unto God," says the original. But when these elect men saw that holy thing which is called the Son of the Highest, they discovered in him a glory all unknown before. Then was his star in the ascendant to them: he became their all in all, and they worshipped with all their hearts. Have you discovered such glory in Christ? " Oh!" says one, " you are always harping upon Christ and his glory. You are a man of one idea!" Precisely so. My one idea is that he is "altogether lovely," and that there is nothing out of heaven nor in heaven that can be compared with him even in his lowest and weakest estate. Have you ever seen as much as that in Jesus? If so, you are the Lord's ; go you, and rejoice in him. If not, pray God to open your eyes until, like the wise men, you see and worship.

Lastly, learn from these wise men that when they worshipped they did not permit it to be a mere empty-handed adoration. Ask yourself, " *What shall I render unto the Lord?* " Bowing before the young child, they offered " gold, frankincense and myrrh," the best of metals and the best of spices; an offering to the King of gold; an offering to the priest of frankincense; an offering to the child of myrrh. Wise men are liberal men. Consecration is the best education. To-day it is thought to be wise to be always receiving; but the Saviour said, " It is more blessed to give than to receive." God judges our hearts by that which spontaneously comes from them: hence the sweet cane bought with money is acceptable to him when given freely. He doth not tax his saints or weary them with incense ; but he delights to see in them that true love which cannot express itself in mere words, but must use gold and myrrh, works of love and deeds of self-denial, to be the emblems of its gratitude. Brothers, you will never get into the heart of happiness till you become unselfish and generous; you have but chewed the husks of religion which are often bitter, you have never eaten of the sweet kernel until you have felt the love of God constraining you to make sacrifice. There is nothing in the true believer's power which he would not do for his Lord: nothing in our substance which we would not give to him, nothing in ourselves which we would not devote to his service.

God give to you all grace to come to Jesus, even though it be by the starlight of this sermon, for his love's sake! Amen.

Christ's Glorious Achievements.   By C. H. Spurgeon.
Cloth, 1s.

London : PASSMORE & ALABASTER, 4, Paternoster Buildings, E.C.

Metropolitan Tabernacle Pulpit.

"SUPPOSING HIM TO BE THE GARDENER."

A Sermon

DELIVERED ON LORD'S-DAY MORNING, DECEMBER 31ST, 1882, BY

C. H. SPURGEON.

AT THE METROPOLITAN TABERNACLE, NEWINGTON.

"Supposing him to be the gardener."—John xx. 15.

I WAS sitting about a fortnight ago in a very lovely garden, in the midst of all kinds of flowers which were blooming in delightful abundance all around. Screening myself from the heat of the sun under the overhanging boughs of an olive, I cast my eyes upon palms and bananas, roses and camellias, oranges and aloes, lavender and heliotrope. The garden was full of colour and beauty, perfume and fruitfulness. Surely the gardener, whoever he might be, who had framed, and fashioned, and kept in order that lovely spot, deserved great commendation. So I thought, and then it came to me to meditate upon the church of God as a garden, and to suppose the Lord Jesus to be the gardener, and then to think of what would most assuredly happen if it were so. "Supposing him to be the gardener," my mind conceived of a paradise where all sweet things flourish and all evil things are rooted up. If an ordinary worker had produced such beauty as I then saw and enjoyed on earth, what beauty and glory must surely be brought forth "supposing *him* to be the gardener"! You know the "him" to whom we refer, the ever-blessed Son of God, whom Mary Magdalene in our text mistook for the gardener. We will for once follow a saint in her mistaken track ; and yet we shall find ourselves going in a right way. She was mistaken when she fell into "supposing him to be the gardener"; but if we are under his Spirit's teaching we shall not make a mistake if now we indulge ourselves in a quiet meditation upon our ever-blessed Lord, "supposing him to be the gardener."

It is not an unnatural supposition, surely ; for if we may truly sing—

> " We a e a garden walled around,
> Chosen and made peculiar ground,"

that enclosure needs a gardener. Are we not all the plants of his right hand planting ? Do we not all need watering and tending by his constant and gracious care ? He says, "I am the true vine : my Father is the husbandman," and that is one view of it ; but we may also sing, " My well-beloved hath a vineyard in a very fruitful hill : and he fenced

No. 1,699.

it, and gathered out the stones thereof, and planted it with the choicest vine "—that is to say, he acted as gardener to it. Thus has Isaiah taught us to sing a song of the Well-beloved touching his vineyard. We read of our Lord just now under these terms—" Thou that dwellest in the gardens, the companions hearken to thy voice." To what purpose does he dwell in the vineyards but that he may see how the vines flourish and care for all the plants ? The image, I say, is so far from being unnatural that it is most pregnant with suggestions and full of useful teaching. We are not going against the harmonies of nature when we are " supposing him to be the gardener."

Neither is the figure unscriptural ; for in one of his own parables our Lord makes himself to be the dresser of the vineyard. We read just now that parable so full of warning. When the " certain man " came in and saw the fig tree that it brought forth no fruit, he said unto the dresser of his vineyard, " Cut it down : why cumbereth it the ground ? " Who was it that intervened between that profitless tree and the axe but our great Intercessor and Interposer ? He it is who continually comes forward with " Let it alone this year also till I shall dig about it and dung it." In this case he himself takes upon himself the character of the vine-dresser, and we are not wrong in " supposing him to be the gardener."

If we would be supported by a type, our Lord takes the name of "the Second Adam," and the first Adam was a gardener. Moses tells us that the Lord God placed the man in the garden of Eden to dress it and to keep it. Man in his best estate was not to live in this world in a paradise of indolent luxury, but in a garden of recompensed toil. Behold, the church is Christ's Eden, watered by the river of life, and so fertilized that all manner of fruits are brought forth unto God ; and he, our second Adam, walks in this spiritual Eden to dress it and to keep it ; and so by a type we see that we are right in " supposing him to be the gardener." Thus also Solomon thought of him when he described the royal Bridegroom as going down with his spouse to the garden when the flowers appeared on the earth and the fig tree had put forth her green figs ; he went out with his beloved for the preservation of the gardens, saying, " Take us the foxes, the little foxes, that spoil the vines : for our vines have tender grapes." Neither nature, nor Scripture, nor type, nor song forbids us to think of our adorable Lord Jesus as one that careth for the flowers and fruits of his church. We err not when we speak of him, " supposing him to be the gardener." And so I sat me still, and indulged the suggested line of thought, which I now repeat in your hearing, hoping that I may open many roads of meditation for your hearts also. I shall not attempt to think out such a subject thoroughly, but only to indicate in which direction you may look for a vein of precious ore.

I.   " Supposing him to be the gardener," we have here THE KEY TO MANY WONDERS in the garden of his church.

The first wonder is *that there should be a church at all in the world ;* that there should be a garden blooming in the midst of this sterile waste. Upon a hard and flinty rock the Lord has made the Eden of his church to grow. How came it to be here—an oasis of life in a desert of death ? How came faith in the midst of unbelief, and hope where all is servile fear, and love where hate abounds? "Ye are of God, little children, and the whole world lieth in the wicked one." Whence this being "of God" where all beside is fast shut up in the devil? How came there to be a people for God, separated, and sanctified, and consecrated, and ordained to bring forth fruit unto his name? Assuredly it could not have been so at all if the doing of it had been left to man. We understand its existence, "supposing him to be the gardener," but nothing else can account for it. He can cause the fir tree to flourish instead of the thorn, and the myrtle instead of the briar; but no one else can accomplish such a change. The garden in which I sat was made on the bare face of the rock, and almost all the earth of which its terraces were composed had been brought up there, from the shore below, by hard labour, and so upon the rock a soil had been created. It was not by its own nature that the garden was found in such a place; but by skill and labour it had been formed: even so the church of God has had to be constructed by the Lord Jesus, who is the author as well as the perfecter of his garden. Painfully, with wounded hands, has he built each terrace, and fashioned each bed, and planted each plant. All the flowers have had to be watered with his bloody sweat, and watched by his tearful eyes: the nail-prints in his hands, and the wound in his side are the tokens of what it cost him to make a new Paradise. He has given his life for the life of every plant that is in the garden, and not one of them had been there on any other theory than "supposing him to be the gardener."

Besides, there is another wonder. *How comes the church of God to flourish in such a clime?* This present evil world is very uncongenial to the growth of grace, and the church is not able by herself alone to resist the evil influences which surround her. The church contains within itself elements which tend to its own disorder and destruction if left alone; even as the garden has present in its soil all the germs of a tangled thicket of weeds. The best church that ever Christ had on earth would within a few years apostatise from the truth if deserted by the Spirit of God. The world never helps the church; it is all in arms against it; there is nothing in the world's air or soil that can fertilise the church even to the least degree. How is it, then, that notwith-standing all this the church is a fair garden unto God, and there are sweet spices grown in its beds, and lovely flowers are gathered by the Divine hand from its borders? The continuance and prosperity of the church can only be accounted for by "supposing him to be the gardener." Almighty strength is put to the otherwise impossible work of sustaining a holy people among men; almighty wisdom exercises itself upon this otherwise insuperable difficulty. Hear ye the word of the Lord, and learn hence the reason for the growth of his church below. "I, the Lord, do keep it: I will water it every moment; lest any hurt it, I will keep it night and day." That is the reason for the existence of a spiritual people still in the midst of a godless and perverse generation. This is the reason for an election of grace in the midst of surrounding vice, and worldliness, and unbelief. "Supposing him to be the gardener," I can see why there should be fruitfulness, and beauty, and sweetness even in the centre of the wilderness of sin.

Another mystery is also cleared up by this supposition. The wonder is *that ever you and I should have been placed among the plants of the Lord.* Why are *we* allowed to grow in the garden of his grace? Why me, Lord? Why me? How is it that we have been kept there, and borne with in our barrenness, when he might long ago have said, "Cut it down: why cumbereth it the ground?" Who else would have borne with such waywardness as ours? Who could have manifested such infinite patience? Who could have tended us with such care, and when the care was so ill-rewarded who would have renewed it so long from day to day, and persisted in designs of boundless love? Who could have done more for his vineyard? who could or would have done so much? Any mere man would have repented of his good intent, provoked by our ingratitude. None but God could have had patience with some of us! That we have not long ago been slipped off as fruitless branches of the vine; that we are left still upon the stem, in the hope that we may ultimately bring forth fruit, is a great marvel. I know not how it is that we have been spared, except upon this ground—"supposing him to be the gardener"; for Jesus is all gentleness and grace, so slow with his knife, so tardy with his axe, so hopeful if we do but show a bud or two, or, perchance, yield a little sour berry—so hopeful, I say, that these may be hopeful prognostics of something better by-and-by. Infinite patience! Immeasurable longsuffering! where are ye to be found save in the breast of the Well-beloved? Surely the hoe has spared many of us simply and only because he who is meek and lowly in heart is the gardener.

Dear friends, there is one mercy with regard to this church which I have often had to thank God for, namely, *that evils should have been shut out for so long a time.* During the period in which we have been together as pastor and people, and that is now some twenty-nine years, we have enjoyed uninterrupted prosperity, going from strength to strength in the work of the Lord. Alas! we have seen many other churches that were quite as hopeful as our own rent with strife, brought low by declension, or overthrown by heresy. I hope we have not been apt to judge their faults severely; but we must be thankful for our own deliverance from the evils which have afflicted them. I do not know how it is that we have been kept together in love, helped to abound in labour, and enabled to be firm in the faith, unless it be that special grace has watched over us. We are full of faults; we have nothing to boast of; and yet no church has been more divinely favoured: I wonder that the blessing should have lasted so long, and I cannot make it out except when I fall into "supposing *him* to be the gardener." I cannot trace our prosperity to the pastor, certainly; nor even to my beloved friends the elders and deacons, nor even to the best of you with your fervent love and holy zeal. I think it must be that Jesus has been the gardener, and he has shut the gate when I am afraid I have left it open; and he has driven out the wild boar of the wood just when he had entered to root up the weaker plants. He must have been about at nights to keep off the prowling thieves, and he must have been here, too, in the noontide heat to guard those of you who have prospered in worldly goods, from the glare of too bright a sun. Yes, *he* has been with us, blessed be his name! Hence all this peace, and unity, and enthusiasm. May we never grieve him so that he shall turn away from as ; but rather let us entreat him, saying, " Abide with us. Thou that dwellest in the gardens, let this be one of the gardens in which thou dost deign to dwell until the day break and the shadows flee away." Thus our supposition is a key to many wonders.

II. Let your imaginations run along with mine while I say that "supposing him to be the gardener" should be A SPUR TO MANY DUTIES.

One of the duties of a Christian is *joy*. That is a blessed religion which among its precepts commands men to be happy. When joy becomes a duty, who would wish to neglect it? Surely it must help every little plant to drink in the sunlight when it is whispered among the flowers that Jesus is the gardener. " Oh," you say, " I am such a little plant ; I do not grow well ; I do not put forth so much leafage, nor are there so many flowers on me as on many round about me !" It is quite right that you should think little of yourself : perhaps to droop your head is a part of your beauty : many flowers had not been half so lovely if they had not practised the art of hanging their heads. But " supposing him to be the gardener," then he is as much a gardener to you as he is to the most lordly palm in the whole domain. In the Mentone garden right before me grew the orange and the aloe, and others of the finer and more noticeable plants ; but on a wall to my left grew common wallflowers and saxifrages, and tiny herbs such as we find on our own rocky places. Now, the gardener had cared for all of these, little as well as great ; in fact, there were hundreds of specimens of the most insignificant growths all duly labelled and described. The smallest saxifrage could say, " He is my gardener just as surely as he is the gardener of the Gloire de Dijon or Maréchal Neil." Oh feeble child of God, the Lord taketh care of you! Your heavenly Father feedeth ravens, and guides the flight of sparrows : should he not much more care for you, oh ye of little faith? Oh little plants, you will grow rightly enough. Perhaps you are growing downward just now rather than upward. Remember that there are plants of which we value the underground root much more than we do the haulm above ground. Perhaps it is not yours to grow very fast ; you may be a slow-growing shrub by nature, and you would not be healthy if you were to run to wood. Anyhow, be this your joy, you are in the garden of the Lord, and, " supposing him to be the gardener," he will make the best of you. You cannot be in better hands.

Another duty is that of *valuing the Lord's presence, and praying for it.* We ought whenever the Sabbath morning dawns to pray our Well-beloved to come into his garden and eat his pleasant fruits. What can we do without him ? All day long our cry should go up to him, "O Lord, behold and visit this vine, and the vineyard which thy right hand has planted." We ought to agonize with him that he would come and manifest himself to us as he does not unto the world. For what is a garden if the gardener never comes near it? What is the difference between it and the wilderness if he to whom it belongs never lifts up spade or pruning-hook upon it? So that it is our necessity that we have Christ with us, " supposing him to be the gardener ;" and it is our bliss that we have Christ walking between our beds and borders, watching every plant, training, tending, maturing all. " Supposing

him to be the gardener," it is well, for from him is our fruit found.
Divided from him we are nothing; only as he watches over us can we
bring forth fruit. Let us have done with confidence in man, let us
forego all attempts to supply facts of his spiritual presence by routine
or rant, ritualism or rowdyism; but let us pray our Lord to be ever present
with us, and by that presence to make our garden grow.

"Supposing him to be the gardener," there is another duty, and that
is, let each one of us *yield himself up entirely to him.* A plant does not
know how it ought to be treated; it knows not when it should be
watered or when it should be kept dry : a fruit-tree is no judge of when it
needs to be pruned, or digged, or dunged. The wit and wisdom of the
garden lieth not in the flowers and shrubs, but in the gardener. Now,
then, if you and I are here to-day with any self-will and carnal judgment
about us, let us seek to lay it all aside that we may be absolutely
at our Lord's disposal. You might not be willing to put yourself
implicitly into the hand of any mere man (pity that you should) ; but,
surely, thou plant of the Lord's right-hand planting, thou mayest put
thyself without a question into his dear hand. "Supposing him to be
the gardener," thou mayest well say, "I would neither have will, nor
wish, nor wit, nor whim, nor way, but I would be as nothing in the
gardener's hands, that he may be to me my wisdom and my all.
Here, kind gardener, thy poor plant bows itself to thy hand; train me
as thou wilt. Depend upon it, happiness lives next door to the spirit
of complete acquiescence in the will of God, and it will be easy to
exercise that perfect acquiescence when we suppose the Lord Jesus to
be the gardener. If the Lord hath done it; what has a saint to say?
Oh thou afflicted one, the Lord hath done it: wouldest thou have it
otherwise? Nay, art thou not thankful that it is even so, because so is
the will of him in whose hand thy life is, and whose are all thy ways?
The duty of submission is very plain, "supposing him to be the
gardener."

One more duty I would mention, though others suggest themselves.
"Supposing him to be the gardener," then *let us bring forth fruit to him.*
I do not address a people this morning who feel no care as to whether
they serve God or not. I believe that most of you do desire to glorify
God ; for being saved by grace, you feel a holy ambition to show forth
his praises who has called you out of darkness into his marvellous light.
You wish to bring others to Christ, because you yourselves have been
brought to life and liberty in him. Now, let this be a stimulus to your
fruit-bearing, that Jesus is the gardener. Where you have brought
forth a single cluster, bring forth a hundred, "supposing him to be the
gardener." If he is to have the honour of it, then labour to do that
which will give him great renown. If our spiritual state were to be
attributed to ourselves, or to our minister, or to some of our fellow
Christians, we might not feel that we were under a great necessity to
be fruitful ; but if Jesus be the gardener, and is to bear the blame or
the honour of what we produce, then let us use up every drop of sap
and strain every fibre, that, to the utmost of which our manhood is
capable, we may produce a fair reward for our Lord's travail. Under
such tutorship and care we ought to become eminent scholars. Doth
Christ train us ? Oh let us never cause the world to think meanly of

our Master. Students feel that their *alma mater* deserves great things of them, so they labour to make their university renowned. And so, since Jesus is tutor and university to us, let us feel that we are bound to reflect credit upon so great a teacher, upon so divine a name. I do not know how to put it, but surely we ought to do something worthy of such a Lord. Each little flower in the garden of the Lord should wear its brightest hues, and pour forth its rarest perfume, because Jesus cares for it. The best of all possible good should be yielded by every plant in our Father's garden, supposing Jesus to be the gardener.

Thus much, then, on those two points—a key to many wonders, and a spur to many duties.

III. Thirdly, I have found in this supposition A RELIEF FROM CRUSHING RESPONSIBILITY. One has a work given him of God to do, and if he does it rightly he cannot do it carelessly. The first thing when he wakes he asks, "How is the work prospering?" and the last thought at night is, "What can I do to fulfil my calling?" Sometimes the anxiety even troubles his dreams, and he sighs, "O Lord, send now prosperity!" How is the garden prospering which we are set to tend? Are we broken-hearted because nothing appears to flourish? Is it a bad season? or is the soil lean and hungry? It is a very blessed relief to an excess of care if we can fall into the habit of "supposing him to be the gardener." If Jesus be the Master and Lord in all things it is not mine to keep all the church in order. I am not responsible for the growth of every Christian, nor for every backslider's errors, nor for every professor's faults of life. This burden must not lie on me so that I shall be crushed thereby. "Supposing him to be the gardener," then, the church enjoys a better oversight than mine; better care is taken of the garden than could be taken by the most vigilant watchers, even though by night the frost devoured them, and by day the heat. "Supposing him to be the gardener," then all must go well in the long run. He that keepeth Israel doth neither slumber nor sleep; we need not fret and despond. I beg you earnest workers, who are becoming depressed, to think this out a little. You see it is yours to work under the Lord Jesus; but it is not yours to take the anxiety of his office into your souls as though you were to bear his burdens. The under-gardener, the workman in the garden, needs not fret about the whole garden as though it were all left to him. No, no; let him not take too much upon himself. I pray you, bound your anxiety by the facts of the case. So you have a number of young people around you, and you are watching for their souls as they that must give account. This is well; but do not be worried and wearied; for, after all, the saving and the keeping of those souls is not in your hands, but it rests with One far-more able than yourself. Just think that the Lord is the gardener. I know it is so in matters of providence. A certain man of God in troublous times became quite unable to do his duty because he laid to heart so much the ills of the age; he became depressed and disturbed, and he went on board a vessel, wanting to leave the country, which was getting into such a state that he could no longer endure it. Then one said to him, "Mr. Whitelock, are you the manager of the world?" No, he was not quite that. "Did not God get on pretty well with it before you were born, and don't you think he will do very well with it when you are dead?" That reflection helped to relieve the good man's mind, and he went back to do his duty. I want you thus to perceive the limit of your responsibility : you are not the gardener himself; you are only one of the gardener's boys, set to run on errands, or to do a bit of digging, or to sweep the paths. The garden is well enough managed even though you are not head manager in it.

While this relieves us of anxiety it makes labour for Christ very sweet, because if the garden does not seem to repay us for our trouble we say to ourselves, "It is not my garden after all. 'Supposing him to be the gardener,' I am quite willing to work on a barren piece of rock, or tie up an old withered bough, or dig a worthless sod ; for, if it only pleases Jesus, the work is for that one sole reason profitable to the last degree. It is not mine to question the wisdom of my task, but to set about it in the name of my Master and Lord. 'Supposing him to be the gardener,' lifts the ponderous responsibility of it from me, and my work becomes pleasant and delightful."

In dealing with the souls of men, we meet with cases which are extremely difficult. Some persons are so timid and fearful that you do not know how to comfort them; others are so fast and presumptuous that you hardly know how to help them. A few are so double-faced that you cannot understand them, and others so fickle that you cannot hold them. Some flowers puzzle the ordinary gardener : we meet with plants which are covered with prickles, and when you try to train them they wound the hand that would help them. These strange growths would make a great muddle for you if you were the gardener; but "supposing him to be the gardener," you have the happiness of being able to go to him constantly, saying, "Good Lord, I do not understand this singular creature; it is as odd a plant as I am myself. Oh, that thou wouldest manage it, or tell me how. I have come to tell thee of it."

Constantly our trouble is that we have so many plants to look after that we have not time to cultivate any one in the best manner, because we have fifty more all wanting attention at the time ; and then before we have done with the watering-pot we have to fetch the hoe and the rake and the spade, and we are puzzled with these multitudinous cares, even as Paul was when he said, "That which cometh upon me daily, the care of all the churches." Ah, then, it is a blessed thing to do the little we can do and leave the rest to Jesus, "supposing him to be the gardener."

In the church of God there is a discipline which we cannot exercise. I do not think it is half so hard to exercise discipline as it is not to be able to exercise it when yet you feel that it ought to be done. The servants of the householder were perplexed when they might not root up the tares. "Didst thou not sow good seed in thy field? From whence then hath it tares?" "An enemy hath done this." "Wilt thou then that we go and gather them up?" "Not so," said he, "lest ye root up the wheat with them." This afflicts the Christian minister when he must not remove a pestilent, hindering weed. Yes, but "supposing *him* to be the gardener," and it is his will to let that weed remain, what have you and I to do but to hold our peace? He has a discipline more sure and safe than ours, and in due time the tares shall know it. In patience let us possess our souls.

And then, again, there is that succession in the garden which we cannot keep up. Plants will die down, and others must be put into their places or the garden will grow bare; but we know not where to find these fresh flowers. We say, "When yonder good man dies who will succeed him?" That is a question I have heard many a time, till I am rather weary of it. Who is to follow such a man? Let us wait till he is gone and needs following. Why sell the man's coat when he can wear it himself? We are apt to think when this race of good brethren shall die out that none will arise worthy to unloose the latchets of their shoes. Well, friend, I could suppose a great many things, but this morning my text is, "Supposing him to be the gardener," and on that supposition I expect that the Lord has other plants in reserve which you have not yet seen, and these will exactly fit into our places when they become empty, and the Lord will keep up the true apostolical succession till the day of his second advent. In every time of darkness and dismay, when the heart sinks and the spirits decline, and we think it is all over with the church of God, let us fall back on this, "Supposing him to be the gardener," and expect to see greater and better things than these. We are at the end of *our* wits, but he is not at the beginning of his yet: we are nonplussed, but he never will be; therefore let us wait and be tranquil, "supposing him to be the gardener."

IV. Fourthly, I want you to notice that this supposition will give you A DELIVERANCE FROM MANY GLOOMY FEARS. I walked down the garden, and I saw a place where all the path was strewn with leaves and broken branches, and stones, and I saw the earth upon the flower-beds tossed about, and roots lying quite out of the ground: all was in disorder. Had a dog been amusing himself? or had a mischievous child been at work? If so, it was a great pity. But no: in a minute or two I saw the gardener come back, and I perceived that *he* had been making all this disarrangement. He had been cutting, and digging, and hacking, and mess-making; and all for the good of the garden. It may be it has happened to some of you that you have been a good deal clipped lately, and in your domestic affairs things have not been in so fair a state as you could have wished: it may be in the Church we have seen ill weeds plucked up, and barren branches lopped, so that everything is *en deshabille*. Well, if the Lord has done it our gloomy fears are idle. "Supposing him to be the gardener," all is well.

As I was talking this over with my friend, I said to him—"Supposing him to be the gardener," then *the serpent* will have a bad time of it. Supposing Adam to be the gardener, then the serpent gets in and has a chat with his wife, and mischief comes of it; but supposing Jesus to be the gardener, woe to thee, serpent: there is a blow for thy head within half a minute if thou dost but show thyself within the boundary. So, if we are afraid that the devil should get in among us let us always in prayer entreat that there may be no space for the devil, because the Lord Jesus Christ fills all, and keeps out the adversary. Other creatures besides serpents intrude into gardens; caterpillars and palmerworms, and all sorts of destroying creatures are apt to devour our churches. How can we keep them out? The highest wall cannot exclude them: there is no protection except one, and that is, "supposing him to be the gardener." Thus it is written, "I will rebuke the devourer for your sakes, and he shall not destroy the fruits of your ground ; neither shall your vine cast her fruit before the time in the field, saith the Lord of hosts."

I am sometimes troubled by the question, What if roots of bitterness should spring up among us to trouble us ? We are all such fallible creatures, supposing some brother should permit the seed of discord to grow in his bosom, then there may be a sister in whose heart the seeds will also spring up, and from her they will fly to another sister, and be blown about till brethren and sisters are all bearing rue and wormwood in their hearts. Who is to prevent this ? Only the Lord Jesus by his Spirit. He can keep out this evil, " supposing him to be the gardener." The root which beareth wormwood will grow but little where Jesus is. Dwell with us, Lord, as a church and people: by thy Holy Spirit reside with us and in us, and never depart from us, and then no root of bitterness shall spring up to trouble us.

Then comes another fear. Suppose the living waters of God's Spirit should not come to water the garden, what then ? We cannot make them flow, for the Spirit is a sovereign, and he flows where he pleases. Ah, but the Spirit of God will be in our garden, " supposing our Lord to be the gardener." There is no fear of our not being watered when Jesus undertakes to do it. " He will pour water on him that is thirsty, and floods upon the dry ground." But what if the sunlight of his love should not shine on the garden ? If the fruits should never ripen, if there should be no peace, no joy in the Lord ? That cannot happen " supposing him to be the gardener ;" for his face is the sun, and his countenance scatters those health-giving beams, and nurturing warmths, and perfecting influences which are needful for maturing the saints in all the sweetness of grace to the glory of God. So, " supposing him to be the gardener " at this the close of the year, I fling away my doubts and fears, and invite you who bear the church upon your heart to do the same. It is all well with Christ's cause because it is in his own hands. He shall not fail nor be discouraged. The pleasure of the Lord shall prosper in his hands.

V. Fifthly, here is A WARNING FOR THE CARELESS, " supposing him to be the gardener." In this great congregation many are to the church what weeds are to a garden. They are not planted by God ; they are not growing under his nurture, they are bringing forth no fruit to his glory. My dear friend, I have tried often to get at you, to impress you, but I cannot. Take heed ; for one of these days, " supposing him to be the gardener," he will reach you, and you shall know what that word meaneth, " Every plant which my heavenly Father hath not planted shall be rooted up." Take heed to yourselves, I pray.

Others among us are like the branches of the vine which bear no fruit. We have often spoken very sharply to these, speaking honest truth in unmistakable language, and yet we have not touched their consciences. Ah, but " supposing him to be the gardener," he will fulfil that sentence : " Every branch in me that beareth not fruit he taketh away." He will get at you, if we cannot. Would God, ere this old year were quite dead, you would turn unto the Lord with full purpose of heart ; so that instead of being a weed you might become a choice flower ; that instead of a dry stick, you might be a sappy, fruit-bearing branch of the vine. The Lord make it to be so ; but if any here need the caution, I pray them to take it to heart at once. "Supposing him to be the gardener," there will be no escaping from his eye; there will be no deliverance from his hand. As "he will throughly purge his floor, and burn up the chaff with unquenchable fire," so he will throughly cleanse his garden and cast out every worthless thing.

VI. Another set of thoughts may well arise as A QUIETUS TO THOSE WHO COMPLAIN, "supposing him to be the gardener." Certain of us have been made to suffer much physical pain, which often bites into the spirits, and makes the heart to stoop: others have suffered heavy temporal losses, having had no success in business, but, on the contrary, having had to endure privation, perhaps even to penury. Are you ready to complain against the Lord for all this? I pray you, do not so. Take the supposition of the text into your mind this morning. The Lord has been pruning you sharply, cutting off your best boughs, and you seem to be like a thing despised, that is constantly tormented with the knife. Yes, but "supposing him to be the gardener," suppose that your loving Lord has wrought it all, that from his own hand all your grief has come, every cut, and every gash, and every slip: does not this alter the case? Hath not the Lord done it? Well, then, if it be so, put your finger to your lip and be quiet, until you **are** able from your heart to say, "The Lord gave and the Lord hath taken away, and blessed be the name of the Lord." I am persuaded that the Lord hath done nothing amiss to any one of his people; that no child of his can rightly complain that he has been whipped with **too** much severity; and that no one branch of the vine can truthfully declare that it has been pruned with too sharp an edge. No; what the Lord has done is the best that could have been done, the very thing that you and I, if we could have possessed infinite wisdom and love, would have wished to have done; therefore let us stop each thought of murmuring, and say, "The Lord hath done it," and be glad.

Especially I speak to those who have suffered bereavement. I can hardly express to you how strange I feel at this moment when my sermon revives a memory so sweet dashed with such exceeding bitterness. I sat with my friend and secretary in that garden some fifteen days ago, and we were then in perfect health, rejoicing in the goodness of the Lord. We returned home, and within five days I was smitten with disabling pain; and worse, far worse than that, he was called upon to lose his wife. We said to one another as we sat there reading the word of God and meditating, "How happy we are! Dare we think of being so happy? Must it not speedily end?" I little thought I should have to say for him, "Alas, my brother, thou art brought very low, for the delight of thine eyes is taken from thee." But here is our comfort: the Lord hath done it. The best rose in the garden is gone. Who has taken it? The gardener came this way and gathered it. He planted it and watched over it, and now he has taken it. Is not this most natural? Does anybody weep because of that? No; everybody knows that it is right, and according to the order of nature, that he should come and gather the best in the garden. If you are sore troubled by the loss of your beloved, yet dry your grief by "supposing him to be the gardener." Kiss the hand that has wrought you such grief? Brethren beloved, remember the next time the Lord comes to your part of the garden, and he may do so within the next week, he will only gather his own flowers, and would you prevent his doing so even if you could?

VII. "Supposing him to be the gardener," then there is AN OUT-LOOK FOR THE HOPEFUL. "Supposing him to be the gardener," then I expect to see in the garden where he works the best possible prosperity: I expect to see no flower dried up, no tree without fruit : I expect to see the richest, rarest fruit, with the daintiest bloom upon it, daily presented to the great Owner of the garden. Let us expect that in this church, and pray for it. Oh, if we have but faith we shall see great things. It is our unbelief that straitens God. Let us believe great things from the work of Christ by his Spirit in the midst of his people's hearts, and we shall not be disappointed.

"Supposing him to be the gardener," then, dear friends, we may expect divine intercourse of unspeakable preciousness. Go back to Eden for a minute. When Adam was the gardener, what happened ? The Lord God walked in the garden in the cool of the day. But "supposing HIM to be the gardener," then we shall have the Lord God dwelling among us, and revealing himself in all the glory of his power, and the plenitude of his Fatherly heart ; making us to know him, that we may be filled with all the fulness of God. What joy is this !

One other thought. "Supposing him to be the gardener," and God to come and walk among the trees of the garden, then I expect he will remove the whole of the garden upward with himself to fairer skies ; for he rose, and his people must rise with him. I expect a blessed transplantation of all these flowers below to a clearer atmosphere above, away from all this smoke and fog and damp, up where the sun is never clouded, where flowers never wither, where fruits never decay. Oh, the glory we shall then enjoy up yonder, on the hills of spices in the garden of God. "Supposing him to be the gardener" what a garden will he form above, and how shall you and I grow therein, developing beyond imagination. "It doth not yet appear what we shall be, but we know that when he shall appear we shall be like him, for we shall see him as he is." Since he is the author and finisher of our faith, to what perfection will he conduct us, and to what glory will he bring us! Oh, to be found in him! God grant we may be! To be plants in his garden, "supposing him to be the gardener," is all the heaven we can desire.

By C. H. SPURGEON.

The Gospel for the People.

Sixty Short Sermons, with a Sketch of Mr. Spurgeon's Life, and Fourteen Portraits and Engravings, with Preface by Pastor Thomas Spurgeon. Cloth Gilt, 5s.

These Short Sermons have been selected from the Series with a view to their being used in Mission Halls, and other similar places. They are about half the length of the ordinary Sermons.

PASSMORE & ALABASTER, 4, Paternoster Buildings, London, E.C.

Metropolitan Tabernacle Pulpit.

A MONUMENT FOR THE DEAD, AND A VOICE TO THE LIVING.

A Sermon

DELIVERED ON LORD'S-DAY MORNING, JANUARY 7TH, 1883, BY

C. H. SPURGEON,

AT THE METROPOLITAN TABERNACLE, NEWINGTON.

"For Moses describeth the righteousness which is of the law, That the man which doeth those things shall live by them. But the righteousness which is of faith speaketh on this wise, Say not in thine heart, Who shall ascend into heaven? (that is, to bring Christ down from above:) Or, Who shall descend into the deep? (that is, to bring up Christ again from the dead.) But what saith it? The word is nigh thee, even in thy mouth, and in thy heart: that is, the word of faith, which we preach; that if thou shalt confess with thy mouth the Lord Jesus, and shalt believe in thine heart that God hath raised him from the dead, thou shalt be saved."—Romans x. 5—9.

You see by this mourning that our church has been bereaved. I have lost a friend tender and true to me, and my heart is too full for utterance.* I scarcely knew what to preach from this morning; but at last I settled in my mind that I would raise a memorial to my departed friend by preaching a sermon which should be connected with himself. Therefore I cast about me, and I considered what subject he would wish me to preach from if he were sitting behind me this morning as he was last Lord's-day. I had no difficulty in answering that question. His life and death pointed in one direction. He was a man of rare common sense, straightforward and downright in his aims, and most pithy in his speech, with such a mixture of mother-wit that he might have been taken for John Ploughman's brother, as indeed he was. He cared nothing for oratory, which I have heard him call "a flash in the pan"; he delighted in the plain, solid gospel of Jesus Christ. I know that he would have said to me,—Give them Christ crucified, and salvation by grace through faith, as plainly as ever you can; for when he was sore sick and in the very agony of death, he repeated as his dying creed—

> "Nothing in my hand I bring:
> Simply to thy cross I cling."

and in his own quaint way he added, "They may talk as much as ever they like, but the whole of it lies in Jack the Huckster's verse—

> 'I'm a poor sinner, and nothing at all;
> But Jesus Christ is my all in all.'"

---

* William Higgs, Esq., for many years a beloved deacon of the church in the Metropolitan Tabernacle, fell on sleep January 3rd, 1883, in his fifty-ninth year.

No. 1,700.

You will find that story in the first volume of my sermons.* In Park-street early in my ministry I told the story, and it did my friend good, and helped to rest his soul all those years ago, so that he remembered it and repeated it at the last. For his sake let me tell it again.

This Huckster Jack was a poor, wicked fellow, who had gone about from village to village, swearing, drinking, huckstering, and perhaps pilfering. Some thought him half-witted, but the story would show his mind to be sound enough. He heard a poor woman sing somewhere—

> "I'm a poor sinner, and nothing at all;
> But Jesus Christ is my all in all."

He remembered the words, and what was better, he felt their sense; and he kept on humming them to himself till God's good Spirit engraved them on his heart. There they were recorded, and Jack was a new man and a saved man. So he essayed to join himself unto the church, but the brethren looked suspiciously at him and enquired, "What is your experience?" He said he had no experience but this—

> "I'm a poor sinner, and nothing at all;
> But Jesus Christ is my all in all."

The good elders very properly asked, "Are you converted? Have you been born again?" and Jack replied, "I do not know much about these things; but this I do know and am sure of—

> 'I'm a poor sinner, and nothing at all;
> But Jesus Christ is my all in all.'"

They put him back for awhile, to try if he would grow in his knowledge, but he never went an inch beyond the first standard. He knew what he did know, and to that he held fast—

> "I'm a poor sinner, and nothing at all;
> But Jesus Christ is my all in all."

Well, they must take him into the church; they could not well refuse a man with such a confession of faith; and when he was in the church, walking with the brethren, he was happier than the rest of them, at which they greatly marvelled, and one said to him, "Brother Jack, don't you sometimes feel doubts and fears?" "Doubts," he said, "what do you mean? I never doubt that

> 'I'm a poor sinner, and nothing at all;'

for I have daily proofs of it, and why should I doubt that

> 'Jesus Christ is my all in all'?

for he says he is, and I must believe him." "Ah, well," said one, "sometimes I enjoy good frames and feelings, and feel very happy, and then I lose them, and sink in spirit." Jack answered, "I never get lower than I am, for I am down at the bottom—

> 'A poor sinner, and nothing at all.'

I cannot get lower than that, can I? But I am also at the top, for

> 'Jesus Christ is my all in all,'

and I cannot get higher than that, can I?" They tried him many ways

---

* See No. 47. "Christ's Prayer for his People."

with their blessed experience, of which you and I have got cartloads, perhaps waggonloads; but he could not be drawn out of his one firm position. They tried him with their various attainments, depressions, anxieties, quibbles, and questions; but still the huckster would not budge. He had bought the truth and would not sell it, and so he stuck to—

> "I'm a poor sinner, and nothing at all;
> But Jesus Christ is my all in all."

The conies are a feeble folk, yet have they their habitations among the rocks: they are safe, but they keep to their hiding place.

Of course our new Perfection brethren, spick and span saints as they are, are not like Jack, they are not "poor sinners, and nothing at all," and I am afraid lest some of them should find out that Jesus Christ is not their all in all. But if you and I are as he was, "poor sinners, and nothing at all," we may, with firm and resolute grip, lay hold upon the other line, "But Jesus Christ is my all in all." Christ's fulness is meant for our emptiness; Christ's righteousness is meant for our sin, salvation is for the lost. When you and I are no longer sinners, Christ is no longer our Saviour; when you and I no more need him, then we shall not have him. Our need is our warrant, and if that be gone, all is gone. Jesus did not bleed and die to be a superfluity to us: he came to meet a grim necessity. As long as we are nothing, Christ is our all in all; we may be sure of that, and that is just the gospel in a nutshell. I want to preach that same gospel this morning, in the hope that in after days this word may be scattered far and wide, and some Jack the Huckster, or some other like him, may find himself to be utterly empty and undone, and may then know that Christ is ordained to be his salvation. Jesus came into the world to save real sinners, not sham sinners; for he is a real, and not a pretended Saviour. He saves those who are always confessors of sin, always needy in themselves, and therefore always glad of him. Even in their best estate the saved ones need their Lord: even if we walk in the light as God is in the light, and have fellowship with him, we still sin, and still the blood of Jesus Christ, his Son, cleanseth us from all sin.

I now plunge into my text. Notice, first, *what Moses said.* Moses said, "That the man which doeth those things shall live by them." Next, *what the gospel says :* "But the righteousness which is of faith speaketh on this wise," and so on. Thirdly, we shall consider *what the Scripture saith :* "Whosoever believeth on him shall not be ashamed." Then, fourthly, we will hear *what experience saith ;* for we may bring in the experience of believers to back up the declarations of God.

I. I invite your earnest attention to the first point—WHAT MOSES SAITH : "Moses describeth the righteousness which is of the law, That the man which doeth those things shall live by them." This is a clear statement. There is no mystery or obscurity about it. You need not go to the universities and earn a degree of D.D. in order to understand this declaration: it is as plain as words can make it. If you wish to be saved by the law you must do its commands and you shall live. The law is written in the ten commandments; you know them; and if you desire to live by them you must keep them. It will not suffice for you to learn those commands by heart, or to write them up in your churches, or to read them over and say, " Lord, have mercy upon us, and incline our hearts to keep this law": all that may be well enough, but it is not to the point. If you are to be saved by the commandments you must do them: that is clear. Moses does not allow any person to dream that under the law he can be saved in any other way than by perfect obedience thereto. " For not the hearers of the law are just before God, but the doers of the law shall be justified." Whatever it is that God has commanded, you must do ; whatever he forbids, you must avoid ; for by such obedience alone can you live.

Mark you, Moses does not tone down the law to suit our fallen state, or talk of our doing our best and God's being satisfied with our imperfect obedience. No, he says only, " He that doeth those things shall live by them." He demands perfect and entire obedience, if life is to come of it. He does not say that if you have broken the law you may still live by some other means. No, if the law is once broken it is all over with you as to salvation thereby: one single fault takes away the possibility of your ever being justified by the law. " He that doeth those things," that is, always, without exception, with all his heart and soul and strength—" he shall live by them"; but nobody else. Be he Jew or be he Gentile, his only righteousness by law must come through the doing of the law. Moses says nothing about wearing phylacteries, or washing hands, or offering incense, or performing ceremonies in order to righteousness. No ; clear, straight, cutting like a sharp razor, he puts before us the single sentence, " He that doeth those things shall live by them."

Judge ye whether any one of us has fulfilled the whole law. To my mind this word of Moses is conclusive that none of us can possibly live by the works of the law. We cannot keep the law now, for we have already broken it : the vase is fractured, and to talk of keeping it entire is nonsense. But even if it were not already broken, should we get through to-morrow with its temptations, bearing such a heart as we have within us, without breaking that perfect and spotless law ? I am sure we should not. You that hope to be saved by your works are indulging a forlorn hope : whatever you may do or be in the future, the past has already ruined you. The way to heaven up the steep sides of Sinai is inaccessible to trembling feet like ours. If you were to be saved by the law you should have begun without sin, continued without sin, and then it would be needful to end without sin. There would not be a moment of your life in which you could be at peace, for there would always be the fear that in some unguarded instant you would transgress, and lose all. But why talk I so ? It is no longer in our power to dream of a perfect, life-long obedience. We went astray from the womb, speaking lies ; we were rebellious to our parents in our childhood, and wayward in our youth ; in our early manhood we were carried about with this passion and with that, and since then all kinds of evils have led us astray. We are as full of evil as an egg is full of meat, and our heart is like a cage of unclean birds. I can say no less. The hope of salvation by works is black despair ; yet we have a set of men on the face of the earth who are always wanting us to preach up this hopeless hope, and urging us to lay this heavy burden upon the shoulders of dying men. They would have us proclaim salvation by the works of the law. This, they say, would at least make men moral and keep them sober : whereas even in this they err against the light; for it has been proved by history that such preaching makes men worse and worse. The idea of salvation by works sits like an awful incubus upon the breast of humanity, and presses out of the soul all hope, thus robbing man of strength to attempt true holiness. When a man has lost all hope he throws the reins upon his neck and runs into all manner of iniquity, judging that he may as well be hanged for a sheep as a lamb.

Clear, then, as possible it must be to every man among us who will think, that if the only way of salvation by the works of the law is by the keeping of the law in its entirety, then that road is closed against us, and the sooner we have done with it the better; for then we shall turn our thoughts in the right direction, and travel on the way which the Lord in great mercy has prepared for us. This is what Moses saith : hear it and be humbled.

II. Now I ask you to listen to WHAT THE GOSPEL SAITH. "The righteousness which is of faith," or believing, "speaketh on this wise, Say not in thy heart, Who shall ascend into heaven ? (that is, to bring Christ down from above :) or, Who shall descend into the deep ? (that is, to bring up Christ again from the dead.) But what saith it? The word is nigh thee, even in thy mouth, and in thy heart: that is, the word of faith, which we preach ; that if thou shalt confess with thy mouth the Lord Jesus, and shalt believe in thine heart that God hath raised him from the dead, thou shalt be saved."

Now observe, first, that *the gospel claims to be like the law in its clearness.* Moses claimed for the law which God had given to the people through him that it was clear, and within the range of their knowledge and understanding. I will read his exact words to you. Turn to Deuteronomy xxx. 11 : "For this commandment which I command thee this day, it is not hidden from thee, neither is it far off. It is not in heaven, that thou shouldest say, Who shall go up for us to heaven, and bring it unto us, that we may hear it, and do it ? Neither is it beyond the sea, that thou shouldest say, Who shall go over the sea for us, and bring it unto us, that we may hear it, and do it ? But the word is very nigh unto thee, in thy mouth, and in thy heart, that thou mayest do it." Now Paul here very adroitly takes these words out of the mouth of Moses, alters them somewhat, and as good as says, "It was the boast of the law that it was clear, known, and accessible to the people ; but much more is this the glory of the gospel." Did not I show you just now that when Moses spoke he did not mystify the matter, but put it plainly, "The man that doeth those things shall live by them." So also the gospel by no means involves itself in obscurity, but says, "Believe and live," quite as distinctly as Moses said, "Do and live." Here you have it, "Believe in the Lord Jesus Christ, and thou shalt be saved." Moses' utterance was single and by itself. He did not say, "Do and thou shalt live, and yet there is another way." No ; under the law it was nothing but "Do and live ; leave undone and die." So the gospel does not propose a second way, and suggest "a larger hope," but it declares with solemn decision, "He that believeth not is condemned already, because he hath not believed in the name of the only begotten Son of God." It is just as clear as ever the law was, and quite as sharply distinct. Herein is no mystery: Jesus Christ came into the world to save sinners, and whosoever believeth in him shall not perish, but have everlasting life. Wrapping everything up into one, the gospel says, "Trust thou in the Lord Jesus Christ, and thy sins shall be forgiven thee, and thou shalt be saved." This believing, or trusting, is the whole of the matter, and neither heaven above nor the abyss beneath will ever reveal another salvation.

I want to call your special attention to the fact that Paul borrows the the words of Moses; for his intent was the ending of all fears. No man among us doubts that if he had performed the law of God the Lord would give him life; but it is equally certain that if we have believed in the Lord Jesus Christ we have eternal life. No trembling sinner doubts but that by the breaking of the law we are condemned: be you equally sure of it, that by not believing you are condemned. As no keeper of the law would have been lost on any ground whatever, so no believer in Christ shall be lost on any ground whatever; as no breaker of the law could escape punishment, so no unbeliever in Christ can be saved. The gospel states its message as clearly as the law. As positively as the law utters its promise and threat, so positively and unalterably doth the gospel deliver its decree. The believer in Jesus shall be saved because he is a believer; and Christ's veracity is staked thereon :—"Verily, verily, I say unto you, He that believeth on me hath everlasting life."

Oh, but this is a very blessed thing to have to say to you. I do not come to-day with a gospel veiled in mystery and shrouded in doubt; I do not bring a message which you cannot understand or receive; neither do I come with "ifs" and "buts" and "peradventures," but with this, "Whosoever shall call upon the name of the Lord shall be saved." "He that believeth and is baptized shall be saved." "Whosoever believeth in him hath everlasting life." This is as certain and clear as the utterance of that dreadful roll of thunder which has just now left on your minds the thought, "He that doeth these things shall live by them."

Let us go a little further. What saith the gospel? Why, next, *it forbids the questions of despair.* "The righteousness which is of faith speaketh on this wise, Say not in thine heart, Who shall ascend into heaven? or, Who shall descend into the deep?" When a man is at length awakened to a sense of sin he cries, "I long to be saved! All that I have and all that I am I would give to escape from the righteous wrath of God. Sirs, what must I do to be saved? Surely it would need that I mount to heaven to own my sin, or dive to hell to bear its punishment. I want a righteousness which would need as much labour to produce as a climb to heaven would need; and I require an expiation for sin as great as though a man were plunged into the abyss itself, and there were made to suffer the divine anger. How is it possible that I can be saved?" This wail of despair takes many forms: one man puts it thus : "What doings can I perform by which I can be saved?

'Could my zeal no respite know,
Could my tears for ever flow,
All for sin could not atone.' "

Another, despairing of deliverance by his doings, runs upon his feelings, and cries, "If I am to be saved, surely I shall need to experience joys like those which are felt by spirits before the throne. If I had a sense of sin as deep as that of lost souls in hell, I could hope that I should be saved." Thus the second man looks to excitements and feelings just as the first looked to works and self-denials. Now, the gospel forbids us to dream in this fashion. Talk not thus. Say not even in thy heart that by these doings or feelings thou canst be saved. Perhaps thou wouldst be ashamed to say it with thy lips; but do not say it at all ; do not say that the way to heaven is hard, or mysterious, or in any degree apart from the simple act of believing. Do not suppose that anything is wanted as to doings or feelings in order to complete the righteousness which is wrought out by the Lord Jesus, and imputed by God to the believer.

Ah, then the heart foolishly cries, "I must know a great deal ; as much as if I had been to heaven and seen for myself, or as if I had dived into the depths and made discoveries there." No, you must not : the gospel is simple; salvation is as plain as a pikestaff; familiar as homespun ; easy as the A B C of your childhood. Say not in thine heart that thou must be educated, trained, and made into a scholar. No, confess yourself a sinner ; trust in the sinner's Saviour, and you are saved.

"Ah, well," says one, "I know I must undergo a singular experience —either I must be carried right away to heaven with delirious delight, or be plunged into the waves of hell in frightful despair." No, my dear friend, do not say that even in your thought. The righteousness of faith lies not in dreams and visions, delusions or depressions : it lies only in reliance upon the work of Jesus finished for you. Go not to the loom to weave a righteousness. The garment is woven already ; put it on ; Christ gives it to you. Dig not into the bowels of the earth to find the gold of salvation. Christ holds it out to you : take it freely, and be rich for ever. So one of the first works of the gospel is silencing the questions of our unbelief.

Next, this precious gospel *translates these questions, and then answers them.* Listen. A voice cries "Who shall ascend into heaven?" The gospel replies, if you did ascend to heaven what would you do there, without Christ, the anointed Saviour? You say, "Who shall descend into the deep?" Listen, man. If you were to descend there, what would you do without him whom God has anointed to save? If you find him it will not much matter where you find him, in heaven or in the deep, for he must be almighty everywhere. Now hearken. Thou sayest, "Who shall ascend into heaven?" the top and bottom of such an ascent must be, "to bring Christ down." Hear this ! Jesus has come down : years ago he left the glories of his Father. Hast thou not heard the tale? Being pure, blazing, glorious Godhead, "Light of lights, very God of very God," on a sudden they found him in a stable hanging on a woman's breast. Angels saw him and wondered. He came down, indeed, when he was born ; and, being down so low as that, he descended to the carpenter's shop, to the weariness of the well's brink, and to a thirst which made him say, "Give me to drink." Lower than that, he descended to being "despised and rejected of men." He was Lord of heaven and earth, and yet they called him Beelzebub, and talked of him as a drunken man and a wine-bibber. Having descended all that length he went lower still. Listen,—angels, you will not weary while I tell the story over again—he went into Gethsemane where he put on the crimson garment of his own bloody sweat; and then to Pilate's hall, where they did falsely accuse him, and spit on him, and scourge him, and make a jest of him; and then to that cross whereon they nailed him in his nakedness, so that he hung in agony, to die in fever and in thirst, till he cried, "It is finished." He descended into the grave, so that he dwelt among the dead! We know not how low he went, but we are told that "he descended into the lower parts of the earth." Oh, my hearer, our salvation lies in this! Not in *our* descending, but in Christ's descending our hope is to be found. Listen to it, lost ones; you need not climb to heaven: Christ has come down from heaven to you; and if you lie among the spiritually dead to-day, or think you do, he has come down to you, and you need not enquire how you can go up to him. No prayers, or tears, are wanted to bring him down: he has already come and is near at hand. You asked, "Who shall descend into the deep?" Now listen. Here is your answer. You need not "bring up Christ again from the dead," for the Lord has risen indeed. His soul scarce descended among the shades before it quitted them for ever; that day he died he was in Paradise, and the thief was with him there as a trophy. Up also his body rose on the light of the third day; and he sojourned for forty days among his disciples. At the close of that period he rose into the air, ascending high. As they watched him rising higher, and yet higher, at last a cloud received him: he has gone up to the Father's throne, as the sinner's Saviour: at the throne he stands to-day to intercede for sinners, and from that throne he bends to comfort those who come to him. Now, your hope lies wholly in what this Son of God did in his descent and ascent. God has brought him again from the dead and exalted him at his own right hand, and this is not for himself, but for all those who trust in him. His death is instead of the death of our souls: his life is the life of our spirits. Now, soul, thou hast nothing to do with asking vain questions; thou hast to accept the result of the Saviour's actual performances. The saving work is done, done by him who was anointed of the Lord to do it. Look to him and salvation is thine. Thy salvation rests in Jesus, rest thou in Jesus. Throw thyself upon him now; even as a babe casts itself upon its mother's breast. Have done with every other confidence. What canst thou need more than to rely upon the Anointed of the Lord?

Now, Paul declares, or rather the gospel speaking for itself declares, *this word of life by faith in the risen Christ to be near us, that is, to be accessible to us.* As your next door neighbour's house is not hard to get at, so neither is salvation by the gospel. It is nigh you; it is nigh you *now:* it will never be nigher than it is at this moment. You may now believe in Christ and live eternally. Difficulty there is none: only believe and thou art saved. It is not a mystical, obscure thing; it is near and familiar. Believe in Christ as you would believe in your friend: believe that he died for sinners, and trust in him for salvation. If God has made you feel yourself a sinner, then Christ is such a Saviour as you need and you may have him at once : the only difficulty lies in the way being so easy that you can hardly think it can be so. Have done with doings, and feelings, and trust yourself with Christ. " The word is nigh thee." It is simple ; indeed, so simple that people try to obscure it in order to understand it. It is such milk for babes that I have known people refuse such plain truth because they were not willing to be treated like little children. Just as I lean all my weight upon this rail. so do I lean my soul wholly upon Christ. If what Christ has done will not save a sinner I am damned ; for I have nothing else to depend upon ; but if it will save, and sure I am that it will, I am saved as surely as Christ has risen from the dead. This is the substance of the matter—Christ saves, and we trust. This is what that word of faith says, even the gospel which we preach. I am afraid we say a great deal at times which rather lumbers and cumbers the gospel than makes it clear. Perhaps I am doing the same this morning, but I do not mean to do it. I mean to let it stand out simply before you, that the incarnation, the life, the death, and the resurrection of Christ are the one foundation upon which we must depend for eternal salvation, and upon that alone ; and if we do so depend we shall most assuredly be saved.

Yet note, that *Paul opens this up into two things.* He says, " If thou shalt confess with thy mouth the Lord Jesus, and shalt believe in thine heart that God hath raised him from the dead, thou shalt be saved.' So there must be confession with the mouth. Do not leave tha. out. Do not suppose that you can be a believer and conceal your faith. As I said the other day, Do not behave like a rat behind the wainscot, only daring to come out in the dark. That is not Christ's way. If you trust in him with your heart, trust him openly, and confess him with your mouth, owning that he is your Lord, and your Saviour. He has put the two things together,—" He that believeth and is baptized shall be saved." The believing and the confession of that believing in God's own way are never to be separated, for " With the heart man believeth unto righteousness, and with the mouth confession is made unto salvation." See ye well to this.

III. Thirdly, let us consider, WHAT THE SCRIPTURE SAITH : " *Whosoever believeth on him shall not be ashamed.*" " Whosoever." Whatever man in all the world, throughout all the ages, shall come and trust himself on Christ shall never be ashamed of having done so. You, dear friend, down the aisle there, if you trust in Christ you shall never be ashamed of your hope. You, up there in the gallery, however guilty you may have been, or however moral you may have been, it matters not, if your one hope is in what Christ has done, you shall never turn round on your dying bed, and cry, " I made a mistake in trusting Christ." You know what Cardinal Bellarmine said : he was a great antagonist of Luther, and thought that we might trust in our works ; but, looking it all over, he admitted that inasmuch as no man could be quite sure that he had done enough good works, it was perhaps best on the whole and safest to trust altogether to the blood and merits of Jesus Christ. I have always felt obliged to the Cardinal for that admission ; because the best is good enough for me, and since trusting in Jesus is the safest, I intend to stick to it even to the end. There is really no other hope, for if you get a little bit of your own works put into the building of your hope, you have just so much rotten timber in the fabric, and that rot will plague the whole house, and turn it into dust at the last. No man that rested in Christ, and Christ alone, ever was ashamed of his hope; and none ever shall be. There is sure ground here. The Rock of Ages never fails.

What else does the Scripture say? It says that *no man is forbidden to believe;* "for there is no difference between the Jew and the Greek: for the same Lord over all is rich unto all that call upon him." There never was a sinner yet to whom God said, "You must not trust my Son": on the contrary, it is written, "Him that cometh to me I will in no wise cast out." What about the doctrine of election? I need not speak about it this morning: I believe it, and rejoice in it: but it is not at all contrary to this precious truth. Read this verse, "All that the Father giveth me shall come to me; and him that cometh to me I will in no wise cast out." Whoever will in the whole world believe in Christ may do so; he is neither too old or too young, or too rich, or too poor, or too wicked, or too moral; if he will but trust Christ he shall be saved, and he is fully allowed and permitted, yea, commanded to believe and live.

Once, again, *though your faith should only be strong enough to lead you to pray, yet it shall save you,* for "Whosoever shall call on the name of the Lord shall be saved." Suppose your faith cannot work miracles; never mind about miracles. Suppose you cannot walk on the sea, like Peter: never mind; you are not called to do it. Can your faith pray? Can it cry? Then call upon the Lord, and you shall be saved. Poor dear heart, if you can but trust Christ, even though the feeblest possible manifestation of it should be the only thing visible, namely, your calling upon God in prayer, it must and shall save you.

IV. Now, I hope I have put it plainly. I have tried my best; and so I close by bidding you hear WHAT EXPERIENCE SAITH. What does experience say about believing in Christ! Experience says, and we are some of us here to say it, that *it is the grandest way of living in the world.* I assure you that I daily find the value of living by faith. In hours of dire distress and great heaviness of spirit, of which I know enough, I prove the power of faith in Jesus. Ah, my Lord, what should I do then if I could not as "a poor sinner, and nothing at all" find Christ to be my "all in all." Fair-weather sailors, who go out in their little painted perfection boats, are people who have had small temptation and little soul-trouble. They are generally gentlemen in good health, with regular incomes and sweet tempers, and so they soon reach their imaginary sinlessness—vain creatures that they are; but you never get any of that among the poor, suffering, tried people of God. In stormy weather our beauty and glory soon turn pale; when the devil meets us face to face, he cracks up our tinsel perfection with a blow. He laughs at all our comeliness, he knows that it is a hollow cheat, a vile sham. In the moments when the soul is in the lowest depths, faith is the only way to live. That mode of living which will do for the depths is safe for the heights.

How blessed it is when a child of God has actually fallen into sin,— God keep us so that we never may,—but if guilt is on the soul, what is a poor creature to do? He can do nothing unless he has learned this precious truth, that he is nothing at all, and Jesus Christ is his all in all. Then he knows that Jesus will blot out his transgressions, and create in him a clean heart, and restore him to himself again, though now, like David, his sin is ever before him.

Yes, and I find a self-denying, Christ-exalting faith to be good in times of jubilation and success. The only way to keep right and humble is to be nothing, and let Jesus be all in all. If God has blessed your ministry or other holy work, the devil whispers, "You are a pretty fellow; you have done wonders"; and up you will go if you are not steadied by the firm conviction that you may not glory, since you are nothing at all in yourself, and your sole help is in Jesus your Lord. When God gives you growth in grace and fruitfulness in good works it will be your safety to be as little as ever you were, and to trust in nothing but the work of the Lord. This blessed faith keeps men down when they are apt to go up, and up when otherwise they would be apt to go down. It is a holy balancing pole: we can walk the narrowest line with this in our hands, and fear no fall. Ourselves nothing, Christ everything—that is it. Keep to it.

Now as to *the test of death*. Does this sort of faith enable men to face death with courage? I have had almost thirty years among you, and God has been very gracious to us, so that we have lost very few comparatively by death; but now many are going home, and, according to the course of nature, many of our honoured brethren and sisters will soon follow. As to those who have been called home, how have they died? I have the deep satisfaction of saying that when our dear brethren and sisters fall asleep they reflect honour upon the gospel which we have preached. Ask those who have seen them die. These dear ones at this hour look back upon me and say, "Go on: preach the same gospel to others; for we found it blessed truth to die upon." Look at our dear, departed brother, Mr. Higgs, the last who has crossed the stream. His sons and daughters will tell you that his death was sad to them, but not to him. He suffered agonizing pain, but his peace was as deep as the sea. He had no uncertainty; he was as sure of his safety as if it had been a matter of calculation by the rules of arithmetic. He knew whom he had believed, and knew what the Lord had done for him, and he could not see a weak point in it all. He spent the whole night in trying to cheer and comfort others: he had no trembling thought about himself. He did not say, "Have pity upon me, have pity upon me, O my friends, for the hand of the Lord hath touched me." No; he knew that Christ was the resurrection and the life, and he was ready to depart. He wished his beloved ones to go to their beds; and since they would stop with him, he desired them to sing." "What shall we sing?" "Sing" said he,—

> "For ever with the Lord,
> Amen, so let it be."

It is hard singing when your father is dying, but it was not hard to him. He bade them read that chapter, "Let not your hearts be troubled"; and, as they read it, he did not take the verses, and apply them to himself. No, he directed the comfort to his dear wife, for she

had greater need of it than he had : his faith was firm.   It was for her
he cared, and for those about him ; as for himself, all was rest.   One
said somewhat roughly to him a fortnight before, " Don't be down-
hearted ; you may get better yet."   " Stop a minute," said he.   " What
do you mean ?   I have never been down-hearted at anything in my
life ; certainly not at the thought of dying.   If it was the Lord's will
that I should die in the street at this moment, I would cheerfully go."
He never said a word more than he felt ; yet that was the style of man.
God send us more like him—men to whom religion is for home consumption.   Not a pretty toy for Sundays, but food to live upon ; a common-sense hope ; a blunt man's religion that he can carry into business.
One reported to me the other day a word which cheered me much.   An
Italian gentleman, who has known me since I have been at Mentone,
was asked, " Are you a Catholic ?"   " No, I am not."   " Are you a
Protestant ? "   " I am not sure, for I know little about it."   " What
are you ? "   " I am of Mr. Spurgeon's religion, which makes people
happy themselves, and causes them to do good to others."   I thank
God he could say that of my religion : it did this for my dear friend—
it made him a happy man, whose pleasure it was to please others : and
now he has passed away in full sunlight into a still brighter noon.
Amen, so let it be.

The top and bottom of the matter is, " Believe in the Lord Jesus
Christ."   Be nothing ; be nobody ; and trust HIM.   Do not believe in
yourself, but believe in Jesus.   Have as many good works as you can cram
into your life, but never tell anybody about them, or think anything
of them.   The best of them are but filthy rags : stow them all away in
the coal-hole, and look to the merits of your Lord for salvation.   Go to
Jesus for everything.   He says, " I counsel thee to buy of me gold
tried in the fire, that thou mayest be rich ; and white raiment, that thou
mayest be clothed."   Take his counsel.   As he whom we sorrow for to-
day could die peacefully, and even merrily, so shall you and I if we rely
on the same Saviour.   When our time comes to depart, we shall just
step aside and say, " Good-bye, dear friends, awhile : we will meet again
in the home of the blessed."   I hear *him* say so at this moment ; and
I answer him, " Dear brother, we will be with you speedily."

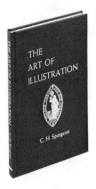

The Art of Illustration
$3.95. SBC rate, $2.65.

A volume of Addresses delivered to the student-
ministers of Spurgeon's school called The Pastor's
College. One doesn't read very far in any of his
books without recognizing Spurgeon as a master
in the use of illustrations. They seem always to
be at the tip of his tongue, just awaiting the signal
to illuminate a text or subject at the appropriate
moment. He thought of illustrations as windows
to let in the light. A very helpful index to the illustrations used in the book is provided, as well
as an index to Scriptures used.

GLADNESS FOR SADNESS.

A Sermon

DELIVERED ON LORD'S-DAY MORNING, JANUARY 14TH, 1883, BY

C. H. SPURGEON,

AT THE METROPOLITAN TABERNACLE, NEWINGTON.

"Make us glad according to the days wherein thou hast afflicted us, and the years wherein we have seen evil. Let thy work appear unto thy servants, and thy glory unto their children. And let the beauty of the Lord our God be upon us: and establish thou the work of our hands upon us; yea, the work of our hands establish thou it."—Psalm xc. 15—17.

To understand this psalm you must observe its black border. Remember the sorrows of Moses, the man of God, who saw a whole generation die in the wilderness, and was himself denied admission to the promised land. The man Moses was greatly afflicted; I might almost call him, as far as his life in the wilderness was concerned, "A man of sorrows, and acquainted with grief." He digged the desert till it became a cemetery, for he lived amid forty years of funerals. This Ninetieth Psalm is saturated with the griefs of a sentenced generation, by whom it could be truly said, "We are consumed by thine anger, and by thy wrath are we troubled." We have in our own case as a church and people a double black border to surround our text this morning; for death has despoiled us a second time. We were last Wednesday burying our honoured deacon, William Higgs, and at the moment of our meeting for that solemn purpose another greatly esteemed deacon, William Mills,* was on a sudden stricken down with paralysis, to linger for a few hours and then to breathe out his soul unto God. I shall not trust myself to speak about him, for this double loss has to a great extent unnerved me; but this I must say, that he was an experienced and mature Christian, and withal a quiet, diligent, loving, gracious servant of our common Master, whose care was the poor of the church, to whom he distributed our alms with discretion and tenderness. It was pleasant to hear from him the story of his Christian experience. His was a calm and lowly walk. Of late, being weakly, he was much at home, and there the Psalms of David, and the Morning and Evening Portions were his comfort. He was always a source of strength to his pastor and his brethren, always of great service to the church, far more so

---

* William Mills, Esq., for many years a beloved deacon of the church in the Metropolitan Tabernacle, was taken to his rest January 12th, 1883, at the age of sixty-two

than the mass of our people will ever know : but of late he ripened and mellowed into an unusual sweetness and spirituality. My last interview with him gave me a high idea of his thorough composure, and his perfect preparedness to commune with the glorified host above. He is gone—gone happily and safely home. He had no pain or struggle, but gradually melted into life eternal. To us who remain one sorrow has succeeded to another, to keep our wound bleeding and smarting. How well did Moses pray, "Return, O Lord, how long? and let it repent thee concerning thy servants." Oh that our God would no more put his hand into the bitter box, as Herbert calls it, but now change his dispensation and revive the spirit of his contrite ones. On our part, as we are made to sympathise with the man of God in this psalm, so let us imitate his example. Like him in multiplied bereavements, let us be like him in grace and faith.

Observe, that the first word of this painful psalm is, "Lord, thou hast been our dwelling place"; as if, touched by the rod, the sufferer remembered his Father. Will the hypocrite always call upon God? Nay, but when God dealeth roughly with him he will kick against the pricks. But the child of God when he is smitten turns to the hand that smote him, and cries, "Show me wherefore thou contendest with me?" If foxes and wolves are prowling about, and the shepherd's dog appears, they fly hither and thither as far away as they can ; but when the dog is sent after the sheep he fetches them back to the shepherd. Trouble drives away the carnal man from his pretended religion; but it gathers the true sheep together, and, being aroused and alarmed, they seek the Good Shepherd. The more of grief we feel the more of grace we need, and the nearer to our Comforter we come. Closer to God! is the cry of the troubled saint.

> "Nearer, my God, to thee!
> Nearer to thee!
> E'en though it be a cross
> That raiseth me ;
> Still all my cry shall be,
> Nearer, my God, to thee!
> Nearer to thee!"

Observe also that this psalm is "a prayer of Moses:" the comfort of a child of God in the darkness is prayer. Adversity, blessed of the Holy Spirit, calls our attention to the promise; the promise quickens our faith; faith betakes itself to prayer ; God hears and answers our cry. This is the chain of a tried soul's experience. Brethren, as we suffer the tribulation, as we know the promise, let us immediately exercise faith, and turn in prayer to God; for surely never did a man turn to God but the Lord also turned to him. If we are set a-praying we may depend upon it the Lord is set on blessing. Blessings are on the way from heaven—their shadow falls upon us even now. I desire at this time to stir you up to a joyful expectancy. These clouds mean rich, refreshing showers. These sharp frosts foretell heavy sheaves. The Lord by the divine Spirit make the words of our text to be our prayer this morning! May the Lord Jesus present our supplication to the Father.

The petition seems to me to be, first, for *proportionate gladness:* "Make us glad according to the days wherein thou hast afflicted us, and the years wherein we have seen evil." And, secondly, our prayer is for *peculiar gladness*, a gladness which is described in the sixteenth and seventeenth verses: "Let thy work appear unto thy servants, and thy glory unto their children. And let the beauty of the Lord our God be upon us: and establish thou the work of our hands upon us; yea, the work of our hands establish thou it."

I. First, then, beloved friends, our prayer this morning as a church and people should be for PROPORTIONATE GLADNESS ; that our God who has filled one scale with grief would fill the other scale with grace till they balance each other. Inasmuch as he has poured out of his vial certain drops of wormwood, we pray him to measure out the like quantity of the consolation of love, whereby our hearts shall be comforted. May our covenant God, who has chastened us heavily, now revive us graciously.

We begin here by noticing that evidently the prayer desires *a gladness of the same origin as the sadness*. The psalm plainly ascribes the sadness to the Lord : " *Thou* turnest man to destruction ; and sayest, Return, ye children of men." " We are consumed by *thine* anger, and by *thy* wrath are we troubled." God is seen in bereavements ; death comes distinctly at his command ; second causes are left behind. Since we have a distinct idea that the sadness comes from God, our text expresses an equally distinct desire that the gladness may come from God. We beg for divine comfort under divine chastening. The words of the prayer are eminently simple and childlike,—" Make us glad." They seem to say, " Father ! Thou hast made us sad; now make us glad ! Thou hast saddened us grievously ; now therefore, O Lord, most heartily rejoice us." The prayer as good as cries, " Lord, no one but thyself can make us glad under such affliction, but thou canst bring us up from the lowest deep. The wound goes too near the heart for any human physician to heal us; but thou canst heal us even to the making of us glad !"

The prayer is full of buoyant hope; for it does not merely say, " Comfort us ; bear us up ; keep our heads above water; prevent us from sinking in despair:" no ; but " Make us glad." Reverse our state: lift us up from the depths to the heights. "Make us glad!" I hear the music of hope drowning the discord of fear ; the songs of a joyous faith rising above the mournful dirges of grief.

The appeal is to the Lord alone. Moses entreats Jehovah himself to kindle the lamps of joy within the tabernacles of Israel. It is healthy sadness which the Lord sends, and it is equally safe gladness which God gives. If we make ourselves merry we may be mere mimics of mirth ; if outward goods make us merry we may be no better than the rich fool in the parable; but if our God makes us glad we may take our fill of delight, and fear no ill consequences. The wine of the Kingdom cheers, but never intoxicates: the bread of God strengthens, but never surfeits. Neither pride, nor worldliness, nor carelessness comes of feasting at the table of our God. Come, then, let us together breathe this prayer: "Make us glad!" Let us paraphrase the expression thus,— " Lord, thou art the maker of all things, make us glad! By thy word thou didst make the light ; make light for us ! Thou wilt new-make these worn-out skies and much-polluted earth ; come, then, and new-make us, and restore unto us the joy of thy salvation ! " The parallel lies much in the source to which both sadness and gladness are ascribed. Lord, make both our summers and our winters, our calms and our storms ; for everything is good which comes from thee, and it is our joy that our times are in thy hand.

But now notice that a *proportion is insisted upon :* " Make us glad according to the days wherein thou hast afflicted us, and the years wherein we have seen evil." This is an original prayer, full of thought and hope. Truly also it is a philosophical prayer ; one which is in accord-ance with the harmonies of nature, and consonant with all the ways of God. I have been told on the Scotch lakes that the depth of the lake is almost always the same as the height of the surrounding hills ; and I think I have heard that the same is true of the great ocean ; so that 'he greatest depth is probably the same as the greatest height. Doubtless, the law of equilibrium is manifest in a thousand ways. Take an instance in the adjustment of days and nights. A long night reigns over the north of Norway ; in these wintry months they do not even see the sun : but mark and admire their summer ; then the day banishes the night altogether, and you may read your Bible by the light of the midnight sun. Long wintry nights find compensation in a perpetual summer day. There is a balance about the conditions of the peoples of differing lands : each country has its drawbacks and its advantages. I believe it is so with the life of God's people : therein also the Lord maintains a balance. " As the sufferings of Christ abound in us, so our consolation also aboundeth by Christ." Some the great Father permits to be little in Israel ; they are none the less dear to him for that. Such are like the minnow which swims a pool proportioned to its size : no great tempest sweeps over the tiny streamlet, its ruffles and its calms suit its little inhabitants. Another of God's children is made for wide service ; he may be compared to leviathan, for whom ocean is prepared ; with billows, tempests, hurricanes, in due proportion. The great Architect draws everything to scale : while some lives are wisely arranged upon a small scale, others are fashioned for wider spheres and made to do business on the great waters ; these have greater tribulations, but they have also greater consolations. God knoweth how to manage for us all, and we have each one a place in his thoughts. Wisdom allots each one his talent and his work, his strength and his trial. What would a sparrow do with an eagle's wing ? Given the eagle's wing and the eagle's eye, there must be a soaring up above the Alps, a com-panionship with winds and lightnings. To the tiny humming-bird God appoints no flight into the upper air, but allots it flowers and sun-shine nearer the ground. He knows the way of his people, and his love is over all.

The good Lord measures out the dark and the light in due propor-tions, and the result is life sad enough to be safe, and glad enough to be desirable. I do not believe that our mortal life is fitly set forth by the Thane's parable, when he said to the Saxon king, " Hast thou marked, O king, when thou art sitting in thy hall, and the fires are lit, and the lamps are burning, how the sparrow comes flying out of the thick darkness, passes through the window, glides into the bright and cheerful light, and then flits out again into the darkness? Such is our life,—an interval of light amidst a long darkness." It is not so. If a believer flits out of the light he glides into the light again; if we traverse a stretch of darkness we may expect an equal breadth of brightness. If to-day we sail a stormy main we may hope to-morrow that the sea will be as glass. We have our changes, but the preponderance of life is not to misery. Rainy days are many, and yet in the long run they are outnumbered by the seasons of fair weather. God makes us glad according to the days wherein he has afflicted us, and the years wherein we have seen evil. It may not be said of God's children that we are a wretched company. Though truly, if in this life only we had hope we should be of all men most miserable; yet since that hope is sure we are of all men the most happy! We shall not say when life is ended here below that it was an evil thing to have lived. We have the promise of the life that now is as well as of that which is to come. "Happy art thou, O Israel," is for the present as well as for the future. God has blessed us, and we are blessed; and it is not for us to speak as if the blessing were in vain.

Now, if it be so, that our gladness and our sadness are balanced, let us accept them by turns with gratitude. Let us notice, further, that *sorrow is the herald of joy.* Did I not tell you but a few Sabbath-days ago how I sat in health and strength and joy in the olive-gardens, and said to my friend,—

> " We should expect some danger nigh
> When we perceive too much delight."

The apprehension was soon justified, as it has often been: but let us not forget the other side of this truth,—we may expect some mercy nigh when we are bowed with heaviest grief. Among the ashes of sorrow we shall find live coals of joy. Grief is God's usher of the black rod, sent to intimate that in the majesty of his grace the Lord is drawing near to us. There will be first to us, even as there was to Israel, the sound of Egypt's chariot-wheels and the cry of her horsemen, and a descent into the depths of the sea: and then shall come the far-resounding, never-forgotten shout of victory. The rage of Pharaoh, and the darkness of the night, and the march through the Red Sea must prepare the way for Miriam's timbrel and the loud refrain, " Sing unto the Lord, for he hath triumphed gloriously; the horse and his rider hath he thrown into the sea." Israel must make bricks without straw before Moses shall come. If I had been a little child among the Israelites I think I should have known, when father set the bitter herbs upon the table, that the lamb was roasting somewhere, and would be set out too. " With bitter herbs shall ye eat it "—and so, if there be bitter herbs, the dainty dish is near. Job did not know, and he cou.d not guess it; but in the light of Job's book we ought to know that the preparation for making a man twice as rich as he was before is to take away all that he has. Oftentimes, in building a bigger house, it is the way of wisdom to clear away the old building altogether. Keeping up the old structure is often an expensive economy; it is better to demolish it. Even so do I believe that the adversities of the saints are to their lasting profit, by removing that which would hinder greater prosperity.

Troubles come clothed in black; but to the eye of faith they carry silver trumpets, and they proclaim the approach of great mercies. God is hastening in the richness of his favour to bless his children : sorrow is the outrider of joy.

A step further, and we have it thus, *sorrow often prepares for joy.* It might not be safe, dear brother, that you should enjoy worldly prosperity at the outset of life. Your adversities in business are meant to teach you the worthlessness of earthly things, so that when you have them you may not be tempted to make idols of them. I am persuaded that many men have been ruined by rising suddenly to fame and power : had they at first been abused and trodden down like mire in the streets, their spirits might have been hardened to endure that sharpest of all tests, namely, human honour; for "as the fining pot for silver, and the furnace for gold; so is a man to his praise." You are not ready yet, dear brethren, to bear the weight of an elevated superstructure : you must be dug out first, and a deep foundation must be laid to bear a lofty building. In the spiritual life God does not run us up with glittering virtues all of a sudden; but deep prostration of spirit and thorough humiliation prepare the under-courses ; and then, afterwards, stone upon stone, as with rows of jewels, we are built up to be a palace for the indwelling of God. Sorrow furnishes the house for joy. The preparation for an eternal heaven is temporary affliction. Jesus has gone to prepare heaven for us ; but he has left his cross behind him that the Holy Spirit may by its means prepare us for heaven. You could not enjoy the rest of Paradise if you had not first known the labours of pilgrimage ; you could not understand the boundless felicity of heaven if your hearts had not been enlarged by the endurance of tribulation. Let not this be forgotten, then,—that our troubles build a house and spread a table for our joys. Did you ever read of a Roman triumph ? Have you ever stood upon the Via Sacra which led up to the Capitol ? There, when the glad day was come, the people crowded all along the road : every house-roof was loaded, the very chimney-tops bore each a man, while along the sacred way the conqueror rode, drawn by white horses, amid the blast of trumpets, and the thundering acclamations of myriads. What glory ! What renown ! Rome's millions did their best to crown their hero. But there had been to him full many a battle before that hour of pride. Victory needs conflict as its preface. The conqueror's scars are his truest decorations, his wounds his best certificates of valour. Because he had been smothered with the dust and defiled with the blood of battle, therefore the hero stood erect, and all men paid him reverence. It must be so in the present condition of things ; no man can wear the garland till he has first contended for it.

"Sure we must fight if we would reign ;
Increase our courage, Lord."

The way to the crown is by the cross : the palm branch cometh not to the idle hand.

"The path of sorrow, and that path alone,
Leads to the place where sorrow is unknown."

Once again, let me say to you, dear friends, there is such a connection between sorrow and joy that *no saint ever has a sorrow but what it has a joy wrapped up in it.* It is a rough oyster, but a pearl lies within those shells if you will but look for it. Do not think I mock at grief by saying that it is the husk of joy : far from it, I would console grief by asserting solemnly that within the black envelope of affliction there is a precious love-token from God : be sure of that. We find the treasure of communion with Christ in the earthen vessel of sorrow. We ask to have fellowship with Jesus in his sufferings; and we cannot do so except we suffer. It is a joy to remember in our woe that by these things we are made like unto our Lord, and conformed unto his image. If there were only this comfort it might suffice to sweeten every suffering.

Beside this, there is generally with sorrow a manifestation of the Lord amid our weakness. I have known many forms of happiness ; but I think, upon the whole, I do consider the purest and sweetest to be that of fainting in weakness upon the breast of Jesus and dying into his life. " Oh to be nothing, nothing, only to lie at his feet ! " To be as a lily broken off at the stalk, and therefore taken up into his hand. This is unutterable happiness. The Lord's love to his poor and afflicted ones is most choice and tender. " He carrieth the lambs in his bosom." Favoured feebleness to be thus laid in the heaven of Jesus's bosom ! I love to cower down under the divine wings like a chick under the hen, finding myself by losing myself in God. I have found it precious to feel that no more strength is left to suffer with, and therefore I must die away into the divine will. Certain is it that in every tribulation there are consolations, even as every night has its own stars. I am sure, dear brothers and sisters, you that grieve most to-day for the departed possess a joy which outweighs your mourning : it is a great sorrow to lose a father, but it is a greater joy to know that your father is not really lost, but translated to the skies. It is a great grief to part with a true brother and fellow labourer, but it is happiness to know that he is promoted to the peerage of the skies. We might each one say of our departed friend, " Let us go, that we may die with him." These good men have the start of us : they are preferred before us : they have first seen the King in his beauty. One of them at least has reached his reward before his spiritual father: he who is my joy and crown is in heaven before me. Verily, there are first that shall be last. Our hold on the invisible is strengthened by the departure of our brethren. We have more in heaven to love, more fraternal meetings to anticipate ; and so we have new links with the eternal. Said I not truly that every sorrow contains a joy ?

Once more, *the day will come when all the sorrows of God's sending will be looked upon as joys.* Hear ye this! By some strange alchemy, known only to " the King eternal, immortal, invisible," our sorrows shall be turned into joys. Ye see this in your own homes,—I quote it because it is the Lord's own metaphor,—a woman when she is in travail hath sorrow because her hour is come; but soon she remembereth no more her travail, for joy that a man is born into the world. Our troubles and travails are sharp, but they will all be forgotten in the joy that will come of them. Before we enter heaven we shall thank God for most of our sorrow ; and when we are once in glory we shall thank him for it all. Perhaps in heaven, among all the things which have happened to us that will excite our wonder and delight, our furnace experience, and the hammer and the file, will take the lead. Sorrow will contribute rich stanzas to our everlasting psalm. Wherefore comfort one another with these words, and breathe the prayer each one to-day, "Make us glad according to the days wherein thou hast afflicted us, and the years wherein we have seen evil." In each case may divine love weigh out the ingredients of a sanctified life according to the art of the apothecary, each one in due proportion.

II. Bear with me while I come to the second part of my subject, which I desire to make eminently practical. The gladness desired is also described : it is PECULIAR GLADNESS. The Psalmist wishes for a fourfold gladness :—the first is *gladness at the sight of God's work.*

Notice ; "THY work." There is always something cheering in God's work. Have you never felt it so? I think you must have done so. When Mungo Park was cheered by that little bit of moss which he picked up in the wilderness, he was but comforted as many of us have been. The flowers of the garden, the wild beauties of the wood, the chance tufts by the roadside, are all God's work, and, therefore, breathe consolation to God's servants. Nature is kindly ; her stars speak light to our hearts; her winds chase away our gloom; and her waves flash with health for us. Nature is a fond foster-mother to the Lord's children, because she is like ourselves, the work of the Lord. When we are in deep tribulation it is a sweet quietus to survey the handiwork of our Father in Heaven. His work in providence, also, is often a consolation to us. Let us but see what God has done for his people and for ourselves in years past, and we are cheered. Trouble itself, when we see it to be God's work, has lost its terror. A certain Persian nobleman found himself surrounded by soldiers, who sought to take him prisoner ; he drew his sword and fought right valiantly, and might have escaped had not one of the company said, "The king has sent us to convey you to himself." He sheathed his sword at once. Yes, we can contend against what we call a misfortune ; but when we learn that the Lord hath done it, our contest is ended, for we joy and rejoice in what the Lord doeth ; or, if we cannot get the length of rejoicing in it, we acquiesce in his will. This is our song :—

> "I would not contend with thy will,
> Whatever that will may decree ;
> But oh, may each trial I feel
> Unite me more fondly to thee."

Brethren, the great comfort which this church wants now is to see God's work in the midst of her revived and glorified. If the Lord will but come among us and save men, and if he will build up and edify his people, and give them help to accomplish their holy service—this will be our richest possible comfort : "Let thy work appear unto thy servants." Lord, our brethren fade away, they go into the shadow land, we see them no more ; but, oh, if we can see thy hand at work among us we shall not be discouraged ! We mourn the loss of our brother's work ; but we will not be disheartened if we see thy work. May the Lord make you to see his work on your own hearts, dear brethren and sisters ; may he make you to see his work in the congregation, in the Sunday-school, and everywhere throughout the world, bringing men to himself; and you will find therein a sovereign balm for all your wounds.

The next consolation is also a very rich one—*gladness at the revelation of God to our children ;—*" and thy glory unto their children." If our God will but make his glory to be seen by our children, what more can we ask ? " I have no greater joy than this, that my children walk in the truth." No better comfort can be found for bereaved mothers than to see their sons and daughters converted. There is a sorrow for those who have departed ; but I could almost say, " Weep not for the dead, neither bewail them,"—for there is a sharper grief by far, and that is our anxiety for those who survive, and yet are dead unto God. Did you ever see a chain-gang of convicts marching to their labour ? I could wish never to see the sad scene again. Suppose that among those convicts there was a boy of yours ! Ah me ! Ah me ! it were better for you that he had never been born. But think of those who are prisoners in the chains of sin. Is there a boy or girl of yours in such bonds ? Oh, then, I am sure you will pray the Lord to rescue you from so sharp a trial, and to set your sons and daughters free from the fetters of iniquity. Pray ye each one fervently, " O Lord, let thy glory as their emancipator appear to my children, and then do what thou wilt." Did you ever visit a condemned cell ? To peep through the gate and to see a man sitting there condemned to die is enough to make one faint. Suppose it were your boy ! Suppose it were your husband ! Suppose it were your brother ! But listen : " He that believeth not is condemned already." Pardon us, dear unconverted relatives, if we say that we feel more sorrow for you living than we do for our gracious ones who are dead ; for yours is a terrible plight, to be even now sitting in the condemned cell, doomed to be taken out to execution before long unless infinite mercy shall grant a free pardon. What dreadful sights must meet the eye upon a battle-field. If I see a man bleeding by a common cut my heart is in my mouth, and I cannot bear the sight : but what must it be to see men dismembered, disembowelled, writhing to and fro in the last agonies of death ! What horror to walk among mounds of dead bodies, and stumble at each step over a human corpse ! Yet, what is natural death compared with spiritual death ? What terror to dwell in the same house with relatives who are dead while they live,—dead unto God. The thought is full of anguish. If God will quicken our spiritually dead ; if he will give life to those who are " free among the slain, as they that go down into the pit," what a consolation we shall find therein ! Did you see that alarming fire the other day ? Did you hear of the hotel in flames, wherein there were many guests, and they were in the upper story, and the flames had grasped the whole edifice, so that numbers perished ? It must be dreadful to see persons at the upper windows of a burning house, and to be powerless to rescue them. But if your child were there, your boy, your girl, or if your husband or your wife were there, or even if anyone you knew were there, your grief would have a double sting about it, and you would cry, " Lord, do what thou wilt with me, but do save those precious lives." Remember, then, that your ungodly friends are in a like condition, and what greater mercy can God bestow upon you than for him to make his glory to be seen by your children in their eternal salvation ?

Therefore I turn your thoughts to that prayer. May you breathe

it now, and may the Lord, for Christ's sake, answer it right speedily,—
" Let thy glory appear unto our children."

The third consolation which Moses here describes is *gladness at beauty bestowed*—" Let the beauty of the Lord our God be upon us." Sorrow mars the countenance and clothes the body with sackcloth ; but if the Lord will come to us and adorn us with his beauty, then the stains of mourning will speedily disappear. Brethren, what a beauty is this which the Lord giveth—" the beauty of the Lord our God!" This comeliness is the beauty of his grace ; for our covenant God is the God of all grace. If the Lord makes us to know that we are his our faces shine. If he fills us with his life and love, then brightness flashes from the eyes, and there is a grace about every movement.

This " beauty" means holiness ; for holiness is the beauty of God. If the Holy Spirit works in you the beauty of holiness, you will rise superior to your afflictions. If this church shall be made the holier by its bereavements, we shall gain much by our losses.

This beauty of the Lord must surely mean his presence with us. As the sun beautifies all things, so does God's presence. When we know that Jesus is with us, when we feel that he is our helper, when we bask in his love, when he abides with us in power, this is the beauty of the saints. If we have Christ in us, Christ with us, we can bear any amount of trouble.

> "I can do all things, or can bear
> All suffering if my Lord be there."

This beauty gives to the believer an attractiveness in the eyes of men : they perceive that we have been with Jesus, and they behold our faces shining like the faces of angels. It is a great thing when a Christian is so happy, so holy, and so heavenly that he attracts others to Christ. and people seek his company because they perceive that he has been in the company of the blessed Lord. God give you this, and if you have it, dear friend, you may forget your sorrows : they are transfigured into joy.

The last comfort that Moses speaks of is *gladness at our own work being established*—" Establish thou the work of our hands upon us ; yea, the work of our hands establish thou it." Do you notice the wonderful blending in the fifteenth and seventeenth verses : there it is, " Let *thy* work appear unto thy servant ;" here it is " Let *our* work be established." Alas, I have heard divines rightly say that salvation is God's work, and then they have harshly added that, in our preaching of the gospel, we make it out to be our own work. Thus they speak hard things against us, and their speech is not after the Lord's mind. Others, again, make out this work to be so much man's work that God is forgotten. Neither of these is correct : we must blend the two : to build up the church and win souls for Jesus is first of all God's work, and then our work. Why should a Christian work to win souls ? Answer : because God works in him to win souls. Remember the verses,—" Work out your own salvation with fear and trembling." Why ? " For it is God that worketh in you to will and to do of his good pleasure." God works to set us working : our work is the result of his work.

Our work is often a very effectual means of comfort to us. On the battle-field of Gettysburg there had been a terrible fight, and among the wounded lay a certain chaplain of the name of Eastman who had been seriously injured in the back by his horse falling upon him. The dark and dreary night came on, and as he lay there in intense pain, unable to rise, he heard a voice at a little distance cry, "O God!" His interest was excited, and he rolled himself over and over through pools of blood, and among the slain, till he reached the side of the dying man, and there lay, talking of Jesus and his free salvation. The man expired in hope, and just then two soldiers came and told Eastman that a captain was dying a little further down the field, and they must carry him there: so he was borne in anguish upon the work of mercy, and while the night wore on he spoke of Jesus to many dying men. Could he have had a surer relief from his pain? I think not. Why, it seems to me that to lie there on his back with nothing to do but moan and groan would have been horrible: but in all his pain and anguish to be carried about to proclaim mercy to dying men made the anguish of an injured back endurable! So is it when you miss a friend, or have lost property, or are heavy in spirit, you shall find your surest comfort in serving God with all your might.

The text prays for our work *that it may succeed:* "Establish thou the work of our hands." Oh, if God will but prosper us in our work for him how happy we shall be! One day this week I had a great lift up out of deep distress when I was informed that a captain was here last Sunday morning, and was so impressed that he found the Saviour, and made the fact known at one of the noonday prayer-meetings, asking for himself that he might be kept faithful to his God. This is good. We do not always see our seed grow so quickly as that. It is wet weather just now, the damp of sorrow is on all things, and so the seed sown in tears is speedily reaped in joy. Is not this something to comfort us? Let us pray God to send us more of it, that by conversions our work may prosper.

Then we pray that our *work may be lasting,*—that is the chief point. I look forward to the future of this church with prayerful, hopeful anxiety! I am not old, not very old at any rate; but I am not all that I was in my earlier days, and mistrust whispers that soon things will decline. The other day a certain great preacher said that after a preacher had been for a while in a place all the heroism, all the earnestness, all the fervour which characterizes new efforts would be gone, and the best thing would be to disband the church, and let them begin again under a new leader. That may look like a practical idea; but I do not quite see it; nor does it commend itself to me as sound and true. If a church is man's work it is dependent upon a man, and when he is gone the best thing we can do with it is to let it dissolve; but I desire to see built up on this spot, by God's hand, a church which will endure till the coming of the Lord. Though dear ones, who seemed to be pillars, are taken away, the Lord will find other pillars; and though just now there are breaches in Zion's wall here and there, yet the wall shall again be repaired, and not a broken place shall remain. If we may see this accomplished we shall be abundantly comforted. "Establish thou the work of our hands upon us; yea, the work of our hands establish thou it." We belong to an established church; established, not by men, but by the Lord. This church will flourish when you and I have passed into our rest. Meanwhile, I beg you to take a deep interest in it, and do all you can for its prosperity. Make it more and more the model of what a church of Christ should be. I long that the truth which I have preached may be established in the earth. They say that Calvinism is at a great discount now : perhaps it is. Yet to me it seems that its free grace spirit is far more spread than ever, and is quietly saturating all true evangelical preaching. If it be so, that the doctrines of grace are now despised, we still hope that we shall live to see them brought to the front again, or, if not, we shall leave behind us such a testimony that in years to come the gospel of the grace of God will be read by thousands.

At this time I beg for the loving help of you all, for the church itself. Our institutions deserve your zeal, and liberality, and prayerfulness ; but do not forget the old house at home, the mother of these efforts. The church itself needs your love, your prayers, your help, your sustenance. I say this to you, my dear friends, who have been with me long—be you this day what you were at first ; be as knit together and as earnest as you were when you had a boy preacher to lead you, and you loved him and helped him to do good service for the Lord. For nearly thirty years God has been with us ; let us begin again from this date and see if we cannot complete the thirty years of blessing, and, if the Lord permits us, let us add another twenty years to it, and make up half-a-century of prosperity. Who knows ? Only let us carefully watch the present and see that nothing declines. Let each one be eager to keep the sacred cause in a healthy condition. God will establish his work upon us from day to day, and this shall be our comfort. Keep everything in the best possible working order. Plead with the Holy Spirit to clothe us with his power. Maintain all forms of holy labour vigorously, and sustain every fund by your spontaneous liberality. Never need pressing, but let each one enquire, " What can I do to keep the church well supplied to God's glory?" I believe this is the way to church comfort. God will comfort Zion, he will comfort all her waste places ; but we must each one take pleasure in her stones, and favour the dust thereof. Close up your ranks. Leave no empty spaces. Let every man stand closer to his fellow : and then " *Forward!*" Forward to a fuller consecration and a braver faith in God. Forward to more grace and higher holiness ; so shall we wipe away our tears, and praise the name of the Lord ; and he will remember us, and by a plenitude of blessing make up to us all that we have lost. A blessing is coming! Be ready for it! Amen.

PORTION OF SCRIPTURE READ BEFORE SERMON—Psalm xc.

HYMNS FROM " OUR OWN HYMN BOOK "—92 (Part I), 73 (Part III), 71 (Part I).

ON LAYING FOUNDATIONS.

A Sermon

DELIVERED ON LORD'S-DAY MORNING, JANUARY 21ST, 1883, BY

C. H. SPURGEON,

AT THE METROPOLITAN TABERNACLE, NEWINGTON.

"And why call ye me, Lord, Lord, and do not the things which I say? Whosoever cometh to me, and heareth my sayings, and doeth them, I will shew you to whom he is like: He is like a man which built an house, and digged deep, and laid the foundation on a rock: and when the flood arose, the stream beat vehemently upon that house, and could not shake it: for it was founded upon a rock. But he that heareth, and doeth not, is like a man that without a foundation built an house upon the earth; against which the stream did beat vehemently, and immediately it fell; and the ruin of that house was great."—Luke vi. 46—49.

THESE parables describe two classes of hearers; but they say nothing of those who are not hearers. Their position and prospects we must infer from what is said of hearers. Our Lord Jesus Christ has come into the world to tell us of the Father's love, and never man spake as he spake, and yet there are many who refuse to hear him. I do not mean those who are far away, to whom the name of Jesus is well-nigh unknown, but I mean persons in this land, and especially in this great and highly-favoured city, who wilfully refuse to hear him whom God has anointed to bring tidings of salvation. Our Lord Jesus is proclaimed, I was about to say, upon the house-tops in this city; for even in their music-halls and theatres Christ is preached to the multitude, and at the corners of our streets his banner is lifted up; and yet there are tens of thousands to whom the preaching of the gospel is as music in the ears of a corpse. They shut their ears and will not hear, though the testimony be concerning God's own Son, and life eternal, and the way to escape from everlasting wrath. To their own best interests, to their eternal benefit, men are dead: nothing will secure their attention to their God. To what, then, are these men like? They may fitly be compared to the man who built no house whatever, and remained homeless by day and shelterless by night. When worldly trouble comes like a storm those persons who will not hear the words of Jesus have no consolation to cheer them; when sickness comes they have no joy of heart to sustain them under its pains; and when death, that most terrible of storms, beats upon them they feel its full fury, but they cannot find a hiding place. They neglect the housing of their souls, and when the hurricane of almighty wrath shall break forth in the world to come they will have no place of refuge. In vain will they call upon the rocks to fall upon them, and the mountains to cover them. They shall be in that day without a shelter from the righteous wrath of the Most High. Alas, that any being who wears the image of man should be found in such a plight! Homeless wanderers in the day of tempest! How my soul grieves for them ! Yet, what excuse will those men invent who have refused even to know the way of salvation? What excuse can the tenderest heart make for them? Will they plead that they could not believe? Yet they may not say that they could not hear ; and faith cometh by hearing, and hearing by the word of God. Oh my friend, if the word of God comes to you, and you decline to hear it, and therefore do not believe in Jesus, but die in your sins, what is this but soul-suicide? If a man die of a disease when infallible medicine is to be had, must not his death lie at his own door? If a man perish of hunger when bread is all around him and others feed to the full, and he will not have it, will any man pity him? Surely not a drop of pity will be yielded to a lost soul wherewith he may assuage the torment of his conscience, for all holy intelligences will perceive that the sinner chose his own destruction. This shall ever press upon the condemned conscience, " You knew the gospel, but you did not attend to it : you knew that there was salvation, and that Christ was the Saviour, and that pardon was proclaimed to guilty men, but you would not afford time from your farm and from your merchandise, from your pleasures and from your sins, to learn how you could be saved. That which cost God so dear you treated as a trifle. Ah, my dear friends, may none of you belong to the non-hearing class. It is not to such that I shall this morning address myself, and yet I could not enter upon my discourse without a word of loving expostulation with them. Let me part with them by quoting the warning word of the Holy Spirit, " See that ye refuse not him that speaketh. For if they escaped not who refused him that spake on earth, much more shall not we escape, if we turn away from him that speaketh from heaven."

Our earnest attention will now be given to those who are hearers of the word, and are somewhat affected by it. All hearers are builders of houses for their souls : they are each one doing something to set up a spiritual habitation. Some of these go a considerable distance in this house-building, and even crown the structure by publicly confessing Christ. They say unto him, " Lord, Lord ": they meet with his followers, and join with them in reverence to the Master's name ; but they do not obey the Lord ; they hear him, but they fail to do the things which he says. Hence they are mistaken builders, who fail in the foundation, and make nothing sure except that their house will come down about their ears. Others there are, and we trust they will be found to be many among us, who are building rightly, building for eternity ; constructing a dwelling-place with basis of rock, and walls of well-built stone, of which the Lord Christ is both foundation and corner-stone.

I am anxious to speak at this time to those who are just beginning to build for eternity. I am indeed happy to know that there are many such among us. May the Holy Spirit bless this sermon to them.

I.   Our first subject will be A COMMON TEMPTATION WITH SPIRITUAL BUILDERS. A common temptation with hearers of the word, according to the two parables before us, is to neglect foundation-work, to get hurriedly over the first part of the business, and run up the building quickly. They are tempted to assume that all is done which is said to be done; to take it for granted that all is right which is hoped to be right; and then to go on piling up the walls as rapidly as possible. The great temptation, I say, with young beginners in religious life, is to scamp the foundation, and treat those things lightly which are of the first importance. The same temptation comes to us throughout the whole of life, but to young beginners it is especially perilous: Satan would have them neglect the fundamental principles upon which their future hope and character are to rest, so that in a future trying hour, from want of a solid foundation, they may yield to evil, and lose the whole of their life-building.

This temptation is all the more dangerous, first, because *these young beginners have no experience.* Even the most experienced child of God is often deceived; how much more the pilgrim who has but just entered the wicket-gate! The tried saint sometimes mistakes that for a virtue which is only a gilded fault, and he fancies that to be genuine which is mere counterfeit; how, then, without any experience whatever, can the mere babe in grace escape deception unless he be graciously preserved? Newly awakened, and rendered serious, earnest hearts get to work in the divine life with much hurry, seizing upon that which first comes to hand, building in heedless haste, without due care and examination. Something must be done, and they do it without asking whether it is according to the teaching of the Lord. They call Jesus "Lord"; but they do what others say rather than what Jesus says. Satan is sure to be at hand at such times that he may lead the young convert to lay in place of gospel repentance a repentance that needs to be repented of, and instead of the faith of God's elect a proud presumption or an idle dream. For that love of God which is the work of the Spirit of God he brings mere natural affection for a minister; and he says, "There, that will do: you must have a house for your soul to dwell in. There are the materials, pile them up." Like children at play upon the beach, the anxious heap up their sand-castles, and please themselves therewith, for they are ignorant of Satan's devices. I am for this cause doubly anxious to save my beloved young friends from the deceiver. The common temptation is, instead of really repenting, to *talk about* repentance; instead of heartily believing, to *say,* "I believe," without believing; instead of truly loving, to talk of love, without loving; instead of coming to Christ, to speak about coming to Christ, and profess to come to Christ, and yet not to come at all. The character of Talkative in Pilgrim's Progress is ably drawn. I have met the gentleman many times, and can bear witness that John Bunyan was a photographer before photography was invented. Christian said of him "He talketh of prayer, of repentance, of faith, and of the new birth; but he knows but only to *talk* of them. I have been in his family, and his house is as empty of religion as the white of an egg is of savour." We have too many such persons around us who are, as to what they say, everything that is to be desired, and yet, by what they are proven to be, mere shams. As tradesmen place dummies in their shops, papered and labelled to look like goods, while yet they are nothing of the sort, so are these men marked and labelled as Christians, but the grace of God is not in them. Oh that you young beginners **may** be on the alert, that you be not content with the form of godliness, but are made to feel the power of it.

There is this to help the temptation too, that *this plan for the present saves a great deal of trouble.* Your mind is distressed, and you want comfort; well, it will comfort you to say, " Lord, Lord," though you do not the things that Christ says. If you admit the claims of Jesus to be Lord, even though you do not believe on him for salvation, and so neglect the main thing which he commands, yet you will find some ease in the admission. He bids you repent of sin, trust his blood, love his word, and seek after holiness; but it is much easier to admire these things without following after them in your life. To feign repentance and faith is not difficult, but genuine godliness is heart-work, and requires thought, care, sincerity, prayerfulness, and watchfulness. Believe me, real religion is no sport. He that would be saved will find it to be no jesting matter. "The kingdom of heaven suffereth violence "; and he that is easy about the thing, and thinks it is nothing more than the conjuror's "Heigh, presto, done," has made a fatal mistake. "Strive," saith Christ, "to enter into the strait gate." The Spirit striveth in us mightily, and often works us to an agony. The crown of eternal glory is not won without fighting, nor the prize of our high calling received without running; yet by just making a holy profession, and by practising an outward form, a man imagines that the same result is produced as by seeking the Lord with his whole heart, and believing in the Lord Jesus. If it were so, there would be a fine broad road to heaven, and Satan himself would turn pilgrim. Believe me, dear hearers, this saving of trouble will turn out to be a making of trouble, and, before matters end, the hardest way will turn out to be the easiest way.

This kind of building without foundation has this advantage to back up the temptation,—*it enables a man to run up a religion very quickly.* He makes splendid progress. While the anxious heart is searching after truth in the inward parts, and begging to be renewed by grace, his exulting friend is as happy as he can be in a peace which he has suddenly obtained without question or examination. This rapid grower never asks, " Has my religion changed my conduct? Is my faith attended by a new nature? Does the Spirit of God dwell in me? Am I really what I profess to be, or am I but a bastard professor after all?" No, he puts aside all enquiry as a temptation of the devil. He takes every good thing for granted, and votes that all is gold which glitters. See how fast he goes! The fog is dense, but he steams through it, heedless of danger! He has joined the church: he has commenced work for God: he is boasting of his own attainments: he hints that he is perfect. But is this mushroom building safe? Will it pass muster in the last great survey? Will it stand should a tempest happen? The chimney-shaft is tall, but is it safe? Ay, there's the rub. This is the question which makes an end of much of the boasting which is all around us. It is better to tremble at God's word than boldly to presume. It is better to be fearful, lest after all we may be castaways, than to harden one's forehead with vain confidence. When a man travels upon a wrong road, the faster he runs the further he will go astray. Remember the advice to hasten slowly, and the old proverb which saith, "The more haste the less speed." If you build quickly because you build without a foundation, your time and toil are thrown away.

How common, how deceptive is this temptation! For the young beginner, the man who is just aroused to seek the Lord, will find *a great many to help him in his mistake*, should he neglect the foundation. Kind, good, Christian friends often, without a thought of doing so, help to mislead seeking souls. "Yes," they say, "you are converted," and so perhaps the person would be if all he said was true; but then it is said without feeling; it comes from the lip only, and does not come from the heart; and therefore it is ruinous to encourage him. A kindly assurance from a Christian friend may breed false confidence, if that assurance was mistakenly given. In these days we do not meet with many Christians who err by dealing too severely with converts; the shot strikes the other target. Our forefathers were possibly too suspicious and jealous; but nowadays we nearly all err in the opposite direction : we are so anxious to see everybody brought to Christ, that our wish may tend to delude us into the belief that it is so. We are so willing to cheer and comfort those who seek the Lord, that we may fall into the habit of prophesying smooth things, and thus shun everything which tends to probe and test, lest it should also discourage. Let us beware lest we cry, "Peace, peace," where there is no peace. It will be a sad thing to breed hypocrites when we were looking for converts. I have heard of one who had been into the Enquiry Room a dozen times, and when on another occasion she was invited to go there she said, "I really do not know why I should go, for I have been told that I was saved twelve times already, and I am not a bit better than before they told me so." It would be better to send some home weeping rather than rejoicing. Many a wound needs the lancet more than the plaster. You may be comforted by well-meant assurances of tender friends, and yet that comfort may be all a lie. I therefore warn you against any peace except that which comes from doing that which Jesus commands, or in other words, against any confidence except that which rests in Jesus only, and is attended with repentance, faith, and a life of obedience to your Lord.

No doubt many are encouraged in slight building by the fact that *so many professors are making a fair show, and yet their building is without foundation.* We cannot shut our eyes to the fact that in all churches there are persons who have no depth of spiritual root, and we are afraid no real spiritual life. We cannot root them up, though we fear that they are tares, for we are assured that we should unavoidably root up the wheat with them, and this our Master forbids. There is nothing about their outward conduct which we could lay hold upon as a proof of their being deceivers, and yet a cold chill runs through us when we talk with them, for they have no warmth, and no life, and nothing of the Lord about them. We miss in their conversation that sweet spirituality, that holy unction, that blessed humility, which are sure to be present when men are truly familiar with the Lord, and have entered into living union with him. People of this order mix up with us in our holy convocations, and when they come across the newly-awakened ones, they talk of divine things in such an off-hand and flippant manner that they do serious mischief.   They speak about conversion as if it were a mere trifle, a matter as easy as kissing your hand ; and so those who are hopeful, and over whom our hearts are yearning, are turned aside by them.   Young people are apt to think, " So-and-so is a member of the church, and he is never very precise.   If a lukewarm profession satisfies him, why should it not satisfy me !"   Ah, my dear friends, but you would not say so in business.   If you knew a man was trading without capital and likely to come to bankruptcy, you would not say, " I may do the same."   If you saw a man venturing into deep water who could not swim, and you felt sure that he would ultimately sink, you would not follow his example and be drowned too.   No, no ; let these frothy professors be beacons to you.   Get away from Mr. Talkative, lest he make you as hollow a drum as himself.   Beware of loose professors, who are as wreckers' lights that lure men upon the rocks. Make sure work for eternity, and bid triflers begone.

Again, there is always at the back of all this an inducement to build without a foundation because *it will not be known, and possibly may not be found out for years.*   Foundation-work is quite out of sight, and the house can be got up and be very useful in a great many ways, and it may stand a good while without the underground work ; for houses without foundations do not tumble down at once ; they will stand for years ; nobody knows how long they may keep up ; perhaps they may even be inhabited with comfort till the last great flood.   Death alone will discover some impostures.   Hence, because the ill-founded house will do for the present, and can be used, and may bring immediate comfort, many people consider it economical to leave out the foundation as a needless superfluity.   If they are questioned as to their vital godliness they grow angry :—" What business have you to enter into my private business ?   Why should you meddle with the secrets of my soul?" Ah, dear friend, if we were cruel to you, and wished you to be deceived, we would hold our tongues, or speak to you with the voice of flattery ; but as we love you, and as we hope to be blessed in years to come through your true and holy consecration to Christ, we are intensely earnest that you should begin aright.   We would have you build that which will not need to be pulled down again, work that will stand when the waters are out and the stream beats vehemently upon it.   I dread that any man should perish without religion, but I dread far more that any man should perish with it, finding his faith to have been false after all.   If you do build, build what is worth building : if you must be builders for your souls, and surely you must, or else be shelterless, then take heed on what foundation you build, and be careful what ye build thereon, lest after all you suffer the loss of all your labour in that last tremendous day.   How sad it will seem to dwell near the gates of heaven, and spend your lives among those who are to be its future inhabitants, and then for want of sincerity and truth to be shut out of the celestial city.   How terrible to find out by experience that there is a back way to the gates of hell even from the gates of heaven.   God grant it be not so with one of us here present.   O ye builders, care not merely for the present, but build for death, and judgment, and eternity !

This part of our discourse is not only for young people, but for us all— for old as well as young.   Depend upon it, there is not one man among us but what has need to search himself, and see whether the foundation of his faith has been truly laid or no.

II. So I advance to the second step, and there we will consider A WISE PRECAUTION WHICH SAFE BUILDERS NEVER FORGET. They dig deep, and never rest till they get a good substantial foundation : they are glad to get to the bottom of all the loose earth and to build on the rock. Let me commend this wise precaution to all of you.

Follow the text and learn to see to your *sincerity*. The Lord Jesus says " Why call ye me, Lord, Lord, and do not the things which I say ? " May the Holy Ghost make you true to the core. Be afraid to say a word more than you feel. Never permit yourself to speak as if you had an experience of which you have only read. Let not your outward worship go a step beyond the inward emotion of your soul. If Christ be truly your Lord you will obey him : if he be not your Lord do not call him so. It is a great point in all your religious thoughts, beliefs, words, and acts to have the heart moving in all. It is an awful thing to make a high profession of sanctity, and yet live in the indulgence of secret vice : such persons will listen to my observation and commend me for my faithfulness, and yet continue in their hypocrisy. This is most painful. These men can speak the Jew's language, and yet the tongue of Babylon is more natural to them : they follow Christ, but their hearts are with Belial. Ah, me ! My soul is sick at the thought of them. Be true ! Be true ! If truth will carry you no further than despair, better that you stop in despair than gain a hope by a lie. Do not live on fiction, profession, presumption. Eat ye that which is good, and feed only upon the truth. Remember that when you build with the wood, hay, and stubble of mere notion you are only gathering materials for your own funeral pile in that day when the fire shall devour all lovers and makers of a lie. Be true as steel ! Every wise builder for his soul must mind that.

The next thing is *thoroughness*. For observe, according to our Lord, the wise builder digged deep. You cannot do a right thing too well. Dig deep if you do dig a foundation. If it be repentance, let it be an intensely earnest repentance, including a vehement hatred of every form of sin. If you make confession before God, confess with your very soul, and not with your lips only : lay bare your spirit before the glance of Deity. If it be faith that you talk of, believe right up to the hilt. Do not go in for that kind of sceptical believing which is so common nowadays. If thou believest, believe : if thou repentest, repent. In the purging of the soul there is nothing like sweeping out every particle of the old leaven of falsehood ; and in bringing in the good things into the heart there is nothing like bringing in everything that Christ prescribes, that of his fulness we may receive, not only grace, but grace for grace, grace upon grace, all the grace that is needed. Be downright in everything. The wise builder dug through the earth, and continued his digging till he reached the rock ; and then he dug into the rock, and struck out a trench wherein he might lay his foundation ; for he could not be content unless he made sure and thorough work of it. Sincerity and thoroughness are fine building-materials.

Next to that add *self-renunciation ;* for that is in the parable. When a man digs a deep foundation he has much earth to throw out. So he that builds for eternity has a great deal to get rid of. Self-trust must go at the beginning; love of sin must follow; worldliness, pride, self-seeking, all sorts of iniquity,—these must be cast aside. There is very much rubbish, and the rubbish must go. You cannot make sure work for eternity without clearing away much which flesh and blood would like to retain. See ye to this, and count the cost.

Then must come *solid principle*. The man who is determined that if he does build he will build securely, digs down to the rock. He says, "I believe in God, he is my helper. I believe in Christ Jesus, and on his atoning sacrifice and living intercession I build my eternal hopes. I also build on the doctrine of grace, for the Lord hath said it,—By grace are ye saved, through faith. I build on Scripture: nothing but the warrant of the word will do for me." What God has said is a rock: what man teaches is mere shifting sand. What a blessed thing it is to get down to the eternal principles of divine verity! You that pick up your religion from your mothers and fathers; you that follow it because it happened to be in the family; what are you worth in the day of trouble? You are blown down like a booth, or a hut of boughs. But you that know what you believe, and why you believe it, you who, when you put your foot down, know what you are standing upon, and are persuaded that you have firm rock beneath you; you are the men who will stand fast when mere pretenders are hurled out of their place. Oh, my dear seeking friends, fix upon true principles, and be not content with falsehood.

These truthful principles must be *firmly adhered to*. Bind your building to the rock. A house will not stand merely because it is *on* the rock; you must get its foundation into the rock. The house must take a grip of the rock, and the rock must grasp the house. The more you can get the house to be a bit of the rock, and the rock, as it were, to grow up into the house, the more secure you are. It is of no use saying, "Yes, I confide in Christ, in grace, in revelation," unless your very life enters into these things, and they enter into you. Hypocrites, Job says, are stolen away in the night; so easily are they removed. The inventor of some new notion comes along, cracks up his novel wares, and silly souls are at once taken in by him. Christ may go, grace may go, and the Bible may go, too: their new master has them wholly in his power. We want not such unsubstantial men; we care not for these speculating builders whose carcases are all around us. We have had enough of castles in the air: we need true men, who will stand fast like the mountains while errors, like clouds, blow over them. Remember the huge shaft at Bradford, and how many were slain by its fall, and let it teach you to hold hard to foundation truths, and never depart from them.

The man in the second parable did not build as he should; what may I say of him? I will say three words. First, he was a man who had *nothing out of sight*: you could see all his house when you looked at it. If you can see all a man's religion at a glance he has no religion worth having. Godliness lies most in secret prayer, private devotion, and inward grace. The wise builder had the most costly part of his house buried in the ground; but the other man showed all that he had above ground. He is a poor tradesman who has no stock but that which he puts into the window. He will not last long who has no capital. He cannot long stand who has no backbone within. Beware of a religion of show.

Next, this man had *nothing to hold to.* He built a house, but it stood upon the loose soil : he easily dug into that, and stuck up his house; but his walls had no holdfast. Beware of a religion without holdfasts. But if I get a grip upon a doctrine they call me a bigot. Let them do so. Bigotry is a hateful thing, and yet that which is now abused as bigotry is a great virtue, and greatly needed in these frivolous times. I have been inclined lately to start a new denomination, and call it "the Church of the Bigoted." Everybody is getting to be so oily, so plastic, so untrue, that we need a race of hard-shells to teach us how to believe. Those old-fashioned people who in former ages believed something, and thought the opposite of it to be false, were truer folk than the present time-servers. I should like to ask the divines of the broad school whether any doctrine is worth a man's dying for it. They would have to reply, "Well, of course, if a man had to go to the stake or change his opinions, the proper way would be to state them with much diffidence, and to be extremely respectful to the opposite school." But suppose he is required to deny the truth? "Well, there is much to be said on each side, and probably the negative may have a measure of truth in it as well as the positive. At any rate, it cannot be a prudent thing to incur the odium of being burned, and so it might be preferable to leave the matter an open question for the time being." Yes, and as these gentlemen always find it unpleasant to be unpopular, they soften down the hard threatenings of Scripture as to the world to come, and put a colour upon every doctrine to which worldly-wise men object. The teachers of doubt are very doubtful teachers. A man must have something to hold to, or he will neither bless himself nor others. Bring all the ships into the pool; but do not moor or anchor one of them ; let each one be free ! Wait you for a stormy night, and they will dash against each other, and great mischief will come of this freedom. Perfect love and charity will not come through our being all unmoored, but by each having his proper moorings and keeping to them in the name of God. You must have something to hold to ; but the builder in the parable had not, and so he perished.

The foolish builder had *nothing to resist outward circumstances.* On summer days his house was a favourite resort, and was considered to be quite as good as his neighbour's in all repects. Frequently he rubbed his hands and said, " I do not see but what my house is quite as good as his, and perhaps a little better the fact is, I had a few pounds to spare which I did not bury in the ground as he did, and with it I have bought many a little ornament, so that my habitation has a finer look than his building." So it seemed; but when the torrent came raging down the mountain side, his building, having nothing wherewith to resist the violence of the flood, fell down at once, and not a trace of it remained, when the storm had ceased. Thus do men fail because they offer no resistance to forces which drive them into sin ; the great current of evil finds in them victims, and not opponents.

III. Thirdly, we will now gather from our text A SET OF ARGUMENTS, URGING US TO TAKE CARE OF THE FOUNDATION. I will glance over these arguments, wishing much that I had time to enforce them. The first is this. We ought to build with a good foundation at the beginning, because otherwise *we shall not build well in any other part of the house.* Bad work in the foundation influences all the rest of the courses. In the Revised Version at the end of the forty-eighth verse instead of, " For it was founded upon a rock," we read, " Because it had been well builded." The house was built well at the bottom, and that led the workman to put in good work all the way up, so that all through " it had been well builded." The other man built badly underground, and did the same up to the roof. When you get into the habit of slovenly work in secret the tendency is to be slovenly in public too. If the underground part of our religion is not firmly laid upon Christ, then in the upper part there will be rotten work, half-baked bricks, mud instead of mortar, and a general scamping of everything. When a great Grecian artist was fashioning an image for the temple he was diligently carving the back part of the goddess, and one said to him, " You need not finish that part of the statue, because it is to be built into the wall." He replied, " The gods can see in the wall." He had a right idea of what is due to God. That part of my religion which no man can see should be as perfect as if it were to be observed by all. The day shall declare it. When Christ shall come everything shall be made known, and published before the universe. Therefore see to it that it be fit to be thus made known.

See, again, that we ought to have good foundations when we *look at the situation whereon the house is to be built.* It is clear from this parable that both these houses were built in places not far from a river, or where streams might be expected to come. Certain parts of the South of France are marvellously like Palestine, and perhaps at the present moment they are more like what the Holy Land was in Christ's day than the Holy Land now is. When I reached Cannes last year I found that there had been a flood in the town. This flood did not come by reason of a river being swollen, but through a deluge of rain. A waterspout seems to have burst upon the hill-side tearing up earth, and rocks, and stones, and then hurrying down to the sea. It rushed across the railway station and poured down the street which led to it, drowning several persons in its progress. When I was there a large hotel—I should think five stories high—was shored up with timber, and was evidently doomed ; for when this stream rushed down the narrow street it undermined the lower courses of the building, and as there were no foundations at all able to bear such a test the whole erection was rendered unsafe. The Saviour had some such case in his mind's eye. A torrent of water would come tearing down the side of the mountain, and if a house was built on the mere earth, it would be carried away directly, but if it were fastened into the rock so that it became part and parcel of it, then the flood might rush all around it, but it would not shake the walls. Beloved builder of a house for your soul, your house is so situated that one of these days there must come great pressure upon it. " How do you know ? " Well, I know that the house wherein my soul lives is pitched just where winds blow, and waves rise, and storms beat. Where is yours ? Do you live in a snug corner ? Yes, but one of these times you will find that the snug corner will be no more shielded than the open riverside ; for God so orders providence that every man has his test sooner or later. It may be that you think yourself past temptation, but the idea is a delusion, as time will show. Perhaps from the very fact that you seem quite out of the way, a peculiar temptation may befall you. Therefore, I do pray you, because of the exposed condition of your life's building, build upon a good foundation.

The next argument is, build deep, because of the *ruin which will result from a bad foundation.* The foolish builder's house was without a foundation. Notice that word, "*without a foundation.*" Write down the expression, and see whether they apply to you or not. What happened to this house without a foundation? The stream beat vehemently on it. The river's bed had long been dry, but suddenly it was flooded, and the torrent rolled with tremendous power. Perhaps it was persecution, perhaps it was prosperity, perhaps it was trouble, perhaps it was temptation, perhaps it was prevalent scepticism, perhaps it was death; but, anyhow, the flood beat vehemently upon that house; and now we read the next word,—" And *immediately it fell.*" It did not stand a prolonged assault, it was captured at once. "Immediately it fell." What! in a minute, all that fair profession gone? "Immediately it fell." Why, that is the man I shook hands with the other Sunday, and called him "Brother," and he has been seen drunk! or he has been in the frivolous assembly, using unhallowed language! or he has become an utter doubter all on a sudden! It is sorrowful work burying our friends, but it is much more sorrowful work to lose them in this fashion: and yet so they vanish. They are gone: even as Job saith "the east wind carrieth him away and he departeth." "Immediately" they fall, and yet we thought so highly of them, and they thought so highly of themselves. "Immediately it fell"; their profession could not endure trial, and all because it had no foundation.

Then it is added, "And the ruin of that house was great." The house came down with a crash, and it was the man's all. The man was an eminent professor, and hence his ruin was all the more notable. It was a great fall because it could never be built up again. When a man dies a hypocrite certainly there is no hope of restitution for him. By the stream the very debris of the ruined house was swept away; nothing was left. Oh, men, if you lose a battle you may fight again and win another; if you fail in business you may start again in trade and realise a fortune; but if you lose your souls the loss is irretrievable. Once lost, lost for ever. There will be no second opportunity. Do not deceive yourselves about that. Therefore, dig deep, and lay every stone most firmly upon the foundation of rock.

For lastly, and perhaps this will be the best argument, *observe the effect of this good, sure building,* this deep building. We read that when the flood beat upon the wise man's house "*it could not shake it.*" That is very beautiful. Not only could it not carry it away, but "it could not shake it." I see the man: he lost his money and became poor, but he did not give up his faith : "It could not shake it." He was ridiculed and slandered, and many of his former friends gave him the cold shoulder; but "It could not shake it." He went to Jesus under his great trial and he was sustained: "It could not shake it." He was very sick and his spirit was depressed within him, but still he held his confidence in Christ: "It could not shake it." He was near to die; he knew that he must soon depart out of this world, but all the pains of death and the certainty of dissolution could not shake him. He died as he lived, firm as a rock, rejoicing as much as ever, nay, rejoicing more, because he was nearer to the kingdom and to the fruition of all his hopes. "It could not shake it." It is a grand thing to have a faith which cannot be shaken. I saw one day a number of beech trees which had formed a wood: they had all fallen to the ground through a storm. The fact was they leaned upon one another to a great extent, and the thickness of the wood prevented each tree from getting a firm hold of the soil. They kept each other up and also constrained each other to grow up tall and thin, to the neglect of root-growth. When the tempest forced down the first few trees the others readily followed one after the other. Close to that same spot I saw another tree in the open, bravely defying the blast, in solitary strength. The hurricane had beaten upon it, but it had endured all its force un-sheltered. That lone, brave tree seemed to be better rooted than before the storm. I thought, "Is it not so with professors?" They often hold together, and help each other to grow up, but if they have not firm personal roothold, when a storm arises they fall in rows. A minister dies, or certain leaders are taken away, and over go the members by departure from the faith and from holiness. I would have you be self-contained, growing each man into Christ for himself, rooted and grounded in love and faith and every holy grace. Then when the worst storm that ever blew on mortal man shall come, it will be said of your faith, " It could not shake it." I beseech you who are now seeking Christ to take care that you build well, that you may stand long in our Zion, steadfast and unmovable. God grant it for Christ's sake. Amen.

Metropolitan Tabernacle Pulpit.

HANDS FULL OF HONEY.

A Sermon

DELIVERED ON LORD'S-DAY MORNING, JANUARY 28TH, 1883, BY

C. H. SPURGEON,

AT THE METROPOLITAN TABERNACLE, NEWINGTON.

"And Samson turned aside to see the carcase of the lion: and, behold, there was a swarm of bees and honey in the carcase of the lion. And he took thereof in his hands, and went on eating, and came to his father and mother, and he gave them, and they did eat: but he told not them that he had taken the honey out of the carcase of the lion."—Judges xiv. 8, 9.

IT was a singular circumstance that a man unarmed should have slain a lion in the prime of its vigour; and yet more strange that a swarm of bees should have taken possession of the dried carcase, and have filled it with their honey. In that country, what with beasts, birds, and insects, and the dry heat, a dead body is soon cleansed from all corruption, and the bones are clean and white: still the killing of the lion, and the finding of the honey, make up a remarkable story. These singular circumstances became afterwards the subject of a riddle; but with that riddle we have no concern at this time. Samson himself is a riddle. He was not only a riddle-maker; but he was himself an enigma very difficult to explain: with his personal character I have at this time little or nothing to do. We are not to-day resting at the house of "Gaius, mine host," where the pilgrims amused themselves with a dish of nuts after dinner; but we are on the march, and must attend to the more important matter of refreshing and inspiriting those who are in our company. Neither are we going to discuss difficulties; but as Samson took the honey without being stung, so would we gain instruction without debate. We have in these days so much to do, that we must make practical use of every incident that comes before us in the word of God. My one design is to cheer the desponding and stir up all God's people to greater diligence in his service. I conceive that the text may legitimately be employed for this purpose. By the help of the divine Spirit, even after this lapse of time, we may find honey in the lion.

The particular part of the incident which is recorded in these two verses appears to have been passed over by those who have written upon Samson's life: I suppose it appeared to be too inconsiderable. They are taken up with his festive riddle, but they omit the far more natural and commendable fact of his bringing forth the honey in his hands and presenting it to his father and mother. This is the little scene to which I direct your glances. It seems to me that the Israelitish hero with a slain lion in the background, standing out in the open road with his hands laden with masses of honeycomb and dripping with honey, which he holds out to his parents, makes a fine picture, worthy of the greatest artist. And what a type we have here of our Divine Lord and Master, Jesus, the conqueror of death and hell. He has destroyed the lion that roared upon us and upon him. He has shouted "victory" over all our foes. "It is finished" was his note of triumph; and now he stands in the midst of his church with his hands full of sweetness and consolation, presenting them to those of whom he says, "these are my brother, and sister, and mother." To each one of us who believe in him he gives the luscious food which he has prepared for us by the overthrow of our foes; he bids us come and eat that we may have our lives sweetened and our hearts filled with joy. To me the comparison seems wonderfully apt and suggestive: I see our triumphant Lord laden with sweetness, holding it forth to all his brethren, and inviting them to share in his joy.

But, beloved, it is written, "As he is, so are we also in this world." All that are true Christians are, in a measure, like the Christ whose name they bear, and it is to his image that we are finally to be conformed. When he shall appear we shall be like him, for we shall see him as he is; and meanwhile, in proportion as we see him now, "we are changed into the same image, from glory to glory, even as by the Spirit of the Lord." The Samson type may well serve as the symbol of every Christian in the world. The believer has been helped by divine grace in his spiritual conflicts, and he has known "the victory which overcometh the world, even our faith." He has thus been made more than a conqueror through him that loved us, and now he stands in the midst of his fellow-men inviting them to Jesus. With the honey in his hands, which he continues still to feast upon, he displays the heavenly sweetness to all that are round about him, saying, "O taste and see that the Lord is good: blessed is the man that trusteth in him." I have before now met with that popular artist Gustave Doré, and suggested subjects to him. Had he survived among us, and had another opportunity occurred, I would have pressed him to execute a statue of Samson handing out the honey: strength distributing sweetness; and it might have served as a perpetual reminder of what a Christian should be—a Conqueror and a Comforter, slaying lions and distributing honey. The faithful servant of God wrestles with the powers of evil; but with far greater delight he speaks to his friends and companions, saying, "Eat ye that which is good, and let your souls delight themselves in sweetness." Set the statue before your mind's eye, and now let me speak about it.

Three touches may suffice. First, *the believer's life has its conflicts;* secondly, *the believer's life has its sweets;* and, thirdly, *the believer's life leads him to communicate of those sweets to others.* Here is room for profitable meditation.

I. First, then, THE BELIEVER'S LIFE HAS ITS CONFLICTS. To become a Christian is to enlist for a soldier. To become a believer is to enter upon a pilgrimage, and the road is often rough: the hills are steep, the valleys are dark, giants block the way, and robbers lurk in corners. The man who reckons that he can glide into heaven without a struggle has made a great mistake. No cross no crown : no sweat no sweet: no conflict no conquest. These conflicts, if we take the case of Samson as our symbol, *begin early* in the life of the believer. While Samson was a child, the Spirit of the Lord moved him in the camps of Dan—see the last verse of the thirteenth chapter ; and as soon as he was on the verge of manhood, he must match himself with a lion. God who intended that his servant should smite the Philistines, and should check their proud oppression of his people Israel, began early to train the hero for his life's conflict. So, when Samson was going to seek a wife, he turned aside into the vineyards of Timnath, and a lion roared upon him. Yes, and the young believer, who as yet has not wrestled with the powers of darkness, will not be long before he hears the roar of the lion, and finds himself in the presence of the great Adversary. Very soon we learn the value of the prayer, " Deliver us from the evil one ! " Most of the Lord's servants have been men of war from their youth up. Without are fightings even when within there are no fears. This early combat with the savage beast was intended by God to let him know his strength when under the influence of the Spirit, and to train him for his future combats with Israel's enemies. He that is to smite the Philistines' hip and thigh with a great slaughter, until he has laid them heaps on heaps by his single prowess, must begin by rending a lion with his naked hands. He was to learn war in the same school as another and a greater hero, who afterwards said, " Thy servant slew both the lion and the bear, and this uncircumcised Philistine shall be as one of them."

Soldiers are made by war. You cannot train veterans or create victors except by battles. As in the wars of armies so is it in spiritual contests: men must be trained for victory over evil by combat with it. Hence " it is good for a man that he bear the yoke in his youth"; for it will not gall his shoulders in after years. It is assuredly a dangerous thing to be altogether free from trouble: in silken ease the soldier loses his prowess. Look at Solomon, one of the greatest and wisest, and yet, I might say, one of the least and most foolish of men. It was his fatal privilege to sit upon a throne of gold and sun himself in the brilliance of unclouded prosperity, and hence his heart soon went astray, and he fell from his high places. Solomon in his early days had no trouble, for no war was then raging, and no enemy worth notice was then living. His life ran smoothly on, and he was lulled into a dreamy sleep, the sleep of the voluptuous. He had been happier far had he been, like his father, called from his earliest days to trial and conflict ; for this might have taught him to stand fast upon the pinnacle of glory whereon the providence of God had placed him. Learn, then, O young brother, that if, like Samson, you are to be a hero for Israel, you must early be inured to suffering and daring, in some form or other. When you step aside and seek for meditation in the quiet of the vineyard a young lion may roar upon you ; even as in the earliest days of your Lord and Master's public service he was led into the wilderness to be tempted of the devil.

These conflicts, dear friends, may often be *very terrible*. By a young lion is not meant a whelp, but a lion in the fulness of its early strength ; not yet slackened in its pace, or curbed in its fury by growing years. Fresh and furious, a young lion is the worst kind of beast that a man can meet with. Let us expect as followers of Christ to meet with strong temptations, fierce persecutions, and severe trials, which will lead to stern conflicts. Do not reckon, thou that art yet putting on thy harness, that thou shalt soon put it off, or that when thou puttest it off it will be quite as bright as it is to-day. It will be dimmed with blood and dust, and battered by many a blow; perhaps thy foe may find a way to pierce it, or at least to wound thee between its joints. I would have every man begin to be a soldier of the cross, but I would at the same time have him count the cost; for it is no child's play, and if he thinks it will be such, he will be grievously disappointed. A young believer will, on a sudden, have a doubt suggested to him of which he never heard before; and it will roar upon him like a young lion; neither will he see all at once how to dispose of it. Or he may be placed in singular circumstances where his duty seems to run counter to the tenderest instincts of his nature ; here, too, the young lion will roar upon him. Or, one for whom he has an intense respect may treat him ill because he is a follower of Christ, and the affection and respect which he feels for this person may make his opposition the more grievous: in this also it is with him as when a lion roareth. Or he may suffer a painful bereavement, or sustain a severe loss; or he may have a disease upon him, with consequent pains and depressions, and these may cast the shadow of death upon his spirit; so that again a young lion roars upon him. Brother, sister, let us reckon upon this, and not be dismayed by it, since in all this is the life of our spirit. By such lessons as these we are taught to do service for God, to sympathise with our fellow Christians, and to value the help of our gracious Saviour. By all these we are weaned from earth and made to hunger for that eternal glory which is yet to be revealed, of which we may truly say, " No lion shall be there, neither shall any ravenous beast go up thereon." These present evils are for our future good: their terror is for our teaching. Trials are sent us for much the same reason that the Canaanites were permitted to live in the Holy Land, that Israel might learn war, and be equipped for battles against foreign foes.

These conflicts come early, and they are very terrible ; and, moreover, they happen to us *when we are least prepared for them.* Samson was not hunting for wild beasts; he was engaged on a much more tender business. He was walking in the vineyards of Timnath, thinking of anything but lions, and " behold," says the Scripture, " a young lion roared against him." It was a remarkable and startling occurrence. He had left his father and mother and was quite alone; no one was within call to aid him in meeting his furious assailant. Human sympathy is exceedingly precious, but there are points in our spiritual conflict in which we cannot expect to receive it. To each man there are passages in life too narrow for walking two abreast. Upon certain crags we must stand alone. As our constitutions differ, so our trials, which are suited to our constitutions, must differ also. Each individual has a secret with which no friend can intermeddle; for every life has its mystery and its hid treasure. Do not be ashamed, young Christian, if you meet with temptations which appear to you to be quite singular: we have each one thought the same of his trials. You imagine that no one suffers as you do, whereas no temptation hath happened unto you but such as is common to man, and God will with the temptation make a way of escape that you may be able to bear it. Yet for the time being you may have to enter into fellowship with your Lord when he trod the wine-press alone, and of the people there was none with him. Is not this for your good? Is not this the way to strength? What kind of piety is that which is dependent upon the friendship of man? What sort of religion is that which cannot stand alone? Beloved, you will have to die alone, and you need therefore grace to cheer you in solitude. The dear wife can attend you weeping to the river's brink, but into the chill stream she cannot go with you; and if you have not a religion which will sustain you in the solitudes of life, of what avail will it be to you in the grim lonesomeness of death? Thus I reckon it to be a happy circumstance that you are called to solitary conflict that you may test your faith, and see of what stuff your hope is made.

The contest was all the worse for Samson, that in addition to being quite alone, "there was nothing in his hand." This is the most remarkable point in the narrative. He had no sword or hunter's spear with which to wound the lordly savage: he had not even a stout staff with which to ward off his attack. Samson stood an unarmed, unarmoured man in the presence of a raging beast. So we in our early temptations are apt to think that we have no weapon for the war, and we do not know what to do. We are made to cry out, "I am unprepared! How can I meet this trial? I cannot grasp the enemy to wrestle with him. What am I to do?" Herein will the splendour of faith and glory of God be made manifest, when you shall slay the lion, and yet it shall be said of you "that he had nothing in his hand"—nothing but that which the world sees not and values not.

Now, go one step further, for time forbids our lingering here. I invite you to remember that *it was by the Spirit of God that the victory was won.* We read, "And the Spirit of the Lord came mightily upon him, and he rent him as he would have rent a kid." Let the Holy Spirit help us in our trouble and we need neither company nor weapon; but without him what can we do? Good Bishop Hall says, "If that roaring lion, that goes about continually seeking whom he may devour, find us alone among the vineyards of the Philistines, where is our hope? Not in our heels, he is swifter than we: not in our weapons, we are naturally unarmed: not in our hands, which are weak and languishing; but in the Spirit of God, by whom we can do all things. If God fight in us, who can resist us? There is a stronger lion in us than that against us."

Here is our one necessity,—to be endowed with power from on high: the power of the Holy Ghost. Helped by the Spirit of God, the believer's victory will be complete: the lion shall not be driven away, but rent in pieces. Girt with the Spirit's power, our victory shall be as easy as it will be perfect: Samson rent the lion as though it were a little lamb, or a kid of the goats. Well said Paul, "I can do all things through Christ that strengtheneth me." Sin is soon overcome, temptations are readily refused, affliction is joyfully borne, persecution is gladly endured when the Spirit of glory and of peace resteth upon us. "With God all things are possible;" and as the believer is with God, it cometh to pass that all things are possible to him that believeth.

If we were surrounded by all the devils in hell we need not fear them for an instant if the Lord be on our side. We are mightier than all hell's legions when the Spirit is mightily upon us. If we were to be beaten down by Satan until he had set his foot upon our breast, to press the very life out of us, yet if the Spirit of God helped us we would reach out our hand, and grasp the sword of the Spirit, which is the word of God, and we would repeat the feat of Christian with Apollyon, when he gave the fiend such grievous wounds that he spread his dragon wings and flew away. Wherefore fear not, ye tried ones, but trust in the Spirit of God, and your conflict shall speedily end in victory. Sometimes our conflict is with past sin. We doubtfully enquire, " How can it be forgiven?" The temptation vanishes before a sight of the dying Redeemer. Then inbred lust roars against us, and we overcome it through the blood of the Lamb, for " the blood of Jesus Christ his Son cleanseth us from all sin." Sometimes a raging corruption, or a strong habit, wars upon us, and then we conquer by the might of the sanctifying Spirit of God, who is with us and shall be in us evermore. Or else it is the world which tempts, and our feet have almost gone ; but we overcome the world through the victory of faith : and if Satan raises against us the lust of the flesh, the lust of the eye, and the pride of life, all at once we are still delivered, for the Lord is a wall of fire round about us. The inward life bravely resists all sin, and God's help is given to believers to preserve them from all evil in the moment of urgent need ; even as he helped his martyrs and confessors to speak the right word when called unprepared to confront their adversaries. Care not, therefore, oh thou truster in the Lord Jesus, how fierce thine enemy may be this day! As young David slew the lion and the bear, and smote the Philistine too, even so shalt thou go from victory to victory. " Many are the afflictions of the righteous, but the Lord delivereth him out of them all." Wherefore, with a lion-like spirit, meet lions which seek to devour you.

II. Now, then, we come to our second head, which is : THE BELIEVER'S LIFE HAS ITS SWEETS. We are not always killing lions, we are sometimes eating honey. Certain of us do both at a time ; we kill lions and yet cease not to eat honey : and truly it has become so sweet a thing to enter into conflict for Christ's sake, that it is a joy to contend earnestly for the faith once delivered to the saints. The same Lord who hath bidden us " quit yourselves like men ; be strong," has also said, " Rejoice in the Lord alway ; and again I say, rejoice."

The believer's life has its sweets, and these are of the choicest : for what is sweeter than honey? What is more joyful than the joy of a saint? What is more happy than the happiness of a believer ? I will not condescend to make a comparison between our joy and the mirth of fools : I will go no further than a contrast. Their mirth is as the crackling of thorns under a pot, which spit fire, and make a noise and a flash, but there is no heat, and they are soon gone out: nothing comes of it, the pot is long in boiling. But the Christian's delight is like a steady coal fire. You have seen the grate full of coals all burning red, and the whole mass of coal has seemed to be one great glowing ruby and everybody who has come into the room out of the cold has delighted to warm his hands, for it gives out a steady heat and warms the body even to its marrow. Such are our joys. I would sooner possess the joy of Christ five minutes than I would revel in the mirth of fools for half a century. There is more bliss in the tear of repentance than in the laughter of gaiety: our holy sorrows are sweeter than the worlding's joys. But, oh, when our joys grow full, divinely full, then are they unspeakably like those above, and heaven begins below. Did you never cry for joy? You say, perhaps, "Not since I was a child." Nor have I; but I have always remained a child as far as divine joy is concerned. I could often cry for joy when I know whom I have believed and am persuaded that he is able to keep that which I have committed to him.

Ours is a joy which will bear thinking over. You can dare to pry into the bottom of it and test its foundation. It is a joy which does not grow stale; you may keep it in your mouth by the year together, and yet it never cloys; you may return to it again, and again, and again, and find it still as fresh as ever. And the best of it is there is no repentance after it. You are never sorry that you were so glad. The world's gay folk are soon sick of their drink; but we are only sorry that we were not gladder still, for our gladness sanctifies. We are not denied any degree of joy to which we can possibly attain, for ours is a healthy, health-giving delight. Christ is the fulness of joy to his people, and we are bidden to enjoy him to the full. Christians have their sweets, and those are as honey and the honeycomb, the best of the best.

Of these joys *there is plenty;* for Samson found, as it were, a living spring of honey, since he discovered a swarm of bees. So abundant was the honey that he could take huge masses of the comb and carry it in his hands, and go away with it, bearing it to others. In the love of Christ, in pardoned sin, in acceptance in the Beloved, in resting in God, in perfectly acquiescing in his will, in the hope of heaven, there is such joy that none can measure it. We have such a living swarm of bees to make honey for us in the precious promises of God, that there is more delight in store than any of us can possibly realise. There is infinitely more of Christ beyond our comprehension than we have as yet been able to comprehend. How blessed to receive of his fulness, to be sweetened with his sweetness, and yet to know that infinite goodness still remains. Perhaps some of you have enjoyed so much of Christ that you could hardly bear any more; but your largest enjoyments are only as tiny shells filled by a single wave of the sea, while all the boundless ocean rolls far beyond your ken. We have exceeding great joy, yea, joy to spare. Our Master's wedding feast is not so scantily furnished that we have to bring in another seat for an extra guest, or murmur to ourselves that we had better not invite at random lest we should be incommoded by too great a crowd. Nay, rather the pillared halls of mercy in which the King doth make his feast are so vast that it will be our life-long business to furnish them with guests, compelling more and more to come in that his house may be filled, and that his royal festival may make glad ten thousand times ten thousand hearts.

Dear friends, if you want to know what are the elements of our joy, I have already hinted at them, but I will for a moment enlarge thereon.

Our joys are often found in the former places of our conflicts. We gather our honey out of the lions which have been slain for us or by us.

There is, first, our sin. A horrible lion that! But it is a dead lion, for grace has much more abounded over abounding sin. Oh, brothers, I have never heard of any dainty in all the catalogue of human joys that could match a sense of pardoned sin. Full forgiveness! Free forgiveness! Eternal forgiveness! See, it sparkles like dew of heaven. To know that God has blotted out my sin is knowledge rich with unutterable bliss. My soul has begun to hear the songs of seraphim when it has heard that note, "I have blotted out thy sins like a cloud, and as thick cloud thine iniquities." Here is choice honey for you!

The next dead lion is conquered desire. When a wish has arisen in the heart contrary to the mind of God, and you have said— "Down with you! I will pray you down. You used to master me ; I fell into a habit and I was soon overcome by you ; but I will not again yield to you. By God's grace I will conquer you ";—I say, when at last you have obtained the victory such a sweet contentment perfumes your heart that you are filled with joy unspeakable ; and you are devoutly grateful to have been helped of the Spirit of God to master your own spirit." Thus you have again eaten spiritual honey.

When you are able to feel in your own soul that you have overcome a strong temptation, the fiercer it was and the more terrible it was the louder has been your song and the more joyful your thanksgiving. To go back to Mr. Bunyan again: when Christian had passed through the Valley of the Shadow of Death during the night, and when he had come entirely out of it and the sun rose, you remember he looked back. (A pause). He was long in taking that look, I warrant you. What thoughts he had while looking back. He could just discern that narrow track with the quagmire on one side and the deep ditch on the other ; and he could see the shades out of which the hobgoblins hooted and the fiery eyes glanced forth. He looked back by sunlight and thought within himself, "Ah me ! What goodness has been with me ! I have gone through all that, and yet I am unharmed !" What a happy survey it was to him ! Ah, the joy of having passed through temptation without having defiled one's garments ! How must Shadrach, Meshach, and Abednego have felt when they stepped out of the fiery furnace, and were not even singed, neither had the smell of fire passed upon them. Happy men were they to have lived in the centre of the seven-times-heated furnace where everything else was consumed. Here again is "a piece of an honeycomb."

We find honey again from another slain lion ; namely, our troubles after we have been enabled to endure them. This is the metal of which our joy-bells are cast. Out of the brass of our trials we make the trumpets of our triumph. He is not the happy man who has seen no trouble ; but "blessed is he that endureth temptation, for when he is tried he shall receive a crown of life that fadeth not away."

Death, too. Oh, the honey that is found in dead death. Death is indeed dead. We triumph over him, and are no more afraid of him than little children are of a dead lion. We pluck him by the beard, and say to him, "O death, where is thy sting ? O grave, where is thy victory ?" We even look forward to the time of our departure with delight, when we shall leave this heavy clay and on spirit wings ascend unto our Father and our God. You see there is rich store of honey for God's people ; and we do not hesitate to eat it. Let others say as they will, we are a happy people, happy in Christ, happy in the Holy Spirit, happy in God our Father. So that believers have their sweets.

III. But the third is the point I want to dwell upon: THE BE-LIEVER'S LIFE LEADS HIM TO COMMUNICATE OF THESE SWEETS. As soon as we have tasted the honey of forgiven sin and perceived the bliss that God has laid up for his people in Christ Jesus, we feel it to be both our duty and our privilege to communicate the good news to others. Here let my ideal statue stand in our midst : the strong man, conqueror of the lion, holding forth his hands full of honey to his parents. We are to be modelled according to this fashion.

And, first, we do this *immediately.* The moment a man is converted, if he would let himself alone, his instincts would lead him to tell his fellows. I know that the moment I came out of that little chapel wherein I found the Saviour, I wanted to pour out my tale of joy. I could have cried with Cennick—

> " Now will I tell to sinners round,
> What a dear Saviour I have found ;
> I'll point to thy redeeming blood,
> And say, ' Behold the way to God ! ' "

I longed to tell how happy my soul was, and what a deliverance I had obtained from the crushing burden of sin. I longed to see all others come and trust my Lord and live ! I did not preach a sermon, but I think I could have told out all the gospel at that first hour. Did not you, my friend, feel much the same ? Did not your tongue long to be telling of what the Lord had done for you ? Perhaps you are one of those proper and retiring people who are greatly gifted at holding their tongues ; and therefore you left the feet of Jesus in silence,—silence which angels wondered at. Is that is why you have held your tongue ever since ? Perhaps if you had begun to speak then you would have continued your testimony to this day. I repeat my assertion that it is the instinct of every newborn soul to communicate the glad tidings which grace has proclaimed in his heart. Just as Samson had no sooner tasted of the honey than he carried a portion of it to his father and mother, so do we hasten to invite our neighbours to Christ. My dear young friend, as soon as ever you know the joy of the Lord, open your mouth in a quiet, humble way, and never allow yourself to be numbered with the deaf and dumb. Let no one stop you from unburdening your heart. Do not follow the bad example of those who have become dumb dogs because of their cowardice at the beginning.

The believer will do this *first to those who are nearest to him.* Samson took the honey to his father and mother who were not far away. With each of us the most natural action would be to tell a brother or a sister or a fellow-workman, or a bosom friend. It will be a great joy to see them eating the honey which is so pleasant to our own palate. It is most natural in a parent at once to wish to tell his children of divine love—have you all done so ? You pray for your children, but many of you would be the means of answering your own prayers if you would

talk with them one by one. This may appear difficult, but once commenced it will soon grow easy: and, indeed, if it be difficult we should
aspire to do it for that very reason. Should we not do many a difficult
thing for him who overcame all difficulties for us ? At the least, do not
deny to your own children the personal testimony of their father or
their mother to the surpassing power of grace and the unutterable sweetness of divine love. Tell it to those who are nearest to you.

The believer will do this as best he can. Samson, you see, brought
the honey to his father and mother in a rough and ready style, going
on eating it as he brought it. If I wished to give honey to my father
and mother I should do it up rather daintily: I would at least put it in
as respectable a dish as our kitchen would afford: but there were no
plates and dishes out there in that Timnath vineyard, and so his own
hands were the only salvers upon which Samson could present the
delicacy,—"he took thereof in his hands, and came to his father and
mother, and he gave them, and they did eat." Perhaps you think, "If
I am to speak to any person upon true religion, I should like to do it in
poetry." Better do it in prose, for perhaps they will take more notice
of your verse than of your subject. Give them the honey *in your hands*,
and if there is no dish they cannot take notice of the dish. "Ay, but
I should like to do it very properly," says one; "it is a very important
matter, I should like to speak most correctly." But my judgment is,
that, as you will not be likely to attain to correct speech all in a
hurry, and your friends may die while you are learning your grammar
and your rhetoric, you had better tell them of Jesus according to your
present ability. Tell them there is life in a look at Jesus. Tell them
the story simply, as one child talks to another. Carry the honey in
your hands, though it drip all round : no hurt will come of the spilling,
there are always little ones waiting for such drops. If you were to
make the gospel drip about everywhere, and sweeten all things, it would
be no waste, but a blessed gain to all around. Therefore, I say to you,
tell of Jesus Christ as best you can, and never cease to do so while
life lasts.

But then Samson did another thing, and every true believer should
do it too: he did not merely tell his parents about the honey, but *he
took them some of it.* I do not read, "And he told his father and
mother of the honey," but I read, "and he took thereof in his hands."
Nothing is so powerful as an exhibition of grace itself to others. Do
not talk about it, but carry it in your hands. "I cannot do that," says
one. Yes, you can, by your life, your temper, your spirit, your whole
bearing. If your hands serve God, if your heart serves God, if your
face beams with joy in the service of God, you will carry grace wherever
you go, and those who see you will perceive it. You will hardly have
need to say, "Come and partake of grace ;" for the grace of God in
you will be its own invitation and attraction. Let our lives be full of
Christ and we shall preach Christ. A holy life is the best of sermons.
Soul-winning is wrought by a winning life more surely than by winning
words.

Take note, also, that Samson *did this with great modesty.* We have
plenty of people about nowadays who could not kill a mouse without
publishing it in the Gospel Gazette; but Samson killed a lion and said

nothing about it. He holds the honey in his hand for his father and mother—he shows them *that;* but we are specially informed that he told not his father or his mother that he had taken it out of the carcase of the lion. The Holy Spirit finds modesty so rare that he takes care to record it. In telling your own experience be wisely cautious. Say much of what the Lord has done for you, but say little of what you have done for the Lord. You need not make much effort to be brief on that point, for I am afraid that there is not much of it, if all were told. Do not utter a self-glorifying sentence. Let us put Christ to the front, and the joy and blessedness that comes of faith in him; and as for ourselves, we need not speak a word except to lament our sins and shortcomings.

The sum of what I have to say is this,—if we have tasted any joy in Christ, if we have known any consolation of the Spirit, if faith has been to us a real power, and if it has wrought in us peace and rest, let us communicate this blessed discovery to others. If you do not do so, mark you, you will have missed the very object for which God has blessed you. I heard the other day of a Sunday-school address in America which pleased me much. The teacher, speaking to the boys, said, "Boys, here's a watch, what is it for?" The children answered, "To tell the time." "Well," he said, "suppose my watch does not tell the time, what is it good for?" "Good-for-nothing, sir." Then he took out a pencil. "What is this pencil for?" "It is to write with, sir." "Suppose this pencil won't make a mark, what is it good for?" "Good-for-nothing, sir." Then he took out his pocket-knife. "Boys, what is this for?" They were American boys, and so they shouted,—"to whittle with,"—that is to experiment on any substance that came in their way by cutting a notch in it. "But," said he, "suppose it will not cut, what is the knife good for?" "Good-for-nothing, sir." Then the teacher asked, "What is the chief end of man?" and they replied, "To glorify God." "But suppose a man does not glorify God, what is he good for?" "Good-for-nothing, sir." That brings out my point most clearly; there are many professors of whom *I* will not say that they are good-for-nothing, but methinks if they do not soon stir themselves up to glorify God by proclaiming the sweetness of God's love it will go hard with them. Remember how Jesus said of the savourless salt "henceforth it is good for nothing." What were you converted for? What were you forgiven for? What were you renewed for? What have you been preserved on earth for but to tell to others the glad tidings of salvation and so to glorify God? Do, then, go out with your hands full of the honey of divine love and hold it out to others.

You must assuredly do good by this; you cannot possibly do harm. Samson did not invite his father and mother to see the lion when he was alive and roaring,—he might have done some hurt in that case, by frightening them, or exposing them to injury; but he settled the lion business himself, and when it came to honey he knew that even his mother could not be troubled about *that;* therefore he invited them both to share his gains. When you get into a soul-conflict, do not publish your distress to all your friends, but fight manfully in God's name; but when you possess the joy of Christ and the love of the Spirit, and grace is abundant in your soul, then tell the news to all around. You cannot do any hurt by such a proceeding: grace does good, and no harm, all its

days. Even if you blunder over it you will do no mischief. The
gospel spilled on the ground is not lost. Good, and only good, must come
of making known salvation by Jesus Christ.

It will be much better for you to tell of the sweets of godliness than
it will be to make riddles about the doctrine of it. Samson afterwards
made a riddle about his lion and the honey; and that riddle ended in
fighting and bloodshed. We have known certain Christians spend their
lives in making riddles about the honey and the lion, by asking tough
doctrinal questions which even angels cannot answer: " Riddle me this,"
they say, and then it has ended in a fight, and brotherly love has been
murdered in the fray. It is much better to bring your hands full of
honey to those who are needy, and present it to them that they may eat
of it, than it is to cavil and discuss. No hurt can come of telling
what the Lord has done for your soul, and it will keep you out of
mischief. Therefore, I would stir up all Christian people to continue
from day to day exhibiting to needy sinners the blessedness of Christ,
that unbelievers may come and eat thereof.

By doing this you will be blessing men far more than Samson could
bless his parents, for our honey is honey unto eternity, our sweets are
sweets that last to heaven, and are best enjoyed there. Call upon others
to taste and see that the Lord is good, and you shall have therein much
joy. You shall increase your own pleasure by seeing the pleasure of the
Lord prospering in your hand. What bliss awaits useful Christians
when they enter into heaven, for they shall be met there by many who
have gone before them whom they were the means of turning to Christ.
I do often inwardly sing when I perceive that I can scarce go into any
town or village but what somebody hunts me up to say to me, " Under
God I owe my salvation to your sermons or to your books." What will
be the felicities of heaven when we shall meet those who were turned to
righteousness by our holding forth the word of life ! Our heaven will
be seven heavens as we see them there. If you have done nothing but
exhibit in your lives the precious results of grace you will have done
well. If you have presented to your companions truths that were
sweetness itself to you, and tried to say in broken accents " Oh that you
knew this peace ! " it shall give you joy unspeakable to meet those in
glory who were attracted to Christ by such a simple means.

God make you all to be his witnesses in all the circles wherein you
move.

PORTION OF SCRIPTURE READ BEFORE SERMON—Psalm xxxiv;
Judges xiv. 5—9.

HYMNS FROM " OUR OWN HYMN BOOK "—146 (Version I.), 507,
145 (Song I.)

ALL JOY IN ALL TRIALS.

A Sermon

DELIVERED ON LORD'S-DAY MORNING, FEBRUARY 4TH, 1883, BY

C. H. SPURGEON,

AT THE METROPOLITAN TABERNACLE, NEWINGTON.

"My brethren, count it all joy when ye fall into divers temptations; knowing this, that the trying of your faith worketh patience. But let patience have her perfect work, that ye may be perfect and entire, wanting nothing."—James i. 2, 3, 4.

JAMES calls the converted among the twelve tribes his brethren. Christianity has a great uniting power: it both discovers and creates relationships among the sons of men. It reminds us of the ties of nature, and binds us with the bonds of grace. Every one that is born of the Spirit of God is brother to every other that is born of the same Spirit. Well may we be called brethren, for we are redeemed by one blood; we are partakers of the same life; we feed upon the same heavenly food; we are united to the same living head; we seek the same ends; we love the same Father: we are heirs of the same promises; and we shall dwell for ever together in the same heaven. Wherefore, let brotherly love continue; let us love one another with a pure heart fervently, and manifest that love, not in word only, but in deed and in truth. Whatever brotherhood may be a sham, let the brotherhood of believers be the most real thing beneath the stars.

Beginning with this word "brethren," James shows a true brotherly sympathy with believers in their trials, and this is a main part of Christian fellowship. "Bear ye one another's burdens, and so fulfil the law of Christ." If we are not tempted ourselves at this moment, others are: let us remember them in our prayers; for in due time our turn will come, and we shall be put into the crucible. As we would desire to receive sympathy and help in our hour of need, let us render it freely to those who are now enduring trial. Let us remember those that are in bonds, as bound with them, and those that suffer affliction as being ourselves also in the body. Remembering the trials of his brethren, James tries to cheer them, and therefore he says, "My brethren, count it all joy when ye fall into divers trials." It is a part of our high calling to rise ourselves into confidence; and it is also our duty to see that none of our brethren despond, much less despair. The whole tendency of our holy faith is to elevate and to encourage. Grace breeds no sorrow, except the healthy sorrow which comes with saving repentance and leads to the joy of pardon: it comes not to make men miserable,

No. 1,704.

but to wipe all tears from their eyes. Our dream is not of devils descending a dreary staircase to hell, but of angels ascending and descending upon a ladder, the top of which leads to the shining throne of God. The message of the gospel is one of joy and gladness, and were it universally understood and received this world would be no longer a wilderness, but it would rejoice and blossom as the rose. Let grace reign in all hearts, and this earth will become a temple filled with perpetual song: and even the trials of life will become causes of the highest joy, so beautifully described by James as " all joy," as if every possible delight were crowded into it. Blessed be God, it is our work, not to upbraid, but to cheer all the brotherhood: we walk in a light which glorifies everything upon which it falls, and turns losses into gains. We are able in sober earnest to speak with the afflicted, and bid them be patient under the chastening hand of God; yea, to count it all joy when they fall into divers trials because those trials will work out for them such signal, such lasting good. They may be well content to sow in tears since they are sure to reap in joy.

Without further preface we will come at once to the text; and observe that in speaking about affliction, for that is the subject of the text, the apostle notes, first, *the essential point which is assailed by temptation*, namely, your faith. Your faith is the target that all the arrows are shot at; the furnace is kindled for the trial of your faith. Notice, secondly, *the invaluable blessing which is thus gained*, namely, the proving of your faith, discovering whether it be the right faith or no. This proof of our faith is a blessing of which I cannot speak too highly. Then, thirdly, we may not overlook *the priceless virtue which is produced* by this process of testing, namely, patience; for the proving of your faith produces patience, and this is the soul's surest enrichment. Lastly, in connection with that patience we shall note *the spiritual completeness which is thus promoted:*—" That ye may be perfect and entire, lacking in nothing." Perhaps you have noticed the little variations I have made in the text; but I am now following the Revised Version, which gives an admirable rendering. I will read it. " Count it all joy, my brethren, when ye fall into manifold temptations; knowing that the proof of your faith worketh patience. And let patience have its perfect work, that ye may be perfect and entire, lacking in nothing."

I. First, let us think a little upon THE ESSENTIAL POINT WHICH IS ASSAILED by temptation or trial. *It is your faith which is tried.* It is supposed that you have that faith. You are not the people of God, you are not truly brethren unless you are believers. It is this faith of yours which is peculiarly obnoxious to Satan and to the world which lieth in the wicked one. If you had no faith they would not be enemies of yours; but faith is the mark of the chosen of God, and therefore his foes become the foes of all the faithful, spitting their venom specially upon their faith. God himself hath put enmity between the serpent and the woman, between the serpent's seed and the woman's seed; and that enmity must show itself. The serpent bites at the heel of the true seed: hence mockings, persecutions, temptations, and trials are sure to beset the pathway of faith. The hand of faith is against all evil, and all evil is against faith. Faith is that blessed grace which is most pleasing to God, and hence it is most displeasing to the devil. By faith God is greatly glorified, and hence by faith Satan is greatly annoyed. He rages at faith because he sees therein his own defeat and the victory of grace.

Because the trial of your faith brings honour to the Lord, therefore the Lord himself is sure to try it that out of its trial praise may come to his grace by which faith is sustained. Our chief end is to glorify God, and if our trials enable us more fully to answer the end of our being it is well that they should happen unto us. So early in our discourse we see reason to count it all joy when we fall into manifold trials.

It is by our faith that we are saved, justified, and brought near to God, and therefore it is no marvel that it is attacked. It is by believing in Christ that we are delivered from the reigning power of sin, and receive power to become the sons of God. Faith is as vital to salvation as the heart is vital to the body: hence the javelins of the enemy are mainly aimed at this essential grace. Faith is the standard bearer, and the object of the enemy is to strike him down that the battle may be gained. If the foundations be removed what can the righteous do? If the cable can be snapped whither will the vessel drift? All the powers of darkness which are opposed to right and truth are sure to fight against our faith, and manifold temptations will march in their legions against our confidence in God.

It is by our faith that we live; we began to live by it, and we continue to live by it, for " the just shall live by faith." Once let faith go and our life is gone; and hence it is that the powers which war against us make their main assault upon this royal castle, this key of the whole position. Faith is your jewel, your joy, your glory; and the thieves who haunt the pilgrim way are all in league to tear it from you. Hold fast, therefore, this your choice treasure.

It is by faith, too, that Christians perform exploits. If men of old wrought daring and heroic deeds it was by faith. Faith is the fighting principle and the conquering principle: therefore it is Satan's policy to slay it even as Pharaoh sought to kill the male children when Israel dwelt in Egypt. Rob a Christian of his faith and he will be like Samson when his locks were cut away: the Philistines will be upon him and the Lord will have departed from him. Marvel not if the full force of the current shall beat upon your faith, for it is the foundation of your spiritual house. Oh that your faith may abide steadfast and unmovable in all present trials, that so it may be found true in the hour of death and in the day of judgment. Woe unto that man whose faith fails him in this land of peace, for what will he do in the swellings of Jordan?

Now, think of *how faith is tried*. According to the text we are said to fall into " manifold temptations " or into " divers temptations "—that is to say, we may expect very many and very different troubles. In any case these trials will be most real. The twelve tribes to whom this epistle was written were a specially tried people, for in the first place they were, as Jews, greatly persecuted by all other nations, and when they became Christians they were cruelly persecuted by their own people. A Gentile convert was somewhat less in peril than a Jewish Christian, for the latter was crushed between the upper and the nether millstones of Paganism and Judaism. The Israelitish Christian was usually so persecuted by his own kith and kin that he had to flee from them, and whither could he go, for all other people abhorred the Jews? We are not in such a plight, but God's people even to this day will find that trial is no sham word. The rod in God's house is no toy to play with. The furnace, believe me, is no mere place of extra warmth to which you may soon accustom yourself: it is often heated seven times hotter, like the furnace of Nebuchadnezzar, and God's children are made to know that the fire burns and devours. Our temptations are no inventions of nervousness nor hobgoblins of dreamy fear. Ye have heard of the patience of Job—his was real patience, for his afflictions were real. Could each tried believer among us tell his own story I do not doubt we should convince all who heard us that the troubles and temptations which we have endured are no fictions of romance, but must be ranked among the stern realities of actual life.

Ay, and note too, that the trials of Christians are such as would in themselves lead us into sin, for I take it that our translators would not have placed the word "temptation" in the text, and the Revisionists would not have retained it, if they had not felt that there was a colouring of temptation in its meaning, and that "trial" was hardly the word. The natural tendency of trouble is not to sanctify, but to induce sin. A man is very apt to become unbelieving under affliction: that is a sin. He is apt to murmur against God under it: that is a sin. He is apt to put forth his hand to some ill way of escaping from his difficulty: and that would be a sin. Hence we are taught to pray, "Lead us not into temptation"; because trial has in itself a measure of temptation, and if it were not neutralized by abundant grace it would bear us towards sin. I suppose that every test must have in it a measure of temptation. The Lord cannot be tempted of evil, neither tempteth he any man; but this is to be understood of his end and design. He entices no man to do evil; but yet he tries the sincerity and faithfulness of men by placing them where sin comes in their way, and does its best or its worst to ensnare them: his design being that the uprightness of his servants may thus be proved, both to themselves and others. We are not taken out of this world of temptation, but we are kept in it for our good. Because our nature is depraved it makes occasions for sin, both out of our joys and our trials, but by grace we overcome the tendency of nature, and so derive benefit from tribulation. Do I not speak to many here who at times feel strong impulses towards evil, especially in the darksome hour when the spirit of evil walks abroad? Have you not been made to tremble for yourselves in seasons of fierce trial, for your feet were almost gone, your steps had well-nigh slipped. Is there any virtue that has not been weather-beaten? Is there any love that has not at times been so tried that it threatened to curdle into hate? Is there any good thing this side heaven which has marched all the way in silver slippers? Did ever a flower of grace blossom in this wretched clime without being tried with frost or blight? Our way is up the river; we have to stem the current, and struggle against a flood which would readily bear us to destruction. Thus, not only trials, but black temptations assail the Christian's faith.

As to what shape they take, we may say this much: the trial or temptation of each man is distinct from that of every other. When God did tempt Abraham he was bidden to take his son, his only son, and offer him upon a mountain for a sacrifice. Nobody here was ever tried in that way: nobody ever will be. We may have the trial of losing our child, but certainly not the trial of having a command to offer him in sacrifice. That was a trial peculiar to Abraham: necessary and useful to him, though never proposed to us. In the case of the young man in the gospels, our Lord Jesus tried him with, " If thou wouldst be perfect, go and sell that thou hast, and give to the poor, and thou shalt have treasure in heaven." Some have dreamed that it must therefore be the duty of everybody to part with their possessions: but this is idle. It would not be the duty of any man to offer up his only son ; and it is not the duty of every man to part with all his goods. These were tests to particular persons ; and others equally special and searching have been applied in other cases. We are not to try ourselves, nor to desire other men's trials ; it will be well if we endure those which the Lord appoints for us, for they will be wisely chosen. That which would most severely test me would perhaps be no trial to you ; and that which tries you might be no temptation to me. This is one reason why we often judge one another so severely, because feeling ourselves to be strong in that particular point we argue that the fallen one must have been strong in that point too, and therefore must have wilfully and earnestly have determined to do wrong. This may be a cruel supposition. We hastily conclude that the temptation must have been as feeble in his case as it would have been in our own ; which is a great mistake, for a temptation which to you or to me would be no temptation at all, may be to another individual, of a peculiar constitution and under singular circumstances, a most fierce and terrible blast from the adversary, before which he falls mournfully, but not with malice aforethought. " Divers trials," says the apostle, and he knew what he said.

And, dear friends, sometimes these divers trials derive great force from their seemingly surrounding us, and cutting off escape: James says,—" Ye *fall into* divers temptations " : like men who fall into a pit, and do not know how to get out ; or like soldiers who fall into an ambuscade ; or travellers in the good old times when two or three footpaths surrounded them and made them feel that they had fallen into bad hands. The tempted see not which way to turn ; they appear to be hemmed in ; they are as a bird that is taken in the fowler's snare. This it is that makes calamity of our manifold temptations, that they hedge up our way, and unless faith finds the clue we wander in a thorny maze.

At times temptation comes suddenly upon us, and so we fall into it. When we were at rest, and were quiet, suddenly the evil came, like a lion leaping from the thicket. When Job's children were eating and drinking in their elder brother's house, then suddenly a wind came from the wilderness, and the patriarch was bereaved: the cattle were ploughing, the sheep were grazing, the camels were at their service, and in a moment, by fire from heaven, and by robber bands, the whole of these possessions vanished. One messenger had not told his story before another followed at his heels ; Job had no breathing time, the blows fell thick and fast. The trial of our faith is most severe when divers trials happen to us when we look not for them. Is it not strange in the light

of these things that James should say, " Count it all joy when ye fall
into divers trials " ?

Those were the days of tumults, imprisonment, crucifixion, sword, and
fire.   Then the amphitheatre devoured Christians by thousands.   The
general cry was " The Christians to the lions ! "   Do you wonder if sometimes the bravest were made to say, " Is our faith really true ?   This
faith which is abhorred of all mankind, can it be divine ?   Has it come
from God ?   Why, then, does he not interpose and deliver his people ?
Shall we apostatise ?   Shall we deny Christ and live, or shall we go on
with our confession through innumerable torments even to a bloody
death ?   Will fidelity answer after all ?   Is there a crown of glory ?   Is
there an eternity of bliss ?   Is there in very deed a resurrection of the
dead ? "   These questions came into men's minds then, and were fairly
faced : the faith of martyrs was not taken up at second hand, or
borrowed from their parents ; they believed for themselves in downright earnest.   Men and women in those days believed in such a way
that they never flinched nor started aside from fear of death ; indeed,
they pressed forward to confess their faith in Jesus in such crowds that
at last the heathen cried, " There must be something in it : it must be
a religion of God, or how could these men so gladly bear their troubles ? "
This was the faith of God's elect, the work of the Holy Ghost.

You see, then, the main point of attack is our faith, and happy is the
man whose shield can catch and quench all the fiery darts of the enemy.

II.   That we may make the text more clear we shall next notice THE
INVALUABLE BLESSING WHICH IS GAINED BY THE TRIAL OF OUR FAITH.
The blessing gained is this, that our faith is tried and proved.   Two
Sabbaths ago I addressed you upon the man whose bad foundations led
to the overthrow of his house ; and I know that many said after the
sermon :—" God grant that we may not be like him : may we have a
firm foundation for our soul to rest on."   Then you went home, and
you sat down and said, " Have I this sure foundation ?   You began to
question, argue, reason, and so on, and your design was a good one.
But I do not reckon that much came of it ; our own looking within
seldom yields solid comfort.   Actual trial is far more satisfactory ; but
you must not try yourself.   The effectual proof is by trials of God's
sending.   The way of trying whether you are a good soldier is to go
down to the battle : the way to try whether a ship is well built is, not
merely to order the surveyor to examine her, but to send her to sea :
a storm will be the best test of her staunchness.   They have built a new
lighthouse upon the Eddystone : how do we know that it will stand ?
We judge by certain laws and principles, and feel tolerably safe about
the structure ; but, after all, we shall know best in after-years when
a thousand tempests have beaten upon the lighthouse in vain.   We
need trials as a test as much as we need divine truth as our food.
Admire the ancient types placed in the ark of the covenant of old : two
things were laid close together,—the pot of manna and the rod.   See
how heavenly food and heavenly rule go together : how our sustenance
and our chastening are equally provided for !   A Christian cannot live
without the manna nor without the rod.   The two must go together.   I
mean this, that it is as great a mercy to have your salvation proved to you
under trial as it is to have it sustained in you by the consolations of the

Spirit of God. Sanctified tribulations work the proof of our faith, and this is more precious than that of gold which perisheth, though it be tried by fire.

Now, when we are able to bear it without starting aside, *the trial proves our sincerity.* Coming out of a trouble the Christian says to himself, " Yes, I held fast mine integrity, and did not let it go. Blessed be God, I was not afraid of threatening ; I was not crushed by losses ; I was kept true to God under pressure. Now, I am sure that my religion is not a mere profession, but a real consecration to God. It has endured the fire, being kept by the power of God."

Next, it proves *the truthfulness of our doctrinal belief.* " Oh, yes," you may say, " I have heard Mr. Spurgeon expound the doctrines, and I have believed them." This is poor work ; but if you have been sick, and found a comfort in those doctrines, then you are assured of their truth. If you have been on the borders of the grave, and the gospel has given you joy and gladness, then you know how true it is. Experimental knowledge is the best and surest. If you have seen others pass through death itself triumphantly you have said, " This is proof to me : my faith is no guess-work : I have seen for myself." Is not this assurance cheaply purchased at any price? May we not count it all joy when the Lord puts us in the way of getting it? It seems to me that doubt is worse than trial. I had sooner suffer any affliction than be left to question the gospel or my own interest in it. Certainly it is a jewel worth purchasing even with our heart's blood.

Next, *your own faith in God* is proved when you can cling to him under temptation. Not only your sincerity, but the divinity of your faith is proved ; for a faith that is never tried, how can you depend upon it ? But if in the darkest hour you have still said, " I cast my burden upon the Lord, and he will sustain me," and you find he does sustain you, then is your faith that of God's elect. If in temptation you cry to God in prayer that you may keep your garment unspotted, and he helps you to do so, then also are you sure that yours is the faith which the Spirit begets in the soul. After a great fight of affliction, when I come forth a conqueror, I know that I do believe in God, and I know that this faith makes me a partaker of covenant blessings; from this I may fairly argue that my faith is of the right kind.

I find it specially sweet to learn *the great strength of the Lord* in my own weakness. We find out under trial where we are most weak, and just then in answer to prayer strength is given answerable to the need. The Lord suits the help to the hindrance, and puts the plaster on the wound. In the very hour when it is needed the needed grace is given. Does not this tend to breed assurance of faith ?

It is a splendid thing to be able to prove even to Satan *the purity of your motives.* That was the great gain of Job. There was no question about his outward conduct, but the question was about his motive. " Ah," says the devil, " he serves God for what he gets out of him. Hast thou not set a hedge about him and all that he has ? His is cupboard love: he cares nothing for God himself, he only cares for the reward of his virtue." Well, he is tried, and everything is taken away, and when he cries, " Though he slay me, yet will I trust in him," when he blesses the taking as well as the giving God, then the devil himself could not have the impudence to accuse him again. As to Job's own conscience, it would be quite settled and confirmed as to his pure love to God."   My brethren, I reckon that the endurance of every imaginable suffering and trial would be a small price to pay for a settled assurance, which would for ever prevent the possibility of doubt. Never mind the waves if they wash you upon this rock. Therefore, when you are tempted, "Count it all joy" that you are tried, because you will thus receive a proof of your love, a proof of your faith, a proof of your being the true-born children of God.

James says "*Count it.*"   A man requires to be trained to be a good accountant; it is an art which needs to be learned. What muddles some of us would make if we had to settle accounts and manage disbursements and incomings without the aid of a clerk! How we should get entangled with balances and deficits! We could much easier spend money than count it. But when a man once knows the science of book-keeping, and gets into the way of it, he readily arrives at the true position of affairs. He has learned to count, and no error escapes his eye. James gives us a ready reckoner, and teaches us in our troubles how to count. He sets before us a different kind of measure from that which carnal reason would use : the shekel of the sanctuary was very different from the shekel in common commerce, and so is the counting of faith far other than that of human judgment. He bids us take our pen and sit down quickly and write at his correct dictation. You were going to write down, "Manifold temptations;" that would be so much on the wrong side: but instead thereof he bids you set down the proving of your faith, and this one asset transforms the transaction into a substantial gain. Trials are like a fire; they burn up nothing in us but the dross, and they make the gold all the purer. Put down the testing process as a clear gain, and, instead of being sorry about it, count it all joy when ye fall into divers trials, for this bestows upon you a proof of your faith. So far there is sufficient ground for counting all trials joy. Now, let us go a little further.

III. Let us think of THE PRICELESS VIRTUE WHICH IS PRODUCED BY TRIAL, namely, patience; for the proof of your "faith worketh patience." Patience! We all have a large stock of it—until we need it, and then we have none. The man who truly possesses patience is the man that has been tried. What kind of patience does he get by the grace of God ? First, he obtains *a patience that accepts the trial as from God without a murmur.* Calm resignation does not come all at once ; often long years of physical pain, or mental depression, or disappointment in business, or multiplied bereavements, are needed to bring the soul into full submission to the will of the Lord. After much crying the child is weaned; after much chastening the son is made obedient to his Father's will. By degrees we learn to end our quarrel with God, and to desire that there may not be two wills between God and ourselves, but that God's will may be our will. Oh, brother, if your troubles work you to that, you are a gainer, I am sure, and you may count them all joy.

The next kind of patience is when experience enables a man *to bear ill-treatment, slander, and injury without resentment.* He feels it keenly, but he bears it meekly. Like his Master, he opens not his mouth to reply, and refuses to return railing for railing. Contrariwise he gives blessing in return for cursing; like the sandal-wood tree which perfumes the axe which cuts it. Blessed is that holy charity which hopeth all things, endureth all things, and is not easily provoked. Ah, friend, if the grace of God by trial shall work in you the quiet patience which never grows angry, and never ceases to love, you may have lost a trifle of comfort, but you have gained a solid weight of character.

The patience which God works in us by tribulation also takes another form, namely, that *of acting without undue haste.* Before wisdom has balanced our zeal we are eager to serve God all in a hurry, with a rush and a spurt, as if everything must be done within the hour or nothing would ever be accomplished. We set about holy service with somewhat more of preparedness of heart after we have been drilled in the school of trial. We go steadily and resolutely about work for Jesus, knowing what poor creatures we are, and what a glorious Master we serve. The Lord our God is in no hurry because he is strong and wise. In proportion as we grow like the Lord Jesus we shall cast aside disturbance of mind and fury of spirit. His was a grand life-work, but he never seemed to be confused, excited, worried, or hurried, as certain of his people are. He did not strive nor cry, nor cause his voice to be heard in the streets. He knew his hour was not yet come, and there were so many days in which he could work, and therefore he went steadily on till he had finished the work which his Father had given him to do. That kind of patience is a jewel more to be desired than the gem which glitters on the imperial brow. Sometimes we blunder into a deal of mischief, making more haste than speed; and we are sure to do so when we forget to pray, and fail to commit our matters into the Divine hands. We may run with such vehemence that we may stumble, or lose our breath: there may be in our random efforts as much undoing as doing, for want of possessing our souls in patience.

That is a grand kind of patience, too, when *we can wait without unbelief.* Two little words are good for every Christian to learn and to practise—pray and stay. Waiting on the Lord implies both praying and staying. What if the world is not converted this year! What if the Lord Jesus does not come to-morrow! What if still our tribulations are lengthened out! What if the conflict is continued! He that has been tried and by grace has obtained the true profit of his trials, both quietly waits and joyfully hopes for the salvation of God. Patience, brother! Is this high virtue scarce with thee? The Holy Spirit shall bestow it upon thee through suffering.

This patience also takes the shape of *believing without wavering,* in the very teeth of strange providences and singular statements, and perhaps inward misgivings. The established Christian says, " I believe my God, and therefore if the vision tarry I will wait for it. My time is not yet come. I am to have my worst things first and my best things afterwards, and so I sit me down at Jesus' feet and tarry his leisure."

Brothers and sisters, if, in a word, we learn *endurance* we have taken a high degree. You look at the weather-beaten sailor, the man who is at home on the sea : he has a bronzed face and mahogany-coloured flesh, he looks as tough as heart of oak, and as hardy as if he were made of iron. How different from us poor landsmen. How did the man become so inured to hardships, so able to breast the storm, so that he does

not care whether the wind blows south-west or north-west? He can go
out to sea in any kind of weather; he has his sea legs on: how did he
come to this strength? By doing business in great waters. He could
not have become a hardy seaman by tarrying on shore. Now, trial works
in the saints that spiritual hardihood which cannot be learned in ease.
You may go to school for ever, but you cannot learn endurance there:
you may colour your cheek with paint, but you cannot give it that
ingrained brown which comes of stormy seas and howling winds. Strong
faith and brave patience come of trouble, and a few men in the church
who have thus been prepared are worth anything in time of tempest. To
reach that condition of firm endurance and sacred hardihood is worth
all the expense of all the heaped-up troubles that ever come upon us from
above or from beneath. When trial worketh patience we are incalculably
enriched. The Lord give us more of this choice grace. As Peter's fish
had the money in its mouth, so have sanctified trials spiritual riches
for those who endure them graciously.

IV. Lastly, all this works something better still, and this is our
fourth head: THE SPIRITUAL COMPLETENESS PROMOTED. "That ye
may be perfect and entire, wanting nothing." Brethren, the most
valuable thing a man can get in this world is that which has most to
do with his truest self. A man gets a good house: well, that is something: but suppose he is in bad health, what is the good of his fine
mansion? A man is well clothed and well fed: that is something: but
suppose he shivers with ague, and has no appetite through indigestion.
That spoils it all. If a man is in robust health this is a far more valuable
boon. Health is far more to be prized than wealth, or honour, or learning:
we all allow that, but then suppose that a man's innermost self is diseased
while his body is healthy, so that he is disgraced by vice or fevered with
passion, he is in a poor plight, notwithstanding that he has such a robust
frame? The very best thing is that which will make the man himself
a better man; make him right, and true, and pure, and holy. When the
man himself is better, he has made an unquestionable gain. So, if our
afflictions tend, by trying our faith, to breed patience, and that patience
tends to make us into perfect men in Christ Jesus, then we may be glad
of trials. Afflictions by God's grace make us all-round men, developing
every spiritual faculty, and therefore they are our friends, our helpers,
and should be welcomed with "all joy."

Afflictions find out our weak points, and this makes us attend to
them. Being tried, we discover our failures, and then going to God
about those failures we are helped to be perfect and entire, wanting
nothing.

Moreover, our trials, when blessed of God to make us patient, ripen
us. I do not know how to explain what I mean by ripening, but there is
a sort of mellowness about believers who have endured a great deal of
affliction that you never meet in other people. It cannot be mistaken
or imitated. A certain measure of sunlight is wanted to bring out the real
flavour of fruits, and when a fruit has felt its measure of burning sun it
developes a lusciousness which we all delight in. So is it in men and
women: a certain amount of trouble appears to be needful to create a
certain sugar of graciousness in them, so that they may contain the rich,
ripe juice of a gracious character. You must have known such men

and such women, and have said to yourselves, " I wish I could be like them, so calm, so quiet, so self-contained, so happy, and when not happy, yet so content not to be happy ; so mature in judgment, so spiritual in conversation, so truly ripe." This only comes to those in whom the proof of their faith works experience, and then experience brings forth the fruits of the Spirit. Dear brothers and sisters, there is a certain all-roundness of spiritual manhood which never comes to us except by manifold temptations. Let me attempt to show you what I mean. Sanctified trials produce a *chastened* spirit. Some of us by nature are rough and untender ; but after awhile friends notice that the roughness is departing, and they are quite glad to be more gently handled. Ah, that sick chamber did the polishing ; under God's grace, that depression of spirit, that loss, that cross, that bereavement,—these softened the natural ruggedness, and made the man meek and lowly, like his Lord. Sanctified trouble has a great tendency to breed *sympathy*, and sympathy is to the church as oil to machinery. A man that has never suffered feels very awkward when he tries to sympathise with a tried child of God. He kindly does his best, but he does not know how to go to work at it ; but those repeated blows from the rod make us feel for others who are smarting, and by degrees we are recognised as being the Lord's anointed comforters, made meet by temptation to succour those who are tempted.

Have you never noticed how tried men, too, when their trouble is thoroughly sanctified, become *cautious and humble?* They cannot speak quite so fast as they used to do : they do not talk of being absolutely perfect, though they are the very men who are Scripturally perfect ; they say little about their own doings, and much about the tender mercy of the Lord. They recollect the whipping they had behind the door from their Father's hands, and they speak gently to other erring ones. Affliction is the stone which our Lord Jesus throws at the brow of our giant pride, and patience is the sword which cuts off its head.

Those, too, are the kind of people who are most *grateful*. I have known what it is to praise God for the power to move one leg in bed. It may not seem much to you, but it was a great blessing to me. They that are heavily afflicted come to bless God for everything. I am sure that woman who took a piece of bread and a cup of water for her breakfast, and said, " What, all this, and Christ too ! " must have been a tried woman, or she would not have exhibited so much gratitude. And that old Puritan minister was surely a tried man, for when his family had only a herring and a few potatoes for dinner, he said, " Lord, we bless thee that thou hast ransacked sea and land to find food for us this day." If he had not been a tried man, he might have turned up his nose at the meal, as many do at much more sumptuous fare. Troubled men get to be grateful men, and that is no small thing.

As a rule, where God's grace works, these come to be *hopeful* men. Where others think the storm will destroy the vessel, they can remember storms equally fierce which did not destroy it, and so they are so calm that their courage keeps others from despair.

These men, too, become *unworldly* men. They have had too much trouble to think that they can ever build their nest in this black forest. There are too many thorns in their nest for them to reckon that this

world can be their home.   These birds of paradise take to their wings,
and are ready to fly away to the land of unfading flowers.

And these much-tempted ones are frequently *the most spiritual men*, and
out of this spirituality comes *usefulness*. Mr. Greatheart, who led the band
of pilgrims up to the celestial city, was a man of many trials, or he would
not have been fit to lead so many to their heavenly rest; and you, dear
brother, if ever you are to be a leader and a helper, as you would wish
to be, in the church of God, it must be by such means as this that you
must be prepared for it.   Do you not wish to have every virtue developed? Do you not wish to become a perfect man in Christ Jesus?   If
so, welcome with all joy divers trials and temptations; fly to God with
them; bless him for having sent them: ask him to help you to bear them
with patience, and then let that patience have its perfect work, and so
by the Spirit of God you shall become "perfect and entire, lacking
in nothing."   May the Comforter bless this word to your hearts, for
Jesus Christ's sake.   Amen.

Portion of Scripture read before Sermon—James i.

Hymns from "Our Own Hymn Book"—734, 750, 716.

A CENTENNIAL HISTORY

OF

SPURGEON'S TABERNACLE

by

ERIC W. HAYDEN

$3.95

At Your Bookstore

THE HEARING OF FAITH.

A Sermon

DELIVERED ON LORD'S-DAY MORNING, FEBRUARY 11TH, 1883, BY

C. H. SPURGEON,

AT THE METROPOLITAN TABERNACLE, NEWINGTON.

"This only would I learn of you, Received ye the Spirit by the works of the law, or by the hearing of faith?"—Galatians iii. 2.

A GREAT delusion is upon the heart of man as to his salvation. His ways are perverse. He does not love the law of God; nay, his mind is opposed to it, and yet he sets up to be its advocate. When he understands the spirituality and severity of the law he reckons it to be a sore burden; and yet, when the gospel is preached, and set forth as the gift of sovereign grace, and he is bidden simply to accept it by an act of faith in Christ Jesus, the man professes great concern about the law, lest it should be made void by the freeness of grace. He takes the broken pieces of the two tables of the law and hurls them at the cross. It is not that man loves the law of God, but that he does not love the God of the law: hence he will resort to any pretence to oppose that way of salvation which God has appointed. Doubtless, if it had been possible for the Lord to have set forth another way of salvation, man would have opposed that also, for he is determined to walk contrary to God. Be that as it may, there is a constant animosity in the minds of unregenerate men against the way of salvation by faith in Christ; and to oppose it they set up the pretence of salvation by the works of the law.

Brethren, in all our hearts there is this natural enmity to God and to the sovereignty of his grace. Hence it is that believers have often to complain of the difficulties of faith. Faith in itself is, or ought to be, the easiest thing in the world: for a creature to believe in its Creator, for a child to believe in his father, ought to be the simplest and most natural thing in the world; but by reason of the corruption that remaineth even in the regenerate there is ever a struggling against this simple way of faith. There are times with the best man when in recollection of his many sins conscience saith, " How canst thou believe that thou art justified and accepted while so much of evil is found in thee?" Unless we cleave to the promise of God and to his free mercy in Christ Jesus it will then go hard with us. The soul of the most sincere and upright man may be driven to despair by a sight of his own imperfections unless he clings to that righteousness by which sinners are justified through faith in Christ Jesus.

No. 1,705.

Beloved, if this warfare is discovered even in the minds of those who are born again, we must not wonder that it rages in the unregenerate. One would have thought that the moment we preached salvation by faith every sinner would have leaped up and accepted it. It is so simple, so easy, that surely every man would wish in this way to be forgiven and justified; instead of which, all the reasoning, all the thoughtfulness, ay, all the cunning of unregenerate human nature is stirred up to fight against the method of deliverance by faith in Christ Jesus. "It is too good to be true," says one. Another cries, "If this be preached it will lead men to think little of moral excellence." A third finds in the doctrine of grace an inducement to inaction; and so on, without end. These cavillings take hundreds of shapes; but after all they come to this: proud sinners must dictate to their offended Lord, and be forgiven on their own terms. It would appear that God does not know the best way of saving men, and men are so wise that they amend his methods! Is not this a refinement of blasphemy? It is a hideous farce to see a rebellious sinner suddenly become jealous about good works, and greatly concerned for public morality. Does it not make laughter in hell to see licentious men censuring the pure gospel of the Lord Jesus, and cavilling at free forgiveness because it might make men less mindful of purity? It makes one sick to see the hypocrisy of legalists.

The reason of this contention lies in the fact that man is not only poor, but proud; not only guilty, but conceited; so that he will not humble himself to be saved upon terms of divine charity. He will not consent to believe God; he prefers to believe in the proud falsehoods of his own heart, which delude him into the flattering hope that he may merit eternal life. Against this wicked spirit our text enters the lists; let us see how it conducts the combat. The argument of the text is a very plain and powerful one. Paul puts it thus: "The Holy Spirit has been received by you Galatians. How did you receive the Holy Spirit,—by the works of the law or by the hearing of faith?" They were bound to admit, each one for himself, that they received the Holy Spirit by faith, and by no other means.

Now, the Holy Spirit is the choicest of all the gifts of God which are received into the soul, and it is by the Spirit the work of the Lord Jesus is known and received. The Holy Spirit is himself the seal of divine favour, and the token that we are at peace with God. I might almost say that the reception of the Holy Spirit is salvation; for when he enters into us we are saved from death in sin, from the love of sin, from the power of sin, and from the terror of sin. When he reigns in the heart, all the graces of a perfect character attend upon him as courtiers upon a king. He becomes the source of life, light, love, and liberty to our souls, and even our bodies he sanctifies. Know ye not that your bodies are the temples of God when the Holy Spirit comes to dwell in them? To whom, then, the Holy Spirit is given salvation is given in the highest sense. But how is that Holy Spirit received? The question is soon answered. He is not received by the works of the law, but by the hearing of faith.

I am going to handle this fact, first, as *an argument of experience for all the people of God*, and, secondly, as *an argument at least of observation for those who are seeking after Christ.* May the Holy Spirit graciously aid us in our discourse.

I. First, then, here is AN ARGUMENT OF EXPERIENCE FOR THE PEOPLE OF GOD.

Before I dwell upon the personal experience of believers who are here present, I would remind you of *the experience of the church of God as it is recorded in the Acts of the Apostles.* The book of the Acts of the Apostles is a confirmation of the correct answer to my text. The disciples were met together after our Lord's ascension, and the Holy Spirit descended upon them : but in what way? Simply by their obeying the command of the Lord Jesus, "who commanded them that they should not depart from Jerusalem, but wait for the promise of the Father, which, saith he, ye have heard of me." The gift was received by the hearing of faith, which led them to united prayer and waiting. They performed no ceremonies, and entered upon no labours : the watchword was, "Tarry ye till ye be endowed with power from on high." The power came that they might work, and not because they had worked. The gift of the Spirit came according to promise, and not according to works. Very speedily the Spirit of God fell upon the people outside, and three thousand of them were converted and baptized. How came the Spirit of God upon Parthians, Medes, and Elamites, and the dwellers in Mesopotamia, and so forth? Was it by the works of the law? No, beloved; but Peter thus preached (Acts ii. 38): "Repent, and be baptized every one of you in the name of Jesus Christ for the remission of sins, and ye shall receive the gift of the Holy Ghost." When the thousands believed in Christ Jesus, and confessed their faith by baptism, the Holy Spirit was given them. So was it also in Samaria : "When they believed Philip preaching the things concerning the kingdom of God, and the name of Jesus Christ, they were baptized, both men and women" : and then we read that the apostle Peter went to them, and these believers received the Holy Ghost: certainly not by the works of the law, but by the hearing of faith were they thus blessed. Turn to the story of Cornelius. That good man had abounded in almsgiving and prayer, and yet the Holy Spirit fell not upon him ; but when the " hearing of faith" came, and they were assembled in the house with one accord to listen to Peter, then the Holy Ghost fell upon all them that heard the word. " And they of the circumcision which believed were astonished, as many as came with Peter, because that on the Gentiles also was poured out the gift of the Holy Ghost. For they heard them speak with tongues, and magnify God. Then answered Peter, Can any man forbid water, that these should not be baptized, which have received the Holy Ghost as well as we?" Was it not the same when Paul went out and preached among the Gentiles ? It was indeed so startlingly so, that the news came to the Hebrew Christians who were at Jerusalem, and no small dissension and disputation was the consequence. Here had been no circumcision, no proselyting to Judaism, no observation of any part of the Mosaic ritual, and yet they heard that the Holy Ghost had fallen upon the Gentiles, who had not even known the law, much less fulfilled it. It needed all Peter's influence to stem the flood. Hear how he puts it : " God made choice among us, that the Gentiles by my mouth should hear the word of the gospel, and believe. And God, which knoweth the hearts, bare them witness, giving them the Holy Ghost, even as he did unto us." The Holy Ghost was received by believing Gentiles in every place where Paul had preached; and hence he could refer to these Galatians and use their experience to correct their errors. The fact that the Holy Ghost is given to the hearing of faith, and not as a reward of works, runs like a silver thread through the whole of the Acts of the Apostles: why, then, should men look to the works of the law for that which was never given except to faith? What an infatuation to look to the mirage when a real well is open at their feet!

Now I come to *your own experience*. You, beloved friends, if you are indeed in Christ Jesus have received the Holy Ghost. But how? Let us go over the list of his operations upon your minds. You received enlightenment by his means, by which you were led to understand the way of salvation, and to behold the glory of God in the face of Jesus Christ. Did you attain to that enlightenment by the works of the law? Was it so in any one case? It has been my privilege to know many of you, and to remember your confession of faith: you told me that when you were seeking salvation by your own works you were blind, and saw not the light; the more you strove and the more you struggled the more intense the midnight grew about you, until you well-nigh despaired. Light came by a look at the Crucified; it came only by "the hearing of faith."

After that, you received peace, which peace, I trust, you enjoy this morning—"the peace of God which passeth all understanding." But did you receive that peace while you were trusting in ceremonies, in baptism, or in the Lord's supper, or in your own works? I know you did not; for true peace of conscience comes not in at that door. Did you obtain peace while you tried to repent so much, to weep so much, to feel so much, or to do so much? Nay, brethren, not an atom of peace ever came to your spirit until you looked away from yourself to the Lord Jesus, of whom you heard that he was able to save even the chief of sinners; and in whom you therefore believed. When faith came peace grew out of it as a fruit of the Holy Spirit.

Since that, you have received the Holy Ghost to help you in your sanctification; but you have obtained no sanctification apart from believing. If you have reached after sanctification by your own efforts, made in unbelief, you have never succeeded. Unbelief works towards sin, and never towards sanctification. Our good works are fruits of sanctification, not causes of it; and if we put the fruit where the root should be we greatly err. If you have gone out to fight against a temptation in your own strength, have you ever returned a conqueror? It has been written of all other believers, "They overcame through the blood of the Lamb"; and this is true of you also. Sanctification does not come to us from self-reliance, but as a work of the Spirit received by faith in Christ. Believing in him, he is "made of God unto us wisdom, righteousness, sanctification, and redemption."

You have had besides, dear friends, another gift of the Holy Spirit, namely, that of communion with God. But did you ever commune with the holy God on the footing of your own goodness? Never. Abraham never spake with Jehovah on legal terms; for when he interceded with the Lord, he said, "I have taken upon me to speak unto the Lord—I that am but dust and ashes." Yet he spake with God in wondrous nearness ; and that is the point of it—to be dust and ashes in your own sight, and yet to commune with God as a friend. This is the daring of faith. This the Lord delights in. David said, "So foolish was I, and ignorant: I was as a beast before thee. Nevertheless I am continually with thee : thou hast holden me by my right hand." A beast in your own esteem, and yet upheld by God himself, and allowed to live in favoured fellowship with him !

Dear friends, there is no communion with God except by faith, without which we cannot even please God. The favourites of heaven are in every case men who believe in God. Faith has the golden key of the ivory palaces. Faith opens the secret chambers of communion to those who love her. The works of the law bring no nearness to God ; in token whereof, none might come near to Sinai, and if so much as a beast touch the mountain it must be stoned or thrust through with a dart.

And you, dear friends, have received the Holy Spirit often as your helper in prayer : " The Spirit also helpeth our infirmity ; " but I am sure it never was by the works of the law. When infirmity has stopped your prayer, and you could not cry as you would, then you have had no room to boast of good works, and yet then the Spirit has made " inter-cession for you with groanings that could not be uttered." Your infirmity made you feel that it was by grace, and by grace alone, that you were helped in your time of need.

Now, as to the Holy Spirit's office of sealing the soul and working full assurance in the heart ; as to the Holy Spirit's being the earnest of the future glory, the pledge of joys to come,—in all these grace reigns, and not merit. He that dwelleth in the least degree upon any phantom merit of his own hath no earnest of the inheritance whatsoever ; in fact, for him there is no inheritance, since an inheritance does not come by works. Neither hath he that trusts in his works any pledge of joys to come ; for he does not know that he has done enough to secure them. Neither can he have any comfortable rest in God ; for his work is not finished, and therefore he cannot rest. You know it, you that have toiled to save yourselves. Every Christian here must confess, " It is even so: we have received everything by faith, and nothing by merit." Well, then, the inference is this: do not pump a dry well. If there be a fountain that is ever-flowing and overflowing, keep to it. Do not commit the double evil of forsaking the fountain of living water, and hewing out to yourselves broken cisterns. Wait you at that door at which you have received everything as yet, and do not go where you have received nothing except it be conviction and condemnation. Look not to Moses to bring you into Canaan: that can only be done by Joshua Jesus.

Now, mark this inference: let every child of God ponder it—*keep you to " the hearing of faith."* When you are under a sense of backsliding, when you feel unworthy to be called God's son, when you have erred and strayed from his ways like a lost sheep, do not rush like a madman to the law, for that would be to leap into the fire ; but still say, " Lord, I believe in thee. As a sinner I trust the sinner's Substitute." Whether you did truly come to Christ at the first or not, is a point which you need not discuss; but begin again. Take with you words and come by faith to Jesus, and say, " Heal my backslidings, receive me graciously, and love me freely." By faith we can be restored, but never by doubting and despairing. We can only come to Christ by faith at first, and we can only return to him in the same way. If you begin to doubt the mercy and love of God to you, you will backslide more and more. Your hope lies in holding on to this—" Be I what I may, yet God has not changed, and there is still forgiveness with him, that he may be feared; therefore will I go with the language of the fifty-first psalm upon my tongue, and the penitence of David in my heart, and I will say, ' Create in me a clean heart, O God, and renew a right spirit within me.'" Stick to your faith in Christ; do not think that the greatness of your sin exceeds his atoning merit; do not doubt but that he will still cleanse you and love you as aforetime.

Suppose you have not backslidden, but yet you are in the presence of a tremendous inward conflict. I will suppose that you are led to question whether you are the children of God at all, and persuaded to doubt your sonship. Now, be resolved to hold on to your faith in your heavenly Father. The devil is saying to you, " If thou be the son of God." Do not yield to his " if." This is the way in which he attacked your Saviour in the wilderness. A question about our sonship is the very point of the devil's sword, and it is dipped in deadly poison; wherefore guard thyself with that word of God, " To as many as received him to them gave he power to become the sons of God, even to as many as believed on his name." Say, " I believe in Jesus Christ my Lord, who died for the ungodly, and in him I am assured of being a child of God." You cannot resist temptation by doubting. Doubting is weakness; in believing is your might. " How can I believe," says one. The elect of God believe: those who are born from above believe their Father's word. If thou canst believe thou shalt win great victories, but if thou cast away thy confidence the battle is lost already. Above all, or over all, carry the shield of faith. Be sure to do this in the evil day, when sin prevails. Is this too hard for you? What, has it come to this, that when you feel you are a saint you can then trust to Christ? That is, you can trust him when you can do without him. Poor sham of faith! The genuine faith is a sinner's faith, which trusts the Saviour when signs, and evidences, and marks are all hidden, and sin and temptation hold the upper seats. To believe that I, a sinner, am forgiven by the free grace of God; that I, a poor, imperfect being, am yet accepted of God—this is faith. May we have power to trust the Lord Jesus in earnest; to trust him with real sin and real unworthiness.

Do this, dear friends, with regard to the whole of your life's struggle. Some begin their religious life in the Spirit by faith, but they fancy that the rest of their spiritual life will have to be by works. They forget that the just shall live by faith. Those who say that though they be children of God they may perish after all have not the true gospel ring about them. If they are children of God, can they perish? How? Why? " Well, we must be watchful and prayerful." Precisely so. But is there no provision made to secure that you shall be watchful and prayerful? If not, then I tell you, brother, you will never get to heaven. You will fail in this watchfulness of yours, and then where are you? My hope of heaven lies in the belief that the Lord Jesus has redeemed me and will keep me. He will make me watchful and prayerful, and work in me by his Spirit all else that is essential to my safety. "I know whom I have believed," and I am not afraid to add, "I am persuaded that he is able to keep that which I have committed unto him until that day." Brothers, it is by such faith that we receive the Spirit, and not by legal works and fears.

At this present moment you are saved by faith alone, are you not? Yes. Then I would persuade you to extend that faith over the whole area of your life. Believe for final preservation. Believe for complete salvation. Is it not written "He that believeth on him hath *everlasting life*"? Can that life which is everlasting come to an end? Can eternal life expire? "Faithful is he that hath called you, who also will do it." "Oh," say you, "I am half afraid to believe so bravely, for it might make me careless." This is a mistake: faith *works* by love, it never tends to sloth. My dear friend, if you look to yourself in any degree your foot is beginning to slip. Put the future where you put the past, namely, into the hands of him that is able to keep you from falling. Believe in Jesus for a life as well as for an hour, and he will keep you with spotless garments to the end. Stand on the sure rock of the Lord's finished work, and not on the dubious ground of your own carefulness. Works done as the efforts of our own strength are poor things; but the work of the grace of God upon our spirit is precious. Let all be of grace, and nothing of self. The two will no more go together than oil and water will mix. Do not try to trust partly in Christ and partly in self: as well yoke an archangel with an emmet, or a cherub with a cricket. Salvation is of the Lord alone from first to last.

Brethren, let us keep in this condition when we are comparing ourselves with other saints of God. I sometimes read biographies which make me cover my face for shame because I fall so far short of the attainments of certain believers. This humbling is good for us. What ought we to do when we feel it? To begin to doubt the Lord, and imagine that the Lord Jesus cannot or will not save *us*? Far from it. Faith should rise by observing what the Lord has done for other poor sinners like ourselves; for he is able to do the same for us. Remember that the safety of the weak and of the strong believer rests upon the same foundation. This may be seen in a figure. On board one of the fine steamboats which flit between England and America I see a strong, hardy, vigorous man. Will he get to America safely? Yes, if the ship does. But see, yonder is a little child which cannot walk, and has to be carried in its mother's arms. Will it reach America safely? Yes, if the ship does. Both the robust man and the puling infant, all being well, will reach their journey's end—if the ship does. Their safety lies in the same place. Their condition does not affect their transit. But is there no difference between the child and the man? Assuredly, a great deal of difference as to many things; but there is no difference about the fact that their passage across the ocean depends upon the steamboat rather than upon themselves. The strong man could not walk across the Atlantic any more than the child could: they are alike incompetent for the passage if left alone, and alike capable of it if placed on board the same vessel. So, if you meet with a great saint, say to yourself, " My honoured brother will get to heaven through Jesus Christ; and I, a poor babe in grace, shall get to heaven in the same way." I want you children of God to feel this.   Are you on board the Covenant transport ?   Does the blood-red flag fly at the mast-head ?   Then, if the meanest believer is not safely carried into port, neither will the strongest child of God reach the fair havens.   If that ship of free grace go down, Peter and Paul must sink as well as ourselves; for we are at sea in the same vessel.   Our confidence is in no measure or sense in what we are, but altogether in what Christ is on our behalf; we depend on Jesus and rest in Jesus by a simple faith, and the brightest of martyrs and apostles has no surer ground to rest on.

When you come to die do not look upon death through the glass of the law ; for if so it will be terrible to you ; but believe this, that to die by faith is to enter into life.   I hardly like to use the word death in such a connection, for it is not dying at all, but " departing out of this world unto the Father."   By faith to die is such sweet work as you, poor Despondency, and you, Much-Afraid, will be able to accomplish as safely as Valiant-for-Truth, or Greatheart himself.   By faith we swallow up death in victory.   They that have served God for fifty years faith-fully and without fault, when they come to die have in every case gathered up their feet in the bed and said, " Into thy hands I commit my spirit."   But never has one of them died pleading his own religiousness and claiming a reward as due to his deserts. Trusting in Jesus is the universal spirit of the most praiseworthy believers.   Well, if they flung every other hope away except that which was presented to them in Christ, you, dear friend, need not hesitate to do the same ; and as they were secure and triumphant, even so shall you be.

This is the argument, then—you have obtained nothing except by the hearing of faith; therefore, keep to the way of faith even to your last hour, for wisdom teaches you so to do.

II.   But now I want to throw all my strength into the second part of the sermon, which is this: I want to use this AS AN ARGUMENT DERIVED FROM OBSERVATION FOR THE USE OF SEEKERS.   I say "observation," but in part it might be called an argument from expe-rience, for at any rate on the negative side it is so.

Listen, dear hearer, you have not yet found rest, you are not yet saved ; and so far you have obtained no advantage by the works of the law. By your own honesty, generosity, and righteousness, you have not been justified, nor have you received a new heart, or any other gift of the Spirit.   Why continue at this unprofitable business ?   Some try church-goings, chapel-goings, Bible-readings, sacraments, forms of prayer, and the like, but nothing comes of it.   Hear how they repeat their Ave Marias, and their Pater Nosters ; and not only Romanists, but so-called Protestants, are puffed up with the hope that by formal worship they will be saved.   But they make no headway, and are still without salvation.   Let me ask you work-trusters, have you any rest ? are you prepared to die ? would you be willing to die at once ? No.   Your position is one of unrest, and fear, and dread.   Why not abandon this vain method of building, for " except the Lord build the house they labour in vain that build it?" Instead of following out your own way of salvation by the works of the law, why not try the Lord's appointed way of the hearing of faith? Has he not said "Hear and your soul shall live"? Are you willing to hear me explain it?

The "hearing of faith": this is the way by which the Spirit of God comes to men. "What kind of hearing," says one, "is that?" Well, to begin with, it is *personal hearing*, listening to the word for yourself. I have heard of one who had a dream in which he thought he stood at the gates of heaven, and his wife with him. She went in, but the porter shut him out, saying, "The other day you said to your wife, ' Mistress, you may go to church and pray for us both,' and now she shall go to heaven for you both, and you must stop outside." Is not that just? There must be a personal hearing. I pray you, do not absent yourselves from the hearing of the word; for "faith cometh by hearing, and hearing by the word of God."

That last sentence reminds me that the hearing *must be the hearing of the gospel*. I wish people were more careful upon that point. You will not receive the Holy Ghost by merely hearing a man talk. He may be eloquent, he may be clever, and he may be pious; but mark you, if he does not preach the gospel, saving faith cannot come of your hearing it. Too many people go to that place of worship which is nearest to their houses, and never mind what is preached so long as there is an attractive service. Oh, sirs, do not thus play the fool with yourselves. The faith that saves you cannot come to you by hearing anything which comes first; it only comes by hearing the testimony of the Spirit to the appointed Saviour.

The right kind of hearing is *an attentive hearing*. There is a great difference between hearing and hearing. If I were to say, "There is a ship going to sail next Tuesday for New Zealand," the most of you would hear it, and think no more of it. But suppose there should be a person here who is in great haste to reach New Zealand, he will catch at my words, and be round in the vestry to make further enquiries. This is the kind of hearing which the gospel requires. You are in one of our great stations, and you hear a person say, "That train is for Exeter." The information is lost upon you, for you are bound for Oxford, and it is as though you heard it not: but suppose you were bound for Exeter, you would catch at the sound, and make use of the news. Now, I am talking about the salvation of man from the power of sin, the salvation of man from the guilt of sin, the preparation of man for a holy life on earth and an eternal life of bliss in heaven: if you have the hearing of faith you will feel that this subject is one which concerns yourself, you will be anxious to know more about it, and you will give your mind to its consideration: this is the sort of hearing by which faith comes. Do not lend your ears to others, but hear for yourself. Go where the gospel is preached, and hear it with both your ears. Drink it in as an ox drinks of the stream. Treasure up every word as the ants store up grain. Test all as goldsmiths test gold; and then receive the truth as babes drink in milk from the breast. This is "the hearing of faith."

"But what is this *faith*," says one, "the hearing of faith?" I will try to work out the idea. You begin with hearing the gospel believing that it comes from God. I suppose nearly everybody here believes the Bible to be the word of God. Very well, when you hear that teaching which is consistent with Scripture, the hearing of faith is to accept it as God's word, and therefore true, and worthy of your reverent attention. The gospel is the voice of God, and it comes by the Spirit of God : a belief of this truth will help you to hear it reverently, and it will prepare your mind to receive it.

Then remember that, if it be God's word, a genuine faith in God knows of no difficulties whatever. A man who believes the Bible to be inspired, just as readily believes that the whale swallowed Jonah, or that Joshua stayed the sun, as he believes that Abraham interceded for Sodom, or that Paul was a prisoner at Rome. Knowing the gospel to be God's testimony we believe it *all*. That is the way in which to hear the gospel. Say to yourself, " This is God's gospel. It is wonderfully grand and good, but it is not therefore a matter of doubt. That I may be saved in one single minute by believing in Jesus ; that every sin I have ever committed, however black, may all be washed away ere the clock ticks again,—these are wonderful things ; but I believe them because the Lord has said so. It is not mine to quibble, question, or cavil ; if there are any difficulties in these great promises, those difficulties belong to God, and not to me. Let the Lord promise what he pleases, I am ready to believe it because he is able to perform his own word."

Then, " the hearing of faith" signifies, further, that we do venture our eternal interests upon the truth of what we hear. I use the word " venture" advisedly. One of our hymns puts it—

> " Venture on him, venture wholly,
> Let no other trust intrude."

I have heard critics object that it is no *venture*, but a certainty, when men trust in Christ. But I venture to assert that, when a man is in trouble of spirit, faith is a venture to him ; it appears to him to be the greatest venture possible. He that saith, " This gospel which I have heard is true, and I will venture my soul upon the truth of it," he is the man who has given to the gospel " the hearing of faith." Let me try to set forth faith yet again :—this bridge is strong enough to carry me over the stream, therefore I am going over the stream upon it. That is real faith. Faith is a most practical principle in daily life. The most of trade hangs on trust. When a man sows wheat he has to scatter it into the furrows and lose it, and he does so because he has faith that God will send a harvest. When the sailor loses sight of the shore, he has to sail by faith ; believing in his compass, he feels safe though he may not see land for weeks. Faith is the hand which receives what God presents to us, and hence it is a simple child-like thing. When a child has an apple offered to him, the child may know nothing about the orchard in which the apple grew, and he may know nothing of the mechanism of his hand and arm, but it is quite enough for him to take the apple. Faith does the most effectual thing for the soul when it takes what God gives : all the rest may be or may not be, faith is the main thing. When God holds out to me salvation by Christ Jesus, I need not ask anything further about it, but just take it to myself and be at once saved, for by faith the Spirit of God is received.

Once more, "the hearing of faith" is when a man hears and accepts the gospel and then holds to it under opposition. When conscience reminds you that you are a guilty man you must still hold to peace by the blood of Jesus. What says the word? It tells you that he that believeth in Jesus is not condemned, and you must believe that word, whatever your own judgment and feelings may say. When the devil, as the accuser of the brethren, howls out, "You cannot be saved; look at your imperfections and transgressions!" then reply, "But I am saved, whatever my imperfections and my sins may be, for it is written, 'He that believeth and is baptized shall be saved.' I have obeyed both precepts, and therefore I shall be saved, despite your rage." Poor sinner, have you not seen that this is the way the Holy Ghost has come to others? Your Christian friends have all told you that this is the way they obtained mercy. Will you not make an attempt in the same way, and hear and believe as a little child? Believe God's word. Do not wish to be anything or to do anything; but just trust in what Jesus is and did. You shall have the Holy Ghost, and you shall feel as you have never felt before, if you will give "the hearing of faith."

I want your attention for a minute while I mention some of the points in the gospel out of which this "hearing of faith" generally comes. What truth is it which men most readily believe?

The first is this. A man says, "I cannot believe"; but he can hear, and he hears that God has sent forth his Son Jesus Christ to be the Saviour of men. "God has sent him," says he, "the offended God has appointed a mediator. Christ does not come as an amateur, but as an ambassador authorized of heaven." "Then," says he, "I will trust him whom God has ordained to be a Saviour."

Next, while listening to the gospel the man hears about the person of the Lord, and sees who he is, namely, that he is God's only-begotten Son, equal and co-eternal with the Father: and yet he is in the fullest sense man, in our nature. I have known many a soul say, "I can trust Jesus, since he is God and able to save me, and man, and thus willing to save me." By that celestial lamp many have seen their way to faith. Oh, that faith may come to you while you are hearing me.

Another very blessed nail on which faith loves to hang all its weight is the sufferings of Christ,—for, being found in fashion as a man, he humbled himself, and became obedient to death, even the death of the cross. See him languishing upon the cruel tree, bleeding out his life for unworthy men, his enemies, that they might live through him. Many and many a time that sight has turned a doubter into a believer. Thousands have seen the cross, and felt that they must believe.

Another nail on which many have learned to hang all their hope has been Christ's risen power. They have heard of him that he is in glory now, at the right hand of God, making intercession for transgressors, and this has been the star of hope to the desponding. Is it not a joy that God also hath highly exalted him, so that he is able to save to the uttermost all that come unto God by him? Myriads of tremblers have felt faith leap up from their hearts like the water from the rock in the wilderness when Christ has been set before them as exalted to be a Prince and a Saviour, giving both repentance and remission of sins. They have been trying to believe before, but now they believe without trying. Trying to believe is a very stupid operation: you cannot do it; minds work not so: but when a man sees a thing to be true he believes it as a matter of course. He is convinced by the blessed fact of Christ's resurrection and ascension that he is able to save, and so he trusts in him to save him. Thus he receives the Spirit.

I have known many that have been led to believe by hearing of the work and grace of the Holy Spirit. They have heard the preacher say that the Holy Spirit can raise men from their death in sin, that he can renew the heart, that he can change the will, and conquer the passions: they have said " Is it so ? Is God himself willing to work with me to make me holy ? Then I will trust him." Thus faith comes.

Sometimes also when we have preached free forgiveness, full redemption, irreversible acceptance, infinite love, boundless grace, unchallengeable justification; when we have declared that the Lord's mercy endureth for ever, and that men have but to look to Jesus and there and then find eternal life,—then faith has dropped on men's minds as dew upon the grass. Our hearers have felt that such tidings must be true, for nobody could have invented them. The gospel has the stamp of Deity upon it, and this commends it to man's heart. Free grace and dying love are worthy of faith, and they win faith. I pray that all of you who are seekers may give up all trying to feel, and trying to work, and trying to be, and may just come and put your trust in Jesus. Then shall you be saved, and then you may work, and feel, and do as much as you like. Then shall you abound in good works, and the more the merrier. Then you shall fight with sin and overcome it; then shall you set up a high standard and reach it; then shall you strive after holiness and manifest it. But do not begin where you ought to leave off. Do not put, as the proverb hath it, the cart before the horse; do not place the top of the house where the foundation ought to be; but as you never did obtain anything by the works of the law, come and try " the hearing of faith," and you shall receive all that you need in Christ Jesus. God grant it, for Jesus' sake. Amen.

PORTION OF SCRIPTURE READ BEFORE SERMON—Galatians iii.

HYMNS FROM " OUR OWN HYMN BOOK "—406, 533, 546.

THE CAST-OFF GIRDLE.

A Sermon

DELIVERED AT THE THURSDAY EVENING LECTURE, BY

C. H. SPURGEON,

AT THE METROPOLITAN TABERNACLE, NEWINGTON.

"Thus saith the Lord unto me, Go and get thee a linen girdle, and put it upon thy loins, and put it not in water. So I got a girdle, according to the word of the Lord, and put it on my loins. And the word of the Lord came unto me the second time, saying, Take the girdle that thou hast got, which is upon thy loins, and arise, go to Euphrates, and hide it there in a hole of the rock. So I went, and hid it by Euphrates, as the Lord commanded me. And it came to pass after many days, that the Lord said unto me, Arise, go to Euphrates, and take the girdle from thence, which I commanded thee to hide there. Then I went to Euphrates, and digged, and took the girdle from the place where I had hid it: and, behold, the girdle was marred, it was profitable for nothing. Then the word of the Lord came unto me, saying, Thus saith the Lord, After this manner will I mar the pride of Judah, and the great pride of Jerusalem. This evil people, which refuse to hear my words, which walk in the imagination of their heart, and walk after other gods, to serve them, and to worship them, shall even be as this girdle, which is good for nothing. For as the girdle cleaveth to the loins of a man, so have I caused to cleave unto me the whole house of Israel and the whole house of Judah, saith the Lord; that they might be unto me for a people, and for a name, and for a praise, and for a glory: but they would not hear."—Jeremiah xiii. 1—11.

GOD'S servants, in the olden time, were very anxious to be understood when they spoke. They were not content because the people listened to them, or because they were to their hearers as "a very lovely song of one that hath a pleasant voice, and can play well on an instrument." They reckoned the people's approval of their style to be proof of its failure. Had it wounded their hearts it would not have gratified their tastes. They wanted the truth to go home to men, so that they could no longer discuss modes of speech, or methods of action, but would be compelled to remember the message, and feel its force. They reckoned that they had done nothing unless they riveted attention, excited thought, and impressed the heart. Oh that all preachers were as solemnly in earnest in all their addresses as Jeremiah was: we might then hope to see more true conversions, and less of the flimsy religion of the day!

The people of Israel and Judah were so sunk in thoughtlessness that it was absolutely necessary to do something more than speak. Prophet after prophet had spoken, "but they would not hear." Even though Jeremiah, the most plaintive of all the prophets, spoke in such melting tones that it must have been difficult to turn away from him with indifference, yet they remained so hardened that God described them, as "this evil people, which refuse to hear my words, which walk in the imagination of their heart." Though the prophet wept, and entreated,

No. 1,706.

and persuaded, yet they regarded him not ; but turned on their heel and
went each one his own way, to his merchandise, to his idolatry, to his
adultery, or to his oppression. Therefore the Lord bade his servants add
to their speech certain symbols which the people would see with their
eyes, which would be talked about as strange things, and so would excite
attention and command consideration. Perhaps by this means the Lord
would extort from some of them a deeper thought, and bring them
penitently to their knees. It is better for preachers to do odd things
than for men to be lost. If plain talk fails we may even use emblems
and signs, for we cannot let the careless ones perish without another
attempt to get at them. Oh that by any means we might save some !

In many instances the prophets were bidden to do singular things, and
among the rest was this : Jeremiah must take a linen girdle and put
it about his loins, and wear it there till the people had noticed what he
wore, and how long he wore it. This girdle was not to be washed ;
this was to be a matter observed of all observers, for it was a part of the
similitude. Then he must make a journey to the distant river Euphrates,
and take off his girdle and bury it there. When the people saw him
without a girdle they would make remarks and ask what he had done
with it; and he would reply that he had buried it by the river of
Babylon. Many would count him mad for having walked so far to get rid
of a girdle : two hundred and fifty miles was certainly a great
journey for such a purpose. Surely he might have buried it nearer home,
if he must needs bury it at all. There was the Jordan : he might have
gone to its bank, and digged a hole, and hidden away the garment there,
if he thought it well to do so. There would be a good deal of talk about
Jeremiah's eccentric conduct, and the more thoughtful would endeavour
to spell out his meaning for they would feel sure that he meant much by
it. Anon, the prophet goes a second time to the Euphrates, and
they say one to another—The prophet is a fool: the spiritual man is
mad. See what a trick he is playing. Nearly a thousand miles the man
will have walked in order to hide a girdle, and to dig it up again. What
next will he do? Whereas plain words might not have been noticed,
this little piece of acting commanded the attention and excited the
curiosity of the people. Blame us not if we sometimes dramatize the
truth : we must win men's hearts, and to do so we dare even run the
risk of being called theatrical. Jeremiah might have been ridiculed as
an actor : but he would not have fretted much under the charge if he
saw that he had succeeded in teaching the people the truth which God
would have them learn. When our young folks cannot learn by books,
we try the kinder-garten method, and we will sooner teach them by toys
than leave them ignorant : even so was it with the old prophets; they
would use emblems rather than leave the people in the dark.

The record of this singular transaction has come to us, and we know
that, as a part of Holy Scripture, it is full of instruction. Thousands
of years will not make it so antique as to be valueless. The word
of the Lord never becomes old so as to lose its vigour ; it is still as
strong for all divine purposes as when first of all Jehovah spoke it.
This Bible is the oldest of instructors, and yet it wears the dew of its
youth : like the sea, it is ancient as the ages, but time has written no
furrow on its brow. It is always venerable, yet ever novel; eternal,

yet always fresh. Even the symbol of Jeremiah, which was so strikingly adapted to his age and time, is quite as well suited to this present year of grace. May the Holy Spirit give us all instruction thereby.

I. And, first, in our text we have AN HONOURABLE EMBLEM of Israel and Judah : we may say, in these days, an emblem of the church of God. I say it is an honourable emblem ; I hardly know of one which is more so except when the church is called a crown of glory, and a royal diadem, or better still, the Bride, the Lamb's wife. The people were compared to a linen girdle with which the prophet in the type girt himself, but which God explains to be *his* girdle, for "as the girdle cleaveth to the loins of a man, so have I caused to cleave unto me the whole house of Israel and the whole house of Judah, saith the Lord."

Notice first, then, that God had taken this people to be *bound to himself* : he had taken them to be as near to him as the girdle is to the Oriental when he binds it about his loins. The eastern merchant or worker does not go out without his girdle : it is an essential part of his dress, keeping all the rest together : and so the Lord declares that he had taken his people and had bound them about himself to be near unto him, and fastened about him, so that he would not go forth without them. Often he speaks of them as "a people near unto him." Had they acted as they should have done, so as to be not only the natural but the spiritual seed of Israel, they would have enjoyed what every true believer may enjoy, namely cleaving unto God as a girdle cleaves unto a man ; for the Lord's own sanctified ones are bound unto God by God himself, so as never to be torn away from him. I invite you, beloved of the Lord, to consider your choice privilege in thus being, as it were, girt about the loins of God. It is a wonderful metaphor. In infinite condescension the Lord has put it so : the believer's place is near his God, in intimate, continuous, open fellowship. What can be more intimately associated with a man's most vital parts than his girdle ? What can be nearer to the life of God than his living people ? The traveller in the East takes care that his girdle shall not go unfastened : he girds himself securely ere he commences his work or starts upon his walk ; and God has bound his people round about him so that they shall never be removed from him. "I in them," saith Christ, even as a man is in his girdle. "Who shall separate us ?" saith Paul. Who shall ungird us from the heart and soul of our loving God ? "They shall be mine, saith the Lord." They are his, and ever shall be his ; neither shall any tear them away from him, for by covenant and by promise are they bound up with the life of God.

Yet remember that there are many who, like the Jewish people, bear the name of Israel, but they are not the true Israel. They are bound about God nominally, as it were, but yet they are not spiritually united to him ; and concerning such this parable tells us much that is worthy of solemn consideration. May the Holy Ghost warn all professors by this instructive image. If we are indeed what we profess to be, then we shall cleave to God for ever, as it is written, "I will put my fear in their hearts, and they shall not depart from me." Our faith will encompass Christ our Lord ; our love will embrace him : our patience will surround him : our hope will encircle him world without end. In all our service we shall endeavour to cleave fast to God. If anything comes between us and God it will be our sorrow, a trouble not to be endured. Nothing shall seduce the faithful from their hold upon God ; for he who bound them about himself will allow no enemy to unloose his girdle. Whatever the world may do by way of bribe, or by way of threatening, we shall hold fast to him, and shall not let him go, and that for this reason —that unchanging love and infinite wisdom have bound us too fast for us to be ungirt again. Because the Lord's own love has bound us to himself, therefore we bind ourselves to him by steadfast covenant.

> "Loved of our God, for him again
> With love intense we burn:
> Chosen of him ere time began,
> We choose him in return."

And, as nothing can separate us from the love of God which is in Christ Jesus our Lord, so nothing shall separate our love from God whom we love in Christ Jesus our Lord. What a privilege this—that the Lord should cause us to cleave unto him, to be unto him for a people, and for a name, and for a praise, and for a glory." Pardon me if I speak feebly, my heart loses utterance in contemplating the gracious imagery here set before us.

But Jeremiah's girdle was a linen one : it was the girdle peculiar to the priests, for such was the prophet ; he was "the son of Hilkiah, of the priests that were in Anathoth." Thus the type represents chosen men as bound to God *in connection with sacrifice.* The people of the Lord are the very girdle of the Most High in this sense, that if there is priestly work to do, he puts us about him, and makes us to be the instruments of this hallowed service. For us our blessed Lord girt himself with a linen girdle, for us he even now is girt about the paps with a golden girdle ; and now for him we also become priests and kings unto God and his continued priestly work among men is done by us. I mean, not by ministers alone, but by all the inheritance of God ; by all the blood-washed ones, by all the regenerate ones; for ye are "a royal priesthood, a peculiar people." God hath made his people to be "a nation of priests," and it is ours to offer sacrifice to God continually, the sacrifice of prayer and thanksgiving. We know of no order of priests save the whole body of the faithful, who present their bodies a living sacrifice, holy, acceptable to God by Jesus Christ. That is why a linen girdle was specified rather than any other. We are bound to the Most High for solemn priesthood to minister among the sons of men in holy things. The Lord Jesus is now blessing the sons of men as Aaron blessed the people, and we are the girdle with which he girds himself in the act of benediction by the gospel.

The girdle also is used by God always *in connection with work.* When eastern men are about to work in real earnest they gird up their loins. Our garments in this country are close-fitting and convenient, but the Oriental's robes would always be in his way whenever he had work to do, if he did not tightly strap them around him. Whenever we read of earnest work to be done we read of this girdle : so when God comes to do work among the sons of men we always hear of this girdle, which girdle we are, or may be, if we are unto God what we ought to be. When the Lord worketh righteousness in the earth it is by means of his chosen ones. When he publishes salvation, and makes known his grace, his saints are around him. When sinners are to be saved it is by his people. When error is to be denounced, it is by our lips that he chooses to speak. When his saints are to be comforted, it is by those who have been comforted by his Holy Spirit, and who therefore tell out the consolations which they have themselves enjoyed. The girdle of the Lord's work-day robes is his people. He saith, "Gather my people unto me ; those that have made a covenant with me by sacrifice." When he comes, not to judgment, for that is his strange work ; but for mercy and salvation, then he comes girt about with his redeemed. Blessed are they whose happy lot it is to be connected with God in his sacred acts, and in all his glorious work of salvation.

I cannot explain my deep emotion, but my heart would utter weighty words, if it could talk without my lips ; for I am awe-stricken at the bare idea of our being used as the girdle of the divine strength, cleaving unto God as a girdle cleaveth unto the loins of a man. How blessed a thing it is to be bound to God, bound for hallowed service ; being set apart for the Master's most personal and honourable use. Blessed are you who were once worthless and useless, but are now made so precious in his sight that you are bound around him for his use in the highest exercises of his grace among the sons of men.

Moreover, the girdle was intended *for ornament.* It does not appear that it was bound about the priest's loins under his garments, for if so it would not have been seen, and would not have been an instructive symbol : this girdle must be seen, since it was meant to be a type of a people who were to be unto God "for a people, and for a name, and for a praise, and for a glory." Is not this wonderful beyond all wonder, that God should make his people his glory ? Yet so it is, for true believers become an ornament unto God, adorning the doctrine of God their Saviour in all things. Is it not written, " Thou shalt also be a crown of glory in the hand of the Lord, and a royal diadem in the hand of thy God " ? Like as when a man puts on his jewels, or a prince puts on his royal attire, so does God regard his elect " as the stones of a crown," and to prove his value of them he arrays himself with his people as with a girdle.

Can it be so, that God is glorified in his saints ? Is it so, that Christ himself is admired *in* them that believe as well as *by* them that believe ? Do we, after all, illustrate the magnificence of God, and show to principalities and powers in the heavenly places what God can do ? Yes, it is so. You can easily perceive what true glory God has in us if we be sincere. Is it not to his honour that we who were disobedient and obstinate and hard-hearted should by his love be subdued to the obedience of the faith ? Does not this show his glory—that we creatures, possessed of the very dangerous possession of a free will, nevertheless, without violating that will, are led to obey his commands with pleasure and delight ? Is it not to the praise of his grace that we who are, under some aspects, the meanest of his creatures, seeing that we have been guilty of such gross sin, are nevertheless set next to himself, and made to be his dear children ? Next to God, the Redeemer, comes man, the redeemed. Yea, God and man are united—wondrously united in the person of the Lord Jesus Christ. What can more grandly set forth the adorable love and goodness of Jehovah ! What great things God has done for us already in having taken us up out of the horrible pit and out of the miry clay! Let this stand as his beautiful girdle—that he passeth by transgression, iniquity, and sin. Let this be his divine adornment—that he is the Lord God, merciful and gracious. Hallelujah! But how much greater things he will yet do for us! I know that he has taken us from the dunghill, but then it follows, "and hath set us among princes, even the princes of his people." We are not always sitting among princes yet, but we shall be elevated to the throne ere long. Our spirits, rid of this clay, shall rise up among spiritual dignities and powers, not second to the most exalted of them, and then shall an astonished universe behold the mercy of the Lord. Yet once more ; when the blast of the archangel shall have aroused the sleeping dead, even these poor material bodies, made like unto Christ's glorious body, shall share the glory of the Son of man. Truly " it doth not yet-appear what we shall be " ; for there are great things yet for men ; and the race of men to whom God has had a special favour shall yet be highly exalted, and have dominion over all the works of his hands, and he shall put all things under his feet. In all this the exceeding riches of divine grace shall be resplendent, and thus man shall be as a jewelled girdle unto the Lord of hosts.

Oh, majesty of love! infinity of grace! Here seraphs may admire and adore. My brethren, beloved in the Lord, muse much upon this figure of a girdle. Silently meditate upon it ; and try to understand it. We are the girdle that God causes to cleave unto his loins, and that no mere poverty-stricken girdle of a beggar, but the girdle of a royal priest, worn by him in sacrifice and labour, and regarded as his ornament and glory. Oh the splendour of Jehovah's love to his people!

II. But now, alas! we have to turn our eyes sorrowfully away from this surpassing glory. These people who might have been the glorious girdle of God displayed in their own persons A FATAL OMISSION. Did you notice it? Thus saith the Lord unto Jeremiah, "Go and get thee a linen girdle, and put it upon thy loins, and *put it not in water.*" Ah, me! there is the mischief : the unwashed girdle is the type of an unholy people who have never received *the great cleansing.* God is pure and holy, and he will wear cleansed garments, but of this garment it is said, "Put it not in water." The priests of Jehovah were continually washing, but of this girdle we read, " Put it not in water."

Now, when a man seems to be bound to God, and to be used of God, if he has never undergone the great cleansing, he will sooner or later come to a terrible end. " If I wash thee not, thou hast no part with me," is a very solemn word from the Lord Jesus himself. Oh, my brothers and sisters, I invite you to meditate upon this for a moment! No nearness to God can save you if you have never been washed by the Lord Jesus. No official connection can bless you if you have never been washed in his most precious blood. No matter though you may seem to be an ornament of the church, and all men may think so, and even good men may bless God for you, if you have never been washed you are not Christ's. If Jesus Christ, your Lord and Master, has never enabled you to say, " We have washed our robes and made them white in the blood of the Lamb," then, the great cleansing having been omitted, you will be shut out of the marriage supper of the Lamb. Oh the terror of that sentence,—" Put it not in water." Surely, this is what Satan desires; his malice cannot exceed the wish that we may never be cleansed from our iniquities! How accursed are those of whom Solomon saith, "There is a generation that are pure in their own eyes, and yet is not washed from their filthiness." If that one, first, perfect washing has never exercised its purifying influence upon you, my brother, it is all in vain for you to bear the vessels of the Lord, and to be thought to be great and to be eminent in his house, for you must be put away. On the spot let each one of us pray, " Wash me, and I shall be whiter than snow." God loves purity, and will not keep unholy men in nearness to himself. Here is the alternative for all professors,—you must be washed in the blood of Christ, or be laid aside; which shall it be?

The prophet was bidden not to put it in water, which shows that there was not only an absence of the first washing, but there was *no daily cleansing.* Take heed, beloved, that you omit not those after-washings which must follow the washing in the blood of the Lamb. When our blessed Lord took a towel and a basin, and went to wash the disciples' feet, he did not perform a superfluous action : Peter was misguided when he said " Thou shalt never wash my feet." It is necessary that we be washed every day. Even " if we walk in the light, as he is in the light, we have fellowship one with another, and the blood of Jesus Christ his Son cleanseth us from all sin." We are constantly defiling our feet by marching through this dusty world, and every night we need to be washed. There is sin within us as well as sin without us; and even if we do not leave our chamber, but have to lie upon a sick-bed all day long, impatience is quite enough to defile our feet, and we greatly need to be cleansed. The first grand washing is never repeated : that great bath does its work so effectually that the putting away of guilt is perfected once for all and for ever. When our Lord bowed his head and gave up the ghost he offered an effectual atonement by which all the guilt of his redeemed was eternally put away. " This man, after he had offered one sacrifice for sins for ever, sat down at the right hand of the Majesty on high" ; and he that hath that one washing " needeth not except to wash his feet." But the footbath is always necessary. Stains of pilgrimage, stains of service, stains of grief, stains of pleasure, stains of our holy things, these must still be put away. What with pride, or doubt, or ill-desire, or imagination, or anger, or forgetfulness, or error, we are always being defiled, and always need to be put in water, and to undergo that washing in water by the word of which the apostle speaks.

If, dear friends, you and I live without washing, we live in a way that renders us unfit for divine service. And have you not found it so ? I know this, that if you suffer a sin to lie on your conscience, you cannot serve God aright while it is there. If you have transgressed as a child, and you do not run and put your head into your Father's bosom and cry, " Father, I have sinned!" you cannot do God's work. The external part of it you may perform, though there will often be a great weakness even there; but as for the spiritual and vital part, it will be sadly deficient. If you try to write the epistle of life with an unwashen hand it will tremble, and every line you write will be in the shaky handwriting of paralysis. " He that has clean hands shall wax stronger and stronger," but the foul hand shall wax weaker and weaker. There must be this washing or there cannot be abundant working. If you do not know yourself to be "accepted in the Beloved," if you do not know yourself to be clean every whit, you will not be happy with God, and when you are not happy with him, your mind will be taken off from work for him to work for yourself. You will be thinking about your own imperfection rather than *his* perfection: the sin of any single day, though it will not destroy you, will grieve you. A stone in your shoe, though almost invisible, will spoil a day's journey. It is not a great rock to grind you to powder; it is only a little stone, but your foot will blister before you have walked many miles. Ah me, how great the pain of a single unconfessed sin! The best thing you can do is to put off your shoe at once, and remove the stone before you again put down your foot. So it is with every little sin : if it is only a thought, if it is only a look the wrong way, go to your Father and get rid of it. Do not live a day out of fellowship with God, nay, nor an hour under the Lord's frown. You know how it is with your dear child when he has done wrong : he does not expect that you will turn him out of doors and say, "You shall not be my child," but he does expect you to be grieved with him ! Children are believers in the "final perseverance" of parental love ; they expect always to be your children ; but if you are a wise father, they do not feel happy when they have done wrong. You have not perhaps found out their disobedience ; but the kiss at night is not half as warm as usual, for they are afraid that father will soon know of their fault and will be angry. When God deals with us as a father who has seen his child's naughtiness, there is no peace or rest in our spirit. Even chastisement, however, is better borne than a sense of having offended. If you gave your naughty child a good whipping at once, it would comfort him, for your displeasure would be over ; but as long as you do not chastise him, but only say, "No, my child, I cannot have dealings with you while you act so ; I have no word of love for you, for you are so wicked,"—then the dear child will be sorely troubled until your anger is over ; he will be ready to break his little heart until you forgive him, and comfort him, saying "I shall put the matter away this time, for I see you are sorry, and I hope you will not behave so badly any more." Brethren, this holy, filial fear of the Lord is not servitude under the law : it is not trying to be saved by what we do ; it is the discipline of the Father's house, and that is what we attend to when we ask for daily washing.

There was a fatal flaw about this girdle ; it had never been washed, and it is a fatal thing if you and I can go from day to day without being cleansed by our blessed Lord. Oh Lord, purge me by thy continual pardon ! Cleanse me this day from every spot, for thy sweet mercy's sake.

But observe, once again, that the more this girdle was used the more it gathered *great and growing defilement.* It was a prophet that wore it, but even with such wear the unwashed girdle began to be spotted and stained ; and as he might not put it into water, the oftener the prophet went out to his daily work,—the more the girdle was used,—the more service it performed, the more worn and dirty it became. It will be just the same with us if no water is applied, and there is no application of the cleansing blood of Christ. Without the atonement, the more we do the more we shall sin. Our very prayers will turn into sin, our godly things will gender evil. We shall be preaching, and when we preach we shall preach our condemnation. We shall gather our class about us, and talk to them of good things, and all the while there will be in our consciences the thought that we are not acting as we talk, or living as we tell them to live, and we shall be growing blacker and more defiled from hour to hour. Oh, Lord, deliver us from this! Save us from being made worse by that which should make us better. Save us from turning even our service into sin, our prayers into abominations, and our psalms into mockery. Let us be thy true people, and therefore let us be washed that we may be clean, that thou mayest gird thyself with us.

III. Very soon that fatal flaw in the case here mentioned led in the third place to A SOLEMN JUDGMENT. It was a solemn judgment upon the girdle, looking at it as a type of the people of Israel.

First, the girdle, after Jeremiah had made his long walk in it, was taken off from him *and put away*. It is an awful thing when God takes off the man that has once appeared to be on him, and lays him aside, as he did Saul when he finally gave him up and took the kingdom from him. Ay, and it is a solemn thing, also, when the Lord takes off the man that has been really bound to him, and for a time lays him aside and says, " I cannot use you : I cannot wear you as mine : I cannot work with you. You can be no ornament to me : you are defiled." He puts away the spoiled girdle : in other words, he works no longer with the backsliding professor. This is a terrible thing to happen to any man. I would rather suffer every sickness in the list of human diseases than that God should put me aside as a vessel in which he has no pleasure, and say to me, " I cannot wear you as my girdle, nor own you as mine before men." That would be a dreadful thing. Is there one here who has come into that condition ? Has the Lord left you to your backsliding ? Learn the lesson of my text ! What you want, my friend, is to be cleansed in the double stream which John of old saw flowing from the Redeemer's riven side. You want spiritual cleansing before the Lord can put you on again, and use you again, and be one with you again ; and before you can be again unto him a praise and a glory. While you are unclean you are dishonouring him, and he must set you aside.

After that girdle was laid aside, the next thing for it was *hiding and burying*. It was placed in a hole of the rock by the river of the captivity, and left there. Many a hypocrite has been served in that way. God has said to his servants, " Put him out of the church ; he is defiled ; " and there has been nothing heard of him any more. He may have been offended at being put aside, and have gone into the world altogether ; and though he once seemed to be as the very girdle of God, yet he has rotted and decayed into corruption and open transgression ; for the raw material of hypocrisy soon decays, and turns into loathesomeness. The worst things are frequently the rot of the best things ; and so the worst characters grow out of those who apparently were once the best.

Thus, then, this girdle is put right away, hidden, and left. God will have nothing to do with it. He has put it aside. And now *the girdle spoils*. It was put, I dare say, where the damp and the wet acted upon it ; and so when, in about seventy days, Jeremiah came back to the spot, there was nothing but an old rag instead of what had once been a pure white linen girdle. He says, " Behold the girdle was marred; it was profitable for nothing." So, if God were to leave any of us, the best men and the best women among us would soon become nothing but marred girdles, instead of being as fair white linen. Alas, for certain goodly professors that did appear to be very fine once, what rotten old rags they come to be when they are put into the hole and left to themselves. We have seen it. They have only been fit at last to be put upon the dust-heap with useless things. They have fallen into such a horrible condition of mind that they can do evil without check of conscience: they have forgotten how to blush. The same persons who did run well (what did hinder them?) are now found, not only sleeping in the harbours of sloth, but rioting in chambers of wantonness. The glorious girdle of God, as the man seemed to be, becomes a mass of rottenness. What does the text say? Let me read the words, for I should not like to say them of myself,—" Behold, the girdle was marred, it was profitable for nothing "; and again in the tenth verse—" Which is good for nothing." So may men become who have not been washed : so will they become unless God, in his infinite mercy, gives them speedily expiation through his Son, renewing by his Spirit.

I desire to profit you all, and so I want to notice how true this is of the real children of God. I could speak this even weeping. There are certain real children of God whom God greatly honoured at one time, so that they were as his girdle; but they became proud, and were soon defiled with other sins besides, and so the Lord has put them away, and has laid them aside from his service. They are still his, but he has put them under discipline, and as a part of that discipline he has cashiered them from his public service. They were once everywhere in the Lord's battles, and now they are nowhere. He knows where he has put them, and there they will remain till their pride is quite gone. When the Lord has effected this purpose his wandering servant will come back with an altered tale, and you shall hear him as he laments himself and cries,—" I do not feel fit to be in God's church. I have walked in such a way that if I were cast off altogether it would be my just deserts. Oh that I may be forgiven." The deep repentance of returning wanderers makes you feel that they are the children of God though they have dis-honoured him, and you welcome their return, saying, " Come with us, and enjoy the means of grace." Alas, they answer—

> " The saints are comforted, we know,
>   Within the house of prayer ;
> We often go where others go,
>   And find no comfort there."

One man sighs, " I have my Sunday-school class, and I teach it, but I do not feel tenderly for the children as I once did. There is no power about me. I am a branch of the tree that appears to have no sap in it. I bear no fruit. Alas," he cries, " I do not enjoy private prayer, and when I pray, and pour out my soul before God, I do not obtain a comfortable answer. I am as one that is forgotten." Is it at all wonder-ful that God frowns when we disobey? The Lord will not hear those who decline to hear him. If we are deaf to his commands he will be deaf to our prayers. You have become defiled, for you have not watched your steps, and now the Lord cannot be in communion with you. You have not been careful, and so the girdle has become foul with public spots and private foulnesses: and the Lord says, "I cannot use that man; I cannot be in fellowship with him. If I should it would ruin him." If God were to be kind and tender to his children when they are living in sin, it would encourage them in evil, and they would go from bad to worse. If a believer grieves God, he must be grieved himself. The heavenly Father takes down the rod, and though it is more pain to him than it is to us, he will not spare us for our crying. Just because he loves us he will lay on his strokes thick and heavy, one after the other, perhaps in sharp affliction, but very often in a continuous and growing loss of all that made us happy and useful. Alas! alas! the girdle is marred: the Lord hath hid it out of his sight!

Oh, what a mercy it is that the Lord can take that girdle and wash it, and make it as good as new, and even better than at the first! He can give back to the man his old joy with an added experience which will make him humble and tender; he can restore his former usefulness, and even increase it by teaching him to deal gently with others that err, and by enabling him to prize and value the mercy of God. Did you ever get into a corner and sing that verse, "Love I much? I've more forgiven. I'm a miracle of grace"? Those sweet lines have often charmed my inmost heart. I have wanted to love my Lord infinitely. I have wished that I could love him as much as seven million hearts put together could love him. I would love him as much as the whole universe could love him. I would I had his Father's love to him, for what do I not owe to him for all his wonderful mercy to me? And do *you* not feel the same? Are not you, also, great debtors to sovereign grace? If you do not at any time kindle with love and gratitude, I am afraid that you are put in the hole with the girdle, and that you are rotting away. Sad case for you!

Certain of God's people are marvellously high-minded: they cannot sit anywhere but in the big arm-chair, or at the head of the table. They cannot mingle with any of us common Christians at all, because they are perfect, and we are a long way from making any claim to such a degree of excellence. Some of the hymns that we are glad to sing are not good enough for them, for they cry, "We hate hymns of this style. They are so below our experience." These are the dons and grandees of the Court of Arrogance. When I see fine professors coming in with the seven league boots on, I am always afraid that they are not God's children at all, because I have never read of any true saints who said much in praise of themselves, and I have read of so many gracious persons whose tone and temper were the very reverse of this lofty boasting. I have seen God's poor little child like Moses in a basket on the Nile, with crocodiles all round ready to devour him, and when I have looked at him, I have always noticed that which the Holy Spirit took pains to record,—"Behold, the babe wept." This was the real Moses: those crystal drops are the tokens of a goodly child. The tears of God's babes are wonderfully precious, and they have great power with him. The dragons of Nilus cannot devour a weeping Moses. "When I am weak, then am I strong." When you are so weak that you cannot do much more than cry, you coin diamonds with both your eyes. The sweetest prayers God ever hears are the groans and sighs of those who have no hope in anything but his love. There is music in our moaning to his kind and tender ears. He can restore you, even though you be as the marred girdle; and when he once puts you on again, you will cleave to his loins more closely than ever, praying that he will bind you fast about him.

But the worst part of it—and this I finish with—is that this relates undoubtedly to many mere professors whom God takes off from himself, laying them aside, and leaving them to perish. And what is his reason for so doing? He tells us this in the text: he says that this evil people *refused to receive God's words.* Dear friends, never grow tired of God's word: never let any book supplant the Bible. Love every part of Scripture, and take heed to every word that God has spoken. Let it all be a divine word to you; for if not, when you begin to pick and choose about God's word, and do not like this, and do not like that, you will soon become like a marred girdle—for the base-hearted professor is detected by his not loving the Father's words.

Next to that, we are told that they *walked in the imagination of their heart.* That is a sure sign of the hypocrite or the false professor. He makes his religion out of himself, as a spider spins a web out of his own bowels: what sort of theology it is you can imagine now that you know its origin. This base professor grows his theology on his own back as the snail produces her shell: he is everything to himself—his own Saviour, his own teacher, his own guide. He knows so much, that if the world would only sit at his feet, it would become a wonderfully learned world in a very short time, so great a Rabbi is he. When a man is so puffed up that his own imagination is his inspiration, and his obstinacy holds him fast in his own opinion, then he has become as the girdle which was taken from the prophet's loins, and put into a hole to rot away.

Upon all this there followed actual transgression,—" *They walked after other gods to serve them and to worship them.*" This happens also to the base professor. He keeps up the name of a Christian for a little while, and seems to be as God's girdle; but by-and-by he falls to worshipping gold, or drink, or lust. Bacchus, or Venus, becomes his deity. He turns aside from the infinitely glorious God, and so he falls from one degradation to another till he hardly knows himself. He becomes as a rotten girdle "which profiteth nothing:" neither God nor man are benefited by him.

The Lord save you, dear friends, from being found insincere in the day when he searches the heart. May he also save us from failing to be washed in the most precious blood. Is not this a fit subject for immediate and continuous prayer? See ye to it.

The Lord bless you for his name's sake. Amen.

PORTIONS OF SCRIPTURE READ BEFORE SERMON—Jeremiah xiii. ;
Psalm xliv.

HYMNS FROM "OUR OWN HYMN BOOK,"—668, 79, 653.

"HEREIN IS LOVE."

A Sermon

DELIVERED ON LORD'S-DAY MORNING, FEBRUARY 18TH, 1883, BY

C. H. SPURGEON,

AT THE METROPOLITAN TABERNACLE, NEWINGTON.

"Herein is love, not that we loved God, but that he loved us, and sent his Son to be the propitiation for our sins. Beloved, if God so loved us, we ought also to love one another."—1 John iv. 10, 11.

THE law commands love; indeed, all its precepts are summed up in that one word "love." More widely read it runs thus: "Thou shalt love the Lord thy God with all thy heart, and with all thy soul, and with all thy strength, and with all thy mind; and thy neighbour as thyself": yet all this amounts only to "Thou shalt love."

But the law by reason of our depravity never produced love. We were commanded to love, but we did no such thing. The spirit that is in us is selfish, and it lusteth to envy and to enmity. Whence come wars and fightings among us? Come they not from our lusts? Since the Fall man has become man's bitterest foe upon the earth, and the world is full of hating, slandering, struggling, fighting, wounding, and slaying: all that law can do is to show the wrong of enmity, and threaten punishment; but it cannot supply an unregenerate heart with a fountain of love. Man remains unloving and unlovable till the gospel takes him in hand, and by grace accomplishes that which the law could not do, in that it was weak through the flesh. Love is winning many hearts to the kingdom of God, and its reign shall extend till love shall rule over the whole earth, and so the kingdom of God shall be set up among men, and God shall dwell among them. At the present moment love is the distinguishing mark of the people of God. Jesus said, "By this shall all men know that ye are my disciples, if ye have love one to another"; and John said, "We know that we have passed from death unto life, because we love the brethren." The man whose spirit is selfish has not the spirit of Christ, and "if any man have not the spirit of Christ he is none of his." The man whose spirit is that of envy and contention is evidently no follower of the lowly and loving Jesus, and those who do not follow Jesus are none of his. They that are Christ's are filled with his love. "Every one that loveth is born of God, and knoweth God. He that loveth not knoweth not God; for God is love." God is the centre of the believer's love; the saints are an inner circle specially beloved, and all mankind are embraced

No. 1.707.

within the circumference of the ring of love. "He that dwelleth in love dwelleth in God, and God in him"; and he alone is a child of God whose spirit is kindly and affectionate, and who seeks, wherever he is, to promote peace, goodwill towards men.

The saints begin with love to God. That must ever hold the highest place; for God is the best and noblest being, and we owe him all our hearts. Then comes, for Jesus' sake, love to all who are in Christ. There is a peculiarly near and dear relationship existing between one child of God and all the rest. Loving him that begat, we love all them that are begotten of him. Should not a child love his brothers with a tender, peculiar affection? This principle of love, once implanted, induces in the heart of the converted man a love towards all mankind. Not that he can take any complacency in the wicked; God himself cannot do that: his holiness abhors all iniquity. The love desired is not the love of complacency, but the love of benevolence; so that we wish well, and to the utmost of our power would do well, unto all those that dwell upon the face of the earth. In this holy charity, this unselfish love, be ye imitators of God as dear children. Our heavenly Father is kind to the unthankful and to the evil, and so must we be; desiring that even the most abandoned may yet be rescued and made right and good. Love desires to create that which is lovable even in the most unlovable of mankind, and God helping the effort, she succeeds.

I hear one say, "This is a vast idea. Are we to love at this rate? Where is the love to come from? Our hearts are narrow, men are unworthy, provocations are numerous, another spirit is abroad in the world: where is this love to come from?—this flood of love which is to cover the tops of the mountains of man's unworthiness?" Hast thou entered into the springs of the sea? or hast thou walked in search of the depths? Yes, by the leadings of God's Spirit we will search out the springs of the sea of love. Only in one place shall we find love enough for our supreme purpose, which is also the purpose of the Lord himself. There is one shoreless ocean into which we may be baptized, and out of which we may be filled until we overflow. Where is the unfailing motive of love? For love is tried, and hardly put to it to hold her own. Can we find a motive that will never fail even towards the most provoking of mankind? Can we find an argument for affection which shall help us in times of ingratitude, when base returns threaten to freeze the very heart of charity? Yes, there is such a motive; there is a force by which even impossibilities of love can be accomplished, and we shall be supplied with a perpetual constraint moving the heart to ceaseless charity.

Come with me, then, in the first place, to notice *the infinite spring of love*—"Herein is love, not that we loved God, but that God loved us;" secondly, let us observe *the marvellous outflow of that love*—"God sent his Son to be the propitiation for our sins;" and then, thirdly, let us notice *the overflow of that love in us*, when it fills our hearts and runs over to others—"Beloved, if God so loved us, we ought also to love one another."

I. First, THE INFINITE SPRING OF LOVE. Our text has two words upon which I would place an emphasis—"*not*" and "*but.*"

The first is "*not.*" "Herein is love, not"—"not that we loved God."

Very naturally many conclude that this means "not that we loved God first." That is not exactly the truth taught here, but still it is a weighty truth, and is mentioned in this same chapter in express words—"We love him because he first loved us" (verse nineteen). The cause of love in the universe is not that man loved God first. No being in existence could love God before God loved him; for the existence of such a being is due to God's previous love. His plans of love were all laid and many of them carried out before we were born; and when we were born we none of us loved God first so as to seek after God before he sought after us, so as to desire reconciliation with God before he desired reconciliation with us. No; whatever may be said about freewill as a theory, it is never found as a matter of fact that any man, left to himself, ever woos his God, or pines after friendship with his Maker. If he repents of sin it is because the Spirit of God has first visited him and shown him his sin; if he desires restoration it is because he has first of all been taught to dread the wrath of God and to long for holiness.

> "No sinner can be beforehand with thee;
> Thy grace is most sovereign, most rich, and most free."

We inscribe a negative in black capital letters upon the idea that man's love can ever be prior to the love of God. That is quite out of the question.

"Not that we loved God." Take a second sense—that is, not that any man did love God at all by nature, whether first or second; not that we, any one of us, ever did or ever could have an affection towards God while we remained in our state by nature. Instead of loving God, man is indifferent to God. "No God," saith the fool in his heart, and by nature we are all such fools. It is the sinner's wish that there were no God. We are atheistical by nature, and if our brain does not yield to atheism, yet our heart does. We wish that we could sin according to our own will, and that we were in no danger of being called to account for it. God is not in all our thoughts, or if he does enter there it is as a terror and a dread. Nay, worse than that: man is at enmity with God by wicked works. The holiness which God admires man hath no liking for; the sin which God abominates has about it sweetness and fascination for the unrenewed heart; so that man's ways are contrary to the ways of God. Man is perverse; he cannot walk with God, for they are not agreed; he is all evil, and God is all goodness, and therefore no love to God exists in the natural heart of man. He may say that he loves God, but then it is a god of his own inventing, and not Jehovah, the God of the Bible, the only living and true God. A just God and a Saviour the natural mind cannot endure: the carnal mind is enmity against God, and is not reconciled to God, neither indeed can be. The unregenerate heart is, as to love, a broken cistern which can hold no water. In our natural state, there is none that doeth good, no, not one; so is there also none that loveth God, no, not one.

We come nearer to John's meaning when we look at this negative as applying to those who do love God. "Not that we loved God,"—that is, that our love to God, even when it does exist, and even when it influences our lives, is not worthy to be mentioned as a fountain of supply for love. The apostle points us away from it to something far more vast, and then he cries, "Herein is love." I am looking for "the springs of the sea," and you point me to a little pool amid the rocks which has been filled by the flowing tide. I am glad to see that pool: how bright! how blue! how like the sea from whence it came! But do not point to this as the source of the great waterfloods; for if you do I shall smile at your childish ignorance, and point you to yon great rolling main which tosses its waves on high. What is your little pool to the vast Atlantic? Do you point me to the love in the believer's heart, and say, "Herein is love!" You make me smile. I know that there is love in that true heart; but who can mention it in the presence of the great rolling ocean of the love of God, without bottom and without shore? The word *not* is not only upon my lip but in my heart as I think of the two things, "NOT that we loved God, but that God loved us." What poor love ours is at its very best when compared with the love wherewith God loves us!

Let me use another figure. If we had to enlighten the world, a child might point us to a bright mirror reflecting the sun, and he might cry, "Herein is light!" You and I would say, "Poor child, that is but borrowed brightness; the light is not there, but yonder, in the sun: the love of saints is nothing more than the reflection of the love of God. We *have* love, but God *is* love. When I think of the love of certain saints to Christ, I am charmed with it; for it is a fruit of the Spirit not to be despised. When I think of Paul the Apostle counting all things but loss for Christ; when I think of our missionaries going one after another into malarious parts of the African coast, and dying for Christ; and when I read the Book of Martyrs, and see confessors standing on the faggots, burning quick to the death, still bearing witness to their Lord and Master,—I do rejoice in the love of saints to their Lord. Yet this is but a streamlet; the unfathomable deep, the eternal source from which all love proceeds, infinitely exceeds all human affection, and it is found in God, and in God alone. "Herein is love, not that we loved God, but that God loved us."

Let us contrast our love to God with his love to us. Dear brethren, we do love God, and we may well do so, since he is infinitely lovable When the mind is once enlightened it sees everything that is lovable about God. He is so good, so gracious, so perfect that he commands our admiring affection. The spouse in the Song, when she thought of her beloved, mentioned all manner of beauties, and then cried, "Yea, he is altogether lovely." It is natural, therefore, that one who sees God should love him. But, now, think of God's love to us: is it not incomparably greater, since there was nothing lovely in us whatever, and yet he loved us? In us there is by nature nothing to attract the affection of a holy God, but quite the reverse; and yet he loved us. Herein, indeed, is love!

When we love God it is an honour to us; it exalts a man to be allowed to love a Being so glorious. A philosopher once wrote that for a man to speak of being the friend of God was too daring, and in the reverence of this thoughtful heathen there was much to admire; for indeed there is an infinite difference between the glorious God and the sinful creature man. Though God in condescension allows us to call him friend, and Jesus says, "Ye are my friends!" yet this is beyond reason, and is a sweet revelation of the Holy Spirit. What an uplifting there is in it for us! On the other hand, God's love to us can add nothing to him; it gives, but receives not. Divine love can have no recompense. That he, the Infinite, should stoop to love the finite; that he the infinitely pure should love the guilty, this is a vast condescension. See, moreover, what it involved; for this love rendered it necessary that in the person of his dear Son God should be "despised and rejected of men," should make himself of no reputation, and should even be numbered with the transgressors. "Herein is love!"

When we love God we are gainers by the deed. He that loves God does in the most effectual manner love himself. We are filled with riches when we abound in love to God; it is our wealth, our health, our might, and our delight. But God gains nothing by loving us. I hardly like to set the two in contrast, for our love is so poor and pitiable a thing as compared with the immeasurable love of God.

It is our duty to love God; we are bound to do it. As his creatures we ought to love our Creator; as preserved by his care we are under obligation to love him for his goodness: we owe him so much that our utmost love is a mere acknowledgment of our debt. But God loved us to whom he owed nothing at all; for whatever might have been the claims of a creature upon his Creator, we had forfeited them all by our rebellion. Sinful men had no rights towards God except the right of being punished. Yet the Lord manifested boundless love to our race, which was only worthy to be destroyed. Oh words! How ye fail me! I cannot utter my heart by these poor lips of clay. Oh God, how infinite was thy love which was given without any obligation on thy part, freely and unsought, and all because thou willest to love—yea, thou dost love because thou art love. There was no cause, no constraint, no claim why thou shouldest love mankind, except that thine own heart led thee so to do. What is man that thou art mindful of him? "Herein is love, not that we loved God, but that God loved us."

I have thus pointed out the well-head of love: let us draw from it, and from none other. If you go into the world and say, "I am to love my fellow-men because I love God," the motive is good, but it is questionable, limited, and variable. How much better to argue—I am to love my fellow-men because God loves me. When my love grows cold towards God, and when by reason of my infirmity and imperfection I am led even to question whether I do love God at all, then my argument and my impulse would fail me if it came from my own love to God; but if I love the fallen because God loved me, then I have an unchanging motive, an unquestionable argument, and a forcible impulse not to be resisted: hence the apostle cried, "The love of Christ constraineth us." It is always well for a Christian to have the strongest motive, and to rely upon the most potent and perpetual force, and hence the apostle bids us look to divine love, and not to our own. "Herein is love," saith he, "not that we loved God, but that God loved us." So far the "not."

Let us turn to the "but." "*But* that he loved us." I have nothing new to say, nor do I wish to say anything new; but I should like you to meditate on each one of these words :—" He loved us." Three words, but what weight of meaning ! " He," who is infinitely holy and cannot endure iniquity,—" He loved us " ; " He," whose glory is the astonishment of the greatest of intelligent beings,—" He loved us." " He," whom the heaven of heavens cannot contain, " loved us." " He " who is God all-sufficient, and needs nothing of us, neither can indeed receive anything at our hands,—" He loved us." What joy lies sleeping here ! Oh, that we could wake it up! What hope, too, for hopeless sinners, because " God loved us." If a man could know that he was loved of all his fellow-men, if he could have it for certain that he was loved by all the angels, doted on by cherubim and seraphim, yet these were but so many drops, and all put together could not compare with the main ocean contained in the fact that " God loved us."

Now ring that second silver bell : " He loved us." I do not think the apostle is here so much speaking of God's special love to his own elect as of his love to men in general. He saw our race ruined in the fall, and he could not bear that man should be destroyed. Lord, what is man that thou dost visit him in love ? Yet he did so visit him. The Lord's love made him lament man's revolt, and cry, " I have nourished and brought up children, and they have rebelled against me" ; whereupon he bade heaven and earth witness to his grief. He saw that sin had brought men into wretchedness and misery, and would destroy them for ever; and he would not have it so. He loved them with the love of pity, with the love of sweet and strong benevolence, and he declared it with an oath : " As I live, saith the Lord, I have no pleasure in the death of him that dieth, but that he turn unto me and live." " Herein is love." But if you and I be reconciled to God we can lay the emphasis, each one for himself, upon this word love, and view it as special, effectual, electing love. Let each believer say, " He loved me, and gave himself for me." Then what force is in my text : " He loved us ": it is not enough that he pitied us, or spared us, or helped us ; but "he loved us." It has often made me rise from my seat to think that God loves me ! I could not sit still and hear the thrilling truth. Such knowledge is too wonderful for me : it is high, I cannot attain unto it. It is sweet to be loved even by a dog ; it is sweet to be loved by a babe ; it is sweet to be loved by a friend; it is sweet to be loved by God's people ; but, oh! to be loved of God, and to know it !—this is paradise. Would a man want any other heaven than to know for certain that he enjoyed the love of God ?

Note the third word. " He loved us,"—" us,"—the most insignificant of beings. There is an anthill somewhere ; it is no matter to you where it is. It teems with ants. Stir the nest, and they swarm in armies. Think of one of them. No ; you do not need to know anything about him! His business is no concern of yours ; so let him go. But that ant, after all, is more considerable to you than you are to God. " All the inhabitants of the earth are reputed as nothing." What are you even in this great city!—one man, one woman in London, in England, in the population of the world,—what a cipher you are ! Yet what is the population of this world compared with the universe ? I suppose that all these stars which we see at night, all the countless worlds within our range of vision, are but as a little dust in a lone corner of God's great house. The whole solar system, and all the systems of worlds we have ever thought of, are but as a drop of a bucket compared with the boundless sea of creation ; and even that is as nothing compared to the infinite God : and yet "He loved *us*"—the insignificant creatures of an hour. What is more, he loved us though in our insignificance we dared to rebel against him. We boasted against him; we cried, "Who is Jehovah ?" We lifted up our hand to fight with him. Ridiculous rebellion ! Absurd warfare! Had he but glanced at us and annihilated us, it would have been as much as we could merit at his hands ; but to think that he should love us,—*love us*, mark you, when we were in rebellion against him. This is marvellous.

Observe that the previous verse speaks of us as being dead in sin. " In this was manifested the love of God toward us, because that God sent his only begotten Son into the world, that we might live through him." Then we were dead, dead to all goodness, or thought or power, of goodness, criminals shut up in the condemned cell ; and yet God loved us with a great love even when we were dead in trespasses and sins. Child of God, God's love to you to-day is wonderful; but think of his love to you when you were far gone in rebellion against him. When not a throb of holy, spiritual life could be found in your entire being; yet he loved you and sent his Son that you might live through him. Moreover, he loved us when we were steeped in sin. Does not our text tell us so ? for he sent his Son to be the propitiation for our sins, and this implies that we needed to be reconciled. Our righteous Judge was angry with us; his righteous wrath smoked against our evil, and yet even then "He loved us." He was wroth with us as a Judge, but yet he loved us : he was determined to punish, and yet resolved to save.

This is a world of wonders ! I am utterly beaten by my text. I confess myself mastered by my theme. But who among us can measure the unfathomable? "Herein is love," that God freely, out of the spontaneous motion of his own heart, should love us. This is the argument for love ; this is the inexhaustible fountain out of which all love must come. If we desire love, may we come and fill our vessels here and bear it out to others. Love springing from our own bosoms is flat, feeble, and scant; but the love of God is a great deep, for ever fresh, and full and flowing. Here are those springs of the sea of which we spake : " Herein is love !"

II. I want your attention a little longer while I speak as best I can upon THE MARVELLOUS OUTFLOW OF THAT LOVE. " Herein is love, not that we loved God, but that he loved us, and sent his Son to be the propitiation for our sins." Beloved, the love of God is seen in creation : he that studies the mechanism of the human frame and of its surroundings will see much of divine kindness therein. The love of God is to be seen in providence: he that watches the loving hand of God in daily life will not need to look far before he sees tokens of a Father's care. But if you want to know when the great deep of God's love was broken up, and arose in the fulness of its strength to prevail over all; if you would see it revealed in a deluge, like Noah's flood, you must wait till you see Jesus born at Bethlehem and crucified on Calvary ; for his mission to men is the divinest manifestation of love.

Consider every word: " He sent his Son." God " *sent.*" Love caused that mission. If there was to be reconciliation between God and man, man ought to have sent to God; the offender ought to be the first to apply for forgiveness; the weaker should apply to the greater for help; the poor man should ask of him who distributes alms; but "Herein is love" that God "sent." He was first to send an embassy of peace. To-day "we are ambassadors for Christ, as though God did beseech you by us: we pray you in Christ's stead, be ye reconciled to God." Oh, the wonder of this, that God should not wait till rebellious men had sent to his throne for terms of reconciliation, but should commence negociations himself!

Moreover, God sent such a One: he "sent *his Son*." If men send an embassy to a great power they select some great one of their nation to wait upon the potent prince; but if they are dealing with a petty principality they think a subordinate person quite sufficient for such a business. Admire, then, the true love of the infinitely gracious God, that when he sent an embassy to men he did not commission an angel nor even the brightest spirit before his throne; but he sent his Son,—oh, the love of God to men! He sent his equal Son to rebels who would not receive him, would not hear him, but spat upon him, scourged him, stripped him, slew him! Yes, "he spared not his own Son, but freely delivered him up for us all." He knew what would come of that sending of him, and yet he sent him.

> "Jesus, commission'd from above,
>   Descends to men below,
> And shows from whence the springs of love
>   In endless currents flow.

> "He, whom the boundless heaven adores,
>   Whom angels long to see,
> Quitted with joy those blissful shores,
>   Ambassador to me!

> "To me, a worm, a sinful clod,
>   A rebel all forlorn:
> A foe, a traitor, to my God,
>   And of a traitor born."

Note further, not only the grandeur of the ambassador, but the tenderness of the relationship existing between him and the offended God. "He sent his Son." The previous verse says, "His only-begotten Son." We cannot speak of God except after the manner of men, for God in all his glory is incomprehensible; but speaking after the manner of men, what must it have cost Jehovah to take his only Son from his bosom to die? Christ is the Father's self; in essence they are one: there is but one God. We do not understand the mystery of the Trinity in unity, but we believe it. It was God himself who came hither in the person of his dear Son: he underwent all: for we are "the flock of God which he hath purchased with his own blood." Remember Abraham with the knife unsheathed, and wonder as you see him obey the voice which says, "Take now thy son, thine only son, Isaac, whom thou lovest, and offer him for a sacrifice." Remember yet again that the Lord actually did what Abraham in obedience willed to do: he gave up his Son! "It pleased the Father to bruise him; he hath put him to grief." Christ's death was in fact God in human form suffering for human sin; God incarnate bleeding because of our transgressions. Are we not now carried away with the streams of love? I speak my best, my brethren; but if my words were what they ought to be they would set your souls on fire. Is not all heaven still astounded at the death of the Only-begotten? It has not recovered from its amazement that the heir of all things should bow his head to death. How can I fitly tell you how much God loved the world when he gave his Only-begotten to die that sinners might live!

Go a step further. "God sent his Son *to be a propitiation*," that is, to be not only a reconciler, but the reconciliation. His sacrifice of himself was the atonement through which mercy is rendered possible in consistency with justice. I have heard men say with scorn that God required a sacrifice before he would be reconciled, as if that were wrong on the part of the Judge of all. But let me whisper in their ears: God required it, it is true, for he is just and holy; but God found it himself. Remember that—Jehovah found the ransom which he demanded. It was himself, his own Son, one with himself, that became the propitiation and the reconciliation. It was not that God the Father was unkind, and could not be placated unless he smote his Son; but that God the Father was so kind that he could not be unjust, so supremely loving that he must devise a way by which men could be justly saved. An unjust salvation would have been none at all. The Lord found the reconciliation—I will not say in the sufferings of Christ, though that is true; I will not say in the death of Christ, though that is true; but I will put it in Scriptural words, and here we have it in 1 John ii. 2: "He"— that is, Jesus himself—"is the propitiation for our sins." The sent One in himself, as well as in all that he did and all that he suffered, is the reconciliation between God and man. "Herein is love!" for in order that there might be peace and love between man and God, God finds the sin-offering, becomes himself the atonement. that love might reign supreme.

What seems to me the most wonderful thing of all is that the Lord Jesus should deal, not only with our sorrow, but with our sin; for "he is the propitiation for our *sins.*" That God should deal with us as to our virtues, if we had any; that he should deal with us as to our love, if we had any, might not seem so difficult; but that he should send his Son to dwell with us as sinners—ay, and to come into contact with our sins, and thus to take the sword, not only by its hilt, but by its blade, and plunge it into his own heart, and die because of it, this is a miracle of miracles. O friends, Christ never gave himself for our righteousness, but he laid down his life for our sins. He viewed us as sinners when he came to save us. "Jesus Christ came into the world to save sinners." If I had not found Christ till this very minute, I hope I should find him now as my mind drinks in this doctrine. By God's Spirit there seems to me to be such a window opened that even despair may see the light, for if the thing which God sent his Son to deal with was the sin of man, then I, even though I am nothing but a mass of loathsomeness and sin, may yet enjoy the infinite love of God. Oh, guilty ones, hear these words, which are more sweet than music, and fuller of delight than all poetry; for even the harps of angels never rise to higher measures than these which I do so poorly and simply rehearse in your ears,—even these glad tidings, that God who made the heavens and the earth, whom ye have offended, wills not that you die, but loves you so greatly that he opens up a road of reconciliation through the body of his own dear Son.   There was no other way by which you could be reconciled to God, for had he reconciled you to a part of himself and not to his justice, you had not been in very truth at all reconciled to God.   It is now to God completely just, holy, whose anger burns against sin ; it is to him that you are reconciled by faith in Christ Jesus, through the laying down of his life for men.   Oh that God would bless this to all who hear the glad tidings!

III.   We come at last to think of the CONSEQUENT OUTFLOW OF LOVE FROM US,—"Beloved, if God so loved us, we ought also to love one another."   Our love then to one another is simply God's love to us, flowing into us, and flowing out again.   That is all it is.   "Herein is love, not that we loved God, but that God loved us," and then we love others.   You have seen a noble fountain in a continental city adorning a public square.   See how the water leaps into the air ; and then it falls into a circular basin which fills and pours out its fulness into another lower down, and this again floods a third.   Hear the merry plash as the waters fall in showers and cataracts from basin to basin !   If you stand at the lower basin and look upon it and say, "Herein is water ;" that is true, and will be true of the next higher one, and so forth ; but if you would express the truth as to where the water really is, you may have to look far away, perhaps upon a mountain's side, for there is a vast reservoir from which pipes are laid to bring these waters and force them to their height that they may descend so beautifully.   Thus the love we have to our fellow-creatures drops from us like the descending silvery cataract from the full basin, but the first source of it is the immeasurable love of God which is hidden away in his very essence, which never changes, and never can be diminished.   Herein is love ?   If you and I desire to love our fellow Christians and to love the fallen race of man, we must be joined on to the aqueduct which conducts love from this eternal source, or else we shall soon fail in love.

Observe, brethren, then, that as the love of God is the source of all true love in us, so a sense of that love stimulates us.   Whenever you feel that you love God you overflow with love to all God's people ; I am sure you do.   It is when you get to doubt the love of God that you grow hard and cold ; but when you are fired with the love of a dying Saviour who gave himself for you, you feel as if you loved every beggar in the street, and you long to bring every harlot to Christ's dear feet ; you cannot help it.   Man, if Christ baptizes your heart into his love, you will be covered with it, and filled with it.

Your love will respect the same persons as God's love does, and for the same reasons.   God loves men ; so will you ; God loves them when there is no good in them, and you will love them in the same way.   Sometimes the wickedness of men kindles in the heart of a true Christian a stronger affection for them.   The deeper down they are the more they want a Saviour.   Did not our Moravian brethren feel when they went out as missionaries that they would prefer to go first to the most barbarous tribes?—for they said, "The more degraded they are the more they need a Saviour."   And should not the missionary spirit make believers feel, if men are sunk until they are as low as brutes, and as savage as devils, that this is the stronger reason for our being eager to bring them to Christ? I hope that abominable spirit which used to come in among Christian people has been kicked away to its father the devil, where it ought to be: I mean the spirit which despises the poor and the fallen. When I have heard people say, "What is the good of looking after such riff-raff?" I have been saddened. The church of God feels that the souls of the meanest are precious,—that to save the most foul, the most ignorant, the most degraded, the most brutalized man or woman that ever lives is an object worthy of the effort of the whole church, since God thought it worthy of the death of Jesus Christ that he might bring sinners dead in sin to live unto himself.

Brothers and sisters, we shall not have grasped the truth unless we feel that our love to men must be practical, because God's love to us was so. His love did not lie pent up like the waters in the secret caverns of the earth, but it welled up like the waters in the days of Noah, when we read that the fountains of the great deep were broken up. In the gift of the Lord Jesus we behold the reality of divine love. When we see the poor we must not say, "Be ye warmed; be ye filled; I am sorry for you"; but we must let our love relieve them from our stores. If we see the ignorant we must not say, "Dear me, the church is neglecting the masses; the church must wake up"; but we must bestir ourselves and struggle ourselves to win sinners. If there be any near you who are degraded, do not say, "I wish somebody would go after them." No; go after them yourself. We have each one a mission: let that mission be fulfilled.

Our love ought to follow the love of God in one point, namely, in always seeking to produce reconciliation. It was to this end that God sent his Son. Has anybody offended you? Seek reconciliation. "Oh, but I am the offended party." So was God, and he went straight away and sought reconciliation. Brother, do the same. "Oh, but I have been insulted." Just so: so was God: all the wrong was towards him, yet he sent. "Oh, but the party is so unworthy." So are you; but "God loved you and sent his Son." Go you and write according to that copy. I do not mean that this love is to come out of your own heart originally, but I do mean that it is to flow out of your heart because God has made it to flow into it. You are one of those basins of the fountain: love has poured into you from above, let it run over to those who are below. Go forth at once, and try and make reconciliation, not only between yourself and your friend, but between every man and God. Let that be your object. Christ has become man's reconciliation, and we are to try and bring this reconciliation near to every poor sinner that comes in our way. We are to tell him that God in Christ is reconciled; we are to say to him, "He is the propitiation for our sins, and not for ours only, but for the sins of the whole world." Mark that word! It tallies with that other, "Behold the Lamb of God, which taketh away the sin of the world." God is now able to deal on gospel terms with the whole race. We need never think that we shall meet with men to whom God will not consent to be reconciled. The propitiation is such that whosoever comes to God shall be received through it. God is always within to receive every soul that comes to him by

Jesus Christ. " God so loved the world, that he gave his only begotten Son, that whosoever believeth in him should not perish, but have everlasting life." Your work and mine is reconciliation, and everything that tends that way.

When we have done all, what then? We shall have nothing whereof to glory. Suppose a man should become so loving that he gave himself wholly up for his fellow-creatures, and actually died for them, would he have anything to boast of? Read my text over again. " Beloved, if God so loved us, we *ought* also to love one another"; so that if you get to the highest point of self-sacrifice you will never be able to boast, for you have only then done what it was your duty to have done. Thus you see the highest grade of Christianity excludes all idea of salvation by works, for when we come up to its utmost pitch, if we give our body to be burned for love, yet still we have done no more than it was our duty to have done, considering the tremendous obligations under which the love of God has laid us.

If you had to manage waterworks for the distribution of water all over this city, and there was a certain pipe into which you poured water, and none ever came out at the other end, do you know what you would do? You would take it out and say, " This does not suit my purpose: I want a pipe that will give out as well as receive." That is exactly what the Lord desires of us. Do not selfishly say, " I want to sit down and enjoy the love of God. I shall never say a word to anybody about Christ. I will never give a poor creature so much as a brass farthing; but I want to sit down and be solaced with the love of God." If you think thus, you are a pipe plugged up; you are of no use; you will have to be taken out of the system of the church; for the system of love-supply for the world requires open pipes, through which love divine may freely flow. May the Lord clear you, and fill you, so that out of you there may continually flow rivers of living water. Amen.

Portion of Scripture Read before Sermon—1 John iv.

Hymns from " Our Own Hymn Book "—199, 782, 803.

A History of Spurgeon's Tabernacle
by Eric Hayden
$3.95. SBC rate, $2.65

The author pastored the Tabernacle when it was rebuilt the third time, necessitated by the damage from Nazi bombs. He is perhaps the greatest living authority on Mr. Spurgeon's life and work. His own grandfather was a member under Spurgeon's ministry. He has updated Spurgeon's own little history of the Tabernacle and added valuable appendixes, making this the best source of information on Spurgeon printed in this century.

Metropolitan Tabernacle Pulpit.

THE HOLY SPIRIT'S THREEFOLD CONVICTION OF MEN.

A Sermon

DELIVERED ON LORD'S-DAY MORNING, FEBRUARY 25TH, 1883, BY

C. H. SPURGEON,

AT THE METROPOLITAN TABERNACLE, NEWINGTON.

"And when he is come, he will reprove the world of sin, and of righteousness, and of judgment: of sin, because they believe not on me; of righteousness, because I go to my Father, and ye see me no more; of judgment, because the prince of this world is judged."—John xvi. 8—11.

THE Apostles had a stern task before them. They were to go into all nations and proclaim the gospel to every creature, beginning at Jerusalem. Remember that only two or three years before they were simple fishermen engaged upon the Galilean lake—men of little or no education, men of no rank or standing. At best they were but Jews, and that nation was everywhere despised, while these peasants were not even men of repute among their own nation. Yet these men were to turn the world upside down. They were told by their Lord that they would be brought before rulers and kings for his sake, and that they would be persecuted wherever they went. They were to proclaim the gospel in the teeth of the imperial power of Rome, the ancient wisdom of Greece, and the fierce cruelties of barbaric lands, and to set up the kingdom of peace and righteousness.

At the very time when they were about to receive their commission, they were also to lose the bodily presence of their great Leader. While he was with them they had felt no fear. If they were puzzled at any time by the Scribes and Pharisees, they resorted to Jesus, and they were rescued from bewilderment. Never man spoke like that man; never did such wisdom and prudence dwell in any mind as dwelt in the mind of Christ. His presence was their ægis, the broad shield behind which they stood securely, whatever shafts might be shot at them by their adversaries. But now that he was to depart out of the world unto the Father they would be deprived of their fortress and high tower; they would be as children bereft of their father, or, at best, as soldiers without a general. Here was a sad case. Work given, and power withdrawn: a battle beginning, and the conquering captain leaving.

How happy was it for these disciples that our blessed Lord could tell them that his going away would be for their gain rather than for their loss; for when he was gone the Spirit of God would come to be an advocate for them and with them, and by his power they would be able

No. 1,708.

to silence all their enemies and achieve their mission. The Holy Spirit was to be their Comforter, that they might not be afraid, and their Advocate, that they might not be baffled. When they spoke, there would be a power within them suggesting their words, a power with those words convincing their hearers, and a power in their hearers causing the word spoken to abide in their memories: that power would be divine, the power of the Holy Ghost, who is one God with the Father and the Son. It is one thing for men to speak, and quite another thing for God to speak through men. The work of proclaiming the gospel to the world was far too great for the twelve; but it was by no means too great for the Spirit of God. Who can limit his power? Is anything too hard for the Lord? The Holy Spirit being their helper, these feeble men were equal to the task which God had committed to their trust. The presence of the Holy Ghost was better for them than the bodily presence of the Lord Jesus. The Lord Jesus could only have been in one place as to his corporeal presence, but the Holy Ghost could be everywhere; the sight of Jesus would but appeal to the senses, but the power of the Holy Ghost touched the heart and wrought spiritual life and saving faith; thus, by his own withdrawal and the sending of the Spirit, our Lord furnished his servants for the conflict.

We will at this time observe what the Holy Spirit did as an Advocate. The passage cannot be fully understood except we give it three renderings; and I do not pretend that even then we shall have pressed from this choice cluster all the generous wine of its meaning. To my mind, it is a compendium of all the work of the Spirit of God. By our three readings we shall see much: first, the Spirit of God goes with the preaching of the gospel to *reprove* men of sin, and so to abash them in the presence of the preacher of righteousness; secondly (and this is a much more blessed result), to *convince* men of sin, and so to lead them to repentance towards God and faith in our Lord Jesus Christ; and, thirdly, the ultimate result of the Holy Spirit's work will be to *convict* men before all intelligent beings of having been guilty of the grossest sin, of having opposed the most perfect righteousness, and of having defied the most glorious judgment. We shall try to see the meaning of the passage through these three windows.

I. First, we believe that a promise is here made to the servants of Christ, that when they go forth to preach the gospel the Holy Ghost will be with them TO REPROVE MEN. By this is meant, not so much to save them as to silence them. When the minister of Christ stands up to plead his Master's cause, another advocate appears in court, whose pleadings would make it hard for men to resist the truth.

Observe how this reproof was given with regard to *sin*. On the day of Pentecost the disciples spoke with divers tongues, as the Spirit gave them utterance. Men from all countries under heaven heard themselves addressed in their native tongues. This was a great marvel, and all Jerusalem rang with it; and when Peter stood up to preach to the assembled multitude, and told the Jews that they had crucified the Holy One and the Just, the signs and wonders wrought by the Spirit in the name of Jesus were a witness which they could not refute. The very fact that the Spirit of God had given to these unlettered men the gift of tongues was evidence that Jesus of Nazareth, of whom they spoke, was no impostor. It was laid down in the old Jewish law, that if a man prophesied and his prophecies did not come to pass, he was to be condemned as a false prophet; but if that which he said came to pass, then he was a true prophet. Now, the Lord Jesus Christ had promised the outpouring of the Spirit, which had also been foretold in reference to the Messiah by the prophet Joel; when, therefore, that mark of the true Messiah was set upon Jesus of Nazareth by the coming of the Holy Spirit and the working of miracles, men were reproved for having refused to believe in Jesus. The evidence was brought home to them that they had with wicked hands crucified the Lord of glory: and so they stood reproved.

All the subsequent miracles went to prove the same thing; for when the apostles wrought miracles the world was reproved of sin because it believed not on Christ. It was not that a few disciples testified to the sin of the race, but the Holy Spirit himself made men tremble as by his deeds of power he bore witness to the Lord Jesus, and exhibited the fact that in crucifying him the world had put to death the incarnate Son of God. Do you not see the terrible power with which the first disciples were thus armed? It was more to them than the rod in the hand of Moses with which he smote Pharaoh with so many plagues. It needed all the wilfulness of that stiff-necked generation to resist the Holy Spirit and refuse to bow before him whom they had pierced ; they were full of malice and obstinacy, but in their secret hearts they were sore put to it, and felt that they were fighting against God.

Do you not see, too, dear friends, how the working of the Holy Spirit with the apostles and their immediate followers was a wonderful rebuke to the world concerning the matter of *righteousness*. Jesus was gone, and his divine example no longer stood out like clear light reproving their darkness, but the Holy Spirit attested that righteousness, and compelled them to feel that Jesus was the Holy One, and that his cause was righteous. The teaching of the apostles, sealed by the Holy Spirit, made the world see what righteousness was as they had never seen it before. A fresh standard of morals was set up in the world, and it has never been taken down: it stands in its place to rebuke, if not to improve. The world was then sunken in the uttermost depths of vice, and even its good men were loathsome; but now another kind of righteousness was exhibited in the teachings of the Lord Jesus, and the Spirit came to set the seal of divine approval thereto, so that if men continued in sin it might be against light and knowledge, for they now knew what was righteousness, and could no longer mistake upon that point. God was with the preachers of a new righteousness, and by divers signs and wonders he attested the cause of the gospel Now, brethren, we also rejoice in this, seeing that the witness of truth is for all time, and we know of a surety that the kingdom which our Lord Jesus has set up among men is divinely sanctioned as the kingdom of righteousness, which in the end shall grind to powder the powers of evil. We are the covenanted servants of a Lord whose righteousness was declared among men by the personal witness of God the Holy Ghost. Are you not glad to be enlisted in such a service? Oh, world! art thou not reproved for resisting such a kingdom?

These twelve fishermen could not of themselves have exhibited a new standard of righteousness among men; they could not on their own account have set before all nations a higher ideal of moral excellence; but when the eternal power and majesty of the Godhead vouched for the righteousness of the Lord Jesus, the course of the apostolic church became like that of the sun in the heavens. "Their line is gone out through all the earth, and their words to the end of the world." None could stand against them; for, as when the morning breaks the darkness flies and the bats and the night-birds hasten away, so when the messengers of mercy proclaimed the righteousness of God, man's hypocrisy and self-glorying fled away.

Then, too, they were made to feel that a *judgment* had come; that somehow the life and the death of Jesus of Nazareth had made a crisis in the world's history, and condemned the way and manner of the ungodly. All historians must confess that the turning point of the race is the cross of Christ. It would be impossible to fix any other hinge of history. From that moment the power of evil received its mortal wound. It dies hard, but from that hour it was doomed. At the death of our Lord the heathen oracles were struck dumb. There had been oracles all over the world, either the product of evil spirits or of crafty priests; but after the Christian era the world ceased to believe in these voices, and they were no more heard. Systems of false worship, so firmly rooted in prejudice and custom that it seemed impossible that they should ever be overthrown, were torn up by their roots by the breath of the Lord. The apostles might have said to all the systems of falsehood, "as a bowing wall shall ye be, and as a tottering fence." Men could not help perceiving that the prince of darkness had been cast down from his undivided power, and that he spake henceforth with bated breath. The seed of the woman had met the old serpent, and in the duel between them he had gained such a victory that the cause of evil was henceforth hopeless.

Moreover, the thought flashed upon humanity more clearly than ever it had done before—that there would be a day of judgment. Men heard and felt the truth of the warning that God would judge the world at the last by the man Christ Jesus. The dim forms of Rhadamanthus on a cloudy judgment seat, and of the assembly before his throne, and of the crowds divided according to their lives, now began to assume another and far more definite shape. It was written on the heart of mankind that there is a judgment to come! Men will rise again; they shall stand before the judgment-seat of Christ to give an account of the things done in the body, whether good or evil. The world heard this, and the tidings have never been forgotten. The Holy Ghost has reproved men by the prospect of judgment.

The Holy Spirit attested the life of Christ, the teaching of the apostles, and all the grand truths that were contained therein, by what he did in the way of miracle, and by what he did in the way of enlightening, impressing, and subduing human hearts. Henceforth man is accused and rebuked by the great Advocate; and all who remain in opposition to the Lord Jesus, remain so in defiance of the clearest proofs of his mission. He who rejects human testimony when it is true is foolish; but he who despises the witness of the Holy Ghost is profane, for he gives the lie to the Spirit of truth. Let him beware lest he so sin against the Holy Ghost as to come under the most terrible of curses ; for it is written of him that speaketh against the Holy Ghost, " he hath never forgiveness."

Brethren, does not that put the apostles in quite a different position from that in which they appeared to be? If we judge according to sense and carnal reason, their adventure was Quixotic, their success was impossible. Everybody would have said to them, " Go back to your nets and to your boats. What can you do against the established system of Judaism in your own country ? And if that be too hard for you, what will you be able to do in other lands ? There are nations that have been tutored in their own learning for thousands of years, and have become adepts in all the arts and sciences ; they have brought all the charms of poetry, and music, and statuary, to support their idolatrous systems : you are fools to think that you unlearned and ignorant men can ever overturn all this." Would not prudence agree with this ? Ay, but if God is in these men, if he that dwelt in the bush at Horeb, and made it burn, though it was not consumed, will dwell in them, and each one of them shall be gifted with a tongue of fire, this is a different business altogether. Surely, he that made the world, could new-make it. He that said, " Let there be light, and there was light," could command light to shine upon the moral and spiritual night.

Thus much upon the first reading of the text. Let us advance to that which will more interest you.

II. The Holy Spirit was to go with the preaching of the word TO CONVINCE MEN of three great prominent truths. This was to be a saving word : they are to be so convinced as to repent of sin, to accept of righteousness, and yield themselves to the judgment of the Lord. Here we see as in a map the work of the Spirit upon the hearts of those who are ordained unto eternal life. Those three effects are all necessary, and each one is in the highest degree important to true conversion.

First, the Holy Ghost is come to convince men of *sin*. It is absolutely necessary that men should be convinced of sin. The fashionable theology is—" Convince men of the goodness of God : show them the universal fatherhood and assure them of unlimited mercy. Win them by God's love, but never mention his wrath against sin, or the need of an atonement, or the possibility of there being a place of punishment. Do not censure poor creatures for their failings. Do not judge and condemn. Do not search the heart or lead men to be low-spirited and sorrowful. Comfort and encourage, but never accuse and threaten." Yes, that is the way of man ; but the way of the Spirit of God is very different. He comes on purpose to convince men of sin, to make them feel that they are guilty, greatly guilty—so guilty that they are lost, and ruined, and undone. He comes to remind them not only of God's loveliness, but of their own unloveliness ; of their own enmity and hatred to this God of love, and, consequently, of their terrible sin in thus ill-using one so infinitely kind. The Holy Ghost does not come to make sinners comfortable in their sins, but to cause them to grieve over their sins. He does not help them to forget their sin, or think little of it, but he comes to convince them of the horrible enormity of their iniquity. It is no work of the Spirit to pipe to men's dancing : he does not bring forth flute, harp, dulcimer, and all kinds of music to charm the unbelieving into a good opinion of themselves; but he comes to make sin appear sin, and to let us see its fearful consequences. He comes to wound so that no human balm can heal: to kill so that no earthly power can make us live. The flowers bedeck the meadows when the grass is green; but lo! a burning wind comes from the desert, and the grass withereth, and the flower thereof falleth away. What is it that makes the beauty and excellence of human righteousness to wither as the green herb? Isaiah says it is " because the Spirit of the Lord bloweth upon it." There is a withering work of the Spirit of God which we must experience, or we shall never know his quickening and restoring power. This withering is a most needful experience, and just now needs much to be insisted on. To-day we have so many built up who were never pulled down; so many filled who were never emptied; so many exalted who were never humbled; that I the more earnestly remind you that the Holy Ghost must convince us of sin, or we cannot be saved.

This work is most necessary, because without it there is no leading men to receive the gospel of the grace of God. We cannot make head-way with certain people because they profess faith very readily, but they are not convinced of anything. " Oh, yes, we are sinners, no doubt, and Christ died for sinners": that is the free-and-easy way with which they handle heavenly mysteries, as if they were the nonsense verses of a boy's exercise, or the stories of Mother Goose. This is all mockery, and we are weary of it. But get near a real sinner, and you have found a man you can deal with: I mean the man who is a sinner, and no mistake, and mourns in his inmost soul that he is so. In such a man you find one who will welcome the gospel, welcome grace, and welcome a Saviour. To him the news of pardon will be as cold water to a thirsty soul, and the doctrine of grace will be as honey dropping from the comb. "A sinner," says one of our songsters, "is a sacred thing: the Holy Ghost hath made him so.' Your sham sinner is a horrid creature ; but a man truly convinced of sin by the Spirit of God is a being to be sought after as a jewel that will adorn the crown of the Redeemer.

Note here, that the Spirit of God comes to convince men of sin, because they never will be convinced of sin apart from his divine advocacy. A natural conscience touched by the Spirit of God may do a good deal in the way of showing a man his faults ; it may thus make him uneasy, and may bring about a reformation of life; but it is only the Spirit of God that to the full extent convinces a man of sin so as to bring forth repentance, self-despair, and faith in Jesus. For what is the sin that you and I are guilty of? Ah, brethren, it were not easy to tell ; but this I know, that the extent of sin is never known till the Spirit of God reveals the secret chambers of the heart's abominations. We do a thousand things that we do not know to be sin till the Spirit of God enlightens us and pleads the cause of holiness in us. What natural man, for instance, ever laments over evil thoughts or desires, or the imaginations which flit across his mind? Yet all these are sins, and sins which cause a gracious heart the deepest distress. If we were never actually to commit evil, yet if we desire to do so, we have already sinned; and if we feel pleasure in thinking of evil, we have already sinned. This poison is in our nature, and shows itself in a thousand ways. The fact that we not only sin, but are by nature sinful, is one which our pride kicks against, and we will not learn it till the Spirit of God teaches it to us. Neither does any man know the exceeding sinfulness of sin till the light falls upon the black mass from the Holy Spirit. Every sin is, as it were, an assault upon God's throne, glory, and life. Sin would dethrone the Most High, and destroy him if it could; but men do not see this. They talk of sin most lightly, and know not that it scatters firebrands and death. I tell you, when the Spirit of God makes a man see sin in its naked deformity, he is horrified. When I saw, or thought I saw, the heinousness of sin, it was intolerable, and I had no rest in my spirit. Some such a sight we must all have, or we shall never look to the Lord Jesus to take away our sin. None but those whose wounds smart are likely to apply for the heavenly balm.

The Holy Spirit dwells upon one point in particular: "of sin, because they believe not on me." None see the sin of unbelief except by his light. For a man thinks, "Well, if I have not believed in Christ, that is a pity, perhaps; but still, I was never a thief, or a liar, or a drunkard, or unchaste. Unbelief is a matter of very little consequence; I can set that square at any time." But the Holy Spirit makes a man see that not to believe in Christ is a crowning, damning sin, since he that believeth not hath made God a liar: and what can be more atrocious than that? He who believes not on Christ has rejected God's mercy, and has done despite to the grandest display of God's love; he hath despised God's unspeakable gift, and trampled on the blood of Christ. In this he has dishonoured God on a very tender point; has insulted him concerning his only-begotten Son. How I wish that the Spirit of God would come upon unbelievers here, and make them see what they are and where they are with regard to the one and only Saviour. How shall they escape who neglect so great salvation? It will not matter how feebly I speak this morning if the Spirit of God will only work by the truth, you will perceive the greatness of your crime, and you will never rest until you have believed on the Lord Jesus, and found forgiveness for your high offence against the bleeding Lamb. So far, then, upon the first operation of the Holy Ghost.

The next work of the Spirit is to convince men of *righteousness;* that is to say, in gospel terms, to show them that they have no righteousness of their own, and no means of working righteousness, and that apart from grace they are condemned. Thus he leads them to value the righteousness of God which is upon all them that believe, even a righteousness which covers sin, and renders them acceptable with God.

Lend me your ears a moment while I call your attention to a great wonder. Among men, if a person is convicted of wrong-doing, the next step is judgment. A young man, for instance, has been in the service of an employer, and he has embezzled money: he is convicted of the theft by process of law, and found guilty. What follows next? Why, judgment is pronounced, and he must suffer penalty. But observe how our gracious God interpolates another process. Truly, his ways are not our ways! "He shall convince of sin ———" The next step would be judgment; but no, the Lord inserts a hitherto unknown middle term, and convinces "of righteousness." Be amazed at this. The Lord takes a man, even when he is sinful and conscious of that sin, and makes him righteous on the spot, by putting away his sin and justifying him by the righteousness of faith, a righteousness which comes to him by the worthiness of another who has wrought out a righteousness for him. Can that be? Brethren, this seems to be a thing so impossible that it needs the Spirit of God to convince men of it. I may now set forth the great plan whereby the Lord Jesus is made of God unto us righteousness; I may show how the Son of God became man that he might fully keep the law of God for us, and that having done so, and having added his passive obedience to his active service, he presented to his Father a complete vindication of his injured law, so that every man that believeth on him shall be delivered from condemnation, and accepted in the Beloved. I might also tell how Christ's righteousness is set to our account, so that faith is reckoned unto us for righteousness, even as was the case with faithful Abraham. Yet all my labour will be in vain till the Spirit shall make it plain. Many hear the gladsome tidings; but they do not receive the truth, for they are not convinced of it. They need to be persuaded of it before they will embrace it; and that persuasion is not in my power. Did I hear one remark, "I cannot see this way of righteousness"? I answer, No, and you never will until the Spirit of God convinces you of it.

Note well the great point of the Spirit's argument,—"Of righteousness, because I go to my Father, and ye see me no more." Our Lord was sent into the world to work out a righteousness, and here he says "I go"; but he would not go till he had done his work. He says also, "I go to my Father"; but he would not go back to his Father till he had fulfilled his covenant engagements. "I go to my Father"; that is, I go to receive a reward and to sit upon my Father's throne; and he could not have received this glory if he had not finished his appointed work. Behold, then, Christ has finished a righteousness which is freely given to all them that believe, and all those who trust in Christ are for his sake regarded as righteous before God, and are in fact righteous, so that Paul saith, "Who is he that condemneth?" His ground for asking that question is the same as that which the Spirit uses in my text. He says, "It is Christ that died, yea rather, that is risen again, who is even at the right hand of God, who also maketh intercession for us." He quotes, as the Holy Spirit does, the resurrection, ascension, and enthronement of the great Intercessor as the proof positive that there is a perfect righteousness for all believing sinners. I know that many will say, "This is making people righteous who are not righteous," and hence they will raise many objections. Just so! This is the glory of God, that he justifieth the ungodly, and saves sinners by Christ. "Blessed is the man unto whom the Lord imputeth not iniquity." "I do not see it," cries one. And our answer is, "We know you do not: we are not in the least surprised that you reject our testimony; we never expected you to receive it unless the arm of the Lord should be revealed, and the Holy Ghost should convince you of righteousness." No man comes to Christ who is not drawn of the Father and enlightened by the Spirit; but if the Spirit convinces you we shall soon hear you sing—

> "Jesus, thy blood and righteousness
> My beauty are, my glorious dress;
> Midst flaming worlds, in these arrayed,
> With joy shall I lift up my head."

Dear people of God, pray hard that the Spirit of God may even now convince unbelievers that the only true righteousness for mortal men is that which comes not by the works of the law, but by the hearing of faith.

But then comes a third point, the Spirit of God is to convince men *of judgment*. To whom is this judgment committed? "The Father hath committed all judgment unto the Son." The true penitent feels that if he had all his sins forgiven him yet it will not serve his turn so long as he lies wallowing in sin. He feels that the great enemy of his soul must be dethroned, or else forgiveness itself will afford him no rest of heart. He must be rescued from the power as well as from the guilt of sin, or else he abides in bondage. He must see the power of evil hewn in pieces before the Lord as Samuel hewed Agag of old. Hearken, O troubled one! You shall be set free, for "the prince of this world is judged." Jesus came to destroy the works of the devil; and on the cross our Redeemer judged Satan, overcame him, and cast him down. He is now a condemned criminal, a vanquished rebel. His reigning power over all believers is broken. He hath great wrath, knowing that his time is short, but that wrath is held in check by his conqueror. In his passion our Lord fought Satan foot to foot, and overcame him, spoiling principalities and powers, and making a show of them openly, triumphing over them in it. Believest thou this? May the Spirit of God convince you of it! O tried believer, the Lord Jesus overthrew the devil for you. He crushed the powers of darkness for you; and believing in him you shall find evil dethroned in you, and all the forces of sin hurled from their high places. You shall overcome through the blood of the Lamb. Again I say, believest thou this? Christ is made of God unto us sanctification; he saves his people from their sins; he makes them holy, and so breaks in pieces their enemy. Though it will cost you many a conflict, and the beaded sweat may in the hour of temptation stand upon your brow, as you fear that you will fall from holiness, yet the Lord shall bruise Satan under your feet shortly, for he has already bruised him under his own feet on your behalf. The Spirit of God is needed to convince our unbelieving hearts that it is even so. Most men dream that they must overcome sin by their own strength. Alas, the strong man armed still keeps the house against our feebleness. You have a pretty piece of work before you if in your own strength you venture on this conflict. I can hear the devil laughing at you even now. This leviathan is not to be tamed by you. Job would say, "Wilt thou play with him as with a bird?" Dost thou think the devil is as easily managed as a woman carries her pet bird on her finger, and puts it to her lip to peck a seed? Canst thou draw out leviathan with a hook? Will he speak soft words unto thee? Wilt thou take him to be a servant for ever? Thine arrows cannot come at him, nor thy sword wound him. "Lay thine hand upon him, remember the battle, do no more." A power divine is needed, and that power is ready to display itself if it be humbly sought.

Many who are convinced of the righteousness of Christ are not yet fully convinced that evil is judged, and condemned, and cast down. They are haunted with the dread that they may yet perish by the hand of the enemy. Oh, my brother, see the need of the Holy Spirit to advocate in thy heart the cause of God and truth, and make thee believe that the Lord Jesus hath supreme power over every enemy. I sometimes meet with a Christian brother who tells me the world is all going to the bad, the gospel is being utterly defeated, Christ is routed, the devil is waving the black flag and shouting victory. I know how terrible is the conflict, but I believe that my Lord Jesus has judged the whole kingdom of evil, and in that fact I see Satan fall like lightning from heaven. Our Lord *must* reign. His enemies must lick the dust. We shall judge the fallen angels at the last great day, and meanwhile a believing life is a life of triumph over the arch enemy. In the power of the Spirit it shall be proven that truth is mightier than error, love is stronger than hate, and holiness is higher than sin; for the Lord's right hand and his holy arm have gotten him the victory. Behold how the ascended Saviour leads captivity captive. See how he comes from Edom, with dyed garments from Bozrah, for he has trodden sin and hell in the winepress, and now he travelleth in the greatness of his strength, speaking in righteousness, mighty to save.

Let me run again over this ground, that we may not overlook anything. Dear friends, those of us who are saved still need the Holy Spirit with us every day to convince us of sin. Good men do at this hour most complacently things which in clearer light they will never think of doing. May the Holy Spirit continually show us layer after layer of sin, that we may remove it; may he reveal to us rank after rank of sin, that we may conquer all its forces. May he especially discover to us the sin of not believing in Christ, for even we have our doubts and fears. After a sermon concerning sin the poor child of God cries out, " I dare not believe. I am afraid I shall be lost after all." This unbelief is another sin. Strange way of escaping from sin by plunging into it! To doubt the Lord is to add sin to sin. No sin is more pernicious than the sin of not believing. Whenever our heart distrusts the Lord we grieve his Spirit; hence we always need the Holy Ghost to convince us of this evil and bitter thing, and to lead us to trust after a childlike fashion. Any mistrust of God's promise, any fear of failure on God's part, any thought of his unfaithfulness, is a crime against the honour of the divine majesty. Oh, convincing Spirit, dwell with me from day to day convincing me of sin, and especially making me to feel that the worst of all evils is to question my faithful Friend.

So, also, may you always have the Spirit of God dwelling with you, convincing you of righteousness. May those of you who are indeed believers never question but what you are righteous before God. We who believe are made the righteousness of God in Christ Jesus: are we assured of this? If so, do not think and talk as if you were still under the curse of the law, for you are no longer in any such condition. "Therefore being justified by faith, we have peace with God through our Lord Jesus Christ." "There is therefore now no condemnation to them which are in Christ Jesus." Oh, may the Spirit of God every day convince you of that; and convince you of it on the ground that Jesus is reigning yonder at the Father's right hand. The interest of each believer in his Lord is clear and sure. If Jesus is there, I am there. If the Father has accepted him, he has accepted me. Do you catch the logic of it ? You are in Christ, you are one with him : as he is so are you in him. Do hold fast to the fact that you are not condemned. How can you be ? You are at the right hand of God in Christ. You condemned ! Why, you are "accepted in the Beloved," for your representative is accepted by God and made to sit upon his throne. Jesus is exalted, not for himself alone, but for all those who believe in him. May the blessed Spirit fully convince you of this grand truth.

And, next, may he convince you of judgment—namely, that you have been judged, and your enemy has been judged, and condemned. The day of judgment is not a thing to be dreaded by a believer. We have stood our trial, and have been acquitted. Our representative has borne the penalty of our sin. Our chastisement is passed : for Jesus has borne it : he was numbered with transgressors. There is now no curse for us : there can be none : heaven, earth, hell cannot find a curse for those whom God has blessed, since the Lord Jesus "was made a curse for us." May the Spirit of God come on you afresh, my dearly beloved, and make you confident and joyful in him who is the Lord our righteousness, by whom evil has been judged once for all!

III. Last of all, let us read our text by rendering it " convict "— " The Spirit of God will CONVICT the world of sin, of righteousness, and of judgment." There is the world. It stands a prisoner at the bar, and the charge is that it is and has been full of sin. In courts of law you are often surprised with what comes out. You look at the prisoner, and he seems to be a quiet, respectable person, and you say, " I should not think he is guilty." But the advocate who has engaged to plead the cause of righteousness stands up and gives an outline of the case ; and you speedily change your mind, until as the evidence proceeds you say to yourself, " That is a villain, if ever there was one." Now hear the Spirit of God. The Spirit came into the world to make all men know that Jesus is the Christ, and he attested that fact by miracles that could not be questioned, miracles without number : he has moreover attested the truth of the gospel by the conversion of myriads, whose happy and holy lives have been a proof that Jesus Christ was indeed sent forth from God. But what did this wicked world do with Christ ? They gave him a felon's death : they nailed him to a cross. By this the world is condemned ! We need no further evidence. The world is convicted : self-condemned by the slaughter of him who was incarnate goodness and unbounded love. The world is base enough to desire to slay its God even when he comes on an errand of love. Take the accused away ! The world's guilt is proven beyond question. The wrath of God abideth on it.

What follows upon this? The trial is viewed from another point. The world has declared that the gospel is not righteous, that the system which our Lord has come to establish is not true. Up to this day the world is continually raising objections, trying to confound believers, and, if possible, to defeat our most holy cause. But the Spirit of God by his teaching proves that the gospel is full of righteousness ; and by all his operations through the word he proves that the gospel is holy, and just, and good, and tends to make men pure, godly, peaceable, and holy. By sanctifying men through the gospel so that they lead gracious lives, the Holy Spirit proves that the gospel is righteous. This process grows more and more complete as time rolls on. Were not the world un-righteous it would long ago have yielded to the holy message and its holy Messenger. But it will be forced to own the truth one day. The Holy Spirit makes the world know that Christ is righteous by flashing into its face the fact that Christ has gone,—gone up to glory, at the right hand of God,—and this could not have been had he not been the righteous One.

When the world shall see Jesus enthroned at the last, and all mankind shall behold the Son of man on the clouds of heaven, what con-viction will seize on every mind! There will be no agnostics then! Not a sceptic will be found in that day! Christ seen at the Father's right hand will end all unbelief!

And then the Spirit of God shall make men see the judgment. Before the day actually comes, they shall perceive that since Christ has judged the devil, since Christ has cast him down from his high places, and his power over the world is already broken, assuredly he will smite all that are in the dominion of Satan, and will not allow one of them to escape. The cause of evil is judged, and its case is desperate. Oh, how the Spirit of God will convict men at that last day when they hear the Judge say, " Come, ye blessed of my Father," or " Depart, ye cursed, into ever-lasting fire."

Men and brethren, will you be convinced by the Holy Spirit now, or will you wait till then ? Shall it be the convincement of grace or the conviction of wrath ? The Spirit bears witness still with us who preach the gospel : will you yield to that gospel, and believe it now? or will you wait until the blaze of the last tremendous day ? Which shall it be ? I think I hear you say, "The gospel is true." Why, then, do you not believe it ? If you confess " sin," why are you not washed from it ? If there be " righteousness," why do you not seek it ? If there be " judgment," why do you not ask to be so cleansed that you need not be afraid of it ? Oh, sirs, the most of men act as if they were born fools. If they were sick, and we had a sure medicine for them, they would rush to us for it. If they were poor, and we brought them gold, they would tread us down in their vehemence to snatch at wealth. But when there is Christ to be had, the divine remedy for sin, Christ to be had as a perfect righteousness, Christ to make them stand securely at the last dread day, they turn their backs upon the heavenly boon. Oh, Spirit of God, win these madmen; bring back these fools and make them sane and wise, for Christ Jesus' sake. Amen.

PORTION OF SCRIPTURE READ BEFORE SERMON—John xvi.

HYMNS FROM " OUR OWN HYMN BOOK "—449, 170, 544.

Metropolitan Tabernacle Pulpit.

THE BEST WAR-CRY.

A Sermon

DELIVERED ON LORD'S-DAY MORNING, MARCH 4TH, 1883, BY

C. H. SPURGEON,

AT THE METROPOLITAN TABERNACLE, NEWINGTON.

"The Lord his God is with him, and the shout of a king is among them."—Numbers xxiii. 21.

IT was a singular spectacle to see the king of Moab and his lords climbing to the tops of the craggy rocks, accompanied by that strange being, the Eastern prophet Balaam. They are seeking to look upon Israel with the evil eye, and flash down curses upon her tents in the plain beneath. You see them gazing down from the mountains upon the encampment in the wilderness below, even as vultures from aloft spy out their prey. They watch with keen and cruel eyes. Cunning and malice are in their countenances. How Balak longs to crush the nation which he fears! They are secretly endeavouring by spell and enchantment to bring evil upon the people whom Jehovah has chosen and led into the wilderness. You see them offering their seven bullocks and their seven rams upon the seven altars which they have set up upon Pisgah's rocks; and Balaam retires to wait until the afflatus shall come upon him, and he shall be able to prophesy. In all probability Moses knew nothing about this at the time; and certainly the people below knew nothing of the foul conspiracy. There lay the tribes in the valley, unaware that mischief was brewing, and quite unable to meet the dark design even if they had been aware of it. What a mercy it was for them that they were guarded by a Watcher, and a holy one, whose eyes can never slumber. How true it is—" I the Lord do keep it; I will water it every moment: lest any hurt it, I will keep it night and day." The Lord's eyes are fixed upon Balaam the hireling, and Balak the son of Zippor : in vain do they weave the enchantment and work the divination; they shall be utterly ashamed and confounded. They were baffled in their machinations, and utterly defeated in their schemes, and that for one single reason: it is written, "JEHOVAH SHAMMAH—the Lord is there. God's presence in the midst of his people is as a wall of fire round about them, and a glory in their midst. The Lord is their light and their salvation, whom shall they fear?

At this present time God has a people, a remnant according to the election of grace, who still dwell like sheep in the midst of wolves. When, as a part of the Lord's church, we look at our surroundings, we

see much that might cause us alarm ; for never, either day or night, is
Satan quiet. Like a roaring lion he goeth about, seeking whom he may
devour: he plots in secret his crafty devices; if it were possible he
would deceive even the very elect. This prince of darkness has on
earth many most diligent servants, compassing sea and land to make
proselytes, laying out all their strength, and using all their craft and
cunning if by any means they may destroy the kingdom of God, and
blot out the truth from under heaven. It is saddest of all to see
certain men who know the truth in some degree, as Balaam did, entering
into league with the adversary against the true Israel. These combine
their arts, and use all possible means that the gospel of the grace of
God, and the church that holds it, may utterly be destroyed. If the
church be not destroyed it will be no thanks to her enemies, for they
would swallow her up quick. When we look upon the signs of the
times our heart grows heavy ; for iniquity abounds, the love of many
waxes cold, many false spirits have gone abroad into the earth, and some
whom we looked upon as helpers are proving themselves to be of
another order. What then? Are we dismayed? By no means, for
that same God who was in the midst of the church in the wilderness
is in the church of these last days. Again shall her adversaries be
defeated. Still will he defend her, for the Lord has built his church
upon a rock, and the gates of hell shall not prevail against her. The
reason of her safety is this :—

> " God in the midst of her doth dwell ;
> Nothing shall her remove ;
> The Lord to her a helper shall,
> And that right early, prove."

Our text declares the grand safeguard of the church of God, ensuring
her against every peril known and unknown, earthly or Satanic :—" Jehovah his God is with him, and the shout of a king is among them."

May the Holy Spirit help me while I try to speak first upon *God's
presence with his people ;* secondly, upon *the results of that presence ;* and,
thirdly, upon *how, by the grace of God, that presence may be preserved
continually amongst us.*

I. First, let me speak a little upon GOD'S PRESENCE AMONG HIS
PEOPLE. It is *an extraordinary presence*, for God's ordinary and usual
presence is everywhere. Whither shall we flee from his presence ? He
is in the highest heaven and in the lowest hell ; the hand of the Lord
is upon the high hills, and his power is in all deep places. This knowledge is too high and wonderful for us : yet everywhere is God, for in
him we live and move and have our being. Still there is a peculiar
presence ; for God was among his people in the wilderness as he was not
among the Moabites and the Edomites their foes, and God is in his
church as he is not in the world. It is a peculiar promise of the
covenant that God will dwell with his people and walk among them.
By the gift of the Holy Spirit the Lord is with us and in us at this hour.
He saith of his church, " Here will I dwell, for I have desired it." This
is much more than God's being about us ; it includes the favour of God
towards us, his consideration of us, his working with us. An active
nearness to bless is the presence of which we speak.

Here we may say with great reverence that God is with his people *in the entireness of his nature.* The Father is with us, for the Father himself loveth us. Like as a father pitieth his children, so the Lord pitieth them that fear him. He is near to us, supplying our needs, guiding our steps, helping us in time, and tutoring us for eternity. God is where his children are, hearing every groan of their sorrow, marking every tear of their distress. The Father is in the midst of his family, acting a father's part towards them. "Lord, thou hast been our dwelling-place in all generations." He is never far from any into whose breasts he has put the spirit of adoption whereby we cry, "Abba, Father!" Come, ye children of God, rejoice in this: your heavenly Father has come unto you, and abides with you. We have also the presence of the divine Son of God. Said he not to his apostles, "Lo, I am with you alway, even unto the end of the world"? Have we not this for our joy whenever we come together, that we meet in his name, and that he still says, "Peace be unto you," and manifests himself unto us as he doth not unto the world. Many of you know most delightfully what it is to have fellowship with God, for "truly our fellowship is with the Father, and with his Son Jesus Christ"; and this fellowship were not ours if we were not made nigh by his precious blood. Very near are we to the heart of Christ: he dwells with us; yea, he is one with us. Peculiarly this presence relates to the Holy Ghost. It is he who represents the Lord Jesus who has gone from us. We have a double portion of Christ's spirit, because we see him now that he is taken up; even as Elisha had a double portion of Elijah's spirit, according to the prophet's saying, "If thou see me when I am taken from thee, it shall be so unto thee"; that is, a double portion of my spirit shall rest upon thee. It was expedient that our Lord and Master should go, that the Spirit might be given. That Spirit once outpoured at Pentecost has never been withdrawn. He is still in the midst of this dispensation, working, guiding, quickening, comforting, exercising all the blessed office of the Paraclete, and being for us and in us God's advocate, pleading for the truth, and for us. Yes, dear friends, the Father, the Son, and the Holy Spirit are in the midst of the true church of God when that church is in a right and healthy state; and if the triune God be gone away from the church, then her banners must trail in the dust, for her warriors have lost their strength. This is the glory of the church of God—to have the grace of the Lord Jesus Christ, and the love of God the Father, and the communion of the Holy Ghost to be her never-failing benediction. What a glory to have Father, Son, and Holy Spirit manifesting the Godhead in the midst of our assemblies, and blessing each one of us.

For God to dwell with us: what *a condescending presence* this is! And will God in very truth dwell among men? If the heaven of heavens cannot contain him, will he abide among his people? He will! He will! Glory be to his name! "Know ye not that your bodies are the temples of the Holy Ghost?" God dwelleth in us. Wonderful word! Who can fathom the depth of this grace? The mystery of the incarnation is equalled by the mystery of the indwelling. That God the Holy Ghost should dwell in our bodies is as extraordinary as that God the Son should inhabit that body which was born of the blessed virgin. Strange, strange is this, that the Creator should dwell in his creatures, that the Infinite should tabernacle in finite beings. Yet so it is; for he has said, " Certainly I will be with thee."

What *an awe* this imparts to every true church of God! You may go in and out of certain assemblies, and you may say, " Here we have beauty! here we have adornment, musical, ecclesiastical, architectural, oratorical, and the like!" but to my mind there is no worship like that which proceeds from a man when he feels—the Lord is here. What a hush comes over the soul! Here is the place for the bated breath, the unsandalled foot, and the prostrate spirit. Now are we on holy ground. When the Lord descends in the majesty of his infinite love to deal with the hearts of men, then it is with us as it was in Solomon's temple when the priests could not stand to minister by reason of the glory that filled the place. Man is set aside, for God is there. In such a case the most fluent think it better to be silent; for there is at times more expressiveness in absolute silence than in the fittest words. " How dreadful is this place! this is none other but the house of God, and this is the gate of heaven." For why? Because Jacob had said, " Surely the Lord is in this place." We regard the lowliest assemblies of the most illiterate people with solemn reverence if God be there: we regard the largest assemblies of the wealthiest and most renowned with utter indifference if God be not there.

This is the one *necessary* of the church: the Lord God must be in the midst of her, or she is nothing. If God be there, peace will be within her walls, and prosperity within her palaces; but if the Lord be not there woe unto the men that speak in his name, for they shall cry in bitterness, " Who hath believed our report?" Woe unto the waiting people, for they shall go away empty! Woe unto the sinners in a forsaken Zion, for them comes no salvation! The presence of God makes the Church to be a joyful, happy, solemn place: this brings glory to his name and peace to his people; but without it all faces are pale, all hearts are heavy.

Brethren, this presence of God is *clearly discerned* by the gracious, though others may not know it. Yet methinks even the ungracious in a measure perceive it,—coming into the assembly they are struck with a secret something, they know not what; and if they do not immediately join in the worship of the present God, yet a deep impression is made upon them beyond any that could be caused by the sound of human speech, or by the grandeur of outward show. They feel awed, and retire abashed. Certainly the devil knows where God is,—none better than he. He hates the camp of which Jehovah is the leader; against it he doubles his enmity, multiplies his plots, and exercises all his power. He knows where his kingdom finds its bravest assailants, and he therefore attacks their head-quarters, even as did Balaam and Balak of old.

Let us look at Balaam for a moment. May we never run in the way of Balaam for a reward; but let us stand in his way for a moment that he may be our beacon. This man had sold himself for gold, and though he knew God and spoke under inspiration, yet he knew him not in his heart, but was willing to curse God's people for hire. He was thwarted in his design because God was there. It is worth our while to see what kind of a God Jehovah is in Balaam's estimation. He describes our God in verse nineteen,—" God is not a man, that he should lie; neither the son of man, that he should repent: hath he said, and shall he not do it? or hath he spoken, and shall he not make it good?" Balaam perceived that the God who was in the midst of his people is not a changeable God, not a false God, not one who promises and forgets, or promises and eats his words, or promises what he cannot and will not perform. The God of Israel is faithful and true, immutable, unchanging : every one of his promises shall be fulfilled : none of his words shall fall to the ground. "Hath he said, and shall he not do it?—hath he spoken and shall it not come to pass ?" What a joy it is to have such a God as this among us,—a promise-making and a promise-keeping God; a God at work for his people, as he has declared he would be; a God comforting and cheering his people, and fulfilling in their experience that which his word had led them to expect. This God is our God for ever and ever : he shall be our guide even unto death.

My dear friends, we sometimes hear men talk of the failure of the church. We are afraid that some churches do fail. Wherever failure occurs, the bottom of it is the absence of the Lord of hosts, for he cannot fail. I heard one, speaking of the district in which he lives, say, " We are a religious people; almost all the people attend a place of worship, but," he added, "I am bound to add that of spiritual life we have few traces. One church has given up its prayer-meetings; another feels that its entertainments are more important than its worship, and another is notorious for worldliness." This is a testimony as terrible as it is common. The worst thing that can be said of any Christian community is this : "Thou hast a name to live and art dead." " Thou art neither cold nor hot." Our Lord Jesus says, " I would thou wert cold or hot. So then because thou art lukewarm, and neither cold nor hot, I will spue thee out of my mouth." A church without life and zeal makes Christ sick; he cannot bear it. He can put up with downright godlessness sooner than with a profession of religion out of which the life and the power are gone, since it has cooled down into lukewarmness. This, then, we should pray for continually—the presence of God in the midst of his people.

> " Great Shepherd of thine Israel
> Who didst between the cherubs dwell,
> And ledd'st the tribes, thy chosen sheep,
> Safe through the desert and the deep :
>
> Thy church is in the desert now ;
> Shine from on high, and guide us through;
> Turn us to thee, thy love restore ;
> We shall be saved, and sigh no more."

II. To whet your desire for this let me pass on to the second head of my subject, which is briefly to describe THE RESULTS OF THIS DIVINE PRESENCE. Some of these results are *mentioned in the context*. One of the first is *leading*—" God brought them out of Egypt " (verse 22). The best critics give us another rendering : " God is bringing them out of Egypt." When God is in the midst of his people he is leading them, so that we may cheerfully sing that song, " He leadeth me ; he leadeth me," and go on with David to word it, " He leadeth me beside the still waters." We want no other leader in the church when we have God;

for his eye and arm will guide his people.   I am always afraid of having human rules in a church, and equally fearful of being governed by human precedents.   I am afraid of power being vested in one, or two, or twenty men; the power must be in the Lord himself.   That church which has God in the midst of it rules itself, and goes right without any other guidance but that which comes of the Holy Spirit's working.   Such a church keeps together without aiming at uniformity, and goes on to victory even though it makes no noise.   That movement is right which is led by God, and that is sure to be all wrong which is led in the best possible way if God be absent.   Organization is all very well, but I sometimes feel inclined to join with Zwingle in the battle when he said, " In the name of the holy Trinity let all loose ; " for when everybody is free, if God be present everybody is bound to do the right.   When each man moves according to the divine instinct in him there will be little need of regulations : all is order where God rules.   Just as the atoms of matter obey the present power of God, so do separate believers obey the one great impelling influence.   Oh, for God to be in the church to lead it : and it shall be rightly guided.   Do not fall in love with this particular system or that, my brother: do not cry up this scheme of working or that !   Get the Spirit of God, and almost any shape that spiritual life takes will be a form of energy suitable for the particular emergency.   God never leads his people wrongly.   It is for them to follow the fiery, cloudy pillar; though it lead them through the sea, they shall traverse it dry-shod ; though it lead them through a desert, they shall be fed ; though it bring them into a thirsty land, they shall drink to the full of water from the rock.   We must have the Lord with us to guide us into our promised rest.

The next blessing is *strength.*   " He hath as it were the strength of an unicorn" (ver. 22).   It is generally agreed that the creature here meant is an extinct species of urus or ox, most nearly represented by the buffalo of the present period.   This gives us the sentence,—" He hath as it were the strength of a buffalo."   When God is in a church, what rugged strength, what massive force, what irresistible energy is sure to be there !   And how untamable is the living force !   You cannot yoke this buffalo to everybody's plough : it has its own free way of living, and it acts after its own style.   When the Lord is with a church her power is not in numbers, though very speedily she will increase ; her power is not wealth, though God will take care that the money comes when it is needed : her power lies in God, and that power becomes irresistible, untamable, unconquerable.   Force and energy are with the Lord.   I do fear me that what many bodies of Christian people need is this force.   Examine yonder religious body: it is huge, but it lacks muscle : it is a fine-looking organization, but soul, sinew, backbone are wanting.   Where God is there is sure to be life-force.   When the Spirit of God descended upon the first saints they began to speak with wondrous power ; and though they were persecuted, they were not subdued.   No bit could be put into their mouths to hold them in, for they went everywhere preaching the word.   Of the true Israel it shall be said—his strength is as the strength of the buffalo : it cannot be controlled or conquered.

The next result is *safety.*   " Surely there is no enchantment against Jacob, neither is there any divination against Israel."   The presence of

God quietly baffles all the attempts of the evil one. I have noticed, dear brethren, in this church, where we have had God's presence in a great measure, that all around us people have gone off to this opinion and to the other fancy, yet our members as a rule have stood firm. Persons say to me, " Do you not sometimes answer the scepticisms of the day ? " I answer, No. They do not come in my way. " Do not modern opinions trouble your church ? " They have not done so. Why ? because God is there, and spiritual life in vigorous exercise does not fall a victim to disease. A gracious atmosphere does not agree with modern doubt. When people fall into that evil they go where the thing is indulged, or at least where it is combated ; where in some way or other they can develop their love of novelty and foster the notion of their own wisdom. Infidelity, socinianism, and modern thought can make no headway where the Spirit is at work. Enchantment does not lie against Israel, and divination does not touch Jacob. If a Church will keep to truth, keep to God, and do its own work, it can live like a lamb in the midst of wolves without being torn in pieces. Have God with you, and not only the evil of doctrinal error but every other shall be kept far from you. There was even when Christ was in the Church a Judas in the midst of it ; and even in the apostles' days there were some that went out from them because they were not of them, for if they had been of them doubtless they would have continued with them ; hence we may not expect to be without false brethren. But the true safety of the Church is not a creed, not an enactment for expelling those who violate the creed ; the presence of God alone can protect his people against the cunning assaults of their foes.

Upon these words " there is no enchantment against Jacob, no divination against Israel," suffer a few sentences. There are still a few foolish people in the world who believe in witchcraft and spells, but ye, beloved, if you love the Lord, throw such nonsense to the winds. Do you not hear people talk about this being lucky and that unlucky ? This notion is heathenish and unchristian. Never utter such nonsense. But even if there were such things as witchcraft and divination, if this house were full of devils and the air swarmed with invisible sprites of an evil sort, yet if we be the people of God, surely there is no enchantment against us. Divination cannot touch a child of God : the evil one is chained. Wherefore be of good courage : if God be for us, who can be against us ?

Further than that, God gives to his people the next blessing, that is, of his so *working among them* as to make them a wonder, and cause outsiders to raise enquiries about them. " According to this time it shall be said of Jacob and of Israel, What hath God wrought ? " Is not that a singular thing ? Here is Balaam with his seven altars, and seven bullocks, and seven rams, and here is Balak, and they are all going to compass some dreadful evil against Israel. The prophet is a man of great skill in the occult arts : and what does God say ? In effect he says,—From this hour in which you try to curse them I will bless them more than ever, until I will make them say, and their enemies say, " What hath God wrought ? " Brethren, there is another question, " What hath Israel wrought ? " I am glad that Israel's work is not my subject just now, because I should make a very wretched sermon out of it ; we have better music in the words, " What hath God wrought ? '

Let me tell, not what *I* have done, but what God has done; not what human nature is, but what God's nature is, and what the grace of God will work in the midst of his people. If God be with us we shall be signs and wonders, until those about us shall say, "What is this that God is doing?" Yes, in you, poor Jacob, wrestling, halting on your thigh, men shall see marvels and cry, "What hath God wrought?" Much more shall it be so with you, my brother Israel, you who have prevailed and won the blessing; you are as a prince with God, and you shall make men enquire, "What hath God wrought?"

When God is with his people he will give them *power of a destructive kind.* Do not be frightened. Here is the text for it: "Behold, the people shall rise up as a great lion, and lift up himself as a young lion"—that is, as a lion in the fulness of his vigour,—" he shall not lie down until he eat of the prey, and drink the blood of the slain." God has put into his church, when he is in it, a most wonderful, destructive power as against spiritual wickedness. A healthy church kills error, and tears in pieces evil. Not so very long ago our nation tolerated slavery in our colonies. Philanthropists endeavoured to destroy slavery; but when was it utterly abolished? It was when Wilberforce roused the church of God, and when the church of God addressed herself to the conflict, then she tore the evil thing to pieces. I have been amused with what Wilberforce said the day after they passed the Act of Emancipation. He merrily said to a friend when it was all done, "Is there not something else we can abolish?" That was said playfully, but it shows the spirit of the church of God. She lives in conflict and victory; her mission is to destroy everything that is bad in the land. See the fierce devil of intemperance how it devours men! Earnest friends have been labouring against it, and they have done something for which we are grateful, but if ever intemperance is put down, it will be when the entire church of God shall arouse herself to protest against it. When the strong lion rises up the giant of drunkenness shall fall before him. "He shall not lie down until he eat of the prey, and drink the blood of the slain." I augur for the world the best results from a fully aroused church. If God be in her there is no evil which she cannot overcome. This crowded London of ours sometimes appals me,—the iniquity which reigns and rages in the lower districts, the general indifference and the growing atheism of the people,—these are something terrible; but let not the people of God be dismayed. If the Lord be in the midst of us we shall do with this as our sires have done with other evils: we shall rise up in strength, and not lie down till the evil is destroyed. For the destructions, mark you, of God's people, are not the destructions of men and women; they consist in the overthrow of sin, the tearing in pieces of systems of iniquity. This it is which God shall help his church to do, he being in the midst of her.

Once more: the results of God's presence are to be seen, not only in the context, but in other matters which we have personally experienced and hope to experience more fully still. Note them. When God is in a church there is *a holy awe* upon the hearts of his people; there is also a childlike trustfulness and hopefulness, and consequent courage and joy. When the Lord is in the midst of his people the ordinances of his house are exceeding sweet; baptism and the Lord's

Supper become divinely painted pictures of our burial in Christ, and of our life through him; the preaching of the word drops as dew and distils as the rain; the meetings for prayer are fresh and fervent; we want to stay in them hour after hour, we feel it such a happy thing to be there. The very house wherein we meet grows beautiful to us; we love the place where our Lord is wont to meet with us. Then work for Christ is easy, nay, delightful; God's people never want urging on, they are eager for the fray, when the Lord is with them. Then, too, suffering for Christ becomes pleasant, yea, any kind of suffering is easily borne.

> " I can do all things, or can bear
> All sufferings, if my Lord be there :
> Sweet pleasures mingle with the pains,
> While his left hand my head sustains."

Then prayer grows abundant all over the church, both in private and in public. Then life is made vigorous; the feeblest becomes as David, and David like the angel of the Lord. Then love is fervent; unity is unbroken; truth is esteemed, and the living of truth in the life is sought after by all the people of God. Then effort is successful; the church enlarges the bounds of her tent, for she breaks forth on the right hand and on the left. Then her seed inherits the Gentiles, and the desolate places are inhabited. Then God gives unto her the holy energy with which she vanquishes nations. When God is with her she becomes like a sheaf of fire in the midst of the stubble, and consumes her adversaries round about. "Fair as the moon, clear as the sun, and terrible as an army with banners," is a church which has God in her midst.

But now notice one thing in my text, and with that I close this description. Where God is, we are told, " *The shout of a king is among them.*" What is the shout of a king? When great commanders are known to have come into a camp what a thrill of joy it causes among their trusty warriors. When the soldiers have been much dejected it has been whispered in their tents—

> " The king has come to marshal us,
> All in his armour dressed,"

and from that moment every man has cheered up. At the sight of the king as he comes riding into the camp the host raises a great shout. What means it? It is a shout of loyal love—they are glad to welcome their leader. So is it with us when we sing—

> " The King himself comes near,"

we are all as glad as glad can be. Those who cannot come out to see their prince, because they are lying on their sick beds in hospital, clap their hands, while even the little children in their mothers' arms join in the general joy. "The king is come," say they, and his presence kindles their enthusiasm till they make the hills ring again. You know how the stern Ironsides felt when Cromwell came along; every man was a hero when he led the way. They were ready for any adventure, no matter how difficult, as long as their great chief was there. That enthusiasm which was inspired by Alexander, and by Napoleon, and by other great commanders, is the earthly image of the spiritual fervour felt by the church when the Lord Jesus is in her midst.

What next ? When the King comes and they have received him with enthusiasm, he cries, "Now is the hour of battle ; " and at once a shout goes up from his warriors who are eager for the fight. When a clan of Highlanders was led to the battle by their chief he had only to show them the enemy and with one tremendous shout they leaped upon them like lions. It is so with the people of God. When God is with us then are we strong, resolute, determined. The charge of the servants of God is as the rush of a hurricane against a bowing wall and a tottering fence. In God is our confidence of victory. With God present no man's heart fails him ; no doubt enters the host. "Be strong, and quit yourselves like men," is the word that is passed round, for their king's eye makes them brave and the presence of his majesty secures them triumph. My brethren, let us cry to God, entreating him to be among us. This it is that you want in your Sunday-schools, in your mission halls, in your street preaching, in your tract distributing ; it is this that I want beyond everything when I have to speak to you in this vast house. If I could hear the sound of my Master's feet behind me I would speak though I were lying upon the borders of the grave ; but if God be gone I am bereft of power. What is the use of words without the Spirit ? We might as well mutter to the whistling winds as preach to men without the Lord. O God, if thou be with us then the shout of a King is among us, but without thee we pine away.

III. Thirdly, let us look at a very important point, and a very practical one too : What can be done for THE SECURING AND PRESERVING OF THE PRESENCE OF GOD WITH THE CHURCH ? This is a matter that would require several sermons to discuss it fully ; but I notice that there is *something even in the conformation of a church* to secure this. God is very tolerant, and he bears with many mistakes in his servants and yet blesses them ; but depend upon it, unless a church is formed at the very outset upon scriptural principles and in God's own way, sooner or later all the mistakes of her constitution will turn out to be sources of weakness. Christ loves to dwell in a house which is built according to his own plans, and not according to the whims and fancies of men. The church ought not to set up as her authority the decrees of men, either living or dead: her ruler is Christ. Associations formed otherwise than according to Scripture must fail in the long run. I wish Christians would believe this. Chillingworth said, " The Bible, and the Bible alone, is the religion of Protestants." That is not true. Certain Protestants have tacked many other things to the Bible ; and they are suffering as the result of their folly, for they cannot keep their church from becoming Popish. Of course they cannot : they have admitted a little leaven of Popery, and it will leaven the whole lump. The dry rot in one part of the house will spread throughout the whole fabric sooner or later. Let us be careful to build on the foundation of Christ, and then let every man take heed how he build thereon ; for even if the foundation is good, yet if he build with hay and stubble the fire will cause him grievous loss.

But next, God will only dwell with a church which is *full of life.* The living God will not inhabit a dead church. Hence the necessity of having really regenerated people as members of the church. We cannot secure this in every case with all our watching: tares will grow among the wheat. But if the admission of unregenerate men is usual, and there are no restrictions, then the Lord will be grieved and leave us. God dwelleth not in temples made with hands : he has nothing to do with bricks and mortar; he dwells in living souls. Remember that text : " God is not the God of the dead, but of the living," and it bears this sense among others, that he is not the God of a church made up of unconverted people. Oh that we may all live unto God, and may that life be past all question.

That being supposed, we next notice that to have God among us we must be *full of faith*. Unbelief gives forth such a noxious vapour that Jesus himself could not stop where it was. His strength was paralyzed :—" He could not do many mighty works there because of their unbelief." Faith creates an atmosphere in which the Spirit of God can work ; meanwhile the Spirit of God himself creates that faith, so that it is all of his own working from first to last. Brothers, sisters, do you believe your God ? Do you believe up to the hilt ? Alas, too many only believe a little ! But do you believe his every word ? Do you believe his grandest promises ? Is he a real God to you, making his words into facts every day of your lives ? If so, then the Lord is among us as in the holy place. Faith builds a pavilion in which her king delights to sit enthroned.

With that must come *prayer*. Prayer is the breath of faith. I do not believe God will ever be long with a church that does not pray : and I feel certain that when meetings for prayer, when family prayer, when private prayer, when any form of prayer comes to be at a discount, the Lord will leave the people to learn their weakness. Want of prayer cuts the sinews of the church for practical working ; she is lame, feeble, impotent, if prayer be gone. If anything be the matter with the lungs we fear consumption : prayer-meetings are the lungs of the church, and anything the matter there means consumption to the church, or at best a gradual decline, attended with general debility. Oh, my brothers, if we want to have God with us, pass the watchword round, " Let us pray." Let us pray after the fashion of the widow who was importunate and would not be repulsed ; remember, it is written, " Men ought always to pray, and not to faint." Where prayer is fervent God is present.

Supposing there is this faith and prayer, we shall also need *holiness of life*. You know what Balaam did when he found he could not curse the people. Satanic was his advice. He bade the king of Moab seduce the men of Israel by the women of Moab that were fair to look upon ; these were to fascinate them by their beauty, and then to invite them to their idolatrous rites, which rites were orgies of lust : he hoped that the lewdness of the people would grieve the Lord and cause him to leave them and then Moab could smite them. He sadly succeeded. If it had not been for Phineas who in holy wrath drove his javelin right through a man and woman in the very act of sin, sparing none in the vehemence of his zeal, Israel had been quite undone. So in a church. The devil will work hard to lead one into licentiousness, another into drunkenness, a third into dishonesty, and others into worldliness. If he can only get the goodly Babylonish garment and the wedge of gold buried in an Achan's tent, then Israel will be chased before her adversaries. God cannot dwell in an unclean church. A holy God abhors the very garments spotted by the flesh. Be ye holy as Christ is holy. Do not take up with this German-silver electrotype holiness, which is so much boasted of nowadays. Do not be deluded into self-righteousness, but seek after real holiness; and if you do find it you will never boast about it: your life will speak, but your lips will never dare to say, " See how holy I am." Real holiness dwells with humility, and makes men aspire after that which yet lies beyond them. Be holy, upright, just, straight, true, pure, chaste, devout. God send us this behaviour, and then we shall keep him among us as long as we live.

Lastly, when we have reached to that, let us have *practical consecration.* God will not dwell in a house which does not belong to him. No, the first thing with anyone of us is to answer this question:—Dost thou give thyself up to Christ, body, soul, and spirit, to live for him and to die for him? Wilt thou give him all that thou hast of talent and ability, and substance, and time, and life itself? Where there is a church made up of consecrated people, there God will remain, and there he will make a heaven below, and there the shout of a king shall be heard, and there his strength shall be revealed, and there his glory shall be seen even as it is beheld on high. The Lord send us this, for Jesus' sake. Amen and Amen.

PORTION OF SCRIPTURE READ BEFORE SERMON—Numbers xxiii.

HYMNS FROM " OUR OWN HYMN BOOK "—907, 114, 149.

INCENSE AND LIGHT.

A Sermon

DELIVERED ON LORD'S-DAY MORNING, MARCH 11TH, 1883, BY

C. H. SPURGEON,

AT THE METROPOLITAN TABERNACLE, NEWINGTON.

" And Aaron shall burn thereon sweet incense every morning : when he dresseth the lamps, he shall burn incense upon it. And when Aaron lighteth the lamps at even, he shall burn incense upon it, a perpetual incense before the Lord throughout your genera-tions."—Exodus xxx. 7, 8.

CERTAIN ceremonies under the law were only of annual celebration; while other matters were of daily observation; and by the daily repeti-tion were intended to be set forth as eminently constant and perpetual. These daily ordinances were to be regarded by the children of Israel as of standing obligation, abiding types of constant necessity, never to be removed so long as the dispensation should last.

When the priest went into the tabernacle he could not enter it without being warned of sin and of sacrifice, for at the entrance of the holy place stood an altar of brass, upon which there was offered every morning a lamb and every evening a lamb. This taught that access to God was not possible except by expiation,— expiation by bloody sacrifice, expiation by the death of a substituted victim, expiation which must continue as long as sin remained. You could not enter even into the first court without the sight of an altar, and blood, and fire : thus showing us that there is no coming to God, even on the ordinary level of Christian expe-rience, apart from the atonement made by our Lord Jesus, who is " the Lamb slain from the foundation of the world." You cannot be heard in penitent prayer, or receive pardon, or commence the life of faith, or be even a babe in grace, except you know the great truth, that the Lord " hath made him to be sin for us, who knew no sin ; that we might be made the righteousness of God in him." Without shedding of blood remission of sin and access to God are out of the question. Paul ascribes our drawing near unto the Lord to our Saviour's perfect sacrifice, for he says, "Ye who sometimes were far off are made nigh by the blood of Christ."

Before the innermost sanctuary there hung a substantial veil, and the entrance into the Holy of Holies was only permitted once in the year. If that veil had been lifted up so that we could enter, we should have found at the door a golden altar, to represent again our Lord Jesus Christ under another aspect ; for on that golden altar there was offered a sweet perfume of precious spices, denoting his perpetual intercession

No. 1,710.

on the behalf of his people, and his enduring merits which are continually being presented by himself before the throne of the Most High. To go within the veil you must pass by the altar of incense. Learn hence that to the door of the inner chamber of communion with God we must approach by the perfect merit of our redeeming Lord. We come not in our own merit; but we are " accepted in the Beloved." If we have ever been favoured with high and holy communion with God, such as he reserves for favoured saints; if we have been enabled to come boldly to the throne of the heavenly grace, and have looked into the tempered brightness of that light which shines above the mercy-seat, we have come only by virtue of the infinite merit of our Lord Jesus. The lowest form of communion in the outer court must be by the sacrifice of Jesus; and the highest form of communion, even that which is most intense and most delightful, is still by Christ: the incense sets forth his merit, and that is not without blood, for once in the year the horns of the altar were smeared with the blood which had been carried within the veil. There was no coming within the veil without passing by the incense altar, even as there is no access to God but by the all-powerful mediation of the Lord Jesus Christ. Let us never forget this. Simple as the truth is, we are apt to pass it by as of no force. I am afraid we are apt to put the most important truths into the background because they seem to be so elementary; but we ought to remember that they are elementary only because they are essential from first to last. Never try to draw near to God in prayer, or praise, or meditation, or Scripture reading, or holy service apart from Jesus Christ, or your attempt must be a failure. Through the wall of fire which surrounds the throne you can only pass by way of the one door, namely, the body and blood of our great Mediator, Sacrifice, and Substitute. Is not that door sufficient? Why should we climb up some other way? If I am very heavy of heart, do not let me try to raise my spirits, and so come in the power of human courage; but let me come just as I am, made bold through him whose comforts delight my soul. If I feel that I have been sinning, do not let me try to get rid of my sin by some other process, and then draw near to God; but let me come, sinner as I am, in the name of the sinner's Saviour, and so draw near to God, having washed my robes and made them white in the blood of the Lamb. Jesus saith, " I am the way": why should we seek another? Have nothing to do with an absolute God; only deal with him through a mediator, and keep to that way, for no man cometh unto the Father but by the Lord Jesus. Oh, ye most experienced and privileged ones, take good note of the golden altar, and whenever ye approach the mercy-seat let the cloud of its incense cover you and perfume your prayers.

Hard by the golden altar, which was nearest to the Holy of Holies, stood the golden candlestick with its seven branches: these two instructive types were set near each other for a purpose which I would open up to-day. This candlestick was a matter of daily ordinance as much as the brazen altar of sacrifice, or the golden altar of incense: it was for continual use and was therefore dressed twice each day. We have a continual want of the precious atonement of Christ, of the intercession of Christ, and of the light of God's Holy Spirit. These are not things for once in a year; these are matters for every day and all the day, and therefore they were attended to both at morning and at evening as if to shut in all the hours of the day within two golden doors. Every morning had its lamb, its burning incense, and its lighted lamp ; and the same pertained to every evening all the year round. Thus all days were fringed and bordered with this three-fold type : even as at this time all our days are sanctified by faith in the effectual expiation, joy in the prevailing intercession, and delight in the clear shining of the Spirit which makes glad all who are in the house.

This morning I desire to call your attention to the conjunction which was established by the divine law between the burning of the incense and the lighting of the lamps : these two things, being both of daily observance, were attended to at the same moment for reasons worthy of our study.

I. And first I call your attention to THE WONDERFUL CO-OPERATION BETWEEN THE INTERCESSION OF CHRIST FOR US, AND THE WORK OF THE HOLY SPIRIT IN US. See how on the grandest scale the incense of intercession and the lamp of spiritual illumination are set side by side. He whose merit brings us life is in divine alliance with him who brings us light : indeed, there is such unity between them that Jesus himself is said to be a light to lighten the Gentiles, and the glory of his people Israel. The grace of our Lord Jesus Christ brings with it the communion of the Holy Ghost, for the Father has joined them together.

Note, *that we have these both revealed in their fulness at the same time.* When our Lord ascended on high to plead before the throne, the Spirit descended to abide in the Church. After the Lord was taken up the disciples received the promise of the Father and were illuminated by the Holy Ghost. Jesus our great High Priest presented the sweet savour of his own person and work before the eternal throne; and then came the Spirit of God as tongues of fire lighting up the sons of men and making them to be as candles of the Lord. Well said the apostle at Pentecost,—"This Jesus hath God raised up, whereof we all are witnesses. Therefore being by the right hand of God exalted, and having received of the Father the promise of the Holy Ghost, he hath shed forth this, which ye now see and hear." I say the two come historically together and we must for ever connect in our meditations the ascended Saviour's intercession and the illumination of the saints by the descended Spirit.

Now, as they were connected historically, so are they *continually connected as a matter of fact.* At this day it is as it was at Pentecost : our Lord hath not ceased to intercede, and the Spirit hath not ceased to illuminate. Herein lies our hope for our own eternal salvation, in the ceaseless plea and the quenchless light. For the working out of that which God is working in us, both to will and to do of his own good pleasure, we have these two guarantees and helps,—the Saviour praying and the Spirit shining. Jesus is pleading, and therefore our faith fails not when Satan sifts us as wheat; the Spirit is working, and therefore the light of our faith is sustained by a secret mystic oil which prevents the enemy from putting it out. This also is our two-fold confidence when we go forth into the world to preach the gospel. Unto the Lord Jesus all power is given in heaven and in earth, and he is " able to save to the uttermost them that come unto God by him, seeing he ever liveth to make intercession for them." The Church of God must succeed in her mission because her errand is the object of the continual prayers of her living Lord. But she has her second help, namely the Comforter who abideth with us and goeth forth with the word that we preach, making it potent for the conversion of the sons of men. We have the incense of Christ's merit pleading with God, and the light of God's Spirit pleading with men : we have Christ as an advocate with God, and the Holy Ghost as an advocate with men. What more is needed? What joy and confidence we ought to feel in the work of the Lord since Jesus is pleading and the Spirit is striving at the same time : the incense rising, filling earth and heaven with its sweetness, and the Spirit brightly shining to the comfort and delight of those who go forth into the darkness with the name of Jesus on their lips. Joy to those who sit in darkness. and in the valley of the shadow of death, for even for them is this seven-fold light shining; and to their dank, pestilential abodes there comes the healing breath of sweet perfume from the Redeemer's merits.

Furthermore, this conjunction, as it is a matter of history, and as it is continuous, *will always be seen by us personally when our prayer is the effectual fervent prayer of a righteous man* that availeth much. It needs the Trinity to make a Christian, it needs the Trinity to make a Christian prayer. The Father must hear us, else of what avail are our cries ? But the ordained Mediator must also stand between us and the Father, presenting his merit like the smoke of sweet incense, or else our prayer can never be accepted of God ; and to come down closer to ourselves, the Spirit of God must also help our infirmities, for we know not what we should pray for as we ought. So that whenever we pray we must have these two in happy conjunction : intercession and enlightenment : incense and light. My prayer as my own prayer is a poor, vain, defiled thing unless Jesus perfumes it ; and it is a poor, dark, blind thing unless the Spirit of God has enlightened it. The Holy Spirit teaches us what to pray for, and how to order our words aright. In his light we see light. We are in the dark till he shines like the golden candlestick, and enables us to see our own need and the fulness of God's grace. It is his light that makes our heart to see the Lord in prayer : so that we seek the Lord by the light of his own Spirit. When prayer is the work of the Spirit in the heart we are absolutely certain that it must succeed, because the Spirit maketh intercession in the saints according to the will of God. The Holy Spirit is one with the Father, and he is most truly God, so that whatever he prompts us to pray for is the same thing which the Father has already decreed and eternally determined to bestow. Our wishes and desires might never succeed with God if they were that and no more, for our thoughts are not his thoughts, neither are our ways his ways : but the thoughts and purposes of God, when these are photographed upon our spirit by the Holy Ghost, are the pictures of that which is assuredly to be, the prophecy of the determinate purpose and foreknowledge of God. What is written in yon sealed book, upon which no human eye can gaze, is transcribed and written by the Spirit of God upon our hearts, and thus we pray for that very thing which God designs to give. There is an assured certainty of success to the prayer that is made in the power of the Spirit of God. While praying in the Holy Ghost we have the petition which we have asked of the Lord.

But then there is our second comfort, that Jesus stands ready to take every prayer of ours, however imperfect in knowledge, however feeble in expression, however marred with sorrow, and he presents the purified and perfected prayer with his own merit, and it is sure to speed. The sins of our holy things are seldom absent, and hence the constant need that we have an Advocate. Blessed be God for that inspired word, "If any man sin, we have an advocate with the Father, Jesus Christ the righteous." True prayer is the offering to God of the merit of the Lord Jesus, and hence it must be accepted. What can be refused to merit such as his? True prayer is presented ever by the Lord Jesus, and hence, again, its certainty of efficacy : how can the Father deny anything to the Well-beloved ? It is written in the book of the Revelation— "And another angel came and stood at the altar, having a golden censer ; and there was given unto him much incense, that he should offer it with the prayers of all saints upon the golden altar which was before the throne. And the smoke of the incense, which came with the prayers of the saints, ascended up before God out of the angel's hand." Can we doubt the success of prayers presented by the angel of the covenant ? Assuredly not. There is such excess of perfection in Christ that it covers all our imperfection. There is such delicious sweetness in Christ to the Father that it effectually destroys the ill savour of anything that comes from us ; and by its power we ourselves become unto God a sweet savour ; and so also are our prayers when they are presented by Jesus Christ. I like to think of the incense, and of the lamp, and, best of all, of the two together, for these two enable me to come boldly to the throne of the heavenly grace to obtain mercy and find grace. Acceptance through sweet savour, and light through divine teaching, are both mine as my soul waiteth upon God, with her expectation turned towards him.

Nor ought I to pass away from this first head without noting that *in God's drawing near to man* there is the same conjunction of incense and light. If the glory of God were to come forth from between the cherubim, if it should come past the veil to be revealed throughout the world, that glory would pass by these two, the golden altar of incense and the golden lamp of light. I mean this : God can have no dealing with men at all except through the merit of Christ and the light of the Spirit. As for the work of our Lord Jesus, you and I believe in the special substitution of Christ for his elect ; what we call " particular redemption " is held most firmly by us ; for we believe that he redeemed us from among men, and that he laid down his life for the sheep. Yet there are many passages of Scripture which speak of the work of Christ as having a universal bearing. He is "the propitiation for our sins, and not for ours only, but for the sins of the whole world." We are told that by the grace of God "he tasted death for every man." Now, the atonement of Christ is many-sided, and may be viewed in very different lights ; and while I trust we shall never even be shaky about the question of his literal and effectual substitution for his own chosen, whereby he offered for them a most sure, effectual, and perfect satisfaction, so that no sin can ever be laid to their charge, yet there is, on the other hand, a general and universal view of his atoning work. God could not have dealt with the world at all in the way of mercy apart from the sacrifice of Christ. The only thing which could have been done with the race of man was to have crushed it out for ever if Christ had not stood for them as an interposer. God was in Christ reconciling the world unto himself. For the sake of the man Christ Jesus God was able to look upon the fallen race in justice, and yet prepare mercy for the guilty. Men owe their lives to the sacrifice of Christ. Men owe the various alleviations of their sorrows by God's gracious tenderness in providence to the sacrifice of Christ. Above all, that free and honest proclamation of salvation to every man that will believe in Christ Jesus is rendered possible by the wondrous, perfect, unlimited, illimitable merit which resided in the person and work of such an one as Jesus our Lord.

The picture before you is a very beautiful one. Here are spices of the most precious kind, made up into a compound such as never was compounded for any other purpose. This divinely-appointed mixture of sweet odours is placed in the censer upon the golden altar—that is to say, eternal acceptance is found in the person of Christ. The incense is kindled with fire from on high. What follows? The spices begin to burn, and up ascends a pillar of smoke. See how it rises high into the clear air, and as it rises it expands like a cloud, covers the sky, is wafted all around, and perfumes the whole air with its own exceeding fragrance. It rises and rises till it enters heaven—yea, and the heaven of heavens; its sacred odour is recognised in every golden street; it fills every chamber of the glorious "house of God not made with hands;" it ascends to the throne of his excellent Majesty, and the Lord is well pleased with it, and again is fulfilled the word which is written concerning the burnt-offering of Noah—"The Lord smelled a sweet savour; and the Lord said in his heart, I will not again smite everything living as I have done." Such is the merit of Christ that through its sweet savour God looks down upon the world and treats it with long-suffering, and tenderness, and mercy. Is it not a blessed picture? As a just and holy God he could not deal with a guilty race except through a mediatorial sacrifice, which should wrap mankind in its cloud of merit, and reconcile the world unto himself.

And now you and I may follow in the track of God, and go out and preach the gospel to every creature without the slightest fear, because the whole air is perfumed with the incense of a Saviour's mediatorial work. Although not perceptible by carnal sense, yet the inward spirit in the soul of the believer perceives the grateful odour of the finished work of the ever-living Saviour sweetening all things, so that now we call nothing common or unclean, but are prepared to deliver our message to the vilest of the vile. God in Christ is kind even to the unthankful and the evil, and wills that supplications, prayers, intercessions, and giving of thanks be made for all men; and that to every creature the gospel should be preached.

We shall not, however, proceed to any practical purpose unless we recollect next that, when God comes to deal with men, it is with the light of the Spirit as well as with the merit of Christ. The golden candlestick is as needful as the golden censer: for God's work among men is ever by his Spirit. He is seeking out his people as the woman sought out her lost piece of money, and it is significant that it is written,

"She did light a candle, and sweep the house." God in his work of salvation comes to men with the candle of his word lighted through the Holy Spirit; and through the teaching of his word from day to day that Spirit shines as from a lantern among the sons of men. If you and I would follow in the track of God, as his dear children imitating him, we must take with us continually the light of the gospel of the glory of God, and by the power and light of his Spirit we must make known to men the unsearchable riches of Christ. To us Jehovah is our light and our salvation, and when we go in his name we must not go without the light. Thus you see we come to God by the incense and the light; and even so doth God come down to man to bless him.

II. Secondly, our text seems to me to teach THE CONNECTION BE-TWEEN PRAYER AND KNOWLEDGE. The golden altar represents inter-cession offered by Christ, and also the prayers of all the saints, which are accepted through his intercession; and as the candlestick stood side by side with it, and represented the light of the Spirit of truth, so must true prayer and true knowledge never be separated.

So I gather, first, that *prayer should be attended with knowledge.* It is ill when men worship they know not what. God is light, and he will not have his people worship him in the dark. When they burn the incense they must also light the lamp. In the Romish Church the mass of the people repeat prayers in an unknown tongue, having no idea of what their meaning may be, and this is both a grievous wrong to the people and a mockery of God. What can be the good of such prayers in the sight of him who seeketh those to worship him who worship him in spirit and in truth? Mere sounds without meaning are not prayer: understanding, desire, and heart must go with every word, or else the prayers are vain repetitions, such as the heathen employ. Supplicants must know what they are asking, or they are not really asking. And you, dear people of God, please notice that the more divine knowledge you get, all things being equal, the more complete will your prayers become. "Grow in grace, and in the knowledge of our Lord and Saviour Jesus Christ": light the lamp at the same time that you kindle the incense.

For instance, when you pray, what prayer can there be without knowing God our Father? How can you pray aright to an unknown God? The more knowledge of God the more correct does prayer become. He that cometh to God must believe that he is, and that he is the rewarder of them that diligently seek him. What prayer can there be apart from the know-ledge of the Lord Jesus Christ? If we know nothing of him by whom we pray, how full of sins of ignorance will our prayers be! It is well also to have a deep, sensible knowledge of sin. Penitential prayers are impossible without this, and how can prayers be accepted if penitence be not mixed with our petitions? We want at the same time that we have the knowledge of sin to have also a knowledge of our own weak-ness. The man who is consciously weak prays for strength; but he who dreams that he is strong will not do so. You need to study your-selves before you pray, so as to ask for those things in which you are most deficient, and for protection against those constitutional tendencies or besetting sins to which you are most subject. The prayer of ignorance is like an arrow shot by a blind man, which is not likely to hit the mark. In proportion as petitions arise from a heart fully instructed in its own necessities they will be likely to ask for the right blessings, and to be prepared aright before the Lord. David wished his prayers to be accepted, and hence he cried, "Let my prayer be set forth before thee as incense."

A supremely excellent piece of knowledge is to know the promises which we are to plead. Here you have the very sinews of prayer. When a man knows the promise suitable to his case, and lays it before God, saying, "Do as thou hast said," he presents the best form of supplication. Remember how Jacob pleaded with the Lord the sacred word of promise, saying, "Thou saidst, I will surely do thee good." When we have looked at all the bearings of the petition so as to make quite certain that it is a petition the fulfilment of which will glorify God ; when we see that it must be consistent with the divine will because of the various statements which God has made in his word, and because of promises which he has given concerning the matter: then, with the lamp shining clearly upon us, we shall kindle the incense the more discreetly and boldly, and both our prayers and our meditations will be the more accepted of the Lord. Do try, especially, dear brethren, you that pray in public, to light the lamps when you kindle the incense. It will be for the good of us all if petitions are thoughtful, suitable, Scriptural, and withal fresh and hearty. Let us never degenerate into repeating the same expressions till they grow to be cant; let us never drop into the use of hackneyed prayers for everything in general and for nothing in particular; but as instructed men, having thought of what we are going to say, having adapted our prayer to our circumstances and needs, let us order our case before the Lord, and fill our mouth with arguments. Burn the incense of prayer in the light of the Spirit of revelation, praying in the Holy Ghost.

But now turn the thought round the other way—*knowledge should always be accompanied by prayer.* Whenever we are taught of God, his teaching almost always comes in connection with prayer; but lest we should solely try to learn and forget to pray, let me remind you of a few particulars. Dear brother, as a Christian thou art a disciple, or student; be also a suppliant. When thou art impressed with the greatness, or the goodness, or the immutability, or the faithfulness of God, straightway turn thine impressions into supplications. Pray the great God to be gracious to thee; ask the unchangeable God to be the same to thee; beg the faithful God to keep his promises to thee; implore the mighty God to uphold thee. As thou learnest more and more of God, place the light near the incense by using thy knowledge in thy pleadings. To employ all thy knowledge as fuel for prayer will be the best way of utilising thy acquirements; it will stamp truth firmly on thy memory, and it will sanctify thy heart.

When thou knowest more of the Saviour pray thy way to him by it, as ships move into haven by their sails. If thou hast seen his manhood, go and plead his sympathy with thee in thy weakness. If thou hast thought more of his Deity, go and worship him more reverently, and pray that his glory may be seen among the sons of men. Whatever point in the unutterable glory of his perfection breaks most upon thy mind, pray most that way; opening thy window towards the sunrising.

So will the Lord teach thee more, and so shalt thou have profited by that which thou hast learned.

If from day to day, my brother, thou learnest more of thy sinfulness, then thou hast more errands with which to come to the mercy-seat; and if thou dost make a new discovery by experience of thy corruption and indwelling sin, fly at once to the throne of grace with thy discovery lest it weigh thee down and drive thee to despondency. Make a ladder of thy needs wherewith to climb nearer to heaven. The more thy necessities the more urgent let thine importunity be. Cry mightily to God because of the greatness of thy poverty. I do not think there is anything in the Scriptures which we cannot pray over. If we learn the devices of the devil, let us pray against them. If we learn the depravity of mankind let us pray God's Holy Spirit to create men's hearts anew. Everything from the first of Genesis to the end of Revelation, when we truly know it, furnishes us with fresh arguments for drawing near to God. Revealed truth is as a church-bell summoning us to come into the presence of the Lord, and bow the knee before him. As you hear a sermon turn it into prayer; even if you find that there is nothing in the sermon, it may benefit you if you pray God to feed his poor famished people. If you will pray all through his discourse every preacher will minister to your edification directly or indirectly. If you are set upon praying by the lighting of the tiniest candle that ever glimmered, there will at least be sweetness in the incense even if there be no brilliance in the lamp.

III. I desire, in the third place, to show SOME SPECIAL PRACTICAL CONNECTION BETWEEN THE INCENSE AND THE LAMP. Let us read the text again: " And Aaron shall burn thereon sweet incense every morning: when he dresseth the lamps, he shall burn incense upon it." So, then, *there should be prayer especially at the dressing of the lamps :* that is to say, when preparing our minds for that ministry by which we enlighten the people among whom we dwell we should be specially earnest in prayer. Preparation for preaching and teaching is most important : God's work is not to be done carelessly as boys shoot arrows at random in their play. We must prepare both by reading and pleading : we must, like the apostles, give ourselves to the word of God and prayer. We are told by ancient Rabbis that when the priest who was appointed for that office went into the holy place he took with him the golden snuffers and the golden snuff dishes, and a vessel full of pure olive oil and by the help of these he attended to the trimming of the golden lamp. There were seven lamps on the candelabra : some of these might have gone quite out during the night; he would have to take away whatever of snuff remained, wipe out the lamp, place a new wick, fill up with fresh oil, and then kindle the flame anew. In another lamp it may be the light was still burning but feebly : he might have simply to snuff it, take away the "the superfluity of naughtiness" in the golden snuff dish and make all things clean and right. Sometimes the light might be burning well and nothing was needed but to replenish it with oil. Thus all was set in order for another day. The like was done in the evening. In the process of trimming lamps there is a measure of offence : snuffs do not give forth a very dainty perfume, and the smear and smell of oil are not altogether of sweet savour; therefore, before he trimmed the lamps, the priest kindled

the incense. No snuff would then be offensive, for the overpowering
fragrance of the incense killed it all and prevented the prevalence of
any odour unfit for the house of God. When we go into our studies to
try and trim our lamps let us remember that our first business is to
pray. Alas, we have much of smoking wick about us ; much negligence,
much ignorance, many mistakes and errors ; and thereby we shall grieve
the Lord if Jesus is not called in to cover all. When we are preparing
in secret to serve the Lord in public we shall make poor work of it if
we do not beforehand draw near to God in prayer. We need that
our garments should be made to smell of myrrh and aloes and
cassia by being covered with the merit of Jesus, or else we shall
offend even while engaged in the holy act of preparing to spread
abroad the light of divine truth. You have to trim your lamps,
brethren and sisters, when you go into the Sunday-school—at least, I
hope you do. I hope you do not run into your class with anything which
first comes to hand: if you do not snuff your candles and feed your
lamps with fresh oil your children will sit in darkness before a lamp
which does not shine. No, there ought to be careful preparation,
according as your time and ability will allow, and above all the
pouring in of the holy oil of the Holy Spirit, by fresh fellowship with
Jesus. In that process one of the chief elements is prayer. Dr. Adam
Clarke used to say to young ministers, "Study yourselves dead, and
then pray yourselves alive again ; " and that is an excellent rule. Work
in your study as if it all depended upon you, and then go forth and
speak, trusting in God because all depends upon him. Remember that
the chief part of all study of God's word must be prayer. This is the
boring-rod and the powder by which we burst open the great rocks of
truth. "To have prayed well is to have studied well," said Martin
Luther, and so most certainly it is ; therefore let none of us when we
dress the lamp forget the incense.

What a double privilege comes of this! This priest, you see, had
thus two things to do for the Lord. If he was called only to light the
lamp, that would have been one happy, blessed service : but if he must
burn the incense too, he has a double portion of honour in thus doubly
serving the Lord his God. So when you are preparing to light up the
people, or preparing to enlighten your children in the class, what a happy
necessity it is which calls upon you at the same time to pray ! It
is one of the greatest privileges of preachers and teachers, that they
are driven to pray more than other people, for they have greater necessities : they have necessities that come upon them because of their office,
and these drive them to more frequent supplication, and so their labours
become a means of grace to their own souls. Let us thank our Lord
Jesus that he hath made us kings and priests unto our God, and that
he permits us both to let our lights shine before men, and our prayers
ascend before God.

One thing more, this burning of the incense was not only at the
dressing of the lamps, but also *at the kindling of the lamps,* when they
began to shine. I want to plead, dear friends, very heartily with you
that when it is my privilege to come here this week and at all other
times to light the lamps, you who are my beloved helpers will take care
to burn the incense at the same time. We need the incense of prayer

more than ever in these latter days. Did you ever notice in Ezekiel xli. 22 that an altar of incense is spoken of, but its dimensions are twice as great as those of the golden altar in the Tabernacle: as if, say some, to teach us that in these gospel times prayer would become more abundant and would be offered up more frequently than ever. The Gentiles have an altar which presents more incense to the Lord than that which was served by Aaron; and inasmuch as it is more purely spiritual it is all the more acceptable with God. The altar mentioned by Ezekiel was of wood, as if to show that our worship is to become more simple, and to be more divested of everything that is pompous and showy: indeed, the altar disappears, and we read, " This is the table that is before the Lord": you will guess the meaning.

Malachi has a glorious prophecy. " For from the rising of the sun even unto the going down of the same my name shall be great among the Gentiles; and in every place incense shall be offered unto my name, and a pure offering: for my name shall be great among the heathen, saith the Lord of hosts." Are you not charmed by the divine prophecy? Will you not, yourselves, help to fulfil it?

We know that this altar of incense meant prayer, because the Jews themselves so interpreted it. In the first chapter of Luke we read of Zacharias, that it was his turn in the order of his course to go into the holy place to offer incense, and it says, " And the whole multitude of the people were praying without at the time of incense." Just so, the offering of incense clearly means prayer, and therefore I plead, that while we are lighting the lamps by preaching the gospel, you will burn the incense by being constantly in prayer. Brethren, pray for us. Paul spake thus; how much more may I? Dismiss me or else intercede for me. Joshua could not prevail except as Moses held up his hands. Our lamp-lighting will not succeed unless you burn the incense. Peter's sermon at Pentecost did not derive its force from Peter's zeal, or from its own eloquence, but from another source. Of course, all the power came from the Spirit of God; but why did the Spirit of God work so mightily on that day? Surely it was because the entire church was earnestly praying while Peter was preaching. " They were all with one accord in one place": nobody was away, they were all there, and when the one man stood up to preach, he might well light three thousand lamps, for all the fervent company of the faithful were causing the incense of prayer to ascend to heaven. I want your prayers for the sermon of to-night. You will not be here, for strangers are invited to occupy your seats; and therefore I beg you in your houses to cry unto the Lord for me that the word may have free course, and that my hearers may feel its power. It might be the most profitable expenditure of time that ever happened to you if you would spend the whole evening in prayer. Beseech the Lord to bring the people to this house; and to bring the right sort of people, rich and poor, believers and infidels, moral people and the depraved. We do not know who will come. Some of them do not know whether they will come themselves or not; but the Lord may influence in various ways those individuals to come whom he designs to bless. Pray that the fish may come in shoals round the boat. When the congregation is gathered, pray that the speaker may be guided of the Holy Spirit to a right theme. The preacher has no manuscript,

so that there is room for the Spirit's guidance, and he may be led to say
what he never thought of saying: the right word may thus be spoken
in the right way, so as to reach the heart.   Then pray that there
may be given the willing ear, the receptive mind, the retentive
memory; that impressions may be made to-night, and at all other times,
such as even Satan cannot remove.   And, oh, pray that many may
decide for God to-night who have been halting between two opinions;
many converted who have not before found the Saviour's face; many
led into the joy of the Lord who have been hitherto of a sorrowful
spirit.   I shall feel it a joyous work to be the lamplighter to-night for
my Master, if I know that I have you at home pleading earnestly on my
behalf.   Give me this aid this morning.   Pray God to bless each word
that has been spoken.   Pray that some poor sinner's soul may be perfumed by the merits of Jesus and illuminated with the light divine; and
it shall be done, for the Lord heareth his people.   We want more and
more to be a praying church, and then we shall be a growing church:
hitherto we have had a great blessing, but the windows of heaven are
wide enough for a greater one to come down through them.   The more
we plead with God, and the more we set forth the light of the gospel,
the more will God be with us, and build up in this place a temple for
his praise.   May his love be with you.   Amen.

PORTIONS OF SCRIPTURE READ BEFORE SERMON—
Exodus xxix. 38—46; xxx. 1—10, 34—38; Hebrews x. 11—22.

HYMNS FROM "OUR OWN HYMN BOOK"—325, 986, 999.

Exposition of the Doctrines of Grace
50¢.

These sermons were delivered by different
speakers, including Spurgeon, at a special Conference held in the Tabernacle when it was first
opened in 1861. It is an excerpt from the 1861
volume of MTP.

Baptismal Regeneration
25¢.

No Spurgeon sermon ever created so much
controversy or reached so wide a circulation as
this one. A "storm of protest" was raised by the
Church of England faithful in opposition to this
"attack" upon their theory of baptismal new birth,
but the protests only served to increase the demand for copies of the message.

Metropolitan Tabernacle Pulpit.

A SERMON TO THE LORD'S LITTLE CHILDREN.

A Sermon

DELIVERED ON LORD'S-DAY MORNING, MARCH 18TH, 1883, BY

C. H. SPURGEON,

AT THE METROPOLITAN TABERNACLE, NEWINGTON.

"I write unto you, little children, because your sins are forgiven you for his name's sake." 1 John ii. 12.
" I have written unto you, little children, because ye know the Father." 1 John ii. 13. (Revised Version.)

PROBABLY you ask, "Why does John say first, 'I write,' and then, 'I have written'?" There is a beautiful touch of nature in this speedy change of tense. John was an extremely old man, and therefore while he says, "I write," he adds, "I have written," as if he felt that it might be the last time that he should take his pen in hand. Very soon with him the present tense would change into the past, and he indicates the fact by changing his mode of speech. Perhaps he even felt that possibly before the letter reached the brethren to whom he addressed it he would be no more among the sons of men. Therefore he says, "I write," indicating that while he was still with them, with warm and loving heart he solemnly exhorted them ; and then he adds, "I have written," as if he had recorded his dying testimony, and left it as his last legacy of love. To us, to-day, John's words run altogether in the past tense,—"I have written ; " but we need not therefore forget that they were the well-considered words of a venerated father in Christ, and that he wrote them as one so near to his departure that he regarded himself as already on the move, and therefore scarcely knew which tense to use. Ah, my brethren, how soon our " I speak " will change into " I have spoken : " let this invest every word with solemnity.

Remember also what order of man John was,—that disciple whom Jesus loved, whose head had leaned on Jesus' bosom, whose eyes had seen the King in his beauty, and whose strengthened gaze had looked within the gates of pearl. This is he who at one time saw the pierced heart of the Well-beloved pouring forth blood and water ; and at another beheld the Lion of the tribe of Judah prevail to take the book and loose the seven seals thereof. It is the apostle of love who says to us, "I write to you," "I have written to you." Let us carefully note what the Spirit saith unto us by his servant John.

Observe that our text is addressed to the " little children." It is thought by many wise interpreters that under this term John includes the whole church of God, and that afterwards he divides that church into two companies—the fathers and the young men: those who under one aspect are all "little children," are under another regarded as young men or fathers. There is very much to support this view in several instances in this epistle. John is evidently addressing all the saints when he speaks of them as "my little children," as, for instance, in the eighteenth verse of the third chapter, and also in the closing verse, "Little children, keep yourselves from idols." Surely, all the saints are included in these exhortations. There is a sense in which every Christian is still a little child, a sense in which he ought to be so,—ever dependent upon the great Father, ever ready to receive the word of the Father without questioning, ever teachable, ever restful in the Father's care, and full of love to him who is his all in all. Of necessity we must ever be children before God; for our finite capacity is so limited that we are mere babes in knowledge in the presence of Infinite wisdom, and as very sucklings in understanding when contrasted with the great Father of spirits. We know enough to make us know that we know very little. The most advanced intellects in the church are but as infants compared with the Ancient of Days. We are of yesterday, and know nothing: with all our experience, with all our study, with all our meditation, with all our illumination, we remain "little children" when measured by the boundless knowledge of the Lord. Ay, I mean the fathers, the men who bring sinners to Jesus, the men who teach others, and are themselves taught of God, even these must each one cry out with Jeremiah, "Ah, Lord God! behold, I cannot speak: for I am a child." I mean the young men who have overcome the wicked one, whose holy valour sets them in the forefront of the battle, where they turn to flight the armies of the aliens. "They are strong," says John; and yet, in the presence of the mighty God of Jacob, what are our champions and our valiant men? Are they not still but as "little children"? It may do us all good to join the infant-class this morning, or, at least, to sit with the boys in the school of grace. Even those who have made the greatest advances in divine grace may do well to "become as little children," that they may still more fully enter into the kingdom of heaven, and have closer fellowship with "the holy child Jesus." It may even be an advance for some who have grown self-willed as they have advanced in knowledge if they will say with David, "Surely I have behaved and quieted myself, as a child that is weaned of his mother: my soul is even as a weaned child." Happy childhood! when it means entire submission to the Father, and sweet delight in his will.

Still, I am inclined to think that in this case John really does divide the entire church into three classes—the babes in grace, or the children, or as one of the words might properly be translated, the boys—those who have not long been born into the family: these are an interesting company. Then follow the young men: these are the second class, and a valued body of Christians they are, in the fulness of their vigour; strong in faith, giving glory to God; mighty in prayer; vehement in action, bold in testimony. May the Lord muster among our hosts a grand array of these vigorous heroes who shall earnestly contend for the faith once delivered to the saints. The fighting power of the church militant must come out of them: these are they that turn the battle to the gate. Blessed is the man that hath his quiver full of them. Then there is the third class; the fathers, the mature, the experienced : these do not quite so much delight in war as the young men do, but at home they diligently care for the household of faith, watching over the feeble, strengthening and comforting them: these are able by their experience to answer gainsayers, to edify the untaught, and to guide the ignorant. Their knowledge is deep, and they are, therefore, able to become teachers of others; they are men of spiritual force, and have come to the full stature of men in Christ Jesus, therefore they are the solid strength of the church. If the young men are the church's arm, these are the church's backbone. We need to have many such, though alas, it is to be feared that our churches are much like the apostolic ones, of which Paul said, "Ye have not many fathers."

This morning I am going to say nothing at all to the young men, nor to the fathers, except so far as they are willing to include themselves under the term of " little children;" and, as we have already said, there is just reason why they should do so. Little children, it is to you I speak this day : I mean you that have newly been converted, whose first cries of repentance are still in our ears. You, I mean, whose grace is feeble ; who are new to everything in the house of God, and as yet need to be fed with the milk of simple elementary truth : you are the little children, dear to the whole family. You, I mean, who are but little in Israel as yet—little in knowledge, little in faith, little in strength, little in service, little in patience ; you cannot as yet keep the watch of the house of the Lord, for you yourselves need to be watched over ; you tremble when you try to stand, and your unaccustomed feet can scarcely bear you along the road without a helping hand ; you are very apt to tumble down, and probably will do so many times before you learn to walk with the fathers, or run with the young men. You little children may by some be thought to be a burden, but the wise among us count you a blessing: the more of you the merrier in the church of God, for ye are the blessed of the Lord, and we are glad to hear your youthful voices in the streets of the New Jerusalem. To you I shall speak this morning, as the Holy Spirit shall enable me. I would say these things to you: First, observe *your privilege*—" I write unto you, little children, because your sins are forgiven you." Then, note *your knowledge*— " I have written unto you, little children, because ye know, or have known, the Father." And thirdly, consider *the precepts addressed to you*. When we get to that point I shall ask you to refer to your Bibles that we may run through the whole of this epistle and see what John has to say to little children. May we receive the word with meekness, that we may grow thereby.

I. First, I want the babes in grace, the weak in faith, the lambs of the flock, to notice THEIR PRIVILEGE. " I write unto you, little children, because your sins are forgiven you for his name's sake." This is a privilege *extremely desired* by the little children. They have but lately felt the burden of guilt ; they still smart under the lashes of conscience ; the Spirit of God has but newly convinced them of sin, of righteousness, and of judgment; and, therefore, above everything, their prayer is, " Father, forgive me." To them the remission of sins stands out as the first and most desirable of all blessings ; and truly they are right in their

estimate; for what possession is there which can be called a blessing at
all until sin be forgiven ?   It matters not how healthy a man may be;
if his conscience be worried with his sin his inmost heart is sick.   It is
small comfort to him to have all the comforts of this life if his heart feels
the gnawings of the undying worm of conscious guilt.   "God be merciful
to me a sinner," comes often from his breast as he beats upon it in the
deep humiliation of his soul; for joy and rest there can be none to him
till he hears the word, "The Lord hath put away thy sin; thou shalt
not die."   To the freshly saved it is a joy worth worlds to have their sins
forgiven; it is a bliss akin to the heaven of angels; and this joy belongs
of right to all the saints, yea, even to the little children in the family
of God.   You were only born again last Sunday, but your sins are
forgiven you.   Perhaps it is only this morning that you have sought your
Saviour's face and have come to believe in him, but your sins are forgiven
you.   This assurance is as sweet to you as a seraph's song.   I could not
have told you a better piece of news.   The pardon of sin is as the pearl
of great price to you in your present stage of spiritual life; you would
have sold all that you had in order to procure it; and now that you have
it your heart is aglow with gratitude.   The wound in your conscience,
so lately raw and bleeding, makes you set so high a price upon the
healing balm of free and full forgiveness.   Far be it from me to stay
your holy joy, and yet the Lord will show you greater things than these.

At your stage of experience pardon is *the most prominent blessing* of
the covenant.   A newly converted man does not know much about
sanctification or union to Christ; perhaps he does not know much about
election, calling, or sealing; but the principal point he dwells upon is
pardon.   It is written in the Creed,—"I believe in the forgiveness of
sins"; and the man who has newly found peace with God by Jesus
Christ repeats that article of the Creed with solemn emphasis.   "I
believe in the forgiveness of sins," says he; for he has just realized it;
and to him it is a boon so great that like the moon amid the stars it
shines as a queen among the blessings of grace.   Pardon of sin seems to
the "little children" to comprehend the whole work of Jesus, and the
whole work of the Holy Spirit too : vast favours lie beyond ; but to him
who has newly crossed the Jordan this one valley of Eshcol fills all the
range of vision, and the soul hardly dreams of any further benediction.
The newly-pardoned does not yet see the innumerable other blessings
which come in the train of forgiveness; he is for the present absorbed
in the hearing of that one sentence, "Go in peace; thy sins which are
many are all forgiven thee."   Well, beloved child, many more blessings
await you; pardon is but an entrance blessing, a welcome at the doorstep: there are rarer joys within the house.   You have become an heir
to a boundless inheritance : all things are yours; heaven, and Christ,
and God are yours; yet I marvel not that at present all your heart is
taken up with a sense of pardoned sin.   I will not disturb you, but I
will rejoice with you.   I will even sit down and sing with you : let this
be our hymn :—

> "Now, oh joy ! my sins are pardon'd,
>   Now I can, and do believe;
> All I have, and am, and shall be,
>   To my precious Lord I give."

Even the full-grown child of God highly values this boon so dear to little children, and although he has received many other mercies beside, yet still it is a chief part of his joy that he has been cleansed from sin and clothed with righteousness. Ay, and our elder brothers, who are now in the king's country, this is a chief point even with them, that they have washed their robes and made them white in the blood of the Lamb; therefore are they before the throne of God, and serve him day and night in his temple. Yes, dear little children, you have obtained a most precious favour in which you do well to rejoice; "your sins are forgiven you for his name's sake."

Here let me observe that the forgiveness of sins is *assuredly the possession of the new beginner* in the divine life. He is as certainly forgiven as he ever shall be. The forgiveness of sins is not a matter of degrees or of growth. It is done in an instant, and done for ever, never to be reversed. The child of God who was born but yesterday is not as completely sanctified as he will be; he is not as completely instructed as he will be; he is not as completely conformed to the image of Christ as he will be; but he is as completely pardoned as the full-grown saint. He that just now passed the gate of pearl,—did you not hear the shout as he entered, like a shock of corn fully ripe that cometh in his season?—he, I say, was not more truly pardoned than you who but an hour ago believed in Christ unto the salvation of your soul. The dying thief had not many minutes found mercy, and yet the Lord Jesus said to him, "To-day shalt thou be with me in paradise": it is plain, therefore, that he had been perfectly cleansed in a moment. To wash in the fountain filled with blood is not a business of weeks and months and years, nor is it to be repeated many times and often; but he that is washed is there and then made whiter than snow, and there is henceforth no defilement upon him. "There is therefore now no condemnation to them that are in Christ Jesus." "I write unto you, little children, because your sins are forgiven you": they are all gone: grace has most effectually removed them from you as far as the east is from the west. The Egyptians at the Red Sea were not destroyed by little and by little; they were not swallowed up in the flood a regiment at a time; the eager depths which had by miracle been divided for a time leaped together, and Pharaoh and his hosts, all of them, were covered, to be seen no more for ever. Sing unto the Lord, for he hath triumphed gloriously. "The depths have covered them; there is not one of them left." The Israelites had but barely set their foot upon the other side of the Red Sea, and yet all their enemies were as completely drowned as when the people entered into the Promised Land: it is even so with you who have believed in Christ but newly, your sins are cast into the depths of the sea. Your iniquities are subdued by the Lord Jesus, who has come to save his people from their sins. Therefore, little children, praise your God, and sing unto his name with all your might,—"Who forgiveth all our iniquities; who healeth all our diseases."

Note, also, that your sins are forgiven you *on the same terms as those of the Apostle*, and the greatest of the saints: "Your sins are forgiven you for his name's sake"; that is, for the sake of Jesus, for the sake of his glorious person, for the sake of his honourable offices, for the sake of his blood-shedding and atoning death, for the sake of his glorious resurrection, for the sake of his perpetual intercession before the throne of God.   Your sins are not forgiven you because of anything you are or hope to be, nor because of anything that you have done or have suffered; you are forgiven for Christ's name's sake, and all the saints of God can say the same. This is a sure ground of hope. Quicksand there is none, but a solid rock is under our foot. Had the pardon been granted for our own work's sake, it might have been reversed upon our disobedience; but as sin is pardoned for Christ's sake, the pardon is irreversible, since there is no change in Christ. Is not this a dainty sweet for the little children. How gladly do I come and sit at the children's table when I see such food placed thereon.

Now notice that *this is the reason why John wrote to you, little children*. People do not generally write letters to little children; but John does, because of these special little ones it can be said, their sins are forgiven them. The moment, then, that a man has his sins forgiven, he is old enough to begin to understand that which is written, and he should become a Bible reader and a Bible searcher: the moment that his sins are forgiven him for Christ's name's sake, he becomes capable of exhortation, and it is his business to attend to what is written to him. If pardoned as criminals we are enlisted as workers. Why, methinks if my sins have been forgiven me, my heaven-born instincts make me ask, " Lord, what wilt thou have me to do? Hast thou done so much for me? Then set me about doing something for thyself. Give me as a privilege the opportunity of serving thee." Therefore, John, knowing that the little children would be eager to obey, has written to them in this epistle certain commands, of which I will speak to you further on. Only, little children, be on the alert to begin at once your work of faith and labour of love.

II. Secondly, I have to speak of THE KNOWLEDGE of these little children. " I have written unto you, little children, because ye have known, or know, the Father." The tiniest babe in the family of God knows the Father. For, first, as we have seen, *his sins are forgiven him.* By whom is that pardon given? Why, by the Father; and, therefore, he that has had his sins forgiven him necessarily knows the Father. When the poor prodigal felt the kisses of his father's love, and saw the best robe adorning his person, then he knew the Father. All the philosophers in the world do not know so much of the Father God as a forgiven sinner knows. I go a little further : if there be any that have never fallen into sin, but are like the ninety and nine just persons who need no repentance, or like the elder brother who had never at any time transgressed his father's commandment, I say that these do not know and cannot know the Father as the forgiven child does; for the Father's heart comes out most fully and expressly when he says, " Bring forth the best robe, and put it on him; and put a ring on his hand, and shoes on his feet. For this my son was dead, and is alive again; he was lost and is found." Then, as he looks up through his tears and sees the ineffable smile of the Father's affection, the forgiven child knows the Father. The very least child of grace, having received the forgiveness of sin, knows the Father in this most important sense.

Moreover, this is a piece of knowledge, dear friends, which the child of God *obtains very early in his spiritual life;* for, whatever a child does not know, he knows his father. Think of your dear little one at home: he cannot as yet read a letter in the book; he knows nothing of the things which his elder brother studies; but he knows his father. He may not know very much about his father; he could not certainly speak to others about his father's business or his father's wealth, but yet he knows him. The child cannot help his father, or understand what his father does; but he knows his father, and would choose him out from among a thousand. See how his eyes twinkle now that father has come home: see him stretch out his little hands: see how eager he is to get into these dear arms! He knows his father, and never forgets that knowledge. Dear child of God, this is a piece of knowledge which you have also; and in this you will yield to none of all the sacred family. Benjamin knows his father with an absolute certainty: he is as sure of it as Reuben the firstborn. We go to school and college, but long before that we know our father: the fear is lest we overlay that precious knowledge with something not worth half as much. Little children, you know God now in your spiritual childhood. You could not preach about him; you could not write a treatise upon his attributes; you could not describe his mighty acts; but you know him by the instinct of a child; and in you is the promise fulfilled, "Israel shall cry unto me, My God, we know thee."

Little children, the result of your knowing God as your Father is that when he is away from you you are in the habit of crying after him. If you cannot feel your Father's love shed abroad in your heart by the Holy Ghost you are miserable, and you hasten to your closet and begin to pray, "Come to me, my Father; manifest thyself to me, for I cannot live without thee." On the other hand, when you do get to your Father you show that you love him by the perfect restfulness of your spirit. In God you are at home. Once get into your Father's arms, you feel quite safe, quite peaceful, quite happy. The presence of God is the paradise of the believer. God is the ultimatum of our desires: we speak of him as "our exceeding joy." If in my Father's love I share a filial part, I ask no more than to know and enjoy it. We say, "Our Father which art in heaven"; we might as truly say, "Our Father, thou art our heaven." Hence we seek after him. "O God, thou art my God; early will I seek thee." Here, then, we have a token that we know the Father, when we weep because he is absent, or rejoice because he is present.

We know the Father, brothers, even we who are but little in Israel, for we love him. Do you not feel that you love God this morning? You might not dare to say so in public, and yet you would die for him. Sooner than renounce your God would you not give up all that you possess? It may be you will never be tried as the martyrs have been; but if you were, can you suppose it possible that you could part with your God? No, your inmost heart loves him; you know it does; and loving him, you are united to him by bonds which cannot be severed. Moreover, we know the Father, for we trust him. Is it not written, "They that know thy name will put their trust in thee"? Can you not trust God with everything? A child has no cares: his father cares for him. A child knows no anxiety: his father bears all the anxiety on his behalf. Is it not so with you? Though you are babes in grace, do you not trust?—trust for time, trust for eternity, trust for your bodies, and trust for your souls? I am sure you do. If you are what you should be, you know the Father, for your faith rests upon him.

This also is true, that you seek to imitate him. It is wonderful how little children imitate their father, perhaps more than grown-up children do, though the influence of example is seen upon them also. The very little ones will try to do everything exactly like father. It must be right, it must be perfect, if father does it ; they make us smile as we see in them ourselves in miniature. Is not this the very thing which you try to do? Though you were converted but a very little while ago, yet you wish to be like Jesus ; you long to be like the Father. Would you not be perfect if you could? If you could, would you not be rid of every sin? If some painful surgical operation could take away from you the black drops of indwelling sin, would you not cheerfully bare your breast to the keenest knife? I know you would. You would die to be rid of sin ; for that is the thing you hate. This proves that you know your Father in heaven, for you are trying to be like him.

And do you not glory in him? Little children when they begin to talk, and go to school, how proud they are of their father! Their father is the greatest man that ever lived : there never was the like of him. You may talk to them of great statesmen, or great warriors, or great princes, but these are all nobodies: their father fills the whole horizon of their being. Well, so it certainly is with us and our Father God.

> " Since no works are like to thine,
> None so glorious, so divine,
> Since whatever gods there be,
> None, O Lord, are like to thee ;
> Let me bow before thy throne,
> And exalt thy name alone."

We cannot make enough of our God. We extol him with all our might. With the blessed virgin we sing, " My soul doth magnify the Lord." What does " magnify " mean? Why, to make great. We feel as if we would make God's name great, and would greaten him in the minds of men, and make them think what a blessed Father we have.

Now, hearken! This is the reason why John has written to you, little children, because he says, " They know enough to understand my letter, for they know the Father." We do not think of writing a letter to a little child. " Ah," says John, " but the Lord's children know their Father"; and he that knows God is capable of any kind of know-ledge. He who knows God is a fit person to be accepted as a disciple of the beloved apostle. I cannot desire a better congregation than a congregation of men that know the Father. What, if they be little children? Well, they can understand anything that I, another child, can have to say, for they know the Father ; and therefore they have an unction from the Holy One, and are able to know spiritual things. To know God is the centre and the circumference of all knowledge. If you know the Father, do you not see the reason why John writes to you? Because, now that you know him, you are bound to love him, to trust him, and to serve him. Having received such knowledge as this, you are bound to impart it as far as you can ; you are bound to live up to it, and to show to all around you what a child of God is, and how different he is from the children of darkness. Thus, then, out of your privilege, and out of your knowledge, there arises an obligation which I trust you will be not slow to acknowledge. Here is a prayer for you :—

> " If I've the honour, Lord, to be
> One of thy happy family,
> On me the gracious gift bestow
> To call thee " Abba, Father " too.
>
> So may my conduct ever prove
> My filial piety and love !
> Whilst all my brethren clearly trace
> Their Father's likeness in my face."

III. Now we come to our third division. Will you kindly follow me with your Bibles, especially you that are "little children," while I commend to you THE PRECEPTS which John has written for your guidance.

First, look at 1 John ii. : " My little children, these things I write unto you, that ye sin not." That is the first precept,—Little children, *sin not*. Children are very apt to get into the mire. Most mothers will tell you, I think, that if there is a pool of mud anywhere within a mile, her first-born joy and comfort will find it out and get into it if he possibly can ; and no matter how often a child is washed he seems always to need washing again : if there is a method by which he can foul his hands and his face, your pretty cherub is most ingenious to find it out. I am afraid this is too much the case with the children of God. There is so much of carnality about us, so much of the old Adam, that the question is not into which sin we fall, but into which sin we do not fall. Alas! we are apt to be proud, though we have nothing to be proud of ; we are prone to despond and doubt our Father, though he never gave us any cause to do so : we are inclined to be worldly, though there is nothing in the world worth loving ; and we have a tendency to grow cold and chill towards God, though he is altogether lovely, and ought to win our warmest affection. We are apt to speak unadvisedly with our lips ; we are apt to be full of foolish thoughts ; we are apt to be self-willed. We find an angry temper rising against some brother of ours whom we ought to love ; and we have not long got over that before we are half afraid to utter a word of rebuke lest we should incur the laughter of the ungodly. Thus do we glide from one sin to another, even as a waterfall descends from rock to rock. As weeds multiply in the soul so do sins spring up in our hearts. We are a mass of faults. Like the pendulum, we swing to the right hand and then to the left : we err first in one way and then in another ; we are ever inclined to evil, and hence the apostle sweetly puts it, " My little children, I write unto you, that ye sin not." Avoid every sin : forsake it altogether. Ask for the grace of God to sanctify you wholly, spirit, soul, and body. Though you are only newly born, yet, my little children, sin not. You will soon lose your comfort if you do. Little children, sin will hurt you, damage you, grieve you, and displease your heavenly Father : it will raise a cloud, behind which his presence will be hidden from you : it will stop your heavenly growth : it will prevent your usefulness. My little children, I earnestly entreat you that ye sin not. Burnt child, dread the fire ! You have just been plucked out of it, do not go back to it. Do not play with sparks; keep clear of every kind of match that might create a flame. Seek after holiness with all your might. Though born but yesterday do not sin to-day. God help you to fulfil this holy precept.

Further on in this second chapter the apostle writes to them again, and tells them (verse 18) that it is the last time, and that there are many antichrists abroad. You will have to run your eye right down the chapter till you come to verse 24, for that is what he says to little children, because there are many antichrists in the world that would seduce them; "*Let that therefore abide in you, which ye have heard from the beginning.*" Little children are very fickle. The toys which they cry for one day they break the next: young minds change with the wind. So, little children, there are many evil ones who will endeavour to seduce you from the truth of God, and as you have a natural instability of mind as yet, for you are only newly converted, it is well to be on your guard against those who would mislead you. Till we are rooted and grounded in the truth, new things have great charms for us, especially if they have about them a great show of holiness and zeal for God. Listen, then, dear children but newly born into the Saviour's family: "Let that therefore abide in you, which ye have heard from the beginning." Alas, even those who are older in grace than you are have shown a sad readiness to be duped by plausible persons who have invented fresh notions and methods. I have lived long enough to have seen a considerable variety of follies and manias in the religious world. They have sprung up, grown great, declined, and vanished. One day it has been one thing, another another. I have lived to see those things justly ridiculed which a few years before were cried up as the wonders of the age. I thank God I have not been moved by any of these periodical fits of frenzy, but have been content to keep to the one old truth which I have gathered from the Scriptures and made my own by experience, and by the teaching of the Holy Spirit. I have not had to tack about, for I have been enabled to steam ahead; and I hope I shall do so to the end. I have no respect for these upstart inventions; but I regard them as so many phases of human delusion. One never knows what will come next; but of this we are pretty sure, that every now and then a new doctrine is brought forth which turns out to be an old heresy with a fresh coat of varnish on it; or else some new method of saving souls is found out, and the work blazes away like a house on fire till it dies out in smoke. Let us not be carried off our feet by every wind of doctrine. We may live to see the present craze ended and another or two after it; only be it ours to be steadfast, immovable. "Little children, let that therefore abide in you, which ye have heard from the beginning:" leave to others the soon-exhausted novelties and do you keep to the eternal unchangeable truth which is taught you in God's word and in your own soul's experience.

Little children, here is a third precept for you, and I want you to put it into your bosom, and carry it home (verse 28). "And now, little children, abide in him." There is a Sabbath portion for you: "*Abide in him.*" Let the truth abide in you, and do you abide in Christ, who is the truth. Little children are very apt to stray: I have known them tempted away from home, to play the truant: they have gone into the fields after pretty flowers, or down by the brook to fish for minnows, and then they have fallen into all sorts of trouble. The best place for a child is at home; and for a babe in grace the best shelter is the Saviour's bosom. "Little children, abide in him." If you forget everything else, I say this morning, lay this up in your hearts, and let none tempt you away from simply trusting your Saviour, sweetly resting in his love, and humbly following on to know more and more of him. "And now, little children, abide in him."

What next? Read on to chapter iii. verse 7 :—" Little children, *let no man deceive you.*" Children are very credulous: they will believe any idle tale if it be told them by a clever and attractive person. Little children, believe your Saviour, but be not ready to believe anybody else. Believe God's word, and stand fast to that; but if sinners entice you, do not consent to them; and if antichrist would teach you false doctrine, close your ear to it. Be as the sheep of whom Jesus said,—"A stranger will they not follow, for they know not the voice of strangers."

Further on (iii. 18) we read: "My little children, *let us not love in word, neither in tongue; but in deed and in truth.*" Little children are apt to let their angry passions rise till they have to be told by Dr. Watts that their—

> "Little hands were never made
> To tear each other's eyes."

And truly we have some Christian children who have been all too quick about this tearing of each other's eyes. They have seen a truth, and some friend they meet with does not see it; therefore they have tried to knock his eyes out to make him see it. That is a faithful description of many Christian controversies. It is idle to attempt to compel another to think as I think by scolding him, and heaping wrath upon him. Let us never do that. Let us love. If you cannot expect anything else of a child you do expect love; and love never seems to be more suitably enshrined than in the heart and mind of a little child. Come, you that are newly brought to Christ, love with all your might. If you cannot fight as soldiers, or work as labourers, yet love the brotherhood; love Christ; love God; love the souls of men; and by love seek to win them to the Saviour who has saved you. Love not in word only, but in deed and in truth.

You have the next word in chapter iv. verse 4—"Ye are of God, little children, *and have overcome them:* because greater is he that is in you, than he that is in the world." Little children are frequently timid: they are sometimes terrified when left alone: they are generally afraid of strangers. Hear, then, ye little children, you are very weak and feeble, but do not be dismayed because of that, for there is a power dwelling in you which is mightier than the power which dwells in the world. Satan dwells in the world, and he is mighty; but God dwells in you, and he is almighty; therefore be not afraid.

> "A feeble saint shall win the day,
> Though death and hell obstruct the way."

Hold you on to faith in the eternal Lord who dwells in you, and you shall never perish, neither shall any pluck you out of his hand.

The last precept to little children is at the end of the epistle. Carefully read the last verse—"Little children, *keep yourselves from idols.*"

Little children are naturally fond of toys and pretty pictures. Anything like pomp and show is sure to please children. How fond they are of soldiers, and banners, and processions, and bands of music, and all that is gay : these are their idols. That is the tendency of many grown-up children that I know of. They admire a fine religion, tasteful, striking, artistic. " Little children, keep yourselves from idols." I would like this text printed over the altars of our Ritualistic neighbours. I need scarcely mention others who have no taste or care for the beautiful, but their toys are all for noise-making, and glitter and flash, a sort of fifth of November all the days of the year. Do not become fascinated with their playthings. Be not led away from the church of God by armies or navies. Alas, the children must now have their play toys in the church, and their toys in the chapel, and some must have their toys in the streets, till one would think with their trumpets and drums that they had just come home from the fair. " Little children, keep yourselves from idols." I do not think you are likely to fall in love with the idols of the heathen and bow down to them ; but there are plenty of other gods which are the idols of one period and the derision of the next. Keep you to Christ. Ask not for pomp and show ; ask not for noise and bluster : ask for nothing but that your sins may be forgiven you, that you may know the Father, and then that you may abide in Christ, and be full of love to all the family of God. Little children, may the Lord Jesus Christ be with you, and may you grow in grace till you come unto the fulness of the stature of men in him. May his grace be upon all them that love him, and wait for his appearing.

PORTION OF SCRIPTURE READ BEFORE SERMON—1 John ii.

HYMNS FROM " OUR OWN HYMN BOOK"—909, 728, 248.

FILLING THE EMPTY VESSELS.

A Sermon

DELIVERED ON LORD'S-DAY EVENING, SEPTEMBER 17TH, 1882, BY

C. H. SPURGEON,

AT THE METROPOLITAN TABERNACLE, NEWINGTON.

"But my God shall supply all your need according to his riches in glory by Christ Jesus."—Philippians iv. 19.

VERY beautiful, to my mind, is the sight of " Paul the aged " immured in his prison at Rome, likely by-and-by to be put to death, but calm, quiet, peaceful, and joyful. Just now he is so happy that a gleam of sunlight seems to light up his cell, and his face shines like that of an angel. He is exceedingly delighted because he has been, in his deep poverty, kindly remembered by the little church at Philippi, and they have sent him a contribution. See how cheerful the man is—I was about to say, how contented; but I drop the word because it falls far short of the mark. He is far more happy than Cæsar overhead in the palace. He is charmed with the love which has sent him this relief. Probably the gift does not come to very much, if estimated in Roman coin; but he makes a great deal of it, and sits down to write a letter of thanks abounding in rich expressions like these :—" I have all things, and abound : I am full, having received of Epaphroditus the things which were sent from you." His heart was evidently greatly touched; for he says, " I rejoiced in the Lord greatly, that now at the last your care of me hath flourished again." See how little a gift may make a good man glad ! Is it not worth while to be free with our cups of cold water to the prophets of the Lord ? Instead of a little money, the brethren and sisters at Philippi receive a boundless blessing, and are enriched by the fervent prayers of the apostle. Hear how earnestly Paul invokes benedictions on the heads of his benefactors. Is it not a blessed state of mind which enables a heart so soon to be full to overflowing ? Some would grumble over a roasted ox, and here is Paul rejoicing over a dinner of herbs.

So great was the disinterestedness of Paul that there was nothing of selfishness about his joy. He did not speak in respect of want, for he knew how to suffer need without complaint; but he looked upon the kindly contribution as a fruit of the grace of God in the Philippians ; a generous proof that they were lifted out of heathen selfishness into Christian love. There was little enough of kindness in the old Roman and Greek world into which Paul went preaching the gospel. Those

were times of great hardness of heart, even to cruel heartlessness. There
was no sort of provision for the poor. If a man was poor, why, that
was his own look out, and he might starve and die. You know
how hardened the people had become through the fights in the amphitheatre, so that the sight of blood produced a fierce delight in their
brutal bosoms, and human suffering was to them rather a thing to be
rejoiced in than to be prevented. There might be here and there a
tender hand that gave an obolus to the poor, but, for the most part,
charity was dead. The voluptuaries of that most degenerate age
planned no hospitals and built no orphanages : they were too intent upon
their gladiators and their mistresses. Self was lord paramount in
Cæsar's court, and all over Roman realms. But here are people at
Philippi thinking about one who had preached the gospel to them,
and who is now suffering. They are moved by a new principle ; love
to God in Christ Jesus has created love to the man whose word has
changed them. They will not abandon him : they will out of their own
slender means cheer his sad condition. There were churches that had
no such bowels of mercy : alas, that so early in the gospel-day holy
charity should be so rare ! There were people whom Paul had blessed
greatly, who even quarrelled about him, and denied that he was an
apostle of Christ ; but not so the beloved church at Philippi. They
had again and again ministered to his necessities, and Paul now rejoices
in them again because he delights to see another instance of the transforming power of the grace of God upon character, so that those who
were once selfish now rejoiced, unprompted and unasked, to send their
offering to him. Was Lydia at the bottom of that subscription ? I
should not wonder : we know that she was open-hearted. Did the jailer
add his full share ? I feel sure of it, for in the prison he courteously
entertained the apostle. These were a generous people, and Paul is happy
in thinking of them. I may here dare to say that I also have had the
like joy over many of you when I have seen how freely you have
given of your substance to the work of the Lord. It would be unfair if
I withheld commendation for liberality from many now before me.
You have rejoiced my heart by your gifts to the cause of God. You
have given up to the measure of your means, and some of you beyond
what we could have asked of you. The gospel has taught you this.
To God be glory that it is so. Continue in the same spirit, that none
may rob me of this joy.

The apostle makes to them an assurance in the following verses that
they shall be abundantly repaid for all that they have done. He says
to them, " *You* have helped me ; but *my God* shall supply you.
You have helped me in *one* of my needs—my need of clothing and of
food : I have other needs in which you could not help me ; but my God
shall supply *all your need*. You have helped me, some of you, out of
your deep poverty, taking from your scanty store ; but my God shall
supply all your need *out of his riches* in glory. You have sent Epaphroditus unto me with your offering. Well and good : he is a most worthy
brother, and a true yoke-fellow ; but for all that God shall send a better
messenger to you, for he shall supply all your needs *by Christ Jesus.*"
He seems to me to make a parallel of his needs with theirs, and of his
supplies from them with their supplies from the Lord. He would seem

to say,—Just as God has through you filled me up, so shall he by Christ fill you up. That is a translation of the Greek which most nearly touches the meaning,—"My God shall *fill up* all your need according to his riches in glory by Christ Jesus."

Will you allow me to make a break here for one instant ? I read you just now the story of the prophet's widow whose children were about to be taken for a debt, and how the oil was multiplied in the vessels which she borrowed, until there was enough to discharge the debt, and sufficient surplus for herself and children to live upon. Now, kindly take that picture, and join it on to this, and we have here, first, *the empty vessels.* Set them out in a row, "all your need." Secondly, *who will fill them up?*—"My God shall fill up all your need." Thirdly, *after what fashion will he do it?*—"According to his riches in glory." Fourthly, *by what means will he do it?*—"By Christ Jesus." Keep the widow and the vessels before you, and let us see the miracle worked over again on a grand scale in our own houses and hearts. May the Holy Spirit make the sight refreshing to our faith.

I. So, then, we will begin our discourse this evening by asking you to SET OUT THE EMPTY VESSELS. "My God shall supply all your need." Bring forth your vessels, even empty vessels not a few. "All your need."

I do not suppose that you are under any great obligation to go out to-night and borrow other people's needs, for you have enough of your own at home—*needs many, and needs varied.* Very well, set them out. Hide none of them away, but put them down one after another, in a long row, all of them. There are needs for your body, needs for your soul ; needs for yourselves, needs for your families ; needs for the present, needs for the future ; needs for time, needs for eternity ; needs for earth, needs for heaven. Your needs are as many as your moments ; as many as the hairs of your head. I suppose it would be useless for me to attempt a catalogue of them : however carefully we made the list we should have to add a host of sundries altogether unmentionable until circumstances suggested them. I could hardly tell you all my own needs, but I know that they are enormous, and increasing with my years. I have needs as a man, as a husband, as a father, as a citizen, as a Christian, as a pastor, as an author—in fact, every position I take up adds to my needs. If I went through my own personal bill of requests I should fill a document like the roll mentioned in the Old Testament, written within and without; and hardly then could I enumerate all my own demands upon the Bank of Heaven. But if I then attempted to take all the thousands that are gathered beneath this roof, and to let each man state his particular wants, where would the computation end ? The sands upon the sea-shore are not more innumerable. Dear ! dear ! we should want a library larger than the Bodleian to hold all the books which could be written of all the needs of the needy congregation now before me. Well, I am not sorry for it, for here is so much the more room for the Lord to work his miracles of bountiful grace. Sometimes, when I have been in need for the work of the Orphanage and the College, and such like things—and these times have occurred—I do solemnly assure you that I have felt a wonderful joy in my spirit. I have watched the ebb of the funds till nearly everything has been gone, and then I have joyfully said to myself, " Now for it ! The vessels are empty ;

now I shall see the miracle of filling them." What wonders the Lord has wrought for me I cannot now tell you in detail; but many of you who have been my faithful helpers know how hundreds and even thousands of pounds have poured in from our great Lord in the moment of necessity. It will always be the same, for the Lord God is the same. Until the funds run low we cannot expect to see them replenished: but when they get low, then will God come and deal graciously with us. Money is, however, our smallest want; we need grace, wisdom, light, and comfort; and these we shall have. All our needs are occasions for blessing. The more needs you have the more blessing you will get. God has promised to fill up all your needs. That is, all your empty vessels will be filled, and therefore the more the merrier. What! the more in need the better? Yes, I would have your faith believe that strange statement: your poverty shall thus be your riches, your weakness your strength, your abasement your exaltation. Your extremity shall be an opportunity that God will use to show the riches of his grace; to your utter exhaustion he will draw near with all the fulness of his inexhaustible grace, and he will replenish you till your cup runs over. He will fill up all your empty vessels. Be not slow to fetch them out from holes and corners, and place them before the Lord, however many they may be. Weep not over the empty jars, but place them out in rows in full expectation of their being filled to the brim.

These empty vessels of yours are, some of them, I have no doubt, *very large, and they even grow larger.* Most of our wants grow upon us. You still pray, "Give us this day our daily bread;" but the one loaf which was a large answer to the prayer when you were single, would not go far at your table now: the quarterns vanish like snow in the sun. You wanted faith fifty years ago, but you want more now, do you not? for you have more infirmities, and perhaps more trials, than in your younger days. I know that, apart from my loving Lord, I am much more needy now than I ever was before. Whatever a man requires in the things of God, usually the older he grows, and the more experience he has, the more he wants it, and the more of it he wants. He needs more love than he had when he was younger, more patience, more resignation, more humility, more charity, more wisdom, more holiness. He desires more faith, and a brighter hope. He wants, in prospect of death especially, more courage, and more bold, simple, child-like confidence in his Saviour. Why, some of us have wants that could not be supplied if we could turn the stars to gold and coin them and pay them away: these could not touch the hunger of the heart and soul. The world itself would be but a mouthful for our spirits' necessity—a drop in the bucket. I know some saints that have grown to be so deeply in debt to their Lord, and to his church, and to the world, that they are over head and ears in it—hopelessly involved in boundless obligation. How can we meet the demands upon us? Our responsibilities are overwhelming. All that some of us have made by our life-long trading is a bigger stock of wants than ever we had before. The vacuum within our spirit expands and enlarges, and we cry out, "More knowledge of the Scriptures; more of Christ; more of grace; more of God; more of the Holy Ghost; more power to serve God." Our oil-vessels would each one hold a sea : and even these are expanding. We want more and more, and the mercy is that the text before us keeps pace with the growth—" My God shall supply all your need : " this includes the big needs as well as the little ones ; it comprehends all that can be as well as all that is ; it warrants us that our growing needs shall all be supplied. Let the vessels expand to their utmost, " Yet my God," says Paul, " shall fill up all those needs of yours."

Certain of our needs, again, are of this extraordinary kind, that *if they were filled up to-night they would be empty to-morrow morning.* Some of our necessities are fresh every morning ; the crop is a daily one, it springs up every moment. The grace I had five minutes ago will not serve me now. Yesterday I may have possessed great love, great faith, great courage, great humility, great joy ; but I need these to-day also, and none can give them to me but my Lord. You had great patience under your last trial. Yes, but old patience is stale stuff. You must grow more of that sweet herb in your garden ; for the trial that is now coming can only be sweetened by the herb content, newly gathered from the garden of your heart and mixed with the bitter water of your afflictions. Our condition apart from our God may be compared to those fabled vessels that we read of in mythology that were so full of holes that, though the fifty daughters of Danaus laboured hard to fill them up, they could never accomplish the task. You and I are such leaky vessels that none but God can ever fill us; and when we are filled none but God can keep us full. Yet so the promise stands, "My God shall supply all your need" : all the vessels shall be filled and shall be kept full.

We have certain needs, dear friends, that are *very pressing*, and perhaps most clamorous at this moment. Some wants are urgent: they must be supplied, and supplied speedily, or we shall perish with hunger, or die of sickness, or wither up in despair. Here let me add a caution : I dare not tell you that God will supply all the needs of everybody, for this promise is to the children of God, and in its most emphatic sense it is only to a certain class even among them. Those persons who profess to be Christians, and when they were well-to-do never helped anybody else, I think the Lord will let them pinch a bit, and know what a con-dition of poverty is like that they may become more sympathetic with the poor. I have known good stewards, and the Lord has sent them more, for they have dealt well with what they had : they have given away their substance by shovelfuls, and the Lord has sent it back by cartloads, and entrusted them with more. Others who have been bad stewards, and have not served their Master well, have lost what they had, and have come to penury. Let us hope that their substance has gone to somebody that will use it better ; but meanwhile they have to pinch, and deservedly so. But, remember, the apostle is speaking to people of a very different character from that. He is speaking to the Philip-pians, and I think that there is point in that pronoun, " My God shall supply all *your* need." You have been generous in helping the Lord's servant, and the Lord will repay you. Up to the measure of your ability you have served his church and helped to carry on his work in the world, and therefore God will supply all *your* need. This is not spoken to hoarding Judas, but to the generous who had voluntarily yielded of their substance when a fit opportunity was given them. Will

any of you bring your need to God and test him by like conduct?
Remember that old promise of his, "Bring ye all the tithes into the
storehouse, that there may be meat in mine house, and prove me now
herewith, saith the Lord of hosts, if I will not open you the windows
of heaven, and pour you out a blessing, that there shall not be room
enough to receive it." There is that scattereth and yet increaseth.
Give, and it shall be given unto you. Oh yes, our gracious God will fill
all the vessels at once, if time presses! If your needs urgently require
to be filled bring them to him.

I began by saying that few of us had any great call to borrow other
people's empty pots ; *yet there are some of us whose main anxiety is
about the vessels that we have borrowed.* We want more oil than others
for this very reason, that we care for others. Certain of us have been
called to a life which intertwists itself with many lives ; we have been led
by grace and providence to take upon ourselves the wants of thousands.
Every genuine warm-hearted Christian does this more or less. We try
to make other men's needs our own needs, by working for the poor, the
ignorant, the sick, the helpless. You that care for our orphan children
may well join with me in prayer that the Lord will fill up all those
empty vessels not a few, which we have borrowed of poor widows. Think
of my hundreds of borrowed vessels in the Orphanage, and of the number
in the College. Blessed be the Lord my God, he will fill up all these.
Those whom we try to help in different ways, especially those we try to
lead to the Saviour, are like the woman's borrowed vessels, and they are
not a few. You have made their spiritual needs your own, you have
come before God to pray for them as for your own soul, and you shall
be heard. You have talked to your neighbours and laid yourself out for
their good as if your own eternal destiny were in their stead : rest you
fully assured that the Lord that filled the borrowed pots in Elisha's
day will also supply your borrowed needs. " My God will fill up all
your needs." It is a blessed word. Bring out your vessels, and see if
it be not true.

I should like to see every Christian here setting out all his vessels in
rows at once, whatever they may be. Do not put your cares away in the
back room and say, "I shall draw them out to-morrow and begin wor-
rying over them." Instead of that, while the oil is flowing, bring them
here before the Lord, that the oil may have free course, and find suitable
storage. Would you limit the miracle? Have you one forgotten want?
Make haste with it! Still the oil is multiplying. Come one! Come all!
Arrange your vessels ; and the Lord will fill up your needs by his grace,
and fill your mouths with a song.

II. Secondly, let us enquire, WHO IS TO FILL THESE VESSELS?
Paul says, "*My God will supply all your need.*"

"My *God!*" Oh, that is grand! It were foolish talking if any other
name were mentioned. God can supply all the needs of his people, for
he is All-sufficient ; but nobody else can. He can do it alone without
help ; for nothing is too hard for the Lord. He is able to number the
myriads of his creatures and attend to the commissariat of them all, so
that not one of them shall lack: " He calleth them all by their names,
by the greatness of his power not one faileth." "They that wait upon
the Lord shall not want any good thing." As for thee, dear brother,

"trust in the Lord and do good, so shalt thou dwell in the land, and verily thou shalt be fed." He that promises to fill up all thy empty vessels is one who can do it: there is no bound to the goodness and power of God.

Then, notice that sweet word which Paul has put before the glorious word "God." He writes,—"*My* God." As Paul looked at the money which the Philippians had sent him, and perhaps at the warm garments that should cover him in the cold, damp jail, he cried, "See how *my* God has supplied *me !* " And then he says, " *My* God shall supply *you.*" This same God, Paul's God—" shall fill up all your need." Wonderfully had God protected Paul from the malice of those who sought for his life. Very wonderfully had he been carried by divine power through unparalleled labours, so that he had been made to triumph in every place in the preaching of the gospel; and thus he had learned from day to day to get a firmer grip of his God, and say, " My God ! " with more and more emphasis. Jehovah was not to Paul the unknown God, but " My God." With God he dwelt, and in him he reposed all his cares. This same God is our God. Think of that, poor friend, in your hour of need. Think of that, you afflicted widow-woman : you have Paul's God to go to. Think of that, dear child of God in trouble : you have the same God as Paul had, and he is as much yours as he was Paul's. His arm has not waxed short, neither has his heart grown hard towards any of his children. "My God," says Paul, "who is also your God, will supply all your need."

Who is this God that will supply all our needs? Paul's God, remember, was and is *the God of providence,* and what a wonderful God that is ! We speak as if we were some very important part of the universe, but really, what are we ? Our little island can scarcely be found upon the globe till you hunt long for it ; what a tiny speck this congregation must be. But God supplies the wants of all the millions of mankind. " Mankind," I said : but I ought to have included all the other creatures, too ;—the myriads of herrings in the sea, the multitudes of birds that sometimes darken the sun in their migrations, the countless armies of worms and insects, strangely supplied we know not how ; and yet " your heavenly Father feedeth them." Is that all the sphere of his providence ? No ; far from it. I suppose that this round world of ours is but one apple in the orchard of creation, one grain of dust in the corner of God's great palace. But all yon orbs, with all the living things that may be peopling every star, he supplies. And how ? " He openeth his hand and supplieth the want of every living thing." See how easy to him is this universal provision : he doth but open his hand and it is done. This is the God that will supply all your need. He calleth the stars by name. He leadeth out Arcturus with his sons. He looseth the bands of Orion. He doeth great things without number ; and shall he not feed and clothe you, O ye of little faith ? Yes, be ye sure of this, the God of providence shall supply all your needs for this life and its surroundings.

If that suffice you not, let me remind you that this God is *the God of grace,* for Paul above all men counted grace to be his treasure : his God was the God of grace. Chiefly he is the God who gave his Son to bleed and die for men. Oh, stand at Calvary and see God's great sacrifice

—the gift of his only-begotten Son ; and when you have marked the wounds of the Well-beloved and seen Jesus die, answer me this question —"He that spared not his own Son, but freely delivered him up for us all, how shall he not with him also freely give us all things ? " What will he deny us who has given up the best jewel that he had, the glorious One that heaven could not match ? There was never the like of Jesus, and yet he bowed his head to die on our behalf. Oh, my dear, dear friends, if you are anxious to-night and vexed with many cares, do think of that. It is the God and Father of our Lord and Saviour Jesus Christ who says that he will fill up all your need. Do you doubt him ? can you ? dare you distrust him ?

Now, take a flight above this present cloud-land and behold *the God of heaven.* Think of what God is up yonder

> " Beyond, beyond this lower sky,
> Up where eternal ages roll,
> Where solid pleasures never die,
> And fruits immortal feast the soul."

Behold the splendour of God ! Gold in heaven is of no account : the streets of that city are all of pure gold like unto transparent glass. The riches and the merchandise of nations are but as rags and rottenness compared with the commonest utensils of God's great house above. There they possess inexhaustible treasures and everything that is precious; for the walls of the New Jerusalem are described as made of twelve manner of precious stones, as if these stones were so common in Immanuel's land that they built the walls therewith. The gates are each one a pearl. What pearls are those ! Is God thus rich ? inconceivably, incalculably rich, so that he clothes the very grass of the field more gloriously than Solomon clothed himself ? What am I at to be of a doubtful mind ? Is he my Father, and will he let me suffer want? What ! I starving and my Father owning heaven ? No, no.

> " He that has made my heaven secure,
> Will here all good provide ;
> While Christ is rich, can I be poor?
> What can I want beside ? "

My precious text is one which, years ago, when we built the Orphanage, I caused to be cut on one of the pillars of the entrance. You will notice it inside the first columns on either side whenever you go there. " My God shall supply all your need according to his riches in glory by Christ Jesus." This I took for the foundation of the Institution, and set my seal to it as true. And it has been so. Time would fail me if I were to tell how often God has interposed there for his numerous family —those children that are cast upon the divine Fatherhood. He has honoured his own promise and our faith, and I believe he always will. There on the forefront of the Orphanage stands also the word—"The Lord will provide." You shall see whether it be not so. As long as that place stands my God shall supply our need, and it shall be a standing encouragement to us all. Think of the far more extensive orphanage of our brother Müller, of Bristol, with those two thousand five hundred children living simply through prayer and faith, and yet as abundantly supplied as the Queen in her palace. Nothing is wanting where God is the Provider. The Lord will supply without fail; let us trust without fear. Go and plead this promise with the Lord your God and he will fulfil it to you as well as to the rest of his saints.

III. Now, thirdly, let us enquire IN WHAT STYLE WILL GOD SUPPLY HIS PEOPLE'S NEEDS ?

He will do it in such style *as becomes his wealth—" according to his riches."* There are several ways of doing most things. There is more than one way of giving a penny to a beggar. You can throw it at him, if you like; or pitch it in the mud as if you threw a bone to a dog; or you may hand it to him in a sort of huff as if you said, "Take it, and be off with you;" or you may drag the coin out of your pocket as unwillingly as if you were losing your eye-tooth. There is yet another way of doing it, namely that which makes the copper turn to gold, by a courteous kindness which expresses sympathy with the poor creature's need. Always give good things in the best way; for your heavenly Father does so.

Now, how does God supply his children? Stingily, miserably, grudging them every pennyworth? Certainly not! I hope that it was never your misery to dine with a grudging man who watched every mouthful that went down your throat as if there was so much the less for him. Why, when one does eat, at whatever table it may be, if it is the commonest fare, one likes a welcome. It is the welcome which makes the covenant invitation so sweet, when you hear the exhortation, "Eat, O friends; drink, yea, drink abundantly, O beloved." One enjoys the welcome of a heart which does all it can: like the Scotchwoman at a great communion meeting when there was nobody to take the people in,—" Come in," said she : "come in; I have room for ten of you in my house, and I have room for ten thousand of you in my heart. Come along with you. Nobody so welcome as you that have been sitting at my Master's table with me." How then does God dispense his favours? How does he fill up the vessels? The way he does it is not according to our poverty, nor according to our desert, "but according to his riches." He gives like a king. Brethren, I must correct myself :—he gives as a God, and as only God can give, according to his own Godlike riches.

Nay, that is not all. He will do it in a style *consistent with his present glory.* It is " according to his riches *in glory,*" which means that, as rich as God is in glory so rich is he in giving. He never demeans himself in the mercies that he gives. He gives according to his rank, and that is the highest conceivable. He gives *so as to bring him new glory.* I never heard of one of his children receiving a great blessing from him, and then saying that it did not glorify God to bestow it. No, no. The more he gives the more glorious he is in the eyes of men ; and he delights to give, that his glory may be seen, and that the riches of his manifested glory may be increased. Withholding would not enrich the Lord of heaven; rather would it impoverish him in glory. But giving enriches him with more revealed glory, and he therefore delights to scatter his bounty.

The fact is, brethren, *God gives gloriously.* The calculations of God —did you ever think of them? Well, let me say that he always calculates so as to leave something to spare, by which to illustrate the infinity of his goodness. I know that it is so. He does not give us just as much light as our eyes can take in, but he floods the world with splendour till we shade our eyes amidst the blaze of noon. After this fashion did his only-begotten Son feed the thousands when he multiplied bread and fish for them to eat. We read that "they did all eat"; no doubt they were hungry enough to do a great deal of that sort of labour. So far so good : but it is added "and were filled." It takes a good deal to fill men who have come a long way into the country and have had nothing to eat for a whole day. But they *were* filled, fainting and famished though they had been. Yes ; but do not stop there :—" And they took up of the fragments twelve baskets full." The Lord always has baskets full of leavings remaining for the waiters. He will be sure to fill all your needs till you have no other need remaining, and have provision on hand for needs not yet arrived. Will the day ever come when we shall say, " Bring yet another need for God to fill," and the answer will be, ' I have no more needs " ? Then the oil of grace will stay ; but it never will till then. Nay, according to what I have said, it will not stop then, but it will go on flowing and flowing, and flowing and flowing, world without end, " according to his riches in glory by Christ Jesus."

The Lord will give enough, enough for all time, enough *of* all, enough *for* all, and more than enough. There shall be no real need of any believer but what the Lord will fill it full, and exceed it. It is a wonderful expression " filled with all the fulness of God ;" it pictures our being in God and God in us. One has illustrated it by taking a bottle, holding it in the sea, and getting it right full,—there is the sea in the bottle. Now, throw it right into the waves, and let it sink, and you have the sea in the bottle and the bottle in the sea. So God enters into us, and as we cannot hold more, he makes us enter into himself. Into the very fulness of Christ are we plunged. What more can the amplest imagination conceive, or the hungriest heart desire? Thus God will supply our needs. Well may you fill others, who are yourselves so filled by God. Well may you serve his cause with boundless generosity when the infinite liberality of God is thus ensured to you.

IV.   Lastly, let us notice BY WHAT MEANS THE LORD FILLS OUR NEEDS? It is " by Christ Jesus." Does God supply all his people's needs by Christ Jesus ?

Yes, first, *by giving them Christ Jesus,* for there is everything in Christ Jesus. Christ is all. The man who has Christ has all things, as saith the apostle, " All things are yours; for ye are Christ's ; and Christ is God's." You will never have a spiritual want which is not supplied in Christ. If you need courage, he can create it. If you need patience, he can teach it. If you need love, he can inspire it? You want washing, but there is the fountain. You require a garment, but there is the robe of righteousness. You would have great wants if you went to heaven without Christ, but you shall not go there without him : even there he shall supply you with everything. He it is that prepares your mansion, provides your wedding-dress, leads you to his throne, and bids you sit there with him for ever. God will supply your eternal needs by giving you Christ.

Moreover, all things shall come to you *by virtue of Christ's merit.* You deserve no good thing, but he deserves it and he says, " Set it to my poor servant's account." You may use Christ's name at the Bank of Heaven freely, for though God might not give his favour to you, he will always give it to his dear, dying, risen, pleading Son. When Jesus' name is quoted all things are yielded by the Father. God will give you all things by Christ: therefore do not go to anybody else after those things. If you have begun in the Spirit do not attempt to be perfected by the flesh. If your only hope is in what Christ has done, stick to that, and add nothing to it. Be this your motto:—

"None but Jesus! None but Jesus!"

Jesus is our all. We are complete in him. We need no *addenda* to the volume of his love. Christ, and Christ alone, shall supply all your need —all your fresh springs are in him. "It pleased the Father that in him should all fulness dwell; and of his fulness have all we received, and grace for grace."

Now, once more, I would to God that some poor soul here that has no faith—that has no good thing about him—would, nevertheless, look over his house and see whether he has not an empty vessel somewhere. All that Christ wants of you, poor sinner, is that you should be empty and come and let him fill you with his grace. Come along with you, just as you are! Bring no good works, no prayers, no anything : but come with all your sins, and follies, and failures, which you may look upon as so many empty pots. Come to Jesus for everything. "But I have scarce a sense of need," say you. Come to him for that too. You must be very needy to be in want of *that*. Come and get it of him. I tell you, soul, you do not want a half-farthing's worth of your own ; for what you think you have will only keep you back from Jesus. Come in all your poverty—a beggar, a king of beggars, come and be made rich by Jesus. You that have not a rag to cover your sin with ; you that are only fit to be put into the devil's dust bin, and thrown away as worthless: come along with you! My Lord Jesus is ready to receive those that Satan himself flings away. If you are such that you cannot find anything in yourself that is desirable, and even your old companions who once cheered you on now think you too mean for them ; yet come into my Master's company, for "this man receiveth sinners." Come with your beggary and bankruptcy : you cannot dig, but to beg be not ashamed, for "My God will supply all your need according to his riches in glory by Christ Jesus."

As for you that have not trusted my Lord, and boast that you can do very well without him, I suppose I must leave you to fight your own way. You declare that you will carry on your own business, and will not be dependent upon God, nor fall into any fanatical ideas, as you are pleased to call them. *But we shall see.* Already we see that the youths do faint and are wearied, and the young men utterly fall. We see that the young lions do lack and suffer hunger, and also that the best-laid plans of wisest men go oft awry, and they that have felt assured that they could fight their own way—even they have come to terrible failure. We shall see how you fare. They that mount up with wings as eagles and are proud and vainglorious, even these go down to destruction so that no flesh hath whereof to glory. As for me, let me wait upon the Lord

God and live by faith in him.   Is it not better to drink of life out of the deep, inexhaustible fulness of God than to go for ever pumping and pumping at your own shallow cisterns which hold no water ?   Self-reliance may be well enough, but God-reliance eclipses it as the sun outshines the stars.   " Oh, rest in the Lord, and wait patiently for him."   " Trust in the Lord, and do good : so shalt thou dwell in the land, and verily thou shalt be fed."   " He shall cover thee with his feathers, and under his wings shalt thou trust : his truth shall be thy shield and buckler."   There is a God, and those who love him and trust him and serve him know that he is a good Master.   Job was slandered by the devil when he came and said, " Does Job serve God for nought ? "   He insinuated that Job made a good thing out of his religion and was moved by selfish motives.   It was a great falsehood, and yet, in a certain sense, it is true.   If anybody says the same of you, admit that it is true ; own that you do make a fine thing out of your religion. God will not let you serve him for nought ; you shall never have to ask the question " What profit is there if we serve God ? "   You shall have his peace, his love, his joy, his supplies, according to his riches in glory by Christ Jesus.   You shall know that in keeping his commandments there is great reward.

Believer, you shall have everything through Christ and nothing without him.   He that trusts not the Saviour, and prays not to him, shall be like Gideon's fleece—when all around it was wet the fleece was dry ; but the man who trusts God and blesses his name shall be like Gideon's fleece, when all around was dry it was full of moisture.   God will not hear a man's prayers except through Christ Jesus, but if that name be mentioned the gates of heaven fly open.   God withholds no real good from the man of God who is in Christ.   But our plea must be Jesus first, and Jesus last, and Jesus in the midst.   We must present the bleeding Lamb before God each morning and each night.   I pray you seek no mercy of God apart from Christ, but lay hold upon God in Christ ; and you have enough for all your need.   May God the Holy Spirit cause you to abide in Christ Jesus for his name's sake.   Amen.

PORTIONS OF SCRIPTURE READ BEFORE SERMON—2 Kings iv. 1—7 ; and Philippians iv.

HYMNS FROM " OUR OWN HYMN BOOK "—84 (Song II.), 23 (First Version), 708.

OTHER SHEEP AND ONE FLOCK.

A Sermon

DELIVERED ON LORD'S-DAY MORNING, MARCH 25TH, 1883, BY

C. H. SPURGEON,

AT THE METROPOLITAN TABERNACLE, NEWINGTON.

"And other sheep I have, which are not of this fold: them also I must bring, and they shall hear my voice; and they shall be one fold, and one shepherd (or more correctly, one *flock*, one shepherd)."—John x. 16.

THIS verse is guarded before and behind by two notable statements. Before it we hear the Master say, "I lay down my life for the sheep," and immediately after it we meet with another grand sentence, "I lay down my life, that I might take it again." The first statement, "*I lay down my life for the sheep*" is the sheet anchor of our confidence when storms assail the vessel of the church. The Lord Jesus has by his death proved his love to his people; and his determination to save them is made clear by his laying down his life for them; therefore doubt and fear should be banished and the very name of despair should be unknown among the Israel of God. Now are we sure of the love of the Son of God to his chosen flock, for we have an infallible proof of it in the laying down of his life for them. Now also are we absolutely certain that Christ's purpose is perpetual: it cannot alter; the Lord Jesus has committed himself to that purpose beyond recall, for the price is paid and the deed is done by which the purpose is to be effected. Beyond this we are hereby assured beyond a shadow of a doubt that the divine purpose will be carried out, for it cannot be that Christ should die in vain. We think it a kind of blasphemy to suppose that his blood should be spilt for naught. Whatever was proposed to be accomplished by the laying down of the life of the Son of God, we feel absolutely certain that it will be fully performed in the teeth of all adversaries; for we are not now speaking of man's design, but of the purpose of God, to which he devoted the heart's blood of his only-begotten Son. We both patiently hope and quietly wait to see the salvation of God, and the performance of all his designs of love; for that death upon the cross is a cause which will surely produce its effect. Christ did not die at a peradventure. The supposition of a Saviour disappointed in the results of his blood-shedding is not to be tolerated for a moment. In darkest times that glorious cross flames with light. No evil event can prevent its efficacy. Still in that sign we conquer. If Jesus has laid down his life for the sheep, then all is well. Rest assured of the Father's love to those sheep; rest assured of the immutability of the **Divine** purpose concerning them, and rest assured of its ultimate achievement. It must not, shall not be that God's own Son shall lay down his life in vain.   Though heaven and earth should pass away, the precious heart's blood of the Son of God shall accomplish the end for which it was so freely poured forth.   Jesus says, " I lay down my life for the sheep," therefore the sheep must live who have been redeemed at such a price as this, and the Shepherd in them shall see of the travail of his soul and shall be satisfied.   So far we are cheered by the vanguard which marches in advance of our text.

But as if the poor, timid people of God would, nevertheless, at times fancy that the purpose of Christ would not be achieved, behold in the rear another sentence, " *I lay down my life that I might take it again.*"   He that died, and so redeemed his people by price, lives that he may himself personally see that they are also redeemed by power. If a man dies to achieve a purpose, you feel sure that his very soul must have been in it : but if that man should rise again from the dead, and still pursue his purpose you would see how resolutely he was set on his design.   If he rose with greater power, clothed with higher rank, and elevated to a more eminent position, and if he still pursued his great object, you would then be more than certain of his never-ending determination to perform his design.   In the risen life of Jesus assurance is made doubly sure : now are we sure that his design must be carried out, nothing can hinder it.   We dare not dream that the Son of God can be disappointed of the object for which he died, and for which he lives again.   If Jesus died for a purpose he will accomplish it ; if Jesus rose for a purpose, he will accomplish it ; if Jesus lives for ever for a purpose, he will accomplish it.   To me this conclusion seems to be past question : and if it be so, it puts the destiny of the sheep beyond all hazard.   Did not Paul argue much in the same way when he said, " For if, when we were enemies, we were reconciled to God by the death of his Son, much more, being reconciled, we shall be saved by his life " ?

If any of you have been cast down by reason of present difficulties, let these two grand texts sound their silver trumpets in your ears.   If you have been looking forth from the windows, and the outlook has seemed to be exceeding dark, take courage, I pray you, from what your Lord has done : his death and resurrection are prophetic of good things to come.   You dare not think that Christ will miss the end of his death : you dare not think that he will miss the purpose of his glory-life : why, then, are you cast down ?   His will shall be done on earth as it is in heaven, as surely as he came from heaven to earth, and has returned from earth to heaven.   His purpose shall be carried out as surely as he died and lives again.   Is not this the secret reason why, when the Lord appeared to his sorrowing servant John, he said to him, " I am he that liveth and was dead and am alive for evermore, amen, and have the keys of death and of hell " ?   Is not the dying and then living Shepherd the safety and the glory of the flock ?   Wherefore comfort one another with these words of your Lord, " I lay down my life for the sheep"; " I lay down my life, that I might take it again."

I.   There are four things in the text itself which **deserve your** attention, for they are full of consolation to minds troubled by the evils of these perilous times. The first is this,—OUR LORD JESUS CHRIST HAD A PEOPLE UNDER THE WORST CIRCUMSTANCES. When he speaks of "other sheep," it is implied that he had certain sheep at the time; and when he says "other sheep have I which are not of this fold," it is manifest that even then the Good Shepherd had a fold. The times were grievously dark and evil, but a few true hearts clustered about the Saviour and by his divine power were protected as in a "fold." It has been supposed that our Lord here alludes to the Jews as "this fold"; but the Jews, as such, were never Christ's fold. He could not have meant to call the Jews around him his fold, for a little further on he exclaims, "Ye believe not, because ye are not of my sheep, as I said unto you." His fold were that little handful of disciples whom by his personal ministry he had gathered, and who stood folded, as it were, about their Good Shepherd. They might be sneered at as a little company, but he saith to his enemies who are standing outside the fold foaming with wrath, "Other sheep I have that are not of this little fold: these you cannot see, but I have them none the less for that; these I must in due time lead, and then there shall be one flock and one Shepherd."

See, then, that the Lord Jesus had a people in the worst times. Doubtless these days are exceedingly dangerous, and I have certain brethren round me who never allow me to forget it, for they play well in the minor key, and dwell most judiciously upon the necessary topic of the general declension of the church and the growing depravity of the world. I would not stop them from their faithful warnings, although I can assure them that, with slight variations, I have heard the same tune for years. Many a time have they afflicted me from my youth up, and it has been good for me. I recollect hearing some thirty years ago that we lived in awful times; and, as nearly as I can recollect, the times have been awful ever since; and I suppose they always will be. The watchmen of the night see everything except the coming of the morning. Our pilots perceive dangers ahead and steer with caution. Perhaps this is as it should be; at any rate, it is better than sleeping in a fool's paradise. Be this as it may, it is clear that the days of our Lord Jesus Christ were emphatically terrible times. No age can be worse than that age which literally crucified the Son of God, crying, "Away with him! Away with him!" Whether the present days are better than those I will not determine, but they cannot be worse. The day of our Lord's first advent was the culmination and the crisis of the world's career of sin; and yet the Good Shepherd had a fold among men in the midnight of history.

There was *a sad lack of vital godliness* in those days. A few godly ones watched for the coming of the Messiah; but they were very few, such as good old Simeon and Anna. A small remnant sighed and cried for the abounding sin of the nation; but the salt was almost gone: Israel was becoming like Sodom and Gomorrah. The choice band of mourners in Zion had not quite died out, but their number was so few that a child might write them. Speaking generally, when the Saviour came to his own, his own received him not. The mass of professing people in that day was rotten throughout; the life of God was gone; it

could not dwell with the Pharisees nor the Sadducees, nor any of the
sects of the times, for they were altogether gone out of the way. The
Lord looked, and there was no man to help or to uphold his righteous
cause : those who professed to be its champions had altogether become
unprofitable. As for the religious teachers, their mouth was become an
open sepulchre, and the poison of asps was under their tongues: and
yet the Lord had a people in Judea even then. On earth there was
still a fold for sheep whom he had chosen who knew the Shepherd's
voice and gathered to his call and followed him faithfully.

It was a time when *will-worship abounded.* Men had given up worshipping God according to the Scriptures, and they worshipped according to their own fancies. Then you might hear the trumpet in every
corner of the street, for Pharisees were distributing their alms. You could
see fathers and mothers neglected, and families broken up because the
scribes had taught the people that if they should say " Corban " they
were free from all obligation to help father or mother. They taught for
doctrines the commandments of men, and the commandments of God
were laid on one side. To wear broad-bordered garments and phylacteries was exalted into a matter of first importance ; while to lie and
cheat were mere trifles. To eat with unwashen hands was thought to
be a crime, but to devour widow's houses was a thing which to the
most self-righteous Pharisee caused no qualm of conscience. The land
was filled with will-worship, and that is one great and growing hindrance nowadays ; but for all that Christ had a fold of his own, and in
it were those who knew his voice, and these, following at his heel, were
enabled to go in and out and find pasture.

It was a day when there was the most *fierce opposition* to the real
truth of God. Our Lord Jesus could hardly open his mouth but they
took up stones to stone him. It was said that he had a devil and was
mad ; and that he was a " gluttonous man and a wine bibber, the friend
of publicans and sinners." The rage of men against Christ was then
boiling at its greatest heat, till at last they took him and nailed him to
the cross because they could not endure that he should live among them.
And yet he had his own in those dreadful times : even then he had his
chosen company for whom he laid down his life, of whom he said to
the Father, "Thine they were, and thou gavest them me ; and they have
kept thy word." To those he spake saying " Ye are they that have
continued with me in my temptations. And I appoint unto you a
kingdom, as my Father hath appointed unto me." Wherefore, beloved, I
gather that though at this time there is a sad decline in vital godliness,
and though will worship sweeps over the land with its tumultuous
waves, and though opposition to the pure truth of Christ is more fierce
than ever ; nevertheless even at this present time there is a remnant
according to the election of grace. Even to-day the answer of God
saith to the complaining prophet, " Yet have I left me seven thousand
in Israel, all the knees which have not bowed unto Baal." Wherefore,
my brethren, in confidence possess ye your souls.

Now, it is to be noticed that this little company of Christ's people he
calls a " fold." Afterwards they were to be a " flock," but while his
bodily presence was with them they were pre-eminently a " fold." They
were few in number, all of one race, mostly in one place, and so

compact that they could fitly be said to be a fold. One glance of the
Shepherd's bodily eye saw them all. Happily, also, they were so
thoroughly distinct from the rest of the world that they were eminently
and evidently folded. Our Lord said of them, "Ye are not of the
world, even as I am not of the world." He had shut them in to himself,
and shut the world out. Within this blessed seclusion they were
perfectly safe, so that their Lord said to the Father, "While I was with
them in the world, I kept them in thy name: those that thou gavest
me I have kept, and none of them is lost, but the son of perdition; that
the scripture might be fulfilled." Whatever their mistakes and faults,
and they were many, yet they did not conform themselves to the
generation among which they dwelt, but they were kept apart as in a
fold while Jesus was with them. In that fold they were protected
from all ill weathers, and from the wolf, and the thief. The Lord's
presence with them was like a wall of fire round about them: they had
only to run to him and he answered all their adversaries, and defended
them from reproach. Like another David, the Lord Jesus guarded his
flock from all the ravening lions that sought to devour them. True,
even in that little fold there were goats, for he himself said, "I have
chosen you twelve, and one of you is a devil." Even then they were
not absolutely pure, but they were wonderfully so ; and they were
marvellously separated from the world, preserved from false doctrine,
and kept from dividing and scattering. Within that fold they were
being strengthened for the future following of their great Shepherd.
They were learning a thousand things which would be useful to
them when afterwards he sent them forth as lambs among wolves;
so that they would be "wise as serpents and harmless as doves,"
because of what they had learned of their Lord. Thus you see that in
the worst times the Lord had a church, I might almost say the best
church. May I not call it so ? for that apostolic church upon which the
Holy Ghost descended was not a whit behind the church of any era that
succeeded it. It was the choice flock of all the flocks of the ages, even
that feeble company of which Jesus said, " Fear not, little little flock ; for
it is your Father's good pleasure to give you the kingdom."

Yet you see one thing is notable here, that when Jesus had thus shut
them all in he would not allow them to become exclusive and glide into a
state of selfish satisfaction. No, he opens wide the door of the sheepfold and cries to them, "Other sheep I have." Thus he checks a
tendency so common in the church to be forgetful of those outside the
fold, and to make one's own personal salvation the sum and substance
of religion. I do not think it wrong to sing—

> "We are a garden wall'd around,
>   Chosen, and made peculiar ground ;
>   A little spot, enclosed by grace
>   Out of the world's wide wilderness."

On the contrary, I judge that the verse is true, and sweet, and ought to
be sung ; but then there are other truths besides this one. To us also
the Shepherd opens the door of the enclosed garden and says, "The
wilderness and the solitary place shall be glad for them, and the desert
shall rejoice and blossom as the rose." The fold is our abode, but it is

not our sole sphere of action; for we are to go forth of it into all the world seeking our brethren. Seeing that our Lord has other sheep which are not of this fold, and these are to be found by him through his faithful people, let us arouse ourselves to the holy enterprise.

> "O, come, let us go and find them
> In the paths of death they roam;
> At the close of the day 'twill be sweet to say,
> 'I have brought some lost one home.'"

Beloved, I shall leave this point when I have said to you,—never despair! The Lord of hosts is with his people. They may be few and poor, but they are Christ's, and that makes them precious. A common sheepfold is not a thing of glory and beauty, four rough walls compose it, and it is but a hovel for sheep; even so the church may appear mean and base in men's eyes; but then it is the sheepfold of the Shepherd-King, and the sheep belong to the Lord God Almighty. There is a glory about this which angels do not fail to see. Here is human weakness, but also divine power. We do not, I fear, estimate the strength of a church aright. I read of three brethren who had to carry on a college when funds were running short. One of them complained that they had no helpers, and could not hope to succeed; but another who had more faith said to his brother, "Do you ask what we can do? Do you say that we are so few? I do not see that we are few; for we are a thousand at the least." "A thousand of us!" said the other, "how is that?" "Why," replied the first, "I am a cipher, and you are a cipher, and our brother is a cipher; so we have three noughts to begin with. Then I am sure the Lord Jesus is ONE: put him down before the three ciphers and we have a thousand directly." Was not this bravely spoken? What power we have when we do but set the great ONE in the front. You are nothing, brother; you are nothing, sister; I am nothing; we are all nothing when we are put together without our Lord: but, oh, if he stands in front of us then we are thousands; and again is it true on earth as in heaven, the chariots of the Lord are twenty thousand, even thousands of messengers, the Lord is among them as in the holy place. Wherefore, my friends, be ye not cast down at any time, but say unto yourselves—We are not even now come to so dark a night as once fell on this world. We are not at this painful moment in such a desperate condition as the church of Christ was in his own day; and if the Lord be spiritually in the midst of us we need not fear though the earth be removed, and the mountains be carried into the midst of the sea, for there is a city which abides for ever, and there is a river the streams whereof shall for ever make her glad. God is in the midst of her, she shall not be moved; God shall help her, and that right early. Wherefore, my fellow-believers, be ye strong and of good courage!

II. But now, secondly, it is clear, for the text teaches it in so many words, that OUR LORD HATH OTHER SHEEP NOT YET KNOWN TO US. He says, "Other sheep I have." I want you to notice that strong expression, "Other sheep *I have*,"—not "I shall have," but "I have other sheep." Many of these sheep were not even in the thoughts of the apostles. I do not think it had crossed the mind of Peter, James, or John that their Lord had any sheep in this poor savage island, then scarcely regarded as being within the borders of the earth. I do not suppose the apostles at that time even dreamed that their Lord Jesus had sheep in Rome. No, their most liberal notion was that the Hebrew nation might be converted, and the scattered of the seed of Abraham gathered together in one. Our Shepherd-King has greater thoughts than the most large-hearted of his servants. He delights to enlarge the area of our love. "Other sheep have I." You do not know them, but the Shepherd does. Unknown to ministers, unknown to the warmest-hearted Christians, there are many in the world whom Jesus claims for his own through the covenant of grace.

Who are these? Well, these "other sheep" were, first, *his chosen;* for he has a people whom he has chosen out of the world, and ordained unto eternal life. "Ye have not chosen me," said he, "but I have chosen you,"—there is a people upon whom his sovereignty has fixed its loving choice from before the foundation of the world. And of these elect ones he says, "I have them." His election of them is the basis of his property in them. These are also *those whom his Father gave him,* of whom he says in another place, "All that the Father giveth me shall come to me": and again, "Of those whom thou hast given me I have lost none." His Father's eternal donation of them seals his title to them. These are the people for whom he peculiarly and especially laid down his life, that they might be *the redeemed of the Lord.* "Christ loved his church, and gave himself for it." These are they that are redeemed from among men, of whom we read, "Ye are not your own, ye are bought with a price." The Lord Jesus laid down his life for his sheep: he tells us so himself, and none can question his own statement. These are those of whom Jesus says "I have them," for on account of these he entered into *suretiship engagements,* even as Jacob undertook the flock of Laban and watched day and night that he should not lose them, and if one had been torn, he would have had to make it good. These sheep represent a people for whom Christ hath entered into suretiship engagements with his Father that he will deliver each one of them safely at the last day of account, not one of them being absent when the sheep shall pass again under the hand of him that telleth them as they will at the last great day. "Other sheep I have," says Christ. How wonderful that he should say, "I have them," though as yet they were far off by wicked works.

What was their state? They were a people without shepherd, without fold, without pasture, lost on the mountains, wandering in the woods, lying down to die, ready to be devoured by the wolf; yet Jesus says, "Other sheep I have, which are not of this fold." They were sheep that had wandered exceeding far, even into the most shameful iniquity, and yet he says, "I have them." Bad as this world is to-day, it must have been far worse in the cruel Roman age as to open vices and unmentionable abominations; and yet these wanderers were the sheep of Christ, and in due time they were delivered from their sins, and fetched away from all the superstition and idolatry and filthiness into which they had wandered. They were Christ's even while they were afar off; he had chosen them, the Father had given them to him, he had bought them, and he determined to have them; nay, he saith, "I have them," and he calls them his own even while they are transgressing and running headlong to destruction.

It seems to me that these were as well known to Christ as those that were in his fold. I think I see him, the Divine Man, standing there confronting his adversaries, and when he has cast his glance upon his foes, I see his eyes going to and fro throughout the whole earth to gaze upon a sight far more pleasant to him. While he speaks his eyes flash with joyous fire as they light upon thousands out of every kindred and people and tongue, and while he quotes to himself the words of the twenty-second Psalm : "All the ends of the world shall remember and turn unto the Lord : and all the kindreds of the nations shall worship before thee. For the kingdom is the Lord's : and he is the governor among the nations. A seed shall serve him; it shall be accounted to the Lord for a generation." He spies out the myriads that are his, and he rejoices before his scornful foes as he sees his growing kingdom which they are powerless to overthrow. Proud, self-righteous men may blindly refuse the leadership of the Lord's anointed Shepherd, but he shall not be without a flock to be his honour and reward. Did not the Lord at that time rejoice in his inmost heart and soliloquize within himself thus—"Though Israel be not gathered, yet shall I be glorious in the eyes of the Lord, and my God shall be my strength"? This led him to say, "Other sheep I have."

In this there is great comfort for God's people who love the souls of their fellow-men. The Lord has a people in London, and he knows them. "I have much people in this city," was said to the apostle when as yet nobody was converted there. "I have them," says Christ; though as yet they had not sought him. Our Lord Jesus has an elect redeemed people all over the world at this time, though as yet they are not called by grace. I know not where they are, nor where they are not; but for certain he has them somewhere, since still it stands true, "Other sheep I have which are not of this fold." This is a part of our authority for going out to find the lost sheep; for we brethren have a right to go anywhere to ask after our Master's sheep. I have no business to go hunting after other people's sheep; but if they are my Master's sheep who shall stop me over hill or dale enquiring, "Have you seen my Master's sheep?" If any say, "You do intrude in this land," let the answer be, "We are after our Master's sheep which have strayed here!" "Excuse our pushing further than politeness might allow, we are in haste to find a lost sheep." This is your excuse for going into a house where you are not wanted, to try and leave your tract and speak a word for Christ: say, "I think my Master has one of his sheep here, and I am come after it." You have received a search-warrant from the King of kings, and therefore you have a right to enter and search after your Lord's stolen property. If men belonged to the devil we would not rob the enemy himself; but they do not belong to him; he neither made them nor bought them, and therefore we seize them in the King's name whenever we can lay hands on them. I doubt not but what there are some here this morning who neither know nor love the Saviour as yet, who nevertheless belong to the Redeemer, and he will yet bring them to himself and to his flock. Therefore it is that we preach with confidence. I do not come into this pulpit hoping that peradventure somebody will of his own free will return to Christ; that may be so or not, but my hope lies in another quarter; I hope that my Master will lay hold of some of them and say, "You are mine, and you shall be mine; I claim you for myself." My hope arises from the freeness of grace, and not from the freedom of the will. A poor haul of fish will any gospel fisherman make if he takes none but those who are eager to leap into the net. Oh, for an hour of Jesus among this crowd! Oh, for five minutes of the great Shepherd's handiwork! When the good Shepherd overtakes his lost sheep he has not much to say to it. According to the parable he says nothing, but he lays hold of it, lays it on his shoulders and carries it home, and that is what I want the Lord to do this morning with some of you whose will is all the other way, whose wishes and desires are all contrary to him. I want him to come with sacred violence and mighty love to restore you to your Father and your God. Not that you will be saved against your will, but your consent will be sweetly gained. Oh, that the Lord Jesus would take you in hand and never let you go again. May he sweetly say to you, "Yea, I have loved thee with an everlasting love, therefore with lovingkindness have I drawn thee."

III. Our third head contains in it much delight. OUR LORD MUST BRING OR LEAD THOSE OTHER SHEEP. "Them also I must bring"— read it, and it will be more accurate, "them also I must lead:" Christ must be at the head of these other sheep, and they must follow his lead —"them also I must lead, and they shall hear my voice." Those who belong to Christ secretly must be openly led to follow him.

First, it is Christ that has to do it, even as he has done it hitherto. The text says, "Them *also* I must bring," and this language implies that those who have already come he has brought. All that were in the fold Christ had brought there, and all that are to be in the fold he must lead there. All of us who are saved have been saved by the mighty power of God in Christ Jesus. Is it not so? Is there anyone among us that came to Jesus without Jesus first coming to him? Surely, no. Without exception we all admit that it was his love that sought us out and brought us to be the sheep of his pasture. Now, as the Lord Jesus has done this for us he must do it for others; for they will never come except he fetch them.

Here comes in that emphatic, imperious "*must.*" The proverb is that "must" is for the king, and the king may say "must" to all of us: but did you ever hear of a "must" that bound the king himself and constrained him? Kings generally do not care to have it said to them you "must;" but there is a king, the like of which king there never was nor shall be for glory and for dominion, and yet he is bound by a "*must*"—the Prince Immanuel saith, "them also I *must* bring." Whenever Jesus says "*must*" something comes of it. Who can resist the omnipotent *must?* Clear out, devils! Clear out, wicked men! Flee, darkness! Die, O death! If Jesus says "*must*" we know what is going to happen: difficulties vanish, impossibilities are achieved. Glory, glory, the Lord shall get the victory! Jesus says of his chosen, his redeemed, his espoused, his covenanted ones, "Them also I *must* bring," and therefore it must be done.

Furthermore, he tells us how he must do it. He says, "They shall hear my voice." So that our Lord is going to save people still by the gospel. I do not look for any other means of converting men beyond the simple preaching of the gospel and the opening of men's ears to hear it—" They shall hear my voice." The old methods are to be followed to the end of the chapter. Our standing orders are,—" Go ye into all the world, and preach the gospel to every creature." We are not commissioned to do anything else but continue to preach the gospel, the selfsame gospel which saved us and which was delivered to us at the beginning. We know of no alterations, enlargements, or amendments to the gospel. We obey and follow one voice, not many voices. One gospel of salvation is to be proclaimed everywhere, and no other work is in our commission.

Then it is added, " They shall hear my voice." It is promised that they shall first lend an attentive ear and then that they shall yield a willing heart to the voice of divine love, and follow Jesus where he leads. "What then," saith one; " suppose I speak in Christ's name, and they will not hear ? " Do not suppose what cannot be! The Scripture says of the chosen sheep,—" they shall hear my voice." The rest remain in their blindness, but the redeemed will hear and see. Do not again say, " Suppose they will not! " You must not suppose anything that is contrary to what Jesus promises when he says, " They shall hear my voice." The graceless may stop their ears if they will, and perish with Christ's voice as a witness against them, but his own redeemed shall hear the heavenly voice and obey it. There is no resisting this divine necessity: Jesus says—" I *must* bring them, and they *shall* hear my voice." It was with this that Paul turned to the Gentiles, and said to the Jews, " Be it known therefore unto you, that the salvation of God is sent unto the Gentiles, and that they will hear it.". He had no fear about the reception the word would meet with ; neither ought we to entertain any, since Christ has a people who must be led, and shall hear the voice of the Bishop and Shepherd of souls.

We have heard it said that " If Christ *must* have his people, what is the good of preaching ? " What would be the good of preaching if it were otherwise ? Why, dear sir, this fact is one great reason why we preach. That which you suppose to be a motive for inaction is the strongest motive for energetic movement. Because the Lord has a people that must be saved we feel an imperious necessity laid upon us to join with him in bringing this people to himself. They *must* come, and we *must* fetch them : Christian brethren, do you not feel that you *must* help in compelling them to come to the wedding-feast? Is it not laid upon you that you *must* go after lost souls, that you *must* speak to them, seeing that you *must* have a hand in bringing these blood-bought ones to Christ by his Holy Spirit?

And again, are there not some in this place who feel a necessity laid upon them also that they *must* come ? Do I not hear some of you saying, " I have stood out a long while, but I *must* come; I have resisted divine grace long enough, and now Christ has laid his hand on me, I *must* come." How I wish that a heavenly " must," a blessed necessity of omnipotent decree may overshadow you, and bear you as a sheep to the fold. Oh that you may now yield yourselves unto God because the love of Christ constraineth you. Submit yourselves unto God, owning the supreme authority of his grace, which shall lead every thought into captivity, that henceforth Christ may reign in your hearts, and put every enemy under his feet. He saith, " Him that cometh to me I will in nowise cast out." "I will trust him," saith one; "I feel I must." Just so; and that trust is a mark of your election of God, for "He that believeth in him hath everlasting life." "Whom he did predestinate them he also called." If he is calling you it is because he did predestinate you; and you may rest quite sure of it, and yield to him with holy joy and delight. As for me, I feel so happy in preaching the gospel, because I am not fishing with a "chance" and a "perhaps" that some may come. The Lord knoweth them that are his, and they shall come. Every congregation is, in this sense, a picked assembly. I felt this morning when I came here that there were so many friends out in the country for the holidays that we should very likely have a thin house. I rejoice that I was altogether out in my reckoning, but even then I thought, God has a people that he will bring whom he means to bless. Here they are, and now while standing here I know that God's word "shall not return to him void, but it shall accomplish that which he pleases, and shall prosper in the thing whereto he hath sent it."

IV. But now, lastly, OUR LORD GUARANTEES THE UNITY OF HIS CHURCH. "Them also I must bring, and they shall hear my voice; and there shall be one fold and one shepherd." We hear a great deal about the unity of the church, and notions upon this subject are rather wild. We are to have the Roman and the Greek and the Anglican church all joined together in one: if they were so, the result would not be worth two-pence; but much evil would come of it. God has, I doubt not, a chosen people amongst all these three great corporations, but the union of such questionable organizations would be a dire omen of mischief to the world: the dark ages, and a worse Popedom than ever, would soon be upon us. The more those three quarrel with each other the better for truth and righteousness. I should like to see the Anglican Church standing at drawn daggers with the Roman, and coming into a more and more open opposition to its superstitions. I would to God that the national church would in all things be delivered from the Pope of Rome and his Antichristian enormities.

Truly, this has been carried out as a matter of fact; there never was but one Shepherd of the sheep yet, even Christ Jesus; and there never was but one flock of God yet, and there never will be. There is one spiritual church of God, and there never were two. All the visible churches up and down the world contain within themselves parts of the one church of Jesus Christ, but there were never two bodies of Christ, and there cannot be. There is one church, and there is one Head of the church: the motto of Christianity is,—one flock and one Shepherd.

As a matter of experience this is carried out in believers. I do not care who the man is, if he is a truly spiritually-minded man he is one with all other spiritually-minded men. Those people in any visible church who have no grace are usually the greatest sticklers for every point of difference and ever particle of rite and form. Nominal professors are soon at war, quickened believers follow after peace Of course, when a man has nothing else but the outside, he fights for it tooth and nail; but a man who loves the Lord, and lives near him, perceives the inner life in others, and has fellowship therewith : that inner life is one in all the quickened family, and compels them to be one in heart.

Set two brethren at prayer, the one a Calvinist and the other an Arminian, and they pray alike. Get a real work of the Spirit in a district and see how Baptists and Pædo-Baptists pull together. Tell out your inward experience and speak of the Spirit's work in the soul, and see how we are all moved thereby. Here is a brother, a member of the Society of Friends, and he likes silent worship; and here is another who enjoys hearty singing; but when they get near to God they do not quarrel over this, but agree to differ: the one says, "The Lord be with you in your holy silence," and the other prays that the Lord may accept his brother's psalm. All who are one with Christ have a certain family feeling, a higher form of clannishness, and they cannot shake it off. I have found myself reading a gracious book which has drawn me near to God, and though I have known that it was written by a man with whose opinions I had little agreement, I have not therefore refused to be edified by him in points which are unquestionably revealed. No, but I have blessed the Lord that, with all his blunders, he knew so much of precious vital truth, and lived so near his Lord. What Protestant can refuse to love the holy Bernard? Was there ever a more consecrated servant of God or a dearer lover of Christ than he? Yet he was most sorrowfully in bondage to the superstitions of his age and of the Romish Church. Are you not all one with him who sang—

> "Jesus, the very thought of thee
> With sweetness fills my breast;
> But sweeter far thy face to see,
> And in Thy presence rest"?

The external church is needful, but it is not *the one and indivisible church of Christ.* Jesus as the life binds his church together, and that life flows through all the regenerate, even as the blood flows through all the veins of the body. Drop the external, and look by faith into the spiritual realm and you will see one flock and one Shepherd.

The practical lesson is, let us belong to that one flock. How are they known? Answer: they are a hearing flock—they hear the Lord and follow his lead. Be you one of those who listen to Christ's voice, and to none besides. Keep to the one Shepherd! How do you know him? It is Jesus: in his feet and hands are nail-prints, and his side bears yet the scar. He it is who leads the one only flock. Follow Jesus and you are right. Follow him everywhere and you are happy. The best way to promote the unity of the church is for all the sheep to follow the Shepherd. If they all follow the Shepherd they will all keep together. Let us go forth and try and do that, and let us long for that happy day when all disputed points shall be settled by all obeying the Lord. Compromises would only mean an agreement to disobey the Lord. Let no man yield a principle under pretence of charity: it is not charity to call falsehood truth. We must follow Jesus fully, and we shall come together. First pure then peaceable is the rule. Oh, when shall the triple banner again float over all,—" *One Lord, one Faith, one Baptism!* " Oh, God the Holy Ghost, forgive us our errors, and bring us to thy truth! Oh, God the Son, forgive us our want of holiness, and renew us in thine own image! Oh, God the Father, forgive us our want of love, and melt us into one family. To the one God be glory, in the one church, for ever and ever. Amen.

Metropolitan Tabernacle Pulpit.

EARNEST EXPOSTULATION.

A Sermon

DELIVERED ON LORD'S-DAY MORNING, APRIL 1ST, 1883, BY

C. H. SPURGEON,

AT THE METROPOLITAN TABERNACLE, NEWINGTON.

"Or despisest thou the riches of his goodness and forbearance and longsuffering; not knowing that the goodness of God leadeth thee to repentance?"—Romans ii. 4.

THE apostle is intensely personal in his address. This verse is not spoken to us all in the mass, but to some one in particular. The apostle fixes his eyes upon a single person, and speaks to him as "Thee" and "Thou." "Despisest *thou* the riches of his goodness and forbearance and long-suffering; not knowing that the goodness of God leadeth *thee* to repentance?" It should ever be the intent of the preacher to convey his message to each hearer in his own separate individuality. It is always a very happy sign when a man begins to think of himself as an individual, and when the expostulations and invitations of the gospel are seen by him to be directed to himself personally. I will give nothing for that indirect, essay-like preaching which is as the sheet lightning of summer, dazzling for the moment, and flaming over a broad expanse, but altogether harmless, since no bolt is launched from it, and its ineffectual fires leave no trace behind. I will give nothing for that kind of hearing which consists in the word being heard by everybody in general, and by no one in particular. It is when the preacher can "Thee" and "Thou" his hearers that he is likely to do them good. When each man is made to say, "This is for me," then the power of God is present in the word. One personal, intentional touch of the hem of Christ's garment conveys more blessing than all the pressure of the crowd that thronged about the Master. The laying of his healing hand upon the individual who was suffering had more virtue in it than all those heavenly addresses which fell from his lips upon minds that did not receive the truth for themselves. I do pray that we may come to personal dealings with the Lord each one for himself, and that the Spirit of God may convince each man and each woman, according as the case may stand before the living God. O my hearer, *thou* art now to be lovingly spoken with: I speak not to *you* as unto many, but unto *thee*, as one by thyself.

Observe that the apostle singled out an individual who had condemned others for transgressions, in which he himself indulged. This

No. 1,714.

man owned so much spiritual light that he knew right from wrong, and he diligently used his knowledge to judge others, condemning them for their transgressions. As for himself, he preferred the shade, where no fierce light might beat on his own conscience and disturb his unholy peace. His judgment was spared the pain of dealing with his home offences by being set to work upon the faults of others. He had a candle, but he did not place it on the table to light his own room; he held it out at the front door to inspect therewith his neighbours who passed by. Ho! my good friend, my sermon is for thee. Paul looks this man in the face and says, " Therefore thou art inexcusable, O man, whoever thou art, that judgest: for wherein thou judgest another thou condemnest thyself; for thou that judgest doest the same things:" and then he pointedly says to him : "Thinkest thou this, O man, that judgest them which do such things, and doest the same, that thou shalt escape the judgment of God ? "   Well did the apostle aim that piercing arrow; it hits the centre of the target and strikes a folly common to mankind. The poet of the night-watches wrote,—

> " All men think all men mortal but themselves."

As truly might I say, " All men think all men guilty but themselves." The punishment which is due to sin the guilty reckon to be surely impending upon others, but they scarce believe that it can ever fall upon themselves. A personal doom for themselves is an idea which they will not harbour : if the dread thought should light upon them they shake it off as men shake snow-flakes from their cloaks. The thought of personal guilt, judgment, and condemnation is inconvenient ; it breeds too much trouble within, and so they refuse it lodging. Vain men go maundering on their way, whispering of peace and safety ; doting as if God had passed an act of amnesty and oblivion for them, and had made for them an exception to all the rules of justice, and all the manner of his courts. Do men indeed believe that they alone shall go unpunished ? No man will subscribe to that notion when it is written down in black and white, and yet the mass of men live as if this were true ; I mean the mass of men who have sufficient light to condemn sin in others. They start back from the fact of their own personal guiltiness and condemnation, and go on in their ungodliness as if there were no great white throne for them, no last assize, no judge, no word of condemnation, and no hell of wrath. Alas, poor madmen, thus to dream ! O Spirit of Truth, save them from this fatal infatuation.

Sin is always on the downward grade, so that when a man proceeds a certain length he inevitably goes beyond it. The person addressed by the apostle first thought to escape judgment, and then he came to think lightly of the goodness, forbearance, and longsuffering of God. He thinks he shall escape in the future, and because of that he despises the present goodness and longsuffering of the Most High. Of course he does. If he does not believe in the terrors of the world to come for himself, he naturally reckons it to be a small thing to have been spared their immediate experience. Barren tree as he is, he does not believe that he will ever be cut down, and therefore he feels no gratitude to the dresser of the vineyard for pleading, " Let it alone yet another year, till I dig about it, and dung it." I wish, as God shall help me, to drive hard at the consciences of men upon this matter. I would be to you, my careless friend, what Jonah was to Nineveh: I would warn you, and bestir you to repentance. Oh that the Holy Ghost would make this sermon effectual for the arousing of every unsaved soul that shall hear or read it!

I. First, let me speak this morning to thee, O unregenerate, impenitent man, concerning THE GOODNESS OF GOD WHICH THOU HAST EXPERIENCED. Thou hast known the goodness, and forbearance, and longsuffering of God. According to the text, "riches" of these have been spent upon unconverted, ungodly men, and upon thee as one of them. Let me speak with thee first, O man, and remind thee how favoured thou hast been of God by being made a partaker of "the riches of his *goodness.*" In many cases this is true of temporal things Men may be without the fear of God, and yet, for all that, God may be pleased to prosper their endeavours in business. They succeed almost beyond their expectation—I mean some of them; probably the description applies to thee. They rise from the lowest position, and accumulate about them the comforts and luxuries of life. Though they have no religion, they have wit, and prudence, and thrift, and so they compete with others, and God permits them to be winners in the race for wealth. Moreover, he allows them to enjoy good health, vigour of mind, and strength of constitution: they are happy in the wife of their youth, and their children are about them. Theirs is an envied lot. Death seems for awhile forbidden to knock at their door, even though he has been ravaging the neighbourhood; even sickness does not molest their household. They are not in trouble as other men, neither are they plagued like other men. Abraham had to prepare a Machpelah, and David mourned over his sons; but these have had to make scant provision for family sepulchre: a hedge has in very deed been set about them and all that they have. I know that it is thus with many who do not love God, and have never yielded to the entreaties of his grace. They love not the hand which enriches them, they praise not the Lord who daily loadeth them with benefits. How is it that men can receive such kindness, and yield no return? O sirs, you are to-day blessed with all that need requires; but I pray you remember that you might have been in the depths of poverty. An illness would have lost you your situation; or a slight turn in trade would have left you bankrupt. You are well to-day; but you might have been tossing to and fro upon a bed of sickness; you might have been in the hospital, about to lose a limb. Shall not God be praised for health and freedom from pain? You might have been shut up in yonder asylum, in the agonies of madness. A thousand ills have been kept from you; you have been exceedingly favoured by the goodness of the Most High. Is it not so? And truly it is a wonderful thing that God should give his bread to those that lift up their heel against him, that he should cause his light to shine upon those who never perceive his goodness therein, that he should multiply his mercies upon ungodly men who only multiply their rebellions against him, and turn the gifts of his love into instruments of transgression.

Furthermore, this goodness of God has not only come to you in a temporal form, O impenitent man, but it has also visited you in a spiritual manner. Myriads of our fellow men have never had an opportunity of knowing Christ. The missionary's foot has never trodden the cities wherein they dwell, and so they die in the dark. Multitudes are going downward, downward; but they do not know the upward road: their minds have never been enlightened by the teachings of God's word, and hence they sin with less grievousness of fault. You are placed in the very focus of Christian light, and yet you follow evil! Will you not think of this? Time was when a man would have to work for years to earn enough money to buy a Bible. There were times when he could not have earned one even with that toil: now the word of God lies upon your table, you have a copy of it in almost every room of your house; is not this a boon from God? This is the land of the open Bible, and the land of the preached word of God: in this you prove the riches of God's goodness. Do you despise this wealth of mercy? Possibly you have enjoyed the further privilege of sitting under a ministry which has been particularly plain and earnest: you have not had sermons preached *before* you, they have been preached *at* you: the minister has seized upon you and tugged at your conscience, as though he would force you to the Saviour. With cries and entreaties you have been invited to your heavenly Father, and yet you have not come. Is this a small thing?

What is more, you have been favoured with a tender conscience. When you do wrong you know it, and smart for it. What mean those wakeful nights after you have yielded to a temptation? What means that miserable feeling of shame? that fever of unrest? You find it hard to stifle the inward monitor, and difficult to resist the Spirit of God. Your road to perdition is made peculiarly hard; do you mean to follow it at all costs, and go over hedge and ditch to hell?

You have not only been aroused by conscience, but the good Spirit has striven with you, and have been almost persuaded to be a Christian. Such has been the blessed work of the Spirit upon your heart that you have at times been melted down, and ready to be moulded by grace. A strange softness has come over you, and if you had not gathered up all your evil strength, and if the devil had not helped you to resist, you had by this time dropped into the Saviour's arms. Oh, the riches of the goodness of God to have thus wooed you, and pressed his love upon you! You have scarcely had a stripe, or a frown, or an ill word from God; his ways have been all kindness, and gentleness, and longsuffering from the first day of your memory even until now. "Despisest thou the riches of his goodness?" O man, answer this, I implore thee.

The apostle then dwells upon the riches of "*forbearance*." Forbearance comes in when men having offended, God withholds the punishment that is due to them; when men, having been invited to mercy, have refused it, and yet God continues to stretch out his hands, and invite them to come to him. Patient endurance of offences and insults has been manifested by God to many of you, who now hear these words of warning. The Lord knows to whom I speak and may he make you, also, know that I am speaking to you, even to you. Some men have gone back to the very sin of which for awhile they repented: they have suffered for their folly, but have turned again to it with suicidal determination. They are desperately set on their own ruin, and nothing can save them. The burnt child has run to the fire again; the singed moth has plunged again into the flame of the candle: who can pity such self-inflicted miseries? They are given over to perdition, for they will not be warned. They have returned to the haunt of vice, though they seemed to have been snatched from the deep ditch of its filthiness. They have wantonly and wilfully returned to their cups, though the poison of former draughts is yet burning in their veins. Yet, despite this folly, God shows forbearance towards them. They have grievously provoked him when they have done despite to his word, and have even turned to laughter the solemnities of his worship, against their own consciences, and to their own confusion: yet when his hand has been lifted up he has withdrawn it in mercy. See how God has always tempered his providence with kindness to them. He laid them low so that they were sore sick, but at the voice of their moaning he restored them. They trembled on the brink of death, yet he permitted them to recover strength; and now, despite their vows of amendment, here they are, callous and careless, unmindful of the mercy which gave them a reprieve.

Did you ever think what is included in the riches of forbearance. There are quick tempered individuals who only need to be a little provoked, and hard words and blows come quick and furious: but, oh, the forbearance of God when he is provoked to his face by ungodly men! By men, I mean, who hear his word, and yet refuse it! They slight his love, and yet he perseveres in it. Justice lays its hand on the sword, but mercy holds it back in its scabbard. Well might each spared one say,—

> " O unexhausted Grace
> O Love unspeakable!
> I am not gone to my own place;
> I am not yet in hell!
> Earth doth not open yet,
> My soul to swallow up:
> And, hanging o'er the burning pit,
> I still am forced to hope."

Our apostle adds to goodness and forbearance the riches of " *long-suffering.*" We draw a distinction between forbearance and long-suffering. Forbearance has to do with the magnitude of sin; long-suffering with the multiplicity of it: forbearance has to do with present provocation; longsuffering relates to that provocation repeated, and continued for a length of time. Oh, how long doth God suffer the ill manners of men! Forty years long was he grieved with that generation whose carcases fell in the wilderness. Has it come to forty years yet with you, dear hearer? Possibly it may have passed even that time, and a half-century of provocation may have gone into eternity to bear witness against you. What if I should even have to say that sixty and seventy years have continued to heap up the loads of their transgressions, until the Lord saith, " I am pressed down under your sins; as a cart that is full of sheaves I am pressed down under you." Yet for all that, here you are on praying ground and pleading terms with God; here you are where yet the Saviour reigns upon the throne of grace; here you are where mercy is to be had for the asking, where free grace and dying love ring out their charming bells of invitation to joy and peace! Oh, the riches of his goodness, and forbearance, and longsuffering. Three-fold is the claim : will you not regard it ? Can you continue to despise it ?

I should like to set all this in a striking light if I could, and there-fore I would remind you of who and what that God is who has exhibited, this goodness, forbearance, and longsuffering to men. Remember how *great* he is. When men insult a great prince the offence is thought to be highly heinous. If anyone should openly insult our own beloved Queen, and continue to do so, all the nation would be clamorous to have the impertinence ended speedily. We cannot bear that a beloved ruler should be publicly insulted. And what think you of the sin which provokes God ? which to his face defies him ? and in his very courts resists him? Shall this always be forborne with ? Is there not a limit to longsuffering ? *Goodness* also adds another item to the provocation ; for we naturally say, " Why should one so good be treated so cruelly ? " If God were a tyrant, if he were unrighteous or unkind, it were not so much amiss that men stood out against him ; but when his very name is love, and when he manifests the bowels of a Father towards his wander-ing children it is shameful that he should be so wantonly provoked. Those words of Jesus were extremely touching when he pointed to his miracles, and asked, " For which of these things do you stone me ? " When I think of God I may well say—for which of his deeds do you provoke him? Every morning he draws the curtain and glads the earth with light, and gives *you* eyes to see it; he sends his rain upon the ground to bring forth bread for man, and he gives *you* life to eat thereof —is this a ground for revolting from him? Every single minute of our life is cheered with the tender kindness of God, and every spot is gladdened with his love. I wonder that the Lord does not sweep away the moral nuisance of a guilty race from off the face of earth. Man's sin must have been terribly offensive to God from day to day, and yet still he shows kindness, love, forbearance. This adds an excessive venom to man's disobedience. How can he grieve such goodness ? How can divine goodness fail to resent such base ingratitude ?

Think also of God's *knowledge ;* for he knows all the transgressions of men. " What the eye does not see the heart does not rue," is a truth-ful proverb ; but every transgression is committed in the very presence of God, so that penitent David cried, " Against thee, thee only have I sinned, and done this evil in thy sight." Transgression is committed in the sight of God, from whose eyes nothing is hidden. Remember also, that the Lord never can forget ; before his eyes all things stand out in clear light, not only the things of to-day, but all the transgressions of a life. Yet for all this he doth forbear. With evil reeking before his face, he is slow to anger, and waiteth that he may be gracious.

All this while, remember, the Lord is great in *power*. Some are patient because they are powerless : they bear and forbear because they cannot well help themselves ; but it is not so with God. Had he but willed it, you had been swept into hell ; only a word from him and the impenitent had fallen in the wilderness, and their spirits would have passed into the realms of endless woe. In a moment the Lord could have eased him of his adversary ; he could have stopped that flippant tongue, and closed that lustful eye in an instant. That wicked heart would have failed to beat if God had withdrawn his power, and that rebellious breath would have ceased also. Had it not been for long-suffering you unbelievers would long since have known what it is to fall into the hands of an angry God. Will you continue to grieve the God who so patiently bears with you ?

Be it never forgotten that sin is to God much more intolerable than it is to us. He is of purer eyes than to behold iniquity. Things which we call little sins are great and grievous evils to him: they do, as it were, touch the apple of his eye. "Oh, do not," he says, "do not this abominable thing that I hate!" His Spirit is grieved and vexed with every idle word and every sensual thought; and hence it is a wonder of wonders that a God so sensitive of sin, a God so able to avenge himself of his adversaries, a God who knows the abundance of human evil, and marks it all, should nevertheless exhibit riches of goodness and forbearance and longsuffering: yet this is what you, my ungodly hearer, have been experiencing many a long year. Here let us pause; and oh that each one who is still unsaved would sing most sincerely the words of Watts:—

> "Lord, we have long abused thy love,
> Too long indulged our sin,
> Our aching hearts e'en bleed to see
> What rebels we have been.
>
> "No more, ye lusts, shall ye command,
> No more will we obey;
> Stretch out, O God, thy conqu'ring hand,
> And drive thy foes away."

II. Come with me, friend, and let me speak to thee of THE SIN OF WHICH THOU ART SUSPECTED. Hear me, unconverted sinner : the sin of which thou art suspected is this,—"Despisest thou the riches of his goodness and forbearance and longsuffering?" The Lord's goodness ought to be admired and to be adored, and dost thou despise it? His goodness ought to be wondered at and told as a marvel in the ears of others, and dost thou despise it? That I may rake thy conscience a little, lend me thine ear.

Some despise God's goodness, forbearance, and longsuffering, because they *never even gave a thought to it.* God has given you life to keep you in being, and he has indulged you with his kindness, but it has not yet occurred to you that this patience is at all remarkable or worthy of the smallest thanks. You have been a drunkard, have you? a swearer? a Sabbath-breaker? a lover of sinful pleasure? Perhaps not quite so; but still you have forgotten God altogether, and yet he has abounded in goodness to you: is not this a great wrong? The Lord saith, " Hear, O heavens, and give ear, O earth : I have nourished and brought up children, and they have rebelled against me. The ox knoweth his owner, and the ass his master's crib: but these my creatures do not know, my favoured ones do not consider." Why, you have no such forbearance with others as God has had with you. You would not keep a dog if it never followed at your heel, but snarled at you: you would not even keep a potter's vessel if it held no water, and was of no service to you; you would break it in pieces, and throw it on the dunghill. As for yourself, you are fearfully and wonderfully made, both as to your body and as to your soul, and yet you have been of no service to your Maker, nor even thought of being of service to him. Still, he has spared you all these years, and it has never occurred to you that there has been any wonderful forbearance in it. Assuredly, O man, thou despisest the long-suffering of thy God.

Others have, perhaps, thought of it, but *have never seriously medi-tated thereon.* When we offend a man, if we are right-minded, we not only note the fact with regret, but we sit down and weigh the matter, and seek to rectify it; for we would not be unjust to any person, and if we felt that we had been acting unfairly it would press upon our minds until we could make amends. But are there not some of you who have never given half an hour's consideration to your relation to your God? He has spared you all this while, and yet it has never occurred to you to enter into your chamber and sit down and consider your conduct towards him. It would seem to be too much trouble even to think of your Creator. His longsuffering leads you to repentance, but you have not repented; in fact, you have not thought it worth your while to con-sider the question at all: you have thought it far more important to enquire, "What shall I eat and what shall I drink?" Bread and broadcloth have shut out the thought of God. Ah me, you will stand at his judgment bar before long—and then? Perhaps ere this week is finished you may have to answer, not to me, but unto him that sits upon the throne; therefore I do implore you now, for the first time give this matter thought. Despise no longer the goodness and long-suffering of God.

This longsuffering is despised, further, by those who have *imagined that God does not take any great account of what they do.* So long as they do not go into gross and open sin, and offend the laws of their country, they do not believe that it is of any consequence whether they love God or not, whether they do righteousness or not, whether they are sober and temperate, or drunken and wanton; whether they are clean in heart by God's Spirit, or defiled in soul and life. Thou thinkest that God is altogether such an one as thyself, and that he will wink at thy trans-gression and cover up thy sin; but thou shalt not find it so. That base thought proves that thou despisest his longsuffering.

Some even get to think that the warnings of love are so much wind, and *that the threatenings of God will never be fulfilled.* They have gone on for many years without being punished, and instead of drawing the conclusion that the longer the blow is in falling the heavier it will be when it does come, they imagine that because it is long delayed the judgment will never come at all; and so they sport and trifle between the jaws of death and hell. They hear warnings as if they were all moonshine, and fancy that this holy Book, with its threatenings, is but a bugbear to keep fools quiet. If thou thinkest so, sir, then indeed thou hast despised the goodness and forbearance and longsuffering of God. Do you imagine that this forbearance will last for ever? Do you dream that at least it will continue with you for many years? I know your secret thoughts: you see other men die suddenly, but your secret thought is that you will have long space and ample time: you hear of one struck down with paralysis, and another carried off by apoplexy, but you flatter yourselves that you will have plenty of leisure to think about these things. Oh, how can you be so secure?

How can you thus tempt the Lord ? False prophets in these evil days play into men's hands and hold out the hope that you may go into the next world wrong, and yet be set right in the end. This is a vile flattery of your wicked hearts ; but yet remember that even according to their maunderings centuries may elapse before this fancied restoration may occur. A sensible man would not like to run the risk of even a year of agony. Half-an-hour of acute pain is dreaded by most people. Can it be that the very men who start back from the dentist's door, afraid of the pinch which extricates an aching tooth, will run the risk of years of misery? Take the future of the impenitent even on this footing, it is a thing to be dreaded, and by every means avoided. I say, these flattering prophets themselves, if rightly understood, give you little enough of hope ; but what will come to you if the old doctrine proves to be true and you go away into everlasting fire in hell, as the Scripture puts it ? Will you live an hour in jeopardy of such a doom ? Will you so despise the longsuffering and forbearance of the Lord?

I will not enlarge and use many words, for I am myself weary of words : I want to persuade you even with tears. My whole soul would attract you to your God, your Father. I would come to close quarters with you, and say,—Do you not think that, even though you fall into no doctrinal error, and indulge no hazy hope as to either restitution or annihilation, yet still it is a dreadful despising of God's mercy when you keep on playing with God, and saying to his grace, " Go thy way for this time ; when I have a more convenient season I will send for thee"? The more gentle God is the more you procrastinate, and the more in tenderness he speaks of pardon the more you transgress. Is this generous? Is it right? Is it wise? Can it be a fit and proper thing to do? Oh, my dear hearer, why will you act thus shamefully? Some of you delight to come and hear me preach, and drink in all I have to say, and you will even commend me for being earnest with your souls ; and yet, after all, you will not decide for God, for Christ, for heaven. You are between good and evil, neither cold nor hot. I would ye were either cold or hot ; I could even wish that ye either thought this word of mine to be false, or else that, believing it to be true, you at once acted upon it. How can you incur the double guilt of offending God and of knowing that it is an evil thing to do so? You reject Christ, and yet admit that he ought to be received by you ! You speak well of a gospel which you will not accept for yourselves ! You believe great things of a Saviour whom you will not have to be your Saviour ! Jesus himself says, " If I tell you the truth, why do you not believe me ? "

" Despisest thou the longsuffering of God?" Dare you do it? I tremble as I think of a man despising God's goodness. Is not this practical blasphemy? Darest thou do it? Oh, if thou hast done it hitherto, do it no more. Ere yon sun goes down again, say within thy heart, " I will be a despiser of God's goodness no longer ; I will arise and go unto my Father, and I will say unto him,—Father, I have sinned. I will not rest until in the precious blood he has washed my sins away."

III. In closing this sermon I desire to remind thee, O ungodly man, of THE KNOWLEDGE OF WHICH THOU ART FORGETFUL. Read my text :

—" Despisest thou the riches of his goodness and forbearance and long-suffering; *not knowing that the goodness of God leadeth thee to repentance ?*" Now there are many here who know as a matter of doctrine that the goodness of God leads them to repentance, and yet they do not know it as a practical truth affecting their lives : indeed, they so act that it is not true to them at all. Yet, if they do not know this they are wilfully ignorant ; not willing to retain in their minds a fact so disagreeable to them. None are so blind as those who will not see : but he who does not see, and yet hath eyes, has a criminality about his blindness which is not found in that of those who have no sight. Dear hearer, whether you know this truth or not, I would remind you that God's patience with you is meant to lead you to repentance. " How ?" say you. Why, first by *giving you an opportunity to repent.* These years, which are now coming to a considerable number with you, have been given you in order that you might turn to God. By the time you were twenty-one you had sinned quite enough ; perhaps you had even then begun to mislead other youths, and to instruct in evil those under your influence. Why did not God take you away at once ? It might have been for the benefit of the world if he had done so ; but yet you were spared till you were thirty. Did not each year of your lengthened life prove that the Lord was saying " I will spare him, for perhaps he will yet amend and think upon his God. I will give him more light, and increase his comforts ; I will give him better teaching, better preaching ; peradventure he will repent." Yet you have not done so. Have you lived to be forty, and are you where you were when you were twenty ? Are you still out of Christ ? Then you are worse than you were; for you have sinned more deeply and you have provoked the Lord more terribly. You have now had space enough. What more do you need? When the child has offended, you say, " Child, unless you beg pardon at once, I must punish you": would you give a boy so many minutes to repent in as God has given you years ? I think not. If a servant is continually robbing you ; if he is careless, slothful, disobedient, you say to him, " I have passed over your faults several times, but one of these days I shall discharge you. I cannot always put up with this slovenliness, this blundering, this idleness: one of these times you will have to go." Have you not so spoken to your female servant, and thought it kind on your part to give her another chance ? The Lord has said the same to you ; yet here you are, a living but impenitent man; spared, but spared only to multiply your transgressions. This know, that his forbearance gives you an opportunity to repent; do not turn it into an occasion for hardening your heart.

But next, the Lord in this is pleased to give *a suggestion to you to repent.* It seems to me that every morning when a man wakes up still impenitent, and finds himself out of hell, the sunlight seems to say, " I shine on thee yet another day, as that in this day thou mayest repent." When your bed receives you at night I think it seems to say, " I will give you another night's rest, that you may live to turn from your sins and trust in Jesus." Every mouthful of bread that comes to the table says, " I have to support your body that still you may have space for repentance." Every time you open the Bible the pages say, " We speak with you that you may repent." Every time you hear a sermon, if it be such a sermon as God would have us preach, it pleads with you to turn unto the Lord and live. Surely the time past of your life may suffice you to have wrought the will of the Gentiles. "The times of your ignorance God winked at, but now commandeth men everywhere to repent." Do not life and death, and heaven and hell, call upon you so to do? Thus you have in God's goodness space for repentance, and a suggestion to repent.

But something more is here; for I want you to notice that the text does not say, "The goodness of God *calleth* thee to repentance," but "*leadeth* thee." This is a much stronger word. God calls to repentance by the gospel; God *leads to repentance* by his goodness. It is as though he plucked at your sleeve and said, "Come this way." His goodness lays its gentle hand on you, drawing you with cords of love and bands of a man. God's forbearance cries, "Why wilt thou hate me? What wrong have I done thee? I have spared thee; I have spared thy wife and children to thee; I have raised thee up from the bed of sickness; I have loaded thy board; I have filled thy wardrobe; I have done thee a thousand good turns; wherefore dost thou disobey me? Turn unto thy God and Father, and live in Christ Jesus."

If, on the other hand, you have not received rich temporal favours, yet the Lord still leads you to repentance by a rougher hand; as when the prodigal fain would have filled his belly with husks, but could not, and the pangs of hunger came upon him; those pains were a powerful message from the Father to lead him to the home where there was bread enough and to spare. "The goodness of God leadeth thee to repentance." Oh, that thou wouldest yield to its sweet leadings, and follow as a child follows the guidance of a nurse. Let thy crosses lead thee to the cross; let thy joys lead thee to find joy in Christ.

Do you not think that all this should *encourage you to repent,* since God himself leads you that way? If God leads you to repentance he does not mean to cast you away. If he bids you repent, then he is willing to accept your repentance, and to be reconciled to you. If he bids you change your mind, it is because his own mind is love. Repentance implies a radical change in your view of things, and in your estimate of matters; it is a change in your purposes, a change in your thoughts and in your conduct. If the Lord leads you that way he will help you in it. Follow his gracious leading till his divine Spirit shall lead you with still greater power and still greater efficacy, till at last you find that he has wrought in you both repentance and faith, and you are saved in the Lord with an everlasting salvation. If "the goodness of God leadeth thee to repentance," then be sure of this, that the goodness of God will receive thee when thou dost repent, and thou shalt live in his sight as his well-beloved and forgiven child.

I close now, but I am sorry so to do, for I have not pleaded one-half as I could have wished. Yet what more can I say? I will put it to yourselves. If you were in God's stead, could you bear to be treated as you have treated him? If you were all goodness and tenderness, and had borne with a creature now for thirty or forty years, how would you bear to see that creature still stand out, and even draw an inference from your gentleness to encourage him in his rebellion? Would you not say, "Well, if my longsuffering makes him think little of sin,

I will change my hand. If tenderness cannot win him, I must leave him; if even my love does not affect him, I will let him alone. He is given unto his evil ways—I will cease from him, and see what his end will be"? O Lord, say not so, say not so unto anyone in this house, but of thy great mercy make this day to be as the beginning of life to many. Oh that hearts may be touched with pity for their slighted Saviour, that they may seek his face! Here is the way of salvation: "Believe in the Lord Jesus Christ, and thou shalt be saved." You know how the Master bade us put it. "Go ye into all the world and preach the gospel to every creature: he that believeth and is baptized shall be saved." First, we are to preach faith, whereby we lay hold on Christ; then baptism, whereby we confess that faith, and own that we are dead and buried with Christ that we may live with him in newness of life. Those are the two points he bids us set before you, and I do set them before you. Weary, but not quite wearied out, O impenitent man, I plead with thee! Though thou hast so often been pleaded with in vain, once more I speak with thee in Christ's stead, and say—Repent of thy sin, look to thy Saviour, and confess thy faith in his own appointed way. I verily believe that if I had been pleading with some of you to save the life of a dog I should have prevailed with you a great while ago. And will you not care about the saving of your own souls? Oh, strange infatuation—that men will not consent to be themselves saved; but foolishly, madly, hold out against the mercy of God which leads them to repentance. God bless you, beloved, and may none of you despise his goodness, and forbearance, and longsuffering.

PORTION OF SCRIPTURE READ BEFORE SERMON—Luke xiii. 1—17, 24—30.

HYMNS FROM "OUR OWN HYMN BOOK"—103, 516, 518.

Might not the distribution of this sermon be useful? If the Christian reader think so, will he favour the preacher by placing copies of it in the hands of persons who need just such appeals. The prayers of God's people are entreated that this discourse may bear fruit unto life eternal.

A DESCRIPTION OF YOUNG MEN IN CHRIST.

A Sermon

DELIVERED ON LORD'S-DAY MORNING, APRIL 8TH, 1883, BY

C. H. SPURGEON,

AT THE METROPOLITAN TABERNACLE, NEWINGTON.

"I write unto you, young men, because ye have overcome the wicked one. . . . I have written unto you, young men, because ye are strong, and the word of God abideth in you, and ye have overcome the wicked one."—1 John ii. 13, 14.

WHEN I preached a short time ago upon John's message to the "little children," I explained why it was that he first said, "I write," and then, "I have written." He is writing: his whole heart is in it, and he cannot help saying that he himself is earnestly writing to those whom he loves so well; but he has scarcely penned the line before he feels that he must alter that present tense and set it in the past, under the form of "I have written." He knows that he must soon be gone from them, and be numbered with those who were, but are not, among living men. These words, then, are the language of a father in Israel still among his children; they are also the words of one who has passed from earth and entered into glory. If what I shall have to say at this time, fairly flowing from the text, shall come to you as Christ's word from his favoured disciple John you will attach the more importance to it, and it will do your hearts the more good. Lifting his head from that dear bosom which gave him unexampled rest he whispers, "I write unto you young men." Looking down from that favoured place which he now occupies so near to the throne of the Lamb, he looks over the battlements of heaven upon us, and cries, "I have written unto you, young men."

In the Christian church there is an order of Christians who have grown so much that they can no longer be called "babes in grace," but yet they are not so far matured that they can be exactly called "fathers." These, who form the middle-class of the spiritual-minded, are styled "young men." Understand that the apostle is not writing here to any according to their bodily age; he is using human age as a metaphor and figure for representing growth in the spiritual life. Age, according to the flesh, often differs much from the condition of the spirit: many old men are still no more than "babes"; some children in years are even now "young men" in grace, while not a few young men are "fathers" in the church while young in years. God has endowed certain of his servants with great grace, and made them mature in their youth: such were Joseph, Samuel, David, Josiah, and Timothy. It is not age according to the family register that we are now to speak about, but age according to the Lamb's book of life.

Grace is a matter of growth, and hence we have among us babes, young men, and fathers, whose position is not reckoned according to this fleeting, dying life, but according to that eternal life which has been wrought in them of the Spirit of God. It is a great mercy when young men in the natural sense are also young men in the spiritual sense, and I am glad that it is largely so in this church. The fathers among us need not be ashamed of their spiritual seed. In speaking to young men in Christ, I am speaking to a numerous body of Christians among ourselves, who make up a very efficient part of the army of Christ in this region. I would ask them not to be either so modest or so proud as to decline to be thus classed. You are no longer weaklings; do not, therefore, count yourselves mere babes, lest you plead exemption from hard service. You are hardly yet mature enough to rank with the fathers; do not forget the duties of your real place under cover of aspiring to another. It is honour enough to be in Christ, and certainly it is no small thing to be in spiritual things a man in the prime of life.

These young men are not babes. They have been in Christ too long for that: they are no longer novices, to whom the Lord's house is strange. They have been born unto God probably now for years: the things which they hoped for at first they have to a large extent realized; they know now what once they could not understand. They are not now confined to milk diet; they can eat meat and digest it well. They have discernment, having had their senses exercised by reason of use, so that they are not so liable to be misled as they were in their infancy. And while they have been longer in the way, so also have they now grown stronger in the way. It is not a weak and timorous faith which they now possess; they believe firmly and stoutly, and are able to do battle for the "faith once delivered to the saints," for they are strong in the Lord and in the power of his might. They are wiser now than they used to be. When they were children they knew enough to save them, for they knew the Father, and that was blessed knowledge; but now they know far more of the word of God which abideth in them through their earnest, prayerful, believing reception of it. Now they have a clearer idea of the breadth and length, and depth and height of the work of redemption, for they have been taught of God. They even venture to enjoy the deep things of God; and the covenant is by no means an unknown thing among them. They have been under the blessed teaching of the Spirit of God, and from him they have received an unction, so that they know all things. In knowledge they are no more children, but men in Christ Jesus. Thus they are distinguished from the first class, which comprehends the babes in Christ.

They are not yet fathers because they are not yet so established, confirmed, and settled as the fathers are, who know what they believe, and know it with a certainty of full assurance which nothing can shake. They have not yet had the experience of fathers, and consequently have not all their prudence and foresight: they are richer in zeal than in judgment. They have not yet acquired the nursing faculty so precious in the church as the product of growth, experience, maturity, and affection; they are going on to that, and in a short time they will have reached it, but as yet they have other work to do more suitable to their vigour. Do not suppose that when we say they are not to be called "fathers," that they are not, therefore, very valuable to the community; for in some senses they are quite equal to the fathers, and in one or two respects they may even be superior to them. The fathers are for contemplation, they study deep and see far, and so they "have known him that is from the beginning"; but a measure of their energy for action may have gone through stress of years. These young men are born to fight; they are the militia of the church, they have to contend for her faith, and to extend the Redeemer's kingdom. They should do so, for they are strong. This is their lot, and the Lord help them to fulfil their calling. These must for years to come be our active spirits: they are our strength and our hope. The fathers must soon go off the stage: their maturity in grace shows that they are ready for glory, and it is not God's way to keep his shocks of corn in the field when once they are fully ripe for the garner—perfect men shall be gathered up with the perfect, and shall enter into their proper sphere. The fathers, therefore, must soon be gone; and when they are gone, to whom are we to look for a succession but to these young men? We hope to have them for many years with us, valiant for the truth, steadfast in the faith, ripening in spirit, and growingly made meet to take their seats among the glorified saints above. Judge ye, dear brethren, whether ye are fairly to be ranked among the young men. Have no regard to the matter of sex, for there is neither male nor female in Christ Jesus. Judge whether ye be fit to be ranked among those whose full-grown and vigorous life entitles them to stand among the effectives of the church, the vigorous manhood of the seed of Israel. To such I speak. May God the Holy Spirit bless the word!

I. The first thing that John notes about these young men is THEIR POSSESSION OF STRENGTH:—"I have written unto you young men, because ye are strong."

These Christians of the middle class are emphatically strong. This does not imply that any measure of spiritual strength was in them by nature; for the Apostle Paul clearly puts it otherwise concerning our natural state saying, "When we were yet without strength, Christ died for the ungodly"; so that by nature we are without strength to do anything that is good and right. We are strong as a wild bull, to dash headlong into everything that is evil: strong as a lion to fight against all that is good and Godlike; but for all spiritual things and holy things we are utterly infirm and incapable; yea, we are as dead men until God the Holy Spirit deals with us.

Neither does the apostle here at all allude to the strength of the body in young men, for in a spiritual sense this is rather their weakness than their strength. The man who is strong in the flesh is too often for that very reason strongly tempted to sins of the flesh; and hence the apostle bids his young friend "flee youthful lusts." Whenever you read the life of Samson you may thank God you had not Samson's thews and sinews; or else it is more than probable that you would have had Samson's passions, and they might have mastered you as they mastered him. The time of life in which a young man is found is full of perils; and so is the spiritual condition of which it is the type. The young man might almost wish that it were with him as with the older man in whom the forces of the flesh have declined, for though age brings with it many infirmities it also has its gain in the abatement of the passions. So you see the young man cannot reckon upon vigour of the flesh as contributing towards real "strength;" he has rather to ask for more strength from on high lest the animal vigour that is within him should drag down his spirit. He is glad to be in robust health that he may bear much toil in the Lord's cause; but he is not proud of it, for he remembers that the Lord delighteth not in the strength of the horse, and taketh not pleasure in the legs of a man.

These young men in grace are strong, first of all, *in faith*, according to that exhortation, "Be strong! fear not!" They have known the Lord now for some time, and they have enjoyed that perfect peace which comes of forgiven sin: they have marked the work of the Spirit within themselves, and they know that it is no delusion, but a divine change; and now they not only believe in Christ, but they know that they believe in him. They know whom they have believed, and they are persuaded that he is able to keep that which they have committed to him. That faith which was once a healing touch has now become a satisfying embrace; that enjoyment which was once a sip has now become a draught, quenching all thirst; ay, and that which was once a draught has become an immersion into the river of God, which is full of water: they have plunged into the river of life and find waters to swim in. Oh what a mercy it is to be strong in this fashion. Let him that is strong take heed that he glory only in the Lord who is his righteousness and strength; but in him and his strength he may indeed make his boast and defy the armies of the aliens. What saith Paul—"I can do all things through Christ that strengtheneth me." My brethren, take good heed that ye never lose this strength. Pray God that you may never sin so as to lose it; may never backslide so as to lose it; may never grieve the Spirit so as to lose it; for I reckon that to be endowed with power from on High, and to be strong in faith, giving glory to God, is the truest glory and majesty of our manhood, and it were sad to lose it, or even to deface it. Oh that all Christians were so much advanced as to enter the enlisted battalion of the Lord's young men.

This strength makes a man strong *to endure*. He is a sufferer, but mark how patient he is! He is a loser in business, and he has a hard task to earn his daily bread, but he never complains, he has learned in every state to be content. He is persecuted, but he is not distressed thereby: men revile him, but he is not moved from the even tenor of his way. He grows careless alike of flattery and calumny; so long as he can please God he cares not to displease men. He dwells on high, and lives above the smoke of human opinion. He bears and forbears. He bows his neck to the yoke and his shoulders to the burden, and has fellowship with Christ in his sufferings. Blessed is that man who is so strong that he never complains of his trials, never whimpers and frets because he is made to share in the humiliations and griefs of his covenant head. He expected to bear the cross when he became a follower of the Crucified, and he is not now made weary and faint when it presses upon him. It is a fair sight to see young Isaac bearing the wood for the sacrifice: young Joseph bearing the fetters in prison with holy joy;

young Samson carrying away the gates of Gaza, bars and all ; and young David praising God with his harp though Saul is feeling for his javelin. Such are the exploits of the young men who count it all joy when they fall into manifold trials for Christ's sake. O young man, be strong ; strong as an iron column which bears the full stress of the building and is not moved.

This strength shows itself, next, in *labouring for Christ.* The young man in Christ is a great worker. He has so much strength that he cannot sit still; he would be ashamed to leave the burden and heat of the day to be borne by others. He is up and at it according to his calling and ability. He has asked his Lord as a favour to give him something to do. His prayer has been, "Show me what thou wouldst have me to do," and having received an answer he is found in the vineyard trenching the soil, removing the weeds, pruning the vines, and attending to such labours as the seasons demand. His Master has said to him, "Feed my sheep," and "Feed my lambs;" and, therefore, you shall see him through the livelong day and far into the night watching over the flock which is committed to him. In all this toil he greatly rejoices, for he is strong. He can run and not be weary ; he can walk and not faint. "By my God have I leaped over a wall," saith he. Nothing is hard to him ; or, if it be, he remembers that the diamond cuts the diamond, and so he sets a harder thing against a hard thing, and by a firm and stern resolution he overcomes. That which ought to be done he declares shall be done in the power of God, and lo, it is accomplished ! Blessed is the church that hath her quiver full of these ; she shall speak with her adversaries in the gate. These are the men that work our reformations ; these are the men who conduct our missions ; these are the men who launch out into the deep for Christ. They make the vanguard of the host of God, and largely compose the main body of her forces. I trust this church has many such. May they yet be multiplied and increased among us, that we may never lack for choice soldiers of the cross, able to lead on the hosts of God.

So, also, are these young men strong *to resist attack.* They are assaulted, but they carry with them the shield of faith wherewith they quench the fiery darts of the enemy. Wherever they go, if they meet with other tempted ones, they spring to the front to espouse their cause. They are ready in the day of battle to meet attacks upon the faith with the sword of the Spirit : they will yield no point of faith, but defend the truth at all hazards. Clad in the panoply of truth, they meet no deadly wound ; for by grace they are so preserved that the wicked one toucheth them not. They resist temptation, and are unharmed in the midst of peril. Do you want a specimen ? Look at Joseph ! Where ten thousand would have fallen he stands in snow-white purity. Joseph as contrasted with David is an instance of how a young man may bring greater glory to God than an older man when assailed by a kindred temptation. Joseph is but young, and the temptation forces itself upon him while he is in the path of duty. He is alone with his temptress, and no one need know of the sin if it be committed ; on the other hand, if he refuses, shame, and possibly death, may await him through the calumny of his offended mistress ; yet he bravely resists the assault, and overcomes the wicked one. He is a bright contrast to the older man, a father in Israel, who went out of his way to compass an evil deed, and committed crime in order to fulfil his foul desire. From this case we learn that neither years, nor knowledge, nor experience can preserve any one of us from sin ; but old and young must be kept by the power of God, or they will be overthrown by the tempter.

Furthermore, these young men are not only strong for resistance, but they are strong *for attack.* They carry the war into the enemy's territory. If there is anything to be done, they are like Jonathan and his armour-bearer, eager for the fray : these are very zealous for the Lord of hosts, and are prompt to undertake toil and travail for Jesus' sake. These smite down error, and set up truth : these believe great things, attempt great things, and expect great things, and the Lord is with them. The archers have sorely grieved them, and shot at them, and hated them ; but their bows abide in strength, for the arms of their hands are made strong by the mighty God of Jacob. One of them shall chase a thousand, and two put ten thousand to flight.

So have I shown you what these young men are : they are strong— strong to believe, strong to suffer, strong to do, strong to resist, strong to attack. May companies of these go in and out among us to fight the Lord's battles, for to this end hath the Lord girded them with strength.

II. Secondly, let us notice that he implies THEIR NEED OF STRENGTH ; for he says, " Ye are strong, and ye have overcome the wicked one." Between the lines of the text I read the fact, that young men who are strong must expect to be attacked. This also follows from a rule of divine economy. Whenever God lays up stores it is because there will be need of them. When Egypt's granaries were full with the supply of seven years of plenty, one might have been sure that seven years of famine were about to come. Whenever a man is strong it is because he has stern work to do ; for as the Israelite of old never had an ounce of manna left over till the morning except that which bred worms and stank, so there never will be a Christian that has a pennyworth of grace left over from his daily requirements. If thou art weak thou shalt have no trial happen to thee but such as is common to men ; but if thou be strong, rest thou assured that trials many and heavy are awaiting thee. Every sinew in the arm of faith will have to be tested. Every single weapon given out of the armoury of God will be called for in the conflict. Christian soldiering is no piece of military pastime ; it is no proud parade ; it means hard fighting from the day of enlistment to the day of reward. The strong young man may rest assured that he has no force to spend in display, no energy which he may use in vapouring and vainglory. There is a heavy burden for the strong shoulder, and a fierce fight for the trained hand.

Why does Satan attack this class of men most ? I reckon, first, because Satan is not always sure that the babes in grace are in grace, and therefore he does not always attack beginners ; but when they are sufficiently developed to make him see who and what they are, then he arouses his wrath. Those who have clean escaped from him he will weary and worry to the utmost of his power. A friend writes to me to enquire whether Satan knows our thoughts. Of course he does not, as God does. Satan pretty shrewdly guesses at them from our actions and our words, and perhaps even from manifestations upon our countenances ; but it is the Lord alone who knows the thoughts of men immediately and by themselves. Satan is an old hand at studying human nature : he has been near six thousand years watching and tempting men and women, and therefore he is full of cunning ; but yet he is not omniscient, and therefore it may be that he thinks such and such a person is so little in grace that perhaps he is not in grace at all ; so he lets him alone : but as soon as ever it is certain that the man is of the royal seed, then the devil is at him. I do not know whether our Lord was ever tempted at Nazareth, while he was yet in his obscurity ; but the moment he was baptized, and the Spirit of God came upon him, he was taken into the wilderness to be tempted of the devil. If you become an avowed servant of God do not think the conflict is over : it is then that the battle begins. Straight from the waters of baptism, it may be, you will have to go into such a wilderness and such a conflict as you never knew before. Satan knows that young men in grace can do his kingdom great harm, and therefore he would fain slay them early in the day, as Pharaoh wished to kill all the male children in Israel. My brethren, you are strong to overthrow his kingdom, and therefore you need not marvel that he desires to overthrow you.

I think it is right that young men should endure hardness, for else they might become proud. It is hard to hide pride from men. Full of strength, full of courage, full of patience, full of zeal, such men are ready enough to believe the wicked one when he whispers that they are perfect; and therefore trial is sent to keep them out of that grievous snare of the evil one. The devil is used by God as a householder might employ a black, smutty scullion to clean his pots and kettles. The devil tempts the saint, and thus the saint sees his inward depravity, and is no longer able to boast. The devil thinks he is going to destroy the man of God, but God is making the temptation work for the believer's eternal good. Far better to have Beelzebub, the god of flies, pestering you, than to become fly-blown with notions of your own excellence.

Besides, not only might this young man be a prey to pride, but he certainly would not bring the glory to God untried that he brings to him when he overcomes temptation. Read the story of Job up to the time when he is tempted. Say you, " We have no story to read." Just so, there was nothing worthy of record, only that his flocks and herds continued to multiply, that another child was born, and so forth. There is no history to a nation when everything goes well ; and it is so with a believer. But when trial comes, and the man plays the man, and is valiant for God against the arch-enemy, I hear a voice from heaven saying, " Write." Now you shall have history—history that will glorify God. It is but right that those who are young men in Christ should endure conflicts that they may bring honour to their Father, their Redeemer, and the Holy Spirit who dwells in them.

Besides, it prepares them for future usefulness, and here I venture to intrude the testimony of my own experience. I often wondered, when I first came to Christ, why I had such a hard time of it when I was coming to the Lord, and why I was so long and so wearied in finding a Saviour. After that, I wondered why I experienced so many spiritual conflicts while others were in peace. Ah, brethren, I did not know that

I was destined to preach to this great congregation. I did not understand in those days that I should have to minister to hundreds, and even thousands, of distressed spirits, storm-tossed, and ready to perish. But it is so now with me that when the afflicted mention their experience I can, as a rule, reply, " I have been there"; and so I can help them, as one who has felt the same. It is meet, therefore, that the young men should bear the yoke in their youth, and that while they are strong they should gain experience, not so much for themselves as for others, that in after days when they come to be fathers they may be able to help the little ones of the family. Take your tribulation kindly, brother: yea, take it gratefully ; thank your King that he puts you in commission where the thick of the battle centres around you. You will never be a warrior if you never enter the dust-clouds where garments are rolled in blood. You will never become a veteran if you do not fight through the long campaign. The man who has been at the head of the forlorn hope is he who can tell what stern fighting means. So be it unto you : may your Captain save you from the canker of inglorious ease. You must fight in order that you may acquire the character which inspires others with confidence in you, and thus fits you to lead your comrades to the fray. Oh, that we may have here an abundance of the young men of the heavenly family who will defend the church against worldliness and error, defend the weaker ones from the wolves that prowl around, and guard the feeble against the many deceivers that waylay the church of God! As you love the Lord, I charge you grow in grace and be strong, for we have need of you just now. Oh, my brethren, take hold on sword and buckler; watch ye, and stand fast ! May the Lord teach your hands to war and your fingers to fight. In these evil days may you be as a phalanx to protect our Israel. The Canaanites, the Hivites and the Jebusites are upon us just now ; war is in all our borders: now, therefore, let each valiant man stand about the King's chariot, each man with his sword upon his thigh, because of fear in the night.

III. Thirdly, the text reminds us of THEIR PROOF OF STRENGTH: they have overcome the wicked one. Then they must be strong ; for a man who can overcome the wicked one is no mean man of war—write him down among the first three. Wicked ones abound ; but there is one crafty being who deserves the name of *the* wicked one: he is the arch-leader of rebellion, the first of sinners, the chief of sinners, the tempter of sinners. He is the wicked one who heads assaults against the pilgrims to Zion. If any man has ever stood foot to foot with him he will never forget it : it is a fight that once fought will leave its scars, even though the victory be won.

In what sense have these young men overcome the wicked one ?

Well, first, in the fact that they have broken right away from his power. They were once his slaves, they are not so now. They once slept beneath his roof in perfect peace : but conscience raised an uproar, and the Spirit of God troubled them, and they clean escaped his power. Once Satan never troubled them at all. Why should he ? They were good friends together. Now he tempts them and worries them, and assaults them because they have left his service, engaged themselves to a new master, and become the enemies of him who was once their god. I speak to many who gladly own that not a bit of them now belongs to the devil, from the crown of their head to the sole of their foot; for Christ has bought them, body, soul, and spirit, with his precious blood, and they have assented to the purchase, and feel that they are not their own, and certainly not the devil's; for they are bought with a price, and belong to him who purchased them. The strong man armed has been turned out by a stronger than he: Jesus has carried the fortress of the heart by storm, and driven out the foe. Satan is not inside our heart now; he entered into Judas, but he cannot enter into us; for our soul is filled by another who is well able to hold his own. The wicked one has been expelled by the Holy One, who now lives and reigns within our nature as Lord of all.

Moreover, these young men have overcome the wicked one, not only in breaking away from his power and in driving him entirely out of possession so that he is no longer master, but they have overcome him in the very fact of their opposition to him. When a man resists Satan, he is victorious over Satan in that very resistance. Satan's empire consists in the yielding of our will to his will; but when our will revolts against him, then already we have in a measure overcome him. Albeit that sometimes we are much better at willing than we are at doing, as the Apostle Paul was; for he said, "To will is present with me; but how to perform that which is good I find not"; yet, still, the hearty will to be clean from sin is a victory over sin; and as that will grows stronger and more determined to resist the temptations of the evil one, in that degree we have overcome sin and Satan. What a blessed thing this is! for fail not to remember that Satan has no weapons of defence, and so, when we resist him, he must flee. A Christian man has both defensive and offensive weapons, he has a shield as well as a sword: but Satan has fiery darts, and nothing else. I never read of his having any shield whatever: so that when we resist him he is bound to run away. He has no defence for himself, and the fact of our resistance is in itself a victory.

But, oh brothers and sisters, besides that, some of us who are young men in Christ have won many a victory over Satan. Have we not been tempted, fearfully tempted? But the mighty grace of God has come to the rescue, and we have not yielded. Cannot you look back, not with Pharisaic boasting, but with gracious exultation, over many an evil habit which once had the mastery over you, but which is master of you no longer? It was a hard conflict. How you bit your lip sometimes, and feared that you must yield! In certain moments your steps had almost gone, your feet had well-nigh slipped; but here you are conqueror yet! Thanks be to God who giveth us the victory through our Lord Jesus Christ. Hear what the Spirit saith to you when John writes to you: because you have overcome the wicked one, he says, "Love not the world, neither the things that are in the world."

Once more, in Christ Jesus we have entirely overcome the wicked one already; for the enemy we have to contend with is a vanquished foe—our Lord and Master met him and destroyed him. He is now destitute of his boasted battle-axe, that terrible weapon which has made the bravest men to quail when they have seen it in his hand. "What weapon is that?" say you. That weapon is death. Our Lord overthrew him that had the power of death, that is, the devil, and therefore

Satan has not the power of death any longer. The keys of death and of hell are at the girdle of Christ. Ah, fiend, we who believe in Jesus shall defeat thee, for our Lord defeated thee! That bruise upon thy head cannot be hidden! Thy crown is dashed in pieces! The Lord has sore wounded thee, O dragon, and never can thy deadly wound be healed! We have at thee with dauntless courage; for we believe the promise of our Lord, that he will bruise Satan under our feet shortly. As certainly as thou wast bruised under the feet of our crucified Lord, so shalt thou be bruised under the feet of all his seed, to thine utter overthrow and contempt. Let us take courage, brothers, and abide steadfast in the faith; for we have in our Lord Jesus overcome the wicked one. We are more than conquerors through him that hath loved us.

IV. Now I close with my fourth point, which is, THEIR SOURCE OF STRENGTH. You have seen their strength and their need of it, and their proof of it; now for the fountain of it. "The word of God abideth in you." I labour under the opinion that there never was a time in which the people of God had greater need to understand this passage than now. We have entered upon that part of the pilgrim path which is described by Bunyan as the Enchanted Ground: the church and the world appear to be alike bewitched with folly. Half the people of God hardly know their head from their heels at this time. They are gaping after wonders, running after a sounding brass and a tinkling cymbal, and waiting for yet more astounding inventions. Everything seems to be in a whirligig; a tornado has set in, and the storm is everywhere. Christians used to believe in Christ as their leader, and the Bible as their rule: but some of them are pleased with lords and rules such as he never knew! Believe me, there will soon come new Messiahs. Men are already pretending to work miracles, we shall soon have false Christs; and "Lo! here" and "Lo! there" will be heard on all sides. Anchors are up, winds are out, and the whole fleet is getting into confusion. Men in whose sanity and stability I once believed are being carried away with one fancy or another, and I am driven to cry, "What next? and what next?" We are only at the beginning of an era of mingled unbelief and fanaticism. Now we shall know who are God's elect and who are not; for there are spirits abroad at this hour that would, if it were possible, deceive even the very elect; and those who are not deceived are, nevertheless, sorely put to it. Here is the patience of the saints; let him look to himself who is not rooted and grounded in Christ, for the hurricane is coming. The signs of the times indicate a carnival of delusions; men have ceased to be guided by the word, and claim to be themselves prophets. Now we shall see what we shall see. Blessed is the sheep that knows his Shepherd, and will not listen to the voice of strangers. But here is the way to be kept steadfast—"The word of God abideth in you."

"*The word of God*"—that is to say, we are to believe in the doctrines of God's word, and these will make us strong. What vigour they infuse into a man! Get the word well into you, and you will overcome the wicked one. When the devil tempted Luther, the Reformer's grand grip of justification by faith made him readily victorious. Keep you a fast hold of the doctrines of grace and Satan will soon give over attacking you, for they are like plate-armour, through which no dart can ever force its way.

The promises of God's word, too, what power they give a man. To get a hold of a "shall" and "will" in the time of trouble is a heavenly safeguard. "My God will hear me." "I will not fail thee nor forsake thee." These are divine holdfasts. Oh, how strong a man is for overcoming the wicked one when he has such a promise to hand! Do not trust yourself out of a morning in the street till you have laid a promise under your tongue. I see people put respirators on in foggy weather; they do not make them look very lovely, but I dare say they are useful. I recommend the best respirator for the pestilential atmosphere of this present evil world when I bid you fit a promise to your lips. Did not the Lord rout the tempter in the wilderness with that promise, "Man shall not live by bread alone, but by every word that proceedeth out of the mouth of God shall man live"? Get the promises of God to lodge within you, and you will be strong.

Then mind the precepts, for a precept is often a sharp weapon against Satan. Remember how the Lord Jesus Christ struck Satan a killing blow by quoting a precept,—"It is written, Thou shalt worship the Lord thy God, and him only shalt thou serve." If the precept had not been handy, wherewith would the adversary have been rebuked? Nor is a threatening at all a weak weapon. The most terrible threatenings of God's word against sin are the best helps for Christians when they are tempted to sin:—How can I do this great wickedness, and sin against God? How should I escape if I turned away from him that speaketh from heaven? Tell Satan the threatenings, and make him tremble. Every word of God is life to holiness and death to sin. Use the word as your sword and shield: there is none like it.

Now notice that John not only mentions "the word of God," but the word of God "in you." The inspired word must be received into a willing mind. How? The Book which lies *there* is to be pleaded *here*, in the inmost heart, by the work of the Holy Ghost upon the mind. All of *this* letter has to be translated into spirit and life. "The word of God abideth in you"—that is, first to know it,—next to remember it and treasure it up in your heart. Following upon this, we must understand it, and learn the analogy of faith by comparing spiritual things with spiritual till we have learned the system of divine truth, and are able to set it forth and plead for it. It is, next, to have the word in your affections, to love it so that it is as honey or the droppings of the honeycomb to you. When this is the case you must and shall overcome the wicked one. A man instructed in the Scriptures is like an armed knight, who when he goes among the throng inflicts many a wound, but suffers none, for he is locked up in steel.

Yes, but that is not all; it is not the word of God in you alone, it is "the word of God *abideth* in you." It is always there, it cannot be removed from you. If a man gets the Bible right into him he is all right then, because he is full, and there is no room for evil. When you have filled a measure full of wheat you have effectually shut the chaff out. Men go after novel and false doctrines because they do not really know the truth; for if the truth had gotten into them and filled them, they would not have room for these day-dreams. A man who truly knows the doctrines of grace is never removed from them: I have heard our opponents rave at what they call the obstinacy of our brethren.

Once get the truth really into you, it will enter into the texture of your being, and nothing will get it out of you. It will also be your strength, by setting you watching against every evil thing. You will be on your guard if the word abides in you, for it is written, "When thou goest it will keep thee." The word of God will be to you a bulwark and a high tower, a castle of defence against the foe. Oh, see to it that the word of God is in you, in your very soul, permeating your thoughts, and so operating upon your outward life, that all may know you to be a true Bible-Christian, for they perceive it in your words and deeds.

This is the sort of army that we need in the church of God—men that are strong by feeding on God's word. Aspire to it, my brethren and sisters, and when you have reached it, then aspire unto the third degree that you may become fathers in Israel? Up to this measure, at any rate, let us endeavour to advance, and advance at once.

Are there any here who are not young men in Christ Jesus because they re not in Christ Jesus at all ? I cannot speak with you this morning, for my time is gone ; but I am distressed for you. To be out of Christ is such an awful thing that a man had better be out of existence. Without God, without Christ—then you are without joy in life or hope in death. Not even a babe in the divine family ! Then know this, that God shall judge those that are without, and when he cometh how swift and overwhelming will that judgment be ! Inasmuch as you would not have Christ in this day, Christ will not have you in that day. Stay not out of Christ any longer ! Seek his face and live, for " he that believeth in him hath everlasting life." May you be enabled to believe in him at this moment, for Jesus' sake. Amen.

Portion of Scripture read before Sermon—1 John ii.

Hymns from "Our Own Hymn Book"—678, 681, 674.

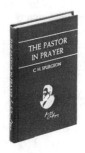

The Pastor in Prayer
$3.75. SBC rate, $2.50.

A choice selection of Spurgeon's audible prayers at the Metropolitan Tabernacle, stenographically recorded and published by popular request. D. L. Moody heard Spurgeon at the Tabernacle and later said, "He seemed to have such access to God that he could bring down the power from Heaven; that was the great secret of his influence and his success." Many thought his praying at the services was even more penetrating of the hearts of hearers than his preaching, if that were possible.

THE BRIDEGROOM'S PARTING WORD.

A Sermon

DELIVERED ON LORD'S-DAY MORNING, APRIL 15TH, 1883, BY

C. H. SPURGEON,

AT THE METROPOLITAN TABERNACLE, NEWINGTON.

"Thou that dwellest in the gardens, the companions hearken to thy voice: cause me to hear it."—Solomon's Song viii. 13.

THE Song is almost ended: the bride and bridegroom have come to their last stanzas, and they are about to part for a while. They utter their adieux, and the bridegroom says to his beloved, "Thou that dwellest in the gardens, the companions hearken to thy voice: cause me to hear it." In other words—when I am far away from thee, fill thou this garden with my name, and let thy heart commune with me. She promptly replies, and it is her last word till he cometh, "Make haste, my beloved, and be thou like to a roe or to a young hart upon the mountains of spices." These farewell words of the Well-beloved are very precious to his chosen bride. Last words are always noticed: the last words of those who loved us dearly are much valued; the last words of one who loved us to the death are worthy of a deathless memory. The last words of the Lord in this canticle remind me of the commission which the Master gave to his disciples or ever he was taken up; when he said to them, "Go ye into all the world, and preach the gospel to every creature." Then, scattering benedictions with both his hands, he ascended into the glory, and "a cloud received him out of their sight." As the sermon progresses you will see why I say this, and you will detect a striking likeness between the commission connected with the ascension and the present adieu, wherein the spiritual Solomon saith to his espoused Solyma, "Thou that dwellest in the gardens, the companions hearken to thy voice: cause me to hear it."

I. We will get to our text at once, without further preface, and we notice in it, first of all, AN APPOINTED RESIDENCE. The bridegroom, speaking of his bride, says, "Thou that dwellest in the gardens." The Hebrew is in the feminine, and hence we are bound to regard it as the word of the Bridegroom to his bride. It is the mystical word of the church's Lord to his elect one. He calls her "Inhabitress of the gardens"—that is the word. So then, dear friends, we who make up the church of God are here addressed this morning under that term, "Thou that inhabitest the gardens."

No. 1,716.

This title is given to believers here on earth, first, by way of *distinction*—distinction from the Lord himself. He whom we love dwelleth in the ivory palaces, wherein they make him glad : he is gone up into his Father's throne, and has left these gardens down below. He came down awhile that he might look upon his garden, that he might see how the vines flourished, and gather lilies ; but he has now returned to his Father and our Father. He watered the soil of his garden with his bloody sweat in Gethsemane, and made it to bear fruit unto life by being himself laid to sleep in the tomb of Joseph of Arimathea; but all this lowly work is over now. He does not dwell in the gardens as to his corporeal presence ; his dwelling-place is on the throne. Jesus has not taken us up with him; he will come another time to do that; but now he leaves us among the seeds and flowers and growing plants to do the King's work until he comes. He was a visitor here, and the visit cost him dear; but he is gone back unto the place whence he came out, having finished the work which his Father gave him : our life-work is *not* finished, and hence we must tarry awhile below, and be known as inhabitants of the gardens.

It is expedient that we should be here, even as it is expedient that he should *not* be here. God's glory is to come of our sojourn here, else he would have taken us away long ago. He said to his Father, " I pray not that thou shouldest take them out of the world, but that thou shouldest keep them from the evil." He himself is an inhabitant of the palaces, for there he best accomplishes the eternal purposes of love ; but his church is the inhabitress of the gardens, for there she best fulfils the decrees of the Most High. Here she must abide awhile until all the will of the Lord shall be accomplished in her and by her, and then she also shall be taken up, and shall dwell with her Lord above. The title is given by way of distinction, and marks the difference between her condition and that of her Lord.

Next, it is given by way of *enjoyment*. She dwells in the gardens, which are places of delight. Once you and I pined in the wilderness, and sighed after God from a barren land. We trusted in man, and made flesh our arm, and then we were like the heath in the desert, which seeth not when good cometh. All around us was the wilderness of this world, a howling wilderness of danger, and need, and disorder. We said of the world at its very best, " Vanity of vanities, all is vanity." Do you remember how you roamed, seeking rest and finding none ? Your way was the path of darkness which leadeth unto death. Then you were poor and needy, and sought water and there was none, and your tongue cleaved unto the roof of your mouth for thirst. Then came the Lord that bought you, and he sought you until he brought you into the gardens of his love, where he satisfied you with the river of the water of life, and filled you with the fruits of his Spirit, and now you dwell in a goodly land : " The fountain of Jacob shall be upon a land of corn and wine ; also his heavens shall drop down dew." Your portion is with the Lord's saints, yea, with himself ; and what can be a better portion ? Is it not as the garden of the Lord ? You dwell where the great Husbandman spends his care upon you and takes a pleasure in you. You dwell where the infinite skill and tenderness and wisdom of God manifest themselves in the training of the plants which his own right hand has planted; you dwell in the church of God, which is laid out in due order, and hedged about and guarded by heavenly power; and you are, therefore, most fitly said to dwell in the gardens. Be thankful: it is a place of enjoyment for you: awake and sing, for the lines have fallen unto you in pleasant places. Just as Adam was put into the garden of Eden for his own happiness, so are you put into the garden of the church for your comfort. It is not a perfect paradise of bliss, but it has many points of likeness to paradise: for God himself doth walk therein, the river of God doth water it, and the tree of life is there unguarded by the flaming sword. Is it not written, "I the Lord do keep it: I will water it every moment; lest any hurt it, I will keep it night and day"? See, beloved, although you are distinguished from your Lord by being here while he is there, yet you are made partakers of his joy, and are not as those who are banished into a salt land to die in desolation. The Lord's joy is in his people, and you are made to have a joy in them also: the excellent of the earth, in whom is all your delight, are made to be the comrades of your sojourning.

The title is also used by way of *employment* as well as enjoyment. Adam was not put in the garden that he might simply walk through its borders, and admire its flowers, and taste its fruits; but he was placed there to keep it and to dress it. There was sufficient to be done to prevent his stagnating from want of occupation. He had not to toil sufficiently to make him wipe the sweat from his brow, for that came of the curse: "In the sweat of thy face shalt thou eat bread:" but still he was not permitted to be idle, for that might have been a worse curse. Even for a perfect man unbroken leisure would not be a blessing. It is essential even to an unfallen creature that he should have work to do—fit work and honourable, seeing it is done by a creature for the great Benefactor who had created him. If we had not our daily tasks to fulfil, rest would corrode into rust, and recreation would soon gender corruption. You and I are set in the garden of the church because there is work for us to do which will be beneficial to others and to ourselves also. Some have to take the broad axe and hew down mighty trees of error; others of a feebler sort can with a child's hand train the tendril of a climbing plant, or drop into its place a tiny seed. One may plant and another may water : one may sow and another gather fruit. One may cut up weeds and another prune vines. God hath work in his church for us all to do, and he has left us here that we may do it. Our Lord Jesus would not keep a single saint out of heaven if there were not a needs-be for his being here in the lowlands, to trim these gardens of herbs, and watch these beds of spices. Would he deny his well-beloved the palm branch and the crown if it were not better for us to be holding the pruning-hook and the spade? A school-book wherewith to teach the little children may be for a while more to our true advantage than a golden harp. To turn over the pages of Scripture wherewith to instruct the people of God may be more profitable to us than to hear the song of seraphim. I say, the Master's love to his own which prompts him to pray, "I will that they also whom thou hast given me be with me where I am, that they may behold my glory," would long ago have drawn all the blood-bought up to himself above, had it not been the fact that it is in infinite wisdom seen to be better that they should abide in the flesh. Ye are the lights of the world, ye are the salt of the earth : shall the light and the salt be at once withdrawn ? Ye are to be as a dew from the Lord in this dry and thirsty land ; would ye be at once exhaled ? Brothers, have you found out what you have to do in these gardens ? Sisters, have you found out the plants for which you are to care ? If not, arouse yourselves and let not a moment pass till you have discovered your duty and your place. Speak unto him who is the Lord of all true servants, and say to him, "Show me what thou wouldest have me to do. Point out, I pray thee, the place wherein I may serve thee." Would you have it said of you that you were a wicked and slothful servant? Shall it be told that you dwelt in the gardens, and allowed the grass to grow up to your ankles, and suffered the thorns and the thistles to multiply until your land became as the sluggard's vineyard, pointed at as a disgrace and a warning to all that passed by? "O thou that dwellest in the gardens !" The title sets forth employment constant and engrossing.

Dear friends, it means also *eminence.* I know many Christian people who do not feel that they dwell in the gardens. They reside in a certain town or village where the gospel may be preached, but not in demonstration of the Spirit and in power. A little gospel is made to go a long way with some preachers. In some ministries there is no life or power, no unction or savour. The people who meet under such preaching are cold of heart and dull in spirit; the prayer-meetings are forgotten ; communion of saints has well-nigh died out ; and there is a general deadness as to Christian effort. Believe me, it is a dreadful thing when Christian people have almost to dread their Sabbath days ; and I have known this to be the case. When you are called to hard toil through the six days of the week you want a good spiritual meal on the Sabbath, and if you get it, you find therein a blessed compensation and refreshment. Is it not a heavenly joy to sit still on the one day of rest, and to be fed with the finest of the wheat? I have known men made capable of bearing great trials—personal, relative, pecuniary, and the like—because they have looked backward upon one Sabbatic feast, and then forward to another. They have said in their hour of trouble,—"Patience, my heart ; the Lord's day is coming, when I shall drink and forget my misery. I shall go and sit with God's people, and I shall have fellowship with the Father and with the Son, and my soul shall be satisfied as with marrow and fatness, till I praise the Lord with joyful lips." But what a sorry case to dread the Sunday, and to mutter, "I shall get nothing next Sunday any more than I did last Sunday except some dry philosophical essay, or a heap of the childish toys and fireworks of oratory, or the same dull mumbling of a mechanical orthodoxy." Oh, brethren and sisters, my text is scarcely meant for those who dwell in such deserts, but it speaks with emphasis to those who dwell where sweet spiritual fruits are plentiful, where odours and perfumes load the air, where the land floweth with milk and honey. If any of you happen to dwell where Christ is set forth evidently crucified among you, and where your hearts do leap for very joy because the King himself comes near to feast his saints and make them glad in his presence, then it is to you that my text hath a voice and a call : "Thou that dwellest in the gardens, in the choicest places of all Immanuel's land, let me hear thy voice."

Yet one more word. The title here employed is not only for eminence but for *permanence.* "O thou that *dwellest* in the gardens." If you are only permitted to enjoy sound gospel teaching now and again, and then are forced to cry, "It may be another twelve months before I shall be again fed on royal dainties." Then you are in a trying case, and you need to cry to God for help : but blessed are those who dwell in the good land, and daily fill their homers with heavenly manna. "Blessed are they that dwell in thy house : they will be still praising thee." No spot on earth is so dear to the Christian as that whereon he meets his Lord. I can understand why the Jew asked of a certain town that was recommended to him as good for business, "Is there a synagogue there?" Being a devout man, and finding that there was no synagogue, he said he would rather remain where trade was dull, but where he could go with his brethren to worship. Is it not so with us? How my heart has longed for these blessed assemblies! Give me a crust and a full gospel rather than all riches and a barren ministry. The profitable hearing of the word is the greatest enjoyment upon earth to godly men. It would be banishment to go where every week's business turned into a mint of money if one were also compelled to be a member of an unhappy, quarrelsome, or inactive church. Our greatest joy is in thee, O Jerusalem! Let our tongue cleave to the roof of our mouth if we prefer thee not above our greatest joy!

> "How charming is the place
> Where my Redeemer God
> Unveils the beauties of his face,
> And sheds his love abroad.
>
> Not the fair palaces,
> To which the great resort,
> Are once to be compared with this,
> Where Jesus holds his court."

Beloved, if you dwell in the gardens you have a double privilege, not only of being found in a fat and fertile place, but in living there continually. You might well forego a thousand comforts for the sake of this one delight, for under the gospel your soul is made to drink of wines on the lees well refined.

This, then, is my first head—appointed residence:—"Thou that dwellest in the gardens." Is not this a choice abode for the Lord's beloved? I leave you to judge how far this describes yourselves. If it be your case, then listen to what the Bridegroom has to say to you.

II. Secondly, let us note the RECORDED CONVERSE: "Thou that dwellest in the gardens, the companions hearken to thy voice." She was in the gardens, but she was not quiet there, and why should she be? God gives us tongues on purpose that they should be used. As he made birds to sing, and stars to shine, and rivers to flow, so has he made men and women to converse with one another to his glory. Our tongue is the glory of our frame, and there would be no glory in its being for ever dumb. The monks of La Trappe, who maintain perpetual silence, do no more than the rocks among which they labour. When God makes bells he means to ring them. It may be thought to be a desirable thing that some should speak less, but it is still more desirable that they should speak better. When the tongue indites a good matter, it is no fault if it be nimble as the pen of a ready writer. It is not the quantity, it is the quality of what we say that ought to be considered.

Now, observe that evidently the spouse held with her companions *frequent intercourse*,—" The companions hearken to thy voice." She frequently conversed with them. I hope it is so among those of you who dwell in this part of Christ's garden. It should be so: " Then they that feared the Lord spake often one to another;" they had not now and then a crack, now and then the passing of the time of day, but they held frequent converse. Heaven will consist largely in the communion of saints, and if we would enjoy heaven below we must carry out the words of the creed in our practice,—" I believe in the communion of saints." Let us show that we do believe in it. Some persons sit still in their pews till the time to go, and then walk down the aisle in majestic isolation, as if they were animated statues. Do children thus come in and out of their father's house with never a word for their brothers and sisters ? I know professors who float through life like icebergs from whom it is safest to keep clear : surely these partake not of the spirit of Christ. It is well when such icebergs are drawn into the gulf stream of divine love and melt away into Christ and his people. There should be among those who are children of the common Father a mutual love, and they should show this by frequent commerce in their precious things, making a sacred barter with one another. I like to hear them making sacred exchanges : one mentioning his trials, another quoting his deliverances ; one telling how God has answered prayer, and another recording how the word of God has come to him with power. Such converse ought to be as usual as the talk of children of one family.

And next, it should be *willing and influential;* for if you notice, it is put here : " Thou that dwellest in the gardens, the companions *hearken* to thy voice." They do not merely hear it, and say to themselves, " I wish she would be quiet," but they hearken, they lend an ear, they listen gladly. I know some Christians whose lips feed many. I could mention brethren and sisters who drop pearls from their lips whenever they speak. We have still among us Chrysostoms, or men of golden mouths ; you cannot be with them for half an hour without being enriched. Their anointing is manifest, for it spreads to all around them. When the Spirit of God makes our communications sweet, then the more of them the better. I like to get sometimes under the shadow of God's best people, the fathers in Israel, and to hear what they have to say to the honour of the name of the Lord. We who are young men feel gladdened by the testimonies of the ancients ; and as for the babes in grace, they look up to the grey-beards and gather strength from their words of experience and grace. If there are any here whose language is such that others delight to listen to it, it is to such that my text is especially addressed ; and when I come to open up the later part of it I want you that have the honeyed tongues, I want you who are listened to with pleasure, to notice how the Beloved says to you, " The companions hearken to thy voice: cause me to hear it." Give thy Lord a share of thy sweet utterances : let thy Saviour's ear be charmed as well as thy companions' ears. Come, speak *to him* as well as to thy brethren, and if there be music in thy voice let that music be for the Well-beloved as well as for thy fellow-servants. This is the very heart of the matter. I cannot help alluding to it even before we have fairly reached that part of the text. The converse of the bride in the gardens was constant, and it was greatly esteemed by those who enjoyed it.

I gather from the text, rather by implication than otherwise, that the converse was *commendable;* for the bridegroom does not say to the spouse, "Thou that dwellest in the gardens, thy companions hear too much of thy voice." No; he evidently mentions the fact with approval, because he draws an argument from it why he also should hear that self-same voice. Brothers, I leave it to yourselves to judge whether your communications with one another are always such as they should be. Are they always worthy of you? What communications have ye had this morning? Can I make a guess? "Nice and fresh this morning." "Quite a change in the weather." Is not this the style? How often we instruct each other about what we all know! When it rains so as to soak our garments we gravely tell each other that it is very wet. Yes, and if the sun shines we are all eager to communicate the wonderful information that it is warm. Dear me, what instructors of our generation we are! Could we not contrive to change the subject? Is it because we have nothing to say of love, and grace, and truth that we meet and part without learning or teaching anything? Perhaps so. I wish we had a little more small change of heavenly converse: we have our crowns and sovereigns for the pulpit, we need groats and pence for common talk, all stamped with the image and superscription of the King of heaven. O Holy Spirit enrich us after this sort. May our communications be such that if Jesus himself were near we might not be ashamed for him to hear our voices. Brethren, make your conversation such that it may be commended by Christ himself.

These communications were, no doubt, *very beneficial.* As iron sharpeneth iron, so does a man's countenance his friend. Oh, what a comfort it is to drop in upon a cheerful person when you yourself are heavy! What a ballast it puts into your ship, when you are a little too merry, to meet with one in sore travail who bids you share his burden and emulate his faith. We are all the better, believe me, when our Lord can praise us, because the companions hearken to our voices.

In fact, our communications with one another ought to be *preparatory* to higher communications still. The converse of saints on earth should be a rehearsal of their everlasting communion in heaven. We should begin here to be to one another what we hope to be to one another world without end. And is it not pleasant to rise from communion with your brethren into communion with the Bridegroom?—to have such talk to one another that at last we perceive that truly our fellowship is with the Father and with his Son Jesus Christ? We thought that we only communed with our brethren; but, lo! we see that the Lord himself is here: do not our hearts burn within us? We two are talking of him, and now we see that he himself is here, opening to us the Scriptures, and opening our hearts to receive those Scriptures in the power of them. Beloved, let us try if we cannot make it so, that as we dwell together as church members, and work together in one common

vineyard, we may be always making our fellowship with each other
a grand staircase of fellowship with the King himself. Let us so talk
that we may expect to meet Jesus while we are talking. How sweet
to hear and see the Master in the servant, the Bridegroom in the
bridegroom's friend, the Head in the members, the Shepherd in the
sheep, the Christ in every Christian! Thus may we rise upon the wings
of hallowed intercourse with holy ones to yet more hallowed intercourse
with the Holy One of Israel.

Thus have we meditated upon two things: we have noted the appointed
residence and the recorded converse. We know what we are talking about.

III. Now comes the pith of the text: INVITED FELLOWSHIP—" The
companions hear thy voice: cause me to hear it." It is beautiful to
hear the Beloved say in effect, " I am going away from you, and you see
me no more; but I shall see you: do not forget me. Though you will
not hear my voice with your bodily ears, I shall hear your voices: therefore speak to me. Unseen I shall feed among the lilies; unperceived I
shall walk the garden in the cool of the day: when you are talking to
others do not forget me. Sometimes turn aside, and when you have
shut to the door, and no eye can see, nor ear can hear, then let me
hear thy voice: it has music in it to my heart, for I died to give you
life. Let me hear the voice of your prayer, and praise, and love."

Now, I note concerning this invitation, first of all, that it is very
loving and condescending to us that the Lord should wish to hear our
voice. I do not wonder that some of you love to hear my voice, because
the Holy Spirit has blessed it to your conversion: but what good has
Jesus ever derived from any of us ? Is it not marvellous that he, the
infinitely blessed, should want to hear our voices when all that he hath
heard from us has been begging, sighing, and a few poor broken hymns ?
You do not want to hear a beggar's voice, do you ? I expect if the man
you have helped a score of times should be to-morrow morning at your
door, you would say, " Dear, dear ; there is that man again." Might
not the Well-beloved say the same of you ? " There she is again : come
on the same errand. Come to confess some new faults, or to ask fresh
favours." But instead of being tired of us our Lord says, " Let me hear
thy voice." O loving Bridegroom ! Must he not love us very truly to
ask us to speak with him ? See, he asks as though he begged it of
us as a favour, " Let me hear thy voice. Thy companions hearken : let
me take a share in their intercourse : they find thy voice pleasant, let it
be a pleasure also to me. Come, do not deny me, thy heart's best
beloved! Do not be silent unto me! Come, speak to me with thine
own sweet mouth."

It is condescending and gracious, and yet how *natural* it is ! How like
to Christ! Love ever seeks the company of that which it loves. What
would a husband say if his wife was seen to be chatty and cheerful to

everybody else, but never spoke to him? I cannot suppose such a case: it would make too sorrowful a household. I should pity the poor, broken-hearted man who should be forced to say, " My beloved, others hear thy voice, and admire it; wilt thou not speak to me, thy husband?" O believer, will you let the Lord Jesus, as it were with tears in his eyes, say to you, " You talk to everybody but to me : you lay yourself out to please everybody but me : you are a charming companion to everybody but to me"? Oh, our Beloved, how ill have we treated thee! How much have we slighted thee! In looking back, I fear there are many of us who must feel as if this gentle word of the Lord had also a sharp side to it. I do remember my faults this day. The text goes like a dagger to my soul, for I have spoken all day long to others, and have had scarce a word for him whom my soul loveth. Let us mend our converse, and henceforth show our Lord a truer love.

We may truly add, that this invitation to fellowship is a *blessed and profitable* request. We shall find it so if we carry it out, especially those of us who are called by God to use our voices for him among the crowds of our companions. I address some brothers and sisters here who are preachers and teachers. What a relief it is, when you have been letting the companions hear your voice, to stop a bit and let Jesus hear it! What a rest to leave the congregation for the closet, to get away from where they criticize you to one who delights in you. What a relief, I say. And what a help to our hearts! Jesus gives us sweet returns if we commune with him, and such as speakers greatly need. The apostles said that they would give themselves to the word of God and to prayer. Yes, we must put those two things together. We shall never fitly handle the word of God without prayer. When we pray we are taught how to speak the word to others. Salvation and supplication are a blessed pair. Put the two together, so that, when you speak to others about salvation, you do it after having baptized your own soul into supplication. " The companions hear thy voice: cause me to hear it: before thou speakest with them speak to me : whilst thou art still speaking with them still speak with me; and when thy speaking to men is done, return unto thy rest and again speak with me."

This invitation is *a many-sided one ;* for when the bridegroom says, " Cause me to hear it," he means that she should speak to him in all sorts of ways. Frequently we should be heard in praise. If thou hast been praising the Lord in the audience of others, turn aside and praise him to his face. Sing thy song to thy Beloved himself. Get into a quiet place and sing where only he can hear. I wish we had more of that kind of music which does not care for other audience than God. Oh, my God, my heart shall find *thee*, and every string shall have its attribute to sing, while my whole being shall extol *thee*, my Lord! The blessed Virgin had none with her but Elizabeth when she sang, " My soul doth magnify the Lord, and my spirit doth rejoice in God my Saviour." Oh, let the Lord hear your voice! Get up early to be alone with him. So let it be with all your complaints and petitions; let them be for Jesus only. Too often we fill our fellow creature's ear with the sad tale of all our care. Why not tell the Lord about it, and have done with it? We should employ our time far more profitably if, instead of murmuring in the tent, we enquired in the Temple.

Speak with Jesus Christ, dear friends, in little broken sentences, by way of frequent ejaculation. The best of Christian fellowship may be carried on in single syllables. When in the middle of business you can whisper, "My Lord and my God!" You can dart a glance upward, heave a sigh, or let fall a tear, and so will Jesus hear your voice! When nobody observes the motion of your lips you may be saying, "My Beloved, be near me now!" This is the kind of fellowship which your Saviour asks of you. He says, "The companions hear thy voice: cause me to hear it. Be sure that when thou speakest with others thou dost also speak with me!"

This is such a blessed invitation that I think, dear friends, we ought to avail ourselves of it at once. Come, what say you? The best Beloved asks us to speak with him, what shall we say at once? Think for an instant! What shall I say? Perhaps I have the start of you, because I have my word ready. Here it is:—"Make haste, my beloved, and be thou like to a roe or to a young hart upon the mountains of spices." "Why," say you, "that is what the church said in the last verse of the Song." Exactly so, and that is what we may wisely say at this moment. We cannot improve upon it. "Come quickly; even so, come quickly, Lord Jesus." Often and often, then, when you are about your business, say, "Come, Lord Jesus! Come quickly!" It is a sweet frame of mind to be in to be willing to invite Christ to come; and whenever you cannot do so let it be a warning to you that you are in dangerous waters. I can imagine a man in business calling himself a Christian about to engage in a doubtful transaction: how is he to discern the danger? Let him ask the Lord Jesus Christ to come while he is doing it. "Oh dear no"; cries one, "I had rather he should not come until that matter had been finished and forgotten." Then be you sure that you are moving in the wrong direction. Suppose you think of going to a certain place of amusement about which you have a question, it is easy to decide it thus:—When you take your seat your first thing should be to bow your head and ask for a blessing, and then say, "Lord, here I sit waiting for thine appearing." "Oh," say you, "I should not want the Lord to come there." Of course you would not. Then do not go where you could not wish your Lord to find you. My text may thus be a monitor to you, to keep you from the paths of the destroyer. Jesus says, "Let me hear thy voice," and let thy voice utter these desires,—" Even so, come quickly; come, Lord Jesus!"

Alas, time reproves me; I must hasten on.

IV. I have a fourth head, which shall be very briefly handled. I find according to the Hebrew that the text has in it a REQUESTED TESTIMONY. According to learned interpreters the Hebrew runs thus: " *Cause to hear me.*" Now, that may mean what I have said, " Cause me to hear;" but it may also mean, " Cause them to hear me." Now hearken; you that are in Christ's garden: make those who dwell in that garden with you to hear from you much about HIM. In the church everyone has a right to talk about the Head of the church. Some of our brethren in this Tabernacle kindly undertake to speak to individuals about their souls, and now and then they receive very sharp rebuffs. What right has he to put such a question? How dare he intrude with personal remarks? What! Is the man poaching? No: these are the Lord's preserves; and the Lord's gamekeepers have a right to do as they are bidden by him. They are not poaching in this place, for they are on the Master's own land. Anywhere inside these four walls you may speak to anybody about Christ, and no man may forbid you. Speak lovingly and tenderly and prudently; but certainly the law of the house is that here we may speak about the Lord of the house. There are some other things you may not talk about, but about the Lord Jesus you may speak as much as you will. In the garden, at any rate, if not in the wild wilderness, let the Rose of Sharon be sweetly spoken of. Let his name be as ointment poured forth in all the church of God.

Again, you, according to the text, are one that can make people hear, so that "the companions hearken to thy voice;" then make them to hear of Jesus. You have the gift of speech: use it for Christ crucified. I always feel regret when a powerful speaker espouses any other cause but that of my Lord. Time was when I used to wish that Milton had been a preacher, and instead of writing a poem had proclaimed the gospel to the multitude. I know better now, for I perceive that God doth not use learning and eloquence so much as knowledge of Christ and plain speech; but still I am jealous of any man who can speak well that he should not give my Lord the use of his tongue. Well-trained tongues are rare things, and they should be all consecrated to Christ's glory. If you can speak to the companions—make them hear about Christ: if you can speak well, make them to hear attractive words about Christ.

If you do not speak about Christ to strangers, do speak to your *companions*. They will hearken to you; therefore let them hearken to the word of the Lord. I have heard of men who called themselves Christians who yet never spoke to their children about their souls, never spoke to their servants nor to their workpeople about Jesus and his love. This is to murder souls. If tongues can bless and do not, then they in effect curse men by their silence. If you have a voice, make the name of Jesus to be sounded out all around you. Many are the voices that strike upon the ear: the world is full of din, even to distraction, yet the name which is above all other names is scarcely heard. I pray you, my brethren, you that are like silver bells, ring out that name o'er hill and dale. As with a clarion, trumpet forth the saving name of Jesus till the deaf hear the sound thereof. Whatever is left out of your testimony, be sure that Christ crucified is first and last in it. Love Christ and live Christ; think of Christ and speak of Christ. When people go away from hearing you preach, may they have to say, "He kept to his subject: he knew nothing but Jesus." It is ill when a man has to say of preachers, "They have taken away my Lord, and I know not where they have laid him." Yet in certain sermons you meet with a little about everything except the one thing. They offer us what we do not need ; but the need of the soul is not supplied. Oh, my brethren, cause Christ to be heard. Hammer on that anvil always: if you make no music but that of the harmonious blacksmith it will suffice. Ring it out with sturdy blows— "Jesus, Jesus, Jesus crucified." Hammer away at that. "Now you are on the right string, man," said the Duke of Argyle, when the preacher came to speak upon the Lord Jesus. It needed no duke to certify that. Harp on that string. Make Jesus to be as commonly known as now he is commonly unknown. So may God bless you as long as you dwell in these gardens, till the day break and the shadows flee away. Amen.

PORTION OF SCRIPTURE READ BEFORE SERMON—Psalm v.

HYMNS FROM "OUR OWN HYMN BOOK"—5, 811, 784.

THE MARVELLOUS MAGNET.

A Sermon

DELIVERED BY

C. H. SPURGEON,

AT THE METROPOLITAN TABERNACLE, NEWINGTON,

On an evening when the regular hearers left their seats to be occupied by strangers.

"I, if I be lifted up from the earth, will draw all men unto me. This he said, signifying what death he should die."—John xii. 32, 33.

JESUS is the spokesman here. He tells of his own death by crucifixion, and of the result which will follow. It appears, then, that our Lord's power to draw all men to himself lies mainly in his death. By being lifted up from the earth upon the cross he was made to die, and so also was he made to draw all men unto himself. There is an attractive power about our Lord's person, and about his life, and about his teaching; but, still, the main attractive force lies in his death upon the cross. Most certainly this is rare and strange; for when a great religious leader dies, a large measure of his personal power is gone. The charm of the man's manner, the impressiveness of his personal conviction, the lofty tone of his daily enthusiasm—these are immense helps to a cause while they are with us: to lose them is a fearful drawback such as makes it perilous for a religious leader to die. Men may remember a leader's life for a time after his death: they will do so most emphatically if he has been eminently good. We say of the righteous,— "Even in their ashes live their wonted fires." From many a tomb there rises a silent voice more eloquent than the choicest speech: " He being dead yet speaketh." But there is a measure and bound to the influence of a mere memory. How often is it the case that, after a little while, the leader having gone, the feebler folk gradually drop away, the hypocritical openly desert, the lukewarm wander, and so the cause dies out. The man's successors desert his principles, or maintain them with but little life and energy, and, therefore, what was once a hopeful effort expires like a dying taper. For a man's work to prosper it is not desirable that he should die. Is it not strange that what is so often fatal to the influence of other men is a gain to our Lord Jesus Christ; for it is by his death that he possesses his most powerful influence over the sons of men? Because Jesus died, he is this day the mightiest ruler of human minds, the great centre to which all hearts are being drawn.

Remember, too, that our Lord Jesus Christ died by a most shameful death. We have come to use the cross as an ornament, and by some it

No. 1,717.

is regarded as an object of reverence; but the cross, to speak **very** plainly, was to the ancients what the gibbet **is to** us—an odious instrument of death for felons—exactly that, and no more. The death of the cross was one never allotted to a Roman citizen except for certain heinous crimes. It was regarded as the death-penalty of a slave. It was not only painful, it was disgraceful and ignominious; and to say that a man was crucified was, in our Lord's time, exactly tantamount to saying in our speech to-day that he was hanged. It means just that; and you must accept the death of the cross with all the shame that can be connected with the gibbet and the tree of death, or else you will not understand what it meant to Jesus and his disciples. Now, surely, if a man is hanged there is an end to his influence among men. When I was looking through all the Bible commentaries in the English language, I found one with a title-page attributing it to Dr. Coke; but on further examination I perceived that it was the commentary of Dr. Dodd, who was executed for forgery. After he had been hanged, of course the publishers could not sell a commentary under his name, and so they engaged another learned doctor to take it under his wing. The man was hanged, and therefore people would not read his book, and you are not at all surprised that it should be so. But herein is a wonderful thing. The Lord Jesus has lost no influence by having been hanged upon the tree; nay, rather it is because of his shameful death that he is able to draw all men unto himself. His glory rises from his humiliation; his adorable conquest from his ignominious death. When he " became obedient unto death, even the death of the cross," shame cast no shame upon his cause, but gilded it with glory. Christ's death of weakness threw no weakness into Christianity; say rather that it is the right arm of her power. By the sign of suffering unto death the church has conquered, and will conquer still. By a love which is strong as death she has always been victorious, and must for ever remain so. When she has not been ashamed to put the cross in the forefront, she has never had to be ashamed; for God has been with her, and Jesus has drawn all men to himself. The crucified Christ has irresistible attractions: when HE stoops into the utmost suffering and scorn even the brutal must relent: a living Saviour men *may* love, but a crucified Saviour they *must* love. If they perceive that he loved them, and gave himself for them, their hearts are stolen away: the city of Mansoul is captured before the siege begins, when the Prince Emanuel uncovers the beauties of his dying love before the eyes of the rebellious ones.

Let us never be ashamed, dear friends, to preach Christ crucified—the Son of God lifted up to die among the condemned. Let those of us who teach in the Sunday-school, or preach at the street corner, or in any other manner try to set forth the gospel, always keep a dying Christ to the front. Christ without the cross is no Christ at all. Never forget that he is the eternal God, but bind with that truth the fact that he was nailed to a Roman gibbet. It is on the tree he triumphed over Satan, and it is by the cross that he must triumph over the world. " I, if I be lifted up from the earth, will draw all men unto me. This he said, signifying what death he should die."

The great truth of the text I have stated to you; let me enlarge thereon.

I. I shall try to speak first upon the ATTRACTIVE FORCE WHICH LIES IN A CRUCIFIED SAVIOUR.

You will observe that it is briefly summed up in these words: *himself* to *himself*. "*I* will draw all men unto *me*." It is not written that Christ will draw all men to the visible church, for the universal profession of our holy faith is slow enough in coming. Certainly the Lord Jesus Christ will not lend himself out to draw men to your sect or to mine. He will draw ever towards truth and righteousness, but not to dead forms or meaningless distinctions; nor to the memories of former wrongs or party victories. If the Lord should draw men to the Cathedral or the Tabernacle, the Abbey or the Chapel, it would be of little service to them unless in each case they found himself. The main thing that is wanted is that they be drawn to himself, and none can draw them to himself but himself. Himself drawing them to himself —this is the soul of the text.

I dare say that you have heard the oft-recounted story of the missionaries among the Greenlanders. Our Moravian brethren, full of fire and zeal and self-denial, went right away among the ignorant folk of Greenland, as those people then were, longing to convert them. Using large prudence, they thought, "These people are so benighted that it cannot be of any use to preach Jesus Christ to them at first. They do not even know that there is a God, so let us begin by teaching them the nature of the Deity, showing them right and wrong, proving to them the need of atonement for sin, and setting before them the rewards of the righteous and the penalties of the wicked." This was judged to be most fit preparatory work. Watch for the result! They went on for years, but had no converts. What was there in all that fine preparatory teaching that could convert anybody? Jesus was being locked out of the Greenlanders' hearts by those who wanted him to enter. But one day one of the missionaries happened to read to a poor Greenlander the story of Jesus bleeding on the cross, and how God had sent his Son to die, "that whosoever believeth in him should not perish, but have everlasting life;" and the Greenlander said, "Would you read me that again? What wonderful words! Did the Son of God die for us poor Greenlanders that we may live?" The missionary answered that it was even so; and, clapping his hands, the simple native cried, "Why did you not tell us that before?" Ah, just so! Why not tell them this at once, and leave it to clear its own path? That is the point to begin with. Let us start with the Lamb of God which taketh away the sin of the world. "God so loved the world, that he gave his only begotten Son, that whosoever believeth in him should not perish, but have everlasting life." To my mind that is the point to begin with and the point to go on with; yes, that is the truth to conclude with, if there can ever be any conclusion to the grand old story of the incarnate God who loved his enemies, and gave himself to die in their stead, that they might live through him. The gospel is Jesus drawing sinners to himself that they might live through him. Dear hearers, do you know what this means? I know that many of you do, and you are happy; for in this knowledge there is life. Would to God that all knew this power of love in Christ—knew it so as to be drawn by almighty love to return that love with all their heart, and soul, and strength. The best thing that can happen to any one

of us is to feel Christ drawing him to Christ, and to find himself
sweetly yielding to the gentle drawing of the Saviour's love.

The text says that Jesus Christ will draw all men unto himself.
Now, all men who hear of Jesus Christ at all are drawn, but they do not
all yield. Some of them pull back, and the most awful thing that ever
happens to a man is when he pulls back till Jesus lets him go. What
a fall is that, when the drawing power is taken away, and the man falls
backward into a destruction which he himself has chosen, having refused
eternal life, and resisted the Saviour's power! Unhappy is the wretch
who strives against his own salvation. Every man that hears the
gospel feels some measure of its drawing power. I appeal to any
one of you who has been accustomed to hear it. Does not Jesus
sometimes tug hard at your conscience-strings, and, though you have
pulled back, yet has he not drawn and drawn again? I remember
how he drew *me* as a child, and, though I drew back from him, yet
did he never let me go till he drew me over the border line. Some
of you must well remember how you were drawn by a mother's gentle
words—by a teacher's earnest pleadings—by a father's admonitions—by
a sister's tears—by a pastor's entreaties. Permit your memories to aid
me. Bring up before your mind's eye the many dear ones who have
broken their hearts to win you for Jesus. Yes, you have been drawn.

I suppose that all of you have felt a measure of that drawing. Why,
it is not merely those that hear the gospel, but whole nations have been
drawn, in other respects, by the all-pervading influence of Jesus and his
love. At this instant the influence of Christianity is being felt in every
corner of the earth to an extent which it is not easy to exaggerate. If I
had an orator's power, I would picture my Saviour casting golden chains
of love over all nations, wherever the missionary goes preaching his
name. The Lord is taming the nations as a man by degrees subdues
wild beasts. Jesus is gradually drawing the heathen to himself. He has
had a long tug at India. That dead weight still lies in the furrow.
But it must come: it must yield. All those that watch it see that if
there is any cause that does make progress in India it is the cause of
Christ. The East appears never to move, but if there be any move it is
Christward. Jesus is drawing China slowly. Japan is being drawn
as in a net. Where the testimony of Christ has been borne the idols
begin to shake, and their priests confess that a change is coming. Every
century sees a marked advance in the world's condition; and we shall
progress at a quicker rate yet when the church wakes up to a sense of
her responsibility, and the Holy Spirit is poured out upon the church
to turn us all into missionaries, causing us all in some way or other to
preach the gospel of Christ. Jesus is drawing, drawing, drawing. When
God meant to scatter the individuals of our race they would not be
scattered: they built a tower to be the centre of union, and only by
their tongues being so changed that they could not understand one
another could their resolve to remain in one company be defeated. But
now, behold, the whole earth has the race of men to cover it: the sons
of Adam dwell in every region, and it is the Father's will to gather
together in one the redeemed of the Lord. Therefore he has set in their
midst the great Shiloh, of whom it was prophesied of old, " To him shall
the gathering of the people be." The roaming races do not answer

to the Father's call; they do not want to come to the elder Brother's rule; but they will have to come, for he must reign. Gentile and Jew, African and European—they shall all meet at the cross, the common centre of our entire manhood; for Christ is lifted up, and he is drawing all men unto him.

But all men are not saved. No, for when drawn they do not come. Yet Christ crucified is drawing some men of all kinds and sorts to eternal life. When Jesus died on the cross it was not for my lord and lady only; nor was it for the working-man alone; it was for all sorts of people.

> "While grace is offered to the prince,
> The poor may take their share.
> No mortal has a just pretence
> To perish in despair."

He that is best taught and instructed has often been drawn to Jesus by the Lord's overpowering charms. Some of the most learned of men have been delighted to come to Christ. But the most illiterate and rude have equally been drawn by Jesus, and it has been their joy to come. I love to hear of the gospel being preached to the poorest of the poor; and so preached that it reaches those who never were reached by it before. God speed every effort by which Jesus is set before the fallen and degraded; so long as it is the gospel, and not mere rant, we wish God-speed to the most irregular of witnesses: our fears begin only when Jesus is no longer in the van. We greatly need to have the gospel preached in the West of London, and so preached that our great ones may receive it, and find life through Jesus Christ. May such a movement soon take place. How I should like to hear of a converted duke telling out the gospel, or a reclaimed knight of the garter proclaiming mercy for the chief of sinners! Why not? And, blessed be God, the Saviour, lifted up, draws all sorts of men to himself—some of every kind; not the Jew alone, as at the first, but the Gentile too.

> "None are excluded hence but those
> Who do themselves exclude.
> Welcome the learned and polite,
> The ignorant and rude."

There is no exclusion of any class or creature from the mercy of God in Christ Jesus. "I, if I be lifted up, will draw all men unto me"; and the history of the church proves how true this is: the muster-roll of the converted includes princes and paupers, peers and potmen.

But what is this force that attracts men to the crucified Saviour? They do come: there is no doubt about it. Look ye, sirs; there is nothing in the world that men will hear so gladly as the gospel. How many years have I stood in this place to preach to a congregation precisely similar to the present! The crowds have been here as regularly as the hours, Sunday after Sunday, morning and evening, year after year. Suppose that I had been appointed to preach upon a scientific subject; could I have gained or held such audiences? I should have been spun out a long while ago if I had been bound to draw upon myself for my matter. If I had preached any other than the doctrine of Christ crucified, I should years ago have scattered my audience to the winds of heaven. But the old theme is always new, always fresh, always attractive. Preach Jesus Christ. That is the recipe for catching men's ears and laying hold upon men's hearts. The name of Jesus is to man's heart the most mighty of charms : man's ear waits for it as the morning hour waits for the sun, or as the parched earth waits for the shower. Ring out the name of Jesus; it is the sweetest carol ever sung. Ring it out without fear or stint, for it is always welcome as the flowers in May : men will never tire of it till the flowers are satiated with sunlight, and the grass grows weary of the dew. The music of that blessed silver bell rings out o'er hill and dale as sweetly as when, on the first Christmas-night, the angels sang, "Glory to God in the highest, and on earth peace, good will toward men." There is about Calvary and its infinite stoop of divine love a power that never dies out, and never will while the world stands. What is it? Whence this universal attractiveness?

Well, first, it is the force of *love*; for Jesus Christ is incarnate love. In him you see one who divested himself of all his glory, that he might save the guilty—who came down upon earth, not seeking wealth and fame, but simply seeking to do good by saving men—who, having laid aside his honour and his glory, at last laid aside his life, and all for love ; for love which met a sad return ; for love which has, however, saved its objects with a great salvation. One of the school-men says that, whenever we know that another person loves us, we cannot help giving back a measure of love in return ; and I believe that the statement is true. Certainly, such love as the love of Christ, when it is told out simply, and men can understand it, is certain to excite an interest, to win a degree of attention, and so to lead up to better things. Full often this love proves its power over observers by transforming them from enemies into friends; and, though they at first despised the Redeemer, his love compels them, at length, to believe and to adore. If I were asked the secret of the attractive power of the crucified Saviour, I should answer that it is invincible love. The only crime that ever could be laid to Jesus' charge was that of which the poet sings—"found guilty of excess of love"—loving beyond all reason, and beyond all bound— loving as none ever loved before ; so that if all the rivers of human love did run together they could not fill such another ocean of love as was in the heart of Jesus the Saviour. This it is—this unique, unrivalled love—which draws men to Jesus. The pierced heart of Christ is a load-stone to draw all other hearts.

No doubt there is also this about the crucified Saviour—that he draws men by *the wonderful rest which his death provides for men.* The most earnest Christian man must sometimes have his doubts as to whether all is right with him. The more sincere a man is the more does he tremble lest he should deceive himself. You, good brother, have your personal anxieties ; certainly I have mine. But when I turn my eyes to Jesus upon the cross, and view the thorn-crown, and the sacred head, and the eyes that were red with weeping, and the hands nailed fast to the wood, and the feet dripping with gore; and when I remember that this shameful death was endured for love of me, I am so quiet and so happy in my spirit that I cannot tell how peacefully my life-floods flow. God *must* forgive my grievous fault, for my Redeemer has so grievously answered for it. When I see Jesus die I perceive that henceforth divine justice is on the sinner's side. How can the Lord God punish the same offence twice—first the Substitute and then the men for whom that Substitute has bled? Christ has bled as substitute for every man that believes in him,—therefore is every believer safe. Oh, brethren, when you are troubled, rest with us, by looking to Calvary: and if the first glance does not quiet you, look, and look, and look again, for every grief will die where Jesus died. Not to Bethlehem, where the stars of Christmas burn, do we look for our greatest comfort, but to that place where the sun was darkened at mid-day, and the face of eternal love was veiled. Because the Lord of life and glory was dying in *iremis*, suffering the most deadly pain for our sakes, therefore his wounds distilled the richest balm that ever healed a sinner's wound. Men know this. Reading their Bibles, they soon find it out. There is no comfort for them against the anger of God, and against their guilty consciences, until they see Christ in their stead, suffering for them. The conscience sees with unspeakable delight the victim provided; she gladly lays her hand on Jesus' head, and sees her sin transferred to him, and punished in him, and thus it findeth rest, like the rest of God. In the expiatory death of Jesus the law is vindicated, and God is "just, and yet the justifier of him that believeth." Dear friends, believe me, Jesus bestows the peerless pearl of perfect rest on every heart that comes to him. He fills the soul so that it has no more longings. You know the horseshoe magnet, and you have seen how rapidly it picks up pieces of iron. Have you ever put a piece of iron right across the two ends of the magnet? You will then have noticed that it ceases to attract anything else. The magnetic circuit is completed, and the magnet rests perfectly quiet, refusing to go beyond its own circle of pure content. When my soul is filled with Jesus he completes the circuit of my soul's passions and longings. He is all my salvation and all my desire. Have you found it so? Has not your soul come to an absolutely perfect rest when it has gotten to Christ? When he himself has drawn you to himself, have you not entered into rest? Because men perceive that such a rest is to be had therefore they come to Christ. He himself uses this as an argument why they should come: remember his cheering words, "Come unto me, all ye that labour and are heavy laden, and I will give you rest." This is part of the attractive force which dwells in a crucified Saviour.

Then I am sure that there is a great attraction about Christ, when we see *the change which he works in men.* Have you known a drunkard become a Christian, or a thief become upright? Have you seen a harlot made chaste? Have you marked any of the modern miracles which are always going on around us in the form of conversions? If you have taken pleasure in these signs and wonders, I know that you have said, "Lord, I, too, will come to thee to be converted." The sight of his power to elevate and sanctify has attracted you to Jesus, and you have fallen at his feet. There is no true, deep, tender, living conversion except through the cross; and therefore those that are taught of God do love to come to Christ, that sin may be conquered in them, that the heart of stone may be taken away, that the heart of flesh may be given, and that they may walk the happy way of holiness, according to the example of their adorable Master.

I could continue thus to show what this attractive force is; but, lest I should weary you, I will only say that it lies much in *his sufferings themselves.* Is it not a strange thing that suffering attracts? Yea, more: lowly suffering conquers; she sitteth as a queen upon her throne, and reigneth by the royalty of her resignation. The ship of the church has ploughed its way through seas of blood; with the blood-red cross at the masthead she has pushed on even in the night, throwing the crimson spray about her. She has never paused because of persecution, affliction, or death: these are the rough winds which fill her sails. No progress is surer than that which comes of holy suffering. The enemies of the church have taken her disciples and burned them; but their deaths yielded a sweet savour of life. It is questionable if a man's influence can be better promoted than by sending him aloft in a chariot of fire. What made us a Protestant nation for so many years? I do not say that we are Protestant now; but what made us enthusiastically Antipapal for so many years? The stakes of Smithfield did it. Men and women stood and saw the martyrs burned; and as they saw them die, they said, "These men are right, and the cause for which they burn is true"; and into the very heart of England martyrdom cast up a way for the Lord Jesus, and he entered there and then into Old England's secret soul. What the martyrs did in their measure, by their bitter death-pangs, is being done on a divine scale by the sufferings of the chief of all martyrs and head of all witnesses. By the agonies of Jesus men's affections are moved and their hearts enthralled.

Are any of you unconverted, and do you wish to be converted? I cannot suggest a better exercise than to read over the story of the death of Christ, as it is told by the four Evangelists. When you have read it once, read it again; and as you read it say, "Lord, I must have a sadly hard heart, or else this would move me to tears. I pray thee, change my heart." Then read the story again; for sure at last it will touch you. God the Holy Spirit blessing you, it will move you, and you will be among the "all men" that shall be drawn to Jesus by his own personal force.

So much, then, about what this force is.

II. Very briefly, my second head is to be—HOW IS THIS FORCE EXERCISED?

This force is exercised through the Holy Spirit. It is the Spirit of God who puts power into the truth about Christ; and then men feel that truth, and come to Christ and live. But our blessed Lord and Master *uses instruments.* The force of Christ's love is sometimes shown to men by those who already love him. One Christian makes many. One believer leads others to faith. To come back to my metaphor of a magnet: you have sometimes seen a battery attached to a coil; and then, if you take a nail and put it on the coil, the nail has become a strong magnet. You notice that the nail turns into a magnet; for you take another nail, and you put it on the end of it and it holds the second nail fast. Now number two is turned into a magnet. Try it. Put a third nail upon it. See, it is held fast! Number three has become a magnet. Try the next nail: it holds on to it like grim death; and now number four has become a magnet. Bring another nail within the influence. Number five has become a magnet. And so it continues. On and on and on the magnetism goes, from one nail to another. But now just go to your battery, and detach one of your wires, and the nails drop off directly, for the coil has ceased to be a magnet, and the nails have ceased to be magnets too. All the magnetism comes from the first place from which it started, and when it ceases at the fountain-head there is an end of it altogether. Indeed, Jesus Christ is the great attractive magnet, and all must begin and end with him. When Jesus lays hold upon us we get hold of a brother, and ere long he turns into a magnet also; thus from one to another the mystic influence proceeds; but the whole of the force abides in Jesus. More and more the kingdom grows, " ever mighty to prevail;" but all the growing and the prevailing come out of him. So it is that Jesus works—first by himself, and then by all who are in him. May the Lord make us all magnets for himself. Jesus says, " I, if I be lifted up, will draw all men unto me," but he leaves room in his figure for the co-working of all grateful hearts.

Jesus draws men *gradually*. Some are brought to Christ in a moment; but many are drawn by slow degrees. The sun in some parts of the world rises above the horizon in a single instant; but in our own country, at this season of the year, it is beautiful to watch the dawn, from the first grey light to the actual break of day. Is it dark, or is it light? Well, it is not quite dark: it is darkness visible. By-and-by there is light. No sun is up as yet, but yet the light increases till the East begins to glow, and the West reflects the radiance: then, by-and-by, up rises the great king of day. So does the Lord bring many to himself by gentle degrees. They cannot tell when they were converted, but they are converted, for they have come to Christ. Rest assured that he will not send you back. Do not say, "I am not converted, for I do not know the moment of the great change." I knew an old lady once who did not know her birthday; but I never told her that she was not born because of that, for there she was. And if you do not know when you were made a Christian, yet, if you are a Christian, it little matters how. If you are really born of God, the date of your new birth is interesting to curiosity but not important to piety. Salvation is often accomplished by a lengthened process. I have heard that when they wanted to bridge a great chasm they shot across the river an arrow or a bullet which drew with it a tiny thread. That was all the communication from bank to bank, and the rolling torrent was far below. Despise not the day of small things! The insignificant beginning was prophetic of grand results. By means of that little thread they drew across a piece of twine; and, when they had safely grasped it on the other side, they bound a small rope to the end of the twine, and they drew the rope across, and then to that rope they tied a cable, and they drew the cable across; and now over that chasm there strides an iron bridge, along which the steam-horse rattles with his mighty load. So does Jesus unite us to himself; he may employ at first an insignificant thread of thought; then a sense of pleasant interest; then some deeper feeling; then a crushing emotion; then a faint faith; then stronger faith; then stronger yet; until, at last, we come to be firmly bound to Christ. Oh, be thankful if you have only a thread of communication between you and Jesus, for it will lead to more.

Something more hopeful will be drawn across the gulf before long: at least, I hunger to see it. Christ's attractions are often very gradually revealed, and their victorious energy is not felt all at once.

Moreover, the cords of our Lord's drawings are very *secret*. You see the swallows twittering round our roofs, hawking in the air, shooting up into the clouds, or flashing by our ear. It is summer, and they are paying us their annual visit. They will be with you for a time, and on a sudden you will see them getting together about the gable of an old house, holding agitated congregations, and evidently discussing matters of importance. The Lord of birds is gently drawing every swallow in England down towards the African coast, and they will all go, without exception, as the secret summons reaches the flying host. They know but little of the way, but their flight is not therefore delayed or its course left to uncertainty. Over thousands of miles of sea and land they pursue their course until they come to their resting-place. And then, next spring, the same power that drew them south-ward will draw them all northward again ; and hither they will come, and we shall hear their joyous twitter, and say to ourselves, "Summer is coming, for here are the swallows again." By a secret power of that order does Jesus draw home the strangers and the foreigners whom his grace has chosen : they say to one another, " Come, and let us go up to the house of the Lord : let us seek the face of the Saviour." The mystic attractions of the power of Christ are secretly drawing many who knew him not ; and now they ask their way to Zion with their faces thither-ward. Look how the sun draws along the planets. He hastens on in his mighty career in space—I know not whither, but drawing with him all the worlds which compose the solar system : all these silently attend his majestic marches. Such is Christ, the great central sun; all his people follow, for he draws. Stand by the seashore and notice what the moon can do. You do not even see her, for it is high noon ; but here comes a wave, and then another, and then another, and the tide rises a little higher to-day than it did yesterday. What is it that causes this pulse of life, these heart-throbs of the deep ? The moon's attractive power is drawing up the waters from the sea. Even so our glorious Christ, in ways unknown to us, draws the hearts of men by his mighty Spirit wherever he pleases. "I, if I be lifted up, will draw all men unto me."

Fail not to observe *how gently* he does it ! The classic heather adored a goddess whom they represented as riding in a chariot drawn by doves. Surely the tenderest mode of impulse—power without force, motion born of emotion ! Certain of us were wafted to Jesus by some such zephyr. We could not but yield ; the softness and tenderness of every touch of Jesus affected us infinitely more than force could possibly have done. Hearts are tender things, and are not to be forced open with crowbars: the doors of the heart open gently to him that holds the key; and who is that but he who made the heart, and bought it with his precious blood ? The gentleness is equal to the power when Jesus draws men to himself !

But, oh, how *effectually !* I thought, as I mused upon my text, that I saw a great whirlpool like the maelstrom in the north of Norway. I thought I saw an enormous whirlpool so huge that all the souls of men, like ships of diverse forms, were being drawn towards it. With strained sight I gazed upon this monstrous death! Woe to those who are sucked in by that dreadful whirlpool, for there is no escape ; the abyss has no bottom, destruction is sure to all who are caught in the tremendous down-rush! Even ships far out at sea on other tacks, though they escape this maelstrom, are hindered in their course by it; for this one monstrous devourer labours to absorb all, and leaves no bay, nor harbour, nor foreign main unaffected by its perpetual draught. As I was thinking of this giant evil, and wondering how I could navigate my own barque so as to avoid this mouth of hell, I saw a hand that had the mark of a nail upon its palm, and lo, it held a mighty magnet which attracted every vessel with a force greater than any born of sea or storm. This magnet attracted many ships so that they flew to it at once, and were gently drawn towards their desired haven in the very teeth of the maelstrom. I saw other vessels in which the mariners hoisted sail to try to escape the influence of this magnet, and even put out their oars to strive to get away ; and some of them did so escape. Alas, they floated farther and farther into the maelstrom's destructive power, to be sucked down to their perdition. These were so besotted that they laboured against mercy, and resolved to be destroyed : we are glad that all are not left to act so madly.

You must have seen an instance of drawing very often down in the river. A grand vessel is bound for the Indies ; but how can it be taken down to the Nore ? It is difficult to move the heavy craft. There it must lie. But here comes a steam-tug. The large vessel hands a rope on board the tug : and now the steam is up. Tug, tug, tug ; the paddle-wheels revolve, and the big ship begins to follow the lead; it is no longer motionless, it will soon be walking the waters as a thing of life. A pleasant sight—the tug draws it gently out to sea, and then leaves it to pursue its distant voyage. Just so may Jesus draw you away from sinful pleasures and from self-righteousness.

III. I shall conclude by drawing one or two lessons. Then I have done. WHAT DOES ALL THIS IMPLY ? "I, if I be lifted up, will draw all men unto me."

Well, it means this first—that *men, by nature, are a long way off from Christ.* You were not born converted. Of that I am sure. Nor were you born a Christian either ; and, though they took you to the font, and said that they made you a " member of Christ, a child of God, and an inheritor of the kingdom of heaven," there was not a word of truth in it, for you were such a child of God that you loved sin, and such a member of Christ that you knew nothing of him, and such an inheritor of the kingdom of heaven that, unless God saves you, you will never get there. I may say of Christians who are made in that way, " Eyes have they, but they see not; mouths have they, but they speak not, neither speak they through their throats ; " and I fear that I must add, " They that make them are like unto them : so is every one that trusteth in them." It is a poor Christianity that is created by such monstrous folly. " Ye must be born again," and ye must be born again of the Spirit of God, or ye cannot enter the kingdom of heaven. Man is a long way off from Christ, and Christ must draw him. Friend, ask him to draw *you.*

I gather another lesson—that *men will not come to Christ unless he draws them.* Sometimes, when I am trying to prepare a sermon to preach, I say to myself, "Why must I take all this trouble?" If men were in their senses they would run to Christ without calling. Why must we put this business so temptingly? Why must we plead? Why must we be so earnest? Because men do not want to come, not even to their own Saviour. They do not wish to have their sins forgiven. They do not wish to be renewed in heart; and they never will come— no, not one mother's son of them—unless he that sent Christ to them shall draw them to Christ. A work of grace in the heart is absolutely necessary before the sacrifice of the Lord Jesus will be accepted by any one of us. Jesus said, "Ye will not come to me that ye might have life." What our Lord said is true to this hour; man has not improved an atom.

But, then, learn another lesson. If there is any man here that Christ is drawing, he need not say, "May I come?" Of course you may, if you feel drawn to come. Are you coming? Come, and welcome. Christ never yet turned away a soul that came to him—not one. "Him that cometh to me, I will in no wise cast out." If he is drawing you, run, for you have Scriptural warrant for so doing. "Draw us : we will run after thee." If to-night you feel any kind of tugging at your heart-strings, do not stay a moment. Come along with you. When God draws then is your time to move. What do the sailors say? "There's a breeze, Jack. Ay, ay, boys. Up with the anchor. Now for every stitch of canvas. We can make headway now." Do you feel any kind of breeze? Is the breath of the Holy Spirit moving upon you in any degree? Do you feel inclined to say, "I will go to Jesus"? Then, fly away with you, like a full-sailed ship before a fair wind; and by God's help may you soon make the port of everlasting salvation.

Let us finish up by saying that, if Christ has said that he will draw, then he will draw to-night. The attractions of the Lord Jesus are continual: he draws, and he will always draw. He is drawing now. Do not pull back, lest his drawing should cease, and you should perish; but rather let your heart sing—

> "He drew me, and I followed on,
> Charmed to confess the force divine."

Oh! Spirit of God, draw men to Jesus. This is the way of salvation: trust Christ, and you are saved. Rely wholly upon what Christ is, and what he has done; and you are saved. In that very act there is a change effected within you which will show itself for ever in your character; for he that believes in Jesus Christ, the Son of God, is born again. The faith which looks to Jesus and the life which lives upon Jesus come together. I cannot tell you which is first—the new birth, or faith. Can you tell me which spoke of a wheel moves first? No. And these are spokes of one and the same wheel. "He that believeth in him hath everlasting life." Oh! believe him. Trust him. Lay hold upon him. Accept him, and go your way; and the mountains and the hills shall break forth before you into singing, and all the trees of the field shall clap their hands.

Amen. So let it be!

CERTAIN SINGULAR SUBJECTS.

DELIVERED BY

C. H. SPURGEON,

AT THE METROPOLITAN TABERNACLE, NEWINGTON.

"And I gave unto Isaac Jacob and Esau: and I gave unto Esau mount Seir, to possess it; but Jacob and his children went down into Egypt."—Joshua xxiv. 4.

THIS passage, though audibly uttered by the mouth of Joshua, is to be regarded as the immediate voice of God. Joshua said unto all the people, "Thus saith Jehovah, God of Israel." Jehovah reminded the tribes, and their elders and judges, of all that he had done, and of all that he had been to them; and from this he challenged their allegiance, requiring that they should henceforth be loyal unto their great Benefactor. Addressing them himself, his argument became all the more impressive. I reverence all Scripture more than tongue can tell, but yet I venerate most of all those portions of the word which are God's own voice,—the thought of Deity interpreted into human speech by Deity itself. The passage now before us, though it reads like a piece of ordinary history, such as might have been composed by a common scribe, has about it a vastness of meaning such as can alone be found in the language of the infinite God. When God inspires David, or Isaiah, or Paul, he teaches us most graciously; but when he condescends to speak himself, how shall we sufficiently reverence the word? We have here, not so much a letter dictated by God, as the actual autograph of the great Father. My text is written with the finger of God. A glory blazes along the lines: the letters are all illuminated: the words glow like the sapphire work of heaven's pavement. Our text has a world of meaning in it. It may, as we notice its plain words and prosaic statements, seem to be a mere common box, but it is in very deed an ark of precious perfumed wood, overlaid with pure gold, and filled with gems and jewels rich and rare. May the Holy Spirit give us eyes wherewith to perceive the treasures which lie before us in these words—"I gave unto Isaac Jacob and Esau: and I gave unto Esau mount Seir, to possess it; but Jacob and his children went down into Egypt."

I. The first thing that I discern here is

HISTORY AND THE HAND OF GOD IN IT.

See: "*I gave;*" and then again, "*I gave.*" It is not merely that

No. 1,718.

Esau and Jacob were born of Isaac and Rebekah, but the Lord says, "*I gave unto Isaac Jacob and Esau.*" How plainly doth this declare that the hand of God is in human history! At first sight history seems a great tangle, a snarl, a confusion; but on looking at it more closely we perceive that it is only in appearance a maze, but in fact a marvellous piece of arrangement, exhibiting perfect precision and never-failing accuracy. Our carnal reason sees the wrong side of the carpet, and it appears to be without design or order; but there is another side to history, and looked at from that standpoint it reveals a pattern wonderful for beauty, displaying wisdom and goodness unparalleled. The histories of nations are, from the human side, little more than a narration of the crimes of kings and the follies of their people; and yet, viewed from another quarter, they are the record of the dealings of God with men,—the story of love's labour to reclaim the lost. Look at Calvary's sacrifice as it rises above all other events; even as this morning I saw the hills and the tops of tall trees standing out above the morning mist. What a sight it is! The cross towering over the ages. Looking down on their sins and sorrows. Calvary—what is it? What but the climax of human iniquity, where man became not so much a regicide, though he slew his King, as a Deicide, for to the utmost of his power he slew his God! On the cross human enmity of God reached its most dread extremity. With wicked hands men crucified and slew the Son of God. Yet it is equally true that on Calvary we see more of the goodness, grace, mercy, justice, and longsuffering of God than anywhere else. The cross is at once our crime and our salvation; an exhibition of man's foulest sin and of God's richest grace. Calvary is of all spots the blackest and the brightest; the place where hell displayed its most deadly power, and yet the very gate of heaven. Thus is all human history, according to its measure and proportion, a bitter sweet. Where man's mischief and misery abound, there do God's goodness and grace much more abound.

We see the hand of God in history very strikingly in the raising up of remarkable men at certain special periods. It is true, as the Lord says, "I gave unto Isaac Jacob and Esau": children are the gift of God. This is true not only of Isaac but of all mortal men. God gave to a worthy couple, George Washington; to another pair, John Howard: and to a third, George Whitefield. Each of these, in his own special way was a divine gift to men. Children are born with differing talents, and varied capacities, but all about them which will make them blessings is the gift of God. I shall not tarry to mention great men whose names mark epochs in history from which men date an increase of light and happiness: but let no man think of these friends and leaders of mankind without admitting the hand of God in their birth, training, disposition, and ability. The greatest blessing which God ever gave to man was the man Christ Jesus; and, under him, the next best blessings are men. You remember the passage, "When he ascended up on high, he led captivity captive, and gave gifts unto men. And he gave some apostles," and so forth. Ascension gifts are sure to be worthy of the occasion, and therefore eminently precious, and lo! these are all men. Within a man; poor, lowly, humble, and even sinful though that man may be in himself, there may lie concealed an almost infinite blessing from the Most High; even as within an acorn sleeps a forest, or within a flint lies light for a nation's watchfires. When the negro slave had borne long years of bondage, and hope of deliverance seemed far away, it was God that gave an Abraham Lincoln, who led the nation onward till " Emancipation" flamed upon its banners. Long before, when England, free in every corner of it, yet held slaves in its colonies, it was God that gave Wilberforce, and raised him up to plead in Parliament the rights of men, till the command went forth—

> " Thus saith Britannia, empress of the sea,—
> ' Thy chains are broken; Africa, be free!'"

In all such acts of righteousness the coming forth of the man at the hour must be attributed to God's own hand. The men themselves may not know wherefore they have come to power: of them it might often be said as the Lord said of Cyrus, "I girded thee, though thou hast not known me." The mighty ones that contend for wrong, and bind the chains, and forge the fetters of the oppressed, do not know the champions who are predestined to overturn them, but God knows, and that is enough. Tyrants have always just cause to be afraid, for every birth may produce a deliverer. Somewhere in a hovel there may sleep in a rude cradle the boy who shall shake the throne of evil. As yet it has always happened in due season that Pharaoh has been confronted by Moses, and the princes of Midian by Gideon. For every Sisera there is a Jael; and for every Goliath a David. The upas tree may increase its deadly shadow, but an axe is sharpening for the felling of it. Evil is a a gourd, and though a man be but a worm, yet he shall destroy that gourd. God is working still in the fashioning—oh, with what mystery! —of his own instruments. In his book are written the members of men who are yet to be, who are now being fashioned in secret by the hand of God; these shall by-and-by appear, and shall lead on the race to a further unloosing of its bonds. I rejoice in the possibilities which lie in birth. As to the One great Seed of the woman we look for our greatest deliverance, so do we in a lower sense look to her seed for the overthrow of many of the doings of the serpent race. That curse which made her in sorrow bring forth children contains enclosed within itself, like a bud in its sheath, the promise of untold benediction. Often at a birth might an age rejoice and sing, " Unto us a child is born: unto us a son is given." Let parents think of this, and dedicate their offspring with many a prayer to the Lord whose gift they are. Let old men think of this, and cry to God to raise up true men to fill the places which they themselves can no longer occupy. Lo! children are a heritage of the Lord. When our sons are a seed that the Lord has blest, blessed is the man that hath his quiver full of them.

Let us bless and praise the Lord, as we look back in history upon God's manifest interference with the course of events by the singular births of men whom he has used to effect his own divine purposes. Nobody denies that the hand of God is in the coming of men for the hour when the hour calls for the men.

So also is the hand of God distinctly to be seen in all great events. If Esau captures Mount Seir, then the setting up of the Edomite dominion, bad as it may have been, is from another point of view a matter in which

God's purpose and design are to be noted, for he says—" I gave Esau mount Seir." Brethren, I believe—and I hope the truth is not too strong for you—that not a tiny bird pecks up a worm from the ground without your Father. A plant does not sprout in the corner behind the wall, and shoot up its flower, and seed, and ripen and decay, apart from the Lord of hosts; much less does an empire rise, flourish, or decline without divine co-operation. When the sere leaf falls from the sycamore in the autumn time, a providence guides the leaf to its place upon the sod ; and when the worm uplifts itself to draw that leaf into the tunnel which it has made, the hand of the Lord directs the burial. In everything that happens, be it small or great, the Lord is present, and his will is done. It is so in all the plottings and manœuvrings of kings and princes and senates, in the stirs of public opinion, in the marchings of armies, and in all that transpires among mortal men. Though the iniquity of man is seen abundantly, yet the overruling power of God is never absent. The world is not left to itself, given over to the lord of misrule; but in all events the hand of God may be perceived by all who care to perceive it. I reckon war to be a huge crime on man's side, but, when battalions have marched against battalions, the destiny of empires, and possibly of the whole race of man, has turned upon the health of a commander, the clearness of his eye, or the quickness of his messenger : yea, the turning aside of a bullet, or the fall of a horse, or the breaking of an axle, has become the pivot of history, the turning point of ages : *and there at the centre the Lord has been surely ready.* Essential points have been secured beyond all question ; perhaps it is more nearly right to say that every turn of the history has been essential, and that the whole of it has been in the hands of the Highest. It is singular how God is seen, both in dangers and preservations, in connection with crises of history. Wellington at Waterloo sat on his horse, Copenhagen, all day long. A friend of mine, well known to most of you, said to him, " I suppose your horse must have been very weary." " No," said the duke, " he was so fresh that when I got off from him he threw his heels into the air, and almost struck my temples. I was not in greater danger all through the battle than at that moment." God had preserved the hero all that live-long day, and we little know what had been the result if a chance slug or ball had carried him off, and yet you see when the red mouth of war was growing silent the Iron Duke was still in jeopardy. Had he been suddenly cut off our island might have become an insignificant province of a vast Napoleonic empire; but he was immortal till his work was done. Above the awful din of war I hear the voice of God : even out of such an evil, which makes earth for the while like hell, the good Lord of all produces good. Masters of armies reckon their hosts, but the Lord of hosts they forget. They plan and scheme—these masters of men, to whom their people are as so much food for powder—but a higher plan overrides their planning. There is a King of kings, and Lord of lords, and he is no silent spectator of what is done, but stretches out his hand to deliver the nations from the power of evil, so that still by his great power the world moves onward to something better. We think of this poor world with great sadness, when we see all the crime and sin which defile it, and yet we join with Galileo in saying, " It does move though ! " Truth makes progress : the right is winning. If we do not see an improvement to-day, or to-morrow, yet take any twenty years, and you will see that the world is moving!—moving on to that grand day when the song shall ascend, Hallelujah, Hallelujah: for the Lord God omnipotent reigneth! As the Lord's hand was in Esau's possession of Mount Seir, so is it in the settlement of every tribe and people, and it is to be seen by all observant eyes in all the great epochs of the history of man.

Yet please to notice that whenever we say this—and I say it pretty plainly—*we never excuse the sin and folly of man*. We speak of predestination and foreknowledge, because we find these truths in Scripture; and they seem to us to be facts in the very nature of things. God knows all that happens; else were he no God, or a poor, blind deity; and if he knows that a certain fact will happen, then it is a fixed and settled thing, depend on that. Nothing happens other than God foreknew would happen, and therefore it is fixed. If I laid aside predestination, yet foreknowledge would be quite enough for me. Something or other is certain to happen, and God knows what that something or other is, and therefore it is fixed; not by blind fate, but still fixed. Yet this fixedness is perfectly consistent with the free agency and responsibilty of man. Man thinks, and resolves, and acts as freely, and as much of his own accord, as if there were no foreknowledge and no God. In the book of the unrevealed everything is written; but the mystic roll is laid up in the archives of heaven, and no man knoweth what is written therein. Down below everything happens according to that book: not a stroke of it is in error, not a mistake is found in a single line, the event happens as it was foreknown: but, still, if there were no such book, man would not be more absolutely free than he is now. I can join heartily with the advocate of free agency when he talks of man's voluntariness in his acts of sin, his wilful choice of evil, his rejection of Christ and of his grace. No man can too thoroughly believe in the wilful guilt of the wicked: at any rate, I will go all lengths in such a belief. I couple with what is called Calvinistic doctrine the other doctrine of free agency and responsibility, which seems to me to be equally true; and if this be judged to be an inconsistency the remark does not stagger me, for I see no inconsistency, and do not believe that any exists. My God is not a mere omnipotent being, who can rule dead materialism, and compel insensible atoms to do his will; but he can rule free agents, leaving them absolutely free, and yet effecting all his purposes with them. God's eternal purposes are accomplished, and yet men remain responsible free agents both in their beginning and in their ending. Do you say that you do not understand how this can be? Neither do I, but I believe it. There are ten thousand other things in nature and history which are too high for me to understand their " how " and " why," and yet I see them ; can I not also make sure of some matters which I do *not* see? It is not for me to profess to comprehend the nature or the ways of the Infinite: if we could comprehend the Lord, he would not be the infinite God. It is because he is beyond me—infinitely beyond such a poor creature as I am—that I all the more reverently adore him. His nature and his acts are alike veiled in mystery, but alike to be had in reverence.

Have you never heard of the insect philosophers: they were midges so small that a man needed a microscope to see them ; but they were very great philosophers for all that, and they set about to describe an elephant ?   One of them hung upon the gigantic creature's ear, and surveyed a small portion of its area, and his theory was that an elephant was a living wall, almost perpendicular : another stood upright somewhere on the creature's back, and he averred that the creature was a vast plain ; while a third, who was perched upon a hair of the animal, propounded the idea that it was a tall shaft. These midge-philosophers had not eyes large enough to take in a whole elephant, and so each one judged from the tiny morsel of hide which came under his own narrow range of observation. Yet these ephemera were nearer the mark with the elephant than our wise men are with the universe, concerning which their first principles, and theories, and hypotheses have usually been a museum of follies.   Yet if philosophers understood the universe, that understanding would not bring their carnal minds within measurable distance of the infinite God. None but the Spirit of God can reveal God to any man, and the man himself must receive a new and spiritual life before he can know what the Spirit teaches.   Who, then, among the worldly-wise may dream of understanding God, when even the spiritual rather embrace him by love than grasp him by understanding?   Let us, therefore, believe what we find to be in God's word, and what we are taught by his Spirit, though it should be far above our heads.   Let us not delay to believe until we can reconcile.   Do you not know that in theology—all the false part of theology—the part on which the sects stand and fight each other—consists of suspension-bridges made of cobwebs, which are intended to bridge the distance between two awful truths which look as if they were divided from each other.   The great rocky truths are in effect accepted by both parties, but the battle waxes hot concerning these cobweb-bridges which were never worth a tithe of the ingenuity which has been wasted upon them.   I hold it true that God is in history, and in everything ; and I read the newspaper that I may see how my heavenly Father governs the world: and this I believe though I most clearly see that men sin wilfully, and wickedly, and voluntarily, and that they are guilty free agents in all their wrong-doing.   These thoughts come to me when I remember the character of Esau, and yet read the Lord's words, " I gave unto Esau mount Seir, to possess it."

To us, dear friends, the hand of God is very visible in our own case. Look at the hand of God that gave to you and to me such *parents* as we have : I mean those of us who have the great delight of having descended from Christian men and women.   Had we anything to do with that ? And yet the greatest part of a man's future depends upon the parents of whom he is born.   No person can deny that our parentage is beyond our own power, and yet to a large extent it colours the whole future of life.   Is not the hand of God in it ?   Why shall one be born of a long succession of drunkards and of thieves, and have within himself an insatiable passion born with him to imitate them ; while another inherits a sound constitution from his parents, and, though he has no tendency to the grace of God, yet he has a tendency to morality, and naturally developes self-restraint and gentle manners?   Do we not see the hand of God in the parents that he gave us ?   I cannot be so blind as to deny my own obligations : I shall for ever bless God that I was given to a godly couple whose delight it was to lead me in the ways of God.

And do we not see the hand of God, again, in our *children* ? Many of us do. Oh! how some of us bless and praise God that ever such sons fell to our lot: we never think of them without delight, for they are living in the service of the Lord Jesus, spending and being spent in the divine Master's service. Look at your children as the gifts of God, and if they are not yet all that you could desire, yet still believe that God has given them to you, even as he says, " I gave Isaac Jacob and Esau." You, dear friends in Christ, united in holy wedlock, may look upon your children as not unclean, but holy, in the sense intended by the apostle when he speaks of the unbelieving wife as sanctified by the believing husband, and adds, "else were your children unclean, but now are they holy." They are not to be viewed as the unhappy fruit of an unhallowed union, but as gifts of God, to be brought up for him, and trained in his fear. They come not as the result of uncleanness, but as gifts from the Lord, to whom marriage is an honourable estate. It were a sad thing if the sight of my child made me blush for shame; but it is a joy to look upon him as, like Samuel, asked of God, and given of God. Bring these gifts of God to God, and say, "Here, Lord, are the children which thou hast given me. Save them of thy grace, since in love thou hast given them to me. These dear ones are favours from thyself, blessings upon which I set great store: O Lord, let thy name be named on them, and let thy grace be glorified in them."

Observe, further, that *the Lord's hand is in all the prosperity which he gives to any.* He says, " I gave unto Esau mount Seir, to possess it." It is by God's allotment that temporal things fall as they do: even the ungodly have their portion in this life by divine grant. It were "vain to rise up early, and to sit up late, and to eat the bread of carefulness," if the Lord did not build the house and prosper the labour. It is he that giveth thee power to get wealth. Our daily bread comes from the granary of Providence. The store most ample, or the measure most scant, must alike be traced to the one all-bountiful hand.

And, once more, *God's hand is to be seen in the place in which we live.* If Esau lives in mount Seir, it is because God appoints him to be there; and if Israel goes down to Egypt, it is for the selfsame reason. If you and I remove from one place to another, it is sweet to see the cloud moving before us, and to know that the Lord directs our way. "The steps of a good man are ordered of the Lord." But I need not instance cases. The hand of the Lord has been with some of us for good from our cradle even until now; and we believe that he who has led us so far will lead us still, until we arrive at the house not made with hands, eternal in the heavens.

II. Secondly, we have another lesson to learn from our text, and that is upon

BIRTH AND ITS DISAPPOINTMENTS.

"*I gave unto Isaac Jacob and Esau,*" twin children born of godly parents. *In that birth there was joy, but sorrow came by it as well as joy.* What joy there was in Isaac's house that day, for we read that it had been a matter of prayer in the family! See Genesis xxv. 21. It had been a grief to Isaac that, married at forty years of age, he had lived twenty years in married life without a child, although he had the promise of a seed. Lo! on a day it happened that Esau and Jacob were born. There was joy; yea, double joy, because two sons had come to build up their father's house. Ah, had they known it, there was grave cause for mingled emotion in that double birth! We read that forty years after Esau married, and he took unto himself two Canaanite wives, "which were a grief of mind unto Isaac and to Rebekah." Yes, we may fondly promise ourselves that children born of godly parents will be an unalloyed comfort to them; and yet it may not be so. Children are certain cares, and doubtful comforts. They may bring to their parents such sorrow that they may be inclined to think the barren happier than the fruitful. Hence it is well for us to leave our hopes of posterity with God; and if we reckon that in a childless house we have missed a great joy, we ought also to reckon that we have missed a mint of trouble by the same fact. Your children are not born in grace, but they are the children of nature; and that being the case, you may have to see in one of them—God grant it may be in no more!—an Esau, yes, a profane person, who will sell his birthright, and become an enemy of the people of God. Esau was born of admirable parents, and so an Esau may be found to your boundless grief in your own family. It has been so aforetime with others, and it may be so with you: the lion's whelp has been found in the sheep's fold, the vulture has been hatched in the dove's nest. There was great hope, certainly, of both boys born in Isaac's house; for we look that godly parents should train up their children in the way that they should go, so that when they are old they may not depart from it: hence both Esau and Jacob were most hopefully started. But Esau was not trainable. He was a wild man, and took his own way, and became a follower of rough sports, "a cunning hunter, a man of the field," and soon he became profane, as often happens to those whose chief pursuits are sporting. Ah, me! Ah, me! How often the brightest hopes have been blasted, and those who appeared to be floating on the current which flows towards heaven have been drifted back and lost on the forlorn shores of unbelief.

It is a great advantage to you, my dear young friend, to have been born into a Christian family; but I charge you, do not trust in it as though it were in itself a guarantee of salvation. Isaac, the beloved of God, has Esau for a son. Mind you that. David had to sorrow over Absalom, and Hezekiah over Manasseh. You may be the Esau of your family. Is it so? May God grant that such a dreadful portion may not be chosen by you! Remember, that your brother who has lived with you, slept with you, and grown with you side by side, may be gracious, and you may remain ungodly. Is it so now? Oh, that the Holy Spirit may come and work upon you till you and your brother are one in Christ, like James and John, Peter and Andrew. Father, do you find a division in your house? Then pray to God, even as Abraham prayed for Ishmael, "Oh, that Ishmael might live before thee!" Pray for your wayward boy. And, oh, you that are in the family, and have through divine mercy become a Jacob and not an Esau, ascribe it all to sovereign grace, and give God the praise; but forget not your brother! While he lives have hope of him, and see what you can do that he also may rejoice in the Lord. But, ah! if we could read the future when we look at our little children, we should rejoice with trembling; and as we cannot read the future, it is fit that we should pray with earnestness. We have prayer often at dying beds; why have we not more prayer in the chamber of birth? Surely, when an immortal spirit starts upon its endless career, it is well for us to cry to God and ask others to join with us in the loving, earnest prayer that the Holy Spirit may cause the newly-born to be born again as soon as they are able to know Jesus and believe in him. There stands the fact: in birth there is joy tempered with godly fear, hope mingled with sacred anxiety, and high advantage which may yet most sadly end in deepened responsibility and increased sin.

III. Thirdly, and very briefly, we have next to view

WORLDLINGS AND THEIR POSSESSIONS.

"*I gave unto Esau mount Seir, to possess it.*" That is to say, Esau, as compared with Jacob, appeared to have the best of it, for he had "mount Seir, to possess it"; but poor Jacob had not a foot of land that he could call his own except the family sepulchre at Machpelah, wherein afterwards he slept the sleep of the righteous.

Why does God so often give possessions to ungodly men? Why do they flourish? Why do they have their portion in this life? Is it not, first, because *God thinks little of these things,* and therefore gives them to those of whom he thinks little? "Why," said Luther, in his day, "the whole Turkish empire is but a basket of husks that God gives to the hogs, and therefore he hands it over to the unbelievers." So, often, wealth and riches are but so much wash, which the great Husbandman gives to the swine on his estate. Something infinitely better is reserved for the Lord's own family. The rich blessing of true grace he reserves for his children and heirs. It shows how little God thinks of kingdoms, and empires, and great riches, for he leaves these full often to the worst of men. How few saints have ever worn crown or coronet! A holy man once said that the kings who have gone to heaven might almost be counted on your fingers. See what small account the Lord makes of the world's best store.

Do you wish that ungodly men should have less? For my part, I am reconciled to their present prosperity, for *it is all they ever will have.* Poor souls, let them have as much of it as they may *here;* they have nothing hereafter. Besides, they have no God; and having no God, it would take a great many fortunes to make a godless man's portion worth a straw. If the graceless could gain all worlds, what use would they be to them when they come to die? Their own souls lost, and no comfort in Christ, and no joy in the Spirit, what have they gained after all? Let the worldlings have the husks. Let none of us ever cry, "I fain would fill my belly with the husks that the swine do eat." Let those have the treasures of this present evil world who have nothing else. Never quarrel with the Lord for saying, "I gave unto Esau mount Seir, to possess it."

Besides, these comforts may lead them to reflect upon God's bounty to them; and at any rate they *ought to move them to repentance.* It is my earnest hope that many an ungodly man, whom God has highly favoured in the things of this life, may be influenced by the Spirit of God to say, "Why should I continue to rebel against God who has been so kind to me? He has prospered me, and taken care of me. Why should I not turn to him, and become his servant?" At any rate, gratitude for

mercies received should produce repentance for sin committed. Worldly
goods have no necessary connection with ungodliness. There is no infection in harvest stores, nor iniquity in the wealth which comes of commerce.
In themselves gold and silver are harmless metals. There have been
men who have enjoyed the abundance of this world, and yet have in-
herited the world to come. Not many great men after the flesh are
chosen ; but there is a great difference between " not *many* " and " not
any." Joseph of Arimathea, and Nicodemus, and the women who
ministered unto Christ of their substance, had a fair measure of the
comforts of this life, and used them for their Lord. It was not Solomon's wealth that brought him down so low : his unrestrained passions were his ruin, else might he have held all his treasures and
held his God too. Pray, therefore, that the rich may be brought to Christ.
Why should not that fish be taken which hath the silver shekel in its
mouth ? Why may not Matthew, the publican, be called from the
receipt of custom ? Is there not yet another Zaccheus to be renewed
by grace ? May not their indebtedness to God be used as a plea with
the wealthy to give themselves to him who has already given them
so much ? It was no fault in Jonah that he felt pleasure under the
shade of his gourd ; the fault lay in making a god of that gourd. There
is no evil in having goods ; but there is great evil in making those
goods our chief good. Yet, brethren, so it is that the men of this world
usually have the most of it ; I do not say the best of it. It is, and always
will be, a mystery as long as the world stands, that the wicked often
flourish and the righteous suffer. Read the Book of Job ; read the
thirty-seventh Psalm ; read the seventy-third Psalm ; and see how holy
men and wise men have been perplexed and troubled by the method of
the divine providence. To see wickedness on a throne and righteousness in a dungeon, pride enshrined in honour, and holiness rolled in the
kennel, is a serious trial of our confidence in God, and yet there are
weighty reasons why it should be so for awhile. Not without wisdom
doth the Lord say, " I gave to Esau mount Seir, to possess it."

IV. Now, comes the fourth point, and a great mystery too. Here
are

THE CHOSEN OF GOD AND THEIR TRIALS.

" I gave unto Esau mount Seir, to possess it; *but Jacob and his children
went down into Egypt.*" That is their portion. They must go down
into Egypt because of famine, and they must suffer there under a
tyrant's iron rod, so that they may become familiar with the drudgery
of slaves. They must be strangers in a strange land, and be sorely
bruised beneath the foot of the oppressor. The escutcheon of their
nation was to be " a smoking furnace and a burning lamp." Moses saw
Israel as well as God when he beheld a bush burning with fire but not
consumed. Is not this a strange thing ? To him whom God loves best
he allots the hardest condition. Esau's sons are dukes, but Jacob's seed
are drudges : Esau reigns, but Israel serves ; Esau set his nest on high,
but Israel crouched by the reeds of the river. The worldling would read
the Scripture as if it said, " As many as I love, I caress and pamper ":
but the Lord speaketh not so : his word is, " As many as I love I
rebuke and chasten." " Whom the Lord loveth he chasteneth, and

scourgeth,"—that is a very hard word—" scourgeth every son whom he receiveth." To carnal reason this seems strange ; faith alone can explain it.

But Israel and his children went down into Egypt, first, for their *preservation*. So God brings his people into trial often to preserve them from the world and its evil influences, from themselves and their natural pride, from Satan and his puffings up. By sorrow and adversity the children of God are driven to their knees, brought near to their great Father, and kept in fellowship with him. Sanctified afflictions are spiritual promotions. The salt and bitterness of sorrow often preserves men from the gall and bitterness of sin.

They went down into Egypt, next, for their *improvement ;* for the family of Jacob was in a mournful condition, and by no means fit to be used of the Lord. The story of Jacob's family is a strangely sad one ; perhaps Scripture does not contain a more mournful page. The evil influence of polygamy is clearly seen, blended with the errors of Laban's house, and envenomed by the foul example of the Canaanites among whom they sojourned. It was time that they should shift their quarters : they were neither getting good nor doing good. It looked as if the patriarch would found an ignorant, quarrelsome, vicious race ; and so they were sent down into Egypt that trouble might teach them better manners. God often thrusts his people into adversity that he may improve them, arouse them, instruct them, and ennoble them. See to it, brethren, that the Lord's design be fulfilled in you to the full. May the fire and the file, the crucible and the flame, work in you a clearance of dross and rust, and make you pure and bright.

They also went down into Egypt for their *education*. The chosen seed needed teaching ; they were getting to be rustic, not to say barbarous, in their manners; acquirements and knowledge were scant among them. They must go down into the seat of ancient learning to acquire arts and sciences, and civilization. In Egypt a race, which else had been a mob, must be consolidated into a nation ; a band of wilful men must be trained to discipline and obedience. The Lord said, " Out of Egypt have I called my son," because Egypt was his school of learning, his drill-ground of discipline. We are ignorant, rebellious, and wilful till the Lord trains us. " Before I was afflicted I went astray ; but now have I kept thy word." The Lord teaches us on the black-board of adversity, and we are often rapped over the knuckles by the stern master. It is wonderful what we learn when we are taken among the thorns. I hardly think that I have learned anything except in affliction ; at least, this I know—I owe more to the hammer, and the anvil, and the file, and the furnace than I do to all the green meads and flowing brooks and singing birds that I have ever seen or heard. I fear that I have learned little beyond that which has been whipped into me; and though I am not fonder of the rod than you are, I confess that such sweet fruit grows on the bitter bough of trial that I would fear to be long without it. Far rather would I weep with the Lord's chosen than laugh with the reprobate. By unhallowed mirth fools grow more foolish, but by sanctified trials wise men become yet wiser. For future usefulness it is well that we bear present sorrow, and like Jacob go down into Egypt.

And they went down to Egypt, again, that *God might display his great power in them.* I would not care to be Esau on Mount Seir when once I see Pharaoh's hosts drowned, and Israel marching through the depths of the sea, and when I hear the song of the Israelitish maidens, and the shouts of the men, " Sing ye to Jehovah, for he hath triumphed gloriously ; the horse and his rider hath he thrown into the sea." It is worth while to go down into Egypt to come out of it with a high hand and an outstretched arm. Oh, the glory of the Lord in his redeemed. Oh, the lofty destiny of the tried people of God! Oh, the sublimity of their lives even now ! There is God in them : there is God about them. He leads the van, and brings up the rear. They are as signs and wonders in their generations. He has blessed them : yea, and they shall be blessed. Little boots it that Esau has Mount Seir for a possession : Israel has her God. No foot of land perhaps you call your own ; you do not know where your next suit of clothes will come from, and God has kept you on short commons, and multiplied your straits and needs : never mind—yours is the lot of the chosen ; for " Jacob and his children went down into Egypt." That is where the story ends, according to my text ; but you know the story does not end there after all ; for out of Jacob and his children came the Star, the Sceptre, and the Throne. The Godhead took up the seed of Israel ; and now to-day he that sprang of Jacob's loins, according to the flesh, sits on the highest throne of God, and reigns supreme. The Shiloh has come, and it matters nothing what Egypt brought of sorrow unto Jacob's seed, seeing that out of them at the last came the King and Saviour of men. If Jesus be ours, the rest is a small affair. Give me Christ, and I ask nothing else. Having faith in Jesus, I can leave all things else with the great Disposer of events. Christ and a crust ; the promise and a parish coat ; grace and an almshouse ! Cannot a saint be more than content with these ?

So have I set before you the varying lots of God's own people and of the wicked. I hope that you are ready to say that you would rather suffer affliction with the people of God than enjoy the pleasures of sin for a season. God help you to make that wise choice, and to make it at once. May his Spirit lead you to take the Lord Jesus to be your all in all. Amen.

Portion of Scripture read before Sermon—Joshua xxiv.

Hymns from " Our Own Hymn Book"—23 (2nd version), 17, 32 (2nd part).

THE TENT DISSOLVED AND THE MANSION ENTERED

A Sermon

DELIVERED ON LORD'S-DAY MORNING, MAY 6TH, 1883, BY

C. H. SPURGEON,

AT THE METROPOLITAN TABERNACLE, NEWINGTON.

"For we know that if our earthly house of this tabernacle were dissolved, we have a building of God, an house not made with hands, eternal in the heavens."— 2 Corinthians v. 1.

PAUL ranks among the bravest of the brave. We note also with admiration how the hero of so many dangers and conflicts, who could glow and burn with fervour, was yet among the calmest and quietest of spirits. He had learned to live beyond those present circumstances which worry and disturb ; he had stolen a march upon the shadows of time, and entered into possession of the realities of eternity. He looked not on the things which are seen, but he set his whole regard on the things which are not seen ; and by this means he entered into a deep and joyful peace which made him strong, resolute, steadfast, immovable. I would to God that we had all acquired Paul's art of being "always confident,"—his habit of having the inward man renewed day by day. The most of us are far too like the insect of the summer hour, which sports away its life of moments among the flowers, and lo ! all is over. Are we not too apt to live in the immediate present which is revealed by the senses? The ox projects no thought upward or beyond: to stand in the cool brook or lie down in the fat pasturage is its all in all; even thus is it with the mass of men, their souls are tethered to their bodies, imprisoned within the circumstances of the day. If we could be completely delivered from the thraldom of things seen and felt, and could feel the full influence of the invisible and the eternal, how much of heaven we might enjoy before the celestial shores are reached !

Paul's life was rough and stormy, yet who might not desire it? Had there been no life to come, he would have been of all men the most miserable, for he was one of the poorest, most persecuted, most despised, most slandered, most wearied, and most suffering of mortals : and yet if I had to put my finger upon happy lives I should not hesitate to select among the foremost the life of the Apostle Paul, for whom to live was Christ. It is also to be specially noted as to his happiness that he had a reason for it. My text begins with the word, "For." Paul is always argumentative, the leaning of his mind is in that direction;

No. 1,719.

hence, if he is cast down he has a reason for it, and if he is calm he can show just cause for his peace. Some religionists are deliriously happy, but they cannot tell you why. They can sing and shout, and dance, but they can give no reason for their excitement. They see an enthusiastic crowd, and they catch the infection: their religion is purely emotional; I am not going to condemn it, yet show I unto you a more excellent way. The joy which is not created by substantial causes is mere froth and foam, and soon vanishes away. Unless you can tell why you are happy you will not long be happy. If you have no principle at the back of your passion your passion will burn down to a black ash, and you will look in vain for a living spark. Some professors have not enough emotion, their hearts are too small, though I cannot say that their heads are too large; but there are others whose hearts are their main force, who are soon on fire, blazing away like shavings and brushwood when first the flame lights upon them; but their brains are an uncertain quantity, never sufficient to manage the furnace of their emotions. It was not so with Paul: he was a well-balanced man. If able to defy the present and rejoice in prospect of the future, he had a solid reason for so doing. I like a man who is fervent and enthusiastic, and yet in his fervour is as reasonable as if he were some cool logician. Let the heart be like a fiery, high-mettled steed, but take care that it is curbed and managed by discretion. An instructed Christian man is rational even in his ecstasies: ready to give a reason for the hope that is in him, when that hope seems to rise above all reason. He is glad, gladdest of the glad, but he knows the why and the wherefore of his gladness; and so he can bear the cruel tests to which the world exposes spiritual joy. The true believer's peace can answer the cavils of men or devils; it can justify itself in its opposition to all appearances. This is a house built upon a foundation, a tree which has a firmly settled root, a star fixed in its sphere ; and thus it is infinitely superior to the house upon the sand, the tree plucked up, the fleeting vapour of mere emotion. May God, the Holy Spirit, instruct us so that we may know the truth out of which solid happiness is sure to grow!

I see in the text before us, first of all, *a catastrophe which Paul saw to be very possible*—" If our earthly house of this tabernacle were dissolved" ; secondly, *the provision which he surely knew to be made* should that catastrophe occur—" We have a building of God, a house not made with hands, eternal in the heavens" ; and thirdly, I shall dwell for a minute or two upon *the value of this knowledge to Paul and to the rest of us in our present trying condition.*

I.   First, then, consider THE CATASTROPHE WHICH PAUL SAW TO BE VERY POSSIBLE: " If our earthly house of this tabernacle were dissolved."

He did not fear that he himself would be dissolved : he had not the slightest fear about that. The catastrophe which he looked forward to is known among us by the name of "death" ; but he calls it the dissolving of the earthly house of his tabernacle; the taking down of his tent-house body. He does not say, " If I were to be destroyed," or " If I were to be annihilated" ; he knows no supposition of that character ; he feels assured that he himself is perfectly safe. There is latent within the text an element of deep quiet as to his real self. "*We* know that if *our* earthly house of this tabernacle were dissolved, *we* have a building of God." The "we" is all unharmed and unmoved; if our house were dissolved *we* should not be undone; if we were to lose this earthly tent we have "a building of God, eternal in the heavens." The real man, the essential self, is out of harm's way; and all that he talks about is the falling to pieces of a certain tabernacle or tent in which for the present he is lodging. Many people are in a great fright about the future, yet here is Paul viewing the worst thing that could happen to him with such complacency that he likens it to nothing worse than the pulling down of a tent in which he was making shift to reside for a little season. He was afraid of nothing beyond that, and if that happened he had expectations which reconciled him to the event, and even helped him to anticipate it with joy.

Paul was not absolutely sure that his body would be dissolved. He hoped that he might be alive and remain at the coming of the Lord, and then he would be changed and be for ever with the Lord, without passing through death. Still, he was willing to leave this in the Lord's hands, and when he saw it to be possible that he should be numbered among the blessed dead who die in the Lord he did not shrink from the prospect, but bravely found a metaphor which set forth the little fear which he entertained concerning it.

The apostle perceived that the body in which he lived *was frail in itself*. Paul was accustomed to make tents. I do not suppose he ever manufactured any very large or sumptuous ones—probably he did not own capital enough for that, but he was a tent worker and mender. The use of tents was common enough among the Roman people in Paul's day. The gentry delighted in bright pavilions which they could set up at pleasure, and the commoner folk found pleasure in spending a part of their time under canvas. Whilst he was sitting writing this letter it is most likely that Paul had a tent or two to repair lying near his hand, and this suggested to him the language of the verse before us. When a tent is newly placed it is but a frail structure, very far removed from the substantiality of a house; in that respect it is exactly like this feeble corporeal frame of ours, which is crushed before the moth. Paul felt that his body would not need any great force to overthrow it; it was like the tent which the Midianite saw in his dream, which only needed to be struck by a barley cake, and lo! it lay along. A house of solid masonry may need a crowbar and a pick to start its stones from their places, but feebler tools will soon overturn a tent and make a ruin of it. The body is liable to dissolution from causes so minute as to be imperceptible—a breath of foul air, an atom of poisonous matter, a trifle, a mere nothing, may end this mortal life. I hope that you and I duly remember the frailty of our bodies. We are not so foolish as to think that because we are in robust health to-day we must necessarily live to old age. We have had among ourselves lately abundant evidence that those who appear to be the healthiest are often the first to be taken away, while feeble persons linger on among us, whose lives are a continued wonder and a perpetual struggle. When we think of the brittle ware whereof our bodies are made it is not strange that they should soon be broken. Is it not a wonderful thing that we

continue to live? much more wonderful than that we should die? Dr.
Watts has wisely said—

> " Our life contains a thousand springs,
>   And dies if one be gone ;
>   Strange! that a harp of thousand strings
>   Should keep in tune so long."

Some small affair interferes with a minute valve or organ of secretion,
mischief is engendered by it, the whole current of life is hindered, and by-
and-by death ensues.   It is a very delicate process by which dust
remains animated; a thousand things can stay that process, and then
our body is dissolved.   Paul, therefore, because he saw his body to be
frail as a bubble, looked forward to the time when the earthly house of
his soul would be dissolved.

When he was writing this epistle *he had many signs about him that
his body would be dissolved.*   His many labours were telling upon him;
he was worn down with fatigue, he was spent in his Master's service.
He was so full of the heavenly fire that he could never rest: after he
had evangelized one city he was forced to hasten to another; if he was
driven out of one village he hurried to the next, for he was eager to
deliver the message of salvation.   He wore himself out with labour,
and he felt, therefore, that the day would come when his body would
give way under the intense excitement of his life-agony.   In addition
to this he endured cold and hunger, and nakedness, and sickness, and
infirmities brought upon him by his missionary self-sacrifice.   He had a
hard time of it as to physical endurance, and I should think there was
scarcely a limb of the man that did not suffer in consequence of the im-
prisonments, scourgings, stonings, and other hardships which he had
suffered.   He felt that one of these days in all probability the house of
his tent would come down through the violence of his persecutors.
Once he most touchingly spoke of himself as "such an one as Paul the
Aged"; and aged men cannot get away from the consciousness that their
body is failing.   Certain crumbling portions warn the old man that the
house is dilapidated; the thatch which has grown thin or blanched tells
its tale.   There are signs about the aged which warn them that their
earthly house was not built to stand for ever; it is a tabernacle or tent
set up for a temporary purpose, and it shows signs of waxing old, and
being ready to pass away.   Hence, then, Paul was led to feel that both
from the natural frailty of the body, and also from the injuries which
it had already sustained, there was before him the evident probability
that the earthly house of his tabernacle would be dissolved.

Besides, Paul's frail body had been *subject to exceeding great perils.*
I saw the other day an encampment of gipsies out upon the common ;
many of this wandering race were sitting under a coarse covering sustained by sticks, I should exaggerate if I called them poles ; and I could
not help feeling that such an abode was all very well on a warm day,
but not at all desirable when the east-wind was blowing, or a shower of
sleet was driving along, or a deluge of rain descending.   The apostle's
body was a tent which was subjected to great stress of weather.   God
had not screened him; though one of the most precious men that ever
lived, yet he was exposed to more danger than almost any other of the

Lord's servants. Here is his own account of the matter;—"Thrice was I beaten with rods, once was I stoned, thrice I suffered shipwreck, a night and a day I have been in the deep; in journeyings often, in perils of waters, in perils of robbers, in perils by mine own country-men, in perils by the heathen, in perils in the city, in perils in the wilderness, in perils in the sea, in perils among false brethren; in weariness and painfulness, in watchings often, in hunger and thirst, in fastings often, in cold and nakedness." Well might he reckon that ere long his poor shepherd's shanty would give way under such rude blasts.

Besides, Paul knew that so *many others whom he had known and loved had already died*, and he gathered from this that he would himself die. There used to sit in this house a brother who has often assured me that he should not die, and that if any Christian man did die it was because he grieved the Lord. I am sorry to say that I have missed that brother for many months; I hope he has not yet disproved his own theory; but I am sure that he will do so sooner or later unless our Lord should hasten his advent. Whenever I meet with an enthusiast who boasts that he shall never die, I find it best to let him wait and see. One fine old Irish clergyman has frequently sought to instruct me in the art of being immortal, and he has been grieved and angry because I never set much store by the long life which he offered me. Though an old man, he assured me that he should never die; he expected in a short time to throw out all the infirmities of his years in the form of a rash, and then he should be as vigorous as ever. Alas! the good rector is buried, and his crazy brain is at rest. It is appointed unto men once to die. I should have thought that since so many of the excellent of the earth have fallen asleep, nobody would ever have been so mad as to raise a question about its being the common lot. Our crowded cemeteries supply ten thousand arguments why each one of us may expect to die in due time. This earthly house of our tabernacle will be dissolved; all things unite to warrant the belief.

Now, brethren, this was all that Paul did expect on the sad side; and truly it is not much. Is it? Certain Swiss peasants not very long ago were feeding their flocks on one of the lofty upland valleys. On one side of the pasturage stood a number of *châlets*, or wooden huts, in which they were accustomed to live during the summer, poor shelters which were left as soon as the winter set in. One day they heard a strange rumbling up in the lofty Alps, and they understood what it meant; it meant that a mass of rock or snow or ice had fallen, and would soon come crushing down in the form of an avalanche. In a brief space their fears were realized, for they saw a tremendous mass come rushing from above, bearing destruction in its course. What did it destroy? Only the old, crazy *châlets:* that was all. Every man of the shepherds was safe, and untouched: the event was rather to them a matter which caused a Te Deum to be sung in the village church below than a subject for mourning and sorrow. They said, "The avalanche is terrible, but it has not slain the aged mother, nor crushed the babe in its cradle: it has injured none of us, but only buried a few hovels which we can soon rebuild." Their case is a picture of ours. The avalanche of death will fall; but O ye saints, when it comes this is all it will do for you—your earthly house will be dissolved! Will you fret over so small a loss? No evil will come nigh to you; the poor hut of the body will be buried beneath the earth, but as for yourself, what will you have to do but to sing an everlasting Te Deum unto him who delivered you from death and danger, and raised you to his own right hand?

It would not long affect a man if his tent should be overthrown; he would shake himself clear of it and come forth; it would not otherwise disturb him. So death shall not affect us for the worse, but for the better; the dissolution of this hampering frame shall give us liberty. To-day we are like birds in the egg; so long as the shell is whole we are not free: death breaks the shell. Does the fledgling lament the dissolution of the shell? I never heard of a bird in its nest pining over its broken shell; no, its thought runs otherwise: to wings, and flight, and sunny skies. So let it be with us. This body will be dissolved: let it be so; it is meet it should be. We have been glad of it while we have needed it, and we thank God for the wondrous skill displayed in it; but when we no longer require it we shall escape from it as from imprisonment, and never wish to return to its narrow bounds. Death, as it pulls away our sackcloth canopy, will reveal to our wondering eyes the palace of the King wherein we shall dwell for ever, and, therefore, what cause have we to be alarmed at it? I have set out the whole catastrophe before you, and surely no believer trembles in view of it.

II. So now we pass on to the second head, THE PROVISION OF WHICH THE APOSTLE PAUL MOST SURELY KNEW. He knew that if his tent-dwelling was overthrown he would not be without a home; he knew that he would not have to open his eyes in a naked condition, and cry, "Woe's me, whither am I to fly? I have no dwelling place." No, he knew that if this tent-house were gone he had "a building of God." Paul was not afraid of going to purgatory: though of late some even among Protestants have in a modified form revived that grim fiction, and have told us that even believers will have much to bear before they will be fit for eternal happiness. The apostle held no such opinion; but, on the contrary, he wrote—"We know that if our earthly house of this tabernacle were dissolved, we have a building of God." He did not expect to be roasted alive for the next thousand years, and then to leap from purgatory to Paradise; but he did expect to go, as soon as ever his earthly house was dissolved, into his eternal house which is in the heavens. He had not even the thought of lying in a state of unconsciousness till the resurrection. He says, "We know that if the earthly house of this tabernacle were dissolved, we have [we have already] a building of God." He says not "we shall have it," but "we have it"; "we know that we have it." The picture seems to me to be as though one of you should dwell in his garden in a tent for a while. Somebody inquires what would happen if a gale of wind should blow your tent away in the night. "Oh," say you, "I have a house over yonder; I should go within doors and live there." What a comfort to know that, whatever occurs to our temporary gear, we have a fixed and settled abode to which we can at once repair. This makes us feel independent of all dangers, and helps us joyfully to welcome the inevitable, come when it may.

What did the apostle mean, however? for this text is said to be a very difficult one. He meant, first—the moment his soul left its body it would at once enter into that house of which Jesus said, "In my Father's house are many mansions: if it were not so, I would have told you." Do you want to know about that house? Read the Book of the Revelation, and learn of its gates of pearl, its streets of gold, its walls of rarest gems, of the river which windeth through it, and of the trees which bear their fruit every month. If after that you desire to know more concerning this house, I can but give you the advice which was given by John Bunyan in a similar case. One asked of honest John a question which he could not answer, for the matter was not opened in God's word; and therefore honest John bade his friend live a godly life, and go to heaven, *and see for himself.* Believe no dreams, but bide thy time, believing in the Lord Jesus, and thou shalt shortly know all about the house not made with hands, eternal in the heavens.

Paul, however, did mean that in the fulness of time he would again be clothed upon with a body. He regarded the waiting time as so short that he almost overlooked it, as men forget a moment's pause in a grand march. Ultimately, I say he expected to be housed in a body: the tent-house which was blown down and dissolved would be developed into a building, so rich and rare as to be fitly called "a building of God, a house not made with hands." This also is our prospect. At this present in this mortal body we groan being burdened, for our spirit is liberated from bondage, but our body is not yet emancipated, although it has been bought with a price. We are "waiting for the adoption, to wit, the redemption of our body," and so "the body is dead because of sin; but the Spirit is life because of righteousness." Our soul has been regenerated, but the body waits for the process which in its case is analagous to regeneration, namely, the resurrection from the dead. Disembodied saints may have to wait a few thousand years, more or less, dwelling in the Father's house above; but there shall come eventually the sounding of the trumpet and the raising of the dead, and then the perfected spirit shall dwell in a body adapted to its glory. The certainty of the resurrection raises us above the dread which would otherwise surround the dissolution of our body. A child sees a man throwing precious metal into a melting pot, and he is sad because fair silver is being destroyed; but he that knows the business of the refiner understands that no loss will come of the process; only the dross of that silver will be taken away, and the pure molten mass poured out into a comely mould will yet adorn a royal table. Well, my brethren, are we assured that to lose this vile body is clear gain since it will be fashioned according to the glorious body of the Lord Jesus?

Let us pass on to *consider how Paul could say he knew this.* This wonderfully enlightened nineteenth century has produced an order of wise men who glory in their ignorance. They call themselves "Agnostics," or know-nothings. When I was a boy it would have seemed odd to me to have met with a man who gloried in being an ignoramus, and yet that is the Latin for that Greek word "Agnostic." Is it not singular to hear a man boastfully say, "I am an ignoramus"? How different is our apostle! He says "we know." Whence came this confidence? How did he know?

First, Paul knew that he had a Father in heaven, for he felt the spirit of sonship; he knew also that his Father had a house, and he was certain that if ever he lost the tent in which he lived he should be sure to be welcomed into his own Father's house above. How do our children know that if ever they are in need of a house they can come home to us? Did they learn that from their tutors at school? No, their childhood's instinct teaches them that our house is their home, just as chickens run under the mother-hen without needing to be trained. Because they are our children they feel that as long as we have a house they have a house too; Paul, therefore, unhesitatingly said, "We know"; and, brethren, we know the same through like confidence in our Father's love. In the house of the many mansions we feel quite sure of a hearty welcome in due time. Shut out from our Father's home we cannot be! Houseless wanderers while our royal Father dwells in his palace we cannot be! We are not merely hopeful on this matter, but certain; and therefore we say, "We know."

Paul knew, again, that he had an elder brother, and that this brother had gone before to see to the lodging of the younger brethren. Paul remembered that Jesus had said, "I go to prepare a place for you, and if I go and prepare a place for you, I will come again, and receive you unto myself, that where I am ye may be also." So Paul had no question whatever; if the Lord had gone to prepare a place there would be a place for him; for he never knew his divine Lord set about anything and fail therein. Can we not all trust our Forerunner? Have we any doubts of him who has entered within the veil as our representative? No; as we are sure that Jesus has passed into the heavens on our behalf, so are we sure that when this tent-house body is dissolved, there remains a rest and home for our souls.

Doubtless, Paul also thought of the Holy Ghost, that blessed One who deigns to live with us in this frail house of clay, which is in many ways an uncomfortable and unsuitable abode for him by reason of the sin which has defiled it. He condescends to dwell in these mortal bodies, and, therefore, when we leave our earthly house he will leave it too; and we are persuaded that a place will be found where we may still abide in fellowship. As our bodies have been honoured to entertain the Holy Ghost we may be sure that in our hour of need he will find an abode for us. He has been our guest, and in his turn he will be our host; this we know, for we know the love of the Spirit. He who has made our body his temple will find a rest for our souls. Thus, from the Father, the Son, and the Holy Ghost, we gather assurance that we shall not wander to and fro unhoused, even though this mortal frame should be dissolved.

Besides, let me tell you something. Paul knew that when he died there was a Paradise prepared, for he had been there already. You remember how he locked up that story till he could keep it no longer, and, then, fifteen years after its occurrence, he let out the blessed secret. Let me read his words, "I knew a man in Christ above fourteen years ago, (whether in the body, I cannot tell; or whether out of the body, I cannot tell: God knoweth;) such an one caught up to the third heaven. And I knew such a man, (whether in the body, or out of the body, I cannot tell: God knoweth;) how that he was caught up into paradise, and heard unspeakable words, which is not lawful for a man to utter."

He says he was taken up to the third heaven; it was, therefore, idle to tell Paul that there was no home for him hereafter, for he had seen the place. "Well," say you, "*I* have not seen it." No; but you fully believe the witness of Paul, do you not? For my own part I am sure that Paul would not say that which is false, and inasmuch as he went into the third heaven or paradise, and saw it, I believe that there is such a place. Remember that this is the place to which the Lord Jesus admitted the dying thief, "To-day shalt thou be with me in paradise." This is the place where Jesus is, and where we shall be with him for ever, when the earthly house of this tabernacle shall be dissolved.

Yet, again, dear brothers and sisters, you and I know that when this earthly tabernacle is dissolved there will be a new body for us, because our Lord Jesus Christ has risen from the dead. In my mind the ultimate answer to my deepest unbelief is the fact of the rising of Jesus from the dead. No matter of history is anything like so well attested as the fact that our Lord was crucified, dead and buried, and that he did upon the third day rise again from the dead. This I unhesitatingly accept as a fact, and this becomes my anchorage. Inasmuch as Jesus is the representative of all who are in him, it is as certain that the believer will rise as that Jesus has risen. The apostle says, "We know," and remembering these grand truths I am sure that his words are not a a bit too strong. Nay, if I knew any word in the English language which would express more assurance than the word to know, I would use it this morning for myself. Much more, then, might the apostle use it for himself.

This we are also sure of, namely, that if our Lord Jesus be alive and in a place of rest he will never leave his chosen and redeemed ones without house or home. Where he has found a throne his people shall find a dwelling. Delightful is our old-fashioned ditty—

> "And when I shall die, Receive me, I'll cry,
> For Jesus has loved me, I cannot tell why;
> But this I do find, we two are so joined,
> He won't be in glory and leave me behind."

There is such an attachment between Christ and the believer; yea, more, such a vital, essential, indissoluble, tender marriage union that separation is impossible. As no man among us would ever be content to see his wife in prison if he could set her free, or to leave her outside in the cold when he could bring her to his fireside in comfort, so Christ, to whom our soul is espoused in eternal wedlock, will never rest until he has brought every one of his own beloved to be with him where he is, that they may behold his glory, the glory which the Father hath given him. No believer in Jesus has any doubts about that. I am sure you can all say, as Paul did, "We know that if our earthly house of this tabernacle were dissolved, we have a building of God, an house not made with hands."

"Ah," says one, "but how is a man to know that *he* has an interest in all this? Suppose I do know that the children of God are thus favoured, how am I to know that I am one of them?" I invite you to self-examination on this point. Dost thou believe in the Lord Jesus

Christ with all thine heart? Then it is written, "He that believeth in me though he were dead yet shall he live. He that liveth and believeth in me shall never die." Having believed in Christ the apostle knew that he was safe; for the promises are to believers, and if any man be a believer every promise of the covenant belongs to him. We obtain further assurance of this by our possessing the new life. Dear friend, have you entered into a new world? Do you feel within you a new heart and a right spirit? Have old things passed away, and have all things become new? Are you a new creature in Christ Jesus? Then it is all right with you: that new life cannot die, your new-born nature must inherit ever-'asting bliss. "Fear not, little flock; it is your Father's good pleasure to give you the kingdom." In addition to this, do you commune with God? do you speak with Christ? None perish who commune with the Father and the Son. Jesus cannot say at the last "I never knew you; depart from me;" for he does know you, and you know him. "Oh," say you, "he knows enough of me, for I am always begging." Just so, go on with that trade; be always a spiritual mendicant. The Lord of love will never cast away a pleading suppliant: he who frequents the throne of grace shall infallibly reach the throne of glory. Beside, does not "the Spirit itself also bear witness with our spirit that we are the children of God?" And if children and heirs, are we afraid of being left naked in the world to come? I hope that many of us have now reached the full assurance of faith, so that we believe and are sure. Can you not say each one for himself,—"I know whom I have believed, and I am persuaded that he is able to keep that which I have committed to him until that day"? These are the ways in which believers know that they are believers, and then by the word of God they know that all things are theirs, so that if their earthly house should fail they would be received into everlasting habitations.

III.   Lastly, as to THE VALUE OF THIS KNOWLEDGE TO US. To be sure that when this body dies all is well, is not that worth knowing? Secularists twit us with taking men's minds away from the practical present that they may dream over a fancied future. We answer that the best help to live for the present is to live in prospect of the eternal future. Paul's confident belief that if his body should be dissolved he would be no loser, kept him from fainting. He knew what the worst would be, and he was prepared for it. Great storms were out, but the apostle knew the limit of his possible loss, and so was ready. All we can lose is the frail tent of this poor body. By no possibility can we lose more. When a man knows the limit of his risk it greatly tends to calm his mind. The undiscoverable and the unmeasured are the worst ingredients of dread and terror: when you can gauge your fears, you have removed them. Our apostle felt that he had been sent into the world with the great design of glorifying God, winning souls, and building up saints, and he was fully resolved to keep to the ministry which he had received. He argues with himself that his most danger-ous course would be to faint in his life-service, for perseverance in his calling could bring with it no greater risk than death, and that he summed up as losing a tent and gaining a mansion. The Roman emperor might strike off his head, or a mob might stone him to death, or he might be crucified like his Master: but he made light of such a fate! It was to him only the coming down of the old tent; it did not affect his undying spirit; he smiled and sang, " For our light affliction, which is but for a moment, worketh for us a far more exceeding and eternal weight of glory. '

The prospect of his heavenly house made his present trials seem very light; for he felt like a man who sojourns for a night at a poor inn, but puts up with it gladly because he hopes to be home on the morrow. If we were trying tent life for a season we should probably cry out, " A fearful draught comes in at that corner! How damp it is under foot! How cramped up one feels!" Yet we should smile over it all, and say, " It will not be for long. We shall soon be in our house at home." Ah, brethren, an hour with our God will make up for all the trials of the way. Wherefore, be of good courage, and press on.

This changed for Paul the very idea of death; death was transformed from a demon into an angel: it was but the removal of a tottering tent that he might enter into a permanent palace. Some of God's own children are much troubled through fear of death, because they do not know what it is. If they were better taught they would soon discover in their present source of sorrow a subject for song. I would like here to say that I have known some of my Master's doubting and fearing servants die splendidly. Do you remember how Mr. Feeble-mind, when he crossed the river, went over dry-shod. Poor soul, he thought he should surely be drowned, and yet he scarcely wet the soles of his feet. I have known men of God go like Jacob all day long weary and faint, feeling banished from their Father's house; and yet when they have laid their head down for their final sleep they have had visions of angels and of God. The end of their journey has made amends for the rough places of the way. It shall be so with you, brother believer. There is usually a dark place in every Christian's experience : I have seen some travel in sunlight almost the whole of the way, and then depart in gloom, and I have thought none the worse of them for it; and I have seen others struggle forward through a fog for the first part of their pilgrimage, and then come out into cloudless day. At one period or another beneath these lowering skies the shadow falls across our way, but surely " light is sown for the righteous, and gladness for the upright in heart."

As I have thought of some of my dear brothers and sisters that I have seen die very sweetly, and I have remembered that they were, in life, lowly and self-distrustful, I have compared them to persons who, when they drink their tea, forget to stir the sugar at the bottom of the cup. How doubly sweet the drink becomes as they near the bottom : they have more sweetness than they can well bear. Would it not be wise to stir the tea at once and enjoy the sweetness from the brim to the bottom? This is the benefit of faith as to the future, for it flavours the present with delight. But what if saints should miss immediate comfort for awhile, how richly will they be compensated! What will it be to open your eyes in heaven! What a joy to fall asleep on the bed of languishing and to wake up amid the celestial Hallelujahs! " What am I ? Where am I ? Ah, my God! my Christ! my heaven! my all! I am at home." Sorrow and sighing shall flee away. Does not this view of things give a transfiguration to death ? O you poor unbelievers, how

I pity you, since you have no such glorious hopes. O that you would believe in the Lord Jesus and enter into life eternal.

Faith had such an effect upon Paul that it made him always calm, and brave. Why should he be afraid of a man that could not do him harm? Even if his persecutor killed him he would do him a service. What had he to fear? This made Paul wise and prudent. He could use his judgment, for he was not fluttered. He was not like some of you that are only a little ill, and straightway you are filled with fright, and so you make yourselves worse than you otherwise would be, so that the doctor has to contend with an affrighted mind as well as a diseased body. He who is calm, restful, happy is already on the road to a cure. He is quiet because he is in his Father's hands, and whether he lives or dies all is well; and this conviction helps the physician to remove his bodily malady. I say again, there is no way to live like learning to die, and he who can afford to be careless whether he lives or dies is the man who will so live as to die triumphantly. Oh, that all of you felt the quiet which comes of trusting in the Lord Jesus. How sad to know that you may die at any moment, and to be unprepared for the change! I do not wonder that you are unhappy: you have good reason for being so. Oh that you were wise, and would make the future sure by faith in the risen Lord.

In Martin Luther's time, and before his era, men who had lived evil lives were often in great fear when they came to die, and in their terror they would send to a monastery and procure a monk's dress in which to be buried. What a foolish fancy! Yet so it was that they hoped to fare better in the day of judgment for being wrapped in brown serge, and covered with a cowl! Be ours a better garment. Here is a wish of holy Rutherford—"His believed love shall be my winding-sheet, and all my grave-clothes; I shall roll up my soul, and sew it up in the web of his sweet and free love." Is not that your idea? It is surely mine! If we are laid to sleep in such a cerecloth, there will be no fear of our waking. It will happen to us as to the man who was laid in Elisha's grave, and at once arose as soon as he touched the prophet's bones. No man can lie dead if wrapped up in the love of Christ, for his love is life. He that has touched the love of Christ has touched the heart of the life of God, and he must live. So let us give ourselves up to that divine love, and trusting in our Lord, let us go onward to eternal bliss till the day break and the shadows flee away : let us triumph and rejoice that there is prepared for us a " building of God, a house not made with hands, eternal in the heavens."

PORTIONS OF SCRIPTURE READ BEFORE SERMON—2 Corinthians iv. 7—18; v. 1—9.

HYMNS FROM "OUR OWN HYMN BOOK"—870, 847, 846.

CHRIST IN YOU.

A Sermon

DELIVERED ON LORD's-DAY MORNING, MAY 13TH, 1883, BY

C. H. SPURGEON,

AT THE METROPOLITAN TABERNACLE, NEWINGTON.

" Christ in you, the hope of glory."—Colossians i. 27.

THE gospel is the grand secret: the mystery of mysteries. It was hidden from ages and from generations, but is now made manifest to the saints. To the mass of mankind it was utterly unknown; and the chosen people, who saw something of it, only perceived it dimly through the smoke of sacrifices and the veil of types. It remained a mystery which wit could not guess nor invention unravel; and it must for ever have continued a secret had not God in his infinite mercy been pleased to reveal it by the Holy Ghost. In a still deeper sense it is even yet a hidden thing unless the Spirit of God has revealed it to us individually, for the revelation of the gospel in the word of God does not of itself instruct men unto eternal life: the light is clear enough, but it availeth nothing till the eyes are opened. Each separate individual must have Christ revealed to him and in him by the work of the Holy Ghost, or else he will remain in darkness even in the midst of gospel day. Blessed and happy are they to whom the Lord has laid open the divine secret which prophets and kings could not discover, which even angels desired to look into.

Brethren, we live in a time when the gospel is clearly revealed in the word of God, and when that word has its faithful preachers lovingly to press home its teachings, let us take care that we do not despise the mystery which has now become a household word. Let not the commonness of the blessing cause us to undervalue it. You remember how in the wilderness the Israelites fed upon angels' food until they had enjoyed it so long, so constantly, and so abundantly that in their wicked discontent they called it "light bread." I fear me that many in these times are cloyed with the gospel like those who eat too much honey. They even venture to call the heavenly word "common-place," and talk as if it were not only " the old, old story," but a stale story too. Are not many hungering after novelties, longing for things original and startling, thirsting after the spiritual dram-drinking of sensational preaching, dissatisfied with Christ crucified, though he is the bread which came down from heaven ?

No. 1,720.

for us, let us keep clear of this folly; let us rest content with the old food, praying from day to day, " Lord, evermore give us this bread." May it never happen to us as unto the Jews of the apostle's time, who refused utterly the word of life; so that the truth became to them a stumbling-block, and those who preached it were compelled to turn to the Gentiles. If we despise the heavenly message we cannot expect to fare better than they did: let us not incur the danger of refusing him that speaks from heaven. If there be life, rejoice in it; if there be light, walk in it; if there be love, rest in it. If the Lord God Almighty has at length set open the treasures of his grace, and put eternal bliss within your reach, stretch out the hand of faith, and be enriched thereby. Turn not your backs upon your God, your Saviour; for in so doing you will turn your backs on eternal life and heaven. God grant that none of you may do this.

In our text we have in a few words that great mystery with which heaven did labour as in travail, that mystery which is to transform this poor world into new heavens and a new earth; we have it, I say, all in a nutshell in the seven words of our text: the riches of the glory of this mystery may here be seen set out to open view—" Christ in you, the hope of glory."

By the assistance of the divine Spirit, I shall speak upon this mystery in three ways: *The essence of it is " Christ"; the sweetness of it is " Christ in you"; and the outlook of it is " the hope of glory."* The words read like a whole body of divinity condensed into a line,—" Christ in you, the hope of glory."

I. The eternal mystery of the gospel, THE ESSENCE OF IT IS CHRIST. I hardly know what is the antecedent to the word "which" here: whether it is " mystery," or " riches," or "glory"; and I do not greatly care to examine which it may be. Any one of the three words will be suitable, and all three will fit best of all. If it be " the mystery," Christ is that mystery: "Without controversy great is the mystery of godliness: God was manifest in the flesh." If it be the word "glory," beyond all question our Lord Jesus wears a " glory as of the Only-begotten of the Father, full of grace and truth." Is he not "the brightness of the Father's glory"? If we take the word " riches," ye have often heard of " the unsearchable riches of Christ," for in him dwelleth all the fulness of the Godhead bodily. Oh, the riches of the grace of God which it hath pleased the Father to impart unto us in Christ Jesus! Christ is the " mystery," the " riches," and the " glory." He is all this; and blessed be his name, he is all this among us poor Gentiles who at first were like dogs, scarce accounted worthy to eat the crumbs from under the children's table, and yet we are now admitted into the children's place, and made heirs of God, joint-heirs with Christ Jesus. Riches of glory among the Gentiles would have sounded like a mockery in the first ages, and yet the language is most proper at this day, for all things are ours in Christ Jesus the Lord.

The essence of this mystery is *Christ himself.* In these days certain would-be-wise men are laboriously attempting to constitute a church without Christ, and to set forth a salvation without a Saviour; but their Babel building is as a bowing wall and a tottering fence. The centre of the blessed mystery of the gospel is *Christ himself in his person.* What a wonderful conception it was that ever the infinite God should take upon himself the nature of man! It never would have occurred to men that such a condescension would be thought of. Even now that it has been done it is a great mystery of our faith. God and man in one person is the wonder of heaven, and earth, and hell. Well might David exclaim, "What is man, that thou art mindful of him? and the son of man, that thou visitest him?" The first thought of the incarnation was born in the unsearchably wise mind of God. It needed omnipotent omniscience to suggest the idea of "Immanuel, God with us." Think of it! The Infinite an infant, the Ancient of days a child, the Ever Blessed a man of sorrows and acquainted with grief! The idea is original, astounding, divine. Oh, that this blending of the two natures should ever have taken place! Brethren, the heart of the gospel throbs in this truth. The Son of the Highest was born at Bethlehem, and at his birth, ere he had wrought a deed of righteousness or shed a drop of blood, the angels sang, " Glory to God in the highest, on earth peace, good will toward men," for they knew that the incarnation had within itself a wealth of good things for men. When the Lord himself took our manhood it meant inconceivable benediction to the human race. "Unto us a child is born, unto us a son is given," and in that child and son we find our salvation. God in our nature can mean for us nothing but joy. How favoured is our race in this respect! What other creature did the Lord thus espouse? We know that he took not up angels, but he took up the seed of Abraham; he took upon him human nature, and now the next being in the universe to God is man. He who was made a little lower than the angels for the suffering of death is this day crowned with glory and honour, and made to have dominion over all the works of Jehovah's hands. This is the gospel indeed. Do not sinners begin to hope? Is there one in your nature who is "Light of lights, very God of very God," and do you not perceive that this must mean good to you? Does not the "word made flesh" dwelling among men arouse hope in your bosoms, and lead you to believe that you may yet be saved? Certainly, the fact of there being such an union between God and man is the delight of every regenerated mind.

Our Lord's person is at this day constituted in the same manner. He is still God and man; still he can sympathize with our manhood to the full, for he is bone of our bone and flesh of our flesh; and yet he can help us without limit, seeing he is equal with the Father. Though manifestly divine, yet Jesus is none the less human; though truly man, he is none the less divine; and this is a door of hope to us, a fountain of consolation which never ceases to flow.

When we think of our Lord we remember with his person *the glorious work which he undertook and finished on our behalf.* Being found in fashion as man he humbled himself and became obedient unto death, even the death of the cross. He took upon himself the form of a servant, and was made in the likeness of sinful flesh, because we had failed in our service, and could not be saved unless another did suit and service on our behalf. The heir of all things girded himself to be among us as one that serveth. What service his was! How arduous! how humble! how heavy! how all-consuming! His was a life of grief and humiliation, followed by a death of agony and scorn. Up to the cross he carried all our load, and on the cross he bore, that we might never bear, his Father's righteous wrath. Oh, what has not Christ done for us? He has cast our sins into the depths of the sea: he has taken the cup which we ought to have drunk for ever, and he has drained it dry, and left not a dreg behind. He has redeemed us from the curse of the law, being made a curse for us; and now he has finished transgression, made an end of sin, and brought in everlasting righteousness, and gone up to his Father's throne within the veil, bearing his divine oblation, and making everything right and safe for us, that by-and-by we may follow him, and be with him where he is. Oh yes, brethren, Christ's person and finished work are the pillars of our hope. I cannot think of what he is, and what he has done, and what he is doing, and what he will yet do, without saying, " He is all my salvation and all my desire."

My brethren, every one of *our Lord's offices* is a well-spring of comfort. Is he prophet, priest, and king? Is he friend? Is he brother? Is he husband? Is he head? Every way and everywhere we lean the weight of our soul's great business upon him, and he is our all in all. Besides, there is this sweet thought, that he is *our representative*. Know ye not that of old he was our covenant head, and stood for us in the great transactions of eternity? Like as the first Adam headed up the race, and stood for us—alas, I must correct myself—*fell* for us, and we fell in him; so now hath the second Adam taken up within himself all his people and stood for them, and kept for them the covenant, so that now it is ordered in all things and sure, and every blessing of it is infallibly secured to all the seed. Believers must and shall possess the covenanted inheritance because Jesus represents them, and on their behalf have taken possession of the estate of God. Whatever Christ is his people are in him. They were crucified in him, they were dead in him, they were buried in him, they are risen in him; in him they live eternally, in him they sit gloriously at the right hand of God, " who has raised us up together, and made us sit together in the heavenly places in Christ Jesus." In him we are "accepted in the Beloved," both now and for ever; and this, I say, is the essence of the whole gospel. He that preaches Christ preaches the gospel; he who does not preach Christ, preaches no gospel. It is no more possible for there to be a gospel without Christ than a day without the sun, or a river without water, or a living man without a head, or a quickened human body without a soul. No, Christ himself is the life, soul, substance, and essence of the mystery of the gospel of God.

Christ himself, again I say, and no other. I have been trying to think what we should do if our Lord were gone. Suppose that a man has heard of a great physician who understands his complaint. He has travelled a great many miles to see this celebrated doctor; but when he gets to the door they tell him that he is out. " Well," says he, " then I must wait till he is in." " You need not wait," they reply, " his assistant is at home." The suffering man, who has been often disappointed, answers, "I do not care about his assistant, I want to see the man himself: mine is a desperate case, but I have heard that this physician has cured the like; I must, therefore, see *him*. No assistants for me." " Well," say they, " he is out; but there are his books; you can see his books." " Thank you," he says, " I cannot be content with his books,

I want the living man and nothing less. It is to him that I must speak, and from him I will receive instructions." "Do you see that cabinet?" "Yes." "It is full of his medicines." The sick man answers, "I dare say they are very good, but they are of no use to me without the doctor: I want their owner to prescribe for me, or I shall die of my disease." "But see," cries one, "here is a person who has been cured by him, a man of great experience, who has been present at many remarkable operations. Go into the inquiry-room with him, and he will tell you all about the mode of cure." The afflicted man answers, "I am much obliged to you, but all your talk only makes me long the more to see the doctor. I came to see *him*, and I am not going to be put off with anything else. I must see the man himself, for myself. He has made my disease a speciality; he knows how to handle my case, and I will stop till I see *him*." Now, dear friends, if you are seeking Christ, imitate this sick man, or else you will miss the mark altogether. Never be put off with books, or conversations. Be not content with Christian people talking to you, or preachers preaching to you, or the Bible being read to you, or prayers being offered for you. Anything short of Jesus will leave you short of salvation. You have to reach Christ, and touch Christ, and nothing short of this will serve your turn. Picture the case of the prodigal son when he went home. Suppose when he reached the house the elder brother had come to meet him. I must make a supposition that the elder brother had sweetened himself, and made himself amiable; and then I hear him say, "Come in, brother; welcome home!" But I see the returning one stand there with the tears in his eyes, and I hear him lament, "I want to see my father. I must tell *him* that I have sinned and done evil in his sight." An old servant whispers, "Master John, I am glad to see you back. Be happy, for all the servants are rejoiced to hear the sound of your voice. It is true your father will not see you, but he has ordered the fatted calf to be killed for you; and here is the best robe, and a ring, and shoes for your feet, and we are told to put them upon you." All this would not content the poor penitent. I think I hear him cry—" I do not despise anything my father gives me, for I am not worthy to be as his hired servant; but what is all this unless I see *his* face, and know that he forgives me? There is no taste in the feast, no glitter in the ring, no fitness in the shoes, no beauty in the robe unless I can see my father and can be reconciled to him." Do you not see that in the case of the prodigal son the great matter was to get his head into his father's bosom, and there to sob out "Father, I have sinned"? The one thing needful was the kiss of free forgiveness, the touch of those dear, warm, loving lips, which said, "My dear child, I love you, and your faults are blotted out." That was the thing that gave his soul rest and perfect peace; and this is the mystery we come to preach to you—God himself drawing near to you in Christ Jesus, and forgiving you all trespasses. We are not content to preach unless Jesus himself be the theme. We do not set before you something about Christ, nor something that belongs to Christ, nor something procured by Christ, nor somebody that has known Christ, nor some truth which extols Christ; but we preach Christ crucified. We preach not ourselves, but Christ Jesus the Lord; and we say to you, never be content till you clasp the Saviour in your arms as Simeon did in the temple. That venerable saint did not pray to depart in peace while he only saw the child in Mary's bosom; but when he had taken the dear one into his own arms, then he said, "Lord, now lettest thou thy servant depart in peace." A personal grasp of a personal Christ, even though we only know him as an infant, fills the heart to the full; but nothing else will do it.

I go a little farther still. As it must be Christ himself, and none other, it must also be *Christ himself rather than anything which Christ gives.* I was thinking the other day how different Christ is from all the friends and helpers that we have. They bring us good things, but Jesus gives us himself. He does not merely give us wisdom, righteousness, sanctification, and redemption; but he himself is made of God all these things to us. Hence we can never do without him. When very ill you are pleased to see the doctor; but when you are getting well you say to yourself, "I shall be glad to see the back of the good man, for that will be a sure sign that I am off the sick list." Ah, but when Jesus heals a soul he wants to see Jesus more than ever. Our longing for the constant company of our Lord is the sign that we are getting well: he who longs for Jesus to abide with him for ever is healed of his plague. We never outgrow Christ; but we grow to need him more and more. If you eat a meal you lose your appetite, but if you feed upon Christ you hunger and thirst still more after him. This insatiable desire after him is not a painful hunger, but a heavenly, pleasant hunger which grows upon you the more its cravings are gratified. The man who has little of Christ can do with little of Christ; but he that gets more of Christ pines for a yet fuller supply. Suppose a wise man were to instruct you: you would learn all he had to teach and then say, "Let him go on and teach somebody else;" but when Jesus teaches we discover so much of our own ignorance that we would fain keep him as our life-tutor. When our Lord taught the two disciples on the road to Emmaus, he opened the Scriptures and he opened their minds until their hearts burned within them. What next? Shall the divine teacher pass on? No, no; they constrain him, saying "Abide with us: it is toward evening, and the day is far spent." The more he taught them the more they wished to be taught. This is ever the way with Christ: he is growingly dear, increasingly necessary. Oh my brothers, you cannot do without him. If you have your foot upon the threshold of pure gold, and your finger on the latch of the gate of pearl, you now need Christ more than ever you did. I feel persuaded that you are of Rutherford's mind, when he cried to have his heart enlarged till it was as big as heaven, that he might hold all Christ within it; and then he felt that even this was too narrow a space for the boundless love of Jesus, since the heaven of heavens cannot contain him, and so he cried out for a heart as large as seven heavens, that he might entertain the Well-beloved. Truly, I am content with what God has given me in all points, save that I long for more of Christ. I could sit down happy if I knew that my portion in the house and in the field would never grow; but I am famished to have more of my Lord. The more we are filled with Christ, the more we feel our own natural emptiness: the more we know of him, the more we long to know him. Paul, writing to the Philippians, when he had been a Christian for many a year, yet says, "That I may know him." **Oh**, Paul, do you not know Christ yet? "Yes," says he, and "No": for he knew the love of Christ, but felt that it surpassed all knowledge. "All the rivers run into the sea, yet the sea is not full": this is not our case in one respect, and yet it is in another, for all the streams of grace and love and blessedness flow into our souls, and we are full; yet, being full, we are longing for more. Not thy gifts, Lord, but thyself: thou, thou art the desire of our hearts.

Christ alone is enough. Mark this. Nothing must be placed with Christ as if it were necessary to him. Some hold a candle to the sun by preaching Christ and man's philosophy, or their own priestcraft. When the blessed rain comes fresh from heaven they would fain perfume it with their own dainty extract of fancy. As for God's blessed air fresh from the eternal hills, they dream that it cannot be right unless by scientific experiments they load it with their own smoke and cloud. Come, clear out, let us see the sun! We want not your rushlights. Away with your gauzes and your fineries, let the clear sunlight enter! Let the holy water drop from heaven; we want not your scented essences. Out of the way, and let the fresh air blow about us. There is nothing like it for the health and strength of the soul. We rejoice in Christ and nothing else but Christ: Christ and no priestcraft; Christ and no philosophy; Christ and no modern thought; Christ and no human perfection. Christ, the whole of Christ, and nothing else but Christ: here lies the mystery of the gospel of the grace of God.

Brethren, what else but Christ can satisfy the justice of God? Look around you when a sense of sin is on you, and the dread tribunal is before your eyes: what can you bring by way of expiation but Christ? What can you bring with Christ? What dare you associate with his blood and merits? Oh, my God, nothing will content thee but thy Son, thy Son alone. What else can quiet conscience? Some professors have consciences as good as new, for they have never been used; but he that has once had his conscience thoroughly exercised and pressed upon with all the weight of sin till he has felt as if it were better for him not to be than to be guilty before God—that man acknowledges that nothing but Christ will ever quiet his agonized heart. See the bleeding Lamb, and you will be pacified! See the exalted Lord pleading his righteousness before the throne; and conscience is even as a weaned child; and all the storm within the spirit is hushed into a great calm. What else will do to live with but Christ? I do not find in times of pain and depression of spirit that I can keep up upon anything but my Lord. The mind can feed at other times on pretty kickshaws and fine confectionery such as certain divines serve out in the form of orations and essays, and the like; but when you are sore sick your soul abhors all manner of earthly meat, and nothing will stay on the stomach but the bread of heaven, even the blessed Christ of God. Think also, when you come to die, what else will do but Christ? Oh, I have seen men die with heaven in their eyes, the eternal Godhead seeming to transfigure them, because they rejoiced in Christ; but a death-bed without Christ, it is the darkening twilight of eternal night: it is the gloomy cave which forms the entrance of the land of darkness. Do not venture on life or death without Jesus, I implore you. "None but Christ, none but Christ," this has been the martyr's cry amidst the fire; let it be ours in life and death.

II. Secondly, we are to consider THE SWEETNESS OF THIS MYSTERY, WHICH IS CHRIST IN YOU. This is a grand advance. I know that there are a great many fishermen here this morning, and I heartily welcome them. When you are out at sea you like to know that there are plenty of fish in the sea all round your boats. It is a fine thing to get in among the great shoals of fish. Yes, but there is one thing better than that. Fish in the sea are good; but the fish in the boat are the fish for you. Once get them in the net, or better still, safe into the vessel, and you are glad. Now Christ in heaven, Christ free to poor sinners is precious, but Christ here in the heart is most precious of all. Here is the marrow and fatness. Christ on board the vessel brings safety and calm. Christ in your house, Christ in your heart, *Christ in you;* that is the cream of the matter, the honey of the honeycomb. Gold is valuable, but men think more of a pound in their pockets than of huge ingots in the Bank-cellar. A loaf of bread is a fine thing, but if we could not eat it, and so get it within us, we might die of starvation. A medicine may be a noble cure, but if it is always kept in the phial, and we never take a draught from it, what good will it do us? Christ is best known when he is Christ *in you.* Let us talk about that a little.

Christ in you—that is, first, *Christ accepted by faith.* Is it not a wonderful thing that Christ Jesus should ever enter into a man? Yes, but I will tell you something more wonderful, and that is, that he should enter in by so narrow an opening as our little faith. There is the sun; I do not know how many thousands of times the sun is bigger than the earth, and yet the sun can come into a little room or a close cell; and what is more, the sun can get in through a chink. When the shutters have been closed I have known him come in through a little round hole in them. So Christ can come in through a little faith—a mere chink of confidence. If you are such a poor believer that you can hardly think of assurance or confidence, yet if you do trust the Lord, as surely as the sun comes in by a narrow crack, so will Christ come into your soul by the smallest opening of true faith. How wise it will be on your part when you see your Lord's sunny face shining through the lattices to say, " I am not going to be satisfied with these mere glints and gleams, I would fain walk in the light of his countenance. Pull up those blinds; let the heavenly sun shine in, and let me rejoice in its glory." Grow in faith, and enlarge your receiving power till you take in Christ into your inmost soul by the Holy Spirit; for it is Christ in you by faith that becomes the hope of glory.

By Christ in you we mean *Christ possessed.* You see nothing is so much a man's own as that which is within him. Do you tell me that a certain slice of bread is not mine, and that I have no right to it? But I have eaten it, and you may bring a lawsuit against me about that bread if you like, but you cannot get it away from me. That question is settled; that which I have eaten is mine. In this case possession is not only nine points of the law, but all the points. When a man gets Christ into him, the devil himself cannot win a suit against him to recover Christ; for that matter is settled beyond question. Christ in you is yours indeed. Men may question whether an acre of land or a house belongs to me; but the meat I ate yesterday is not a case of property which Chancery or any other court can alter. So, when the believer has Christ in him, the law has no more to say. The enclosure made by faith carries its own title-deeds with it.

It means, too, *Christ experienced* in all his power. There may be a valuable medicine that works like magic to expel a man's pains, and cure his diseases; but it is of no efficacy till it is within him! When it commences to purify his blood, and to strengthen his frame, he is in a fair way to know it without depending upon the witness of others. Get Christ in you, curing your sin, Christ in you filling your soul with love to virtue and holiness, bathing your heart in comfort, and firing it with heavenly aspirations,—then will you know the Lord. Christ believed in, Christ possessed, Christ experienced, Christ in you, this is worth a world.

Moreover, Christ in us is *Christ reigning*. It reminds me of Mr. Bunyan's picture of Mansoul, when the Prince Immanuel laid siege to it, and Diabolus from within the city strove to keep him out. It was a hard time for Mansoul then ; but when at last the battering rams had broken down the gates, and the silver trumpets sounded, and the prince's captains entered the breach, then on a day the prince himself did ride down the city's streets, while liberated citizens welcomed him with all their hearts, hung out all their streamers, and made the church towers rock again as the bells rang out merry peals, for the king himself was come. Up to the castle of the heart he rode in triumph, and took his royal throne to be henceforth the sole lord and king of the city. Christ in you is a right royal word. Christ swaying his sceptre from the centre of your being, over every power and faculty, desire and resolve, bringing every thought into captivity to himself, oh, this is glory begun, and the sure pledge of heaven. Oh for more of the imperial sovereignty of Jesus! it is our liberty to be absolutely under his sway.

Yes, and then Christ in you is *Christ filling you*. It is wonderful, when Christ once enters into a soul, how by degrees he occupies the whole of it. Did you ever hear the legend of a man whose garden produced nothing else but weeds, till at last he met with a strange foreign flower of singular vitality. The story is that he sowed a handful of this seed in his overgrown garden, and left it to work its own sweet way. He slept and rose, and knew not how the seed was growing till on a day he opened the gate and saw a sight which much astounded him. He knew that the seed would produce a dainty flower and he looked for it ; but he had little dreamed that the plant would cover the whole garden. So it was : the flower had exterminated every weed, till as he looked from one end to the other from wall to wall he could see nothing but the fair colours of that rare plant, and smell nothing but its delicious perfume. Christ is that plant of renown. If he be sown in the soil of your soul, he will gradually eat out the roots of all ill weeds and poisonous plants, till over all your nature there shall be Christ in you. God grant we may realize the picture in our own hearts, and then we shall be in Paradise.

It may sound strange to add that Christ in you *transfigures the man till he becomes like Christ himself*. You thrust a bar of cold, black iron into the fire, and keep it there till the fire enters into it. See, the iron is like fire itself—he that feels it will know no difference. The fire has permeated the iron, and made it a fiery mass. I should like to have seen that bush in Horeb before which Moses put off his shoes. When it was all ablaze it seemed no longer a bush, but a mass of fire, a furnace of pure flame. The fire had transfigured the bush. So it is with us when Christ enters into us : he elevates us to a nobler state ; even as Paul saith " I live, yet not I, but Christ lives in me." Jesus sanctifies us wholly, spirit, soul, and body, and takes us to dwell with him in the perfect state above.

Christ in you,—how can I explain it? We are the little graft and he is the strong and living stem. We are laid to him, bound to him, sealed to him, and when there is nothing between the new shoot and the old tree, at last the sap flows into the graft, and the graft and the tree are one. Ye know right well how Christ enters into us and becomes our life.

Christ in you means power in you. A strong man armed keeps his house till a stronger than he comes, and when the stronger enters the first tenant is ejected by the power of the new comer, and kept out by the same means. We were without strength till Christ came, and now we war with principalities and powers, and win the victory.

Christ in you! Oh, what bliss! what joy! The Bridegroom is with us, and we cannot fast : the King is with us, and we are glad. When King Charles went to live at Newmarket it is said that a most poverty-stricken village became a wealthy place ; truly when Christ comes to dwell in our hearts our spiritual poverty suddenly turns to blessed wealth.

Christ in you! What a wonder it is that he should deign to come under our roof! Lift up your heads, O ye gates, and be ye lifted up, ye everlasting doors, that the King of glory may come in. See the honour which his entrance brings with it! He glorifies the place where his foot rests even for a moment. If Jesus doth but enter into your heart, his court comes with him : honour, and glory, and immortality, and heaven, and all other divine things follow where he leads.

" Oh," says one, " I wish he would come and dwell in me." Then, be humble, for he loves to dwell with him that is humble and of a contrite spirit. Next, be clean ; for if they must be clean that bear God's vessels, much more they that have Christ himself in them. Next, be empty ; for Christ will not live amid the lumber of self, and pride, and carnal sufficiency. Learn abundantly to rejoice in Christ, for he who welcomes Christ will have him always for a guest. Jesus never tarries where he is not desired. If his welcome is worn out, away he goes. Oh, desire and delight in him ; hunger and thirst after him ; for Christ delights to dwell with an eager people, a hungry people, a people who value him, and cannot be happy without him.

Surely I have said enough to make you feel that the sweetness of true godliness lies in having Christ in you.

III. Thirdly, we are to consider that THE OUTLOOK OF ALL THIS IS " CHRIST IN YOU THE HOPE OF GLORY." Last Sunday morning, as best I could in my feebleness, I spoke to you about the time when this earthly house of our tabernacle shall be dissolved, when we shall find that we have a building of God, a house not made with hands, eternal in the heavens ; but this morning's text goes a little further : it speaks of glory, which is a hope for soul as well as body. Why glory ! Glory ?

Surely that belongs to God only. To him alone be glory. Yes, but Christ has said, " Father, I will that they also whom thou hast given me be with me where I am, that they may behold my glory"; and he also says, " And the glory which thou hast given me I have given them." Think of it. Glory for us poor creatures! Glory for you, sister; glory for me! It seems a strange thing that a sinner should ever have anything to do with glory when he deserves nothing but shame. We are neither kings nor princes, what have we to do with glory? Yet glory is to be our dwelling, glory our light, glory our crown, glory our song. The Lord will not be content to give us less than glory. Grace is very sweet : might we not be content to swim for ever in a sea of grace? But no, our Lord " will give grace and glory."

> " All needful grace will God bestow,
> And crown that grace with glory too."

We shall have glorified bodies, glorious companions, a glorious reward, and glorious rest.

But how know we that we shall have glory ? Why, first, he that has come to live in our hearts, and reigns as our bosom's Lord, makes us glorious by his coming. His rest is glorious : the place of his feet is glorious. He must mean some great thing towards us, or he would never dwell in us. I saw a fine carriage stopping the other day at a very humble hovel; and I thought to myself, " that carriage is not stopping there to collect rent, or to borrow a broom." Oh, no; that lady yonder is calling round and visiting the poor, and I doubt not she has taken in some nourishment to an invalid. I hope it was so : and I am sure my Lord Jesus Christ's carriage never stops at my door to get anything out of me: whenever he comes he brings countless blessings with him. Such a one as he is, God over all, blessed for ever, it cannot be that he took our nature, unless with high designs of love unsearchable. Thus we nourish large expectations upon the food of solid reason. I am sure our Lord Jesus would never have done so much if he had not meant to manifest the immeasurable breadth and length of a love which is beyond imagining. What he has done already surprises me even to amazement. I think nothing can appear strange or hard to believe, let him do what he may in the future. If the Scriptures tell me my Lord is going to fill me with his own glory, and to set me at his own right hand, I can believe it. He who went to the cross for me will never be ashamed of me: he who gave me himself will give me all heaven and more: he that opened his very heart to find blood and water to wash me in, how shall he keep back even his kingdom from me ? O sweet Lord Jesus, thou art indeed to us the hope, the pledge, the guarantee of glory. Friend, do you not feel that Christ in you is the dawn of heaven ?

Besides this, Christ is he that has entered into covenant with God to bring his people home to glory; he has pledged himself to bring every sheep of his flock safe to his Father's right hand, and he will keep his engagement, for he never failed of one covenant promise yet.

Moreover, this we do know, that the Christ who is come to live with us will never be separated from us. If he had not meant to stop he would not have entered our heart at all. There was nothing to tempt him to come, and if in sovereign grace he deigned to live in the poor cottage of our nature, then, brethren, he knew what he was about : he had counted the cost, he had foreseen all the evil that would be in us and about us, and when he came, he came with the intent to stay. Someone asked another the other day, " What persuasion are you of ? " and the answer was, " I am persuaded that neither life, nor death, nor things present, nor things to come, shall separate us from the love of God which is in Christ Jesus our Lord." Are not you of that persuasion, brother? If so, you can see how Christ in you is the hope of glory.

Why, look ye, sirs, Christ in you is glory. Did we not show that just now? " Lift up your heads, O ye gates, and be ye lifted up, ye everlasting doors, that the King of glory may come in ! " You have heaven in having Christ, for Christ is the biggest part of heaven. Is not Christ the soul of heaven, and having him you have glory ? What is more, having gotten Christ, Christ's glory and your glory are wrapped up together. If Christ were to lose you, it would be a great loss to you, but a greater loss to him. If I can perish with Christ in me, I shall certainly be a fearful loser, but so will he, for where is his honour, where his glory if a believer perishes ? His glory is gone if one soul that trusts in him is ever cast away. Wherefore comfort yourselves with this word, Christ in you means you in glory, as sure as God lives. There is no question about that. Go your ways and rejoice in Christ Jesus, and let men see who it is that lives in you. Let Jesus speak through your mouth, and weep through your eyes, and smile through your face : let him work with your hands and walk with your feet, and be tender with your heart. Let him seek sinners through you ; let him comfort saints through you ; until the day break and the shadows flee away.

PORTION OF SCRIPTURE READ BEFORE SERMON—Colossians i.

C. H. Spurgeon's Popular Books.

GLORY!

A Sermon

DELIVERED ON LORD'S-DAY MORNING, MAY 20TH, 1883, BY

C. H. SPURGEON,

AT THE METROPOLITAN TABERNACLE, NEWINGTON.

"Who hath called us unto his eternal glory."—1 Peter v. 10.

A FORTNIGHT ago, when I was only able to creep to the front of this platform, I spoke to you concerning the future of our mortal bodies:* "We know that if our earthly house of this tabernacle were dissolved, we have a building of God, a house not made with hands, eternal in the heavens." On the next Sabbath day we went a step further, and we did not preach so much about the resurrection of the body as upon the hope of glory for our entire nature,† our text being, "Christ in you, the hope of glory." Thus we have passed through the outer court, and have trodden the hallowed floor of the Holy Place, and now we are the more prepared to enter within the veil, and to gaze awhile upon the glory which awaits us. We shall say a little—and oh, how little it will be—upon that glory of which we have so sure a prospect, that glory which is prepared for us in Christ Jesus, and of which he is the hope! I pray that our eyes may be strengthened that we may see the heavenly light, and that our ears may be opened to hear sweet voices from the better land. As for me, I cannot say that I will speak of the glory, but I will try to stammer about it; for the best language to which a man can reach concerning glory must be a mere stammering. Paul did but see a little of it for a short time, and he confessed that he heard things that it was not lawful for a man to utter; and I doubt not that he felt utterly non-plussed as to describing what he had seen. Though a great master of language, yet for once he was overpowered; the grandeur of his theme made him silent. As for us, what can we do, where even Paul breaks down? Pray, dear friends, that the Spirit of glory may rest upon you, that he may open your eyes to see as much as can at present be seen of the heritage of the saints. We are told that "eye hath not seen, neither hath ear heard, neither have entered into the heart of man, the things which God hath prepared for them that love him." Yet the eye has

---

* No. 1,719. "The Tent Dissolved and the Mansion Entered."

† No. 1,720. "Christ in You."

Nos. 1,721-2.

seen wonderful things. There are sunrises and sunsets, Alpine glories
and ocean marvels which, once seen, cling to our memories throughout
life; yet even when nature is at her best she cannot give us an idea of
the supernatural glory which God has prepared for his people. The ear has
heard sweet harmonies. Have we not enjoyed music which has thrilled
us? Have we not listened to speech which has seemed to make our
hearts dance within us? And yet no melody of harp nor charm of
oratory can ever raise us to a conception of the glory which God hath
laid up for them that love him. As for the heart of man, what strange
things have entered it! Men have exhibited fair fictions, woven in the
loom of fancy, which have made the eyes to sparkle with their beauty
and brightness; imagination has revelled and rioted in its own fantastic
creations, roaming among islands of silver and mountains of gold, or
swimming in seas of wine and rivers of milk; but imagination has never
been able to open the gate of pearl which shuts in the city of our God.
No, it hath not yet entered the heart of man. Yet the text goes on
to say, "but he hath revealed it unto us by his Spirit." So that heaven
is not an utterly unknown region, not altogether an inner brightness
shut in with walls of impenetrable darkness. God hath revealed joys
which he has prepared for his beloved; but mark you, even though they
be revealed of the Spirit, yet it is no common unveiling, and the reason
that it is made known at all is ascribed to the fact that "the Spirit
searcheth all things, yea, the deep things of God." So we see that the
glory which awaits the saints is ranked among the deep things of God,
and he that would speak thereof after the manner of the oracles of God
must have much heavenly teaching. It is easy to chatter according to
human fancy, but if we would follow the sure teaching of the word of
God we shall have need to be taught of the Holy Spirit, without whose
anointing the deep things of God must be hidden from us. Pray that
we may be under that teaching while we dwell upon this theme.

There are three questions which we will answer this morning. The
first is, *what is the destiny of the saints?*—"Eternal glory," says the
the text. Secondly, *wherein doth this glory consist?* I said we would
answer the questions, but this is not to be answered this side the pearl-
gate. Thirdly, *what should be the influence of this prospect upon our
hearts?* What manner of people ought we to be whose destiny is eternal
glory? How should we live who are to live for ever in the glory of the
Most High?

I. First, WHAT, THEN, IS THE DESTINY OF THE SAINTS? Our text
tells us that God has "called us unto *his eternal glory.*" "Glory!"
does not the very word astound you? "Glory!" surely that belongs to
God alone! Yet the Scripture says "glory," and glory it must mean,
for it never exaggerates. Think of glory for us who have deserved
eternal shame! Glory for us poor creatures who are often ashamed of
ourselves! Yes, I look at my book again, and it actually says "glory"
—nothing less than glory. Therefore so must it be.

Now, since this seems so amazing and astonishing a thing, I would so
speak with you that not a relic of incredulity may remain in your hearts
concerning it. I would ask you to follow me while we look through
the Bible, not quoting every passage which speaks of glory, but mentioning
a few of the leading ones.

This glory has been promised. What said David ? In the seventy-third Psalm and twenty-fourth verse we meet with these remarkable words: "Thou shalt guide me with thy counsel, and afterward receive me to glory." In the original Hebrew there is a trace of David's recollection of Enoch's being translated; and, though the royal Psalmist did not expect to be caught away without dying, yet he did expect that after he had followed the guidance of the Lord here below the great Father would stoop and raise up his child to be with himself for ever. He expected to be received into glory. Even in those dim days, when as yet the light of the gospel was but in its dawn, this prophet and king was able to say, " Thou shalt afterward receive me to glory." Did he not mean the same thing when in the eighty-fourth Psalm, verse eleven, he said, " The Lord will give grace and glory: no good thing will he withhold from them that walk uprightly"? Not only no good thing under the name of grace will God withhold from the upright, but no good thing under the head of glory. No good of heaven shall be kept from the saints ; no reserve is even set upon the throne of the great King, for our Lord Jesus has graciously promised, " To him that overcometh will I grant to sit with me in my throne, even as I also overcame, and am set down with my Father in his throne." " No good thing," not even amongst the infinitely good things of heaven, will God " withhold from them that walk uprightly." If David had this persuasion, much more may we who walk in the light of the gospel. Since our Lord Jesus hath suffered and entered into his glory, and we know that we shall be with him where he is, we are confident that our rest shall be glorious.

Brethren, it is *to this glory that we have been called.* The people of God having been predestinated, have been called with an effectual calling—called so that they have obeyed the call, and have run after him who has drawn them. Now, our text says that he has " called us unto his eternal glory by Christ Jesus." We are called to repentance, we are called to faith, we are called to holiness, we are called to perseverance, and all this that we may afterwards attain unto glory. We have another Scripture of like import in 1 Thessalonians ii. 12 :—" Who hath called you unto his kingdom and glory." We are called unto his kingdom according to our Lord's word, " Fear not, little flock ; for it is your Father's good pleasure to give you the kingdom." We are called to be kings, called to wear a crown of life that fadeth not away, called to reign with Christ in his glory. If the Lord had not meant us to have the glory he would not have called us unto it, for his calling is no mockery. He would not by his Spirit have fetched us out from the world and separated us unto himself if he had not intended to keep us from falling and preserve us eternally. Believer, you are called to glory; do not question the certainty of that to which God has called you.

And we are not only called to it, brethren, but *glory is especially joined with justification.* Let me quote Romans viii. 30 :—" Moreover whom he did predestinate, them he also called : and whom he called, them he also justified: and whom he justified, them he also glorified." These various mercies are threaded together like pearls upon a string: there is no breaking the thread, no separating the precious things. They are put in their order by God himself, and they are kept there by his eternal and irreversible decree. If you are justified by the righteousness of Christ, you shall be glorified through Christ Jesus, for thus hath God purposed, and so must it be. Do you not remember how salvation itself is linked with glory? Paul, in 2 Timothy ii. 10, speaks of " the salvation which is in Christ Jesus with eternal glory." The two things are riveted together, and cannot be separated.

The saved ones must partake of the glory of God, for *for this are they being prepared every day.* Paul, in the ninth of Romans, where he speaks about the predestinating will of God, says in the twenty-third verse : " The vessels of mercy, which he had afore prepared unto glory." This is the process which commenced in regeneration, and is going on in us every day in the work of sanctification. We cannot be glorified so long as sin remains in us ; we must first be pardoned, renewed, and sanctified, and then we are fitted to be glorified. By communion with our Lord Jesus we are made like to him, as saith the apostle in 2 Corinthians iii. 18 :—" But we all, with open face beholding as in a glass the glory of the Lord, are changed into the same image from glory to glory, even as by the Spirit of the Lord." It is very wonderful how by the wisdom of God everything is made to work this way. Look at the blessed text in 2 Corinthians iv. 17, where Paul says, " For our light affliction, which is but for a moment, worketh for us a far more exceeding and eternal weight of glory ; " where he represents that all that we can suffer, whether of body or of mind, is producing for us such a mass of glory that he is quite unable to describe it, and he uses hyperbolical language in saying, "a far more exceeding and eternal weight of glory." Oh, blessed men, whose very losses are their gains, whose sorrows produce their joys, whose griefs are big with heaven! Well may we be content to suffer if so it be that all things are working together for our good, and are helping to pile up the excess of our future glory.

Thus, then, it seems we are called to glory, and we are being prepared for it ; is it not also a sweet thought that *our present fellowship with Christ is the guarantee of it?* In Romans viii. 17 it is said, " If so be that we suffer with him, that we may be also glorified together." Going to prison with Christ will bring us into the palace with Christ ; smarting with Christ will bring us into reigning with Christ; being ridiculed, and slandered, and despised for Christ's sake will bring us to be sharers of his honour, and glory, and immortality. Who would not be with Christ in his humiliation if this be the guarantee that we shall be with him in his glory? Remember those dear words of the Lord Jesus, "Ye are they which have continued with me in my temptations. And I appoint unto you a kingdom, as my Father hath appointed unto me." Let us shoulder the cross, for it leads to the crown. "No cross, no crown:" but he that has shared the battle shall partake in the victory.

I have not yet done, for there is a text, in Hebrews ii. 10, which is well worthy of our consideration : *we are to be brought to glory.* It is said of our Lord that it "became him, for whom are all things, in bringing many sons unto glory, to make the captain of their salvation perfect through sufferings." See, beloved, we are called to glory, we are being prepared for it, and we shall be brought to it. We might despair of ever getting into the glory land if we had not One to bring us there, for the pilgrim's road is rough and beset with many foes; but there is a "Captain of our salvation," a greater than Bunyan's Greatheart, who is conducting the pilgrim band through all the treacherous way, and he will bring the "many sons"—where?—"*unto glory*," nowhere short of that shall be their *ultimatum*. Glory, glory shall surely follow upon grace; for Christ the Lord, who has come into his glory, has entered into covenant engagements that he will bring all the "many sons" to be with him.

Mark this, and then I will quote no more Scriptures: *this glory will be for our entire manhood*, for our body as well as for our soul. You know that text in the famous resurrection chapter; in 1 Cor. xv. 43 Paul speaks of the body as being "sown in dishonour," but he adds, "it is raised in glory;" and then, in Philippians iii. 21, he says of our divine Lord at his coming, "Who shall change our vile body, that it may be fashioned like unto his glorious body, according to the working whereby he is able even to subdue all things unto himself." What a wonderful change that will be for this frail, feeble, suffering body! In some respects it is not vile, for it is a wonderful product of divine skill, and power, and goodness; but inasmuch as it hampers our spiritual nature by its appetites and infirmities, it may be called a "vile body." It is an unhandy body for a spirit: it fits a soul well enough, but a spirit wants something more ethereal, less earth-bound, more full of life than this poor flesh and blood and bone can ever be. Well, the body is to be changed. What alteration will it undergo? It will be rendered perfect. The body of a child will be fully developed, and the dwarf will attain to full stature. The blind shall not be sightless in heaven, neither shall the lame be halt, nor shall the palsied tremble. The deaf shall hear, and the dumb shall sing God's praises. We shall carry none of our deficiencies or infirmities to heaven. As good Mr. Ready-to-Halt did not carry his crutches there, neither shall any of us need a staff to lean upon. There we shall not know an aching brow, or a weak knee, or a failing eye. "The inhabitant shall no more say, I am sick."

And it shall be an impassive body, a body that will be incapable of any kind of suffering: no palpitating heart, no sinking spirit, no aching limbs, no lethargic soul shall worry us there. No, we shall be perfectly delivered from every evil of that kind. Moreover, it shall be an immortal body. Our risen bodies shall not be capable of decay, much less of death. There are no graves in glory. Blessed are the dead that die in the Lord, for their bodies shall rise never to know death and corruption a second time. No smell or taint of corruption shall remain upon those whom Jesus shall call from the tomb. The risen body shall be greatly increased in power: it is "sown in weakness," says the Scripture, but it is "raised in power." I suppose there will be a wonderful agility about our renovated frame: probably it will be able to move as swiftly as the lightning flash, for so do angels pass from place to place, and we shall in this, as in many things else, be as the angels of God. Anyhow, it will be a "glorious body," and it will be "raised in glory," so that the whole of our manhood shall participate of that wonderful depth of bliss

which is summed up in the word—"glory." Thus I think I have set
before you much of what the word of God saith upon this matter.

II.   Secondly, may the Holy Spirit help me while I try very hesitat-
ingly and stammeringly to answer the enquiry, WHEREIN DOTH THIS
DESTINY CONSIST?

Do you know how much I expect to do?   It will be but little.   You
remember what the Lord did for Moses when the man of God prayed—
"I beseech thee show me thy glory!"   All that the Lord himself did
for Moses was to say, "Thou shalt see my back parts; but my face shall
not be seen."   How little, then, can we hope to speak of this glory!
Its back parts are too bright for us: as for the face of that glory, it shall
not be seen by any of us here below, though by-and-by we shall behold it.
I suppose if one who had been in glory could come straight down from
heaven, and occupy this platform, he would find that his discoveries
could not be communicated because of the insufficiency of language to
express such a weight of meaning.

The saints' destiny is *glory*.   What is glory, brethren?   What is it, I
mean, among the sons of men?   It is generally understood to be fame,
a great repute, the sound of trumpets, the noise of applause, the sweets
of approbation among the crowd and in high places.   The Queen of
Sheba came from afar to see glory of Solomon.   What was that glory,
brethren?   It was the glory of a rare wisdom excelling all others:
it was the glory of immense riches expended upon all manner of magnificence and splendour.   As for this last glory, the Lord says of it
that a lily of the field had more of it than Solomon; at least, "Solomon
in all his glory was not arrayed like one of these."   Yet that is what
men mean by glory—rank, position, power, conquest—things that make
the ears of men to tingle when they hear of them—things extraordinary
and rare.   All this is but a dim shadow of what God means by glory;
yet out of the shadow we may obtain a little inkling of what the substance must be.   God's people shall be wise, and even famous, for they
shall "shine as the stars for ever and ever."   God's people shall be rich;
the very streets of their abode are paved with gold exceeding rich and
rare.   God's people shall be singularly honoured; there shall be a glory
about them unrivalled, for they shall be known as a peculiar people, a
royal priesthood, a race of beings lifted up to reveal their Maker's
character beyond all the rest of his works.

I reckon that glory to a saint means, first of all, *purified character*.
The brightest glory that really can come to anyone is the glory of
character.   Thus God's glory among men is his goodness, his mercy, his
justice, his truth.   But shall such poor creatures as we are ever have
perfect characters?   Yes, we shall one day be perfectly holy.   God's
Holy Spirit, when he has finished his work, will leave in us no trace of
sin: no temptation shall be able to touch us, there will be in us no
relics of our past and fallen state.   Oh, will not that be blessed?   I was
going to say it is all the glory I want—the glory of being perfect in
character, never sinning, never judging unjustly, never thinking a vain
thought, never wandering away from the perfect law of God, never vexed
again with sin which has so long been my worst enemy.   One day we
shall be glorious because the devil himself will not be able to detect
a fault in us, and those eyes of God, which burn like fire and read the

inmost secrets of the soul, will not be able to detect anything blameworthy in us. Such shall be the character of the saints that they shall be meet to consort with Christ himself, fit company for that thrice Holy Being before whom angels veil their faces. This is glory!

Next, I understand by "glory" *our perfected manhood.* When God made Adam he was a far superior being to any of us. Man's place in creation was very remarkable. The Psalmist says, "For thou hast made him a little lower than the angels, and hast crowned him with glory and honour. Thou madest him to have dominion over the works of thy hands; thou hast put all things under his feet: all sheep and oxen, yea, and the beasts of the field; the fowl of the air, and the fish of the sea, and whatsoever passeth through the paths of the seas." No king among men in these days could rival Adam in the garden of Eden : he was indeed monarch of all that he surveyed, and from the lordly lion down to the tiniest insect of all, living creatures paid him willing homage. Can we ever rise to this last honour ? Brethren, listen, "It doth not yet appear what we shall be, but we know that when Christ shall appear we shall be like him, for we shall see him as he is." Is there any limit to the growth of the mind of a man ? Can we tell what he may reach ? We read of Solomon that God gave him largeness of heart as the sand of the sea : God will give to his people glory that will include in it more largeness of heart than Solomon ever knew. Then shall we know even as we are known by God. Now we see, but it is "through a glass darkly," but then we shall see "face to face." You have met with men of great intellect and you have looked up to them : but assuredly the smallest babe in Christ when he shall reach heaven shall have a greater intellect than the most profound philosopher who has ever astounded mankind by his discoveries. We shall not always be as we are to-day, contracted and hampered because of our little knowledge, and our slender faculties, and our dull perceptions. Our ignorance and prejudice shall vanish. What a man will become we can scarcely tell when he is remade in the image of God, and made like unto our divine Lord who is "the firstborn among many brethren." Here we are but in embryo : our minds are but the seeds, or the bulbs, outof which shall come the flower and glory of a nobler manhood. Your body is to be developed into something infinitely brighter and better than the bodies of men here below : and as for the soul, we cannot guess to what an elevation it shall be raised in Christ Jesus. There is room for the largest expectation here, as we conjecture what will be the full accomplishment of the vast intent of eternal love, an intent which has involved the sacrifice of the only-begotten Son of God. That can be no mean design which has been carried on at the expense of the best that heaven itself possessed.

Further, by "glory" and coming to glory I think we must understand *complete victory.* Dwelling in the age of the Romans, men said to themselves, as they read the Scriptures, "What does the apostle mean by 'glory'?" and they could scarcely help connecting it with conquest, and the return of the warrior in triumph. Men called it glory in those days when valiant warriors returned from fields of blood with captives and spoil. Then did the heroes ride through the streets of Rome, enjoying a triumph voted them by the senate. Then for the while the

men of war were covered with glory, and all the city was glorious
because of them. As Christians, we hate the word "glory" when it is
linked with wholesale murder, and girt in garments rolled in blood;
but yet there is a kind of fighting to which you and I are called, for
we are soldiers of the cross; and if we fight valiantly under our great
Captain, and rout every sin, and are found faithful even unto death,
then we shall enter glory, and receive the honour which belongs to men
who have fought a good fight, and have kept the faith. It will be no
small glory to obtain the crown of life which fadeth not away. Is not
this a full glory if we only place these three things together, a purified
character, a perfected nature, and a complete victory?

An invaluable ingredient in true glory is *the divine approval.* "Glory"
among men means approbation: it is a man's glory when he is honoured
of his Queen, and she hangs a medal on his breast, or when his name is
mentioned in the high court of Parliament, and he is ennobled for what
he has done. If men speak of our actions with approval, it is called
fame and glory. Oh, but one drop of the approbation of God has more
glory in it than a sea full of human praise; and the Lord will reward his
own with this holy favour. He will say, "Well done, good and faithful
servant," and Christ before the universe will say, "Come, ye blessed of
my Father." Oh, what glory that will be! They were despised and
rejected of men, they "wandered about in sheepskins and goatskins;
destitute, afflicted, tormented;" but now God approves them, and they
take seats among the peers of heaven, made noble by the approbation
of the Judge of all. This is glory with an emphasis, substantial glory.
One approving glance from the eye of Jesus, one accepting word from
the mouth of the Father, will be glory enough for any one of us, and
this we shall have if we follow the Lamb whithersoever he goeth.

But this is not all: children of God will have *the glory of reflecting
the glory of God.* When any of God's unfallen creatures shall wish to
see the greatness of God's goodness, and mercy, and love, they that
dwell in heaven will point out a glorified saint. Whenever any spirit
from far-off regions desires to know what is meant by faithfulness and
grace, some angel will reply, "Go and talk with those who have been
redeemed from among men." I believe that you and I will spend much of
eternity in making known to principalities and powers the unsearchable
riches of the grace of God. We shall be mirrors reflecting God; and in
us shall his glory be revealed. There may be myriads of races of pure
and holy beings of whom we have never heard as yet, and these may
come to the New Jerusalem as to the great metropolis of Jehovah's
universe, and when they come there they will gaze upon the saints as
the highest instances of divine grace, wisdom, power, and love. It will
be their highest pleasure to hear how eternal mercy dealt with us unworthy ones. How we shall delight to rehearse to them the fact of the
Father's eternal purpose, the story of the incarnate God—the God that
loved and died, and the love of the blessed Spirit who sought us in the
days of our sin, and brought us to the cross foot, renewing us in the
spirit of our minds, and making us to be sons of God. Oh, brothers and
sisters, this shall be our glory, that God shall shine through us to the
astonishment of all.

Yet I think glory includes somewhat more than this. In certain cases a man's *glory lies in his relationships.* If any of the royal family should come to your houses you would receive them with respect; yes, and even as they went along the street they would be spied out, and passers-by would say, "That is the prince!" and they would honour the son of our good Queen. But royal descent is a poor business compared with being allied to the King of kings. Many angels are exceeding bright, but they are only servants to wait upon the sons. I believe that there will be a kind of awe upon the angels at the sight of men; when they see us in our glory they will rejoice to know our near relation to their Lord, and to fulfil their own destiny as ministering spirits appointed to minister to the heirs of salvation. No pride will be possible to the perfected, but we shall then realize the exalted position to which by our new birth and the divine adoption we have been raised. "Behold what manner of love the Father hath bestowed upon us that we should be called the sons of God." Sons of God! Sons of the Lord God Almighty! Oh what glory this will be!

Then there will be connected with this the fact that *we shall be connected with Jesus in everything.* For do not you see, brethren, it was because of our fall that Christ came here to save men; when he wrought out a perfect righteousness, it was all for us; when he died, it was all for us; and when he rose again, it was all for us? And what is more, we lived in Christ, we died in him, we were buried in him and rose in him, and we shall ascend into heaven to reign with him. All our glory is by Christ Jesus and in all the glory of Christ Jesus we have a share. We are members of his body; we are one with him. I say, the creatures that God has made, when they shall come to worship in the New Jerusalem will stand and gaze at glorified men, and with bated breath will say one to another "These are the beings whose nature the Son of God assumed! These are the chosen creatures whom the Prince of heaven bought with his own blood." They will stand astonished at the divine glory which will be manifested in beings emancipated from sin and hell and made heirs of God, joint-heirs with Jesus Christ. Will not even angels be surprised and awed as they look on the church and say to one another, "This is the bride, the Lamb's wife!" They will marvel how the Lord of glory should come to this poor earth to seek a spouse and that he should enter into eternal union with such a people. Glory, glory dwelleth in Immanuel's land! Now we are getting near to the centre of it. I feel inclined, like Moses, to put off my shoes from off my feet, for the place whereon we stand is holy ground, now that we are getting to see poor bushes like ourselves aglow with the indwelling God, and changed from glory unto glory.

And yet this is not all, for there in heaven *we shall dwell in the immediate presence of God.* We shall dwell with him in nearest and dearest fellowship! All the felicity of the Most High will be our felicity. The blessedness of the triune Jehovah shall be our blessedness for ever and ever. Did you notice that our text says, "He hath called us unto *his* glory"? This outshines everything: the glory which the saints will have is the same glory which God possesses, and such as he alone can bestow. Listen to this text:—"Whom he justified them *he* also glorified." He glorifies them, then! I know what it is to glorify God, and so do you, but when we poor creatures glorify God it is in a poor way, for we

cannot add anything to him.   But what must it be for God himself to
glorify a man!   The glory which you are to have for ever, my dear
believing brother, is a glory which God himself will put upon you.
Peter, as a Hebrew, perhaps uses a Hebraism when he says " *his* glory:"
it may be that he means the best of glory that can be, even as the Jews
were wont to say—" The trees of God," when they meant the greatest
trees, or " the mountains of God," when they intended the highest
mountains; so by the glory of God Peter may mean the richest, fullest
glory that can be.   In the original the word " glory " has about it the
idea of " weight," at which the apostle Paul hints when he speaks of a
" weight of glory."   This is the only glory that has weight in it, all else
is light as a feather.   Take all the glories of this world, and they are
outweighed by the small dust of the balance.   Place them here in the
hollow of my hand, all of them : a child may blow them away as thistle-
down.   God's glory has weight; it is solid, true, real, and he that gets
it possesses no mere name, or dream, or tinsel, but he has that which
will abide the rust of ages and the fire of judgment.

The glory of God!   How shall I describe it!   I must set before you
a strange Scriptural picture.   Mordecai must be made glorious for his
fidelity to his king, and singular is the honour which his monarch
ordains for him.   This was the royal order.   " Let the royal apparel be
brought which the king useth to wear, and the horse that the king
rideth upon, and the crown royal which is set upon his head : and let
this apparel and horse be delivered to the hand of one of the king's
most noble princes, that they may array the man withal whom the king
delighteth to honour, and bring him on horseback through the street of
the city, and proclaim before him, Thus shall it be done to the man
whom the king delighteth to honour."   Can you not imagine the surprise of the Jew when robe and ring were put upon him, and when he
found himself placed upon the king's horse.   This may serve as a figure
of that which will happen to us : we shall be glorified with the glory of
God.   The best robe, the best of heaven's array, shall be appointed
unto us, and we shall dwell in the house of the Lord for ever.

Highest of all our glory will be *the enjoyment of God himself.*   He
will be our exceeding joy : this bliss will swallow up every other, the
blessedness of God.   " The Lord is my portion," saith my soul.   " Whom
have I in heaven but thee ? and there is none upon earth that I desire
beside thee."   Our God shall be our glory.

Yet bear with me, I have left out a word again: the text has it,
" Unto his *eternal* glory."   Ay, but that is the gem of the ring.   The
glory which God has in reserve for his chosen will never come to an
end : it will stay with us, and we shall stay with it, for ever.   It will
always be glory, too ; its brightness will never become dim; we shall
never be tired of it, or sated with it.   After ten thousand thousand
millions of years in heaven our happiness shall be as fresh as when it
first began.   Those are no fading laurels which surround immortal
brows.   Eternal glory knows no diminution.   Can you imagine a man
being born at the same time that Adam was created and living all these
thousands of years as a king like Solomon, having all he could desire ?
His would seem to be a glorious life.   But, if at the end of seven thousand
years that man must needs die, what has it profited him ?   His glory is

all over now: its fires have died out in ashes. But you and I, when we once enter glory, shall receive what we can neither lose nor leave. Eternity! Eternity! This is this the sweetness of all our future bliss. Rejoice, ye saintly ones! Take your harps down from the willows, any of you who are mourning, and if you never sang before, yet sing this morning —" God has called us unto his eternal glory," and this is to be our portion world without end.

III. I can only find time for a few words upon the concluding head, which is—WHAT INFLUENCE SHOULD ALL THIS HAVE UPON OUR HEARTS?

I think, first, it ought to excite *desire* in many here present that they might attain unto glory by Christ Jesus. Satan, when he took our blessed Lord to the top of an exceeding high mountain, tempted him to worship him by offering him the kingdoms of the world and all the glories thereof. Satan is very clever, and I will at this time take a leaf out of his book. Will you not fall down and worship the Lord Jesus when he can give you the kingdom of God and all the glory thereof, and all this, not in pretence, but in reality? If there was any force in the temptation to worship Satan for the sake of the glory of this world, how much more reason is there for urging you to worship the Son of God that you may obtain his salvation with eternal glory! I pray the Holy Ghost to drop a hot desire into many a poor sinner's breast this morning that he may cry, " If this glory is to be had, I will have it, and I will have it in God's way, for I will believe in Jesus, I will repent, I will come to God, and so obtain his promise."

Secondly, this ought to move us to the feeling of *fear*. If there be such a glory as this let us tremble lest by any means we should come short of it. Oh, my dear hearers, especially you that are my fellow members, brother church officers, and workers associated with me, what a dreadful thing it will be if any one of us should come short of this glory! Oh, if there were no hell, it would be hell enough to miss of heaven! What if there were no pit that is bottomless, nor worm undying, nor fire unquenchable, it would be boundless misery to have a shadow of a fear of not reaching to God's eternal glory! Let us therefore pass the time of our sojourning here in fear, and let us watch unto prayer and strive to enter in at the strait gate. God grant we may be found of him at last to praise and honour!

If we are right, how this ought to move us to *gratitude*. Think of this, we are to enjoy " his eternal glory"! What a contrast to our deserts! Shame and everlasting contempt are our righteous due apart from Christ. If we were to receive according to our merits, we should be driven from his presence and from the glory of his power. Verily, he hath not dealt with us after our sins, nor rewarded us according to our iniquities; for, after all our transgressions, he has still reserved us for glory, and reserved glory for us. What love and zeal should burn in our bosoms because of this!

Last of all, it should move us to a dauntless *courage*. If this glory is to be had, do we not feel like the heroes in Bunyan's picture? Before the dreamer there stood a fair palace, and he saw persons walking upon the top of it, clad in light, and singing. Around the door stood armed men to keep back those who would enter. Then a brave

man came up to one who had a writer's ink-horn by his side, and said,
" Set down my name ; " and straightway the warrior drew his sword, and
fought with all his might, until he had cut his way to the door, and then
he entered, and they within were heard to sing—

> " Come in, come in,
> Eternal glory thou shalt win."

Will you not draw your swords this morning, and fight against sin, till
you have overcome it? Do you not desire to win Christ, and to be
found in him? Oh, let us now begin to feel a passion for eternal
glory, and then in the strength of the Spirit, and in the name of Jesus,
let us press forward till we reach it. Even on earth we may taste
enough of this glory to fill us with delight. The glory which I have
described to you dawns on earth though it only comes to its noontide in
heaven : the glory of sanctified character, the glory of victory over sin,
the glory of relationship to God, the glory of union with Christ,—
these are all to be tasted in a measure here below. These glories send
their beams down even to these valleys and lowlands. Oh, to enjoy
them to-day and thus to have earnests and foretastes of glory. If we
have them let us go singing on until we reach the place where God's
eternal glory shall surround us. Amen.

PORTION OF SCRIPTURE READ BEFORE SERMON—Philippians iii.

HYMNS FROM " OUR OWN HYMN BOOK "—92 (Part I.), 869, 879.

The Pilgrim Fathers of New England
by John Brown $3.95.

This 352-page book has been proclaimed as the
very best history of our nation's original settlers
as it is written from the Christian point of view.
Every patriotic American will thrill to the account
of how God's providence brought about the establishment of this nation.

THE FIRST SETTING UP OF THE BRAZEN SERPENT.

A Sermon

DELIVERED ON THURSDAY EVENING, MAY 10TH, 1883, BY

C. H. SPURGEON,

AT THE METROPOLITAN TABERNACLE, NEWINGTON.

"And they journeyed from mount Hor by the way of the Red sea, to compass the land of Edom: and the soul of the people was much discouraged because of the way. And the people spake against God, and against Moses, Wherefore have ye brought us up out of Egypt to die in the wilderness? for there is no bread, neither is there any water; and our soul loatheth this light bread. And the Lord sent fiery serpents among the people, and they bit the people; and much people of Israel died. Therefore the people came to Moses, and said, We have sinned, for we have spoken against the Lord, and against thee; pray unto the Lord, that he take away the serpents from us. And Moses prayed for the people. And the Lord said unto Moses, Make thee a fiery serpent, and set it upon a pole: and it shall come to pass, that every one that is bitten, when he looketh upon it, shall live. And Moses made a serpent of brass, and put it upon a pole, and it came to pass, that if a serpent had bitten any man, when he beheld the serpent of brass, he lived."—Numbers xxi. 4—9.

I HAVE frequently expounded to you the type of the brazen serpent as our Lord interprets it in the third of John. I thought it meet to-night to take that type in its connection and look at the original circumstances which led to the setting of it up; for while the general doctrine of looking for salvation to Christ as the brazen serpent is always to be preached, and is most usefully set forth in the midst of the unconverted, yet I take it that its original institution teaches us much which ought not to be overlooked. It is very clear that this type has its first voice to the people of God, for it was amongst Israel—amongst the nominal people of God—that this brazen serpent was first needed and first set up; and while the instruction which it gives is wide as the universe, for whosoever looks shall live, nevertheless it has an inner circle to which it first of all addresses itself, and these are the professed members of the church of God.

The Book of Numbers might be called, without any impropriety, "Moses's Pilgrim's Progress." It contains a full account of the progress of the pilgrims through the wilderness until they came to the promised land. And, like Bunyan's "Pilgrim's Progress," it is not alone a history of any one person or nation, but it is the picture of the life of all God's people. Probably no one amongst us will pass through all the troubles of the Israelites, so as to become in one person an epitome of all wilderness experience; and yet even this may be, for so it was with David, and so it has been with others by whom the Lord would instruct his church. This, however, is exceptional; but, take the whole of us together as the church of God, and you will find that our lives are mirrored, pictured, and foreseen in the travels of God's chosen people from the land of Egypt to Canaan. I am afraid that many of us can see ourselves even in the passage before us ; ay, not only those of us who are young and raw in spiritual things, but certain of us who have been for many years following in the divine track, and are hoping by-and-by to enjoy our portion in the better country. If even Moses and Aaron erred on the road, I fear there are very few of us who can read the story without crying, " I do remember my faults this day."

The passage before us occurred almost at the end of Israel's wanderings. They had been now for forty years in the wilderness, and they had come within sight of the promised land. They had only to cross the mountains of Edom, and to get through the passes of Seir, and they would have been at once in the land which floweth with milk and honey. But the Edomites would not permit them the privilege of passing along the highway, and so, as Israel must not fight his brother Esau, they were called upon to go round his border and to come down to an arm of the Red Sea by a long and weary march, when they seemed to be on the border of their covenanted inheritance. If this happened at the end of their marches, let none of us presume upon our experience and knowledge. May the Holy Spirit help us while we learn caution from this inspired history, for these things happened unto them for our instruction.

I. I call your attention, first of all, to their DISCOURAGEMENT. " *The soul of the people was much discouraged because of the way.*" Assuredly there are times when God's servants become discouraged. To their shame, let us say it. To *our* shame let us confess it. It is by faith that we live, but as discouragement is the opposite of faith, it does not help our life. It is generally the fruit of unbelief; and so by discouragement we cease to live a healthy and vigorous life, and we begin to faint. Yet even those of God's children who have had much experience in the divine way at times give way to discouragement.

The reason may be found in various things. Occasionally it springs out of *disappointment.* It was a serious disappointment to the Israelites to see the land over there within a day's march, or less, and yet for Edom to say, " I will come out against thee with the sword. Thou shalt not pass through my border." It seemed like having the cup at the lip, and being denied a draught. It was a grievous trial, after all those years, to have come so close, and then to be forced to march back to the Red Sea. How tantalizing to see the land, as through a wall of crystal, and yet to be unable to put foot upon it! It was a bitter disappointment; and there may be like trials in store for us. Possibly some of my Master's servants have entertained the notion that they have made amazing progress in the divine life, and just then an event has occurred which showed them their own weakness, and they have been forced to weep in secret places and upbraid themselves, saying, " After all this, am I no better than to be cast down about a trifle? Have I suffered so much, and yet is my progress so small?"

> " I thought that in some favoured hour,
> My Lord would answer my request,
> And, by his love's subduing power,
> Would slay my sins and give me rest.

> " Instead of this, he made me feel
> The hidden evils of my heart,
> And let the angry powers of hell
> Assault my soul in every part."

We ask to have our waters purified, and lo! we are stirred till all the mud which was quiet in the bottom of our soul is made visible, and pollution appears everywhere. Yet may not this be the nearest and surest way to purity? this making us see the secret depravity of our hearts? Yet what a disappointment! I thought I was something, and now I perceive that I am nothing. I had half hoped that I was perfect, and now I see my secret imperfections and lustings more clearly than ever.

> " The truth is easy to repeat;
> But when my faith is sharply tried
> I find myself a learner yet,
> Unstable, weak, and apt to slide."

We thought that we were climbing into full assurance, and lo, we descend into the valley of humiliation. Yes, we did taste of the honey of bold confidence, and we said, " I know whom I have believed, and I am persuaded that he is able to keep that which I have committed to him against that day; " and now we hardly know whether we are the people of God at all. We have with trembling to repeat our first step, and turn our eye to the bleeding Saviour, hoping as poor sinners to find salvation in him. This want of progress is a dreadful thing, and yet it has happened to many till they have dropped all idea of boasting, and have said with the apostle, " Not as though I had already attained." They have felt like men beginning a race, although they have been running that race for many a patient year. Such disappointment ofttimes costs the child of God much discouragement because of the way.

It was not, however, merely disappointment; it was much else. It was the *unfriendliness of those who ought to have been most brotherly.* Surely Edom ought to have granted his brother Israel the small privilege of passing through the country, seeing it was the near way to Canaan. It would not have cost Esau anything. Israel promised to pay if they even drank of the water of his wells. But, no, they must submit to this unkindness. I have known people of God much discouraged by the unfriendliness of those whom they thought to be their brethren and sisters in Christ. They went to them for sympathy, and they received rebuffs. They looked to them for help in the time of depression, and it was denied them. They said, " Surely, my brethren will comfort me "; but they cried in the end, like Job, " Miserable comforters are ye all." Then have they sighed, " It was not an enemy, then I could have borne it; but it was one who was my equal, my acquaintance. We went to the house of God in company.' You know the story of David's desertion by his friend, and of our Lord's betrayal by Judas; and you are well aware how often heartbreak has come to the best of men through the unfriendliness of those whom they looked upon as sure to render them kindness. The people were much discouraged because of the way, for it was blocked up by an unbrotherly brother. May the Lord s people learn great tenderness to one another, for sometimes we may say thoughtlessly that which will inflict a ragged wound. Let us be loving and tender as a nurse with a child, remembering the gentleness of the Father, and the tenderness of Jesus, and the compassion of the Holy Spirit. Alas, that it should be often true that the souls of the people of God may be much discouraged because of the absence of Christian love! Resolve that it shall not be *your* fault.

Undoubtedly, however, the soul of the people was much discouraged because of *the length of the way.* The nation had been forty years on the march. They had stopped for considerable periods at different encampments, but still they never knew how long they should be in one spot. They were like swallows, always on the wing. It is true their life was full of mercy, but at the time mentioned in our text they were not in the humour to notice mercy, they were more inclined to notice discomfort, and to complain that the way was so long that they were downright weary of it. They had hoped years before to have reached the goodly land, and now they must change their direction, and go all round the Edomite country: this was tiresome, and tried their patience till it quite failed.

To certain of God's people old age has brought much of heaviness by reason of its infirmities and afflictions. They often sigh, " Why are his chariots so long in coming? " They are willing in the spirit to abide the Master's will, but the flesh is weak, and they wonder whether the Lord has quite forgotten them. Why has he not taken them home? Why does he keep them lingering in this banishment, so far off from the dear Father's house? Do you not hear them mournfully sing—

> " O when shall we at once go up,
>   Nor this side Jordan longer stop,
>   But the good land possess?
>   When shall we end our lingering years,
>   Our sorrows, sins, and doubts, and fears—
>   A howling wilderness " ?

Oh, my dear brother, if your length of years has become a burden, God grant that you may not be discouraged. May you be " such a one as Paul the aged," and bear up under all the growing weaknesses of your years, bringing forth fruit in your old age. Be not cast down, for the Master will come, and will not tarry. He has not forgotten his servants: he will give them their penny at sundown. The ripe sheaf shall not be left in the field too long. Your Lord will come and receive you unto himself, that where he is you may be also. Quietly hope, and patiently wait for the salvation of God. And yet, no doubt, the length of the way has discouraged full many a true pilgrim.

Then, there was the *fatigue of the way*, for journeying through that wilderness was by no means an easy business, especially along the shore of the gulf. Very rugged to this day is the pathway there. The road is full of hills and valleys, and rugged ravines and sharp stones, and weary sands. Travelling there is as bad as travelling well can be. To some of God's own children life is no parade upon a level lawn, but rough marching and deep wading. They have to take the bleak side of the hill; the wind blows upon them, and the sleet is driven in their eyes, and their home is but a cold harbour to them. Even their bed seems to have a stone for its pillow. We know certain of God's people who, what with poverty and ill-health, with ungenerous relations, with persecution, with hard labour, and with short commons, find from day to day that the pathway to heaven lies through briars and thorns, over dark mountains and through black forests. Do you much marvel that their souls are discouraged because of the way?

I think I hear somebody saying, "Well, now, I don't like all this. *I* do not get discouraged, and *I* do not find the road to be rough." Dear brother, be thankful that you do not ; but let me warn you not to judge others. If you are like great bullocks, full of strength, do not get pushing with horn and shoulder those who happen to be the weak cattle; for the Lord takes note of haughty looks and proud words. When any of his saints grow so strong and stomach-full that they despise the tried ones, they are likely themselves to smart for it. The rule of our God and King is this—" He hath filled the hungry with good things, but the rich he hath sent empty away." This I do know both by observation and experience—that there are many true pilgrims who will enter the King's country triumphantly at the last, who, nevertheless, are occasionally much discouraged because of the way.

And yet, brethren, I am not going to make any excuse for discouragement in myself, nor would I try to make it for you. You do not want to have any excuse made for you, do you? After all, these Israelites were a highly favoured people. What if they were driven to wind around the land of Edom? Yet the Lord went before them; and is not that man happy who marches where Jehovah leads? Tell us that God has chosen the way, and we do not want to know more about it. " He led them forth by a right way." Depend upon that. There could be no mistake where infinite wisdom led the van.

Now, brother, you are discouraged, you say, because of the way; but whose way is it? Have you chosen your own way and wilfully run against your duty and against the providence of God? Well, then, I say nothing about the consequences of such conduct, for they must be terrible. But if you have endeavoured to follow the Lord fully, and if you have tried to keep the path of his statutes, then it must be well with you. Why are you discouraged? Judge not by the sight of the eyes, nor by the hearing of the ears : let faith sit on the judgment-seat, and I am sure she will give forth this verdict—" If the Lord wills it, it is well. If Jehovah leads the way, the road must be right."

Besides that, not only did God lead them, but God carried them. He says himself that he bare them on eagle's wings : for though the ways were often rough, yet it is wonderful to remember that their feet did not swell, neither did their garments wax old upon them, all those forty years. Though it was a wilderness, yet their bread was daily given them; and though it was a land of drought, yet the smitten rock with its waters followed them, and they knew nothing of drought. How could they be better off than to have heaven for their granary, the rocks for their wine-cellars, and God himself for their Provider. They were gentlemen commoners upon the bounty of Jehovah. They were honourable pensioners of the King of kings. What could they desire which he had not supplied? What city was lit up at night with a pillar of fire, as their great canvas city was enlightened? With what other people did God dwell? Where else did he walk in the midst of their abodes, and manifest himself as he did unto Israel? Instead of being discouraged, they had every cause to be doubly grateful and glad. Led of God, fed of God, taught of God, guarded of God,—what better lot could they imagine ?

Besides, dear friends, though they were so very long in getting to Canaan, yet they would get there if they would only believe their God. God would surely bring them in. To every faithful one he would say, "Thou shalt stand in thy lot in the end of the days." Though the unbelievers among them perished, and their carcases fell in the wilderness, yet even to such of them as repented there was this sweet thought, that though nothing more than God's work might appear unto his servants, yet his glory would be seen by their children, and the next generation should surely enter into the land. Come, let us be of good comfort, then, for the same reasons. We also shall reach our Father's house in due time. We shall get home, and our home-coming shall not be too late for the marriage supper of the Lamb. The Lord knoweth the way of the righteous. He is steering us from day to day by infallible wisdom, and, despite these stormy seas, we shall yet cast anchor in the fair havens whither our Lord has gone. "So shall we be for ever with the Lord. Wherefore comfort one another with these words." The Lord is doing us no hurt. The Lord is denying us no good. He is making even evil things to work together for good, for our good; and we have no proper ground for discouragement. Apparent ground for fear there is in plenty, but real ground there is none.

> " Your harps, ye trembling saints,
> Down from the willows take :
> Loud to the praise of love divine:
> Bid every string awake."

II. In the case of the Israelites this discouragement came to a great head, for it led to COMPLAINT; and that is our second point. "And the people spake against God, and against Moses, Wherefore have ye brought us up out of Egypt to die in the wilderness ? for there is no bread, neither any water; and our soul loatheth this light bread." This was a bitter and wicked complaint.

We are in a sad case, dear brethren, when our discouragements at last reach such a point that we begin to complain of our God; for the complaints that come at these times are such as God is not likely to bear with. When God's people are in real trouble, he is longsuffering and tender towards his afflicted; but with the froward he shows himself froward. When the people complained of thirst, the Lord sweetened the waters of Marah for them; when they were hungry, he gave them bread from heaven; but when, having nothing justly to complain of, they merely grumbled because they were discouraged, he dealt with them severely, and sent the fiery serpents among them which bit many of them, so that much people of Israel died. Beware of a murmuring spirit. God will pity our wants, but he will punish our whims.

Some of us have need to be cautioned against letting the spirit of discouragement hurry us on to quarrelling with God and questioning his love. It is ill for a saint to strive with his Saviour. When these people made their first complaint, it was a singular one. It was a complaint about having been brought out of Egypt. "Wherefore have ye brought us up out of Egypt to die in the wilderness ?"

Well, but first of all, they ought not to complain of being brought up out of Egypt, for that was a land of bondage where their male children had to perish in the river, and where they themselves longed to die, for life had become intolerable; and yet, you see, they are complaining that they were brought up out of Egypt to die in the wilderness, as they said. Is it not possible that our rebellious hearts may even complain of God's mercy? For want of something to murmur at, discouraged ones will pick holes in the goodness of God. What a pity that it should be so! Brothers, if we are believers in Christ, we have been redeemed from bondage; we have been brought into a separated condition and made to be the people of God. Shall we ever complain of *that?* Suppose it brings upon us derision, loneliness, unkindness; suppose it entails upon us loss and self-denial; suppose it involves us in many difficulties; are we going to flinch because of these? God forbid! Did we not count the cost when first we started out from Egypt? And having counted the cost, will we now draw back from the fight? Nay, but in the name of God we will struggle until we have won the victory, and it shall never be a complaint against God that he brought us up out of Egypt. He will not let us die in the wilderness. We cannot believe it, and we will not let our soul say so.

> "Determined to save, he watched o'er my path
> When, Satan's blind slave, I sported with death;
> And can he have taught me to trust in his name,
> And thus far have brought me to put me to shame?"

I cannot believe it. Lie down, O dog of doubt! Lie down, O cur of unbelief! If thou hast no better bark than this, be quiet? Oh, for God's grace to stop complaining at once. Our God never forgave a soul to let that soul fall from grace. Christ never bought a soul with his blood, to make it one of his, and then to let it slip through his fingers into perdition. The Lord has never led us through so many trials and temptations to suffer us, after all, to be shipwrecked and cast away. If he had meant to destroy us he would not have showed us such things as these. Let us not become so peevish as to talk about dying in the wilderness, when the fact is the Lord is making signs and wonders of us by causing us to live in the wilderness.

Next, look at their complaint of having no food;—"There is no bread, neither is there any water." It was a great falsehood. There was bread, they had to admit that fact in the next breath: but then they did not call the manna "bread." They called it by an ugly name in the Hebrew. The water, too, was not muddy and thick like the water of the Nile; it was bright, clear, pure water from the rock; and therefore they would not call it water. They wanted water with substance in it which would leave grit between their teeth, and as the stream which leaped from the flinty rock was pure crystal they would not call it water. Have you not known people to whom God has given great mercy, and yet they have talked as if they were quite deserted. Unbelief is blind, just as surely as faith is far-seeing. Unbelief enjoys nothing, just as faith rejoices in everything. He that believes finds sweetness in the manna: "the taste thereof was as wafers made with honey"; but he that has no faith finds nothing pleasant even in "the corn of heaven," but says "there is no bread."

Only think of anybody saying, "Our soul loatheth this light bread"! It was a diet that was very easy of digestion, and kept them in good health; and yet they pined for heavy, lumpy food. They began to wish for leeks, and garlic, and onions—something rank and strong, and less refined than "angels' food." They sighed for the meat that they ate in Egypt; they hankered after a coarse and dangerous diet. God knew that it was not proper food for them in the blazing desert, and he gave them instead the best possible nourishment; and now they cry, "Oh, there is nothing substantial in it. It does not make you feel as if you were full." They found fault with that which they ought to have commended. Men really need that which is sufficient, that which will sustain the frame, that which will enable them to continue in health and strength; but these murmurers recollected the rough stuff they used to eat among the brick-kilns, and they wished to feel full and overblown as they had now and then felt in Egypt. Thus they fell to complaining against God without excuse.

Are there any here in that state? Are you so discouraged that you do not want to live by faith any longer,—it seems too unsubstantial? Are you tired of praying, "Give us day by day our daily bread"? You would like a nice lump sum in the bank instead, and plenty of the cares and snares of wealth. And is it so that you are no longer content with the old gospel? It is so easy of digestion that you pine for a hard morsel—a piece of cast-iron philosophy to lie on your mind for years to come. You want a bit of indigestible modern thought that will remain within you like the cucumbers of Egypt, which were not so soon gone as the manna of heaven. You crave for leeks, and garlic, and onions—something sensational, remarkable, though by no means comformable to the pure taste of those who are born of the Spirit. Is it not strange how men who call themselves Christians run after that kind of meat: and of the real good gospel, which is able to save the soul, and to build it up, they begin to say, "It is worn out; we have heard this one thing so often. You see it is just the same old-fashioned manna; we want more variety. We demand that which is novel, which will commend itself to our advanced intellectual condition by its metaphysical subtlety." That is the style. I see the spirit everywhere, and it comes across us all in some form or other—complaining of what God provides in providence, complaining of what God provides in the Bible, complaining of what the Holy Ghost provides in his divine operations. We look out, like the Athenians, for some new thing: we do not know what we want. When the grumbling humour is on us we complain of anything and everything, as did these Israelites: they complained of God, they complained of Moses; they complained of the manna. They would have been ready to complain of Aaron; but, fortunately for him, he had been dead a month or so, and so they poured the more gall upon Moses. To men in this state nothing is right: nothing can be right. The whole world is turned upside down, and if it was again turned the other way it would be just as wrong—perhaps more wrong than ever. You smile, I see, at this. Well, you may smile if you like, brethren, but it is a thing to weep over; for I remember a text that says, "The Lord heard their murmurings." That is the solemn point in the matter. We are pleased that God should hear our prayers; it is that which we long for: but is it not terrible that God should hear our murmurings? There are two things that God always hears. Mark this! The first is the voice of faith, and the second is the voice of unbelief: for, as much as God loves faith, so much God loathes unbelief. When we are strong in faith the Lord can do anything with us and for us, and he can make us equal to all difficulties, so that we can say with the apostle, " I can do all things through Christ which strengtheneth me." But when we give way to unbelief Christ himself can do nothing with us, as it is written:—" He could not do many mighty works there because of their unbelief."

Do you not feel sorry, then, that you ever murmured and complained, since your God heard it all? What is more, as the Lord usually answers the prayers of faith, so he often answers the prayers of incredulity. I have heard a brother cry out because of his small and bearable trouble, and I have known the Lord answer his impatience with great trials. If children cry for nothing, they ought to have something to cry for ; and, if we get discouraged when there really is no reason for it, we shall probably be answered with astonishing tribulations. If we begin complaining when we ought to be singing it is likely enough that we shall have grave cause for crying out; for is it not written concerning the Lord, " With the froward thou wilt show thyself froward "? When we walk tenderly, submissively, and quietly, and when we say with David, " My soul is even as a weaned child," then the Lord walks very gently and comfortably toward us, and our path is smoothed by his love; but the Lord has said, " If ye walk contrary to me, I will walk contrary to you." Wherefore, brethren, if we be discouraged in any way, let us pray that we may not venture further in that ill way, nor begin to rail against the Lord and his providence. May we go back to confidence and joy and faith, but not go on till we fall into the ditch of murmuring, and lie there waiting for yet worse things.

III. The Lord ere long sends upon murmurers PUNISHMENT. This is our third head. We read that as soon as the people found fault with Moses, and with God, and with the manna, " the Lord sent fiery serpents among the people, and they bit the people, and much people of Israel died." Fiery serpents were ready at the divine call; the Lord never lacks means of chastisement. There was no interval between the sin and the suffering, for the fault was wanton and inexcusable.

Will God send fiery serpents among his own people? These were the tribes that ate of the manna, and the people that " drank of the rock that followed them, which rock was Christ." These were the Lord's visible church in the wilderness, and though not all spiritually his children, yet they were types of his chosen, representatives of the whole believing family.

Well, brethren, the Lord in fatherly anger may send fiery serpents among a doubting and quarrelsome people, and so those who bite with fault-finding may find themselves bitten.

These fiery serpents come in different forms. Sometimes they may be *new trials*. The Israelites, as far as I know, had never seen these seraphs, or burning ones, before. They seemed to fly up out of the sand and bite them or ever they were aware, and then the venom entered into their blood, and made it scald them till they seemed to be a mass of fire from head to foot, burning with fierce pain, and ready to die. It was dreadful to be marching through the midst of fiery flying serpents. The Lord deliver us from that. But he may send to us if we grow peevish a fresh and novel affliction, a crooked trial which will twist and wriggle about us—a sudden grief which will poison the fountain of our life: and this may hastily fly at us, as a chastisement for not having believed in God under much happier circumstances.

In some Christians these fiery serpents may be *the uprisings of their own corruptions.* I have known the corruptions of a child of God to be quiet and still for a long period. They have been there, but they have been forced to hide away like thieves that dare not come out in daylight; and the child of God has hence enjoyed rest. But the good man has been discouraged, and has fallen to complaining, and then these inward corruptions have broken forth upon him and compassed him about like bees, innumerable, and quick to sting. Some of us know what this means : we have been put to a dead stand with our lively inbred sins which we thought were dead : suddenly they have revived within us, and we had to fight against them for dear life.

Or, it may be, that God will let *Satan* loose upon us if we disbelieve. Truly we cannot want any worse fiery serpents than the suggestions and insinuations of the devil. Oh, brother, if you have ever met Satan and fought him foot to foot, you know by your scars what a terrible adversary he is. Why, he will insinuate thoughts into our breasts which never came from our own minds and never would have come—blasphemous thoughts of an infernal kind; and these he would have us accept as our own. He will throw his bombs into our souls, and then tell us that these are of our own making. He will make us doubt the existence of God, the inspiration of Scripture, the deity of Christ, the truth of the gospel, the fact of the resurrection—in fact, he will make us doubt doctrines for which we would lay down our lives. These are his impieties, and not our own thoughts at all; but, like serpents of fire, their sting is terrible. All the while our enemy will beat the great hell drum concerning our past sins, and try if he can to drown the voice of mercy and of that precious blood which " speaketh better things than that of Abel." Thus he would drive us to despair.

Ah, these fiery serpents ! Brethren, it is much better to be tried with poverty and pain than to be molested by the infernal thoughts that come from Satan. It were better for us to lie down crushed like the very dust beneath our feet, and every particle a pang, than to be filled with the desperate thoughts that Satan is able to inject into the mind. Beware, I pray you, of complaining, you that are getting to be at all discouraged. Return to your childlike faith. " Cast not away your confidence which hath great recompense of reward," lest you slide by your unbelief down into complaining, and then by your complaining hatch fiery serpents out of the ground on which you tread.

IV. But now, fourthly, here comes the REMEDY. What is to be done when Israel is bitten with fiery serpents ?

Well, the first thing is *confession.* They went to Moses, and cried, " We have sinned." Oh, that is a sweet art—that art of confession: it empties the bosom of most perilous stuff! Nothing seems to me to be more hideous than to confess your sins to a man like yourselves. I should think that to sit down to a priest's ear, and to pour into it all the filth of your soul, and answer every question that he may care to propound to you, must be one of the most fearful ordeals through which a human mind can pass.   I know that Satan is very ingenious as to the means by which to deprave men, and rob them of the last particle of modesty, so as to make them capable of every crime; but I should think that oracular confession is his last and darkest invention for depraving the soul beyond all common defilement.   It must be the most fearful process of saturating with evil through which the mind can pass.   But to confess sin into the ear of Christ is quite another thing.   To get alone with him, and to tell him all our transgressions and temptations—this is as great a blessing as the other is a curse.   There is no fear that we can pollute *him;* and every blessing comes of emptying out ourselves before him who is able to take away all sin by reason of his precious blood.   Our first business is to hasten away to our great High-priest, and tell him that we have sinned.

The second help was that *Moses prayed* for the people.   So our great cure against fiery serpents, horrible thoughts, and temptations, is inter-cession.   " If any man sin, we have an advocate with the Father, Jesus Christ the righteous."   If we have grown downhearted and dis-couraged, and have sinned by unbelieving utterances, let us go with our poor, little, trembling faith, and ask the blessed go-between, the Divine Interposer, to stand before God on our behalf, and pray for us that our transgressions may be blotted out.   Oh, what a sweet thing it is to have this Advocate!   Come, you that are the Lord's people and yet are transgressors, come and rejoice in this—that he maketh inter-cession for transgressors, and that he is therefore able to save unto the uttermost.

But now comes the great remedy.   After their confession and the prayer of their mediator, the Lord bade Moses make *a brazen serpent,* and lift it up, that they might look upon it and live.   Beloved, when I first came to Christ as a poor sinner, and looked to him, I thought him the most precious object my eyes had ever lit upon; but this night I have been looking to him while I have been preaching to you, in remem-brance of my own discouragements, and my own complainings, and I find my Lord Jesus dearer than ever.   I have been seriously ill, and sadly depressed, and I fear I have rebelled, and therefore I look anew to him, and I tell you that he is fairer in my eyes to-night than he was at first. It is a delightful thing that there should be a fountain open for sinners to wash in; but I will tell you something that is more charming still,— there is a fountain for the house of David and for the inhabitants of Jerusalem for sin and uncleanness.   That fountain is not for outcasts only, but for the saints, for the citizens of Jerusalem, for the house of David.   " If we walk in the light as God is in the light, and have fellowship one with another,"—do we sin still?   Ay, that we do, even then; but " the blood of Jesus Christ, his Son, cleanseth us from all sin." In our lowest condition this is our cleansing.   In our highest condition this is still our cleansing.   The first time a poor sinner comes up out of the ditch, with his own clothes abhorring him, he is made white through Christ's blood the moment he believes in Jesus; and mark this, when he enters heaven and stands before the blaze of the supernal glory, it shall still be said of him and of his fellows, " They have washed their robes, and made them white in the blood of the Lamb." The brazen serpent healed me when first I saw the Lord ; and the brazen serpent heals me to-night, and shall do so till I die. " Look and live " is for saints as well as for sinners. For you, ye ungodly ones,

> "There is life for a look at the Crucified One."

But equally is this true for you who belong to Jesus, but have grieved his Holy Spirit. Ye that have gone aside from your faith, and have begun disputing with your God, and complaining of providence, there is life for you, too, in the Saviour lifted up. There are not two ways of salvation—one for sinners and another for saints. There are not two grounds on which we stand—the ground of the sinner saved and the ground of the saint saved. No, the same basis is under each foot; we each sing—

> " Rock of ages, cleft for me,
> Let me hide myself in thee !"

This is the language of the man who has served his God for half a century, and preached the gospel like a Luther or a Calvin, just as certainly as it must be the language of the trembling sinner, guilty and condemned before the living God.

Do you not see where the brazen serpent fitly comes in according to Scripture? At the end of the pilgrimage, just before they are going to cross the Jordan, then Israel sees the serpent of brass. Then the people sin, and then is there revealed to them in all its splendour that blessed type of Christ,—"And as Moses lifted up the serpent in the wilderness, even so must the Son of man be lifted up: that whosoever believeth in him should not perish, but have eternal life." " Should not perish !" as if even a believer had about him that which would make him perish if he did not still look to the appointed cure. Jesus is lifted up that saints might not perish, but might persevere in grace unto everlasting life. How is our spiritual life rendered everlasting but by the continuance of that look? We are to be looking still to Jesus as long as we live. " Looking unto Jesus, the author and finisher of our faith." Ever looking; ever looking. God keep us looking if we have looked, and bring us to look to Jesus if we have never looked; and to his name be praise for ever and ever. Amen.

PORTION OF SCRIPTURE READ BEFORE SERMON—Numbers xx. 14;
xxi. 9.

By C. H. SPURGEON.

The Most Holy Place.

Sermons on the Song of Solomon. By C. H. SPURGEON. Containing 52 Sermons delivered in the New Park Street Chapel and the Metropolitan Tabernacle, Newington. Cloth Gilt, 7s.

PASSMORE & ALABASTER, Paternoster Buildings; and all Booksellers.

"KNOCK!"

A Sermon

DELIVERED ON LORD'S-DAY MORNING, MAY 27TH, 1883, BY

C. H. SPURGEON,

AT THE METROPOLITAN TABERNACLE, NEWINGTON.

"Knock, and it shall be opened unto you."—Matthew vii. 12.

I HAVE no doubt that, taken very strictly, the three exhortations of this verse—which, indeed, are but one—were first of all intended for God's believing people. It was to his disciples that the Lord said, "Cast not your pearls before swine;" and perhaps certain of them who were poor in spirit might turn round and say, "Lord, we have few pearls; we are too poor to have the treasures of thy grace so plentifully. Thou hast bidden us not to give that which is holy unto dogs; but holiness is rather a thing we seek after than possess." "Well," saith the Lord, "you have only to ask and have; ye have not because ye ask not; you have only to seek and you will be sure to find, for holy things, like rare pearls, are to be discovered if you look for them: you have only to knock and spiritual secrets shall open to you, even the innermost truth of God." In each exhortation our Lord bids us pray. Beloved, let us abound in supplication. Depend upon it that failure in prayer will undermine the foundation of our peace and sap the strength of our confidence; but if we abound in pleading with God we shall grow strong in the Lord, and we shall be happy in his love, we shall become a blessing to those around us. Need I commend the mercy-seat to you who wait before it? Surely prayer must have become such a joy to you, such a necessity of your being, such an element of your life, that I hardly need press it upon you as a duty, or invite you to it as a privilege. Yet still I do so, because the Master does it by a triple exhortation. A threefold cord is not easily broken—let not my text be neglected by you. Let me urge you to repeated, varied, ever intensifying prayer: ask! seek! knock! Cease not to ask till you receive; cease not to seek till you find; cease not to knock till the door is opened unto you.

In these three exhortations there would appear to be a gradation: it is the same thought put into another shape, and made more forcible. *Ask*—that is, in the quiet of your spirit, speak with God concerning your need, and humbly beg him to grant your desires: this is a good

No. 1,723.

and acceptable form of prayer. If, however, asking should not appear to succeed, the Lord would arouse you to a more concentrated and active longing; therefore let your desires call in the aid of knowledge, thought, consideration, meditation, and practical action, and learn to *seek* for the blessings you desire as men seek for hid treasures. These good things are laid up in store, and they are accessible to fervent minds. See how you can reach them. Add to asking the study of the promises of God, a diligent hearing of his word, a devout meditation upon the way of salvation, and all such means of grace as may bring you the blessing. Advance from asking into seeking. And if after all it should still seem that you have not obtained your desire, then *knock*, and so come to closer and more agonizing work; use not alone the voice, but the whole soul; exercise yourself unto godliness to obtain the boon; use every effort to win that which you seek after; for remember that doing is praying; living to God is a high form of seeking, and the bent of the entire mind is knocking. God often giveth to his people when they keep his commandments that which he denies to them if they walk carelessly. Remember the words of the Lord Jesus, how he said, "If ye abide in me, and my words abide in you, ye shall ask what ye will, and it shall be done unto you." Holiness is essential to power in prayer: the life must knock while the lips ask and the heart seeks.

I will change my line of exposition and say: ask as a *beggar* petitions for alms. They say that begging is a poor trade, but when you ply it well with God no other trade is so profitable. Men get more by asking than by working without prayer. Though I do not discommend working, yet I most highly commend praying. Nothing under heaven pays like prevailing prayer. He that has power in prayer has all things at his call. Ask as a poor mendicant who is hungry and pleads for bread. Then seek as a *merchant* who hunts for goodly pearls, looking up and down, anxious to give all that he has that he may win a matchless treasure. Seek as a servant carefully looking after his master's interests and labouring to promote them. Seek with all diligence, adding to the earnestness of the beggar the careful watchfulness of the jeweller who is seeking for a gem. Conclude all by knocking at mercy's door as *a lost traveller* caught out on a cold night in a blinding sleet knocks for shelter that he may not perish in the storm. When you have reached the gate of salvation ask to be admitted by the great love of God, then look well to see the way of entering, seeking to enter in; and if still the door seem shut against you, knock right heavily, and continue knocking till you are safely lodged within the home of love.

Once again, ask for what you want, seek for what you have lost, knock for that from which you are excluded. Perhaps this last arrangement best indicates the shades of meaning, and brings out the distinctions. Ask for everything you need, whatever it may be: if it be a right and good thing, it is promised to the sincere asker. Seek for what you have lost; for what Adam lost you by the Fall, for what you have lost yourself by your neglect, by your backsliding, by your want of prayer: seek till you find the grace you need. Then knock. If you seem shut out from comfort, from knowledge, from hope, from God, from heaven, then knock, for the Lord will open unto you. Here you need the Lord's own interference: you can ask and receive, you can seek and find; but you cannot knock and open,—the Lord must himself open the door, or you are shut out for ever. God is ready to open the door. Remember, there is no cherub with fiery sword to guard this gate, but, on the contrary, the Lord Jesus himself openeth, and no man shutteth. But now I must drop this line of things, for my desire is to use the text in reference to those who are not yet saved.

Last Lord's-day, when we preached upon glory, we had before us the end of the pilgrim way. It was a very, very happy time; for in meditation we reached the suburbs of the Celestial City, and we tasted of eternal glory. This morning I thought we would begin at the beginning, and enter in at the wicket gate which stands at the head of the way to heaven. Mr. Bunyan, in his "Pilgrim's Progress," says, "Now over the gate there was written, ' Knock, and it shall be opened unto you.'" His ingenious allegory is always as truthfully instructive as it is delightfully attractive. I concluded that this should be my text. If it be thought worthy to be written over the gate at the entering in of the way of life it must have a great claim upon the attention of those who have not yet started for glory, but are anxious to do so. May God the Holy Ghost instruct and quicken them while we hear the Lord from within his palace saying, "Knock, and it shall be opened unto you."

I. First, then, dear friend, whoever you are, if you are desirous of entering into eternal life, I would expound to you the inscription over the gate, by saying, first, THE DOOR OF MERCY MAY APPEAR TO YOU TO BE CLOSED AGAINST YOU. That is implied in the text: " Knock, and it shall be opened unto you." If to your consciousness the door stood wide open, there would be no need of knocking; but since in your apprehension it is closed against you, it is for you to seek admission in the proper way by knocking.

To a large extent this apprehension is the result of your own fears. You think the gate is closed because you feel it ought to be so; you feel that if God dealt with you as you would deal with your fellow-men, he would be so offended with you as to shut the door of his favour once for all. You remember how guilty you have been, how often you have refused the divine call, and how you have gone on from evil to evil, and therefore you fear that the Master of the house has already risen up and shut to the door. You fear lest like the obstinate ones in Noah's day you will find the door of the ark closed, and yourself shut out to perish in the general destruction. Sin lieth at the door, and blocks it. Your desponding feelings fasten up the gate of grace in your judgment. Yet, it is not so. The gate is not barred and bolted as you think it to be; though it may be spoken of as closed in a certain sense, yet in another sense it is never shut. In any case it opens very freely; its hinges are not rusted, no bolts secure it. The Lord is glad to open the gate to every knocking soul. It is closed far more in your apprehension than as a matter of fact; for the sin which shuts it is removed so far as the believing sinner is concerned. Had you but faith enough, you would enter in at this present moment; and if you did once enter in, you would never be put out again, for it is written, " Him that cometh to me I will in no wise cast out." If you could with holy courage take leave and licence to come in, you would never be blamed for it. Fear

and shame stand in the sinner's road, and push him back; and blessed
is he whose desperate need forces him to be bold.

One thing we should remember when we fear that the door is closed
against us, namely, that *it is not so fast closed as the door of our hearts
has been.* You know the famous picture of "The Light of the World."
It seems to me to be one of the finest sermons the eye has ever looked
upon. There stands the Ever-Blessed, knocking at the door of the soul,
but the hinges are rusted, the door itself is fast bolted, and wild briars
and all kinds of creeping plants running up the door prove that it is long
since it was moved. You know what it all means; how continuance in sin
makes it harder to yield to the knock of Christ, and how evil habits
creeping up one after another hold the soul so fast that it cannot open
to the sacred knocking. Jesus has been knocking at some of your
hearts ever since you were children; and still he knocks. I hear his
blessed hand upon the door at this moment: do you not hear it? Will
you not open? He has knocked long, and yet he knocks again. I am
sure that you have not knocked at mercy's door so long as incarnate
mercy has waited at your door. You know you have not. How, therefore, can you complain if there should be an apparent delay in answering
your prayers? It is but to make you feel a holy shame for having
treated your Lord so ill. Now you begin to know what it is to be kept
waiting, what it is to be a weary knocker, what it is to cry "my head is
wet with dew and my locks with the drops of the night." This will
excite you to repentance for your unkind behaviour, and also move you
to love the more intensely that gentle Lover of your soul who has shown
such patience towards you. It will be no loss to you that the door
was shut for awhile, if you do but gain a penitent heart and a tender
spirit.

Let me, however, warn you that *the door can be closed and kept
shut by unbelief.* He that believeth entereth into Christ when he
believeth: he that cometh in by the door shall be saved, and shall go
in and out and find pasture; so our Lord says in the tenth of John.
"He that believeth in him hath everlasting life," there is no question
about that; but we read on the other hand, "So then they could not
enter in because of unbelief." Forty years the tribes were in the wilderness, going towards Canaan, yet they never reached the promised land
because of unbelief. And what if some of you should be forty years
attending this means of grace? Coming and going, coming and going,
hearing sermons, witnessing ordinances, and joining with God's people
in worship: what if after all the forty years you should never enter in
because of unbelief? Souls, I tell you if you lived each one of you as
long as Methusaleh, you could not enter in unless you believed in Jesus
Christ. The moment you have trusted him with your whole heart and
soul you are within the blessed portals of the Father's house, but however many years you may be asking, seeking, and knocking, you will never
enter in till faith comes, for unbelief keeps up the chain of the door, and
there is no entering in while it rules your spirit.

Do you, however, complain that you should have to knock? *It is
the rule of the Most High.* Am I addressing any who have been earnestly praying for several months? I can sympathize with you, for that
was my case, not only for months, but even for years: through the

darkness of my mind and my cruel misapprehensions of the Lord, I did not find peace when first I began to ask for it, although I also sought with much earnestness, going to the house of God every time I could, and reading the Bible daily with a burning desire to know the right way. I did not enter into peace till I had knocked long and heavily. Hearken, therefore, to one who knows your trouble, and hear from me the voice of reason. Ought we to expect to enter into the glorious house of mercy without knocking at its door? Is it so with our own houses? Can every straggler carelessly saunter in? Is it not God's way in the world to give great blessings, but always to make men knock for them? We want bread out of the earth, but the farmer must knock at the door of the earth with his plough and with all his instruments of agriculture ere his God will hand him out a harvest. Is anything gained in this world without labour? Is it not an old proverb, "No sweat, no sweet: no pains, no gains: no mill, no meal"? And may we not expect in heavenly things that at least these great mercies should be prayed for with fervency before they can be bestowed? It is the usual rule with God to make us pray before he gives the blessing. And how could it be otherwise? How could a man be saved without prayer? A prayerless soul must be a Christless soul. The feeling of prayer, the habit of prayer, the spirit of prayer are parts of salvation. Unless it can be said of a man, "Behold, he prayeth!" how can there be any sort of hope that he knows his God, and has found reconciliation? The prodigal did not come home dumb, neither did he enter his father's house in sullen silence. No, but as soon as he saw his father, he cried, "Father, I have sinned against heaven." There must be speech with God, for God gives not a silent salvation.

Besides, *to make us knock at mercy's gate is a great blessing to ourselves* upon the spot. It is a going to school for us when we are set to plead with God for awhile without realised success. It makes a man grow more earnest, for his hunger increases while he tarries. If he obtained the blessing when first he asked for it, it might seem dog cheap; but when he has to plead long he arrives at a better sense of the value of the mercy sought. He sees also more of his own unworthiness as he stands outside mercy's gate, ready to swoon away with fear; and so he grows more passionately earnest in pleading; and, whereas he did but ask at first, he now begins to seek, and he adds cries and tears and a broken heart to all the other ways of his pleading. Thus the man, by being humbled and aroused, is getting good by means of his sorrow while he is kept for a while outside the gate. Beside that, he is increasing his capacity for the future. I believe I never could have been able to comfort seekers in their anguish if I had not been kept waiting in the cold myself. I have always felt grateful for my early distress because of its after results. Many men, whose experiences are recorded in books which are invaluable in the Christian library, never could have written those books if they had not themselves been kept waiting, hungry and thirsty, and full of soul-travail, ere the Lord appeared to them. That blessed man, David, who always seems to be—

"Not one, but all mankind's epitome"

—the history of all men wrapped up in one—how he pictures himself as

sinking in the miry clay! Lower and lower did he go till he cried out
of the depths, and then at last he was taken up out of the horrible
pit, and his feet were set on a rock that he might tell to others what the
Lord had done for him. Your heart wants enlarging, dear sir. The
Lord means to prepare you to become a more eminent Christian by
expanding your mind. The spade of agony is digging trenches to hold
the water of life. Depend upon it, if the ships of prayer do not come
home speedily it is because they are more heavily freighted with
blessing. When prayer is long in the answering it will be all the
sweeter in the receiving, like fruit which is well ripened by hanging
longer on the tree. If you knock with a heavy heart you shall yet sing
with joy of spirit; therefore, be not discouraged because for a while you
stand before a closed door.

II. Secondly, A DOOR IMPLIES AN OPENING. What is a door meant
for if it is always to be kept shut? The wall might as well have
remained without a break. I have seen certain houses and public
buildings with the form and appearance of doors where there were none;
the sham doorway being made for architectural purposes; but nothing
is a sham in the house of the Lord. His doors are meant to open: they
were made on purpose for entrance; and so the blessed gospel of God is
made on purpose for you to enter into life and peace. It would be of
no use to knock at a wall, but you may wisely knock at a door, for it is
arranged for opening. You will enter in eventually if you knock on,
for *the gospel is good news for men*, and how could it be good news if it
should so happen that they might sincerely come to Christ and ask
mercy, and be denied it? I fear that the gospel preached by certain
divines sounds rather like bad news than good news to awakened souls,
for it requires so much feeling and preparation on the sinner's part that
they are not cheered nor led to hope thereby. But be you sure that
the Lord is willing to save all those who are willing to be saved in
his own appointed way. A dear brother beautifully said in prayer on
Monday night—" Thou, O Lord, art perfectly satisfied with the Lord
Jesus, and if we are satisfied with *him*, thou art satisfied with us."
That is the gospel put into a few words. God is satisfied with Christ,
and if you are satisfied with Christ, God is satisfied with you. This is
glad tidings to every soul that is willing to accept the atonement made,
and the righteousness prepared by the Lord Jesus.

Dear friend, *this gospel must be meant to be received by sinners*, or else
it would not have been sent. " But," saith one, " I am such a sinner."
Just so. You are the sort of person for whom the news of mercy is
intended. A gospel is not needed by perfect men; sinless men need
no pardon. No sacrifice is wanted if there is no guilt: no atonement
is wanted where there is no transgression. They that are whole need
not a physician, but they that are sick. This door of hope which God
has prepared was meant to be an entrance into life, and it was meant to
open to sinners, for if it does not open to sinners it will never open at
all; for we have all sinned, and so we must all be shut out unless it
be of free grace for those who are guilty.

I am sure this door *must open to those who have nothing to bring with
them*. If you have no good works, no merits, no good feelings, nothing
to recommend you, be not discouraged, for it is to such that Jesus Christ

is most precious, and therefore most accessible, for he loves to give himself to those who will prize him most. A man will never have Christ while he has enough of his own; but he that is consciously naked, and poor, and miserable is the man for Christ's money, he it is that has been redeemed by price. You may know the redeemed man, for he feels his bondage, and owns that he must remain therein unless the redemption of Christ be applied for his deliverance.

Dear friends, that door of hope will be opened to you though you may be ignorant, and weak, and quite unable to fulfil any high conditions. When the text says, "*Knock*, and it shall be opened unto you," it teaches us that *the way of winning admission to the blessing is simple*, and suitable to common people. If I have to enter in by a door which is well secured, I shall need tools and science. I confess I do not understand the art; you must send for a gentleman who understands picklocks, "jemmies," and all sorts of burglarious instruments: but if I am only told to knock, fool as I am at opening doors, I know how to knock. Any uneducated man can knock if that is all which is required of him. Is there a person here who cannot put words together in prayer? Never mind, friend; knocking can be done by one who is no orator. Perhaps another cries, "I am no scholar." Never mind, a man can knock though he may be no philosopher. A dumb man can knock. A blind man can knock. With a palsied hand a man may knock. He who knows nothing of his book can still lift a hammer and let it fall. The way to open heaven's gate is wonderfully simplified to those who are lowly enough to follow the Holy Spirit's guidance, and ask, seek, and knock believingly. God has not provided a salvation which can only be understood by learned men; he has not prepared a gospel which requires half-a-dozen folio volumes to describe it: it is intended for the ignorant, the short-witted, and the dying, as well as for others, and hence it must be as plain as knocking at a door. This is it,—Believe and live. Seek unto God with all your heart and soul, and strength, through Jesus Christ, and the door of his mercy will certainly open to you. The gate of grace is meant to yield admission to unscientific people since it shall be opened to those who knock.

I am sure this door will open to you, because *it has been opened to so many before you*. It has been opened to hundreds of us now present. Could not you, dear brothers and sisters, stand up and tell how the Lord opened the gate of his salvation to you? That door has opened to many in this house during the last few weeks. We have seen persons coming forward to tell how the Lord has been pleased to give them an entrance into his mercy, though at one time they were afraid that the door was shut, and they were ready to despair. Well, if the door has been so often opened for others, why should it not turn on its hinges for you? Only knock, with faith in God's mercy, and before long it shall yield to your importunity.

It is for God's glory to open his door of grace, and that is one reason why we are sure he will do so. We cannot expect him to do that which would be derogatory to his own honour, but we do expect him to do that which will glorify his sacred attributes. It will greatly honour the mercy, the patience, the love, the grace, the goodness, the favour of God if he will open the door to such an undeserving one as you are; wherefore knock. Knock since God delights to give; knock at a door which every time it turns on its hinges unveils his greatness; knock with holy confidence at this present moment, for "it shall be opened unto you." It is a door which seems closed, but because it is a door, it must be capable of being opened.

III. Thirdly, knock, for A KNOCKER IS PROVIDED. When persons can be admitted by knocking, a knocker is usually placed on the door; and if not, we often see the words, NO ADMITTANCE. Before bells became so common the habit of knocking at the door was well-nigh universal, and people were accustomed to make the door resound with their blows. There was a nail-head for the knocker to drop upon, and people used to smite it so heavily that it became remarked that such blows on the head were killing, and hence arose the mirthful proverb, "as dead as a door-nail." It betokens a hearty kind of knocking, which I would have you imitate in prayer. Knock at heaven's gate as earnestly as people knocked at doors in the olden times. Have you not had knocks at your own doors which could be heard all through the house? Some of our friends are vigorous, and knock as if they meant coming in. It may be that gentle folks give such tender taps that they are not heard by the servants, and so they have to wait; but these I am speaking of never fall into that error, for they so startle everybody that people are glad to let them in, for fear they should thunder a second time. In this style let us pray: let us plead in downright fashion, and never cease till we gain admission.

I have said that the Lord has provided a knocker. What is this knocker? First of all, it may be found in *the promises of God*. We are sure to speed well when we can plead a promise. It is well to say unto the Lord, "Do as thou hast said." What force abides in an appeal to the word, the oath, and the covenant of God. If a man presents to another a promissory note upon the day on which it is due he expects to receive the amount stated therein. God's promises are bills of exchange, and he will duly honour them. He was never known to dishonour a bill yet, and he never will do so. If you can only quote a promise applicable to your condition, and spread it before the Lord in faith, and say, "Remember this word unto thy servant upon which thou hast caused me to hope," you must obtain the blessing. Pleading the promise gives such a knock at the gate of heaven that it must be opened.

The great knocker, however, is *the name of the Lord Jesus Christ*. If a person were to call upon you in the name of some dearly-beloved son who is far away, if he brought you due credentials, and a letter, saying, "Father. treat the bearer well for my sake," you would be sure to show him kindness; and if the aforesaid person was authorized to receive a promised amount in the name of your son, would you not hand out the money? Now, when we go to God and plead the name of Christ, it means that we plead the authority of Christ, that we ask of God as though we were in Christ's stead. and expect him to give it to us as if he were giving it to Jesus. That is something more than pleading for Christ's sake. I suppose the apostles at first did plead with God for Christ's sake, but Jesus says to them, "Hitherto ye have asked nothing *in my name.*" It is a higher grade of prayer, and when we get to pleading Christ's name with the Father, then do we gloriously prevail. At a Primitive Methodist meeting a person was trying to pray, but did not get on at it, and presently a voice was heard from the corner of the room, " Plead the blood, brother ! plead the blood !" I am not very fond of such interruptions, yet this was to be commended, for it gave the right note, and set the pleader in his right place. Plead the precious blood of Jesus Christ, and you have knocked so that you must be heard.

" Alas !" says one, " I see the knocker, for I know something of the promises and of the person of our Lord, but how am I to knock ? " With the hand of faith. Believe that God will keep his promise ; ask him to do so, and thus knock. Believe that Jesus is worthy, whose name you are pleading, and so knock in confidence that God will honour the name of his dear Son. " Alas ! my hand is so weak," say you. Then remember that the Holy Spirit helpeth our infirmities. Ask him to put his hand upon your hand, and in that fashion you will be able to knock with prevailing vehemence. I beseech you knock with all the strength you have, and knock often. If you are not in Christ, my dear hearer, do not give sleep to your eyes nor slumber to your eyelids till you have found him. If you have prayed once, go and pray again ; and if you have prayed ten thousand times, yet still continue in prayer. Knock with all your might, with all the vigour of your spirit ; plead as for life ; knock at the door as a man would knock who saw a wolf ready to spring upon him. Knock as one would knock who found himself ready to die of cold outside the door. Throw your whole soul into the work. Say unto the Lord, " I beseech thee have mercy upon me, and have mercy upon me now. I faint, I die, unless thou manifest thy love to me and take me into thy house and heart, that I may be thine for ever." " Knock, and it shall be opened unto you." There is the knocker.

IV. Next, to you who are knocking at the gate A PROMISE IS GIVEN. That is more than having a door before you, or a knocker to knock with. The promise is above the gate in plain words. Read it. You are growing faint and weary ; read the promise, and grow strong again. " Knock, and it shall be opened unto you." Observe how plain and positive it is with its glorious " shall " burning like a lamp in the centre of it. In letters of love the inscription shines out amidst all the darkness that surrounds you, and these are its words, " It shall be opened unto you." If you knock at the door of the kindest of men you see no such promise set before you, and yet you knock, and knock confidently ; how much more boldly should you come to the door of grace when it is expressly declared, " It shall be opened unto you"!

Remember that this promise was *freely given.* You never asked the Lord for such a word, it was uttered by spontaneous goodness. You did not come and plead with Jesus for a promise that you should be heard in prayer. Far from it—you did not even pray. Perhaps you have been living in the world forty years, and have never truly prayed at all ; but the Lord out of his overflowing heart of generous love has made this promise to you, " Knock, and it shall be opened unto you." Wherefore do you doubt ? Do you think he will not keep his word ? A God who cannot lie, who was under no necessity to promise, freely, out of the greatness of his divine nature, which is love, says to a poor sinner, " Knock, and it shall be opened unto you." Oh, be sure of this, that he means it; and till heaven and earth shall pass away his word shall stand, and neither you nor any other sinner that knocks at his door shall be refused admittance.

This inscription has encouraged many to knock: when they have been ready to faint and give up all further seeking, they have read again the cheering lines, " Knock, and it shall be opened unto you," and they have taken heart and made the gate resound again. Now, do you think God will tantalize us, that he will make fools of us, that he will excite hopes in poor sinners, for the mere sake of disappointing them? Will he induce you to knock by his promise, and then laugh at you? Did the God of mercy ever say, " I called and you came; I stretched out my hands and you drew near to me, and yet I will mock at your calamity, and laugh when your fear cometh"? Why, a bad man would scarcely speak so: such an act would be more like Satan than God. Do not tolerate the thought that the God of all grace could treat a seeker thus; if it ever crosses your mind, thrust it away and say, " He that taught me to pray has thereby bound himself to answer prayer. He will not invite me to knock in vain! Therefore, I will knock again, only this time more vigorously than ever, relying upon his word and his truth." Oh, that you may never stop your knocking till salvation's door is entered by you! The promise of the Lord was given freely, and on the strength of that promise we knock, therefore we are sure that the Lord will not deny his trusting servants.

The mercy is that *this promise is meant for all knockers*—" Knock, and it shall be opened unto *you*." The Lord has not denied to you, my hearer, the privilege of praying, or declared that he will not answer your requests. You may knock, and you may expect to see the door open. I know the blessed doctrine of election, and I rejoice in it; but that is a secret with God, while the rule of our preaching is,—" Preach the gospel to every creature." I would, therefore, say to each one here, " Knock, and it shall be opened unto *you*." The Lord knows who will knock, for " the Lord knoweth them that are his." But knock, my friend, knock now, and it will soon be seen that you are one of God's chosen ones. Remember the story of Malachi, the Cornishman. When a Methodist friend had some money to give him he smilingly said, " Malachi, I do not think I shall give you this money, because I do not know whether you are predestinated to have it. Will you tell me whether you are predestinated to have it or not?" Malachi replied, " You put the money in my hand, and I will tell you." As soon as Malachi had the sum in hand he knew that he was predestinated to have it; but he could not know before he had it in possession. So the secret counsel of the Lord is revealed to our faith when it gets Christ in possession, and not before. Knock at once. If you are predestinated to enter, I know you will knock, and knock till you are admitted, for so it stands, and no exception is made to it—" Knock, and it shall be opened unto you." It is a rule with the Lord that to him that knocketh it shall be opened.

Blessed be God, this text of mine shines out as if printed in stars, and *it continues to shine from day-dawn of life to set of sun.* As long as a man lives, if he knocks at God's door, it shall be opened unto him. You may have been long a rebel, and you may have heaped up your sins till they seem to shut out all hope from you, but still knock at Christ, the door, for an opening time will come. Even if it were with thine expiring hand, if thou couldst knock at mercy's gate it would open to thee; but put not off thy day of knocking because of God's long-suffering mercy; rather to-day knock, knock now while sitting in the pew, and if you are not answered immediately, as I trust you will be, yet go home, and there in secret cry unto the Lord, " I will not let thee go except thou bless me. I am lost unless thou find me; I am lost unless I find my Saviour and Lord, I am not playing at prayer now, my very soul means it; I must have Christ or else I die just as I am; I cast myself upon him, and trust his atoning sacrifice. Oh, manifest thyself to me as a pardoning God!" I will be bound for God as a hostage that he will answer you. I sought the Lord, and he heard me; and since then I have never doubted of any living soul but that if he too will seek the Lord through Jesus Christ he will certainly be saved. Oh, that you would try it! The Lord move you thereto by his own blessed Spirit.

V. So I close with one more point. When the door opens IT WILL BE A GLORIOUS OPENING TO YOU. "Knock, and it shall be opened." What will come of it then? Immediately you who have knocked will enter. If you have knocked in sincerity, the moment you see Christ as a Saviour you will accept him as your Saviour. Enter into Christ by faith. Behold, he sets before you an open door, and no man can shut it. Do not hesitate to enter in. Hitherto you have thought there were many difficulties and obstacles in your way, but indeed it is not so—Believe and live. When, in answer to your knocking, you see the door move, then arise, and tarry not.

Remember that the opening of that door will not only give you entrance, but it will ensure you *safety*. He who once enters into Christ is safe for ever. Only pass beneath that blood-besprinkled portal, only rest in the house of the Well-beloved, and you shall go no more out for ever. The life which he bestows is eternal, therefore you shall not die. The destroying angel, whenever he may take his flight, must pass you by. Only believe, and you are saved; only trust Christ with your whole heart, and soul, and strength, and salvation has come unto your house, and you have come unto the house of salvation.

But then there shall come to you more of blessing yet, for yours shall be *the adoption*. Once entered in you shall abide in the mansion of grace, no more a stranger or a guest, but like a child at home. You shall sit at the Father's table and eat and drink as a son, a heir, a joint-heir with Christ. Yours shall be the liberty, the plenty, the joy of the great house of love. At God's right hand there are pleasures for evermore, and these shall be your heritage. Yes, and more than that; when you have once entered into the house of love you shall have access to its inner chambers. Even the vestibule of God's house is a place of safety, but afterwards the Master of the house shall take you into curious rooms, and show you his treasures, and open to you his storehouses, so that you shall go from grace to grace, from knowledge to knowledge, and glory to glory, by continued progress. All this can only be understood by experience, and that experience can only be obtained by knocking.

I want to say this, and I have done. Some people think if they have begun to pray, and are a little in earnest, that this is enough. Now, praying is not an end, it is only a means. Knocking is not the ultimatum: you must enter in. If any of you are seeking, I am glad of it; if you are knocking, I am glad of it; but if you say, "I am perfectly satisfied to stand outside the door and knock," then I am grieved for you. You are foolish to the last degree, because you are resting in the means as if they were the end. You must enter by the door or else knocking will be labour in vain. Would any of you be content to visit a friend, and merely to stand for an hour or two outside of his door knocking. Did you ever say, "I do not want anything more: I shall sit down comfortably on the doorstep, and then get up and have another knock or two?" Knocking would not give you a dinner, nor do your business for you. Knocking is only the way of entrance, but if you stop at knocking it is poor work. The most earnest praying is only a way of getting to Christ: the gospel itself is, "Believe in the Lord Jesus Christ, and thou shalt be saved." Come, then, to Christ. If you find the door shut, knock. But oh, remember, the door is not really shut; it is only so in your apprehension! Heaven's gate stands open night and day. At once believe and live. Trust in the merit of Jesus Christ, and you are clothed with it: trust in the blood of Christ, and you are washed in it. Faith saves in an instant. It touches Jesus, and the healing virtue pours forth from his garment's hem: faith steps over the threshold, and the soul is safe. The Lord grant that you may enter in at once, and then it shall be our joy, and the angels' joy, and the great Father's joy, for ever and ever, to see you rescued from destruction!

PORTION OF SCRIPTURE READ BEFORE SERMON—Matthew vii.

HYMNS FROM "OUR OWN HYMN BOOK"—5, 605, 607.

SUPPOSING HIM TO HAVE BEEN IN THE COMPANY.

A Sermon

DELIVERED ON LORD'S-DAY MORNING, JUNE 3RD, 1883. BY

C. H. SPURGEON,

AT THE METROPOLITAN TABERNACLE, NEWINGTON.

"Supposing him to have been in the company."—Luke ii. 44.

ALL who were present on the occasion are sure to remember our meditation upon, "Supposing him to be the gardener." Although it was only supposition, and evidently a mistake, yet it yielded us most profitable thought. Here is another supposition, a mistake again—a mistake which yielded a good deal of sorrow to those who made it; and yet in the hands of God's Spirit it may bring forth profitable instruction to us as we think it over.

I. We will begin our discourse by saying that THIS WAS A MOST NATURAL SUPPOSITION. That the child Jesus should have been in the company returning to Nazareth was a most likely thing. When the Jews came up from their different allotments once in the year to Jerusalem, they formed family groups at their first starting, and then as they got a little on the road these groups combined and made larger bands; and as the roads approached to Jerusalem, the people gathered into great caravans: thus they went up to the House of God in company. It must have been a delightful season, especially if they sang those " Psalms of degrees " which are supposed to have been written for such pilgrims. What with prayer, and praise, and holy conversation, and with the prospect of meeting together in Jerusalem, the throne of the great King, they must have been happy bands of pilgrims. It was natural enough that, when all was over at Jerusalem, the child Jesus should return home: knowing the time when his parents would return, he would be ready to start with them, and failing to meet with them he would join the company with which he came, and so go back to Nazareth.

His parents did not expect to find him wandering alone: they looked for him in the company. Jesus was a child who loved society. He was not stoical, and thus selfishly self-contained; and he was not sullen, avoiding society. He did not affect singularity. In the highest sense he was singular, for he was "holy, harmless, undefiled, separate from sinners"; but throughout his life he never aimed at singularity either

No. 1,724.

in dress, food, speech, or behaviour. He grew up to be a man among men, mixing with them even at weddings and funerals : no man was more truly human than the man Christ Jesus. It is to be believed that as a child he was like other children in all things but sin ; even as a man he was like other men in all but evil. Jesus was not one whose company would be shunned because of his ill manners ; rather would it be courted because of the sweetness of his disposition. He would not make himself disagreeable, and then crown that disagreeableness by stealing away from those whom he had vexed. They knew the sweetness of their dear child's character and the sociableness of his disposition, and there-fore they supposed him to have been in the company. This supposition would even more readily occur to us, knowing what we know about him, which is more than his parents knew ; for we know that of old his delights were with the sons of men, we know that he often came among men in angel form before his incarnation, and that when he came into the world he came seeking men. As a man he never seemed happier than when he was in the midst of his disciples, or surrounded by publicans and sinners, or feeding famishing crowds. He was so great a lover of mankind that he loved to be "in the company." Living and working in such a city as this, with all its millions, the burden is enough to break one's heart as we consider the city's sin, its irreligion, its neglect of God. It is sweet to hope that he who loved to be "in the company" when he was here, will certainly come and bless these throngs of men. If ever a physician was wanted, it is in this vast hospital ; if ever a shepherd was needed, it is among these perishing sheep. Jesus has such a love to the sons of men, and such a wish to gather them to himself, that even now his redeeming work is done he is still ever with us. He has been lifted up, and now he draws all men to himself ; and therefore do we expect to find him in the centre of these throngs. Those who go into the dense masses of humanity may expect this same Jesus to be with them in full power to save. Rescue the perishing, and he will be in the company. It was a most natural supposition, because of the sweetness and friendliness of his temper, that they would find Jesus in the company.

They never suspected that he would be found in any wrong place. No thought ever crossed their minds that he would be found in any haunt of vice, or in any assembly of vanity, though such could have been found in Jerusalem. We *do* expect to meet our Lord amid the throng of perishing men and women, seeking and saving them ; but we know that we shall not find him among those who find pleasure in noisy laughter and lawless mirth. We never look for Jesus in the theatre or the drinking saloon : it would be profanity to suppose him there. We never look for him where a question of morals might be raised, for he is un-defiled. We expect to find him where his people meet for worship ; we look for him where honest men are labouring hard for their daily bread, or where they lie suffering his Father's will ; but we never dream of his being found where the world, the flesh, and the devil hold supreme control. Let his example be followed by us : let us never go where our Master would not have gone. There are some places where we cannot suppose him to have been ; in those places let it not be supposable that we can be. Let us go only where we can remain in fellowship with our divine Master, and where we should be happy to be found if he were suddenly to come in his kingdom. Let us judge of where we may go by enquiring, " Would Jesus have gone there?" and if he would not have gone, let our feet refuse to carry us that way.

II. But, secondly, THIS SUPPOSITION BROUGHT THEM GREAT SORROW ; from which I gather that we ought, with regard to the Lord Jesus Christ, to leave nothing as a matter of supposition. By supposing him to have been in the company, they were made to miss him, and to seek him sorrowing for three days. Why did they lose sight of him at all? Why did they not abide with him? We may not blame them, for *he* did not : but, at any rate, they fell into days and nights of trouble by supposing something about him. Do not suppose anything about Jesus at all. Do not suppose anything about his character, his doctrine, or his work ; go in for certainty on such points. I have heard of a German who evolved a camel out of his own inner consciousness ; what kind of a camel it was I do not know : but many persons evolve a Christ out of their own imaginations. Do not so; for if you do this you will make to yourselves a Christ nothing like Jesus; it will be a mere image, a false Christ, an idol Christ. No human thought could ever have invented our Saviour. We put it to all those who doubt the inspiration of the four evangelists—would they kindly write us a fifth evangel? Would they even suggest another action of Jesus which would fit into the rest and be of the same order? They cannot do it. The whole conception of Jesus is original and divine. It is not possible that the most ingenious fancy can add anything to the life of Christ which would square with that which is recorded. If you chance to read the *Prot-evangelion*, or *the Gospel of the Infancy*, which are spurious narratives of the childhood of Jesus, you will throw them into the fire and say at once, " These do not fit in with the records of the true evangelists : these stories are ludicrously unlike the child Jesus." In fact, all the books which pretend to be a part of the canon will be detected and rejected at once by the simplest reader who is thoroughly versed in the four evangelists. Do not, therefore, *suppose* anything concerning Jesus, but read the word of God and see what is revealed about him. Never clip the King's coin, but accept it as it is minted in all its purity and preciousness. Add not to the perfect word, lest plagues be added to you. What the Holy Ghost has written concerning the man Christ Jesus, the everlasting Son of God, receive humbly, but do not import suppositions into your theology. This has been the cause of the division of the church into sects : the bones of contention have not been truths revealed, but fictions imagined. I may invent one theory, and another man another, and we shall each fight for his theory. An hypothesis is set up and supported by the letter of Scripture, though not by the spirit of it ; and straightway men begin to differ, dispute, and divide. Let us lay aside all suppositions, for these things will only bring us sorrow in the end. Let us believe in the real Jesus as he is revealed in the Scriptures, and as the Holy Ghost graciously enables us to behold him in the glass of the word.

" Supposing him to have been in the company." This supposition caused them great sorrow. Again, I say, beloved, do not take anything about Jesus at haphazard and peradventure. Let this truth apply to your personal dealing with him; as, for instance, do not suppose him to be *in your hearts*. Do not suppose that because you were baptized in infancy you are therefore in Christ and Christ in you. That is a dangerous supposition. Do not say, "But I have been baptized as a professed believer, and therefore Jesus is in my heart." The inward grace is not tied to the outward sign. Water baptism does not convey the Spirit of God. Blessed are they who, having the Spirit, can use the ordinance to their profit; but do not suppose that the grace of God is tied to any outward rite. Do not say, "I have eaten at the communion table, and therefore Jesus is in my heart." You may eat and drink at his table, and yet never know him, and he may never know you. Outward ceremonies convey no grace to graceless persons. Do not take it for granted that because you are admitted into a Christian church, and are generally accepted as being a believer, that therefore you must needs be so. I dread lest any of you should think your church membership to be a certificate of salvation. It was not given to you with that view; we judged favourably of your conduct and profession, but we could not read your heart. Do not even suppose that grace must necessarily be in your souls because you have been professing Christians for a great many years, for the lapse of time will not turn falsehood into truth. It is difficult to know how long hypocrisy can be kept up, or how far a man may be self-deceived; it is even possible that he may die with his eyes blinded through the exceeding deceitfulness of sin. Do not suppose that Jesus is in your heart because you are an elder, or a deacon, or a pastor. I will not make any supposition in my own case, for woe is unto me if, after having preached to others, I myself should be a castaway! Such things have happened: Judas was one of the twelve. Men have been sweet of voice, and yet bitter of heart: they have been taught in the word of God as to the letter thereof, but they have not known the power of the everlasting Spirit, and so they have perished. Verily, I say unto you, in Christ's name, unless the Spirit of God do actually rest upon each one of us personally, it will be all in vain for us to suppose that he is in our hearts because of professions and ordinances, for the supposition may be a damning falsehood, and may lull us into a fatal slumber. How terrible to be taken out to execution with our eyes bandaged by a supposition!

Again, dear friends, do not ever *suppose* that Christ is *in our assemblies* because we meet in this house. Do not go up to a place of worship and say Jesus is sure to be there. He may not have been there for many a day. Is it not sad that out of the tens of thousands of assemblies held on this day there will be many in which Jesus will not be present; for his gospel will not be preached, or if preached, it will not be set forth in the living power of the Holy Ghost? Christ is not present where he is not honoured. All your architecture, all your millinery, all your music, all your learning, all your eloquence are of small account; Jesus may be absent when all these things are present in profusion; and then your public worship will only be the magnificent funeral of religion, but the life of God will be far away. It brings great sorrow in the long run to a church if they take it for granted that Jesus must be among them. Our question every Sunday morning ought to be, "What think ye, will *he* come to the feast?" for if he does not come to the feast it will be the mockery of a festival, but no bread will be on the table for hungry souls. We must have our Lord in our company or we will break our hearts over his absence. We desire his presence even in the smallest prayer-meeting, and in our minor gatherings when we meet to consult as to his work. If he arouses us by his Spirit, and discovers to us that he was not in our former meetings, we will seek him sorrowing, as his father and mother did.

Once more, let us not take it for granted that the Lord Jesus is necessarily with us *in our Christian labours.* Do we not too often go out to do good without special prayer, imagining that Jesus must surely be with us as a matter of course? Perhaps we thus conclude because he has been with us so long, or because we feel ourselves fully equipped for the occasion, or because we do not even think whether he is with us or not. This is perilous. If Jesus is not with us, we toil all the night and we take nothing; but if Jesus is with us, he teaches us how to cast the net, and a great multitude of fishes are taken. If Jesus be not with us, we are like Samson when his hair was shorn: he went out as at other times thinking to smite the Philistines hip and thigh, as he had done before, but as Watts puts it, he—

> "Shook his vain limbs with vast surprise,
> Made feeble fight, and lost his eyes."

So shall we be defeated if we imagine that we can now succeed without fresh divine assistance; the fact being that we ought to seek the Lord in prayer before the smallest Christian engagement, and then we may reap in it the most important result of our lives. You are going to see a poor bedridden old woman; do not attempt to comfort this king's daughter without first seeking the presence of "the Consolation of Israel." You are going to teach your Sunday-school class this afternoon; you have taken it so many times that you get your dinner and walk off to the school scarcely thinking enough about what you are doing to breathe a prayer for your Lord's help? Is this right? Can you afford to waste one single Sabbath afternoon, or one opportunity to speak for Jesus? and yet it will be wasted if he be not with you. Some of your children may be dead before next Sunday, or never come to the class again; go not even once without your Lord. Do not sit down to teach as if you had Jesus at your command, and were sure that of necessity he must succeed your endeavours. He will withdraw from us if we fall into a careless, prayerless habit. Why was he not with his mother that day? Truly he had to be about the business of his heavenly Father, but why did he permit his human mother to miss him? Was it not because she needed to be taught, as well as the rest of us, the value of his company. Perhaps, if we never missed him, we might not know how sweet he is. I can picture Mary, when she had lost the dear child, weeping floods of tears. Then she began to understand what old Simeon meant when he said, "Yea, a sword shall pierce through thine own heart also." The sword was piercing her heart even then to prepare her for three other days in which she would mourn him as dead with still bitterer grief. See how she enquired everywhere, "Have ye seen him?" She reminds me of the spouse in the Song, "Saw ye him whom my soul loveth?" I think I see her going through the streets, and saying at the close of the day, " I sought him, but I found him not." Everywhere the same question, " Saw ye him whom my soul loveth ?" but she gets no tidings of him. Peace is all unknown to her till she finds him. But, oh, how precious he was in her eyes when at last she discovered him in the temple. How careful she was of him afterwards, how happy to think that no harm had come to her dear charge! If you and I ever lose the society of Christ in our service we will go to him, and cry, " My Lord, do not leave me again. What a fool I am if thou art not my wisdom! How weak I am if thou art not my strength! How worse than silent I am if thou art not mouth to me! How heartless is all my talk, and how flat it falls upon the hearers' ears, if thou art not the spirit and the life of all my speaking!" Oh, if all our preaching and teaching were in the power of the presence of our divine Master, how different it would be!

Do, then, learn the lesson, brethren, as I desire to learn it for myself, that we must not take anything for granted about Jesus. We must make sure work concerning eternal things, for if these be allowed to slip, where are we? Grasp the truth, and know that it is the truth. Never be satisfied with " ifs," and " buts," and " I hope so," and " I trust so," but make sure of Christ! If you are not sure about the health of your body, yet be sure about your being in Christ, and so healthy in soul. If you are not sure about the solvency of your firm, if you are not sure about the deeds of your estate, if you are not sure about your marriage lines, yet at least be sure that you have Jesus within your heart. If you have any doubt to-day, give no sleep to your eyes nor slumber to your eyelids until the Holy Ghost himself hath sealed upon your spirit the certainty that Jesus is yours. Thus have I used the supposition in two ways.

III. Now for a third lesson : THE SUPPOSITION made by these two good people MAY INSTRUCT US. Let us use it at this time, and turn to " Supposing him to have been in the company."

I speak now to children who are hearing this sermon. This is for you. Jesus was about twelve years old, and you are of much the same age. Suppose he had been in the company returning to Nazareth. How would he have behaved himself? Think of Jesus as an example for yourselves. I am sure when the whole company sang a psalm that bright-eyed boy *would have been among the sweetest singers:* he would have sung most heartily the praises of God his Father. There would have been no inattention or weariness in him when God was to be praised. Among the most devout worshippers you would number the holy child. Therefore, dear children, whenever you come in among God's people, give your whole hearts to the worship: pray with us and sing with us, and endeavour to drink in the truth which is spoken, for so will you be like the holy Jesus. Let all boys and girls pray that among God's people they may behave as Jesus would have done.

I feel persuaded that Jesus would have been found in that company *listening to those who talked of holy things;* especially would he have been eager to hear explanations of what he had seen in the temple. When the conversation turned upon the Paschal lamb, how that dear child, who was also "the Lamb of God, which taketh away the sin of the world," would have listened to it! I think I see his sweet face turned towards those who spoke of the sprinkled blood. He would surely have said, "What mean ye by this ordinance?" He would have been anxious to share with the grown-up people all the solemn thoughts of the day. So whenever you come up to the house of God try and learn all that you can from all the teaching of God's word. Seek good company, and learn by it. Have a deaf ear to those who speak wickedly, but always be ready to listen to everything about your God, your Saviour, your faith, and the heaven where you hope to dwell.

I feel sure also that if he had been in the company going home *he would have been the most obliging, helpful, pleasing child* in all the company: if anybody had needed to have a burden carried, this boy of twelve would have been the first to offer, as far as his strength allowed; if any kindly deed could be done, he would be first in doing it. He grew in favour both with God and men because he laid himself out to be everybody's servant. Mary's son won the love of all around, for he was so unselfish, kind, gentle, and willing. He did all that he could to make others happy; and blessed are those boys and girls who learn this lesson well. Oh, children, you will be happy yourselves if you live to make others happy! Act thus to your parents, brothers and sisters, friends and schoolfellows, and you will in this be like Jesus.

I am sure, also, that Jesus would not have done in that company as too many boys are apt to do. *He would not have been mischievous, noisy, annoying, and disobedient;* but he would have been a comfort and delight to all about him. No doubt but he would have been the liveliest and most cheerful boy in the whole company, but yet he would not have been rough, coarse, wilful, or cruel. There would have been no quarrelling where he was; his very presence would have bred peace amongst all the children that were with him. I should like you to think over all that Jesus would have done and would not have done, and then I should be glad to see you acting as he did. Take this little word home with you, dear children,—Ask yourselves often, *what would Jesus do?* for what Jesus would have done is the best rule for you.

And now to you elder folks, "supposing him to have been in the company," and you had been in the company, I will warrant there is not one father or mother but what *would have been willing to care for him.* Every matron here says, "I would have taken him under my wing." You say that honestly, do you not? You mean it, I am sure. Well, you have an opportunity of proving that you are sincere; for Jesus is still in our company. You can find him in the form of the poor. If you would have watched over *him,* relieve their wants; do it to the least of these, and you have done it unto him. You can find Jesus in the form of the sick; visit them. I wish more of God's people would addict themselves to calling upon the sick, visiting them in their loneliness, and cheering them in their needs. As you say you would have taken care of Jesus, prove it at once by remembering his words, "I was sick, and ye visited me." If you would have taken care of Jesus, you can show it by caring for the young, for every young child comes to us under the guardian care of him who said, "Suffer the little children to come unto me, and forbid them not." You that spend your leisure in seeking to bless the young are proving that, if you had been in that company, you would have taken care of the child Jesus. Above all, consider the orphans; for, had he been in that company, he would have been practically an orphan, for he would have lost for a while both father and mother. Many among you have such fond maternal hearts that you would have said, "I must look after that bright, beautiful boy who is now without parents. Evidently he has lost them. Come here, child, come here!" You would have felt a joy to have kissed him, and folded him to your bosom. Prove it by looking after orphan children wherever they are, and let each represent to you the Jesus of that day as he would have been had his parents' supposition been correct. Let us see that the love you feel to Jesus when you read your Bibles is not mere emotion or sentiment, but that practical principle lies at the back of it, and this day affects your life and conduct. So far have we gone, and I hope not altogether without profit. May the Spirit of God help us yet further.

IV. But now I change the line of our thought altogether for a little while. Forget the child Jesus now, and let me use the words concerning Jesus in the fulness of his power. SUPPOSING HIM TO BE IN OUR COMPANY IN ALL HIS GRACIOUS INFLUENCE, what then? Then, brethren, first, *how happy* will such company be! For with Christ known to be in their company saints cannot but be glad. You may have seen a picture representing certain of the martyrs sitting in prison together. They are to be burned by-and-by, and they are comforting each other. Now, supposing him to have been in their company, as I doubt not he was, I could wish to have been there even at the price of sharing their burning —would not you? Or see, a few poor people met together in a cottage talking about Jesus, as people seldom do now; Jesus is there, and their hearts are burning within them! How favoured they are! If their hearts might otherwise have been sad, yet supposing him to be in the company, how restful all the mourners become; how light every burden grows, how every aching heart rejoices, for in his presence there is fulness of joy. Get but Christ into your family circle and it is a ring of delight.

Supposing Jesus to be in the company next *how united* his people will all become! Whenever Christian people fall out, it is because Jesus is not in the company. Whenever there is a lack of love, whenever there is a lack of forbearance, when people fall to fault-finding and quarrelling one with the other, my heart says to me, "Supposing him to have been in the company, they would not have acted so." They would have looked at *him*, and straightway have forgiven one another. Nay, they would hardly have had need to forgive, for they would neither have given nor taken offence, but their hearts would have flowed together in one common stream. The sheep are scattered everywhere upon the hills till the shepherd comes, but they know his voice, and they gather to his person. Jesus is the centre and the source of unity, and when we have him reigning in his full glory in the midst of the church divisions and schisms will cease to be.

"Supposing him to have been in the company," how *holy* they would all grow. Sin dies as Jesus looks upon it, and men's wayward passions yield to his sweet sway. How *devout* would all hearts be "supposing him to be in the company!" What prayer there is, and what praise! There is no hurrying over morning devotion, no falling asleep at the bedside at night when Jesus is in our company. Then our heart is praying all day long, and we delight to pray together for his coming and his kingdom.

How *teachable* we are, too, when Jesus is in the company, opening the Scriptures and opening our hearts; and what sweet *communion* we enjoy. How souls go out to his soul, and hearts to his heart, and how are we knit together in the one Christ! How happy, how united, how holy is the company supposing Jesus to be in it.

When Jesus is in the company how *lively* they all are. Why, in these warm mornings some seem half inclined to fall asleep, even in the house of prayer—"The spirit truly is willing, but the flesh is weak." But when Jesus is in the company the spirit triumphs over the flesh, and we feel full of life, and power, and energy in the divine service. When our hearts burn within us because of his words our bodies cannot freeze. When the soul is quickened by his presence, then the whole man is aroused. As when the sun rises his light wakes thousands of sleepers, though no voice is heard, so the smiles of Jesus arouse a sleeping church, and stir it to zeal and energy.

If Jesus be in the company, how *earnest* we grow! How zealous for his glory! How intent to win souls! I am afraid it is because Jesus is not in the company that we allow many sinners to go by us without a warning, and we neglect fine opportunities for serving our Lord. You have heard of holy Mr. Payson, the American divine, a man who walked with God in his ministry. He was out one day with a brother minister who had to make a call at a lady's house, and Payson went in with him. The lady pressed them both to stay to tea. She was not a Christian woman, and Payson had other business, and therefore he demurred; but as she pressed him very earnestly he sat down, and invoked the divine blessing, which he did in terms so sweet and full of holy unction that he impressed everybody. The lady waited upon him with great attention, and when he rose up to go he said to her, "Madam, I thank you much for your great kindness to me; but how do you treat my Master?" A work of grace was wrought in that lady by the question; she was brought to Jesus; she opened her house for preaching, and a revival followed. Now, if Jesus had not been with Payson, what had become of that woman? I fear that we go in and out among dying men and women, and we let them perish—yes, we let them be damned without an effort for their salvation, and all because we have not obeyed the voice which speaks to us as it did to Abraham, "I am God Almighty, walk before me, and be thou perfect." We shall never be perfected as the servants of God except we walk in his conscious presence; but if we walk before him, and he is with us, then shall we be earnest in the winning of souls.

I am sure, dear friends, that if Jesus be in the company then we shall be *confident*, and all doubts will vanish. How firmly shall we believe because we are living in fellowship with "the Truth"! How *safely* we shall be guarded against temptation, even as the sheep are safe from the wolf when the shepherd is near! What blessed, heavenly lives shall we lead! Surely, it will be small change for us to rise from earth to heaven if Jesus be always in the company, in the family, and in the business; in our labours and recreations, in our joys and sorrows.

V. Lastly, I want to dwell, for just a minute, by way of touching the conscience, upon the reflection that JESUS HAS BEEN IN THE COMPANY, whether we have seen him or not. I want you now to look back upon what he has seen in your company, supposing him to have been there, when you were disputing the other night. Yes, a point of doctrine had come up, and you differed over it. Did you not wax very warm, my brother, even so as to grow red in the face? Did you not go away from that friend with whom you disputed almost hating him? You know you did. Supposing Jesus to have been in the company, he did not smile on that dispute. He was there, and he was grieved at the way in which you remembered his doctrine but forgot his spirit. Had you perceived his presence you would have put your argument much more sweetly, and you would have spoken, not for the sake of beating your friend in argument, but for the sake of instructing him and glorifying your Lord. You know that you did not yield a point you ought to have yielded; you knew you were wrong at the time, but your friend pushed you hard, and you said to yourself, " I will not give way, though I feel that he is right." Although I suppose that we shall differ about many points till the Lord comes, yet when differences arise they will present fair opportunities for holy charity and mutual edification, and these will gladly be seized if Jesus be in the company. When next we argue let each one say, "Jesus is in this company; therefore, while we speak up for what we believe to be true, let us do it in a loving spirit." Our arguments will not lose force by being steeped in love. Truth is never stronger than when it walks with charity.

Then, again, it may be that some little time ago certain of you were acting in such a way that no common observer could have seen any difference between you and worldlings. You were out in business, dealing with one who was trying to do his best for himself, and you were trying to do your best for yourselves. Do I blame you? Not for being prudent and circumspect; but I hope you will blame yourselves for going far beyond this. You did nothing which I may style dishonest—but did you not sail dreadfully near the wind? You stated something which I must not call a lie, but still it was not true as you meant it to be understood: was it? Business men too often aim at getting undue advantage of each other: it is "diamond cut diamond," and rather worse at times. If Christian men in all their dealings would suppose Jesus to be in the company, how it would change their manners. Think of Jesus on this side the counter along with you who sell, and on that side of the counter along with you who buy. You both need his presence, for the buyer is generally quite as intent upon cheating as the seller; he wants the goods for less than they are worth, and the seller therefore baits the hook for him. Trade is growing rotten right through, but the blame is not all on one side. When persons must have goods far below the price for which they can be produced, they must not marvel if they find that they are sold an inferior article which looks well enough, but turns out to be worthless. Oh, that you Christian people would always suppose Jesus to be in your company.   I can hardly imagine Judas cheating John with Jesus looking on ; nor Philip trading hardly with the lad who had the barley loaves.   Should not our dealings among the sons of men be such as Jesus can approve?   He is our Master and Lord; let us imitate him, and do nothing that we shall be ashamed for him to look upon.

Do not accuse me of being personal this morning, for if you do, I will plead guilty.   If the cap fits, you wear it.   The other day you were in company, and certain persons were talking profanely, or was it scepticism which they vented?   And you, as Christ's disciple, heard them, and what did you do?   Did you bear witness for the truth ?   They made a joke—it was not over clean, but you laughed !   Did you not?   But, alas, you said nothing for your Lord!   Yet he was in the company, seeing all !   You had several opportunities, but you did not put in a word for truth and holiness.   Now, supposing Jesus to have been in the company, I think he must have been sorely grieved.   Surely your Lord must have thought, " What ! all this said against me, and never a word in reply from him whom I redeemed with my own blood ! "   Was not this Peter over again in his denials of his Lord ?   You did not deny him with oaths and cursing, but the same cowardly spirit ruled you.   Oh, if you had but come out in your true colours !   You do not know what an influence you might have had for good.   If we set the Lord Jesus Christ always before us, should we not be brave to testify and quick to defend ?

Think, again, of those evenings when a few friends meet together : are they not often a waste of time ?   " Supposing him to have been in the company," as he really is, do you think the evenings should be spent as they frequently are ?   Dr. Chalmers, a truly devout man, tells us that once at a nobleman's house he spent an evening with various friends, and talked over the question of the cause and cure of pauperism—a subject most suitable for conversation.   An aged Highland chieftain among the company listened with great attention to the Doctor, for Chalmers was master of the subject.   Surely they had not spent the evening amiss : but in the night an unusual noise was heard, and a heavy groan.   The chieftain was dying.   In a few minutes he was dead, and Dr. Chalmers stood over him, the picture of distress.   " Alas," he cried, " had I known that my friend was within a few minutes of eternity I would have preached to him and to you Christ Jesus and him crucified."   With how much more reason may many Christians repent of their conversation !   How bitterly may they look back upon wasted hours !   Supposing Jesus to have been in the company, how often must he have been grieved by our frivolities !   Do you not think that it is greatly to our discredit as Christian people that we should so often meet and so seldom pray ?   The happiest evenings that Christians spend are when they talk even upon secular subjects in a gracious manner, and do not fail to rise to holier themes, and mingle prayer and thanksgiving with their talk.   Then when they retire they feel that they have spent the evening as Jesus would approve.

Did I not hear the other day of some Christian friend who was going to give up working for Christ? and of a dozen Christian friends who were going to break up, and no more go on with their holy service for Jesus ?   One was going to leave the Sunday-school in which he had been for years; another was going to allow a weak church to break up and go to pieces, for he had grown tired of working under discouragements: another said, "I have had my turn, let somebody else do the work now." Supposing Jesus to have been in the company, do you think that such observations pleased him? If Jesus were perceived among us, would any one of us turn his back in the day of battle? No, brethren, since Jesus is with us, let us serve him as long as we have any being. Recollect John Newton's speech when they told him that he was too old to preach: the venerable man exclaimed, "What, should the old African blasphemer cease to preach while there is breath in his body? Never!" Do not suffer any difficulty, or infirmity, to prevent your persevering in the service of Jesus in some form or other, and when you do feel as if you must leave the ranks, suppose him to be in the company, and march on! Forward, brethren! Jesus leads the way! Forward, for his presence is victory! God bless you, dear friends, and all this day may Jesus be in the company to make it a hallowed Sabbath to your souls. Amen.

PORTION OF SCRIPTURE READ BEFORE SERMON—Luke ii. 40—52; xxiv. 13—35.

HYMNS FROM "OUR OWN HYMN BOOK"—166, 766, 797.

Campbellism—Its History and Heresies
by Bob L. Ross $2.00.
    Deals with the controversial aspects of the doctrines and practices fostered by the Disciples of Christ and Church of Christ groups. Especially helpful in refuting erroneous teaching regarding the significance of baptism.

IMITATORS OF GOD.

A Sermon

DELIVERED ON LORD'S-DAY MORNING, JUNE 10TH, 1883, BY

C. H. SPURGEON,

AT THE METROPOLITAN TABERNACLE, NEWINGTON.

"Be ye therefore followers of God, as dear children."—Ephesians v. 1.

WE shall read the text as it should more properly be translated: " Be ye therefore imitators of God, as beloved children." Upon the word *imitate* our discourse will hinge.

The division into chapters is often most unfortunate, and in this case it causes a break in a passage which in its sense is one and indivisible. The apostle had said, " Be ye kind one to another, tenderhearted, forgiving one another, even as God for Christ's sake hath forgiven you. Be ye *therefore* imitators of God, as dear children." He has forgiven you, therefore imitate him. It is a pity to have divided the argument from the conclusion.

Here, while your minds are fresh, let me remind you that this is Hospital Sunday, and let me add that my text is an argument, and a powerful one, for helping those houses of mercy. Your Lord would have you kind one to another and tenderhearted; but how can we be kind and tenderhearted if the sick poor are not cared for ? When all the machinery and all the medical skill are waiting to relieve the suffering poor, it is a crying shame that beds in hospitals should be unused because of want of funds ; yet this is sadly the case, and several of those grand institutions are running into debt. We may ourselves have no surgical skill, or nursing art, but we can each give of our substance to aid those whose lives are consecrated to the Christ-like work of healing. We cannot be kind and tenderhearted unless we give according to our ability to such noble institutions as our hospitals. Preachers generally put the application at the end of a discourse, but on these warm days you are apt to grow tired, and therefore I put the application at the beginning, that you may not give faintly and scantily when the sermon is over. All sorts of religionists are contributing to the common fund, and we must not be lacking. When the box comes round, " be ye imitators of God, as dear children," in the largeness of your liberality and the freeness of your gifts.

The apostle urges us to give and forgive. If ye be imitators of God, give, for he is always giving. Give, for if he were not to give, our lives

No. 1,725.

would end; give, for he giveth unto all men liberally and upbraideth not, and every good gift and every perfect gift is from above. Be ye imitators of God, the constant, generous Giver, who spared not his own Son. Thanks be to his name for that unspeakable gift! Then comes that which to most men is a harder task, but which to a Christian man is a delight—I mean to forgive. God for Christ's sake hath forgiven us; he has blotted out our transgressions like a cloud, and cast our sins into the depth of the sea, plunging them into oblivion; therefore, let us forgive most freely all that have done us wrong, so that when we bow our knee we may say without hypocrisy, " Forgive us our trespasses as we forgive them that trespass against us." Let giving and forgiving be two prominent features of our lives as Christians—giving to the needy and forgiving the guilty; giving to such as ask of us, and forgiving such as offend us. By these two things let us show that we walk in love as Christ also hath loved us. He has given himself for us, and through his precious blood we are forgiven our iniquities; let us, therefore, blend giving and forgiving into one God-like life, imitating our God. This is our Father's commandment, let it be our delight.

I. With this as a preface, let us now come closely to the text, and let us CONSIDER THE PRECEPT here laid down—" Be ye imitators of God, as dear children."

I note upon this precept, first, that *it calls us to practical duty*. Many precepts of the word of God are thought by men of the world to be unpractical, but even in those instances they are in error, for the result and outcome of such precepts produces the practical holiness which all profess to desire. In this instance there can be no cavil at the too spiritual, sentimental, or speculative character of the text; there can be no question as to the eminently practical character of the exhortation —" Be ye imitators of God, as dear children," for it points to action, continued action of the best kind. " Be ye imitators "—that is, do not only meditate upon God and think that you have done enough, but go on to copy what you study. Meditation is a happy, holy, profitable engagement, and it will instruct you, strengthen you, comfort you, inspire your heart, and make your soul steadfast; but you may not stop at meditation, you must go on to imitation of the character of God. Let your spiritual life not only bud and blossom in devout thought, but let it bring forth fruit in holy act. Be not satisfied with feeding the soul by meditation, but rise up from the banquet and use the strength which you have gained. Sitting at the feet of Jesus must be succeeded by following in the footsteps of Jesus.

Neither does the text say to us, " Be ye admirers of God." This we ought to be, and shall be if we are true Christians. The pure in heart who alone can truly see God are filled with a reverent admiration of him. With the angels, every gracious heart exclaims, " Holy, holy, holy, Lord God of hosts." " There is none holy as the Lord " (Sam. ii. 2). When the best of men are compared with the Lord their holiness is not to be mentioned. " Who is like unto thee, O God, glorious in holiness?" But we cannot rest satisfied with rendering such admiration: we must prove that we do really admire by closely copying. The world's proverb is that " imitation is the sincerest form of flattery "; I shall alter it, and adapt it to a higher use. Imitation of God is the sincerest form of admiring him; neither can we believe that you know God, and are at all charmed with his holiness, unless you endeavour, as he shall help you, to imitate him as dear children.

Neither does the text even stay at adoration, though that is a sublime height. Adoration springs out of meditation and admiration, and is a very high and noble exercise of the mind. Perhaps we rise to the highest possible service of God on earth when we are adoring him: this is the engagement of saints and angels before his throne, and never are we nearer heaven than when we follow the same occupation here below. Beloved, let your whole lives be adoration. Not only on Sabbaths, and at certain hours, and in your assemblies, but everywhere adore by good works—a manner of worship which is as real and acceptable as the most reverent public service. Remember that "to obey is better than sacrifice,"—holy living outshines all other solemnities. To love is to adore; to obey is to praise; to act is to worship. If ye are imitators of God as dear children your adoration will be proved to be sincere. Worship unattended by imitation is feigned; true adoration dwelleth not in words only, but as it comes from the heart so it affects the entire nature and shows itself in the daily behaviour. Let us spread our adoration over all the day, till from the moment when we open our eyes till we close them again at night, we shall be practically worshipping the Lord by reverencing his law, delighting in his commandments, and imitating his character. It is clear that the precept before us is eminently practical. You who boast in being such practical men give heed to this !

Next, *this precept treats us as children*, treats us as what we are; and if we are lowly in heart we shall be thankful that it is worded as it is. Some men are very high and mighty; measured by their own rod they are great men, and hence they must be original, and strike out a path for themselves. You are not commanded to do anything of the kind : the path is laid down for you—" Be ye imitators." This is a similar doctrine to that which we teach to boys at school. You, my boy, are not to invent a system of writing; yours is a much easier task, keep to your copy, imitate every letter, ay, every turn and twist of your master's hand. Scholars can only learn by imitation, and we are all scholars. It may be something to aspire to be the head of a school of painting; but the first thing for the young artist to do is to copy. He who cannot copy cannot originate ; depend upon that. I have heard great outcries about young preachers imitating, but I would suggest that, in their early efforts, this is not blameworthy. What more natural than that Timothy should at first be much influenced by Paul's manner of speech ? How could a man become an artist if he did not attach himself to some school of painting, and sit under a certain master ? He may be of the French school, or the Italian school, or the Flemish school, but he must begin as a follower even if he grows up to be a leader. When he has been well trained, and has done much work, he may outgrow his master and become an original, but he must begin as a careful copyist. Here you are invited to become imitators ; but the Master is such an one that you will never be able to learn all that he can teach, and so strike out a better path. Though you be immortal, yet throughout eternity you will never advance beyond your model; for it is written, " Be ye imitators of God." Listen to me, ye aspiring minds: if ye must needs be original, the most wonderful originality in this world would be for a man's character to be a precise copy of the character of God: in him there would be novelty indeed, for he would be like him whose name is is called " Wonderful." When our Lord Jesus exhibited on earth the character of God, his life was so original that the world knew him not; they were puzzled and amazed at the sight of One who was so like unto the Father. His life struck men as being the most singular thing they had ever seen; and if we are close copyists of God our characters will also stand out in relief, and we shall each one be "a wonder unto many." You see it is a humbling exhortation which only men of child-like spirit are likely to regard. Wisely does the Scripture address it only to such—" Be ye therefore imitators of God, as dear children": if you are not his children you cannot imitate him, and you will not even desire to do so.

Observe next, that while it thus humbles us, *this precept ennobles us;* for what a grand thing it is to be imitators of God! It is an honour to be the lowliest follower of such a leader. Time has been when men gloried in studying Homer, and their lives were trained to heroism by his martial verse. Alexander carried the Iliad about with him in a casket studded with jewels, and his military life greatly sprung out of his imitation of the warriors of Greece and Troy. Ours is a nobler ambition by far than that which delights in battles; we desire to imitate the God of peace, whose name is love. In after ages, when men began to be a less savage race, and contests of thought were carried on by the more educated class of minds, thousands of men gloried in being disciples of the mighty Stagyrite, the renowned Aristotle. He reigned supreme over the thought of men for centuries, and students slavishly followed him till a greater arose, and set free the human mind by a more true philosophy. To this day, however, our cultured men remain copyists, and you can see a fashion in philosophy as well as in clothes. Some of these imitations are so childish as to be deplorable. It is no honour to imitate a poor example. But, oh, beloved, he who seeks to imitate his God has a noble enterprise before him: he shall rise as on eagle's wings. We are copying infinite goodness; we seek after moral perfection. We are to be "blameless and harmless, the sons of God without rebuke"; but as God is infinitely more than that, so are we to rise above mere innocence into actual holiness. To refrain from evil is not enough, we must be filled with all goodness by the Spirit of God. Is not this a mark worth aiming at? Judge ye what that grace must be which is to raise us to this height! O angels, what happier task could be laid before *you?* What higher ambition can *you* know? God's only-begotten Son, who is this day Lord of all, weareth his Father's image in his glory, even as on earth he was such a copy of God that he could truly say, "he that hath seen me hath seen the Father." "I do always," said he, "the things that please him." The perfect Son of God is as his Father in holiness. You see your calling, brethren; to a high place in the rank of intelligences you are bidden to ascend by God himself. In this respect take your seats in the highest room. Imitate, but note well that ye do not select an imperfect example: " Be ye imitators of God, as dear children."

While it ennobles us, *this precept tests us*—tests us in many points.
" Be ye imitators of God;" this tests our knowledge. A man cannot
imitate that which he has never seen. He who does not know God
cannot possibly imitate him. Do you know God, my hearer? Have
you turned unto him with repentance? Have you ever spoken with him
in prayer? Have you had fellowship with him in Christ? Can you
say, " I have set the Lord always before me"? You cannot possibly
follow a copy except you fix your eye upon that copy, and have some
intelligent knowledge of what it is. We must have a spiritual idea of
God or we cannot imitate him; hence the need of the Holy Ghost.
How can we know the Lord unless the Spirit reveal him in us?

What is more, this precept tests our love. If we love God, love will
constrain us to imitate him; but we shall not do so from any other
force. We readily grow somewhat like that which we love. In married
life persons who have truly loved, though they may begin with great
dissimilarity, will gradually be conformed to one another in the process
of years. Likeness is the natural product of love; and so if we love
God truly we shall by very force of that love through his blessed Spirit
grow more and more like unto him. If we do not love the Lord we
shall not follow him, but if we truly love him we shall cry with David,
" My soul followeth hard after thee; thy right hand upholdeth me."

Our text does even more than this: it tests our sincerity. If a man
is not really a Christian he will take no care about his life ; but in the
matter of close copying a man must be careful; a watchful care is implied
in the idea of imitation. You cannot copy a document without being
intent to read and mark each word. If I sit down to write an article
out of my own mind, I have nothing to do but to make my own track,
and there is my work, such as it is: but if I have to copy from a book,
then I must needs look to each line, and I must read it over attentively,
for otherwise I may misrepresent the writer whose language I transcribe.
In copying from nature how careful the artist has to be at every touch,
or he will fail in his picture. If a sculptor is producing a replica of an
ancient statue, he must keep his eyes open and follow every line and
mark. My friend, you cannot imitate God if you are one of that sort of
Christians who are habitually in a condition between sleeping and waking,
with one eye a little open and the other closed. Such men live a slovenly
life, and attempt a sort of happy-go-lucky religion, which may be right or
which may be wrong, but its character they cannot tell, for they run with
their neighbours, and never examine for themselves. Such people live
at random, and never take a day's life at night and examine it to see
its faults ; thus sin grows upon them like weeds in a sluggard's garden.
Such persons, playing at hit or miss with holiness, are sure to come short
of it ; but he that is in earnest will give his prayerful thought and anxious
desire to it, that he may become in very deed a successful imitator of
God. He will also call in the aid of the Holy Spirit, and thus be led
into holiness.

Moreover, the precept tests us as to our spirit whether it be of the
law or of the gospel. " Be ye imitators of God, as dear children" :
not as slaves might imitate their master—unwillingly, dreading the
crack of his whip; but loving, willing imitators, such as children are.
You do not urge your children to imitate you; they do this even in

their games. See how the boy rides his wooden horse, and the girl
imitates her nurse.   You see the minister's little boy trying to preach
like his father; and you all remember the picture of the tiny girl with
a Bible in front of her and an ancient pair of spectacles upon her nose,
saying, "Now I'm grandmamma." They copy us by force of nature:
they cannot help it. Such will be the holiness of the genuine Christian.
He is born from above, and hence he lives above. His imitation of God
springs out of his relationship to God. Holiness must be spontaneous,
or it is spurious. We cannot be driven to holiness like a bullock
to his ploughing; we must delight in the law of God after the
inward man. "Be ye imitators of God, as dear children," because you
do not wish for anything better than to be like your Father, and have
no ambition in the world that approaches your aspiration to be holy even
as God is holy, according to that word, "Be ye perfect even as your
Father which is in heaven is perfect." Have you that filial spirit?
Have you a burning love to holiness? or is sin your delight, and God's
service a weariness? Where your pleasure is there your heart is. If
you love evil you are not the children of God at all, and cannot imitate
him nor render to him any acceptable service whatever. The Lord
make us to be imitators of him, even as children from a natural bent
copy their parents.

While it tests us, *this precept greatly aids us.* It is a fine thing for a
man to know what he has to do, for then he is led in a plain path because
of his enemies. What a help it is to have a clear chart, and a true
compass! We have only to ask,—"What would our heavenly Father
do in such a case?" and our course is clear. As far as we are capable
of imitating the Lord our pathway is plain. We cannot imitate God in
his power, or omnipresence, or omniscience; certain of his attributes are
incommunicable, and of them we may say—they are high and we cannot
attain to them: but these are not intended in the precept. Creatures
cannot imitate their Creator in his divine attributes, but children
may copy their Father in his moral attributes. By the aid of his divine
Spirit we can copy our God in his justice, righteousness, holiness, purity,
truth, and faithfulness. We can be tenderhearted, kind, forbearing,
merciful, forgiving; in a word, we may walk in love as Christ also hath
loved us. To know what to do is a great aid to a holy life. This puts
us into the light, while the poor heathen gropes in darkness, for his false
gods are monsters of vice which he may not dream of imitating.

Another blessing is that it backs us up in our position; for if we do
a thing because we are imitating God, if any raise an objection it does
not trouble us, much less are we confounded. We did not expect when
we commenced a holy life that everybody would applaud us, but we
reckoned that they would criticize us; and so, when their censure comes,
we are supported by the consideration that those who blame the imitation find fault with the copy,—if, indeed, the imitation be well done. He
who follows God minds not what the godless think of his way of life. A
clear conscience is our portion when we have in all things endeavoured
to please God.

I will leave my first head when I have made one more observation:
this precept is greatly for our usefulness—"Be ye imitators of God, as
dear children." I do not know of anything which would make us so

useful to our fellowmen as this would do. What are we sent into the world for? Is it not that we may keep men in mind of God, whom they are most anxious to forget? If we are imitators of God, as dear children, they will be compelled to recollect that there is a God, for they will see his character reflected in ours. I have heard of an atheist who said he could get over every argument except the example of his godly mother: he could never answer that. A genuinely holy Christian is a beam of God's glory and a testimony to the being and the goodness of God. Men cannot forget that there is a God so long as they see his servants among them, dressed in the livery of holiness. We ought not only to be reminders of the careless, but teachers of the ignorant by our walk and conversation. When they look us up and down, and see how we live, they ought to be learning somewhat of God. Holy men are the world's Bibles: they read not the Testament, but they read our testimony.

Brethren, a close imitation of God would make our religion honourable. The ungodly might still hate it, but they could not sneer at it; nay, the more candid among unbelievers, perceiving our holiness to be the result of our faith, would say nothing against it. The name of Christ would not be so evil spoken of if our lives were not so faulty. Holiness is true preaching, and preaching of the most successful kind. What a support it is to the preacher when he has a people around him who are daily witnessing for God at home and in business. If the pastor can turn to his church and say, "See, here, what the doctrines of grace can do! See in the lives of our church-members what the Spirit of God can produce"; then he will have an unanswerable argument wherewith to silence gainsayers. Doth not the Lord say, "Ye are my witnesses?" Are we not detained in this world on purpose that we may bear testimony to our Lord? How can we bear forcible witness for him unless our lives are pure? An unclean professor is a fountain of scepticism, and a hindrance to the gospel. To be useful we must be holy. If we would bless men as God blesses them, we must live as God lives. Therefore, "Be ye imitators of God, as dear children." Thus much upon the precept.

II. Secondly, I invite you, dear friends, as we are helped of God's Spirit to WEIGH THE ARGUMENT. The argument is this, "Be ye imitators of God, *as dear children.*"

First, *as children.* It is the natural tendency of children to imitate their parents: yet there are exceptions, for some children are the opposite of their fathers, perhaps displaying the vices of a remoter ancestor. Absolom did not imitate David, nor was Rehoboam a repetition of Solomon. In the case of God's children it is a necessity that they should be like their Father; for it is a rule in spirituals that like begets its like. Those who live wickedly are the children of the Wicked One: no proof is wanted, you may take it for granted: life is the evidence of nature. Those who live godly and righteously in Christ Jesus, believing in him, are God's children; and though the godly sin, yet they do not love sin, nor remain without repenting of it. Holiness of life is the proof of regeneration, neither can we accept any other. "By their fruits ye shall know them," is a rule of universal application. God's children *must* be like him. With all their faults and failings there must be about their lives as a whole a likeness to God. The copy may be blurred, but it is a copy. I say to any man here who bears the name of Christian and professes to be a child of God, either be like your Father or give up your name. You remember the old classic story of a soldier in Alexander's army whose name was Alexander, but when the battle was raging he trembled. Then Alexander said to him, "How canst thou bear the name of Alexander? Drop thy cowardice, or drop thy name." So say I to those who are unholy, unclean, impure, unkind, ungracious: be like God, or cease to bear the name of a child of God. What need is there that thou shouldest aggravate thy sin by pretending to a character which thou dost not possess! Be like Christ, or be not called a Christian. Do not play the Judas unless thou hast a mind to be a second "son of perdition."

The argument, then, is that if we are children we should imitate our Father; but it is also said "as *dear* children." Read it as "*children beloved.*" Is not this a tender but mighty argument? How greatly has God loved us in that he permits us to be his children at all. "Behold, what manner of love the Father hath bestowed upon us, that we should be called the children of God." A "behold" is placed there, as if it were a thing of wonder. Do you not wonder at it in your own case that you should be called a child of God? Behold the love which chose you when you were dead in trespasses and sins, and quickened you into the life of God! Do you not remember the text—"As many as received him, to them gave he power to become the sons of God, even to them that believe on his name"? What love was that which revealed itself in your new birth and your adoption, giving you thus the nature and the status of a child of God! Furthermore, since you have been a child, was there ever such kindness received by a child from a father as you have received? Behold, he dealeth with you as with sons. You could not wish for God to improve upon his dealings with you, since he acts towards you as he uses to do unto those that love his name. Behold how he has borne with your ill manners! How he has put up with your mistakes and your forgettings! how he has cared for you in all your cares, helped you in all your difficulties, and pardoned you in all your sins! I do not know what *you* have to say, my brother, but this I can say, I am filled with admiration at the love of God to myself. I have been a child greatly beloved of his Father. His love to me is wonderful; I am a deep debtor to his grace. Are you not the same? Then imitate your Father, for the more the love of a child to his Father the more his admiration of his Father, and the stronger his desire to be like him in all things. Let it be so with you.

However, this word "*as dear children*" bears yet another meaning. Children differ. A father loves all his children, but he cannot be said in all respects to love them all alike, for some force him to love them beyond the rest. You have one dear son who lies nearest your heart. What a sweet child he is! You have got another boy;—he is your child, and you love him, and do your best with him, but he is an awkward bit of stuff. He gives you little pleasure, and you are not particularly anxious to have him about you all day long. The first child loves you with all his heart and strives to please you. How obedient he is! How content and happy! In all things he is a comfort in the house. Your heart binds its tendrils about your Joseph more closely than about the wayward boy : you do not make a favourite of him, and so excite the jealousy of the others ; yet you must own to a nearer and dearer love than usual when you think of him. You cannot help your heart clinging to him; his behaviour is such that he is the son of your right hand, and he has a tender place in your soul,—in a word, he is one of those whom the text calls, "dear children." Just so the Lord has certain *dear* children. Master Trapp says, "God hath but a few such children." I am afraid that the quaint old commentator is correct, and that few imitate the Lord as they should. Yet some of the Lord's children give themselves up wholly to him, are watchful and tenderly obedient, and walk in such closeness with him that they deserve the title of "dear children." Brethren, aim at this. Here happiness lies ; here heaven lies this side of heaven ! To be not only children, but *dear* children, is to antedate eternal bliss. Our Lord Jesus had disciples, but of some he said, "Then are ye my disciples indeed." Be such. May the Holy Spirit make you such ! Around us there are troops of third-rate Christians : oh, for more first-class believers ! We have many who appear to come into the Father's house at mealtimes to get a bit of bread, and then they are off again into the world. I counsel you in one thing to be like the elder brother, to whom his father said, "Son, thou art ever with me, and all that I have is thine." "Blessed are they that dwell in thy house." Oh, to be of David's mind: "I will dwell in the house of the Lord for ever." Be ye imitators of God, then, in so high a sense that ye become dear children, whose one thought is how to please their father, whose sorrow it is to grieve him, whose beauty it is to be like him.

III. In the third place, I desire, dear friends, to SUGGEST ENCOURAGEMENTS. Did I hear one cry, "Oh, sir, this imitation of God is beyond us. How are we to be copyists of God ?" I will encourage you by giving hints, which you can work out for yourselves.

First, *God has already made you his children.* I speak to you that are believers : you are God's sons and daughters. The greater work is done. If you are to be imitators of God, as dear children, you must first be his children : that is already accomplished. You could not have made yourselves children of God, but he has done that for you. "Beloved, now are we the sons of God." It must be a much easier thing to imitate the Father than to become a child. You might adopt a child, and call it yours, but you could not make it really your offspring, do what you might; but the Lord has "begotten us again unto a lively hope." We are "born, not of blood, nor of the will of the flesh, nor of the will of man, but of God"; and by this new birth we are renewed in his image. Hence the greater part of the task, the insurmountable hill of difficulty, is over, and that which remains is but our reasonable service. Should not the child imitate his father ? Will he not do so naturally ?

Next remember that *God has given you his nature already.* Does not Peter speak of our being "partakers of the divine nature, having escaped the corruption which is in the world through lust" ? It remains for you to let the new nature act after its own manner. A well of living water is within you, sing ye unto it, "Spring up, O well." Let the holy thing that has been born in you now occupy the throne, and subdue the body of this death. Pray God it may. It seems to me a small thing to let the new nature have scope and freedom compared with the giving of that nature. A clean heart and a right spirit have been bestowed, let these show themselves in clean lives and right feelings. The living and incorruptible seed will produce a harvest of good works, water it with your prayer and watchfulness. If anything doth hinder it, repent and do your first works.

Next, *the Lord has given you his blessed Spirit to help you.* "Likewise also the Spirit helpeth our infirmity." Never forget that. Things impossible with men are possible enough to the Spirit of God. We have the Spirit abiding in us, vitalizing our whole nature. The most beautiful harp you ever saw has no music in itself, but must be struck by the fingers of a musician ; but the Holy Spirit makes us into living harps, which from themselves pour forth a natural and spontaneous melody. Is not this marvellous ? We have not to look abroad for power to be holy, for the Spirit of God abideth in us, and worketh in us, creating in us "the spirit of power and of love and of a sound mind." Oh, to be filled with the Spirit of God! Meanwhile, it is no small help in the imitation of God to have the anointing of the Holy One, and to be instructed by him. The Holy Spirit is the Spirit of God, and hence he can teach us to imitate God ; he is also the Spirit of holiness, and none can the better promote our holiness. Be of good cheer! With such a Helper you cannot be defeated.

Again remember, dear friend, that *the Lord allows you to commune with himself.* If we had to imitate a man, and yet could not see him, we should find it hard work ; but in this case we can draw nigh unto God ; some of us can shut the closet door and be alone with God when we will, we can even walk with God all the day. What better conditions could we be under for imitating our God? Nearness to God brings likeness to God. The more you see God the more of God will be seen in you. You know the Persian story of the scented clay. One said to it, "Clay, whence hast thou thy delicious perfume ?" It answered : "I was aforetime nothing but a piece of common clay, but I lay long in the sweet society of a rose till I drank in its fragrance and became perfumed myself." Oh, if you dwell much with God in seasons of retirement, and abide with him in all the affairs of life, you will be changed into his image. As surely as the type will make its impress upon the paper, and the seal will stamp itself upon the wax, so will the Lord impress himself upon you, and stamp his image upon you if you dwell in him.

This ought also to inspire you with ardour to remember that you have to imitate God or you cannot go to heaven, for this is one of the main delights of heaven, to be like Christ because we shall see him as he is. "They are without fault before the throne of God." His name shall be in their foreheads ; that is to say, the character of God shall be most conspicuous in them. Surely that which is to be our destiny eternally should be our desire to-day. We should strive after holiness according to his working who worketh in us mightily. We must become close copyists of God that we may enjoy everlasting communion with him. May his Spirit work us to that end.

IV. Now by turning our subject a little round we shall CLOSE WITH CERTAIN INFERENCES. I have hitherto spoken only to saints, but here is an inference for seekers. "Be ye imitators of God, as dear children:" what do I infer from this? I infer that *God is ready to forgive those who have offended him.* O you that have never been pardoned, listen to this: the Lord must be ready to forgive. We are to make God our pattern, but if God were unwilling to forgive he could not be a pattern to us. We are to be ready to pass by the offences of others, therefore if God is set forth as our example he must certainly be more ready to forgive than any of us can be. O you that are covered with sin to-day, I would urge you to catch at this fact. Suppose I were to bid you imitate your earthly father in frankly and freely forgiving all who vexed him; then you might reply "Do you know my father?" If I answered "Yes," you would say, "Is he really a fair example of patience and forgiveness? for I offended him some time ago, and I have always been afraid to go to him, lest he should refuse to receive me." If I could answer, "Yes, your father is an example that you may safely follow in that respect," then you would reply, "I will go home to him and tell him that I desire his forgiveness, and am sorry to have caused him pain." O poor sinners, you do not know what a forgiving spirit the heavenly Father has. He gave his Son Jesus that he might be able to pass by our sins and yet be the righteous Judge of men. There have been good men in the world who have delighted to pass by offences. Some here present have been taught of the Lord till it has become easy and pleasurable to overlook injuries and forget wrongs; but our heavenly Father is much more kind, and with far more delight blots out the sinner's iniquities. They said of Cranmer that he was more than ready to forgive, for he always returned good for evil. It was a common saying, "Do my lord of Canterbury an ill turn, and he will be your friend as long as you live." That was fine; but my lord of Canterbury was nothing in gentleness compared with the Father of our Lord and Saviour Jesus Christ. The holy Leighton, also, was of such a gentle spirit that one day when he went out for a walk and came back he could not get into his own house, for it was locked up, and his servant had gone away for a day's fishing without leave or notice. All the good man said was, "John, next time you go fishing, please to let me know, or at least leave me the key, so that I may open the door." That was all. If even men have come up to such a degree of patience, much more will you find longsuffering in God. Oh, trembler, do believe that our Father in heaven is willing to forgive you. You backsliders, you great sinners, have right thoughts of God, and come to him at once for reconciliation. There is forgiveness with him. "He delighteth in mercy." "The Lord is good, and ready to forgive."

Christian friends, is there one among you who thinks God will not keep his promise to him. Now, listen. God is an example to us, therefore *he will surely keep his word.* He must be faithful and true, for you are bidden to copy him. If God could be false to his word we could not be exhorted to imitate him, and therefore we are sure that he is faithful and true, because we are bidden to imitate him closely. You may be sure that every word of his will shall stand fast, for he would have us righteous and upright in all our ways. "God is not unrighteous to forget your work and labour of love which ye have showed towards his name."

Another inference—only a hint at it—is, if you are told to be "imitators of God, as dear children," then you may depend upon it *the Lord is a dear Father*. The dear children of God have a dear Father. We may rest assured that he will be kind and tender to us, since he would have us loving towards himself. I know you are heavy in spirit at this time: I know you are depressed and troubled; but your Father is kind and good. Believe it if you cannot see it. If reason says that he deals somewhat harshly with you, for he chastens you, remember that this is his way with his beloved. Has he not said, "As many as I love I rebuke and chasten"? These stripes are seals of love. Chastisement is a high proof of wise affection. Your heavenly Father is much better to you than you are to him. He is dearer, and kinder, and more loving as a Father than you have been as a child to him. Rejoice in your Father though you cannot rejoice in yourself.

Lastly, when the text says, "Be ye imitators of God," it bids us keep on imitating him as long as we live: therefore I conclude that God will always be to us what he is. He will continue in his love since he makes that love the example of ours. God will persevere in bringing us home to heaven, for he teaches us to persevere, and make this a part of our likeness to himself. The Lord will not turn away his heart from us ; he will not fail nor be discouraged : having begun to make us meet for heaven he will never stay his hand till that work is done. Wherefore rest ye upon the immutable goodness of your Father, and pray for grace evermore to imitate him until ye come to see his face. May his presence be with you, and may he give you rest. Amen.

PORTION OF SCRIPTURE READ BEFORE SERMON—Ephesians v.

HYMNS FROM "OUR OWN HYMN BOOK"—136, 651, 645.

BUYING WITHOUT MONEY.

A Sermon

DELIVERED ON LORD'S-DAY MORNING, JUNE 17TH, 1883, BY

C. H. SPURGEON,

AT THE METROPOLITAN TABERNACLE, NEWINGTON.

" He that hath no money; come ye, buy, and eat."—Isaiah lv. 1.

THERE is a semicolon in our translation, but we need not take notice of it. It should not be there, since the text is the second of two parallel sentences arranged according to the method of Hebrew poetry.

> " Ho, every one that thirsteth, come ye to the waters,
> And he that hath no money, come, buy, and eat."

We have before us the figure of a merchant selling his wares, and crying like a chapman in the market, "Ho!" To attract attention he calls aloud, "Come! Come! Come!" three several times; and he adds to this the cry of "Buy! Buy!" Shall the Great King thus liken himself to a trader in the market earnest to dispose of his goods? It is even so, and I therefore call upon you to admire the mercy of the Lord.

In the fifty-third and fifty-fourth chapters this Divine Merchantman has been spreading out his wares. What treasures they are! Look to the fifty-third chapter: what see you there? Behold that pearl of great price, *the Lord Jesus Christ.* Behold him wounded for our transgressions, and bruised for our iniquities. This is so costly a treasure that heaven and earth could not match it. Where else should we find a sacrifice for sin, a justifier of many? This anointed One of God, upon whom the chastisement of our peace was laid—who would not have him to be his Saviour? Surely with such a treasure to display we ought not to cry long for buyers, for every truly wise man will exclaim, "This is what I need: a Saviour, and a great one. An atonement for sin is the one thing needful to me." To this you are invited in these words, " He that hath no money, come, buy, and eat."

In the fifty-fourth chapter the Divine Merchantman sets forth the rare possession of *his everlasting love.* Read from verse seven, " For a small moment have I forsaken thee; but with great mercies will I gather thee. In a little wrath I hid my face from thee for a moment; but with everlasting kindness will I have mercy on thee, saith the Lord thy Redeemer. For the mountains shall depart, and the hills be

No. 1,726.

removed; but my kindness shall not depart from thee, neither shall the covenant of my peace be removed, saith the Lord that hath mercy on thee." What more can be set forth to win men's hearts? First, a full atonement and now love everlasting, making a covenant confirmed by oath. Shall there be need often to cry, "Come and buy," when such celestial wares are displayed before us?

Added to this, we see a little further on the blessing of *heavenly edification.* Notice the eleventh verse:—" I will lay thy stones with fair colours, and lay thy foundations with sapphires. And I will make thy windows of agates, and thy gates of carbuncles, and all thy borders of pleasant stones." This is rare building, is it not? There should be a quick market for such an array of choice things: sapphires and agates— what would you have more? Here are all manner of precious stones, and all of these given freely! The only terms are "everything for nothing! Heaven for the asking!" All the treasures of God are freely bestowed upon the sons of men who are willing to accept them as gifts of grace.

As if this were not enough, the Lord brings out a fourth blessing, namely, *everlasting* safety by faith: "In righteousness shalt thou be established: thou shalt be far from oppression; for thou shalt not fear: and from terror; for it shall not come near thee. No weapon that is formed against thee shall prosper; and every tongue that shall rise against thee in judgment thou shalt condemn." Security is worth infinitely more than gold. To be protected by Divine wisdom from every possible harm is the portion of believers in Jesus. To be saved, and made safe for ever, is not this worth worlds? Never was there a market like the gospel market; and never were such wares spread out before the eyes of men as those which are here presented to you. I shall therefore with the more hopefulness speak to those who have not yet been buyers, and urge upon you the invitation of the text, " He that hath no money, come ye, buy, and eat."

In handling this text we shall notice, first, *the description* of the buyer, "He that hath no money"; secondly, *the selection* of this particular buyer—why is he invited beyond all others? Thirdly, *the invitation* to purchase, "Come, buy, and eat"; and fourthly, we shall add *the assurance* that this gospel market is no deception, for these things are really to be had.

I. First, then, here is A DESCRIPTION of the buyer. I believe he is here this morning. I hope he will recognise his own portrait, though it is by no means a flattering one. It is truth itself, a photograph taken by the sunlight of heaven. It is the portrait of a poor, penniless, broken-down creature reduced to the extremity of want: here it is— "He that hath no money."

Of course, by this is meant among other things the man who literally has no money. Among the Jews of our Lord's day there existed an idea that a man who had money was at a great advantage with regard to heavenly things, so that when the Lord said "How hardly shall they that have riches enter into the kingdom," they exclaimed with wonder, "Who then can be saved?" as if they thought that if the rich could not be easily saved then none could be. The word of God contains nothing to encourage such a notion. The rich man is never extolled in the Old Testament, but he is often spoken of most slightingly. It is the glory of the Messiah that "the poor have the gospel preached unto them," and it is the glory of the gospel that it is freely provided by the bounty of God for the beggar on the dunghill. Let no man's heart fail him this day because he saith "Silver and gold have I none." Having nothing, you may yet possess all things. You are at no dis-advantage in God's market because your pocket is empty : you may come penniless and bankrupt and receive the exceeding riches of his grace. But we understand the reference of the text to be mainly spiritual, and so the portrait here is that of a man who has no spiritual money, no gold of goodness, no silver of sanctity,—he it is that is invited to come and buy the wine and milk of heaven.

His fancied stock of natural innocence is spent. At first he thought himself to be pure as the newly fallen snow, forgetting the question— How can he be clean that is born of a woman? They told him that he was made "a member of Christ, a child of God, and an inheritor of the kingdom of heaven" while he was yet a babe; and thus he was led to think that he had started life's business with a respectable stock-in-trade. He knows better now; he has seen this fancied goodness melt away like the mist of the morning. He has gone, like the prodigal, into the far country, and there he has wasted his substance till not a groat remains. If he searches himself through and through he cannot find a relic of innocence ; the whole head is sick and the whole heart faint: from the sole of the foot even to the head he is all wounds, and bruises, and putrefying sores. There is no health in him. Innocence is utterly gone, if it was ever there.

He thought that he had accumulated some little savings of good works ; but *his imaginary righteousness turns out to be counterfeit.* Had he not been honest? had he not been sober? had he not attended a place of worship, and repeated forms of prayer? Did not all this make up a little fortune of righteousness? He thought so, but then he was ignorant and deluded : he knows better now, for he has found out that all his righteousness is base metal : he could not pass a penny's worth of it in the shop of his own conscience, much less in the market of heaven; he knows that it would at once be detected, and nailed to the counter. He finds that his silver is white metal of the basest sort, and that his gold is a sham : he has not the face to offer it anywhere ; yea, he is so afraid of being seized by justice as a coiner that, like a wise man, he has hidden his sham righteousness in the earth, and has run away from it. He is now more afraid of his righteousness than of his unrighteousness. He would think it just as possible for him to be saved by cursing and swearing as by the merit of his own works. His good works are in ill odour with his conscience, for he sees them to be defiled within and without with sin : a rottenness is in the bones of his righteousness, and thus he is without merit of any sort. See his poverty : his original stock is gone, and all his savings have melted away!

He is in a still worse plight, for he is also too poor to get anything : *the procuring power is gone,* for he has "no money." Now that he has come into his sober senses he would repent, but he cannot find a tender heart; he would believe, but he cannot find faith. He has no money ; that is to say, nothing wherewith he can procure those good things which are necessary unto salvation and eternal life. He sees them all before him, like many a poor man who walks the streets of London, and sees just what he wants behind the glass of the shop window; but he puts his hand into his pocket, and despairingly passes on, for he has no money. As without money nothing is to be bought in the world's mart, so is this poor man afraid that no blessing of grace can ever be his because he has no good thing to offer, no righteousness to give in exchange. If God would sell him even a pennyworth of righteousness he has not the penny to buy it with; and if the Lord would pardon all his sins for one sixpennyworth of holiness, he has not so much as that to offer—he has no money.

Moreover, *his stock with which to trade is gone.* Money makes money, and he that has a little to begin with may soon have more; but this man, having no stock to start with, cannot hope to be rich towards God in and by himself. He cannot open the smallest shop, or sell the most trifling wares, for he has no money to start with. Even the poorest will buy a few matches and hawk them about the streets, but this poor creature has "no money," and cannot even invest a twopence in goods. He has no power even to think aright, much less to act aright, so as to become pleasing to God: he is as much without strength as without merit. Not only is he without good, but he appears to himself to be without power to get good. He is a broken trader who cannot again try his fortune, for he has "no money." He is worse than a common beggar, for he does not even know how to beg—" We know not what we should pray for as we ought." He needs even to be taught how to beg. What a pass to come to!

There is your portrait, my poor friend! Do you recognise it? I hope you do. I hear you say, "Yes, that is myself. I am without money." Then to you the word of this salvation is sent—" He that hath no money, come, buy, and eat."

" No money!" Then *he cannot pay his old debts.* His sins rise up before him, but he cannot make amends for them. What a long file is needed to hold the record of his debts; it must be deep as the bottomless pit, and high as heaven. He owes ten thousand talents, and has " nothing to pay": he has not a stiver, he has no money whatever! He is reduced to bankruptcy, and cannot pay a farthing in the pound.

Moreover, *he cannot meet his present expenses.* Poor man! he must live; he must eat the bread of heaven, and he must drink of the water of life: but he has nothing with which to procure these good things. His soul hungereth, yea, even fainteth after the mercy of God, but he has no price with which to procure it. This day he would pluck his eyes out to be pleasing with God; but he has nothing to offer which the Lord could accept. He is reduced to such beggary that like the prodigal he cries, " I perish with hunger."

He cannot face the future. He hardly dares to think of it; and yet the thought of it will come in. He remembers the needs which will surround him on a dying bed, and the terrible demands of the resurrection morning when the ringing trump shall introduce him to the dread Assize, and he shall stand before his God to render his account. He knows that he cannot answer him for one sin of a thousand. He dreads the thought of the world to come! He has nothing with which to meet the demands of the eternal future. He has "no money," nothing that will pass current in the day of judgment. He is brought to the last stage of spiritual destitution ; poverty has come upon him like an armed man. This is a terrible plight to be in; yet I wish that every sinner here might be reduced to it, for when he is so reduced and brought low, grace will come in, and the tide will turn.

The only hope for a man who has "no money" must be outside himself. It is idle for him to look into his own coffers : he must look away from himself ; and his only chance in thus looking is to appeal to charity, and plead for mercy's sake. He cannot buy—it is only God's mercy that talks about his buying : he must beg, he must entreat for love's sake. This is an essential part of spiritual poverty ; and I would that every unregenerate person knew that in him there dwelleth no good thing, and that he were convinced that he must look out and look up for salvation, and that upon the ground of mercy, since he cannot expect to obtain any blessing upon the footing of justice, or as a matter of debt.

This is the man who is called to buy heaven's wine and milk. Do you want a fuller portrait of him? Look at the twenty-first verse of the fourteenth of Luke's gospel, where he that made the feast said, "Bring in hither the poor and the maimed and the halt and the blind." This man is so poor that he cannot buy bread, so maimed that he cannot run for it, so halt that he cannot stand up to receive it, and so blind that he cannot see it ; yet such a person we are to bring into the royal banquet of mercy. If you would like another photograph turn to Revelation iii. 17, 18 : "Thou knowest not that thou art wretched, and miserable, and poor, and blind, and naked." This portrait was taken by John, who had an eagle's eye, and saw deep into the inward misery of the heart. To the "wretched, and miserable, and poor, and blind, and naked," the Lord says, "I counsel thee to buy of me gold tried in the fire, that thou mayest be rich; and white raiment, that thou mayest be clothed, and that the shame of thy nakedness do not appear ; and anoint thine eyes with eyesalve, that thou mayest see." Gospel riches are sent to remove our wretchedness, and mercy to remove our misery. It is to these wretches, these blind beggars, these naked vagrants, that the gospel is sent. This day I have to present the promise of God and the exhortation of mercy to those who have failed in life, who are down at the heel, broken and crushed. Oh, you utterly lost ones, to you is there opened a door of hope. The Lord has come into the market, and he bids you buy of him without money and without price.

II. Now a minute or two upon the second point : THE SELECTION of the buyer. It is a strange choice, and it leads to a singular invitation, "He that hath no money ; come, buy, and eat." In the streets round about this Tabernacle, especially on a Saturday evening, you may note the salesmen standing before their shops, and crying out vociferously, "Buy! Buy! Buy!" No one can refuse to hear their noise ; but if they knew that a person had no money, I think they would save their breath so far as he is concerned. They want ready-money customers, and plenty of them. What would be the use of crying, "Buy! Buy!" to a man whose purse is empty? Yet these are the very persons whom the Lord selects, and to them he cries, "Come, buy, and eat." What is the reason?

Well, first, *these need mercy most.* Oh, poor souls, when the Lord Jesus looks on you he does not look at what you have, but at what you have not. He does not look at your excellences, but at your necessities. He is not looking out for man's fulness but for man's emptiness. The Lord Jesus never gave himself for our righteousness; but he "gave himself for our sins." Salvation is by grace, and it is presented to those who are lost, for they are the people whom it will suit: how should those who are not lost value salvation? I say that God selects the most poverty-stricken first because this character most needs his pitying love. The greatness of your necessity is that which gives you a first call from the God of all grace. Not merit, but demerit; not desert of reward, but desert of wrath, is the qualification for mercy.

Again, this character is chosen because *he is such an one as will exhibit in his own person the power of divine grace.* If the Lord Jesus Christ takes one that is wretched, and miserable, and poor, and blind, and naked, and if he satisfies all his necessities by being riches for his wretchedness, comfort for his misery, wealth for his poverty, eyes for his blindness, and raiment for his nakedness, then all the world will see what a great Saviour he is, and how wonderfully his salvation meets the necessities of the case. If you and I were only little sinners I do not see how Christ could be anything but a little Saviour to us; and if he only met our smaller wants, a small supply would suffice. Ah, friends, it pleased the Father that in him should all fulness dwell, and he wills that this fulness should be seen. When he takes a man whose needs are as large as the sea, whose wants are as many as the sands on the shore, whose danger is deep as the bottomless pit, and whose sin is black as Tophet's midnight; and when he makes that man into a child of God and an heir of heaven, ah, then all intelligences are amazed, and cry out, "What a Saviour is this! What precious blood is this! What a fulness this must be which satisfies such immeasurable wants!" As it is one end of Christ's work to glorify divine grace, therefore he calls first upon those who have the most need, for in them his grace will be best displayed.

Next, *the Lord Jesus delights to make evident the freeness of his grace.* Now, if those were first called who have the money of merit, it might be imagined that they had paid their way: but if those are called who have no good thing in them, it is clear that grace is free. When a poor wretch cannot do a stroke of work, or contribute a button to you, then your lodging him must be of pure charity, and nothing else. The Lord Jesus is very jealous of the freeness of his grace: he will not let a sixpence of our merit cross his hand, lest we should glory in our flesh, and think that we have made Jesus rich.

If you ask me yet again why is he that hath no money so expressly called, I would answer, because *he is the kind of man that will listen.* The man who is needy is the man that will hearken to the tidings of a full and free supply. It is the guilty man who loves to hear of pardon, it is the bond-slave whose ear is charmed with the word "redemption." If you are no sinner you will not care about a Saviour. Only real sinners rejoice in a real atonement. The Lord sends the gospel to every creature under heaven; but he knows, as we do, that the most of men will not regard it, for they fancy that they need it not: but if there is one that has no merit or claim he will listen with eagerness to the tidings of mercy for him. He that hath no money is the man for Christ's money. He that is shivering in his nakedness will rejoice to be clothed. A wretched sinner jumps at mercy like a hungry fish leaping at the bait. When a soul is empty then it longs for the fulness of Christ, but not till then. Full souls quarrel over honeycombs, they are not sweet enough for them ; but to the hungry man even every bitter thing is sweet. A man who is conscious of sin will not quibble about the way of grace, but if pardon is to be had he will have it at once : whoever may be silent, you will hear his voice crying aloud, "Thou Son of David, have mercy on me !"

Let me add that such an empty, penniless soul, when he does get mercy, *will prize it and praise it.* He that has been shut up in the dark for years values the light of the sun. He that has been a prisoner for months, how happy he is when the prison doors are opened, and he is at liberty again ! Let a man once get Christ, who has bitterly known and felt his need of him, and he will prize him beyond all things, and find his sole delight in him. The impotent man at the beautiful gate of the temple, when his ankles received strength, walked, ay, and ran, ay, and leaped. He leaped, praising God, before all the people. He could not do enough to show his delight and his gratitude. Oh, for a few leaping Christians. The Lord Jesus loves us to prize the mercy which cost him so dear. Shall he die on the tree and give us blessings to treat with contempt ? No, no. We will love him much because of his priceless gifts to us. Therefore the Well-beloved delights to invite those who manifestly have no merit, and no spiritual power, because he knows that when they taste of his love they will overflow with praise to his name for ever and ever. You have heard of the old woman who said that if ever she got to heaven the Lord Jesus Christ should never hear the last of it ; many of us are of that mind : we shall never praise the Lord sufficiently throughout eternity. If I do but once cross the golden threshold, and stand within the pearly gate, my heart, my soul, my tongue shall extol my Redeemer world without end. This shall be the one and only contention among the birds of Paradise, who shall sing the most sweetly to the praise of infinite compassion. None of us will yield the palm in that contest ; we will see which can sink lowest in sense of obligation, which can rise highest in adoring love. Singers are wanted for the celestial choirs and there are no voices so sweet as those which have known the force of spiritual hunger and thirst : these take the *alto* notes, and sing "Glory to God in the highest."

In any case, be the reason what it may, it is clear that there are special invitations issued for the royal feasts, and these are all directed to those whose need has reached the extremity of distress.

But I may not linger. How I wish that I knew how to preach ! I long with my whole heart to use great plainness of speech. I would not utter a single sentence which would seem to have the wisdom of words in it. I aim not at fine language, but only to get at poor sinners' hearts. Oh that I could bring the sinner to his Saviour. Oratory has been the curse of the Christian church ; it has hidden the cross under roses, and taken men's minds away from Christ. To strain after eloquence when preaching the gospel is a sin worthy of eternal destruction. To point the sinner to Christ must be our sole desire. Pray for me, brethren and sisters, as I go on, for I need aid from the Holy Ghost.

III. I have now in the third place to notice THE INVITATION. The man who has no money is to *come, buy, and eat.* It looks odd to tell a penniless man to come and buy, does it not? and yet what other word could be used? Come and *buy,* has a meaning of its own not to be otherwise expressed.

In buying there are three or four stages, and the first is *desiring to have* the thing which is exhibited. The man who buys has first the wish that the property in the article should be vested in himself. Will you not desire that Christ, that forgiveness, that eternal life, that salvation should become yours? Do you not long for the Lord to grant it to you? Men in the streets, as I have said before, cry " Buy! buy!" because buying means business. They are not unwilling that people should stop and look at their goods—they even ask them to walk in and see for themselves; but they aim at finding buyers and not gazers. If a man were to come into the shop and turn over all the goods, and never purchase anything, the tradesman would begin to cry, " Buy! buy!" with quite another accent; for he does not want a crowd to look at him, but he wants people to buy of him. Many of you who are here this morning have only come to hear what the preacher has to say, and to criticise his style and language; I pray you rise to something better than that. Come, and *buy!* Let us do business this morning for God, and for our own souls. Do not waste the precious market-day of the Sabbath. People come and go, and hear sermons, and read books, and all for a sort of amusement; they do not come to downright business with the Lord. See, how they select striking sentences and cull sparkling and delightful extracts, and take notes of telling anecdotes; but all this is comparatively wasting time. "Come, *buy!* Buy! Buy!" Do you mean business? Then, come and buy. Do not stand huckstering by the year together. Come to terms, and make an end of hesitation. If you have no desire you will not buy, and I shall effect no sales. Again I cry, " Come, buy, and eat." Oh that the Spirit may work in you that strong desire without which no man will ever buy! Alas! there are thousands who have a wish to understand the gospel, but because they do not care to come to serious dealings. Perhaps you have read the story of a governor of one of the American States who called at an hotel where there was a coloured waiter, who was well known to hold Calvinistic opinions, and was, therefore, made the butt for many a jest. So the Governor said to him, " Sam, you do not really believe that doctrine of election, do you?" " 'Deed I do, sah," said he. " Well, then," replied the Governor, "tell me whether I am elect or not." " Sah," said the negro, " I did not know you were a candidate, and I know nothing about a man's being elected if he has not put up for it." Now, that is common sense. It is a business-like way of answering an absurd question. Certain people who are not even candidates for heaven will yet shelter themselves behind wrong ideas of predestination—playing with the blessings of grace instead of desiring them. Have you not seen a man with a pack stand at a door trying to sell a few trinkets to a servant. He does not mind half-an-hour's talk about his goods; but when at last he finds that the maid does not mean buying, see how he shuts up his boxes, folds up his packages, and indignantly takes himself off, saying by his gestures, " I wish I had not wasted so much time over you." It is just so with earnest preachers; they grow sick at heart when they see that men will not come to business. They cry, "Who hath believed our report?" and are anxious to carry their heavenly burden to another people. Oh, dear hearers, let us not have to shake off the dust of our feet for a testimony against you! Oh, that you would hunger and thirst after Christ and his salvation, and then we should soon do a trade with you.

"*Buy*":—This means next to *agree to terms*, for there cannot be any purchasing, however much the buyer desires to buy and the seller to sell, till they agree to terms. Now, our difficulty with God's goods is this: whereas ordinarily the buyer cannot be brought *up* to the seller's price, in our case we cannot get men *down* to God's price. They *will* persist in offering something or other as a price. They talk to us thus— " I cannot be saved, for I do not see any good thing in myself. Sir, if I had a deep sense of need, then I could be saved"; or, " Sir, if I could pray better"; or, "Sir, if I had more repentance, or more love, I could then believe in Jesus." Oh, yes, if you had a price in your hand, you would pay for heaven's blessings, would you not? But then, you see, they are not presented to you upon such terms. Price is out of the question. God's terms are that there shall be no terms of purchase at all: you are to be nothing, and Jesus is to be your all in all. When you will come down to that, then take the goods, the bargain is made; eternal life is yours.

The next thing in a purchase is that, when the terms are carried out, *the buyer appropriates the goods to himself.* If I buy a thing it is mine, and I take it into my possession. You do not see a man buy a thing and then leave it behind him for the seller to do as he likes with it. In the things of God you are to appropriate the blessing to yourself. Put out the hand of faith, and say, " Here is Christ for a sinner. I am a sinner, and I take Christ to be my Saviour. Here is washing for the filthy: I am filthy, and I wash. Here is a robe of righteousness for the naked: I am naked, I take the raiment to be mine." Make Christ your own, and he has made you his own. Take the Lord by an appropriating act of faith to be yours for ever, and the bargain is struck.

But the text says a little more than that—it says, " Buy, *and eat*" as much as to say, make it yours in the most complete sense. If a man buys a loaf of bread it is his: but if he eats it, then all the lawyers in the world cannot dispute him out of it—he has it by a possession which is not only nine points of the law, but all the law. When a poor soul hath confidence enough to take Christ and to live upon him as his own, saying, " This Christ is able to save me, I take him into me and I am saved," why, the devil himself cannot unsave you. What is to divide him from Christ? There is the bath, and I wash therein and am clean: what then? Who can obliterate the fact that I have washed? The righteousness of Christ is bestowed upon me, and put on by me, who can tear off that glorious dress? Christ fed upon is ours beyond all question. No method of possession is more sure and safe than that of eating what you have bought. Feed, then, on Christ, the bread of heaven, and though you be in yourself the poorest of the poor, yet he is yours for ever and ever.

See, then, the blessed invitation, the whole of God's mercy in Christ, infinite love and boundless compassion are to be had for no price at all; they are freely given to every man who has no money with which to procure them. The height of love meets the depths of poverty and fills them up. He that has nothing is invited to have all things, for he is the person for whom they were provided in the eternal purposes of God.

IV. I conclude now by saying a few things by way of ASSURANCE, to show that this is all real and true, and no make-believe. Every needy, thirsty soul may have this day all the grace of God. Oh, may the Spirit of God make him willing, he shall have all the blessings of the covenant of grace to be his own for ever and ever! This is no sham: there is an honest offer made to everyone who is conscious of soul-poverty!

For, first, *it is not God's way to mock men.* He hath himself declared, " I said not unto the seed of Jacob, seek ye my face in vain." God has not said one thing in one place and another in another to contradict himself. He has not in the Scriptures bidden men come to him with the promise that he will not cast them out, all the while meaning of some of them that he will cast them out. No, there are no exceptions made in the promises of God to empty sinners who come to him. You must not dream of exceptions which do not exist. Jesus says " Him that cometh to me I will in no wise cast out," and this includes all who come. I am speaking to some this morning who have come across the Atlantic and are not yet saved: you may have been careless and thoughtless all your lives, but if you come to Jesus Christ this morning he will not refuse you his salvation. Many have come in from the country to-day: oh, that this may become their spiritual birthday! Come to the Lord Jesus Christ, my friend, and he will welcome you. He never did reject one, and he never will. He will not find pleasure in tantalizing you. He is too good, too true, to become a deceiver even to one poor lonely seeker. His word of promise to you is true and real: every word is full of meaning, sweeter meaning than you dream of. Grace shall be had by you at once if you will but take it " without money and without price." Men mock men, but God never deludes. We may say of him " Thy word is truth."

Note that these mercies must be really meant to be given gratis to the poor, because *God is under no necessity to sell his benefits.* He is not impoverished: he is so rich that none can add anything to his wealth. All things are his, therefore he must give freely, since it would be beneath his all-sufficiency to be chaffering for compensation, or demanding a price at a creature's hand. He means the penniless to have everything for nothing, since nothing can be imagined to be a price to him. If a poor tradesman began to give away his goods you would say, " There is some trick about this "; but when the Most High God, the possessor of heaven and earth, who has everything, freely gives to us, then there can be no design for his own advantage : his motive must be pure compassion.

There is no adequate price that we could bring to God for his mercy;

how could there be? Would it be mercy if it could be bought? Grace is without price because it is priceless. You can buy gold if you will: there is some medium of exchange for the purchase of every finite thing; but what medium of exchange could there be for the purchase of infinite blessings? Huge heaps of such things as the native Africans call money would be of no value to us, and what self-righteous men call merit is utterly despicable to God. Is there any comparison between a man's giving all his wealth and the possession of eternal glory? No comparison can be instituted between metals and spiritual joys. As you cannot bring any price, I do pray you believe that God is honest when he declares that he will give you pardon of sin and all the blessings of his grace of God without money and without price. You cannot have them otherwise; do believe that he means you to receive them by grace.

Remember that Jesus must be meant for sinners, for *if sinners had not existed there never would have been a Saviour.* When the Lord Jesus Christ set up in business to save he must have known that there was no sphere for his operations except among sinners, and hence he entered on his office with the view of saving sinners. If a doctor comes into a town, and there is nobody ill, and it is certain that nobody ever will be ill, he had better drive off somewhere else: he will do most business where there is most sickness. When Christ Jesus became a soul-physician he had his eye on the spiritually sick, and on them alone. They are the patients who make up his practice, and they only. If, then, thou art sick even unto death, put thy case into the hands of Christ, for he will heal thee.

Remember, too, that it must be true that God will give these blessings to men who have no merits, and will bestow them as gifts, because *Jesus himself is a gift.* Did anybody ever dream of buying Christ? Stand at the foot of the cross and say to yourself, " Could I ever have procured this vast display of love by any merit of mine? Could I have done anything which could have merited that the Son of God should become man, and that being found in fashion as a man he should die such a death as this for me?" Salvation must be a gift, for Jesus is a gift. Away with your sacraments, your ceremonials, your prayers, your alms, your good works, if these are made the brass pence with which you hope to buy such inestimable things as pardon, sonship, heaven! Salvation is seen to be such when it is given to those who have no money of their own.

Beside that, *Christ is all.* Men have no notion what Christ is when they talk of getting ready for Christ, or bringing something to him. What would you bring to Christ? Everything is in Christ, and therefore you cannot bring anything to him. " Oh, but," say you, " I must come with a broken heart." I tell you no, you must come *for* a broken heart. " Oh, but I must come with a sense of need." I tell you that a true sense of need is his work in you. True repentance and a sense of need spring from his grace, and you must get them from him without money and without price. "Ah, but I must *be* something." Say, rather, you must be nothing. We cannot drill this into men's brains: nay, if we were to use steam power to work upon the mind, we could not get this thought fixed in their proud hearts. They will cling to merit, they must *be* something, *feel* something, *say* something, *do* something. Out of the way with your somethings! Subside into nothingness. The Spirit of God brooded of old over chaos, so that order was clearly his work; and when the mind seems to be all chaos and darkness, then the Spirit of God is sure to work, and the Lord's voice is heard, saying, "Let there be light!" Go to the Lord Jesus just as you are, you will never be better—you may be worse; go now, just as you are, to Jesus, and buy and eat without money, means, or merit.

One thing more I would say, and that is the gospel of Jesus Christ is blessedly free from all clogging conditions, because *all supposed conditions are supplied in Christ Jesus.* We have heard of men advertising to give things away, but when you read the advertisement carefully you find that you are to pay after all : the gospel is not so, its freedom is real. Many a good thing is to be had, but when you see how it is to be obtained, you say to yourself "the conditions shut me out :" but the conditions of eternal life shut no man out who needs to be saved and wills to be saved. Over the gate of heaven is written "Come, and welcome." But you remind me that it says "Buy," and you insist upon it that therefore you must pay. Not so ; salvation is paid for already : all the paying has been done by him who opened his veins to find the only price that is current in heaven—the sin-atoning blood. If price may be spoken of—that price was all paid long before you were born Nearly nineteen hundred years ago on Calvary's cross the purchasing work was done, and Jesus bowed his head and said, "It is finished." Will you add to that which is finished ? Will you tag on your rags to the Lord's glistering cloth of gold, and add your base farthings to the infinite price which he poured forth so lavishly at the foot of the Eternal Throne ? Oh, do not so. To yoke you with Christ can never be. You and Christ together! An archangel and an emmet would make a better pair than you yoked with Christ. Nay, my friend, sink, sink, sink ; by a mighty descent sink to nothing, and let Jesus rise, rise, rise, till he fills the whole horizon of your thoughts and hopes, for then are you saved. Let us sing—

> "'Tis done! the great transaction's done;
> I am my Lord's, and he is mine :
> He drew me, and I follow'd on,
> Charm'd to confess the voice divine."

PORTION OF SCRIPTURE READ BEFORE SERMON—Isaiah lv.

HYMNS FROM "OUR OWN HYMN BOOK"—487, 496, 233.

THE VOICE FROM THE CLOUD AND THE VOICE OF THE BELOVED.

A Sermon

DELIVERED ON LORD'S-DAY MORNING, JUNE 24TH, 1883, BY

C. H. SPURGEON,

AT THE METROPOLITAN TABERNACLE, NEWINGTON.

" While he yet spake, behold, a bright cloud overshadowed them : and behold a voice out of the cloud, which said, This is my beloved Son, in whom I am well pleased ; hear ye him. And when the disciples heard it, they fell on their face, and were sore afraid. And Jesus came and touched them, and said, Arise, and be not afraid."—Matthew xvii. 5, 6, 7.

IT is exceedingly important to have clear evidences of the truth of our holy religion. Sometimes, I dare say, you have wished that God would speak out of heaven in your hearing, or that he would work some extraordinary marvel before your eyes, that you might know beyond all question the truth of the gospel of Jesus. This desire for signs and wonders is no new thing. Ah, my dear friends, we know not what we ask, nor what we desire ; for if such a voice were to come to us out of the excellent glory, we are made of the same flesh and blood as Peter, and James, and John, and it would therefore produce the same effect upon us as upon them : we should fall upon our faces, and be sore afraid. Spirituals must grow out of spirituals : saving faith can never be produced by carnal sight and hearing. The Holy Ghost can work faith in us apart from any form of miracle ; and miracle alone can never create a spiritual faith. Do we wish to receive a sign in order to confirm our belief in God ? Suppose that we had it, we should soon need to have it repeated, for unbelief dies hard. I cannot tell how often we should need to hear the voice out of the cloud ; but certainly life would soon become a misery to us, for we should be so frequently lying on our faces, so often cast into a swoon of fear, that we should be shattered, and nervous, and incapable of the ordinary duties of life. Like Israel at Sinai, we should begin to entreat that the Lord would not speak to us any more. The fact is that the voice of God, as absolute God, is too awful, too majestic, for mortal ears, and the sight of overwhelming miracles would put such a strain upon the human mind that it is better for us to be without them. It is plain from the example of Israel in the wilderness that even the lowest form of grace does not grow out of frequent miracles, for the tribes fell into every form of evil, though they lived on miracles, and even ate and drank the result thereof. Not signs

No. 1,727.

and wonders without, but a new heart within, is the grand cure for unbelief.   Christ in you is the hope of glory and the death of doubt:
anything else will fall short of your need.

According to our text, what is wanted is, not an audible voice of God to
confirm the evidences of our religion, but the touch and the voice of Christ
to make us conscious within ourselves of the power of him to whom God
bears witness.   Not external, but internal evidences are what we need.
The best evidences in the world are what we call experimental, such as
grow out of actual experience.   It is a better thing for a man to live
near to Christ, and to enjoy his presence, than it would be for him to be
overshadowed with a bright cloud, and to hear the divine Father himself speaking out of it.   The voice out of the cloud would but dismay
and distract: the voice of Christ would cheer and comfort, and at the
same time would be an equally powerful assurance to us of the divinity
of the whole matter.   Assurance is the thing which we so much desire,
and we can better obtain it by personal test than by any external witness.
Brethren, the most profitable thing for me at any rate is not so much to
study evidences or to seek them, as to enjoy the gospel itself by personal
contact with the Christ of God.   You may be told that this is the bread
of heaven, but you will not know it, however heavenly the voice, one
half so vividly as if you eat thereof and live: then shall you know when
Jesus touches you and bids you " be not afraid."   A miraculous interposition would crush as well as convince; a spiritual visitation and a
consoling word will convince as certainly, and it will comfort at the same
time.

The verses which I have selected seem to me to teach us just this—
that even the voice of God the Father would need to be supplemented
by the voice and by the touch of our Lord Jesus Christ the incarnate
Son, or else we should not be so assured as to become active witnesses
for gospel truth.   To preach Christ we must hear Christ; no other voice
will suffice unless he speak to us.

This morning I propose to treat the subject thus: first, *let us hear
the voice out of the cloud;* and then, secondly, *let us hear the voice of
Jesus.*   May the Holy Spirit sweetly enable us to hearken diligently in
each case.

I.   First: LET US HEARKEN TO THE VOICE THAT SPEAKETH OUT
OF THE CLOUD.

Observe at the outset the words, "*Behold, a bright cloud overshadowed
them.*"   When God draws near to man it is absolutely necessary that
his glory should be veiled.   No man can see his face and live.   Hence
the cloud, in this instance, and in other cases; hence that thick veil
which hung over the entrance to the most holy place; hence the need of
the incense to fill that place with smoke when the high priest once in
the year went within the veil; hence above all the need of the body
and the manhood of Christ that the Godhead may be softened to our
view.   The God shines graciously through the man, and we behold the
brightness of the Father's glory without being blinded thereby.   There
must be a cloud.   Yet it was a *bright* cloud which in this case yielded
the shadow, and not a thick darkness like that which became the canopy
of Deity at the giving of the law.   Then Mount Sinai was altogether on a
smoke, and the Lord sat enthroned amid thick darkness.   On other

occasions we read, " He made darkness his secret place; his pavilion round about him were dark waters and thick clouds of the skies"; but now on Tabor, where God bears peaceful witness to his well-beloved Son he veils himself in a brightness significant of his good pleasure towards the sons of men.

There were but three who saw this glory of the Transfiguration, and heard the Father's voice; such signs are not for unholy eyes and ears. There were sufficient to bear complete witness, for " the testimony of two men is true," and " in the mouth of two or three witnesses the whole shall be established." It is not needful that you and I therefore should see the transfigured Saviour: the fact of the transfiguration is quite as sure as if we did see it, for three men saw it of whose truthfulness we have no question. It is not needful that these ears should hear the attesting words of the divine Father, for those three apostles heard him speak, and they bore witness thereof by their honest lives and martyr deaths. We know that their witness is true, and to us to-day there is an absolute certainty of belief that the Lord God Almighty did with an audible voice declare Jesus of Nazareth to be his Son, in whom he is well pleased. The testimony of honest men is all that we can have about most things, and we are accustomed to accept it and act thereon ; in this case we may be as sure as if we had ourselves been there, and had ourselves seen and heard.

It is a very instructive fact that *the utterance of God out of the cloud was made up of words out of Scripture.* We are told, " If any man speak, let him speak as the oracles of God ; " and what honour has the Father put upon holy Scripture here! He did but utter three brief sentences, and each of them might be called a quotation. The Lord God is the master of language, for he is the creator of tongues ; he need not, therefore, confine himself to language used by prophets and seers in the volume of inspiration, and because he did so in this instance we conclude that he intended to put special honour upon the words of Scripture. The occasion was most august, yet no better words are needed by the Lord himself concerning his own Son than those recorded in former ages in the pages of Holy Writ. First the Father said, " This is my beloved Son." Turn to Psalm ii. 7, and there you read, " Thou art my Son." Then the Father said, " In whom I am well pleased." Look to Isaiah xlii. 1, and there you will read of our Lord that he is called " Mine elect, in whom my soul delighteth." This passage is quoted in Matthew xii. 18 in a rather different form—" In whom my soul is well pleased," thus showing how nearly the words agree in all respects. Then comes the last word, " Hear ye him," which is a repetition of Deuteronomy xviii. 15, where Moses saith, " The Lord thy God will raise up unto thee a Prophet from the midst of thee, of thy brethren, like unto me; unto him ye shall hearken"; or as Stephen puts it, " him shall ye hear." The words of Moses are as much imperative as prophetic, and contain the sense,—" hear him." So that this voice of the Lord utters three Bible words, and surely if the Lord speaks in the language of Scripture, how much more should his servants? We preach best when we preach *the word of God.* We may be confident in what we say when we preach the truth in the words which the Holy Ghost teacheth, and endeavour to convey the mind of the Holy Ghost in his own words.

I take it that the scripturalness of the divine witness is noteworthy, and full of instruction.

Coming to the words themselves, the Father said, "*This is my beloved Son.*" "*This.*" As if he called their attention away from Moses and Elias and said, "*This* is he of whom I speak to you. He is above the law and the prophets, he is my Son." There was a question among the Jews who the Messiah should be: they believed in the Messiah, but they did not know when he would come, nor where, nor how; and hence, when he did come, they made a mistake and missed him. Here the great Father points to Jesus of Nazareth, who is the son of Mary as to his flesh, and he says, "*This* is my beloved Son." It is a word of demonstration and distinction, by which he marks him out from all others as his own nearest and dearest one. By this also he points him out as being present there and then; not as yet to come, but as actually with them, their Master and friend. "*This* is my beloved Son." It is not a finger pointing into history, but a hand laid upon the true Messiah, who in very flesh and blood stood before them, of whom they afterwards said, "We were eyewitnesses of his majesty. For he received from God the Father honour and glory, when there came such a voice to him from the excellent glory, This is my beloved Son, in whom I am well pleased. And this voice which came from heaven we heard, when we were with him in the holy mount." In this very place, upon this Tabor, Jesus stood among them, and the Father pointed him out, saying, "*This* is my beloved Son." They could make no mistake whatever about the person: the word of the Lord so distinctly pointed him out.

While it thus pointed him out personally as being present it separated him from all others, and set him apart by himself as the sole and only one. "*This* is my beloved Son," and no one else may claim that title. Truly, other sons are the Lord's by adoption and regeneration, but none are such in the sense in which the Lord said, "*This* is my beloved Son." Beyond all others and in a special sense he is "the only begotten Son." "Unto which of the angels said he at any time, Thou art my son, this day have I begotten thee?" We do not understand, we cannot understand, the doctrine of the eternal filiation of the Son of God. I suppose it to be well-nigh profane to endeavour to look into that sublime mystery: a holy delicacy forbids; and besides, the glory is too bright: we lack the eyes which could perceive anything in such a blaze of light. This, however, we may observe: namely, that Jesus is not the Son of God so that the idea exactly tallies with sonship among men, for he is coequal and coeternal with the Father: and he is himself called "the Mighty God, the everlasting Father." He is not of fewer years than the Father, for "in the beginning was the Word." Concerning this matter we may sing,—

> "Thy generation who can tell,
> Or count the number of thy years?"

Yet doubtless sonship is the nearest approach to the great mystery which could be found among human similitudes, and the word "Son" is the nearest description that could be given in human language. Hence the Father, looking at Jesus and at none other beside him, says of him, and of him only, "This is my beloved Son." He says, "I proceeded forth and came from God." He is "the only begotten Son," which is in the bosom of the Father. Oh, dear friends, how we ought to fix our gaze upon Jesus! His is a most singular personality, the wonder of wonders, for he is Son of God as truly as he is Son of man. Verily, he is man, and we err not when we so think of him, for he both suffered and died: yet verily he is God, for he liveth for ever and ever, and upholdeth all things by the word of his power.

"This is *my Son*." Moses and Elias were his servants—Jesus alone was his *Son*. By his being thus called *Son* we are taught that Jesus is of the same nature as God—is indeed God. A man is the father of a man; a man is not the father of that which he makes with his own hands, such as a statue or a painting; but a man is the father of another who is of the same nature as himself, and the Lord Jesus Christ is of the same nature as God in all respects—a true Son. The Lord Jesus Christ is equal in nature to the Father, and therefore he counts it not robbery to be equal with God, and he receives the same honour and worship as the Father, as saith the Scripture, "that all men should honour the Son even as they honour the Father. He that honoureth not the Son honoureth not the Father which hath sent him."

A son bears the likeness of his father, and assuredly the Lord Jesus is described as "the brightness of his Father's glory and the express image of his person"; so that he said himself, "He that hath seen me hath seen the Father." "He is the image of the invisible God:" in him is the Godhead better seen than in all the works of creation.

Not only is there a likeness between them, but there is a perpetual union: "I and my Father are one." "I am in the Father," said Christ, "and the Father in me." This leads to continual communion with each other, and a participation in plans and designs. "The Son can do nothing of himself, but what he seeth the Father do: for what things soever he doeth, these also doeth the Son likewise. For the Father loveth the Son, and sheweth him all things that himself doeth." The Lord Jesus was for ever in the bosom of the Father, and he saith, "All things are delivered unto me of my Father: and no man knoweth the Son, but the Father; neither knoweth any man the Father, save the Son, and he to whomsoever the Son will reveal him." It was with the Son of God that the Father took counsel when he said, "Let us make man in our own image, after our likeness." Our Lord knows and reveals the inmost heart of the Father; yea, the being and essence of God, unknown to all besides, are with him, for he himself is "God over all, blessed for ever, Amen." Let us never, brethren, think of the Lord Jesus without the lowliest reverence of him as very God of very God, co-equal, co-eternal with the Father. While we call him Master and Lord let us take care that we render unto him the glory which is due unto his name. There must be no trifling with him, nor with the things which he speaks, for he is Lord of all, and to him every knee shall bow, and every tongue shall confess that he is Lord to the glory of God the Father.

For a minute let me dwell upon this declaration. "This is my Son." Does it not teach us the great love of God to us guilty creatures? "He spared not his own Son." You perceive the love of Abraham to God when he is ready to offer up Isaac at the Lord's bidding. Remember the words, "Take now thy son, thine only son, Isaac, whom thou lovest, and offer him for a burnt-offering." This is just what the great Father did for us; and yet we were his enemies, living in alienation and in open rebellion against him. Hear, O heavens, and wonder, O earth! he spared not his own Son, but freely delivered him up for us all! "Herein is love, not that we loved God, but that God loved us, and sent his Son to be the propitiation for our sins." What gratitude this should create! What devotion it should bring! "This is my Son." When you see Jesus on Tabor or on Calvary, you see God giving himself to us, that we might not perish, but have everlasting life.

Does the Father say, "This is my Son"? What a Saviour this must be! How confidently may you and I trust him! If the Lord Jesus Christ be no common person, but nothing less than God himself, who shall doubt his power to save? If he be God's only-begotten Son, how safely we may trust our souls' affairs in his almighty hands! He is indeed "a Saviour, and a great one!" "It pleased the Father that in him should all fulness dwell." What an Intercessor have we! So dear to him with whom he pleads, for he is his beloved Son! What a sacrifice have we that may well cover all our sin, for "he gave himself for us, an offering and a sacrifice to God, for a sweet smelling savour." However black our sin, and however deep our despair, we may readily rise out of it and say, "Verily, there is salvation here!" If the Son of God has made his own person the price of our redemption, then are we indeed redeemed, and none can hold us in bondage.

One thing more is worthy to be noted here. If the Father says, "This is my Son," observe the graciousness of our adoption! With such a Son the Lord had no need of children. He did not make us his children because he needed sons, but because we needed a father. The infinite heart of the Father was well filled by the love of the Only-begotten. There was enough in Jesus to satisfy the love of the divine Father, and yet he would not rest till he had made him "the firstborn among many brethren." Herein we ought to admire exceedingly the grace of God. "Behold what manner of love the Father hath bestowed upon us that we should be called the sons of God." When a man is childless, and desires an heir, it may be that he adopts a child to fill the vacancy which exists in his house; but the heavenly Father had no such want, for he saith, "This is my beloved Son." Our adoption is, therefore, not for his gain, but for ours: it is a matter of divine charity, arising out of the spontaneous love of God. Thanks be unto the Father evermore!

Do you remind me that I have left out one word? The Father said, "This is my *beloved* Son." I have by no means forgotten it, for though I cannot speak as I would upon that word yet it is exceedingly sweet in my ears. "This is my *beloved* Son." We none of us know how much beloved our Lord is of the Father. We love our children, we love them as our own souls, we could not measure our affection for them; but still we are finite and so are our children, and the finite to the finite yields but a finite love; but here is an Infinite Father with an Infinite Son, and he loves him infinitely. Why should he not? He is most near to him: his own Son. Why should he not? He is in all things like unto him in nature, dignity, character, and glory. Why should he not? For he in all things doth his will. Jesus said "And he that sent me is with me: the Father hath not left me alone; for I do always those things that please him." If we had such a son as God has in Jesus then we should love him indeed, for there has been nothing in the Son throughout eternity which is in the least opposed to the Father's mind. These are wonderful words of the man Christ Jesus— "Therefore doth my Father love me, because I lay down my life, that I might take it again." When Solomon speaks of wisdom, which is but another name for our Lord Jesus, he represents him as saying, "The Lord possessed me in the beginning of his way, before his works of old. I was set up from everlasting, from the beginning, or ever the earth was. When he gave to the sea his decree, that the waters should not pass his commandment: when he appointed the foundations of the earth: then I was by him, as one brought up with him: and I was daily his delight, rejoicing always before him." He has been in the bosom of the Father from of old; and when he left the bosom of the Father it was to do his Father's will and to be obedient to him even unto death. His will and his Father's will are perfectly joined together in one spirit, and therefore we cannot fathom the depths of love which are indicated in these words which came from the Father who himself is love: he, looking at his own Son, saith plainly, "This is my beloved Son." Oh that we might have grace to trust without wavering in this glorious Son of God!

Permit me now to introduce to you the second of the sentences: "*In whom I am well pleased.*" I have heard it quoted, "With whom I am well pleased." The alteration cannot be tolerated: it robs the language of half its sense. True, God is pleased with Christ, but that is not all that he says here: he is pleased *in* him, which means not only that God is eternally, infinitely pleased with Jesus Christ himself, but that God himself is reconciled and pleased as we view him in his Son. I thought this over last night till my heart seemed ready to dance for joy, for I thought—"then, however much I have displeased the Father, my Lord Jesus, who stands for me, has pleased him more than I have displeased him. Mine is finite sin, but his is infinite righteousness. If my sins have vexed the Lord God, yet Christ's righteousness has pleased him more. I cannot be more than finitely displeasing to God, but Jesus is infinitely pleasing to him; and if he stands in my room, and place, and stead, then the pleasure which the Father derives from his Son is greater than the displeasure which he has ever felt towards me." My brethren, how displeased the great God has been with men. He said that it repented him that he had made men upon the earth. That was a striking expression which is used in Genesis vi. 6: "It grieved him at his heart." He seemed to grow so weary of man's wanton wickedness that he was sorry that he ever made beings capable of so much evil. Yet he is so well content with his beloved Son, who has assumed our nature, that we read of him, "The Lord is well pleased for his righteousness' sake: he will magnify the law, and make it honourable." (Is. xlii. 21). The Lord looks down upon those who are in Christ with an intense affection, and loves them even as he loves the Son, for that is the meaning of this word, "In whom I am well pleased." All who are in Christ Jesus are pleasing to God; yea, God in Christ looks with divine satisfaction upon all those who trust his Son: he is not only pleased, but *well* pleased. If you are pleased with Jesus, God is pleased with you: if you are in the Son, then you are in the Father's good pleasure. Out of Christ there is nothing but divine displeasure for you. Concerning you who are out of Christ, it is written, "The Lord will take vengeance on his adversaries." Who can stand before his indignation? Who can abide the fierceness of his anger? He cannot look on sin without hatred. He says of sinners, "My soul loathed them, and their soul also abhorred me." There is no peace between a Christless soul and God, neither can there be. But when a poor sinner by faith enters into Christ, then such is the Father's delight in Christ's person, that he delights in all that are in him. Jesus said, "The Father himself loveth you." God is pleased with every hair of Christ's head: the meanest member of Christ's body is delightful to the Father. If I am pleased with a man, I am not angry with his foot or with any part of him. So, then, if I am a member of Christ, if I am joined unto him by a living, loving, lasting union, then I am well-pleasing unto God, because Jesus is well-pleasing to him. Indeed, the Scripture speaketh of all saints as one with Christ; they are so perfectly joined unto him that they are one body with him, and God has not hatred to some part of the body and love to another part of it. Is Christ divided? It cannot be. The Father is well pleased with the entire mystical body for the sake of Jesus Christ its head. I wish I could speak at length upon this; but I might weary you upon this close and sultry day, when your spirit truly is willing but your flesh is weak. Oh, the charm of this voice of God! Each word has a divine emphasis upon it. It is not the voice of man, but of the Eternal himself. "This is my beloved Son, in whom I am well pleased."

Consider, next, the third word, which is, "*Hear ye him*" Listen to what he says; remember it carefully; endeavour to understand it; heartily accept and believe it; confidently trust in it, and cheerfully obey it. All these precepts are wrapt up in the expression "Hear ye him"; as we could prove if there were time available. "Hear ye him": it is as if the Father said, "You need not hear Moses any longer; hear ye *him*. You need not listen to Elias any more; hear ye my Son." There are thousands of priests in the world who say, "Hear us"; but the Father says "Hear *him*." Many voices clamour for our attention: new philosophies, modern theologies, and old heresies revived, all call to us and entreat us to hearken, but the Father says, "Hear *him*." As if he said, "Hear him and none besides." Does any man claim to be a successor of Christ? The Father speaks of no succession, but bids us, "Hear *him*." If Jesus were dead and his prophetic office extinct we might hear others; but since he liveth, we hear the celestial voice rolling along the ages and distinctly crying, "Hear ye *him*." Brethren beloved, do not hear *me* as though I spake of myself, for I have no more claim upon your attention than any other man. I speak faultily, for I know but in part, and prophesy in part. So far as I speak my own mind, I speak in vanity; but if I speak the words of Christ, and the truth which the Spirit of God has revealed, then it is no longer I that speak, but

Christ himself that speaks, and then you are bound by the word from the Father, which saith, " Hear ye *him.*" Oh, to be content with hearing Christ, and letting other voices go away into the eternal silence. Is he God's Son? Then "hear him." Is he God's beloved Son? Then " hear him." Is the Father well pleased with him ? Then " hear him." Is the Father well pleased in him, and with you in him? Then " hear him." What less can you do? Ought you not to do this always, and with all your might? Peter, you need not build the tabernacles : the Father bids you hear Jesus, your Lord. It is better to hear Christ, that is, to believe his teaching and obey it, than it would be to build cathedrals for him, much more such frail tents as Peter intended. Peter, you need not cumber yourself with much serving, and play the Martha ; you will do better if you sit at his feet with Mary and *hear* him. The highest honour we can render to Christ as a prophet is to hear him, trusting him in his promises and obeying him in his precepts. Jesus came on purpose to teach, and we are in our best position for adoration when we lend him our ears and hearts, and are determined to believe what he says, and to do what he commands.

" This is my beloved Son ; hear ye him." It does seem to me as if the great Father said, " *I* have spoken to you once, with my own voice, and I see you fall upon your faces with fear ; evidently you cannot bear my immediate presence. I see your faces blanched with fright ; you lie prone upon the ground, stiff with dismay : I will speak no more directly from myself ; I have made my beloved Son your Mediator ; hear *him.*" The Psalmist David said, " The voice of the Lord is powerful ; the voice of the Lord is full of majesty. The voice of the Lord shaketh the wilderness ; the Lord shaketh the wilderness of Kadesh." Is it not gracious on his part that he should no more speak with us himself, but reveal himself by his Son, whose name is " *the Word of God*"? Remember what Israel said at Sinai to Moses, the typical mediator : " Speak thou with us and we will hear ; but let not God speak with us, lest we die." To this the Lord replied to Moses, " They have well said all that they have spoken." The Lord recognized at once the need of a mediator, and he finds us one in the person of the Well-beloved as he says, " Hear ye *him.*" It is like Pharaoh saying to those who came for corn, " Go unto Joseph." This day God saith to men, " Come not to me at the first : go to my Son. No man cometh to the Father but by Jesus Christ his Son. I will not speak with you, for you are but dust and ashes, and you would be overwhelmed by the thunder of my voice. Hear ye HIM." Blessed ordinance of that gracious One who knoweth our frame and remembereth that we are dust ! He hath spoken to us by his Son : let us incline our ear and come unto him, let us hear that our soul may live.

This links on the first part of my discourse to the second, upon which I will speak as briefly as I can, though the subject might well demand a full sermon.

II. Secondly, LET US HEAR THE VOICE OF JESUS. The Father himself has sent us to Jesus, and unto Jesus let us go.

" When the disciples heard it, they fell on their face, and were sore afraid. And Jesus came and touched them, and said, Arise, and be not afraid." Dear friends, I think you will be cured of desiring miracles, and of wishing to hear voices from God, if you well consider the effect of the Divine voice upon these favoured apostles. You could not bear the voice divine any better than they could; if, indeed, so well. I hope that you will now be content with what the Father recommends to you, namely, that you hear his beloved Son Jesus Christ our Lord. The apostles, one would have thought, needed not to have been afraid, for they were holy men; engaged in the best possible business, and in the company of their Lord who was their protector and friend; and yet such is the amazing power of the glory of God upon the human mind that they fell on their faces. So was it with Job, and Daniel, and Isaiah, and Habakkuk, and all such holy men: the presence of the Lord filled them with fear and trembling and self-abhorrence.

See how Jesus acts to his three disciples. We might have thought that they would have hastened to their Lord. Why did they not? Why did they not cry out to him, "Master, we perish"? Why did not Peter say, as he did on another occasion, "If it be thou, bid me come unto thee"? No; they are overpowered, bewildered, confounded: the glory of the Lord has laid them on their faces as dead, and a sore fright is upon them. Then the incarnate God, their Lord and yet their brother, interposes his sacred ministry. First, *he comes to them*. Wycliffe's version puts it, "He came nigh." He approached to them; for any distance is painful when a heart is afraid. Jesus came near to the affrighted three. This is the beauty of our Lord Jesus Christ, that he comes so near to us, poor troubled ones, when we are overwhelmed with the glory of God and our own sense of sin. "The man is near of kin unto us: one of our next kinsmen." God, the glorious, must ever seem to be far off as to our weakness, however near he comes to us in condescending grace. He is in heaven, and we upon earth; he is the Creator, and we are the creatures of an hour. The Lord Jesus comes so very near to us because he bears our nature, and is 'bone of our bone and flesh of our flesh. We may be familiar with him, and yet incur no censure. Little children climbed his knee, and he said, "Suffer the little children to come unto me." We feel that we may come where children are welcomed; yea, we rejoice that when we cannot come to him, our Lord Jesus comes to us, and when our weakness makes us fall upon the ground, he stoops over us to help us up. His sympathy makes him quick to draw near, and calm our troubled breasts. When a child falls, how fast the mother runs to set it on its feet again. Yet she is not more in haste than Jesus, who leaves not his own to remain long in their distress. He draws very near to his poor, fainting, swooning disciples. He will not leave them comfortless, he will come unto them. He is the same Christ at this hour as in the days of his flesh: he is still in the habit of visiting his people and manifesting himself to them as he doth not to the world. Brothers, do not ask evidence any more; do not begin searching books to find out arguments and reasons. Ask Jesus to come to you: his presence will stand in stead of all reasoning, and be better far. Communion with Christ supplies the soul with irresistible arguments as to his being, his love, his power, his Godhead. Actual nearness to him clothes the mind with a coat of mail which wards off every arrow of unbelief. Let Christ come to us, and questions and doubts are heard no more. Quibblings are nailed to his cross; insinuations fall dead at his feet. This assurance works in an infinitely better manner than if out of yon black cloud God himself were to speak to us in thunder-tones.

When Jesus came, the next thing he did was, *he touched them.* This is to me most precious: as they lie there all fainting he touches Peter, and touches James, and touches John, just as in after days we read, "He laid his right hand upon me, saying unto me, Fear not." That was his way of healing those diseased with leprosy. The blind man he touched and gave him sight, and the dead maiden was thus revived. Oh, the power of his touch! Our touch of Jesus saves us; what will not his touch of us do? We are so much made up of feeling, after all, that we want to know that the Lord really feels for us, and will enter so tenderly into our case as to touch us. That touch reassures our fainting hearts, and we know our Lord to be Emanuel, God with us. Sympathy! This is the meaning of that human touch of a hand which is nevertheless divine. Oh, how sweetly Christ has touched us by being a partaker in all that is human! He touched us everywhere: in poverty, for he had not where to lay his head: in thirst, for he sat by the well and said, "Give me to drink:" in anguish, for he was betrayed by his friend. He has touched us in depression of spirit, for he cried, "My soul is exceeding sorrowful even unto death." He is touched with a feeling of our infirmities, "for he was tempted in all points like as we are." An absolute God does not seem to touch us with a fellow-feeling : he pities us as a father pitieth his children, yet in this he is above us, and our fears prevent our reaching up to him: for tenderest sympathy in adversity a brother must be born, and Jesus is that brother. We are frail and sinful; and Jesus touches us in both respects, for he has taken our flesh and carried away our sins. He was "numbered with the transgressors," thus he touched transgressors; and he became frail even as we are, until at last he said, "I am a worm, and no man"; thus he touched our infirmities. Dear friends, nothing so cheers the heart as the divine touch of Christ, for if you have felt it you will bear witness that contact with his wondrous person is like life from the dead. Virtue comes out of Christ to us when his garment's hem and our finger meet. The contact of grace on his part and faith on our part brings into us strength, light, joy, and all else that is laid up in Jesus to meet our wants. The hand of Jesus is laid upon us, and in the strength which it gives a man might dash through hell and climb to heaven. Ezra said, "I was strengthened as the hand of the Lord my God was upon me." Touched with the almighty Sufferer's sacred sympathy, we glory in tribulation, and triumph in death. Is not this more effective evidence of the truth of the gospel and of the commission of Christ than if the Lord God should again speak out of a cloud? To feel the wondrous power of Christ strengthening our hearts, surely this is the most certain witness.

Next time you read of the Red Sea, and of God's dividing it for his people, and drowning Pharaoh in the deep waters, do not say to yourself, " I wish I had been there!" but pray God to make a way for you through your troubles, and to dry up the Red Sea of your sins, and lead you into Canaan. Pardoned sin will make you rejoice in him. It must have been a fine demonstration of God's glorious majesty when he sent a thick darkness over all the land, even darkness that might be felt. For my part, I count it a more-to-be desired demonstration of the power of God when he took away my thick darkness and brought me into his marvellous light. When he turned all the waters of Egypt into blood, so that they loathed to drink of the river, it was a sure proof that God was there ; but to my soul it was a more assuring proof when he turned my water into wine, and made my ordinary life to become like the life of those in heaven by his sovereign grace. He has raised us up together from the depths of our natural ruin, and made us sit together in the heavenly places,—is not this as great a proof of his power and Godhead as when he raised up Israel from the brick-kilns, and set his people free ? It was a sure proof of God's being in Egypt when he called for the frogs, and they came, even into the king's chambers ; but what a proof of his being with us is given to our mind when the Lord sweeps out of our soul all the frogs of fear that used to croak within us, even in the king's chambers of devotion and communion. We could not worship God for their croaking, but everywhere we were defiled and disturbed with doubts and fears, and when Jesus comes and clears them all away it is a kindlier proof and more effectual to the heart than a thousand plagues could be. So there were two actions of Christly sympathy— Jesus came near, and touched them.

But always the great thing with Jesus is his word—*he spake to them.* He is the Word, and as the Word he proves his Godhead. " Where the word of a king is, there is power." Jesus, after he had touched them, said, " Arise, be not afraid." Precious word ! " Arise, be not afraid." When the word of Jesus Christ comes with power to our discouraged souls, and we are made strong in confidence, then we are persuaded of the truth of the gospel. When we are disabled from the divine service through fear, and Jesus renews our strength by saying, " Arise," so that we are able to work again, then do we believe and are sure, " The joy of the Lord is our strength." Whenever the blessed Comforter reveals Christ to us so that we are cheered and made glad in the midst of our tribulations, then we need not ask for signs and wonders, nor for voices speaking out of the cloud : it is enough, the truth is sealed in our consciences. The voice of Christ is better far than all other manifestations, for it does not leave us swooning with fear, but sends us out to fight the battles of the Lord.

This is the sum of what I have spoken unto you. Ask not signs and wonders which God will not give ; but " Hear ye him." Listen to Jesus by faith, and your personal experience of his presence shall be to you all that you need by way of assurance. Live on Christ, live in Christ, live with Christ, and this shall be better to you than visions or bright clouds, or celestial voices, or all supposable evidences. This shall make your spirit leap and your heart rejoice, till the day break and the shadows flee away, and you see God, even the Father, face to face in glory. May the grace of our Lord Jesus Christ be with you evermore. Amen.

PORTIONS OF SCRIPTURE READ BEFORE SERMON—Matthew xvii. 1—9 ; II. Peter i. 10—21.

HYMNS FROM " OUR OWN HYMN BOOK" —251, 292, 289

Metropolitan Tabernacle Pulpit.

THE WORKS OF THE DEVIL DESTROYED.

A Sermon

DELIVERED ON LORD'S-DAY MORNING, JULY 1ST, 1883, BY

C. H. SPURGEON,

AT THE METROPOLITAN TABERNACLE, NEWINGTON.

"For this purpose the Son of God was manifested, that he might destroy the works of the devil."—1 John iii. 8.

IN this chapter John makes a sharp and clear division of mankind into two classes. He gives not even the slightest hint that there is, or ever was, or ever can be a third class; but he describes men as being the children of God or else the children of the devil, and tells us how the two classes are made manifest (see verse 10). Now, this distinction would not have been drawn by John so sharply if it had not existed; for he was a man of most loving heart and gentle spirit, and if he could somewhere or other have found a space for neutrals, or what I call "betweenites," or people who come in midway between saints and sinners, I am sure he would have done it. No one could suspect John of want of charity, and therefore as *he* was convinced that no middle position was possible, we may be quite clear upon that point, and at once dismiss every theory which is meant to flatter the undecided. At this day the world is still divided into children of God and children of the evil one. This distinction ought never to be forgotten; and yet thousands of sermons are preached in which it is quite ignored, and congregations are commonly addressed as if they were all the people of God. How shall we preach the truth if we begin by assuming a lie? Yet to assume that all our hearers are Christians is to begin with an error. Is it not highly probable that men will be built up in falsehood if the very truth which is addressed to them is put in a false way? No, my hearers, we cannot talk to you as all the people of God, for you are not; some of you are the children of the wicked one, and though it may not be pleasant to be told so, yet it is no business of ours to please you. Our duty is to preach so as to please God and benefit the souls of men, and that can only be effected by an honest enunciation of matters of fact. There is a definite and fixed line in the sight of God between the living and the dead, between those who are born again and those who abide in their fallen estate; between the spiritual and the carnal, between the believing and the unbelieving. There is a gulf fixed between the two orders of men, which, blessed be God, can be passed, but which nevertheless divides the whole race as though a vast chasm

No. 1,728.

had opened up in their midst, and set them apart from each other, separating them into two camps.

This important distinction ought to be observed in public prayer; and this is a point in which we are dissatisfied with most liturgies, because they are necessarily composed with the view of suiting both saints and sinners, and, as a necessary result, they are not suitable for either. The joyous notes of confidence which are becoming in the children of God are left out because the ungodly could not use such expressions of exultant faith; while, on the other hand, the wailing notes which are most suitable to anxious souls are put into the mouths of men who by the grace of God have long ago found their Saviour. Men walking in full fellowship with the Lord are not correctly described as "miserable sinners," neither is it theirs to pray as if they had never found pardon and life in Christ Jesus. It is impossible that public prayer should be suitable for a mixed congregation unless a portion of it is evidently for such as fear the Lord, and another portion for such as do not fear him. I suppose it would be difficult, if not impossible, to compose a liturgy for common use upon strictly truthful principles; and yet that order of public prayer which ignores the distinction between the regenerate and the unregenerate must inevitably be mischievous to the souls of men. In this matter the servant of the Lord must discern between the precious and the vile, or he cannot be as God's mouth.

If this distinction is to be thought of in preaching and in public prayer, it should be specially considered in our personal religion. We ought to know whose we are and whom we serve. We ought to know the differences which the Lord has made by grace, and whether or not he has made us to differ from the unrenewed. Every man in trade wishes to be sure of his position, whether he is prospering or not ; and surely we ought each one to know our position in that one great enterprise of life which if it finds us bankrupt at the last must leave us so for ever. It is of the utmost importance for a man to know whether he has been enlightened or abideth in darkness, whether he is the slave of sin or the Lord's free man. Each man should know that he is either saved or lost, pardoned or condemned : he may not sit down in peace in the deceitful hope that though he may not be a child of God, he is nevertheless no heir of wrath, for it cannot be; he is one thing or the other at this moment. Every one is under the wrath of God unless he has believed in Jesus, and so has become accepted in the Beloved. Two seeds there are, and only two—the seed of the woman and the seed of the serpent, and you, my friend, belong to one or other of these. John sums up the vital distinction when he writes, " He that hath the Son hath life; and he that hath not the Son hath not life. And we know that we are of God, and the whole world lieth in wickedness."

Let this stand as the preface of the sermon, for the spirit of it will run through my whole discourse.

And now I come to the words of the text itself : " For this purpose the Son of God was manifested, that he might destroy the works of the devil." We shall speak of four things : *the works of the devil; the purpose of God; the manifestation of the Son of God ;* and *the experience within ourselves* of the meaning of this text. Oh, for the aid of the Holy Spirit, that we may think aright and speak with power.

I.   First, then, let us say a little upon THE WORKS OF THE DEVIL.

This very strong expression is descriptive of *sin*; for the preceding sentence so interprets it. I will read the whole verse:—" He that committeth sin is of the devil; for the devil sinneth from the beginning. For this purpose the Son of God was manifested, that he might destroy the works of the devil,"—that is, that he might destroy *sin*.

This name for sin is first of all *a word of detestation*.   Sin is so abominable in the sight of God and of good men that its various forms are said to be " the works of the devil."   Men do not like the idea of having any connection with the devil, and yet they have a most intimate connection with him until they are made anew by the Spirit of God. When it was supposed in a superstitious age that a man had commerce with the devil he was abhorred or feared, and most properly so : he that is in league with Beelzebub has forfeited all right to honour.   Yet let every man know that if he lives in sin his actions are called by the Holy Spirit "the works of the devil."   Satan is "the spirit that now worketh in the children of disobedience."   Think of that, ye ungodly ones, the devil is at work in you, as a smith at his forge.   Is it not a shocking thought that if I am living in sin I am the bondslave of Satan, and I am doing his work for him ?   If the devil be in the heart the whole life will be more or less tainted by the presence of that arch-enemy of God and man.   Do not laugh at sin, then ; do not dare to trifle with it, for it is dangerous and deadly, because it is of the devil, from whom no good thing can ever come.   Oh, if men could but see the slime of the serpent upon their pleasurable sins, the venom of asps upon their dainty lusts, and the smoke of hell upon their proud and boastful thoughts, surely they would loathe that which they now delight in !   If sin connects us with the devil himself, let us flee from it as from a devouring lion.   The expression is a word of detestation : may it enter into our hearts and make sin horrible to us.

Next, it is *a word of distinction :* it distinguishes the course of the ungodly man from the life of the man who believes in the Lord Jesus. For he that is of God doeth the works of God—his life is the work of God, it is a life which has much that is God-like about it, and he is upheld by the power of God, the ever blessed Spirit.   But the ungodly man's life is very different—he lives for himself, he seeks his own pleasure, he hates all that oppose him, he is up in arms against the Lord, and his truth, and all that is pure and good : his spirit is not the spirit of God, but of the evil one.   There is a radical distinction between the gracious and the graceless, and this comes out in their works : the one works the works of God and the other the works of the devil.   I know that this doctrine is not pleasant, but it is true, and therefore it must be plainly stated.   I hear one say, " Look at me ; am I a child of the devil ?   I may not be much of a saint ; but I am no worse than many of your professing Christians."   I answer, that such may be the case ; for professing Christians are sometimes horrible hypocrites, but what has that to do with you ?   Ah, my friend, their perishing will not help your salvation.   If you are not trusting in Christ and living under the power of his love, you may be as good as a hypocrite, or even better, and yet you may be widely different from a real Christian.   If you have not the life of God in you, you cannot do the works of God.   The mineral cannot rise into the vegetable of itself, it would require another touch from the creative hand ; the vegetable cannot rise into the animal unless the Creator shall work a miracle; and, even so, you as a carnal man cannot become a spiritual man by any spontaneous generation ; the new life must be imparted to you by the quickening Spirit. The distinction of your works from those of the real believer in Christ is as great as that between the works of the devil and the works of God; and this may show you how great the distinction of the natures must be by which these different fruits are produced.

The language before us is, next, *a word of descent.* Sin is "of the devil," it came from him; he is its parent and patron. Sin is not so of the devil that we can lay the blame of our sins upon him, for that is our own. Thou must not blame the tempter for tempting thee to do that which without thy will he could not make thee do. He may tempt thee, but that would be no sin of thine if thy will did not yield thereto. The responsibility lies with thy will. The devil has plenty of sin of his own to answer for, and yet he is often made a pack-horse to carry loads of evil which are none of his. Mother Eve taught us that art when she said, "The serpent beguiled me, and I did eat"; and since then men have become wonderfully proficient in the science of excuse-making, frequently imputing their own guilt to the devil's guile. Yet sin in a sadly true sense does come of the devil. He first introduced it into the world. How or when he himself first sinned and fell from being an angel of light to become the apostle of darkness we will not conjecture. Many have thought that the pride of his lofty station, or envy of the foreseen glories of the Son of man, may have overthrown him ; but, at any rate, he kept not his first estate, but became a rebel against his Lord, and the active promoter of all evil. Being expelled from heaven for his wickedness, he desired to wreak his revenge upon God by alienating the human race from its obedience. He saw what an interest the Creator had taken in man, and therefore judged that he could grieve him greatly by seducing man from obedience. He perceived that the Maker, when he formed the earth, did not rest; when he had made birds and fishes, did not rest ; when he had made sun, moon, and stars, did not rest; but when he had fashioned man, he was so well content that then he took a day of rest, and consecrated it for ever to be a Sabbath. Thus was God's unresting care for man made manifest. "Surely," said the evil one, "if I can turn this favoured being into an enemy of God, then I shall bring dishonour upon the name of the Most High, and have my revenge." Therefore he alighted in the garden, and tempted our first parents, thus opening the gate by which sin entered into the world with all its train of woe. In that sense sin is truthfully described as being the work of the devil. He brought the flame which has caused so great a burning. Since then he has been in some degree the author of sin by often tempting men. I doubt not that he suggests to many a sinner the delights of the flesh, and the pleasures of self; and that he shuts the eye of conscience to the truth, and hardens the heart against the threatenings of God. Under these influences men doubtless rush into wild extravagances of evil, willingly yielding themselves to be led captive at his will. Doubtless, Satan not only suggests sin to men, but as one spirit influences another spirit, he influences men strongly towards that which is evil, and blinds them against that which is good. "Lead us not into temptation, but deliver us from the evil one," is a prayer which plainly connects the evil one with temptation, as we know that he is connected with it as a matter of fact. This is his constant employment, to be tempting one way or another the sons of men. Hence sin is the work of the devil, but not so that it excuses us; it is our work because we willingly yield: let us be thoroughly ashamed of such work when we find that the devil has a hand in it. May Almighty God deliver us from the mighty spirit of evil!

Consider, next, that we have here *a word of description.* The work of sin is the work of the devil because it is such work as he delights in. What are the works of the devil? They are such actions as are like himself, and exhibit his nature and spirit. Open your eyes, and you will surely see "the works of the devil;" they are everywhere in this poor world. The earth is defiled with his horrible productions. How delightful it is to take a survey of the works of God! The wise man saith, "The works of the Lord are great, sought out of all them that have pleasure therein." I heard of a good man who went down the Rhine, but took care to read a book all the way, for fear he should have his mind taken off from heavenly topics by the beauties of nature. I confess I do not understand such a spirit—I do not want to do so. If I go into an artist's house I do that artist a displeasure if I take no notice of his works under the pretext that I am quite absorbed in himself. Why not enjoy the objects in which our heavenly Father has set forth his wisdom and power? There is nothing in any of the works of God to defile, debase, or carnalize the soul. Delight yourself in all your heavenly Father's handiwork, and make it to be a ladder by which you climb to himself. But what a very different contemplation is that which lies before us in the works of the devil! Ah, me, what a picture for a painter here—the works of the devil! Yet surely, brush and colour would altogether fail. Oh, evil one, how cunning are thy works; in malice hast thou made them all; the earth is full of thine abominable things!

Look abroad in the world and you see *atheism*: men made by God deny his existence. They could not stand upright and speak if he did not enable them to do so, and yet they cry, "There is no God!" Into what a condition must an intelligent mind be brought ere it can vent such folly! Surely this must come from that arch-fiend who above all things desires that there should be no God! See, also, how much there is of *ignorance* abroad, a leaden night of ignorance of God and of his Son. Is not this the work of the prince of darkness? Note also the abounding *unbelief* of truth which would be believed at once if men's minds were pure, of truth which is salvation to those who accept it, and yet is rejected by many as if it were injurious to them. Whence comes all this *indifference* to God and his grace, and what is the origin of all this plague of *doubting* which is now upon us? Is it not of the same character as that which abode in the serpent's heart when he whispered, "Hath God said?" and, again, "Ye shall not surely die." Here is the liar that is from the beginning still producing a host of lies against God himself. What is *idolatry*, which we see everywhere abroad, not only

among the heathen, but among those who call themselves Christians,—
the worship of visible symbols instead of the spiritual adoration of the
unseen Spirit? It must have come from Satan, who has made himself
the god of this world, setting himself up to be God's rival. Things
offered to idols are offered to devils, for a mere idol is nothing in the
world; its evil lies in its representing a principle which is opposed
to the one true, invisible God. The superstitions which degrade
humanity, which are an insult to our manhood, all these are most
pleasing to Satan, and approved of by him, and so they are fitly
described as "the works of the devil." And what, my brethren, is
blasphemy—that common profanity which pollutes our streets?
Who could have taught men wantonly, and for no purpose whatever, to use the foul and filthy language that is so common nowa-
day? This must be the speech of pandemonium, the dialect of hell.
And what is *pride*, my brethren, pride in a creature that will die? pride
in a sinful worm?—the pride of dress, the pride of life, the pride of
talent? What are those haughty looks? what are those presumptuous
words? what are those contemptuous glances,—what are all these things
but works of the devil? He whom Milton describes as thinking it
"better to reign in hell than serve in heaven," he surely is the great
fomenter of all pride among mankind. As for *deceit*, so current everywhere, and, worst of all, religious deceit, formalism, and *hypocrisy*,
whence come these but from the bottomless pit—from him who transforms himself into an angel of light? Are not all liars his dear children?
My list is long enough: but I see a numerous brood hatched beneath
the wings of *hate*: envy, strife, wrath, bitterness, malice, revenge. These
are as fiery flying serpents in this wilderness, inflaming men's blood. I
see these accursed evils rousing nations into war, dividing communities
with discords, embittering families that else might be full of love; yea,
making men to be the worst enemies of men. These come from him who
is a murderer from the beginning, and is the aider and abetter of all
hatred and strife. What a busy being he has been! How he has toiled
incessantly day and night to set up a kingdom of hate in opposition to
the empire of eternal love! With what diligence he has smothered the
world with a pall of darkness, so that men sit down to weep and rise up
to torment one another. Ah me, what mischief this unclean spirit has
wrought! His works are evil, only evil, and that continually. He has
led the human race to become accomplices in his treason against the
majesty of heaven, allies in his rebellion against the sovereignty of God
Most High. The works of the devil make up a black picture: it is a
thick darkness over all the land, even a darkness that may be felt.

II. But now, secondly, and much more joyously, let us consider THE
PURPOSE OF GOD—" For this purpose the Son of God was manifested,
that he might destroy the works of the devil."

Ring out sweetly all the silver bells of earth, and all the golden harps
of heaven; God has purposed that the terrible work of the devil upon
the earth shall be every atom of it destroyed. Yes, mark that word
" *destroyed*," not limited, nor alleviated, nor neutralized, but destroyed.
Oh, men and brethren, what could you and I do against such a power
as Satan; so malicious and so strong, and withal so cunning and subtle,
and apt to deceive? Who among us can loosen his works, and cast his

cords from us? But if God has purposed it, verily the purpose of Jehovah shall stand! If this be the divine decree, tremble, O Tophet, and thou, Beelzebub, for there shall come an end to all thy works, if God hath purposed to destroy them!

The work which lies in this purpose is assuredly *a divine work*. The Lord who can create can certainly destroy. Destruction lies in the hand of Omnipotence, and is a prerogative of the Eternal One. Destruction of forces so terrible must come from the Lord alone. What could you and I do in this business? Ourselves originally under Satan's power, ourselves destroyed, could we destroy the destroyer? The image of God in us has been marred by the work of Satan; could we restore that image? Enmity to God has been created in our hearts by Satan; could we while yet enemies tear out that enmity? No, another hand must make us friends, a hand outside of us. That which has been done by the powers of darkness must be undone by the eternal light, or else it will remain for ever. It is a divine work, this destruction of the works of the devil, and herein lies our hope of its being accomplished.

And there is, to my mind, about it the idea of *a conquering work*. When are the palaces and the fortifications of great kings destroyed? Not till the kings themselves have been overthrown in fair fight; but when their power is broken, then it is that the conquerors raze the castle and burn the stronghold. Glory be unto Jehovah, it is his purpose to win such a victory over the Prince of Darkness that every work of his shall be destroyed. "Come, behold the works of the Lord, what desolations he hath made in the earth; he breaketh the bow, and cutteth the spear in sunder; he burneth the chariot in the fire." Thy right hand, O Lord, has dashed in pieces the enemy. Our Almighty Champion has come forth with a shout of victory to divide the spoil with the strong. The arch-enemy is vanquished, and therefore his works are to be destroyed!

This means also *a complete work*. The product of evil is not to be cut down for a time and left to grow again. The tree of the forest is felled by the axe, but the root remaineth, and at the scent of water it will bud and send forth branches; but the purpose of God is utterly to *destroy* the works of the devil, and destroyed they shall be. In the heart of man, when God begins his work, he does not cease till he hath utterly destroyed all sin, yea, the very tendency and possibility of sin; and then he conducts the purified spirit up to his right hand, having neither spot or wrinkle, nor any such thing. In the world, also, do not doubt it, oh ye soldiers of Christ, who are ready to turn your backs in the day of battle, he will yet drive sin out of its entrenchments; the habitations of cruelty shall become the temples of adoration: all people shall bow before the Lord, and there shall be a new heaven and a new earth wherein dwelleth righteousness. Up from this poor planet there shall ascend, like smoke from a great golden altar of incense, the perpetual hallelujahs of a ransomed race, redeemed by blood and power from all the rule of the enemy. Glory be to God, he hath purposed it, and he will accomplish it.

It is a complete work and *a conclusive work;* for the Lord Jesus will so break the head of the old dragon, that he shall never wear the crown again. Christ has come, not to fight a battle with Satan which shall continue throughout all ages, but to win a victory which shall so crush the power of evil that it shall not molest the world again. The powers of darkness upon this earth hang out their flags and ring out the clarions of victory, but they are too fast. Wait a little while, and he that will come shall come, and will not tarry; and when he cometh he shall lead captivity captive; and the reign of goodness, and truth, and love shall be established for ever and ever. Rebellion shall not rise up a second time. Oh, how glorious is the text:—"For this purpose the Son of God was manifest, that he might destroy the works of the devil." Sin in every shape and form the Lord shall destroy from off the face of the earth for ever.

III. Thirdly, our text plainly tells us how this is to be done: By THE MANIFESTATION OF THE SON OF GOD. "For this purpose the Son of God was manifested." The work of the devil was so clever, the foundations of it were so deeply laid, and the whole thing had such a semblance of omnipotence about it, and was, indeed, in itself so strong, that no champion was found in heaven or on earth that could hope to destroy it. It never entered Satan's thoughts that God himself could deign to suffer and to die. He said within himself,—"If I can make man so to offend God that he must justly be incensed against him, then I shall have done the work effectually. If I can make man a rebel, God's infinite holiness cannot overlook his rebellion, and he must punish him, and so I shall have made for God a perpetual race of enemies, and he will have lost the love of myriads of his creatures." He did not know the boundless love and wisdom of Jehovah. Even his angelic intellect could never have conceived the matchless plan of atonement by a sacrifice, propitiation by substitution. The blessed fact of the Son of God becoming manifest in human flesh, and dying in human form, to destroy the works of the devil, entered not into a creature's mind. Yet this was always in God's purpose, for the better display of his divine attributes. Behind, and under, and over the works of the devil the Lord had ever the design that this evil should be permitted that he might baffle it with love, and that the glory of his grace might be revealed.

My text has in it to my mind a majestic idea, first, of the difficulties of the case,—that the Son of God must needs be manifested to destroy the works of the devil; and then, secondly, of the ease of his victory. Have you been abroad at midnight when darkness has been all about you, dense and palpable? Not a star was visible, the moon had forgotten to shine; you could scarce see your hand when you held it before your eyes. The blackness seemed to be not only above, beneath, and around, but also within you. You were embedded in a thick, heavy, sensible ebon mass. How could all this be scattered? What power could uplift the pall and scatter the mass? Lo, in the east old Sol has lifted up his head, and the black walls have vanished: not a wreck remains, the works of darkness are destroyed by the manifestation of the light. That is the thought of the text—"For this purpose the Son of God was manifested." Uprising from his divine retreat in the silences of eternity, he appeared in human form, and thereby scattered and utterly destroyed the works of darkness. Let us see how this was done.

First, Christ's manifestation, even *in his incarnation*, was a fatal blow to the works of Satan. Did God come down to men? was he incarnate in the infant form that slept in Bethlehem's manger? Then the Almighty has not given up our nature to be the prey of sin. Despair may not be! If one is born on earth who is divine as well as human, then joy unto thee, O race of Adam! Hear ye not the song, " Glory to God in the highest, and on earth peace, goodwill toward men"? It cannot be that the race is given up to perpetual night if the Son of God is manifested in such fashion as this.

Next, look to *the life of Christ on earth,* and see how he there destroyed the works of the devil. It was a glorious duel in the wilderness when they stood foot to foot—the champions of good and evil! How dexterously the evil one played his weapons! how cunningly he tempted the Christ of God! But the Lord Jesus used the sword of the Spirit, and " It is written," " It is written," " It is written," struck home till the evil one spread his dragon wings and fled away, for he had found his victor. Evil spirits had taken possession of human forms: legions of devils were established in men; but the Lord Jesus Christ had only to speak the word, and away they fled, glad to leap into swine, and rush into the sea, to escape from his presence. They knew that he had come who was ordained " to destroy the works of the devil."

All our Lord's preaching, all his teaching, all his labour here below was in order to the pulling away the corner stone from the great house of darkness which Satan had built up.

But oh, dear friends, it was in *his death* that Jesus chiefly overthrew Satan and destroyed his works. Satan built upon this—that man had become offensive to God and God must punish him; that punishment was his hope for the continuance of alienation. Behold, the august Son of God takes the offender's place! Marvel of marvels, the Judge stands where the criminal should have stood and is "numbered with the transgressors!" Behold, the wrath of God falls upon his Wellbeloved, and Jesus suffers, that he may reconcile man to his God, and heal the breach which sin had caused. The deed was done. Man is no more offensive to heaven, for one glorious man's boundless merit has put away the demerit of the race. Jesus has, by his unutterable beauties, removed the deformities of all who are in him. By his obedience unto death the law is vindicated, justice is honoured, grace is glorified. Man, accepting this great sacrifice, loves and adores the Father who ordained it, and so the works of the devil in his heart are destroyed.

Our Lord's *rising again,* his ascension into glory, his sitting at the right hand of the Father, his coming again in the latter days—all these are parts of the manifestation of the Son of God by which the works of the devil shall be destroyed. So also is *the preaching of the gospel.* If we want to destroy the works of the devil our best method is to manifest more and more the Son of God. Preach up Christ and you preach down the devil. All kinds of reforms are good, and we are on the side of everything that is pure, and honest, and temperate, and righteous; still, the best Reformer is the Christ of God. The one medicine for man's moral sickness is the cross, and nothing but the cross. Preach the crucified Saviour; preach the incarnate God; preach Christ full of forgiveness and love, reconciling the world unto himself and you have applied the best remedy to the sore. Only be it never forgotten that Jesus destroys the works of darkness *by his Spirit.* It is the Spirit of God who puts divine energy into the sacred word. When the Spirit manifests Christ in a man then the works of darkness are destroyed in that man. When Christ is manifested in a nation then the works of Satan begin to fall in that nation; and in proportion as the Holy Ghost shall more and more reveal Christ to hearts and consciences, bringing them into obedience to the faith, in that degree shall the works of Satan be destroyed.

Lastly, on this point, our blessed Lord is manifested in his eternal power and kingdom as *enthroned*, in order to destroy the works of the devil; for " the government shall be upon his shoulders, and his name shall be called Wonderful, the mighty God, the Father of the ages." He is such a father, and the age is made to feel his forming hand. Kings, presidents, parliaments, poets, leaders, and such like—these are powers visible; but there is over them all a power invisible. A late philosopher asserted that amid all the confusion of affairs he could see a power over all which works towards righteousness. There is such a power: there is a King of kings and a Lord of lords; and who is he? It is he of whom we read, " The father hath committed all things into his hands." He is ruling, he is reigning even now, and, despite our unbelief, things are moving on. God is being glorified, his kingdom is coming; the ultimate destruction of evil on the earth is sure, and the eternal reign of the right and of good is certain. " The Lord reigneth ; let the earth rejoice ; let the multitude of isles be glad thereof." Enthroned at the right hand of the Eternal, Jesus sits, the man of love, the crucified : he has reassumed his eternal glory and sovereignty, and without his bidding shall not a dog move his tongue. The dominion is with the Son of God, and he shall end the reign of evil. Glory be to his name for ever and ever !

IV. Lastly, I would come close home to each dear friend as we utter a few words of inquiry as to THE EXPERIENCE OF ALL THIS IN OURSELVES. Has the Son of God been manifested to you to destroy the works of the devil in you ? Come to the point, and look at home ! At first there was in your heart an *enmity to God;* for " the carnal mind is enmity against God." Is that enmity destroyed ? Has the love of God in Christ Jesus appeared to you in such a way that you can truly say you no longer hate God, but love him ? Though you do not love him as you wish to do, yet your heart is toward him and you desire to be like him, and to be with him for ever. This is a good beginning; the Son of God has destroyed your enmity ; you have seen the love of of God in Christ, and your rebellion against God has ceased.

The next work of the devil which usually appears in the human mind is *self-righteous pride.* The man says, " I am no enemy to God, I am righteous; if I am not perfect, yet I am tolerably good. God ! I thank thee that I am not as other men are. I do this and I do that, and I do not do the other." This is our natural boasting, but the Son of God destroys it. Has the Son of God destroyed all your self-righteousness ? It is a precious lot of rags; but we so constantly practise the art of patching and mending that we dream that we are clothed in royal apparel. Have all those rags gone from you ? Has a strong wind

blown them right away ? Have you seen your own natural nakedness ?
Why, if I were to talk about my own righteousness, I should be a fool
and a liar in one. I have no righteousness of my own; I dare not
dream of such a thing. Is that your case? Then the Lord Jesus
Christ has been manifested to destroy in you the works of the devil.
That is a pretty name for your righteousness, is it not? It deserves
that name, for the best righteousness of man, when it is set up in
opposition to the righteousness of Christ, deserves small compliments;
it is one of the works of the devil.

When the Lord has destroyed self-righteousness in us, the devil
generally sets us forth another form of his power, and that is *despair*.
" Ah," says he, " you see what a sinner you are—God will never be
reconciled to you! There is no forgiveness for you!" Oh, that ever
he should have the impudence to make a man believe so gross a
slander of such a God as ours, whose very name is love, and who gave
his Son to die for sinners ! But, if the Lord Jesus Christ has been
manifested to you, despair has gone, that work of the devil has been all
destroyed, and now you have a humble hope in God, and a joy in his
mercy. Though you speak sometimes with bated breath, yet your doubt
is about yourself, not about your Lord. You know whom you have
believed, and you know that he is a God that passeth by transgression,
iniquity, and sin. Thus three sets of works of the devil are gone already
—enmity is gone, self-righteousness is gone, and despair is gone.

What next? Have you any *unbelief* in your heart as to the promises
of God ? That is a favourite work of the devil: unbelief is one of
his darling children. Now, I beseech you, do not say, " I must always
feel this unbelief." No. Down with it ! Christ was manifested to
destroy the works of the devil. Grind your cutlasses, and cut down
these doubts ! All mistrusts must die. Not one of them must be
spared. Hang them up before the face of the sun!

Jesus has not come that he may lock up our sins, and keep them quiet,
hidden away in a dark corner; he has come to *destroy* them. Israel
was not to make a league with the Canaanites, as they unwisely did with
the Gibeonites; but they were to sweep out the entire race, root and
branch. Thus must sin be exterminated and extirpated. Cry to the
Lord Jesus Christ that you may never tolerate the sin of unbelief,
and look upon it as a pitiable infirmity. No: it is a grievous sin;
war to the knife with it; the Son of God is manifested that it may be
utterly destroyed. Happy is that man who no longer doubts his God,
but exercises the Abrahamic faith which staggers not at the promise
through unbelief !

Do fleshly lusts arise in your heart, my brother ? In whose heart do
they not arise ? The brightest saint is sometimes tempted to the foulest
vice. Yes, but he yields not thereto. By the grace of God he says,
" Christ is manifested to destroy the works of the devil." He will not
play with these things and dally with them, and let them be his De-
lilah, for he knows that they will cost him his eyes, even if they do not
ruin his soul. He cries, " Away with them!" It is not meet even to
mention these vile things; they are works of the devil, and to be
destroyed.

My brother, do you quickly become angry ? I pray God you may be angry and sin not; but if you are of a hasty temper, I entreat you to overcome it. Do not say, "I cannot help it." You must help it, or rather Christ must destroy it. It must not be tolerated. Does your anger ever intensify into hate? Do you ever feel envious of those who are better off than yourself, or better than yourself? Does that envy ever lead you to think harshly of them, to indulge yourself in suspicions that are groundless concerning them? Oh, for the sword of the Lord and of Gideon! Slay all these Midianites, for Christ is revealed on purpose to clear the heart of the whole brood of them. God is love, and he that dwelleth in love dwelleth in God; and hate and ill-will must not live! Every form of evil must fall; destruction is meted out to them all. Every idol must be broken.

Oh, brethren, there is to be in every true believer the ultimate abolition of sin. What a prospect this is! The cutting up of the very roots of evil! The sooner the better. The day shall come when every child of God shall be transformed and transfigured into the likeness of Christ, and shall be without fault before the throne of God. This is already foreshadowed upon us, for the outlines are drawn in the fact that we hate all sin, and long after perfect holiness. The great Father has put his mark upon the lump of clay, and we can see from the rough draft that he will fashion it and form it into the perfect image of his dear Son. After that image we are struggling. It is begun in us by the power of the Spirit of God, and he will not fail nor be discouraged till the purpose of God shall be accomplished, and all the works of Satan in us shall be destroyed. This robs death of all dread: the prospect of being totally free from sin makes us welcome even the grave, if by that road we are to come to the home of the perfect. Meanwhile, let us seek after sanctification; let us labour after holiness, and let us abound in it to the glory of God. Despite our failures and mistakes let us pursue holiness! Taking it by the heel, let us keep close to it. So may the Lord enable us for Jesus' sake. Amen.

PORTION OF SCRIPTURE READ BEFORE SERMON—1 John iii.

HYMNS FROM "OUR OWN HYMN BOOK"—373, 680, 428.

"BEGINNING AT JERUSALEM."

A Sermon

DELIVERED ON THURSDAY EVENING, JUNE 14TH, 1883, BY

C. H. SPURGEON,

AT THE METROPOLITAN TABERNACLE, NEWINGTON.

" And that repentance and remission of sins should be preached in his name among all nations, beginning at Jerusalem."—Luke xxiv. 47.

THE servants of God were not left to originate a gospel for themselves, as certain modern teachers appear to do, nor were they even left to map out their mode of procedure in the spreading of the glad tidings. They were told by their great Master *what to preach*, and *where to preach it*, and *how to preach it*, and even *where to begin to preach it.* There is ample room for the exercise of our thought in obeying Christ's commands; but the worldly wise in these days call no one a thoughtful person who is content to be a docile follower of Jesus. They call themselves " thoughtful and cultured " simply because they set up their own thoughts in opposition to the thoughts of God. It were well if they would remember the old proverb—" Let another praise thee, and not thine own lips." As a rule those who call themselves " intellectual " are by no means persons of great intellect. Great minds seldom proclaim their own greatness. These boasters are not satisfied to be " followers of God, as dear children," but must strike out a path for themselves; this reveals their folly rather than their culture. We shall find use for every faculty which we possess, even if we are endowed with ten talents, in doing just as we are bidden by our Lord. Implicit obedience is not thoughtless: on the contrary, it is necessary to its completeness that heart and mind should be active in it.

I. Ye that would faithfully serve Christ note carefully how he taught his disciples WHAT THEY WERE TO PREACH. We find different descriptions of the subject of our preaching, but on this occasion it is comprised in two things—*repentance and remission of sins.* I am glad to find in this verse that old-fashioned virtue called *repentance.* It used to be preached, but it has gone out of fashion now. Indeed, we are told that we always misunderstood the meaning of the word " repentance"; and that it simply means a " change of mind," and nothing more. I wish that those who are so wise in their Greek knew a little more of that language, for they would not be so ready with their infallible statements. True, the word does signify a change of mind, but in its Scriptural connection it indicates a change of mind of an unusual

No. 1,729.

character. It is not such a fitful thing as men mean when they speak of changing their minds, as some people do fifty times a day; but it is a change of mind of a deeper kind. Gospel repentance is a change of mind of the most radical sort—such a change as never was wrought in any man except by the Spirit of God. We mean to teach repentance, the old-fashioned repentance, too; and I do not know a better description of it than the child's verse:—

> " Repentance is to leave
> The things we loved before,
> And show that we in earnest grieve
> By doing so no more."

Let every man understand that he will never have remission of sin while he is in love with sin; and that if he abides in sin he cannot obtain the pardon of sin. There must be a hatred of sin, a loathing of it, and a turning from it, or it is not blotted out. We are to preach *repentance as a duty.* "The times of this ignorance God winked at, but now commandeth all men everywhere to repent." "Repent, and be baptized every one of you in the name of Jesus Christ for the remission of sins." He that has sinned is bound to repent of having sinned: it is the least that he can do. How can any man ask God for mercy while he abides in his sin?

We are to preach *the acceptableness of repentance.* In itself considered there is nothing in repentance deserving of the favour of God; but, the Lord Jesus Christ having come, we read, "He that confesseth and forsaketh his sin shall find mercy." God accepts repentance for the sake of his dear Son. He smiles upon the penitent sinner, and puts away his iniquities. This we are to make known on all sides.

We are also to preach *the motives of repentance*—that men may not repent from mere fear of hell, but they must repent of sin itself. Every thief is sorry when he has to go to prison: every murderer is sorry when the noose is about his neck: the sinner must repent, not because of the punishment of sin, but because his sin is sin against a pardoning God, sin against a bleeding Saviour, sin against a holy law, sin against a tender gospel. The true penitent repents of sin against God, and he would do so even if there were no punishment. When he is forgiven, he repents of sin more than ever; for he sees more clearly than ever the wickedness of offending so gracious a God.

We are to preach *repentance in its perpetuity.* Repentance is not a grace which is only to be exercised by us for a week or so at the beginning of our Christian career: it is to attend us all the way to heaven. Faith and repentance are to be inseparable companions throughout our pilgrimage to glory. Repenting of our sin, and trusting in the great Sinbearer, is to be the tenor of our lives; and we are to preach to men that it must be so.

We are to tell them of *the source of repentance,* namely, that the Lord Jesus Christ is exalted on high to *give* repentance and remission of sins. Repentance is a plant that never grows on nature's dunghill: the nature must be changed, and repentance must be implanted by the Holy Spirit, or it will never flourish in our hearts. We preach repentance as a fruit of the Spirit, or else we greatly err.

Our second theme is to be *remission of sins.* What a blessed subject is this! To preach the full pardon of sin—that it is blotted out once for all; the free pardon of sin—that God forgives voluntarily of his own grace; free forgiveness for the very chief of sinners for all their sins, however black they may be; is not this a grand subject? We are to preach a final and irreversible remission; not a pardon which is given and taken back again, so that a man may have his sins forgiven and yet be punished for them. I loathe such a gospel as that, and could not preach it. It would come with an ill grace from these lips. But the pardon of God once given stands for ever. If he has cast our sin into the depths of the sea it will never be washed up again. If he has removed our transgressions from us as far as the east is from the west, how can they return to condemn us? Once washed in the blood of the Lamb we are clean. The deed is done: the one offering has put away for ever all the guilt of believers.

Now this is what we are to preach—free, full, irreversible pardon for all that repent of sin, and lay hold on Christ by faith. O servants of the Lord, be not ashamed to declare it, for this is your message!

II. Next to this, we are told WHERE IT IS TO BE PREACHED. The text says that repentance and remission of sins should be preached in his name *among all nations.* Here, then, we have the divine warrant for missions. They are no speculations, or enthusiastic dreams: they are matters of divine command. I daresay you have heard of what the Duke of Wellington said to a missionary in India who was questioning whether it was of any use to preach the gospel to the Hindoos. "What are your marching orders?" said this man of discipline and obedience. "What are your marching orders?" that is the deciding question. Now the marching orders are, "Go ye into all the world and preach the gospel to every creature." What a wonder it is that the church did not see this long before. After her first days she seems to have fallen asleep, and it is scarcely a hundred years ago since in the providence and grace of God the church began to wake to her high enterprise. We are to preach the gospel everywhere: missions are to be universal. All nations need the preaching of the word. The gospel is a remedy for every human ill among all the races that live upon the face of the earth. Some out of all nations shall receive it; for there shall be gathered before the eternal throne men out of every kindred, and nation, and tongue. No nation will utterly refuse it: there will be found a remnant according to the election of grace even among the most perverse of the tribes of men.

We ought to preach it to every creature, for it is written that it behoved to be so. Read the forty-sixth verse: "Thus it is written, and thus it behoved Christ to suffer, and to rise from the dead the third day: . . . and that repentance and remission of sins should be preached among all nations." Brethren, there was a divine necessity that Christ should die, and an equally imperative *must* that he should arise again from the dead; but there is an equally absolute necessity that Jesus should be preached to every creature under heaven. It behoves to be so. Who, then, will linger? Let us each one, according to his ability and opportunity, tell to all around us the story of the forgiveness of sin through the Mediator's sacrifice to as many as confess their sin and forsake it. We are bidden to preach repentance of sin and faith in our Lord Jesus Christ, let us not be slow to do so.

III. But this is not all. We are actually told HOW TO PREACH IT. Repentance and remission are to be preached *in Christ's name.* What does this mean? Ought we not to learn from this that we are to tell the gospel to others, because *Christ orders us to do so?* In Christ's name we *must* do it. Silence is sin when salvation is the theme. If these should hold their peace, the stones would cry out against them. My brethren, you must proclaim the gospel according to your ability: it is not a thing which you may do or may not do at your own discretion; but you *must* do it if you have any respect for your Saviour's name. If you dare pray in that name, if you dare hope in that name, if you hear the music of joy in that name, then in the name of Jesus Christ preach the gospel in every land.

But it means more than that. Not only preach it under his orders, but preach it *on his authority.* The true servant of Christ has his Master to back him up. The Lord Jesus will seal by threatening or by grace the word of his faithful messengers. If we threaten the ungodly, the threatening shall be fulfilled. If we announce God's promise to the penitent, that promise shall be surely kept. The Lord Jesus will not let the words of his own ambassadors fall to the ground. "Lo, I am with you alway," says he, "even to the end of the world. Go ye therefore and teach all nations." You have Christ with you : teach the nations by his authority.

But does it not mean, also, that *the repentance and the remission which are so bound together come to men by virtue of his name?* Oh, sinner, there would be no acceptance of your repentance if it were not for that dear name ! Oh, guilty conscience, there would be no ease for you through the remission of sin if it were not that the blessed name of Jesus is sweet to the Lord God of hosts ! We dare preach pardon to you in his name. The blood has been shed and sprinkled on the burning throne : the Christ has gone in within the veil, and stands there "able to save to the uttermost them that come unto God by him, seeing he ever liveth to make intercession for them." Salvation in his name there is assuredly, and this is our glory ; but "there is none other name given under heaven among men whereby we must be saved." That name has a fulness of saving efficacy, and if you will but rest in it, you shall find salvation, and find it now.

Thus you see we are not bidden to go forth and say—We preach you the gospel in the name of our own reason; or we preach you the gospel in the name of the church to which we belong, or by the authority of a synod, or a bishop, or a creed, or a whole church. No, we declare the truth in the name of Christ. Christ has set his honour to pawn for the truth of the gospel. He will lose his glory if sinners that believe and repent are not saved. Dishonour will come to the Son of God if any man repenting of sin is not accepted before God. For his name's sake he will not cast away one that comes to him. O chief of sinners! he will receive you if you will come. He cannot reject you; that were to be false to his own promise, untrue to his own nature.

Be sure then that you preach in Christ's name. If you preach in your own name it is poor work. A man says to me, "I cannot tell a dead sinner to live. I cannot tell a blind sinner to see. I cannot invite an insensible sinner; it is absurd; for the sinner is altogether without strength." No, dear sir, I do not suppose you can do so while you speak according to carnal reason. Does the good man say that God has not sent him to bid the dead arise? Then let him not do it. Pray let him not try to do what God never sent him to do. Let him go home and go to bed; he will probably do as much good asleep as awake. But as for me, I am sent to preach in Jesus' name, "Believe and live," and therefore I am not slow to do so. I am sent on purpose to say, "Ye dry bones, live," and I dare do no otherwise. No faithful minister who knows what faith means looks to the sinner for power to believe, or looks to himself for power; but he looks to the Master that sent him for power; and in the name of Christ he says to the withered hand, "Be stretched out," and he says to the dead, "Come forth!" and he does not speak in vain. Oh, yes, it is in Christ's name that we fulfil our office! We are miracle-workers: he endows us with *his* power if in faith we tell out his gospel. All of you who try to speak the gospel may do it without fear of failure; for the power lies in the gospel and in the Spirit who goes with it, not in the preacher or in the sinner. Blessed be the name of God, we have this treasure in earthen vessels, but the excellency of the power is of God, and not of us. So he tells us, then, what to preach, and where to preach it, and how to preach it.

IV. Now, I shall ask your attention to the principal topic of the present discourse, and that is, that he told his disciples WHERE TO BEGIN.

I have heard of a Puritan who had in his sermon forty-five main divisions, and about ten subdivisions under every head. He might be said largely to divide the word of truth, even if he did not rightly divide it. Now, I have nine subheads to-night, and yet I hope I shall not detain you beyond the usual time. I cannot make fewer of them and give the full meaning of this sentence—" Beginning at Jerusalem." The apostles were not to pick and choose where they should start, but they were to begin at Jerusalem. Why?

First, because *it was written in the Scriptures that they were to begin at Jerusalem*: "Thus it is written, and thus it behoves, that repentance and remission of sin should be preached in his name among all nations, beginning at Jerusalem." It was so written: I will give you two or three proofs. Read in the second chapter of Isaiah, at the third verse: "Out of Zion shall come forth the law, and the word of the Lord from Jerusalem." Isaiah's word would have fallen to the ground if the preaching had not begun at Jerusalem; but now, to the very letter, this prediction of the evangelical prophet is kept. In Joel, that famous Joel who prophesied the descent of the Spirit and the speaking of the servants and the handmaidens, we read in the second chapter, at the thirty-second verse, "In mount Zion and in Jerusalem shall be deliverance;" and again in the sixteenth verse of the third chapter of the same prophet— "The Lord shall roar out of Zion, and utter his voice from Jerusalem." As if the Lord were as a strong lion in the midst of Jerusalem, and as if the sounding forth of the gospel was like the roaring of his voice, that the nations might hear and tremble. How could those promises have been kept if the gospel had begun to be preached in the deserts of

Arabia, or if the first church of Christ had been set up at Damascus?
Note another passage. Obadiah in his twenty-first verse says, " Saviours
shall come up on mount Zion." Who were these saviours but those
who instrumentally became so by proclaiming the Saviour Jesus Christ.
And Zechariah, who is full of visions, but not visionary, says in his
fourteenth chapter at the eighth verse, " Living waters shall flow out
of Jerusalem," and then he describes the course of those waters till they
flowed even unto the Dead Sea, and made its waters sweet. Because
the Bible said so, therefore they must begin at Jerusalem, and I call your
attention to this, for our Lord Jesus was particular that every jot and
tittle of the Old Testament should be fulfilled. Do you not think that
this reads us a lesson that we should be very reverent towards every
sentence of both the Old and the New Testaments ; and if there be
anything taught by our Lord ought not his people to consider well, and
act according to the divine ordinance ? I am afraid that many take
their religion from their parents, or from the church that is nearest to
them, without weighing it. " I counsel thee to keep the King's commandment." Oh, that we may be more faithful servants of the Lord ;
for if we are faithful we shall be careful upon what men call small
points, such as the doctrine of baptism, the manner of the Lord's Supper,
or this small point of where the gospel should be first preached. It
must begin at Jerusalem and nowhere else ; for the Scripture cannot be
broken. See ye to it, then, that ye walk according to the word of God,
and that ye test everything by it. " To the law and to the testimony :
if they speak not according to this word, it is because there is no light
in them." So much on that first head.

Secondly, I suppose that our Lord bade his disciples begin to preach
the gospel at Jerusalem, because *it was at Jerusalem that the facts which
make up the gospel had occurred.* It was there that Jesus Christ died,
that he was buried, that he rose again, and that he ascended into
heaven. All these things happened at Jerusalem, or not far from it.
Therefore the witness-bearing of the apostles must be upon the spot
where if they lie they can be confuted, and where persons can come
forward and say, " It was not so ; you are deceivers." If our Lord had
said, " Do not say anything at Jerusalem. Go away to Rome and begin
preaching there," it would not have looked quite so straightforward as
it now does when he says, " Preach this before the scribes and the
priests. They know that it is so. They have bribed the soldiers to
say otherwise, but they know that I have risen." The disciples were to
preach the gospel in the streets of Jerusalem. There were people in
that city who were once lame, and who leaped like a hart when Jesus
healed them. There were men and women there who ate of the fish and
the bread that Jesus multiplied. There were people in Jerusalem who
had seen their children and their friends healed of dreadful diseases.
Jesus bids his disciples beard the lion in his den, and declare the gospel
on the spot where, if it had been untrue, it would have been contradicted
with violence. Our Lord seemed to say, " Point to the very place where
my death took place. Tell them that they crucified me ; and see if they
dare deny it. Bring it home to their consciences that they rejected the
Christ of God." Hence it was that, coming to the very people who
had seen these things, the preaching of Peter had unusual force about

it : in addition to the power of the Holy Spirit there was also this—that he was telling them of a crime which they had newly committed, and could not deny : and when they saw their error they turned to God with penitent hearts. I like this thought—that they were to begin at Jerusalem, because there the events of the gospel occurred. This is a direction for you, dear friend : if you have been newly converted, do not be ashamed to tell those who know you. A religion which will not stand the test of the fireside is not worth much ! " Oh," says one, " I have never told my husband. I get out on a Thursday night, but he does not know where I am going, and I steal in here. I have never even told my children that I am a believer. I do not like to let it be known. I am afraid that all my family would oppose me." Oh, yes ; you are going to heaven, round by the back lanes. Going to sneak into glory as a rat crawls into a room through a hole in the floor ! Do not attempt it. Never be ashamed of Christ. Come straight out and say to your friends, " You know what I was ; but now I have become a disciple of Jesus Christ." Begin at Jerusalem : it was your Lord's command. He had nothing to be ashamed of. There was no falsehood in what he bade his disciples preach, and therefore he did as good as say, " Hang up my gospel to the light. It is nothing but truth, therefore display it before mine enemies' eyes." If yours is a true, genuine, thorough conversion, I do not say that you are to go up and down the street crying out that you are converted ; but on due occasions you must not hide your convictions. Conceal not what the Lord has done for you, but hold up your candle in your own house.

The third reason why the Lord Jesus told them to begin at Jerusalem may have been that *he knew that there would come a time when some of his disciples would despise the Jews,* and therefore he said—When you preach my gospel, begin with them. This is a standing commandment, and everywhere we ought to preach the gospel to the Jew as well as to the Gentile ; Paul even says, " to the Jew first." Some seem to think that there ought to be no mission to the Jews—that there is no hope of converting them, that they are of no use when they are converted, and so on. I have even heard some who call themselves Christians speak slightingly of the Jewish people. What ! and your Lord and Master a Jew ! There is no race on earth so exalted as they are. They are the seed of Abraham, God's friend. We have nobles and dukes in England, but how far could they trace their pedigree ? Why, up to a nobody. But the poorest Jew on earth is descended lineally from Jacob, and Isaac, and Abraham. Instead of treating them with anything like disrespect, the Saviour says, " Begin at Jerusalem." Just as we say, " Ladies first," so it is " the Jew first." They take precedence among races, and are to be first waited on at the gospel feast. Jesus would have us entertain a deep regard to that nation which God chose of old, and out of which Christ also came, for he is of the seed of Abraham according to the flesh. He puts those first who knew him first. Let us never sneer at a Jew again ; for our Lord teaches us the rule of his house when he says, " Begin at Jerusalem." Let the seed of Israel first have the gospel presented to them, and if they reject it we shall be clear of their blood. But we shall not be faithful to our orders unless we have taken note of Jews as well as of Gentiles.

The fourth reason for beginning at Jerusalem is a practical lesson for you. *Begin where you are tempted not to begin.* Naturally these disciples would have said one to another when they met, " We cannot do much here in Jerusalem. The first night that we met together the doors were shut for fear of the Jews. It is of no use for us to go out into the street; these people are all in such an excited frame of mind that they will not receive us; we had better go up to Damascus, or take a long journey and then commence preaching; and when this excitement is cooled down, and they have forgotten about the crucifixion, we will come and introduce Christ gradually, and say as little as we can about putting him to death." That would have been the rule of policy—that rule which often governs men who ought to be led by faith. But our Lord had said, " Beginning at Jerusalem," and so Peter must stand up in the midst of that motley throng, and he must tell them, " This Jesus whom ye have with wicked hands crucified and slain is now risen from the dead." Instead of tearing Peter to pieces they come crowding up, crying, " We believe in Jesus : let us be baptized into his sacred name." The same day there were added to the church three thousand souls, and a day or two afterwards five thousand were converted by the same kind of preaching. We ought always to try to do good where we think that it will not succeed. If we have a very strong aversion to a certain form of Christian work, instead of taking that aversion as a token that we are not called to it, we may regard it as a sign that we ought at least to try it. The devil knows you, dear friend, better than you know yourself. You see, he has been longer in the world than you have, and he knows a great deal more about human nature than you do; and so he comes to you, and he reckons you up pretty accurately, and says, " This brother would be very useful in a certain sphere of labour, and I must keep him from it." So he tells the brother that he is not called to it, and that it is not the sort of thing for him, and so on; and then he says to himself, " I have turned aside one foe from harming my cause." Yonder is a good sister. Oh, how much she might do for Christ, but Satan guides her into a work in which she will never shine; while the holy work which she could do right well is dreaded by her. I heard a beautiful story last Wednesday, when I was sitting to see inquirers, and I cannot help mentioning it here, for it may be a suggestion to some Christian who is present. A brother, who will be received into the church, was converted in the following way. He came up to London, and worked in a certain parish in the West-end. He was at work on a sewer, and a lady from one of the best houses in the West-end came to the men that were making the sewer and said, " You men, come into my servants' hall and eat your dinners. I will give you either tea or coffee with your meal, and then you will not have to go into the public-house." Some of them went in, but others did not. So the next day the lady came out, and said, " Now, I know that you think my place too fine for you. You do not like to come : so I have come out to fetch you in. While this sewer is being done I should like you to eat your dinners in my house." She got them all in; and when they had done their dinners and drank their tea or coffee she began to talk to them about Jesus Christ. The work was a month or so about, and it was every day the same. Our friend does not know the lady's name, but he knows the name of Jesus through her teaching. Friends, we lose hosts of opportunities; I am sure we do. Many ways of doing good have never occurred to our minds, but they ought to occur to us; and when they do occur we should use them. Let us crucify the flesh about this. Let us overcome natural timidity. Let us in some way or other begin at Jerusalem, which is just where we thought that we never could begin.

Now, fifthly. We are getting on, you see. " Beginning at Jerusalem," must surely mean *begin at home.* Jerusalem was the capital city of their own country. You know the old proverb, " The cobbler's wife goes barefoot." I am afraid that this proverb is verified by some Christians. They do a deal of good five miles off home, but none at home. I knew a man who used to go out with preachers every night in the week, and try to preach himself, poor soul that he was; but his children were so neglected that they were the most wicked children in the street, and they grew up in all manner of vice. The father was prancing about and looking after other people, and did not care for his own family. Now, if you are going to serve Christ to the very ends of the earth, take care that you begin at home. Dear parents, need I urge you to look to your own children? It is a great joy to me to know that the members of the church for the most part do this. When a dear sister came to me on Wednesday night with three of her children, making four that had come within the last six weeks, I felt grateful to God that parents were looking after their offspring. But if any of you are in the Sabbath-school, and never have a Sabbath-school at home; if any of you talk to strangers in the aisles, but are neglecting your own sons and daughters—oh, let it not be so! The power of a father's prayers with his arms about his boy's neck I know full well. The power of a mother's prayers with her children all kneeling round her is far greater with the young than any public ministry will be. Look well to your children: begin at Jerusalem.

Begin with your servants. Do not let a servant live in your house in ignorance of the gospel. Do not have family prayer merely as a matter of form, but let it be a reality. Do not have one person working for you to whom you have never spoken about his or her soul.

Begin with your brothers. Oh, the influence of sisters over brothers! I have a friend—a dear friend, too—who has long been a man of God, but in his young days he was a very loose fellow, and often he was all the night away from home. His sister used to write letters to him, and frequently while half tipsy he has read them under the street lamp. One letter which he read cut him to the quick. His sister's grief about him was too much for him, and he was compelled to seek and find the Saviour. Well has the sister been rewarded for all her love to him. Oh, dear friends, begin at Jerusalem! Begin with your brothers and sisters.

Begin with your neighbours. Oh, this London of ours! It is a horrible place for Christian people to live in! Round about this neighbourhood scarcely can a decent person remain by reason of the vice that abounds, and the language that is heard on every side. Many of you are as much vexed to-day as Lot was when he was in Sodom. Well, bear your witness. Do not be dumb dogs, but speak up for your Lord and Master wherever you are. Look at our dear brother Lazenby, who entered a workshop where none feared the Lord, and has been the means of bringing all in the shop to God. Another shop has felt his influence, and the first recruit has come to join the church: I should not wonder if the whole of the workmen in the second shop should come, too. The Lord grant it. It is marvellous how the gospel spreads when men are in earnest, and their lives are right. God make you so to live that you show piety at home.

Then, sixthly, *begin where much has been already done.* Begin at Jerusalem. It is hard work, dear friends, to preach to certain people: they have been preached to so long, like the people at Jerusalem. They know all about the gospel, it is hard to tell them anything fresh, and yet they have felt nothing, but remain wedded to their sins. The Jerusalem people had been taught for centuries in vain; and yet Christ's disciples were to speak to them first. We must not pass the gospel-hardened; we must labour for the conversion of those who have enjoyed privileges but have neglected them, those who have had impressions and have crushed them out, those who seem now as if they had sealed their own death-warrants and would never be saved. Do not hesitate to go to them. The Lord has done much already: it may be that he has laid the fire, and you are to strike the match and set it all alight. Many people have a love to the gospel, a love to the house of God, a love to God's people, and yet they have no saving faith. What a pity! Do not hesitate to address them. I think I hear you say, "I would rather go and preach to the outcasts." So would I; but you and I are not allowed to pick our work. Virgin soil yields the best harvest; and if a man might choose a congregation that is likely to be fruitful, he might well select those that have never heard the word before. But we have not our choice. The Saviour's disciples were to begin where the prophets had prophesied, and had been put to death; where sinners had rejected God's voice times out of mind. Therefore do not pass by your fellow-seatholders. Perhaps you say, "Sir, I have spoken to them a great many times, but I cannot make anything of them." No, *you* cannot; but God can. Try again. Suppose that for twenty years you were to sit in this Tabernacle side by side with an unconverted person, and you were to speak to that person twice every Sunday and twice in the week, and all the twenty years it should be in vain; yet if the individual was brought to Christ at last would not his conversion repay you? Is your time so very precious? Is your ability so very great? Oh, my dear friend, if you were an archangel it would be worth while for you to work a thousand years to bring one soul to Christ! A soul is such a precious jewel that you would be abundantly rewarded if a century of service only brought you one conversion. Wherefore, in working for Christ, do not hesitate to go to those who have refused the gospel hitherto, for you may yet prevail.

Seventhly, *begin where the gospel day is short.* If you ask me where I get that thought, it is from the fact that within a very short time Jerusalem was to be destroyed. The Romans were to come there to slay men, women, and children, and break down the walls and leave not one stone upon another. And Christ's disciples knew this; wherefore their Lord said, "Begin at Jerusalem." Now, then, if you have any choice as to the person you shall speak to, select an old man. He is near his journey's end, and if he is unsaved there is but a little bit of candle left by the light of which he may come to Christ. Choose the old man, and do not let him remain ignorant of the gospel. Fish him up at once, for with him it is now or never, since he is on the borders of the grave. Or when any of you notice a girl upon whose cheek you see that hectic flush which marks consumption—if you notice during service the deep "churchyard" cough—say to yourself, "I will not let you go without speaking to you, for you may soon be dead." How many a time have I seen a consumptive at Mentone apparently getting better; but I have noticed him rise from dinner with his handkerchief to his mouth and soon they have whispered, "He died of hæmorrhage"—suddenly taken off. When you meet with a pining case, do not wait to be introduced, but introduce yourself; and tenderly, gently, quietly, lovingly say a word about coming to Christ at once. We ought speedily to look up those whose day of grace is short. Perhaps, also, there is a stranger near you who is going far away to a distant land, and may never hear the gospel again; therefore, if you have an opportunity, take care that you avail yourself of it, and reason with him for Jesus at once. Begin at Jerusalem : begin where the day of grace is short.

Eighthly, begin, dear friend, *where you may expect opposition.* That is a singular thing to advise, but I recommend it because the Saviour advised it. It was as certain as that twice two are four that if they preached Christ in Jerusalem there would be a noise, for there were persons living there who hated the very name of Jesus, for they had conspired to put him to death. If they began at Jerusalem they would arouse a ferocious opposition. But nothing is much better for the gospel than opposition. A man comes into the Tabernacle to-night, and as he goes away he says, " Yes, I was pleased and satisfied." In that man's case I have failed. But another man keeps biting his tongue, for he cannot endure the preaching. He is very angry: something in the doctrine does not suit him, and he cries, " As long as I live I will never come here again." That man is hopeful. He begins to think. The hook has taken hold of him. Give us time, and we will have that fish. It is no ill omen when a man gets angry with the gospel. It is bad enough, but it is infinitely better than that horrible lethargy into which men fall when they do not think. Some are not good enough even to oppose the gospel of Jesus Christ. Be hopeful of the man who will not let you speak to him, he is one that you must approach again; and if, when he does let you speak to him, he seems as if he would spit on you, be grateful for it. He feels your words. You are touching him on a sore place. You will have him yet. When he swears that he does not believe a word of what you say, do not believe a word of what *he* says; for often the man who openly objects secretly believes. Just as boys whistle when they go through a churchyard in order to keep their courage up, so many a blasphemer is profane in order to silence his conscience. When he feels the hook, like the fish, the man will drag away from it. Give him line. Let him go. The hook will hold, and in due time you will have him. Do not despair. Do not think it a horrible thing that he should oppose you ; you should rather be grateful for it, and go to God and cry that he will give you that soul for your hire. Begin courageously where you may expect opposition.

And, lastly, to come to the meaning which Mr. John Bunyan has put upon the text in his famous book called "The Jerusalem Sinner Saved," I have no doubt that the Saviour bade them begin at Jerusalem, *because the biggest sinners lived there.* There they lived who had crucified him. The loving Jesus bids them preach repentance and remission to them. There he lived who had pierced the Saviour's side, and they that had plaited the crown of thorns, and put it on his head. There dwell those who had mocked him, and spat upon him ; therefore the loving Jesus, who so freely forgives, says, "Go and preach the gospel first to them." The greatest sinners are the objects of the greatest mercy. Preach first to them. Are there any such here? My dear friend, we must preach the gospel first to you because you want it most. You are dying; your wounds are bleeding; the heavenly surgeon bids us staunch your wounds first. Others who are not so badly hurt may wait awhile, but you must be first served lest you die of your injuries. Should not this encourage you great sinners to come to Jesus, when he bids us preach to you first ?

We are to preach to you first because, when you have received him, you will praise him most. If you are saved you will encourage others to come, and you will cheer up those who have come already. We shall be glad to get fresh blood poured into the veins of the church by the conversion of big sinners who love much because they have had much forgiven. Therefore, we are to come to you *first.* Will you not come to Christ at once? Oh, that you would believe in him! Oh that you would believe in him to-night! To you is the word of this salvation sent. You old sinners—you that have added sin to sin, and done all you can do with both hands wickedly—you that have cursed his name—you that have robbed others—you that have told lies—you that have blackened yourselves with every crime, come and welcome to Jesus. Come to Christ and live at once. Mercy's door is set wide open on purpose that the vilest of the vile may come ; and they are called to come first. Just as you are, come along with you. Tarry not to cleanse or mend, but now "believe on the Lord Jesus Christ and thou shalt be saved." This night if you believe in Jesus you shall go out of these doors rejoicing that the Lord has put away your sin. To believe is to *trust*—simply to trust in Christ. It seems a very simple thing, but that is why it is so hard. If it were a hard thing you would more readily attend to it ; but being so easy you cannot believe that it is effectual. But it is so : faith does save. Christ wants nothing of you but that you accept what he freely presents to you. Put out an empty hand, a black hand, a trembling hand ; accept what Jesus gives, and salvation is yours.

Thus have I tried to expound "Beginning at Jerusalem," O that my Lord would begin with *you.* Amen.

PORTION OF SCRIPTURE READ BEFORE SERMON—Matthew xxviii.

HYMNS FROM "OUR OWN HYMN BOOK"—486, 537.

Metropolitan Tabernacle Pulpit.

A CURE FOR UNSAVOURY MEATS: OR, SALT FOR THE WHITE OF AN EGG.

A Sermon

DELIVERED ON THURSDAY EVENING, JULY 5TH, 1883, BY

C. H. SPURGEON,

AT THE METROPOLITAN TABERNACLE, NEWINGTON.

"Can that which is unsavoury be eaten without salt? or is there any taste in the white of an egg?"—Job vi. 6.

THIS is a question which Job asked of his friends, who turned out to be so unfriendly. Thus he battles with those "miserable comforters" who inflamed his wounds by pouring in verjuice and vinegar instead of oil and wine. The first of them had just opened fire upon him, and Job by this question was firing a return shot. He wanted the three stern watchers to understand that he did not complain without cause. If he had spoken bitterly, it was because he suffered grievously. He was in great bodily pain; he was enduring great mental depression; and at the same time he had been smitten with poverty and bereavement; he had, therefore, reason for his sorrow. He had no comforts left, and every arrow of grief was sticking in his flesh: if he did groan, he had something to groan for. His were not sorrows which he had imagined; they were real and true, and hence he asks this question first, "Doth the wild ass bray when he hath grass? or loweth the ox over his fodder?" If these creatures lift up their notes of complaint, it is when they are starving. When the wild ass cannot find a mouthful of grass anywhere, then his complaint is heard far and near. When the ox at the stall has no fodder—when he is fastened there, and no husbandman brings him provision—then he lows, and there is good reason for his bellowing. Job seems to say, "I do not complain without cause. If I still enjoyed my former comforts, or even a tithe of them, you should hear no voice of murmuring from me. But I am tried to the utmost. I am grievously afflicted, and there is overflowing cause for my moanings." He had lost all care to breathe; the zest of life was gone; no joy remained to make existence worth the having. He was like one who finds no flavour in his food, and loathes the morsel which he swallows. That which was left to him was tasteless as the white of an egg; it yielded him no kind of comfort; in fact, it was disgusting to him. He was fed, he says, upon meat which yielded

No. 1,730.

him no solace. "The things that my soul refused to touch are as my sorrowful meat." Therefore, he virtually asks his friends, "How can you expect me to eat such meat as this without sighs and tears? Can that which is unsavoury be eaten without salt? Is there any taste in the white of an egg?" He means that everything about him had lost its flavour, and life had become dull and dreary to him, and therefore they must not wonder that he uttered words of complaint.

The speech, also, to which Job had listened from Eliphaz the Temanite did not put much sweetness into his mouth; for it was devoid of sympathy and consolation. If you read it at home you will see that it was worthy to be the first of a singular selection of galling utterances. Job, we must admit, was sufficiently acid himself, and abundantly sarcastic; but his friends produced the irritation, and took care always to repay him double for all his wormwood. For every hard speech of his they returned compound interest. They grieved and vexed his upright soul till he said no more than the truth when he cried, "Miserable comforters are ye all." Here he tells them that Eliphaz had administered unto him unsavoury meat without salt;—mere whites of eggs, without taste. Not a word of love, pity, or fellow-feeling had the Temanite uttered. He had spoken as harshly and severely as if he were a judge addressing a criminal who was suffering no more than he deserved. Looking at the speech, and looking at all his surroundings, poor Job feels that he has very unsavoury meat to eat, and he asks them whether they expect him to eat it without salt. They have given him something that is no more gratifying to him than the white of an egg, and he enquires if they really think that he can accept this at their hands, and thank them for their treatment.

We may now forget the much-tortured patriarch Job, and apply this text to ourselves. "Can that which is unsavoury be eaten without salt? or is there any taste in the white of an egg?" Three thoughts arise out of it.

I. The first point will be this, that A WANT OF SAVOUR IS A VERY GREAT WANT in anything that is meant for food. I am not going to deliver a cookery lecture, and so I shall not enlarge upon the passage so far as it refers to the bread upon our table, or the food which we eat and drink. Everybody knows that all kinds of animal life delight in food that has a flavour in it; and even "dumb driven cattle" will turn away from dry, flavourless food, and will go a long way to find something that has a juice and a taste in it which suits the palate which God has created in them. It is exactly the same with regard to the food of our souls. It is a very great fault with a sermon when there is no savour in it. It is a killing fault to the people of God when a book contains a good deal of what may be true, but yet lacks holy savour—or what, in other words, we call "unction." Somebody says, "Tell us what unction is." I can much more easily tell you what it is not. You know a discourse when there is savour in it; and you also know when a sermon is dry, sapless, marrowless; and yet you could not state the difference in words. Some sermons could not even be suspected of anything like unction, their authors would sneer at you if you accused them of it; but salt is still to be had; the fat things, full of marrow, are not quite out of the market yet. But what kind of savour is that which we expect in a sermon?

I answer, first, it is *a savour of the Lord Jesus Christ.* Years ago, before ministers grew so wise as to question the inspiration of Scripture, and renounce the doctrine of atonement, there used to be men in the country whose ministry was full of savour to the people of God. There were numbers of Christians in London who would go to the north, or go to the south, or go to the east, or go to the west to hear such preachers, and count it a great feast to listen to them. What was there about them? Were they great critics? I do not suppose that the good men ever read a work on criticism. Were they profoundly learned? Assuredly they were not. Profoundly learned brethren were preaching in churches and chapels where there were more spiders than people. Those who displayed their learning and rhetoric had empty places, but these men were followed by multitudes, and wherever they spoke the places were too strait for them. Those who did not know the reason said one to another, " What is there about these men? We do not see any peculiar talent." And there was not much. " We do not see any profound learning." And there was none to see. " We do not hear anything of advanced thought and liberal ideas." No, these good men were innocent of these modern diseases. Yet there are people of God to-night, now grey-headed, who recollect the happy hours they spent, and the joyful seasons they knew while hearing these men, and how they journeyed home perhaps seven or eight or ten miles from such a sermon, and only wished they could go again the next night, when their labour was done, to be fed again. What was it that made this preaching so attractive, so edifying? What drew the Lord's people so far? What evoked such enthusiasm? Why, it was that the preacher spoke of his Lord, and never wandered from the cross. When we were children we learned Dr. Watts's catechism of the Bible; and I remember one question—" Who was Isaiah? " and the answer was, " He was that prophet who spoke more of Jesus Christ than all the rest." Who were these men, then, that were followed by God's people so earnestly? They were men that spoke more of Jesus Christ than all the rest. You have read Dr. Hawker's Morning and Evening Portions, perhaps? I do not suppose that you have learned much of fresh exposition from them, or that you have been struck with any great originality of idea in them; but if you have read them profitably you have said to yourself, " Well, this one point there is in Hawker,— his subject is Christ on the first of January, Christ on the last of December, and Christ all the other days of the year." He speaks of nothing else but Christ. He seems to bring forth the Lord Jesus in his portions every day as a matter of course, just as your maid always puts the bread on the table, whatever else she does not place there. So it was with Hawker and men like him, Christ crucified, was their all in all. Their dear Lord and Master was never long absent from their discoursing. If they preached doctrine, it was "the truth as it is *in Jesus.*" If they preached experience, it was "to know *him* and the fellowship of his sufferings." And if they went into practice, as they did, their idea of holiness was to be made like to Jesus and to follow him without the camp, bearing his reproach. Now, I do not believe a sermon can have savour in it unless it has Christ in it, for he has the savour of all good ointments, and there is no sweetness without him. What shall we say of him? "Thy name is as ointment poured forth; therefore the virgins love thee." His name is so fragrant that it perfumes heaven itself: Jehovah smells a savour of rest in the name, and person, and work of his well-beloved Son. Therefore an essential to savoury meat is that it shall have Christ in it. He has said, "My flesh is meat indeed, and my blood is drink indeed," and there is no meat and no drink that has such savour in it as this. Oh, that we might hear more of a crucified Christ in all our places of assembly!

The next necessity to secure savour is a devout spirit in the preacher— a *savour of devotion*. I am trying to explain savour by not attempting a definition, but by noticing its accompaniments. Why, those men who have now gone to heaven, whom you used to hear, seemed to be praying while they preached: their sermons were devotions as well as discourses; their rhetoric was rapture, their oratory was emotion. Their preaching came from the heart; but it came also from "the deep that lieth under," that secret reservoir of everlasting truth which is opened up by the Spirit to those who know the Lord, and to none else. They could say, "All my fresh springs are in thee"; they drew up the truth which they preached out of this deep, out of the very heart of God. They preached the gospel of grace as men that knew it, loved it, lived on it. It was no irksome task to them to speak of Christ, and grace, and pardon, and covenant faithfulness. You could not always see traces of elaboration or even of preparation about their utterances; but you could see something better—the sparkling salt of grace. If the midnight oil had not smeared their sermons, the unction of the Spirit had anointed them. Their heart was inditing a good matter, for they spake the things which they had made touching the King. They spake with such cheerfulness and reverence that it was good to hear them. They spake with profound belief that what they said was infallibly true, for had they not received it fresh from the Spirit of God? Coming from their heart, it went to your heart, and by their realizing faith you were helped to believe it joyfully. It is an ill sign when the teacher of truth does not himself believe it; for thus he becomes a virtual spreader of error. David said, "I believed: therefore have I spoken." Do you not believe, brother? Then go home and be quiet till you do. At least, do not come into the pulpit until you know what your Lord would have you say. Woe to the man who lets the smoke of undried wood come from off his hearth and blow into poor seekers' eyes. We want live coals from off the altar, and the less doubt-smoke the better. Where a man has evidently been with God to learn the truth, and has been baptized into the everlasting spirit of that truth, and therefore speaks what he does know and testifies what he has seen in the fear of the living God, there is a savour about his witness, and the saints discern it gladly. This holy savour cannot be imitated or borrowed; it must come of personal assurance. It is a holy thing, and the composition thereof is known only to the great Giver of all spiritual gifts, the Lord himself. It is a holy anointing oil, which comes not on man's flesh, and is far removed from all carnality. It never comes on any man except as it descends from him who is "the Head," and so drops even to the skirts of his garments. From Christ alone the true anointing comes, and blessed is he who is made partaker with him.

Very well, then, as food without savour is an evil and undesirable sort of food, so is all Christian teaching unacceptable if it lack the savour of Christ, and of devotion.

Another matter goes to make up sweet savour in a discourse, and that is, a *savour of experience.* You used to delight in those men because they had tasted and tested the doctrines which they preached. The younger brethren were somewhat at a discount, because you said, " That good brother speaks fluently, but he cannot have experienced so much as the man of God under whom I have now sat for many years." You prefer to have the truth spoken to you by one who has felt for himself the renewing, upholding, and comforting power of divine grace ; and I cannot blame you for your liking. If the preacher has done business on great waters, in deep soul trouble, or personal affliction, so much the better for you. If he is one who loves much because much has been forgiven him, so much the better for you. If he is a man conscious of his own infirmity and weakness, who speaks humbly of himself as out of the very dust, though he speaks confidently the word from heaven, so much the better for you. Such experience puts a kind of spice into the food which he presents to you. It is so in all our communications one to another. We do not speak with certainty of edification unless we speak of what we have ourselves enjoyed. I have been greatly benefited by hearing an aged blind man stand up and tell of the faithfulness of God to himself. I have been much encouraged at times by hearing a poor but gracious woman near to the gates of death telling with tears in her eyes of the goodness of the Lord to her. Testimonies from such people have weight in them. These people do not play at religion. Poor and tried people, people with aches and pains, people who have none of this world's comforts, people on the borders of the grave, tell us of the great Father's love, and when they do so there is great force of conviction in their testimony. We attach weight to every word they say because their experience is taken into consideration. I never heard a man who spoke more to my soul than dear Mr. George Müller. The sermon that I heard from him was like an address to a Sunday-school, it was so simple and unadorned ; but then there was the man behind it—that simple-hearted child of God, who has believed the promises, and has gone on doing wonders such as astonish all beholders. That man has no more doubt about God's answering his prayers than he has about twice two making four—why should he have ? He acts out the truth which he has received—why should he not ? Entertaining no modern questions and no ancient questions either, he triumphs by knowing the truth and living the truth, and rejoicing in the truth. Such a man is a pattern and example to us all, and there is a precious savour in what he utters, because he speaks experimentally of truths which he has carried out in his own life.

Thus three things help to make up savour in sermons—Christ as the doctrine, devotion as the spirit, and experience as adding weight to testimony.

But these three things are not the whole of it. There is a sacred something : it is not nameless, for I will name it by-and-by : it is a heavenly influence which comes into man, but which has no name among the things that belong to men. This sacred influence pervades the speaker, flavouring his matter, and governing his spirit, while at the same time it rests upon the hearer so that he finds his mind awake, his faculties attentive, his heart stirred.   Under this mysterious influence the hearer's spirit is in a receptive condition, and as he hears the truth it sinks into his soul as snow-flakes drop into the sea.   He finds himself warmed, and cheered, and comforted, and stirred up, as fainting men are wont to be when refreshed after a long fast.   Now, what is this? Whence comes this savour?   In a word, it cometh of *the Holy Ghost*. The Holy Spirit bears witness with the word upon the quickened heart and conscience of the people of God, and that word becomes life, light, and power to them.

All this we greatly need; and if we have it not, what shall we do? I have often trembled as I have come to preach here lest I should have to speak among you without the help of the Divine Spirit.   It would be much better to be silent.   I could almost wish that we had the liberty of our Quaker friends just to sit still until we feel that we are moved to speak; for sometimes we might do better to wait without a spoken word for the hour and a half rather than for one of us to talk without the guidance of the Spirit of God.   Pray much, beloved, that there may be a great deal of dew about—that heavenly showers may fall on us and on all the churches of God.   Let our belief in the Holy Ghost never become a mere compliment which we feel bound to pay him; but in deep and reverent sincerity may we own that he is the great worker in the church—the real actor and doer of the wondrous works of quickening, saving, and comforting.   Let us wait upon him with lowly spirits, feeling that we can do nothing without him, but that if he be with us then all is well.

Take away from any preaching or any teaching Christ as the subject, devotion as the spirit, experience as the strength of testimony, and the Holy Ghost as being all in all, and you have removed all the savour; and what is left?   What can we do with a savourless gospel?   "Can that which is unsavoury be eaten without salt?   Is there any taste in the white of an egg?"   They said of a brother the other day, that he liked savoury doctrine.   "He had a sweet tooth," they said.   It was said in scorn; but if there is anything to be scoffed at in that matter I desire to be a partaker in the reproach, for I have a sweet tooth myself.   I like such books as have savour in them; and I protest to you that whatever scorn it brings upon me, that the majority of modern books seem to me to be fit for nothing but to be burned.   The old theology has the sweetness and the savour in it which the people of God delight in, and I for one mean to stick to it; for I cannot eat the white of your eggs; I cannot endure your unsavoury meat.   I must hear of the electing love and covenant purpose of the Father—this is savoury meat such as my soul loveth.   I must have teaching full of Christ and the doctrines of grace and the Holy Spirit, or my soul will die of famine.   This is my first head.

II.   Our second remark is this.   I find a rendering given to the text, which, if it be not absolutely accurate, nevertheless states an important truth, namely, that THAT WHICH IS UNSAVOURY FROM WANT OF SALT MUST NOT BE EATEN.   I shall only mention this second head as a note of caution.   A word to the wise suffices.

There is a great deal in this world which is unsavoury for want of salt: I mean *in common conversation.* Alas, it is easy to meet with people—and even people wearing the Christian name—whose conversation has not a particle of salt in it. Nothing that tends to edification is spoken by them. Their talk has an abundance of gaiety, but no grace in it. They exhibit any amount of frivolity, but no godliness. In other conversation there is information weighty and solid upon common matters; but there is a lack of that spirit which God's people desire to live in, for the Lord Jesus is forgotten. Someone said to me the other day, " When we were young people, we knew many good old folk who used to meet together and talk about the Lord Jesus Christ by the hour together, and we used to sit and wonder whether we should ever join in such talk as that. But where do you hear it now ? " So I said to him, " I hope that we can hear it in a great many places." " Ah," said he, " I do not meet with it. I find that the ordinary talk among professors has not much in it for the helping of souls onward towards heaven." I do not profess to form a judgment on this matter, but I will say this—that it is a great pity if holy converse be a scarce commodity; and it is well for you and for me to get away from that conversation which does not benefit us. If there is no salt in conversation, it will be unsavoury to a true Christian spirit, and the less he has of it the better.

Again, there is some talk in the world—I hope not among professors —which has no salt in it even of common morality; and consequently it corrupts, and becomes impure and obnoxious. Old Trapp says, somewhat roughly, that it is full of maggots, and that is perhaps what Job meant. That is to say, many persons use coarse allusions, and evil suggestions: to such things shut your ears. Things are often said which sparkle, but the flash is born of decay. The wit which owes its pungency to sin is of the devil. The brilliance which comes of corruption is not for holy eyes. Oh, child of God, never tolerate it in your company ! If it be not in your power to stop evil communications, remove yourself out of their reach. It is not for us to associate with those whose lips are cankered with lascivious words. We have enough within these gunpowder hearts to make us afraid to go near the forge when the sparks are flying about. Let us keep ourselves from ever permitting corrupt communication to proceed out of our own lips: that would be horrible indeed. Let us avoid all company wherein the purity of a renewed heart would be in danger of taint. Yet I fear me that in our daily avocations we shall have grave cause to watch against the things which are unsavoury and corrupt, for the preserving salt is not so abundantly used in these days as it ought to be.

Now, *the same thing is true,* not only of common conversation, but *of a great deal of modern teaching.* Have nothing to do with teaching that is tainted with heresy, brethren. If a man's discoursing has not salt enough in it to keep false doctrine out of it, it is not the kind of food for you. Clean provender is not so scarce that you need to eat carrion. Some like their meat rather high, and there are hearers who are inclined to a preacher who has a sniff of heresy about him ; but, as for us, our taste conducts us where salt is found. Where grace is lacking we are not eager to be feeding.   The banquets of truth need not be supplemented by the tables of error.

But I shall not dwell upon this, because I require all my time for the third head.

III. The third point is, that THERE ARE CERTAIN THINGS IN THE WORLD WHICH NEED SOMETHING ELSE WITH THEM. " Can that which is unsavoury be eaten without salt? or is there any taste in the white of an egg?"

There are many things in this world which we cannot tolerate by themselves : they need seasoning with them.   One of the first of these may read us a lesson of prudence; that is, *reproof.*   It is a Christian duty to reprove a brother who is in a fault, and we should speak to him with all gentleness and quietness, that we may prevent his going farther into evil, and lead him back to the right way.   But will you please remember, brothers and sisters, that the giving of reproofs is dainty work, and needs a delicate hand.   It was said of good Andrew Fuller that frequently he gave a rebuke so severely that it reminded you of one who saw a fly upon his brother's forehead, and seized a sledge hammer to knock it off.   It is the habit of some brethren to do everything forcibly ; but in this case one needs more love than vigour, more prudence than warmth, more grace than energy.   Some persons have a very quick eye for the faults of others, and they have a ready tongue to descant upon them when they perceive them ; to all which they add a tendency to exaggerate the importance of the fault.   Now, these brethren always reprove in a wrong way.   Listen.   One of them cries,—"Come here, brother !   Come here.   Let me take that beam out of your eye." The aforesaid " beam " is really only a mote; and the brother who is addressed becomes indignant at such injustice, and will not have his eye touched at all.   Why destroy your own influence by such unwisdom? If the mote can be removed, well and good ; but if you will ruin the eye in the process, would it not be better to let it alone ?   We have known persons who, to spread truth, have killed love, which is truth's life. They wish to set a brother right in doctrine, and, in order that his sight may be clearer, they knock his eye out, and call it "controversy."   It is one thing to be " valiant for the truth," and quite another thing to be bitter for your own opinion.   Rebuke, however kindly you put it, and however prudently you administer it, will always be an unsavoury thing : therefore, salt it well. Think over it. Pray over it. Mix kindness with it. Rub the salt of brotherly love into it. Speak with much deference to your erring friend, and use much tenderness, because you are not faultless yourself. Speak acknowledging all the excellences and virtues of your brother which may, after all, be greater than your own ; and try, if you can, to wrap up what you have to say in gentle words of praise for something else wherein the friend excels. Express the rebuke in one of your Master's sentences, if you can find one that will exactly fit. Give your patient the pill silver-coated with gentleness; it will be received the more willingly and have none the less efficacy. If you speak unkindly, the reproved one may turn round upon you in anger, and if you ask him why he is wroth, he may answer, " Can that which is unsavoury be eaten without salt? or is there any taste in the white of an egg?"   Do not expect your neighbour to eat your eggs without salt.   Do not expect him to receive your words of rebuke without the true kindliness of voice and spirit which will act as salt. Be not silent about sin, but be not harsh in your rebuke of it. Savour your admonitions with affection, and may the Lord make them acceptable to those who need them.

Now for other matters which many people do not like by themselves; I mean, *the doctrines of the gospel.* The true doctrines of the gospel never were popular, and never will be; but there is no need for any of us to make them more distasteful than they naturally are. The human heart especially revolts at the sovereignty of divine grace. Man is a king, so he thinks, and when he hears of another king he straightway grows rebellious. Man would have God bound hand and foot to give his mercy as man likes; and when the Lord defies the bond and declares, " I will have mercy on whom I will have mercy, and I will have compassion on whom I will have compassion," man burns with wrath. When the Lord saith, " It is not of him that willeth or of him that runneth, but of God who showeth mercy," man is up in arms. He will not brook the divine prerogative. It becomes us who preach this doctrine to take care that we do not add needless offensiveness to it. No one of the doctrines of grace is palatable to man naturally. He does not like the truth of total depravity. Over that he grows exceeding wroth. He calls it a libel upon the nobility of human nature. I have often read of human nature as a noble thing; but I am sorry to say that I have never seen it in that aspect. I am told that our fallen nature is sublime, and that we defame mankind when we speak of them as altogether fallen and say, " There is none that doeth good, no, not one." It is little wonder that this is unsavoury to carnal pride. As to the doctrine of justification by faith alone, Mrs. Toogood stamps her foot at such teaching—is she to be none the better for all her good works? Mr. Good-Enough gnashes his teeth at the idea that human merits cannot save. He cannot endure to hear that we must be saved by faith in Jesus Christ, and that the most moral and excellent need Christ quite as much as the most depraved and abandoned. Carnal minds have no taste for the gospel: they rave against the system of theology that glorifies God. Man wants to be the great Man, and he would have God to be the little god, and then he will be satisfied; but if God be set on high as filling all in all, then straightway many are offended.

Brothers and sisters, since we want people to receive these doctrines, what must we do? We must mix an abundance of salt with them. If the gospel be distasteful we must add a flavouring to it. What shall it be? We cannot do better than flavour it with holiness! Where there is a holy life men cannot easily doubt the principles out of which it springs. If it be so that men and women are kindly, generous, tender, affectionate, upright, truthful, Christ-like, because of the doctrines they hold, then the world begins to think that there must be truth in those doctrines. The evangelical school must always draw its strongest arguments first from the gospel, and next from the lives of its believers; and if we cannot point to those who profess this faith as being famous for holiness, what will the world say? In former ages holy living has been our battle-axe and weapons of war. Look at the Puritanic age. To this day it is the stumbling-block of infidelity. In these times it is very common to laugh at the

Puritans, and to say that their faith is outworn, and that we have got beyond their teaching; and yet the very same men who say this cannot read Carlyle's writings without marvelling at Oliver Cromwell, and the great men who trooped around him.   Do they never say to themselves, Upon what meat did these men feed that they have grown so great? They cannot turn to the lives of the Puritans without reading how they saturated all England with godliness, till as you passed down Cheapside in the morning you would have noticed that there was scarcely a single house in which the blinds were not drawn down because the inhabitants were at family prayer.   The whole land felt the force of truth and righteousness through these men—these poor, benighted, foolish Puritans, whom our boys fresh from college call by ill names.   In their contests for truth the Puritans were as mighty as Cromwell's Ironsides in the days of battle, when they drove the foe before them like chaff before the wind. Then there followed an age of drivelling, in which our Nonconformity existed, but gradually dwindled down, first into Arminianism, and then into Unitarianism, until it almost ceased to be.   Men know that it was so, and yet they would act it all over again.   They read history, and yet demand that the old doctrine should again be given up, and the experiment be tried again of starving our churches with human philosophies.   Oh, fools, and slow of heart!   Will not history teach them?   No, it will not if the Bible does not.   If they hear not Christ and his apostles, neither will they believe even though another Unitarian ghost should pass before their eye.   Surely evil days are near, unless the church shall again clasp the truth to her heart.

But I diverge.   The point I had in hand was this—that in the case of the Puritans their doctrines were rendered respectable and forceful by their glorious lives ; and it must be so now.   Holy living must salt our doctrines.   We must be like Christ that men may believe what we have to say about Christ.

Now, a third egg which cannot be eaten without salt is *affliction*. Afflictions are very unsavoury things.   I think I hear one say, " I should not mind any affliction except the one which now oppresses me." Brother, you speak as other foolish brethren have done before you. This has been my language in my turn.   Somebody sitting next to you would not mind your affliction at all ; at least, he thinks so; it is his own cross which is so galling.   The loads borne by people in yonder street have no great weight for you ; but if you had to carry a sack of flour yourself, the sack would prove very heavy.   We all know the weight of our own burden, but we underestimate that of others.   People in trouble know where their own shoe pinches ; yet other people's shoes pinch too, and other people's crosses are weighty.   " No affliction for the present seemeth to be joyous, but grievous."   Afflictions are unsavoury meat.   What is to be done with them, then?   Why, let us salt them, if we can.   Salt your affliction with patience, and it will make a royal dish. By grace, like the apostle, we shall " glory in tribulations also."   Look at those who endure constant infirmities.   Do you know any?   I do. A dear sister has been blind many years, and yet I do not know a happier woman than she is.   She has more visions of joy than the most of us, though her eyes are closed to the light of the sun.   I know a brother in the ministry who has lost his sight almost entirely ; but he preaches more sweetly than ever he did; he has become a seer in our Israel, enjoying a depth of insight into truth which few possess. Truly the lame take the prey! Some that are deaf hear the voice of their Master better than others. And so infirmities become things to glory in, since Christ's power the better rests upon us.

It is so when the Lord gives grace to the poor man and he becomes contented with his lot. Has he not far greater joy than the rich man who still craves for more? Many of God's poor prisoners in the martyr days were happier in prison than ever they were out of it: in the days of the Covenanters, when they worshipped God on the bleak hill or by the moss side, the Lord was specially near to them. When those times had passed away, and they went to kirk decorously, and sat with the congregation undisturbed, they said, "Ah, man, the Lord was not here to-day as he was out on the brae and on the hill-side." The Master was transfigured before his disciples among the mists of the glens. Then he wore no veil over his face, but he revealed himself so clearly that the sanctuary among the hills was none other than the house of God and the very gate of heaven. The Lord salted their afflictions with his presence, and with the abundant power of the Holy Ghost, and so they enjoyed a sweet savour in them. It is even thus with you and me.

> "I can do all things, or can bear
> All sufferings, if my Lord be there:
> Sweet pleasures mingle with the pains,
> While his left hand my head sustains."

There now, brother, do not go on eating that egg without salt; no longer say to yourself, "Here is nothing but the white, with no taste in it. I cannot bear to eat such loathsome food." Put the salt in, brother: put the salt in, sister. Have you been forgetting that salt? Have you failed to ask of the Lord grace equal to your day?—grace to see that "all things work together for good to them that love God"? Be forgetful no longer, but throw in a pinch of salt; then the tasteless thing will go down comfortably enough, and you will bless the name of the Lord for it.

I will not detain you longer to speak about *persecution*, though that is another unsavoury article, with which salt of consolation is much to be desired.

But, lastly, there is *the thought of death.* Is not death an unsavoury thing in itself? The body dreads dissolution and corruption, and the mind starts back from the prospect of quitting the warm precincts of this house of clay, and going into what seems a cold, rarefied region, where the shivering spirit flits naked into mystery untried. Who likes to sit down and think of his last hour,—the corpse, the coffin, and the shroud? The spade, and the mattock, and the falling clods make poor music for gay minds? Who cares for charnel houses? Oh, but dear friends, thoughts of death, when they are salted, are among the richest, daintiest things that ever come to the believer's table; for what is it to die? Is it not to end our pilgrimage, and come to the place where the many mansions be? Is it not to quit the storm-tossed seas for the Fair Havens where all is bliss for ever? Death strips the soul of its garments, and by itself this seems a trying process; but season it well, and you will long for evening in order to undress, that you may rest with God. Salt it well, and you will almost grow impatient of your length of days, and look for your last hours as children do for their holidays, when they may go home. Salt it well, and your heart will grow like hers whose husband tarries away, and she reckons how long it will be before he will come home again to her house and to her heart. You will cry, " Why are his chariots so long in coming?" I have known saints to salt their thoughts of death until they were transfigured into antepasts of heaven, and they began to drink of that wine of the kingdom which the Beloved will drink new with us in the day of his appearing. Oh, happy spirits who can do this! " What salt," say you, " shall I mingle with my thoughts of death ?" Why the thought that you cannot die: since because *he* lives you shall live also. Add to it the persuasion that though you be dead, yet shall you live. Thoughts of the resurrection and the swinging open of the pearly gates, and of your entrance there ; thoughts of the vision of the Well-beloved's face ; thoughts of the glory that shall be yours for ever and ever at his own right hand—these are the things with which to savour your meditations among the tombs.

As for you that are not in Christ, you *must* eat this unsavoury meat, and there will be no salt with it. I see you put it away from you. You say, " No, I do not mean to think of death." Oh, man, but you will have to die, and it may be full soon. Oh, woman, you will have to die ; the seeds of death are in your bosom now. As surely as you live, you will have to die ; and after death the judgment. This is the meat which will be laid in your dish, and there will be no leaving it. This is the white of the egg, and you must even down with it, whether you will or no. It has no taste which your palate can enjoy ; it has no savour about it but that of fear. Ah, when your conscience awakes, what will you do with the burning thought that, dying, you must go where hope can never come ? O soul, if you pass out of this world as you are, you can never see the face of God with joy, but you must be driven from his presence and from the glory of his power to know what that meaneth—" Where their worm dieth not, and their fire is not quenched." They say that everlasting does not mean ever lasting. What then ? Are the righteous to perish after a while ? In these two sentences the same word must mean the same thing—" These shall go away into everlasting punishment, but the righteous into life eternal." If eternal life lasts for ever, so must eternal punishment. When the righteous cease to be, the wicked will cease to be ; when the godly cease their joy, the ungodly will cease their misery ; but not till then. That is unsavoury meat for you. The Lord help you to salt it, even yet, by believing in Jesus, and so finding eternal salvation. Amen.

PORTION OF SCRIPTURE READ BEFORE SERMON—Psalm cxvi.

HYMNS FROM "OUR OWN HYMN BOOK"—758, 34, 716.

ACCEPTED OF THE GREAT FATHER.

A Sermon

DELIVERED ON LORD'S-DAY MORNING, JULY 15TH, 1883, BY

C. H. SPURGEON,

AT THE METROPOLITAN TABERNACLE, NEWINGTON.

" He hath made us accepted in the beloved."—Ephesians i. 6.

A FEW Sabbath mornings ago I spoke to you upon those memorable words of the great Father, " This is my beloved Son, in whom I am well pleased." We now go a step farther, and see how the love of God to his beloved Son overflows, and runs like a river of life to all those who are in Christ Jesus. To him he saith, " This is my beloved Son," and then he turns to all who are in union with him and says, " These also are my beloved for his sake." As believers we are assured by the text that we are " accepted *in the Beloved*," to the praise of the glory of God's grace. Why is that peculiar title here used? It might have been said, we are accepted in Christ, or accepted in the Mediator; there must be some motive for giving him this special name in this place. The motive is declared to be that we may praise the glory of divine grace. God did not want for a beloved when he made us his beloved: his heart was not pining for an object; his affections were not lone and desolate. His only-begotten Son was his delight, and there was room enough in him for all the Father's love; it was *we* that needed to be loved, and so the Beloved is mentioned that we may remember the unselfishness of divine grace. He makes us his beloved, but he had a Beloved before.

We are also reminded that we are " accepted in the Beloved" to let us know that God has not shifted his love—his first Beloved is his Beloved still. We have not supplanted his dear Son, nor even diverted a beam of love from him. The Lord has called us beloved who were not so, and made us a people who were not a people; but he has not withdrawn a grain of love from Jesus, whom he still calls " mine elect, in whom my soul delighteth." All the infinite love of God still flows to Jesus, and then to us in him. It pleased the Father that to him a fulness of love should be given, that out of it we might each one receive. God's love to us is his love to his Son flowing in a hundred channels. For his sake he makes the wedding-feast, and we are the happy guests who sit at the table. Not for our sakes is this done, but for Jesus' sake, that so it might be all of grace. His perpetual

No. 1,731.

acceptance with God is our acceptance, that nothing legal, nothing whereof we might boast, might be mingled with the work of sovereign grace.

We are "accepted in the Beloved." Do you not love that sweet title? Is it not the highest quality of the acceptance, that it comes through such an One? He is beloved in the highest conceivable degree by the Father, and in this you imitate the great God, for to you also the Lord Jesus is altogether lovely. He is your Beloved as well as God's Beloved, and this is one proof that you are accepted; for all who truly love the Son are approved by the Father. Thus saith the Scripture: "Because he hath set his love upon me, therefore will I deliver him: I will set him on high because he hath known my name." Is Christ your Beloved? Then, as he is the Father's Beloved, you and the Father have evidently come to a sweet agreement; you have come to look at things from the same standpoint as the glorious Jehovah; the Lord and you evidently have a mutual interest in one common person—the incarnate God. Your recognition of Christ as your Beloved is thus a sure proof that you are accepted in the Beloved. See you not this? It is because he is the Father's Beloved that the Father loves you in him, and because he is your Beloved therefore you have an evidence within yourself that you have come to an agreement with the Father, and so to an acceptance by him. I delight in being *accepted* all the more because therein I am still further linked with him who joins God and man in one grand affection.

God's love of his dear Son covers all believers, as a canopy covers all who come beneath it. As a hen covereth her chickens with her wings, so God's love to Christ covers all the children of promise. As the sun shining forth from the gates of the morning gilds all the earth with golden splendour, so this great love of God to the Well-beloved, streaming forth to him, enlightens all who are in him. God is so boundlessly pleased with Jesus that in him he is altogether well pleased with us. Oh, the joy of this blending of our interests with those of the Well-beloved! I scarcely know whither I am borne even by a single word of my precious text.

Let this stand for our preface, and now let us come close to our subject, upon which I do not desire so much to descant myself as to lead you individually to meditate, and personally to feed. I would much rather put the text into your mouths as a sweet fruit from the garden of the Lord, most mellow and ripe, than be judged myself to handle it well. I seek not to exhibit my own skill in words, but I long that you may be refreshed with the marrow and fatness of the choice word. I desire that you may this morning experimentally enjoy the precious drop of honey from the rock Christ Jesus which is contained in the four words— "Accepted in the Beloved." Oh that the Holy Spirit may make you enter into the treasures which they contain!

I. I will begin by treating the text by way of CONTRAST. Brethren and sisters, the grace of God hath made us to be this day "accepted in the Beloved"; but it was not always so. As many of us as have, through grace, believed in Christ are now, to a certainty, at this very moment "accepted in the Beloved"; but in times past it was very different. It is not a matter of question, nor of imagination, nor of sentiment;

but a matter of fact, declared by the Holy Ghost himself, that the Lord hath "made us accepted in the Beloved"; but it was far otherwise a little while ago. What a contrast is our present condition of acceptance to our position under the law through Adam's fall. By actual sin we made ourselves to be the very reverse of accepted, for we were utterly refused. It might have been said of us, "Reprobate silver shall men call them, because God hath rejected them." Our way was contrary to God's way, our thoughts were not his thoughts, our hearts were not according to his heart. Oh, if he had dealt with us then after our sins what must have become of us? At that time we were condemned, "condemned already," because we had not believed on the Son of God. We had no acceptableness before God; he could take no complacency in us; his pure and holy eyes could not look upon us, we were so full of everything that provoked him to jealousy; but now we are—(oh, let me pronounce it like music!)—"accepted in the Beloved." The criminal is now a child, the enemy is now a friend, the condemned one is now justified. Mark, it is not said that we are "acceptable," though that were a very great thing, but we are actually accepted; it has become not a thing possible that God might accept us, but he has accepted us in Christ. Lay this to your soul, and may it fill you with delight. The Lord has chosen you: he has received you to himself, and set his love upon you, and his delight is in you now. What a contrast from what you were a season ago in your own consciousness, in your own judgment. Refresh your memories a little. If you passed through the same state of mind as I did, you loathed your very selves in the sight of God; you felt that God must abhor you, for you abhorred yourselves; you saw sin to be exceeding sinful, and that sinful thing was permeating your entire being, saturating your thoughts, putrefying your aims, making you to be corrupt and offensive in the sight of the Most High. I know I felt that if the Lord swept me away with the besom of destruction, and cast me into the lowest hell, I well deserved it. But now that condemnation is no more to be dreaded; we receive not the spirit of bondage, but the spirit of adoption. Lift up your eyes out of the thick darkness, and behold the light. You, who in your own judgment were cast away for ever; you, who thought that the Lord would never be favourable to you, nor blot out your sins, are this day accepted, "accepted in the Beloved." No contrast could be more sharp and clear, and no reflections could be more joyful than this contrast suggests to the heart.

Think, again, of the contrast between what you are now and what you would have been had not grace stepped in. Left out of Christ as we then were, we might at this time have been going from sin to sin, revelling and rioting in it, as so many do: we might at this moment have been sinning with a high hand, finding even in the Sabbath-day a special opportunity for double transgression. In our daring rebellion we might have been crying, "The better the day the better the deed," and so might have shown how completely we had thrown off the yoke of allegiance to the great King. Ay, by this time we might have been dead, as the result of our own sins. The measure of our iniquity might have been full, and we might have been in hell. Be startled, my soul, at this thought, that nothing but infinite longsuffering has kept thee out of the pit that is bottomless, "where their worm dieth not, and their fire is not quenched."

But, brothers, we are not in hell, and, what is more, we never shall be, for those iron gates can never close upon a soul that is " accepted in the Beloved," and that is our condition now.   We have fled for refuge to the hope set before us, and now no more need we be in terror of the great white throne and the righteous Judge, and the stern sentence, " Depart, ye cursed."   Clinging to the cross, and beholding ourselves covered with the righteousness of Christ, we know that we are saved, and, what is far more, we are *accepted*.   This blessed fact is true of those who might have been among the damned.   Our laments might have been going up to-day amidst the wailings of the wretched who are eternally cast away from hope ; and now, instead thereof, we lift the joyful song of praise unto our God, and bless and magnify his name in whom we are accepted this day.   Oh, my soul, sing thou thine own song to thy Beloved—

> " Just as thou art—how wondrous fair,
> Lord Jesus, all thy members are!
> A life divine to them is given—
> A long inheritance in heaven.

> "Just as I was I came to thee,
> An heir of wrath and misery ;
> Just as thou art before the throne,
> I stand in righteousness thine own.

> " Just as thou art—nor doubt, nor fear,
> Can with thy spotlessness appear ;
> Oh timeless love! as thee, I'm seen,
> The ' righteousness of God in him.' "

One more point I cannot quite pass over, and that is, the contrast between what we now are and all we ever could have been in the most favourable circumstances apart from the Beloved.   If it had been possible for us out of Christ to have had desires after righteousness, yet those desires would all have run in a wrong direction ; we should have had a zeal of God, but not according to knowledge, and so, going about to establish our own righteousness, we should not have submitted ourselves to the righteousness of God.   We should have been weaving a righteousness of our own with heavy labour, which would have proved no better when completed than a cobweb that could never conceal our nakedness.   At this moment the prayers we offered would never have been received at the throne ; the praises we presented would have been an ill savour unto God ; all that we could have aimed to accomplish in the matter of good works, had we striven to our utmost, would have been done in wilfulness and pride, and so must necessarily have fallen short of acceptance.   We should have heard the voice of the Eternal saying, " Bring no more vain oblations; incense is an abomination unto me ";. for out of Christ our righteousness is as unacceptable as our unrighteousness, and all our attempts to merit acceptance increase our unworthiness. Oh, strive as ye will, ye self-righteous ; labour as ye may after a righteousness of your own, what can come of it but confusion ?   Whence is it that the people labour as in the very fire ?   This shall they have at the Lord's hands—they shall lie down in sorrow.   The bed is shorter than that a man may stretch himself on it, and the covering is narrower than that a man may wrap himself in it.   Woe is unto the man who is out of

Christ, wherever he may be. In any case the wrath of God abideth on him. But we are not out of Christ, we are not striving in vain, we are not spending our strength for naught, for here is the blessed contrast, we are " accepted in the Beloved."

A touch of the black pencil brings out the bright lights, and therefore I have laid on these shades. Such were some of you, but now ye are washed, now ye are sanctified, now ye are justified, now ye are " accepted in the Beloved." All glory be unto the grace by which we have received this heavenly benefit.

II. Secondly, we will say a little by way of EXPLANATION, that the text may sink yet deeper into your hearts, and afford you richer enjoyment. Recollect, brethren, that once we were pitied of God as poor, lost, self-destroyed creatures : that was in a degree hopeful. We were chosen of God while in that pitiable condition, and although forlorn, wretched, and ruined, yet were we marked by his electing love —this was still more encouraging. Then came a time of dealing with us, and we were pardoned, our transgressions were put away, we were renewed in the spirit of our minds by the Holy Ghost, and the righteousness of Christ was imputed to us, and at length burst forth the light of this word, " He hath made us accepted in the Beloved." Much went before this, but, oh, what a morning without clouds rose upon us when we knew our acceptance and were assured thereof. Acceptance was the watchword, and had troops of angels met us we should have rejoiced that we were as blest as they.

Understand that this acceptance comes to us entirely as a work of God—" He *hath made* us accepted in the Beloved." We never made ourselves acceptable, nor could we have done so, but he that made us first in creation, hath now new made us by his grace, and so hath made us accepted in the Beloved.

That this was an act of pure grace there can be no doubt, for the verse runs thus, " *Wherein* he hath made us accepted in the Beloved"— that is, in his grace. There was no reason in ourselves why we should have been put into Christ, and so accepted ; the reason lay in the heart of the Eternal Father himself. He will have mercy on whom he will have mercy, and by this will we were saved. To the great First Cause we must ever trace the motive for our acceptance. Grace reigns supreme. It is a gracious acceptance of those who but for grace had been rejected. Do notice this, and dwell upon the truth, glorifying God therein. Again, our acceptance is " *in the Beloved.*" It is only as we are in Christ that we are accepted. Let no man steal out of Christ, and then say, " God has accepted me." Nothing of the kind. If the Lord views you apart from Christ, whoever you may be, you are a thing to be consumed, and not to be accepted. " In the Beloved," that is, as it were, within the gates of the city of refuge. You must abide within that wall of fire of which the cross is the centre, or else you are not accepted. You must remain within the arms of the Well-beloved, living in the very heart of Christ, and then you shall know yourself to be " accepted in the Beloved." For Christ's sake, and because you are a part of him, you shall be approved of the Father. He has taken you into covenant union, so that you can say with the favoured apostle, " Truly our fellowship is with the Father and with his Son Jesus Christ." Therefore the

Father accepts you, because he cannot dissociate you from his Son, nor his Son from you, nor think of Christ without you, nor of you without Christ ; hence it is you are " accepted in the Beloved." That explains the words.

The following remarks may make the sense somewhat more transparent. No man, my brethren, can be accepted of God while he is guilty of sin, so that our acceptance in the Beloved involves the fact that our sin at this moment is for ever put away. Covered is our unrighteousness, and therefore from condemnation we are free, and we are accepted. Realize this truth. It does not require any oratory to set it forth ; it needs only that your faith should fully apprehend it. Realize that you are forgiven to-day. With your eye upon the wounds of Christ, say unto your soul by the Spirit, " I am without spot or wrinkle in the sight of God ; for Christ hath washed me whiter than the driven snow." He has said of his people, " Ye are clean every whit." Rejoice in this. You could not be accepted if he had not made you clean, for the filthy are not accepted of the Lord.

Neither could God accept a man devoid of righteousness. A mere colourless person, whose sin was forgiven, but who had no righteousness, could not be acceptable with him. I cannot suppose the existence of such a being ; but if there were such, he would be like one who was neither cold nor hot, and must be spued out of God's mouth. He that is accepted with God must be positively righteous. Very well, then, if he has made believers " accepted in the Beloved," they that believe in Christ are righteous in the sight of God. Mark you, they are not righteous with a sham righteousness, an imaginary, fictitious righteousness ; no, the righteousness which is of faith is the most real righteousness under heaven. The righteousness of works may be questioned, but the righteousness of faith cannot be, for it is the righteousness of God himself. Now drink that in. Do not let me hold it up, and show you what a draught it is ; but drink it up for yourselves. You are righteous in Christ, or else you could not be accepted. Sin is gone, and righteousness is positively yours.

Now to come back again. If we be indeed " accepted *in the Beloved*," does it not show how close, how real our union with the Beloved must be ? Do we even share in Christ's acceptance with God ? Then we are one with him in everything. Here is a father who has no particular interest in such and such a woman, but his son takes to himself that woman to be his wife, and now the loving father says, " That woman is my daughter," and so she is received into his love for his son's sake. He says to her ; " You are my dear son's wife ; therefore you are my daughter, and dear to me, and welcome to my house at any time." Thus it is with the great God. He says to us, whom Christ has espoused unto himself, that we may be his bride in blessed conjugal union for ever and ever, " Come to my heart, my children, for he is my Son, and I love you for his sake ; I accept you in him." Is not that a wonderful union, closer than the marriage bond, which causes us to share in Christ's righteousness, so that the holy God can say to us who are sinful by nature, " You are acceptable to me because of your connection with my Son " ? If a woman of base character were married to the best of men it would not make her acceptable. A father would scarcely know what to do with such a daughter-in-law: we should try and carry out our relationship as far as we could with all kindness, but we could hardly say that such a person brought into our family by marriage would be acceptable to us; but, oh, the Lord sees his people so wrapped up in Christ that he must accept them in him. If I accept a man, I cannot quarrel with his little finger; if I accept a man, I accept his whole body: and so, since the Father accepts Christ, he accepts every member of his mystical body. If I am one with Christ, though I be but as it were only the sole of his foot, and exposed often-times to the mire of the streets, yet, because the glorious Head is accepted, the meanest member joined in living union to that Head is accepted too. Is not this glorious? Can you get a firm hold of it? Unless you intelligently grasp its full significance you will not heartily enjoy this unspeakable privilege. But if your faith receives and welcomes it, you will not need any further explanation. You are "accepted in the Beloved," and it is clear that there is a blessed union between you and Christ. The acceptance which the Father gives to Christ he gives to you. Now, see if you can measure it. How acceptable is Christ to God? Must it not be an infinite acceptance? for it is an infinite Being infinitely accepting an infinitely holy and well-pleasing One, and then accepting us who are in him with the self-same acceptance. Oh, how acceptable is every believer to the eternal Father in Christ Jesus!

III. Can we get a step farther? Will the Holy Spirit help us while I say a few words by way of ENLARGEMENT? If we are "accepted in the Beloved," then, first, our persons are accepted: we ourselves are well-pleasing to him. God looks upon us now with pleasure. Once he said of men that it repented him that he had made them, but now when he looks at his people he never repents that he made us; he is glad he made us, he takes delight in us. Look at your own children; sometimes they grieve you, but still you are pleased with them; it is a pleasure to have them near you; and if they are long out of your sight you grow anxious about them. They are coming home for their holidays soon: they are glad to return home, and I am sure their mothers are glad at the thought of seeing them again. Our Father is as truly pleased with us: our very persons are accepted of God. He delights in us individually; he thinks of us with joy, and when we are near to him it gives pleasure to his great heart.

Being ourselves accepted, the right of access to Him is given us. When a person is accepted with God he may come to God when he chooses; he is one of those sheep who may go in and out and find pasture; he is one of those courtiers who may come even to the royal throne and meet with no rebuff. No chamber of our great Father's house is closed against us; no blessing of the covenant is withheld from us; no sweet smile of the Father's face is refused us. He that accepted us gives us access into all blessings. "See, I have accepted thee concerning this thing also." You remember the story of King Ahasuerus and his poor trembling spouse Esther, how she ventured in at peril of her life, for if her royal lord and master did not stretch out the golden sceptre then the guards that stood about the throne would cut her down, the queen royal though she was, for daring to come unbidden into the despot's presence ; but to-day, when you and I come to God, we have no fear of that kind, because we are accepted first ; he hath already stretched out to us the golden sceptre, and he bids us come boldly. All is well between us and him. We have access with boldness into this grace wherein we stand.

And, being accepted ourselves, our prayers are also accepted. Children of God, can you sincerely believe this ? Do you not sometimes pray as if you were beggars in the street, pleading with unwilling persons to give you a gratuity of coppers ? I believe many children of God do so ; but when we know we are "accepted in the Beloved" we speak to God with a sweet confidence, expecting him to answer us. To us it is no surprise that our heavenly Father should hear our prayers. He does it so often and so generously that we expect him to do so always. It is a way of his to hear the prayers of the Well-beloved. When unaccepted men pray they pray unaccepted prayers, but when accepted men plead with God he says, " In an acceptable time have I heard thee, and in a day of salvation have I succoured thee." When God delights in men he gives them the desires of their hearts. Oh, the splendour of that man's position who is " accepted in the Beloved!" To him the Lord seems to say, " Ask what thou wilt, and it shall be given to thee, not even to the half of my kingdom, but my kingdom itself shall be thine : thou shalt sit with me upon my throne." Oh, the blessedness of being " accepted in the Beloved," because the acceptance makes our prayers to be as sweet incense before the Lord !

It follows, then, as a pleasant sequence, that our gifts are accepted, for those who are accepted with God find a great delight in giving of their substance to the glory of his name. I know that when money is wanted for the church of God, and one of the brethren goes round to collect the offerings, the subjects of the kingdom are wont to say, " Here comes the tax-gatherer again." Yes, that is what the subjects say. Oh, but when the children are about, they cry, " Here is another opportunity of presenting an offering to our Father, a welcome occasion of proving that our love to him is pure, without greed or grudging." They clap their hands to think that they may come before the Lord with their sacrifices. Their only question is, " Will he accept it ? Oh, what would I not give if I did but know that he would accept it ! " Many a poor woman will take her two mites, and not more stealthily than joyfully cast them into the treasury, as she says, " Will he really accept them when dropped into the offering-box ; will he even know about them ? " And some of God's children get schemes into their heads of doing great things for God, but they say, " May I not after all be working for myself? May it not be that pride and vain-glory so leaven my labours that ' the odour of a sweet smell,' like to that ' sacrifice acceptable ' which the Philippians presented, will be all a-wanting." Nay, my friends, my helpers in every good work, you need not ask that question if he has accepted you, for the accepted man brings an accepted offering. It is wonderful how God sees good things in his people where we cannot see them. He saw in Abijah some good thing towards the Lord God of Israel when perhaps no one else saw it. Mistress Sarah once made a rather naughty speech; yet there was one good word in it. I doubt very much if any one of us would have been quick enough to discern it. Yet the Holy Spirit picked out that one word, and put it into the New Testament to her praise. She spoke unbelievingly as to her bearing a child at her advanced age, though the promise was pronounced that she should bring forth a son. She said "Shall it be, I being old, my lord being old also?" This was a bad speech, but we are somewhat startled to read in the New Testament, " As Sarah also obeyed her husband, calling him lord." If God can find a speck of good in us he will. Then let us try what we can do for him. Here is a great lump of quartz, but if the Lord can see a grain of gold he will save the quartz for the sake of it. He says, " Destroy it not, for a blessing is in it." I do not mean that the Lord deals thus with all men. It is only for accepted men that he has this kind way of accepting their gifts. Had you seen me, when a young man, and an usher, walking through the streets with rolls of drawings from a boys' school, you would have guessed that I considered them of no value and fit only to be consigned to the fire ; but I always took a great interest in the drawings of my own boy, and I still think them rather remarkable. You smile, I dare say, but I do so think, and my judgment is as good as yours. I value them because they are his, and I think I see budding genius in every touch, but you do not see it because you are so blind. I see it since love has opened my eyes. God can see in his people's gifts to him and their works for him a beauty which no eyes but his can perceive. Oh, if he so treats our poor service, what ought we not to do for him? What zeal, what alacrity should stimulate us ! If we are ourselves accepted our sacrifices shall be acceptable. The Almighty will permit us to be called his servants, and we shall find his blessing resting on all that we do. If the tree be good the fruit is good. As is the man so is his strength ; and as is his prestige, so is his power. " Accepted in the Beloved " has for its accompaniment " God hath accepted thy works."

IV. We have thus pursued our train of thought in a contrast, an explanation, and an enlargement; let us now indulge in a few REFLECTIONS.

" Accepted in the Beloved." May not each believer talk thus with himself—I have my sorrows and griefs, I have my aches and pains, and weaknesses, but I must not repine, for God accepts me. Ah me ! How one can laugh at griefs when this sweet word comes in, "accepted in the Beloved." I may be blind, but I am " accepted in the

Beloved :" I may be lame, I may be poor, I may be despised, I may be persecuted, I may have much to put up with in many ways, but really these troubles of the flesh count for little or nothing to me since I am "accepted in the Beloved."

I have to mourn over a multitude of infirmities and imperfections, and there is never a day but what when night comes on I have repenting work to do, and feel compelled to fly to the precious blood again for a renewed sense of pardon. Yes, but I am "accepted in the Beloved." Ah me, I have been struggling with this evil and that, and I hope I have got the victory, though I have had many a wound in the battle: yes, but I am "accepted in the Beloved." I have just now been blaming myself for my shortcomings, and mourning over my many slips and failures : yes, but I am "accepted in the Beloved." I am speaking for you, or at least I am trying to interpret your meditations : I want you to let this blessed fact go down sweetly with you, that whatever may be the trials of life, whatever the burdens that oppress you, whatever the difficulties of the way, whatever the infirmities of the body, whatever the frailties of the mind, yet still, as being "in the Beloved" you are accepted. Oh, will you not be accepted when you stand where golden harps ring out perpetual hallelujahs, where every robe is spotless, and every heart is sinless ? Yes, but you will not be a jot more accepted *then* than you are now, in all this noise, and strife, and turmoil of everyday life, for you are "accepted in the Beloved" *now*. Is not this present grace in the highest perfection ? What more can you have till you behold the unveiled face of infinite love. Drink down that truth, I pray you.

Let a further reflection be added also to the sweetness of your enjoyment. Think of who it is that doth accept you. It is no common person who admits us to his favour: it is the God whose name is Jehovah, the jealous God. "Holy, holy, holy," cry the seraphim unceasingly, and nothing that is defiled can ever enter his palace-gates, nor can his heart endure the thought of iniquity, and yet it is he that hath accepted you. Did your brethren cast you out ? Did your friend condemn you ? Did your own heart accuse you ? Did the devil roar upon you ? What matters it, for he hath accepted you. "Who shall lay anything to the charge of God's elect ? It is God that justifieth. Who is he that condemneth ?" He hath made us "accepted in the Beloved," and if that be so, we need not fear what men can do unto us.

Now, just think again, he has made you "accepted in the Beloved." He, that is, God, has accepted you in Christ. Would you have liked any other way of acceptance one half as well ? For my part, I had infinitely rather receive everything through Christ than reach it from myself. Mercy seems so much the sweeter and the better from the fact that it all comes from that dear, pierced hand. If I were this day accepted in myself, I should fear that I might lose my acceptance, for I am a poor, changeable being, but if I am "accepted in the Beloved," then the Beloved will never change, and I always must and shall be accepted, come what may. Is not this a word to die with? We will meet death and face his open jaws with this word, "Accepted in the Beloved." Will not this be a word to rise with amidst the blaze of the great judgment-day? You wake up from your tomb, lift up your eyes, and ere you gaze upon the terrors of that tremendous hour, you say, "I am accepted in the Beloved," what can then fill you with alarm? For ever and ever, as the cycles of eternity revolve, will not this be the core and centre of heaven's supremest bliss, that still we are "accepted in the Beloved"? I hear strange theories nowadays of what may happen to the saints: they tell us the sinners will die out, or be restored, or something else; for they are not content with the Scripture teaching of eternity, but must needs invent strange notions about the punishment of the ungodly. Then they begin to picture new destiny for saints too, and the heaven of our fathers has sad doubts cast on it. I care not for their dreams, for I am "accepted in the Beloved." It matters nothing what all the eternities can reveal: he that is accepted in Christ, and eternally one with him, has nothing before him at which he need tremble.

My time is gone: I heard the warning bell just now, and so I must forbear to amplify on the many reflections that spontaneously flow out of our text; all fitted to stifle anxious care, to sweeten mortal life, and to set our souls a-longing for the home which is above where so hearty a welcome awaits us.

V. And now I wish to finish with this one PRACTICAL USE. If it be so that we are "accepted in the Beloved," then let us go forth and tell poor sinners how they can be accepted too. Are you, to-day, though unconverted, anxious to be found right at last? Listen, friend. If you want to be accepted, you must accept. "And what," do you ask, "must I accept?" You must accept Christ as the free gift of God; you must accept Christ as God's way of accepting you, for if you get into Christ you are accepted. The guiltiest of the guilty *may be* accepted in Christ: no matter how great and grievous their transgressions may have been, the atoning sacrifice can take all their guilt away, and the perfect righteousness can justify the most heinous sinner before God. You may be accepted. Listen. If you come to Christ now and trust him you *will be* accepted. Never did one come to Christ to be rejected. You shall not be the first. Try it; and though you came into this house condemned you shall go out accepted, if you come now and hide in those dear wounds of his as doves do hide them in the clefts of the rocks. Listen again. It is not only that *you may be* accepted; it is rather that *you will be* accepted, *you cannot but be* accepted in Christ:

there is no sort of fear nor possibility that you shall come to Christ and be cast out. Christ must change, truth must change, God must change towards his Well-beloved, he must cease to love him ere he could refrain from loving a soul that is in him. Guilty as you are, come to Christ this morning. Come, despise not the exhortation, for you must be accepted; it cannot but be that you should be accepted if you come. And you shall be accepted *at once.* If at this moment you are as vile as vile can be, if while I speak you know that you are black as hell's dark night, yet the moment that you come to Christ you are "accepted in the Beloved." Trust him: trust him. Have you done so? Your sin is gone; righteousness is imputed; you are saved.

And, then, to close, if you get into Christ you shall be accepted as long as you are in Christ, and as the grace of God will never let you go out of Christ you shall be accepted for ever, "accepted in the Beloved" world without end. If that be the verdict of this day it shall be the verdict of every day till days shall be no more; the hope for you dying, the song for your rising again, the verdict which shall be given out when the great assize shall sit, and you shall be tried for your life for the last time. They that sit in judgment shall say, "Let that man go; he is accepted in the Beloved." If thou believest in Jesus it shall be so; it is so; it shall be so for ever and ever. God bless you all by his good Spirit, for Christ's sake. Amen.

Portion of Scripture read before Sermon—Ephesians 1.

Hymns from "Our Own Hymn Book"—427, 554, 397.

Price 3s. 6d. Cloth Gilt.
"FARM SERMONS."
By C. H. SPURGEON.

"In this book there is compressed, we venture to say, more valuable counsel to Farmers, Graziers, Shepherds, etc., than can be found in the same compass in any other volume. In it Mr. Spurgeon shows how many-sided his preaching is, how general his knowledge of the ways of men and of nature, and how felicitous in illustrating divine truth, and how honest and pungent are his suggestions. There is no part of agriculture overlooked in his range of subjects, and through the whole he walks with the Great Teacher, drawing lessons of infinite importance from every department of rural life, and from every act of those who live by the soil. Happy the farmer who follows his advice, and useful the preacher who learns from these 'Farm Sermons' how to instruct his hearers in his country parish."—*From* "*The (American) Preacher and Homiletic Monthly.*"

Passmore & Alabaster, 4, Paternoster Buildings; and all Booksellers.

Metropolitan Tabernacle Pulpit.

IN HIM: LIKE HIM.

A Sermon

DELIVERED ON THURSDAY EVENING, MAY 17TH, 1883, BY

C. H. SPURGEON,

AT THE METROPOLITAN TABERNACLE, NEWINGTON.

"He that saith he abideth in him ought himself also so to walk, even as he walked."—1 John ii. 6.

"HE that *saith* he abideth in him:"—that is exactly what every Christian does say. He cannot be a Christian unless this be true of him, and he cannot fully enjoy his religion unless he assuredly knows that he is in Christ, and can boldly say as much. We must be in Christ, and abidingly in Christ, or else we are not saved in the Lord. It is our union with the Christ that makes us Christians: by union with him as our life we truly live,—live in the favour of God. We are in Christ, dear brethren, as the manslayer was in the city of refuge: I hope that we can say we abide in him as our sanctuary and shelter. We have fled for refuge to him who is the hope set before us in the gospel; even as David and his men sheltered themselves in the caves of Engedi, so we hide ourselves in Christ. We each one sing, and our heart goes with the words—

"Rock of ages, cleft for me,
Let me hide myself in thee."

We have entered into Christ as into the shadow of a great rock in a weary land, as guests into a banquet-hall, as returning travellers into their home. And now we abide in Christ in this sense, that we are joined to him : as the stone is in the wall, as the wave is in the sea, as the branch is in the vine, so are we in Christ. As the branch receives all its sap from the stem, so all the sap of spiritual life flows from Christ into us. If we were separated from him, we should be as branches cut off from the vine, only fit to be gathered up for the fire, and to be burned. So that we abide in Christ as our shelter, our home, and our life. To-day we remain in Christ, and hope for ever to remain in him, as our Head. Ours is no transient union ; while he lives as our Head we shall remain his members. We are nothing apart from him. As a finger is nothing without the head, as the whole body is nothing without the head, so should we be nothing without our Lord Jesus Christ. But we are in him vitally, and therefore we dare ask the question, "Who shall separate us from the love of God which is in Christ Jesus our Lord?"

No. 1,732.

Beloved, since we, then, are the people who say that we abide in him, it is upon us that the obligation of the text falls: we ought ourselves also so to walk even as he walked. A Bible *ought* has great weight with a conscientious man. Ought it to be so? Then it shall be so, God helping me. If we *say*, we must *do*. If we talk, we must walk, or it will be mere talk. If we make the profession of abiding in Christ, we must prove it by our practice of walking with Christ. If we say that we are in Christ and abide in him, we must take care that our life and character are conformed to Christ, or else we shall be making an empty boast. This is true of every man who says he is in Christ, for the text is put in the most general and absolute manner: be the man old or young, rich or poor, learned or simple, pastor or hearer, it is incumbent upon him to live *like* Christ if he professes to live *in* Christ.

The first thing about a Christian is initiation, initiation into Christ: the next thing is imitation, the imitation of Christ. We cannot be Christians unless we are in Christ; and we are not truly in Christ unless in him we live and move and have our being, and the life of Christ is lived over again by us according to our measure. "Be ye imitators of God, as dear children." It is the nature of children to imitate their parents. Be ye imitators of Christ as good soldiers, who cannot have a better model for their soldierly life than their Captain and Lord. Ought we not to be very grateful to Christ that he deigns to be our example? If he were not perfectly able to meet all our other wants, if he were an expiation and nothing else, we should glory in him as our atoning sacrifice, for we always put that to the front, and magnify the virtue of his precious blood beyond everything: but at the same time we need an example, and it is delightful to find it where we find our pardon and justification. They that are saved from the death of sin need to be guided in the life of holiness, and it is infinitely condescending on the part of Christ that he becomes an example to such poor creatures as we are. It is said to have been the distinguishing mark of Cæsar as a soldier that he never said to his followers "Go!" but he always said "Come!" Of Alexander, also, it was noted that in weary marches he was sure to be on foot with his warriors, and in fierce attacks he always was in the van. The most persuasive sermon is the example which leads the way. This certainly is one trait in the Good Shepherd's character, "when he putteth forth his own sheep he goeth before them." If Jesus bids us do anything, he first does it himself. He would have us wash one another's feet; and this is the argument—"Ye call me Master and Lord, and ye say well; for so I am. If I, then, your Lord and Master, have washed your feet, ye also ought to wash one another's feet." Shall we not do as he does whom we profess to follow? He has left his footprints that we may set our feet in them. Will we not joyfully fix our feet upon this royal road?

That is our theme at this time. We do many of us say that we are in Christ: let us hear how obliged we are by this to walk even as he walked. Oh, Holy Spirit, let us feel the weight of the sacred obligation!

But I stop a minute. I know that there are some here who cannot say that they are in Christ. Then, if you are not in Christ, you are out of Christ; and out of Christ your position is dangerous, terrible, ruinous.

If we saw a man hanging over a deep pit, if we saw a man exposed to a sea of fire, and likely to perish in it, all our tenderest emotions would begin to flow, and we should pray in an agony of spirit, " Oh, God, save this man from danger!" My brethren, there are some among us to-night who are in the utmost danger; in a most emphatic sense they are lost already, for they are without God, and without Christ, strangers to the commonwealth of Israel. Oh, my hearers, how shall I speak of you without tears? Poor souls, abiding under the wrath of God! Poor souls! The mercy is that you are not past hope. There is an arm that can reach you: there is a voice that calls you—calls you even now; hear it: " Look unto me, and be ye saved, all the ends of the earth; for I am God, and besides me there is none else." Can you not even now give one look to him who died for you? Will you not turn the eye of faith that way, and trust him who was nailed to the tree on your behalf? God grant that you may, and then I may include you also in the blessed instruction of the text. " He that saith he abideth in him, ought himself also so to walk, even as he walked."

I. I shall first of all ask you to CONSIDER HOW THIS OBLIGATION IS PROVED. Let us spend a few minutes over the question, Why ought we to walk as Jesus did?

When we read the word "ought," if we are honest men, we begin to look about us and to make enquiries as to the reason and the measure of this obligation. An "ought" is a compulsion to a true heart. There is a "needs be " to every godly man that he should do what he ought.

What, then, is the ground upon which this " ought " is fixed?

First, *it is the design of God* that those who are in Christ should walk as Christ walked. It is a part of the original covenant purpose; for " whom he did foreknow he also did predestinate to be conformed to the image of his Son." That is the drift of the plan of grace, the aim of the covenant. Grace looks towards holiness, that there should be a people called forth to whom Christ should be the elder brother, the first-born among many brethren. You certainly have not had the purpose of God fulfilled in you, dear friend, unless you have been conformed to the image of his dear Son. " He hath chosen us in Christ Jesus before the foundation of the world, that we should be holy and without blame before him in love." This is the aim of election; this is the object of redemption; this is the fruit of calling; this is the concomitant of justification; this is the evidence of adoption; this is the earnest of glory; that we should be holy, even as Christ is holy, and in this respect should wear the lineaments of the Son of God. He hath given his own Son to die for us, that we may die to sin; he has given him to live that we may live like him. In every one of us the Father desires to see Christ, that so Christ may be glorified in every one of us. Do you not feel this to be an imperative necessity to be laid upon you? Would you have the Lord miss his purpose? You are chosen of God to this end, that you should be " a chosen generation, a royal priesthood, a holy nation, a peculiar people, zealous of good works," and what is this but that you should walk even as he walked?

Observe, again, another point of this necessity: *it is necessary to the mystical Christ* that we should walk as he walked, for we are joined unto the Lord Jesus in one body. Now, Christ cannot be made a monster:

that would be a blasphemous notion. And yet if any man had eyes, ears, hands, or other members that were not conformable to the head, he would be a strange being. The mouth of a lion, the eye of an ox, the feathers of a bird—these things would have no consistency with the head of a man. We read of the image in Nebuchadnezzar's dream, that it had a head of fine gold, but legs of iron, and feet part of iron and part of clay. Surely, Christ's spiritual body is not compounded of such discordant elements. No, no. He must be all of a piece. The mystical body must be the most beautiful and precious production of God; for the church is Christ's body, "the fulness of him that filleth all in all." And shall that mysterious fulness be something defiled, deformed, full of sin, subject to Satan? God forbid! "As he which hath called you is holy, so be ye holy," and as your HEAD is holy, so be ye, as members of his body, holy too. Ought it not to be so? Does anybody raise a question? Does not every member of Christ, by the very fact that he is joined to him by living union, feel at once that he must walk even as Christ walked?

And this, beloved, again, must all be *the fruit of the one Spirit that is in Christ and in us.* The Father anointed Christ of old with the same anointing which rests on us in our measure. The Holy Spirit descended upon him, and rested upon him, and we have an unction from the same Holy One. The Spirit of God has anointed all the chosen of God who are regenerated, and he dwelleth with them and in them. Now, the Spirit of God in every case works to the same result. It cannot be supposed that the Spirit of God in any case produces unholiness: the thought were blasphemy. The fruit of the Spirit is everything that is delightful, right, and good towards God, and generous towards man. The Spirit of God, wherever he works, works according to the mind of God; and God is hymned as "Holy, holy, holy," by those pure spirits who know him best. He is altogether without spot or trace of sin, and so shall we be when the Spirit's work is done. If, then, the Spirit of God dwell in you (and if it do not, you are not in Christ), it must work in you conformity to Christ that you should walk even as he walked.

Perhaps further argument is not needed; but I would have true Christians remember that this is one *article of the agreement which we make with Christ when we become his disciples.* It is taken for granted that when we enter the service of Jesus we by that act and deed undertake by his help to follow his example. "Whosoever doth not bear his cross, and come after me, cannot be my disciple." "Take my yoke upon you, and learn of me, and ye shall find rest unto your souls." You know, if any man love Christ, he must follow him :—"If ye love me, keep my commandments." When we took Christ's cross to be our salvation we took it also to be our heavenly burden. When we yielded ourselves up to Christ to be saved by him, we in spirit renounced every sin. We felt that we had come out from under the yoke of Satan, and that we made no reserve for the lusts of the flesh that we might obey them, but bowed our necks to the yoke of the Lord Jesus. We put ourselves into Christ's hands unreservedly, and we said, "Lord, sanctify me, and then use me. Take my body and all its members; take my mind and all its faculties; take my spirit and all the new powers which thou hast bestowed upon me with it; and let all these be thine. Reign in me; rule me absolutely, sovereignly, always and alone. I do not ask to be my own, for I am not my own, I am bought with a price." After we have learned the grand truth that, "if one died for all, then all died," we infer that "Christ died for all, that we that live might not henceforth live unto ourselves, but unto him that died for us, and rose again." Are we not, then, to be true to this blessed compact? "I do remember my faults this day," says one. Ay, but remember also the vows that still engage you. Do not desire to escape from the sacred bond. This day remember the Lord to whom you dedicated yourself in the days of your youth, perhaps long years ago, and again entreat him to take full possession of the purchased possession, and hold it against all comers, for ever. So it ought to be. He that says, "I am in him" ought also so to walk even as he walked. Obey the sacrifice of Jesus, yield yourselves as living sacrifices; by your hope of being saved by him put your whole being into his hands to love and serve him all your days.

For, once more, inasmuch as we are in Christ, we are now bound to live to Christ's glory, and this is a great means of glorifying Christ. What can we do to glorify Christ if we do not walk even as he walked? If I came and preached to you, and if I had the tongues of men and of angels, yet if I did not seek to do as my Master did, what avails all that I can say? It is but "sounding brass and a tinkling cymbal." You know what men say to unholy preachers: they bid them be silent or be consistent. Unholy ministers are a derision, and a scoff, and a by-word. And so it is with unholy Christians, too. You may teach your children at home, or teach them in the Sunday-school class; but if they see your lives to be Christless, prayerless, godless, they will not learn any good from you. They will rather learn from what you *do* amiss, than from what you *say* that is right. Do you blame them that it is so? Are not actions far more forcible than words? Suppose you church-members are unjust in your trade; suppose that in your common conversation you are loose; suppose that in your acts you are licentious or untrue; what does the world say of your Christianity? Why, it becomes to them a thing of contempt. They sniff at it. It is so much dung and sweepings of the street to them, and so it ought to be. In the early ages some of the worst opponents of Christianity used to wing their shafts with the inconsistencies of Christian professors, and they were wise in their generation. One of them said, "Where is that catholic holiness of which we have often heard so much?" and another said, "We heard of these people that they love their Christ, and love other men so that they would even die for love of their brethren; but many of them do not love as well as the heathen whom they despise." I dare say there was a good deal of slander and scandal in what they said; but I am also afraid that, if it were said to-day, there would be a vast deal of sorrowful truth in it. Christian love is by no means so plentiful as it might be, nor holy living either. Is not this the thing that weakens the preaching of the gospel—the want of living the gospel? If all the professed Christians who live in London really walked as Christ walked, would not the salt have more effect upon the corrupt mass than the stuff which is now called salt seems to have? We preach here in the pulpit; but what can we do, unless you preach yonder at home? It is you preaching in your shops, in your kitchens, in your nurseries, in your parlours, in the streets, which will tell on the masses. This is the preaching—the best preaching in the world, for it is seen as well as heard. I heard one say he liked to see men preach with their feet; and this is it, "they ought also so to *walk* even as Christ walked." No testimony excels that which is borne in ordinary life. Christ ought to be glorified by us, and therefore we ought to be like him, for if we are not, we cannot glorify him, but must dishonour him.

Now, that is my first point. Consider how this obligation is proved, and when you have weighed the argument pray the Holy Ghost to make you yield to its gentle pressure.

II. Now, secondly, CONSIDER WHEREIN THIS WALKING WITH CHRIST AS HE WALKED CONSISTS. Here is a wide subject. I have a sea before me with as much sailing room as Noah in the ark. I can only just point out the direction in which you should sail if you would make a prosperous voyage.

First, brothers, to put it all together in one word, the first thing that every Christian has to see to is *holiness.* I will not try at any great length to explain what that word means, but it always sounds to me as if it explained itself. You know what wholeness is—a thing without a crack, or flaw, or break ; complete, entire, uninjured, whole. Well, that is the main meaning of holy. The character of God is perfectly holy : in it nothing is lacking; nothing is redundant. When a thing is complete it is whole, and this applied to moral and spiritual things gives you the inner meaning of "holy." When a man is healthy, perfectly healthy, in spirit, soul, and body, then he is perfectly holy; for sin is a moral disorder, and righteousness is the right state of every faculty. The man whose spiritual health is altogether right is right towards God, right towards himself, right towards men, right towards time, right towards eternity. He is right towards the first table of the law, and right towards the second table. He is an all-round man ; he is a whole man, a holy man. Truth is within him ; truth is spoken by him ; truth is acted by him. Righteousness is in him; he thinks the right thing, and chooses that which is according to the law of uprightness. There is justice in him; he abhors that which is evil. There is goodness in him; he follows after that which will benefit his fellow-men. I cannot spare time to tell you all that the word "holy" means ; but if you wish to see holiness, look at Christ. In him you see a perfect character, an all-round character. He is the perfect one ; be ye like him in all holiness.

We must go a little into detail; so I say, next, one main point in which we ought to walk according to the walk of our great Exemplar is *obedience.* Our Lord Jesus Christ took upon himself the form of a servant; and what service it was that he rendered ! "He was a son; yet learned he obedience by the things that he suffered." And what obedience that dear Son of God rendered to the Father! He did not come to do his own will, but the will of him that sent him. He yielded himself up to come under law to God, and to do the Father's will. Now in this respect we ought also to walk even as he walked. We have not come into the world to do what we like, to possess what we choose, or to say, "That is my notion, and therefore so shall it be." Sin promised freedom, and brought us bondage; grace now binds us, and ensures us liberty. Obedience is the law of every spiritual nature. It is the Lord's will that in his house his word should be the supreme law, for so only can our fallen natures be restored to their original glory. Set the wandering stars in their spheres, and rule them by the majestic sway of the sun, and then they will keep their happy estate, but not else. Understanding, heart, life, lip, everything, is now to enter into the service of God, even the Father, and it is to be ours to say, " Lord, show me what thou wouldst have me to do." Surely, beyond any other quality, we see in the career of the Son of God the perfection of self-abnegation. No man was ever so truly free as Jesus, and yet no man was so fully subservient to the heavenly will. Never saw these seas a pilot so able to steer according to his own judgment, and never one so carefully to follow the channel as marked down in the chart. His was the unique originality of absolute obedience. Dear friends, you see how it ought to be with you also. It is ours to walk in cheerful subservience to the mind of the Father, even as Jesus did. Does this strike you as an easy thing? It is child's work, certainly; but assuredly it is not child's play.

Such a life would necessarily be one of great *activity*, for the life of Jesus was intensely energetic. The life of Christ was as full as it could hold. After he had been developed and disciplined by thirty years of seclusion, he showed himself among men as one moved to vehemence with love: " he was clad with zeal as with a cloak." From the day of his baptism till his death he went about doing good. It is wonderful what was packed into about three years: each action had a world of meaning within its own self, and there were thousands of such acts ; each sermon was a complete revelation, and every day heard him pour forth such sermons. His biography is made up of the essence of life. Some one remarks that it is wonderful that he did not begin his active life when he was younger. We reply, that it is beautiful that he did not, because he was not called to it, and he was best obeying the Father by living in obscurity. Those thirty years at Nazareth were thirty wonderful years of obedience—obedience tested by obscurity, patience, restraint, and perhaps dulness. Who among us would find such obedience easy ? Would we not far rather rush into notice and make to ourselves a name ? Some of us, perhaps, never learned the obedience of being quiet—but it is a wonderful one. Oh, for more of it ! Do we know the obedience of being hidden when our light seems needed ?—the obedience of going into the desert for forty years, like Moses, with nothing to do but wait upon God till God shall put us in commission ? There is a wonderful service in waiting till the order comes for us actively to be at it. Samuel said, " To obey is better than sacrifice ;" it is in fact better than anything which we can possibly present to God. But when our Lord was at length loosed from his obscurity, with what force he sped along his life-way. How he spent himself! It was a candle burning not only at both ends, but altogether. He not only had zeal burning at his heart, but, like a sheet of flame, it covered him from head to foot. There is never an idle hour in the life of Christ. It is wonderful how he sustained the toil. Perhaps he measured out his zeal and his open industry by the fact that he was only to be for a short time here below. It might not be possible to others that they should do as much as he did in so short a space, because they are intended to live longer here, and must not destroy future usefulness by present indiscretion : but still, activity was the rule of our Master's existence. At it, always at it, altogether at it, spending and being spent for his Father; such was his mode of walking among men. Oh, friends, if we, indeed, are in him, we ought also so to walk even as he walked! Wake up, you lazy ones!

Next, we ought to walk as Christ did in the matter of *self-denial*. Of course, in this work of self-denial we are not called to imitate Christ in offering up ourselves as a propitiatory sacrifice. That would be a vain intrusion into things which are his peculiar domain. The self-denials which we practise should be such as he prescribes us. There is a will-worship which is practised in the Church of Rome of self-denials which are absurd, and must, I think, be hateful in the sight of God rather than pleasing to him. Saint Bernard was a man whom I admire to the last degree, and I count him to be one of the Lord's choice ones; yet in the early part of his life there is no doubt that he lessened his powers of usefulness to a large extent by the emaciation which he endured, and the way in which he brought himself to death's door. At times he was incapable of activity by reason of the weakness which he had incurred through fasting, and cold, and exposure. There is no need to inflict useless torture upon the body. When did the Saviour thus behave himself? Point me to a single mortification of a needless kind. Enough self-denials come naturally in every Christian man's way to make him try whether he can deny himself in very deed for the Lord's sake. You are thus tested when you are put in positions where you might get gain by an unrighteous act, or win fame by withholding a truth, or earn love and honour by pandering to the passions of those about you. May you have grace enough to say, "No; it cannot be. I love not myself, but my Lord. I seek not myself, but Christ. I desire to propagate nothing but his truth, and not my own ideas": then will you have exhibited the self-denial of Jesus. These self-denials will sometimes be hard to flesh and blood. And then in the Church of God to be able to give all your substance, to devote all your time, to lay out all your ability—this is to walk as Jesus walked. When weary and worn, still to be busy; to deny yourself things which may be allowable, but which if allowable to you would be dangerous to others—this also is like the Lord. Such self-denial as may be helpful to the weak you ought to practise. Think what Christ would do in such a case, and do it; and, whenever you can glorify him by denying yourself, do it. So walk as he did who made himself of no reputation, but took upon himself the form of a servant, and who, though he was rich, brought himself down to poverty for our sakes, that we might be rich unto God. Think of that.

Another point in which we ought to imitate Christ most certainly is that of *lowliness*. I wish that all Christians did this. When I see some Christian women dressed out—well, like women of the world, though not with half a worldling's taste, and when I see men so big that they cannot speak to poor people, as if they were made of something better than ordinary flesh and blood; when I notice a haughty, high, hectoring disposition anywhere, it grates upon my feelings, and makes me wonder whether these blunderers hope to go to the heaven of the lowly. The Lord Jesus would never have been half as big as some of his followers are. What great folk some of his disciples are, as compared with him! He was lowly, meek, gentle, a man who so loved the souls of others that he forgot himself. You never detect in the Lord Jesus Christ any tendency towards pride or self-exaltation. Quite the reverse : he is ever compassionate and condescending to men of low estate.

And then note again another point, and that is his great *tenderness*, and gentleness, and readiness to forgive. His dying words ought to ring in the ear of all who find it hard to pass by affronts, "Father, forgive them, for they know not what they do." Did he not set us an example of bearing and forbearing ? "Who, when he was reviled, reviled not again." For every curse he gave a blessing. You cannot be Christians if this spirit of love is foreign to you. "Oh," say you, "we endorse the confession." I do not care. You must love your enemies, or you will die with the Creed in your throats. "Oh," say you, "we are regular in our pews, hearing the gospel." I do not care ; you must forgive them that trespass against you, or you will go from your pews to perdition. "Oh, but we have been baptized, and we come to the communion." I do not care even about that ; for unless you are made meek and lowly in heart you will not find rest unto your souls. Pride goeth not before salvation, but before destruction ; and a haughty spirit is no prophecy of elevation, but the herald of a fall. Take care, take care, you that say that you are in Christ ; you ought also to walk in all the lowliness and in all the tenderness of Christ, or else at the end you will be discovered to be none of his. Hard, cruel, unrelenting, iron-hearted professors will no more go to heaven than the hogs they fatten.

There is one little big word which tells us more than all this about how Christ walked, and that is the word "*love.*" Jesus was incarnate love. "God is love," but God is a spirit, therefore if you wish to see love embodied, look at Christ. He loves the little children, and suffers them to come to him. He loves the widow, and he is tender to her, and raises her dead son. He loves the sinners, and they draw near to him. He loves all sinful and tempted and tried ones, and therefore he comes to seek and to save. He loves the Father first, and then for the Father's sake he loves the myriads of men. Do you love nobody ? Do you live within yourself ? Are you immured within your own ribs ? Is self all your world ? Then you will go to hell. There is no help for it ; for the place of unloving spirits is the bottomless pit. Only he that loves can live in heaven, for heaven is love : and you cannot go to glory unless you have learned to love, and to find it your very life to do good to those about you.

Let me add to all this, that he who says that Christ is in him ought also to live as Christ lived in secret. And how was this ?

His life was spent in abounding *devotion*. Ah, me ! I fear I shall condemn some here when I remind them of the hymn we just now sang—

> "Cold mountains and the midnight air
> Witnessed the fervour of his prayer."

If the perfect Christ could not live without prayer, how can such poor imperfect ones as we are live without it ? He had no sin within him, and yet he had need to pray. He was pure and holy, and yet he must needs wait upon God all day long, and often speak with his Father ; and then when the night came, and others went to their beds, he withdrew himself into the wilderness and prayed.   If the Lord Jesus be in you, you must walk as he walked in that matter.

And, then, think of his delight in God.   How wonderful was Christ's *delight in his God!*   I can never think of his life as an unhappy one. He was, it is true, "a man of sorrows and acquainted with grief"; but still there was a deep spring of wondrous happiness in the midst of his heart, which made him always blessed; for he said to his Father, "I delight to do thy will, O my God!   Yea, thy law is within my heart."   He delighted in God.   Many a sweet night he spent in those prayer-times of his in fellowship with the Father.   Why, it was that which prepared him for the agony of his bloody sweat, and for the "Why hast thou forsaken me?"   Those love-visits, those near and dear communings which his holy heart had with the Father were his secret meat and drink.   And you and I also must delight in God.   This charming duty is far too much neglected.   Strange that this honey should so seldom be in men's mouths!   Listen to this text, "Delight thyself also in the Lord, and he shall give thee the desires of thine heart." Many a man says, "I should like to have the desires of my heart." Brother, here is the royal road thereto, the King's ascent to his treasury —"Delight thyself also in the Lord."   But, listen.   It is very likely you would not obtain the desire that is now in your heart if you did that ; for he that delights himself in God rises above the desires of the flesh and of the mind, and comes to desire that which God desires, and therefore it is that he wins the desire of his heart.   But, oh, the pleasure, the joy, the bliss of delighting in God !   How many times have I sung to myself that last dear stanza of the psalm, wherein the inspired poet sings—

> " For yet I know I shall him praise,
>   Who graciously to me,
>   The health is of my countenance,
>   Yea, mine own God is he."

Oh, what a pleasure !   "Mine own God is he."   Rich men glory in wealth, famous men in valour, great men in honour, and I in "mine own God."   There is nothing about God but what is delightful to a saint.   The infinite God is infinitely delightful to his people.   Once get really to know God and to be like him, and even his sternest attributes —his power, his justice, his indignation against sin—will come to be delightful to you.   Those men who are cavilling at what God does, questioning over what God has revealed, do not know him, for to know him is to adore him.   Oh, brethren, let us find our pleasure, our treasure, our heaven, our all, in the Lord our God, even as our Lord Jesus did.   In this thing let us walk even as he walked.

I have not quite done.   Dear friends, we ought to walk in holy *contentment.*   Jesus was perfectly content with his lot.   When the foxes had holes and the birds of the air had nests, and he had not where to lay his head, yet he never murmured, but found rest in pursuing his life-work.   The cravings of covetousness and pinings of ambition never touched our Lord.   Friends, if you do, indeed, say that you abide in him, I pray you be of the same contented spirit.   "I have learned," said the apostle, as if it were a thing which had to be taught, "in whatsoever state I am, therewith to be content."

In a word, Christ lived above this world; let us walk as he walked. Christ lived for God, and for God alone; let us live after his fashion. And Christ persevered in such living; he never turned aside from it at all; but as he lived so he died, still serving his God, obedient to his Father's will, even unto death. May our lives be a mosaic of perfect obedience, and our deaths the completion of the fair design. From our Bethlehem to our Gethsemane may our walk run parallel with the pathway of the Well-beloved! Oh, Holy Spirit, work us to this sacred pattern!

III. I close now by saying, in the last place, CONSIDER, dear friends, WHAT IS NEEDFUL TO ALL THIS.

First, it is needful to have *a nature like that of Christ.* You cannot give out sweet waters so long as the fountains are impure. "Ye must be born again." There is no walking with Jesus in newness of life unless we have a new heart and a right spirit. See to it, dear friends, that your nature is renewed—that the Holy Ghost has wrought in you a resurrection from among the dead; for, if not, your walk and conversation will savour of death and corruption. A new creature is essential to likeness to Christ: it is not possible that the carnal mind should wear the image of Jesus.

That being done, the next thing that is necessary is *a constant anointing of the Holy Spirit.* Can any Christian here do without the Holy Spirit? Then I am afraid that he is no Christian. But, as for us, we feel every day that we must cry for a fresh visitation of the Spirit, a renewed sense of indwelling, a fresh anointing from the Holy One of Israel, or else we cannot walk as Christ walked.

And then, again, there must be in us a *strong resolve* that we will walk as Christ walked; for our Lord himself did not lead in that holy life without stern resolution. He set his face like a flint that he would do the right; and he did the right. Do not, I pray you, be led astray by thoughtlessly following your fellow-men: it is a poor, sheepish business, that running in crowds. Dare to be singular; dare to stand alone. Stand to it firmly that you will follow Christ. A Christian man in a discussion attempted to defend the truth, but his opponent grew angry, and cried out vehemently again and again, "Hear me! Hear me!" At last the good man answered, "No, I shall not hear you, nor shall you hear me; but let us both sit down and hear the word of the Lord." And that is the thing to do, brethren, to be hearing Christ and following *him*; not I to learn of you, nor you of me, but both of Christ: so shall we end all controversy in a blessed agreement at his feet. God help us to get there.

And so, once again, I add that if we want to walk as Christ walked, we must have much *communion with him.* We cannot possibly get to be like Christ except by being with him. I wish that we could rise to be so much like the Saviour that we should resemble a certain ancient saint who died a martyr's death, to whom the world said, "What are you?" He said, "I am a Christian." They asked, "What trade do you follow?" And he said, "I am a Christian." They inquired, "What language do you speak?" And he said, "I am a Christian." "But what treasures have you?" said they; and he replied, "I am a Christian." They asked him what friends he had, and he said, "I am a

Christian;" for all he was, and all he had, and all he wished to be, and all he hoped to be, were all wrapped up in Christ. If you live with Christ you will be absorbed by him, and he will embrace the whole of your existence : and, in consequence, your walk will be like his.

Take care that you do not in all things copy any but Christ ; for if I set my watch by the watch of one of my friends, and he sets his watch by that of another friend, we may all be wrong together. If we shall, each one, take his time from the sun, we shall all be right. There is nothing like going to the fountain-head. Take your lessons in holiness, not from a poor erring disciple, but from the infallible Master. God help you to do so.

A person has written to me this morning to say that he has painted my portrait, but that he cannot finish it until he sees me. I should think not. Certainly you cannot paint a portrait of Christ in your own life unless you see him—see him clearly, see him continually. You may have a general notion of what Christ is like, and you may put a good deal of colour into your copy ; but I am sure you will fail unless you see the grand original. You *must* get to commune with Jesus. You know what we did when we went to school. Our schoolmasters were not quite so wise then as schoolmasters are now. They wrote at the top of the page a certain line for us to follow, and a poor following it was. When I wrote my first line I copied the writing-master's model, but when I wrote the next line I copied my copy of the top line ; so that when I reached the bottom of the page I produced a copy of my copy of my copy of my copy of the top line. Thus my handwriting fed upon itself, and was nothing bettered, but rather grew worse. So one man copies Christ, perhaps ; a friend who hears him preach copies *him*, and his wife at home copies the hearer, and somebody copies her ; and so it goes on all down the line, till we all miss that glorious hand-writing which Jesus has come to teach us. Keep your eye on Christ, dear brother. Never mind me: never mind your friend : never mind the old doctor that you have been hearing so long. Look to Jesus, and to him alone. We have had our sects and our divisions all through that copying of the lines of the boys, instead of looking to the top line that the Master wrote. "He that saith he abideth in him ought himself also so to walk even as he walked." May the Spirit of God cause us to do it! Amen and Amen.

PORTION OF SCRIPTURE READ BEFORE SERMON.—1 John ii.

HYMNS FROM " OUR OWN HYMN BOOK."—425, 262, 646.

ON HUMBLING OURSELVES BEFORE GOD.

A Sermon

DELIVERED BY

C. H. SPURGEON,

AT THE METROPOLITAN TABERNACLE, NEWINGTON.

"Humble yourselves therefore under the mighty hand of God, that he may exalt you in due time."—1 Peter v. 6.

PRIDE is so natural to fallen man that it springs up in his heart like weeds in a watered garden, or rushes by a flowing brook. It is an all-pervading sin, and smothers all things like dust in the roads, or flour in the mill. Its every touch is evil as the breath of the cholera-fiend, or the blast of the simoom. Pride is as hard to get rid of as charlock from the furrows, or the American blight from the apple-trees. If killed it revives, if buried it bursts the tomb. You may hunt down this fox, and think you have destroyed it, and lo! your very exultation is pride. None have more pride than those who dream that they have none. You may labour against vainglory till you conceive that you are humble, and the fond conceit of your humility will prove to be pride in full bloom. It apes humility full well, and is then most truly pride. Pride is a sin with a thousand lives; it seems impossible to kill it, it flourishes on that which should be its poison, glorying in its shame. It is a sin with a thousand shapes; by perpetual change it escapes capture. It seems impossible to hold it; the vapoury imp slips from you, only to appear in another form and mock your fruitless pursuit. To die to pride and self one would need to die himself.

Pride was man's first sin, and it will be his last. In the first sin that man ever committed there was certainly a large admixture of pride, for he imagined that he knew better than his Maker, and even dreamed that his Maker feared that man might grow too great. It has been questioned whether pride was not the sin by which the angels fell when they lost their first estate: I will not go into any controversy upon that subject; but there was certainly pride in the sin of Satan and pride in the sin of Adam. This is the torch which kindled hell and set the world on fire.

Pride is a ringleader and captain among iniquities: it attaineth unto the first three of Satan's champions. It is a daring and God-defying sin, arraigning divine justice, as Cain did; challenging Jehovah to combat, as Pharaoh did; or making self into God, as Nebuchadnezzar

No. 1,733.

did. It would murder God if it could, that it might fill his throne. While it is first to come, and first in horrible supremacy, it is also last to go. As Paul said, "The last enemy that shall be destroyed is death." I think I might say that the last enemy but one is pride, for even at our death-bed pride will be found in attendance. In his last moments John Knox had a sharp conflict with self-righteousness though he had preached against it with all his might, and knew, with a clearness seldom given to men, that salvation is of the Lord alone. Even within an hour of glory he had to make a stand against that vile thing, the pride of the human heart. Many others of the Lord's valiant ones have been sorely assailed by the same crafty foe, which shoots with feathered flatteries shafts of destruction. In the most quiet minds the deadly calm of self-conceit may be found. Our hearts are deceitful above all things, and in nothing less to be trusted than in this matter of pride. Even while we breathe out our souls unto God it will attempt to puff us up ;—yes, it will puff up poor dying worms ! Brothers and sisters, for certain, you and I are in danger of pride ; possibly we are even now victims of it : let us be on our guard, for it may be ruining us without our knowledge even as the moth in secret eats up the garment, or as unseen rust cankers the hidden treasure.

Let pride lodge where it may, it does its entertainer great mischief, for it bars out the favour of God, " God resisteth the proud." It must be sent adrift ere God can visit us with favour, for no grace comes to the proud, " but he giveth grace unto the humble." Humility is the grace that attracts more grace. As money makes money, so humility increases humility, and with it every other spiritual gift. If you would have much grace have much humility. God hath assistance for the humble, but resistance for the proud. You know how he fought Pharaoh. What blows he struck at the haughty monarch! He would have him down from the pinnacle of defiance one way or another, and make him learn in bitterness the answer to his own insolent question, " Who is the Lord ?" Remember how Nebuchadnezzar had to eat grass like an ox because he spake with haughty tongue. Wherever God sees pride lifting itself on high, he resolves to level it with the dust. He draws his bow, he fits his arrow to the string, and pride is the target that he shoots at. The more pride enters into the Christian's heart the less grace will enter there, and the more opposition from God will come there; for pride is never so hateful to God as when he sees it in his own people. If you see disease in a stranger you are very sorry, but if you discover its symptoms in your own child your grief is much more deep. A viper is loathsome anywhere; but how it would make you start if you saw the head of one of those creatures peeping out from the bosom of a beloved friend ! So pride is detestable anywhere, but it is worst in those whom the Lord loves best. If God sees pride in a David he will smite him till he ceases from his high thoughts; or if it be in a Hezekiah he will abase him ; and be you sure that if the Lord sees pride in you he will smite you; ay, smite you again and again till you wait humbly at his feet.

All this I have given by way of preface, but I think it is also an argument which may run before the words of the text, and strengthen them, " Humble yourselves *therefore* under the mighty hand of God."

I shall handle the text, not at any great length, but for practical purposes in three or four ways. May the Holy Spirit bless the discourse.

I. First, our text is evidently intended to bear upon us IN OUR CHURCH LIFE.

We will use it in that respect. Observe that Peter has been speaking to the elders, and telling them how they should behave themselves in the flock over which they are set as overseers. Then he speaks to the younger members, and he says, "Submit yourselves unto the elder." He says to all church-members, " All of you be subject one to another, and be clothed with humility"; and it is in the same context that he writes, "Humble yourselves therefore under the mighty hand of God." I am, as a member of a church, not to seek honour to myself, but I am to walk humbly. I am not to make it in any respect the object of my Christian life to be esteemed among my fellow-Christians so as to have influence over them, and to take the lead among them. I am to have far humbler motives than that. I am to think very little of myself, and to think so much of others that I admire all that I see of God's grace in them, and am glad to learn from them as well as to help them in their progress to heaven. Each one of us should think little of himself and highly of his brethren. I cannot say that all of us as Christians are clothed with humility as we should be. I am afraid that, from the preacher down to the most obscure member, we may, everyone of us, listen with awe to the injunction, " Humble yourselves under the mighty hand of God," and confess that we fall short of this command. Yet I may honestly add that in this church I have seen more submissiveness, and deference to others, and less of ambitious self-esteem than anywhere else in the world. I have spoken nothing less than bare justice when I have said this. Let all the world know that as a pastor I can in this point praise the people of my charge beyond any that I have ever heard of. I am not apt to judge too favourably ; I speak as I have seen, and this is my honest testimony. We owe our union and prosperity under God to the readiness of most of the brethren to do anything and everything for Christ, without considering ourselves.

Now, true humility in our church relationship will show itself in our *being willing to undertake the very lowest offices for Christ.* Some cannot do little things : they must be ordained to great offices, or they will sulk in indolence. Genuine humility makes a man think it a great honour to be a doorkeeper in the house of God, or to be allowed to speak a word to a little child about Jesus, or even to wash the saints' feet. I am sure, brethren, that those who are not willing to fulfil the lesser offices will never be used by Christ to mind the greater duties. Humility is a qualification for greatness. Do you know how to be little ? You are learning to be great. Can you submit ? You are learning to rule. My symbolic sketch of a perfected Christian would be a king keeping the door, or a prince feeding lambs, or, better still, the Master washing his disciples' feet.

The next point of humility is, that *we are conscious of our own incompetence to do anything aright.* He who can do all things without Christ will end in doing nothing. The man who *can* preach without divine aid cannot preach at all. The woman who *can* teach a Bible-class cannot teach a Bible-class. Human ability without the grace of

God is only puffed-up inability. Those of you who, apart from supernatural help, feel quite sufficient for any kind of holy service are miserably deluded. Self-sufficiency is inefficiency. The fulness of self is a double emptiness. He that has no sense of his weakness has a weakness in his sense. I believe, brethren and sisters, that any man whom God uses for a great purpose will be so emptied out that he will wonder that ever God uses him in the least degree; and he will be ready to hide his head, and long to get out of public notice, because he will feel himself to be utterly unworthy of the favour which God manifests towards him. I do not believe that God ever fills a cup which was not empty; or that he ever fills a man's mouth with his word while that man has his mouth full of his own words. Humble yourselves *therefore* under the mighty hand of God : if you desire that the Holy Spirit should bless you, be purged from your own spirit. The way to rise into God is to sink in your own self : as our Lord Jesus descended into the depths, that he might rise above all things and fill all things, so we, in our imitation of him, must descend to the uttermost that we may rise to the highest.

This humility will show itself, next, in this—*that we shall be willing to be ignored of men.* There is a craving in the heart of many to have what they do written upon tablets, and set up in the market-places. I once heard a professing Christian complain bitterly that he had been ignored. He had been a Sunday-school teacher for years, and yet he had never been publicly mentioned by anyone. Did he make that a complaint? He might far rather have rejoiced in his quietude. The fierce light of public notoriety is not much valued by those upon whom it falls. I wish some people would ignore *me*—at least, all next week, so much at least as not to call to see me, or write me a letter, or name me in the papers. I would be happy as all the birds in the air to be ignored, if I might be let alone, and allowed peacefully to work for God with his sweet smile to cheer me in my loneliness. Oh, to be a little ant, allowed to labour on at God's bidding, receiving nothing of men but the high privilege of being let alone! A saintly soul was wont to pray, " Grant me, O Lord, that I may pass unnoticed through the world ! " It seems to me to be one of the highest delights of life for people to permit you to work for God without being interrupted by their praises or censures. When I have seen a certain great artist at work, I have only peeped at him from a corner, and have kept out of his sunshine : I am quite sure he did not want me to express my valueless opinion about his glorious creations. To have people for ever talking about you, for you, and against you is one of the wearinesses of mortal life ; and yet some people sigh for the fuss that others would be glad to be rid of. Yes, so it is. It is but a little thing that certain friends have done, but they would like much made of it : their slender alms must be published at the corners of the streets, their prosy speech must be reported in all papers. Oh, brothers, do not let us care about its being known that we have done our part. Let it be done as to God, and in God's sight ; and then, as to what our fellow-mortals shall say, let us have scant concern ; for, if we live on human praise, we shall grow not only proud, but vain, which, if it be not more wicked, is certainly more silly. Serve God, and do not wish to have a trumpet blown before you.   Never cry with Jehu, " Come, see my zeal for the Lord of hosts."   Go on serving God year after year, though you be altogether unknown, feeling it quite sufficient that you have by the grace of God served your generation and honoured your Redeemer. This would be a great attainment in our church life if we could reach to it.

Brethren, we want humility, all of us, in our church life, in the sense of *never being rough, haughty, arrogant, hard, domineering, lordly ;* or, on the other hand, factious, unruly, quarrelsome, and unreasonable. We should endeavour to think very carefully of those who are poorest, for fear we should hurt their feelings ; and very noticeably of those who are obscure, lest we should seem to despise them.   It is ours never to take offence, and to be most cautious never to cause it even by inadvertence. He that is set as a leader in the church of God, let him be the person that is most ready to bear blame, and least ready to give offence : let him say, " You may think what you please of me, but I shall lay myself out to do you good, and to be your servant for Christ's sake." The lower you can stoop the greater is your honour.   In the eye of wisdom no piece of furniture in the house of God has greater dignity than the doormat. If you are willing to let others wipe their feet on you, then shall Christ Jesus take pleasure in you, for you are a partaker of his lowly mind.   Even for your own sake it will be wise to occupy a humble place, for in the vales the streams of peace are flowing. The mountains are the playground of the storm, but in the quiet villages the dove finds her shelter. If you would escape from ill-will, and live peaceably with all men, practise the maxims of an influential man, who, when asked after the Revolution how he managed to escape the executioner's axe, replied, " I made myself of no reputation, and kept silence."

I am speaking to a number of young men who have begun to speak for Jesus Christ in the church : let me earnestly entreat them to take great notice of my text,—" Humble yourselves under the mighty hand of God."   Recollect, you cannot do any good except " the mighty hand of God" be with you ; therefore be humble, and look to that hand for all success.   Feel it to be a wonderful thing that the mighty hand of God should ever use *you* ; therefore lie very low in that hand, and beneath that hand, for thus you may claim the promise that he will exalt you in due time. If you are willing to look after a few poor people in a village, and to do your duty thoroughly well among a lowly company, you shall have a larger sphere ere long. If you are satisfied, young brother, to stand in the corner of the street and talk about Jesus Christ to a few rough folk, you shall find hundreds of hearers by-and-by. If you are willing to be nothing, God will make something of you.   The way to the top of the ladder is to begin at the lowest round.   In fact, in the church of God, the way up is to go down ; but he that is ambitious to be at the top will find himself before long at the bottom. "He that exalteth himself shall be abased ; but he that humbleth himself shall be exalted." Suffer, my younger brethren, this word of exhortation.

II.   And now, secondly, I will use the text in quite another way—in reference to OUR BEHAVIOUR IN OUR AFFLICTIONS.   Here let every tried believer listen to the counsel of the Holy Ghost.

Certain of us are never long together without affliction and trial: like salamanders, we live in the flame, passing from fire to fire. As by a succession of shafts we descend into the heart of the earth, going down from woe to woe; we had need learn the way of these dark places. Frequently our heavenly Father's design in sending trial to his children is to make and keep them humble; let us remember this, and learn a lesson of wisdom. The advice of Peter is that we should humble ourselves. Many people have been often humbled, and yet they have not become humble. There is a great difference between the two things. If God withdraws his grace and allows a Christian man to fall into sin, that fall humbles him in the esteem of all good men; and yet he may not be humble. He may never have a true sense of how evil his action has been; he may still persevere in his lofty spirit, and be far from humility. When this is the case the haughty spirit may expect a downfall. The rod will make blue wounds when pride abates not at gentler blows. The most hopeful way of avoiding the humbling affliction is to humble yourself. Be humble that you may not be humbled. Put yourself into a humble attitude, and draw near to God in a lowly spirit, and so he will cease from his chiding.

And do this, first, by *noticing whether you have been guilty of any special sin of pride*. You are suffering: let the rod point out to you wherein you have erred through pride. I believe that David was afflicted in his children because he had been proud of his children, and had indulged them. When there is a breakage in the house, it is generally the idol that is broken. Usually our sins lie at the roots of our sorrows. If we will repent of the sin, the Lord will remove the sorrow. Have you been tried in your worldly possessions? Were you ever puffed up by them? Is your health failing? Did you never glory in your bodily strength? Are you deceived? Were you never boastful of your own wisdom? Are you mourning over a failure in character? Did you not once dream that you were past temptation? Look into your affliction till you see, as in a glass, what was the thing you were proud of, and then take the idol down from its pedestal, humble yourself before God, and henceforth worship him alone.

In your affliction humble yourself by *confessing that you deserve all that you are suffering*. Is it poverty?—then, dear child of God, own that you deserve poverty because of your love of the world. Is it physical pain? Then own how every erring member deserves to smart. It is a great thing to have wrung out of us the confession that our chastisement is less than our deservings, and that the Lord is not dealing with us after our sins, nor rewarding us according to our iniquities. Is there a bereavement in the house? Then, I pray you, acknowledge that if God were to visit you, as he did Job, and take all your children away at a stroke, yet still you deserve it at his hands. Confess that the chastening hand is not dealing too severely with you. Humble yourself, and then you will not quarrel with your grief.

But, more than that, humble yourself so as to *submit entirely to God's will*. Ask the Holy Spirit to help you in this act of self-humiliation while you meekly kiss the rod. Bow yourself before the mighty hand of God, ready to receive yet harder blows if God so pleases; for when your will entirely yields to the will of God, it is highly probable that either the affliction will be removed, or else the sting of it will be taken away. Down, brother, down in the dust as low as ever you can get. God is evidently dealing with you as with a son; and a son's wisdom lies in cheerful submission to parental discipline. When a child is under his father's chastening hand, it will not help him to kick, and quarrel, and say ill words: his best hope lies in submitting absolutely to his father's good pleasure. When that is done the chastisement will soon end. Humble yourself therefore under the mighty hand of God. Yield up your will so as to have no suit-in-law against the Lord, no difference as to his goodness, not even if the evil you dread should actually come, and come in the worst form. Submit to the Lord's will as the rush bends to the wind, or as the wax yields to the seal. Pray against the calamity which moves you to fear, but let your petition always end with "Nevertheless, not as I will, but as thou wilt." Ask that you may not be obliged to drink the bitter draught, but do not upset the cup, nor push it away. There let it stand, while you for the moment supplicate for its removal; and when there comes no answer to your prayer, then take it up meekly, put it to your lips resolutely, and drink right on, even as your Master drank his cup and drained it to the dregs. This needs the help of the Holy Spirit, and truly he waits to help us: he delights to aid us in such holy acts of submission. Nothing is better for us in our time of tribulation than to bow ourselves in lowliest obeisance before the hand of God.

Dear friend, what can be the use of striving against the hand of the Lord? It is a mighty hand: we cannot resist it, even if we are wicked enough to attempt rebellion. If affliction is to come it will come, and come with all the greater sharpness because we refuse to yield. If God appoints a trial, we cannot escape it. What can be the use of our striving against divine decrees? It will only make our sorrow the more severe. When the ox kicks out against the goad the iron enters the deeper into its flesh; but when the bullock hastens on its way, sensitive to the least touch, the driver scarcely urges it again. The tender, sensitive horse scarcely receives a stroke from the whip; he feels it too much: but the mule that will not move is struck again and again for his obstinacy. So will it be with us. We can make rods for ourselves by wilfulness. Oh foolish fingers, which prepare prickles for our own pillows! Humble yourself, therefore, under the mighty hand of God, and by-and-by, brother, you shall be exalted to consolation and prosperity. Your affliction shall bring forth the comfortable fruits of righteousness. You shall come out of the furnace purified and refined. You shall have more knowledge, more grace, more zeal, more of every excellence, as the result of sanctified trial; but all this must come by obedient resignation. A rebellious heart comes out of affliction worse rather than better. Submit, and you shall be so exalted by your affliction that you shall bless God for it, and feel that you would not have missed the trouble for ten thousand pounds if you could have done so. Heavy tribulation shall bring with it unspeakable preferment. You shall be exalted to a higher degree in the peerage of Christianity by battling with adversities. Therefore, I pray you, humble yourselves under the hand of God.

III. Thirdly, I am going to use the text in another way. IN OUR

DAILY DEALINGS WITH GOD, whether in affliction or not, let us humble ourselves under his hand, for so only can we hope to be exalted.

It is a blessed thing whenever you come to God to come wondering that you are allowed to come, wondering that you have been led to come ; marvelling at divine election, that the Lord should ever have chosen you to come ; wondering at divine redemption, astonished that such a price should have been paid that you might be brought nigh to God. It is well to draw near to God weighed down with gratitude that ever the Holy Spirit should have deigned to work effectual calling upon you. Humble yourself under the mighty hand of divine grace, which has brought you into the family of love, and constantly say, "Why me, Lord ? Why me ?" A grateful walk is a gracious walk, and there is no gratitude where there is no humility. Never trace the difference between yourself and others to your own free-will, nor to any betterness of your natural disposition, but entirely to the mercy and grace of God, which have been freely bestowed on you. Let grace be magnified by your grateful heart !

When you are doing this be very humble before God, because you have not made more improvement of the grace that he has given you. You are chosen, but you are not as choice as you ought to be ; you are redeemed, but you are not so much your Lord's as you ought to be ; you are called, but you are still too deaf to the divine call ; you are blessed, enriched, instructed, adopted, comforted, with heaven before you and everything prepared on the road thither ; but what a poor return have you made ! Always feel thus humbled in reference to your God and his grace. When you are doing most, and God is using you most, always feel that if you had been fit for it he might have done much more by you—that if you had been meet to be used he might have used you far more extensively. Thus you will always see cause for humility even when you discern abounding reason for gratitude. Walk always so with God that when you stand on the highest point you still feel, "I might have been higher but for my own fault. I have not, because I have not asked, or because I have asked amiss. I have not become as rich as I might have been in spiritual things, because I have not been as diligent in my Lord's business, or as fervent in spirit, or as abundant in serving God as I ought to have been.

Next, humble yourself, dear brother, under the hand of God by feeling your own want of knowledge whenever you come to God. Do not think that you understand all divinity. There is only one body of divinity, and that is Christ himself ; and who knoweth him to the full? When even his love, which is the plainest point about him, passeth knowledge, who shall know Christ in all his fulness ? Come before God to be instructed in the knowledge of your God and Saviour. Do not think that you understand providence, for I am sure that none of us do. We sometimes think that we could manage things a great deal better than they are managed. Many farmers would not have appointed that heavy shower for this afternoon, and yet that downpour was essential to the general well-being of the universal kingdom. I cannot tell why, but it was so. Everything that comes by God's appointment is a cog in the wheel of providence, and if that cog were gone, the machinery would be out of order. The Lord does all things wisely : only a vile pride will suspect otherwise. Consider, O man, that you do *not* know : God only knows. Little children sometimes think they are wise, but they know nothing: wisdom is with their father, not with them. Let us be content to humble ourselves under the hand of God as poor know-nothings, satisfied that he knows what is best for us. This humility is the vestibule of knowledge, the corner-stone of true philosophy. Commence with a confession of ignorance, or you will never be taught of the Lord. It cannot be hard to confess this when the mighty hand of the Lord is seen and felt.

One point concerning which I should like everyone of us to humble ourselves under the hand of God is about our little enjoyment of divine things. The elder brother in the parable said, " Lo, these many years do I serve thee, neither transgressed I at any time thy commandment : and yet thou never gavest me a kid, that I might make merry with my friends." So have I known certain sincere Christian men fall into a horribly legal state of mind. They have always been very regular in their living, constant in their religious observances, and persevering in their prayers, and yet they have never had much joy: but they see a poor soul, just saved from sin, full of delight, and they envy him, and cry out, " Why is a fuss made over such a sinner, when I have been all these years a Christian, and my brethren have never made any rejoicing over me ? There is no music and dancing about me ! Thou never gavest me a kid that I might make merry with my friends." I do not know how we could make a fuss over some of the elder brothers : they would not bear it, they would be angry, and enquire, in hard and surly tones, what these things meant. Music and dancing are things too trivial for their solid souls. They stand outside and grumble, and we cannot warm them into a revival spirit. They are freezing outside the door of our happy home. Must they always stand there ? How divinely sweet was the father's answer to that naughty elder brother ! He said to him, "Son, thou art ever with me, and all that I have is thine." That is to say, " You live in my house. You are with me as my own dear son. Everything I have is yours by heirship. Your brother had his portion, and he spent it, but all that remains to me is yours." Hence his short commons had been of his own appointing. If he had not made merry with his friends it was his own fault. Is it not much the same with us if we have been dull and melancholy ; I mean those of us who are believers? Are not all things ours? Come, let us humble ourselves under the hand of God, because we have not made merry with our friends. You growling Christians—if you growl it is because you *will* growl ; there is nothing to murmur at. You who never have a happy day, who never have any of the fervours and enthusiasms of young beginners : whose fault is that? It is your own. You might have anything in the Father's house. You have a right to rare music and dancing, for you are ever with God, and all that he has is yours. It is meet that we should make merry and be glad ; and if we are dull at the business of holy merry-making, let us humble ourselves under the hand of God because of our despondencies and mistrusts. O my soul, if thy ceilings are painted with black instead of vermilion, blame thyself alone, and not thy God.

I am sure, dear friends, if any of us will go over our daily lives we shall find plenty of reasons for humbling ourselves under the hand of God. It is really dreadful how a man can serve God nobly and do great things and yet in a certain matter he may fail sadly. A grand old prophet is that Jonah, going through the streets of Nineveh, and bravely delivering the Lord's warning. Whoever did the like? "Yet forty days and Nineveh shall be overthrown" is the word which he hurls into the face of princes. Grand man! One, yet a conqueror of myriads! Yes! But look at him a day or two after! Call that a grand man, sitting there crying because the cucumber that grew up over his head is withered! fretting because a worm has devoured a gourd! He is angry, and he says that he does well to be angry about a bower of melon-leaves. Dear me, that a man can be so great in noble things and so little in a trifling matter! How many have like cause to be humble before God! Observe that good man: he bore the loss of his property with holy resignation, but he lost his temper because a button was gone from his linen. Such a thing has often happened. Do I put it so that you smile at it? It would be better to weep over it. As you think about yourselves, my brethren, recollect the causes that you have to be humble under the hand of God because of the gross weakness by which you have shown the natural depravity of your heart, and the faultiness of your nature apart from the strengthening Spirit of God.

Humble yourselves therefore under the hand of God as creatures under the hand of the Creator. We are the clay, and thou our potter, O Lord: it becomes us to be lowly. Humble yourselves under the hand of God as criminals under the hand of their judge. Cry, "Against thee, thee only, have I sinned, and done this evil in thy sight: that thou mightest be justified when thou speakest, and be clear when thou judgest." Humble yourselves under the hand of God—as chastened children under a father's rod—for he chastens us for our profit, and right well do we deserve each smarting blow. Humble yourselves under the mighty hand of God, lastly, as servants under their Lord's word. Ask no questions about your Master's command, but go and do it; and when he rebukes you for shortcomings answer not again, but accept the reproof with bowed head and tearful eye, acknowledging that his rebuke is well deserved. Humble yourselves thus, dear brethren, in your daily lives, and God will exalt you in due time.

IV. I finish by using my text with all the earnestness my soul can feel in reference to the unconverted part of this audience IN OUR SEEK-ING FORGIVENESS AS SINNERS. Oh, tender Spirit of God, help me now.

The text was not originally meant for the ungodly, but it may fitly be applied to them. If you would find grace in God's sight and live, dear unconverted hearers, you must humble yourselves under the mighty hand of God. So you want to be saved, do you? The way of salvation is, "Believe in the Lord Jesus Christ." "But," you say, "I cannot understand it." Yet it is very simple; no hidden meaning lies in the words: you are simply bidden to trust Jesus. If, however, you feel as if you could not do that, let me urge you to go to God in secret and own the sin of this unbelief; for a great sin it is. Humble yourself. Do not try to make out that you are good. That will be fatal, for it will be a falsehood which will shut the gate of grace. Confess that you are guilty. When a man is clearly and manifestly guilty, it is of no use his standing before the judge and begining to urge his own merit: his best course is to cast himself upon the mercy of the court. It is *your* only course, dear soul, the only one that can avail you. Know that you have transgressed, and feel that it is so. Sit down and think over the many ways in which you have done wrong, or failed to do right. Pray God to break you down with deep penitence. It is no waste of time to dig out foundations when you build a house, and it is no superfluity to labour after a deep sense of sin.

When your sin is confessed, then acknowledge that if justice were carried out towards you, apart from undeserved grace, you would be sent to hell. Do not cavil at that fact. Do not entertain sceptical questions as to whether there is a punishment for sin, and as to what it will be; but own that, whatever it is, you deserve it. Do not fence with God or quarrel with Scripture; but as his word declares that the wicked shall be cast into hell with all the nations that forget God, own that you deserve to be so dealt with; for you *do* deserve it. When this is acknowledged you are on the road to mercy. You have almost obtained mercy when you have fully submitted to justice. You have in a measure received grace when you are brought to own your sin and the justice of its penalty.

Then, next, accept God's mercy in his own way. Do not be so vain as to dictate to God how you ought to be saved. Be willing to be saved by free grace through the blood of Jesus Christ; for that is God's way. Be willing to be saved by faith in Jesus Christ, for that also is God's way. If your unbelief begins to ask, "How can it be, and why should it be?" cease from such questions. Humble yourself and say, "God says it is so, and therefore it must be so;" if God says, "Believe, and be saved," I will believe and be saved; and if he says, "Trust Christ, and live," I will trust Christ and live. If a man had forfeited his life, but should be told by the court that he shall have pardon freely given to him if he will freely accept it—he would be a fool if he began to enquire, "But is this according to law? Is this according to precedent? What may be the effect of this pardon?" and so on. These enquiries are for the court, not for the prisoner. My dear man, you do not want to hang yourself, do you? Yet some men argue against their own souls, and labour to find out reasons why they should not be saved. If this perverse ingenuity could but be taught right reason, and men would strive to find out why they should at once yield themselves to God's way of salvation, they might enter into comfort and rest much sooner. O cavilling sinner, let thy artful doubts and reasonings be nailed with Jesus to the tree. Be a little child, and come and believe in the salvation which is revealed in Jesus Christ. Trust Christ to save you, and he will do it, as he has saved so many of us, to the praise of the glory of his grace.

"Ah," say you, "I have done this, but I cannot get peace." Then, dear friend, sink lower down! sink lower down! Did I hear you say, "Alas, Sir, I want to get comfort." Cease from that. Do not ask for comfort; ask for forgiveness, and that blessing may come through your greater discomfort. Sink lower down! Sink lower down! There is a point at which God will surely accept you, and that point is lower down. "Oh," you say, "I think I have a due sense of sin." That will not do. I want you to feel that you have *not* a due sense of sin, and come to

Jesus just so. "Oh, but I do think that I have been brokenhearted."
I should like to see you lower than that, till you cry, "I am afraid I
never knew what it is to be brokenhearted." I want you to sink so
low that you cannot say anything good of yourself; nay, nor see
an atom of goodness in yourself. When you look inside your heart
and can see nothing but that which would condemn you; when you
look at your life and see everything there that deserves wrath;
then you are on the road to hope. Come before God a criminal,
in the prison dress, with the rope about your neck. You will be saved,
then. When you confess that you have nothing of your own but sin—
when you acknowledge that you deserve to die, and to be cast away
for ever—God in infinite pity will let you live through faith in Christ
Jesus. Many years ago a certain prince visited the Spanish galleys,
where a large number of convicts were confined, chained to their oars
to toil on without relief;—I think nearly all of them condemned to a
life sentence. Being a great prince, the King of Spain told him that he
might in honour of his visit set free anyone of the galley-slaves he
chose. He went down among them to choose his man. He said to one,
"Man, how did you come here?" He replied that false witnesses swore
away his character. "Ah!" said the prince and passed on. He went
to the next, who stated that he had done something that was wrong, certainly, but not very much, and that he never ought to have been condemned.
"Ah!" said the prince, and again passed on. He went the round, and
found that they were all good fellows—all convicted by mistake. At
last he came to one who said, "You ask me why I came here. I
am ashamed to say that I richly deserve it. I am guilty, I cannot for
a moment say that I am not: and if I die at this oar, I thoroughly
deserve the punishment. In fact, I think it a mercy that my life is
spared me." The prince stopped and said, "It is a pity that such
a bad fellow as you should be placed amongst such a number of innocent
people. I will set you free." You smile at that; but let me make you
smile again. My Lord Jesus Christ has come here at this time to set
somebody free. He has come here at this time to pardon somebody's
sins. You that have no sins shall have no pardon. You good people
shall die in your sins. But, oh, you guilty ones, who humble yourselves
under the hand of God, my Master thinks that it is a pity that you
should be among these self-righteous people. So come right away, and
trust your Saviour, and obtain life eternal through his precious blood;
and to him shall be glory for ever and ever. Amen.

PORTION OF SCRIPTURE READ BEFORE SERMON—1 Peter iv.

HYMNS FROM "OUR OWN HYMN BOOK"—605, 704, 564.

A GOSPEL WORTH DYING FOR.

A Sermon

DELIVERED ON LORD'S-DAY MORNING, AUGUST 12TH, 1883, BY

C. H. SPURGEON,

AT EXETER-HALL.

"To testify the gospel of the grace of God."—Acts xx. 24.

PAUL says that, in comparison with his great object of preaching the gospel, he did not count even his life to be dear to himself; yet we are sure Paul highly valued life. He had the same love of life as other men, and he knew besides that his own life was of great consequence to the churches, and to the cause of Christ. In another place he said, "To abide in the flesh is more needful for you." He was not weary of life, nor was he a vain person who could treat life as though it were a thing to fling away in sport. He valued life, for he prized time, which is the stuff that life is made of, and he turned to practical account each day and hour, "redeeming the time because the days are evil." Yet he soberly said to the elders of the church at Ephesus that he did not regard his life as a dear thing in comparison with bearing testimony to the gospel of the grace of God. According to the verse before us the apostle regarded life as a race which he had to run. Now, the more quickly a race is run the better: certainly, length is not the object of desire. The one thought of a runner is how he can most speedily reach the winning-post. He spurns the ground beneath him; he cares not for the course he traverses except so far as it is the way over which he must run to reach his desired end. Such was life to Paul: all the energies of his spirit were consecrated to the pursuit of one object—namely, that he might everywhere bear testimony to the gospel of the grace of God; and the life which he lived here below was only valued by him as a means to that end. He also regarded the gospel, and his ministry in witnessing to it, as a sacred deposit which had been committed to him by the Lord himself. He looked upon himself "as put in trust with the gospel;" and he resolved to be faithful though it should cost him his life. He says he "desired to fulfil the ministry which he had received of the Lord Jesus Christ." Before his mind's eye he saw the Saviour taking into his pierced hands the priceless casket which contains the celestial jewel of the grace of God, and saying to him—"I have redeemed thee with my blood, and I have called

No. 1,734.

thee by my name, and now I commit this precious thing into thy hands, that thou mayest take care of it, and guard it even with thy heart's blood. I commission thee to go everywhere in my place and stead, and to make known to every people under heaven the gospel of the grace of God." All believers occupy a somewhat similar place. We are none of us called to the apostleship, and we may not all have been called to the public preaching of the word of God; but we are all charged to be valiant for the truth upon the earth, and to contend earnestly for the faith once delivered to the saints. Oh, to do this in the spirit of the apostle of the Gentiles! As believers, we are all called to some form of ministry; and this ought to make our life a race, and cause us to regard ourselves as the guardians of the gospel, even as he that bears the colours of a regiment regards himself as bound to sacrifice everything for their preservation.

Paul was a true hero; a hero of even a nobler stamp than those brave Greeks whose stories still stir the blood and fire the soul. Their heroism to a large extent depended upon public note, the present approval of their fellow-citizens, or upon the animal excitement of the battle-field; but Paul's heroism, so far as man was concerned, was self-contained, deliberate, and as sure to display itself in the solitude of a dungeon as in the assembly of the faithful. He was parting with his weeping friends, and going forward to trials of unknown intensity, but he was altogether unmoved by fear, and advanced on his way without a question. His leave-taking of the elders irresistibly reminds me of the old historian's record of Epaminondas the Theban general who, when he was mortally wounded by a Spartan spear, the head of which remained in his flesh, bade his friends leave it alone a little, "for" said he, "I have lived long enough if I die unconquered;" and when they told him that the battle was won, and that his comrades were victorious, he bade them draw out the head of the spear, that his life might end. One observed to him that he had fallen but that he had not lost his shield, and that the victory was won; to which he replied with his last breath, "Your Epaminondas thus dying doth not die." So Paul has lived long enough if the gospel is prospering in its course, and though he lays down his life he does not die if his ministry is fulfilled. Let me read you his words, and you shall judge if they have not this heroic ring. "And now, behold, I go bound in the spirit unto Jerusalem, not knowing the things that shall befall me there: save that the Holy Ghost witnesseth in every city, saying that bonds and afflictions abide me. But none of these things move me, neither count I my life dear unto myself, so that I might finish my course with joy, and the ministry, which I have received of the Lord Jesus, to testify the gospel of the grace of God."

We shall this morning first of all inquire, *what was this gospel which Paul judged to be worth dying for?*—" the gospel of the grace of God." When we have made that inquiry, I think we shall be prepared for another; if we cannot die for it, *how can we live for it?* and then, thirdly, I shall press this consecration upon you by answering the question—*Why should we?* Oh, that the Holy Spirit may work in us the holy devotion and self-sacrifice of Paul!

I. First, then, our enquiry this morning is, WHAT WAS THIS GOSPEL

FOR WHICH PAUL WOULD DIE? It is not everything called "gospel" which would produce such enthusiasm, or deserve it. For, my brethren, we have gospels nowadays which I would not die for, nor recommend anyone of you to live for, inasmuch as they are gospels that will be snuffed out within a few years. It is never worth while to die for a doctrine which will itself die out. I have lived long enough to see half-a-dozen new gospels rise, flourish, and decay. They told me long ago that my old Calvinistic doctrine was far behind the age, and was an exploded thing; and next I heard that evangelical teaching in any form was a thing of the past, to be supplanted by "advanced thought." I have heard of one improvement upon the old faith and then of another; and the philosophical divines are still improving their theology. They have gone on advancing and advancing, till heaven knows and perhaps hell knows what next they will advance to; but I am sure I do not. I would not die for any one of all the modern systems. I should like to ask broad church divines whether there is any positive doctrine in the Bible at all; and whether any form of teaching could for a moment be judged worth dying for; and whether the martyrs were not great fools to die for truths which might be valuable to them, but which the advance of thought has cast into disuse. Those men and women who went to Smithfield and were burnt quick to the death for Christ, were they not fools every one of them to die for a set of ideas which "modern thought" has quite exploded? I do verily think that to our modern divines there is no such thing as fixed truth, or that, if there be, they are not sure of having yet reached it. They have digged, and digged, and digged: look at the dark pits of unbelief which they have opened; but they have not come to the rock yet. Wait a little longer; they may one of these days find out something solid; but as yet they have only bored through layers of sand.

Yet there used to be a gospel in the world which consisted of facts which Christians never questioned. There was once in the church a gospel which believers hugged to their hearts as if it were their soul's life. There used to be a gospel in the world which provoked enthusiasm and commanded sacrifice. Tens of thousands have met together to hear this gospel at peril of their lives. Men, to the teeth of tyrants, have proclaimed it, and have suffered the loss of all things, and gone to prison and to death for it, singing psalms all the while. Is there not such a gospel remaining? Or are we arrived at cloud-land, where souls starve on suppositions, and become incapable of confidence or ardour? Are the disciples of Jesus now to be fed upon the froth of "thought" and the wind of imagination, whereon men become heady and high-minded? Nay, rather, will we not return to the substantial meat of infallible revelation, and cry to the Holy Ghost to feed us upon his own inspired word?

What is this gospel which Paul valued before his own life? It was called by him "the gospel of the grace of God." That which most forcibly struck the apostle in the gospel was that it was a message of *grace*, and of grace alone. Amid the music of the glad tidings one note rang out above all others and charmed the apostle's ear; that note was grace—the grace of God. That note he regarded as characteristic of the whole strain: the gospel was "the gospel of the grace of God." In these days that word "grace" is not often heard; we hear of moral duties, and scientific adjustments, and human progress; but who tells us of "the grace of God" except a few old-fashioned people who will soon be gone? As one of those antiquated folk I am here this morning, and I shall try to sound out that word "GRACE" so that those who know its joyful sound shall be glad, and those who despise it shall be cut to the heart. *Grace* is the essence of the gospel. *Grace* is the one hope for this fallen world! *Grace* is the sole comfort of saints looking forward for glory! Perhaps Paul had a clearer view of grace than even Peter, or James, or John; and hence he has so much larger space in the New Testament. The other apostolic writers excelled Paul in certain respects; but Paul as to his depth and clearness in the doctrine of grace stood first and foremost. We need Paul again, or at least the Pauline evangelism and definiteness. He would make short work of the new gospels, and say of those who follow them, " I marvel that ye are so soon removed from him that called you into the grace of Christ unto another gospel, which is not another; but there be some that trouble you, and would pervert the gospel of Christ."

Let me try to explain in a brief manner how the gospel is the good news of grace.

The gospel is an announcement that God is prepared to deal with guilty man on the ground of free favour and pure mercy. There would be no good news in saying that God is just; for, in the first place, that is not news,—we know that God is just; the natural conscience teaches man that. That God will punish sin and reward righteousness is not news at all; and if it were news, yet it would not be good news, for we have all sinned, and upon the ground of justice we must perish. But it is news, and news of the best kind, that the Judge of all is prepared to pardon transgression, and to justify the ungodly. It is good news to the sinful that the Lord will blot out sin, cover the sinner with righteousness, and receive him into his favour, and that not on account of anything he has done, or will ever do, but out of sovereign grace. Though we are all guilty without exception, and all most justly condemned for our sins, yet God is ready to take us from under the curse of his law, and give us all the blessedness of righteous men, as an act of pure mercy. Remember how David saw this and spake of it in the thirty-second Psalm :—" Blessed is he whose transgression is forgiven, whose sin is covered. Blessed is the man unto whom the Lord imputeth not iniquity, and in whose spirit there is no guile." This is a message worth dying for, that through the covenant of grace God can be just, and yet the justifier of him that believeth in Jesus; that he can be the righteous Judge of men, and yet believing men can be justified freely by his grace through the redemption that is in Christ Jesus. That God is merciful and gracious, and is ready to bless the most unworthy, is a wonderful piece of news, worth a man's spending a hundred lives to tell. My heart leaps within me as I repeat it in this Hall, and tell the penitent, the desponding, and the despairing that, though their sins deserve hell, yet grace can give them heaven, and make them fit for it: and *that* as a sovereign act of love, altogether independent of their character or deservings. Because the Lord hath said, " I will have mercy on whom I will have mercy, and I will have compassion on whom I will have compassion," there is hope for the most hopeless. Since "it is not of him that willeth, nor of him that runneth, but of God that showeth mercy" (Romans ix. 16), there is an open door of hope for those who otherwise might despair. It is as though there had been held a great assize, and the judge had passed from county to county, and a number of prisoners had been condemned, and there remained nothing further in the course of justice but that their sentences should be carried into execution. Lo, suddenly, by the silver trumpets of messengers clothed in silken apparel, it is proclaimed that the king has discovered a method by which, without violating justice, he can deal with the condemned in pure mercy, and so grant them free pardon, immediate jail-delivery, and a place in his majesty's favour and service. This would be glad tidings in the condemned cells, would it not? Would you not be glad to carry such news to the poor prisoners? Ah, Paul, I can understand your getting into a holy excitement over such a revelation as that of free grace. I can understand your being willing to throw your life away that you might tell to your fellow sinners that grace reigns through righteousness unto eternal life.

But the gospel tells us much more than this, namely, that in order to his dealing with men upon the ground of free favour, God the Father has himself removed the grand obstacle which stood in the way of mercy. God is just; that is a truth most sure; man's conscience knows it to be so, and man's conscience will never rest content unless it can see that the justice of God is vindicated. Therefore, in order that God might justly deal in a way of pure mercy with men, he gave his only-begotten Son, that by his death the law might receive its due, and the eternal principles of his government might be maintained. Jesus was appointed to stand in man's stead, to bear man's sin, and endure the chastisement of man's guilt. How clearly doth Isaiah state this in his fifty-third chapter! Man is now saved securely, because the command-ment is not set aside, nor the penalty revoked; all is done and suffered which could be exacted by the sternest justice, and yet grace has her hands untied to distribute pardons as she pleases. The debtor is loosed, for the debt is paid. See a dying Saviour, and hear the prophet say, "The chastisement of our peace was upon him, and with his stripes we are healed." Here, too, everything is of grace. Brethren, it was grace on God's part to resolve upon devising and accepting an atonement, and especially in his actually providing that atonement at his own cost. There is the wonder of it: he that was offended himself provides the reconciliation. He had but one Son, and sooner than there should be any obstacle in his way as to dealing with men on the footing of pure grace, he took that Son from his bosom, allowed him to assume our frail nature, and in that nature permitted him to die, the just for the unjust, to bring us to God. You admire Abraham's giving up his son to God; much more admire Jehovah's giving up his Son for sinners. "Herein is love, not that we loved God, but that he loved us, and sent his Son to be the propitiation for our sins." This, then, is the gospel of the grace of God—that God is able, without injustice, to deal with men in a way of pure mercy, altogether apart from their sins or their merits, because their sins were laid upon his dear Son Jesus Christ, who hath offered to divine justice a complete satisfaction, so that God is glorious in holiness and yet rich in mercy. Ah, beloved Paul, there is something worth preaching here.

In the gospel there is also revealed a motive for mercy which is in agreement with the grace of God. There is always needed in the action of every wise man a competent motive ; men do not act without reason if they are reasonable men. The same is true with God, the highest of all intelligences : he acts upon the highest reasons. His motive for dealing with men on the footing of free grace is the revealing of his own glorious character. He says : "Not for your sakes do I this, saith the Lord God, be it known unto you : be ashamed and confounded for your own ways, O house of Israel." He works the wonders of his grace "to the intent that now unto the principalities and powers in heavenly places might be known by the church the manifold wisdom of God, according to the eternal purpose which he purposed in Christ Jesus our Lord." He finds a motive in his own nature and mercy since he could not find it anywhere else. He will deal with guilty men according to the sovereignty of his will, "to the praise of the glory of his grace wherein he hath made us accepted in the Beloved." He saves men that his own beloved Son Jesus Christ may be magnified and extolled, and be very high, and that his Holy Spirit may be honoured in the new-creating of rebellious natures. Listen to this, ye that feel your guilt : God is able without infringement of his justice to deal with you on the footing of pure grace, and he has found a reason for so doing, a reason which will apply as much to the worst of men as to the best. If it be for his own glory's sake that he saves guilty sinners, then is a window opened by which light can come to those who sit in the thickest gloom of despair.

In order to the accomplishment of the designs of grace it was necessary further that a gospel message should be issued full of promise, encouragement, and blessing ; and truly that message has been delivered to us ; for that gospel which we preach to-day is full of grace to the very brim. It speaks on this wise,—Sinner, just as you are, return unto the Lord, and he will receive you graciously and love you freely. God hath said, "I will be merciful to their unrighteousness, and their sins and their iniquities will I remember no more." For Christ's sake, and not because of any agonies, or tears, or sorrows on your part, he will remove your sins as far from you as the east is from the west. He saith, "Come now, and let us reason together : though your sins be as scarlet, they shall be as white as snow ; though they be red like crimson, they shall be as wool." You may come to Jesus just as you are, and he will give you full remission upon your believing in him. The Lord says to-day, "Look not within, as though you would search for any merit there ; but look unto me, and be ye saved. I will bless you apart from merit, according to the atonement of Christ Jesus." He says, "Look not within as though you looked for any strength for future life : I am become both your strength and your salvation ; for when you were yet without strength, in due time Christ died for the ungodly." The gospel invitation is, "Ho, every one that thirsteth, come ye to the waters, and he that hath no money ; come ye, buy, and eat ; yea, come, buy wine and milk without money and without price." Come and welcome, ye lame, ye halt, ye blind, ye wandering, ye foul, ye miserable. You are invited, not because you are good, but because you are evil ; not because you are hopeful, but because you are hopeless. The gospel message is of grace, because it is directed to those whose only claim is their need. The whole have no need of a physician, but they that are sick. Christ came not to call the righteous but sinners to repentance. Come, therefore, ye morally sick; ye whose brows are white with the leprosy of sin; come and welcome, for to you is this free gospel proclaimed by divine authority. Assuredly such a message as this is worth any exertion for its spreading, and it is so blessed, so divine, that we may gladly pour out our blood to proclaim it.

Further, brethren: that this gospel blessing might come within the reach of men, God's grace has adopted a method suitable to their condition. "How can I be forgiven?" saith one, "tell me truly and quickly!" "Believe in the Lord Jesus Christ, and thou shalt be saved." God asks of you no good works, nor good feelings either, but that you be willing to accept what he most freely gives. He saves upon believing. This is faith: that thou believe that Jesus Christ is the Son of God, and that thou trust thyself with him; "But as many as received him, to them gave he power to become the sons of God, even to them that believe on his name." If thou believest, thou art saved. Salvation "is of faith that it might be of grace, to the end the promise might be sure to all the seed."

Dost thou say, " But faith itself seems beyond my reach"? Then, in the gospel of the grace of God we are told that even faith is God's gift, and that he works it in men by his Holy Spirit; for apart from that Spirit they lie dead in trespasses and sins. Oh, what grace is this, that the faith which is commanded is also conferred! "But," saith one, "if I were to believe in Christ and have my past sins forgiven, yet I fear I should go back to sin; for I have no strength by which to keep myself for the future." Hearken! the gospel of the grace of God is this, that he will keep thee to the end—that he will preserve alive within thee the fire which he kindles, for he saith, "I give unto my sheep eternal life"; and again he saith, "The water that I shall give him shall be in him a well of water springing up unto everlasting life." The sheep of Christ shall never perish, neither shall any pluck them out of Christ's hand. Dost thou hear this, thou guilty one—thou who hast no claim upon God's grace whatever? His free grace comes to thee, even to thee; and if thou art made willing to receive it, thou art this day a saved man, and saved for ever beyond all question. I do say it again, this is a gospel so well worth the preaching that I can understand Paul saying, "Neither count I my life dear unto myself, so that I might finish my course with joy, and the ministry which I have received of the Lord Jesus, to testify the gospel of the grace of God." I read in an old book a dream of one who was under concern of soul. He fell asleep and dreamed that he was out in the wilds in a terrible storm. The lightnings flamed around him, and the voice of the thunder made the earth to rock beneath him. He looked eagerly around for a shelter. He ran to the first house before him, but he was denied admittance. He that dwelt there was named *Justice,* and he said in angry tones, "Get thee gone—I cannot shelter a criminal, a traitor to his King and God!" He fled to the next house, and it turned out to be the mansion of *Truth.* Truth came to the door with calm but stern countenance, and said, "Thou art full of falsehood, thou canst not sojourn here." He fled to the home of *Peace*, which stood near, and hoped that there perhaps he might be housed from the storm; but Peace said, "Begone! there is no peace, saith my God, unto the wicked." He could not then tell what to do, for the storm waxed yet more furious: when lo! he saw a portal over which was written "*Mercy*." "Ay," said he, "this is the place for me, for I am guilty." The door was open and he was welcomed there. To that house I invite you. Come in and be at rest. You who cannot as yet be harboured by justice, or peace, or truth, may come to mercy, and receive abundant grace.

Do you seem inclined to accept the way and method of grace? Let me test you. Some men think they love a thing and yet they do not, for they have made a mistake concerning it. Do you understand that you are to have no claim upon God? He says, "I will have mercy on whom I will have mercy, and I will have compassion on whom I will have compassion." When it comes to pure mercy, then no one can possibly urge a claim; in fact, no claim can exist. If it be of grace it is not of debt, and if of debt it is not of grace. If God wills to save one man, and another be left to perish in his own wilful sin, that other cannot dare to dispute with God. Or if he do, the answer is—" Can I not do as I will with my own?" Oh, but you seem now as if you started back from it! See, your pride revolts against the sovereignty of grace. Let me beckon you back again. Though you have no claim, there is another truth which smiles upon you; for, on the other hand, there is no bar to your obtaining mercy. If no goodness is needed to recommend you to God, since all must be pure favour which he gives, then also no badness can shut you out from that favour. However guilty you may be, it may be God may show favour to you. He has in other cases called out the chief of sinners; why not in your case also? At any rate, no aggravation of sin, no continuance in sin, no height of sin, can be a reason why God should not look with grace upon you; for if pure grace and nothing else but grace is to have sway then the jet black transgressor may be saved. In his case there is room for grace to manifest its greatness. I have heard men make excuse out of the doctrine of election, and they have said, "What if I should not be elected?" It seems to me far wiser to say, "What if I should be elected?" Yea, I am elected if I believe in Jesus; for there never was a soul yet that cast itself upon the atonement of Christ but what that soul was chosen of God from before the foundation of the world.

This is the gospel of the grace of God, and I know that it touches the heart of many of you. It often stirs my soul like the sound of martial music, to think of my Lord's grace from old eternity, a grace that is constant to its choice, and will be constant to it when all these visible things shall disappear as sparks that fly from the chimney. My heart is glad within me to have to preach free grace and dying love: I can understand why crowds met at dead of night to hear of the grace of God. I can understand the Covenanters on the bleak hills listening, with sparkling eyes, as Cameron preached of the grace of the great King! There is something in a free-grace gospel worth preaching, worth listening to, worth living for, and worth dying for!

II. This brings me to the second head: you and I are not called to

die for it just yet; let us see to-day that we live for it. How can we
live for this gospel of the grace of God?

I answer, first, if anybody here is to live for this gospel, he must
have received it from God, and he must have received a call to minister
or serve for it. He must feel himself under bonds to hold and keep
this gospel; not so much because he has chosen it, but because it has
chosen him. I forget who it was, but a quaint old minister was once
told that he could not preach in a certain pulpit if he held the doctrines
of grace. "Well," said he, "I think I might be allowed to preach
there, for I can truly say that I do not hold the doctrines of grace, the
doctrines of grace hold me." That might be rather a quibble, but
there is a grand truth in it. When a man picks and selects his creed,
the probabilities are that by-and-by he will pick again, and will select
another next time. There is about the love which constitutes our domestic bliss a something of necessity: our beloved one was chosen by us,
but yet we could not help it, we were carried away and overborne, and
so our marriage came to pass. It was not altogether choice, there was
a mystic power that enchained our hearts; and I am sure it is so with
the doctrines of grace if we believe them,—we chose them with a willing
soul, but yet we were under constraint, and could do no other. To me
there is but one form of doctrine; I know no other. Brethren, I
cannot be of any other faith than that which I preached nearly twenty-
nine years ago on this platform. I think I have read as much as most
men, and I know most of the maunderings of advanced thinkers; but I
have never come into their secret, and I never can. I abhor the very
idea of an advance upon the gospel which Paul preached. I am to-day
what I was when, as a youth, I preached to crowds in this Hall. I
have progressed in my theology not so much as the tithe of an inch. I
hope I preach better and with more experimental knowledge of the
truth ; but that which I preached thirty-three years ago I preach to-day.
You know the story of the boy who stood upon the burning deck because
his father said, "Stand you there"; and I desire to imitate his steadfastness. Other boys might be much wiser than he was, but his wisdom
was obedience. I prefer obeying God to being wise with my own
wisdom. The gospel which the Bible has revealed, and the Holy Ghost
has taught me, I must preach, and no other. I am incapable of
believing the novelties of the hour. I must abide in my old faith. I
would say with Luther, "I cannot help it, so help me God!" I know
no other gospel to-day than that which I knew when I first believed in
Jesus. I know that by grace we are saved through faith, and that not
of ourselves,—it is the gift of God: what more do I need to know?
You shall leave this rock, if you like, my brother, for you may be able
to swim; but I must stop where I am, for I should drown. When the
crack of doom shall be heard, I shall be here, God helping me, believing
the gospel of the grace of God and none other creed. I hope there is
something in adhesiveness and pertinacity which will help to preserve,
if not to spread the gospel. Steadfastness at this particular time has a
special value, and I urge you to it; to the gospel which ye have
received, to the gospel of the grace of God, I implore you to stand fast
so long as you live.

But the next thing Paul did was to make it known. Wherever he went he published the gospel. This is what we must do. "Oh," says one, "I cannot make it known." Why not? "I could not tell out the gospel." Why not? "Why, I am a person of mean appearance, and I do not suppose people would pay me any respect." Just what they said about Paul—"his personal presence is weak." "Oh, but I am no speaker." Just so, that also is what they said of Paul—"His speech is contemptible." "Oh, but if I were to say anything, I could not adorn it with a figure of speech, or illustrate it with a simile; I could not even quote a bit of poetry, to make it fine." Paul also used home-spun. He says, "We use great plainness of speech." Many of the other teachers were great orators, but Paul always fought shy of oratory; he stood up and allowed the truth to flow out of his mouth freely, in its own way; and I do believe at the present moment we want a race of preachers who will not be fine, or scholarly, or rhetorical, or sensational; men of whom you will say when you have heard them—"I cannot make out why people flock to hear such a ministry. All that they can go for is *what* the man says; for he does not say it grandly, he does not seem as if he wanted to do so, he appears only concerned to get his message out of his own heart, and get it into the people's hearts." That is just what Paul did. Do you not think that you could tell the gospel out in his fashion? "Oh, but I have so many infirmities." Yes, Paul said he gloried in infirmities because the power of Christ the more clearly rested on him. When he had done preaching the people could not say, "Oh, we understand why we felt it so; you see Paul practises all the graces of manner. We quite understand why his speech penetrated our hearts; he has such a melodious, bell-like voice. We can understand why we like to hear him; he has such expressive eyes, they look into our souls." Now, Paul, in all probability, had weak eyes; according to his name he was a short man; and it is likely that he spoke very plainly. Yet he never felt sorry that it was so; on the contrary, he believed that in his weakness he was strong, for the power of Christ rested upon him. He hoped also that for this very reason their faith would not stand in the wisdom of man, but in the power of God. Brothers and sisters, we are all qualified, if this be the case, to go and tell to others the gospel of the grace of God.

Yet further, Paul desired to *testify* to the gospel. Now, to testify is something more than to proclaim; it means to bear personal witness to the truth. Paul was specially qualified to testify; was he not? When he preached he frequently told that story about the fierce persecutor who was on the way to Damascus, and was suddenly struck down—a persecutor who had never asked to be saved by grace, who had no free-will towards Christ, but who had a very strong will against him, and was haling men and women to prison, and compelling them to blaspheme, being exceeding mad against them. Oh how sweetly Paul told out the gospel of the grace of God when he said, "The Lord appeared to me by the way." "I obtained mercy, that in me first Jesus Christ might show forth all longsuffering for a pattern to them which should hereafter believe on him to life everlasting." Friend, cannot you tell of your conversion, and let men know how free grace came to you when you looked not for it?

Nor would Paul end there; for he would often tell his consolations, how the gospel had comforted him when he had been stoned, and tried by false brethren, and yet had been upheld by the grace of God. Paul could tell also of his heavenly joys: how often he had been exceedingly lifted up, and made to triumph in Christ by feeding upon the gospel of the grace of God. His personal experience of its power over himself was that which he used as the great instrument and argument for spreading the gospel—for this is the meaning of testifying.

My friend, if the gospel has done nothing for you, hold your tongue or speak against it; but if the gospel has done for you what it has done for some of us, if it has changed the current of your life, if it has lifted you up from the dunghill and made you to sit as on a throne, if it is to-day your meat and your drink, if to your life it is the very centre and sun,—then bear constant witness to it. If the gospel has become to you what it is to me, the light of my innermost heart, the core of my being, then tell it, tell it wherever you go; and make men know that even if *they* reject it it is to you the power of God unto salvation, and will be the same to every man that believeth.

III. My time is gone, but yet I must detain you a minute while I remind you of reasons WHY WE, MY BRETHREN, SHOULD LIVE TO MAKE KNOWN THE GOSPEL OF THE GRACE OF GOD.

First, because *it is the only gospel in the world*, after all. These mushroom gospels of the hour, which come and go like a penny newspaper, which has its day and then is thrown aside, have no claim on any man's zeal. These changing moons of doctrine, what are they doing for England? They are doing much evil in this city—they are alienating the mass of the people from going to any place of worship at all. Why should they come to hear uncertainties? Why should they come merely to be taught their duty, and to be moralized, and so on? Men are not led to assemble in multitudes by such poor attractions. I do not know that I should go across the street Sunday after Sunday merely to hear a moral essay. I might as well stay at home and read the paper. But to hear the gospel of the grace of God is worth many a mile's walk, and if it were plainly set forth in all our churches and chapels I warrant we should see very few empty pews: the people would come and hear it, for they always have done so. It is your grace-less gospel which starves the flock till they forsake the pasture: it is your Socinian reasoning which leads men to treat ministry and public worship with contempt. The old gospel is a sweet savour which attracts the masses. When Whitefield sounded it forth, what common was big enough to hold the thousands? Man wants something that shall cheer his heart in the midst of his labour, and give him hope under a sense of sin. As the thirsty need water, so does man want the gospel of the grace of God. And there are no two gospels in the world any more than there are two suns in the heavens. There is but one atmo-sphere for us to breathe, and one gospel for us to live by. "Other foundation can no man lay than that which is laid, Jesus Christ the righteous." Therefore tell out the gospel, lest men die for lack of the knowledge of it.

Do it, next, because *it is for God's glory*. Do you not see how it glorifies God? It lays the sinner low; it makes man nobody, but God is all-in-all. It sets God on a throne, and trails man in the dust; and then it sweetly leads men to worship and reverence the God of all grace, who passeth by transgression, iniquity, and sin—therefore spread it.

Spread it, because thus you will *glorify Christ.* Oh, if he should come on this platform this morning, how gladly would we all make way for him! how devoutly would we adore him! If we might but see that head, that dear majestic head, would we not all bow in worship? And if he then spoke, and said, "My beloved, I have committed to you my gospel; hold it fast as ye have received it! Give not way to the notions and inventions of men, but hold fast the truth as ye have received it; and go and tell my word, for I have other sheep that are not yet of my fold, who must be brought in; and you have brothers that yet are prodigals, and they must come home": I say, if he looked you each one in the face, and addressed you so, your soul would answer, "Lord, I will live for thee! I will make thee known! I will die for thee if needs be to publish the gospel of Jesus Christ."

Now, if you and I arouse ourselves this day, and God's Holy Spirit shall help us so to do, and we begin to proclaim the gospel of the grace of God, do you know what I think is sure to happen? I prophesy the best results. They tell us that all sorts of evils are growing strong, and brethren, darkly prophetic, tell us that awful times are coming—I cannot tell you how dreadful they are to be. Popery is to come back according to some, and once again the harlot of the Seven Hills is to dominate over all the earth. Is she? We shall see. If you boldly proclaim the gospel I tell you it will not be so. If the gospel of the grace of God be fully and fairly preached it cannot be so. Listen to what John saw—"I saw another angel fly in the midst of heaven having the everlasting gospel to preach unto them that dwell on the earth, and to every nation, and kindred, and tongue, and people, saying with a loud voice, fear God and give glory to him." Do you see that angel? Observe what follows! Close behind him flies another celestial herald. "And there followed another angel, saying, Babylon is fallen, that great city, because she made all nations drink of the wine of the wrath of her fornication." Fly, angel of the everlasting gospel! Fly, for as surely as thou dost speed thy flight, that other angel will follow who shall proclaim the downfall of Babylon, and of every other system that opposeth itself to the grace of the Lord God Almighty! The Lord stir you up for his name's sake. Amen.

PORTIONS OF SCRIPTURE READ BEFORE SERMON—Psalm xxxii.; Romans iii. 9—31; iv. 1—8.

HYMNS FROM "OUR OWN HYMN BOOK"—100, 980, 546.

THE DOCTRINES OF GRACE DO NOT LEAD TO SIN.

A Sermon

DELIVERED ON LORD'S-DAY MORNING, AUGUST 19TH, 1883, BY

C. H. SPURGEON,

AT EXETER-HALL.

" For sin shall not have dominion over you : for ye are not under the law, but under grace. What then? shall we sin, because we are not under the law, but under grace? God forbid."—Romans vi. 14, 15.

LAST Sabbath morning I tried to show that the substance and essence of the true gospel is the doctrine of God's grace—that, in fact, if you take away the grace of God from the gospel you have extracted from it its very life-blood, and there is nothing left worth preaching, worth believing, or worth contending for. Grace is the soul of the gospel : without it the gospel is dead. Grace is the music of the gospel : without it the gospel is silent as to all comfort. I endeavoured also to set forth the doctrine of grace in brief terms, teaching that God deals with sinful men upon the footing of pure mercy : finding them guilty and condemned, he gives free pardons, altogether irrespective of past character, or of any good works which may be foreseen. Moved only by pity he devises a plan for their rescue from sin and its consequences—a plan in which grace is the leading feature. Out of free favour he has provided, in the death of his dear Son, an atonement by means of which his mercy can be justly bestowed. He accepts all those who place their trust in this atonement, selecting faith as the way of salvation, that it may be all of grace. In this he acts from a motive found within himself, and not because of any reason found in the sinner's conduct, past, present, or future. I tried to show that this grace of God flows towards the sinner from of old, and begins its operations upon him when there is nothing good in him : it works in him that which is good and acceptable, and continues so to work in him till the deed of grace is complete, and the believer is received up into the glory for which he is made meet. Grace commences to save, and it perseveres till all is done. From first to last, from the "A" to the "Z" of the heavenly alphabet, everything in salvation is of grace, and grace alone; all is of free favour, nothing of merit. "By grace are ye saved through faith; and that not of yourselves: it is the gift of God," "So then it is not of him that willeth, nor of him that runneth, but of God that sheweth mercy."

No sooner is this doctrine set forth in a clear light than men begin to

No. 1,735.

cavil at it. It is the target for all carnal logic to shoot at. Unrenewed minds never did like it, and they never will ; it is so humbling to human pride, making so light of the nobility of human nature. That men are to be saved by divine charity, that they must as condemned criminals receive pardon by the exercise of the royal prerogative, or else perish in their sins, is a teaching which they cannot endure. God alone is exalted in the sovereignty of his mercy ; and the sinner can do no better than meekly touch the silver sceptre, and accept undeserved favour just because God wills to give it :—this is not pleasant to the great minds of our philosophers, and the broad phylacteries of our moralists, and therefore they turn aside, and fight against the empire of grace. Straightway the unrenewed man seeks out artillery with which to fight against the gospel of the grace of God, and one of the biggest guns he has ever brought to the front is the declaration that the doctrine of the grace of God must lead to licentiousness. If great sinners are freely saved, then men will more readily become great sinners ; and if when God's grace regenerates a man it abides with him, then men will infer that they may live as they like, and yet be saved. This is the constantly-repeated objection which I have heard till it wearies me with its vain and false noise. I am almost ashamed to have to refute so rotten an argument. They dare to assert that men will take license to be guilty because God is gracious, and they do not hesitate to say that if men are not to be saved by their works they will come to the conclusion that their conduct is a matter of indifference, and that they may as well sin that grace may abound.

This morning I want to talk a little about this notion ; for in part it is a great mistake, and in part it is a great lie. In part it is a mistake because it arises from misconception, and in part it is a lie because men know better, or might know better if they pleased.

I begin by admitting that the charge does appear somewhat probable. It does seem very likely that if we are to go up and down the country, and say, "The very chief of sinners may be forgiven through believing in Jesus Christ, for God is displaying mercy to the very vilest of the vile," then sin will seem to be a cheap thing. If we are everywhere to cry, "Come, ye sinners, come and welcome, and receive free and immediate pardon through the sovereign grace of God," it does seem probable that some may basely reply, "Let us sin without stint, for we can easily obtain forgiveness." But that which looks to be probable is not, therefore, certain: on the contrary, the improbable and the unexpected full often come to pass. In questions of moral influence nothing is more deceptive than theory. The ways of the human mind are not to be laid down with a pencil and compasses; man is a singular being. Even that which is logical is not always inevitable, for men's minds are not governed by the rules of the schools. I believe that the inference which would lead men to sin because grace reigns is not logical, but the very reverse ; and I venture to assert that, as a matter of fact, ungodly men do not, as a rule, plead the grace of God as an excuse for their sin. As a rule they are too indifferent to care about reasons at all; and if they do offer an excuse it is usually more flimsy and super-ficial. There may be a few men of perverse minds who have used this argument, but there is no accounting for the freaks of the fallen understanding. I shrewdly suspect that in any cases in which such rea-soning has been put forward it was a mere pretence, and by no means a plea which satisfied the sinner's own conscience. If men do thus excuse themselves, it is generally in some veiled manner, for the most of them would be utterly ashamed to state the argument in plain terms. I question whether the devil himself would be found reasoning thus— "God is merciful, therefore let us be more sinful." It is so diabolical an inference, that I do not like to charge my fellow-men with it, though our moralist opposers do not hesitate thus to degrade them. Surely, no intelligent being can really persuade itself that the goodness of God is a reason for offending him more than ever. Moral insanity produces strange reasonings, but it is my solemn conviction that very rarely do men practically consider the grace of God to be a motive for sin. That which seems so probable at the first blush, is not so when we come to consider it.

I have admitted that a few human beings have turned the grace of God into lasciviousness ; but I trust no one will ever argue against any doctrine on account of the perverse use made of it by the baser sort. Cannot every truth be perverted ? Is there a single doctrine of Scripture which graceless hands have not twisted into mischief? Is there not an almost infinite ingenuity in wicked men for making evil out of good ? If we are to condemn a truth because of the misbehaviour of individuals who profess to believe it, we should be found condemning our Lord himself for what Judas did, and our holy faith would die at the hands of apostates and hypocrites. Let us act like rational men. We do not find fault with ropes because poor insane creatures have hanged them-selves therewith ; nor do we ask that the wares of Sheffield may be destroyed because edged tools are the murderer's instruments.

It may appear probable that the doctrine of free grace will be made into a license for sin, but a better acquaintance with the curious working of the human mind corrects the notion. Fallen as human nature is, it is still human, and therefore does not take kindly to certain forms of evil—such, for instance, as inhuman ingratitude. It is hardly human to multiply injuries upon those who return us continued benefits. The case reminds me of the story of half-a-dozen boys who had severe fathers, accustomed to flog them within an inch of their lives. Another boy was with them who was tenderly beloved by his parents, and known to be so. These young gentlemen met together to hold a council of war about robbing an orchard. They were all of them anxious to get about it except the favoured youth, who did not enjoy the proposal. One of them cried out, "*You* need not be afraid : if our fathers catch us at this work, we shall be half-killed, but your father won't lay a hand upon *you*." The little boy answered, "And do you think because my father is kind to me, that therefore I will do wrong and grieve him ? I will do nothing of the sort to my dear father. He is so good to me that I cannot vex him." It would appear that the argument of the many boys was not overpoweringly convincing to their companion : the opposite conclusion was quite as logical, and evidently carried weight with it. If God is good to the undeserving, some men will go into sin, but there are others of a nobler order whom the goodness of God leadeth to repentance. They scorn the beast-like argument—that the more loving God is, the more rebellious we may be; and they feel that against a God of goodness it is an evil thing to rebel.

By-the-way I cannot help observing that I have known persons object to the evil influence of the doctrines of grace who were by no means qualified by their own morality to be judges of the subject. Morals must be in a poor way when immoral persons become their guardians. The doctrine of justification by faith is frequently objected to as injurious to morals. A newspaper some time ago quoted a verse from one of our popular hymns—

> " Weary, working, plodding one,
>   Why toil you so ?
> Cease your doing ; all was done
>   Long, long ago.
>
> " Till to Jesus' work you cling
>   By a simple faith,
> ' Doing' is a deadly thing,
>   ' Doing' ends in death."

This it styled mischievous teaching. When I read the article I felt a deep interest in this corrector of Luther and Paul, and I wondered how much he had drunk in order to elevate his mind to such a pitch of theological knowledge. I have found men pleading against the doctrines of grace on the ground that they did not promote morality, to whom I could have justly replied, " What has morality to do with you, or you with it?" These sticklers for good works are not often the doers of them. Let legalists look to their own hands and tongues, and leave the gospel of grace and its advocates to answer for themselves.

Looking back in history, I see upon its pages a refutation of the oft-repeated calumny. Who dares to suggest that the men who believed in the grace of God have been sinners above other sinners ? With all their faults, those who throw stones at them will be few if they first prove themselves to be their superiors in character. When have they been the patrons of vice, or the defenders of injustice ? Pitch upon the point in English history when this doctrine was very strong in the land; who were the men that held these doctrines most firmly ? Men like Owen, Charnock, Manton, Howe, and I hesitate not to add Oliver Cromwell. What kind of men were these ? Did they pander to the licentiousness of a court ? Did they invent a Book of Sports for Sabbath diversion ? Did they haunt ale-houses and places of revelry ? Every historian will tell you, the greatest fault of these men in the eyes of their enemies was that they were too precise for the generation in which they lived, so that they called them Puritans, and condemned them as holding a gloomy theology. Sirs, if there was iniquity in the land in that day, it was to be found with the theological party which preached up salvation by works. The gentlemen with their womanish locks and essenced hair, whose speech savoured of profanity, were the advocates of salvation by works, and all bedabbled with lust they pleaded for human merit; but the men who believed in grace alone were of another style. They were not in the chambers of rioting and wantonness; where were they ? They might be found on their knees crying to God for help in temptation; and in persecuting times they might be found in prison, cheerfully suffering the loss of all things for the truth's sake. The Puritans were the godliest men on the face of the earth. Are men so inconsistent as to nickname them for their purity, and yet say that their doctrines lead to sin?

Nor is this a solitary instance—this instance of Puritanism; all history confirms the rule : and when it is said that these doctrines will create sin, I appeal to facts, and leave the oracle to answer as it may. If we are ever to see a pure and godly England we must have a gospelized England : if we are to put down drunkenness and the social evil it must be by the proclamation of the grace of God.   Men must be forgiven by grace, renewed by grace, transformed by grace, sanctified by grace, preserved by grace ; and when that comes to pass the golden age will dawn ; but while they are merely taught their duty, and left to do it of themselves in their own strength, it is labour in vain. You may flog a dead horse a long while before it will stir : you need to put life into it, for else all your flogging will fail. To teach men to walk who have no feet is poor work, and such is instruction in morals before grace gives a heart to love holiness. The gospel alone supplies men with motive and strength, and therefore it is to the gospel that we must look as the real reformer of men.

I shall fight this morning with the objection before us as I shall find strength. The doctrine of grace, the whole plan of salvation by grace, is most promotive of holiness. Wherever it comes it helps us to say, " God forbid," to the question, " Shall we sin, because we are not under the law, but under grace ? " This I would set out in the clear sunlight.

I wish to call your attention to some six or seven points.

I.   First, you will see that the gospel of the grace of God promotes real holiness in men by remembering that THE SALVATION WHICH IT BRINGS IS SALVATION FROM THE POWER OF SIN. When we preach salvation to the vilest of men, some suppose we mean by that a mere deliverance from hell and an entrance into heaven. It includes all that, and results in that, but that is not what we mean. What we mean by salvation is this—deliverance from the love of sin, rescue from the habit of sin, setting free from the desire to sin. Now listen. If it be so, that that boon of deliverance from sin is the gift of divine grace, in what way will that gift, or the free distribution of it, produce sin?   I fail to see any such danger. On the contrary, I say to the man who proclaims a gracious promise of victory over sin, " Make all speed : go up and down throughout the world, and tell the vilest of mankind that God is willing by his grace to set them free from the love of sin and to make new creatures of them." Suppose the salvation we preach be this :—you that have lived ungodly and wicked lives may enjoy your sins, and yet escape the penalty—that would be mischievous indeed ; but if it be this,—you that live the most ungodly and wicked lives may yet by believing in the Lord Jesus be enabled to change those lives, so that you shall live unto God instead of serving sin and Satan,—what harm can come to the most prudish morals ? Why, I say spread such a gospel, and let it circulate through every part of our vast empire, and let all men hear it, whether they rule in the House of Lords or suffer in the house of bondage. Tell them everywhere that God freely and of infinite grace is willing to renew men, and make them new creatures in

Christ Jesus. Can any evil consequences come of the freest proclamation of this news ? The worse men are, the more gladly would we see them embracing this truth, for these are they who most need it. I say to every one of you, whoever you may be, whatever your past condition, God can renew you according to the power of his grace ; so that you who are to him like dead, dry bones, can be made to live by his Spirit. That renewal will be seen in holy thoughts, and pure words, and righteous acts to the glory of God. In great love he is prepared to work all these things in all who believe. Why should any men be angry at such a statement? What possible harm can come of it? I defy the most cunning adversary to object, upon the ground of morals, to God's giving men new hearts and right spirits even as he pleases.

II. Secondly, let it not be forgotten as a matter of fact that THE PRINCIPLE OF LOVE HAS BEEN FOUND TO POSSESS VERY GREAT POWER OVER MEN. In the infancy of history nations dream that crime can be put down by severity, and they rely upon fierce punishments ; but experience corrects the error. Our forefathers dreaded forgery, which is a troublesome fraud, and interferes with the confidence which should exist between man and man. To put it down they made forgery a capital offence. Alas for the murders committed by that law! Yet the constant use of the gallows was never sufficient to stamp out the crime. Many offences have been created and multiplied by the penalty which was meant to suppress them. Some offences have almost ceased when the penalty against them has been lightened.

It is a notable fact as to men, that if they are forbidden to do a thing they straightway pine to do it, though they had never thought of doing it before. Law commands obedience, but does not promote it ; it often creates disobedience, and an over-weighted penalty has been known to provoke an offence. Law fails, but love wins.

Love in any case makes sin infamous. If one should rob another it would be sufficiently bad ; but suppose a man robbed his friend, who had helped him often when he was in need, everyone would say that his crime was most disgraceful. Love brands sin on the forehead with a red-hot iron. If a man should kill an enemy, the offence would be grievous ; but if he slew his father, to whom he owes his life, or his mother, on whose breasts he was nursed in infancy, then all would cry out against the monster. In the light of love sin is seen to be exceeding sinful.

Nor is this all. *Love has a great constraining power towards the highest form of virtue.* Deeds to which a man could not be compelled on the ground of law, men have cheerfully done because of love. Would our brave seamen man the life-boat to obey an Act of Parliament ? No, they would indignantly revolt against being forced to risk their lives ; but they will do it feeely to save their fellow-men. Remember that text of the apostle, " Scarcely for a righteous (or merely just) man will one die : yet peradventure," says he, " for a good (benevolent) man some would even dare to die." Goodness wins the heart, and one is ready to die for the kind and generous. Look how men have thrown away their lives for great leaders. That was an immortal saying of the wounded French soldier. When searching for the bullet the surgeon cut deeply, and the patient cried out, " A little lower and you will touch the

Emperor," meaning that the Emperor's name was written on his heart. In several notable instances men have thrown themselves into the jaws of death to save a leader whom they loved. Duty holds the fort, but love casts its body in the way of the deadly bullet. Who would think of sacrificing his life on the ground of law? Love alone counts not life so dear as the service of the beloved. Love to Jesus creates a heroism of which law knows nothing. All the history of the church of Christ, when it has been true to its Lord, is a proof of this.

Kindness also, working by the law of love, has often changed the most unworthy, and therein proved that it is not a factor of evil. We have often heard the story of the soldier who had been degraded to the ranks, and flogged and imprisoned, and yet for all that he would get drunk and misbehave himself. The commanding officer said one day, "I have tried almost everything with this man, and can do nothing with him. I will try one thing more." When he was brought in, the officer addressed him, and said, "You seem incorrigible: we have tried everything with you; there seems to be no hope of a change in your wicked conduct. I am determined to try if another plan will have any effect. Though you deserve flogging and long imprisonment, I shall freely forgive you." The man was greatly moved by the unexpected and undeserved pardon, and became a good soldier. The story wears truth on its brow: we all see that it would probably end so.

That anecdote is such good argument that I will give you another. A drunkard woke up one morning from his drunken sleep, with his clothes on him just as he had rolled down the night before. He saw his only child, his daughter Millie, getting his breakfast. Coming to his senses he said to her, "Millie, why do you stay with me?" She answered, "Because you are my father, and because I love you." He looked at himself, and saw what a sottish, ragged, good-for-nothing creature he was, and he answered her, "Millie, do you really love me?" The child cried, "Yes, father, I do, and I will never leave you, because when mother died she said, ' Millie, stick to your father, and always pray for him, and one of these days he will give up drink, and be a good father to you'; so I will never leave you." Is it wonderful when I add that, as the story has it, Millie's father cast away his drink, and became a Christian man? It would have been more remarkable if he had not. Millie was trying free grace, was she not? According to our moralists she should have said, "Father, you are a horrible wretch! I have stuck to you long enough: I must now leave you, or else I shall be encouraging other fathers to get drunk." Under such proper dealing I fear Millie's father would have continued a drunkard till he drank himself into perdition. But the power of love made a better man of him. Do not these instances prove that undeserved love has a great influence for good?

Hear another story: In the old persecuting times there lived in Cheapside one who feared God and attended the secret meetings of the saints ; and near him there dwelt a poor cobbler, whose wants were often relieved by the merchant; but the poor man was a cross-grained being, and, most ungratefully, from hope of reward, laid an information against his kind friend on the score of religion. This accusation would have brought the merchant to death by burning if he had not found a means of escape. Returning to his house, the injured man did not change his generous behaviour to the malignant cobbler, but, on the contrary, was more liberal than ever. The cobbler was, however, in an ill mood, and avoided the good man with all his might, running away at his approach. One day he was obliged to meet him face to face, and the Christian man asked him gently, " Why do you shun me? I am not your enemy. I know all that you did to injure me, but I never had an angry thought against you. I have helped you, and I am willing to do so as long as I live, only let us be friends." Do you marvel that they clasped hands? Would you wonder if ere long the poor man was found at the Lollards' meeting? All such anecdotes rest upon the assured fact that grace has a strange subduing power, and leads men to goodness, drawing them with cords of love, and bands of a man. The Lord knows that bad as men are the key of their hearts hangs on the nail of love. He knows that his almighty goodness, though often baffled, will triumph in the end. I believe my point is proved. To myself it is so. However, we must pass on.

III. There is no fear that the doctrine of the grace of God will lead men to sin, because ITS OPERATIONS ARE CONNECTED WITH A SPECIAL REVELATION OF THE EVIL OF SIN. Iniquity is made to be exceeding bitter before it is forgiven or when it is forgiven. When God begins to deal with a man with a view of blotting out his sins and making him his child, he usually causes him to see his evil ways in all their heinousness ; he makes him look on sin with fixed eyes, till he cries with David, " My sin is ever before me." In my own case, when under conviction of sin, no cheering object met my mental eye, my soul saw only darkness and a horrible tempest. It seemed as though a horrible spot were painted on my eyeballs. Guilt, like a grim chamberlain, drew the curtains of my bed, so that I rested not, but in my slumbers anticipated the wrath to come. I felt that I had offended God, and that this was the most awful thing a human being could do. I was out of order with my Creator, out of order with the universe ; I had damned myself for ever, and I wondered that I did not immediately feel the gnawing of the undying worm. Even to this hour a sight of sin causes the most dreadful emotions in my heart. Any man or woman here who has passed through that experience, or anything like it, will henceforth feel a deep horror of sin. A burnt child dreads the fire. " No," says the sinner to his tempter, " you once deceived me, and I so smarted in consequence, that I will not again be deluded. I have been delivered, like a brand from the burning, and I cannot go back to the fire." By the operations of grace we are made weary of sin ; we loathe both it and its imaginary pleasures. We would utterly exterminate it from the soil of our nature. It is a thing accursed, even as Amalek was to Israel. If you, my friend, do not detest every sinful thing, I fear you are still in the gall of bitterness ; for one of the sure fruits of the Spirit is a love of holiness, and a loathing of every false way. A deep inward experience forbids the child of God to sin : he has known within himself its judgment and its condemnation, and henceforth it is a thing abhorrent to him. An enmity both fierce and endless exists between the chosen seed and the serpent brood of evil : hence the fear that grace will be abused is abundantly safeguarded.

IV. Remember also that not only is the forgiven man thus set against sin by the process of conviction, but EVERY MAN WHO TASTES OF THE SAVING GRACE OF GOD IS MADE A NEW CREATURE IN CHRIST JESUS. Now if the doctrine of grace in the hands of an ordinary man might be dangerous, yet it would cease to be so in the hands of one who is quickened by the Spirit, and created anew in the image of God. The Holy Spirit comes upon the chosen one, and transforms him: his ignorance is removed, his affections are changed, his understanding is enlightened, his will is subdued, his desires are refined, his life is changed—in fact, he is as one new-born, to whom all things have become new. This change is compared in Scripture to the resurrection from the dead, to a creation, and to a new birth. This takes place in every man who becomes a partaker of the free grace of God. "Ye must be born again," said Christ to Nicodemus; and gracious men are born again. One said the other day, "If I believed that I was eternally saved, I should live in sin." Perhaps *you* would; but if you were renewed in heart you would not. "But," says one, "if I believed God loved me from before the foundation of the world, and that therefore I should be saved, I would take a full swing of sin." Perhaps *you* and the devil would; but God's regenerate children are not of so base a nature. To them the abounding grace of the Father is a bond to righteousness which they never think of breaking: they feel the sweet constraints of sacred gratitude, and desire to perfect holiness in the fear of the Lord. All beings live according to their nature, and the regenerated man works out the holy instincts of his renewed mind: crying after holiness, warring against sin, labouring to be pure in all things, the regenerate man puts forth all his strength towards that which is pure and perfect. A new heart makes all the difference. Given a new nature, and then all the propensities run in a different way, and the blessings of almighty love no longer involve peril, but suggest the loftiest aspirations.

V. One of the chief securities for the holiness of the pardoned is found in the way of CLEANSING THROUGH ATONEMENT. The blood of Jesus sanctifies as well as pardons. The sinner learns that his free pardon cost the life of his best Friend; that in order to his salvation the Son of God himself agonized even to a bloody sweat, and died forsaken of his God. This causes a sacred mourning for sin, as he looks upon the Lord whom he pierced. Love to Jesus burns within the pardoned sinner's breast, for the Lord is his Redeemer; and therefore he feels a burning indignation against the murderous evil of sin. To him all manner of evil is detestable, since it is stained with the Saviour's heart's blood. As the penitent sinner hears the cry of, "Eloi, sabachthani!" he is horrified to think that one so pure and good should be forsaken of heaven because of the sin which he bore in his people's stead. From the death of Jesus the mind draws the conclusion that sin is exceedingly sinful in the sight of the Lord; for if eternal justice would not spare even the Well-beloved Jesus when imputed sin was upon him, how much less will it spare guilty men? It must be a thing unutterably full of poison which could make even the immaculate Jesus suffer so terribly. Nothing can be imagined which can have greater power over gracious minds than the vision of a crucified Saviour denouncing sin by all his wounds, and by every falling drop of blood. What! live in the sin which slew Jesus? Find pleasure in that which wrought his death? Trifle with that which laid his glory in the dust? Impossible! Thus you see that the gifts of free grace, when handed down by a pierced hand, are never likely to suggest self-indulgence in sin, but the very reverse.

VI. Sixthly, a man who becomes a partaker of divine grace, and receives the new nature, is ever afterwards A PARTAKER OF DAILY HELPS FROM GOD'S HOLY SPIRIT. God the Holy Ghost deigns to dwell in the bosom of every man whom God has saved by his grace. Is not that a wonderful means of sanctifying? By what process can men be better kept from sin than by having the Holy Spirit himself to dwell as Vicegerent within their hearts? The Ever-blessed Spirit leads believers to be much in prayer, and what a power for holiness is found in the child of grace speaking to the heavenly Father! The tempted man flies to his chamber, unbosoms his grief to God, looks to the flowing wounds of his Redeemer, and comes down strong to resist temptation. The divine word also, with its precepts and promises, is a never-failing source of sanctification. Were it not that we every day bathe in the sacred fountain of eternal strength we might soon be weak and irresolute; but fellowship with God renews us in our vigorous warfare with sin. How is it possible that the doctrines of grace should suggest sin to men who constantly draw near to God? The renewed man is also by God's Spirit frequently quickened in conscience; so that things which heretofore did not strike him as sinful are seen in a clearer light, and are consequently condemned. I know that certain matters are sinful to me to-day which did not appear so ten years ago : my judgment has, I trust, been more and more cleared of the blindness of sin. The natural conscience is callous and hard; but the gracious conscience grows more and more tender till at last it becomes as sensitive as a raw wound. He who has most grace is most conscious of his need of more grace. The gracious are often afraid to put one foot before another for fear of doing wrong. Have you not felt this holy fear, this sacred caution? It is by this means that the Holy Spirit prevents your ever turning your Christian liberty into licentiousness, or daring to make the grace of God an argument for folly.

Then, in addition to this, the good Spirit leads us into high and hallowed intercourse with God, and I defy a man to live upon the mount with God, and then come down to transgress like men of the world. If thou hast walked the palace floor of glory, and seen the King in his beauty, till the light of his countenance has been thy heaven, thou canst not be content with the gloom and murkiness of the tents of wickedness. To lie, to deceive, to feign, as the men of the world do, will no longer beseem thee. Thou art of another race, and thy conversation is above them : "Thy speech betrayeth thee." If thou dost indeed dwell with God, the perfume of the ivory palaces will be about thee, and men will know that thou hast been in other haunts than theirs. If the child of God goes wrong in any degree, he loses to some extent the sweetness of his communion, and only as he walks carefully with God does he enjoy full fellowship ; so that this rising or falling in communion becomes a sort of parental discipline in the house of the Lord. We have no court with a judge, but we have home with its fatherhood, its smile and its rod. We lack not for order in the family of love, for our Father dealeth with us as with sons. Thus, in a thousand ways, all danger of our presuming upon the grace of God is effectually removed.

VII. THE ENTIRE ELEVATION OF THE MAN WHO IS MADE A PAR-TAKER OF THE GRACE OF GOD is also a special preservative against sin. I venture to say, though it may be controverted, that the man who believes the glorious doctrines of grace is usually a much higher style of man than the person who has no opinion upon the matter. What do most men think about? Bread-and-butter, house-rent and clothes. But the men who consider the doctrines of the gospel muse upon the everlasting covenant, predestination, immutable love, effectual calling, God in Christ Jesus, the work of the Spirit, justification, sanctification, adoption, and such like noble themes. Why, it is a refreshment merely to look over the catalogue of these grand truths! Others are as children playing with little sand-heaps on the seashore; but the believer in free grace walks among hills and mountains. The themes of thought around him tower upward, Alps on Alps ; the man's mental stature rises with his surroundings, and he becomes a thoughtful being, communing with sublimities. No small matter this, for a thing so apt to grovel as the average human intellect. So far as deliverance from mean vices and degrading lusts must in this way be promoted, I say, it is no small thing. Thoughtlessness is the prolific mother of iniquity. It is a hopeful sign when minds begin to roam among lofty truths. The man who has been taught of God to think will not so readily sin as the being whose mind is buried beneath his flesh. The man has now obtained a different view of himself from that which led him to trifle away his time with the idea that there was nothing better for him than to be merry while he could. He says, "I am one of God's chosen, ordained to be his son, his heir, joint-heir with Jesus Christ. I am set apart to be a king and priest unto God, and as such I cannot be godless, nor live for the common objects of life." He rises in the object of his pursuit : he cannot henceforth live unto himself, for he is not his own, he is bought with a price. Now he dwells in the presence of God, and life to him is real, earnest, and sublime. He cares not to scrape together gold with the muck-rake of the covetous, for he is immortal, and must needs seek eternal gains. He feels that he is born for divine purposes, and enquires "Lord, what wouldst thou have me to do ? " He feels that God has loved him that his love may flow forth to others. God's choice of any one man has a bearing upon all the rest : he elects a Joseph that a whole family, a whole nation, nay, the whole world, may be preserved alive when famine had broken the staff of bread. We are each one as a lamp kindled that we may shine in the dark, and light up other lamps.

New hopes come crowding on the man who is saved by grace. His immortal spirit enjoys glimpses of the endless. As God has loved him in time, he believes that the like love will bless him in eternity. He knows that his Redeemer lives, and that in the latter days he shall behold him ; and therefore he has no fears for the future. Even while here below he begins to sing the songs of the angels, for his spirit spies from afar the dawn of the glory which is yet to be revealed. Thus with joyous heart and light footstep he goes forward to the unknown future as merrily as to a wedding-feast.

Is there a sinner here, a guilty sinner, one who has no merit, no claim to mercy whatever; is there one willing to be saved by God's free grace through believing in Jesus Christ? Then let me tell thee, sinner, there is not a word in God's book against thee, not a line or syllable, but everything is in thy favour. "This is a faithful saying, and worthy of all acceptation, that Christ Jesus came into the world to save sinners," even the chief. Jesus came into the world to save thee. Only do thou trust him, and rest in him. I will tell thee what ought to fetch thee to Christ at once, it is the thought of his amazing love. A profligate son had been a great grief to his father; he had robbed him and disgraced him, and at last he ended by bringing his grey hairs with sorrow to the grave. He was a horrible wretch of a son: no one could have been more graceless. However, he attended his father's funeral, and he stayed to hear the will read: perhaps it was the chief reason why he was there. He had fully made up his mind that his father would cut him off with a shilling, and he meant to make it very unpleasant for the rest of the family. To his great astonishment, as the will was read it ran something like this: "As for my son Richard, though he has fearfully wasted my substance, and though he has often grieved my heart, I would have him know that I consider him still to be my own dear child, and therefore, in token of my undying love, I leave him the same share as the rest of his brothers." He left the room; he could not stand it, the surprising love of his father had mastered him. He came down to the executor the next morning, and said, "You surely did not read correctly?" "Yes I did: there it stands." "Then," he said, "I feel ready to curse myself that I ever grieved my dear old father. Oh, that I could fetch him back again!" Love was born in that base heart by an unexpected display of love. May not your case be similar? Our Lord Jesus Christ is dead, but he has left it in his will that the chief of sinners are objects of his choicest mercy. Dying he prayed, "Father, forgive them." Risen he pleads for transgressors. Sinners are ever on his mind: their salvation is his great object. His blood is for them, his heart for them, his righteousness for them, his heaven for them. Come, O ye guilty ones, and receive your legacy. Put out the hand of faith and grasp your portion. Trust Jesus with your souls, and he will save you. God bless you. Amen.

PORTION OF SCRIPTURE READ BEFORE SERMON—Romans vi.

HYMNS FROM "OUR OWN HYMN BOOK"—136, 980, 645.

Metropolitan Tabernacle Pulpit.

THE KING'S WEIGHINGS.

A Sermon

DELIVERED ON LORD'S-DAY MORNING, AUGUST 26TH, 1883, BY

C. H. SPURGEON,

AT EXETER-HALL.

"Talk no more so exceeding proudly; let not arrogancy come out of your mouth: for the Lord is a God of knowledge, and by him actions are weighed."—1 Samuel ii. 3.

IT is very beautiful to see how the saints of old time were accustomed to find comfort in their God. When they came into sore straits, when troubles multiplied, when helpers failed, when earthly comforts were removed, they were accustomed to look to the Lord and to the Lord alone. Thus Hannah thinks of the Lord, and comforts herself in his name. By this means they were made strong and glad: they began to sing instead of sighing, and to work wonders instead of fainting under their burdens, even as here the inspired poetess sings, "My heart rejoiceth in the Lord, mine horn is exalted in the Lord." To them God was a reality, a present reality, and they looked to him as their rock of refuge, their helper, and defence, a very present help in time of trouble. Can we not at the outset learn a valuable lesson from their example? Let us do as they did; let us lean upon our God, and stay ourselves upon him when heart and flesh are failing. Does not the apostle say, "Rejoice in the Lord alway: and again I say, Rejoice"? There is always cause for thankfulness that the Lord liveth; and that he is what he is, for "there is no rock like our God"; and that he is ready still to lay bare the arm of his strength on the behalf of them that serve him. Oh, believer, the fountain of your joy is never dried up! If, like Jonah, your gourds are withered, yet your God is living; if, like Job, your goods have been plundered, yet the highest good is still your own. Are the rivers dry? Yet is this ocean full. Are the stars hidden? Yet the heavenly sun shines on in his eternal brightness. You have a possession that is unfading, a promise that is unfailing, a protector who is unchanging. Though you dwell in a faithless world, you also dwell in a faithful God. Your trials are present, and so is your helper, who hath said, "I will never leave thee, nor forsake thee." As the bird to the woods, and the cony to the rock, so let your soul flee away unto the Lord your refuge. "Straightforward makes the best runner": do not beat the bush, and go about to friends and cry, "Have pity upon me! Have pity upon me!" but "turn you to the stronghold, ye prisoners of hope." As for the son of man whose breath is in his nostrils, wherein

No. 1,736.

is he to be accounted of? Men are vanity in the hour of distress. Miserable comforters are they all. "Cursed be the man that trusteth in man, and maketh flesh his arm" : the heath in the desert which sees neither dew nor rain is the fit image of this spiritual idolater. "Blessed is the man that trusteth in the Lord, and whose hope the Lord is. For he shall be as a tree planted by the waters, and that spreadeth out her roots by the river, and shall not see when heat cometh." Oh, learn to live upon the Lord alone!

Hannah, who was once a woman of a sorrowful spirit, had so learned to delight herself in God, that she could dwell upon the different points of the divine character with joyful adoration. Like others of God's instructed people, she was very happy in the thought of God's *holiness*. Notice the second verse: "There is none holy as the Lord." I have heard many persons praise the Lord for his goodness, but it is a far higher and surer mark of grace when a man can praise the Lord for his holiness. Is it not noteworthy that in heaven, the abode of happiness, which happiness springs mainly out of the presence of their God, the adoration of the blessed chiefly tends to this point, the reverent celebration of his holiness? We read of the seraphim, "And one cried unto another, and said, Holy, holy, holy, is the Lord of hosts : the whole earth is full of his glory." We read again in the Revelation concerning the living creatures, "They rest not day and night, saying, Holy, holy, holy, Lord God Almighty, which was, and is, and is to come." Are you conscious that you are unholy? Then, O believer, rejoice that God is holy! Are those around you unholy? Is your soul among lions? Do you dwell among those that are set on fire of hell? Yet say, as the Lord Jesus did, "Thou art holy, O thou that inhabitest the praises of Israel." Does it seem as if unholiness covered all things, breaking forth like a flood, and deluging the earth with its black and filthy waters? Yet the Lord sitteth upon the throne of his holiness, and cutteth asunder the cords of the wicked. Let this be our song in the night : "There is none holy as the Lord."

Hannah also tuned her heart to celebrate the *power* of Jehovah, saying, "Neither is there any rock like our God." One of the leading ideas in the metaphor of a rock is strength, abiding endurance, unmoving stability, unconquerable power. Let us also rejoice in the Lord God Almighty, and delight in the mighty God of Jacob, the Lord strong and mighty, the Lord mighty in battle. Even his finger brought plagues upon the Egyptians ; and as for his hand, it utterly overthrew them. The Lord God omnipotent is the joy of his people ; for the Lord is our strength and song, he also has become our salvation. He shall surely show himself strong on the behalf of all them that put their trust in him. Fly, then, O timid soul, to the covert of Jehovah's wings! Abide under the shadow of the Almighty, and his divine power shall cause thee to lie down in safety. Oh, for a well-tuned harp to celebrate these two attributes so terrible to the ungodly, so full of exultation to those who are saved by grace!

Hannah touched, in her rapturous hymn, upon the *wisdom* of the Lord, and sang thus, "For the Lord is a God of knowledge," or of "knowledges ;" for every kind of knowledge is with him. We are not among those who impiously ask, "How doth God know?—

and is there knowledge in the Most High?" We are assured that nothing past, present, or future is hidden from the eternal eye. In his knowledge there is no error, and to it there is no limit. The Lord knoweth them that are his, and he knoweth the way that they take. He knoweth how to deliver his people, and when to bring them out of the furnace. Reverently do we worship the Lord and say, "O Lord, thou hast searched me, and known me. Thou knowest my downsitting and mine uprising, thou understandest my thought afar off. Thou compassest my path and my lying down, and art acquainted with all my ways. For there is not a word in my tongue, but, lo, O Lord, thou knowest it altogether. Thou hast beset me behind and before, and laid thine hand upon me. Such knowledge is too wonderful for me ; it is high, I cannot attain unto it." Let us rejoice that our God is not unconscious, or ignorant ; and when our own ignorance grieves us, let us rejoice that the Lord will teach us, and what we know not now we shall know hereafter.

Hannah also derived comfort from the fact that God is strictly *just ;* for she says with delight, "By-him actions are weighed." It is to this that I would turn your attention. May the Holy Spirit direct our meditations. Justice is a very terrible attribute to the unforgiven, to those who are not justified by the righteousness of Christ, and even on God's own people it turns a heart-searching glance at times.

I. The staple of our discourse will consist of a consideration of THE PROCESS OF DIVINE JUDGMENT, which is continually going on : " The Lord is a God of knowledge, and by him actions are weighed." The figure of weighing suggests a thorough testing, and an accurate estimating of the matters under consideration. Solomon saith, " All the ways of a man are clean in his own eyes; but the Lord weigheth the spirits." God sees men's actions, notes them, thinks upon them, and deliberately forms an estimate of them. " For the ways of man are before the eyes of the Lord, and he pondereth all his goings."

Our first note here shall stand thus,—*this is not as man dreams.* Many imagine that God takes no note of what is done among the sons of men ; indeed, their God does not appear to be a personal, intelligent existence, at all; or, if intelligent, they boast that he is too great to mark the trivial actions of men : that is to say, in order to make God great, they would make him blind. Their idea of his greatness would seem to be loftiness, impassiveness, and a measure of ignorance: our notion of greatness is the reverse; we believe in a great God to whom all things are known and by whom the least matters are observed. Our God is neither unobservant nor indifferent. " He humbleth himself to behold the things that are in heaven, and in the earth!" He is constantly observant of all that is done in heaven above, in the earth beneath, and in all deep places. Each movement of the tiniest worm upon the sea bottom is marked by him, together with the migration of fishes, the flight of birds, and the falling of the sear leaves. There are no forces so minute as to be beneath his notice, no movements so rapid as to escape his observation; and the Psalmist says, " Yea, the darkness hideth not from thee; but the night shineth as the day: the darkness and the light are both alike to thee." The atheist cries, " No God"; and he who would deny to God universal knowledge is twin brother to

him. As good have no God as a God who does not know. " Jehovah
is a God of knowledge, and by him actions are weighed."

This text plainly rebukes those who say—God is too merciful to take
much account of what we do, poor creatures that we are, shot out of the
back of a tumbril into the midst of a society all in chaos, which tempts
us to indulge the passions of our nature. They dream that God will
surely wink at such inconsiderable things as the actions of men ; but
surely it is not so, since it is written, " The Lord is a God of knowledge,
and by him actions are weighed." The Lord our God is merciful, but
this mercy is consistent with the severest justice : he pardons sin, and
yet he never suffers it to go unpunished. Strange as the statement
may seem, the Lord never ceases to be the righteous Judge, even when
he is passing by transgression. The great and glorious God does not
forgive sin because he does not know of it, or does not remember how
sinful it is ; but this is the wonder of his mercy, that he blots out the
sins of his people with the fullest knowledge of their foulness. After
having weighed sin, noted its motive, marked its meaning, and considered its consequences, the Lord nevertheless forgives it for Jesus'
sake. Do not fall into any error on this point, or imagine that the
Lord thinks little of human guilt, and therefore readily pardons it. No.
" The Lord is a God of knowledge, and by him actions are weighed."

Consider, next, that this form of procedure *is not as man judges*. By
men actions are judged flippantly, but "by God actions are weighed."
By men actions are more frequently counted. Such a man has done
this, and that, and that, and that, and that; what a wonderful man he
is ! Yes, but by God human deeds are not so much measured in the bushel
as weighed in the scale. A man's life may be made up of countless
bubbles, each one brilliant as the rainbow ; but what a collapse there
will be when the Lord comes with the balances to weigh the deeds done
in the body ! By men actions are frequently measured as to apparent
bulk, and persons placed in certain positions bulk very largely upon
the public mind ; their doings fill the newspapers, though they are
empty enough in themselves. You scarcely get a day's issue of a
journal but what something is reported of a man of mark : not that
what he has done is by any means surprisingly good, or wise, or
benevolent, but it is done by him, and therefore it must be emblazoned.
Men and women must have something to talk about, and certain persons
are selected for observation, and therefore to their lives an exaggerated
importance is attached. Let no such person delude himself: at the
bar of divine justice the acts of princes and peasants, of lords and
labourers, shall have an equal trial, and shall be tested in the selfsame
scales. Apparent greatness shrivels before the divine balance. Measure
a cloud by its volume and it is vast ; but condense it, and how small
is the weight of the water ! When our lives shall be freed from
vapour, and judged by their solid contents, how small will some of us
appear !

Constantly men measure actions by their brilliance. Oh, it was a
splendid action ; it was so dashing, so unlooked for, so extraordinary !
Was it right and pure and holy ? If not, the light of genius cannot
save it from condemnation. He who gave £10,000 to a fund did a
brilliant act of charity ; and yet the legacy may not have weighed so

much as the two mites that made a farthing which were all the poor widow's living. He who silently adores the Lord may have given him a greater weight of praise than he whose charming voice led the great congregation. The godly life of a poor bedridden woman may have been more highly esteemed of the Lord than the flaming eloquence of the great preacher. Ah me! how easily are we deceived by appearances! but not so the Lord; for "by him actions are weighed."

Men are exceedingly apt to measure actions by their consequences. How wrong it is to measure actions by results, rather than by their own intrinsic character! A man upon the railway neglected to turn a switch, but by the care of another no accident occurred. Is he to be excused? Another man was equally negligent, certainly not more so; but in his case the natural result followed—there was a collision, and many lives were lost. This last man was blamed most deservedly, but yet the former offender was equally guilty. If we do wrong and no harm comes of it, we are not thereby justified. Yea, if we did evil and good came of it, the evil would be just as evil. It is not the result of the action but the action itself which God weighs. He who swindles and prospers is just as vile as he whose theft lodged him in prison. He who acts uprightly, and becomes a loser thereby, is just as honoured before God as if his honesty had led on to wealth. If we seek to do good and fail in our endeavour, we shall be accepted for the attempt, and not condemned for the failure. You have all admired Grace Darling because of her gallant act in rescuing mariners from a wreck; but suppose she had not saved a single sailor, and had been herself drowned, would she not have been equally a heroine? Of course she would. Her success had nothing to do with the excellence of her design; the moral weight of her conduct lay in the self-sacrificing courage which led her on such a howling, murky night to risk her life upon the cruel waters for her unknown fellow-men. Had she been swallowed up by the remorseless deep, her action would have weighed as much before the throne of God as when she landed the saved ones at the lighthouse. If a man gives his life to convert the heathen, and he does not succeed, he shall have as much reward of God as he who turns a nation to the faith. Two ministers have laboured in the same field: the first preached the gospel faithfully, but saw scant results; the second, following him, found the rough work done, and reaped full sheaves from the field. The thoughtless are apt to think the second man greatly superior to the first, but it is not so: one soweth and another reapeth. When God comes to weigh the actions of men, he may give greater praise to the sower than to the reaper.

We have odd ways of measuring up our fellow-men—odd, I mean, as compared with our self-measurement. Usually we have two sets of weights—one for ourselves, and a second for our friends. When we place ourselves in the scale we weigh pretty heavily: we are full weight, and a little bit over. It is very different with our fellow-men: they may really weigh more than we do, but we adjust the machine in such a way that it is greatly to their disadvantage. I am not an admirer of the machine called a "steel-yard," for it is singularly easy to fix it according to your wishes; and certainly our estimates of others are as easily affected by prejudice. But by God "actions are weighed" truly, honestly, righteously, and the result is very different from the judgment of men.

I would now have you note that *this weighing is a very searching business.* "By him actions are weighed." A man enters a goldsmith's shop and says, "Here is old gold to sell. See, I have quite a lot of it." "Yes," says the goldsmith, "let me weigh it." "Weigh it? Why, look at the quantity; it fills this basket." What is the goldsmith doing? Looking for his weights and certain acids by which he means to test the metal. When he has used his acids, he puts the trinkets into the scale. "You are not going to buy by weight?" "I never buy in any other way," says the goldsmith. "But there is such a quantity." "That may be, but I buy by weight." It is always so with God in all our actions: he estimates their real weight. We may hammer out our little gold, and make a great show of it, but the Lord is not mocked or deceived. Every dealing between us and God will have to be by a just balance and standard-weight.

And in what way will he weigh it? The weights are somewhat of this sort. The standard is *his just and holy law,* and all which falls short of that is sin. Any want of conformity to the law of God is sin, and by so much our acts are found wanting. Remember this, ye who would justify yourselves.

The Lord also enquires how much of *sincerity* is found in the action. You acted in such a manner, and therein you were right; but did you do this in pretence, or from force, or in sincerity and in truth? In worship did you heartily adore? In charity did you give cheerfully? Did your heart go with your voice and hand? You prayed so long; did your heart truly pray? You attended so many religious services, but did you personally attend them, or did you send your chrysalis there, and leave the living thing at home? Yes, you did preach the truth; but did you believe it in your own soul? You did give your gold; was it with the motive of doing good, or that your name might be in the list, or because it would not look well for your name to be left out? That which is not done sincerely has no weight in it. It is weighed in the balances and found wanting.

The Lord also weighs actions according to their *motives.* He asks not only what you did, but why you did it? Was self the motive force? The preacher weighs his sermon this morning, and asks his conscience whether he seeks alone the glory of God. Will not you, my brethren, weigh what you are doing in this world? To what end are you living? What wind is filling your sails? You have been kept from outward transgressions; your life has been moral and pure in the sight of men; but have you lived for God's glory? Have you sought to obey God and please him? Have you been moved by love to God and man? Have you been in heart God's servant? If not, if another motive has ruled you, his servant you are whom you have obeyed. The motive which lies at the fountain-head colours all the streams of action, and God who judges us not according to what is done externally, but according to what is meant internally will make short work of a great multitude of human virtues. When you cannot find a fault with a day's life as to what you have outwardly done, it may yet be faulty all through because of the reason which actuated you. When you sum up your actions at night, pride may lean over your shoulder and whisper, "You have done well to-day!" At such a time it may be well for conscience to arouse itself and ask, "But was this done purely for the Lord's glory, and in dependence upon his grace?" An ill motive will poison all.

Another mode of judging is by our *spirit* and temper. If we live proudly, our actions lose weight. If we act from envy and illwill, we fall short. If we are flippant, inconsiderate, prayerless, we spoil all. The odour of actions is a great thing ; if they are not steeped in grace, they miss acceptance. An inch of grace has more weight in it than a mile of nature. To be in the fear of the Lord is solid living; all else is froth.

Sometimes actions may be weighed by the *circumstances* which surround them. Men are not to be considered good if their surroundings forbid their being what they would like to be. "As a man thinketh in his heart, so is he." Yonder man has been strictly truthful. Yes ; but he could not have made a sixpence by being false, or it may be he would have lied heavily. Another man is placed where the whole custom of his trade is knavery, and he takes a firm stand, and at great risk refuses to swerve from strict integrity. Now, this second man will bear weighing, but the first will not. Are not some children so carefully brought up from their childhood, happily for them, that their character is never discovered until they get out into life, and are tempted? and then it is seen that the truthful boy was a little hypocrite, and the thoughtful girl was as frivolous as any of the giddy throng. So you see that the fruit of tender culture may not always be what it should be or what it seems to be. It is wonderful how amiable we all are until we are irritated. What a deal of patience we have when we have no sickness to bear! I had enough and to spare till my pains multiplied, and then my stock ran very low. I am afraid that most of us have a great quantity of fictitious goodness which arises out of our favourable circumstances, and has no other foundation. Now God judges with this before him, for he places some men amid peculiar difficulties, and others in positions of special advantage ; and this he takes into account in the weighing. Some men cannot run in the crooked road because they are lame and inactive ; let them not lay a flattering unction to their souls and dream that they excel in goodness. Many a man thinks himself a Joseph, and the only reason is that no Potiphar's wife has tried him : many a man has never been an Achan because no wedge of gold or goodly Babylonish garment has come in his way. Multitudes of men are honest because they never had a chance of making a grand haul by setting up a bubble company—which is the modern mode of thieving. The lion in the Zoological Gardens is very good because he is behind iron bars, and many a man's goodness owes more to the iron bars of his position than to his own heart and motive.

Another weight to put in the scale is this,—Was there any *godliness* about your life ? I may be speaking to men in Exeter Hall whose lives are such that they think themselves examples, and yet their lives are spoiled from end to end by a grievous flaw. This point must be enquired into. You are to be weighed by God, and this will be the main matter—Has God been recognised in your life? O sirs, I fear that many are fitly described by David—" God is not in all their thoughts."

They have lived from childhood to manhood, and from manhood to old age, but God has not been considered in any of their actions; they have had great respect to society and to the law of the land; but if there had been no God, they would not have acted otherwise than they have done : God has not been an active agent in the influences which have moved their conduct. Now that life has wandered from its true end which has not God for its leading star. If thou hast not lived to thy God, to whom hast thou lived? Thou art his creature: hast thou never served thy Creator? Thou sayest that Christ is thy Redeemer; but how has he redeemed thee if thou livest unto thyself, and not as one that is bought with a price? This is the enquiry to test us all—Is God the main object of our living? do we throw ourselves with intensity into the pursuit of that which will glorify his blessed name? If not, the scales of the sanctuary will soon discover that we are sadly wanting.

Once more—have we lived by *faith*? for without faith it is impossible to please God; and if there be no faith in our life then are we nothing worth. Hear me, O man, and answer these questions: Hast thou believed in God, and done anything because of that believing in him? Hast thou trusted in Jesus Christ as thy Saviour, and has this faith cleansed thy way and purged thy thoughts? Hast thou believed the promises of God and his covenant, and has thy life been ordered according to this belief? If not, thou art weighed and rejected. Without faith in him whom God hath sent thou canst not be acceptable with God.

Thus, you see, in different ways God searches deeply into the life of man, and woe to that man who cannot bear the weighing: the greater his pretensions the more terrible his dismay when the scales refuse him.

This weighing of our lives must be exceedingly accurate because it is *done personally by God himself*. Notice my text : "The Lord is a God of knowledge, and *by him* actions are weighed." One might not mind the text if it said actions are weighed by Gabriel; for he is fallible; an angel might make mistakes, and he might wink and be partial; but when it is written that by God himself actions are weighed, O man, there is no possibility of bribing this great tester of thy life! He will judge righteous judgment. He is a God of knowledge, and therefore he knows not only thine outward deeds, but thy secret designs and desires. Moreover, he knows the standard of right; with him are the weights and the scales. Therefore knowing what our actions are, and what they ought to be, he readily enough discovers our discrepancies and mistakes, and there will be no possibility of our escaping his infallible decision. I wonder we are so ready to deceive ourselves as we are; I wonder that so many count it worth their while to deceive their fellow-Christians and their ministers. It is a poor ambition to live a life of deceit. Be what you seem to be, and seem to be what you are. But oh, if we could cheat ourselves throughout life, and deceive all those who watch us, yet we should never once have deceived God, "for by him actions are weighed" so accurately, that never a mistake is made! Ah me! I fear that many professors live a life of utter falsehood, comforting themselves with a lie. I once heard a story (I do not know if it is true) of an old banker who said to his son to whom he bequeathed the business, "This is the key of our large iron safe : take great care of it. The bank depends upon that safe ; let the people see that you have such a safe, but never open it unless the bank should be in the utmost difficulty. The bank went on all right as long as the iron safe was fast closed, but at last there came a run upon it, and in his greatest extremity the young gentleman opened it, and he found in it—nothing at all. That was the stock of the bank : poverty carefully concealed, imaginary wealth winning confidence, and living on the results. Are there not many persons who all their lives long are doing a spiritual banking business, and deriving a considerable income of repute from that which will turn out to be mere nothing? Beware of driving a trade for eternity upon fictitious capital, for failure will be the sure result. Time tries most things, but eternity tries all. Who among us would care to trade without a capital? Who would go to sea in a rotten boat painted to look seaworthy? How wise it is to invite divine inspection that we may not be deceived! What a dreadful thing it is that so many professing Christian people are never willing to open the iron safe ! They do not want to know whether all is right between God and themselves ; they prefer to go on saying, " Peace, peace." They love the lullaby of "It is well; it is well." Preach sweetly-comforting sermons, and they will be well content; and truly they might wisely be content if it were not written, " By him actions are weighed." God will not be charmed by our self-approving songs : he will weigh us and our actions, and reveal us before the sun.

Again, I want you to notice that this weighing *is carried on at this present time*—" By him actions *are* weighed." Not only shall they be weighed at the last great day, but every minute they are being weighed. How mean must a hypocrite feel to himself if he believes that he has never once deceived God! He knelt in prayer, but he did not pray ; God knew that he did not, and perceived the insult. At service-time he sang with the assembly, but his heart was never in communion with God, and the Lord knew it. He never established a repute with heaven. His conduct was understood at all times, and he was always branded as false-hearted. A man has joined the Christian church ; he has risen in esteem till he has become an officer among his brethren ; yet all the while he never was converted, grace was never in his soul : does he think that God is taken in by him? Let him not be deceived. The Lord has gone on weighing all his acts as they have happened, and he has put them all aside as of short weight. As at the Bank all moneys are put through a process by which the light coins are detected, so evermore our life passes over the great weighing-machine of the Lord's justice, and he separates that which is short in weight from that which is precious, doing this at the moment as infallibly as at the judgment-day.

" By him actions are weighed." Please remember, dear hearers, that *this is true of all of us*—not of open sinners only, but of those who are considered saints. You are getting old I see, my friend, but not too old to have your actions weighed. Old age is venerable, but it cannot screen you from inspection. "Oh," said an old man the other day, "you can trust *me; I* am past temptation." Grey hairs should not talk such nonsense ; you can be tempted still ; and your actions are still weighed as well as those of that silly boy whom you blame for his rashness. And you, good sir, who have been a professor of religion for forty years, and who when you rise up to pray stand like a cedar in the garden of God, your actions are still examined, and if you are rotten at heart, it is no matter how green you seem to be with the verdure of apparent grace, you will in due time be detected and destroyed. The preacher here is being daily weighed, and he knows it ; and so are all the members of the church ; and however excellent our outward lives may be, we must still pass through the testing-house. Not one of us shall escape from the upright judgment of the Most High.

And one day, to conclude this point, *the King's weighings will be published*—set up where men and angels shall read them. Oh, can you bear it that the whole of the secrets of your soul should be made public in the market-place of the universe ; that the actions which seemed so admirable should have their secret motives searched out and should be seen to be leprous with selfishness ? Can you endure to have your secret sins laid bare ; your private designs, deep intentions, and evil purposes set out in the open daylight ? Can you bear to have your envyings, jealousies, plottings, lyings—all held up to public gaze ? With what shame will the wicked cover their faces when all their hidden things shall be read out and published through the streets of the universe ! Then shall they be ashamed and confounded, while everlasting contempt shall be poured upon them. Most of all will the men be ashamed who came into the Church of God and wore Christ's livery, and were servants of Satan all the while ; and of these most of all the ministers who climbed into pulpits, professing to preach Christ, and all the while declared their own vain thoughts instead of the gospel of salvation. How will men gaze on the unmasked ! When the visors are knocked off, and all their masquerade shall be over, how will men despise the hypocrites ! They looked like kings, but, behold, the puppets were nought but beggars ! They seemed pure and holy, but a ray from the sun of truth has revealed their ulcered inner life, and all holy intelligences shrink from them. Oh, what discoveries there will be in that day when the record of the King's weigh-house shall be read of men and angels !

II. It is now time for me to observe THE HUMBLING NATURE OF THIS CONSIDERATION. "Talk no more so exceeding proudly ; let not arrogance come out of your mouth ; for the Lord is a God of knowledge, and by him actions are weighed."

The fact of divine judgment on ourselves should for ever prevent our insulting over others. When you see anyone found out in wrong-doing, do not act as if you were his executioner. When you pass by a person who has lost his or her character, do not straighten your back and disdainfully regard him as the mire of the streets. Do not act the part of the very superior person. "By him actions are weighed." Your actions are none too good. Perhaps there is not so much difference between you and the person whom you condemn, if all were known. You and the sinful one are not the least alike as to your outside wrappings and labellings, for you are labelled "saint," and she is labelled "a fallen woman"; but if all were known, and all is known by God, the man without fault himself who would dare to cast the first stone is not sitting in your seat. Ah, how the fact that we are ourselves to be judged should make us speak with bated breath when we are tempted to judge others! Let us not judge one another any more, for the Judge is at the door, and "by him actions are weighed." Let us leave judging to the Judge. Let everyone look to himself, and let no man despise his neighbour.

Next, I think we must give up all idea of speaking proudly in the presence of God. Our good works, what are they when weighed? They look very pretty indeed as we set them out in array; but when God puts them into the scales they look very different. We thought we did weigh something, but in the scale we seem turned into feathers. Our good works are high up in the air, and we are disappointed to see that the law is not uplifted by all that we have done. I remember a good man who said when he was dying that he once began to separate his good works from his bad works, but he found them so much like one another in the light of eternity, that he ceased separating them, and threw them all over, and determined to float to heaven on the cross of Christ. This was wisely done, for our best things are so stained with sin, and the whole of a holy life is worth so little in the way of merit, that the short cut of the whole matter is just to cry, "God be merciful to me a sinner," and rest ourselves on Jesus Christ alone.

Dear friend, if ever you have had the weighing process carried on in your own heart I know you have given up all hope of being saved by your own merit or strength. If conscience has been awakened, and if the law has fulfilled its office upon you, you have given up all idea of appearing before God in your own righteousness. The man who boasts that he is perfect in the flesh either fails to weigh himself at all, or else he is in great need of a visit from the inspector, for his weights and scales are sadly out of repair. It is very easy to appear perfect if you have an imperfect standard to measure by: but when the Lord himself weighs us by the law, we cry out, "Who can understand his errors?" We have nothing whereof to glory before God. The perfect character of our Lord Jesus Christ shuts our mouths as to all self-congratulation, and compels us to fall at his feet in deep humiliation. May the Lord carry on the weighing process in your consciences till you glory only in the Lord, and every false, pretentious thing is banished for ever.

III. In closing, let us briefly consider THE POSITION IN WHICH ALL THIS LEAVES US. If God weighs our actions and we are thereby found wanting, and can only cry, "Guilty" in his sight, what then? Then we are in God's hands. That is where I wish every one of my hearers to feel himself to be.

But who is the Lord? First, according to Hannah, he is a *God of salvation*. "My spirit hath rejoiced in thy salvation." Salvation for sinners, salvation for the guilty, salvation for those that are weighed in the balance and found wanting; free pardon, full remission, gracious acceptance, even for the worst and vilest: this is the gospel of the blessed God. How sweet to be in the hands of a God who is able to save, and delights to save, and makes it his glory to save!

Next, according to Hannah's song, he is *the God who delights in reversing the order of things*. He throws down those who are on high, and sets up those that are down. "He hath filled the hungry with good things; and the rich he hath sent empty away." Is not that a hint to you to be empty, to be hungry, to be poor and needy? If God is going to pick men from the dunghill and set them among princes, even the princes of his people, then the surest road to princely preferment is consciously to take your place on the dunghill. If the shields of the mighty are broken, but the weak are girded with strength, then it is wise to be weak before the Lord. Down, pride! Down! Down! Humble yourselves under the mighty hand of God, and he shall exalt you in due time.

Once more, this God is one who *delights to carry on strange processes in the hearts of his people*. "The Lord killeth, and maketh alive: he bringeth down to the grave, and bringeth up. The Lord maketh poor, and maketh rich; he bringeth low, and lifteth up." See! This is God's way of making men live—he kills them. This is God's way of giving them resurrection—he brings them to the grave: this is God's way of making men rich—he first makes them poor; this is God's way of lifting men up—they are first brought down. Are you brought down this morning? Be of good courage: this is the royal road to comfort in Christ Jesus. Is the Holy Ghost making you conscious of sin? He does so that you may be conscious of pardon. Do you feel condemned? The Lord condemns you now that you may not be condemned with the world. Are you black, and foul, and vile in your own sight? It is that you may wash and be whiter than snow through the Lord Jesus. Oh, how I rejoice to meet with a real sinner! Sham sinners are a vexation, but those who are really and truly so are precious in our sight. We hear of the *bonâ-fide* traveller: give me the *bonâ-fide* sinner.

> "A sinner is a sacred thing ;
> The Holy Ghost has made him so."

He who is made to feel that he is truly lost is well-nigh saved. Christ died for such. "This is a faithful saying, and worthy of all acceptation, that Christ Jesus came into the world to save sinners." O thou who art really a sinner, catch at that word!

God grant you may find salvation now, for Jesus' sake. Amen.

PORTIONS OF SCRIPTURE READ BEFORE SERMON—1 Samuel ii. 1—10; Psalm cxiii.; Luke i. 46—55.

HYMNS FROM "OUR OWN HYMN BOOK"—103, 690, 560.

Metropolitan Tabernacle Pulpit.

JOHN'S FIRST DOXOLOGY.

A Sermon

DELIVERED ON LORD'S-DAY MORNING, SEPTEMBER 2ND, 1883, BY

C. H. SPURGEON,

AT EXETER-HALL.

"Unto him that loved us, and washed us from our sins in his own blood, and hath made us kings and priests unto God and his Father; to him be glory and dominion for ever and ever. Amen."—Revelation i. 5, 6.

JOHN had hardly begun to deliver his message to the seven churches, he had hardly given in his name and stated from whom the message came, when he felt that he must lift up his heart in a joyful doxology. The very mention of the name of the Lord Jesus, "the faithful witness, and the first begotten of the dead, and the Prince of the kings of the earth," fired his heart. He could not sit down coolly to write even what the Spirit of God dictated: he must rise; he must fall upon his knees; he must bless and magnify, and adore the Lord Jesus. This text is just the upward burst of a great geyser of devotion. John's spirit has been quiet for awhile, but on a sudden the stream of his love to Jesus leaps forth like a fountain, rising so high that it would seem to bedew heaven itself with its sparkling column of crystal love. Look at the ascending flood as you read the words, "Unto him that loved us, and washed us from our sins in his own blood, and hath made us kings and priests unto God and his Father; to him be glory and dominion for ever and ever. Amen."

Now, in the matter of this bursting out of devotion at unexpected times, John is one among the rest of the apostles. Their love to their divine Master was so intense that they had only to hear his footfall and their pulse began to quicken, and if they heard his voice, then were they carried clean away: whether in the body or out of the body, they could not tell, but they were under constraint to magnify the Saviour's name; whatever they were doing they felt compelled to pause at once, to render direct and distinct homage unto the Lord Jesus by adoration and doxology. Observe how Paul breaks forth into doxologies: "Now unto him that is able to do exceeding abundantly above all that we ask or think, according to the power that worketh in us, unto him be glory in the church by Christ Jesus throughout all ages, world without end. Amen." Again: "Now unto the King eternal, immortal, invisible, the only wise God, be honour and glory for ever and ever. Amen." The like is true of Jude, who cries: "Now unto him that is able to keep you from falling, and to present you faultless before the presence of his

No. 1,737.

glory with exceeding joy, to the only wise God our Saviour, be glory and majesty, dominion and power, both now and ever. Amen." The apostles overflowed with praise.

This explains to me, I think, those texts which bid us "rejoice evermore," "bless the Lord at all times," and "pray without ceasing": these do not mean that we are always to be engaged in devotional exercises, for that would cause a neglect of other duties. The very apostle who bids us "pray without ceasing," did a great many other things beside praying; and we should certainly be very faulty if we shut ourselves up in our private chambers, and there continued perpetually upon our knees. Life has other duties, and necessary ones; and in attending to these we may render to our God the truest worship: to cease to work in our callings in order to spend all our time in prayer would be to offer to God one duty stained with the blood of many others. Yet we may "pray without ceasing," if our hearts are always in such a state that at every opportunity we are ready for prayer and praise; better still, if we are prepared to make opportunities, if we are instant in season and out of season, and ready in a moment to adore and supplicate. If not always soaring, we may be as birds ready for instant flight: always with wings, if not always on the wing. Our hearts should be like beacons made ready to be fired. When invasion was expected in the days of Queen Elizabeth, piles of wood and combustible material were laid ready on the tops of certain hills, and watchmen stood prepared to kindle the piles should there be notice given that the ships of the enemy were in the offing. Everything was in waiting. The heap was not made of damp wood, neither had they to go and seek kindling; but the fuel waited for the match. The watch-fire was not always blazing, but it was always ready to shoot forth its flame. Have ye never read, "Praise waiteth for thee, O God, in Sion"? So let our hearts be prepared to be fired with adoring praise by one glimpse of the Redeemer's eyes; to be all on a blaze with delightful worship with one touch from that dear, pierced hand. Anywhere, wherever we may be, may we be clad in the robes of reverence, and be ready at once to enter upon the angelic work of magnifying the Lord our Saviour. We cannot be always singing, but we may be always full of gratitude, and this is the fabric of which true psalms are made.

This spontaneous outburst of John's love is what I am going to preach upon this morning. First of all I shall ask you to consider *the condition of heart out of which such outbursts come*, and then we will look more closely at *the outburst itself;* for my great desire is that you and I may often be thus transported into praise, carried off into ecstatic worship. I long that our hearts may be like Eolian harps through which each wind as it sweeps on its way makes charming music. As roses are ready to shed their perfume, so may we be eager to praise God; so much delighting in the blessed exercise of adoration that we shall plunge into it when colder hearts do not expect us to do so. I have read of Mr. Welch, a minister in Suffolk, that he was often seen to be weeping, and when asked why, he replied that he wept because he did not love Christ more. May not many of us weep that we do not praise him more? Oh that our meditation may be used of the Holy Spirit to help us in that direction!

I. First, let us look at THE CONDITION OF HEART OUT OF WHICH OUTBURSTS of adoration arise.

Who was this man who when he was beginning to address the churches must needs lay down his pen to praise the Saviour ? We will learn the character of the man from his own devout language. We shall see his inmost self here, for he is carried off his feet, and speaks out his very heart in the most unguarded manner. We shall now see him as he is, and learn what manner of persons we must be if, like him, we would overflow with praise. It would be easy to talk at great length about John from what we know of his history from other parts of Scripture ; but at this time I tie myself down to the words of the text, and I notice, first, that this man of doxologies, from whom praise flashes forth like light from the rising sun, is first of all *a man who has realized the person of his Lord.* The first word is, " Unto *him; " and* then he must a second time before he has finished say, " To *him* be glory and dominion." His Lord's person is evidently before his eye. He sees the actual Christ upon the throne. The great fault of many professors is that Christ is to them a character upon paper ; certainly more than a myth, but yet a person of the dim past, an historical personage who lived many years ago, and did most admirable deeds, by the which we are saved, but who is far from being a living, present, bright reality. Many think of Jesus as gone away, they know not whither, and he is little more actual and present to them than Julius Cæsar or any other remarkable personage of antiquity. We have a way, somehow, a very wicked way it is, of turning the facts of Scripture into romances, exchanging solidities for airy notions, regarding the august sublimities of faith as dreamy, misty fancies, rather than substantial matters of fact. It is a grand thing personally to know the Christ of God as a living existence, to speak into his ear, to look into his face, and to understand that we abide in him, and that he is ever with us, even to the end of the world. Jesus was no abstraction to John ; he loved him too much for that. Love has a great vivifying power: it makes our impressions of those who are far away from us very lifelike, and brings them very near. John's great, tender heart could not think of Christ as a cloudy conception; but he remembered him as that blessed One with whom he had spoken, and on whose breast he had leaned. You see that is so, for his song rises at once to the Lord's own self, beginning with, " *Unto* HIM."

He makes us see Jesus in every act of which he speaks in his doxology. It runs thus : " Unto *him* that loved us." It is not " Unto the love of God," an attribute, or an influence, or an emotion ; but it is " Unto *him* that loved us." I am very grateful for love, but more grateful to him who gives the love. Somehow, you may speak of love and eulogize it ; but if you know it only in the abstract what is it ? It neither warms the heart nor inspires the spirit. When love comes to us from a known person, then we value it. David had not cared for the love of some unknown warrior, but how greatly he prized that of Jonathan, of which he sang, " Thy love to me was wonderful, passing the love of women !" Sweet is it to sing of love; but sanctified hearts delight still more to sing, " Unto *him* that loved us."

So, too, with the washing from sin. It is enough to make us sing

of pardoning mercy for ever and ever if we have been cleansed from
sin;" but the centre of the joy is to adore him "that washed us from
our sins in his own blood." Observe that he cleansed us, not by some
process outside of himself, but by the shedding of his own blood of
reconciliation. It brings the blood-washing into the highest estimation
with the heart when we look into the wounds from whence the atonement
flowed, when we gaze upon that dear visage so sadly marred, that brow
so grievously scarred, and even peer into the heart which was pierced by
the spear for us to furnish a double cleansing for our sin. "Unto him
that washed us." The disciples were bound to love the hands that took
the basin and poured water on their feet, and the loins which were girt
with the towel for their washing; and we, brethren, must do the same.
But as for the washing with his own blood, how shall we ever praise
him enough? Well may we sing the new song, saying, "Thou art worthy,
for thou wast slain, and hast redeemed us to God by thy blood." This
puts body and weight into our praise when we have realized *him*, and
understood how distinctly these precious deeds of love as well as the love
itself come from him whose sacred heart is all our own.

So, too, if we are "kings and priests," it is Jesus who has made us so.

> "Round the altar priests confess:
> If their robes are white as snow,
> 'Twas the Saviour's righteousness
> And his blood that made them so."

Our royal dignity and our priestly sanctity are both derived from him. Let
us not only behold the streams, but also consider the source. Bow before
the blessed and only Potentate who doth encrown and enthrone us, and
extol the faithful high-priest who doth enrobe and anoint us. See the
divine actor in the grand scene, and remember that he ever liveth, and
therefore to him should we render perpetual glory. John worships the
Lord himself. His mind is not set upon his garments, his crowns, his
offices, or his works, but upon himself, his very self. "I SAW HIM," says
the beloved apostle, and that vision almost blotted out the rest. His
heart was all for Jesus. The censer must smoke *unto him*, the song
must rise *unto him;*—unto himself, unto his very self.

I pray that every professor here may have a real Christ, for otherwise
he will never be a real Christian. I want you to recognize in this
realization of Christ by John this teaching,—that we are to regard our
holy faith as based on facts and realities. We have not followed
cunningly-devised fables. Do you believe in the divine life of Christ?
Do you also believe that he who is "very God of very God" actually
became incarnate and was born at Bethlehem? Do you put down the
union of the Godhead with our humanity as an historical fact which has
the most potent bearing upon all the history of mankind? Do you
believe that Jesus lived on earth and trod the blessed acres of Judæa,
toiling for our sake, and that he did actually and really die on the
behalf of sinners? Do you believe that he was buried, and on the
third day rose again from the dead? Are these stories in a book
or facts in the life of a familiar friend? To me it is the grandest fact
in all history, that the Son of God died and rose again from the dead,
and ever lives as my representative. Many statements in history are

well attested, but no fact in human records is one half as well attested as the certain resurrection of Jesus Christ from the dead. This is no invention, no fable, no parable, but a literal fact, and on it all the confidence of the believer leans. If Christ is not risen, then your faith is vain; but as he surely rose again, and is now at the right hand of God, even the Father, and will shortly come to be our judge, your faith is justified, and shall in due season have its reward. Get a religion of facts and you will have a religion which will produce facts by operating upon your life and character; but a religion of fancies is but a fancied religion, and nothing practical will come of it.

To have a real, personal Christ is to get good anchor-hold for love, and faith, and hope. Somehow men cannot love that which is not tangible. That which they cannot apprehend they do not love. When I was about to commence the Orphanage at Stockwell, a gentleman who had had very large experience in an excellent orphanage, said to me, " Begin by never expecting to receive the slightest gratitude from the parents of the children, and you will not be disappointed;" for, said he, " I have been connected with a certain orphanage," which he mentioned, " for a great many years, and except in the rarest case I have never seen any tokens of gratitude in any of the mothers whose children have been received." Now, my experience is very different. I have had a great many grips of the hand which meant warm thanks, and I have seen the tears start from the mother's eye full often, and many a grateful letter have I received because of help given to the orphan children. How do I explain the difference? Not that our Orphanage has done more than the other; but the other Orphanage is conducted by a Committee with no well-known head, and hence it is somewhat of an abstraction; the poor women do not know who is to be thanked, and consequently thank nobody. In our own case the poor people say to themselves, " Here is Mr. Spurgeon, and he took our children into the Orphanage." They recognize in me the outward and visible representative of the many generous hearts that help me. They know me, for they can see me, and they say, " God bless you," because they have someone to say it to. There is nothing particular about me, certainly, and there are others who deserve far more gratitude than that which comes to me; but it does come to me because the poor people know the name and the man, and have not to look at a mere abstraction. Pardon the illustration: it suits my purpose well. If you have a Christ whom you cannot realize you will not love him with that fervent affection which is so much to be desired. If you cannot reach the Lord in your mind, you will not embrace him in your heart; but if you have realized the blessed Master, if he has become a true existence to you, one who has really loved you and washed you from your sins, and made you a king and a priest, then your love must flow out towards him. You cannot resist the impulse to love one who has so truly loved you, and is so well known to you.

This also gives foothold to faith. If you know the Lord Jesus you feel that you can trust him. " They that know thy name will put their trust in thee." Those to whom Christ has become a well-known friend do not find it difficult to trust him in the time of their distress. An unknown Christ is untrusted; but when the Holy Spirit reveals Jesus he also breeds faith. By the same means, your hope also becomes vivid, for you say, "Oh, yes; I know Jesus, and I am sure that he will keep his word. He has said, 'I will come again and receive you unto myself;' and I am sure that he will come, for it is not like him to deceive his own chosen." Hope's eyes are brightened as she thinks of Jesus and realizes him as loving to the end; in him believing, she rejoices with joy unspeakable and full of glory. To love, to trust, to hope, are all easy in the presence of a real living Christ; but if, like the disciples at midnight on the Galilean lake, we think him to be a mere spectre or apparition, we shall be afraid, and cry out for fear. Nothing will suffice a real Christian but a real Christ.

Next, the apostle John, in whom we note this outburst of devotion, was a man *firmly assured of his possession* of the blessings for which he praised the Lord. Doubt has no outbursts; its chill breath freezes all things. Oh for more assurance! Nowadays we hear Christian people talk in this way:—"Unto him that we hope has loved us, and that we humbly trust has washed us, and that we sometimes believe has made us kings, unto him be glory." Alas! the doxology is so feeble that it seems to imply as little glory as you like. The fact is, if you do not know that you have a blessing, you do not know whether you ought to be grateful for it or not; but when a man knows he has covenant mercies, that divine assurance which the Holy Ghost gives to Christians works in him a sacred enthusiasm of devotion to Jesus. He knows what he enjoys, and he blesses him from whom the enjoyment comes. I would have you, beloved, know beyond all doubt that Jesus is yours, so that you can say without hesitation, "He loved me and gave himself for me." You will never say, "Thou knowest all things; thou knowest that I love thee," unless you are first established upon the point that Jesus loves you; for "we love him because he first loved us." John was certain that he was loved, and he was furthermore most clear that he was washed, and therefore he poured forth his soul in praise. Oh to know that you are washed from your sins in the blood of Jesus! Some professors seem half afraid to say that they are cleansed; but oh, my hearer, if you are a believer in Jesus, the case is clear, for "there is now no condemnation to them that are in Christ Jesus"! "He that believeth in him hath everlasting life." "He that believeth in him is justified from all things from which he could not be justified by the law of Moses." "Ye are clean," saith Christ. "He that is washed needeth not save to wash his feet, but is clean every whit;" and "Ye are clean."

> "O how sweet to view the flowing
>   Of the Saviour's precious blood!
> With divine assurance, knowing
>   He has made my peace with God."

This well-grounded assurance will throw you into ecstasy, and it will not be long before the deep of your heart will well up with fresh springs of adoring love. Then shall you also praise the Lord with some such words as these: "Unto him that loved us, and washed us from our sins in his own blood, to him be glory and dominion for ever and ever. Amen."

Once more. I think we have brought out two points which are clear enough. John had realized his Master, and firmly grasped the blessings which his Master brought him; but *he had also felt*, and was feeling very strongly, *his communion with all the saints*. Notice the use of the plural pronoun. We should not have wondered if he had said, " Unto him that loved *me*, and washed *me* from my sins in his own blood." Somehow there would have been a loss of sweetness had the doxology been so worded, and it would have hardly sounded like John. John is the very mirror of love, and he cannot live alone, or rejoice in sacred benefits alone. John must have all the brotherhood round about him, and he must speak in their name, or he will be as one bereft of half himself. Beloved, it is well for you and me to use this " us " very often. There are times when it is better to say " me," but in general let us get away to the " us "; for has not our Lord taught us when we pray to say, " Our Father which art in heaven. Give us this day our daily bread ; forgive us our trespasses," and so on ? Jesus does not bid us say, " My Father." We do say it, and it is well to say it; but yet our usual prayers must run in the " Our Father " style ; and our usual praises must be, " Unto him that loved *us*, and washed *us* from our sins." Let me ask you, beloved brethren, do you not love the Lord Jesus all the better and praise him all the more heartily because his grace and love are not given to you alone? Why, that blessed love has embraced your children, your neighbours, your fellow church-members, myriads who have gone before you, multitudes that are round about you, and an innumerable company who are coming after ; and for this we ought to praise the gracious Lord with unbounded delight. It seems so much the more lovely,—this salvation, when we think of it, not as a cup of water of which one or two of us may drink, but as a well of water opened in the desert, ever flowing, ever giving life and deliverance and restoration to all who pass that way. " Unto him that loved us." Oh, my Lord, I bless thee for having loved me ; but sometimes I think I could adore thee for loving my wife, for loving my children, and all these dear friends around me, even if I had no personal share in thy salvation. Sometimes this seems the greater part of it, not that I should share in thy compassion, but that all these poor sheep should be gathered into thy fold and kept safe by thee. The instinct of a Christian minister especially leads him to love Christ for loving the many ; and I think the thought of every true worker for the Lord runs much in the same line. No man will burst out into such joyful adoration as we have now before us unless he has a great heart within him, full of love to all the brotherhood ; and then, as he looks upon the multitude of the redeemed around about him, he will be prompted to cry with enthusiastic joy :

" To him that lov'd the souls of men,
    And wash'd us in his blood,
To royal honours raised our head,
    And made us priests to God ;

" To him let every tongue be praise,
    And every heart be love !
All grateful honours paid on earth,
    And nobler songs above ! "

Thus much upon the condition of heart which suggests these doxologies.

II. Secondly, let us look at THE OUTBURST ITSELF. It is a doxology, and as such does not stand alone : *it is one of many.* In the Book of the Revelation doxologies are frequent, and in the first few chapters they distinctly grow as the book advances. If you have your Bibles with you, as you ought to have, you will notice that in this first outburst only two things are ascribed to our Lord. " To him be glory and dominion for ever and ever." Now turn to the fourth chapter at the ninth verse, and read, " Those living creatures give glory and honour and thanks to him that sat on the throne." Here we have three words of honour. Run on to verse eleven, and read the same. " Saying, thou art worthy, O Lord, to receive glory and honour and power." The doxology has grown from two to three in each of these verses. Now turn to chapter v. 13. " And every creature which is in heaven, and on the earth, and under the earth, and such as are in the sea, and all that are in them, heard I saying, Blessing, and honour, and glory, and power, be unto him that sitteth upon the throne, and unto the Lamb for ever and ever." Here we have four praise-notes. Steadily but surely there is an advance. By the time we get to chapter vii. 12, we have reached the number of perfection, and may not look for more. " Blessing, and glory, and wisdom, and thanksgiving, and honour, and power, and might, be unto our God for ever and ever. Amen." If you begin praising God you are bound to go on. The work engrosses the heart. It deepens and broadens like a rolling river. Praise is somewhat like an avalanche, which may begin with a snow-flake on the mountain moved by the wing of a bird, but that flake binds others to itself and becomes a rolling ball : this rolling ball gathers more snow about it till it is huge, immense ; it crashes through a forest ; it thunders down into the valley ; it buries a village under its stupendous mass. Thus praise may begin with the tear of gratitude ; anon the bosom swells with love ; thankfulness rises to a song ; it breaks forth into a shout; it mounts up to join the everlasting hallelujahs which surround the throne of the Eternal. What a mercy it is that God by his Spirit will give us greater capacities by-and-by than we have here! for if we continue to learn more and more of the love of Christ which passeth knowledge we shall be driven to sore straits if confined within the narrow and drowsy framework of this mortal body. This poor apparatus of tongue and mouth is already inadequate for our zeal.

> " Words are but air and tongues but clay,
> But his compassions are divine."

We want to get out of these fetters, and rise into something better adapted to the emotions of our spirit ; I cannot emulate the songsters of Immanuel's land though I would gladly do so ; but as Berridge says—

> " Strip me of this house of clay,
> And I will sing as loud as they."

These doxologies occur again and again throughout this book as if to remind us to be frequent in praise ; and they grow as they proceed, to hint to us that we also should increase in thankfulness.

Now, this outburst *carried within itself its own justification.* Look at it closely and you perceive the reasons why, in this enthusiastic manner, John adores his Saviour. The first is, "Unto him that *loved* us." Time would fail me to speak long on this charming theme, so I will only notice briefly a few things. This love is in the present tense, for the passage may be read, "Unto him that loveth us." Our Lord in his glory still loves us as truly and as fervently as he did in the days of his flesh. He loved us before the world was, he loveth us now with all his heart, and he will love us when sun, and moon, and stars have all expired like sparks that die when the fire is quenched upon the hearth and men go to their beds. "He loveth us." He is himself the same yesterday, to-day, and for ever, and his love is like himself. Dwell on the present character of it and be at this moment moved to holy praise.

He loved us first before he washed us : "Unto him that loved us, and washed us." Not "Unto him that washed us and loved us." This is one of the glories of Christ's love, that it comes to us while we are defiled with sin—yea, dead in sin. Christ's love does not only go out to us as washed, purified, and cleansed, but it went out towards us while we were yet foul and vile, and without anything in us that could be worthy of his love at all. He loved us, and then washed us : love is the fountain-head, the first source of blessing.

Think of this as being a recognizable description of our Lord—"Unto him that loved us." John wanted to point out the Lord Jesus Christ, and all he said was, "Unto him that loved us." He was sure nobody would make any mistake as to who was intended, for no one can be said to love us in comparison with Jesus. It is interesting to note that, as John is spoken of as "that disciple whom Jesus loved," so now the servant describes the Master in something like the same terms : "Unto him that loved us." No one fails to recognize John or the Lord Jesus under their several love-names. When the apostle mentioned "him that loved us," there was no fear of men saying, "That is the man's friend, or father, or brother." No ; there is no love like that of Jesus Christ: he bears the palm for love; yea, in the presence of his love all other love is eclipsed, even as the sun conceals the stars by his unrivalled brightness.

Again, the word "him that loved us," seems as if it described all that Christ did for us, or, at least, it mentions first the grandest thing he ever did, in which all the rest is wrapped up. It is not, "Unto him that took our nature ; unto him that set us a glorious example; unto him that intercedes for us ;" but, "Unto him that loved us," as if that one thing comprehended all, as indeed it does.

He loves us : this is matter for admiration and amazement. Oh, my brethren, this is an abyss of wonder to me! I can understand that Jesus pities us ; I can very well understand that he has compassion on us; but that the Lord of glory loves us is a deep, great, heavenly thought, which my finite mind can hardly hold. Come, brother, and drink of this wine on the lees, well refined. Jesus loves you. Grasp that. You know what the word means in some little degree according to human measurements, but the infinite Son of God loved you of old, and he loves you now! His heart is knit with your heart, and he cannot be happy unless you are happy.

Remember, he loves you with his own love according to his own nature. Therefore he has for you an infinite love altogether immeasurable. It is also like himself, immutable; and can never know a change. The emperor Augustus was noted for his faithfulness to his friends, whom he was slow in choosing. He used to say, "Late ere I love, long ere I leave." Our blessed Lord loved us early, but he never leaves us. Has he not said, "I will never leave thee, nor forsake thee"? The love of Jesus is a pure, perfect, and divine love: a love whose heights and depths none can measure. His nature is eternal and undying, and such is his love. He could not love you more; he will never love you less. With all his heart and soul and mind and strength he loves you. Come; is not that a grand excuse, if excuse is wanted, for often lifting up our hearts and voices in hearty song unto the Lord? Why should we not seven times a day exult before him, saying, "Unto him that loved us, and washed us from our sins in his own blood, and hath made us kings and priests unto God and his Father, to him be glory and dominion for ever and ever. Amen"? Oh for new crowns for his blessed brow! Oh for new songs for his love-gifts ever new! Praise him! Praise him, all earth and heaven!

Then the apostle passes on to the second reason why he should thus magnify the Lord Jesus by saying, "And washed us from our sins in his own blood." "Washed us." Then we were foul; and he loved us though we were unclean. He washed *us* who had been more defiled than any. How could he condescend so far as to wash *us*? Would he have anything to do with such filthiness as ours? Would that sublime holiness of his come into contact with the abominable guilt of our nature and our practice? Yes, he loved us so much that he washed us from our sins, black as they were. He did it effectually, too: he did not try to wash us, but he actually and completely washed us from our sins." The stains were deep and damnable; they seemed indelible, but he has "washed us from our sins." No spot remains, though we were black as midnight. "Wash me, and I shall be whiter than snow," has been realized by every believer here. But think of how he washed us—"with his own blood." Men are chary of their own blood, for it is their life; yet will brave ones pour it out for their country or for some worthy object; but Jesus shed his blood for such unworthy ones as we are, that he might by his atonement for ever put away the iniquity of his people. At what a cost was this cleansing provided! Too great a cost I had almost said. Have you never felt at times as if, had you been there and seen the Lord of glory about to bleed to death for you, you would have said, "No, my Lord, the price is too great to pay for such a one as I am"? But he has done it; brethren, his sin-atoning work is finished for ever: Jesus has bled, and he has washed us, and we are clean beyond fear of future defilement. Shall he not have glory for this? Will we not wish him dominion for this?

> "Worthy is he that once was slain,
>   The Prince of Peace that groan'd and died;
>   Worthy to rise, and live, and reign
>   At his Almighty Father's side."

Does not this doxology carry its justification in its own bowels? Who can refuse to praise at the remembrance of such grace as this?

Nor is this all. The Lord that loved us would do nothing by halves, and therefore when he washed us in his own blood, he "made us kings." What is that? Are we kings this morning? We do not feel our crowns as yet, nor perhaps grasp our sceptres as we might, but the Lord has made us a royal priesthood. We reign over our own selves, and that is a dominion which is hard to gain, indeed, impossible without grace. We walk like kings among the sons of men, honoured before the Lord and his holy angels—the peerage of eternity. Our thoughts, our aims, our hopes, and our longings are all of a nobler kind than those of the mere carnal man. Ours is a nature of a higher order than theirs, since we have been born again of the Spirit. Men know us not because they know not our Lord; but we have a heritage they have not, and we have prepared for us a crown of life which fadeth not away. The Lord has made us kings and endowed us with power before his presence, yea he has made us rich since all things are ours. We read of the peculiar treasures of kings, and we have a choice wealth of grace. He has made us even now among the sons of men to possess the earth and to delight ourselves in the abundance of peace.

Furthermore our Lord has made us priests. Certain men impiously set up to be priests above the rest of the Lord's people. As Korah, Dathan, and Abiram are they, and they had need fear lest they and their evil system should go down into the pit. Whoever they may be, all the people of God are priests. Every man that believes in Jesus Christ is from that moment a priest, though he be neither shaven nor shorn, nor bedecked in peculiar array. To the true believer his common garments are vestments, every meal is a sacrament, every act is a sacrifice. If we live as we should live, our houses are temples, our hearts are altars, our lives are an oblation. The bells upon our horses are holiness unto the Lord, and our common pots are as the bowls before the altar. It is the sanctification of the Holy Spirit which gives men a special character, so that they are the priesthood of the universe. The world is dumb, and we must speak for it: the whole universe is as a great organ, but it is silent; we place our fingers on the keys, and the music rises towards heaven. We are to be priests for all mankind. Wherever we go we are to teach men, and to intercede with God for them. In prayer and praise we are to offer up acceptable oblations, and we are ourselves to be living sacrifices, acceptable unto God by Jesus Christ our Lord. Oh, what dignity is this! How you and I are bound to serve God! Peter Martyr told Queen Elizabeth: "Kings and queens are more bound to obey God than any other persons; first as God's creatures, and secondly as his servants in office." This applies to us also. If common men are bound to serve God how much more those whom he has made kings and priests unto his name!

What does the doxology say? "To him be glory and dominion." First, "To him be glory." Oh, give him glory, my beloved, this morning! Do I address any that have never yet accepted Christ's salvation? Accept it now, and thus give your Saviour glory. Have you never trusted Jesus to save you? The best, the only thing you can do to give him glory is to trust him now, sinner as you are, that he may remove your transgressions. Are you saved? Then, dear brother, give him glory by speaking well of his name, and by perpetual adoration.

Glorify him in your songs, glorify him in your lives.   Behave yourselves as his disciples should do, and may his Spirit help you.

But the doxology also ascribes to him dominion. My heart longs for Jesus to have dominion. I wish he might get dominion over some poor heart this morning which has hitherto been in rebellion against him! Yield thee, rebel! Yield thee to thy Sovereign and Saviour! "Kiss the Son, lest he be angry, and ye perish from the way, when his wrath is kindled but a little." To him be dominion over hearts that have never submitted to him; and assuredly to him be fullest dominion over hearts that love him. Reign, my Lord, reign in my bosom more and more; cast out every enemy and every rival; reign supreme, and reign eternally. Set up thy throne also more and more conspicuously in the hearts and lives of all who call themselves Christians. O my brethren, ought it not to be so? Is it not clear to you that since he has loved and washed us he should have dominion over us? Ah! let him have dominion over the wide, wide world, till they that dwell in the wilderness shall bow before him, and his enemies shall lick the dust. Reign for ever, King of kings and Lord of lords.

Then it is added, let him have glory and dominion "for ever and ever." I suppose we shall have some gentlemen coming up to prove that "for ever and ever" only means for a time. They tell us that everlasting punishment means only for a time, and, of course, everlasting life must mean just the same, and this praise must also have a limit. I mean not so, nor do you, beloved. I pray that our Lord may have endless glory, eternal dominion. I pray that Christ's power and dominion may be over this generation, and the next, and the next, until he cometh, and then that it may be said, "The Lord shall reign for ever and ever." Hallelujah! As long as there is wing of angel or song of man; as long as God himself shall live, may the Lord Jesus Christ that loved us and washed us have glory and dominion.

Now we have come to the last word of the text. It finishes up with "Amen."   "For ever and ever.   Amen."   Can you heartily say "Amen" to this?   Do you wish Christ to have glory and dominion for ever and ever? If you know he loved you, I am sure you do; if you know he washed you, I am sure you do. Now let our beating hearts in solemn silence say, "Amen"; and when we have done that, do you think you could join with one voice with me and say it out aloud, like thunder?   Now, "Unto him that loved us, and washed us from our sins in his own blood, and hath made us kings and priests unto God and his Father, to him be glory and dominion for ever and ever.   Amen;" and "Amen" yet again.   (Here the great congregation joined aloud with the preacher.)   The prayers of David the son of Jesse were ended when he came to that, and so may ours be, and so may this morning's service be.   God bless you through his adorable Son. Amen and Amen.

PORTIONS OF SCRIPTURE READ BEFORE SERMON—Revelation i.

HYMNS FROM "OUR OWN HYMN BOOK"—427, 337, 317.

Metropolitan Tabernacle Pulpit.

"GLORY BE UNTO THE FATHER."

A Sermon

DELIVERED ON LORD'S-DAY MORNING, SEPTEMBER 9TH, 1883, BY

C. H. SPURGEON,

AT THE METROPOLITAN TABERNACLE, NEWINGTON.

"Blessed be the God and Father of our Lord Jesus Christ, who hath blessed us with all spiritual blessings in heavenly places in Christ: according as he hath chosen us in him before the foundation of the world, that we should be holy and without blame before him in love."—Ephesians i. 3, 4.

LAST Lord's-day I finished the morning services at Exeter Hall with a sermon upon John's choice doxology, "Unto him that loved us and washed us from our sins in his own blood, to him be glory and dominion for ever and ever. Amen." I felt, therefore, that it would be most fitting to open this series of services with another doxology; and as the last was in praise of the Second Person of the divine Unity, this is to the honour and glory of the Adorable Person of the Father. May God, who gave his servants a praiseful spirit so that their epistles abound with doxologies, give the like spirit of joyous thankfulness to us at this time, that we may all say from the very bottom of our hearts, "Amen" to our text, "Blessed be the God and Father of our Lord Jesus Christ." Of praise, we may say what was said concerning salt in the Scripture, "without prescribing how much." Oh to praise and pray without ceasing! May the Holy Spirit work in us perpetual thanksgiving!

Observe well, that the same word is used in reference to our wish towards God and God's act towards us:—"Blessed be the God and Father of our Lord Jesus Christ, who hath blessed us." It is a very striking thing that our poor pebble-stones of wishes should be valued so much that the same word should be used in reference to them as in reference to the priceless diamonds of grace which the Lord hath bestowed upon us. We bless God because he blesses us. "Bless the Lord, O my soul, and forget not all his benefits."

Now, it is easy to understand how the Father of mercies, from whom every good and perfect gift proceeds, really blesses us; but how can we be said to bless him?—and what is the distinction between that and praising him? For there is such a distinction, since we read, "All thy works shall praise thee, O Lord, and thy saints shall bless thee." Praise rises even from lifeless objects, as they display the power and wisdom of their Creator; but intelligence, will, and intent are needful for blessing God. Praise is the manifestation of our inward reverence and esteem,

No. 1,738.

it adores and magnifies; but in blessing God we think well of him, and wish well to him, and desire that others may do the same. In blessing God there is the desire to do good to God even as he doth to us, if it were possible for us to do so. We fail in the power wherewith to accomplish such a desire, but it is well that it is in our hearts. God cannot actually receive anything from us for his own enrichment or increase; for all things that we can do for him are his already, and they must be done in his strength, so that when all is done it must be said, "Of thine own have we given thee." Neither can we add to his splendour or his happiness; for he is by nature inconceivably glorious and infinitely blessed: yet if such an increase were within our power, we would gladly render it. If all things were ours, we would lay them at his feet; and such things as we have, though we cannot give them directly to him, yet we give them to his cause, and to the poor of his people. What saith the Psalmist, "O Lord, thou art my God; my goodness extendeth not to thee, but to the saints that are in the earth, and to the excellent, in whom is all my delight." We are happy that, in assisting the needy believer, we are blessing the Lord. There is also a considerable measure of blessing God in such prayers as these: "Hallowed be thy name. Thy kingdom come. Thy will be done in earth, as it is in heaven." When we gladly ascribe unto the Lord glory, and power, and dominion, we are blessing him. When we wish other men to love and serve the Lord, and do him homage, we are blessing him. When we desire to love him more ourselves, and feel our hearts burn with aspirations after fellowship with him, we are blessing him. When we are zealous to make known the truth of the gospel which glorifies God, and to make known his Son in whom especially he is revealed, we are blessing God. In sacred silence, when the heart cannot translate her emotions into words, and hardly into thoughts, we can bless the Lord. In rendering unto God such things as we can render, and in asking evermore the still larger question, "What shall I render unto the Lord for all his benefits toward me? we are blessing him. If we cheerfully await his bidding, and count it a delight to stand with girded loins, crying, "What wouldst thou have me to do? Hast thou an errand for these willing feet? Here am I; send me." Then are we in effect blessing our Lord. Can you sing from your soul—

> "There's not a lamb among thy flock
> I would disdain to feed;
> There's not a foe before whose face
> I'd fear thy cause to plead?"

Then are you in that state of heart in which all that is within you blesses God's holy name. Blessed be God. We would make him better known, and so increase his manifest glory, wishing all the while that we could do a thousand times more. May our hearts be at this time filled with high ideas of the goodness and greatness of the Lord, and so may our souls be ready to burst forth in praise, eager for service, and bowed in reverent adoration. "Bless the Lord, O house of Israel: bless the Lord, O house of Aaron: bless the Lord, O house of Levi: ye that fear the Lord, bless the Lord. Blessed be the Lord out of Zion, which dwelleth at Jerusalem. Praise ye the Lord."

May we be stirred up to bless the Lord by the teaching of our text.

I. Here we have, first of all, GOD THE FATHER VIEWED ARIGHT. "Blessed be the God and Father of our Lord Jesus Christ." When the divine Father is viewed aright *he becomes the object of our gratitude,* not of our dread. Instead of trembling before him as before an austere judge, we rejoice in him as a tender Father. He is no more to us the Thunderer of Sinai, but the Father of our spirits. Among the ignorant it is too much the custom to ascribe every mercy to the Lord Jesus Christ, and to think that he is all kindness and gentleness, while the Father is full of stern justice and severity; but it is not so. God is love, and that love dwells equally in each of the sacred Three. Our Lord Jesus Christ comes to us by reason of the love of the Father: "thanks be unto God for his unspeakable gift." "God so loved the world, that he gave his only-begotten Son." In every act of the Lord Jesus he reveals the tenderness and grace of the Father to us. He says, "He that hath seen me hath seen the Father," and "I say not that I will pray the Father for you, for the Father himself loveth you." "Behold what manner of love the Father hath bestowed upon us." The love of the Father is in all respects equal to the love of the Son. We must never for a single moment in our minds set one person of the Holy Trinity before another. We must believe in "the love of the Spirit," and speak of "our Lord Jesus Christ himself and God, even our Father which hath loved us." Let us never fall into the mistaken idea that the atoning sacrifice of Christ was intended to make an angry God willing to be merciful. Far otherwise is it: Jesus dies not to create mercy in God's heart, but to open a way for the exercise of the mercy which was there from all eternity. To our apprehension God may seem changed when we realize the great reconciliation, but in very deed he was always full of grace. God's love went forth towards his chosen before the Saviour died, and because he loved them, therefore he gave his Son to die for them. Let us see in this death of our Redeemer not the cause, but the result of God's love; and let us magnify the Father who spared not his own Son, but freely delivered him up for us all. "Herein is love, not that we loved God, but that he loved us, and sent his Son to be the propitiation for our sins." Is not the Father from this point of view the object of our love, and praise, and blessing? "Blessed be the God and Father of our Lord Jesus Christ." Let us cast out the fear which hath torment; let us no longer stand afar off, but draw nigh unto God with childlike confidence and hearts aglow with ardent love. May the Lord direct our hearts into the love of God.

Next, if we would view the Father aright we must regard him *as the God of our Lord Jesus Christ.* This is a wonderful title. We sing often—

"The God of Abraham praise,"

and truly it is blessed to view God as the God of Abraham, but how much more as the God of our Lord Jesus Christ! Jesus, after his resurrection, called him "My Father, and your Father: my God, and your God"; and when he was in the act of expiring, he cried, "My God, my God, why hast thou forsaken me?" To our Lord Jesus as man, the Father was God, and he worshipped him and served him. How frequently Jesus drew near to God in prayer! How constantly he rendered obedience to him! Our Lord also says of himself in the twenty-second Psalm—"I will declare thy name unto my brethren: in the midst of the congregation will I praise thee." Thus did our Mediator bow before the throne, and own to the truth then present, "My Father is greater than I." I delight to think that God is now dealing with his people as the God of our Lord Jesus Christ; for what blessings are there which God would not give to the Son of the Highest, that holy thing that was born of Mary? How greatly must God bless him, the perfect man Christ Jesus, of whom it is written in the psalm: "Thou lovest righteousness, and hatest wickedness: therefore God, thy God, hath anointed thee with the oil of gladness above thy fellows." God, I say, is dealing with his own chosen as he dealeth with the perfectly obedient One. By the obedience of one many are made righteous, and treated as such; and we among the many are accepted in the Beloved. It is the God of Jesus Christ who hath blessed us with all spiritual blessings in heavenly places, and to him Paul prayed for the Ephesians, "That the God of our Lord Jesus Christ, the Father of glory, may give unto you the spirit of wisdom and revelation in the knowledge of him." You remember how the tribes of Israel were blessed by the God of Jacob for their father's sake: even so are we blessed by the God of Our Lord Jesus Christ according to the measure in which he would bless his spotless Son Jesus. Think then of the infinite Jehovah as the God of our Lord Jesus, and therefore the God of his redeemed people.

The text title is "*The Father of our Lord Jesus Christ*," which may respect the double filiation of Christ. First, as to his Godhead: there is that mysterious sonship which we cannot understand, but which is nevertheless clearly revealed. He is the Father of our Lord Jesus Christ as Jesus is God. And then there is that second sonship which belongs to Christ as man, in which again he is said to be the Son of God. "God sent forth his Son, made of a woman." The Father thrice said, "This is my beloved Son, in whom I am well pleased." The great work of expiation is over, and "now is the Son of God glorified," and the Father manifests his unbounded love to his Son; let it then be a matter of great joy to us that the Father loves his people even as he loves his Son, and blesses us as he blesses him. Even as Jacob blessed Ephraim and Manasseh because of his love to Joseph, even so the great Father lays his mighty hand in benediction upon all his chosen, and blesses the very least believer as he blesses his Son Jesus. He who hath highly exalted his Son Jesus, to whom he stands in a double sense in the relation of a Father, has also prepared a throne in glory for all who are in Christ.

"The Father of our Lord Jesus Christ!" How endearing and attractive is the name! If we can view the Father in that light, we shall be able to approach him with firmer confidence, we shall rejoice in him with greater joy. Note that the text contains a possessive pronoun: it saith, not "The God and Father of the Lord Jesus Christ," but "of *our* Lord Jesus Christ," who is ours in this particular sense, that he is our federal Head. Just as the first Adam headed up the race, and we stood or fell in him, even so the second Adam headed up and comprehended within himself all the chosen, and we who can claim that Christ is ours are for that reason able to claim all that belongs to Christ, for our heavenly Bridegroom endows us with all his possessions. "It pleased the Father that in him should all fulness dwell; and of his fulness have all we received, and grace for grace." Jesus says, "All things that the Father hath are mine," and the Spirit saith, "All things are yours"; and therefore we may rejoice with joy unspeakable and full of glory. Believers, are you not one with Christ? Then Christ's God is your God, Christ's Father is your Father. "Ye are members of his body, of his flesh, and of his bones"; for this cause did he leave his Father and cleave unto the church, that he might be one flesh with her. All believers are heirs of God, joint-heirs with Jesus Christ.

This is the true view of the Father: he is our Father, our God, our Saviour's Father, our Saviour's God. Let us delight ourselves in him, and magnify and bless his name.

II. We come, secondly, to notice THE BLESSING WHICH COMES FROM THE FATHER AS VIEWED BY FAITH. "Blessed be the God and Father of our Lord Jesus Christ, who hath blessed us with all spiritual blessings in heavenly places in Christ." *The blessing of God even the Father has fallen from all eternity upon all who are in Christ,* and that in the most copious manner, for the one blessing includes "all spiritual blessings." This is a very pleasant thing to me, because there can be no blessing like that of God. "I wot," said one of old, "whom he blesseth is blessed." Satan may curse you; you may already be suffering the curse of the Fall; but, if God blesses you, what of all this? Let but the Lord say, "I have blessed him," and who can stay it, or who can reverse it? The blessing of God maketh rich, safe, happy. When he commands the blessing, it is life for evermore. Why, it means an infinite blessing, the blessing of one omnipotent to fulfil his word; omniscient to carry it out in every place; immutable, so that it never can be reversed; eternal, so that it shall stand for ever and ever. The blessing of God! What must it be? As is God, such is his blessing. Who that dives deepest into it can fully comprehend all its meaning? The blessing of God the Father is a true and real blessing: he speaketh not a lie nor a vanity. Hath he said, and shall he not do it? Hath he commanded, and shall it not stand fast? The blessing of God! How sure, how effectual! Oh, to receive it! He that hath it, though he be in poverty, he is rich; though he be in sorrow, he is consoled; though in shame, he hath honour; though he lie a-dying, he shall revive; though he were dead, yet shall he live. Such a blessing as this is enough to turn a dungeon into a paradise, a hell into heaven; and if it fall upon the most desponding and despairing, it must make their hearts to dance for joy.

I have already told you *this is the blessing of the God and Father of our Lord Jesus Christ;* and I would remind you that it was the custom of fathers to give blessings to their sons. All through the Old Testament we find patriarchs, when about to die, calling their children together, and pronouncing a blessing upon them. I should have liked to have received the blessing of Abraham, or Isaac, or Jacob; but what must be the blessing of the Father of our Lord Jesus Christ as he lays his hand upon each one of our poor unworthy heads, and says, " Surely, blessing I will bless thee " ? Jacob could not bless the beloved Joseph after the fashion in which the Lord blesses his beloved Son and those who are in him.

You could not desire a greater blessing than you have at this day, for the text says, " He hath blessed us with all spiritual blessings in heavenly places in Christ." I would call your attention very particularly to the fact that it is here stated that *God has already given the blessing.* Strictly speaking, I suppose it should be read, " God blessed us with all spiritual blessings in Christ Jesus"; and he continues still to do the same. Do you seek a blessing from God? He has pronounced it already upon you. Do you require anything? You have it : it is given to you in the covenant of grace. Like as when the Lord blessed Abraham he gave him the land of Canaan, so has he given to you all covenant blessings. You have only to ask of the Lord, and he will give you to enjoy each blessing, according as it will be for your good. No good thing will the Lord withhold from you. All you now have to do is by prayer and faith to grasp and enjoy the mercy, for he hath said —" For this good thing will I be enquired of by the house of Israel to do it for them." " Alas !" says one, " I have some blessings, but need many more." This is your unbelief, for all spiritual blessings are pronounced upon you. Yours are the precious things of heaven, the dew and the deep which coucheth beneath. The chief things of the ancient mountains and the precious things of the everlasting hills are yours, and no part of your inheritance shall be rent away from you. A boundless blessing the eternal Father has pronounced upon you as you are in Christ Jesus : he hath spoken it, and he will make it good. When therefore you are in need, bow the knee, and say, " My Father, thou hast given me this already in Christ, now therefore fulfil this word unto thy servant, whereon thou hast caused me to hope." When Jacob rose up from his father's bedside he knew that Isaac's blessing was upon him, and even so the benediction of the Father is on every believer. Rise up, thou heir of heaven ; shake thyself from the dust, for the God and Father of our Lord Jesus Christ has blessed thee out of the fulness of his heart, and thou art blessed indeed. *The benediction is as comprehensive as your needs;* if you lack all things, behold all things are here.

Notice, *the apostle here dwells mainly upon all spiritual blessings :* does he therefore exclude temporal mercies ? Nay, brethren, the greater secures the less. Doubtless Paul thought the comforts of time and sense to be so secondary compared with spiritual blessings in heavenly places, that he thought it no wrong to omit them or consider them to be included while he lifted up his praise in this verse to the Father for his spiritual gifts : for he that gives us the gold of spiritual blessings will never deny us the silver of temporal blessings. He that gives us heaven will surely give us all that is needful on the road thither. Abraham gave gifts to his sons by Keturah and sent them away, but to Isaac he gave the inheritance, which is described as "all that he had." Spirituals are the best gifts : the heritage given to the firstborn. Delight yourselves in spiritual things, for this will mark the distinction between you and the carnal man who has his portion in this life, whereas the believer's motto is, "The Lord is my portion." Look at the worldling. If his barns are full of corn, and his presses bursting with new wine, then he is happy, for he cares not for spiritual things, and his soul's poverty does not trouble him. You and I are of another quality : spirituals are our first demand, and without them we are undone. Our covetousness is for much of the Spirit's gifts and graces—much love, much faith, much holiness, much communion with the Father and the Son, and the temporals we can leave with our heavenly Father, who knows that we have need of all these things. We shall have enough spending money on the road to glory ; for he who has guaranteed to bring us there will not starve us by the way. Spiritual blessings are such as concern our spirit, which is our nobler part ; they have a fulness about them which can never dwell in the disappointing riches of earth, and they are of a substantial and enduring nature, which widely separates them from the shadows of mere carnal delight. Every mouth may eat of the bread of the body, but truly blessed are they that eat bread in the kingdom of God. Every dog as he runs may drink of Nilus, but to drink of the river of the water of life is another matter. Spiritual blessings are for spiritual men, for they only can appreciate or even perceive them : they are a prepared portion for a prepared people. They range from the first painful sense of sin up to the sinless perfection of eternal glory, and all these blessings are pronounced upon the head of each heir of salvation. Shall we not laud and magnify the Father for this? These are the good and perfect gifts which are from above, and come from the unchanging Father of lights ; to him be glory in the church throughout all ages for ever and ever.

These blessings are ours personally, for he hath blessed *us*. It is not upon the clouds that the blessing falls, but upon individuals. "He loved me, and gave himself for me." The Lord hath said to his people, "Ye are the blessed of the Lord and your offspring with you." Personal appropriation is the main thing that we need ; all else lies ready to our hand. Nothing more could be provided, nothing more need to be desired ; but we need faith to take to ourselves the heavenly provision, and for lack of it we go hungering in the midst of plenty. Brethren, there is no need for this. We do not well to sit with the lepers at Samaria's gate when we have but to arouse ourselves and find abundant provision for ourselves and all the King's household.

Furthermore, note well that our heavenly Father has blessed us with all spiritual blessings *in heavenly places* in Christ. Spiritual blessings are heavenly things ; they come from heaven, they lead to heaven, they are of a heavenly nature, and are such as are enjoyed in heaven itself. You may read the text either as heavenly *places* or heavenly *things*, and be equally correct. It is a wonderful thing that, even here on earth, the saints enjoy and experience heavenly blessings ; for a new nature is a heavenly thing, and love, and joy in God, and rest, and safety, and acceptance in the Beloved are all heavenly things. If you read it "places," it is equally true that heaven and all its mansions are ours, and we have already taken possession of them in Christ Jesus, our representative and forerunner. When God made the covenant with Abraham which gave to him the land of Canaan, Abraham had not yet a foot of land that he could call his own, and when he died he only possessed a cave for burial; but yet, in truth, according to the decrees of heaven, the land of Canaan belonged to Abraham and his seed; for had not the Lord said, "Unto thy seed have I given this land, from the river of Egypt unto the great river, the river Euphrates?" They had the title-deeds of it, though for a while the Canaanites held it as tenants upon lease. Now, all the spiritual blessings which belong to the heavenly estate at this moment are the property of the heirs of heaven; and God hath said to each one of them, "Lift up now thine eyes, and look from the place where thou art northward, and southward, and eastward, and westward: for all the land which thou seest, to thee will I give it." The blessings laid up in reserve for those who love God are secured to them in the covenant made with Christ, and we wait only for the time when the Lord our God shall surely bring us into the purchased possession. All things needful for the heavenly life are already secured to the people of God in Christ Jesus, in whom also they have obtained an inheritance. My brother, does not this lift you up, and make you feel yourself to be a different man? You thought you had only a little grace, but all spiritual and heavenly blessings are yours. You never dreamed that you could touch heaven so closely; but heaven has a wide sweep, and is to be found not only in glory above, but in grace below. For God has made us kings even now—we are already in the kingdom of heaven, and upon heavenly manna we are fed at this day. Where Christ is, there is heaven, and he is in our hearts. The sun is above, but inasmuch as his light and heat are here, we say that we sit in the sun and bask in the sun; even so, though the presence of Jesus is in glory, yet we enjoy on earth that sacred revelation of God which is the centre and essence of heaven. Present grace is heaven begun in the soul. He that dwelleth in love dwelleth in God and God in him; what more can heaven be? Even now "he hath raised us up together, and made us sit together in heavenly places in Christ Jesus." That which God has given to us is not bounded by the narrow horizon of this present visible world, but he has given to us all heavenly things most richly to enjoy; the boundless glories of eternity even now belong to us by virtue of the Father's benediction, which he has pronounced on us in Christ Jesus. Only here let me enquire whether you belong to the company upon whom the divine blessing rests. Are you seeking to be saved by your own works? Then you are not saved by grace through Christ Jesus. Are you without faith in Christ? Then the heavenly blessing does not belong to you. The inheritance is secured to a seed who are by faith the children of faithful Abraham, born not after the flesh but after the Spirit. Can you say, I do believe in Jesus Christ, and fix my trust upon the promises of a faithful God? Then take possession of the covenant provision and be glad in the Lord.

We must not fail to note that the plenitude of spiritual and heavenly blessings *only comes to us in Christ.* It is not in ourselves that these boons are vested: we hold them by virtue of our union with the Lord Jesus. He is that golden casket in which the treasures of the covenant are enclosed and secured. He is our Trustee, holding the heritage for us; and this is the form of our tenure,—"joint-heirs with Christ." How precious then is our union with him! Of what vital importance is it to be bound up in the bundle of life with him! As without him we can do nothing, so without him we can possess nothing. In him we have already received a thousand blessings in actual experience, and in him there is laid up a boundless supply for future enjoyment.

At the thought of this let our hearts sing hallelujahs. In the spirit of sonship let us reverence the Father of our spirits who is also the Father of mercies, and the God of all consolation. Blessed, for ever blessed, be the Lord God of heaven and earth, for his unutterable goodness to his chosen in the person of his dear Son. Let us sing unto him :

> " O measureless might!
> Ineffable love!
> While angels delight
> To hymn thee above,
> The humbler creation,
> Though feeble their lays,
> With true adoration
> Shall lisp to thy praise."

III. Thirdly and briefly let us observe THE FIRST OUTFLOW OF THESE HEAVENLY BLESSINGS. The fountain of eternal love burst forth in our election—"According as he hath chosen us in him before the foundation of the world." Consider these words one by one. The first is, *he hath chosen:* God has a will and a choice in the matter of salvation. Some people do not like this doctrine, but they must have it whether they like it or not, or else they must reject the word of inspiration. Is man's will to be deified? Is the whole result of the scheme of salvation to depend upon the creature's choice ? God forbid. The Father has made a choice of some men unto eternal life, these he has given to his Son Jesus; all these the Lord Jesus has redeemed with his own blood, and pledged himself to bring them to glory. Has he not said, "All that the Father giveth me shall come to me?" God has made a choice, then, and you who are believers in Christ may rest assured that you are the objects of this choice. The Lord himself gave you your faith, and brought you into living union with Jesus; do you not bless him for this? It seems to me that here is something for which to praise and bless the Father world without end.

Carefully note that *election shapes everything:* the Father has blessed us with all spiritual blessings, "According as he hath chosen us in Christ." All the grace of earth and the glory of heaven come to us in accordance with the eternal choice. There is not a single boon that comes from the blessed hand of the divine Redeemer but is stamped with the mark of God's electing love. We were chosen to each mercy, and each mercy was appointed for us. If we will not have the Father's election we cannot have his blessing, for his gifts are plainly stated to be according to his choice: they come because of the choice, and they prove the choice ; they should therefore remind us of our election, and call forth our sweetest songs. They should make us ask with David " Whence is this to me ? " A man who is elect of God ought to sing the praises of God both day and night, for he is chosen to show forth the praises of Jehovah.

The next word is "he hath chosen *us.*" Herein is grace indeed. What could there be in us that the Lord should choose *us?* Some of us feel ourselves the most unworthy of the unworthy, and we can see no trace of a reason for our being chosen. So far from being choice men in our own esteem, we feel ourselves by nature to be the very reverse. But if God has chosen *us* then let our hearts love him, our lips extol him, our hands serve him, and our whole lives adore him.

> " Loved of my God, for him again
>   With love intense I burn :
> Chosen of thee ere time began,
>   I choose thee in return."

Then we are told *he has chosen us in Christ Jesus.* He first chose Christ as the head and then looked through Christ upon us and chose us to be members of Christ's mystical body. We are none of us chosen apart from Jesus Christ ; but we are chosen in Christ, loved in Christ, given to Christ, united to Christ, and accepted in Christ. This is a blessed way of being chosen ; for none can separate us from Christ, and consequently till the Father changes his choice of Christ, he cannot and will not reverse his choice of his people. Until Christ ceases to be God's elect, the Father can never cast away those who are chosen in Christ Jesus.

Moreover, we are told the time when this choice was made :—*Before the foundation of the world.* This is the earliest conceivable period. When this earth was fitted up for man we do know, for the Scriptures inform us, but how many ages elapsed before it was furnished for our race, we do not know ; yet long before that period the Father had chosen his people. The foundation of the world may mean its first creation, when it was spoken out of nothing : that must be ages of ages ago, but before that the Father chose us. Remember those words " who hath saved us, and called us with an holy calling, not according to our works, but according to his own purpose and grace, which was given us in Christ Jesus before the world began." Before sun and moon had been created, or any of the visible things were formed, God had set his heart upon his people in Christ and ordained them to eternal life in him. God's love is no novelty. His choice is no sudden act. Blessed doctrine ! I know of none which, if rightly considered, has a greater tendency to draw out the intense affection and reverent admiration of human hearts. Did the Lord of glory choose me from before the foundation of the world ; then I choose him with all my heart to be my Lord, my all. Did he love me from of old ? Then I will love him with all my soul and strength, and pray that my heart may be enlarged to love him more. This is mentioned here in order that you may bless the Father : let there now flow from your hearts a mighty stream of gratitude which shall cover your whole being and bear your lives along in the channel of obedience. Come, my heart, bless the Father at this moment and never cease from his praise while life and being last or immortality endures.

IV. Fourthly and lastly, our text reminds us of another cause for praise, namely, the DESIGNED RESULT OF ALL THIS BLESSING : " That we should be holy and without blame before him in love." *It is God's eternal design that his people should be holy,* and this purpose he has pursued at infinite cost. This is the design of all the blessings which the Father has given us in Christ. All these favours are a call to us to be holy, and each one has a tendency to promote our sanctification. When you grow in grace, and faith, and hope, and joy, all that growth is towards holiness. Always think of that, and bless God for your graces by manifesting their influence in your conduct. Bless God for increased knowledge and deepened experience, for he has designed by these to sanctify you more fully to himself. There is something practical in every boon that comes from the Father's hand, and you should pray to him that you may by each one conquer sin, advance in virtue and perfect holiness in his fear. The ultimate end of election is the praise of the glory of divine grace, but the immediate and intermediate end is the personal sanctification of the chosen. We are chosen unto holiness.

The Father chose us to himself that we might be *without blame* before him in love. He would have us blameless, so that no man can justly find fault with us ; and harmless, so that our lives may injure none but bless all. Holiness is, however, more than this. We are called to be made whole by being healed of the disease of sin, and by having all our broken powers reunited into one harmonious whole. This restored nature is to be wholly consecrated to God, and thus to become holy before God. Oh that we may realize God's object in election even at this time, and so make our calling and election sure! Let us mightily strive after this, and never rest till we have it.

But notice where and what kind of holiness this is : holy and blameless *before him*. I have met with several people who say they are perfectly holy ; but I believe they are under a delusion, and I feel sure that those who watch them will not long think them perfect. This perfection of theirs is according to their own vain ideas and conceited notions, and not according to the judgment of the Lord, who searches the heart. Perfection in the flesh is a lie : I believe it to be one of the grossest falsehoods ever palmed on foolish minds. It would be something to be holy and blameless before the devil as Job was. It would be something to be perfect before the eyes of men who are so ready to criticize us ; but to be blameless *before him* who reads our thoughts and sees our every failure in a moment—this is an attainment of a far higher order. Oh, to be spotless and faultless ! Let us bless God that he is aiming every day to make us holy and blameless before himself ; and he will do it, for his purpose never fails. He has wrought it in a large measure in all his saints, and he will perfect that which he has begun. This is the goal towards which we are running, that we may attain to the complete likeness of Christ. Courage, brethren, it is yet beyond us, but he that hath begun the good work in us will perform it unto the day of Christ. We shall one day be without fault before the throne of God.

To conclude, we are to be holy and blameless before him *in love*. Love is the anointing oil which is to be poured on all the Lord's priests ; when he has robed them in their spotless garments, they shall partake of the unction of love. When he has delivered us from all sin, one choice thing shall be seen in us, and that is love—abounding love. "God is love ; and he that dwelleth in love dwelleth in God, and God in him." As we love we live unto God. Perfect life will be perfect love. Judge of your sanctification by this—Do you grow in love to God ? Do you also increase in love to the brethren ? If your heart grows hard with the proud notion that you are somebody by reason of your high attainments, and that the poor little saints around you are unworthy even to unloose the latchets of your shoes, you are not growing in holiness. Do you love poor sinners more? For if your heart does not grow tender you are not growing holy. What a blessed thing it would be to be saturated with love! They said of Basil, that he was a pillar of fire because of his zeal. I wish it could be said of us that we were flames of fire because of our love. Oh, to love our neighbour as ourselves, thinking no evil! "Oh," says one," we should be imposed upon!" That would be no harm compared with being hardened by selfishness. "But we should be illtreated and defrauded." Suppose we were; it would be better than being miserly and cruel. The worst of ills is hate, the best of blessings is love. When we become incapable of selfishness, and get right away from unkindness of heart and uncharitableness of thought, Christ will be living in us and we in him, and then we shall be fulfilling the purpose of electing love and the design of the innumerable spiritual blessings which are already given us in Christ Jesus. To this let us all aspire. Let brotherly love continue. Let us love each other more than we have ever done, and join our hands anew in a firm league of concord. Let us love the universal church of Christ. Let our hearts burn with ardent affection towards the perishing multitudes of men, that we may bring them to put their whole trust in Jesus and live. May the Father deal with us according to his riches in glory by Christ Jesus, and to Father, Son, and Holy Ghost be glory for ever and ever. Amen.

PORTIONS OF SCRIPTURE READ BEFORE SERMON—Ephesians i.

HYMNS FROM "OUR OWN HYMN BOOK"—152, 195, 198.

BANKRUPT DEBTORS DISCHARGED.

A Sermon

DELIVERED ON LORD'S-DAY MORNING, SEPTEMBER 16TH, 1883, BY

C. H. SPURGEON,

AT THE METROPOLITAN TABERNACLE, NEWINGTON.

"And when they had nothing to pay, he frankly forgave them both."—Luke vii. 42.

THE two debtors differed very considerably in the amounts which they owed: the one was in arrears five hundred pence, and the other fifty. There are differences in the guilt of sins, and in the degrees of men's criminality. It would be a very unfair and unrighteous thing to say that all men are exactly alike in the extent of their transgression. Some are honest and upright, kind and generous, even though they be but natural men: while others appear to be of a malicious, envious, selfish disposition, and rush into evil, sinning, as it were, with both hands greedily. The man who is moral, sober, and industrious is only a fifty pence debtor as compared with the vicious, drunken blasphemer whose debt is written at five hundred pence. Our Saviour recognizes the distinction, because it exists and cannot justly be overlooked. There are distinctions among unconverted men, very great distinctions. One of them, a young man, came to Jesus, and he had so many fine traits in his character that the Lord looking upon him loved him; whereas when the Pharisees gathered about him our Lord looked round upon them with indignation. The soil, which was none of it yet sown with the good seed, yet varied greatly, and some of it was honest and good ground before the sower came to it. Sinners differ from each other.

But I call your particular notice to this fact—that though there was one point of difference in the two debtors, there were three points of similarity; for they were both debtors: and so all men have sinned, be it little or be it much: and, secondly, they were both alike bankrupt, neither of them could meet his debt; the man who owed fifty pence could no more pay than he who owed five hundred pence, so that they were both insolvent debtors. But what a mercy it is that they were alike in a third point! for "when they had nothing to pay," their creditor "frankly forgave them both."

Oh, my dear hearers, we are all alike in the first two things! Oh that we might be all of us alike in this last point, that the Lord our God may grant to every one of us the free remission of sins according to the riches of his grace through Christ Jesus! Why should it not be so,

Nos. 1,739-40.

since Jesus is exalted on high to give repentance and remission of sins? There is forgiveness with God. He delighteth in mercy. He can cast all our sins into the depths of the sea, that they may not be mentioned against us any more for ever. While we are compelled to go together two-thirds of the road, what a pity it would be that we should be divided in the third portion of it! That first two-thirds of the road is a very muddy, boggy piece of way, and we sorrowfully wade along it in company,—all in debt and all of us unable to pay; but that next part of the road is well-made, smooth, and good for travellers, and it leads into the gardens of felicity. Oh that we may traverse it, and find the free pardon of God! Oh for free remission for all of us without exception! Why not? God send it of his great mercy at this good hour! To that end I wish to speak with you, dear friends; for I believe that the Lord Jesus has somewhat to say unto you, and I pray that your hearts may be open to him, crying gladly, "Master, say on!"

Our first point for consideration is, *their bankruptcy*—"they had nothing to pay"; the second is, *their free discharge*—"he frankly forgave them both"; and the third is, *the connection between these two things:* for that little word "when" marks the connection—"*when* they had nothing to pay, he frankly forgave them both."

I. First, let us think of THEIR BANKRUPTCY. This was their condition. They were unquestionably in debt. If they could have disputed the creditor's claim, no doubt they would have done so. If they could have pleaded that they were never indebted, or that they had already paid, no doubt they would have been glad to have done so; but they could not raise a question; their debt could not be denied. Another fact was also clear to them, namely, that they had nothing to pay with. No doubt they had made diligent search; they had turned out their pockets, their cash-boxes, and their lockers, and they had found nothing; they had looked for their household goods, but these had vanished piece by piece. They had nothing at home or abroad that they could dispose of. Things had come to such a pass with them that they had neither stock nor money, nor anything in prospect which they could draw upon: they were brought to the last extremity, reduced to absolute beggary. Meanwhile, their great creditor was pressing them for settlement. That idea lies in the heart of the text. The creditor had evidently brought his over-due accounts, and had said to them, "These claims must be met. There must be an end to this state of affairs; your accounts must be discharged." They were just brought to this condition—they must confess the debt, and they must also humbly acknowledge that they had nothing to meet it with: the time for payment had come, and it found them without a penny. No condition could be much more wretched.

So far I have stated the parable, and it most truly sets forth *the condition* of every man who has not come to Jesus Christ and so received the frank forgiveness of his sins. Upon this we will enlarge. We are all by nature and by practice plunged in debt, and this is the way in which we came to be so. Hear it and mark it well. As God's creatures we from the very first owed to him the debt of obedience. We were bound to obey our Maker. It is he that made us, and not we ourselves; and we were, therefore, bound reverently to recognize our Creator, affectionately to worship him, and dutifully to serve him. This is an obligation so natural and reasonable that nobody can dispute it. If you are the creatures of God, it is nothing more than right that you should honour him. If you receive daily the breath in your nostrils and the food that you eat from him, then you are bound to him by the ties of gratitude, and should do his will.

But, dear friends, we have not done his will. We have left undone the things we ought to have done, and we have done the things we ought not to have done, and so we have come in a second sense into his debt. We now stand liable to penalty, yea, we are condemned already. There is due from us to God, in vindication of his broken law, both suffering and death; and in the word of God we find that the righteous penalty for sin is something utterly overwhelming. "Fear him," saith Christ, "which is able to destroy both soul and body in hell." Yea, I say unto you, fear him! Very terrible are the metaphors and symbols by which the Holy Spirit sets forth the misery of a soul upon which the Lord pours forth his fiery indignation. The pain of loss and pain of woe which sin at last brings upon guilty men are inconceivable: they are called "the terrors of the Lord." There is not one among us, apart from the Lord Jesus Christ, but what owes to God's law a debt which eternity cannot fully meet, even though it be crowded with agonizing regrets. A life of forgetfulness of God and breaking of his law must be recompensed by a future life of punishment. That is where we stand: can any man be at rest while this is his condition before God? We are debtors: the debt is overwhelming; it brings with it consequences tremendous to the last degree.

And we are utterly unable to make any amends for this. If he should meet with us and call us to account we cannot answer him one of a thousand. We cannot excuse ourselves, and we cannot by any possibility render to him his righteous due. If any think they can, let me remind them of this, that to cancel the debt which we owe to God we must pay it all. God demands, righteously demands, from us the keeping of his entire law. He tells us that he that is guilty in one point is guilty of all: for God's law is like a fair vase of alabaster, lovely in its entireness; but if it be chipped in any part, it may not be presented in his court; the least flaw in it mars its perfection and destroys its value. A perfect obedience to a perfect law is that which is required by the justice of the Most High; and is there any one of us who can render it, or who can attempt to pay the penalty due for not rendering it? Our inability to obey comes of our own fault, and is part of our crime. Ah me! may none of us ever have to bear the penalty! To be banished from his presence, and from the glory of his power! to be cast away from all hope and light and joy for ever! Why, there are those at this moment in the abyss of woe who have for thousands of years endured the heavy hand of justice, and yet their debt remains undischarged even now; for they have yet to appear before the judgment-seat of Christ at the last day and answer for their transgressions. It is certain that to meet the whole payment is impossible; neither in the form of obedience, nor in the form of penalty, may we ever hope to meet it—it would be all in vain to make the attempt.

Remember, too, that if there is anything that we can do for God in the way of obedience it is already due to him. All that I can do if I love God with all my heart and soul and strength, and my neighbour as myself, throughout the rest of my life, is already due to God : I shall but be discharging new duties as they occur—how will this affect old disobediences? In what way can I cleanse myself from my former stains by the resolve that I will not be defiled with fresh ones? If your hand be blood red can you make it clean by the mere resolution that you will not plunge it again into the dye? You know it is not so : past sin cannot be removed by future carefulness.

> " Could my tears for ever flow,
> Could my zeal no respite know,
> All for sin could not atone ;
> Christ must save, and Christ alone."

We have nothing with which to meet our liabilities because everything that we can possibly earn or obtain in the future is already due to justice, and so we have nothing left unmortgaged, nothing of our own.

Moreover, the debt is immense and incalculable! Fifty pence is but a poor representation of what the most righteous person owes ; five hundred pence is but an insignificant sum compared with the transgressions of the greater offenders. Oh, friends, when I think of my life it seems to be like the sea, made up of innumerable waves of sin ; or like the sea-shore, constituted of sands, that cannot be weighed nor counted. My faults are utterly innumerable, and each one deserving death eternal. Our sins, our heavy sins, sins against light and knowledge, our foul sins, our repeated sins, our aggravated sins, our sins against our parents, our sins against all our relationships, our sins against our God, our sins with the body, our sins with the mind, our sins of forgetfulness, our sins of thought, our sins of imagination—who can reckon them up in order unto God ? Who knoweth the number of his trespasses ? Now, to think that we can ever meet such a debt is indeed to bolster up ourselves with a notion that is utterly absurd :—we have nothing to pay.

Moreover, I go a little further. Even if these sins were somewhat within compass, and if we were not indebted for the future as to all we even can do, yet what is there that we can do? Does not Paul say of himself that he was not sufficient to think anything of himself? Did not the Lord tell his Israel of old, " From me is thy fruit found " ? Did not Jesus say to his disciples and even to his apostles, " Without me ye can do nothing " ? Then, O bankrupt sinner, what is there good that you can do of yourself ? You must first of all get the good work from God before you can perform it yourself. It is true you are to " work out your own salvation with fear and trembling"; but what must come first ? Read the passage, " For it is God which worketh in you both to will and to do of his good pleasure." If the Lord does not work salvation in us, we cannot work it out. Every good thing in man is the work of God, the produce of the Spirit of God operating upon the heart and mind. Men are dead in trespasses and sins, dead to all that is holy and acceptable with God, and life itself is a gift. What then can sinners do ? Their bankruptcy is utter and entire ; and this is true of every man that is still out of Christ—he is a debtor, and he has nothing to pay.

This being the case, I want to spend a minute in noticing *certain temptations* to which all bankrupt sinners are much subject. One of these is to try and forget their spiritual estate altogether. Some of you here to-day have never given serious thought to your souls and to your condition before God. It is an unpleasant subject. You suspect that it would be still more unpleasant if you looked into it. You want amusement, something to while away the time, because you do not care to examine into the state of your heart before God. Solomon exhorts the diligent man to know the state of his flocks, and look well to his herds; but he that is careless and idle would rather leave such enquiries, and let things go as they please. The man who is going backward in business has no pleasure in stock-taking. " Oh," says he, " don't bring me my books ; I shall not sleep at nights if I look into *them*." He knows that he is sinking lower and lower, and will soon be a ruined man; and the only way in which he can endure his life is to drive dull care away by drink, or by going into company, or idle amusement. He labours to beguile the hours that he may conceal from himself his true condition. But what a fool he is! Would it not be infinitely wiser if he would look the thing in the face and have it out, and know his actual state? Such ignorance as he chooses is not bliss to a right-hearted man, but suspense and misery. I have often prayed this prayer —" Lord, let me know the very worst of my case," for I do not wish to entertain a hope that will at last deceive me. Disappointment will be bitter in proportion as false hope was sweet. This is the temptation of the bankrupt soul, to shut its eyes to unwelcome truth. The ostrich is fabled when hunted to bury its head in the sand, and conceive that the huntsman is gone when he is no longer seen. But he is not gone : the unseen danger is quite as real as if it stared us in the face. However forgetful you may be, God does not forget your sins.

Another temptation to a man in this condition is to make as good a show as he can. A man who is very near bankruptcy is often noticed for the dash he cuts. What a horse he drives as he comes up to business! What fashionable parties he gives! Just so, he desires to keep up his credit as long as ever he can. He is going to make a smash of it by-and-by, but for a season he assumes the airs of my lord, and everybody near him imagines that he has money enough and to spare. The governor of a besieged city threw loaves of bread over the wall to the besiegers, to make them believe that the citizens had such large supplies that they could afford to throw them away; yet they were starving all the while. There are some men of like manners; they have nothing that they can offer unto God, but yet they exhibit a glittering self-righteousness. Oh, they have been so good, such superior people, so praiseworthy from their youth up; they never did anything much amiss ; there may be a little speck here and there upon their garments, but that will brush off when it is dry. They make a fair show in the flesh with morality and formality, and a smattering of generosity. Besides, they profess to be religious: they attend divine service, and pay their quota of the expenses. Who could find any fault with such good people? Just so ; this profession is the fine horse and trap with which they too are cutting a dash just before going through the court. There is nothing at all in you, and there never was, if you are as nature has made you; wherefore then do you try to brazen it out, and make yourself to seem somewhat when you are nothing. You may by this means deceive yourself, but certainly you will not deceive God.

Another temptation which lurks in the way of a bankrupt sinner is that of making promises of what he will do. Men in debt are generally very promising men; they will pay next week for certain; but when that next week comes, they meant the next week further on, and then payment shall be doubly certain; yet they put in no appearance even then, or, if they do, they give a bill. Is not that a precious document? is it not as good as the money itself? They evidently think so, for they feel quite as easy as if they had really paid that debt. But when the bill falls due, what then? It falls, never to rise again. Ah me! a bill is often just a lie with a stamp on it. So will debtors go on as long as they can. This is what every sinner does before he becomes cleared by the sovereign grace of God. He cries, "I mean to do better." Never mind; tell us no more what you mean to do, but do it. To promise and vow so falsely is only adding to your sins! "Oh! but you know I do not intend to go on in this way always. It is a long lane that has no turning. I shall pull up short one of these days, and then you will see." What shall we see? What we shall see; and that will not be much. Yes. We shall see the dew of promise disappear, and the morning cloud of resolution pass away. Dear sir, you cannot raise our hopes now. Neither God nor man will trust you; you have promised these twenty years, and in no one year have you made a real move in the right direction. You have not lied unto men only, but unto God, and how will you answer for it? Know you not that every promise that you make to God which you do not keep is a great addition to your transgressions, and helps to fill up the measure of your iniquities? Give up the way of lying, I pray you.

Another temptation is, always to ask for more time—as if this was all that was needed. When the debtor, in another parable, was arrested, he said to his creditor, "Have patience with me, and I will pay thee all." We cannot pay any of our debt to-day, and yet dote upon to-morrow. Yes, it does seem such a relief to get a little longer time; somehow a vague shadowy hope seems to pervade the months to come. The sinner cries, "Go thy way for this time; when I have a convenient season, I will call for thee." It is not convenient just now, but do wait a little bit, a suitable hour will come. With this temptation Satan has destroyed multitudes of men, tempting them to ask for more time, instead of coming up to the mark at once and asking for immediate pardon. What are the fabled virtues of to-morrow? Why do men dote upon the unknown future? To immediate decision I would press you at this moment; and may God by his divine Spirit deliver you as a bird from the hand of the fowler, that you may no longer procrastinate and waste your life in disobedient delay.

This being the temptation, let me hint to those of you who are bankrupt what *your wisdom* is. It is your wisdom to face the business of your soul. Your soul-matters are the most important things you will ever have on hand, for when your wealth must be left, and your estate shall see you no more, and when your body is dead, your soul will still be living in eternal happiness or endless woe; therefore, do not let your state in reference to God have the go-by. It is the most important matter; give it the first place. Settle this business before you attend to anything else.

Take care that you face it, like an honest man, and not as one who makes the best of a bad story. Though it be bad, yet still the best thing you can do is to go right through with it in truth and soberness before the Lord. Hope lies that way. Do not let your danger be concealed like a thief who hides in the good man's cupboard till the hour to rob his house. Suffer not the sparks to smoulder where they may consume your all. Quench the fire before you sleep. When you face the matter, be very true and sincere with yourself and with God; because you are not now dealing with creditors who may be cheated, but you are dealing with One who knows the secret thoughts and intents of your heart. Before God nothing but truth can stand; the painted hypocrite is spied out immediately. The Lord takes off all masks, and men stand before him as they really are, and not as they would seem to be; so be true with yourself. Do not take your pen and write down sixty if you owe a hundred; but put the fair hundred down. Tricks and falsehoods had better be put away once for all when you deal with God.

One thing more: it will be your wisdom to give up all attempts to pay, because you have nothing to pay with. Do not delude yourself into the idea that you will pay one day, for you never will. Do not make the slightest attempt at paying, for you cannot do it; but take quite another course, plead absolute poverty, and appeal to mercy. Say, " Lord, I have nothing, I am nothing, I can do nothing. I must throw myself upon thy grace." Of this grace I am now going to speak. May I so speak as to encourage you who are bankrupts to come to the Lord, that he may frankly forgive you all.

II. Our second head is, THEIR FREE DISCHARGE. " He frankly forgave them both." What a blessing they obtained by facing the matter! These two poor debtors, when they went into the office, were trembling from head to foot, for they had nothing to pay, and were deeply involved; but see! they come out with light hearts, for the debt is all disposed of, the bills are receipted, the records are destroyed. Even thus the Lord has blotted out the handwriting that was against us, and has taken it out of the way, nailing it to his cross.

In this free discharge I admire, first of all, *the goodness* of the great creditor. What a gracious heart he had! What kindness he showed! He said, " Poor souls, you can never pay me, but you need not be cast down because of it, for I freely cancel your debts." Oh, the goodness of it! Oh, the largeness of the heart of God! I was reading of Cæsar the other day. He had been at fierce war with Pompey, and at last he conquered him, and when he conquered him he found among the spoil Pompey's private cabinet, in which were contained letters from the various noblemen and senators of Rome who had sided with him. In many a letter there was fatal evidence against the most eminent Romans, but what did Cæsar do? He destroyed every document. He would have no knowledge of his enemies, for he freely forgave them and wished to know no more. In this Cæsar proved that he was fit to govern the nation. But look at the splendour of God when he puts all our sins into one cabinet, and then destroys the whole. If the sins of his people be sought for they cannot now be found. He will never mention them against us any more for ever. Oh, the goodness of the infinite God, whose mercy endureth for ever! Bow before that goodness with joy.

But, then, observe *the freeness* of it—"He frankly forgave them both." They did not stand there and say, "Oh, good sir, we cannot pay," and plead and beg, as for their lives; but he freely said to them, "You cannot pay, but I can forgive. You ought never to have got into my debt, and you ought not to have broken your promises to me; but behold, I make an end of all this weary business: I freely blot out all your obligations!" Did not this open a fountain in their eyes? Did they not hasten home to their wives and children, and tell them that they were out of debt, for the beloved creditor had forgiven it all most freely? This is a fair picture of the grace of God. When a poor sinner comes to him bankrupt, he says, "I forgive you freely: your offence is all gone. I do not want you to earn a pardon by your tears, and prayers, and anguish of soul. You have not to make me merciful, for I am merciful already; and my dear Son Jesus Christ has made such a propitiation that I can be just and yet can forgive you all this debt. Therefore, go in peace."

Furthermore, this debt was *fully* discharged. The creditor did not say, "Come, my good fellow, I will take fifty per cent. off the account if you find the remainder." As they had nothing wherewith to pay, they would not have been a bit the better if he had reduced them ninety per cent. If he had taken half the debt, the one would have owed two hundred and fifty and the other twenty-five; but still their case would have been hopeless, since they had not a farthing of their own. Now the Lord, when he blots out his people's sin, leaves no trace of it remaining. My own persuasion is that when our Lord Jesus died upon the cross he made an end of all the sins of all his people, and made full and effectual atonement for the whole of those who ever shall believe in him. I can sing with all my heart—

> "Here's pardon for transgressions past,
> It matters not how black their cast;
> And, O my soul, with wonder view,
> For sins to come here's pardon too!"

All the sin of believers has been once for all carried into the wilderness of oblivion by our great Scapegoat, and none shall ever find a sin wherewith to condemn one soul of the chosen band. There is no debt left against a believer: no, not one single pennyworth of debt remains upon the score. Does not the Spirit of God himself ask the question, "Who shall lay anything to the charge of God's elect?" The Lord has frankly forgiven their debt, and he has not done so in part, but as a whole. As for our sins, "the depths have covered them;" "there is not one of them left." Hallelujah!

Observe that it was a very *effectual* forgiveness too. The only person that can forgive a debt is he to whom the debt is due. God only can forgive sin, seeing it is a debt to him. What think you of those folk who are said to be able to forgive you for a shilling? Why, I say that to pay them their fee would be elevenpence three farthings and another farthing thrown away. When you have got their forgiveness what is the good of it? Suppose I were to forgive you for injuries done by you to the Queen, of what value would my forgiveness be? He against whom I have transgressed is the only one that can pronounce my pardon; but if he absolves me, how effectual is the sentence! When the creditor said, "I freely forgive you both," why, the deed was done: his lips had power, he had finished the debt by his word. And so when the Lord Jesus Christ is looked unto by the eye of faith, there comes a voice from his dear wounds which cries to the poor trembling bankrupt sinner, "Your sins, which are many, are all forgiven. I have blotted out your sins like a cloud, and like a thick cloud your iniquities." What an effectual pardon it is! How it charms the heart, and lulls every fear to rest! He frankly, he fully, he freely, he effectually forgave them both.

And I believe that when this is done, I may add another adjective— it is an *eternal* discharge. That creditor could never summon those debtors again for debts which he had remitted. He could never think of such a thing with any show of justice. He had frankly forgiven them, and they were forgiven. God does not play fast and loose with his creatures, and forgive them and then punish them. I never shall believe in God's loving a man to-day, and casting him away to-morrow. The gifts and calling of God are without repentance on his part. Justification is not an act which can be reversed, and followed with damnation. No; no; "whom he justified, them he also glorified."

> "If sin be pardoned I'm secure,
> Death has no sting beside;
> The law gave sin its damning power,
> But Christ my ransom died."

By his death our Redeemer effectually swept away sin once for all, and all the curse of the law he removed. In the offering of bullocks and lambs there was a continual remembrance made of sin, for the blood of bulls and of goats could not take away sin; but the apostle writes, "This Man, after he had offered one sacrifice for sins for ever, sat down on the right hand of God," because his work was effectually and eternally done.

Only one more remark on this point: this frank forgiveness *applied to both the debtors*—"he frankly forgave them both." The man that owed only fifty pence needed a free discharge as truly as the debtor who owed five hundred; for though he was not so deep in the mire, yet he was as truly in the slough. If a man was lying in prison for debt, as men used to do under our old laws, if he only owed fifty pounds he was shut within walls just as closely as the greater debtor who owed fifty thousand; and he could no more get out without the payment or forgiveness of his smaller liability than the bigger debtor could. A bird held by a string is as much a prisoner as a bull that is tied by a rope. Now, you good people who have always tried to do your duty, and are numbered with the fifty pence debtors, you must confess that you have become somewhat indebted to God by committing a measure of sins. Take note that you cannot be saved except by the free forgiveness of God through the precious blood of Christ. The fifty pence debtor must obtain his discharge by grace alone. It is also a most blessed thing to perceive that he forgave the five hundred pence debtor with equal freeness. Perhaps I have some here, men and women, who have never made any pretence of being good, who from their childhood have gone from bad to worse. There is a possibility of free and instantaneous forgiveness for you at this moment. You that are over head and ears in debt to God can be freely forgiven by the same Lord who forgives the smaller debtors. When a man has his pen in his hand, and is writing receipts, it takes him no more trouble to write a receipt for five hundred pounds than it does for a bill of fifty—the same signature will suffice : and when the Lord has the pen of his Spirit in his hand, and he is about to write upon a conscience the peace which comes of reconciliation, he can write upon one as well as upon another. Ho, you with a little bill, bring it here that infinite grace may write upon it " CANCELLED ! " Ho, you with a more weighty account, come and place it near that gracious right hand, for though your bill be never so long and heavy, the hand of Infinite Love can write " CANCELLED " in a moment ! My joy overflows at having such a gospel to preach to you : whatever your guilt, my gracious God is ready to forgive you for Jesus' sake, because he delighteth in mercy.

III. I now beg your very special attention to the last point, and that is THE CONNECTION BETWEEN THIS BANKRUPTCY AND THIS FREE DISCHARGE. It is said " *When* they had nothing to pay, he frankly forgave them both." There is a time when pardon comes, and that time is when self-sufficiency goes. If any person in this place has in his own conscience come to this point, that he feels he has nothing to pay, he has come to the point at which God is ready to forgive him. He that will own his debt, and confess his own incapacity to meet it, shall find that God frankly blots it out. The Lord will never forgive us until we are brought to the starvation of pride and the death of boasting. A sense of spiritual bankruptcy shows that a man has become *thoughtful;* and this is essential to salvation. How can we believe a thoughtless person to be a saved man ? If we so think about our state as to mourn our sin and feel its wickedness, and if we have made a close search into our hearts and lives, and find that we have no merit and no might, then are we prepared in all thoughtfulness to say, " In the Lord have I righteousness and strength." Must there not be serious thought before we can hope for mercy ? Would you have God save us while we are asleep, while we are giddy, frivolous, trifling, and without concern about our sin ? Surely that would be giving a premium to folly ! God acts not so. He will have us know the seriousness of our danger, for else we shall treat the whole matter with lightness; and *we* shall miss the moral effect of pardon, while *he* will be robbed of his glory.

Next, when we come to feel our bankruptcy we then *make an honest confession,* and to that confession a promise is given—" he that confesseth his sin shall find mercy." The two debtors had owned to their debts, and they had also openly confessed, though it must have gone against the grain a bit, that they could not pay. They humbled themselves before their creditor, and then he said, " I frankly forgive you." If one of these debtors had bounced and bragged, " Oh, we can pay ; " in all probability he would have been sent to prison. As for you, poor trembler, I do not know where you are this morning, but here is comfort for you : when you go unto God in your chamber and cry,

"Lord, have mercy upon me, for I am guilty, and I cannot justify myself before thee, nor offer any excuse to thee:" then it is that he will say, "Be of good cheer; I have put away thy sin; thou shalt not die." When you have nothing to pay and confess your insolvency, the debt shall be wiped out. When you are brought to your worst, you shall see the Lord at his best.

It is in their utter destitution that *men value a discharge.* If God were to give his mercy to every man at once, without his ever having had any sense of sin at all, why men would count it cheap and think nothing of it. "God is merciful," is a common saying everywhere; and it is such a bit of valueless talk with them, that they let it roll glibly out as if it were no matter. They do not worship him for his mercy or serve him for his grace. They say, "Oh, God is merciful," and then they go on to sin worse than ever; the idea has no effect upon their hearts or lives; they have no esteem for that mercy of which they speak so freely. So the Lord takes care that the sinner shall know his need of mercy by feeling the pinch of conscience and the terror of the law. If I may so speak, he puts in the sheriff's officer, and makes a distraint upon the soul by convincing the man of sin, of righteousness, and of judgment. The Lord puts an execution into the heart, and then it is, when the poor creature cries, "I have nothing to pay with," that free discharge is given by the Lord, and heartily prized by him to whom it comes. When our account is long and heavy, it is a blessed thing to see the Lord write "Cancelled," and to behold the whole mountain of debt swallowed up in the sea of love. Christ is precious when sin is bitter. Is it not wise on God's part that the cancelling of the debt shall come just when we have nothing to pay, and therefore are prepared to prize a free forgiveness?

Under conviction a poor soul *sees the reality of sin and of pardon.* My dear hearer, you will never believe in the reality of forgiveness till you have felt the reality of sin. I remember when I felt the burden of sin, and though but a child, my heart failed me for anguish, and I was brought very low. Sin was no bugbear to scare me; it was a grim reality; as a lion it tore me in pieces. And now, to-day, I know the reality of pardon: it is no fancy, no dream, for my inmost soul feels its power. I know that my sins are forgiven, and I rejoice therein; but I should never have known the real truth of this happy condition if I had not felt the oppressive load of sin upon the conscience. I could not afford to play at conversion, for sin was an awful fact in my soul. Our heavenly Father does not wish us to use lightness in a matter concerning which Jesus shed his blood, and so he brings us into trouble of soul, and afterwards into a vivid realization of free grace. He lets the whip fall on our shoulders until we bleed again, and this makes us weary of the slavery of sin. He sets conscience and the law upon us, and these two gaolers thrust us into the inner dungeon, and make our feet fast in the stocks. All this prepares us for the delivering power which shakes the prison walls, and looses our bonds, and for the tender love which washes our stripes and sets meat before us.

I do believe that the Lord will give us our quittance when we have got to our last farthing, and not till then, because *only then do we look to the Lord Jesus Christ.* Ah, my dear friends, as long as we have anything else to look to, we never will look to Christ. That blessed port into which no ship did ever run in a storm without finding a sure haven is shunned by all your gallant vessels : they will rather put into any port along the coast of self-deceit than make for the harbour which is marked out by the two lighthouses of free-grace and dying love. As long as a man can scrape the meal-barrel and find a little in it, as long as he can hold up the oil-cruse, and it drips, if it only yields a drop in a week, he will never come to Christ for heavenly provision. As long as he has one rusty counterfeit farthing hidden away in the corner of his till, the sinner will never accept the riches of redeeming love; but when it is all up with him, when he has nothing in the parlour, nothing in the kitchen, nothing in the cellar, when there is neither stick nor stock left, then he prizes Jesus and his salvation. We break to make. We are emptied to be filled. When we cannot give, God can forgive. If any of you have any goodness of your own you will perish for ever. If you have anything you can trust to of your own you will be lost as sure as you are living men and women; but if you are reduced to sore extremity, and God's fierce wrath seems to burn against you, then not only may you have mercy, but mercy is yours already.

> " 'Tis perfect poverty alone
>   That sets the soul at large ;
> While we can call one mite our own
>   We get no full discharge.
>
> But let our debts be what they may,
>   However great or small,
> As soon as we have nought to pay
>   Our Lord forgives us all."

Blessed are ye poor, for ye shall be rich! Blessed are ye hungry, for ye shall be fed! Blessed are ye that are empty, for ye shall be filled! But woe unto you that are rich and are increased in goods, and have need of nothing, and boast of your own goodness! Christ has nothing to do with you, and we have nothing to preach to you except this—"They that be whole need not a physician." The heavenly Surgeon did not come to save those who have no need of saving. Let those who are sick prick up their ears and hear with delight, for the Physician is come with a special eye to them. Are you a sinner? Then Christ is the Saviour of sinners. Join hands with him by faith, and the work is done: you are saved for ever! God bless you, for Christ's sake. Amen.

Portions of Scripture read before Sermon—Psalm xxxii.;
Luke vii. 36—50.

Hymns from "Our Own Hymn Book"—136 (Part II.), 504, 546.

Metropolitan Tabernacle Pulpit.

THE EXETER-HALL SERMON TO YOUNG MEN.

A Sermon

DELIVERED ON LORD'S-DAY EVENING, SEPTEMBER 2ND, 1883, BY

C. H. SPURGEON,

AT EXETER-HALL.

" O Lord, truly I am thy servant ; I am thy servant, and the son of thine handmaid : thou hast loosed my bonds."—Psalm cxvi. 16.

I HAVE been wondering whether I might correctly say that I would preach to-night as a young man to young men. It is precisely what I should like to do, but can I do it? You are young men, I see, to a very large extent; but I wonder whether I am a young man myself. I have two opinions upon it in my own mind. Sometimes I feel very old. When I look in the glass and see the hairs that have turned white upon my head, I suspect that I cannot be a young man; when I feel weary with my work and worn with sickness, I am persuaded that years are telling upon me; yet when I recover from sickness I feel young again, and when cheerful spirits and vivacity return I half hope that I may still be a young man. I must not, however, deceive myself, for when I come to calculate and tally all up, I confess that if youth be essential to membership with the Young Men's Christian Association I could not expect to be voted in. I am a little under fifty, and I am a grandfather; and so I do not think that I can call myself a young man. Very well; I will not take upon myself airs, and pretend to be what I am not, nor will I affect to be quite in your position upon the life-chart. I am not old, however. I suppose that I am just in the middle passage, and, as a man in the centre of life, I may venture to-night to give some little instruction and advice to you who are at its beginning. I have received a lot of advice myself in former years, and have borne it pretty patiently. Everybody has advised me. I must honestly own that I have not followed all their advice, or else I had not been here. But now I think that I shall take my turn, and see whether I may not give a little advice; and the advice, such as it is, shall come out of my own experience. I do not expect you blindly to follow it, for I have confessed that I have not always accepted everybody's counsel myself. Only give me a hearing : gather the good of what I say into vessels, and throw the bad away. Before I get quite away from being a young man I will try to talk with those who so lately were my comrades : before I shake hands with the old men, and ask for a seat among them, I would have a word with those who are coming upon the scene of action to fill our places.

I may say honestly at the very beginning that I want so to preach to-night that every man here who is not yet a servant of the Lord may at least desire to become one, and that very many may actually enlist in the service of our great Lord and Master on this very spot. Why not? I shall be thrice happy, and they will be thrice happy too, if such should be the case. Hence I have taken a text which I can repeat on my own behalf as sincerely as the Psalmist could for himself: "O Lord, truly I am thy servant; I am thy servant, and the son of thine handmaid: thou hast loosed my bonds."

I. I begin, then, dear young men, by COMMENDING THE SERVICE OF GOD TO YOU. I want you to enter it, and therefore I commend it.

When a young man starts in life he is apt to enquire of an older person in this fashion—" I should like to get into such a business, but is it a good one; you have been in it for years, how do you find it?" He seeks the advice of a friend who will tell him all about it. Some will have to warn him that their trade is decaying, and that there is nothing to be done in it. Others will say that their business is very trying, and that if they could get out of it they would; while another will answer for his work, "Well, I have found it all right. I must speak well of the bridge which has carried me over. I have been able to earn a living, and I recommend you to try it." I come here at this time on purpose to give my own experience, and therefore *I wish to say concerning the service of the Lord that I have never regretted that I entered it.* Surely, at some time or other, in these thirty-three years since I put on Christ's livery and became his servant, I should have found out the evil if there had been anything wrong in the religion of Jesus. At some time or other I should have discovered that there was a mistake, and that I was under a delusion. But it has never been so. I have regretted many things which I have done, but I have never regretted that I gave my heart to Christ and became a servant of the Lord. In times of deep depression—and I have had plenty of them—I have feared this and feared the other, but I have never had any suspicion of the goodness of my Master, the truth of his teaching, or the excellence of his service: neither have I wished to go back to the service of Satan and sin. Mark you, if we had been mindful of the country from whence we came out, we have had many an opportunity to return. All sorts of enticement have assailed me, and siren voices have often tried to lure me upon the rocks; but never, never since the day in which I enlisted in Christ's service have I said to myself, "I am sorry that I am a Christian; I am vexed that I serve the Lord." I think that I may, therefore, honestly, heartily, and experimentally recommend to you the service which I have found so good. I have been a bad enough servant, but never had a servant so lovable a Master or so blessed a service.

There is one thing, too, which will convince you that in my judgment the service of God is most desirable: *I have great delight in seeing my children in the same service.* When a man finds that a business is a bad one, you will not find him bringing up his boys to it. Now, the greatest desire of my heart for my sons was, that they might become the servants of God. I never wished for them that they might be great or rich, but, oh, if they would but give their young hearts to Jesus! This I prayed for most heartily. It was one of the happiest nights of my life when I baptized them into the name of the Father, and of the Son, and of the Holy Ghost, upon profession of their faith; and now, while I am speaking to you, one is preaching in New Zealand, and another at Greenwich; and my heart is glad that the gospel which the father preaches, the sons are preaching too. If my Lord's service had been a hard one, I should have said to these lads, "Don't you take to it. God is a hard Master, reaping where he has not strawed: I went into the service blindly, but I warn you to avoid it." My conduct has been the reverse of this, and thus I have given you hostages in the persons of my sons for my honest love to my Master and Lord: I do without reserve commend to you the service of the Lord Jesus Christ; for if you enter it, you will wish your sons and daughters to enter it; and it will be your ambition that to the latest generation all your house may fear and serve God.

I would add this more of personal testimony: so blessed is the service of God, that *I would like to die in it!* When I have been unable to preach through physical pain, I have taken my pen to write, and found much joy in making books for Jesus; and when my hand has been unable to wield the pen, I have wanted to talk about my Master to somebody or other, and I have tried to do so. I remember that David Brainerd, when he was very ill, and could not preach to the Indians, was found sitting up in bed, teaching a little Indian boy his letters, that he might read the Bible; and so he said, "If I cannot serve God one way, I will another. I will never leave off this blessed service." This is my personal resolve, and verily, there is no merit in it, for my Lord's service is a delight. It is a great pleasure to have anything to do for our great Father and Friend, and most affectionately, for your own good, I commend the service of God to you.

I think of it now in the following lights, and therefore I commend it to you for four reasons:

To serve God is the most reasonable thing in the world. It was he that made you: should not your Creator have your service? It is he that supports you in being: should not that being be spent to his glory? Oh, sirs, if you had a cow or a dog, how long would you keep either of them if it were of no service to you? Suppose it were a dog, and it never fawned upon you, but followed at everybody else's heel, and never took notice of *you*—never acknowledged *you* as its master at all: would you not soon tire of such a creature? Which of you would make an engine, or devise any piece of machinery, if you did not hope that it would be of some service to you? Now, God has made you, and a wonderful piece of mechanism is the body, and a wondrous thing is the soul; and will you never obey him with the body or think of him with the mind? This is Jehovah's own lament: "Hear, O heavens, and give ear, O earth: for the Lord hath spoken, I have nourished and brought up children, and they have rebelled against me. The ox knoweth his owner, and the ass his master's crib: but Israel doth not know, my people doth not consider." To have lived to be one-and-twenty without God is a terrible robbery; how have you managed it? To have lived to be thirty or forty, and never to have paid any reverence to him who has kept the breath in your nostrils, without which you would have been a loathsome carcase in the grave long ago, is a base injustice; how dare you continue in it? To have lived so long, and, in addition to that, to have often insulted God; to have spoken against him; to have profaned his day; to have neglected his Book; to have turned your back on the Son of his love—is not this enough? Will you not cease from such an evil course? Why, there are some men who cannot bear five minutes' provocation, nay, nor five seconds' either. It is "a word and a blow" with them; only the blow frequently comes first. But here is God provoked by the twenty years at a stretch—the thirty, the forty, the fifty years right on; and yet he bears patiently with us. Is it not time that we render to him our reasonable service? If he has made us, if he has redeemed us, if he has preserved us in being, it is but his due that we should be his servants.

And let me notice, next, that *this is the most honourable service that ever can be.* Did you say, " Lord, I am thy servant "? I see, coming like a flash of light from heaven, a bright spirit, and my imagination realizes his presence. There he stands, a living flame. It is a seraph fresh from the throne, and what does he say? " O Lord, I am thy servant." Are you not glad to enter into such company as this? When cherubim and seraphim count it their glory to be the servants of God, what man among us will think it to be a mean office? A prince, an emperor, if he be a sinner against God, is but a scullion in the kitchen compared with the true nobleman who serves the Lord in poverty and toil. This is the highest style of service under heaven: no courtier's honour can rival it. Knights of the Garter or what else you like lose their glories in comparison with the man whom God will call servant in the day of the appearing of our Lord and Saviour Jesus Christ. You are in grand company, young friend, if you are a servant of God.

And let me note, again, that *this service is full of beneficence.* If I had to engage in a trade, I should like to spend my time and strength in a pursuit which did no hurt to anybody, and did good to many. Somehow, I do not think that I should like to deal in deadly weapons— certainly not in the accursed drink. I would sooner starve than earn my bread by selling that or anything else that would debase my fellow-men, and degrade them below the level of brute beasts. It is a grand thing, I think, if a young man can follow a calling in which he may do well for himself, and be doing well to others at the same time. It is a fine thing to act as some have done who have not grown rich by grinding the faces of poor needlewomen, or by stinting the wage of the servant behind the counter, but have lifted others up with them, and as they have advanced, those in their employment have advanced also. That is a something worth living for in the lower sphere of things. But he that becomes a servant of God is doing good all along, for there is no part of the service of God which can do any harm to anybody. The service of the Lord is all goodness. It is good for yourself, and it is good for your fellow-men; for what does God ask in his service but that we should love him with all our heart, and that we love our neighbour as ourselves? ·He who does this is truly serving God by the help of his Spirit, and he is also greatly blessing men. I say, it is a most beneficent work to engage in; and therefore it is that I commend it to you— for its reasonableness, its honourableness, and its beneficence.

And there is another thought. *It is the most remunerative work under heaven.* "Not always to-day," someone may say. Yet I venture to say, "Always to-day." To serve God is remunerative *now.* How so? Certainly not in hard cash, as misers rightly call their gold; but in better material. A quiet conscience is better than gold; and to know that you are doing good is something more sweet in life than to know that you are getting rich or famous. Have not some of us lived long enough to know that the greater part of the things of this world are so much froth upon the top of the cup, far better blown away than preserved? The chief joy of life is to be right with yourself, your neighbour, your God. And he that gets right with God—what more does he want? He is paid for anything that he may suffer in the cause of God by his own peace of mind. There was a martyr once in Switzerland standing barefooted on the fagots, and about to be burnt quick to the death—no pleasant prospect for him. He accosted the magistrate who was superintending his execution, and asked him to come near him. He said, "Will you please to lay your hand upon my heart. I am about to die by fire. Lay your hand on my heart. If it beats any faster than it ordinarily beats, do not believe my religion." The magistrate, with palpitating heart himself, and all in a tremble, laid his hand upon the martyr's bosom, and found that he was just as calm as if he was going to his bed rather than to the flames. That is a grand thing! To wear in your button-hole that little flower called "heart's-ease," and to have the jewel of contentment in your bosom—this is heaven begun below: godliness is great gain to him that hath it.

But, listen. I think that all that we can get in this world is paltry, because we must leave it, or it must leave us in a very short time. I am addressing now a congregation of young men. Young men—but in how very short a time, if you all live, will your hair be powdered with the grey of age! In how brief an interval will the whole company now gathered in Exeter Hall be gathered in the grave! How short life is! How swift is time! The older we get the faster years fly. That only is worth my having which I can have for ever. That only is worth my grasping which death cannot tear out of my hand. The supreme reward of being a servant of God is hereafter; and if, young man, you should serve God and you should meet with losses here for Christ's sake, you may count these "light afflictions which are but for a moment," and think them quite unworthy to be compared with the glory that shall be revealed; for there is a resurrection of the dead; there is a judgment to come; there is a life eternal; there is a heaven of unutterable splendour; there is a place in that heaven for everyone of us who become true servants of the living God.

I think that I hear somebody saying, "Well, I do not want to be a servant." You cannot help it, my friend: you cannot help it. *You must be a servant of somebody.* "Then I will serve myself," says one. Pardon me, brave sir, if I whisper in your ear that if you serve yourself you will serve a fool. The man who is the servant of himself—listen to this sentence—the man who is the servant of himself is the slave of a slave; and I cannot imagine a more degrading position for a man to be in than to be the slave of a slave. You will assuredly serve some-body. You will wear fetters, too, if you serve the master that most men choose. Oh, but look at this city—this city full of free men; do the most of them know real liberty? Look at this city full of "free-thinkers." Is there any man that thinks in chains like the man who calls himself a free-thinker? Is there any man so credulous as the man that will not believe the Bible? He swallows a ton of difficulties, and yet complains that we have swallowed an ounce of them. He has much more need of faith of a certain sort than we have, for scepticism has far harder problems than faith. And look at the free-liver, what a bondage is his life? "Who hath woe? who hath redness of eyes" but the slave of strong drink? Who has rottenness in the bones but the slave of his passions? Is there any wretch that ever tugged in the Spanish galley, or any bondsman beneath the sun, that is half such a slave as he who will be led to-night of his lusts like a bullock to the slaughter, going to his own damnation, and even to the ruin of his body, while he makes himself the victim of his own passions? If I must be a slave, I will be a slave to Turk or savage, but never to myself, for that were the nethermost abyss of degradation. You must be a servant to somebody; there is no getting through the world without it, and if you are the servant to yourself, your bondage will be terrible. "Choose you this day whom ye will serve," for serve ye must. Every man must get him to his task, whether he be peer or pauper, millionaire or beggar. Kings and queens are usually the most wearied servants of all. The higher men climb, the more they have to serve their fellow-men. You must serve. Oh, that you would enter the service of your God!

There is room in it. Other places are crowded. Hundreds of young men go from shop to shop, and beg for the opportunity to earn a livelihood; I lament that in many instances they beg in vain. Some of you wear the boots from off your feet in trying to get something to do: how anxiously do I desire that you may find the employment you seek! But there is room in the service of God, and he is willing to receive you. And let me tell you that, if you enter his service, *it will help you in everything that you have to do in this life.* They say that a Christian man is a fool. Ah! proud opposers, though we say not the same to you, we might, perhaps, with truth think so. I have seen many believers in Jesus whom it would have been very dangerous to deal with as with fools, for very soon he that dealt with them in that fashion would have found that he made a great mistake. They are not always fools who are called so; they are such sometimes who use those names. I like a Christian man to be all the better in every respect for being a Christian. He should be a better servant and a better master. He should be a better tradesman and a better artisan. Surely, there is no poet whose minstrelsy excels that of the poet of the sanctuary: Milton still sits alone. There is no painter that should paint so well as he who tries with his brush to make immortal the memorable scenes in which great deeds were done. That which you can now do well you might do better by becoming a servant of God.

Thus would I commend my Master's service with all my heart. Are there any here who will enlist in it? for, if so, I have a second point to dwell on very briefly. I lift the flag and bid you rally to it, but first hear me patiently.

II. My second point is A WORD OF CAUTION. Did you notice that

David said, " O Lord, *truly* I am thy servant." " Truly." The word of
caution is, If you become the servant of God, become the servant of
God *truly*. God is not mocked. It is the curse of our churches that we
have so many merely nominal Christians in them. It is the plague of
this age that so many put on Christ's livery, and yet never do him a
hand's turn. Oh, if you serve God, mean it! If a man serves the devil,
let him serve the devil; but if he serves God, let him serve God. Some
people serve their business very actively, but not their God. There was,
years ago, a brother who used to pray at the prayer-meeting occasionally
in a low tone, as if he had no lungs left. Seldom could you hear
what he said, and if you listened and strained your ear there was still
nothing to hear. I thought that the brother had a bad voice, and so
I never called on him to pray any more. But, stepping one day into his
shop, I heard him say in a commanding voice, " John, fetch that half-
hundred!" " Oh, dear ! " I thought, " that is the kind of voice he has in
his business, but when he comes into the service of God, that little squeak
is all he can give." Laugh again, sirs ! Laugh again ! It deserves to
be laughed at. But is there not much of this hypocrisy abroad ? God
is to have the cheese-parings of a man's life, and he flings these
down as if they were all that God was worth. But as for the world,
that is to have the vigour of his life and the cream of his being. God
does not want nominal servants; nor do I invite them in his name
to-night. " O Lord, truly I am thy servant," said David ; and he that
does not mean to be *truly* God's servant, let him not pretend to be one
at all.

If you would be God's servant, then *count the cost*. You must leave
all others. " Ye cannot serve God and mammon." Ye cannot serve
Christ and Belial. He is not God's who is not God's only.

You must enter upon God's service also *for life;* not to be sometimes
God's servant and sometimes not—off and on. Have you never heard
of the child who was asked by the district visitor, " Is your father a
Christian ?" The child replied, " Yes, sir, father is a Christian, but he
is not doing much at it just now." Oh, how many Christians there are
of that sort ! They profess to be Christians, but they are not doing
much at it. If you become the servant of God you must be his servant
every day and all the day for ever and ever.

> " 'Tis done, the great transaction's done :
> I am my Lord's, and he is mine,"

must be a covenant declaration which must stand true throughout the
entire life. And if you become the servant of God *you must cease from
every known sin*. You cannot give one hand to Christ and another to
Satan. You must give up the dearest sins. Sweet sin must become bitter.
If sins are like right hands or right eyes they must be cut off or plucked
out, and you must follow Christ fully, giving him all your heart, and
soul, and strength ; for if it be not so, you cannot be his disciple.
So much by way of caution. I am very brief on that, but take it as
though it were said at length.

III. I want now to offer COUNSEL IN THE MATTER OF DISTINCT
CONFESSION IF YOU BECOME THE SERVANT OF CHRIST. " I am thy

servant," says David ; and then he puts it over again, "I *am* thy servant."

Now, I want every young man here who is a Christian to make it known by an open avowal of his discipleship. I mean that there should not be one among us who follows the Lord Jesus Christ in a mean, sneaking, indistinct, questionable way. It has become the custom of many to try to be Christians and never say anything about it. This is beneath contempt. But I urge you true servants of Christ to "out with it," and never to be ashamed, because if ever a bold profession was required it is required now. You may not be burned at the stake for saying that you are a Christian, but I believe that the old enmity to Christ is not removed, and a true believer will still be called upon to take up the cross. In many a house in London a young man will have to run the gauntlet if he is known to be a Christian. Run the gauntlet, then ! You have an honourable opportunity. It is a grand thing to be permitted to endure reproach for Christ's sake ; and you should look at it as a choice privilege that you are counted worthy not only to believe in the Lord Jesus Christ, but also to suffer for his sake. Nowadays the world wants decided men. Everywhere it seems to be imagined that you may believe what you like, or believe nothing ; and do as you like, or do nothing, and the result will be all the same both to the unbeliever and the man of faith. But it is not so. It is time for the out-and-out servant of the Lord to put down his foot and say, "I have believed ; therefore have I spoken. I am a Christian, and while I leave you to your individual liberty I mean to have mine, and I mean to exercise that liberty by being openly and unquestionably on the side of Christ, and on the side of that which is pure, and sober, and right, and true, and good."

Is not this well deserved by Christ? Oh, if he never was ashamed of us we never ought to be ashamed of him ! If the Lord of life and glory stooped to die for us, could we ever stoop at all even if we rolled into the mire or dropped into the grave for him ? Surely, our blessed Lord deserves to be followed by heroes. Every man in the presence of the cross-bearing Jesus should feel that to take up his cross and follow Christ is the simplest and most natural thing that can be; and he should resolve in God's strength that he will do it, and continue to obey the Lord, though all the world should ridicule. Let me tell you that *it is the easiest thing* to do, after all : as compared with compromise it is simplicity itself. I have known many young Christians that have come up to London, and they have determined that they would serve God if they could, but that they would keep it very quiet, and so they have attempted to be Christians on the sly : but they have failed. If you are a genuine Christian it will be found out as surely as you are a living man. If you go down to Mitcham when the lavender is ripe, you may shut all your windows, but you will find that the perfume of the lavender will get into your house somehow. Christianity has a perfume about it which will spread abroad, so that all in the house enquire, "What is all this?" The wicked wags will whisper that you are "a Christian young man"; and if you have not come out at first it will be very hard for you afterwards. Begin as you mean to go on, young man. Do not hide your flag and try to sail under false colours, for both good and bad will be against you in that case. You will be hunted from place to place if the dogs find that you will run : you will make rare sport for the hunters if you take to your heels. Come straight out and let them do their best or their worst. Live a most consistent life, and the other young fellows will know whereabouts you are. They will soon reckon you up, and if you are sincere before long they will let you alone : and if they do not, forbearance is still yours. If they continue to persecute you, so much the worse *for them;* for you, by your quiet, holy life, will make them feel that it is hard for them to kick against the pricks. But, anyhow, do come out bravely. Some of you young fellows are like rats behind the wainscot : you do not mind coming out of a night to eat the crumbs on the floor, but there you are, back again directly : I mean that you will join in religious exercises if it is not known to the shop, but you would not for the world become suspected of real religion. Is that how true Christians should act? No; put on your livery. "But I do not care about joining a church," says one. Very likely; but do you not know that it is found to be a convenient and proper thing in warfare that a soldier should wear regimentals? At first Oliver Cromwell's Ironsides were dressed any-how and everyhow; but in the *mêlée* with the Cavaliers it sometimes happened that an Ironside was struck down by mistake by the sword of one of his own brethren, and so the general said, "You wear red coats, all of you. We must know our own men from the enemy." What Cromwell said he meant, and they had to come in their red coats, for it is found essential in warfare that men should be known by some kind of regimental. Now, you that are Christ's, do not go about as if you were ashamed of his Majesty's service. Put on your red coats : I mean come out as acknowledged Christians. Unite with a body of Christian people, and be distinctly known to be Christ's. How are the ordinances of the Lord's house to be sustained if every man is to go to heaven alone by the back way? Come out boldly. If any man wants to laugh at a Christian, step out, and say, "Laugh at me. If anybody wants to abuse a fellow, and call him a hypocrite, a Presbyterian, a Methodist, come on! I am ready for you." If you have once done that, and come right out on the straight, you shall find it the easiest thing in life to bear the reproach of Christ.

And oh, remember, young men, that if you should meet with any reproach for Christ, *a reward awaits you.* Shall I tell you a parable? There was once a king's son who went upon a journey incognito, and he journeyed into a far country, but there he was ill-treated, and because of his language and his appearance the people of the land set him in the pillory, which was of old the place of scorn. They set him there, and the mob gathered round him, and threw all kinds of filth and ordure upon him. This prince unknown must needs be pelted thus, and made as the offscouring of all things. But there was among them one man who loved the prince, and who recognized him, and determined to bear him company. He mounted the pillory and stood by his side, and wiped his face with his handkerchief, and whenever he could he put himself in the way of the mire and dirt that he might catch it and screen the prince from it. Years went on, and it came to pass that the prince was back in his kingdom in all his glory, and the courtiers were standing

round about the throne. This man who had been a poor man in his
own country was summoned to the court, and when he arrived at the
palace, the prince saw him, and said to the peers of the realm, "Stand
aside and make way for this man. He was with me when I was ill-
treated and scorned, and now he shall be with me in my glory, chief
among you here." Do you not know the story of how our sweet Lord
Jesus came down to earth and suffered many things, and how he was
despised and rejected of men? Young man, are you the man who
would wipe his blessed face and share his shame, and take half turns
with the man of Nazareth in all the obloquy and scorn? Are you that
man? Then there shall come a day when the great Father on his throne
shall spy you out and say, "Make a lane, ye angels! Stand back,
seraphim and cherubim! Make way for this man. He was with my Son
in his humiliation, and now he shall be with him in his glory." Will
you receive that mark of honour? Not unless you are prepared to
put on the badge of Christ, and say, "I am his servant and his
follower from this day to life's end." God help you to do it! O Holy
Spirit, lead scores of young men now to shoulder the cross!

IV. And so, lest I weary you, I CLOSE BY CONGRATULATING SOME
OF YOU who are God's servants UPON YOUR FREEDOM, for that is the
last part of the text. "Truly I am thy servant; I am thy servant, and
the son of thine handmaid: *thou hast loosed my bonds.*"

Oh, but this is a grand thing—this loosing of the bonds. Were you
ever in bonds? Did you ever feel *the bonds of guilt?* Are you
believing in Christ: then those bonds are loosed, for your sin is forgiven
you for Christ's sake, and you are delivered from all condemnation.
Oh, will you not love him who has loosed your bonds? Were you,
dear friend, ever in *the bonds of despondency* and despair on account
of sin? Did you ever sit and sigh because you thought that there was
no salvation for you? And did the Lord Jesus Christ appear to you as
your crucified Saviour? And did you trust in him, and feel the bonds
of despondency broken? Happy day for you! I remember it well
myself. Oh, then, will you not follow him that has loosed your bonds?
Now, you are clean delivered from the bonds of guilt and despair, you
are also saved from *the power of sin.* The habits that were your masters
are now destroyed. The lusts that lorded it over you are now slain;
and you are free. Will you not wish to be bound to Christ henceforth
because he has loosed your bonds? I know some men in this world
who talk a great deal about being free, but they are always in chains.
There is a man I know for whom the devil makes a nauseous mixture;
at least, to me it is very nauseous; and he says, "Drink a quart of it;"
and he drinks. "Drink another," says the devil; and he does so.
"Drink another," says the devil; and his brain begins to reel, and he
is all on fire. "Drink it," says the devil; and he lets it run down his
throat, for he is in chains. I know another who, against his better
self, will go into sin, which he knows to be sin, and knows to be
injurious to him. Yet he goes in a silly manner and harms himself
more and more. He is led by the nose by the devil, and he says that
he cannot resist. He is a slave in the worst sense. Oh, blessed is the
man who can say, "Thou hast loosed my bonds: no evil habit enslaves
me now, no passion controls me, no lust enchains me!" Young friend, if

you can stand up and say, "I am free from myself: I am no longer the slave of sin!"—you are a blessed man, and you may well be God's servant for ever!

What a mercy it is to be delivered from *the bonds of the fear of man!* Some young men dare not call their souls their own for fear of their employers. A great many more are dreadfully in fear of the young man who sleeps in the next bed. Oh, dear, they dare not do what is right! Poor babies that they are, they must ask permission to keep a conscience! When they are about to do anything they are always saying, "What will So-and-so think of it?" Does it matter to any true man what all the world thinks about him? Has he not risen out of that? Is he still a serf? "Go," says the brave man; "think what you will, and say what you will. If I serve God, I am no servant of yours; by your censures I shall not fall, as by your praises I shall not rise." Be afraid of such a thing as I myself, and ask the leave of another man what I shall think, what I shall believe, what I shall do! I will die first! When God brings a man to know himself, and to be his servant, he sets him free from this cowardly crime of being afraid of a man that shall die.

So, too, he sets him free from all *the maxims and customs of the world.* Young man, when you go into business, they will tell you that you must do so-and-so, because it is "the custom of the trade." "Why," say you, "it is lying!" You will be told that it is not exactly lying, because your customer is used to your tricks, and quite understands that a hundred means eighty, and the best quality means a second-class article. I am told that half the business in London is robbery in some form or another if the customs of the trade are not understood. If it be so that it is all understood, it might just as well be done honestly for the matter of that, and it would pay as well. Yet, somehow, men feel as if they must do what others have done, or else they will be out of the race. Slaves! Serfs! Be honest! He is not free that dares not be honest. Shall I not speak my mind? Shall I not act out my integrity? If I cannot, then I cannot say with David, "Thou hast loosed my bonds."

Lastly, what a blessing it is when God frees us from *the fear of death!* "Thou hast loosed my bonds." What will it matter to you, young man, if you become the servant of God by faith in Jesus Christ whether you live or die? If you die early, so much the sooner in heaven. If you live long, so much the longer in which to serve your God on earth. Give your heart to Christ; trust your salvation in those dear hands that were pierced for sinners; thus become the servant of God, and you shall be provided for, for his children shall not lack. You shall be led, guided, taught, educated, prepared for heaven; and one of these bright days a convoy of celestial spirits shall think it an honour to be permitted to bear your joyful spirit up to the throne of God.

Who will be the servant of the Most High, then? I always wish when I have done with sermons that I could preach them over again, because I have not done well enough; but all I care to preach for is that I may touch your hearts. I would not care a snap of the fingers to be an orator, or to put sentences prettily. I want to put the truth so that some young man will say, "I will serve God." I remember young men that began life when I began, that are now—I will not say what. Ah! I remember hearing their names mentioned as models, they were such fine young men, and had just gone up to London. Yes, and they are to-night, if not in jail, in the workhouse. It all came about in this way: the young man sent word home to his mother what the text was on the Sunday, yet he had not been to hear a sermon at all. He had been to some amusement, to spend a happy day: wherever he went he had neglected the house of God; and by-and-by there was a little wrong in his small accounts—just a little matter; but that man could not pick himself up again, once having lost his character. There was another. There was nothing wrong in his accounts, but his habits were loose. By-and-by he was ill. Who could wonder? When a man plays with edged tools he is very likely to cut himself. It was not long before he was so sickly that he could not attend to business, and ere long he died; and they said—I fear it was true—that he killed himself by vice. And that is how thousands do in London. Oh, if you become the servant of God this will not happen to you! You may not be rich; you may not be famous; you may not be great: you need not want these things. They are gilded vanities full often. But to be a man—to the fulness of your manhood; to be free and dare to look every other man in the world in the face, and speak the truth, and do the right; to be a man that can look God in the face because Christ has covered him with his glorious righteousness—this is the ambition with which I would fire the spirit of every young man before me; and I pray God that the flame may burn in his life by the power of the divine Spirit. Come then, brethren, bow your heads and say, "We will be servants of the living God henceforth and for ever." God grant it, for Jesus Christ's sake. Amen and Amen.

PORTION OF SCRIPTURE READ BEFORE SERMON—Psalm cxvi.

HYMNS FROM "OUR OWN HYMN BOOK"—416, 562, 555.

Sermons in Candles
$3.75. SBC rate, $2.50

He once made the remark to his students that a preacher could find enough illustrations in a single tallow candle to last six months. They did not show too much faith in this, so Mr. Spurgeon set out to prove his point. The result: this little book, using candles as a basis for many valuable lessons of practical and spiritual importance. You-'ll be held in rapt attention.

Metropolitan Tabernacle Pulpit.

"LET NOT YOUR HEART BE TROUBLED."

A Sermon

DELIVERED ON LORD'S-DAY MORNING, SEPTEMBER 23RD, 1883, BY

C. H. SPURGEON,

AT THE METROPOLITAN TABERNACLE, NEWINGTON.

"Let not your heart be troubled: ye believe in God, believe also in me. In my Father's house are many mansions: if it were not so, I would have told you. I go to prepare a place for you. And if I go and prepare a place for you, I will come again, and receive you unto myself; that where I am, there ye may be also. And whither I go ye know, and the way ye know."—John xiv. 1—4.

WE may well feel glad that God's people, whose lives are recorded in the Old and New Testaments, were men of like passions with ourselves. I have known many a poor sinner pluck up hope as he has observed the sins and struggles of those who were saved by grace, and I have known many of the heirs of heaven find consolation as they have observed how imperfect beings like themselves have prevailed with God in prayer, and have been delivered in their time of distress. I am very glad that the apostles were not perfect men; they would then have understood all that Jesus said at once, and we should have lost our Lord's instructive explanations; they would also have lived above all trouble of mind, and then the Master would not have said to them these golden words, "Let not your heart be troubled."

It is, however, most evident from our text that it is not according to our Lord's mind that any of his servants should be troubled in heart. He takes no delight in the doubt and disquietude of his people. When he saw that because of what he had said to them sorrow had filled the hearts of his apostles, he pleaded with them in great love, and besought them to be comforted. As when a mother comforteth her child, he cried, "Let not your heart be troubled." Jesus saith the same to you, my friend, if you are one of his downcast ones. He would not have you sad. "Comfort ye, comfort ye my people; speak ye comfortably to Jerusalem," is a command even of the old dispensation, and I am quite sure that under this clearer revelation the Lord would have his people free from heartbreak. Has not the Holy Ghost especially undertaken the work of comfort in order that it may be effectually done? Trials depress the hearts of God's children, for which the most tender ministry fails to afford consolation; and then it is most sweet for the failing comforter to remember the unfailing Comforter, and to commit the case of the sorrowful spirit into the divine hands. Seeing that one Person of the blessed Trinity

No. 1,741.

has undertaken to be the Comforter, we see how important it is that our hearts should be filled with consolation. Happy religion in which it is our duty to be glad! Blessed gospel by which we are forbidden to be troubled in heart!

Is it not a thing greatly to be admired that the Lord Jesus should think so carefully of his friends at such a time? Great personal sorrows may well be an excuse if the griefs of others are somewhat overlooked. Jesus was going to his last bitter agony, and to death itself, and yet he overflowed with sympathy for his followers. Had it been you or I, we should have asked for sympathy for ourselves. Our cry would have been, "Have pity upon me, O my friends, for the hand of God hath touched me!" But, instead of that, our Lord cast his own crushing sorrows into the background, and bent his mind to the work of sustaining his chosen under their far inferior griefs. He knew that he was about to be "exceeding sorrowful, even unto death"; he knew that he should soon be in an agony through bearing "the chastisement of our peace;" but ere he plunged into the deep, he must needs dry the tears of those he loved so well, and therefore he said most touchingly, "Let not your heart be troubled."

While I admire this condescending tenderness of love, I at the same time cannot help adoring the marvellous confidence of our blessed Lord, who, though he knows that he is to be put to a shameful death, yet feels no fear, but bids his disciples trust implicitly to him. The black darkness of the awful midnight was beginning to surround him, yet how brave his word—"Believe also in me!" He knew in that threatening hour that he had come forth from the Father, and that he was in the Father and the Father in him; and so he says, "Ye believe in God, believe also in me." The calm bearing of their Master must have greatly tended to confirm his servants in their faith.

While we see here his confidence as man, we also feel that this is not a speech which a mere man would ever have uttered had he been a good man; for no mere creature would thus match himself with God. That Jesus is a good man few question; that he must be God is therefore proven by these words. Would Jesus bid us trust in an arm of flesh? Is it not written—"Cursed be the man that trusteth in man, and maketh flesh his arm"? Yet the Holy Jesus says, "Ye believe in God, believe also in me." This association of himself with God as the object of human confidence in the time of trouble, betokens a consciousness of his own divine power and Godhead; and it is a mystery in whose difficulties faith takes pleasure, to see in our Lord Jesus the faith of a man for himself, and the faithfulness of God for others.

Come then, dear friends, close up to the text, and may the Spirit of God be with us! I will read the text again very distinctly. Ask that you may feel the words even more powerfully than the apostles felt them; for they had not yet received the Comforter, and so they were not yet led into all truth; in this we excel them as they were that night: let us therefore hopefully pray that we may know the glory of our Lord's words, and hear them spoken into our very soul by the Holy Spirit. "Let not your heart be troubled: ye believe in God, believe also in me. In my Father's house are many mansions: if it were not so, I would have told you. I go to prepare a place for you. And if I go and prepare a place for you, I will come again, and receive you unto myself; that where I am, there ye may be also. And whither I go ye know, and the way ye know."

These words are in themselves much better than any sermon. What can our discourse be but a dilution of the essential spirit of consolation which is contained in the words of the Lord Jesus? Now let us, first, *taste of the bitter waters of heart-trouble;* and, secondly, let us *drink deep of the sweet waters of divine consolation.*

I. First, then, LET US TASTE OF THE BITTER WATERS. "Because I have said these things unto you, sorrow hath filled your heart." I would not confine the comfort to any one form of affliction, for it is a balm for every wound; but still it will be well to enquire what was the particular trouble of the disciples? It may be that some of us are passing through it now, or we may be plunged in it ere long.

It was this—*Jesus was to die:* their Lord, whom they sincerely loved, was about to go from them by a shameful, painful death. What tender heart could bear to think of that? Yet he had told them that it would be so, and they began to remember his former words wherein he had said that the Son of man would be betrayed into the hands of wicked men, and would be scourged and put to death. They were now to pass through all the bitterness of seeing him accused, condemned, and crucified. In a short time he was actually seized, bound, carried to the high priest's house, hurried to Pilate, then to Herod, back again to Pilate, stripped, scourged, mocked, insulted. They saw him conducted through the streets of Jerusalem bearing his cross. They beheld him hanging on the tree between two thieves, and heard him cry, "My God, my God, why hast thou forsaken me?" A bitter draught this! In proportion as they loved their Lord they must have deeply grieved for him: and they needed that he should say, "Let not your heart be troubled." To-day those who love the Lord Jesus have to behold a spiritual repetition of his shameful treatment at the hands of men; for even now he is crucified afresh by those who account his cross a stumbling-block and the preaching of it foolishness. Ah me! how is Christ still misunderstood, misrepresented, despised, mocked, and rejected of men! They cannot touch him really, for there he sits enthroned in the heaven of heavens; but as far as they can, they slay him over again. A malignant spirit is manifested to the gospel as once it was to Christ in person. Some with coarse blasphemies, and not a few with cunning assaults upon this part of Scripture, and on that, are doing their best to bruise the heel of the seed of the woman. It is a huge grief to see the mass of mankind pass by the cross with averted eyes as if the Saviour's death was nothing—nothing at least to them. In proportion as you feel a zeal for the Crucified, and for his saving truth, it is wormwood and gall to live in this age of unbelief. Christ Jesus is nailed up between the two thieves of superstition and unbelief, while around him gathers still the fierce opposition of the rude and the polished, the ignorant and the wise.

In addition to this, the apostles had for an outlook the expectation that *their Lord would be away from them.* They did not at first understand his saying, " A little while, and ye shall not see me: and again, a little while, and ye shall see me, because I go to the Father." Now it dawned upon them that they were to be left as sheep without a shepherd; for their Master and head was to be taken from them. This was to them a source of dread and dismay: for they said to themselves, " What shall we do without him? We are a little flock; how shall we be defended when he is gone, and the wolf is prowling? When the Scribes and Pharisees gather about us, how shall we answer them? As for our Lord's cause and kingdom, how can it be safe in such trembling hands as ours? Alas for the gospel of salvation when Jesus is not with us!" This was a bitter sorrow: and something of this kind of feeling often crosses our own hearts as we tremble for the ark of the Lord. My heart is sad when I see the state of religion among us. Oh for an hour of the Son of man in these darkening days! It is written, " There shall come in the last days scoffers "; and they have come, but, oh, that the Lord himself were here in person! Oh, that the Lord would pluck his right hand out of his bosom, and show us once again the wonders of Pentecost, to the confusion of his adversaries, and to the delight of all his friends. He has not come as yet! Well-nigh two thousand years have rolled away since he departed, and the night is dark, and there is no sign of dawn. The ship of the church is tossed with tempest, and Jesus is not come unto us. We know that he is with us in a spiritual sense; but, oh, that we had him in the glory of his power! Surely he knows our need and the urgency of the times; yet are we apt to cry, " It is time for thee, Lord, to work; for they make void thy law."

But they felt a third grief, and it was this: that *he was to be betrayed by one of themselves.* The twelve were chosen men, but one of them was a devil and sold his Lord. This pierced the hearts of the faithful—" the Son of man is betrayed." He is not taken by open seizure, but he is sold for thirty pieces of silver by one whom he entrusted with his little store. He that dipped with him in the dish had sold him for paltry gain. This cut them to the heart, even as it did the Master himself; for our Lord felt the treachery of his friend. Of this bitter water the faithful at this hour are made to drink: for what see we at this day? What see we in various places but persons that are reputed to be ministers of the gospel whose main business seems to be to undermine our holy faith, and batter down the truths which are commonly received in the Christian church? Certain of them preach as if they were ordained not of God, but of the devil; and anointed not by the Holy Spirit, but by the spirit of infidelity. Under the banner of "advanced thought," they make war upon those eternal truths for which confessors contended and martyrs bled, and by which the saints of past ages have been sustained in their dying hours. It is not an enemy; then we could have borne and answered it. If the outward and avowed infidel attacks inspiration, let him do so. It is a free country, let him speak; but when a man enters our pulpits, opens the sacred volume, and denies that it is inspired, what does he there? How does his conscience allow him to assume an office which he perverts? To make him a shepherd who is a wolf; to make him a dresser of the vineyard who, with his axe, cuts up the very roots of the vines;—this is an incomprehensible folly on the part of the churches. It is a dagger to every believing heart that Judas should be represented in the Christian church by so many of the professed ministers of Christ. They betray their Master with a kiss.

Then there came another pang at the back of this; for one of them, though true-hearted and loyal, would that night *deny his Lord.* Peter, in many respects the leader of the little company, had been warned that he would act the craven and vehemently deny his Lord. This is bitterness indeed, of which those that love the church of God are compelled full often to drink, to see men whom we cannot but believe to be the disciples of Jesus Christ carried away by temptation, by fear of man, or by the fashion of the times, so that Christ and his gospel are virtually denied by them. The fear of being thought dogmatic or puritanic closes many a mouth which ought to be declaring him to be the Son of God with power, and extolling his glorious majesty in defiance of all that dare oppose him. The hearts of some who best love Jesus grow heavy at the sight of the worldliness and lukewarmness of many of his professed followers. Hence it seems to me to be a most seasonable hour for introducing you to the sweet waters of our text, of which I bid you drink till every trace of bitterness is gone from your mouth: for the Master saith to you, even to you, "Let not your heart be troubled: ye believe in God, believe also in me."

II. Under our second head LET US DRINK OF THE SWEET WATERS and refresh our souls.

First, in this wonderful text our Master indicates to us the true means of comfort under every sort of disquietude. How puts he it? " Let not your heart be troubled "—*believe.* Kindly look down your Bibles, and you will see that this direction is repeated. He says in the opening of the eleventh verse, " Believe me"; and then, again, in the second clause, " Believe me." I thought as I tried to enter into the meaning of this sacred utterance that I heard Jesus at my side saying thrice to me, "Believe me! believe me! believe me!" Could any one of the eleven that were with him have disbelieved their present Lord? He says, " Believe me! believe me! believe me!"—as if there was great need to urge them to faith in him. Is there no other cure, then, for a troubled heart? No other is required. This is all-sufficient through God. If believing in Jesus you still are troubled, believe in him again yet more thoroughly and heartily. If even that should not take away the perturbation of your mind, believe in him to a third degree, and continue to do so with increasing simplicity and force. Regard this as the one and only physic for the disease of fear and trouble. Jesus prescribes, " Believe, believe, believe in *me!* " Believe not only in certain doctrines, but in Jesus himself—in him as able to carry out every promise that he has made. Believe in him as you believe in God. One has been at times apt to think it easier to believe in Jesus than in God, but this is a thought of spiritual infancy; more advanced believers find it not so. To a Jew this was certainly the right way of putting it, and I think to us Gentiles it is so also, when we have been long in the faith; for we get to believe in God as a matter of course, and faith in Jesus requires a further confidence. I believe in God's power in creation: he can make what he wills, and shape what he has made. I believe in his power in providence, that he can bring to pass his eternal purposes, and do as he wills among the armies in heaven and among the inhabitants of this lower world. I believe concerning God that all things are possible unto him.　Just in that way I am called upon to believe in Jesus that he is as omnipotent in power and as sure in his working as the Lord from whom come all the forces of nature; and just as certain to accomplish his purposes as God is to achieve his design in the works of providence.　Relying upon the Saviour with the implicit faith which every right-minded man renders towards God, we shall only give our Lord the faith which he justly claims.　He is faithful and true, and his power can effect his promise: let us depend trustfully upon him, and perfect peace shall come into our hearts.　These disciples knew that the Saviour was to be away from them, so that they could not see him nor hear his voice.　What of that?　Is it not so with God, in whom we believe?　"No man hath seen God at any time"—yet you believe in the invisible God working all things, sustaining all things.　In the same manner believe in the absent and invisible Christ, that he is still as mighty as though you could see him walking the waves, or multiplying the loaves, or healing the sick, or raising the dead.　Believe him, and sorrow and sighing will flee away.

Believe in him as ever living, even as you believe in the eternity of God.　You believe in the eternal existence of the Most High whom you have not seen, even so believe in the everlasting life of the Son of God. Ay, though you see him die, though you see him laid in the grave, yet believe in him that he has not ceased to be.　Look for his reappearance, even as ye believe in God.　Yea, and when he is gone from you, and a cloud has received him out of your sight, believe that he liveth, even as God liveth; and because he lives, you shall live also.　You believe in the wisdom of God, you believe in the faithfulness of God, you believe in the goodness of God; "Even as ye believe in God," saith Jesus, "believe also in me."　Faith in Jesus Christ himself as an ever-living and divine Person, is the best quietus for every kind of fear.　He is the "King Eternal, Immortal, Invisible," "the Wonderful, Counsellor, the mighty God, the everlasting Father, the Prince of Peace;" and therefore you may safely rest in him.　This is the first ingredient of this priceless comfort.

But now our Lord proceeded to say that though he was going from them *he was only going to his Father's house.*　"In my Father's house are many mansions."　Ay, but this was sweet comfort.　"I am going," said he, "and on my way you will see me scourged, bleeding, mocked, and buffeted; but I shall pass through all this to the joy and rest, and honour of my Father's house."　God is everywhere present, and yet as on earth he had a tabernacle wherein he specially manifested himself, so there is a place where he in a peculiar manner is revealed.　The temple was a type of that matchless abode of God which eye hath not seen; we call it heaven, the pavilion of God, the home of holy angels and of those pure spirits who dwell in his immediate presence.　In heaven God may be said in special to have his habitation, and Jesus was going there to be received on his return to all the honour which awaited his finished service.　He was, in fact, going home, as a son who is returning to his father's house, from which he had gone upon his father's business.　He was going where he would be with the Father, where he would be perfectly at rest, where he would be above the assaults of the wicked ; where he would never suffer or die again ; he was going to reassume the glory which he had with the Father or ever the world was. Oh, if they had perfectly understood this, they would have understood the Saviour's words, " If ye loved me, ye would rejoice, because I said, I go unto the Father." Imagination fails to picture the glory of our Lord's return, the honourable escort which heralded his approach to the Eternal City, the heartiness of the welcome of the Conqueror to the skies. I think the Psalmist gives us liberty to believe that, when our Lord ascended, the bright ones of the sky came to meet him, and cried, " Lift up your heads, O ye gates; and be ye lift up, ye everlast- ing doors; and the King of glory shall come in." May we not believe of bright seraphs and ministering angels that—

> " They brought his chariot from on high
>   To bear him to his throne;
>   Clapped their triumphant wings, and cried,
>   ' The glorious work is done.' "

"He was seen of angels." They beheld that " joyous re-entry," the opening of the eternal doors to the King of Glory, and the triumph through the celestial streets of him who led captivity captive and scat- tered gifts among men. They saw the enthronement of Jesus who was made a little lower than the angels for the suffering of death, but was then and there crowned with glory and honour. These are not things of which these stammering lips of mine can speak, but they are things for you to consider when the Spirit of the Lord is upon you. Muse upon them for your delectation.

Jesus has gone by the way of Calvary up to his Father's house: all his work and warfare done, he is rewarded for his sojourn among men as man. All the shame which his work necessitated is now lost in the splendour of his mediatorial reign. Ye people of God, be no more troubled, for your Lord is King, your Saviour reigns! Men may still scoff at him, but they cannot rob him of a ray of glory! They may reject him, but the Lord God omnipotent has crowned him! They may deny his existence, but he lives! They may rebelliously cry, " Let us break his bands asunder, and cast his cords from us," but the Lord hath set his King upon his holy hill of Zion, and none can thrust him from his throne. Hallelujah! "God hath highly exalted him, and given him a name which is above every name : that at the name of Jesus every knee should bow." Wherefore let not your hearts be troubled by the noise of controversy, and the blasphemy and rebuke of an evil age. Though there be confusion as when the sea roareth and the fulness thereof, and the wicked foam in their rage against the Lord and against his anointed, yet the Lord sitteth upon the flood, the Lord sitteth King for ever. Again let us say, " Hallelujah! " The Prince hath come unto his own again; he hath entered into his Father's palace; the heavens have received him. Why should we be troubled ?

Thirdly, our Lord gave his servants comfort in another way : *he gave them to understand by implication that a great many would follow him to the Father's house.* He did not only assure them that he was going to his Father's house, but he said, " In my Father's house are many man- sions." These mansions are not built to stand empty. God doeth nothing in vain; therefore it is natural to conclude that a multitude of spirits, innumerable beyond all count, will rise in due time to occupy those many mansions in the Father's house. Now I see in this great comfort to them, because they doubtless feared that if their Lord was absent his kingdom might fail. How would there be converts if he were crucified? How could they expect, poor creatures as they were, to set up a kingdom of righteousness on the earth? How could they turn the world upside down and bring multitudes to his feet whom he had purchased with his blood, if his conquering right arm was not seen at their head? The Lord Jesus in effect said, "I am going, but I shall lead the way for a vast host who will come to the prepared abodes. Like the corn of wheat which is cast into the ground to die, I shall bring forth much fruit, which shall be housed in the abiding resting-places." This is one part of our comfort at this hour. Little boots it how men fight against the gospel, for the Lord knoweth them that are his, and he will ransom by power those redeemed by blood. He has a multitude according to the election of grace whom he will bring in. Though they seem to-day to be a small remnant, yet he will fill the many mansions. This stands fast as a rock—"All that the Father giveth me shall come to me; and him that cometh to me I will in no wise cast out." They boast that "they will not come unto Christ;" but the Spirit of God foresaw that they would reject the salvation of the Lord. What said Jesus to those like them? "Ye believe not, because ye are not of my sheep, as I said unto you. My sheep hear my voice, and I know them, and they follow me: and I give unto them eternal life." The wicked unbelief of men is their own condemnation; but Jesus loses not the reward of his passion. We fling back into the faces of the despisers of Christ the scorn which they pour upon him, and remind them that those who despise him shall be lightly esteemed, their names shall be written in the earth. What if *they* come not to him? it is their own loss, and well did he say of them, "No man can come to me except the Father which hath sent me draw him." Their wickedness is their inability and their destruction. They betray by their opposition the fact that they are not the chosen of the Most High. But "the redeemed of the Lord shall come to Zion with songs and everlasting joy upon their heads." "He shall see of the travail of his soul, and shall be satisfied." This matter is not left to the free will of man, so that Jesus may be disappointed after all. Oh no, "they will not come unto him, that they may have life;" but they shall yet know that the eternal Spirit has power over the human conscience and will, and can make men willing in the day of his power. If Jesus be lifted up he will draw all men unto him. There shall be no failure as to the Lord's redeeming work, even though the froward reject the counsel of God against themselves. What Jesus has bought with blood he will not lose; what he died to accomplish shall surely be performed; and what he rose again to carry out shall be effected though all the devils in hell and unbelievers upon earth should join in league against him. Oh, thou enemy, rejoice not over the cause of the Messiah; for though it seem to fall it shall arise again!

But our Lord went much further, for he said, "*I go to prepare a place for you.*" I think he did not only refer to the many mansions for our spirits, but to the ultimate *place* of our risen bodies, of which I will speak before long. In our Lord's going away, as well as in his continuance in his Father's presence he would be engaged in preparing a place for his own. He was going that he might clear all impediment out of the way. Their sins blocked the road; like mountains their iniquities opposed all passage; but now that he is gone, it may be said, "The breaker is come up before them, and the Lord on the head of them." He hath broken down every wall of partition, and every iron gate he hath opened. The way into the kingdom is opened for all believers. He passed through death to resurrection and ascension to remove every obstacle from our path.

He went from us also to fulfil every condition: for it was absolutely needful that all who entered heaven should wear a perfect righteousness, and should be made perfect in character, seeing no sin can enter the holy city. Now the saints could not be perfected without being washed in his precious blood, and renewed by the Holy Spirit; and so the Saviour endured the death of the cross; and when he arose he sent us the sanctifying Spirit, that we might be fitted for his rest. Thus he may be said to have prepared the place of our rest by removing from its gateway the sin which blocked all entrance.

He went away also that he might be in a position to secure that place for all his people. He entered the glory-land as our Forerunner, to occupy the place in our name, to take possession of heaven as the representative of all his people. He was going that he might in heaven itself act as Intercessor, pleading before the throne, and therefore be able to save to the uttermost all that come to God by him. He was going there to assume the reins of Providence, having all things put under his feet, and having all power given to him in heaven and in earth he might bless his people abundantly. By being in heaven our Lord occupies a vantage-ground for the sure accomplishing of his purposes of love. As Joseph went down into Egypt to store the granaries, to prepare for Israel a home in Goshen, and to sit upon the throne for their protection, so hath our Lord gone away into the glory for our good, and he is doing for us upon his throne what could not so advantageously have been done for us here.

At the same time, I am inclined to think that there is a special sense in these words over and above the preparing of heaven for us. I think our Lord Jesus meant to say, "I go to prepare a place for you" in this sense—that there would in the end be a place found for their entire manhood. Mark that word, "*a place*." We are too apt to entertain cloudy ideas of the ultimate inheritance of those who attain unto the resurrection of the dead. "Heaven is a state," says somebody. Yes, certainly, it is a state; but it is *a place* too, and in the future it will be more distinctly a place. Observe that our blessed Lord went away in body; not as a disembodied spirit, but as one who had eaten with his disciples, and whose body had been handled by them. His body needed a "*place*," and he is gone to prepare a place for us, not only as we shall be for a while, pure spirits, but as we are to be ultimately—body, and soul, and spirit. When a child of God dies, where does his spirit go? There is no question about that matter: we are informed by the inspired apostle—"absent from the body, present with the Lord." But that is a spiritual matter, and something yet remains. My spirit is not the whole of myself, for I am taught so to respect my body as to regard it as a precious portion of my complete self—the temple of God. The Lord Jesus Christ did not redeem my spirit alone, but my body too, and consequently he means to have a "place" where I, this person who is here, in the wholeness of my individuality, may rest for ever. Jesus means to have a place made for the entire manhood of his chosen, that they may be where he is and as he is. Our ultimate abode will be a state of blessedness, but it must also be *a place* suited for our risen bodies. It is not, therefore, a cloud-land, an airy something, impalpable and dreamy. Oh, no, it will be as really a place as this earth is a place. Our glorious Lord has gone for the ultimate purpose of preparing a suitable place for his people. There will be a place for their spirits, if spirits want place; but he has gone to prepare a place for them as body, soul, and spirit. I delight to remember that Jesus did not go as a spirit, but in his risen body, bearing the scars of his wounds. Come, you that think you will never rise again, you who imagine that the scattering of our dust forbids all hope of the restoration of our bodies; we shall go where Christ has gone, and as he has gone. He leads the way in his body, and we shall follow in ours. Ultimately there shall be the complete redemption of the purchased possession, and not a bone shall be left in the regions of death, not a relic for the devil to glory over. Jesus said to Mary, "Thy brother shall rise again;" he did not need to say thy brother's spirit shall live immortally; but thy brother shall "rise again," his body shall come forth of the tomb. Well might the apostles' hearts be comforted when they learned the blessed errand upon which their Lord was going!

The next consolation was *the promise of his sure return* : "If I go away to prepare a place for you, I will come again." Listen, then! Jesus is coming again. In the same manner as he ascended he will return—that is, really, literally, and in bodily form. He meant no play upon words when he so plainly said, without proverb, "I will come again," or more sweetly still, "I go away and come again *unto you*." This is our loudest joy-note, "Behold, he cometh!" This is our never-failing comfort. Observe that the Saviour, in this place, says nothing about death, nothing about the peace and rest of believers till he is come ; for he looks on to the end. It is not necessary to put every truth into one sentence ; and so our Lord is content to mention the brightest of our hopes, and leave other blessings for mention at other times. Here the consolation is that he will come, come personally to gather us in. He will not send an angel, nor even a host of cherubim to fetch us up into our eternal state; but the Lord himself will descend from heaven. It is to be our marriage-day, and the glorious Bridegroom will come in person. When the Bride is prepared for her Husband, will he not come to fetch her to his home ? O beloved, do you not see where our Lord's thoughts were ? He was dwelling upon the happy day of his ultimate victory, when he shall come to be admired in all them that believe. That is where he would have his people's thoughts to be ; but alas! they forget his advent. The Lord shall come ; let your hearts anticipate that day of days. His enemies cannot stop his coming ! "Let not your heart be troubled." They may hate him, but they cannot hinder him ; they cannot impede his glorious return, not by the twinkling of an eye. What an answer will his coming be to every adversary! How will they weep and wail because of him! As surely as he lives he will come; and what confusion this will bring upon the wise men who at this hour are reasoning against his Deity and ridiculing his atonement! Again I say, " Let not your heart be troubled " as to the present state of religion; it will not last long. Do not worry yourselves into unbelief though this man may have turned traitor, or the other may have become a backslider, for the wheels of time are hurrying on the day of the glorious manifestation of the Lord from heaven! What will be the astonishment of the whole world when with all the holy angels he shall descend from heaven and shall glorify his people!

For that is the next comfort—*he will receive us.* When he comes he will receive his followers with a courtly reception. It will be their marriage reception; it shall be the marriage supper of the Son of God. Then shall descend out of heaven the new Jerusalem prepared as a bride for her husband. Then shall come the day of the resurrection, and the dead in Christ shall rise. Then all his people who are alive at the time of his coming shall be suddenly transformed, so as to be delivered from all the frailties and imperfections of their mortal bodies : " The dead shall be raised incorruptible, and we shall be changed." Then we shall be presented spirit, soul, and body "without spot, or wrinkle, or any such thing " ; in the clear and absolute perfection of our sanctified manhood, presented unto Christ himself. This is the sweetest idea of heaven that can be, that we shall be with Christ, that we shall see him, that we shall speak to him, that we shall commune with him most intimately, that we shall glorify him, that he will glorify us, and that we shall never be divided from him for ever and ever. " Let not your heart be troubled," all this is near at hand, and our Lord's going away has secured it to us.

For this was the last point of the consolation, that when he came and received his people to himself *he would place them eternally where he is, that they may be with him.* Oh, joy! joy! joy! unutterable joy! Can we not now, once for all, dismiss every fear in the prospect of the endless bliss reserved for us ?

> "See that glory, how resplendent!
>   Brighter far than fancy paints!
> There in majesty transcendent,
>   Jesus reigns, the King of saints.
> Spread thy wings, my soul, and fly
> Straight to yonder world of joy.
>
> Joyful crowds, his throne surrounding,
>   Sing with rapture of his love ;
> Through the heavens his praises sounding,
>   Filling all the courts above.
> Spread thy wings, my soul, and fly
> Straight to yonder world of joy."

The Lord talks to us as if we now knew all about his goings and doings; and so we do as far as all practical purposes are concerned. He says, " Whither I go ye know." He is not gone to a place unknown, remote, dangerous. He has only gone home. " Whither I go ye know." When a mother sends her boy to Australia she is usually troubled because she may never see him again; but he replies, "Dear mother, the distance is nothing now, we cross the ocean in a very few weeks, and I shall speedily come back again." Then the mother is cheered; she thinks of the ocean as a little bit of blue between her and her son, and looks for him to return, if need be. So the Saviour says, "Whither I go ye know." As much as to say—"I told you, I am going to your own Father's house, to the mansions whither your spirits will soon come, and I am going for the blessed purpose of making it ready to receive you in the entirety of your nature. You are thus made to know all about my departure and my business. I am going to a glorious place which eye hath not seen, but my Spirit will reveal it to you. You know where I am going, and you know also the way by which I am going—I am going through suffering and death, through atonement and righteousness: this is the way to heaven for you also, and you will find it all in me. You shall in due time enter heaven by my atonement, by my death, by my sacrifice, for 'I am the way.' You know the way; but remember it is only the way, and not the end. Do not imagine that the wicked can make an end of me; but believe that Christ on the cross, Christ in the sepulchre, is not the end, but the way." This, beloved, is the way for us as well as for our Lord. He could not reach his crown except by the cross, nor his mediatorial glory except by death: but that way once made in his own person is open for all who believe in him. Thus you know where the Lord has gone, and you know the road; therefore, be encouraged, for he is not far away; he is not inaccessible; you shall be with him soon. "Let not your heart be troubled."

Oh, brave Master, shalt thou be followed by a tribe of cowards? No, we will not lose heart through the trials of the day. Oh, holy Master, thou didst meet thy death with song, for "after supper they sang a hymn:" shall not we go through our griefs with joyful trust? Oh, confident Lord, bidding us believe in thee as in God himself, we do believe in thee, and we also grow confident. Thine undisturbed serenity of faith infuses itself into our souls, and we are made strong. When we hear thee bravely talking of thy decease which thou hadst to accomplish at Jerusalem, and then of thy after-glory, we also think hopefully of all the opposition of ungodly men, and, waiting for thine appearing, we solace ourselves with that blessed hope. Make no tarrying, O our Lord! Amen.

SPIRITUAL KNOWLEDGE AND ITS PRACTICAL RESULTS.

A Sermon

DELIVERED ON LORD'S-DAY MORNING, SEPTEMBER 30TH, 1883, BY

C. H. SPURGEON,

AT THE METROPOLITAN TABERNACLE, NEWINGTON.

> "For this cause we also, since the day we heard it, do not cease to pray for you, and to desire that ye might be filled with the knowledge of his will in all wisdom and spiritual understanding; that ye might walk worthy of the Lord unto all pleasing, being fruitful in every good work, and increasing in the knowledge of God."— Colossians i. 9, 10.

FOR the church that was at Colosse Paul gave hearty thanks to God for many most important blessings, especially for their faith, their love, and their hope. It would be a very useful exercise to our hearts if we would often give thanks to God for the gifts and graces which we discover in our Christian brethren. I am afraid we are more inclined to spy out their faults, and to suppose that we deplore them, than we are to discern the work of the Holy Spirit in them, and from the bottom of our hearts to give thanks to God for them. Paul felt encouraged by what he saw in the Colossian believers to pray to God to enrich them yet further. It should be our desire that our best brethren should be better, and that those who are most like Jesus should be still more completely conformed to his image. We cannot more wisely show our love to our friends than by first acknowledging the grace which is in them, and then by praying that God may give them more. Paul, as with an eagle eye, surveyed the church at Colosse, which he loved so well, and he noted that it was somewhat lacking in knowledge. The Colossian brotherhood differed considerably from the church at Corinth, which abounded in talent, and was enriched with all knowledge. The Colossians had fewer gifted brethren among them who could act as teachers, and, though this was no fault of theirs, it impoverished them in the matter of knowledge, and as Paul would not have them come behind in any desirable attainment, he therefore prayed for them that they might be filled with knowledge in all wisdom and spiritual understanding. If you read this epistle through, you will observe that Paul frequently alludes to knowledge and wisdom. To the point in which he judged the church to be deficient he turned his prayerful attention. He would not have them ignorant. He knew that spiritual ignorance is the constant source of error, instability, and sorrow; and therefore he desired that they might be soundly taught in the things of God. Not that they were destitute of saving knowledge already, for he says in the sixth

No. 1,742.

verse that they "knew the grace of God in truth," and that they had brought forth fruits meet for salvation; but saving knowledge, though it be the most essential attainment, is not the only knowledge which a Christian should seek after. He longs to be useful as well as to be safe. Being himself delivered out of darkness he strives to bring others into the marvellous light of grace. Paul would have his brethren thoroughly furnished for sacred service, knowing the will of the Lord themselves, and able to teach others. He desired for them that they might possess comforting knowledge, strengthening knowledge, edifying knowledge, sanctifying knowledge, directing knowledge; so that they might be ready for all the trials, duties, and labours of life.

Upon this subject I am led to make four observations, and to enlarge upon each of them. May the Holy Spirit by this discourse build us up in the knowledge of God.

I. My first subject is THE GREAT VALUE OF INTERCESSORY PRAYER; for as soon as Paul felt his heart burning with love to the saints at Colosse, and had heard of the work of the Spirit among them, he began to show his love by lifting up his heart in prayer for them. He did that for them which he knew would bless them.

Notice, that intercessory prayer is a very *important part of the work of Christians for one another.* We are not sent into the world to live unto ourselves, but we are members of one body, and each member is expected to contribute to the health and the comfort of the whole. It is true we cannot all preach, but we can all pray; we cannot all distribute alms from our substance, but we can all offer prayer from our hearts. In temporal things we may not be able to enrich the church for lack of substance; but if we fail to bless the church by our prayers it will be for lack of grace. Whatever you fail in, dearly beloved,—and I pray that you may in nothing come behind,—yet do not fail in prayer for all the saints, that every blessing may abound towards them.

Intercessory prayer is to be esteemed as an *invaluable proof of love,* and as the creator of more love. The man who will truly pray for me will certainly forgive me readily if I offend him; he will relieve me if I am in necessity; and he will be prepared to assist me if I am engaged in a service too hard for me. Give us your earnest prayers, and we know that we live in your hearts. How sweet it is to be permitted thus to manifest our love to one another! When our hand is palsied we can still pray; when our eye grows dim we can see to pray; when by sickness we are altogether laid aside we can still pray; and when we meet with cases in which we are unable to help, and yet are moved with sympathy for a brother, our sympathy can always find one open channel, for we can pray, and by prayer call in the aid of one whose help is effectual. Therefore, by your love to your Lord, and to all those who are in him, I beseech you abound in intercessory prayer, as the apostle did.

Intercessory prayer, again, is most valuable, because it is an *infallible means of obtaining the blessings* which we desire for our friends. It is not in vain that we ask, for it is written, "Everyone that asketh receiveth." It is not in vain that we intercede for others, for the Lord delights to answer such petitions. The unselfish devotion which pleads as eagerly for others as for itself is so pleasing to the Lord that he puts great honour upon it. If we desire any blessing for our friends our best course is to pray: even if we would have them to be filled with knowledge in all wisdom our safest course is to pray that it may be so. Of course, we must not forget to instruct them and to aid them in their own studies as far as lieth in our power, for every honest prayer supposes the use of all proper means; but the instruction which we offer will be of no service unless we first bring down the blessing of God upon it, that thereby our friends may be made willing to learn, and may receive the truth not as the word of man, but as from the Lord himself. None but spiritual teaching will nourish spiritual life. The Holy Ghost must teach divine truth to the heart, or it will never be truly known. Whatsoever thou wisely desirest for thy friend go about to get it for him, but hasten first to the throne of grace. If thou wouldst have thy friend converted, if thou wouldst have him strengthened, if thou wouldst have him taught of God, if thou wouldst have him quickened to a nobler life, and elevated to a higher consecration, do him this great service—take his case before the Lord in prayer; and in so doing thou hast gone the wisest way to work to enrich him.

Note, brethren, for I am keeping to my text closely, that such intercessory prayer will be all the more valuable if it is our *immediate resort*. The apostle says, " Since the day we heard it, we do not cease to pray for you." He began to pray at once. Whenever you perceive the work of the Spirit in any heart, pray at once, that the holy change may proceed with power. Whenever you discover any lack in a brother begin on the day you hear of it to pray that his lack may be supplied. There should be no delaying of prayer. " He gives twice who gives quickly " is a human proverb, but I believe that when we pray speedily we shall often find that God in answering quickly gives us a double blessing. Usually he shall win worldly riches who is the most diligent in the pursuit of them, and assuredly he shall be richest towards God who is most diligent in supplication. Linger not a minute, speed thee to the mercy-seat. Now is the accepted time; the Lord waits to be gracious to thee. The Lord indicates to thee what thy prayer shall be by the news which thou hast just heard of thy friend ; therefore, bring his case at once before the throne of grace. Divine providence has brought the needful subject for prayer under thy notice; therefore, this day begin to pray about it.

Our prayers will be all the more valuable if they are *incessant as well as immediate*. "We cease not," said Paul, "to pray for you since the day we heard it." "Oh," says one, "was Paul always praying for the Colossians from the day he heard of their welfare? It may have been months and years ; did he never cease to pray?" I answer, he was always praying for them in the sense which he explains: he adds, "and to desire." Now, desire is the essence of prayer ; in fact, desire is the kernel of prayer, and the vocal expressions which we call by the name of prayer are often but its shell ; inward desire is the life, the heart, the reality of prayer. Though you cannot always be speaking in prayer, you can always be desiring in prayer. The miser is always desiring riches, though he is not always talking about his gold and silver ; and the man who loves his fellow-men, and desires their profit, is really always praying for their benefit, though he is not always lifting up his voice in supplication. "Since the day we heard it," saith Paul, "we do not cease to pray for you." The act of prayer is blessed, the habit of prayer is more blessed, but the spirit of prayer is the most blessed of all; and it is this that we can continue for months and years. The act of prayer must, from force of circumstances, be sometimes stayed; but the habit of prayer should be fixed and unvarying; and the spirit of prayer, which is fervent desire, should be perpetual and abiding. We can hardly realize the value to the church and to the world of that intercessory prayer which ceases not day nor night, but without fail ascends before the Lord from the whole company of the faithful, as the incense ascended from the altar.

Dear friends, our intercessory prayer will be all the more precious if it is an *intense expression unto God.* I suppose that by the use of the word "desire" here, the apostle not only explains how he continued to pray, but in what manner he prayed—with "desire." Remember how our Lord puts it—"with desire have I desired to eat this passover with you before I suffer." I wish we could always say "with desire have I desired in prayer. I did not repeat a merely complimentary benediction upon my friends, but I pleaded for them as for my life; I importuned with God; I offered an effectual inwrought prayer, which rose from the depths of my heart to the heights of heaven, and obtained an audience with God." Fervency is a great essential for victorious prayer. God grant us to be importunate, for then we shall be invincible.

One more observation, and I have done with this. Intercessory prayer is increased in value when it is not from one person alone, but is offered in *intimate union with other saints.* Paul says, "We also," not "I only," but "*We* also, since the day *we* heard it, cease not." If two of you agree as touching anything concerning the kingdom, you have the blessing secured to you by a special promise of God. Remember how Abraham prayed for the cities of the plain, but succeeded not until Lot also added his supplication for Zoar. Then the little city was spared. I compare Abraham's intercession to a ton weight of prayer, and poor Lot's I can hardly reckon to have been more than half an ounce, but still that half ounce turned the scale. So here is Paul, and with him is youthful Timothy, who, compared with Paul, is inconsiderable; yet Paul's prayer is all the more effectual because Timothy's prayer is joined with it. Our Lord sent out his servants by two and two, and it is well when they come back to him in prayer two and two. I commend to you, brethren and sisters, the habit of frequent prayer together. When a Christian friend drops in, his visit will perhaps end in mere talk unless you secure its spiritual profit by at least a few minutes spent in united prayer. I frequently during the day, when a friend comes in upon the Master's business, say, "Let us pray before you go," and I always find the request is welcomed. Such prayers do not occupy much time, and if they did, it might be well spent; but such united supplications oil the wheels of life's heavy wain, and cause it to move with less of that creaking which we too often hear. "I alone" is certainly a good word in prayer; but "we also" is a better one. Let us link hands and intercede for our brethren and the whole church of God.

Thus have I expatiated upon the excellences which increase the value of intercessory prayer. Use much this heavenly art. It is effectual for ten thousand ends. It turneth every way to bless the church. Brethren, pray for us, pray for all saints, pray for all sinners, and by so doing you will be the benefactors of your age.

II. Our second observation from the text is this—we learn here THE PRECIOUSNESS OF SPIRITUAL KNOWLEDGE ; for all this earnest, ceaseless prayer is offered for this end, " That ye might be filled with the knowledge of his will in all wisdom and spiritual understanding." Here let us speak of the usefulness and blessedness of that spiritual knowledge for which the apostle and his friend cried incessantly unto the Lord.

First, consider the *men* for whom this knowledge is desired. They are saints and faithful brethren, of whom we read that they " knew the grace of God in truth," and were " bringing forth fruit " unto God. For those who know the Lord already we must not cease to pray. They are not beyond the need of our prayers while they are in this life. We may pray for those who know nothing of the Lord, that he would open their blind eyes ; but even those who have been taught of God already are in need of our supplications that they may learn yet more. We have great encouragement to pray that they may be filled with all knowledge, since the Lord has already done so much for them. We dare not say in this case that a little knowledge is a dangerous thing, for a little knowledge of the things of God may suffice to save the soul ; but more knowledge is a most desirable thing for those who have that little knowledge. Pray therefore for them. Let not your prayers plead only and altogether for the unconverted, but entreat for our young converts that they may be further edified. It will be an ill day when we are so engaged in seeking lost sheep that we forget the lambs. It would be very mischievous for us to neglect our work at home in order to carry on warfare with the adversary abroad. No, let us cry to God daily in prayer that the stones lately quarried may be built up upon the one foundation, and embedded in the walls of the church of God unto eternal glory. We desire life for the dead, health for the living, and maturity for the healthy. For the deeper instruction of our younger brethren let us pray.

Of this desirable knowledge, what is the *measure ?* We desire for them " that they may be filled with the knowledge of his will." " Filled "—this is grand scholarship, to have the mind, and heart, and the whole of our manhood filled with knowledge. Paul would not have a believer ignorant upon any point : he would have him filled with knowledge, for when a measure is full of wheat there is no room for chaff. True knowledge excludes error. The men that go after false doctrine are usually those who know little of the word of God ; being untaught they are unstable, ready to be blown about with every wind of doctrine. If you leave empty spots in your minds unstored with holy teaching, they will be an invitation to the devil to enter in and dwell there. Fill up the soul, and so shut out the enemy. Paul desired the Colossian saints to be filled—filled up to the brim with the knowledge of God's will. Brethren, we would have you know all that you can know of God's truth. Rome flourishes by man's ignorance, but the New Jerusalem rejoices in light. No knowledge of the revealed will of God can ever do you any harm if it be sanctified. Do not be afraid of what they call "high doctrines," or the "deep things of God." They tell us that those things are secrets, and therefore we ought not to pry into them. If they are secrets, there is no fear that anybody can pry into them; but the truths revealed in the word are no longer secrets, seeing that they are revealed to us by the Spirit of God, and as far as they are revealed it should be our desire to understand them, so as to be filled with the knowledge of them.

Let us try to know divine truth more and more intimately. You know a man, for you pass him in the streets with a nod; you know another man far better, for you lodge in the same house with him; you know him best of all when you have shared his trouble, partaken in his joy, and have, in fact, had fellowship with him by blending your two lives in one common stream of friendship. When you learn a spiritual truth endeavour to know it out and out; to know its foundation and upbuilding; to know it by the application of the Spirit to your own soul so that you are filled with it. You may have knowledge in the brain, but it may not run into your spirit, so as to penetrate, and permeate, and saturate your spirit, till you are filled therewith. Oh, to get the gospel into one's entire nature, and to be like the waterpots of Cana, filled up to the brim! Lord, fill thy poor children with the knowledge of thy will!

This makes me notice what the *matter* of this knowledge is; "filled with the knowledge of his will." What is that? It means the revealed will of God. Paul would have the Colossians know what the Lord has revealed, as far as human mind could grasp it, whether it were doctrine, precept, experience, or prophecy. How well it is to know the preceptive will of God. Our prayer should daily be, "Lord, what wilt thou have me to do?" Lord, teach me what is sin, and what is righteousness, that I may discern things which are excellent. Whereas there are questions in the church of God itself upon what the will of the Lord is, Lord help me not to care to know what is the will of this learned doctor, or what is the will of a certain assembly, but what is the Lord's will. "To the law and to the testimony," this is our touchstone. Our desire is to be filled with the knowledge of the Lord's will so as to do it without fail. Especially would we know the will of God, as it constitutes the gospel; for Jesus says, "This is the will of him that sent me, that every one which seeth the Son, and believeth on him, may have everlasting life." Oh, to know his will in that respect most clearly, so as to go and tell it out on all sides, that men may know the way of life, and may be led into it by our word! Once more we read in 1 Thessalonians iv. 3: "This is the will of God, even your sanctification." Oh, to be filled with the knowledge of the Lord's will till you know what sanctification means, and exhibit it in your daily life! It is yours to teach men what God means by holiness. Your mission is not fulfilled, and the will of God is not accomplished unless you are sanctified. This it is with which we need to be filled.

Know anything, know everything that is worth knowing. "That the soul be without knowledge is not good." Never attempt to run side by side with the agnostic whose glory it is that he knows nothing; but let it be your delight to know all that can be learned out of the Book of the Lord, by the teaching of the Holy Ghost. Concentrate your faculties upon the will of God. Here dive into the deeps and climb up to the heights, and be afraid of nothing; ask the Holy Spirit to saturate you with truth, as Gideon's fleece was wet with the dew of heaven, as the golden pot was filled with manna, or as Jordan is filled in the time of harvest, when it overfloweth all its banks.

Still we have not done, for we must now notice the *manner* as well as the matter of this knowledge: "in all wisdom and spiritual understanding." Wisdom is better than knowledge, for wisdom is knowledge rightly used. Knowledge may find room for folly, but wisdom casts it out. Knowledge may be the horse, but wisdom is the driver. When a man hath knowledge it is like the corn which is laid in the barn; but wisdom is the fine flour prepared for food. We want Christian people not only to know, but to use what they know. Happy is he who knows what to do at the right time! Many people are very knowing half an hour after it is too late; but to be filled with wisdom is to be able at once to apply knowledge rightly in difficult cases. Wisdom enables you to bring your knowledge practically to bear upon life, to separate between the precious and the vile, to deal with your fellow Christians in their different conditions, and to deal with sinners and those that are without. You need wisdom so to conduct your affairs that nothing therein shall scandalize the weak, or bring dishonour upon the name of Christ; for mere knowledge will not suffice for this. Knowledge is the blade, wisdom is the full corn in the ear. Knowledge is the cloth, but wisdom is the garment. Knowledge is the timber, but wisdom hath builded her house. May all our knowledge be sanctified by grace and attended with the guidance of the Spirit that we may become wise to know what the will of the Lord is.

"All wisdom," saith the apostle—many-handed wisdom, wisdom of all sorts, wisdom that will serve you in the shop, wisdom that will be useful in the counting-house, wisdom that will aid the church of God, and wisdom that will guide you if you are cast among the vilest of mankind. May you "be filled with knowledge in all wisdom."

But that wisdom which operates without must be attended by a spiritual understanding which is powerful within. I hardly know how to explain this: it is an inward knowledge of truth, the knowledge of the inward parts of things. It is a spiritual discernment, taste, experience, and reception of truth, whereby the soul feeds upon it, and takes it into herself. We know many men who know much but understand nothing. They accept implicitly what they are taught, but they have never considered it, weighed it, estimated it, found out the roots of it, or seen the heart of it. Oh, to have in the church men full of spiritual understanding! These can say that they have tasted and handled the good word of life, and have proved and tested the truth as it is in Jesus. You know how it was with the sacrifices of old: a man who was poor brought turtle-doves or pigeons, and of these we read of each bird, " The priest shall cleave it with the wings thereof, but shall not divide it asunder:" but a man who was rich in Israel brought a bullock or a sheep, and this offering was not only cleft down the middle, but further divided, and the fat and the " inwards " are mentioned in detail. The poorer sacrifice represents the offering of the uninstructed; they have never rightly divided the word of God, and know not its fulness of meaning;

but the man who is rich in grace is comparable to him who brought his
bullock; for he can enter into detail and see the secret meanings of the
Word.   There is a deep which lieth under, and he that is taught of the
Lord shall find it.   "The secret of the Lord is with them that fear
him; and he will show them his covenant;" and blessed are they that
are taught of the Lord so as to read the mystery of his grace!

Here, then, is a grand petition for us.   To go back to our first head,
let our intercessory prayers go up for all our brethren.   Lord, teach
them thy word.   Let them know thy book from cover to cover, and let
the truths therein revealed enter into them until they are filled to
the brim : then grant thou them the skill to use in daily life the knowledge which thy Spirit has imparted, and may they more and more in
their inmost souls be guided into all truth, that they may comprehend
with all saints what are the heights, and depths, and know the love of
Christ which passeth knowledge.

III.   Now, thirdly, let us see in the text a lesson concerning THE
PRACTICAL RESULT OF SPIRITUAL KNOWLEDGE.   Paul prays for his
friends "that ye might be filled with the knowledge of his will in all
wisdom and spiritual understanding ; that ye might walk worthy of the
Lord unto all pleasing."   See, see the drift of his prayer—"that ye
may walk."   Not that ye might talk, not that ye might sit down and
meditate, and enjoy yourselves, but "that ye might walk."   He aims at
practical results.

He desires that the saints may be instructed so that they may *walk
according to the best model.*   By walking worthy of the Lord Jesus we
do not understand in any sense that he expected them to possess such
worthiness as to deserve to walk with the Lord; but he would have
them live in a manner that should be in accordance with their communion with Christ.   You would not have a man walk with Christ
through the streets to-day clothed in motley garments, or loathsome with
filth: would you?   No, if a man be a leper, Christ will heal him before
he will walk with him.   Let not a disciple walk so as to bring disgrace
upon his Lord!   When you walk with a king, you should be yourself
royal in gait ; when you commune with a prince you should not act the
clown.   Dear friends, may you know so much of Jesus that your lives
shall become Christ-like, fit to be put side by side with the character
of Jesus, worthy of your perfect Lord.   This is a high standard, is it
not?   It is always better to have a high standard than a low one,
for you will never go beyond that which you set up as your model.   If
you get a low standard you will fall below even that.   It is an old
proverb, "He that aims at the moon will shoot higher than he that
aims at a bush."   It is well to have no lower standard than the desire
to live over again the life of the Lord Jesus—a life of tenderness, a.
life of self-sacrifice, a life of generosity, a life of love, a life of honesty,
a life of holy service, a life of close communion with God.   Mix all
virtues in due proportion, and that is the life of Jesus towards which
you must press forward with all your heart.

Next, the apostle would have us get knowledge in order that we may
so live as to *be pleasing to our best friend*—"worthy of the Lord unto all
pleasing."   Is not that beautiful ?   To live so as to please God in all
respects!   Some live to please themselves, and some to please their

neighbours, and some to please their wives, and some to please their children, and some live as if they wished to please the devil; but our business is to please him in all things whose servants we are. Without faith it is impossible to please him; so away with unbelief! Without holiness no man shall see him, much less please him; therefore let us follow after holiness, and may the Lord work it in us. "Unto all pleasing"—so that we may please God from the moment we rise in the morning to the time when we lie down, ay, and please him even when we are asleep: that we may eat and drink so as to please him; that we may speak and think so as to please him; that we may go or stay so as to please him; that we may rejoice or suffer so as to please him—" walking worthy of the Lord unto all pleasing." Oh, blessed man, whose life is pleasing to God in all respects! The apostle Paul desires that we may be filled with knowledge to this very end. If I do not know the will of God how can I do the will of God? At least, how can there be anything pleasing to God which is ignorantly done without an intent to do his will? I fear that many children of God grieve their heavenly Father much through sins of ignorance—an ignorance in which they ought not to remain a single day. Be it clearly understood that sins of ignorance are truly sins. They have not about them the venom and the aggravation which are found in sins against light and knowledge, but still they are sins; for the measure of our duty is not our light, but the law of God itself. If a man pleads that he follows his conscience, yet this will not excuse his wrong-doing if his conscience is an unenlightened conscience, and he is content to keep it in the dark. You are to obey the will of the Lord: that will is the standard of the sanctuary. Our conscience is often like a deficient weight, and deceives us; be it ours to gather a clear knowledge of the word, that we may prove what is that perfect and acceptable will of God. The law makes no allowance for errors committed through false weights; when a man says, "I thought my weights and measures were all right," he is not thereby excused. The law deals with facts, not with men's imaginations; the weights must actually be correct, or the penalty is exacted; so is it with conscience, it ought to be instructed in the knowledge of the divine will, and if it is not so, its faultiness affords no justification for evil. Hence the absolute necessity of knowledge in order to true holiness. God grant us grace to know his will, and then to obey it "unto all pleasing."

Look at the text again—" That ye might walk worthy of the Lord unto all pleasing, being fruitful." Paul would have us *producing the best fruit*. Without knowledge we cannot be fruitful; at least in the points whereof we are ignorant we must fail to bring forth fruit. Therefore would he have us to be right well taught, that we may abundantly produce fruit unto God's glory. He says, "fruitful in every good work"; and this means much. He desires us to be as full of good works as we can hold. Some are hindered in this because they do not know how to set about holy service. How can a man be fruitful as a preacher if he does not know what to preach? True, he may preach the elementary doctrine of the cross, but even that he will be apt to set forth in a blundering manner. For certain, a man cannot teach what he does not know. The zealous, but untaught man, would be much more fruitful if he had a clearer understanding of divine things. In daily life, if in knowledge you are ignorant as to the things of God, you will be ready to become the prey of any false teacher who may chance to pick you up. In hundreds of ways ignorance will make you run risks, lose opportunities of usefulness, and fall into dangerous mistakes. Knowledge is food to the true heart, and strengthens it for the Lord's work. Oh, to have knowledge placed like good soil around the roots of the soul, to fertilize the mind, that thus the clusters of usefulness may be as large as those of Eshcol: beautiful, plentiful, sweet, and full. May our Lord, the King of Israel, to whom the vineyard belongs, receive an abundant reward for all his labour for the vines which he has planted.

There is another note in this verse which I beg you to notice. Paul would have them cultivate *a comprehensive variety of the best things.* He says—" Fruitful in *every* good work." Here is room and range enough—"in every good work." Have you the ability to preach the gospel? Preach it! Does a little child need comforting? Comfort it! Can you stand up and vindicate a glorious truth before thousands? Do it! Does a poor saint need a bit of dinner from your table? Send it to her. Let works of obedience, testimony, zeal, charity, piety, and philanthropy all be found in your life. Do not select big things as your special line, but glorify the Lord also in the littles—"fruitful in every good work." You never saw in nature a tree which yielded all sorts of fruit, and you never will. I have seen a tree so grafted that it produced four kinds of fruit at one time, but I remarked that it was a poor business in reference to two of the varieties; for one of the grafts, more natural than the others to the parent stem, drew off the most of the sap, and flourished well, but robbed the other branches. The second sort of fruit managed to live pretty fairly, but not so well as it would have done on its own stem. As for the third and fourth, they were mere attempts at fruit of the smallest size. This tree was shown to me as a great curiosity; it is not likely that practical gardeners will be encouraged by the experiment. But what would you think of a tree upon which you saw grapes, and figs, and olives, and apples, and all other good fruits growing at one time? This is the emblem of what instructed believers will become: they will produce all sorts of goodness and graciousness to the honour of their heavenly Father. I have no doubt that you will naturally abound most in certain good works for which you have the largest capacity, but still nothing ought to come amiss to you. In the great house of the church we want servants who will not be simply cooks or housemaids, but general servants, maids of all-work, prepared to do anything and everything. I have known persons in household employment in England who would not do a turn beyond their special work to save their masters' lives: these are a sort of servants of whom the fewer the better. In India this is carried to a ridiculous extreme. The Hindoo water-bearer will not sweep the house, nor light a fire, nor brush your clothes—he will fetch water, and nothing else: you must, therefore, have a servant for each separate thing, and then each man will do his own little bit, but he will not go an inch beyond. When we enter into Christ's church we should come prepared to wash the saints' feet, or bear their burdens, or bind up their wounds, or fight their foes, or act as steward, or shepherd, or nurse. It has been well said that if two angels in heaven were summoned to serve the Lord, and there were two works to be done, an empire to be ruled, or a crossing to be swept, neither angel would have a choice as to which should be appointed him, but would gladly abide the will of the Lord. Let us be equally prepared for anything, for everything by which fruit can be produced for the Well-beloved.

Why is it that some are not fruitful in this comprehensive way? Because they are not filled with knowledge in all wisdom. When a man says, "You ask me to do the lowest work! Don't you know that I am a man of remarkable ability who should have higher work to do?" I venture to assert that he is an ignorant man. Self-assertion is ignorance on horseback. You have probably read of a certain renowned corporal in the American service a century ago. A general as he rode along saw a body of men endeavouring to lift timber. They were short-handed, and the work lagged, but their famous corporal stood by ordering them about at a magnificent rate. The general passed and said, "Why don't you lend them help and put your shoulder to it?" "Why, sir," said the great little officer, "how can you think of such a thing? Do you know who I am? I am a corporal!" The general got off his horse, pulled off his coat, and helped to move the timber, and by his judicious help the soldiers achieved their task. Then he turned to the high and mighty gentleman and said, "Mr. Corporal, next time you want a man to do such work as this you can send for me : I am General Washington." Just so the Lord Jesus Christ if he were here would gladly do a thousand things which his poor little servants are too great to touch. I know you, dear brother, you are too experienced, too old, too learned to help the Sunday-school! I know you are too respectable to give away a tract! Pray get out of such ignorant ways of thinking, and ask to be useful in all possible ways. If you have done a little, do much; if you have done much, do more; and when you have done more, ask for grace to proceed to the highest possible degree of usefulness for your Lord.

IV. And now, fourthly, notice THE REFLEX ACTION OF HOLINESS UPON KNOWLEDGE. We have only a few moments left; let my few words sink into your hearts. "Fruitful in every good work"—what then? "increasing in the knowledge of God." Look at that. It seems, then, that *holiness is the road to knowledge.* God has made it so. If any man will do his will he shall know of the doctrine. If you read and study, and cannot make out the meaning of Scripture, get up and do something, and it may be, in the doing of it, you shall discover the secret. Holiness of heart shall increase the illumination of your mind.

Will you kindly observe that *this knowledge rises in tone?* for Paul first prayed that they "might be filled with the knowledge of God's will"; but now he implores for them an increase in the knowledge of God himself. Oh, blessed growth, first to know the law, and then to know the Law-giver! first to know the precept, and then to know the mouth from which it comes! This is the height of knowledge, to see Christ and know the Father, and learn how to say from the heart, "Truly our fellowship is with the Father, and with his Son Jesus Christ."

I would call your willing attention to another thought. The apostle, if he is to be judged according to his outward language, often utters impossible things, and yet his every sentence is not only full of deep meaning, but is strictly correct. Notice his language here : in the ninth verse he says, " that ye might be filled with the knowledge of his will." Can anything go beyond this? The vessel is filled right up to the brim, what can it have more? Yet the apostle says, "increasing in the knowledge of God." What can that mean? If the mind is full to the brim, how can it receive more? If the man is full of knowledge, how can his knowledge increase? Can there be any increase after that? I propose to you the riddle. Here is the answer of it: Make the vessel larger, and then there can be an increase. This solution of the difficulty requires no great wit to discover it. So that Paul plainly teaches us here that, if we have so increased in knowledge as to be full, *he would have us increased in capacity to know yet more;* he would have our manhood enlarged, our powers of reception increased, that we might grow from being children to be young men, and from young men to be fathers, and so may be filled—filled, always filled with all the fulness of God! The Lord grant unto us to perceive with humility, that if we are already full of knowledge, we can still advance, for we "have not yet attained." Let no man think that he can go no further. " There is," says Augustine, " a certain perfection according to the measure of this life, and it belongs to that perfection that such a perfect man should know that he is not yet perfect." To that I heartily subscribe. There is a certain fulness to be found in this life according to the measure of a man, and it belongs to that fulness that the man should know that he can yet increase in knowledge. Holy Bernard says "he is not good at all who doth not desire to be better." I also subscribe to that saying. Some might become good if they were not puffed up with the fancy of their own perfection. Others are somewhat commendable, but will never grow because they judge themselves to be full-grown already. I would have you filled, and yet have room for more : filled with all knowledge, filled with all holiness, filled with the indwelling Spirit, filled with God, and yet increasing in knowledge, in holiness, in likeness to God, and in all good things evermore to his glory. The Lord add his blessing for Jesus' sake. Amen.

PORTION OF SCRIPTURE READ BEFORE SERMON—Colossians i.

HYMNS FROM "OUR OWN HYMN BOOK"—178, 648, 646.

A LOVING ENTREATY.

A Sermon

DELIVERED ON LORD'S-DAY MORNING, OCTOBER 7TH, 1883, BY

C. H. SPURGEON,

AT THE METROPOLITAN TABERNACLE, NEWINGTON.

"Put me in remembrance: let us plead together: declare thou, that thou mayest be justified."—Isaiah xliii. 26.

WE shall mainly dwell upon the first invitation of the text: "Put me in remembrance."

If you will cast your eye upon the Scripture itself you will be struck with its singular position. It makes a paradox of the most striking kind if you read it in connection with the preceding clause: "I, even I, am he that blotteth out thy transgressions for mine own sake, and will not remember thy sins. Put me in remembrance." This looks like a contradiction; but, as a wise teacher will win attention by dark sayings, so doth the word of God abound in expressions by which thought is excited, and the lesson is more deeply impressed upon the mind. Many are the paradoxes of the prophets, and of the Lord and leader of all the prophets. Who can read without attention two such sentences as these in succession—"I will not remember thy sins"; "Put me in remembrance"? The use of such paradoxes in Scripture needs no sort of apology. Man is a living riddle. Does any man understand himself? He may think he does, but by this conceit he betrays his ignorance. The sinner is a paradox, and the saint is a double paradox. I say it is meet and right that the Holy Spirit should thus use paradoxical expressions, because those whom he addresses have paradoxes lying deep in their nature, and so the speech is congruous to the listener.

In this verse man is invited to draw near to God. Those same men of whom God saith that he was weary of them are bidden to plead with him. "Thou hast made me to serve with thy sins, thou hast wearied me with thine iniquities;" and yet it is evident that in another sense the Lord was not weary of them, for he calls upon them to come to a conference with him, saying, "Put me in remembrance: let us plead together." This approach to God is the way of our salvation. The first thing that must be done with some men is to make them think of God at all, and the best thing that can be done with any man is to draw him nearer and yet nearer to the great Father of spirits. "It is good for me to draw near to God," said one who knew right well what he was speaking of; and every man who does not yet

No. 1,743.

understand such an utterance will find it to be true if he will test it. Here is a commandment with promise :—" Draw nigh to God, and he will draw nigh to you." Here is another,—" Seek ye the Lord while he may be found, call ye upon him while he is near: let the wicked forsake his way, and the unrighteous man his thoughts: and let him return unto the Lord, and he will have mercy upon him; and to our God, for he will abundantly pardon." Nearness to God is evidently the hope of the seeker. For the prodigal in the distant country the most essential thing was that he should arise and go unto his father. It would have been of little use for him to have washed himself from the filth of the swine-trough, or to have broken off his acquaintance with the citizens of that country; he could never be right while he dwelt so far from his father's house. The most sober and secluded life in the far country would not have satisfied the cravings of his heart, any more than the husks would have filled his belly: true, it would have been some improvement upon spending his living riotously, but it would have wrought no change in his soul, and given no rest to his heart. The remedy is the father's kiss, the father's bosom, the father's house, the father's love. Understand my text, then, however paradoxical it may seem, as being a genuine invitation on the part of a gracious God to the most provoking of men. Though they have acted so wickedly that he may well be tired of them, he presses them to hold converse with him. If anything has been charged upon them in error, he is willing to hear their complaints,—only he longs that they will not keep at a sullen distance. God grant that the invitation may be accepted by those of you to whom it will this morning be addressed.

We shall regard our text thus :—First, it is *a humbling challenge,*—" Put me in remembrance: let us plead together." Secondly, as we cannot answer the challenge, we will put another sense upon the words and accept it in *an amended version;* such as penitence can carry out ; and, thirdly, we shall see in it *a practical suggestion;* perhaps more than one. May the Holy Ghost enable us to learn the lessons and carry out the suggestions!

I. First, then, our text appears before us as A HUMBLING CHALLENGE. God had punished Israel on account of sin. Israel was not penitent, but in self-righteousness judged that the Lord was harsh and severe. " Come, then," says God, " come and plead your suit with me. Put me in remembrance of any virtues on your part which I may be supposed to have overlooked. If I have misjudged you, if you have not really been neglectful of my service and worship, let the matter be rectified. If really you have a righteousness of your own, put me in remembrance of it."

On looking back we find that the Lord had charged his people with *neglect of prayer :* " But thou hast not called upon me, O Jacob." This is the charge which we are compelled to bring against all unconverted men and women : you do not call upon God, you live without sincere and fervent prayer. Perhaps you offer a form of prayer ; but that is nothing if your heart goes not with the words. This is rather to mock God than truly to call upon him. But come now; if there be any mistake in this charge, disprove it! If you have earnestly called upon the Lord through Christ Jesus, if you have been diligent in seeking his face, and yet he has turned his back upon you—testify against him. It will be a new thing under the sun to find a praying heart rejected at the throne of grace. I know you cannot deny the accusation of prayerlessness. If you are Christless you are prayerless. If you have received no mercy it is because you have not sought it at the mercy-seat.

Next the Lord charged it upon Israel that they had *not delighted in him*—" Thou hast been weary of me, O Israel." Is not this a charge which cannot be denied? You men and women who are not regenerate and have never received the pardon of your sin, is it not true that you are weary of God? You readily enough grow tired of a sermon in which we try to speak of him, though you would listen for hours to a silly tale. You become tired of the Sabbath-day. What a weariness it is! You are weary of the Bible; how little do you read it! a foolish novel suits you better. If you hear Christians talking wisely and seriously of the things of Christ, you have no liking for their words ; you would rather listen to a comic song. To you the house of God is the temple of dulness, and the worship of God is bondage. As for God himself, you will not allow yourself to remember him, he is not in all your thoughts. You sometimes think that even heaven itself would be a weary place for you if it were full of the praising and adoring of God, and communion with him. Can you deny this? If you can, you are invited to state your innocence before the Lord. But I know that in truth you cannot raise the question; for there is within your mind an unquestionable aversion to the service of God; in fact, you would feel happier if there were no God, and if thoughts of eternity never intruded themselves. Take heed lest your aversion become mutual, and God should say, "My soul lothed them, and their soul also abhorred me."

The Lord had also said that these people *did not honour him*—" Thou hast not brought me the small cattle of thy burnt offerings; neither hast thou honoured me with thy sacrifices." It may be you have presented no tokens of love to the Lord at all; or, on the other hand, you may have brought sacrifices, but you have not honoured God by them. You have given that you might be known to give, or because others did so, but not with the view of honouring God. You come and sit with his people and join in their songs, but you do not seek the glory of God thereby ; nor is this the main object of your daily life, you know it is not. Yet if it be so, if any unconverted man can say that whether he eats or drinks, or whatsoever he does, he seeks to do all to the glory of God, this ought to be known. It would be a new thing under the sun. In truth, it would prove that the man was converted, and had been renewed in the spirit of his mind by the grace of God. But it is not so,—you have not honoured the name of your Creator and Benefactor, you have robbed him of the glory due unto his name.

Moreover, the Lord charged Israel that they *did not love him*—" Thou hast bought me no sweet cane with money, neither hast thou filled me with the fat of thy sacrifices." No token of love had been presented, but they had made the Lord to serve with their sins. The purchase of calamus with money had not come into their thoughts. They could not afford it, they said ; but when they were worshipping their false gods they could find money enough—" They lavish gold out of the bag,

and weigh silver in the balance." So there are men who cannot afford
to give anything to the cause of God or Christian charity, but for their
sinful pleasures they can waste their substance. No sacrifice is too
expensive for a man's lusts: he will do anything that he may live a
merry life, which merry life consists in rebellion against God. This
proves that man has no love in his heart to God. O sinner! didst thou
ever feel a tear start to thine eyes at the thought of God's being dis-
honoured? Didst thou ever humble thyself before God because thou
hast thyself dishonoured him? Is his word dear to thee? Is there
music in the sweet name of Jesus to thine ear? Nay, it is not so.
Thou knowest thou art dead to all this. He challenges thee to plead
thine innocence if thou canst. Darest thou take up the glove? Prove
that thou hast loved him. Put him in remembrance of thy kindly deeds
and zealous acts. Thou hast none to bring to remembrance. Thy heart
has had no delight in the Lord thy God.

The Lord again challenges them upon the charge that they *had not
obeyed him:* "Thou hast made me to serve with thy sins"—thou hast
made me a very slave with thy waywardness. "Thou hast wearied me
with thine iniquities,"—God's patience was tried to the utmost with
their wanton wickedness. Is not this charge true—sadly true of many?
Oh, you that have never accepted Christ, nor cast yourselves at his dear
feet, you have by this wilful refusal of love insulted the mercy of the
Lord. You have had no respect to his law, you have not checked
yourself because you were likely to offend, you have not stirred yourself
up to please the Lord. Ah no! you have lived as if you were your
own masters. If it be not so, you are now challenged to vindicate your
characters. Do not set up a lying defence, but speak the truth. "Put
me in remembrance," saith he. If you have abounded in prayer, if
you have delighted in God, if you have sought his honour, if you
have loved him, if you have obeyed him, then set out your righteousness before the sun, and be not afraid. But you are not innocent
before the Lord. Therefore humble yourselves, confess your guilt, and
cover your face before the Lord. The Lord would thus humble you that
you may repent, and that he may fulfil his word to you,—" I, even I,
am he that blotteth out thy transgressions for mine own sake, and will
not remember thy sins."

The challenge before us is occupied not only with the ways of man,
but with the ways of God; for the Lord here asserts of himself, "I
have not caused thee to serve with an offering, nor wearied thee with
incense." That is to say, God is no hard taskmaster, he is not an
austere man, gathering where he has not strawed. The commandments
of God are essential justice: you could not improve upon them: no law
could be more for our benefit than that which he has given us. The
service of God is no bondage. Ask his children how they find it.
When they take his yoke upon them and learn of him, they find rest
unto their souls. His ways are ways of pleasantness, and all his paths
are peace. Perfect obedience is heaven. If God has treated you like
slaves, if he has exacted of you more than his right, if he has made your
heart heavy with endless labours, then say so, and state your grievance
in solemn converse with God. Only do speak with him. But who that
is in his senses will say that the service of God is anything but liberty?

O beloved! when God forbids us anything it is because he knows it would be for our harm; and when God-commands us to do anything it is because he knows that it is for our soul's welfare and eternal good. The moral law is the mirror of right: the will of the Lord as therein revealed commends itself so thoroughly to the conscience of man that he cannot wage an honest warfare with it: it is "true and righteous altogether." If we are upright in our judgments our desire will be, "Oh that my ways were directed to keep thy statutes!" If we offend against the law it is not because it is unreasonable, unjust, or unkind. His yoke is easy, and his burden is light. It is so, most surely so. Though I feel myself quite unable worthily to plead the cause of God as I would desire, I could stand here and weep because of the manner in which his creatures treat him. I feel ashamed of myself that I can so coldly vindicate his cause, which deserves a far better advocate than I can be. But have ye not, ye that are ungodly, have ye not treated the Lord shamefully? Have ye not forgotten him who never forgets you? Have you not turned your backs on your Benefactor and your Friend? Have you not refused the service which would have afforded your souls a deep delight? Have you not quarrelled with your mercies, and fought against heaven itself? It is surely so. If you have anything to plead to the contrary, argue it with your Maker; only do not continue to keep away from him. Turn unto him and answer his appeal, "Put me in remembrance: let us plead together: declare thou, that thou mayest be justified."

II. I hope you will be prepared to follow me while our penitence suggests AN AMENDED VERSION; I do not mean an alteration of the words, but of the sense. Let us take the text as our consciousness of guilt desires to read it. There are certain things which God in great love invites us to bring before his memory. What are these? Let me tell you. If you cannot take up his challenge, and prove your personal righteousness, let the charges stand, with your silence as an assent to them; and now plead with him and put him in remembrance of matters which may serve your turn, and lead to your forgiveness.

First, put the Lord in remembrance of *that glorious act of amnesty and oblivion* which in sovereign grace he has proclaimed to the sons of men in the preceding verse. Come, now, all guilty and defiled, and say to him, "Lord, though my iniquities testify against me, I rest upon thy forgiving word, 'I, even I, am he that blotteth out thine iniquities for mine own sake, and will not remember thy sins.'" Remember that God has not forgotten to be gracious, neither has he changed a single declaration of his mercy. Still, he would have you remind him of them as earnestly as if he had forgotten them. It is not for the refreshment of *his* memory, but of *yours*, that he wishes you now to put him in remembrance. Never will you find a safer position as a sinner than kneeling at the mercy-seat, pleading such words as these—"Come now, and let us reason together, saith the Lord: though your sins be as scarlet, they shall be as white as snow; though they be red like crimson, they shall be as wool." "I will be merciful to their unrighteousness, and their sins and their iniquities will I remember no more." "If we confess our sins, he is faithful and just to forgive us our sins, and to cleanse us from all unrighteousness." At once, with tears and broken language, put the Lord in remembrance of his gracious promises, and say, " Remember thy word unto thy servant, upon which thou hast caused me to hope." Cry to him after this fashion, " Lord, do as thou hast said. Here is one who is full of iniquity. I pray thee cleanse me. If I had no transgressions thou couldst not blot them out; but here they are; I beseech thee blot them out according to thy word! Behold, I put thee in remembrance of thy word. O Lord, let me hear thee say—— ' Thy sins, which are many, are forgiven.' "

That done, proceed to put the Lord in remembrance of your sins. Make an open unreserved acknowledgment unto the Lord. Tell him that you have transgressed. Say, with the returning prodigal, " I have sinned against heaven, and before thee, and am no more worthy to be called thy son." Hide nothing, for nothing can be hid: conceal nothing, for it cannot be concealed. Be sure your sin will find you out; therefore, find out your sin, and surrender it into the hand of the great God, that he may deal with it. Especially put the Lord in remembrance of this—that you have sinned against one who has continued to pardon you, and therefore you have sinned in a most cruel and ungrateful manner. It puts an exceeding heinousness into sin, that it is an offence against one who so freely forgives it. The Lord might long ago have cast us into hell, and yet he spares us—shall we find in this a liberty to offend yet more? " He hath not dealt with us after our sins; nor rewarded us according to our iniquities;" and this fact makes perseverance in rebellion a scarlet sin.

Confess this also, that you have continued by your sins to go away from him who invites you to return, and promises you a welcome reception. Remember, if you are still out of Christ it is not because God has made you so. He takes an oath, " As I live, saith the Lord God, I have no pleasure in the death of the wicked; but that the wicked turn from his way and live." He will not have your damnation laid at his door. He saith expressly, " O Israel, thou hast destroyed thyself;" and the tender Saviour cries, " Ye will not come to me, that ye might have life." Own the truth of this. Though you may have foolishly boasted of your free will aforetime, now be humbled about that wicked will of yours which threatens to be your destruction. On your knees cry to the Lord for the pardon of offences against his mercy, and the forgiveness of provocations against his long-suffering. He invites you to do it; therefore he saith, " Put me in remembrance."

When you have done this, if your spirit is much depressed, and your heart is driven to despair by a sense of your guilt, then I would advise you to put the Lord in remembrance of *the extraordinary reason which he gives for pardoning sin :*—" I, even I, am he that blotteth out thy transgressions *for mine own sake.*" Say unto him thus: " Lord, there is no reason in me why thou shouldst spare me, but do it for thine own sake—for thy love's sake, for thy mercy's sake. Thou hast said that thou delightest in mercy; Lord, delight thyself in having mercy upon me. It is to thy glory to pass by transgression: it makes to the Lord Jesus Christ a great name when he puts away the guilt of men; Lord, I pray thee now for thine own sake, for thy Son's sake, to cast a veil over all my former iniquities, and let me be reconciled unto thee by the death of thy Son." I fear, dear hearers, that I do not speak this as I ought to speak it. I wish I could weep over you while I plead with you. I implore you at once honestly and affectionately to obey the exhortation of the text. Come, I beseech you, hear your Father say, "Put me in remembrance : let us plead together." Put the Lord in remembrance of his sovereign grace, and of his all-sufficient power to bless. Put him in remembrance that he has taken the vilest of the vile and washed them in the blood of Jesus ; that he has taken the hardest and most obdurate hearts, and softened them to the praise of the glory of his grace; and then add, "Lord, do all this in me, that I too may magnify thy gracious name!"

When you have gone as far as that in putting God in remembrance, I would with much affection advise you to plead *the Lord's purpose and intent* revealed in the twenty-first verse : "This people have I formed for myself; they shall shew forth my praise." Say, "Lord, I am thy poor creature. Thou hast made me ; even my very body is fearfully and wonderfully made ; and the mysterious thing which dwells within me which I call my soul, is also the creature of thy power. Hast thou not made me for thyself? Wilt thou not have a desire to the work of thine own hands ? Lord, come and bless me! Sinner as I am, and utterly undeserving, yet I am thy creature ; do not fling me upon the dunghill. If thou wilt forgive me, Lord, might I not praise thee? Is there not room somewhere for me to give thee thanks ? In earth, or in heaven, may I not yet render to thee some little service, and magnify thy name? Now, Lord, I do dishonour thee while I live in sin, but I shall glorify thee if thou make me holy. I am as a worthless vessel, only fit to be cast with the broken potsherds, of no use to God or man, and scarce of use even to myself, but in my person I beseech thee fulfil thy word, 'This people have I formed for myself; they shall shew forth my praise.'" This is good arguing. After this fashion obey the word— "Put me in remembrance : let us plead together."

If that does not ease you, go a little further back in the chapter till you come to the nineteenth verse—"Behold, I will do a new thing ; now it shall spring forth ; shall ye not know it? I will even make a way in the wilderness, and rivers in the desert. The beast of the field shall honour me, the dragons and the owls : because I give waters in the wilderness, and rivers in the desert, to give drink to my people, my chosen." Plead that *published declaration!* Say, "Lord, thou hast said, 'I will do a new thing :' it will indeed be a new thing if I am saved. I am driven to such self-abhorrence, that if ever I am saved I shall be a leading wonder among thy miracles of grace.

> "Saved!—the deed shall spread new glory
> Through the shining realms above!
> Angels sing the pleasing story,
> All enraptured with thy love!"

It may be you can say—"Lord, I have been sighing, and crying, and groaning now by the month together, and I can find no peace. Oh, if thou wilt but put a new song into my mouth, the dragons and the owls that saw me in my gloom shall open their eyes and be astonished, and honour the Lord God of Israel!" You have come to be familiar in your gloom with strange company, comparable to the dragons and the owls;

therefore cry unto your Redeemer, "Lord, save me, and the owls will hoot no longer, or if they do, they will hoot to thy praise; and the very dragons that all men dread shall become comfortable things, and begin to magnify thy name, as said the Psalmist, 'Praise him ye dragons, and all deeps.'" I know some who might say, "Lord, it will fill all the workshop with wonder if I shall rejoice in Jesus. All my friends and companions will wonder that I should become happy and holy through sovereign grace. I am the very last person they would have thought to see converted. Then will they know what thine arm can do, and confess that this is the finger of God. Men that could not open their mouths except to blaspheme the Lord, shall stand awe-struck and astonished as they see what a brand is plucked from the burning."

You see I have tried to help you in obeying this word—"Put me in remembrance;" but I cannot do the work for you. Dear unconverted hearers, you must yourselves make confession and plead for your lives. This pleading must be wrought in you by the Spirit of God; and if it be, I could almost wish to be a mouse in your chamber, that I might listen to you while you are putting the gracious Father in remembrance of his promises, and of the glory which will come to his name if he will save you. Specially should I like to hear you begin thus—"Lord, remember thine only-begotten Son. Hast thou not declared that it is a faithful saying and worthy of all acceptation that Christ Jesus came into the world to save sinners? I am a sinner; Lord, save me! Oh, remember Gethsemane, remember Calvary, remember the bloody sweat, remember the wounds of thy Well-beloved, remember the cry, 'It is finished!' and give him to see of the travail of his soul in me! Give me as a spoil to the Risen One, that in me he may see the reward for his pains!" That is the style of pleading. This will ere long bring you rest and ease. God help you not only to hear me now with attention, but to go and see to the doing of it. I fear and tremble lest my labour should be lost through your failing to come to the mark. In vain do you listen if you do not obey.

III. So this brings me to the last point, which is this : our text affords us some PRACTICAL SUGGESTIONS.

If the Lord says to us, "Put me in remembrance," then, in the first place, it is very clear that *we ought to remember these things ourselves.* We cannot put another in remembrance of a thing which we ourselves forget. Come, then, let us for a time remind ourselves of certain matters which we are prone to cast behind us. Going over the same ground which I have traversed before, I shall make no apology, since my desire is that God's Spirit may impress it on your hearts.

Oh, you that are not saved, remember the years in which you have lived without prayer! What a wonder that you have been permitted to live at all! Morning light and evening shade, and yet no prayer! Mercies on the table, mercies in the family, mercies to your body, mercies to your soul, and yet no prayer! Sermons heard, exhortations given, gentle entreaties all thrown away, for still there has been no prayer! "Thou hast not called upon me, O Jacob." It is not good to take our sins in the lump, but to set them out in detail one after the other. Here is a God ready to pardon, and we would not even ask for forgiveness. Here is a God waiting to be gracious, and we have kept him waiting these forty years. Here is mercy's door before us, and we will not knock, though there is a promise that it shall be opened to every knocker. Here is Jesus himself knocking at our door till his head is wet with dew, and his locks with the drops of the night, and yet we will not open! Remember that! Let this transgression come before us, and cause us deep repentance and self-humiliation.

Remember next, for your own humbling, how weary you have been of God. I went over that just now; but think of it! Here is a creature that cannot endure to think of its creator. Here is one that has daily fed at the table of a friend, and yet he never gives that friend a good word. Living where God's works are all around you so that you cannot help but see them, when even the night doth but unveil a new scene of wonder as it shows to you the stars that were hidden by day, yet you can look upon all that wondrous scene and yet refuse to see your God! You were tired of God, did not want to hear about him, wished there were no God and no eternity, and that you could just enjoy yourself like as the beasts do who live only in the present. Ah me! Think of this, and so let your sin come to remembrance—you have been willing rather to be a beast than to serve God, and be like the angels.

Some I would earnestly urge to remember long years of neglect of God's service, with all their niggardliness to the cause of God, all their want of love to God, all the many times in which they have hardened their hearts, stopped their ears, and refused the warnings and invitations of their Saviour. Such memories might be used of the Holy Spirit for their conviction. Oh, dear, unconverted hearers, am I speaking the truth about you or not? God forbid I should bring a false accusation against any man! I am not charging you now with the blacker and more open sins, for perhaps you are innocent of them, but yet this is the sin of sins—forgetfulness of God, weariness of his service, refusal to receive the salvation of his Son. "This is the condemnation, that light is come into the world, and men love darkness rather than light." You think of your business, and yet the great business of your salvation causes you no concern. Think of that: you put your dying body beforethe immortal soul. You are full of care and anxiety about matters which relate only to a span of time, and yet you care not for your eternal interests. Can you justify this? Are you in your senses? Why do you act so foolishly? There is a God whose smile is heaven and whose frown is hell, and yet you ignore his existence, and neither seek him nor serve him. I know I plead but badly, but my cause is a good one, and if you are right at heart you will feel its force. Ought not the wrongs done to God to be owned and forsaken? Say, dear hearer, "I do remember my faults this day, and remembering them I will arise and go unto my Father, and put him in remembrance that I may be forgiven." My faith sees the Lord standing here blotting out the debts of all who will bring them to his remembrance. Come, bring your bills! Hand in the record of your debts to justice! Spread them now before the face of the Lord, not that he may condemn you for them, but that he may stamp them with the atoning blood and say, "I have blotted out thy sins." Do not hesitate to put the Lord in remembrance of them, for then he promises to forget them. I am sure if I could stand here to-morrow and exercise the power to remit all debts by giving a receipt in full for them all, if the one condition were that each debtor would produce his schedule of debts, no one would be backward in doing so. You who owe anything would search your files, rake out your drawers, and look in every place to find out every unpaid account, so as to have them all blotted out. I pray you do so in this spiritual business. Bring your sins to remembrance by humble acknowledgment and penitent confession, for "if we confess our sins, he is faithful and just to forgive us our sins." O Spirit of God, support this appeal to these my hearers, and send it home to the hearts of thy chosen, that they may confess their iniquities unto thee and be saved this day!

A second practical suggestion is this : since the text says, "Put me in remembrance : let us plead together," it is time that we should now *begin our pleading with God*. He saith, "Come now, and let us reason together"; let us not be so unreasonable as to refuse. I am once more going over the same ground, just as schoolmasters do with their pupils, teaching the same lesson over again that it may be thoroughly learned. I do so long for the troubled sinner to find the way of peace at once, that I would beseech him to begin pleading with God at this moment. Plead thus : "Lord, there stands thy word, 'I am he that blotteth out thy transgressions' : I entreat thee make that word true to me!" Appealing to the faithfulness of God is a grand argument. To lay hold of God by his promise is the main part of the art of wrestling in prayer. No grip of the covenant angel is half so sure as that which faith gets when she seizes a promise. This is, as it were, the skirt of Jehovah's robe ; blessed is he that can hold it; for it will never rend away. He that holds a promise holds the God who gave it, and he shall not trust the promise in vain. "Hath the Lord said, and will he not do it?" Plead it, then :—"Lord, thou hast said that thou dost forgive sin, I pray thee forgive mine. Hadst thou never promised pardon, I could never have dreamed of gaining it; but since thou hast promised it, I dare not doubt thy word. My blackest, foulest, filthiest sins can be washed away, for thou tellest me that all manner of sin and of blasphemy shall be forgiven unto men. I urge thine own word as my sole claim. I implore thee to carry out thine own word." We read that out of Christ's mouth there goeth a two-edged sword ; may not his word of promise be to us as a sword with which we may overcome even mercy itself, conquering heaven by heaven's own weapons? Oh that you may have faith enough to try this at once !

Be sure you do not forget to use in your pleading that verse about God's being honoured by the dragons and the owls. Say, "Lord, this very room in which I have cried to thee of late for mercy bears witness to my sighs and groans and deep sorrows ; but if thou wilt grant me grace it shall ring with thy praises. I have dwelt spiritually with owls and dragons, but if thou wilt forgive me these shall honour thee. Lord, if thou do but set me free thou hast won a new singer for the choirs of earth and for the orchestra of heaven. Oh, my Saviour, I know my poor praises cannot make thee more glorious, for thou art divinely great, but still such as they are they shall be laid at thy feet."

Next plead with the Lord that he will have won thy heart by his grace. He evidently desires it, for he complains, "Thou hast bought me no sweet cane with money, neither hast thou filled me with the fat of thy sacrifices." Does God care for calamus? Does he delight in burning fat? Ah no! but he does care to see his people making a self-sacrifice, to prove their love, by presenting something to their Lord which cost them dear. He condescends to accept at their hands their love-tokens, and he takes much pleasure therein. Now tell him, "Lord, I am not worthy of thine acceptance, but still, if thou wilt but save me, I will be all thine own, and all that I have shall be laid upon the altar. Lord, I must love thee! I have nothing whereof to glory in that love, for how can I help it? I am under constraint to love thee, because thou hast first loved me. I am a captive to grace; I am bound hand and foot by the cords of thy love. When I have dared to entertain a hope that thou wouldst look upon me in mercy, I have felt my stony heart dissolve, and my soul has gone out after thee with strong desire. If thy great love will indeed stoop to me, and to the putting away of all my sin, then my whole heart shall be bound to thee for ever, and I will magnify thy name as long as I have any being." This is good pleading; be sure you use it with deep sincerity and true humility.

Then plead the argument which lies in the word "for mine own sake." Cry, "Lord, do save me for the glory of thine own name, that men may know how gracious thou art. There is room in me for the display of all the wonders of thy love, for I have been one of the chief of sinners. O Lord, prove the power of the cleansing blood of Jesus by washing me, that I may be whiter than snow. I have shown a harder heart than most of my fellows. Oh that thy Spirit would display the energy of his operations by turning this stone to flesh! Lord, I have been unbelieving, yea, desperately full of doubt and unbelief, Oh, demonstrate in me the truth that faith is the gift of God! If thou savest all the world beside me and save not me, there will be a note lacking in the music of thy mercy; for in some respects I stand alone, a special sinner. But, Lord, if thou save me thou wilt put thy finger on a string that will give forth a note such as can come from no other string in all the universe. Thou wilt have saved the most worthless of all, the one who can do least for thee in return. Thou wilt have shown how gratuitous is thy mercy by bestowing it upon one who has no past merit, no present worth, no future hope of doing great things for thee." Thus plead with God, and may the Wonderful, the Counsellor direct thy pleading till thou dost prevail.

Finish all pleadings with the argument of the precious blood, for that shall prevail where all else is driven back. "I believe in the forgiveness of sins": thousands say this when they repeat the creed; they do not feel that they are sinners, and therefore they find it very easy to believe in forgiveness. But, believe me, when a man knows and feels that he is in very deed a sinner before God, it is a miracle for him to believe in the forgiveness of sins; nothing but the omnipotence of the Holy Ghost can work this faith in him. When you really know what it is to be lost and condemned, so that you receive sentence of death in your own conscience, then it is a brave thing to believe in pardoning grace. Some of us remember when it seemed like mocking us for people to say, "Believe, Believe!" for we felt that it was one thing to *say* "I believe," and quite another thing to possess the faith of God's elect. When God the Holy Ghost comes to reveal Jesus to us, and the poor empty sinner is plunged into Christ's fulness, then there is glory to God both from the sinner's faith, and from the object of that faith. God is magnified in the work of grace, for it is his from top to bottom. In the heart of the saved one is heard the voice, " I, even I, am the Lord; and beside me there is no saviour." Lofty looks are laid low, and boasting is excluded. Humility rules the mind, and obedience walks hand in hand with it. Then do renewed hearts cry, " O Lord our God, other lords beside thee have had dominion over us: but by thee only will we make mention of thy name."

Thus have I tried to plead with you for the Lord, wishing only your good and his glory. I am very conscious of my own weakness, much more so, perhaps, than ever I was in my life, but yet I expect to succeed with many of you. What am I apart from the Spirit of all grace? What am I but as a sounding brass and as a tinkling cymbal? And yet I am not feebler than other servants of God in this respect, for we are all nothing apart from the Spirit.

> " Till God diffuse his graces down,
> Like showers of heavenly rain,
> In vain Apollos sows the ground,
> And Paul may plant in vain."

Blessed be God we shall not plant in vain, for he is with us! Some of you have received the message, and I shall hear from you soon. Let it sink into the spirits of all of you. Do you feel any degree of softness creeping over you? Yield to it. It is the blessed Spirit now inclining you to relent, making you feel serious and thoughtful, and anxious and desirous. Bow before his heavenly breath as the rush by the river yields to the wind! Yours shall be the benefit, but to the sweet Spirit of love, together with the Father and the Son, shall be glory for ever and ever. Amen, and Amen.

PORTION OF SCRIPTURE READ BEFORE SERMON—Isaiah xliii. 14—23; xliv. 1—8.

HYMNS FROM "OUR OWN HYMN BOOK"—257, 579, 589.

"Till He Come"
$3.95. SBC rate, $2.65.

A volume of twenty-one messages delivered at the observance of the Lord's Supper (not published in the MTP services). Covers a wide range of subjects, but all related to the atoning work of Christ of which the bread and cup are the simple yet significant symbols.

Metropolitan Tabernacle Pulpit.

WHERE THE "IF" LIES.

A Sermon

DELIVERED ON LORD'S-DAY MORNING, OCTOBER 14TH, 1883, BY

C. H. SPURGEON,

AT THE METROPOLITAN TABERNACLE, NEWINGTON.

"Jesus said unto him, If thou canst believe, all things are possible to him that believeth."—Mark ix. 23.

I BELIEVE that our own Authorized Version conveys to the mind of the reader the sense intended by the Evangelist; it is, however, exceedingly probable that in exact words the Revised Version is nearer to the original. It runs thus—"And Jesus said unto him, If thou canst! All things are possible to him that believeth." Our own Version better expresses the sense to the general reader, and the main object of a translation is to give the meaning. The father of the lunatic child had said to our Lord, "If thou canst do anything, have compassion on us, and help us;" and our divine Master virtually replies, "The 'if thou canst' lies not with me, but with thee. It is not if *I* can, but if *thou* canst." Thus you see the word "believe" is implied if not actually expressed. Jesus would certainly go as far as ever the man's faith could go; but as the rule of the kingdom is, "According to thy faith, so be it unto thee," the man's unbelief would hamper the Lord in his working. If the suppliant could be rid of unbelief, Jesus would get rid of the devil from his child. The difficulty of casting out the demon lay mainly in the want of faith in the father. Let it, then, be understood as the teaching of this text, that the difficulties in the way of souls that would be saved do not lie with Jesus Christ, but with themselves. They need never ask the question, "Can Jesus forgive?" or "Can he renew?" there is a prior question—Canst thou believe that he can forgive, and that he can renew? If God's grace enables thee to say, "I can and do believe that Jesus can work in me according to the full measure of my need," then all difficulty has vanished. Thy faith is the shadow of the coming blessing, the token of the Lord's favour towards thee. When thy faith believes in Christ's omnipotence, he is omnipotent to thee, for "all things are possible to him that believeth."

I long at this time to get at some here who cannot get at Christ. I would to God that by his Spirit I may deal with their difficulties, so as to remove them once for all, so that they may come just as they are, and put their trust in Jesus, and find eternal life this day.

No. 1,744.

I. The first subject we shall speak about is the vital question—
WHAT IS BELIEVING? After all these hundreds of years of gospel
preaching, is this question necessary? I believe it is so necessary that,
if faith were explained in every sermon, it would not be too often spoken
of. It is a good rule that every tract ought to contain the gospel;
and it ought to be put in the plainest way, for still, despite all the
gospel teaching which is around us, nothing is so little known or so
little understood as faith in the Lord Jesus Christ. I am also bound
to admit that many explanations of faith are no explanations, but tend
to make the subject darker than it was before ; and I am fearful lest my
own explanation should be of the like order. Certainly, I will do my
best to avoid such a catastrophe, for I will speak very plainly.

Let us take the man before us as an example, and from him let us
see what faith is. This man evidently believed that Jesus was a healer,
for he says, " I brought my son unto thee." He would not have brought
his son to Jesus if he had not felt some measure of confidence in him.
*It is a good beginning of faith to know that if I am saved it must be through
Jesus Christ alone ;* it is well to be aware that the salvation of the soul
must come from the work of Jesus, and from no one else, since no other
name is given among men whereby we must be saved. This man had
also some slight faith in Christ's willingness to help him. It may not
have been very strong, but still it was there, or else he would not have
laid the stress of his prayer upon the Lord's power ; he did not say
" if thou wilt thou canst," but " if thou canst do anything, have compassion on us, and help us." Looking up into that blessed face so full
of singular tenderness, the man felt that he might say, " Have compassion on us." From some persons we could not ask compassion or
fellow-feeling, because they do not appear to have any ; they wear a
harsh look, and a chill air surrounds them ; but the Saviour was not
so ; the man felt that Jesus was full of compassion : his suit was that
this compassion would show itself to him and his son. *It is a good
beginning to saving faith if thou believest that Jesus is willing to save
thee.* I trust that many of you have advanced as far as this.

What is it really and savingly to believe in Jesus ? The suppliant
father had not yet reached that point of faith which would secure the
miracle : more was needed ; what was it ? *He needed to believe in Christ's
power in reference to his own case.* The point in which his faith failed
was our Lord's power as to the special case now before him, for he said
—" If thou canst do anything." Before you condemn the anxious
father for his doubt, let me remind you that his son was in a very evil
plight, and our Lord had just caused him to remember and review the
sad features of the case. The father had sorrowfully dilated upon the fact
that " wheresoever the spirit taketh him, he teareth him : and he foameth,
and gnasheth with his teeth, and pineth away ;" and then he had further
told the Lord that the youth had suffered thus ever since he was a child ;
and he had gone still more into detail, saying, " Ofttimes it hath cast him
into the fire, and into the waters, to destroy him." After that painful
detail he added his pitiful "If thou canst." Do you wonder at it?
Jesus seems to tell him, " If thou canst believe in the teeth of all this,
then thou shalt see the salvation of God." It is very easy to say, " I
believe" when you have no sense of your sin, and no consciousness of

your danger. It is the easiest thing in the world to say, "Yes, Christ can save me," when you do not really believe that you need saving. Faith, where there is no present sense of need, is but the image of faith, and not the grace which saves the soul. This is the question: *can you, my dear hearer, at this moment trust Jesus to save you, though you feel that you are full of sin?* Can you say, "Lord, I am possessed with the spirit of evil: I am under bondage to him, and have been so since I was a child? I have been driven to one sin and so cast into the fire, and then I have been hurled into the opposite sin, and so thrown into the water: I have been rent with passion, and torn with evil desires; I have sinned against light and knowledge, I have sinned against love and mercy; I have sinned in thought, and word, and deed; I have sinned grievously and continually, and yet I believe that thou canst pardon me, and that thou canst make me a new creature. Wicked as I am, I believe that thou canst drive sin from the throne of my heart and cause me to love thee and to serve thee all my days." If thou canst believe in Jesus after this fashion he will save thee, yea he has saved thee. If thou, as an undeserving sinner, canst so honour the mercy of God as to believe that through Christ Jesus he can blot out thy sin, it shall be done unto thee: only remember that this confidence must not come unto thee because of thy forgetfulness of thy sin, but whilst thou art conscious of it and humbled on its account. If I persuade myself that I am merely a sinner in name, then I shall only find Jesus to be a saviour in name. If I am not such a sinner as to deny that I am a sinner, but pay the Lord the compliment of saying, "Oh, yes, I am a sinner; we are all sinners," then I am a sham sinner, and I shall become a sham believer, and the true Saviour will have nothing to do with me. Jesus came to save that which is really and truly lost. The downright sinner, who dares not deny his guilt, is the object of the Lord's saving search. In the teeth of thy conscious guilt, canst thou believe that Jesus can wash thee and renew thee? Then thou hast one main element of the faith which saves.

Yet, mark you, if this man could by any possibility have believed in Christ's power to save his son and yet had refused to bring him to Jesus for healing, he would have missed one of the essentials of true faith. For, hark. *If thou wouldst get to the very heart and bowels of faith, thou hast it here: it is to trust the Lord.* Trust! trust! that is the word. To believe that Christ is able to save thee is an essential, but to put thyself into his hands that he may save thee, is the saving act. Believe Christ's word to be true; then appropriate that word unto thyself as spoken to thee: believe that it is true to thee, and rest in the truth of it—that is saving faith. To see Christ as such a Saviour as thou needest, able and willing to save thee, is a right good sight, but thou must also take this Saviour to be thine. Say heartily, "Into that hand which was nailed to the cross I commit my guilty soul, hoping and believing that Jesus will forgive all my trespasses, and cause me to love all that is true and holy henceforth and for ever."

> "Thou canst, thou wilt (I dare not doubt),
> Th' indwelling demons chase;
> I trust thy power to cast them out,
> I trust thy pardoning grace."

He that trusts in Jesus is saved.   I said not, "he *shall be* saved," but
he *is* saved.   "He that believeth in him hath everlasting life."   " He that
believeth in him is justified from all things, from which he could not be
justified by the law of Moses."

Will you please to notice about this man's faith that *it was not perfect
faith.*   Though it obtained for him the healing of his son, it was weak
faith, and for its weakness he was blamable; but the faultiness of his
faith was not the destruction of his faith.   A feeble faith can receive a
mighty Saviour, even as a beggar with a palsied hand can receive a
golden gift.   An heir to an estate has as good a title to it when he is
a child as he will have when he is grown up, and even so little faith
possesses the inheritance, though as yet it be a babe.   The anxious
father had to cry, " Lord, help my unbelief," but that unbelief, confessed and lamented, did not shut him out of the blessing.   The unbelief which lingers around our faith is a thing to be got rid of by the
help of Christ, but still it will not destroy the virtue of the faith which
we possess.   So, dear friend, if thy faith in Jesus Christ amounts to
this, that thou believest him able to save, and thou dost therefore trust
him, thou art a saved man, even though thou mayest be staggered with
a host of fears, and troubled with a multitude of sins.   Thy faith hath
saved thee, go in peace ; for that faith of thine shall grow from a
mustard-seed into a far-spreading tree.   I would that thou couldst take
Jesus up into thine arms as Simeon did, for then wouldst thou say with
full assurance, " Mine eyes have seen thy salvation."   But if thou canst
not do so much as that, at least stretch out thy finger and touch the
hem of the Lord's garment; for if thou dost but touch his clothes thou
shalt be made whole.   The faintest contact with the ever-blessed Christ
will open up a way by which saving power will flow out of him into
thee.   Oh, how blessed it is to think that God hath ordained this plain
way of faith for poor sinners!   It is of faith that it might be of grace,
to the end that the promise might be sure to all the chosen seed.

*This faith in the Lord Jesus ought to be to each one of us the easiest
thing in all the world.*   If we were what we ought to be it would never
occur to us to doubt our Lord Jesus ; and our shameful unbelief of him
is the most conclusive evidence of our need of him, for we must have
become grievously wrong in heart to be forced to admit that we find it
difficult to believe in Jesus.   What an insult to him!   What a crime
on our part!   Remember the whole story of grace and blush for your
wicked unbelief.   God, the ever-blessed, whom we had offended, sent
his dear Son to be made in the likeness of sinful flesh, and he dwelt
here among us as our brother, friend, and helper.   In the fulness of
time he took upon himself our sin and sorrow, and went up to the
cross with the awful load of our guilt.   Though still the well-beloved
Son of the Father, he suffered even unto death in the room and
stead of his people, and God's record concerning him is that he has
set him forth as the propitiation for sin.   God has accepted his atonement, will not sinners accept it?   This is the Saviour; God has ordained
him such : will not the sinner agree that Jesus should save him?   If
not, why not ?   If we were not fallen to the uttermost degree of
depravity we should cry out with delight, " Lord, we believe.   Blessed
be the dear name of Jesus, our Substitute, we can and do trust him.

We are quite sure if the Lord God has made Jesus to be his salvation to the ends of the earth he must be a perfect salvation; therefore we accept him with joy and delight." But this is the curse of our nature, the innate vice of our hearts, that we cannot believe our God, thus making him a liar. Oh, the horror of suspecting his truth whom angels adore with veiled faces! Oh, the daring presumption of questioning the promise of a faithful God! It is horrible, horrible, horrible to the last degree to mistrust the Almighty Father, to doubt his bleeding Son! There ought to be no room for an "if" when we know that in the Lord Jesus all fulness dwells. I am not at this moment speaking to those who reject the word of God, and deny the Deity of Christ: I can understand their position, and deal with them another time; but I am now speaking to you who accept this Bible as God's word, and unquestioningly believe that Jesus Christ is divine: to you I say that your refusal to put your trust in him is without excuse; at least, I cannot find an excuse for you. Remember those telling words of the Lord Jesus—"If I tell you the truth, why do you not believe me?" If you believe Jesus to be the Son of God and the Saviour of men, why do you not trust your own soul with him? Why not at this moment confide in him whom you admit to be worthy of your trust?

II. I have tried thus to explain the nature of faith. I will now, in the second place, deal with the startling question, How IS IT THAT FAITH CAN BE DIFFICULT? It certainly is difficult to some. It cannot be so in itself, yet many in trouble of heart find it to be so, and those that labour to bring them to Christ, find themselves sore put to it.

Why, first, *it is difficult to get the very idea of faith into some men's minds*—not only difficult for them to believe, but even to know what it is to believe. I have met with persons who have attended a place of worship regularly twenty or thirty years, and yet they have never made the discovery that faith is a childlike trust in Jesus. I, as a lad, was taught this blessed secret by the Spirit of God; but it was at the first a great wonder to me that I should have attended evangelical ministries for years, and yet should not have known what was meant by believing in Christ. That simple truth broke in upon my mind like a new revelation. I had read the Bible; there was no part of it with which I was not acquainted, and yet even from that blessed book I had not learned what believing in Christ meant. Is not this singular? It is remarkable, and yet it is a general fact. We try by illustrations, by anecdotes, by parables, to drill the notion of faith into men; but we cannot even get it into their heads, much less into their hearts. Martin Luther complained that he thought he must take the Bible and bang it about his hearers' heads because he could not get them to see its clear teaching as to justification by faith. This idea of believing is alien to men's minds, and it can only dwell there by forcing its way against the tendency of human nature. Again, I say, that this is a sad proof of human depravity, since in itself it is no difficult idea: it is the simplest thought that can be uttered or accepted. Trust thou thy salvation with Christ, and Christ will save thee, is a lesson which a babe may learn. Still, the unregenerate do not think so: they muddle it all up, and stick to their belief that faith is something to be felt, or seen, or done, or suffered. To trust their God, to rely upon the atonement of his Son—this is not to their mind, and so their foolish heart is darkened, and they cannot see the way which lies straight before them.

When we get that thought into our hearers' heads, then there comes the next difficulty, *to make them believe that faith can save them.* It seems so difficult to believe this *because the way is so easy.* They say— What! am I, after thirty, forty, fifty years of sin, to be delivered from all the punishment of my transgressions by simply trusting to the Lord Jesus Christ? If you were to tell them that they must go to a desert and live there as hermits on berries and cold water for the rest of their natural lives, they would believe the message. If they were bidden to scourge themselves with whips of wire, they could expect some good result from such suffering, but not from mere believing. If they were to look at the idea of propitiating God by their personal suffering, it would soon become impossible of belief; yet for a time they incline to it rather than to the doctrine of salvation by trust in the great Substitute. Hideous imaginings, despairings, and dreads are also looked upon hope- fully by many; they hope that by deep feelings they may arrive at forgiveness, and may force their way to heaven by the gates of hell; but to trust Christ, and to believe the promise of God, is a thing too simple for them; they fear that safety is not to be found so soon! Ah! poor soul, if the prophet had bid thee do some great thing, wouldst thou not have done it? How much rather then when he saith to thee, " Believe and live? "

I wish you would change your opinion as to what faith really is, for it is by no means so insignificant a matter as you suppose. Simple as it is there lies within it great excellence and value. Faith in God is the divinest exercise of the mind. To believe in God and his Christ is to be reconciled to God and restored from enmity. We are in unison of heart with those we trust. To believe your God is to worship him: the essence of worship is faith. For a poor sinner to trust the Lord gives him more honour than the cherubim can bring him with their loftiest notes of praise. In the teeth of all my sin and sinfulness, with a thorough sense of my guilt, I believe that the blood of Jesus has saved me—is not this true praise? To confess scarlet sins, and yet to say, " Wash me, and I shall be whiter than snow," gives unto the Lord great glory for his mercy and his power. Yet the doctrine of " Believe and live " startles poor sinners because it is too easy!

When they get over the idea of its extreme ease, *they say to them- selves, " This news is certainly too good to be true.* Do I really understand you, sir, that if I trust the Lord Jesus now I am at once delivered from sin and am made a new creature in Christ? " Yes, you understand my teaching if that is the sense you find in my words. Yet you say it is too good to be true. Do you not see how poorly you think of your God? I know that pardoning grace is infinitely above your deservings or thoughts; but then does not the Lord say of himself, " As the heavens are higher than the earth, so are my ways higher than your ways, and my thoughts than your thoughts? " Grace may be too good for you to expect, but it is not too good for God to bestow. Oh that you would think better of God than you have done, and say of his amazing grace, " It is just like him! " Sing with me these words—

> " Who is a pardoning God like thee ?
>   Or who hath grace so rich and free ? "

Salvation pitched in such a key as this, given freely to whosoever believeth in Jesus! Why, that is like the Lord, and we will accept it as having the divine stamp and impress upon it. He forgives like a God, and this does not stagger our faith, but confirms it.

Then, again, men are astounded by *the rapidity of justification*. Shall fifty years' sinning be forgiven in a moment? Shall an instant's believing end the guilty past, and commence a holy future? It is even so; in one instant a man begins a course of believing which introduces him into a new world. What is strange about this? Is it not God's way to do wonders in a short time? He took but a week to fit up the earth for man; nay, six days sufficed, and on the seventh he rested. To make the light in which we rejoice, only needed for the Lord to say, "Let there be light." In the case before us our Lord only said to the demon, "I charge thee, come out of him, and enter no more into him," and the deed was done. If we had all time at our disposal, we could not work such wonders, but to God there are no limits as to length or brevity of time. A thousand years are to him as one day, and one day as a thousand years. He speaks, and it is done. Think of it—salvation in a moment! The moment a sinner believes he lives unto God, and his trespasses are forgiven. Oh sinner! why shouldest thou doubt it? Yet we cannot get the conscience-stricken one to believe it.

If we lead our friends out of this difficulty, they plunge into another. *They cannot be satisfied with the word of God alone as the ground for their faith.* Why do I believe that I am saved? I know that I am saved because the word of God says, " He that believeth in him hath everlasting life;" and I do believe in Jesus, and therefore I have everlasting life. " But," saith one, " if I had that word applied to me with power, then I could and would believe it." Just so; but until then you refuse to believe the promise of God, and treat him as a liar! God must needs give you some pledge or bond beyond his promise, because his word is not good enough for you, though you admit that even with a good *man* his word is his bond. You cannot trust your God. "Oh, but if I had a dream." Just so. You would have more faith in a silly dream, perhaps caused by indigestion, than you have in the solemn word and written promise of God. " Oh, sir, but if an angel were to speak to me, I could believe." Just so; and if God does not choose to send the angels, what then? Then he is not to be believed, but treated as a liar. What is this but saying, " Lord, thou shalt bow to my whims, or else I will not believe a word thou sayest?" Is it come to this? Dare you demand signs of God? Then let me ask you—Is this Book God's word? Say "No," and I can understand your conduct; but if you believe, as I know you do, that this is the very word of God, how dare you disbelieve? If all the angels in heaven were to march by me in a file, and assure me that God would keep his word, I should say, " I did not require you to tell me that, for the Lord never fails to be as good as his word." God is so true that the witness of angels would be a superfluity. If my father were to make a statement, I certainly should not call in his servant to confirm it. If this book be dictated by the Holy Spirit, it is ours to believe it without demanding confirmations or applications. Let us say, "That word is true, for God hath said it. Jesus Christ came into the world to save sinners: I am a sinner, and I trust him to save me. Inasmuch as the word says, 'To as many as received him, to them gave he power to become the sons of God, even to them that believe on his name;' I do believe on his name, and therefore I have the power and privilege to become a child of God, and a child of God I am. God says so: that is enough for me." We cannot get men to see that the word of the Lord is surer than all signs and wonders—they want something in addition.

If we compel them to own that the word of God is the only and sufficient basis of faith, *they straightway begin to look at their own believing as if it were the Saviour.* They cry, "My faith is so weak; my faith is so variable; my faith is so shaken," and so forth. It is as if those who were bidden to look to the brazen serpent had, instead thereof, tried to see their own eyes. Here is a child thirsty, and there is a flowing fountain; you give the child a cup that it may drink of the water. The child does not go to the fountain, but is so pleased with its empty cup that it tries to satisfy its thirst out of it. What a foolish child! Or suppose it should refuse to go to the fountain because the cup was of earthenware, or of tin, would not that be a strange way for a thirsty child to act? A child needs the cup to drink out of, but it cannot drink out of an empty cup. Faith is the cup, but Christ is the fountain. Faith is a secondary thing compared with Christ. We must have faith to be as the finger with which we touch the hem of the Master's garment, but the finger does not work the cure. Shall I refuse to touch because perhaps I have not washed my finger clean, or it has no gold ring upon it; or there are traces of rheumatism upon it? To attach so much importance to the finger as to refuse to touch Christ's garment with it would be insanity. Do not mind your finger: touch the garment's hem. Sinner, get you to Christ somehow, anyhow; for if you get to him you will live. It is not, after all, the greatness nor the perfection of your faith, it is *his* greatness and *his* perfection which is to be depended on.

Then the next trial is, that we cannot get troubled sinners *to see the difference between their faith and its fruits.* "I would believe in Christ," says one, "if I were as holy as So-and-So, who is a believer, but then you see I am a sinner." Now mark, dear friend, that the person of whom you speak in that fashion does not think himself to be one particle more deserving than you are. If you talk to that good man he will tell you that whatever holiness you can see in him is the work of grace, and that at the first he came to Jesus just as you must come, that is, as a sinner. Faith produces holiness; but when we come to Jesus, at the first we come as unholy persons, and as such he receives us. Suppose that I have a number of bulbs which I am told will produce most remarkable flowers; if I believe the statement I shall take care to have them properly planted. The gardeners are beginning to put such things into pots, that they may have hyacinths and other fair flowers in the winter and early spring. Suppose that I resolve not to plant my bulbs, because I use my own eyesight, and come to the conclusion that as I cannot see a hyacinth or even the beginnings of one in any of the bulbs, therefore there can be no use in planting them. Why, everyone would tell me that in this matter I must go by faith, and plant my hyacinth in order that I may in due time see it bloom. "That bulb will yield a beautiful blue flower," says one. I answer that it is a brown, dried-up sort of onion, and that I shall throw it on the dunghill, for I can see no bud or flower in it. What a simpleton I should be if I talked so! Though I cannot *see* it, yet there is, closely compacted and quietly hidden away within that bulb, a slumbering thing of beauty which will wake up at the call of spring. Even so, if thou believest in Christ, there is a holy life packed away within thy faith, and it will gradually develop itself. Even within a feeble faith there are the elements of ultimate perfection. If thou dost truly trust Christ, thy preparation for glory has begun. As the king was hidden in the oak so is Christ hidden in true faith. Do not, however, expect to see all this at the first : look to the root now and the growth will follow. You are not to come to Christ because you are healed, but to get healing ; your faith must be a sinner's faith before it can be a saint's faith. Trust Christ while yet you are foul, lost, and undone, and he will wash, save, and restore you.

Still we find the awakened ones clinging to the idea that they must be something or feel something before they may trust Jesus. We cannot get them to see that the whole of their salvation lies in Jesus Christ and in Jesus Christ alone. We cannot wean them from some sort of reliance upon their own feelings, or weepings, or prayers, or Bible-readings, or some other form of working. Why, they will even look to their own faith rather than to Jesus Christ alone. Know ye not that our Lord has offered a full atonement for sin, and brought in a perfect righteousness for his people ? His propitiation is to be accepted as full and complete, and his righteousness we are to wear as our own. Our whole trust must go to the perfect work of our Lord, it must not even rest on our faith. To trust in our own trusting would be absurd. A wounded man has healing ointment given him and a piece of linen with which to bind on the ointment ; now, if he were to wrap the linen around the wound and leave out the healing agent, he could not expect a cure. Faith is the linen whereon the ointment of Christ is spread, and we must not put it out of its due place and order, or we shall be making it a rival to Christ. Oh, that I could clear up some of the difficulties with which men surround themselves, so that they would consent to look out of themselves to Jesus only !

III. We must now speak to the last point. Oh, you that are seeking rest, dwell upon each word as it is now lovingly delivered to you. WHAT IS IT THAT CAN MAKE FAITH EASY ? The Holy Spirit alone can do that ; but he does so by bringing certain truths to remembrance. Faith is rendered easy to a man by the Holy Spirit when, first of all, he sees clearly *the infallible certainty of the sacred record ;* and this is the record that God gave concerning his Son, that he that believeth in him hath everlasting life. Is this Bible true or not ? I believe in every letter of it : I accept it as God's word in the most unreserved sense, and so do you to whom I now speak. Well, if that be so, then it remains no longer difficult to believe what is plainly taught in this book. If God hath spoken then questions are ended. It may be a hard saying, it may be a dark saying ; it may seem to be too good to be true ; but what of that ? Do we dare to question the Lord ? He is not a man that he should lie, nor the Son of man that he should repent. He has said that whosoever believeth in Jesus shall not perish, but have everlasting life; and if we have so believed, eternal life is ours.

The next thing that the Spirit of God helps us to see is *the applicability of that record to ourselves :* that is to say, we read, " Jesus Christ came into the world to save sinners," and we conclude that, as we are just such, we may look to him to save us. We read, " Come unto me, all ye that labour and are heavy laden, and I will give you rest." We labour and are heavy laden, and therefore we come, and he gives us rest. We read that " in due time Christ died for the ungodly"; and knowing that we are ungodly, we yet take heart and come to him who justifies the guilty through his righteousness. We read again, " Whosoever will, let him take the water of life freely." We feel that to will is present with us, and therefore we freely take the living water. We read once more, " Go ye into all the world, and preach the gospel to every creature; " and as we are creatures, we conclude that the gospel has something to say to us. On one or other of these accounts we see that the gospel is directed to us, and so we receive it. It is better for us that the promise should be directed to us in terms of character than that it should mention our actual names. Is your name John Brown ? Well, if the gospel came in a letter to you, directed to John Brown, what might you not say if you were tempted to doubt ? You would think to yourself that there are many more John Browns besides yourself, and therefore the message might not be for you. If it was directed to your address, you might then fear that another John Brown once lived at that house, before you were born, and so you would fear to appropriate the message lest it should prove to be out of date. Even supposing that your name was there, and the address, and the date, you might be mistrustful enough to fancy that there was a mistake, or that some other person of your name had used your address for the day. If you mean to ride on the back of unbelief any fancy will do for a saddle. But when the promise comes "to him that believeth in Jesus," there can be no question that it is ours if we believe. We read, " If we confess our sins, God is faithful and just to forgive us our sins ;" is it not clear that if we have confessed our sins, mercy is ours ? It is a blessed thing for us when the Spirit of God leads us to see that the gospel is free to all who are made willing to receive it.

Another thing that makes faith easy is when the Spirit of God shows us *the glory of Christ's person.* Our Saviour is truly God, and this fact helps us to believe in him. It strikes me that the poor anxious father may have been much helped to believe in our Lord by that peculiar majesty which shone about him through his having just come down from the mount of transfiguration. It was a very hard case which exercised the poor man's mind, and therefore our Lord appeared to him with an unusual splendour—a splendour of which we read— " when they saw him they were amazed." A sight of our Saviour's face helped the trembler to cry, "Lord, I believe." Oh, if the Spirit of God will lead you to read the Scriptures till you get a clear idea of the Godhead and perfect manhood of the Lord Jesus, you will feel that everything is possible with an Almighty Saviour. " Is anything too hard for the Lord?" Our Lord is gone up unto his glory, and he is able to save unto the uttermost them that come unto God by him. Oh, could you but grasp the idea that he who asks your trust is the Son of the Highest, who has all power in heaven and in earth, you could not, you would not withhold your confidence! As for myself, knowing beyond all doubt my Lord's divinity it seems easy enough to rely upon him. I have told you before what John Hyatt said on his dying bed, when his deacons said, " Mr. Hyatt, can you trust your soul with Christ now?" " One soul!" said he, "I could trust a million souls with him if I had them." Even so could I trust the Lord Jesus not only with my soul, but with all the destinies of earth and heaven, time and eternity. Every child of God may safely say that. I could trust Jesus with all the souls that ever lived or shall live, if they were all mine. Surely, he is able to keep that which we have committed to him.

Another great help to faith is to perceive *the completeness of the divine work and sacrifice of the Lord Jesus.* He took our sin upon himself, and in his own body on the tree was made sin for us, that we might be made the righteousness of God in him. Only let your eyes behold the Son of God suffering the death-agony for guilty man, and you must believe in his power to redeem. I have thought that if men had been more sinful than they are, and if they were a million times as numerous as they are, and if every star that studs the midnight sky were a world, and all crowded full of sinners, yet the sacrifice of God himself must from the glory of his nature be such a vindication of the law that it might well suffice as a reason for forgiving a rebel universe! Shall the infinitely holy suffer for the guilty? Shall the Eternal take upon himself humanity, and bow his head to death? Then the sacrifice must possess such boundless efficacy that none may fear that it will fall short of their need. No limit can be set to the power which lies in the divine expiation. My God, I see that thou hast given thine own Son to die, and surely in his precious blood there is more than sufficient reason for my faith in thee.

If that does not lead you to believe perhaps the Spirit of God will go to work in another way. Some have been helped to believe in Jesus by *the sight of others converted, justified, and made happy.* When someone like yourself is saved you take courage. " I have been a thief," says one.

> " The dying thief rejoiced to see
> That fountain in his day;
> And there may you, though vile as he,
> Wash all your sins away."

" I have been an adulterer," saith one. Alas! so was David, but he said, " Wash me, and I shall be whiter than snow." " I have been a murderer," sobs a third. So was Manasseh, who shed innocent blood very much. " But I have been a persecutor and a blasphemer." So was Saul of Tarsus, yet he obtained mercy. " But I seem to have far more of the devil in me than anybody else." So had Mary Magdalene, out of whom Christ cast seven devils. You think you are a sinner all by yourself, but there have been others like you, and the door through which others have passed into mercy is open for you. If I had been a little rabbit in the day when Noah brought the living creatures into the ark, I do not think I should have been troubled about whether there was room for me to enter the ark; but if I had been so timid I should have forgotten all my fears when I saw the elephant come up and his mate with him, and had seen them go tramping through the door. Then I should have known assuredly that there was room for me. Oh, you who have been kept moral and upright, and therefore are not outwardly great sinners, surely you may enter where the chief of sinners have found ready admission. The salvation of others is often a sweet encouragement to sinners to trust in Christ.

Lastly, I will tell you one thing which will make you trust him, and that is, *desperation as to all other hopes*. It is a singular thing that despair is often the mother of faith, but the mother dies when the child is born. We were many of us led to believe in Jesus because we had nothing else to trust in. When we are driven to the last extremity, then it is we come to Jesus, and take him to be our all in all. A boy was awakened in a house which had taken fire. He could be seen from the street, poor child, and his danger was great indeed. He rushed to the window: his father stood below and called to him to drop into his arms; but it was a long way down, and the child was afraid. He clung to the window, but dared not drop. Do you know what made him let go his hold and fall into his father's arms? There came a burst of fire out of the window and scorched him, and then he dropped directly. I wish that some of you would get just such a touch of the fires of despair as to compel you to say:

> "I can but perish if I go;
> I am resolved to try,
> For if I stay away I know
> I must for ever die."

Years ago one of our students was greatly emaciated with what seemed to be consumption. He had heard of a certain medicine which was said to be useful in such cases, but he had no faith in it. When he was growing worse and worse I said, " Brother, you are at death's door; try that man's stuff. There may be something in it. At any rate, nothing else does you any good." He took the medicine through sheer despair, of all other prescriptions, and God blessed it to him so that he is alive at this day. He would never have tried the remedy if he had not felt that there was no other hope. Even so, it will be well for you to be driven into a corner as to your soul's estate, that you may believe in Christ Jesus and say with his disciples in old time, " To whom shall we go? Thou hast the words of eternal life." Here is a closing verse for you to sing at home by yourself

> " A guilty, weak, and helpless worm,
> On Christ's kind arms I fall ;
> He is my strength and righteousness,
> My Jesus and my all."

PORTION OF SCRIPTURE READ BEFORE SERMON—Mark ix. 2—29

HYMNS FROM " OUR OWN HYMN BOOK"—249, 498, 551.

Metropolitan Tabernacle Pulpit.

ABIJAH, OR SOME GOOD THING TOWARDS THE LORD.

A Sermon

DELIVERED ON LORD'S-DAY MORNING, OCTOBER 21ST, 1883, BY

C. H. SPURGEON,

AT THE METROPOLITAN TABERNACLE, NEWINGTON.

"And all Israel shall mourn for him, and bury him: for he only of Jeroboam shall come to the grave, because in him there is found some good thing toward the LORD God of Israel in the house of Jeroboam."—1 Kings xiv. 13.

JEROBOAM had proved false to the Lord who had placed him upon the throne of Israel, and the time was come for his overthrow. The Lord, who usually brings forth the rod before he lifts the axe, sent sickness into his house: his son Abijah was sore sick. Then the parents bethought them of an old prophet of God, and desired to know through him what would happen to the child. Fearful lest the prophet should denounce plagues upon him and his child if he knew that the enquirer was the wife of Jeroboam, the king begged the Egyptian princess whom he had married to disguise herself as a farmer's wife, and so get from the man of God a more favourable answer. Poor foolish king, to imagine that a prophet who could see into futurity could not also see through any disguise with which his queen might surround herself! So anxious was the mother to know the fate of her son, that she left his sick-chamber to go to Shiloh to hear the sentence of the prophet. Vain was her clever disguise! the blind prophet was still a seer, and not only discerned her before she entered the house, but saw the future of her family. She came full of superstition to be told her fortune, but she went away heavy, having been told her faults and her doom.

In the terrible tidings which the prophet Ahijah delivered to this wife of Jeroboam, there was only one bright spot, only one word of solace; and I am greatly afraid that it gave no kind of comfort to the heathen queen. Her child was mercifully appointed to die, for in him there was "found some good thing toward Jehovah, God of Israel." As an Egyptian, it is not likely that she appreciated the meaning of that sentence; probably she thought it of very small importance that her child should have regard towards the God of his people. She saw not the light which was full of joy. In what an unhappy condition is that person who cannot derive comfort from the salvation of his own child! Yet there are many men and women in such a state. They care nothing for the souls of their own offspring. It would bring no joy to them if they saw all their children walking in the truth; nor

Nos. 1,745-6.

does it cause them any concern to see them otherwise. To see them sharp in business, or fair in countenance, is their main ambition; but to have them beloved of the Lord is no matter of desire. Poor souls, their own carnality overflows and saturates their family! To some it would even cause anger and wrath to see their children turning to the Lord; they so despise true religion that, if their sons and daughters were converted, they would rather hate them than love them the more. Such is the alienation which sin works in the human mind, that it will in some instances curdle human affection into enmity, at the sight of the grace of God. That which should increase love has even created loathing. As Saul sought to slay Jonathan because he loved David, so do some hate their children because they love Jesus. Such persons make curses out of their blessings. They put bitter for sweet and sweet for bitter, darkness for light and light for darkness; and therefore that which ought to be their comfort and joy becomes a source of disquietude. But, beloved, I think I could say of the most of us here present, that if we did but know of a surety that there was in our child some good thing toward Jehovah, God of Israel, we would be perfectly content to leave all the rest of his case at the absolute disposal of the Lord. If such a child should die, it would be well; for it is much better to have a child in heaven than to have one on earth breaking our heart by his wicked ways: and if such a child shall live, what happy prospects open up before us, that as his years advance, he will grow in knowledge, and in favour both with God and man! Certify us of this, that there is in the young mind some good thing toward the Lord God of Israel, and we reckon that the grand matter is secured, and all else is regarded by us as a mere matter of detail. We will bless the Lord let him send what he will to our children, so long as he has chosen them to be his own, and has put his fear in their hearts. This wretched wife of Jeroboam went her way in utter misery; for that sentence which would have been a sweet solace to us, had little or no charm for her. Oh the sinfulness of that heart which finds no comfort in the salvation of the soul of a dying child!

This morning we are going to look into the little that we know of the young prince Abijah. We know nothing more of him than the text tells us. His name was a suitable one. A good name may belong to a very bad man; but in this case a gracious name was worthily worn. He called God his Father, and his name signifies that fact. " Ab," you know, is the word for " Father," and " Jah " is " Jehovah,"—Jehovah was his father. I would not have mentioned the name had not his life made it true. Oh, you who bear good Bible names, see that you do not dishonour them!

I. I shall ask you first of all to follow me in studying the character of this prince while I say, LET US HERE ADMIRE WHAT WE CANNOT PRECISELY DESCRIBE.

And I mean, first, by that, that *there was in this child " some good thing toward the Lord God of Israel;* " but what was it? Who shall define it? A boundless field for conjecture opens before us. We know there was in him *some* good thing, but what form that good thing took we do not know. Tradition has made assertions, but as these are mere inventions to fill up a gap, they are scarcely worth mentioning here. Our own reflections will, probably, be as near the mark as these improbable traditions Perhaps the obscurity was intentional. We may learn much from the silence of Scripture: we are not told precisely what the good thing was, because any good thing towards the Lord is a sufficient sign of grace. Where there is some good thing towards the Lord God, every good thing is present in seed and essence. The "some good thing" which is so fully developed as to be seen and noted is an index of the presence of all the rest, since the grace of God is not divided, but is present as a whole. God's blessings come in groups; and if some good thing be apparent, all others which are really vital and essential are there. Though the child's *faith* is not mentioned, we are sure that he had faith in the living God, since without it nothing in him would have been good towards God; for " without faith it is impossible to please God." He was a child believer in Jehovah, the God of Israel: perhaps his mother left him at his own request to go to the Lord's prophet about him. Many false prophets were around the palace: his father might not have sent to Shiloh, had not the boy pleaded for it. The child believed in the great invisible God, who made the heavens and the earth, and he worshipped him in faith. I should not wonder, however, if in that child his *love* was more apparent than his faith; for converted children more usually talk of loving Christ than they do of trusting in him : not because faith is not in them, but because the emotion of love is more congenial to the child's nature than the more intellectual act of faith. The heart is large in the child, and therefore love becomes his most conspicuous fruit. I have no doubt this child showed an early affection towards the unseen Jehovah, and a distaste for the idols of his father's court. Possibly he displayed a holy horror of the worship of God under the figure of a calf. Even a child would have intelligence enough to perceive that it must be wrong to liken the great and glorious God to a bullock which hath horns and hoofs. Perhaps the child's refined nature also started back from those base priests of the lowest of the land whom his father had raked together. We do not know exactly the form it took, but there it was: "some good thing" was in the child's heart towards Jehovah, God of Israel.

Carefully note that it was not merely a good inclination which was in him, nor a good desire, but a really good, substantial virtue. There was in him a true and substantial existence of grace, and this is far more than a transient desire. What child is there that has not at some time or other, if it has been trained in the fear of God, felt tremblings of heart and desires towards God? Such goodness is as common as the early dew; but alas! it passeth away quite as speedily. The young Abijah possessed something within him sufficiently real and substantial to be called a "good *thing;* " the Spirit of God had wrought a sure work upon him, and left within him a priceless jewel of grace. Let us admire this good thing, though we cannot precisely describe it.

Let us admire, also, that this "some good thing " should have been in the child's heart, for *its entrance is unknown.* We cannot tell how grace entered the palace of Tirzah and gained this youthful heart. God saw the good thing, for he sees the least good thing in any of us, since he has a quick eye to perceive anything that looks toward himself. But how did this gracious work come to the child? We are not told, and this silence is a lesson to us. It is not essential to us to know how a child receives grace. We need not be painfully anxious to know when, or where, or how a child is converted; it may even be impossible to tell, for the work may have been so gradual that day and hour cannot be known. Even those who are converted in riper years cannot all describe their conversion in detail, much less can we expect to map out the experience of children who have never gone into outward sin, but under the restraints of godly education have kept the commandments from their youth up, like the young man in the gospel narrative. How came this child to have this good thing in his heart? So far we know: we are sure that God placed it there; but by what means? The child, in all probability, did not hear the teaching of the prophets of God; he was never, like young Samuel, taken up to the house of the Lord. His mother was an idolatrous princess, his father was among the most wicked of men, and yet the grace of God reached their child. Did the Spirit of the Lord operate upon his heart through his own thoughts? Did he think over the matter, and did he come to the conclusion that God was God, and that he must not be worshipped as his father worshipped him, under the image of a calf? Even a child might see this. Had some hymn to Jehovah been sung under the palace wall by some lone worshipper? Had the child seen his father on that day when he lifted up his hand against the prophet of Jehovah at the altar of Bethel, when suddenly his right hand withered at his side? Did the tears start from the boy's eye when he saw his father thus paralyzed in the arm of his strength? and did he laugh for very joy of heart when by the prophet's prayer his father was restored again? Did that great miracle of mercy cause him to love the God of Israel? Is it a mere fancy that this may have been so? A withered right hand in a father, and that father a king, is a thing a child is pretty sure to be told of, and if it be restored by prayer the wonder would naturally fill the palace, and be spoken of by everybody, and the prince would hear of it. Or what if this little child had a godly nurse? What if some girl like her that waited upon Naaman's wife was the messenger of love to him? As she carried him to and fro, did his nurse sing him one of the songs of Zion, and tell him of Joseph and Samuel? Israel had not yet so long forsaken her God as to be without many a faithful follower of the God of Abraham, and by some one of these sufficient knowledge was conveyed to the child to become the means of conveying the love of God to his soul. We may conjecture with considerable probability, but we may not pretend to be sure that it was so, nor is there any need that we should be. If the sun be risen it matters little when the day first dawned. Be it ours when we see in children some good thing to rest content with that truth, even if we cannot tell how it came there. God's electing love is never short of means to carry out its purpose: he can send his effectual grace into the heart of Jeroboam's family, and while the father is prostrate before his idols the Lord can find a true worshipper for himself in the king's own child. "Out of the mouths of babes and sucklings hast thou ordained strength because of thine enemies." Thy footsteps are not always seen, O God of grace, but we have learned to adore thee in thy work, even when we discern not thy way.

This "good thing" is described to us in the text in a certain measure.

It was a "good thing towards Jehovah, the God of Israel." The good thing looked towards the living God. In children there often will be found good things towards their parents: let these be cultivated—but these are not sufficient evidences of grace. In children there will sometimes be found good things towards amiability and moral excellence: let all good things be commended and fostered, but they are not sure fruits of grace. It is towards God that the good thing must be that saves the soul. Remember how we read in the New Testament of repentance towards God and of faith in our Lord Jesus Christ. The way the face of the good thing looks is a main point about it. There is life in a look. If a man be travelling away from God every step he takes increases his distance from him; but if his face be toward the Lord he may be only capable of a child's tottering step, but yet he is moving nearer and nearer every moment. There was some good thing in this child *towards God*, and that is the most distinguishing mark of a truly good thing. The child had love, and there was in it love to Jehovah. He had faith, but it was faith in Jehovah. His religious fear was the fear of the living God; his childlike thoughts and desires, and prayers, and hymns went towards the true God. This is what we desire to see not only in children, but in adults: we wish to see their hearts turned to the Lord, and their minds and wills moving towards the Most High. Strange that it should be wonderful for the creature man to look towards his Creator! and yet it is so. Indeed there is no surer sign of a renewed heart than when a man exclaims, " I will arise and go to my Father."

In this dear child that "good thing" wrought *such an outward character that he became exceedingly well beloved.* We are sure of that, because it is said, " All Israel shall mourn for him." He was probably the heir to his father's crown, and there were godly but grieved hearts in Israel that hoped to see times of reform when that youth should come to the throne; and perhaps even those who did not care about religion, yet somehow had marked the youth, and observed his going in and out before them, and had said, " He is Israel's hope; there will be better days when that boy becomes a man"; so that when Abijah died he alone of all his race received both tears and a tomb; he died lamented, and was buried with respect, whereas all the rest of Jeroboam's house were devoured with dogs and vultures. It is a very blessed thing when there is such a good thing in our children that they come to be beloved in their little spheres. They have not all the range which this young prince enjoyed so as to secure universal admiration; but still the grace of God in a child is a very lovely thing, and it draws forth general approbation. I do not know how it is with you, but youthful piety is a very touching thing to me ; I see the grace of God in men and women with much thankfulness, but I cannot perceive it in children without shedding tears of delight. There is an exceeding beauty about these rosebuds of the Lord's garden; they have a fragrance which we find not in the fairest of earth's lilies. Love is won for the Lord Jesus in many a heart by these tiny arrows of the Lord, whose very smallness is a part of their power to penetrate the heart. The ungodly may not love the grace which is in the children, but since they love the children in whom that grace is found, they are no longer able to speak against religion as they otherwise would have done. Yea more, the Holy Spirit uses these children for yet higher ends, and those who see them are often impressed with desires for better things. Once again, let us admire what we cannot precisely describe ; for I have not ventured upon any precise description, but I have closely followed the words of the text.

The piety of this young child was every way of the right kind. It was inward and sincere, for the "good thing" that is spoken of was not found about him, but "in him." He did not wear the broad phylactery, but he had a meek and quiet spirit. He may not have been much of a speaker, else it might have been said "He has spoken good things concerning the God of Israel;" he may have been a timid, retiring, almost silent boy, but the good thing was "*in* him." And this is the kind of thing which we desire for every one of our friends, a work of grace *within*. The grand point is not to wear the garb, nor use the brogue of religion, but to possess the life of God *within*, and feel and think as Jesus would have done because of that inner life. Small is the value of external religion unless it be the outcome of a life within. True grace is not as a garment, to be put on and taken off; but it is an integral part of the person who possesses it. This child's piety was of the true, personal, inward kind : may all our children have some good thing *in* them!

We are told by our text that this good thing "was found" in him : this means that it was discernible in him, discernible without much difficulty, for the expression "found" is used even when it does not imply any great search. Does not the Lord say, "I am found of them that sought me not?" Zealous, child-like piety soon shows itself ; a child is usually far less reticent than a man; the little lip is not frozen by cold prudence, but reveals the heart. Godliness in a child appears even upon the surface, so that persons who come into the house as visitors are surprised by the artless statements which betray the young Christian. There were many in Tirzah who could not help knowing that this child had in him some good thing towards Jehovah. They may not have cared to see it, they may have hoped that it would be crushed out of him by the example of the court around him, but still they knew that there it was, they had found it without difficulty.

Still, the expression does bear another shade of meaning : it implies that when God, the strict heart-searcher, who trieth the reins of the children of men, visited this child he found in him somewhat unto praise and glory : "some good thing" was discovered in him by those eyes which cannot be deceived. It is not all gold that glitters, but that which was in this child was genuine metal. Oh that the like may be true of each of us when we are tried as by fire! It may be that his father was angry with him for serving Jehovah ; but whatever his trial may have been, he came out of it unharmed.

The expression suggests to me somewhat of the idea of surprise. How did this good thing get into the child? "In him there is *found* some good thing,"—as when a man findeth a treasure in a field. The farmer was thinking of nothing but his oxen, and his acres, and his harvest, when on a sudden his plough laid bare a hidden treasure : he found it where it was, but how it came to be there he could not tell. So in this child, so disadvantageously placed, to the surprise of everybody there was found some good thing toward the Lord God of Israel. His conversion, you see, is veiled in mystery. We are not told of the grace in his heart what it was, nor whence it came, nor what special actions it produced, but there it was, *found* where none expected it. I believe that this case is typical of many of the elect children whom God calls by his grace in the courts and alleys of London. You must not expect that you shall jot down their experience, and their feelings, and their lives, and total them all up; you must not reckon to know dates and means specifically, but you must take the child as we have to take Abijah, rejoicing to find in him a little wonder of grace with God's own seal upon him. The old prophet in the name of the Lord attested the young prince as a true-hearted follower of the Most High; and in like manner the Lord sets his attesting mark of grace on regenerated children, and we must be content to see it, even if some other things be wanting. Let us welcome with delight those works of the Holy Spirit which we cannot precisely describe.

II. Now, changing the line of our thought a little, I come to a second remark : in this case LET US HEARTILY PRIZE WHAT WE ARE TOO APT TO OVERLOOK.

First, *let us heartily prize " some good thing " towards the Lord God of Israel whenever we perceive it.* All that is said of this case was that there was in him "some good thing;" and this reads as if the divine work was as yet only a spark of grace, the beginning of spiritual life. There was nothing very striking in him, or it would have been more definitely mentioned. He was not an heroic follower of Jehovah, and his deeds of loyalty to God are not written, because by reason of his tender years he had neither power nor opportunity to do much which could be written. Inasmuch as we read that in him was " some good thing," it is implied that it was not a perfect thing, and that it was not attended with all the good things one might wish for. Many good things were missing, but " some good thing " was manifest, and therefore the child was accepted and by divine love rescued from an ignoble death. Do you not think that there is a tendency with many Christian people when they are talking with enquirers to look for *every* good thing in them, instead of looking for *some* good thing in them ? Here is a person professing to be converted ; he is evidently sincere and honest, and therefore he is very cautious not to say more than he feels, and this makes him say little, and that little tremblingly. You put him a question which everybody ought to be able to answer; but this nervous one fails to answer it, and therefore by a severe judgment it is thought that he is ignorant and unenlightened. Cold prudence decrees that a person who cannot answer such a question cannot be a child of God, and little allowance is made for timidity and flutter of mind. Suppose the enquirer could answer the question and a dozen others, might he not still be a deceiver ? Is it not sufficient for you that there is some good thing in him, even though he has no great stock of knowledge and very slender power of expression. Grace grows ; the grain of mustard seed becomes a tree, the little leaven leavens the whole lump. " Some good thing " will by-and-by breed every good thing ; the life of God is sure to conquer the whole nature. And ought we not to be much more hopeful than we are, and at the same time more tender, more gentle, more considerate ? Does

God bid his prophet say that this child shall escape the judgment that was to come upon Jeroboam's family because there was some good thing in him ?   Ought we not to conclude that if we see some good thing in any towards God, towards his Christ, towards eternal things, it is a token to us not to condemn but to commend, not to judge with severity but to treat with kindness and care ?   I fear that in many a case harshness has wrought serious mischief to those who were with all their hearts coming to Jesus.   That harshness may have been thought to be fidelity by him who exercised it, and perhaps it was; but there is such a thing as mistaken fidelity, and faithfulness is not the only virtue needed by a soul-winner.   I would not have you err, brethren and sisters beloved, when you are talking with seekers by whispering in their ears, "Peace, peace," when there is no peace; but on the other hand I would not have you sin against the child by a hard, suspicious manner, and by demanding more of a youthful heart than the Lord Jesus would have looked for.   There is a happy medium ; may God help us to follow it,—hoping but not flattering, examining with care but not chilling with suspicion.   Again I say, let us prize anything we see of Christ, anything we see of the Spirit's work in anyone who comes before us, being satisfied that all is well so long as we can see "some good thing toward the Lord God of Israel."

Further, I am afraid we are too apt to overlook "*some good thing*" *in a child.* "Oh, only a child !"   Pray, what are you ?   You are a man ; well, I suppose that a man is a child who has grown older, and has lost many of his best points of character.   A child is at no disadvantage in the things of God from being a child, for " of such are the kingdom of heaven."   Men have to grow back into children before they enter the kingdom at all.   If there be some good thing, it ought not to be doubted and thought to be questionable because it is in a child ; for in Holy Scripture it is very common to find good things in children. Do we not find some good things in Joseph while he was still a youth ? in Samuel, with whom God spake while he was yet a young child ? in David, who, as a boy, slew the giant Goliath ? in Obadiah, the governor of the house of Ahab, who said to Elijah, " I thy servant fear the Lord from my youth " ? in King Josiah, who wrought so great a reformation in Judah ? in young Timothy, who knew the Scriptures from his youth ? Was there not also early piety in John ? of whom Jerome says that one reason why our Lord loved John better than the other apostles was because he was younger than the rest.   I am not sure of that, but there is a peculiar child-likeness about John which might well attract the closest fellowship of the holy child Jesus.   Do not, therefore, be surprised to find grace in children, but look for it eagerly.   Why should we not have Samuels and Timothies among us ?   Do not let us trample pearls under our feet by refusing to see the Lord's work of grace in children.   Watch for grace in them as sentinels watch for the first gleams of the morning ; I say watch for it more than they that watch for the morning.

Another thing we are apt to overlook, and that is, "*some good thing*" *in a bad house.* This was the most wonderful thing of all, that there should be a gracious child in Jeroboam's palace.   The mother usually sways the house, but the queen was a princess of Egypt and an idolater.   A father has great influence, but in this case Jeroboam sinned and made Israel to sin.   It strikes me as a wonder that he should make Israel to sin but could not make his child to sin.   All the land feels the pestilent influence of Jeroboam, and yet close at his feet there is a bright spot which sovereign grace has kept from the plague ; his firstborn child, who naturally would imitate his father, is the very reverse of him—there is found in Jeroboam's heir "some good thing toward Jehovah, God of Israel."   In such a place we do not look for grace, and are apt to pass it by.   If you go to the courts of our great cities, which are anything but palatial, you will see that they swarm with the children of the poor, and you hardly expect to see grace where sin evidently abounds.   In the fever-dens and pestilent alleys of the great city you hear blasphemy and see drunkenness on all sides, but do not therefore conclude that no child of God is there ; do not say within yourself, "The electing love of God has never pitched upon any of these."   How do you know ?   One of those poor little ragged children playing on a dustheap may have found Christ in the Ragged-school, and may be destined to a place at Christ's right hand.   Precious is that gem, though cast amidst these pebbles.   Bright is that diamond, though it lie upon a dunghill.   If in the child there is "some good thing toward the Lord God of Israel," he is none the less to be valued because his father is a thief and his mother is a gin-drinker.   Never despise the most ragged child.   A clergyman in Ireland, ministering to a little Protestant congregation, noticed for several Sundays, standing in the aisle near the door, a very ragged boy, who listened to the sermon most eagerly.   He wished to know who the boy could be, but he always vanished as soon as the sermon was over.   He asked a friend or two to watch, but somehow the boy always escaped, and could not be discovered.   It came to pass one Sunday that the minister preached a sermon from this text, "His own right hand and his holy arm hath gotten him the victory," and after that time he missed the boy altogether.   Six weeks elapsed, and the child did not come any more, but a man appeared from the hills, and begged the minister to come and see his boy, who was dying.   He lived in a miserable hovel up in the mountains.   A six-mile walk in the rain, through bogs and over hills, and the minister came to the door of the hut.   As he entered, the poor lad was sitting up in bed, and as soon as he caught sight of the preacher he waved his arm and cried out, " His own right hand and his holy arm hath gotten him the victory." That was his closing speech on earth, his dying shout of triumph.   Who knows but in many and many a case the Lord's right hand and holy arm have gotten him the victory, despite the poverty and the sin and the ignorance that may have surrounded the young convert ?   Let us not therefore despise grace wherever it is, but heartily prize what we are apt to overlook !

III.   Lastly, LET US CAREFULLY CONSIDER WHAT WE CANNOT FULLY UNDERSTAND.   I want you first to consider the very singular fact which you cannot understand, *that holy children should be often placed in ungodly families.*   God's providence has arranged it so, yet the consequences are painful to the young believer.   You would think that if God loved a child he would not suffer it to be born unto Jeroboam's court, and that he would not send his own chosen down into a back slum to be surrounded by everything that will grieve its tender heart; and yet God does send his dear children into such places. Why is this?

Well first they are God's protest against sin where no other protest would be heard—a tender touching message from God to let the ungodly know that there is something better than the sin in which they wallow. Holy children are as angels amid demons, by their innocence rebuking sin. Does not God send children there also to make a display of his divine grace, that we may see that he chooses whom he wills and takes one of a family according to his good pleasure? Does he not also show us that he can keep grace alive in the most unlikely places where all things war against the soul? The grace of God can live where you and I would die. The life of grace can continue under conditions which threaten death. Some of the brightest and most gracious people have been found where there was nothing to keep them, but everything to hinder them. Does not the Lord permit this to show what his grace can do? and is it not intended to be an encouragement to each of us to be faithful? for if this dear child could be faithful to God with such a father and mother, and in such a court, ought you and I to be afraid? Oh, you big man, let a child shame you—you were afraid to speak out before your work-mates the other day! What a coward you must be, when this child displayed his love to the Lord God of Israel where all opposed!

Is it not remarkable how God distributes his people, as we scatter salt? He sets one of them down in each den of evil. Saul the king is a great rebel against God; but close at his side is Jonathan: thus the sweetest flower that ever bloomed is found growing near the roughest bramble that could be found. What a sty of filthiness was the court of Ahab! and yet he had for his chamberlain Obadiah, who hid the servants of God by fifties in a cave, and fed them from Jezebel's table; Nebuchadnezzar must not be left without three holy champions who can go into the fire for God. Look at Belshazzar drinking wine out of the cups of the sanctuary, and yet a Daniel is employed in his court. Even in the court of Ahasuerus, Esther is placed to confront that wicked Haman. Oh, I think there is never an Uz without a Job, nor a Chaldea without an Abraham, nor a Sodom without a Lot, nor an Egypt without a Moses, nor a house of Eli that has gone astray without some little Samuel sent of God to bear his protest. Think over the ways of God to man and admire what you cannot understand.

The next thing that we cannot understand is this, *that God's dear little children who love him should often be called to suffer.* We say, " Well, if it was my child I should heal him and ease his sufferings at once." Yet the Almighty Father allows his dear ones to be afflicted. The godly child of Jeroboam lies sick, and yet his wicked father is not sick, and his mother is not sick; we could almost wish they were, that they might do the less evil. Only one godly one is in the family, and he lies sick! Why was it so? Why is it so in other cases? You shall see a gracious child a cripple, you shall see a heavenly-minded girl a consumptive: you shall often see the heavy hand of God resting where his eternal love has fixed its choice. There is a meaning in all this, and we know somewhat of it; and if we knew nothing we would believe all the same in the goodness of the Lord. Jeroboam's son was like the fig of the sycamore tree, which does not ripen till it is bruised : by his sickness he was speedily ripened for glory. Besides, it was for his father's good and his mother's good that he was sick; if they had been willing to learn from the sorrow, it might have greatly blessed them. It did drive them to the prophet of God. Oh, that it had driven them to God himself! A sick child has led many a blinded parent to the Saviour, and eyes have thereby been opened.

There is something more remarkable still, and that is *that some of God's dearest children should die while they are yet young.* I should have said let Jeroboam die and his wife too, but spare the child. Ay, but the child must go : he is the fittest. His departure was intended to give glory to God's grace in saving such a child, and making him so soon perfect. It was to be the reward of grace, for the child was taken from the evil to come ; he was to die in peace and be buried, whereas the rest of the family would be slain with the sword and given to the jackals and the vultures to tear in pieces. In this child's case his early death was a proof of grace. If any say that converted children ought not to be taken into the church, I answer, how is it the Lord takes so many of them into heaven ? If they are fit for the one, they surely are fit for the other ? The Lord, in infinite mercy, often takes children home to himself, and saves them from the trials of long life and temptation ; because not only is there grace in them, but there is so much more grace than usual that there is no need for delay, they are ripe already for the harvest. It is wonderful what great grace may dwell in a boy's heart : child piety is by no means of an inferior kind, it is sometimes ripe for heaven.

Once more, it does strike me as a very singular thing *that such a child as this should die and yet produce no effect whatever on his parents ;* for neither Jeroboam nor his wife repented of their sins because their child was taken home to God. I may be addressing some here who have lost a darling in whom the grace of God was from his youth. Do you mean to lose the benefit of such a costly experiment upon your heart? Shall such bitter medicine be given to you in vain ? Why, there is a great power for good about a living child, much more ought there to be about a dying one. A sailor landed in New York one day, and he said to himself, " I'll have a fine time of it before I go to sea again." It was Sunday morning, and in the madness of his wickedness he went up to a girl who was going to her class, and he spoke to her mocking and wicked words. She turned round and looked at him with her beautiful, sad eyes, and said, " Sir, you will have to meet me at the bar of God ! " The sailor started back, turned on his heel, and made the best of his way to his vessel that he might get out of temptation. He said afterwards, " I never had such a broadside in my life as that girl gave me ; she raked me fore and aft, and swept by the board every sail and spar with which I had got ready for a wicked cruise." He went on his knees, repented of his sins, and found the Saviour. Shall a strange child have such power by its look and word, and shall not your own child impress you by its death ? A father was swearing dreadfully one day : he had often been rebuked for it but never felt the rebuke ; but on that occasion using a most horrible expression to his wife, his little daughter in fright ran behind the door and began to cry. She sobbed aloud until her father heard her. He said to her, "What are you crying for?" "Please, father," she said, and kept on crying. He cried out roughly, "I will know what you are crying about;" and the child replied, "Dear father, I was crying because I am so afraid you will go to hell, for teacher says that swearers must go there." "There," said the man, "Dry your eyes, child—I will never swear any more." He kept his word, and soon he went to see where his daughter had learned her holy lesson. Now, if children living among the roughest can by their tears win the victory, your dear child, with whose curls you used to play, but who has now been taken home to heaven, ought to touch your heart if you are not following in the way to glory! Your child beckons you from above and bids you "come up hither." Will you turn away? There is but one way: it is by faith in Jesus that men are saved. May Christ the Lord lead you to it now if you are unconverted, and may there this day be found in you "some good thing towards the Lord God of Israel." Amen.

THE DEVIL'S LAST THROW.

A Sermon

DELIVERED ON LORD'S-DAY EVENING, JUNE 10TH, 1883, BY

C. H. SPURGEON,

AT THE METROPOLITAN TABERNACLE, NEWINGTON,

On an evening when the regular hearers left their seats to be occupied by strangers.

" And as he was yet a coming, the devil threw him down, and tare him."—Luke ix. 42.

OUR Lord Jesus Christ taught the people much by his words, but he taught them even more by his actions. He was always preaching, his whole life was a heavenly discourse on divine truth ; and the miracles which he wrought were not only the proofs of his deity, but the illustrations of his teaching. His wonders of mercy were, in fact, acted sermons, truths embodied, pictorial illustrations appealing to the eye, and thus setting forth gospel teaching quite as clearly as vocal speech could have done. When we read of the miracles of our Lord, we should not only accept them as proofs of his Deity, and seals of his commission, but as instructions as to the manner of his gracious working. What he did of old to the bodies of men should be received as a prophecy of what he is to-day prepared to do to the souls of men. I am sure I shall not be straining the meaning of the text, or the intention of the miracle, if, instead of preaching about the youth possessed of the devil, and dwelling only upon that wonderful display of power, I endeavour to show that there are parallel cases at this time in the world of mind. Jesus is able to work in the unseen spirit-world miracles such as were foreshadowed by those which he wrought in the visible natural world.

I suppose that we have never seen Satanic possession, although I am not quite sure about it ; for some men exhibit symptoms which are very like it. The present existence of demons within the bodies of men I shall neither assert nor deny ; but certainly, in our Saviour's day it was very common for devils to take possession of men and torment them greatly. It would seem that Satan was let loose while Christ was here below that the serpent might come into personal conflict with the appointed seed of the woman, that the two champions might stand foot to foot in solemn duel, and that the Lord Jesus might win a glorious victory over him. Since his defeat by our Lord, and by his apostles, it would seem that Satan's power over human bodies has been greatly limited ; but we have still among us the same thing in another and worse shape, namely, the power of sin over men's minds. That this is akin to the power of the devil over the body is clear from holy Scripture. "The God of this world hath blinded the eyes of them that believe not." "The spirit that now worketh in the children of disobedience," says the apostle Paul. Satan works in all ungodly men, as a smith at his forge ; do you wonder that they sometimes curse and swear ? These are only the sparks from the forge below, flying out of the chimney. The evil one is found co-operating with evil natures, finding fire for their tinder, blowing up the flame that is within them, and in every way assisting them, and exciting them to do evil ; so that, albeit men are not possessed of devils in the sense in which they were so in Christ's day, yet the evil one still has power over them and leads them whithersoever he desires. Do we not constantly meet with persons of this kind ? I do. I know passionate men in whom the fiercest of devils appear to rave and rage; and I could point out others whose love of lying betrays the presence of the father of lies. One blasphemes and uses such filthy language that we are sure his tongue is set on fire of hell, even if the prince of devils is not ruling it. A man says, "Drink is ruining me, body and soul. I know that it is shortening my life. I have had delirium tremens, and I know that I shall have it again if I continue as I am ; but I cannot leave the drink. Sometimes the craving comes over me, and I seem as if I must swallow the intoxicating draught, whether I will or no." Whether this is the devil, or whether it is altogether the man himself, I am not going to argue; but the drink-devil, whose name is legion, is certainly among us to this day, and we hear persons tell us that they are anxious to escape from its power, and yet they return to it, rushing to intoxication as the swine rushed into the sea when the demons had entered into them.

Need I mention another form of this evil in the shape of unchastity ? How many a man there is—alas, it is true of women too !—struggling against a fierce passion, and yet that passion conquers them ; the unclean desire comes upon them like a hurricane bearing all before it, and they yield to it as the sere leaf yields to the blast. Nay more, they rush into a sin which they themselves condemn, of which already they have tasted the bitter fruit : they could not be more eager for it if it were the purest of all enjoyments. As the moth dashes again into the candle which has burned its wings, so do men hurry into the vice which has filled them with misery. They are possessed and domineered over by the spirit of lust, and return to their crimes as the oxen return to the stream.

I need not go further into details, for one man falls into sin in one way, and another falls after quite a different fashion. All devils are not alike—though they are alike evil. Anger differs from lust, and profligacy laughs at covetousness, yet are they all of one brood, privates in the same dreadful legion. Men practise differing sins, but their sins all manifest the same evil power. Unless Christ has set us free we are all in some shape or other under the dominion of the prince of darkness, the master of the forces of evil.

This poor young man of whom we are to talk to-night was brought into a most horrible condition through the influence of a Satanic spirit.

He was a lunatic : reason had been dethroned. He was an epileptic, so that if left alone he would fall into the fire or into the water. You have yourself seen persons in fits of epilepsy, and you know how dreadful would be their danger if they were taken in a fit in the middle of a street, or by the side of a river. In this youth's case the epilepsy was only the means by which the demon exercised his power, and this made his condition seven-fold worse than if it had been simply a disease. This afflicted one had become deaf and dumb besides, and very violent, so that he was capable of doing a great deal of mischief. In all the Holy Land there was only one who could do anything for him ! There was one name by which he could be cured, and only one. It was the name of Jesus. The Lord Jesus had disciples who had wrought miracles in his name, but they were baffled by this extraordinary case. They tried what they could do, but they were utterly defeated, and gave up the task in despair ; and now there remained only one person beneath the canopy of heaven that could touch this child's case and drive out the devil. Only one person could now answer the poor father's prayers : every other hope was dead. That is just the state in which we are : there is but one name under heaven whereby we must be saved. Many are the pretended salvations, but only one is real.

> " There is a name high over all,
> In hell, and earth, and sky.
> Angels and men before it fall,
> And devils fear and fly."

That one name is the name of Jesus, the Son of God, to whom all power is given. He is God, and can deliver any man from the dominion of evil, whatever form it may have assumed, and however long established the dominion may be. Cure besides there is none. Nothing else can rescue a man from the thraldom of his sin but the word of Jesus. When the word of power is spoken from his divine mouth all things obey ; but none out of the ten thousand voices of earth can deliver us from evil. We are shut up to heaven's unique remedy : God grant that, being so shut up, we may avail ourselves of it.

This poor lad, although nobody could cure him save Jesus, had a father that loved him, and nobody could tell the sorrow of that father's heart because of his poor son. The father had a sharp struggle to get his son to the disciples, for epileptic persons who are also insane are hard to manage. I cannot tell how many round about assisted to hold him, all pitying the poor creature. Alas, the Lord Jesus Christ was away ! The parent's heart was heavy when he found that the great Healer to whom he looked was for a while absent. But when Jesus came down from the mountain-top the poor demoniac had this one great advantage—that he had friends to aid in bringing him to Christ. I hope that all here who are not saved are privileged with relationship to some friend who seeks their salvation. Perhaps it is a wife who cannot bear that her husband should remain out of Christ, or a husband who pines till his spouse is turned unto the Lord, and in either case it is a great help. How often a mother bears a secret anguish in her breast for her unconverted sons and daughters ! I have known a sister in the family to be the only one who knew the Lord, and she has pleaded with the Lord day and night, entreating him to bless the whole of her household. Frequently a servant in the house becomes its best helper, or it may be a neighbour who has seen the ungodly conduct of his neighbours never ceases to pray for them. When some few get together to bring a specially hard case before Jesus, it is blessed work : for desperate cases grow hopeful under the influence of prayer. Come, ye saved ones, pray with me now for these unrenewed sinners, that at this moment they may feel the power of our Lord Jesus.

I. So, then, my first point shall be, that OUR HOPES ARE ALL AWAKENED. Here is a poor youth, but bad as he is. terribly possessed as he is, he is coming to Christ! Prayer has been offered for him by his father, and Jesus is near. All looks well! We will take the case of a sinner who is in a similar condition : prayer has been offered for him, and that prayer has, in some measure, been heard. We have in this congregation, I trust, some who are coming to Christ, and I am right glad of it. Coming to Christ is not the best possible condition, for the best condition is to have already come to him. For a hungry man to be coming to a dinner is not enough : he must actually reach the table and eat. For a sick man to be coming to an eminent physician is hopeful, but it is not enough; he must get to that physician, take his medicine, and be restored. That is the point. To be coming to Christ is not enough : you must actually come to him, and really receive him ; for to such only does he give power to become the sons of God.

This poor child was coming, and so are some here: that is to say, they have begun to hear the gospel with attention. They did not aforetime go anywhere on the Sabbath ; nor did they get up very early on a Sunday morning. I can see a man who seldom rose on a Sunday morning, and when he did, he read his newspaper. You might see him any time before one o'clock in his shirt-sleeves. Half this city of London is in that condition every Sunday morning, because they look upon the day as simply their own day, and not the Lord's-day. They have very short memories, and do not "remember the sabbath-day to keep it holy:" they forget all about its being the Lord's-day, and do not reverence it. This is shameful conduct towards God. If a man on the road were to meet with a poor beggar, and give him six out of seven shillings which he had with him, the beggar would be a wicked wretch if he afterwards knocked the man down and stole the other shilling. Yet there are multitudes of people to whom God gives six days out of seven, and nothing will satisfy them but they must have the seventh all to themselves, and rob God of it. The man I refer to is repenting of this wrong, and so you see him coming upon the Sunday morning to hear the gospel. He hears it very attentively ; he leans forward to catch every word, and he treasures up what he hears.

We are sure that he is coming to Christ, for when he gets home he reaches down his Bible. He has begun to read the Word of God in an earnest way. He thought at one time that it was about the dullest book in the world. He even dared to turn it into a jest, and all because he never read it; for those who deny the inspiration of Scripture are almost always people who have never read it for themselves. It is a book which carries conviction within itself to candid minds when they carefully peruse it. Assuredly this man is coming to Christ, for he searches the Scriptures.

I feel sure he is coming to Christ, for he has begun to mend in many respects. He has dropped his frequent attendance at his usual place of worship, namely, the public-house. He keeps more at home, and is therefore sober. Plenty of people in London need no bell to fetch them into the temples of their gods. We see in some of our churches and chapels persons going in twenty minutes or half-an-hour after service begins; but look at the temples of Bacchus at one o'clock, and at six in the evening, and see how punctual are his votaries! The worshippers of liquid fire stand outside till the shrine is opened; they are afraid of being late; they are so thirsty that they long for the time of the deadly libation. Drink seems to be the water of life to them, poor creatures that they are! But now our friend of whom we are so hopeful is not seen waiting at the posts of the doors—the "Blue Posts," I mean. Thank God, he is looking to another fountain for comfort.

Note also that he has dropped his blasphemy and his unchastity. He is a purer man in mouth and body than he used to be. He is coming to Christ. But, as I said, coming is not enough. The thing is really to reach the Lord Jesus and to be healed by him. I pray you, do not rest short of this.

Still, this is all hopeful, very hopeful. The man is a hearer; he is also a reader of the Scriptures; he has begun to mend a bit; and now he is a thinker, too, and begins to be a little careful about his soul. While he is at his labour, you can see that there is something working in his brain, though once it was filled with vanity and wickedness. He has a weight, too, at his heart, a burden on his mind; he is evidently in earnest; so far as he knows the teaching of Scripture he is deeply affected by it. He has learned that he will not cease to exist when he dies; but that he will continue to be when yonder sun becomes black as a burnt-out coal. He knows that there will be a day of judgment, when throngs upon throngs, yea, all the dead, shall stand before the judgment-seat of Christ to give an account of the things which they have done in the body; he thinks this over, and he is alarmed. He chews the cud upon divine truth, and finds time for solitary meditation. That man is coming to Christ, for there is no better evidence of the face being set towards Christ and heaven than a thoughtful state of mind.

And I have heard—of course, I cannot tell, for I was not there to see —I have heard, I say, that the other night he began to pray. If so, I know that he is coming to Christ, for prayer is a sure token. He has not yet cast himself fully at the feet of Jesus, but he cries, "Lord, save me." He is coming, and I am as glad as the birds on a spring morning. The angels are watching; they are leaning from the battlements of heaven to see whether it will end rightly, and you and I are very hopeful, especially those of us who have been praying for this man; for since we see that there is some change in him, and he begins to think and pray, we look for his salvation, as men look for flowers when April showers are falling. So, you see, our hopes are excited.

II. And now I will read the text again,—"As he was yet a coming, the devil threw him down, and tare him." By this OUR FEARS ARE

AROUSED. What a sight it must have been! Here is the poor father bringing his lunatic son, and friends are helping him; they are getting him near the Saviour, and he is just coming to him who can cure him, when, on a sudden, he is taken in a fearful fit, worse than he had ever suffered before. He is cast down, thrown about, dashed to and fro; he wallows on the ground: he seems to be flung up and down as by an unseen hand, we fear that he will be torn to pieces. See! he falls down like a dead man, and there he lies. As the crowd gathers around him, people cry, "He is dead." Does it not seem a dreadful thing that when hope was at its brightest all should be dashed aside?

I have observed this thing scores of times: I might say, I think without exaggeration, hundreds of times. I have seen men, just when they were beginning to hear and beginning to think, taken on a sudden with such violence of sin, and so fearfully carried away by it, that if I had not seen the same thing before I should have despaired of them; but, having often seen it, I know what it means, and I am not so dismayed as a raw observer might be; though I must confess that it half breaks my heart when it happens to some hopeful convert whom I hoped to receive into the church, and to rejoice over. We mourn when we hear that the man who was somewhat impressed has become worse than aforetime, and has gone back to the very vice from which we had rescued him. The case runs on the same lines as our text— "As he was a coming, the devil threw him down, and tare him."

How does the devil do this? Well, we have seen it done in this way:—When the man had almost believed in Christ, but not quite, Satan seemed to multiply his temptations around him, and to bring his whole force to bear upon him. There is a wicked man in the shop, and the devil says to him, "Your mate is beginning to be serious: ridicule him. Tempt him all you can. Treat him to strong drink. Get him away to the theatre, the music-hall, or the brothel." It is wonderful how the ungodly will lay all kinds of traps for one who is escaping from his sins. They are fearfully set on keeping him from Christ. This is a free country, is it not? A wonderfully free country when a Christian man in the workshop has to run the gauntlet for his very life to this day. A man may swear, and drink, and do what he likes that is detestable, and never is there a word of rebuke for him; but the moment he begins to be serious and thoughtful the wicked are down upon him like so many dogs on a rat. The devil finds willing servants, and they worry the poor awakened one; is there any wonder that, as he has not yet found Christ and is not yet saved, he should for the time be carried away by these assaults, and feel as if he could not go further in the right road?

I have known in addition to all this that Satan has stirred up the anxious one's bad passions. Passions that lay asleep have suddenly been aroused. Moreover, the man has become thoughtful, and from that very fact doubts which he never knew before have come upon him. He begins to mend, and now he finds a difficulty in getting his needle through where the rent was made. He finds that tearing is easier work than mending, and that running into sin is a much more easy thing than rising out of the black ditch into which he has fallen. So now, what with those about him tempting him, his bad passions responding to the temptation, and his doubts overclouding everything, it is not a marvellous thing that the poor creature grows worse before he gets better. The disease which before had been concealed in more hidden and vital parts, seems to be thrown out upon the surface, and the sight is sickening. This, however, is not always a bad sign. Doctors rather prefer it to an inward festering.

So have I seen it when men have been coming to Christ; their boat has been tossed with tempest, and they have been driven far out upon a raging sea.

Yes, and I will tell you what I have seen. I have seen a man almost converted—well-nigh a believer in Christ, on a sudden become more obstinate in his opposition to the gospel than ever he was before. A man that was quiet and harmless and inoffensive before has, under the influence of Satan, just when we hoped the best things of him, turned round in a rage against the people who sought to do him good, and he has spoken opprobriously of the gospel which a little while before he seemed anxious to understand. Sometimes such persons act as if they were reckless and profane; just as boys, when they go through a graveyard, whistle to keep their courage up. Many a man says big things against the gospel when he is pretty nearly caving in, and he does not like anybody to know that he is beaten. He is coming to Jesus; but still he does not want anybody to see that he is so, and therefore he pretends to an opposition which is not sincere. Have you not discovered that a man is never so violent against a thing as when he is unwillingly convinced of the truth of it? He has to try and demonstrate to himself that he does not believe it by being very loud in his declarations: a secret something in his soul makes him believe, and he is mad because he cannot resist the inward conviction.

Do not be astonished—you that are trying to bring men to Christ—if it should often happen that these lunatics break loose—that these epileptics have a worse fit just before Christ cures them than ever you knew them to have had before.

I will describe the usual way in which the devil throws men down and tears them. You need not listen to this unless you like, because it does not relate to all of you here; but it is true of a sufficient number to render it needful for me to speak of it. It is a very curious thing that if there is a poor soul in London that is well-nigh insane through despair of heart he wants to talk to me. I am often sore burdened by the attempt to sympathize with the distracted. I do not know why they should be attracted to me, but they come to tell me of their evil state of mind—people who have never seen me before. This fact gives me a wide field of actual practice and careful observation. I frequently meet with persons who are tempted with blasphemous thoughts. They have not yet laid hold on Christ, but they are trying to do so; and at this stage of their experience most horrible thoughts pass through their minds. They cannot prevent it: they hate the thoughts, and yet they come, till they are ready to lose their reason. I will tell you what happened to me. I was engaged in prayer alone in a quiet place one day when I had just found the Saviour, and while I was in prayer a most horrible stream of blasphemies came into my mind, till I clapped my hand to my mouth for fear that I should utter any one of them. I was so brought up that I do not remember ever hearing a man swear while I was a child ; yet at that moment I seemed to know all the swearing and blasphemy that ever was in hell itself; and I wondered at myself. I could not understand whence this foul stream proceeded. I wrote to my venerable grandfather who was for sixty years a minister of the gospel, and he said to me,—" Do not trouble about it. These are no thoughts of yours ; they are injected into your mind by Satan. The thoughts of men follow one another like the links of a chain, one link draws on another; but when a man is in prayer the next natural thought to prayer is not blasphemy ; it is not, therefore, a natural succession of our own thoughts. An evil spirit casts those thoughts into the mind." I read also in an old book what they used to do years ago in our parishes in the "good old times" when nobody had any sense of humanity. If a poor wretch came to a parish begging, they whipped him through the place and sent him on to his own parish. Thus should we treat these diabolical thoughts. Whip them by hearty penitence, and send them off to where they came from, back to their own parish, which is far down in the deeps. Thoughts of this sort, seeing you loathe them, are none of yours. Do not let Satan lay his brats at your door, but send them packing. Perhaps when you know this, it may help to break the chain ; for the devil may not think it worth his while to worry you in this way any more, when he cannot by this means lead you to despair : he seldom wastes his time in spreading nets when the bird can see them. Therefore, tell Satan to begone, for you can see him, and you are not going to let him deceive you. It may be he will take the hint and begone.

When this does not answer, I have known Satan to throw the coming sinner down and tear him in another way. "There," says he, "did you not hear the preacher speaking about election ? You are not one of the elect." "Perhaps I am not," says one. Perhaps you are, say I, and I think that whether you are one of the elect or not, you had better come, on the ground that Jesus says—"Him that cometh to me I will in no wise cast out." If you come, he will not cast you out, and then you will find that you are one of the elect. You need not trouble about predestination : you will see that clearly enough very soon. If any man had a ticket to go to a meeting, and he said, "I do not know whether I am ordained to get in or not," I should think it very probable that he was not ordained to enter if he sat at home in the chimney-corner and did not make the attempt to go ; but if, having his ticket, he walked to the place and went in, I should feel sure that he was ordained to go in. You will know your election when you have obeyed your calling. Go you to Christ because you are commanded and invited, and leave the deeper question to be answered by the facts.

Satan will throw men down and tear them in another way. "Ah !" says he, "you are too big a sinner." I make short work of that. No man is too big a sinner. "All manner of sin and of blasphemy shall be forgiven unto men."

"Oh but," says Satan, "it is too late." Another lie of his. It is never too late so long as we are in this world, and come to Jesus for pardon. Generally in the case of young people he puts the clock back, and says "It is too soon"; and then when they get old he puts the clock on, and says "It is too late." It is never too late as long as Jesus lives, and the sinner repents. If a sinner were as old as Methuselah, if he came to Christ and trusted him he would be saved.

"Oh but," the devil says, "it is no use your trying at all. The gospel is not true." Ay, but it is true, for some of us have proved it. I could bring before you to-night, if it were necessary, men and women who lived in sin and wallowed in it, and yet the Lord Christ has saved them by his precious blood. They would rejoice to tell you how they have been delivered from the reign of sin by faith in Jesus, though they could never have delivered themselves. The gospel is true. Our converts prove it. Conversion is the standing miracle of the church; and while we see what it works every day in the week, we are confident and sure. When men that were passionate, dishonest, unchaste, covetous, become holy, gracious, loving, pure, generous, then we know that the gospel is true by the effect which it produces. A lie would never produce holiness and love. Out of the way, devil! It is all in vain for you to come here with your falsehoods; we know the truth about you, and about the gospel, and you shall not deceive us.

And then the devil will come with this—"It is of no use. Give it up; give it up." Many and many a man who has been on the brink of eternal life, has been thrown down and torn with this, "It is of no use; give it up. You have prayed, and you have not been answered: never pray again. You have attended the house of God, and you have become more miserable than ever: never go again. Ever since you have been a thinking man and a sober man, you have had more trouble than ever you had. See," says the devil, "what comes of your religion." Thus he tries to induce the newly awakened to give it up. But oh, in God's name let me implore you do not turn from it, for you are on the brink of the grand discovery. Another turf turned, and there is the golden treasure. After all your striving—your long striving —never give up the search until you have found your Saviour; for your Saviour is to be found. Trust in him this night, and he is yours for ever.

III. I shall not detain you much longer. But as our hopes have been awakened and our fears have been aroused, let us look on the scene till OUR WONDER IS EXCITED. Did you notice when I was reading in the ninth chapter of Mark, how Jesus healed this poor child? He did *heal* him, he healed him of all that complication, healed him of the devil's domination, healed him of the epilepsy, healed him of being deaf and dumb, healed him of being a lunatic, healed him of pining away; and in one moment that young man was completely saved from all his ills. He could speak; he could hear; he was cured of his epilepsy, and was no more a lunatic, but a happy rational being. The whole thing was done at once. Wonder, and never leave off wondering!

"Can a man be changed all at once? It must take a long time," says one. I admit there are certain qualities which come only by education and patient watchfulness. There are certain parts of the Christian character that come of culture, and must be watered with tears and prayer. But let me assure you, not as a matter of theory, but as a matter which I have seen for thirty years, that a man's character may be totally changed in less time than it takes me to tell you of it. There is such power in

the name of Christ that, if that name be preached and the Spirit of
God applies it, men can be turned right round. There can be a total
reversal of all their conduct, and, what is more than that, of all their
inclinations, and desires and wishes, and delights and hates; for God can
take away the heart of stone and give a heart of flesh. The child of darkness can be translated into the kingdom of light. The dead heart can be
quickened into a spiritual existence, and that in a single moment, by
faith in Jesus Christ. When that poor epileptic child was healed,
it is said that the people were amazed. But how much greater will be
our amazement if we see the Lord Jesus work such a miracle upon you!
You have struggled to get better, you have prayed to get better, and all
seems to be unavailing. Now, just trust Christ, the blessed Son of
God who reigns in heaven, who died for sinners, and now lives for
sinners. Only trust him, and this blessed deed is done. you become a
new creature in Christ Jesus, and commence a holy life which shall
never end. This wonder can be performed *now*.

This cure was perfected at once, and it remained with the youth.
The most charming point about it was that the Lord Jesus said, "Thou
dumb and deaf spirit, I charge thee, come out of him, and enter no
more into him." Enter no more into him—there is the glory of it!
Though the epileptic fit was ended, yet the young man would not have
been cured if the devil had returned to take possession of him again.
The Saviour's cures endure the test of years. "Enter no more into him"
preserved the young man by a life-long word of power.

I never dare to preach to anybody a temporary salvation. "Believe
in the Lord Jesus Christ and thou shalt be saved," not for to-night merely,
but for ever. When God saves a man he *is* saved: not for weeks and
years, but eternally. If Christ turns the devil out of him he shall enter
into that man no more for ever. Now, this is a salvation that is worth
your having, and worth my preaching. A temporary, I had almost said,
a trumpery salvation, that saves a man for a few months and then lets
him perish, is not worth preaching or having; but that which so makes a
man new as to put into him "a well of water springing up into everlasting life"—that is worth worlds. I will tell you a story of Christmas
Evans which I like to tell on this point. Christmas Evans was once
describing the prodigal's coming back to his father's house, and he said
that when the prodigal sat at the father's table his father put upon his
plate all the daintiest bits of meat that he could find; but the son sat
there and did not eat, and every now and then the tears began to flow.
His father turned to him and said, "My dear son, why are you unhappy?
You spoil the feasting. Do you not know that I love you? Have I not
joyfully received you?" "Yes," he said, "dear father, you are very
kind, but have you really forgiven me? Have you forgiven me altogether,
so that you will never be angry with me for all I have done?" His
father looked on him with ineffable love and said, "I have blotted
out thy sins and thy iniquities, and will remember them no more
for ever. Eat, my dear son." The father turned round and waited
on the guests, but by-and-by his eyes were on his boy, they could
not be long removed. There was the son weeping again, but not
eating. "Come, dear child," said his father, "come, why are you
still mourning? What is it that you want?" Bursting into a

flood of tears a second time, the son said, "Father, am I always to stop here? Wil. you never turn me out of doors?" The father replied, "No, my child, thou shalt go no more out for ever, for a son abides for ever." Still the son did not enjoy the banquet; there was still something rankling within, and again he wept. Then his father said, "Now, tell me, tell me, my dear son, all that is in thy heart. What do you desire more?" The son answered, "Father, will you *make* me stop here? Father, I am afraid lest, if I were left to myself, I might play the prodigal again. Oh, constrain me to stay here for ever!" The father said, "I will put my fear in thy heart, and thou shalt not depart from me." "Ah! then," the son replied, "it is enough," and merrily he feasted with the rest. So I preach to you just this—that the great Father when he takes you to himself will never let you go away from him again.

Whatever your condition, if you trust your soul to Jesus, you shall be saved, and saved for ever.

> "Once in Christ, in Christ for ever :
> Nothing from his love can sever."

"But what if we fall into great sin?" says one. You shall not abide in great sin. You shall be kept and preserved by that same power which has begun the good work, for it will surely carry it on even to the end.

Just two or three sentences and I have finished. I have been speaking about the devil throwing some down and tearing them when they are coming to Christ. Are there any of you who do not know anything about it? Well, I am glad that you do not. If you come to Christ without being thrown down and torn I am glad of it. I have endeavoured to help those that are terribly tormented; but if you are not so tried, do not wish to be. There were here this morning two or three of the good fish-people from Newhaven, and when I saw them in their picturesque costumes they reminded me of a story that I heard about an old fish-wife who used to live near Edinburgh. A young man visited her, and began speaking to her about her soul. She was going out, and she took up her great load of fish to carry on her back, much more than most men would like to carry. The young man said to her, "Well, you have got a great burden there, good woman. Did you ever feel a spiritual burden?" She put down her load and said, "You mean that burden which John Bunyan speaks about in the *Pilgrim's Progress*, do you not?" "Yes," he said. "Well," she said, "I felt that burden before you were born, and I got rid of it, too ; but I did not go exactly the same way to work that John Bunyan's pilgrim did." Our young friend thought that she could not be up to the mark to talk so, for he fancied that John Bunyan could not make a mistake. "Well," she said, "John Bunyan says that Evangelist pointed the man with the burden on his back to the wicket-gate, and when he could not see the gate, Evangelist said, 'Do you see that light?' And he looked till he thought he saw something like it. 'You are to run that way—the way of that light and that wicket gate.' Why," she said, "that was not the right direction to give a poor burdened soul. Much good he got out of it ; for he had not gone far before he fell into the Slough of Despond, up to his neck in the mire, and had like to have been swallowed up. Evangelist ought to have said, ' Do you see that cross? Do not run an inch, but stand where you are, and look to that; and as you look your burden will be gone. I looked to the cross at once and lost my load.' " "What!" said the young man, "did you never go through the Slough of Despond?" "Yes," she said, "I have been through it far too many times ; but let me tell you, young friend, that it is a deal easier to go through the Slough of Despond with your burden off than it is with your burden on." There is much blessed truth in this story. Do not any of you be saying to yourselves, "How I wish I could get into the Slough of Despond!" If you say that, you will get in, and then you will say, "How I wish I could get out of the Slough of Despond!" I have met with persons who fear that they never were saved because they have not experienced much terror. I meet with others who say that they cannot be saved because they experience too much terror. There is no pleasing people. Oh that they would look to Jesus whether or no ! After I was preaching Jesus Christ from this platform once, there came a man into the vestry who said to me, " Blessed be God that I entered this Tabernacle. I come from Canada, sir. My father, before he found true religion had to be locked up in a lunatic asylum, and I always thought that I must undergo a similar terror before I could be saved." I said, " No, no, my dear friend, you are to believe in the Lord Jesus Christ, and if you do that, despond or not despond, you are a saved man." This gospel I preach to you. Believe in the Lord Jesus Christ. Trust him quietly, humbly, simply, immediately. Trust him to make you a holy man—to deliver you from the power of the devil and the power of sin, and he will do it : I will be bound for him that he will keep his word. Jesus is truth itself, and never breaks his word. He never boasts that he can do what he cannot do. He has gone into heaven, and he is therefore "able to save them to the uttermost that come unto God by him, seeing he ever liveth to make intercession for them." Only trust him. Trust him to overcome the evil you have to fight with. You will conquer it, man, if you will only trust Jesus. Woman, there is hope for you if you will trust the wounded, bleeding, dying, risen, living Saviour. He will battle for you, and you shall get the victory.

God bless you, everyone, and may we all meet in heaven to praise the Son of God for ever and ever.

By C. H. SPURGEON.
THE GOSPEL FOR THE PEOPLE.

Sixty Short Sermons, with a Sketch of Mr. Spurgeon's Life, and Fourteen Portraits and Engravings, with Preface by Pastor Thomas Spurgeon. Cloth Gilt, 5s.

These Short Sermons have been selected from the Series with a view to their being used in Mission Halls, and other similar places. They are about half the length of the ordinary Sermons.

LONDON : PASSMORE AND ALABASTER, PATERNOSTER BUILDINGS ; and all Booksellers.

MARVELLOUS! MARVELLOUS!

A Sermon

DELIVERED ON LORD'S-DAY MORNING, OCTOBER 28TH, 1883, BY

C. H. SPURGEON,

AT THE METROPOLITAN TABERNACLE, NEWINGTON.

"Thus saith the LORD of hosts ; If it be marvellous in the eyes of the remnant of this people in these days, should it also be marvellous in mine eyes? saith the LORD of hosts."
—Zechariah viii. 6.

GOD sent his servant Zechariah with a promise that Jerusalem should be rebuilt, and that it should enjoy a time of great peace and prosperity. Instead of men being slain in battle in the prime of their days, old men and old women were to dwell in the streets of Jerusalem, " every man with his staff in his hand for very age ": and whereas war had often cut off the women and the children, the promise further added, " the streets of the city shall be full of boys and girls playing in the streets thereof." Everything was to be prosperous in the land around, so as to bring plenty into the city,—" For the seed shall be prosperous ; the vine shall give her fruit, and the ground shall give her increase, and the heavens shall give their dew ; and I will cause the remnant of this people to possess all these things." It was a sweet assurance, and it ought to have made them very happy, but it did not.

When this gracious promise came, it startled the people, for it seemed past belief. The unbelievers did not say point blank, " This promise is not true," but deep in their hearts they thought as much. It is not the general habit of unbelief among God's people to give a flat contradiction to his promises : we are hardly honest enough to our own thoughts to express them with deliberate plainness of speech : even unbelief loves to wear some cobweb covering or other, that its naked deformity may not appear. Our reverence for the Lord will not permit us distinctly to give him the lie ; but it comes to much the same thing, for in our heart of hearts we deny the truthfulness of his word. The remnant of Israel said, " How can this thing be? In these days, in these troublous days, in these threatening days, how can Jerusalem be made to prosper? Former hopes have been disappointed : we see no better signs of the times, and doubtless if our hopes be now raised they will again be disappointed. How can the city rise from its ashes? We can hardly think it possible : at any rate, it will be marvellous, extremely difficult, exceedingly unlikely, indeed, impossible." They did not say

No. 1,747.

at once, "It will not be"; but they said, "It will be a marvellous thing"; by which they meant that it was not in the least likely.

You who carry Bibles with you which have the marginal readings, will notice that in the margin there is the word "difficult," and the text may be read thus, "Thus saith the Lord of hosts; If it be difficult in your eyes, should it also be difficult in mine eyes?" This is the only instance in which the word "difficult" occurs in our version of the Bible, and in this case it is only to be found in the margin. There is too much of God in the Bible for difficulties to live in it. I should be very glad if I could always put the word "difficult" into the margin of my life, and never let it stand in the substance of it. I wish my faith would banish it. Difficulty does crop up now and then through unbelief: but where God manifests himself, difficulty vanishes. Leave it in the margin, brother! Leave it in the margin; let it not be read in the annals of your actual life. A brave self-reliance blots the word *difficult* out of its dictionary, and a full God-reliance may much more safely do so. If God be for us, all things can be accomplished. Things impossible with men are possible with God. The remnant of Israel said, "It will be difficult"; and then they softened the words a little, and said, "It will be marvellous in our eyes"; still it came to this at the bottom, that they did not believe the word of the Lord. They could not conceive how the promise could be fulfilled, and therefore because it surpassed their conception, they supposed that the Lord was equally non-plussed and perplexed. Because the restored prosperity of Jerusalem would be a great wonder, they doubted if it could ever be accomplished. Yet, blessed be the name of the Lord, it was accomplished; for "though we believe not, he abideth faithful; he cannot deny himself."

It certainly was a marvellous thing that Jerusalem, after having been so dreadfully destroyed, should again lift up its head and enjoy a little period of sunlight; but we are called upon to believe in even greater wonders—wonders of a spiritual kind which are more difficult of belief than material miracles. I am going to talk about what to every intelligent and awakened mind will be the greatest wonder of all, namely, the possibility of our salvation by faith which is in Christ Jesus. Satan will assail you who are saved, and you who are seeking to be saved, and he will aim a blow at your faith. If he does not dare to tell you in his own native tongue of point blank lying that the promise which the gospel makes to the believer is false, yet he will lead you to think it highly improbable, too good to be true, too wonderful ever to happen; in a word, he will make it appear marvellous in your eyes, and he will hint that it is incredible. So this morning I am going, first, to speak upon *carnal reasoning*, how it runs; secondly, to offer *a correction to that reasoning* by pointing out an untruth which lies at the bottom of it; and, thirdly, I will try, in conclusion, to dwell upon the truth of the matter, and see if we cannot enjoy some *right reasoning*. O blessed Spirit of grace, teach our reason right reason at this hour, and make us to perceive all things in the light of truth!

I. Here we have before us a specimen of CARNAL REASONING. The Jews of those days said, "It is difficult; it will never be performed. It is marvellous in our eyes; it will never happen." This kind of speech comes from men as soon as they begin to think about their souls, and to desire the salvation of the Lord. We inform them in God's name that whosoever repents of sin and confesses it, and believes in Jesus Christ, shall receive immediate pardon; and this good news surprises them, as well it may. Straightway the old serpent begins to hiss out a doubt, and they ask, "How can it be? Can a man receive in one moment forgiveness for fifty years of sin? How can his conscience be cleared by the simple act of believing in Christ? How can the record of a life of evil be blotted out at once?" Assuredly it does not seem probable to a troubled mind; reason decides that it must be very difficult; common sense assents that it is a marvellous affair altogether, and the poor awakened hearts conclude that the promise of full, free, and present forgiveness cannot be true. Thus they push the promise of God concerning pardon on one side as a good thing which is quite past belief.

Then comes the blessing of renewal of heart, such as God speaks of in the covenant-promise, "A new heart also will I give them, and a right spirit will I put within them." Our hearer understands that upon his believing in Jesus he is born again, and becomes a new creature, with new likes and new hates, an entirely altered being; but understanding the promise is one thing, and believing it is another. A new heart the awakened one desires, but he considers it too great a marvel. He asks, "Can the Ethiopian change his skin, or the leopard his spots? Can I who have been accustomed to do evil learn to do well? It will be marvellous indeed if such a sinner as I should be turned into a saint; if such a rebel as I should become a loyal subject of King Jesus! Such a conversion will be most extraordinary. I do not think it can be carried out." He knows that he cannot subdue his own stubborn will, nor conquer his own unruly passions; and therefore he concludes that the thing is improbable, and not to be looked for. Thus another choice covenant-promise is thrown on one side by unbelief, and the man sits down in self-created despair, under the persuasion that a new birth for him would be too marvellous a thing to expect.

Even if the awakened soul proceeds as far as believing in the first two blessings, unbelief comes to him in another way, for this thief is sure to meet the traveller to Zion again and again. The Lord has promised that the righteous shall hold on his way, and he that hath clean hands shall wax stronger and stronger; and Christ has declared that the living water which he gives shall be no transient boon, but shall be in a man a well of water springing up into everlasting life. "Oh! but," says the tempted one, "how can I hope to persevere to the end? I shall be one of these days tempted so strongly that I shall be carried off my feet. What with indwelling sin and a cunning tempter, and a world full of evil, I cannot hope to endure to the end. I shall one day fall by the hand of the enemy. Do you assure me that the righteous shall hold on their way? Then it will be marvellous: it must be so difficult that I fear it is improbable, if not impossible." Thus unbelief pushes on one side another covenant blessing.

Further on there comes to the man who has been helped to persevere for a while the promise that he shall ultimately be presented faultless before the presence of God with exceeding joy: this promise is assailed

in the same manner. The serpent of unbelief leaves its slimy trail upon
everything. We are told that a day shall come when the believer shall
be without spot or wrinkle or any such thing, made meet to dwell
with the angels in light, ay, and to dwell with God himself for ever:
and straightway the soul is tempted to think this wonderful effect of
grace to be impossible. When we remember how often we have been
worsted by the enemy, how frail, how fallible we are, and how fierce
and subtle is our adversary, we dare not hope that we shall see him
utterly defeated and his power broken to pieces. We dwell upon the
fact that it will be very marvellous; indeed, the more we think of it
the more marvellous it becomes in our eyes; and, alas! unbelief leaps
upon the back of our wonder, and we judge that the blessing can never
be ours. Thus another promised blessing is thrown under the table.
In fact, each mercy of God's covenant is looked at, wondered at, and
then renounced, not because it is undesirable, but because it is so good,
so rich, so full. O wretched unbelief which makes the excellence of
the favour into a reason for refusing it! Help us, O Holy Spirit, to
believe our Lord, and no more reason in this evil fashion!

I have known children of God in the time of their great trial, when they
have been surrounded with afflictions, oppressed with poverty, and
depressed in spirit, to become quite incredulous as to the possibility of
deliverance. They ask, " How can God cause our bread to be given us
and our water to be sure *now?* Can he bring us out of such sore trouble
as this? We know that he has been gracious to his people in other
instances, but our case is one of peculiar difficulty: surely our Lord has
forsaken us quite, our God will be gracious no more." This cometh of
reasoning, falsely so called. When we see no passage through our
straits we are sadly apt to conclude that God sees none. He has
promised that with every trial he will make us a way of escape; but we
doubt his word. Like the unbelieving lord in the Book of Kings, we say,
" If God would make windows in heaven, might such a thing be?" Have
you never said that, my brother, in your spirit? Dear sister, has not
the evil one whispered such a word in your ears in dark times? Have
you not fancied that at last you have passed beyond the reach of divine
help, and will surely perish? In this way carnal reason is sure to
argue, and rob God of his glory, and our souls of consolation. It has
been so from the beginning, that while doubting God we cover our unbelief with an evil sophistry, but this sophistry does not avail to remove
the mischievous tendencies of our mistrust. Unbelievers by this
wicked reasoning are left in their spiritual death, while believers are
hampered and sorely wounded. O accursed unbelief, this is thy false
argument, " It is marvellous, and therefore it cannot be true!" We
answer thee that because it is marvellous it is all the more likely to be
true.

II. Secondly, we will now aim our arrows at the dark spot in this
carnal argument, which makes it all to be false; or, in other words,
we will CORRECT THIS REASONING.

First, let us note that when because the blessing promised is marvellous, we therefore doubt the promise of God concerning it, *we must
have forgotten God.* " If it be marvellous in your eyes, saith the Lord
of hosts, is it therefore marvellous in mine eyes?" God himself puts it

so, and there is but one answer to the question. My text is a very singular one, for it is hedged in with the name of the Lord, and with a double "thus saith the Lord of hosts." It begins with "Thus saith the Lord of hosts," and it finishes up with, "saith the Lord of hosts," as if twice to bring to our memory that God is, and that God has made a promise, and that this Promiser is Jehovah the great and powerful, the Lord of all, who has countless armies at his beck and call. This unbelief forgets, and hence her error.

To come to our one subject, that of your own salvation, you hear the promise of eternal life in Christ Jesus, and your mind replies, "It is marvellous, it is difficult." Do you not see that you are looking at it as if *you* had made the promise? From that standpoint it would be indeed difficult, even to impossibility. But whose promise is it? It is not yours, but God's. If you were to promise to give yourself eternal life, and to keep yourself to the end, and sanctify yourself perfectly, what a foolish person you would be to undertake what you could not possibly perform! But it is not *your* promise; it is God's promise. Is anything too hard for the Lord? Do look at it in that light. It is a marvellous promise for you to receive, but the God who spake it knew what he was saying, and he knew that he had power to perform it. It is the promise of God, "who alone doeth great wonders": remember that.

And remember, next, that God does not look to you to fulfil his promises. Do not fall into such a foolish imagining. If you make a promise yourself, it is your own business to carry it out: is it not? And if God makes a promise that he will save a sinner, whose work is it to save that sinner? Why, it is the work of the God who made the promise. It is written, "He that believeth in him hath everlasting life." "Marvellous," say you; but who says it? Why, God. Then it is God's department to make it true. If you would but remember this, that the pardon of sin is God's business, that the renewing of the heart is God's business, that the keeping of the saint to the end is God's business, that the sanctifying and perfecting of all believers is God's business, then you would find it more easy to believe. Can anything surpass the power of God? Did you ever hear of the Lord being baffled in his designs? Can it be possible that he has promised what he is not able to perform?

The false reasoning which cries—"It is marvellous, and therefore impossible," ignores altogether the fact that God is a marvellous Being, and that if his promise is marvellous, it is like himself. He is a great God and his power and wisdom are infinite: can anything surpass his ability? Would you have the infinite God confine his promises and gifts to common-place matters? Would it be seemly that the Lord, who is infinite in resources, should do nothing but what you can understand? O sirs, you forget the Eternal, and therefore doubt the promise: do so no more.

And, further, the error which vitiates the argument of carnal reason takes another shape. There is here, as far as the Lord is thought of at all, *an underestimate of God.* The Lord puts this very plainly in our text—"If it be marvellous in the eyes of the remnant of this people in these days, should it also be marvellous in mine eyes?" You are judging God as if he were like yourself; you have been calculating divine

possibilities by the scale of your own capacity; you have lowered God
to the limit of your understanding, you have narrowed him to your
notion of what he can do; and thus you degrade his greatness to your
littleness, his wisdom to your folly, his power to your weakness. The
deed of salvation is marvellous with you; but it is not strange with God,
to whom it has been the great thought of eternity, towards which he
causeth all things to move. Everything in wonder depends upon the
person affected by it: a trader goes to Africa, he takes with him a
looking-glass, and you see the chiefs gather around, and with wonder
they gaze upon their own pleasing countenances in the mirror. It is
marvellous to them ; it becomes the talk of the tribe; but that looking-
glass is not marvellous to the trader who brought it there. A musical-
box is set playing, and a whole village of negroes gather about it,
unanimously believing that it must be at least a spirit, if not a God.
To them it is a great marvel, and they expect the white man to marvel
too, for they measure his capacity by their own: yet their wonderful
thing is to an Englishman a mere simplicity. Shall we set it down for
certain that what is a wonder to us is a wonder to God? This would be
absurd. The Lord can do exceeding abundantly above all that we ask
or even think: there is no bounding his power, no searching of his
understanding. "But my sin," say you, "who is to subdue it?"
Not you, certainly; but the Lord of hosts is able to overcome the power
of sin. Do not measure God by yourself. "But my trouble, who can
bring me through it?" Nobody can, except the everlasting God, who
fainteth not, neither is weary. The end of the creature is the starting-
place of the Creator. The limit of our power is soon reached; but the
wings of the morning could not bear us beyond the power divine.
Whatsoever the Lord wills is accomplished; be sure of that.

When we begin to doubt whether God will love us to the end, is it
not measuring God's patience by our impatience ? Is there not a calculating of God's immutability by our mutability ? Because we change
and grow weary, shall we fancy that the Lord also changes ? Is there
variableness and turning with the great Father of lights ? Hath not the
Lord declared, " I am God ; I change not; therefore ye sons of Jacob are
not consumed ? "

When we doubt God's wisdom by questioning whether he can find a
way of keeping his word and helping us, is it not because our little
knowledge is exhausted and our plans broken down, and therefore we
conclude that God's plans will break down too, and his invention will
fail to contrive our deliverance? But, beloved, it is not so. The
Lord's way is in the whirlwind, and the clouds are the dust of his feet.
His footsteps are not seen, but he walketh on the sea, he rideth on the
wings of the wind. He everywhere hath sway, and all things answer
to his purpose and accomplish his designs. Leave off doubting, and
believe that the Lord's thoughts are as high above your thoughts as the
heavens are above the earth.

It is at bottom our pride which makes us judge the Lord to be like
ourselves. If you degrade God to be like to man it is because you
idolize man, and make him like to God. Who are you, you creature of
an hour? Who are you, you creeping insect upon the bay leaf of
existence? Who are you, poor mortal, that to-day is, and to-morrow is

shovelled back into mother earth, that you should begin to measure God? Go, measure heaven with your span, weigh the Alps in scales, and the Andes in balances, and hold the Atlantic in the hollow of your hand, and when you have done these things know that you are not at the beginning of the measurement of the wisdom, the power, the truth, and the goodness of the Lord. This, however, is the fault of carnal reasoning, that it judges the Lord of hosts by the miserable standard of human weakness.

Do you not see, dear friends, that if we begin to say that God's promise is so marvellous that it cannot be performed, *we do the infinite God high dishonour?* You dishonour his power by imagining that a difficulty has arisen which he cannot meet. You suppose a power greater than God, since it baffles and defeats him. What is this but to set up another god? It is a fault charged upon Israel of old as a very provoking crime, that they limited the Holy One of Israel. Oh that we may never be guilty of this offence! But you do worse than that, for I can suppose God to bear the dishonour of his power being limited, but it is far worse practically to insinuate that he boasts beyond his line. I tremble as I say that unbelief accuses the Lord of vain boasting. When a man promises you what he knows he cannot perform, what opinion do you form of him? You say at once, " Why, the man is a boaster; he is big at talking, but small at performing." Will you insinuate that of the Lord God? Has it come to this, that you dare criticize your Maker? Do you dare insinuate that the infinite Jehovah has promised to a sinner what he is incapable of giving him? He says, " Believe on the Lord Jesus Christ, and thou shalt be saved ;" and you say, " No, I could not be saved." Does God, then, speak beyond his ability? Does he promise what he is not able to perform? This is a form of blasphemy from which may we be cleansed through the blood of our Lord Jesus.

Or is it that you dream that God does not know his own strength? What! Is the Almighty ignorant? Is the only wise God unaware of his own power? Does he not know what he can do? I will not say that a man brags when he promises what he cannot perform, provided that he is unaware of his inability, for in such a case he blunders through ignorance or conceit of himself. Dost thou dare charge either of these upon God? Far from me be such an evil thought. I feel this morning that if all your sins were mine, yet since the Lord has promised pardon to him that believeth, I could and would believe over the head of all that mass of sin. Yea, if all the iniquities of all the men that ever lived were laid upon my soul, yet upon that assurance, " The blood of Jesus Christ his Son cleanseth us from all sin," I would even venture my soul's hope of salvation, and make sure of success. If the Lord has given a promise to his people that he will keep them to the end, and that they shall not perish, then he will keep them to the end without fail. Why, brothers, if our road to heaven were thick with devils, so that they stood like blades of wheat in a corn-field, yet we should be able to force a lane right through the serried host, the Lord Jehovah being our helper. If all the powers that are, or were, or can be, were to raise themselves up against the promise of God, in the name of God would we defy and defeat them. The word of the Lord makes us more than conquerors. David said of old,

" They compassed me about like bees ; yea, they compassed me about, but in the name of the Lord I will destroy them." What can stand against the feeblest man that lives if he has God's promise to back him ? The Lord can do just what he wills, whoever may oppose : wherefore let us fling away this folly of ours in supposing that, because a work of grace is marvellous in our eyes, it is therefore marvellous in the eyes of the Lord. That which is difficult with us is easy with him. There is a radical mistake at the bottom of all this wicked, unbelieving reasoning— it leaves out the Lord altogether, or degrades him below the glory of his Godhead.

III.   We have reached the third division of our discourse, and here let us practise a little RIGHT REASONING.

I invite any here who are troubled with doubts about the promise of God to follow me in a few simple considerations.

First, *it is quite clear that for our salvation marvels must be wrought.* It will be a wonder in all ages for any one of us to attain to glory : it will need the omnipotence of God to renew, preserve, and perfect us.   It is a rule with regard to miracles that God is very economical with them.   In the Romish Church you have miracles in abundance, such as they are ; but they are for the most part needless parades of power. When St. Denis, after his head was cut off, picked it up in his hands and walked a thousand miles with it, the dear good man might as well have saved himself and his head the unsightly pilgrimage.   When the blood of St. Januarius liquefies, or a Madonna winks, it may be interesting, but one does not see the necessity for either performance. The God of the Scriptures has no hand in such miracles ; they are not of the same order as those which are wrought by his right hand.   Our Lord never uses a miracle where the same thing could be done by the ordinary processes of nature ; but whenever a miracle is requisite, a miracle is forthcoming,—there is no stint of power though there is no wasteful display of it.   I argue, then, that if it is necessary for you to be saved in order that God's promise may be kept, you shall be saved ; and if in order to this, marvels are needed, marvels will happen.   The Lord reserves no strength when it is needful to expend it for the fulfilment of his promises ; if omnipotence must make bare its arm, it shall be bared.   The Lord led his people Israel to the Red Sea : perhaps if the Egyptians had not come up, it might have been possible to make rafts to ferry them across the gulf, and we are sure it would have been done if it had been the best way of achieving the Lord's design ; but when the Egyptians were so close behind that you could hear the neighings of their horses, and almost feel the hot breath of their vengeful masters, then there remained no ordinary way for the people of God to escape, and lo ! the mighty depths yawned before the tribes, and a road was opened through the heart of the sea that the people of God might pass through.   So it shall be with you : if to forgive your sin needs a miracle of grace, believe in the Lord Jesus Christ, and the miracle of grace is done.   If to change thy nature needs the miraculous power of the Holy Spirit, if thou believest in the Lord Jesus Christ, the Spirit waiteth to work that great change . nay, he has wrought the change, and thy faith is the evidence of it.   If it shall need all the power of God to keep one of his children to the end, all that power shall be seen in him ; for though God worketh not miracles till they are needed, he is not slow to do so when the case demands them. He will shake earth and heaven to complete the salvation of his chosen. Therefore, if a deed of grace be marvellous in thine eyes, say to thyself, "Marvellous as it is, nothing short of it will avail, and therefore it shall be done." It was marvellous that God should become man; but as there was no salvation for us apart from Immanuel God with us, Jesus was born of a woman. It is marvellous that the Son of God should die; but as there was no salvation apart from his death, he died upon the cross. If the Lord has given a promise it must be carried out cost what it may, for his name is "God that cannot lie." If there is no way of bringing a saint to God except by the Holy Ghost's dwelling in him, which is a great wonder, then the Holy Ghost shall dwell in him; for the many sons must be brought unto glory, and if marvels are needed as many as the hairs on their heads, so many marvels there shall be.

A second little bit of reasoning may tend to comfort some of you, namely, that, *after all, marvellous things are the rule with God.* I say not miracles, although it is difficult to draw the line between the ordinary processes of God's working and the extraordinary ones, for the ordinary are extraordinary, and his extraordinary deeds can hardly be more marvellous than his daily operations. All the works of God in creation are marvels. Take the telescope and search out the stars. Assuredly an "undevout astronomer is mad." When we perceive somewhat of the multitudes of worlds that God has made, their vast distances, the proportions of their bulk, the regularity of their orbits, and the rapidity of their motions, we discover that the great machinery of nature is ordered by infinite skill. "It is the Lord's doing," and it is marvellous in our eyes. Surely, that God who flings the stars about with both his hands can give us our daily bread. If he makes worlds to fly off like sparks from the anvil of his omnipotence, he can make new creatures in Christ Jesus. If he keeps all those heavenly lamps shining so brightly for centuries, he can sustain grace in the hearts of his people without difficulty. But now, if you have done with the telescope, please put it by, and let me lend you a microscope. Look at a butterfly from your garden; nay, you need not trouble to examine the whole creature, a portion of a broken wing will suffice for your astonishment. Here is a spider's eye! Are you not surprised? This is the petal of a flower—what amazing beauty! Take but a single portion of a minute blood-vessel, and study it awhile. I hear you say, "I never could have believed it; this glass reveals to me such wonders that I am utterly astounded." God is as great in the little as in the great: he is God everywhere. If a man carefully fashions a needle it appears to be exquisitely smooth and polished. Ah! it is only bright because your eye is dim. Put it under the glass. It is transformed into a rough bar of iron. No works of man will bear to be examined with a microscope; but you may search the Lord's work with the utmost care. The commonest, plainest, simplest, most ordinary creation of God is perfect. Since, then, all nature teems with marvels, why put aside a promise of God because it involves a marvel? Is such conduct reasonable?

However, if you have read through all the page of nature, which I am sure you have not, I would invite you to peruse the book of providence, and see what marvels are there. I will give you no illustrations, because your own life will probably furnish you with such. If not, look at the history of any country: see how wondrously God has wrought out his everlasting purposes of justice or of mercy in each land. The story of providence contains a world of wonders. Why, then, should you doubt the promise of God because it involves a marvel? Rather believe it for that very reason. I think there is good reasoning in all this.

Follow me yet a little further, when I say that *you must be prepared to abandon altogether the religion of our Lord Jesus Christ if you make it a rule to disbelieve the marvellous.* The greatest marvel that I ever heard of is this—" Great is the mystery of godliness ; God was manifest in the flesh." How the infinite could become one with the finite, so that the babe at Bethlehem should be the Mighty God, I cannot tell, and I think you cannot. Are you prepared to forego the incarnation of Christ? For if you are not, you must not refuse to believe in any act of God because it is marvellous, for it cannot be more marvellous than God in human flesh.

Think again: it is a cardinal doctrine of Christianity that the dead will rise again ; that at the sounding of the trump of God they that are in their graves will rise to be judged in their bodies. Is not this a marvel? Stand in a cemetery, and ask the question, " Can these dry bones live?" Do you believe in the resurrection? Then you must never set aside any promise of God because it involves a marvel. You also believe, according to the word of the Lord, that this world will one day be the home of God's glory, for there shall be new heavens and a new earth wherein dwelleth righteousness, and the travail of the groaning creation shall come to an end, and this world shall be made anew a temple for the Lord. What an extraordinary thing this will be! yet you believe it. Do not therefore ever doubt a single promise that God makes either to saint or sinner because it contains a marvel.

Yet, again, I want you to follow me in another thought, namely, that *greater marvels have been already wrought than any which your salvation and mine will henceforth involve.* Brothers, if it had been whispered to some one of us that God would take upon himself human form and dwell among men, we should have looked much astonished ; but if the prophet had added, " In that form he will be despised and spit upon, and hung up to die a felon's death, because he will bear the sin of man, which will be laid upon his perfect person, so that he will be made a curse for us," we should have said, " No, that cannot be." Beloved, it has been ; atonement has been accomplished. Christ has borne the load of his people's sins up to the cross, and he has hurled that weight from his shoulders into his own sepulchre, and left it there buried for ever. No wonder like this remains to be done: the greatest deed is finished. The renewal of our nature, and the forgiveness of our sin, are but little things compared with what Christ has already done. That he should now save his people seems to me not at all extraordinary ; it would be more extraordinary that he should die, and not save those for whom he died. Having paid the ransom price for his heritage, it is but a natural consequence that it should be set free. The greater wonder has already amazed angels, and principalities, and powers. Oh, think not, though

I for lack of time have passed lightly over this miracle of miracles, the death of our blessed Lord, that there is not much more to be said of this great wonder! Why, in dying, our Lord destroyed death, and cried, "Where is thy sting?" In rising again, he burst the bands of the sepulchre, and opened a way to life to all believers: in ascending the starry road, he led captivity captive, and took possession of heaven in the name of all his redeemed; and now, this day, he that was despised and rejected has all power given to him in heaven and in earth on our behalf. These great wonders have been finished, and registered in heaven; it only remains for us simply to receive the result of them by believing in Christ Jesus our Lord. To deliver us from the wrath to come is now comparatively but a small marvel. Compared with the griefs and death of the Son of God nothing great remains. Think of that, and let your faith be encouraged.

I will not detain you except to remind you of the sweet thought that *the more marvels there may be in our salvation the more glorifying it will be to God.* Do think of that. The more difficult it will be to save you, the more glory to God when he has achieved it. Your sin washed away will only demonstrate the power of the precious blood of Jesus; your hard, stubborn will subdued, will only prove the might of the love of Christ upon your soul. Your trials, and temptations, and weaknesses, and infirmities will only glorify that almighty strength which is working in you to produce your ultimate perfection. Believe the promise all the more because it is so wonderful; and therefore so honouring to the Lord. Do not let the marvel stagger you: let it encourage you. Say, "If this involved nothing wonderful, I could not think it came from God; but inasmuch as it is great and high it is all the more worthy of a God." Make the difficulties of the Bible a help to your faith, and let the greatness of grace render you the more hopeful of receiving it.

Lastly, let me say, whenever you have any doubts and fears, do *turn away your mind from the thing that is promised to the faithful Promiser.* We want larger ideas of God altogether. If we had them we should find it easy to believe his word. I remember when a boy being taken to see the residence of one of our nobility, and the good friend who took me noticed my astonishment at the largeness of the house. I was amazed at it, having never seen anything like it, and so I said, "What a house for a man to live in!" "Bless you, boy," said he, "this is only the kitchen!" I was only looking at the servants' apartments, and was astonished at the grandeur thereof; but the mansion itself was a far nobler affair. Oftentimes when you see what the Lord has done, you are ready to cry out, "How can all this be? His goodness, his mercy, is it as great as this?" Rest assured that you have only seen a little of his goodness, as it were the kitchen of his great house: you have not seen the palace of the Most High, where he reveals his full power and splendour.

You know the story of the warrior, who, having led his men into a difficult position, went round at night to their tents. He said to himself, "If they are all in good heart we shall fight well to-morrow, but certainly this defile needs all our valour: I should like to know the spirit of my men." Going round the camp secretly, he heard in a tent some half-dozen soldiers conversing, and one of them above the rest was just saying, " I think our general has made a great mistake this time: look at the enemy: they have so many cavalry, so many infantry and guns, and so forth." He added up all the force of the enemy, and another soldier chimed in, " What do you suppose our strength to be ?" So the other calculated—so many footmen, so many horsemen, so many artillerymen, and so on. He was just going to total it up, and make a very small concern of the whole, when the general drew aside the canvas of the tent and said, " And pray, my man, how many do you count me for ?" Did all the general's skill, and valour, and renown count for nothing? He who had won so many fights could he not win again? Just so the Lord Jesus Christ, whenever we begin summing up our strength, or rather our weakness, seems to appear and say, " How many do you count me for?" O sirs ! you have not counted the Lord Jesus at the millionth part of what he is; nay, the firmest believer here has not yet reached the trailing skirts of the garments of divine omnipotence. Let us enlarge our minds. Come, blessed Spirit, reveal Christ in us, and let us thus know more of God, and trust him better, and let nothing be unbelievingly marvellous in our eyes, since nothing can be too hard for the Lord. God bless you. Amen.

PORTIONS OF SCRIPTURE READ BEFORE SERMON—Numbers xi. 1—23·
2 Kings vii.

HYMNS FROM " OUR OWN HYMN BOOK."—186, 192, 686.

Metropolitan Tabernacle Pulpit.

JEHOVAH HATH SPOKEN : WILL YE NOT HEAR?

A Sermon

DELIVERED ON LORD'S-DAY MORNING, NOVEMBER 4TH, 1883, BY

C. H. SPURGEON,

AT THE METROPOLITAN TABERNACLE, NEWINGTON.

"Hear ye, and give ear ; be not proud : for the LORD hath spoken. Give glory to the LORD your God, before he cause darkness, and before your feet stumble upon the dark mountains, and, while ye look for light, he turn it into the shadow of death, and make it gross darkness. But if ye will not hear it, my soul shall weep in secret places for your pride ; and mine eye shall weep sore, and run down with tears, because the LORD's flock is carried away captive."—Jeremiah xiii. 15—17.

IN this chapter Jeremiah had proclaimed the judgment of God against his sinful people under two very striking figures. Israel had been to God what a girdle is to a man ;* the people had been bound closely about him in his great love and favour ; but on account of their sin the Lord would put them away, and they should be hidden by the Euphrates till their beauty was marred ; till, in fact, like a rotten girdle, their whole state had become decayed. "Thus saith the Lord, After this manner will I mar the pride of Judah, and the great pride of Jerusalem." Then he spake to them by a second parable—"Every bottle shall be filled with wine";—and he showed how God's wrath would come upon the people to fill them with a judicial drunkenness, so that they should become besotted, and in their delirium should strive one with another to their mutual undoing. The Lord declared that thus he would "dash them one against another, even the fathers and the sons together." Thus, under two homely but exceedingly terrible figures, Jeremiah preached the law to the people, that they might be humbled under a sense of sin. Had they but felt the force of this teaching they would have begun to mourn for their sin, and, under dread of wrath, they would have cried for mercy. Taking it for granted that this might be the case, though, alas! it did not so happen, the Lord gave to his prophet an interval for proclaiming mercy. After those two great thunder claps of judgment came a gracious shower of grace.

The prophet, in what we may venture to call an evangelistic style, exhorts the people, and addresses to them the characteristic gospel precept,—"Hear ye, and give ear; for Jehovah hath spoken." His words remind us of Isaiah's exhortation—"Incline your ear and come unto me: hear, and

---

* See Spurgeon's Sermon, No. 1,706, entitled "The Cast-off Girdle."

No. 1,748.

your soul shall live;" and again—"Hearken diligently unto me, and eat ye that which is good." Under the gospel "faith cometh by hearing, and hearing by the word of God;" and so Jeremiah doth, as it were, in these verses preach the gospel to the backsliding house of Judah. This is ever God's design in threatening judgment; he desires to prepare the people for his grace. I would take up the prophet's strain by the help of the Lord, praying to be a partaker of his earnest and tender Spirit. Oh, that to-day those who have never heard the voice of the Lord in the inward parts of their being may hear it and live! O Holy Spirit, work thou to that end!

I. We will enter upon our subject at once, for there is much to speak of. The first head will be this: listen, O my hearers, with deep attention, for THERE IS A REVELATION. Read the text—"Hear ye, and give ear; be not proud: *for the Lord hath spoken.*" If the Lord had not spoken, the silence would have deepened and established your natural darkness, and if you had been inquiring after God your heart would have cried, "Oh, that he would break this dreadful silence!" How sad would have been our estate if we had to seek after God if haply we might find him! Shall man by searching find out God? Who among us could reason ourselves into the knowledge of the Lord? or imagine the thoughts of his mind? But here you have the great source of comfort and instruction—"Jehovah hath spoken." Is not this a just call for the attention of all his creatures?

The voice which we are bidden to hear is *a Divine voice*, it is the voice of him that made the heavens and the earth, whose creatures we are. Jehovah hath spoken! If it were but the voice of prophets apart from their Master, it might be but a slight sin to refuse what they say; but since Jehovah hath spoken, shall men dare to be deaf to him? Shall they turn away from him that speaketh from heaven? He that spake us into being hath spoken to our being. He by whose word the heavens stand, and at whose word both heaven and earth shall pass away, hath spoken, and his voice is to the sons of men. It is God who says, "I have written to him the great things of my law." The sacred Scriptures are the record of what God hath spoken: receive them with the reverence which they deserve as coming from God only, and as being, therefore, pure truth, fixed certainty, and unerring right.

It is a word most *clear and plain*, for Jehovah hath *spoken.* He might have taught us only by the works of his hands, in which the invisible things of God, even his eternal power and Godhead are clearly seen. What is all creation but a hieroglyphic scroll, in which the Lord has written out his character as Creator and Provider? But since he knew that we were dim of sight and dull of comprehension, the Lord has gone beyond the symbols and hieroglyphs, and used articulate speech such as a man useth with his fellow: Jehovah hath *spoken!* A man may act before us his mind in emblems, and we may fail to perceive his meaning; but when he speaks, we understand his communications by language, since such modes of expression are suitable to the human intellect. Speech is the fit manner of commerce between mind and mind, and it is, therefore, most delightful that the all-glorious Jehovah should stoop from writing in starry letters across the sky, and from mirroring his form in tempests on the sea, and *speak* with us as a man speaketh with his friends. Jehovah is no dumb deity: he hath spoken to us in sweet and chosen words by his Spirit. Oh, when there is a testimony so clear and plain that he who runs may read, well may the prophet exhort us, saying, "Hear ye, and give ear; for Jehovah hath spoken." Let it not be said of us, as of the sinners long ago, "I spake unto you, rising up early and speaking, but ye heard not; and I called you, but ye answered not."

Moreover, I gather from the expression in the text that the revelation made to us by the Lord is *an unchangeable and abiding word.* It is not to-day that Jehovah *is speaking,* but Jehovah *hath spoken:* his voice by the prophets and apostles is silent now, for he hath revealed all truth which is needful for salvation. The Lord might fitly say to us this day; "What I have written I have written." He changeth not his word, but though heaven and earth pass away, his word abideth. We are not living in a period of gradual revelation, as some imagine: Jehovah hath spoken, and he openeth not his mouth a second time. He hath closed the canon of Scripture with a curse upon him that shall add to or take from the words of the book of this prophecy. Jehovah hath spoken! You have not to go on making discoveries of new truth outside of Scripture; your duty lies in diligently receiving the completed testimony of the Lord God, for the word of the Lord is perfect, converting the soul. He has fully told you your relation to your God, and the way by which you may be reconciled to him, and be at peace. "Add thou not unto his words, lest he reprove thee, and thou be found a liar." Jehovah hath spoken; and it is written in his law, "Ye shall not add unto the word which I command you."

Beloved, this revelation is pre-eminently *a condescending and cheering word.* The Lord might without a word have trodden us down to destruction when we sinned against him; he might have left us to that natural testimony which is borne upon the face of creation, and which is also reflected in the conscience of all men, and when we rejected these testimonies he might have allowed us to travel on in tenfold night. But instead thereof, in the plenitude of his grace, Jehovah hath spoken; and be it ever remembered that while of old he spoke in sundry times and divers manners by the prophets, he hath in these last times spoken unto us by his Son. The very fact that the great God speaks to us by his Son indicates that mercy, tenderness, love, hope, grace, are the burden of his utterance. His Son Jesus is full of grace and truth, and therefore that which he now speaks to us is not only truth, but grace; it is truthful grace and gracious truth which God speaks to us by Jesus Christ. Oh, the richness of that message, the height and depth of love which it contains! Who can refuse to listen to the heavenly music of mercy? The Lord's voice on the first day of creation said, "Let there be light," and there was light, and now this second voice, this voice to the spiritual world, gives us light, and life, and love, and every needful, conceivable, desirable boon. The words of God, as they are recorded in this Book, have a fulness unfathomable about them: they are spirit and life. In Christ, by whom he speaks, there is hid all the treasures of wisdom and knowledge. The prophet asked no more than was perfectly reasonable when he said, "Hear, and give ear; for Jehovah hath spoken." When the kings who dwell at the utmost ends of the earth hear that Jehovah hath spoken, they would do well to quit their thrones and make a journey, like the Queen of Sheba, to hear of the divine wisdom. If all workmen should throw down their tools, and say, "We will hear what God the Lord shall speak," and if merchants should close their shops and counting-houses for awhile, and come together without delay crying, "Everything must stop till we have heard what the Lord has spoken;" would it be any more than right reason would suggest to thoughtful and right-minded men? O sirs, if God has spoken, every ear should surrender itself to attention, for surely never could the sense of hearing be more honourably and profitably employed. Jehovah hath spoken, and his word is true: "The grass withereth, and the flower thereof falleth away: but the word of the Lord endureth for ever. And this is the word which by the gospel is preached unto you." There is a way of salvation arranged and determined of the Lord; it is not to be guessed at, but we are to learn it from infallible wisdom: Jehovah hath spoken. There is an atonement prepared, provided, designated, and set forth; we have not to search for it, or add to it: Jehovah hath spoken. There is no point of necessity, nor even of real interest to the heart of man, but what Jehovah hath spoken upon it; and if there be any truth upon which he has not spoken, it is because it is to his glory to conceal the thing, and for our profit that we do not pry into it. Upon all that is essential to our full preparation for our eternal destination, Jehovah hath spoken. He hath said it, and here it is recorded; in the volume of the Book it is written, and blessed are they that read and keep the words of the Book of this prophecy.

II. Secondly—and I have already anticipated it—since there is a revelation, IT SHOULD BE SUITABLY RECEIVED. If Jehovah hath spoken, then all attention should be given; yea, double attention, even as the text hath it, "*Hear ye, and give ear.*" Hear, and hear again: incline your ear, hearken diligently, surrender your soul to the teaching of the Lord God; and be not satisfied till you have heard his teaching, have heard it with your whole being, and have felt the force of its every truth. "Hear ye," because the word comes with power, and "give ear," because you willingly receive it. Oh, brothers, I fear that we give far more attention to the distracting voices of the world than to the soul-satisfying voice of the God of all grace. How eager men are after the treasure which melts before their eyes—how they will drink in every syllable by which they may learn how to be rich; but when God speaketh, who brings in both his hands eternal and abiding riches, men are deaf as the adder, careless as the beasts of the field. He saith, "I have called, and ye refused; I have stretched out my hand, and no man regarded." Is this right or wise? Surely, if Jehovah speaks we are bound by all that is just, and good, and grateful to wait in reverent silence till we know his mind. Let a general hush go through the universe, and let all ears with solemn reverence await the sound of the voice of the Lord.

Then it is added, as if by way of directing us how suitably to hear this revelation—"*Give glory to Jehovah your God.*" There ought to be in hearing and reading the revelation of God a constant giving of glory to the Lord. His speaking is a manifestation of his glory, as when the sun ariseth his light is spread abroad; you and I are to reflect that light even as the valleys rejoice in his brightness of the noontide. Let us stand, as it were, this morning to be shone upon by the Lord, ready

everyone of us, to reflect that light which cometh from on high.   Give
glory to God at once by worthily hearing his gospel.   How is that to be
done ?

Stand thou still, and hear the word of the Lord.   Glorify the Lord
by *accepting* whatsoever he saith unto thee as being infallibly true.
Believe in the Lord your God, so shall ye be established ; believe his
prophets, so shall ye prosper.   Know what the Lord has said, and let it
stand to thee as sure and steadfast truth.   Seek for no further reasons
to sustain thy faith ; but let "Thus saith the Lord" stand to thee
in the stead of all arguments.   To me a sentence of Scripture is the
essence of logic, the proof positive, the word which may not be questioned.
Eyes and ears may be doubted, but not the written word, inspired
of the Holy Ghost.   Blessed are those who sit at Jesus' feet and
receive of his words.   It is our wisdom to know nothing of ourselves,
but to be taught of the Holy Ghost ; and to think nothing of ourselves,
but to have the mind of God, and think after him whose thoughts
are as high above our thoughts as the heavens are above the earth.   We
give glory to God in reference to revelation when we receive it, every
jot and tittle of it, and bow our minds before it.   In these days this
virtue is lightly esteemed, for the Saviour's words are still true,—" He
that loveth me not keepeth not my sayings."   In all its length and
breadth, whatsoever the Lord saith we believe ; and we desire to know
neither less nor more than he has spoken.

We must receive the word, however, in a hearty and honest manner
so as to act upon it.   We must therefore *repent of the sin* which the
Lord condemns, and turn from the way which he abhors ; we must
loathe the vice which he forbids us, and seek after the virtue which he
commands.   We give glory to God when we penitently confess that we
have broken his holy law, and grieve because we have so done.   Did
not Joshua bid Achan give glory to God by confession of his sin ? and
so must we.   By confession we glorify God's justice, omniscience, and
truth, and yet further we glorify his mercy when, confessing sin, we ask
for pardon through Jesus Christ our Lord.   Thus should every human
being receive the revelation of God bringing forth fruits meet for repentance.   Thy light hath shone upon me, O my God, and therefore I
see my darkness !   O remove it !   Thou hast lighted a candle, and by
its light I discover my spots and stains, and I acknowledge them in thy
sight,—" Against thee, thee only, have I sinned, and done this evil in
thy sight: that thou mightest be justified when thou speakest, and be
clear when thou judgest."   Thus humbling ourselves on account of sin
we receive the word of God aright, and give God glory.

But we must go further than repentance and the acceptance of the truth
as truth, we must further reverence the gracious voice of God when he
bids us believe on Christ and live.   He has couched that message of
love in so blessed a form that he who does not accept it must be wantonly malicious against God and against his own soul.   For the Lord
does not demand that by penances and acts of mortification, and feelings
of misery and despair, we are to purge ourselves from sin ; but he has
graciously declared—" He that believeth on him is not condemned."
" Believe on the Lord Jesus Christ, and thou shalt be saved."   If
Jehovah has spoken in such a manner, if the sum and substance of what

he has spoken is that " God hath set forth his Son Jesus Christ to be a
propitiation through faith in his blood," then we must and will give ear
to him.   He saith, " Come now, and let us reason together, saith the
Lord : though your sins be as scarlet, they shall be as white as snow ;
though they be red like crimson, they shall be as wool."   If this be the
heavenly word, how can we refuse to hear it with our whole hearts ?
Give glory to the Lord by answering, " Lord, I joyfully obey thy call.
I am glad of a Saviour, glad of the atoning blood, glad to cast myself at
those dear feet that were nailed to the cross for me, and to find in the
Lord Jesus my salvation and my all."   This is the way in which we
ought to receive this revelation, and we ought to go on to *complete
obedience.*   We should humbly inquire, " Lord, what further wouldst thou
have me know, what further wouldst thou have me do ?   Is there still
left in me a part of my nature unsubdued, I would humble myself under
thy mighty hand.   Is there in me anything unrenewed, of pride revolting,
or of the flesh rebelling, then conquer it in me, for I desire thy word
to be my rule, my law, my guide.   O that my ways were directed to keep
thy statutes !   I wish in all things to be obedient to thy gracious will."
There is no part of God's word at which the human mind should kick.   If
our hearts were in a right state we should fling open all the doors of
our mind, and say, " Come in, O sacred truth, come in !   Thou art
welcome to my heart of hearts since thou comest from my God."   If
Jehovah speaks ought we not instead of cavilling, and questioning,
and disputing, and raising difficulties, just to say, " Speak, Lord, for thy
servant heareth" ?   When the Lord says to us, " Seek ye my face," our
heart should at once reply, " Thy face, Lord, will I seek."   I think that
point is clear.   There is a revelation, and that revelation ought to be
suitably received.

III.   But thirdly, PRIDE IN THE HUMAN HEART PREVENTS SUCH A
RECEPTION.   The text runs, " Hear ye, and give ear ; *be not proud :* for
the Lord hath spoken."   And further on the prophet says—" If ye will
not hear it, my soul shall weep in secret places *for your pride."*   The
prophet here puts his finger upon the blot.   Why is it, my dear hearers,
that there are any among you this day who have heard God's word year
after year and yet have not received it ?   The secret reason is your pride.
Perhaps pride prompts you indignantly to deny the accusation.

In some it is the *pride of intellect.*   They do not wish to be treated like
children ; they are not content to receive the kingdom of God as a little
child, and so when Jesus says, " Except ye be converted, and become
as little children, ye shall not enter into the kingdom of heaven,"
they reply that they intend to think out a gospel for themselves.   To lay
the inventiveness of thought on one side, and simply to believe what Jesus
teaches, is not to their mind ; they will not humble themselves to a fact so
little self-exalting.   Well, sirs, if you shut the door of the kingdom against
yourselves because you are too wise to enter, be this known unto you, that
the poor have the gospel preached to them, and that they receive it ; and
that God hath hid these things from the wise and prudent, and hath revealed them unto babes.   Things that are despised, hath God chosen, and
things that are not, to bring to naught the things that are : that no flesh
may glory in his presence.   If your wisdom is greater than the wisdom
of God, it were better for you to be foolish.   If you will destroy yourself

to indulge your own conceit, well, so it must be ; but the day shall come in which your regret shall know neither measure nor end.   Oh, let none of us be so proud as to lift up ourselves in opposition to that which Jehovah hath spoken!

In some others it is the *pride of self-esteem.*   " No," say they, " this gospel which we have heard so often is too simple—we are capable of something more elaborate.   It humbles us, it represents us as fallen, as depraved ; it says·that we can do nothing, it lays us in the very dust, it makes nothing of us : it excludes all hope of boasting and glorying : we cannot stoop so low.   Salvation by grace, is it?   Then free grace, sovereign grace is not to our mind.   We care not to be saved like paupers ; we care not to be freely forgiven as those who have nothing to pay.   That no composition will be accepted, not even a farthing in the pound of our own merit—is a doctrine too lowering to our dignity."   They set the gospel on one side because it sets them on one side.   They are too great to be saved.   O sirs, if ye must be proud, at least do not throw away your souls to indulge that propensity.   Surely, something less costly may suffice for a sacrifice to the demon of vain glory.   It is a dreadful thing that men should think it better to go to hell in a dignified way than to go to heaven by the narrow road of a child-like faith in the Redeemer. Those who will not stoop even to receive Christ himself and the blessings of eternal life deserve to perish.   God save us from such folly. It may well make us weep to think that any man should be so far gone astray from right reason as to throw away eternal bliss in order to walk with haughty steps through this poor life.

Some have a *pride of self-righteousness.*   They are good, they have kept the commandments from their youth up : they have attended to religion, they have seen to it that all rites and ceremonies have been duly performed upon them, and they thank God that they are not as other men are.   This righteousness of theirs is a garment respectable enough for them to wear, and therefore they reject the righteousness of God.   O ye proud, I would to God ye knew that ye are naked, and poor, and miserable.   I would ye understood that your fig-leaf righteousness will never cover your nakedness in the sight of God, for if ye knew this ye would seek after the perfect righteousness of Christ, and be robed and adorned therewith.   While sin ruins many in the outside world, I fear self-righteousness ruins more among those who attend places of worship.   They say " we see," and therefore their eyes are not opened : they cry " we are clean," and therefore they are not washed from their iniquity.   Oh that they would cease from this vanity, and give glory to the Lord their God, instead of taking glory themselves ?   How can they believe while they seek honour one of another ?

In some, too, it is the *pride of self-love.*   They cannot deny their lusts.   To cut off right-hand sins, and pluck out right-eye iniquities, cannot be endured by them.   Their hearts are set upon a certain evil pleasure, and they cannot give it up.   The gospel of Jesus Christ demands of those who receive it that they shall be saved not *in* their sins, but *from* their sins ; it comes to give us renewal as well as rest, purity as well as pardon, sanctity as well as safety ; and there are many who, because of their foolish self-indulgence, cannot deny themselves any seeming joy, but must needs fill themselves with the poisoned sweets which delight the flesh. O friend, I wish that this pride were taken from thee, and that it seemed wisdom to thee to deny thyself life itself for the present rather than miss the hope of life eternal.

The *pride of self-will* also works its share of ruin among men. "Who is the Lord, that I should obey his voice?" is the cry of many beside Pharaoh. The unrenewed heart virtually says—"I shall not mind these commands. Why should I be tied hand and foot, and ruled, and governed? I intend to be a free thinker and a free liver, and I will not submit myself." Just so, and you are free to lose all hope of heaven, my friend, free to destroy yourself. If this be your choice, then who is to hinder you in it? I know that I cannot. Oh, that the Lord will lead you to a better mind. Would God the Lord that he would change your will and renew your heart. But if you are so proud that you reject the testimony of God against yourself, then who is to blame when you fall into eternal destruction? Who is to blame but yourself? So I pass from mournfully considering this great evil which prevents the revelation of God from being properly received.

IV. Fourthly, HENCE THERE COMES AN EARNEST WARNING. The prophet has put it—"Give glory to the Lord your God, before he cause darkness, and before your feet stumble upon the dark mountains." I desire to explain this with deep humiliation of spirit on my own part, and with much trembling lest anyone of you should ever by experience know the truth of these words. Listen, my friend, thou who hast rejected God and his Christ till now. *Thou art already out of the way*, among the dark mountains. There is a King's highway of faith, and thou hast refused it; thou hast turned aside to the right hand or to the left, according to thine own imagination. Being out of the way of safety, *thou art in the path of danger even now*. Though the sunlight shines about thee, and the flowers spring up profusely under thy feet, yet thou art in danger, for there is no safety out of the King's road. If thou wilt walk according to his bidding thou shalt be quiet from fear of danger, for no lion shall be there; but inasmuch as thou art now thine own keeper and thine own law, and thou followest in thine own ways, thou art in great peril. The unbeliever is condemned already, because he has not believed on the Son of God. Escape, I pray thee, while thou mayest, and enter upon that one road which is strait and narrow, but leadeth unto life eternal—the way of faith in Jesus.

If thou wilt still pursue thy headlong career, and choose a path for thyself, I pray thee remember that *darkness is lowering around thee*. The day is far spent! Around thy soul there are hanging mists and glooms already, and these will thicken into the night-damps of *bewilderment*. Thinking but not believing, thou wilt soon think thyself into a horror of great darkness. Refusing to hear what Jehovah has spoken, thou wilt follow other voices, which shall allure thee into an Egyptian night of confusion. Thou wilt go on meditating and ex-cogitating, or criticizing and trifling, till thou art enveloped in a cloud of doubts, wrapped as in a dense smoke of speculation, and well nigh smothered in exhalations of unbelief. Thou shalt not know what to do, nor what to think, nor what to say, nor whither to betake thyself, for thou wilt have renounced thy guide and quenched thy torch. At the same time, it may be, there will come upon thee a darkness of *distress:*

thou wilt be sick and sorry, thou wilt be faint and weary, thou wilt be tried and troubled, and thy soul will see no help or deliverance. To which of the saints wilt thou turn? Upon whom wilt thou call in the day of thy calamity, and who will succour thee? Then thy thoughts will dissolve into vanity, and thy spirit shall melt into dismay. " Thus saith the Lord, Behold, I will make thee a terror to thyself, and to all thy friends." Thou shalt grope after comfort as blind men grope for the wall, and because thou hast rejected the Lord and his truth, he also will reject thee and leave thee to thine own devices.

Meanwhile, there shall overcloud thee a darkness bred of thine own *sin and wilfulness*. Thou shalt lose the brightness of thine intellect, the sharp clearness of thy thought shall depart from thee, professing thyself to be wise thou shalt become a fool. Thou shalt no longer be able to boast thyself because of the clearness of thy judgment, but thou shalt find thy conceptions thrown into confusion. Thou shalt ask of others, but they shall know no more than thyself, or if they know thou shalt not understand what they tell thee. Thou shalt be in an all-surrounding, penetrating blackness. Hence comes the solemnity of this warning, "Give glory to the Lord your God, before he cause darkness." While as yet you have not absolutely turned away from the truth and rejected God's word, accept it in your heart by a living faith, and give him glory, lest by continuing a procrastinator and a halter between two opinions, thou be gradually made to slide by little and by little away from the brightness of the truth, till thou be shut up in a sevenfold night, out of which there shall be no escape.

For after that darkness there comes a *stumbling*, as saith the text, "before your feet stumble upon the dark mountains." He who is going to think out his own way apart from revelation, will meet with mysteries which he cannot surmount. There are mysteries in revelation, but these rise before us like hills of light; while to those who trifle with the word of the Lord there shall arise mountains of gloom. I care not what philosophy you take, whether it be old or new, openly profane or faintly sprinkled with Christianity, you will never get rid of mystery— it is essential to the limited capacity of the human mind confronted by boundless truth. There must be difficulties in every man's way, even if it be a way of his own devising ; but to the man that will not accept the light of God, these difficulties must necessarily be dark mountains with sheer abysses, pathless crags, and impenetrable ravines. He has refused the path which wisdom has cast up, and he is justly doomed to stumble where there is no way. Beware of encountering mysteries without guidance and faith, for you will stumble either into folly or superstition, and only rise to stumble again. Those who stumble at Christ's cross are like to stumble into hell.

There are also dark mountains of another kind which will block the way of the wanderer—mountains of dismay, of remorse, of despair. Woe to that man who finds himself travelling at midnight, without a guide, without a road, amid tremendous mountains, impassable to human feet. Ah, when a man comes into the land of doubt, which is a land of darkness, as darkness itself, and of the shadow of death, without any order, and where the light is as darkness—how terrible his case ! I say no more—thank God, my hearers, you are not there yet ! Therefore hearken to Jehovah's voice, and give glory to God ere he send a thick darkness over all your soul, even darkness that may be felt, and your feet stumble, never to rise again.

After that stumbling there will come bitter *disappointment.* The man finding that he cannot discover his way sits down awhile, and says to himself, " I will wait till the moon rises, or the day dawns. Many before me have come to a pause ; no doubt light will come." He looks and looks and looks again, but all in vain, for thus saith the prophet, "While ye look for light, he turns it into the shadow of death." Dread word—*death!* Terrible shade which death casts over men's minds! That shadow is coming on the man as years advance, and he has no light with which to dispel it. The physician cannot remove the death shadow—the disease is incurable. The sinner's face is pale with anguish, and his heart melts like wax in the midst of his bowels, for the shadow now upon him chills him to the marrow of his bones! What will he do now that the arrow is rankling in his heart? What will he do now that eternal night is descending? He cowers down and waits; but nothing comes except the thickening of the death shadows, amid the weeping of those whom he must leave. He is anticipating the weeping and wailing and gnashing of teeth, which are to be his endless portion.

And now a *paralyzing despair* seizes him, for God makes the darkness to be "gross darkness," black, palpable, as it were a solid thing. The man is shut up, and he cannot come forth ; the darkness is within the chambers of his soul, it is in his brain, it is in his heart, he is drowning in a black sea. Meet ending this for one who hated the light ! Oh, I pray you, before any of you pass into that state, give glory to God, and receive his word. I beseech you believe ere your doubt has utterly destroyed you. Accept the witness of God before you become hardened in scepticism.

I do not know what may ever happen to me in this life; perhaps it shall come to pass that I may be visited with severe physical infirmities, and possibly these may cause me mental depression and anguish; but this one thing I know, I have committed my mind, my heart, my whole intellectual nature to his keeping who has promised to preserve his own. I desire to believe nothing but what he tells me, to do nothing but what he bids me, and to yield myself to no influence but that which he ordains for my direction ; and, therefore, it seems to me that having done this for many a day I can with unstaggering confidence say at the last, "Father, into thy hand I commit my spirit." I think I may confidently hope to cast anchor for ever in that haven which is no new refuge to me, but the daily roadstead of my soul. Can a man be more safe as to his soul's condition than when he has ceased from depending upon himself and has taken the great Lord to be the Shepherd at whose heel he follows ? What shield can so well protect you as the divine faithfulness ? Under what rock can you find such shelter as under the truthfulness of God ? I am at a pass with all new ideas in religion : I will have none of them. If that grand old Book fail me, I am content to fail ; if the Lord shall desert me, I resign myself to be deserted : if God himself doth lie then there is an end of all things, and we all alike flounder in chaos. We tolerate no such fears. Believing in God I am not fearful of the future. Neither dark mountains nor dark death can cause the believer to stumble, for he cries, " I know whom I have believed, and I am persuaded that he is able to keep that which I have committed unto him against that day." But oh, if God be true, what will become of you who will not hear him? If the Bible be true, what must be your portion who pretend to be wiser than the Holy Ghost? You must assuredly wander into that endless captivity from which there can be no redemption.

V. So now I have to close, but not till I have delivered my burdened heart once more. If the people would not submit to God, the prophet determined what *he* would do. THERE REMAINS FOR THE FRIENDS OF THE IMPENITENT BUT ONE RESORT. The loving prophet cries, "If ye will not hear it, my soul shall weep in secret places for your pride; and mine eye shall weep sore, and run down with tears, because the Lord's flock is carried away captive." He cannot do anything more, he has no other message to deliver. He cannot hope that God will brook their insults and invent another way of saving them. He has told them the truth, and if they refuse it he will lay no flattering unction to their souls. He will deliver the word of the Lord once more, and if they again refuse he will go home to mourn for them even as Samuel mourned for Saul when the Lord had put him away. Observe that he does not say in the first clause, " my eyes shall weep," but "my soul shall weep." Bitter tears make red the eyes, but what must be the brine of those tears which are wept by the soul itself—a soul in anguish over wilful men who persist in destroying themselves!

Those soul-sorrows showed themselves in floods of tears which drenched the prophet's cheeks; for he loved the people, and could not bear to look upon the ruin which was coming upon them. Like our Lord in later times, the prophet beheld the city and wept over it: he could do no less, he could do no more. Alas, his sorrow would be unavailing, his grief was hopeless. *He* could not help those who would not be helped by God. If they refused to hear, he does not speak to them of " a larger hope " yet to be revealed, another season of probation, or a future revelation which would override the present word. Ah no, he loved men too well to invent for them fools' paradises; he dared not imitate the old serpent in the garden by insinuating—" Ye shall not surely die." I fear that the garments of many modern divines are steeped in the blood of souls whom they are deluding with their " larger hope," which is but a larger snare of Satan. Jeremiah had a brave though tender heart; he did not truckle to men, and sing pretty ditties to them, as preachers nowadays are prone to do; but he told them they would stumble in the darkness, and that nothing remained for him but to sigh out his soul over their ruin. Let us each one learn to sympathize with this holy man :—

> " Arise, my tenderest thoughts, arise,
> To torrents melt my streaming eyes;
> And thou, my heart, with anguish feel
> Those evils which thou canst not heal.

> " See human nature sunk in shame;
> See scandals pour'd on Jesu's name;
> The Father wounded through the Son;
> The world abused, and souls undone.

"See the short course of vain delight
   Closing in everlasting night;
   In flames that no abatement know,
   Though briny tears for ever flow."

Observe that the prophet did not expect to obtain sympathy in this sorrow of his. He says, "My soul shall weep *in secret places* for your pride." He would get quite alone, hide himself away, and become a recluse. Alas, that so few even now care for the souls of men! Many ignore their danger, forgetting or else denying it, and few mourn over the ungodly and seek,

"With cries, entreaties, tears to save,
   To snatch them from the fiery wave."

Hearts are hardened, pride is flattered, falsehoods are cried up; and what can the faithful do but seek to their God alone, and weep in secret places? Solitude and weeping are a poor solace, and yet there is no other.

This also puts a pungent salt into the tears of the godly, that the weeping can do no good, since the people refuse the one and only remedy. Jehovah has spoken, and if they will not hear *him* they must die in their sins. O sirs, if you will not have Christ, if all the saints in the world prayed for you, yea, all the saints that ever lived, or ever shall live—if they all prayed for you, and if in one great river the tears of the whole church flowed on for ever, they could not help you nor bring you hope of salvation. You must have Christ or die, you must believe in the Lamb of God or perish everlastingly. Stands it so according to the Scripture? Then none can change it. Do not dash yourselves against this rock! Fall not upon this stone!

What a burden it is that so many should cause us this unnecessary sorrow, for if men turned to God our joy would exceed all bounds. O my hearers, why will you distress me? Turn ye, turn ye, why will ye die? What excuse can you urge for your folly in choosing to perish? What motive can be strong enough to make you leap into the fire when Christ is waiting to be gracious to you? We have labour enough in preparing and delivering our weighty messages, without the added grief of seeing you reject them to your own destruction. Our throes of heart are sometimes grievous enough before we preach a sermon lest we should not preach aright: why must we be driven to this further misery? We exhaust ourselves while pleading with you: why should we have to sit down in sorrow because you will not believe our report? O blessed Spirit of God, touch all hearts this day, for Jesus' sake. Amen.

PORTION OF SCRIPTURE READ BEFORE SERMON—Jeremiah xiii. 1—17;
John i. 1—18.

HYMNS FROM "OUR OWN HYMN BOOK,"—92 (Part 1), 100, **97**.

Metropolitan Tabernacle Pulpit.

A LUTHER SERMON AT THE TABERNACLE.

A Sermon

Delivered on Lord's-day Morning, November 11th, 1883, by

C. H. SPURGEON,

AT THE METROPOLITAN TABERNACLE, NEWINGTON.

"But the just shall live by his faith."—Habakkuk ii. 4.

This text is three times employed by the apostle Paul as an argument. Read Romans i. 17, Galatians iii. 11, and Hebrews x. 38: in each of these cases it runs, "The just shall live by faith." This is the old original text to which the apostle referred when he said, " As it is written, The just shall live by faith." We are not wrong in making the inspiration of the Old Testament to be as important as that of the New; for the truth of the gospel must stand or fall with that of the prophets of the old dispensation. The Bible is one and indivisible, and you cannot question the first Testament and retain the New. Habakkuk must be inspired, or Paul writes nonsense.

Yesterday, four hundred years ago, there came into this wicked world the son of a miner, or refiner of metals, who was to do no little towards undermining the Papacy and refining the church. The name of that babe was Martin Luther: a hero and a saint. Blessed was that day above all the days of the century which it honoured, for it bestowed a blessing on all succeeding ages, through " the monk that shook the world." His brave spirit overturned the tyranny of error which had so long held nations in bondage. All human history since then has been more or less affected by the birth of that marvellous boy. He was not an absolutely perfect man, we neither endorse all that he said nor admire all that he did; but he was a man upon whose like men's eyes shall seldom rest, a mighty judge in Israel, a kingly servant of the Lord. We ought oftener to pray to God to send us men—men of God, men of power. We should pray that, according to the Lord's infinite goodness, his ascension gifts may be continued and multiplied for the perfecting of his church; for when he ascended up on high he led captivity captive, and received gifts for men, and " he gave some, apostles; and some, prophets; and some, evangelists; and some, pastors and teachers." He continues to bestow these choice gifts according to the church's necessity, and he would scatter them more plentifully, mayhap, if our prayers more earnestly ascended to the Lord of the harvest to thrust forth labourers into his harvest. Even as we believe in the crucified Saviour for our personal salvation, we ought to believe in the ascended Saviour for the perpetual enriching of the church with confessors and evangelists who shall declare the truth of God.

I wish to take my little share in commemorating Luther's birthday, and I think I can do no better than use the key of truth by which Luther unlocked the dungeons of the human mind, and set bondaged hearts at liberty. That golden key lies in the truth briefly contained in the text before us—"The just shall live by his faith."

Are you not a little surprised to find such a clear gospel passage in Habakkuk; to discover in that ancient prophet an explicit statement which Paul can use as a ready argument against the opponents of justification by faith? It shows that the cardinal doctrine of the gospel is no new-fangled notion; assuredly it is not a novel dogma invented by Luther, nor even a truth which was first taught by Paul. This fact has been established in all ages, and, therefore, here we find it among the ancient things, a lamp to cheer the darkness which hung over Israel before the coming of the Lord.

This also proves that there has been no change as to the gospel. The gospel of Habakkuk is the gospel of our Lord Jesus Christ. A clearer light was cast upon the truth by the giving of the Holy Ghost, but the way of salvation has in all ages been one and the same. No man has ever been saved by his good works. The way by which the just have lived has always been the way of faith. There has not been the slightest advance upon this truth; it is established and settled, evermore the same, like the God who uttered it. At all times, and everywhere, the gospel is and must for ever be the same. "Jesus Christ the same yesterday, and to day, and for ever." We read of "the gospel" as of one; but never of two or three gospels, as of many. Heaven and earth shall pass away, but Christ's word shall never pass away.

Noteworthy also is it, not only that this truth should be so old, and should continue so unchanged, but that it should possess such vitality. This one sentence, "The just shall live by his faith," produced the Reformation. Out of this one line, as from the opening of one of the Apocalyptic seals, came forth all that sounding of gospel trumpets, and all that singing of gospel songs, which made in the world a sound like the noise of many waters. This one seed, forgotten and hidden away in the dark mediæval times, was brought forth, dropped into the human heart, made by the Spirit of God to grow, and in the end to produce great results. This handful of corn on the top of the mountains so multiplied that the fruit thereof did shake like Lebanon, and they of the city flourished like grass of the earth. The least bit of truth, thrown anywhere, will live! Certain plants are so full of vitality, that if you only take a fragment of a leaf and place it on the soil, the leaf will take root and grow. It is utterly impossible that such vegetation should become extinct; and so it is with the truth of God—it is living and incorruptible, and therefore there is no destroying it. As long as one Bible remains, the religion of free grace will live; nay, if they could burn all printed Scriptures, as long as there remained a child who remembered a single text of the word, the truth would rise again. Even in the ashes of truth the fire is still living, and when the breath of the Lord bloweth upon it, the flame will burst forth gloriously. Because of this, let us be comforted in this day of blasphemy and of rebuke,—comforted because though "the grass withereth, and the flower thereof falleth away: but the word of the Lord endureth for ever. And this is the word which by the gospel is preached unto you."

Let us now examine this text, which was the means of enlightening the heart of Luther, as I shall tell you by-and-by.

I. I shall in the outset make a brief observation upon it: A MAN WHO HAS FAITH IN GOD IS JUST. "The just shall live by his faith;" the man who possesses faith in God is a just man: his faith is his life as a just man.

He is "just" in the gospel sense, namely, that having the faith which God prescribes as the way of salvation, he is by his faith justified in the sight of God. In the Old Testament (Gen. xv. 6) we are told concerning Abraham that "he believed in the Lord; and he counted it to him for righteousness." This is the universal plan of justification. Faith lays hold upon the righteousness of God, by accepting God's plan of justifying sinners through the sacrifice of Jesus Christ, and thus she makes the sinner just. Faith accepts and appropriates for itself the whole system of divine righteousness which is unfolded in the person and work of the Lord Jesus. Faith rejoices to see him coming into the world in our nature, and in that nature obeying the law in every jot and tittle, though not himself under that law until he chose to put himself thereon our behalf; faith is further pleased when she sees the Lord, who had come under the law, offering up himself as a perfect atonement, and making a complete vindication of divine justice by his sufferings and death. Faith lays hold upon the person, life, and death of the Lord Jesus as her sole hope, and in the righteousness of Christ she arrays herself. She cries, "The chastisement of my peace was upon him, and by his stripes I am healed." Now, the man who believes in God's method of making men righteous through the righteousness of Jesus, and accepts Jesus and leans upon him, is a just man. He who makes the life and death of God's great propitiation to be his sole reliance and confidence is justified in the sight of God, and is written down among the just by the Lord himself. His faith is imputed to him for righteousness, because his faith grasps the righteousness of God in Christ Jesus. "All that believe are justified from all things, from which ye could not be justified by the law of Moses." This is the testimony of the inspired word, and who shall gainsay it?

But the believer is also just in another sense, which the outside world better appreciates, though it is not more valuable than the former. The man who believes in God becomes by that faith moved to everything that is right, and good, and true. His faith in God rectifies his mind, and makes him just. In judgment, in desire, in aspiration, in heart, he is just. His sin has been forgiven him freely, and now, in the hour of temptation, he cries, "How then can I do this great wickedness, and sin against God?" He believes in the blood-shedding which God has provided for the cleansing of sin, and, being washed therein, he cannot choose to defile himself again. The love of Christ constraineth him to seek after that which is true, and right, and good, and loving, and honourable in the sight of God. Having received by faith the privilege of adoption, he strives to live as a child of God. Having obtained by faith a new life, he walks in newness of life. "Immortal principles forbid the child of God to sin." If any man live in sin and love it, he has not the faith of God's elect; for true faith purifies the soul. The faith which is wrought in us by the Holy Ghost is the greatest sin-killer under heaven. By the grace of God it affects the inmost heart, changes the desires and the affections, and makes the man a new creature in Christ Jesus. If there be on earth any who can truly be called just, they are those who are made so by faith in God through Jesus Christ our Lord. Indeed, no other men are "just" save those to whom the holy God gives the title, and of these the text says that they live by faith. Faith trusts God, and therefore loves him, and therefore obeys him, and therefore grows like him. It is the root of holiness, the spring of righteousness, the life of the just.

II. Upon that observation, which is vital to the text, I dwell no longer, but advance to another which is the converse of it, namely, that A MAN WHO IS JUST HAS FAITH IN GOD. Else, let me say, he were not just; for God deserves faith, and he who robs him of it is not just. God is so true that to doubt him is an injustice: he is so faithful that to distrust him is to wrong him—and he who does the Lord such an injustice is not a just man. A just man must first be just with the greatest of all beings. It would be idle for him to be just to his fellow-creatures only; if he did a wilful injustice to God, I say he would be unworthy of the name of just. Faith is what the Lord justly deserves to receive from his creatures: it is his due that we believe in what he says, and specially in reference to the gospel. When the great love of God in Christ Jesus is set forth plainly it will be believed by the pure in heart. If the great love of Christ in dying for us is fully understood it must be believed by every honest mind. To doubt the witness of God concerning his Son is to do the sorest injustice to infinite love. He that believeth not has rejected God's witness to the gift unspeakable and put from him that which deserves man's adoring gratitude, since it alone can satisfy the justice of God, and give peace to the conscience of man. A truly just man must, in order to the completeness of his justness, believe in God, and in all that he has revealed.

Some dream that this matter of justness only concerns the outer life, and does not touch man's belief. I say not so; righteousness concerns the inner parts of a man, the central region of his manhood; and truly just men desire to be made clean in the secret parts, and in the hidden parts they would know wisdom. Is it not so? We hear it continually asserted that the understanding and the belief constitute a province exempt from the jurisdiction of God. Is it indeed true that I may believe what I like without being accountable to God for my belief? No, my brethren; no single part of our manhood is beyond the range of the divine law. Our whole capacity as men lies under the sovereignty of him that created us, and we are as much bound to believe aright as we are bound to act aright: in fact, our actions and our thinkings are so intertwisted and entangled that there is no dividing the one from the other. To say that the rightness of the outward life sufficeth is to go clean contrary to the whole tenor of the word of God. I am as much bound to serve God with my mind as with my heart. I am as much bound to believe what God reveals as I am to do what God enjoins.

Errors of judgment are as truly sins as errors of life. It is a part of our allegiance to our great Sovereign and Lord that we do yield up our understanding, our thought, and our belief to his supreme control. No man is right until he is a right believer. A just man must be just towards God by believing in God, and trusting him in all that he is, and says, and does.

I see not also, my dear friends, what reason there is for a man to be just towards his fellow-men when he has given up his belief in God. If it comes to a pinch, and a man can deliver himself by a piece of dishonesty, why should he not be dishonest if there be no higher law than that which his fellow-men have made, no judgment-seat, no Judge, and no hereafter? A few weeks ago a man deliberately killed his employer, who had offended him, and as he gave himself up to the police, he said that he was not in the least degree afraid nor ashamed of what he had done. He admitted the murder, and owned that he knew the consequences very well; he expected to suffer about half-a-minute's pain upon the gallows, and then there would be an end of him, and he was quite prepared for that. He spoke and acted in consistency with his belief or his non-belief; and truly there is no form of crime but what becomes logical and legitimate if you take away from man faith in God and the hereafter. That gone, break up your commonwealth; there is nothing to hold humanity together; for without a God the moral government of the universe has ceased, and anarchy is the natural state of things. If there be no God, and no judgment to come, let us eat and drink, for to-morrow we die. If necessary, let us thieve, lie, and kill. Why not? if there be no law, no judgment, and no punishment for sin. I forget —nothing can be sinful; for if there be no lawgiver, there is no law; and if there be no law, then there can be no transgression. To what a chaos must all things come if faith in God be renounced. Where will the just be found when faith is banished? The logically just man is a believer in some measure or other; and he that is worthy to be called " just" in the scriptural sense, is a believer in the Lord Jesus Christ, who is made of God unto us righteousness.

III. But now I come to the point upon which I mean to dwell. Thirdly, BY THIS FAITH THE JUST MAN SHALL LIVE.

This is at the outset *a narrow statement;* it cuts off many pretended ways of living by saying, " The just shall live *by faith.*" This sentence savours of the strait gate which standeth at the head of the way—the narrow way which leadeth into life eternal. At one blow this ends all claims of righteousness apart from one mode of life. The best men in the world can only live by faith, there is no other way of being just in the sight of God. We cannot live in righteousness by self. If we are going to trust to ourselves, or anything that cometh of ourselves, we are dead while we so trust; we have not known the life of God according to the teaching of Holy Writ. You must come right out from confidence in everything that you are or hope to be. You must tear off the leprous garment of legal righteousness, and part with self in any and every form. Self-reliance as to the things of religion will be found to be self-destruction; you must rest in God as he is revealed in his Son Jesus Christ, and there alone. The just shall live by faith; but those who look to the works of the law are under the curse, and cannot live before God. The same is also true of those who endeavour to live by sense or feeling. They judge God by what they see : if he is bountiful to them in providence, he is a good God; if they are poor, they have nothing good to say of him, for they measure him by what they feel, and taste, and see. If God works steadily to a purpose, and they can see his purpose, they commend his wisdom; but when they either cannot see the purpose, or cannot understand the way by which the Lord is working unto it, straightway they judge him to be unwise. Living by sense turns out to be a senseless mode of life, bringing death to all comfort and hope.

> "Judge not the Lord by feeble sense,
> But trust him for his grace,"

for only by such trust can a just man live.

The text also cuts off all idea of living by mere intellect. Too many say, " I am my own guide, I shall make doctrines for myself, and I shall shift them and shape them according to my own devices." Such a way is death to the spirit. To be abreast of the times is to be an enemy to God. The way of life is to believe what God has taught, especially to believe in him whom God has set forth to be a propitiation for sin; for that is making God to be everything and ourselves nothing. Resting on an infallible revelation, and trusting in an omnipotent Redeemer, we have rest and peace; but on the other unsettled principle we become wandering stars, for whom is appointed the blackness of darkness for ever. By faith the soul can live, in all other ways we have a name to live and are dead.

The same is equally true of fancy. We often meet with a fanciful religion in which people trust to impulses, to dreams, to noises, and mystic things which they imagine they have seen : fiddle-faddle all of it, and yet they are quite wrapt up in it. I pray that you may cast out this chaffy stuff, there is no food for the spirit in it. The life of my soul lies not in what I think, or what I fancy, or what I imagine, or what I enjoy of fine feeling, but only in that which faith apprehends to be the word of God. We live before God by trusting a promise, depending on a person, accepting a sacrifice, wearing a righteousness, and surrending ourselves up to God—Father, Son, and Holy Ghost. Implicit trust in Jesus, our Lord, is the way of life, and every other way leads down to death. It is a narrowing statement, let those who call it intolerance say what they please; it will be true when they have execrated it as much as it is now.

But, secondly, this is *a very broad statement*. Much is comprehended in the saying—"the just shall live by his faith." It does not say what part of his life hangs on his believing, or what phase of his life best proves his believing : it comprehends the beginning, continuance, increase, and perfecting of spiritual life as being all by faith. Observe that the text means that the moment a man believes he begins to live in the sight of God : he trusts his God, he accepts God's revelation of himself, he confides, reposes, leans upon his Saviour, and that moment he becomes a spiritually living man, quickened with spiritual life by God the Holy Ghost. All his existence before that belief was but a form of death : when he comes to trust in God he enters upon eternal life, and is born from above. Yes, but that is not all, nor half; for if that man is to continue living before God, if he is to hold on his way in holiness, his perseverance must be the result of continued faith. The faith which saves is not one single act done and ended on a certain day: it is an act continued and persevered in throughout the entire life of man. The just not only commences to live by his faith, but he continues to live by his faith: he does not begin in the spirit and end in the flesh, nor go so far by grace, and the rest of the way by the works of the law. "The just shall live by faith," says the text in the Hebrews, "but if any man draw back, my soul shall have no pleasure in him. But we are not of them who draw back unto perdition; but of them that believe to the saving of the soul." Faith is essential all along; every day and all the day, in all things. Our natural life begins by breathing, and it must be continued by breathing: what the breath is to the body, that is faith to the soul.

Brethren, if we are to make advance and increase in the divine life, it must still be in the same way. Our root is faith, and only through the root comes growth. Progress in grace comes not of carnal wisdom, or legal effort, or unbelief; nay, the flesh bringeth no growth unto the spiritual life, and efforts made in unbelief rather dwarf the inner life than cause it to grow. We become no stronger by mortifications, mournings, workings, or strivings, if these are apart from simple faith in God's grace; for by this one sole channel can nourishment come into the life of our spirit. The same door by which life came in at the first is that by which life continues to enter. If any man saith to me, " I once lived by believing in Christ; but I have now become spiritual and sanctified, and therefore I have no longer any need to look as a sinner to the blood and righteousness of Christ:" I tell that man that he has need to learn the first principles of the faith. I warn him that he has drawn back from the faith; for he who is justified by the law, or in any other way beside the righteousness of Christ, has fallen from grace, and left the only ground upon which a soul can be accepted with God. Ay, up to heaven's gate there is no staff for us to lean upon but faith in the ever-blessed Saviour and his divine atonement. Between this place and glory we shall never be able to live by merits, or live by fancies, or live by intellect; we shall still have to be as children taught of God, as Israel in the desert depending wholly on the great Invisible One. Ours it is for ever to look out of self, and to look above all things that are seen; for " the just shall live by his faith." It is a very broad sentence, a circle which encompasses the whole of our life which is worthy of the name. If there be any virtue, if there be any praise, if there be aught that is lovely or of good repute, we must receive it, exhibit it, and perfect it by the exercise of faith. Life in the Father's house, life in the church, life in private, life in the world, must all be in the power of faith if we are righteous men. That which is without faith is without life; dead works cannot gratify the living God; without faith it is impossible to please God.

I beg you to notice, in the third place, what *a very unqualified state-ment* it is. " The just shall live by his faith." Then, if a man have but a little faith, he shall live; and if he be greatly just, he shall still live by faith. Many a just man has come no further than striving after holiness, but he is justified by his faith: his faith is trembling and struggling, and his frequent prayer is, "Lord, I believe; help thou mine unbelief;" yet his faith has made him a just man. Sometimes he is afraid that he has no faith at all; and when he has deep depression of spirits, it is as much as he can do to keep his head above water; but even then his faith justifies him. He is like a barque upon a stormy sea: sometimes he is lifted up to heaven by flashing waves of mercy, and anon he sinks into the abyss among billows of affliction. What, then, is he a dead man? I answer, Does that man truly believe God? Does he accept the record concerning the Son of God? Can he truly say, "I believe in the forgiveness of sins," and with such faith as he has does he cling alone to Christ and to none beside? Then that man shall live, he shall live by his faith. If the littleness of our faith could destroy us how few would be numbered with the living? "When the Son of man cometh, shall he find faith on the earth?" Only here and there, and now and then, a Luther appears who really does believe with all his heart. The most of us are not so big as Luther's little finger: we have not so much faith in our whole souls as he had in one hair of his head: but yet even that little faith makes us live. I do not say that little faith will give us the strong, and vigorous, and lion-like life which Luther had; but we shall live. The statement makes no distinction between this and that degree of faith, but lays it down still as an unquestionable truth, "the just shall live by faith." Blessed be God, then, I shall live, for I do believe in the Lord Jesus as my Saviour and my all. Do you not also believe in him?

Ay, and is it not singular that this unqualified statement should not mention any other grace, as helping to make up the ground on which a just men lives? "The just shall live by his faith:" but has he not love, has he not zeal, has he not patience, has he not hope, has he not humility, has he not holiness? Oh, yes, he has all these, and he lives *in* them, but he does not live *by* them, because none of these so intimately connects him with Christ as does his faith. I will venture to use a very homely figure, because it is the best I can think of. Here is a little child, a suckling. It has many necessary members, such as its eyes, its ears, its legs, its arms, its heart, and so forth, and all these are necessary to it; but the one organ by which the tiny babe lives is its mouth, by which it sucks from its mother all its nourishment. Our faith is that mouth by which we suck in fresh life from the promise of the ever-blessed God. Thus faith is that which we live by. Other graces are needful, but faith is the life of them all. We do not undervalue love, or patience, or penitence, or humility, any more than we depreciate the eyes or the feet of the babe. Still, the means of the life of the spiritual man is that mouth by which he receives divine food from the truth revealed by the Holy Ghost in sacred Scripture. Other graces produce results from that which faith receives, but faith is the Receiver-General for the whole isle of man.

This, dear friends, to proceed a little further, is *a very suggestive statement,*—"The just shall live by his faith;" because it wears so many meanings. First, the righteous man is even to exist by his faith, that is to say, the lowest form of grace in a righteous character is dependent upon faith. But, brother, I hope you will not be so foolish as to say,—

"If I am but a living child of God, it is all I want:" no, we wish not only to have life, but to have it more abundantly. See yonder man rescued from drowning; he is yet alive, but the only evidence of it is the fact that a mirror is somewhat bedewed by his breath: you would not be content to be alive for years in that poor fashion, would you? You ought to be grateful if you are spiritually alive even in that feeble way; but still we do not want to remain in a swooning state, we wish to be active and vigorous. Yet even for that lowest life you must have faith. For the feeblest kind of spiritual existence that can be called life at all, faith is needful. The just who barely live, who are feeble in mind, who are scarcely saved, are nevertheless delivered by faith. Without faith there is no heavenly life whatever.

Take the word "life" in a better sense, and the same will apply; "The just shall live by his faith." We sometimes meet with very poor persons who say to us in a pitiful tone, "Our wages are dreadfully scant." We say to them, "Do you really live upon so small a sum?" They answer, "Well, Sir, you can hardly call it living; but we exist somehow." None of us would wish to live in that style if we could help it. We mean, then, by "life," some measure of enjoyment, happiness, and satisfaction. The just, when they have comfort, and joy, and peace, have them by faith. Thank God, peace of heart is our normal state, because faith is an abiding grace. We sing for joy of heart and rejoice in the Lord, and blessed be the Lord this is no novelty to us; but we have known this bliss, and still know it by faith alone. The moment faith comes in the music strikes up: if it were gone the owls would hoot. Luther can sing a psalm in spite of the devil; but he could not have done so if he had not been a man of faith. He could defy emperors, and kings, and popes, and bishops while he took firm hold upon the strength of God, but only then. Faith is the life of life, and makes life worth living. It puts joy into the soul to believe in the great Father and his everlasting love, and in the efficacious atonement of the Son, and in the indwelling of the Spirit, in resurrection, and eternal glory: without these we were of all men most miserable. To believe these glorious truths is to live—"The just shall live by his faith."

Life also means strength. We say of a certain man, What life he has in him: he is full of life, he seems all alive. Yes, the just obtain energy, force, vivacity, vigour, power, might, life—by faith. Faith bestows on believers a royal majesty. The more they can believe, the more mighty they become. This is the head that wears a crown; this is the hand that wields a sceptre; this is the foot whose royal tread doth shake the nations; faith in God links us with the King, the Lord God Omnipotent.

By faith the just live on when others die. They are not overcome by prevalent sin, or fashionable heresy, or cruel persecution, or fierce affliction: nothing can kill spiritual life while faith abides—"The just shall live by faith." Continuance and perseverance come this way. The righteous man when he is put back a while is not baffled; and when he is wounded by enemies, he is not slain. Where another man is drowned, he swims; where another man is trampled under foot, he rises and shouts victoriously,—" Rejoice not over me, O mine enemy. If I fall, yet shall I rise again!" In the fiery furnace of affliction he walks unharmed through faith. Ay, and when his turn comes to die, and, with many tears his brethren carry his ashes to the tomb, "he being dead yet speaketh." The blood of righteous Abel cried from the ground to the Lord, and it is still crying adown the ages, even to this hour. Luther's voice through four hundred years still sounds in the ears of men, and quickens our pulses like the beat of drum in martial music: he lives, he lives because he was a man of faith.

I would sum up and illustrate this teaching by mentioning certain incidents of Luther's life. Upon the great Reformer gospel light broke by slow degrees. It was in the monastery that, in turning over the old Bible that was chained to a pillar, he came upon this passage—"The just shall live by his faith." This heavenly sentence stuck to him; but he hardly understood all its bearings. He could not, however, find peace in his religious profession and monastic habit. Knowing no better, he persevered in penances so many, and mortifications so arduous, that sometimes he was found fainting through exhaustion. He brought himself to death's door. He must make a journey to Rome, for in Rome there is a fresh church for every day, and you may be sure to win the pardon of sins and all sorts of benedictions in these holy shrines. He dreamed of entering a city of holiness; but he found it to be a haunt of hypocrites and a den of iniquity. To his horror he heard men say that if there was a hell Rome was built on the top of it, for it was the nearest approach to it that could be found in this world; but still he believed in its Pope and he went on with his penances, seeking rest, but finding none. One day he was climbing upon his knees the Sancta Scala which still stands in Rome. I have stood amazed at the bottom of this staircase to see poor creatures go up and down on their knees in the belief that it is the very staircase that our Lord descended when he left Pilate's house, and certain steps are said to be marked with drops of blood; these the poor souls kiss most devoutly. Well, Luther was crawling up these steps one day when that same text which he had met with before in the monastery, sounded like a clap of thunder in his ears, "The just shall live by his faith." He rose from his prostration, and went down the steps never to grovel upon them again. At that time the Lord wrought him a full deliverance from superstition, and he saw that not by priests, nor priestcraft, nor penances, nor by anything that he could do, was he to live, but that he must live by his faith. Our text of this morning had set the monk at liberty, and set his soul on fire.

No sooner did he believe this than he began to live in the sense of being active. A gentleman, named Tetzel, was going about all over Germany selling the forgiveness of sins for so much ready cash. No matter what your offence, as soon as your money touched the bottom of the box your sins were gone. Luther heard of this, grew indignant, and exclaimed, "I will make a hole in his drum," which assuredly he did, and in several other drums. The nailing up of his theses on the church door was a sure way of silencing the indulgence music. Luther proclaimed pardon of sin by faith in Christ without money and without price, and the Pope's indulgences were soon objects of derision. Luther lived by his faith, and therefore he who otherwise might have been quiet, denounced error as furiously as a lion roars upon his prey. The faith that was in him filled him with intense life, and he plunged into war with the enemy. After a while they summoned him to Augsburg, and to Augsburg he went, though his friends advised him not to go. They summoned him, as a heretic, to answer for himself at the Diet of Worms, and everybody bade him stay away, for he would be sure to be burned; but he felt it necessary that the testimony should be borne, and so in a wagon he went from village to village and town to town, preaching as he went, the poor people coming out to shake hands with the man who was standing up for Christ and the gospel at the risk of his life. You remember how he stood before that august assembly, and though he knew as far as human power went that his defence would cost him his life, for he would, probably, be committed to the flames like John Huss, yet he played the man for the Lord his God. That day in the German Diet Luther did a work for which ten thousand times ten thousand mothers' children have blessed his name, and blessed yet more the name of the Lord his God.

To put him out of harm's way for a while a prudent friend took him prisoner, and kept him out of the strife in the castle of Wartburg. There he had a good time of it, resting, studying, translating, making music, and preparing himself for the future which was to be so eventful. He did all that a man can do who is outside of the fray; but "the just shall live by his faith," and Luther could not be buried alive in ease, he must be getting on with his life-work. He sends word to his friends that he who was coming would soon be with them, and on a sudden he appeared at Wittenberg. The prince meant to have kept him in retirement somewhat longer, but Luther must live; and when the Elector feared that he could not protect him, Luther wrote him, " I come under far higher protection than yours; nay, I hold that I am more likely to protect your Grace than your Grace to protect me. He who has the strongest faith is the best Protector." Luther had learned to be independent of all men, for he cast himself upon his God. He had all the world against him, and yet he lived right merrily : if the Pope excommunicated him he burned the bull; if the Emperor threatened him he rejoiced, because he remembered the word of the Lord, " The kings of the earth set themselves, and the rulers take counsel together. He that sitteth in the heavens shall laugh." When they said to him, " Where will you find shelter if the Elector does not protect you ?" he answered, " Under the broad shield of God."

Luther could not be still; he must speak, and write and thunder; and oh! with what confidence he spoke ! Doubts about God and Scripture he abhorred. Melancthon says he was not dogmatical; I rather differ from Melancthon there, and reckon Luther to be the chief of dogmatists. He called Melancthon the "soft treader," and I wonder what we should have done if Luther had been Melancthon, and had trodden softly, too. The times needed a firmly assured leader, and faith made Luther all that for years, notwithstanding his many sorrows and infirmities. He was a Titan, a giant, a man of splendid mental calibre and strong physique; but yet his main life and force lay in his faith. He suffered much in exercises of the mind and through diseases of body, and these might well have occasioned a display of weakness; but that weakness did not appear; for when he believed, he was as sure of what he believed as of his own existence, and hence he was strong. If every angel in heaven had passed before him and each one had assured him of the truth of God, he would not have thanked them for their testimony, for he believed God without the witness of either angels or men : he thought the word of divine testimony to be more sure than aught that seraphim could say.

This man was forced to live by his faith, for he was a man of stormy soul, and only faith could speak peace to him. Those stirring excitements of his brought on him afterwards fearful depressions of spirit, and then he needed faith in God. If you read a spiritual life of him you will find that it was hard work sometimes for him to keep his soul alive. Being a man of like passions with us, and full of imperfections, he was at times as desponding and despairing as the weakest among us ; and the swelling grief within him threatened to burst his mighty heart. But both he and John Calvin frequently sighed for the rest of heaven, for they loved not the strife in which they dwelt, but would have been glad peacefully to feed the flock of God on earth, and then to enter into rest. These men dwelt with God in holy boldness of believing prayer, or they could not have lived at all.

Luther's faith laid hold upon the cross of our Lord, and would not be stirred from it. He believed in the forgiveness of sins, and could not afford to doubt it. He cast anchor upon Holy Scripture, and rejected all the inventions of clerics and all the traditions of the fathers. He was assured of the truth of the gospel, and never doubted but what it would prevail though earth and hell were leagued against it. When he came to die his old enemy assailed him fiercely, but when they asked him if he held the same faith his "Yes" was positive enough. They needed not to have asked him, they might have been sure of that. And now to-day the truth proclaimed by Luther continues to be preached, and will be till our Lord himself shall come. Then the holy city shall need no candle, neither light of the sun, because the Lord himself shall be the light of his people ; but till then we must shine with gospel light to our utmost. Brethren, let us stand to it that as Luther lived by faith even so will we ; and may God the Holy Ghost work in us more of that faith. Amen and Amen.

PORTION OF SCRIPTURE READ BEFORE SERMON—Galatians iii.

HYMNS FROM "OUR OWN HYMN BOOK,"—46 (Vers. II.), 690, 533.

THE LUTHER SERMON AT EXETER-HALL.*

A Sermon

DELIVERED ON LORD'S-DAY EVENING, NOVEMBER 11TH, 1883, BY

C. H. SPURGEON,

AT EXETER-HALL.

"For in Jesus Christ neither circumcision availeth anything, nor uncircumcision; but faith which worketh by love."—Galatians v. 6.

PAUL makes a clean sweep of that trust in the externals of religion which is the common temptation of all time. Circumcision was a great thing with the Jew, and oftentimes he trusted in it; but Paul declares that it availeth nothing. There might be others who were glad that they were not Jews, but Paul declares that their uncircumcision availeth no more than its opposite. Certain matters connected with godliness are external, and yet they are useful in their places: especially is that the case with baptism and the Lord's supper, the assembling of ourselves together, the reading of the word, and public prayer and praise. These things are proper and profitable; but none of them must be made in any measure or degree the ground of our hope of salvation; for this text sweeps them all away, and plainly describes them as availing nothing if they are made to be the foundations of our trust.

In Luther's day superstitious confidence in external observances had overlaid faith in the gospel; ceremonies had multiplied excessively under the authority of the Pope, masses were said for souls in purgatory, and men were actually selling indulgences for sin in the light of day. When God raised up Martin Luther, who was born four centuries ago, he bore emphatic testimony against salvation by outward forms and by the power of priestcraft, affirming that salvation is by faith alone, and that the whole church of God is a company of priests, every believer being a priest unto God. If Luther had not affirmed it, the doctrine would have been just as true, for the distinction between clergy and laity has no excuse in Scripture, which calls the saints, "God's *kleros*"— God's clergy, or heritage. Again we read, "Ye are a royal priesthood." Every man that believes in the Lord Jesus Christ is anointed to exercise the Christian priesthood, and therefore he need not put his trust in another, seeing the supposed priest is no more than any other

---

* Having already preached a Luther sermon of somewhat like tenor in the morning of the day, I have considerably altered this discourse, that the reader may not find so much repetition as there would otherwise have been.

man. Each man must be accountable for himself before God. Each one must read and search the Scriptures for himself, and must believe for himself, and when saved, he must offer up himself as a living sacrifice unto God by Jesus Christ, who is the only High Priest of our profession. So much for the negative side of the text, which is full of warning to this Ritualistic age.

The chief testimony of our great Reformer was to the justification of a sinner in the sight of God by faith in Jesus Christ, and by that alone. He could fitly have taken this for his motto, " In Jesus Christ neither circumcision availeth anything, nor uncircumcision ; but faith which worketh by love." He was in the Augustinian monastery at Wittenberg troubled and perturbed in mind ; and he read there, in an old Latin Bible, this text,—"The just shall live by faith." It was a new idea to him, and by its means spiritual light entered his soul in some degree ; but such were the prejudices of his up-bringing, and such the darkness of his surroundings, that he still hoped to find salvation by outward performances. He therefore fasted long, till he was found swooning from hunger. He was exceedingly zealous for salvation by works. At last he made a pilgrimage to Rome, hoping to find there everything that was holy and helpful : he was disappointed in his search, but yet found more than he looked for. On the pretended staircase of Pilate, while in the act of climbing it upon his knees, the Wittenberg text again sounded in his ear like a thunder-clap : " The just shall live by faith." Up he started and descended those stairs, never to grovel upon them again. The chain was broken, the soul was free. Luther had found the light ; and henceforth it became his life's business to flash that light upon the nations, crying evermore, " The just shall live by faith." The best commemoration which I can make of this man is to preach the doctrine which he held so dear, and you who are not saved can best assist me by believing the doctrine, and proving its truth in your own cases. May the Holy Ghost cause it to be so in hundreds of instances.

I. First, let us inquire WHAT IS THIS FAITH ? We are always talking about it ; but what is it ? Whenever I try to explain it, I am afraid lest I should confuse rather than expound. There is a story told concerning John Bunyan's " Pilgrim's Progress." Good Thomas Scott, the Commentator, wrote notes to it : he thought the " Pilgrim's Progress " a difficult book, and he would make it clear. A pious cottager in his parish had the book, and she was reading it when her minister called. He said to her, " Oh, I see, you are reading Bunyan's ' Pilgrim's Progress.' Do you understand it ? " She answered innocently enough, " Oh, yes, sir, I understand Mr. Bunyan very well, and I hope that one day I shall be able to understand your explanations." I am afraid lest you should say when I have done, " I understand what faith is, as I find it in the Bible, and one day, perhaps, I may be able to understand the preacher's explanation of it." Warned by this, I will speak as plainly as I can.

And first, it is to be remembered that faith is not a mere creed-holding. It is very proper to say, " I believe in God the Father Almighty, Maker of heaven and earth," and so forth ; but you may repeat all that and be no "believer" in the Scriptural sense of that term. Though the creed be true, it may not be true to you ; it would have been the same to you if the opposite had been true, for you put the truth away like a paper in a pigeon-hole, and it has no effect upon you. "A very proper doctrine," you say, "a very proper doctrine," and so you put it to sleep. It does not influence your heart, nor affect your life. Do not imagine that the professing an orthodox creed is the same thing as faith in Christ. A truthful creed is desirable for many reasons; but if it be a dead, inoperative thing, it cannot bring salvation. Faith is belief of the truth; but it is more.

Again, faith is not the mere belief that there is a God, though that we must have, for we cannot come to God except we "believe that he is, and that he is a rewarder of them that diligently seek him." We are to believe *in* God—that he is good, blessed, true, right, and therefore to be trusted, confided in, and praised. Whatever he may do, whatever he may say, God is not to be suspected, but believed in. You know what it is to believe in a man, do you not? to believe in a man so that you follow him, and confide in him, and accept his advice? In that same way faith believes in God—not only believes that he is, but finds rest in his character, his Son, his promise, his covenant, his word, and everything about him. Faith livingly and lovingly trusts in her God about everything. Especially must we believe in what God has revealed in Scripture —that it is verily and indeed a sure and infallible testimony to be received without question. We accept the Father's witness concerning Jesus, and take heed thereto "as unto a light that shineth in a dark place."

Faith has specially to believe in him who is the sum and substance of all this revelation, even Jesus Christ, who became God in human flesh that he might redeem our fallen nature from all the evils of sin, and raise it to eternal felicity. We believe *in* Christ, *on* Christ, and *upon* Christ; accepting him because of the record which God has given to us concerning his Son, that he is the propitiation for our sins. We accept God's unspeakable gift, and receive Jesus as our all in all.

If I wanted to describe saving faith in one word, I should say that it is *trust*. It is so believing God and so believing in Christ that we trust ourselves and our eternal destinies in the hands of a reconciled God. As creatures we look up to the great Father of spirits; as sinners we trust for the pardon of our sins to the atonement of Jesus Christ; as being weak and feeble we trust to the power of the Holy Spirit to make us holy and to keep us so; we venture our eternal interests in the vessel of free grace, content to sink or swim with it. We rely upon God in Christ. The word employed to set forth faith in the Scriptures sometimes signifies to lean. We lean with all our weight upon our God, in Jesus Christ. We hang upon Christ as a vessel hangs upon the nail. "Recumbency" was a term by which the old Puritans used to describe faith—a lying, or leaning upon, something out of ourselves. Guilty as I am, I believe God's word, that "the blood of Jesus Christ his Son cleanseth us from all sin:" trusting to that blood I know that I am cleansed from all sin. God sets forth Christ to be a propitiation; we believe that he is a propitiation, and we take him to be *our* propitiation; by that appropriation our sin is covered and we are free. Faith is the grasping, the appropriating, the receiving into one's self, of the Lord Jesus Christ. I sometimes illustrate it by that passage of Paul where he says, "The word is nigh thee, even in thy mouth." When a morsel is in your mouth, if you desire to possess it so as never to lose it, what is the best thing to do? *Swallow it.* Let it go down into the inward parts. Now the word that we preach is, according to the Apostle, "in thy mouth"; suffer it then to go down into thy heart, and thou shalt find it true that "with the heart man believeth unto righteousness; and with the mouth confession is made unto salvation." This is the faith which saves the soul.

II. In the second place we will consider, WHY FAITH IS SELECTED AS THE WAY OF SALVATION?

I would remind you that if we could not answer this question it would not matter; for since the Lord has appointed believing as the way of grace it is not ours to challenge his choice. Beggars must not be choosers: let us trust, if so the Lord ordains.

But we can answer this question in a measure. First, it is clear that *no other way is possible.* It is not possible for us to be saved by our own merits, for we have broken the law already, and future obedience, being already due, cannot make up for past defects.

> "Could my tears for ever flow,
> Could my zeal no respite know,
> All for sin could not atone:
> Thou must save, and thou alone."

The road of good works is blocked up by our past sins, and it is sure to be further blocked up by future sins: we ought therefore to rejoice that God has commended to us the open road of faith.

God has chosen the way of faith *that salvation might be by grace.* If we had to do anything in order to save ourselves, we should be sure to impute a measure of virtue to our own doings, or feelings, or prayers, or almsgivings, and we should thus detract from the pure grace of God. But salvation comes from God as a pure favour—an act of undeserved generosity and benevolence, and the Lord will, therefore, only put it into the hand of faith, since faith arrogates nothing to herself. Faith, in fact, disowns all idea of merit, and the Lord of grace therefore elects to place the treasure of his love in the hand of faith.

Again, it is of faith *that there may be no boasting;* for if our salvation be of our doings or feelings, we are sure to boast; but, if it be of faith, we cannot glory in self. "Where is boasting then? It is excluded. By what law? of works? Nay: but by the law of faith." Faith is humble, and ascribes all praise to God. Faith is truthful, and confesses her obligation to the sovereign grace of God.

I bless the Lord that he has chosen this way of faith, because *it is so suitable for poor sinners.* Some among us to-night would never have been saved if salvation had only been prepared for the good and righteous. I stood before my God guilty and self-condemned. No youth ever had a keener sense of guilt than I had. When I was convinced of sin I saw my thoughts and desires to be vile in the sight of God, and I became vile in my own eyes also. I was driven to despair; and I know that I could never have been cheered by any plan of salvation except that which is of faith. The covenant of works by reason of our weakness affords us no suitable way of hope at any time, but under certain circumstances we see this very vividly. Suppose that you were in the last article of death, what good works could you do? Yonder dying thief found it a happy thing that by faith he could trust the Crucified One, and before set of sun could be with him in Paradise.   Faith is a way suitable for sinners, and especially for sinners who are soon to die; in some sense we are all in that condition, and some of us peradventure are especially so ; for what man among us knows that he will see to-morrow's dawn ?

I bless God again that the way of salvation is by faith, because *it is a way open to the most unlearned.*   What fine theology we get now-a-days—deep thinking they call it.   The men go down so deep into their subjects, and so stir the mud at the bottom, that you cannot see them and they cannot see themselves.   I apprehend that teachers of a certain school do not themselves know what they are talking about.   Now, if salvation were only to be learned by reading through huge folios, what would become of multitudes of poor souls in Bow, and Bethnal Green, and Seven Dials?   If the gospel had consisted of a mass of learning, how could the unlearned be saved?   But now we can go to each one of them and say, " Jesus died."

> " There is life in a look at the Crucified One ;
> There is life at this moment for thee."

However little you may know, you know that you have sinned; know, then, that Jesus has come to put away sin, and that whosoever believeth in him is immediately forgiven, and enters into life eternal.   This brief and blessed gospel is suitable to all cases, from princes to peasants, and we wonder not that faith was selected as the way of salvation.

III.   But now, thirdly, I want to say a good deal to-night upon another question, How DOES FAITH OPERATE?   For according to our text, it is " Faith *which worketh* by love."   It is a living, labouring, loving faith which alone saves the soul.   I cannot tell you what hard things I have heard about this doctrine of salvation by faith.   They say that it is immoral.   I have heard immoral men say so, and surely they ought to know.   They say that it will lead to sin ; and those who say so would, I should think, be rather pleased with it for that reason if they believed their own statement.   I have never heard a holy man charge faith with leading him into sin.   I know no man that follows after God and lives near to him who is under fear that faith in God will tempt him to transgress.   The fact is, faith does nothing of the kind ; its action is most distinctly the reverse.   Like the prudent wife in the Proverbs, faith will do a man good and no harm all the days of his life.

First, *it touches the mainspring of our nature by creating love within the soul.*   What is wanted now for the degraded classes in London ? Sanitary regulations ?   Certainly, if they are not allowed to be a dead letter for the want of some one to carry them out.   New houses?   By all manner of means : the more the better.   Lower rents ?   Assuredly, for no one has a right to get an excessive rent for unhealthy accommodation.   Higher wages ?   Certainly, we could all of us do with a little more. Many other things are wanted.   While yonder gin-palaces remain at the corners of the streets you will not make much headway in uplifting the masses ; and I suppose the drink-shops will always flourish while the taste for drink remains.   Suppose the licensed poison-shops were shut up, would that suffice ?   I think not.   There are men and women in London, and thousands of them, who, if they were put into the cleanest houses, and were a mile off a gin-shop, would still drink and still turn their houses into piggeries. What is wanted? Oh, if you could make Christians of them! Suppose they could be born again. Suppose they could be made to love the things which they now hate, and hate the things which they now love. New hearts and right spirits are the need of London's outcasts. How can these be produced? In the hand of God the Holy Ghost, this is exactly what faith works in the heart. Here is a watch. "It wants cleaning." Yes, clean it. "It does not go now. It wants a new glass." Well, put in a new glass. "It does not go any the more. It wants new hands." Get new hands by all means. Still it does not go. What is the matter with it? The maker says that it needs a mainspring. There's the seat of the evil: nothing can be right till that is rectified. Set all other matters going, but do not forget that the mainspring is the chief part of the business. Faith supplies the soul with a powerful spring of action. It says to the man, "Thou art forgiven through the blood of Christ who died for thee: how dost thou feel towards him?" The man replies, "I love the Lord for redeeming me." Loving Jesus, the man has now within his soul the seed of every good. He will become a holier and a better being; for he has begun to love, and love is the mother of holiness. Is any service in the world like the service of love? You have a servant in your house, fawning and obsequious; but if you were to reduce his wages, he would show you the rough side of his tongue and seek another situation. You do not expect any more of him than that, and if you did, you would not get it. How different was an old servant I have heard of, who, when his master went down in the world, was content with half-pay; and when he was sorrow-fully told that he must go, for his master could not afford him clothes, he made his old ones last him, for he would not leave his master in his old age. He would rather have earned bread for his old master than have left him. He was an attached servant worth his weight in gold: there are few such servants now-a-days, for there are not many such masters. This kind of service cannot be purchased; but its price is above rubies. When the Lord leads us to believe in Jesus, we become henceforth his loving servants, and serve him not for reward, but out of gratitude. It is no longer with us so much work and so much pay; we do not fear the threat of hell for disobedience, nor do we look to heaven as won by works. No, no; our salvation is a free gift. It is furnished for us through infinite love and supreme compassion, and therefore we return our heart's warmest affection. Our heart clings to that dear side which was opened for us. We feel a tender love to those dear pierced feet; we could kiss them every day. Those blessed hands of the Crucified! If they do but touch us, we are strengthened, honoured, comforted. Jesus is altogether lovely to us, our bosom's lord. Faith, instead of being a poor, paltry thing, as some imagine, is the grandest cause of love, and so of obedience and holiness.

Know, again, that *faith puts us into a new relation.* We are bound by nature to be the servants of God; but faith whispers in our ear, " Say ' Our Father,' " and when the heart has received the Spirit of adoption, the aspect of service is entirely changed: mercenary service is succeeded by loving obedience, and our spirit is altered. To become an heir of God, a joint-heir with Jesus, is to elevate work into delight, labour into fellowship with God. The law is no fetter to a child of God: it is his delight. *Faith removes from the soul that form of selfishness which aforetime seemed necessary.* So you hope to be saved by what you do, do you? May I ask you, friend, whom you are serving in all this? I will tell you. You are serving yourself. All that you do is to win happiness for yourself. How, then, are you serving God? You are living a selfish life, though it be tinged with the colour of spirituality. What is done by you in the matter of religion has no object but that *you* may be saved, and go to heaven. Your most zealous work is all for self. Suppose I say to you, "I know that I am saved: I know that Jesus has put away my sin: I know that he will not permit me to perish;"—why, then there is room in my case for the service of the Lord because of what he has done for me. Now I have not myself to save I have Christ to serve. Gratitude is the motive of the gospel, and under its power unselfish virtue is possible, but not upon the ground of legal service. Pure virtue, it seems to me, is a sheer impossibility till a man is saved, because it always must partake till then of the low and grovelling view of benefiting himself by what he is doing. When once the great transaction is done, and you are saved, then you are lifted up into a nobler sphere, and you say,

" Then why, O blessèd Jesu Christ,
Should I not love thee well?
Not for the hope of winning heaven,
Nor of escaping hell ;

" Not with the hope of gaining aught,
Not seeking a reward :
But as thyself hast lovèd me,
O ever-loving Lord,

"So would I love thee, dearest Lord,
And in thy praise will sing :
Solely because thou art my God,
And my Eternal King."

Hence faith inspires us with a higher motive than the law can suggest. *Faith soon creates love to man ;* for, if the Lord Jesus has saved you, my brother, you will speedily desire that others may be saved also. You have tasted of this honey, and the sweetness upon your own tongue constrains you to invite others to the feast. He who has been brought into the liberty of free grace would set free every captive sinner if he could.

When well worked out, *faith means harmony with God.* It creates an agreement with the divine will, so that whatever pleases God pleases us. If the Lord should set the believer on a dunghill with Job, he would still bless his name. Faith agrees with the divine precept which it desires to obey, with the divine doctrine which it desires to know and publish ; yea, whatsoever is of God faith saith, "It is the Lord, let him command, teach, or do what seemeth him good."

I have shown you that faith is not the trifling principle which its deprecators describe as "Only believe." Oh, that they knew what it is only to believe. It is the setting free of the mind from fetters. It is the dawn of heaven's own day. It is a lifelong struggle, this "Only

believe." It is "the work of God, that ye believe on him whom he
hath sent."

Brethren, I believe that *a humble, persevering faith in God is one of
the highest forms of adoration that ever reaches the throne of God.*
Though cherubim and seraphim salute the Lord with their "Holy, holy,
holy"; though the whole host of shining ones surround the throne with
perpetual hallelujahs, there is no more hearty reverence given to God
thereby than when a poor sinner, black as night, cries believingly, "Wash
me, and I shall be whiter than snow." To believe in the pardon of sin
is a wonderful adoration of the mercy and power of God. To believe
in a constant providence is a sweet way of worshipping God in his
power and goodness. When a poor labourer in his cottage, needing
bread for his children, kneels down and cries, "Lord, it is written, 'Thy
bread shall be given thee, and thy water shall be sure,' I believe thy
word, and therefore I look to thee in my necessity," he renders a
homage to the truth and faithfulness of God such as Gabriel could not
give, for he never knew the pinch of hunger. To believe that God will
keep us to the end and raise us to his glory is more honouring to God
than all the hymns of the glorified. From us dying sons of earth, when
we confide in his promise, there arises up to heaven incense of a sweet
smell, acceptable to God by Jesus Christ.

To my mind there is also this about faith—that it has a marvellous
power over God. Do you ask me to retract that expression? Let it
stand. I will explain it. Faith overcomes the Highest upon his throne.
Faith in an inferior can hold a superior fast. Some years ago I was
walking in the garden one evening, and I saw a stray dog about whom
I had received information that he was in the habit of visiting my
grounds, and that he did not in the least assist the gardener, and therefore his attentions were not desired. As I walked along one Saturday
evening meditating upon my sermon, I saw this dog busily doing
mischief. I threw my stick at him, and told him to go home. But
what do you think he did? Instead of grinding his teeth at me, or
hurrying off with a howl, he looked at me very pleasantly, took up my
stick in his mouth and brought it to me, and then, wagging his tail, he
laid the stick at my feet. The tears were in my eyes: the dog had beaten
me. I said, "Good dog! Good dog; you may come here when you
like after that." Why had the dog conquered me? Because he had
confidence in me, and would not believe that I could mean him any
hurt. To turn to grander things: the Lord himself cannot resist
humble confidence. Do you not see how a sinner brings, as it were,
the rod of justice to the Lord, and cries, "If thou smite me, I deserve
it; but I submit to thee." The great God cannot spurn a trustful
heart. It is impossible. He were not God if he could cast the soul away
that implicitly relies on him. This is the power of faith, then, and I marvel
not that the Lord should have chosen it, for believing is a thing most
pleasing to God. O that you would all trust him! God lifts his sword
against you—run into his arms. He threatens you—grasp his promise.
He pursues you—fly to his dear Son. Trust at the foot of the cross in
his full atonement, and you must be saved.

IV. Now, I am going to finish in a way suitable to this Luther
memorial. You have heard a great deal about Luther's preaching salva-

tion by faith alone. Now, LET US TURN TO LUTHER'S LIFE, and see what Luther himself meant by it. What kind of faith did Luther himself exhibit by which he was justified?

First, in Luther's case, faith led him to *an open avowal of what he believed.* Luther did not mean to go up to heaven by the back stairs, as many young men hope to do. You wish to be Christians on the sly, so as to escape the offence of the cross. Luther did not refuse to confess Christ and take up his cross and follow him. He knew that he who with his heart believeth, must also with his mouth make confession, and he did so right nobly. He began teaching and preaching the truth which had enlightened his own soul. One of his sermons displeased Duke George of Saxony; but as it saved a lady of high rank Luther did not fret. He was not the man to conceal truth because it was dangerous to avow it. Tetzel came with his precious indulgences, and his releases for souls in purgatory. Thousands of good Catholics were indignant; but no one would bell the cat. Luther called Tetzel " servant of Pope and of the devil," and declared, " As he came among us practising on the credulity of the people, I could not refrain from protesting against it, and opposing his odious career." Without mincing words, or attempting to speak politely, Luther went at him fearless of consequences. He believed in the blessings of grace " without money and without price," and he did not conceal his convictions. He nailed his theses to the church door where all might read them. When astronomers require a new constellation in the heavens let it be " the hammer and nails." O you who make no profession, let this man's outspoken faith rebuke you!

His *dauntless valour for truth* caused him to be greatly hated in his own day with a ferocity which has not yet died out. Luther is still the best hated man in certain quarters. Witness the vile tracts which have been produced during the last fortnight, to the disgrace of the press which they defile. I can say no worse nor better of them than that they are worthy of the cause in whose interest they are issued. Mention the name of Luther and the bond-slaves of Rome gnash their teeth. This intense ill-feeling proves Luther's power. Young men, I do not know what your ambition may be; but I hope you do not wish to be in this world mere chips in the porridge, giving forth no flavour whatever. My ambition does not run in that line. I know that if I have no intense haters, I can have no intense lovers; and I am prepared to have both. When right-hearted men see honest love of truth in a man, they cry, " He is our brother. Let him be our champion." When the wrong-hearted reply, " Down with him ! " we thank them for the unconscious homage which they thus pay to decision of character. No child of God should court the world's approbation. Certainly Luther did not. He pleased God, and that was enough for him.

His faith was of this kind also—that it moved him to *a hearty reverence for what he believed to be Holy Scripture.* I am sorry that he was not always wise in his judgment of what the Bible contains; but yet to him Scripture was the last court of appeal. If any had convinced Luther of error out of that book, he would gladly have retracted; but that was not their plan, they simply said, " He is a heretic; condemn him or make him retract." To this he never yielded for an instant. Alas, in this age numbers of men are setting

up to be their own inspired writers. I have been told that every man
who is his own lawyer has a fool for his client; and I am inclined to
think that, when any man sets up to be his own Saviour and his own
revelation, much the same thing occurs. That conceited idea is in
the air at this present: every man is excogitating his own Bible. Not
so Luther. He loved the sacred book! He fought by its help. It was
his battle-axe and his weapon of war. A text of Scripture fired his
soul; but the words of tradition he rejected. He would not yield to
Melancthon, or Zwingle, or Calvin, or whoever it might be, however
learned or pious; he took his own personal faith to the Scripture, and
according to his light he followed the word of the Lord. May many
a Luther be in this place!

The next thing I note was *the intense activity of his faith.* Luther did
not believe in God doing his own work, so as to lie by in idleness himself.
Not a bit of it. A disciple once said to Mahomet, "I am going to turn
my camel loose, and trust in providence." "No," said Mahomet,
"trust in providence, but tie up your camel carefully." This resembled
Oliver Cromwell's Puritan precept, "Trust in God, but keep your
powder dry." Luther believed above most men in keeping his powder
dry. How he worked! By pen, by mouth, by hand; he was energetic
almost beyond belief. He seemed a many-handed man. He did works
which would have taxed the strength of hundreds of smaller men. He
worked as if everything depended upon his own activity, and then he
fell back in holy trust upon God as though he had done nothing. This
is the kind of faith which saves a man both in this life and in that which
is to come.

Again, *Luther's faith abounded in prayer.* What supplications they
were! Those who heard them tell us of his tears, his wrestlings, his
holy arguments. He would go into his closet heavy at heart, and remain
there an hour or two, and then come forth singing, "I have conquered,
I have conquered." "Ah," said he one day, "I have so much to do to-
day that I cannot get through it with less than three hours' prayer." I
thought he was going to say, "I cannot afford to give even a quarter of
an hour to prayer;" but he increased his prayer as he increased his
labour. This is the faith that saves—a faith that lays hold on God and
prevails with him in private supplication.

His was a faith that *delivered him entirely from the fear of man.*
Duke George is going to stop him. "Is he?" said Luther. "If it were
to rain Duke Georges I would go." He is exhorted not to go to Worms,
for he will be in danger. If there were as many devils in Worms as
there were tiles on the house-tops he would be there. And he was
there, as you all know, playing the man for the gospel and for his God.
He committed himself to no man, but kept his faith in God pure and
unmingled. Popes, emperors, doctors, electors were all as nothing to
Luther when they stood against the Lord. Be it so with us also.

His was a faith that made him risk all for the truth. There seemed
no hope of his ever coming back from Worms alive. He was pretty sure
to be burned like John Huss; and the wonder is that he escaped.
His very daring brought him safety from peril. He expressed his regret
that the crown of marytrdom would, in all probability, be missed by him;
but the faith which is prepared to die for Jesus was within him. He

who in such a case saves his life shall lose it, but he that loses his life for Christ's sake shall find it unto life eternal.

This was the faith that made Luther a man among men, and *saved him from priestly affectations.* I do not know whether you admire what is thought to be very superior religion: it is a thing of beauty, but not of use; it ought always to be kept in a glass case; it is made up for drawing-rooms and religious meetings, but would be out of place in a shop or on a farm. Now, Luther's religion was with him at home, at the table as well as in the pulpit. His religion was part and parcel of his common life, and that life was free, open, bold, and unrestrained. It is easy to find fault with him from the superfine standpoint, for he lived in an honest unguardedness. My admiration kindles as I think of the hearty openness of the man. I do not wonder that even ungodly Germans revere him, for he is all a German, and all a man. When he speaks he does not take his words out of his mouth to look at them, and to ask Melancthon whether they will do; but he hits hard, and he has spoken a dozen sentences before he has thought whether they are polished or not. Indeed, he is utterly indifferent to criticism, and speaks what he thinks and feels. He is at his ease, for he feels at home: is he not everywhere in his great Father's house? Has he not a pure and simple intent to speak the truth and do the right?

I like Luther with a wife and children. I like to see him with his family and a Christmas-tree, making music with little Johnny Luther on his knee. I love to hear him sing a little hymn with the children, and tell his pretty boy about the horses in heaven with golden bridles and silver saddles. Faith had not taken away his manhood, but sanctified it to noblest uses. Luther did not live and move as if he were a mere cleric, but as a brother to our common humanity. After all, brethren, you must know that the greatest divines have to eat bread and butter like other people. They shut their eyes before they sleep, and they open them in the morning, just like other folks. This is matter of fact, though some stilted gentleman might like us to doubt it. They feel and think like other men. Why should they seem as if they did not? Is it not a good thing to eat and drink to the glory of God, and show people that common things can be sanctified by the word of God and prayer? What if we do not wear canonicals, and so on? The best canonicals in the world are thorough devotion to the Lord's work; and if a man lives aright, he makes every garment a vestment, every meal a sacrament, and every house a temple. All our hours are canonical, all our days holy days, every breath is incense, every pulse music for the Most High.

They tell us that Luther ignored good works. It is true he would not allow good works to be spoken of as the means of salvation; but of those who professed faith in Jesus he demanded holy lives. *Luther abounded in prayer and charity.* What an almsgiver Luther was! I fear he did not at all times duly regard the principles of the Charity Organization Society. As he goes along, if there are beggars he empties his pockets for them. Two hundred crowns have just come in, and, though he has a family about him, he cries, "Two hundred crowns! God is giving me my portion in this life." "Here," says he to a poor brother minister, "take half. And where are the poor? Fetch them in. I must be rid of this!" I am afraid that his Catherine was forced at times to shake her head at him; for, in truth, he was not always the most economical husband that might be. In almsgiving he was second to none, and in all the duties of life he rose far beyond the level of his age. Like all other men he had his faults; but as his enemies harp on that string, and go far beyond the truth, I need not dwell upon his failings. I wish that the detractors of Luther were half as good as he. All the glory of his grand career be unto the Lord alone.

Lastly, Luther's faith was a faith that *helped him under struggles that are seldom spoken of.* I suppose that never man had greater soul-conflict than Luther. He was a man of heights and depths. Sometimes he went up to heaven and he sang his hallelujahs; and then he went down again into the abyss with his "misereres." I am afraid that, great, vigorous man that he was, he had a bad liver. He was grievously afflicted in body in ways which I need not mention; and he was sometimes laid aside for months together, being so racked and tortured that he longed to die. His pains were extreme, and we wonder how he endured them so well. But ever between the attacks of illness Luther was up again preaching the word of God. Those desperate struggles with the devil would have crushed him but for his faith. The devil seems to have been constantly assailing him, and he was constantly assailing the devil. In that tremendous duel he fell back upon his Lord, and, trusting in Omnipotence, he put Satan to rout.

Young men, I pray that a Luther may spring up from your ranks. How gladly would the faithful welcome him! I, who am more a follower of Calvin than of Luther, and much more a follower of Jesus than of either of them, would be charmed to see another Luther upon this earth.

God bless you, brethren, for Christ's sake. Amen.

PORTION OF SCRIPTURE READ BEFORE SERMON—Galatians iii.

HYMNS FROM "OUR OWN HYMN BOOK"—46 (Ver. I.), 554, 686.

Now ready. Price One Penny Each.

SPURGEON'S ILLUSTRATED ALMANACK for 1884,

CONTAINING

Articles by the Editor and other Writers, Texts of Scripture selected for Meditation for every Day in the Year, Metropolitan Tabernacle Directory, &c.

JOHN PLOUGHMAN'S SHEET ALMANACK for 1884.

Suitable for Cottage Homes, Workshops, Mission Halls, &c.

PASSMORE & ALABASTER, 4, Paternoster Buildings; and all Booksellers.

Metropolitan Tabernacle Pulpit.

FATHERS IN CHRIST.

A Sermon

DELIVERED ON LORD'S-DAY MORNING, NOVEMBER 18TH, 1883, BY

C. H. SPURGEON,

AT THE METROPOLITAN TABERNACLE, NEWINGTON.

"I write unto you, fathers, because ye have known him that is from the beginning."
. . . . "I have written unto you, fathers, because ye have known him that is from the beginning."—1 John ii. 13, 14.

OBSERVE the difference in the two verses : John first says, "I write," and then, "I have written." When in two former discourses* I preached upon the beloved apostle's address to the young men and the children, I gave you as full an interpretation of this difference as I could command, and I need not now repeat it. Certain additional thoughts occur to me, which I will give you, that the matter may be still clearer. The apostle John says, "I write," and by-and-by, "I have written ;" this shows, I think, *the importance of his subject.* If he has already written upon it, he must think it to be a very necessary and valuable truth if he writes upon it yet again. A man does not discourse repeatedly upon the same subject if he be a man full of matter, as this inspired writer was, unless he feels that it is of necessity that he return again and again to his subject till he has impressed it upon the minds of his audience. Hence the apostle is not ashamed to say in effect,—" I write this, though you need not remind me that I have written it before, for I feel it to be wise so long as I am in this tabernacle to put you in remembrance of what I have said unto you." Nails which are important to a structure must be driven in with diligence. Foundation stones should be laid with scrupulous care ; and truth, which is fundamental, should be repeated by the teacher till the disciple has learned it beyond all fear of ever forgetting it.

This form of speech also reveals *the unchanging conviction of the writer,* who, having written once, is glad to write the same things again. This shows a mind made up and decided, from which proceeds consistent testimony. In these fickle times certain of our public teachers must feel unable to say of any one subject, "I write," and "I have written ;" for before the ink is dry they have need to blot out what they have put upon paper, and to write an amended version of their religious ideas.

---

* No. 1,711, "A Sermon to the Lord's Little Children" ; No. 1,715, "A Description of Young Men in Christ."

No. 1.751.

Scarcely for a month at a stretch do these loose thinkers abide in one stay : they are such wandering stars that no chart could ever mark their position for three weeks together. They might say, " I write, but bless you, dear people, I do not know what I wrote six months ago. Very probably my former opinion is not now true, for all things are flowing on, and my head is swimming with the rest. I am a man of progress; for ever learning, and never coming to the knowledge of the truth. Blot out what I wrote a year ago, and read with care what I write to-day." To which we reply,—Dear sir, we cannot take much notice of what you write now, because in all probability in another week or two you will retract it all, or improve it from off the face of the earth. Neither shall we pay much attention to you then, for you will probably be on the move as soon as ever you have said your say. We decline to learn what we shall have to unlearn. We will wait in our present knowledge until you have reached something certain for yourself. Perhaps in twenty years' time, when you have pitched your gipsy tent, it may be worth our while to hear where it is; but we do not commit ourselves even to that promise : for as the progress you are now making is into deeper darkness, you will probably end in sevenfold night.

I rejoice, dear friends, in the fixity of the Christian's faith : I know nothing of improvements and growths in the gospel of the Lord Jesus, which is summed up in these words, " Jesus Christ the same yesterday, and to day, and for ever." I believe that God the Holy Ghost has given us in the Scriptures a perfect and entire revelation which is to be received by all Christians without addition or diminution. I do not believe that apostles, martyrs, confessors, and teachers have been living for these nineteen hundred years upon falsehoods : I prefer the faith of saints in glory to the day-dreams of those whipper-snappers who now-a-days claim to lead us by their " thought." Our mind is that of David when he said, " I hate vain thoughts." Well saith the Scripture, " The Lord knoweth the thoughts of man that they are vanity." If it be a question of thinking we can think as well as they can, and our thoughts about the modern theology are full of sorrowful contempt. Peradventure the doctrine is new, though even this we doubt; but if it be new it is not true, for truth must necessarily be as old as the everlasting hills. We observe that the word " meditation " is now seldom used, and " thought " is the modern idol. Just so: we meditate on revealed truth; but this notion of *thought* sets aside truth, and sets up mere fancy. We refuse to be of this vagrant party of thinkers; we are of the settled race of believers. We can say—What we have written, we still write; what we have preached, we still preach : for inasmuch as we have preached that which is revealed in Holy Scripture, to that truth we stand and shall stand, God helping us. If we live a thousand years, at the close of life we shall have nothing more nor less to say than the fixed, immutable, eternal truth of God. We hope to understand the truth better, but we shall never discover better truth.

"I write," and "I have written," also indicate *the abiding need of men:* they require the same teaching from time to time. I suppose that John alludes to his Gospel when he says, " I have written," and now, a little later, he writes his Epistle, and says " I write"—giving in each case the same teaching. Men's natures are still the same, men's spiritual conflicts and dangers are still the same, and hence the same truth is suitable, not only from day to day, but from century to century. There is but one food for soul hunger, and but one help in spiritual danger. The true teacher evermore comes to men with the same truth, because men continue to have the same dangers, necessities, sorrows, and hopes. The fathers who needed that John should write to them previously, still needed that he should write to them the selfsame thing. Though they may have grown more fatherly, they have not outgrown apostolic teaching. The former truth is good for our latter days. Many years ago, when some of us were mere boys, we listened to the gospel of Jesus, and our heart leaped as we embraced it; it was the life and joy of our spirit; and now to-day, after having advanced far in the divine life, if we hear one of those simple sermons that first brought us to Christ, concerning the precious blood of Jesus and child-like faith in him, it suits us quite as well as in those early days. I have noticed with regard to well-grown Christian people, that when I have given a purely evangelical discourse, meant only for sinners, and not at all designed for the edifying and comforting of full-aged saints, they have sucked it in with as much delight as if they were themselves newly converted. After all, though you and I are not now fed upon milk, yet a draught of milk is still most refreshing. Though we can now digest the solid meat of the kingdom, yet the children's bread has lost none of its relish in our esteem. The elementary truths are still sweet to our hearts; ay, sweeter than ever they were. Though we have advanced to the higher courses of the edifice of holy knowledge, yet we never cease to look with intense delight upon those foundation-truths which concern our Lord Jesus. We cleave with full purpose of heart to him of whom the Lord God has said, " Behold, I lay in Zion for a foundation a stone, a tried stone, a precious corner stone, a sure foundation." Jesus remains to us " elect, precious," and we know it will be so with us till life's latest hour.

From this text I am to preach principally to the fathers, and as the church has not many fathers I may be supposed to have a slender audience; but yet this is hardly so, since I hope and trust that the area of the sermon's influence will include young men; for you, my brethren, aspire to reach the front rank, and to be numbered among the fathers. Even to you who are little children, the text has its word of instruction; for you will be glad to hear what the fathers know, since you hope ere long to know the same. The life of God is so much the same in all stages that the word which is profitable to fathers has a use for babes, and that which is spoken to little children has a voice in it for young men. May God the Holy Ghost bless this word to the hearts of all his people!

Concerning the fathers, I am going to inquire three things this morning. First, *who are they?*—" You fathers." Secondly, *what is their peculiar characteristic?*—" Ye have known him that is from the beginning." And, thirdly, *what is the message to them?*—" I have written unto you, fathers." What is it that John has written to fathers in the church of God?

I. First, WHO ARE THE FATHERS?

We usually associate that idea somewhat with age; but we must take care that we do not make a mistake here, because age in grace, albeit that it may run parallel with age in nature in many cases, does not always do so. In the church of God there are children who are seventy years old. Yes, little children displaying all the infirmities of declining years. It is not a pleasant sight to see grey-headed babes, yet I must confess I have seen such, and I have even been glad that I could dare to go the length of hoping that they were babes in Christ. One would not like to say of a man of eighty that he had scarcely cut his wisdom-teeth, and yet there are such ; scarcely out of the nurse's arms at sixty years of age, needing just as much care and comfort as sucklings at the breast. On the other hand, there are fathers in the church of God, wise, stable, instructed, who are comparatively young men. The Lord can cause his people to grow rapidly, and far outstrip their years. David as a lad was more of a father in God than Eli in his old age. Growth in grace is not a time growth. In eternal matters years count for little. The Lord gives subtlety to the simple, to the young men knowledge and discretion. Solomon was wise while yet young ; in some respects wiser than when he was old. Some youths have been like Joseph, men with God before they were men among men. Joseph, we are told in our translation, was more loved by Jacob than any of his brethren, " because he was the son of his old age"; this can hardly be a correct rendering, for Benjamin, who was born sixteen years later, was far more entitled to be so called. Another interpretation, which seems to me more correct, signifies that he was *a son of the Elders*, and implies that while he was a child he was an associate of elderly persons, and was himself so thoughtful, serious, and well-instructed as to be an elderly child, a child-man, full of unusual wisdom and prudence. Josephs are still sent into the church now and then, and the Lord greatly blesses his people by their means. Oh, for more of them! From their early youth they have a discernment of God's word, and a quickness of apprehension wonderful to notice. More than that, I have even observed a depth of experience within a very short time granted to certain young believers, so that though they were but youths in age they were fathers in piety. Nevertheless, as a usual thing, it is to be expected that advancement in grace should be accompanied with advancement in years, and it is so often so that we are wont to call those who are fit to look after the souls of others " the elders of the church," not necessarily because they are old men, but because they are instructed in the things of God. These are the fathers, then, men who have aged in grace, have come to the full development of their spiritual manhood, and have been confirmed in that development by the test of time and trials. Believers when they have in the course of years shown themselves able both to labour and to suffer, are fitly ranked among fathers. Why do we call the early writers the fathers of the church? Not, I think, because we owe more to their teaching than to those of a later period, but because they were the first men, the pioneers, the vanguard, and so the fathers of the church. The first and earliest members of a church will become fathers in due time if they continue in the faith, grounded and settled : their years of persevering holiness entitle them to respect. Paul mentions with honour certain persons, saying, " Who also were in Christ before me." There is an honour in having been a soldier of Christ for a long time. It was no small praise of his disciples when Jesus said of them, "Ye have been with me from the beginning." With the idea of fathers we so far associate that of age that we hope and expect that believers who have been in Christ long have well learned their lesson, and have come to a fulness of growth in the things of God. Judge ye, Christian brethren, whether ye can rank yourselves among the fathers; and if ye are not able to do so, yet press onward towards it. I make bold to say that in this church there is a larger proportion of this class of Christians than I have ever seen elsewhere, and for this I thank God with all my heart, for they are of the utmost service to our host.

"Fathers," again, are *persons of maturity*, men who are not raw and green; not fresh recruits, unaccustomed to march or fight, but old legionaries who have used their swords on others, and are themselves scarred with wounds received in conflict. These men know what they know, for they have thought over the gospel, studied it, considered it, and having so considered it have embraced it with full intensity of conviction. Usually we mean by "fathers" men who have become deve oped in grace, mature in character, decided in conviction, clear in statement, and accurate in judgment. These can discern between things that differ, and are not deceived by the philosophies which allure the ignorant. They know the voice of the Shepherd, and a stranger will they not follow. The younger folk may be bewitched so that they do not obey the truth; but these are not fascinated by error. New converts in their difficulties resort to these fathers; for doubts which bewilder the beginner are simplicity itself to those who are taught of the Lord. These are the watchmen on the walls who detect where insidious doubt is creeping in, where deadly error under the guise of truth is slily undermining the faith of the church: to that end the Lord has instructed them and given them to have their senses exercised to discern between good and evil. Among them are men who have understanding of the times to know what Israel ought to do. If you are such fathers, dear brethren, I rejoice in you: if you are not such as yet, aspire to this eminence, and pray the Lord that you may not be long before you arrive at the ripeness and sweetness which belong to mellow Christians who are prepared for the great ingathering.

"Fathers," again, are *men of stability and strength*. If burglars are planning to attack a house they care little about the children, and make small account of the boys; but if fatherly men are about, the thieves are not eager for an encounter. Even thus the arch-deceiver has hope of injuring the church by deceiving the little children and the young men; but the stalwart men of God, who walk in the midst of the household, looked up to by everybody, are not so readily blown to and fro. As the Spartans pointed to their citizens as the real walls of Sparta, so do we point to these substantial men, as under God the brazen walls and bulwarks of the church. Men who are well taught, confirmed, experienced, and trained by the Spirit of God are pillars in the house of our God. It may be said of each of them, "He keepeth himself so that the evil one toucheth him not." These are men-at-arms, who know how to wear the armour which God has provided, and to use the sword of the Spirit, which is the word of God. These are men of strong faith and firm

convictions, men of decision and courage, men of prudent action, in
no hurry through fear, and under no excitement through false hope.
These are not men that retract, or shuffle, or evade; but witnesses who
are faithful and true, imparting confidence to the feebler sort by their
calm defiance of the foe.   Oh, that all Christians would grow into such
solid saints.   Many light, frothy, chaffy minds come into the church,
and give us untold trouble to keep them right, and infinitely more
trouble because they will not be kept right.   Oh, for more men of such
a sort that if the whole world went wrong they would still abide by the
right; men who cannot be carried away by superstition, let it adorn
itself with all the beauties of art; men who cannot be borne down
by Scepticism either, let it flaunt all the pomp of its pretended culture
and wisdom.   These fathers know and are sure, and have learned to be
on their own accounts determined and unyielding; for they will not stir
beyond "It is written," nor tempt eternal ruin by building upon the
shifting quicksands of the hour.   At this moment there is large need
for a phalanx of invincibles.   Be ye steadfast, unmovable, always
abounding in the work of the Lord.

But there is something more than this in Christian fatherhood.   The
fathers of the church are men of heart, who *naturally care for the souls
of others.*   It is upon the father that the weight of the household falls:
he goes forth in the morning to his daily labour, and he returns at
night with the fruit of his toil for the support of the household.   It is
not for himself that he lives, but for that dear family which is gathered
about him.   He is not wholly comprised within his own personal self,
for he lives in all the house: he lives especially in his children.   Their
suffering or their want would be his suffering and his want.   His heart
has grown larger than when he was a child or a young man; for now
his heart beats in all that household, of which he is the life.   It is a
grand thing when Christian men and Christian women come to this,
that they are not perpetually thinking of their own salvation, and of
their own souls being fed under the ministry, but they care most of
all for those who are weak and feeble in the church.   During a service
their thoughts go out for those assembled.   They are anxious as to
how that stranger may be impressed by the sermon; how yonder anxious
spirit may be comforted, how a backsliding brother may be restored,
how one who is growing somewhat chill may be revived.   This paternal
care betokens a true father in the church.   May the Lord multiply
among us those who feel it to be their life-work to feed the flock of
Christya.

Having this care upon him the father *comes to be tender*; he par-
takes somewhat of the tenderness of a mother, and thus is called a
nursing-father.   A true father, such as fathers should be, has a tender
love for all the little ones.   He would not hurt them; nothing would
be more painful to him than to grieve them; on the contrary, he
studies to give them pleasure, and lays himself out for their good.   It is
a great blessing to the church when the leading spirits are loving; not
rough and uncouth, domineering or hectoring, but gentle and Christ-
like.   Oh, my brothers, who take the lead, let us bear and forbear, and
put up with a thousand trying things from our Master's children whom
he has committed to our care.   Let us make ourselves the servants of

all. Is not the father the labourer for the children? Does he not lay up for them? Is not his superiority best seen by his doing more for the family than anybody else? This is how Christians grow great, by making themselves greatly useful to others. If you are the slave of all, willing to do anything so that you can but help them, and make them happy and holy, this is to be a father in the church of God. Sympathetic care and hearty tenderness are gifts of the Holy Spirit, and will bring you a happiness which will richly compensate you for your pains.

Not yet have I quite reached the full meaning of a father; for the father is *the author, under God, of the being of his children;* and happy is a church that has many in it who are spiritual parents in Zion, through having brought sinners to Christ. Happy are the men by whose words, and acts, and spirit, and prayers, and tears, men have been begotten unto God through Jesus Christ our Lord. What an honour it is to be such a father! Some of us have been filled with this joy till it has well-nigh broken our hearts even to think of it; for the Lord has fulfilled to us the promise which he made to Abraham when he bade him lift up his eyes to the stars, and said, "So shall thy seed be." This cannot fall to the lot of all; but in the church of God every man should pray that he may not be barren or unfruitful. May we all be soul-winners; not the minister alone, not the Sunday-school teachers alone; but each one without exception! Why should not each saint bring some one to the Lord Jesus? At least, by our united prayers and godly living, by our united testimony and fidelity, let us labour for the increase of Messiah's kingdom. I hardly think we can put any one among the fathers until he has won some heart for Jesus.

Thus have I described the fathers. They are never very numerous —they are never so numerous as they ought to be. Paul saith, "Yet have ye not many fathers;" but wherever they are, they are the strength of the church. I have seen in the army a number of veterans marching in front, an ornament and an honour to the whole company. Your short-service men come and go, but these tried men stick to the colours, and are the backbone of the regiment. If a tough bit of fighting has to be done, you must rely upon such as these. Like Napoleon's Old Guard, they cannot be shaken or driven back; the smell of powder does not alarm them, nor yet the whistling of the shot, nor the roar of the artillery : they have seen such things before. They can also bide their time and wait, which is a great thing in a soldier; and when at last they are bidden to charge, they leap like lions on their prey, and the enemy is driven before them. Such men we have in the church of God, and such we need; men that are not flattered by opposition, nor made to lose their heads by excitement. They believe in God, and if others doubt, they are not infected by their folly. They know; they are certain; they have put their feet down, and will not move from their persuasion. When the time comes for action, they are ready for it; and throw their whole weight so heartily into the war that every charge tells. God send us regiments more of these in this evil day and preserve to us such as we have!

II. Secondly. WHAT IS THE PROMINENT CHARACTERISTIC OF A FATHER IN CHRIST? Read the text. "I write unto you, fathers, because *ye have known him that is from the beginning."* He repeats the expression without alteration.

Observe here *the concentration of their knowledge.* Twice he says, "Ye have known him that is from the beginning." Now, a babe in grace knows twenty things: a young man in Christ knows ten things; but a father in Christ knows one thing, and that one thing he knows thoroughly. It is very natural for us at first to divide our little stream into many rivulets ; but as we grow grey in grace we pour it all into one channel, and then it runs with a force efficient for our life-work. I trust I know many doctrines, many precepts and many teachings; but more and more my knowledge gathers about my Lord, even as the bees swarm around their queen. May it come to this with us all,—" I determined not to know anything among you, save Jesus Christ, and him crucified." May all our knowledge be focused as with a burning-glass upon this one point. May the adorable person of him that was from the beginning fill the entire horizon of our thought. Oh, to have one heart, one eye, for our one Lord, and for him alone.

Note, next, *the peculiarity of their knowledge as to its object* : they know " him that was from the beginning." Do not the babes in Christ know the Lord Jesus ? Yes, they do; but they do not know him in his full character. They know him as having forgiven their sins, and that is much, but it is not all. Yonder is the blessed Christ, and I, a poor sinner, look to him just as he comes to me, and I am lightened, and become one of his little children. Yes, and as I grow and become a young man, I approach nearer to Jesus, and get another view of him ; for I overcome the Wicked One even as he did, and thus I stand side by side with him in the conflict. But if I come to be a father I enter into fellowship with the great Father himself ; for it is union with God the Father that makes a man a father in God. Then do we, as it were, not only look toward Jesus as coming to save, but we look on Christ from the Father's point of view. The sinner sees Jesus coming to him, but the Father sees Jesus as sent from him. When we grow in grace we, in our measure, see Jesus from God's point of view ; that is to say, we see him as "him that was from the beginning," and in due time was manifested to take away sin. " These are ancient things," says one. Just so ; but fathers are also ancient men, and the deep things of God are suitable to them. Believers see Christ in a fashion similar to their own. I scarcely need allude to that which I have often mentioned to you, that every man in the Old Testament who saw the Lord saw him in a character like his own. Abraham, the pilgrim, saw Christ as a pilgrim. Jacob, the struggler, saw the covenant angel wrestling with him through the night. Moses, the representative of a people tried as by fire and yet continuing, saw the Lord as a burning bush. Joshua, the valiant warrior, saw the captain of the Lord's host as a man with a sword drawn in his hand. The three holy children saw the Son of God in the burning, fiery, furnace, even as they were themselves. When you become a father in Christ you see Christ from the Father's point of view ; not as newly come to save, but as " from the beginning " the Saviour of men.

The father in grace rejoices to behold the Lord Jesus as God : he beholds the glory of his adorable person as for ever with the Father or ever the earth was. He knows that without him was not anything made that was made, and therefore beholds him as fashioning everything upon the anvil of his power. He knows that "His goings forth were of old, from everlasting," and he delights to see him planning the salvation of his chosen in the beginning. A glorious sight it is. The grown believer meditates upon the covenant,—the settlements of grace in the old eternity. Poor babes in Christ are frequently stumbled by the mysterious truth of God—high doctrine they call it: but when a man grows to be a father he loves covenant truth, and feeds on it. It is one mark of advanced grace that the sublime truths which concern eternity are increasingly valued. In gracious maturity the Christian sees the blessed persons of the Divine Trinity entering into a compact for the salvation of men, and he sees the Son of God himself from the beginning acting as the representative of his elect, and taking upon himself to answer on their behalf to the Father. He sees the Eternal Son there and then becoming the sponsor and the surety for his chosen, engaging to pay their debt and make recompense to the injured justice of God on account of their sins. He sees that covenant even from of old ordered in all things and sure in the hand of him that was from the beginning.

There is one point that the father in Christ delights to think upon, namely, that the coming of Christ into the world was not an expedient adopted after an unavoidable and unforeseen disaster in order to retrieve the honour of God; but he understands that the whole scheme of events was planned in the purpose of divine wisdom for the glorifying of Christ, so that from the beginning it was part of Jehovah's plan that Jesus should take upon himself human nature, and should manifest in that nature all the attributes of the Father. It was the original plan that the incarnate God should reveal infinite grace and boundless love by laying down his life for sinners, "the just for the unjust, that he might bring us to God." The Only-begotten Son is not introduced into the divine economy as an afterthought; but the whole arrangement is shaped with an eye to him who was before all things, and for whom all things were created. It pleased the Father that he should lift up creation by uniting the creature and the Creator in one person; and that he should ennoble our nature, which is a combination of the spiritual and the material, by assuming a body, and bearing that body to the throne of God. O matchless plan, by which the redeemed are ennobled, and God himself is glorified! Oh, fathers, if you have ever seen this, I know that you will say: "The preacher does not half describe it." No, he does not: he wishes that he could; but neither time nor ability are present with him. Still, I delight in the everlasting glories of the Lord Jesus, who was from the beginning. Greatly dear to my own heart are the "chief things of the ancient mountains, and for the precious things of the lasting hills." I believe in my Lord Jesus Christ as second to none, but as the King and Lord from the beginning, who, though he was despised and rejected of men, yet still is God over all blessed for ever, and will be so for ever and ever. Though "the heathen rage, and the people imagine a vain thing," Jehovah has set his Son as King upon his holy hill of Zion, and God's decree shall stand. He that is Alpha shall be Omega: he that is from the beginning shall be to the end

King of kings and Lord of lords. My heart cries, " Hallelujah." Oh,
ye fathers, cry " Hallelujah " with me!

Yes, but I want to notice again, that *this knowledge is in itself special:*
the knowledge itself is remarkable as well as the object of the knowledge. " Ye have *known* him." A dear servant of Christ on this
platform the other evening sat beside me : he belonged to quite another
part of the church of Christ, but he said to me of such and such a
person, " You know, dear brother, he is one that knows the Lord ; he is
not merely a Christian, but he knows our Lord : you and I know what
that means, do we not ? " I could only look at him with a deep look of
loving appreciation. Yes, we do know the Lord as a living, bright
reality, a daily friend, councillor, and companion. True fathers in grace
meditate upon Christ ; they feed upon Scripture, press the juice of it,
and inwardly enjoy the flavour of it. People say they have a sweet tooth.
It is a good thing to have a sweet tooth for the Lord Jesus Christ. They
not only know the Lord by much meditation upon him, but they know
him by actual intercourse : they walk with him, they talk with him.
Such saints are more with Christ than with any one else ; to no one do
they tell so much as they have told to him ; and no one has ever told
them so much as Jesus tells them ; for "the secret of the Lord is with
them that fear him ; and he will show them his covenant." Ask them,
" Who is your nearest friend ? " and they will reply, " The Well-beloved
is my next of kin, my dearest companion." They know the Lord by
intercourse, and they have come to know him now by having an intense
sympathy with him. They feel as Jesus does about matters, and so
they know him ; his tender pity for sinners stirs their hearts, not in the
same degree, but yet in like manner according to their measure. They
often feel as if they could die for sinners. One of these fathers said,
" I could wish myself accursed from Christ, for my brethren, my kinsmen
according to the flesh." They look upon matters not from man's standpoint, but from Christ's point of view, and hence they understand much
of the Lord's ways which aforetime were dark to them. He who very
deeply sympathizes with a man knows him well. Learning by faith
to sit still and believingly wait the event, these fathers calmly expect
that all things will work together for good to them ; and hence they
understand the unbroken serenity of the heart of Jesus, and know him
in his joys as well as in his sorrows. Such saints know what it is to
weep over the city with Jesus, and to rejoice over returning sinners with
the good Shepherd ; yea, they know what it is to sit down with him on
his throne expecting till his enemies be made his footstool. They are
calm with Jesus, for they have drunk in the meaning of the text, " He
must reign." Yes : he must reign ; he must reign ; till all his enemies
shall be under his feet. This knowing him that is from the beginning
is the chief characteristic of the father in Christ.

III. Thirdly, dear friends, WHAT IS THE MESSAGE TO THE FATHERS ?
I would indicate that message very briefly, by referring you to the
context. John has been saying to you, dear fathers, and indeed to all
of us who are in Christ, that we should *love one another.* If you are
truly fathers you cannot help loving all the family : the fatherly instinct
is love, and fathers in Christ should be brimful of it. Little ones should
be induced by our loving spirit to come around us, feeling that if nobody

else loves them we do, if nobody else cares for them we do. I have known a father in Christ to whom a convert would speak much more readily than he would to his own earthly father or mother. I suppose they see an invitation in the faces of these fathers. I do not quite know how they find it out, but somehow converts feel that such an one is a man whom they could address, or a woman whom they could talk with. These fathers and mothers in Israel are full of love, and their speech betrays the fact. I know some men who are like great harbours for ships: a soul tossed with tempest makes for them as for a harbour. Breaking hearts say, " Oh, that I could tell him my trouble, and get his prayers." May you and I be just such persons, and may the Holy Spirit use us for the good of our fellows.

The next message immediately succeeds the text: "*Love not the world*, neither the things that are in the world." Oh, dear fathers, you must not love the world, for it passeth away, and this is specially true of you. If any Christian man might love the world, and I hope none will do so, certainly the fathers may not. You know so much of Christ that you may well despise the world ; and you are so soon going home that you ought to set little store by these fleeting things. You have all the marks of what they call declining years—I call them ascending years : you will soon be gone from the world and its changing vanities, therefore do not set your love on earthly treasures. Hold wealth with a loose hand, be ready to depart, for depart you soon will. Before the morning watch you may be gone to your Father's house on high. " Love not the world."

Another duty of fathers is also mentioned here. While they are not to love the world they must take care that they *do not fall victims to any of the lusts of this present evil world,* such as the lust of the flesh. Can fathers ever fall that way? Ah me ; we have to speak very solemnly and admit that the most advanced saint still needs to be warned against the lust of the flesh, the indulgence of appetites which so readily lead men to sin. Then there is the lust of the eye. David fell into that when he repined because of the prosperity of the wicked, and was obliged to confess, " So foolish was I, and ignorant." He looked at the prosperous wicked till he began to fret himself about them. That lust of the eye, in desiring more for yourself and envying those that have more—never let it happen to a father. And the pride of life— that thirsting to be thought respectable, that emulation of others, that struggling after honour and such like—this must not be in a father. You are men, and must put away childish things. My dear and honoured brethren, fall not a prey to vanities : these toys are for the children of the world, not for you who are so near to the glory of the Lord. You are grown ripe in grace, and will soon enter heaven, live accordingly. Let all earthly things lie like babies' baubles beneath your feet, while you rise to the manhood of your soul.

The next exhortation to the fathers is that they should *watch*, for, says the apostle, " Ye have heard that antichrist shall come, even now are there many antichrists." Oh, valiant fathers, keep ye watch and ward. I marvel much that members of churches agree to the choice of ministers who are not sound in the faith, nay, who do not seem to have any faith at all. How comes this about? We used to have in our

Baptist churches substantial men who would as soon have brooked Satan at their own table as an unsound preacher in the pulpit.   There used to be a company in the north of Scotland called "The Men."   Why, if heresy had been preached before them, they would have been as provoked as Janet Geddes when she threw her cutty stool at the head of the preacher.   They would not have endured these modern heresies as the present effeminate generation is enduring them.   Let the new theologians have liberty to preach what they like on their own ground, but not in our pulpits.   Alas! the leading members in many churches are Christians without backbones, molluscous, spongy; snails I would call them, only they have not the consistency of a snail's shell.   They are ready to swallow any mortal thing if the preacher seems clever and eloquent.   Cleverness and eloquence—away with them for ever!   If it is not the truth of God, the more cleverly and eloquently it is preached the more damnable it is.   We must have the truth and nothing but the truth, and I charge the fathers in Christ all over England and America to see to this.   Get ye to your watch-tower and guard the flock, lest the sheep be destroyed while they are asleep.

Lastly, it is the duty of the fathers to *prepare for the coming of the Lord.*   How beautifully it is put in the twenty-eighth verse, " Abide in him ; that, when he shall appear, we may have confidence, and not be ashamed before him at his coming."   It is addressed to you all, for you are all little children, but it is specially incumbent upon those of you who are fathers.   Arouse all your faculties!   Watch for the coming of the Lord, and keep your loins well girded.   Jesus may come to-day ; this Sabbath may be the last Sabbath of this dispensation : yet he may not come for ten thousand years for aught I know ; therefore weary not if you wait through a long night.   Say not that he delayeth his coming, for he will return at the day appointed.   Only let us hold fast that which we have received, and stand waiting for the midnight cry, He will come, he will not tarry ; therefore go ye forth to meet him.

" Hold the fort, for I am coming,
    Jesus signals still :
Wave the answer back to heaven,
    By thy grace we will."

Amen.

PORTION OF SCRIPTURE READ BEFORE SERMON—1 John ii.

HYMNS FROM " OUR OWN HYMN BOOK "—249, 217, 412.

MOURNERS, INQUIRERS, COVENANTERS.

A Sermon

DELIVERED ON LORD'S-DAY MORNING, NOVEMBER 25TH, 1883, BY

C. H. SPURGEON,

AT THE METROPOLITAN TABERNACLE, NEWINGTON.

"In those days, and in that time, saith the LORD, the children of Israel shall come, they and the children of Judah together, going and weeping: they shall go, and seek the LORD their God. They shall ask the way to Zion with their faces thitherward, saying, Come, and let us join ourselves to the LORD in a perpetual covenant that shall not be forgotten."—Jeremiah l. 4, 5.

THE previous part of this chapter declares the overthrow of Israel's cruel oppressor: "Babylon is taken, Bel is confounded, Merodach is broken in pieces." The Assyrian and Babylonian power had been the great tyrant of the ages, and the Lord had employed it for the chastening of his people, until at last Israel and Judah had been carried away captive to the banks of the Euphrates, and the land of their fathers knew them no more. This was the mournful song of the exiles, "By the rivers of Babylon, there we sat down, yea, we wept, when we remembered Zion." What a turn would come! In the day when God would reckon with Babylon, and punish the haughty people for their cruelties and oppressions, then should Israel and Judah come to their own again. "In those days, and in that time," there would be hope for the down-trodden: the Lord would keep his appointments of grace to the hour, and at the time determined Israel should be free. "Surely the least of the flock would draw out the enemy," and escape from his power. God doth devise means for bringing back his banished ones, and among those ways we usually see the overthrow of their conquerors. When, therefore, the Lord deals with Babylon in a way of vengeance it is that he may deliver his own people. See how the two things are joined together in the eighteenth and nineteenth verses,— "Therefore thus saith the Lord of hosts, the God of Israel; Behold, I will punish the king of Babylon and his land, as I have punished the king of Assyria. And I will bring Israel again to his habitation, and he shall feed on Carmel and Bashan, and his soul shall be satisfied upon mount Ephraim and Gilead." When Pharaoh is drowned, Israel is saved; when Sihon and Og are slain, the Lord's mercy to his people is seen to endure for ever. The destruction of Amalek is the salvation of

No. 1,752.

I

Jacob, and the overthrow of Babylon is the restoration of Jerusalem. It was a very wonderful thing that a nation so crushed and scattered as the Jews were should come back from captivity: it was a very marvellous instance of divine power and faithfulness, as it is written —" For Israel hath not been forsaken, nor Judah of his God, of the Lord of hosts; though their land was filled with sin against the Holy One of Israel."

I will not talk much with you concerning the Chaldeans and the Jews, but I would speak concerning ourselves. We, too, by nature are in banishment, far off from our God and the abode of his glory. We are not what we ought to have been, for the Lord did not make us to be sinners, but to be his happy and obedient creatures: our present lost estate is not our true state, we are banished through coming under the power of our great adversary; sin has carried us into captivity, we are in the far country, away from the great Father's house. It is a great blessing when the times come, and they have come, when there is an opportunity and an invitation to return. To-day the power of the adversary is broken, and we may flee out of the Babylon of sin. A greater than Cyrus has opened the two-leaved gates, and broken the bars of iron in sunder, and proclaimed liberty to the captives. We may now return to our God and freely enjoy the holy and happy as~~ciations which belong to the City of our God.

At such times, when the Lord is leading men to seek his face, questions arise, anxieties abound, and difficulties multiply. The lost tribes could not come back from Babylon by merely thinking of it the way was long and dangerous, the paths were unknown and difficult, and they who came back to Zion found the journey to be no promenade of pleasure or parade of pomp. It is so with the Lord's banished when he gives them a heart and a will to return to him; they are not, therefore, restored to the Father's house at once: they may have to persevere through months of weary pilgrimage before they come to their desired abode. As I have said, returning times are anxious times; men wander thoughtlessly, but they do not return without grave thought and serious consideration. I earnestly desire to be the means in the hand of God of answering questions, removing fears, and clearing the way for those who have begun to seek the Lord. They mourn, and I would fain comfort them; they ask the way, and I would gladly direct them; they long to join themselves unto the Lord, and I would help them. Last Sabbath morning was given to the fathers of the church, let this be given to the beginners in the divine life. May the Holy Spirit give us thoughts and words which may lead the seeker into the way of peace.

Every one who is really seeking the Lord desires to be sure that he is seeking aright; he is not willing to take anything for granted, since his soul is of too much value to be left at hazard. He does not even believe in his own judgment of himself, but when he thinks his face is towards Zion, he still asks the way. He inquires, " Are my feelings like those of the truly penitent ? Am I believing as those do who are justified by faith ? Am I seeking the Lord in a manner which will be pleasing to him ?" They have so long been as lost sheep, going from mountain to hill, that they have forgotten their resting places, therefore in then confusion they are afraid of going wrong again, and so they inquire with eager anxiety. Perhaps we may show them from this Scripture how others sought and how others found, and this may be a guide and a comfort to them ; for albeit there are differences of operation, and all do not come to Christ with equal terrors, or with equal joys, yet there is a likeness in all the pilgrims to the holy city. " As in water face answereth to face, so the heart of man to man ; " the experience of God's people in its root principles is evermore the same. All coming sinners endure like griefs, and pass through similar struggles: the same desires, the same fears, the same hopes, and by-and-by the same realizations are to be found in all those who seek unto the Lord their God.

Looking carefully at the text, we perceive that those who came back to Zion by God's gracious leadership, were first *mourners ;* secondly, *inquirers ;* and thirdly, *covenanters ;* for they ended by joining themselves unto the Lord in a perpetual covenant.

I. To begin at the beginning, the Lord's restored ones during the processes of grace were first of all MOURNERS : " In those days, and in that time, saith the Lord, the children of Israel shall come, they and the children of Judah together, going and weeping: they shall go, and seek the Lord their God." Oh, my hearer, after all your sins I will not believe that you are truly coming to God if there is not about you a great *sorrow for sin and a lamenting after the Lord.* Some seekers are made to drink of this bitter cup very deeply ; the wine of astonishment is long kept to their lips ; their sense of sin is terrible, even to anguish and agony. I know that there are others who do not taste this bitterness to the same degree ; but it is in their cup, for all that, only the sweet love of Christ is revealed to them so soon and so fully that the healthful wormwood of penitence is veiled beneath the exceeding sweetness of gracious pardon. The clear shining in their case so soon follows the rain that they scarcely know that there has been a shower of grief. Surely, in their case the bitterness is passed ; yet is it truly there, only the other ingredient of intense delight in God's mercy swallows up all its sharpness. Oh, friends, you cannot imagine the Jews returning from captivity without bewailing the sins which drove them into the place of their exile. How could they be restored to God if they did not lament their former wicked estrangement ? Shall the Lord press to his bosom an impenitent transgressor ? How can there be peace to an offender so long as his offences are not repented of ? While the heart feels no compunction concerning its wanderings, no mourning over its guilt, no grief at having grieved the Lord, there can be no acceptance with God. There must be a shower in the day of mercy : not always a long driving rain causing a flood, but the soft drops must fall in every case. There must be tenderness toward God if we expect reconciliation with God. The heart must cry, " How could I have sinned against so good a Lord ! How could I have stood out against his love ! How could I have refused my Saviour and his abounding grace ! My God forgive me !" These confessions, if truly made,cannot be spoken without sighs and sorrows ; the multitudes of our sins cannot be thought of without a moving of the soul and a measure of heart-break. Is it not written, " They shall look on him whom they have pierced, and shall mourn for him, and be in bitterness as one that is in bitterness for his firstborn "? A look at Christ gives life, and it also produces the tokens of that life, among which we find godly sorrow, which worketh repentance not to be repented of. Even a sense of pardon does not exclude this holy mourning: on the contrary, it increases it. The more certain we are that we are forgiven, the more do we loathe the sin which caused the Saviour to bleed and die. The more sure we are of the divine favour, the more intensely do we regret the fact of our having been enemies to the infinitely gracious God. Of all the ransomed it is written, "They shall come with weeping, and with supplications will I lead them."

Observe that this mourning in the case of Israel and Judah was so strong that *it mastered other feelings*. Between Judah and Israel there was an old feud. They were brethren, and it ought not to have been so; but they had become bitter adversaries of each other. Yet now that they return unto the Lord, we read, " The children of Israel shall come, they and the children of Judah together." O happy union in a common search for God! One of the first results of holy sorrow for sin is to cast out of our heart all forms of enmity and strife with our fellowmen. When we are reconciled to God we are reconciled to men. I have seen those who had been fired with mutual hatred loving each other when they have been alike under the power of the Spirit of God, and bowed down with contrition. I am sure if you were to go forward as a sincere inquirer to ask the way to heaven, if you met your worst enemy at the door, and he said to you, " I am seeking mercy of God for my transgressions," you would grasp each other's hands and weep together. If a man, professing to be a penitent, drew back at the sight of another who also came penitently to Christ, and said, " I can have nothing to do with him," I should unhesitatingly declare him to be a hypocrite; or even if he were sincere, I should have to tell him that to a certainty the Lord could not and would not accept his repentance or grant him peace. If thou wilt not forgive thy brother, how shall God forgive thee? Durst thou pray, "Forgive us our trespasses," if thou canst not forgive thy brother his trespasses? A penitent sense of our own provocations of God will prevent our being provoked with men. As Aaron's rod swallowed up all other rods, so a sincere sorrow for sin will remove all readiness to take offence against our fellow-sinners. In the secret chambers of their souls the truly penitent say, " Everything that I have against any man is gone now, for I remember nothing but that I have offended against my God. If the Lord will forgive my wrong, everything I have had to bear from others shall be as the small dust of the balance, not worthy to be considered or thought of in the day of infinite grace."

I am trying so to preach that I may help you who are seeking the Lord to discover whether you are coming aright. This shall be one simple test to you—you cannot be coming home to your Father unless there is some degree of mourning for sin, some smiting upon the breast, some bemoaning of yourself because of your iniquities; and again, for certain, you cannot be coming to the Lord aright unless there is a blotting out altogether from your heart of every offence that every man may have committed against you in past times. Judah and Israel, when the Lord has mercy on them, forget their enmity, and recognize the brotherhood which they ought never to have forgotten. If I am speaking to any who are seeking the Lord, but seem to make small progress to the light, I entreat them to inquire whether sins of enmity and wrath may not be lying at the door and blocking the way of grace. Hasten to forgive freely, fully, heartily, and then pray, " Forgive us our trespasses as we forgive them that trespass against us." A family dis-agreement may seem to be a little thing, but it may be holding many in the deadly bonds of the evil one. Be reconciled to thy brother, or thou canst not be reconciled to thy God.

Keeping close to the text, we notice again that the exiles on their return *were mourning while marching.* Observe the words—" going and weeping." We might have thought, perhaps, that when they began to go to their God, so much light would break in upon them that they would cease to weep: but no, it is "going and weeping." A true heart that is coming to God takes the road by Weeping-Cross: it feels its sin, its guilt, its undesert, and it therefore mourns. The closet is sought out and prayer is offered; but in the supplication there is a dove's note, a moaning as of one sorrowing for love. When the prayer is over, there is a dissatisfaction with the prayer, a smiting on the breast, as much as to say, " I pray but coldly compared with the way in which I ought to pray. I look not to Christ as I ought, but look half askance, I fear, at something else besides the cross." An honestly believing soul is fearful lest it should be mistaken in its faith. A truly praying heart is jealous of its own prayer, lest it should ask amiss. Probably no prayer is more sincere than that which is followed by deep regret that it is not more fervent: in the fact that the pleader is dissatisfied with his cry lies a proof that the Lord is satisfied with it. Our humility is the water-mark which proves our prayer to be genuine. If we think well of our prayers, and imagine that we have almost a right to be heard, we shall make a fruitless visit to the mercy-seat. We may not claim of God as a matter of justice those boons which are pure gifts of mercy. The Lord had no respect unto Cain and his sacrifice, because there was no reference to sin, no type of atonement, no confession of guilt in that which he pre-sented. Publicans confessing sin are justified rather than self-satisfied Pharisees. When a sense of sin leads to prayer, the prayer itself appears to be another cause for repentance, because of the sin which mingles with it. He who feels a humbling sorrow while he seeks his God is coming aright. Now the seeker opens his Bible, and sits down to read the promise, and as he reads he thinks what great mercy there is in it; but he adds, "Alas! how evil has been my life, since I have grieved the Lord of love." Then the tears flow like the water which gushed from the smitten rock; for as the believer sees that pardon is real and that it is meant for him he is all the more melted down with penitential sorrow. This is his song:—

" Thy mercy is more than a match for my heart,
Which wonders to feel its own hardness depart ;
Dissolved by thy goodness, I fall to the ground,
And weep to the praise of the mercy I've found."

Having grasped the promise, and having looked to Christ and seen

himself forgiven, the sincere soul continues to draw nearer and nearer
to his God, and yet all the while he is filled with self-accusations and
humblings on account of sin. While he cries, " Blessed be the God of
my salvation, who has delivered me from my iniquities;" he also
mourns within himself, exclaiming, " Alas! that I should have so transgressed and grieved his Holy Spirit! I am ashamed at having rejected
such wondrous love!" Thus " Going and mourning" depicts a gracious
blending of activity and repentance.

Turning the text round, we read not only of " going and weeping,"
but also of weeping and going. The holy grief here intended does not
lead to sitting still, for it is added " they shall go." That word " weeping" is sandwiched in between two goings—" going and weeping ; they
shall go and seek the Lord." To sit down and say, " I will sorrow for
my sin, but never seek a Saviour," is an impenitent pretence of repentance, a barren sorrow which brings forth no cleansing of the life, and no
diligent search after the Lord. Such a sorrow is the first dropping of
that dread shower of remorse which will fall upon the soul for ever.
Remorse is the never-dying worm and the fire unquenchable. No doubt
all that are now lost lament that they have brought themselves into
such a ruin, but that lamentation is no evidence of reconciliation with
God; many have a kind of repentance for having brought themselves
into a condemmed condition ; but this is not genuine repentance if it
stands alone. When the prodigal cries, " I will arise and go to my
Father," then a work of grace is certainly begun, but not till then. It
is not enough to say, " I perish with hunger"; but when there follows
upon it, " I will arise, and go to my Father, and will say unto him,
Father, I have sinned," then we have reached the true turning point—
salvation has come to our house. True mourning for sin leads the sinner to the cross. When thou talkest about repentance, if thy repentance
be with thy back to the cross, away with thy repentance. If thou art
trusting to thy tears, and sorrows, and griefs, and not trusting to
the blood of Jesus Christ, thou art trusting in a vain show. Vanity
of vanities : thy tears shall scald thee, if thou trustest in them, and thy
groans shall be the echoes of thy death-sentence if thou reliest on
them. That repentance in which a guilty man dares to fix his confidence shall be swept away as a thing that lacks the salt which would
make it acceptable with God. The way to repent is with your eye
upon the sacrifice, viewing the flowing of the sin-atoning blood, marking every precious drop, gazing into the Redeemer's wounds, and
believing in the love which in death opened up its depths unsearchable.
All the while we must be saying, " My God, my God, I groan within
myself that such a sacrifice should have been required by my atrocious
transgressions against thee." This is the holy mixture which is needed
—going and weeping, but still going and seeking the Lord.

We must not pass over that last word, " They shall go *and seek the
Lord their God.*" This, dear hearer, shall be a guide to you as to
whether your present state of feeling is leading you aright. What is it
you are seeking ? " I am seeking," says one, " I am seeking peace."
May you soon obtain it, and may it be real peace ; but I am not sure of
you. " I am seeking," says another, " the pardon of sin." Again, I
pray that you may find it ; but I am not sure of you. If another shall

reply, "I am seeking the Lord; for I desire above all things to have him for a friend, though to him I have been an enemy"; then I have good hope of him. I rejoice over the heart which is crying, "I want to see my Father's face, and hear him say, 'I have blotted out thy sins;' I want to dwell with God, to serve him, to obey him, to grow like him. There has been a quarrel between him and me, and other lords have had dominion over me, but now I desire that he shall be my Lord and King, and myself his loyal humble servant, and his beloved child. I hunger and thirst after God!" You see, brethren and sisters, we require a great many things in order to be saved, and yet one thing is needful. I would represent it in this form:—Here is a little child, picked up from the gutter, diseased and filthy, unclad, unfed; and if you ask me to make out a catalogue of what the child wants you must give me a sheet of foolscap paper to write it all down, and then I fear I shall leave out many things. I will tell you in one word what that poor infant requires —it wants its mother. If it gets its mother it has all it needs. So to tell what a poor sinner wants might be a long task; but when you say that he wants his heavenly Father you have said it all. This was what the prodigal needed, was it not? He needed his Father, and when he came to his Father all his necessities were supplied. Oh, souls, you are seeking aright if you are seeking your God. Nothing short of this will suffice. This may greatly aid you to judge whether you are in the right way or no.

So you see, first of all, the returning exiles were mourners.

II. Secondly, these mourners became INQUIRERS. We read in the second verse of our text, "They shall ask the way to Zion with their faces thitherward." They knew something, that is clear, for they turned their faces in the right direction; but having been born and nurtured in Babylon the road to Jerusalem had never been trodden by them, the route was strange and new. They knew within a little the quarter in which Zion lay, and they looked that way; but they did not know all about the road: how should they? The saving point about them was that *they were not ashamed to confess their ignorance*. Minds that the Lord has touched are never boastful of their wisdom. There are many persons in the world who would be converted if they could but consent to be taught by God's word and Spirit; but they are such wise people, they know too much to enter the school of grace. Jesus tells such, "Except ye be converted, and become as little children, ye shall not enter into the kingdom of heaven." A sense of ignorance is the doorstep of wisdom. He shall never know who is not willing to confess that he does not know. These exiles did confess their ignorance; they knew a little, but they felt that they had much more to learn before they could stand in the temple of God in happy fellowship with him.

It is clear from their asking their way that *these inquirers were teachable*. They not only yielded to be instructed, but they were eager to be taught; and therefore they asked for information. It is a hopeful sign when children ask questions; if we can get them to desire knowledge, the desire will be more valuable than the knowledge itself. The way nowadays is to cram the memory; but if our youths could be brought to hunger for knowledge, and to ask questions, their minds would be much more effectually benefited. It is a great mercy for a poor seeking sinner to have a teachable spirit, so as to pray, " Lord Jesus, write thy gospel upon my heart. Here it is, ready to be written on. Only tell me what thou wouldst have me to do. I make no reservation—I am willing, by thy help, to do it; or if there be nothing to be done but to sit at thy feet, tell me that, and I will do this as thy grace enables me." This teachable spirit is a great benefit to any man: it is in fact a precious fruit of the Spirit. "They shall ask the way to Zion:" they shall therefore be conscious of ignorance, and they shall be willing to be taught; these are good characteristics, such as God accepts.

More than this, *they will be anxious although they are right:* "they shall ask the way to Zion, with their faces thitherward"—they are travelling in the right direction, and yet they ask the way. They have looked westward from Babylon, towards Jerusalem: they have taken up the westward position, which in their case had a hopeful meaning in it. They are setting out for the land of Canaan as their first father did when he left Chaldea; and as they have no map of the road they ask for the way which leads from banishment to the city of their God. They are right, for their faces are Zionward, and one proof of it is that they are anxious to keep right, or to be set right. You who are certain that you are right are very liable to be wrong, but those who make every inquiry of the word of God, of the servants of God, and of their fellow travellers are in all probability pursuing the right road. He that has never raised a question about his condition before God had better raise it at once. The fullest assurance of faith we can ever attain will never excuse us from the duty of self-examination. When a man is most surely prospering in business, it will be wise for him to keep his accounts with care; if he does not attend to the state of his affairs we shall suspect that his prosperity is a pleasing delusion which he dares not disturb. He who is most sure that he is right before God is most willing to look within; and he that will not search his own heart, but takes it for granted he is safe, may take my word for it that he is in a perilous condition. It is a strange thing that when men set their faces in the right way, they become careful and serious, and deeply concerned, for they feel that their eternal destiny is not a thing to trifle with.

At the same time, note concerning those that are coming to the Lord and his people, that *they are questioning, but they are still resolved.* They ask their way to Zion, but they have set their faces like flints in that direction. They ask how they can be right with God, not as a matter of curiosity, but because they mean to be at peace with him : by God's grace nothing shall turn them aside from their God and his temple, and hence their anxiety to be surely right. They do not raise questions by way of quibbling that they may have an excuse for sitting still, but they question because they are in downright earnest. True penitents will have Christ or die. Therefore with solemn resolve, lest perchance they should be misled, they ask their way, determined to walk therein.

Though they ask the way, we may remark further that *they know whither they are going.* They ask their way *to Zion.* They wish to know how they can become fellow-citizens with the people of God, how they can behold

the great sacrifice, how they can eat the true passover, how they can be
accepted worshippers of Jehovah, and how they can enjoy fellowship
with him: they ask their way with understanding, for they know what
their heart is seeking. They ask their way, not to somewhere or other,
but to Zion; not to some imaginary blissful shore that may be or may
not be, but they seek God's own dwelling-place, God's own palace,
God's own sacrifice. They ask boldly too, for they are not ashamed to
be found inquiring; and when they are informed, their faces are already
that way, and therefore they have nothing to do but to go straight on.
May God grant us myriads of such inquirers! Observe the right order:
first they sought the Lord, and then they asked their way to Zion. First
God, and then God's people; first the Master of the house, and then the
house of the Master; first that you may become his child, secondly that
you may be put among the children. We pray the Holy Spirit to teach
you this order well: first give yourself to the Lord, and afterwards to
us by the word of God.

III. Now we come to the last matter: these inquirers become
COVENANTERS, for they said one to another, " Come and let us join ourselves to the Lord in a perpetual covenant that shall not be forgotten."
Oh, that word " covenant "! I can never pronounce it without joy in
my heart. It is to me a mine of comfort, a mint of delight, a mass of
joy. Time was when theology was full of covenant truth; nowadays
these grand old doctrines are laid aside by our wise men as too common-
place for their enlightened minds. I do not believe that some modern
preachers could say " covenant "; they could not frame to pronounce it
aright. The doctrine of the " covenant" is a kind of Shibboleth by
which we may know the man of God from the false prophet. Let the
people of God take no delight in the man who does not delight in the
covenant of grace. I rejoice in those old Scotch books about the
covenant: covenant truth was so inwrought into the Scotch heart that
Scottish peasants as well as divines talked about it perpetually. You
remember the good old cottager's grace over her porridge. I cannot
repeat it in pure Doric, but it ran like this:—" Lord, I thank thee for
the porridge, I thank thee for an appetite for the porridge, but I thank
thee most of all that I have a covenant right to the porridge." Only
think of that, a covenant right to the porridge. Does not the promise
say, " Thy bread shall be given thee and thy waters shall be sure?" God
has given to his children a covenant right to be fed in this life with
daily bread, else we might not pray for it. In the day in which the
Lord put us into the covenant by personal experience, he said, " No
good thing will I withhold from them that walk uprightly," and consequently he promised the porridge, and any other provision which he
judged to be " food convenient for us." If we are in poverty it sweetens
everything if we can feel that our food and raiment must come to us,
for the Lord has covenanted to supply all our needs. We pray the Lord,
" Give us this day *our* daily bread." How came it to be *ours?* Why,
because it was guaranteed us in the covenant: covenant provision has
made it ours, and therefore we may ask for it as ours. Have I any right
to ask God for what is not mine in Christ Jesus? As sinners we sue for
mercy and crave for the sake of grace; but when we come to be children,
we can also appeal to other attributes, and especially to faithfulness,

which is a great covenant security. We can now say, " My Father,
since I am thy child I am an heir of God, joint-heir with Jesus Christ;
therefore give me of the fulness which thou hast treasured up in him on
my behalf." The upper springs are ours, and the nether springs shall
not be withheld.

> " He who hath made my heaven secure
>   Will here all good provide.
>   Since Christ is rich, can I be poor ?
>   What can I want beside ? "

Returning to the text, from which I have diverged a little: these
inquirers become covenanters, for we read that *they seek to be joined
unto the Lord*—" Come and let us join ourselves to the Lord." The
mischief of our fallen state arose from our trying to be distinct and
independent of our God. The younger son said, " Give me the portion
of goods that falleth to me." See, he has received his share in ready-
money and off he goes to the far country. What does he do when he
penitently returns? Why he joins himself to his Father. Nothing in
the house is his, he has had his portion of goods long ago ; but he lives
at home because he is one with his Father, and cannot be shut out from
the house of his Father. He is in communion with his Father, and so
he is a partaker of all his Father's goods. O that word, " joint-heirs " !
What security and sweetness dwell in it. It is a grand thing to be an
heir of God, but it makes it so much surer to be " joint-heirs with
Christ." We have such fellowship with Jesus, that we share all that
Jesus has : our title to all good things lies in Jesus, and in our being
one with him. " Come and let us join ourselves to the Lord." Now,
dear hearts, are you willing to be one with Christ, and so to be one
with the Father? Is not this the one thing you long for, that you may
be so at peace with God through Jesus Christ that you may be joined
with him? You are a right-hearted seeker, in fact, you have found the
Lord already, or else you would not find it in your heart to use such an
expression as seeking to be joined unto the Lord.

Next, notice *for how long a time this covenant is to be made*—" Let
us join ourselves to the Lord in a perpetual covenant." In our English
army of late they have enlisted "short time " men. A good brother came
to join the church last week who is in the Reserve, and I said to him,
" You are not coming to unite with us for two sixes, the first six with
the colours and the other six as a reserve man,—you have come, I hope,
to fight under the colours as long as life lasts." " Ay, sir," he said, " I
give myself up to the Lord for ever." No salvation is possible except
that which saves the soul for ever. It must be an everlasting salvation or no salvation. And yet some professors try to be off and on
with God : they are wonderfully good on the Sabbath ; but they slip
their regimentals off on Sunday night, and there is no accounting for
them during the week. I do not know where these double-faced people
are to be found on a Monday night, but I fear they are up to no good. These
chameleons change their colour according to the light they are in. Their
religion is a sort of play-acting, a kind of masquerade. Beware of a
religion which you can put on and off. In the Capitol at Rome I saw one
of the Roman Emperors, and I remembered well his majesty's brutal

text describes *a serious plight*, mentions *a special interference*, and
s *a singular reason* for that interference. When we have spoken
ach of these, we shall close by giving you *a suitable advice*. May
irit of God bless the discourse.

First, then, taken in connection with the verses which precede it,
t describes a class of men and women who are in A SERIOUS PLIGHT.
se people suffer under two evils. First, they are sick through
r they need to have their health restored; and, secondly, they are
ed for their sin by the chastisements of the Lord, so that there is
ity for their wound to be healed. They are afflicted with the
per of evil, and also by dismal disquietude of conscience. They
roken God's commandments, and now their own bones are broken.
have grieved their God, and their God is grieving them.

us carefully look at the first part of their sad condition: *they
k with sin*, and that disease is one which, according to the fifth and
verses, brings great pain and trouble into men's minds when they
to their senses, and know their condition before God. At first,
y numbs the conscience, and its tendency is to sear it as with a
on. It may be compared to a stroke of paralysis, which, when it
pon a man's body, takes away from him all pain, and makes him
dead in the parts which it affects. Sin paralyzes the consciences
ungodly. At first they do not know it to be an exceeding great
they trifle with it; it is a basilisk, whose very look is poisonous,
t they sport with it as though it were a bird. It is a deadly
e, causing the soul to be full of leprosy, and yet men will exhibit
rks of it as though they were the spots of God's children. But
while, when the conscience is awakened by judgments, or aroused
d's word, then this disease ceases to stupefy, and becomes the
of intolerable pain. Read these words: "For thus saith the
We have heard a voice of trembling, of fear, and not of peace.
now, and see whether a man doth travail with child? wherefore
ee every man with his hands on his loins, as a woman in travail,
faces are turned into paleness?" The fiercest form of bodily
here selected as the type of the anguish caused by strong con-
of sin. Believe me, there can be nothing in the world so terrible
feel sin without feeling pardon; to know yourself to be guilty, and
know how to get the guilt removed. Conviction without faith is
rthly hell. Brethren, you have many of you felt it, and you know
eath itself, if there were no hereafter, would be preferable to life
the pressure of guilt. "The spirit of a man will sustain his
ity; but a wounded spirit who can bear?" Sin is a disease of
irit, which embitters the central fountain and wellspring of our
ll gall and wormwood flavour all things. Sin felt and known is a
le kill-joy: as the Simoom of the desert smites the caravan with
, and as the Sirocco withers every herb of the field, so does a sense
dry up peace, blast hope, and utterly kill delight. If those who
ne are oppressed with the disorder of sin, they will rejoice greatly
ey dwell upon the words of our text, "I will restore health unto
and I will heal thee of thy wounds."

is disease, moreover, is not only exceedingly painful when the con-
e is smarting, but it is altogether incurable, so far as any human

---

countenance; soon after I saw the gentleman looking very different; I should not have recognized his imperial highness at all if it had not been for the name: the fact is, they had put another wig on him. Oddly enough, certain of those statues are so carved that a series of stone head-dresses can be put upon them; and this makes a mighty difference in their appearance. I am afraid that to some professors their religion is a wig, which so wonderfully changes them when they put it on or take it off, that you would not think they were the same people. A real man of God has his religion interwoven into the warp and woof of his being; he could not be other than he is whatever his circumstances might be. Said one, "I hate such a man; he shall not come to my house; for I hear he is never ten minutes in a room but he begins to talk about religion." Such a man the world may hate; but such a man the Lord loves. Oh, that our godliness may be as our eyes, our mouth, our countenance, our heart, our life, never to be parted with, but for ever essential to ourselves. May we now join ourselves to the Lord in a *perpetual* covenant! The covenant of life requires a life-long covenant. We do not take grace upon a terminable lease; it is an entailed inheritance, an immortal, eternal possession.

Note, further, that this joining to God these covenanters intended to carry out in a most solemn way; "let us join ourselves to the Lord in a perpetual"—agreement? or promise? No. "*Covenant*" is the word. It is a profitable thing for the soul to covenant with God. Dr. Doddridge gives a form of personal covenant in his "Rise and Progress," and I have been told that some persons have written it out and even signed it with their blood. I believe that such a formal transaction may lead a soul into bondage. This covenanting is not to be performed quite so literally, but that it should be done *really* I do believe. That a man should give himself to the Lord in set and solemn form at some time in his life I believe to be a great help to his after persever-ance; and if he will renew his covenant every now and then it may greatly help to his keeping it. In the ordinance of baptism we have the best visible setting forth of that covenant. Circumcision set forth the taking away of the filth of the flesh; but baptism sets forth the death and burial of the flesh itself; we see in it the emblem of our death and burial with our Lord. The believer thereby says, "Now I am come to an end of my old life, for I am dead and buried," and he becomes henceforth as one who has risen with Christ, to walk in newness of life. By that solemn act the believer has covenanted that Christ shall be his life, and that his old self, being dead and buried, shall no more rule and reign. I have known some believers, and I think they did wisely, take a part of a day for the special object of giving themselves anew to the Lord. They have said, "Lord, I do this day, as a poor sinner, solemnly put my trust in thy word, and in thy Son, and in his atoning sacrifice; and, doing this, I feel that I am not my own, for I am bought with a price; and I now ask for grace that from this day forward I may be wholly thine. Not only I, but my wife, and my children, and my substance, and all that I have I give to thee, my Lord, admitting that nothing which I have was ever mine, but always thine. I pray that thou wilt be my God for ever and ever, and be my guide even unto death, and that after death thou wilt receive me to glory." Such a covenant as this will bear to be looked back upon and repeated. You can gladly say—

> "High heaven that heard my solemn vow,
> That vow renewed shall daily hear,
> Till in life's latest hour I bow,
> And bless in death a bond so dear."

You are coming to the Lord rightly, my dear friend, if you are yielding body, soul, and spirit unto him to be his for ever. There is no fear about your safety when you join yourself unto the Lord by a perpetual covenant.

One word more remains to be spoken: those who came mourning and inquiring, when they became covenanters felt that they had a nature very apt to forgetfulness of good things, and so a part of what they desired in their covenanting with God was "a perpetual covenant *that shall not be forgotten.*" God will never forget, yet may you pray, "Lord, remember me when thou comest into thy kingdom." The fear is lest *you* should forget. What is your view of that possibility? Would it not be terrible? Think it over, and say, "If I should ever forget the Lord Jesus, if I should ever forget my obligations for his great salvation, and for the good hope of eternal life which he has given me, it would be infamous! God grant I may die sooner than deny my Lord!" Whither could we go for comfort if we had forgotten our God? What would remain for us but everlasting despair? Let us therefore pray the Lord that it may be a perpetual covenant, that shall never, never, not even for an hour be forgotten. Ask the Lord to write this covenant upon the fleshy tablets of your heart, that it may be there for ever. O Zion, if I forget thee let my right hand forget her cunning! Sooner than I should forget thee, O my God, suffer me speedily to die! Let me not live to become so false, so wicked, as under stress of infirmity or temptation, even for a moment to turn aside from thee! Beloved brother, take hold on Christ this morning with a renewed grip, and say, "Lord, thou knowest all things; thou knowest that I love thee: suffer me not to forsake thee. Hold thou me up, and I shall be safe. I would be thine living, thine dying, and thine for ever and ever." Thus desiring and pleading, all will be well with you. May the God of the everlasting covenant bless you. Amen.

PORTION OF SCRIPTURE READ BEFORE SERMON—Isaiah lx.

HYMNS FROM "OUR OWN HYMN BOOK"—176, 965, 605.

Metropolitan Taberna

BLESSED PROMISES FOR DYIN

A Sermon

DELIVERED ON LORD'S-DAY MORNING, DEC

C. H. SPURGEC

AT THE METROPOLITAN TABERNACLE,

"For I will restore health unto thee, and I will heal th Lord; because they called thee an Outcast, saying, This is after."—Jeremiah xxx. 17.

THE promises of this verse will be exceedingly their personal need of them; but those who boas sick nor wounded will take no interest in this co who are charmed with themselves will see no Physician. I have heard of certain hungry tra the wilderness, and came upon a bag which they yield them a seasonable supply of food. The door by starvation, and eagerly opened the bag, nothing but pearls, which they poured out co desert sand as things of no use to them. E hungering and thirsting after the things of this are taken up with carnal appetites, carnal sorro will reject as worthless the priceless promises o that they are of no immediate use to him. another sort, let his heart hanker after unsearch pine for eternal love, then are his views of thing to buy the pearl of great price he would glad Oh, you that are sick at heart, here is a word fo all grace: Jehovah Rophi himself says, "I w thee." Oh, you that have felt the shafts of G souls, here is a word from him who healeth th bindeth up their wounds: "I will heal thee of Lord." Here is music for your ear, honey for for your heart. But if you feel you have no no weakness and no spiritual need, then the wor will pass over your ear as a meaningless sound, Neither shall we wonder at this, for the who physician, but they that are sick: healthy me medicines and remedies, for they feel no need my audience, but improves it; for, while it dri it draws the needy to a more careful listening.

Nos. 1,753-4.

skill is concerned. We are told in the twelfth verse, " Thus saith the Lord, Thy bruise is incurable, and thy wound is grievous." It would be much easier to heal a man's body of leprosy than to heal a man's soul of sin. It is a disease which takes such fast hold upon the nature, and so entirely impregnates the mind with a deadly virus, that it abides in the very essence of manhood, and can only be removed by a miracle. It is far more possible for the Ethiopian to change his skin, or the leopard his spots, than for a man who is accustomed to do evil to learn to do well; especially to love to do well, and find a pleasure in it. If this were a matter of custom, or practice only, it might be fought with and overcome, but inasmuch as it is a matter of nature, and the whole head is sick, and the whole heart faint with it, no human power can possibly effect a cure. Some have wept over sin, but tears are a poor lotion for a disease which penetrates to the core of the heart. Others have shut themselves up alone, and retired as hermits to escape from evil by solitude; but they have found no secret place which evil could not enter. Whither shall we flee from the presence of sin? When it has once laid hold upon our nature, if we take the wings of the morning, and fly to the uttermost parts of the sea, our depravity will still be with us. If we cover ourselves with multiplied midnights, sin will only be the more completely in its element. Where can we fly, and what can we do, to escape from this terrible force, this ever-present mischief? This poison has penetrated all our nature, so that we must confess :—

> " It lies not in a single part,
> But through my frame is spread;
> A burning fever in my heart,
> A palsy in my head."

Neither body, soul, nor spirit is free from its taint. At all hours it is our curse and plague; over all places it casts its defiling influence; in all duties it injures and hinders us. To those who know this there is a music sweeter than marriage-bells in these words,—" I will restore health unto thee, and I will heal thee of thy wounds." The incurable shall be cured; the insatiable malady shall be stayed.

Further on we are told that this disease is one for which there is neither surgeon nor medicine:—" There is none to plead thy cause, that thou mayst be bound up: thou hast no healing medicines. Why criest thou for thine affliction? thy sorrow is incurable for the multitude of thine iniquity: because thy sins were increased, I have done these things unto thee." What a disease this must be for which there is no physician, since the direst forms of human disease have found each one its specialist, who has at least attempted to perform a cure; but here is a sickness for which there is no physician. Bad men do not pretend to heal the disease of sin; they do not even consider it to be a disease, and they care not to make men holy. Good men are very far from thinking that they can conquer sin in others, for they cannot even overcome it in themselves, and therefore they never set up to be physicians in such a case as this. No human hand can bind up this wound: no earthly skill can touch this deeply-seated complaint: it is past all mortal surgery. Yea, and the prophet adds, " There is no healing medicine": none has ever been known. The question is often asked, " Is there no balm in Gilead? Is there no physician there?"

The answer to that question is, No, there is no balm in Gilead;
there never was. Balms for soul-mischiefs do not grow in the fields
of Gilead, nay, nor on Carmel and Sharon. Physicians of sin-sick souls
are not to be found beneath the skies : the other question proves it,—
"Why then is not the health of the daughter of my people recovered?"
If there were balms and physicians for her disease she would have been
healed long ago ; but neither salve nor surgeon can be found among the
sons of men. Search through all the lore of the ancients, and you
shall discover no remedy for sin: examine all the inventions of the
moderns, and you shall light upon no physic for the love of evil.
Nothing can touch it save one thing, and that is not of earth. The
Lord from heaven, upon the cross, did bleed a balm that can cure this
wound, and by his death he was the death of this disease; but apart
from him no one can bind up our wounds, or mollify them with ointment.
He is the one and only good Samaritan for the spiritually bruised: he
alone hath wine and oil suitable for our wounds. Are my hearers
brought to feel this? Are there any here who have not yet found out
God's way of salvation, but still are well aware that they have none of
their own? I am thankful you are brought so far; may you not be
long before you go much further, and find the Lord Jesus able to heal
you of every disease. You are for ever lost unless you go to him, for
your sickness is unto death, your wound is breeding corruption, and none
can give you health for your sickness, or healing for your wound, but
the Lord Jesus, who is able to save unto the uttermost.

> "When wounded sore the stricken soul,
>   Lies bleeding and unbound,
> One only hand, a pierced hand,
>   Can salve the sinner's wound."

This disease is exceeding dangerous, because it insinuates itself into
the heart, and takes up its abode there. If apparently it be for a time
driven out, it returns when we least expect it. Like the tree which is
cut down, it will sprout again; at the scent of water it will bud. It
annoys us in every way; it hinders our aspirations, for how to perform
that which we would, we find not; it robs us of comfort, and makes us
groan, being burdened; it enters into our holiest things, chills our
prayers, freezes our praise, and hampers our usefulness. It is evil,
only evil, and that continually. How gracious is it on God's part, to
pity a creature infected with this vile distemper! How good of him
to regard our iniquity rather as a sickness to be healed than as a crime
to be punished!

I told you of a double mischief in this plight, and the second
mischief is that this person *has been wounded for his sin.* His wounds
are of no common sort, for we are told in the fourteenth verse
that God himself has wounded him. The Lord says, " I have wounded
thee with the wound of an enemy, with the chastisement of a cruel one,
for the multitude of thine iniquity; because thy sins were increased."
God in infinite mercy determines to make the sinner see and feel the
evil consequences of his sin; and in doing this he makes deep wounds,
such as an enemy would give who felt no pity, but only wished to
cause pain. The Lord knows that in this work slightness is of no
avail, and therefore he strikes home, and cuts deep. He does not play

with consciences, but his chastisement is so severe that men think him cruel. There is such a thing as cruel kindness, and the opposite to it is a loving cruelty, a gracious severity. When the Lord brings sin to remembrance, and makes the soul to see what an evil it has committed in transgressing against God, then the wound bleeds, and the heart breaks. You could not tell the blows of our greatest Friend from those of our worst enemy if you only judged by present feeling. Under the Lord's hand the soul is well-nigh driven to despair. Vain hopes are dashed in pieces like potsherds, false lights are quenched in gloom, and joys are ground to powder. It is in love that the Lord thus judges us, and chastens us that we should not be condemned with the world. The smart is sharp, but salutary. The Lord wounds that he may heal, he kills that he may make alive. His storms wreck us upon the rock of salvation, and his tempests drive us into the fair havens of lowly faith. Happy are the men who are thus made unhappy; but this for the present they know not, and therefore they need the promise, "I will heal thee of thy wounds, saith the Lord."

The blows are not only on the conscience, but when God is in earnest to make men flee from their sins, he will smite them anywhere and everywhere. He takes away the delight of their eyes with a stroke; the child, the husband, the wife, or the friend is laid low; for the Lord will fill our houses with mourning sooner than leave us in carnal security. He takes away the silver and the gold, for he will make us beggars sooner than leave us to worship the idols of the world. The oil vat is burst, and the barn is burned; for he will not permit us to bury our souls in earthly things. He brings the body into sickness, and the mind into distress; health departs, and the robust worker is stretched upon a sick bed; he groans and moans under the hand of God. God is in all this smiting most cruelly, according to the short-sighted judgment of men; but in very truth he is tender and gracious, and is working out the eternal good of the sufferers. Like as the surgeon uses a sharp knife, and cuts far down into the flesh when he would eradicate some deadly ulcer, even so does the Lord in true severity wound the heart until he gets at the roots of our self-love.

Surely, a man is in a wretched plight when he is diseased with sin, and then bruised by divine chastisement, but, it may be, he adds to this wounds inflicted by himself, for falls into sin are falls that break the bones. Many a man will have to go limping to his grave because of his transgressions. Doubtless David did so: he never recovered what he lost when he sinned with Bathsheba. Much pain comes of broken bones, especially when you have broken them yourself, through your own folly. When you cannot trace an affliction to second causes, nor look upon it as an affliction from God, but when you hear conscience whisper, "Thou hast procured this unto thyself," then the wormwood is mixed with gall, and the suffering knows no solace. If thou be poor because thou hast squandered thy substance; if thou be sick because thou hast indulged thine appetites or passions, who can say thee a word of cheer? If thou hast lost godly friends whom thou didst once despise, if thou art by sore sickness prevented from going up to the house of the Lord, which was formerly a weariness to thee, is there not a special sharpness in thy grief?

Now, put these three things together—bones broken through thine own sin, God dealing with thee in the way of chastisement, and sin felt in the conscience like a grievous disease ; and I think I said not too much when I described the soul as in a serious plight. God help the man who is in such a case, for none else can. The comfort is that the Lord Jesus does help such, for so his gracious promise runs, " I will restore health unto thee, and I will heal thee of thy wounds." May the Holy Spirit bless this first head to many of you !

II.   Our second consideration fitly falls under the title of A SPECIAL INTERFERENCE.   The poor creature is in desperate dolour; but the God of pitying love comes in, and I beg you to notice the result.

This interference is, first of all, *divine*.   "*I* will restore health unto thee, and *I* will heal thee of thy wounds."   The infinite Jehovah alone can speak with that grand *Ego*, and say, " I will," and again, " I will." No human physician who was worthy of the name would speak thus. He would humbly say, " I will attempt to give you health ; I will endeavour to heal your wounds ; " but the Lord speaks with the positiveness of omnipotence, for he has the power to make good his words.   All others fail; but the Lord will do it.   Thou canst not heal thyself ; but the Lord will heal thee.   And who is this great " I " that speaks so exceeding boldly ?   It is none other than he that made the heavens and the earth, and sustaineth all things by the power of his hand ; it is the " I AM," the everlasting Jehovah, whose word has boundless power in it.   He appears in the moment of man's extremity, and when there is no helper, his own arm brings salvation.   Blessed be the Lord who forgiveth all our iniquities, who healeth all our diseases.

Note, that since this interference is divine it is *effectual*.   The Lord effectually heals all those on whom he lays his hand.   How could it be otherwise ?   What can baffle the Lord ?   Can anything perplex infinite wisdom?   Is anything difficult to almighty power?   " If it be marvellous in thine eyes, should it also be marvellous in mine eyes ? saith the Lord of hosts."   He speaks, and it is done ; he commands, and it stands fast.   When therefore God says, " I will restore health unto thee," health will visit the wretch who lies pining at death's door. When he says, " I will heal thee of thy wounds," the deep cuts and gashes are closed up at once.   Glory be to the name of the Beloved Physician!   Poor, troubled heart, where are you this morning ?   Do you say, " Nobody can cure me ? "   Thou sayest truly if thou wilt make one exception, and that exception is thy God.   I tell thee he can heal thee now, so that the bones which he has broken shall rejoice.   He can take away this disease of yours, and give you back wholeness as though your flesh were the flesh of a little child, and you shall be clean ; only have faith in him.   He that made you can make you anew.   Do you believe this?

Observe that this interposition performs a work which is most *complete*, for it meets the two-fold mischief.   " I will restore health unto thee : "—That is a great matter.   When a man grows healthy he can bear a wound or two without being too much overburdened ; but God does nothing by halves, for having restored health he then adds " I will heal thee of thy wounds."   He will heal both disease and wound.   There is no condition into which the heart can sink but what the Lord is equal to the raising of it from the depths. If thou art in the borders of Hades, and on the verge of hell, yet as long as thou hast not passed the iron gates of death thy salvation is possible with God, ay, simple and sure with God if thou wilt but trust in his well-beloved Son. What a mercy it is that the Redeemer does not half save us, and leave us to finish the work ! He does not commence and do a part of the cure, and then say, " I must leave nature to work out the rest." No ; the cure is absolutely complete : " I will restore health unto thee, and I will heal thee of thy wounds." Oh, sick and wounded one, go just as thou art, and throw thyself at Jesus' feet, and say unto him, " Keep thy promise, Lord : I am come with thy word in my mouth and in my heart ; be as good as thine own declaration, and restore health to *me*, and heal *me* of my wounds."

Notice, too, how sovereignly *free* this promise is. It does not say, "I will restore health unto thee if——." No, there is no "if ;" and there is no mention of a fee. Here is healing for nothing. Jesus comes to give us health without money and without price, without pence or penance, without labour or merit. I admire, for my part, the splendid, unconditional character of this promise made by Jehovah to his covenant people. Its tenor is, " I will." There is no sort of condition or demand. " Perhaps " is banished: "peradventure" is not so much as hinted at. Come, poor guilty soul, thou who hast no claim on God, come and plead the divine, "I will." Thou canst not have a better hand-hold of the covenant angel in wrestling with him. God's promise is an unconquerable plea : to use it well will put thee among the invincibles. Come then, I pray thee, and just say, " Lord, it is so written in thy word ; therefore, write it, I pray thee, on the page of my experience."

Notice that, although it be thus free and unconditional, yet it is now a matter of covenant *certainty*, for God has made the promise, and he cannot turn from it. To every guilty sinner, conscious of his guilt, who will come and confess it before God, this promise is made to-day, " I will restore health unto thee, and I will heal thee of thy wounds." To you, dear fellow-sinners, as much as unto Judah and Israel of old, is this promise sent : if you will bring your sorrow and your sin before the eye of the all-merciful Father, and plead the precious blood of Christ. No sick one shall be shut out from this hospital of love. If, like Job, the sinner is covered with sores from head to foot; and if he only feels at home when he sits on a dunghill, and begins to scrape himself with a potsherd, yet the Lord says, " I will heal thee." If thy sin has made thee loathsome to thyself, till thou criest out with one of old, " My wounds stink and are corrupt," still is the Lord Jesus able to save thee; nay, he promises to save thee. Grasp thou the promise by the hand of faith, and thou shalt be made whole. All manner of sin and of iniquity shall be forgiven unto men; ay, and all tendencies to sin, and all taint of iniquity, shall be removed from men if they will trust the power and promise of the faithful Lord. Sinner, his touch can make thee clean at once. Trust thou that hand, I say, and the miracle shall be wrought.

III. But now I come to a third point, which is this—A SINGULAR REASON. " I will restore health unto thee, and I will heal thee of thy wounds, saith the Lord; *because they called thee an Outcast, saying, This is Zion, whom no man seeketh after.*" God never finds a reason for mercy in the sinner's supposed goodness. He looked upon this sick one, and he could not find a redeeming feature of beauty by which the blessing might be won; therefore, he did not look at the sinner at all, except to pity him. Is it not a singular thing that the Lord will sooner *find a reason for mercy in the lying mouths of the wicked* than he will attempt to find it in the supposed righteousness of those who count themselves righteous? He says not " Because you were holy," or " Because you had good desires;" but " Because *they* called thee an outcast." Who were they? Why, the jeerers, and mockers, and blasphemers: the Lord actually transforms the venom of asps, which was under the tongues of the malicious, into a reason for his mercy. This clearly shows how God hates the very notion of man's merit; but it also shows that he will find a reason for mercy somewhere. They called poor Zion, when God seemed to have given her up, " an outcast ;" they said, " Nobody goes to Jerusalem now : there was a temple there once, but it is a wretched heap now : princes dwelt there once, but now the inhabitants of Jerusalem are a set of beggars; no man cares to mix with them; they are the world's castaways." *This roused the Lord's pity.* " Oh," he said, " has it come to this? Have they dared to call my beloved ' an outcast,' and say that no man seeketh after her? Then I will seek her, and heal her, and restore her, for I cannot endure such tauntings." Now, if there is a poor sinner in the world, upon whom other sinners, who are just as bad in their heart, begin to vent their scorn, and say, " She is an outcast; " then the God of mercy seems to say, " Who are you that you should talk like this? You are as vile yourselves, and yet you dare to look down upon this poor, selected one, as if she were so much worse than you. Therefore, I will save that despised one, and will have mercy upon the rejected." God's tastes and man's differ very much. Whom man despises God delights in ; and whom man delights in God despises. It often happens that when a transgressor has been put out of the synagogue Jesus finds him directly. When certain offenders happen to transgress in a particular way, which particular way is scouted and denounced by the bulk of ungodly people, then like so many hounds they unite to hunt the wretched being to death, but the Lord Jehovah interposes to save; as if he would say, " Why do you this, ye hypocrites? Wherefore do ye denounce those whose sins are no viler than your own ? " I believe the Lord Jesus often stands as he did with the woman taken in adultery, and cries, " He that is without sin among you, let him first cast a stone at her." Still he convicts men in their consciences, and still in sweetness of mercy turns to the poor, condemned one, and says, " Neither do I condemn thee: go, and sin no more." Where are you, poor hunted sinner? You are somewhere or other in the crowd, I know. They told you yesterday that they would never associate with you any more. You do not deny your wickedness: still, it is not for your fellow-sinners to be hard with you, for they are not your judges. By faith take this promise to thyself: " I will restore health unto thee, because they called thee an outcast." Thou mayest get a good deal out of it if thou hast but faith to do so. Now that the world has cast thee out, the church shall take thee in: now that the devil seems tired of thee, Christ shall begin with thee: now that the door is shut against thee by those who once delighted in thee, Christ's door is open to receive thee. "Because they called thee an outcast" *he* calls thee to approach him.

But this is not the full meaning of the text. I think it means that *God's jealousy is aroused* against those who despise his people, and speak ill of them. Whatever Zion might be, it was still the palace of God: however guilty Jerusalem might have become, it was still the holy city, the dwelling-place of the great King. The Lord, for a while, when he was very angry with Jerusalem, on account of its great *iniquity*, gave it over to the destroyer, and it was laid waste and burned with fire; but when he heard the heathen everywhere saying, "As for those people, they are outcasts, and as for that city, no man seeks after it:" then the Lord said to himself, "But they are my people, and I will not have them called outcasts; and this is my city, and I will not have it said that no man seeks after it. Her name shall be called Hephzibah, and her land Beulah, for the Lord delighteth in her." His love burned like fire, and kindled into a flame of jealousy, and he said, "I will restore health to her, and shut the mouths of her adversaries." It is one thing for a father to chasten his boy; but if, when he is out in the streets, a stranger begins to kick him, his father declares that it shall not be. He arouses himself to defend his child, the same child that just now he smote so heavily. A man might complain of his wife if she had vexed him, but I suppose the quickest way to put him in good temper with her would be for somebody else to find fault with her. "What business is that of yours?" says he; "I will not have my wife abused: no man shall speak against her in my presence." That is a fair parallel to the case of our God. He will chasten his people in measure, but the moment that their enemies call them outcasts he turns his anger another way and releases his people. Oh, how blessedly does good come out of evil! How graciously he causes the wrath of man to praise him. He restores health to Zion, and heals her wounds because she is called an outcast.

I always have great hope for the entire Church of Christ when the ungodly begin to rail and revile. They say, "Christianity has lost its power; the Church is an old effete institution; no people of culture and intelligence keep to the old book and the old faith. The religion of Jesus is a by-word and a proverb among learned men." Therefore, I am confident that God will return to his Church, and magnify his truth. As surely as he lives he will give us bright days and glorious days, because they call his true Church an outcast, whom no man seeketh after. I like to read in man's black book, for man's revilings will lead to the speedier fulfilment of God's glorious promises.

> "Let Zion's foes be fill'd with shame;
> Her sons are bless'd of God;
> Though scoffers now despise their name,
> The Lord shall break their rod.

> "Oh, would our God to Zion turn,
> God with salvation clad;
> Then Judah's harps should music learn,
> And Israel be glad."

Appropriate the text personally any of you who have been made to feel that you are outcasts. One said to me the other day, talking of her sin, and of her repentance, "Yet, sir, I am an outcast." That word pierced my heart like a dagger. I said, "Yes, but the Church of Christ was made on purpose to be a home for outcasts: here is a new household for you, new brothers and sisters for you, a new future for you; for now you are one of the solitary ones whom the Lord will set in families."

Some of us were never called outcasts by other people, but we thought ourselves such. I once felt like Cain, as if God had set a mark upon me never to bless me; like an outlaw, condemned, and cast away; but when I reached that point the Lord's mercy revealed itself to me. He seemed to say, "Because thou hast called thyself an outcast, therefore will I restore health unto thee, and I will heal thee of thy wounds."

I should like to say a word that would be comforting to poor hearts that are greatly down-trodden. I do not feel able to preach at all, for I am weak and weary; but I always find when I am weak the Lord says somewhat by me which is just the thing wanted by some poor devil-hunted soul that cannot find rest. I think the Lord puts the trumpet out of order on purpose to draw from it a different note from what it gives when it is in proper condition,—a note that may precisely suit some weary ear that could not hearken to any other sound. May the Holy Spirit cause it to be so now.

IV. I am going to finish in the fourth place, by giving A LITTLE SUITABLE ADVICE. I will suppose that I have those before me who have felt their disease and their wound, and have been healed by the God of mercy. I would recommend them to attend to certain matters. The first thing is, *take care that you live very near your Physician.* I notice that patients come up from the country when they are suffering with serious complaints, and they take lodgings near a medical man who is in high esteem for such cases as theirs. They leave the comforts of home, and let their business go, because life is precious, and they need a helper close at hand. No one blames them for this; in fact we count them wise; let us learn wisdom from their example. Now, the Lord has healed your wound, and restored health to you, therefore abide in him; never leave him, nor live far away from him, for this old disease of yours may break out on a sudden, and it will be well to have the Healer close at hand. It will be best to entertain him constantly beneath your roof, and within your heart; for his presence is the wellspring of health to the soul. Abide perpetually with Christ, and then the sun shall not smite you by day, nor the moon by night: dwelling in the secret place of the Most High, there shall no evil befall you, neither shall any plague come nigh your dwelling. This disease of sin may cause eruptions when we least expect it; when we suppose that the evil leaven will work no more it may suddenly gather force, and the whole body of our nature will be in a ferment with iniquity. The danger is near, abide therefore near your security. Live with him who renews your youth like the eagle's, and restores your soul.

I recommend you often to put yourself under his searching examination. Go to this great Physician, and ask him to look into your hidden parts, to search you, and try you, and see what wicked way may be in you, that he may lead you in the way everlasting. A man may have a deadly disease upon him and scarcely be aware of it, because no skilled person has looked upon him, and observed his symptoms; and in spiritual things this is a common mischief, to which multitudes fall a prey. Invite, therefore, the eyes of the Lord Jesus, for in our most honest searches we miss much, and we are naturally prejudiced in our own favour, so that we are pretty sure to give a verdict on our own side; and this may lead to final and fatal self-delusion. If we intrust the search to him whose eyes are as a flame of fire we shall not be deceived.

I recommend you from personal experience to *consult with this Doctor every day.* It is a wise thing before you go downstairs into the world's tainted atmosphere to take a draught of his *Elexir Vitæ.* in the form of renewed faith in him. I am sure at night it is an admirable thing to purge the soul of all the perilous stuff which has accumulated through the day by full confession and renewed confidence.

Lay bare your case before him; conceal nothing; beg of him to deal with you according to his knowledge of your case. Make a clean breast that Christ may make a sure cure. Conceal no symptom however threatening, but tell him all the truth. He cannot be deceived; do not attempt it, but unbosom every secret thing before his all-surveying gaze. Entreat him to search both thoughts and affections, designs and motives. The ill may gather in secret places unless his discerning eye shall detect the growing danger, and prevent it by immediate action.

Then I should very strongly recommend you always to *obey the prescriptions of the great Healer.* "Whatsoever he saith unto you, do it." Do not follow a part of his orders, and neglect the rest. The Lord Jesus must be received as a whole, or not at all. Say not "This is non-essential;" for such a speech is flat rebellion. I do not believe in any words of our Lord being non-essential. They may not be essential to our salvation, but every word of Christ is essential to our spiritual health; neither can we disregard the least of his precepts without suffering loss through our disobedience. Be very careful that you follow the Lamb whithersoever he goeth; no other kind of walking is safe in such a world as this. Do what he bids you, as he bids you, and it shall be well with you.

Take care also to *exercise great confidence in this Physician.* Rely upon him without stint or question. Your cure is working wondrously when you trust in Jesus heartily. Never doubt the Saviour's power to make you perfectly whole. Our Lord never can be baffled; though all diseases should meet in one person he would overcome them all. Stick to this with unyielding assurance. Let not the devil force you to doubt the boundless power of your Lord. When our Lord Jesus set up to be a Saviour, he understood the work upon which he entered. His is no 'prenticed hand. He has never had a failure yet. Never did a soul trust him for salvation and remain unsaved; and you shall not be the first to defeat his skill. Trust him with all your heart. There is no cause to doubt. Distrust is what you have to fear; faith is your strength.

When you are healed, as I trust you are already, *speak well of your Benefactor.* Make a point of going round to your neighbours, if you find them sick, and telling them how you have been healed; thus will you make to your Lord a name of honour and renown. Tell out among all men what the Lord has done for you. I know you can tell them that story though you are no orator. When you were restored from sickness the other day, you were quite able to inform your friends as to that new medicine which acted like a charm, and you found a tongue to speak well of your doctor; and I am sure you have ability enough to declare the wonderful works of the Lord in your case. "Oh, but I could not embellish the tale!" Do not attempt to embellish it; for that would only spoil it. Tell the story as simply as possible. I think it is of Mr. Cecil that I have read the following incident. A friend came from some distance to inform him of a medicine which was to relieve him of his disorder. This friend told him all about it, and having done so, entered into conversation upon the current matters of the day. The result was that Mr. Cecil was greatly interested in the talk, and when his friend was gone, he quite forgot every ingredient of the wonderful medicine. Beware of allowing the many things to drive the one thing needful out of your friend's mind. When we preach fine sermons our hearers say, "That was prettily put. They do not so much notice what we taught as how we taught it; and this is a great evil. Even so if you go and talk about your salvation to your neighbour, and narrate it eloquently, she will say, "Mrs. So-and-so has been here, and told me about her conversion in such beautiful language; I do not know that I ever heard such elegant sentences; it was most delightful to hear her." What did she say? "I do not know what she said, but it was very beautiful." Thus many a sermon or Sunday-school address is overlaid and buried under its own robes. Pity that those we seek to bless should be more taken up with our pretty words than with our adorable Master. I hope I have not this morning fallen into the evil which I lament. Lest I should have done so in any measure I would make my text my banner, and display it again. The Lord has said, "I will restore health unto thee, and heal thee of thy wounds." I believed that word when I was sick and wounded, and "the Lord was ready to save me: therefore we will sing my songs to the stringed instruments all the days of our life in the house of the Lord."

PORTION OF SCRIPTURE READ BEFORE SERMON—Jeremiah xxx.

HYMNS FROM "OUR OWN HYMN BOOK"—103 (Part I.), 472, 475.

THE BLIND MAN'S EYES OPENED; OR, PRACTICAL CHRISTIANITY.

A Sermon

DELIVERED ON LORD'S-DAY EVENING, AUGUST 12TH, 1883, BY

C. H. SPURGEON,

AT EXETER-HALL.

"Jesus answered, Neither hath this man sinned, nor his parents: but that the works of God should be made manifest in him. I must work the works of him that sent me, while it is day: the night cometh, when no man can work.—John ix. 3, 4.

OBSERVE, dear friends, how little disconcerted our Lord Jesus Christ was by the most violent opposition of his enemies. The Jews took up stones to stone him, and he hid himself from them; but almost the moment after, when he had passed, perhaps, through a single court, and was sufficiently out of range to be unobserved of them, he stood still and fixed his eyes upon a blind beggar who had been sitting near the temple gate. I am afraid that the most of us would have had no heart to help even the most needy while ourselves escaping from a shower of stones; and if we had attempted the work, moved by supreme compassion, we should have gone about it blunderingly, in a great hurry, and certainly should not have talked calmly and wisely, as the Saviour did when he answered his disciples' question, and went on to discourse with them. One of the things worthy to be noticed in our Lord's character is his wonderful quiet of spirit, especially his marvellous calmness in the presence of those who misjudged, and insulted, and slandered him. He is reviled often, but never ruffled; he is in deaths oft, but always full of life. No doubt he felt keenly all the contradictions of sinners against himself, for in a passage in the Psalms which refers to the Messiah we read, "Reproach hath broken my heart;" yet the Lord Jesus did not permit his feelings to overcome him, he was quiet and self-possessed, acting with a profound disregard of the calumnies and assaults of his bitter enemies.

One reason, I take it, for his being so self-contained was that he was *never elated by the praise of men*. Take my word for it, for I know it, that if you ever allow yourself to be pleased by those who speak well of you, to that extent you will be capable of being grieved by those who speak ill of you. But if you have learned (and it is a long lesson for the most of us) that you are not the servant of men, but of God, and that therefore you will not live upon the breath of men's nostrils if they praise you, and you will not die if they denounce you—then you will be strong, and show that you have come to the stature of a man in Christ Jesus. If the great Master's head had been turned by the hosannas of the multitude, then his heart would have sunk within him when they cried, " Crucify him, crucify him." But he was neither lifted up nor cast down by men: he committed himself unto no man because he knew what was in man.

The innermost reason for this quiet of heart was *his unbroken communion with the Father.* Jesus dwelt apart, for he lived with God : the Son of man who came down from heaven still dwelt in heaven, serenely patient because he was raised above earthly things in the holy contemplations of his perfect mind. Because his heart was with his Father, the Father made him strong to bear anything that might come from men. Oh, that we all could wear this armour of light, the celestial panoply of communion with the High Eternal One. Then we should not be afraid of evil tidings, or of evil occurrences, for our hearts would be fixed on the sure rock of Jehovah's unchanging love.

There was perhaps another reason for our Saviour's wonderful composure when he was attacked with stones, namely, that *his heart was so set upon his work* that he could not be turned away from it whatever the unbelieving Jews might do. The ruling passion bore him on through danger and suffering, and made him calmly defy all opposition. He had come into the world to bless men, and he must bless men. The Jews might oppose him for this reason and for that, but they could not turn the current of his soul from the river-bed of mercy along which it rushed like a torrent. He *must* do good to the suffering and the poor, he cannot help it; his face is set like a flint towards his life-work. It had become his meat and his drink to do the will of him that sent him; and so, when they took up stones, although he withdrew himself a little, yet as he only wished to preserve his life to do good, he returned to his life-work without a moment's delay. Stones cannot drive him from his gracious pursuits. As we have seen a parent bird, chased away a moment from its nest, return to it the instant the intruder had withdrawn, so do we see our Lord come back to his holy work almost before he is out of the sight of his would-be murderers. Yonder sits a blind man, and Jesus is at once at his side to heal him. They will overtake thee, O Christ ! They will seek to slay thee ! There are more stones in their cruel hands. Thy haters hurl their missiles fiercely, and they will be upon thee in a moment ! What cares he for that ? No craven spirit can make him overlook an occasion for glorifying the Father. That blind man must be attended to, and at all hazards he stops to deal with him in love. If you and I become completely taken up with zeal for God, and with the desire to win souls then nothing will daunt us. We shall bear anything, and not seem to have anything to bear; we shall hear slander as though we heard it not, and endure hardship as though there were none to endure. As an arrow from a bow, shot by an archer strong, defies the opposing wind, and speeds forward to the white of the target, so shall we fly forward towards the great object of our compassionate ambition. Happy is that man whom God has launched like a thunderbolt from his hand, who must go on and fulfil his destiny; happy that it is his vocation to bring sinners to the Saviour's feet. O blessed Spirit, lift us up to dwell in God, and so to sympathize with his fatherly compassion that we may heed neither stones, nor sneers, nor slanders, but become absorbed in our self-denying service for Jesus' sake !

Let that stand for an introduction. The Saviour in his worst and lowest estate, when near to death, thinks of nothing but the good of men. When cruel eyes are spying him out that they may slay him he has an eye for the poor blind ; there is no stone in his heart towards the sorrowful even when stones are flying past his ears.

I. So I introduce you to-night to the first topic of the present discourse, which is THE WORKER. I give that as a well-earned title to the Lord Jesus Christ. He is *the* worker, the chief worker, the example to all workers. He came into the world, he says, to do the will of him that sent him, and to finish his work. On this occasion, when he is pursued by his enemies, he is still a worker—a wonder-worker with the blind man. There are many in this world who ignore sorrow, who pass by grief, who are deaf to lamentation, and blind to distress. The easiest thing that I know of to do with this wicked, wretched City of London, is not to know much about it. They say that half the world knows not how the other half lives : surely if it did know, it would not live so carelessly as it does, or be quite so cruel as it is. There are sights in this metropolis that might melt a heart of steel, and make a Nabal generous. But it is an easy way of escaping from the exercise of benevolence to shut your eyes and see nothing of the abject misery which is grovelling at your feet. "Where ignorance is bliss it is folly to be wise ; " so said some easy-going ignoramus of old time. If beggars are importunate, then passers-by must be deaf. If sinners are profane, it is a simple matter to stop your ears, and hurry on. If this blind man must needs sit and beg at the gate of the temple, then those who frequent the temple must just slip by as if they were as blind as he. Crowds pass by and take no notice of him. Is not that the way with the multitude to-day ? If you are in trouble—if you are suffering heart-break, do they not ignore you, and go their way to their farm and to their merchandise, though you lie down and starve ? Dives finds it convenient to remain ignorant of the sores of Lazarus. It is not so with Jesus. He has a quick eye to see the blind beggar if he sees nothing else. If he is not enraptured with the massive stones and the beautiful architecture of the temple, yet he fixes his eyes upon a sightless mendicant at the temple gate. He is all eye, all ear, all heart, all hand, where misery is present. My Master is made of tenderness: he melts with love. O true souls who love him, copy him in this, and ever let your hearts be touched with a fellow feeling for the suffering and the sinning.

There are others who, though they see misery do not diminish it by warm sympathy, but increase it by their cold logical conclusions. "Poverty," they say—"yes: well: that of course is brought on by drunkenness and by laziness and by all sorts of vice." I do not say that it is not so in many cases; but I do say that the observation will not help a poor man to become either better or happier: such a hard remark will rather exasperate the hardened than assist the struggling. "Sickness," say some,—"oh, no doubt, a great deal of sickness is caused by wicked habits, neglect of sanitary laws," and so on. This also may be sadly true, but it grates on a sufferer's ear. A very kind and pleasing doctrine to teach in the wards of our hospitals! I would recommend you not to teach it till you are ill yourself, and then perhaps the doctrine may not seem quite so instructive. Even Christ's disciples, when they saw this blind man, thought that there must be something particularly wicked about his father and mother, or something specially vicious about the man himself, which God foresaw, and on account of which he punished him with blindness. The disciples were of the same spirit as Job's three comforters, who, when they saw the patriarch on a dung-hill, bereft of all his children, robbed of all his property, and scraping himself because he was covered with sores, said, "Of course he must be a hypocrite. He must have done something very dreadful, or he would not be so grievously afflicted." The world will still stick to its unfounded belief that if the Tower of Siloam falls upon any men they must be sinners above all sinners upon the face of the earth. A cruel doctrine, a vile doctrine, fit for savages, but not to be mentioned by Christians, who know that whom the Lord loveth he chasteneth, and even his best beloved have been taken away on a sudden. Yet I do see a good deal of this cruel notion about, and if men are in trouble, I hear it muttered, "Well, of course they brought it on themselves." Is this your way of cheering them? Cheap moral observations steeped in vinegar make a poor dish for an invalid. Such censures are a sorry way of helping a lame dog over a stile—nay, it is putting up another stile for him so that he cannot get over it at all. Now I mark this of my Lord—that it is written of him that he "giveth to all men liberally, *and upbraideth not.*" When he fed those thousands in the wilderness it would have been most just if he had said to them, "Why did you all come out into the wilderness, and not bring your provision with you? What have you to do out here without something to eat? You are unthrifty, and deserve to hunger." No, no, he never said a word of the sort, but he fed them, fed them all, and sent them home filled. You and I are not sent into the world to thunder out commandments from the top of Sinai: we are come unto Mount Zion. We are not to go on circuit as if we were judge and hangman rolled into one, to meet all the sorrow and misery in the world with bitter words of censure and condemnation. If we do so how different we are from that blessed Master of ours who says not a word by way of rebuke to those who seek him, but simply feeds the hungry, and heals all those who have need of healing! It is easy to criticize, it is easy to upbraid, but ours should be the higher and nobler task of blessing and saving.

I notice yet again that there are certain others who, if they are not indifferent to sorrow, and do not pitch upon some cruel theory of condemnation, nevertheless speculate a good deal where speculation can be of no practical service. When we get together there are many questions which we like to raise and dispute upon which are of no practical value whatever. There is the question of the origin of evil. That is a fine subject for those who like to chop logic by the week, without making enough chips to light a fire for cold hands to warm at. Such was the subject proposed to the Saviour—foreseen guilt, or hereditary taint—"Who did sin, this man, or his parents?" How far is it right that the sin of parents should, as it often does, fall upon the children?

I could propose to you a great many topics equally profound and curious, but what would be the use ? Yet there are many in the world who are fond of these topics, spinning cobwebs, blowing bubbles, making theories, breaking them, and making more. I wonder whether the world was ever blessed to the extent of a bad farthing by all the theorizings of all the learned men that have ever lived. May they not all be put down under the head of vain janglings ? I would rather create an ounce of help than a ton of theory. It is beautiful to me to see how the Master breaks up the fine speculation which the disciples are setting forth. He says somewhat shortly, " Neither hath this man sinned, nor his parents," and then he spits on the ground, and makes clay, and opens the blind man's eyes. This was work, the other was mere worry. "Father," said a boy, "the cows are in the corn. How ever did they get in ? " " Boy," said the father, " never mind how they got in, let us hurry up and get them out." There is common sense about that practical proceeding. Here are these people sunken in vice, and steeped in poverty. Postpone the inquiries—How did they get into this condition ? What is the origin of moral evil ? How is it transmitted from parent to child ? Answer those questions after the day of judgment, when you will have more light ; but just now the great thing is to see how you and I can get evil out of the world, and how we can lift up the fallen and restore those who have gone astray. Never let us imitate the man in the fable who saw a boy drowning, and there and then lectured him upon the imprudence of bathing out of his depth. No, no, let us land the boy on the bank, dry him and dress him, and then tell him not to go there again, lest a worse thing come unto him.

I say that the Master was no speculator ; he was no spinner of theories ; he was no mere doctrinalist ; but he went to work and healed those that had need of healing. Now, in this, he is the great example for us all in this year of grace. Come, what have we ever *done* to bless our fellow men ? Many of us are followers of Christ, and, oh, how happy we ought to be that we are so ! What have we ever *done* worthy of our high calling ? " Sir, I heard a lecture the other night," says one, " upon the evils of intemperance." Is that all you did ? Has any action come of that brilliant oration and of your careful attention to it ? Did you straightway try to remove this intemperance by your example ? " Well, I shall think of that, sir, one of these days." Meanwhile what is to become of these intemperate ones ? Will not their blood lie at your door ? " I heard the other day," says one, " a very forcible and interesting lecture upon political economy, and I felt that it was a very weighty science, and accounted for much of the poverty you mention." Perhaps so : but political economy in itself is about as hard as brass ; it has no bowels, or heart, or conscience, neither can it make allowance for such things. The political economist is a man of iron, who would be rusted by a tear, and therefore never tolerates the mood of compassion. His science is a rock which will wreck a navy, and remain unmoved by the cries of drowning men and women. It is as the simoon of the desert which withers all it blows upon. It seems to dry up men's souls when they get to be masters of it, or rather are mastered by it. It is a science of stubborn facts, which would not be facts if we were not so brutish. Political economy or no political economy, I come back to my point—What have. you *done* for others? Do let us think of that, and if any of us have been dreaming day after day what we would do "*if*," let us see what we can do now, and, like the Saviour, get to work.

Yet that is not the point which I am driving at. It is this. If Jesus be such a worker, and no theorizer, then what a hope there is to-night for some of us who need his care! Have we fallen? Are we poor? Have we brought ourselves into sorrow and misery? Do not let us look to men or to ourselves. Men will let us starve, and then they will hold a coroner's inquest over our body to find why we dared to die, and so necessitated the paying for a grave and a coffin. They will be sure to make an inquiry after it is all over with us; but if we come to Jesus Christ, he will make no inquiry at all, but receive us and give rest unto our souls. That is a blessed text, "He giveth to all men liberally, *and upbraideth not.*" When the prodigal son came home to his father, according to all propriety, as people would do nowadays, the father should have said to his son, "Well, you have come home, and I am glad to see you, but what a state you are in! How did you get into this condition? Why, you have scarcely a clean rag on your back! How is it you have become so poor? And you are lean and hungry : how comes this about? Where have you been? What have you done? What company have you kept? Where were you a week ago? What were you doing the day before yesterday at seven o'clock?" His father never asked him a single question, but pressed him to his bosom, and knew all about it by instinct. He came as he was, and his father received him as he was. The father seemed, with a kiss, to say, "My boy, bygones are bygones. You were dead but you are alive again ; you were lost but you are found, and I inquire no further." That is just how Jesus Christ is willing to receive penitent sinners to-night. Is there a street-walker here? Come, poor woman, as you are, to your dear Lord and Master, who will cleanse you of your grievous sin. "All manner of sin and blasphemy shall be forgiven." Is there one here who has transgressed against the rules of society, and is pointed at as especially sinful? Yet, come, and welcome, to the Lord Jesus of whom it is written, "This man receiveth sinners, and eateth with them." The physician never thinks it scorn to go among the sick; and Christ never felt it shame that he looks after the guilty and the lost. Nay, write this about his diadem—"The Saviour of sinners, even of the very chief :" he counts this his glory. He will work for you, not chide you. He will not treat you with a dose of theories, and with a host of bitter objurgations ; but he will receive you just as you are into the wounds of his side, and hide you there from the wrath of God. Oh, blessed gospel that I have to preach to you! May the Holy Spirit lead you to embrace it. So much concerning the worker.

II. Now, the second thing is THE WORK-ROOM. Every worker needs a place to work in. Every artist must have a studio. Did Christ have a studio? Yes, he came to do very wonderful works—the works of him that sent him : but what a strange, strange place, the Lord found to do his work in! and yet I do not know that he could have found any other. He resolved to work the works of God, and he selected the fittest place for so doing. One of the works of God is *creation*. If Jesus is to perform this work among men he must find out where something is missing which he can supply by a creating act. Here are two eyes without the proper light-receiving apparatus: here there is room for Jesus to create eyes and sight. He could not have created eyes in my head or in yours had we been present, for eyes are there already, and more eyes would be unsuitable for us. In the blind beggar of the temple there was room for Jesus to produce that which was lacking in the curious mechanism of the eye; the blind eye was, therefore, his workshop. If there were eyeballs, they were completely sightless, and had been so from the man's birth; and this gave the occasion for Jehovah Jesus to say, "Let there be light!" If that man's eyes had been like yours and mine, clear and bright and full of light, there would have been no space for our Lord's divine operation; but since he was still in the darkness which had been about him from his birth, his eyes afforded space wherein the power of the Almighty might be manifested by a work so wonderful that since the world began it had never been heard that any one had opened the eyes of a man who was born blind. The man was blind for this reason —"That the works of God should be made manifest in him." Oh, but that is a blessed thought if you will think it over! Apply it to yourself. If there is anything wanting in you there is room for Christ to work in you. If you are naturally perfect, and there is no fault in you, then there is no room for the Saviour to do anything for you; for he will not gild refined gold, nor lay enamel on the lily. But if you suffer from some great deficiency, some awful lack that makes your soul sit in darkness, *your* necessity is Christ's opportunity, your need of grace supplies his need of objects for his pity. Here is room for the Saviour to come and display his pity towards you, and you may be sure he will soon be with you. Even so, come Lord Jesus.

Then, again, it was not only this man's deficiency of sight, but it was this man's ignorance which required Almighty aid. It is a work of God not only to create, but to *illuminate*. The same power which calls into existence also calls into light, whether that light be natural or spiritual. It is a divine work to enlighten and regenerate the heart. This man was as dark in mind as he was in body—what a grand thing to enlighten him in a double sense! He did not know the Son of God, therefore he did not believe in him, but asked in wonder "Who is he, Lord, that I might believe on him?" Jesus Christ came to work in this man the knowledge of God, the life of God—in a word, salvation; and because the man was destitute of these things, there was room in him for the Saviour's skill and power. Friend, is that your case? Are you unconverted? Then there is space in you for the Redeemer to work by converting grace. Are you unregenerate? Then there is space in you for the Spirit of God to work regeneration. All these spiritual deficiencies of yours—your ignorance and your darkness—shall be turned by infinite love into opportunities for grace. If you were not lost, you could not be saved. If you were not guilty, you could not be pardoned. If you were not sinful, you could not be cleansed. But all your sin, and sorrow, by a strange mystery of love, is a sort of qualification of yourself for Christ to come and save you. "That is putting it," says one, "in a new light to me." Accept that new light, and be comforted, for it is gospel light, and intended to cheer the despairing. You have said, " There is nothing in me ; " therefore it is clear that there is room for Christ to be your all in all. You see there cannot be two all-in-alls: there can be but one, and as you do not pretend to the title Jesus will wear it. All the space that you occupy in your own esteem takes so much away from the glory of the Lord Jesus ; and if you are nothing, then the whole house is left for the Saviour. He will come and fill up all your inward vacuum with his own dear self and be glorious in your eyes for ever.

I may venture to say to-night that all affliction may be regarded in the same manner as affording opportunity for the mercy-work of God. Whenever you see a man in sorrow and trouble, the way to look at it is, not to blame him and inquire how he came there, but to say, " Here is an opening for God's almighty love. Here is an occasion for the display of the grace and goodness of the Lord." This man being blind gave the Lord Jesus opportunity for the good work of giving him his sight, and that work was so great a wonder that all around were obliged to remark it and admire it. The neighbours began to inquire about it ; the Pharisees had to hold a conclave over it ; and though nearly nineteen centuries have slipped away, here are we at this hour meditating upon it. That man's opened eyes are enlightening our eyes at this hour. The Bible would not have been complete without this touching and teaching narrative : if this man had not been born blind, and if Christ had not opened his éyes, all generations would have had the less light. We ought to be glad that this man was so grievously afflicted, for thereby we are graciously instructed. If he had not been sightless we had not seen the great sight of birth-blindness chased away by him who is the Light of men. So I think I may say to all afflicted ones here to-night, Do not kick at your afflictions : do not be excessively troubled by them, or utterly cast down by them ; but hopefully regard them as openings for mercy, gates for grace, roadways for love. The valley of Achor shall be to you a door of hope. That mighty worker of whom I have been speaking will find a workshop in your affliction, and therein he will fashion monuments of his grace. Glory in your infirmities, that the power of Christ may rest upon you. Rejoice that as your tribulations abound, so also shall your consolations abound by Christ Jesus. Ask him to make all things work together for your good and for his glory, and so it shall be.

I leave that thought of the workshop when I have added that I do believe that sin itself has somewhat of the same aspect as affliction, for it makes room for the mercy of God. I hardly dare say what Augustine said : when speaking of the fall and of the sin of Adam, and looking to all the splendour of grace that followed after it, he said " *Beata culpa* "— happy fault—as if he thought that sin had furnished such opportunities for the unveiling of the grace of God, and so displayed the character of Christ, that he even dared to call it a happy fault. I will not venture upon such an expression, I scarcely dare do more than repeat what that great master in Israel once said ; but I do say, that I cannot imagine an occasion for glorifying God equal to the fact that man has sinned, since God has given Christ to die for sinners. How could that unspeakable gift have been bestowed if there had been no sinners? The cross is a constellation of divine glory brighter than creation itself.

> " For in the grace that rescued man,
> His noblest form of glory shines ;
> Here on the cross 'tis fairest writ
> In precious blood and crimson lines."

How could we have known the heart of God? How could we have understood the mercy of God? If it had not been for our sin and misery, how could such forbearance and love have been displayed? Come, then, guilty ones, take heart, and look for grace. As a physician needs the sick that he may exert his healing power, so does the Lord of mercy need you that he may show what grace he can bestow. If I were a physician, and desired a practice, I should not inquire for the healthiest parish in England, but for a position where the sick would fill my surgery. If all I sought was to do good to my fellow men I should desire to be in Egypt or some other land visited by cholera, or plague, where I could save human life. The Lord Jesus Christ looking over this throng to-night, seeks not for those who are good, or think themselves so, but for the guilty, who know their sinnership and bemoan it. If there be here a sinner, leprous and defiled; if there be here a soul from head to foot sick with the incurable disease of sin, the Lord Christ, the mighty worker, looks on him, for in him he finds a laboratory wherein he may work the works of him that sent him.

III. You will bear with me now if I pass on, in the third place, briefly to notice THE WORK-BELL.

You hear early in the morning a bell which arouses the workers from their beds. See how they troop into the streets, swarming like bees hastening to or from the hive. You see them going forth to labour, for the bell is ringing. There was a work-bell for Christ, and he heard it. Then he said, " I must work; I must work; I must work." What made him say that? Why, the sight of that blind man. He no sooner saw him than he said, " I must work." The man had not asked anything, nor uttered a sound; but those sightless orbs spake eloquently to the heart of the Lord Jesus, and rang aloud the summons which Jesus heard and obeyed, for he himself said, " I must work."

And why must he work? Why, he had come all the way from heaven on purpose to do so. He had come from his Father's throne to be a man on purpose to bless men, and he would not cause his long descent to go for nothing. He must work; why else was he here where work was to be done?

Besides, there were impulses in his heart which we need not stop now to explain, which forced him to work. His mind, his soul, his heart, were all full of a force which produced perpetual activity. Sometimes he selected a route when he was travelling because " he must needs go through Samaria." Sometimes he went after men because he said, "Other sheep I have, which are not of this fold: them also I must bring." There was a sort of instinct in Christ to save men, and that instinct craved gratification and could not be denied. "I must work," he said. The sight of those blind eyes made him say "I must work;" and he thought of that poor man—how for twenty years and more he had lived in utter darkness—how he had not been able to enjoy the beauties of nature, or look his loved ones in the face, or earn his daily bread; and he pitied the sorrows of the man in a life-long darkness. Moreover, as he recollected how that man's soul had also been shut up like a prisoner in a dungeon by reason of gross ignorance, he said, "I must work, I must work." You see they are after him with stones, but he stops, for he says "I must work. They may stone me if they will, but I must work. I hear the summons and I must work."

Now learn this lesson, all ye followers of Christ. Whenever you see suffering, I hope you will each one feel "I must work, I must help." Whenever you witness poverty, whenever you behold vice, say to yourself, "I must work, I must work." If you are worthy of the Christ whom you call leader, let all the necessities of men impel you, compel you, constrain you to be blessing them. Let the world which lieth in the wicked one arouse you; let the cries of men of Macedonia awaken you, as they say "Come over and help us!" Men are dying, dying in the dark. The cemetery is filling, and hell is filling too. Men are dying without hope; and are passing into the eternal night. "I must work." They cry,—Master, spare thyself: incessant labour will wear thee down and bring thee to thy grave. But see! see! see! Perdition swallows crowds, they go down alive into the pit! Hark to their doleful cries! Lost souls are being shut out from God. "I must work." Oh, that I could lay my hand—or, better far, that my Master would lay his pierced hand on every true Christian here and press it upon him until he cried out, "I cannot sit here. I must be at work as soon as this service is done. I must not only hear, and give, and pray, but I must also work."

Well, that is a grand lesson; but I do not mean it to be the chief one, for I am looking out for those who long to find mercy and salvation. What a blessing it is for you, dear friend, if you want to be saved, that Christ *must* save! There is an impulse upon him that he must save. I know you say, "I cannot pray. I cannot feel as I wish to do." Never mind about that: the matter is in abler hands. You see, this man did not *say* a word: the sight of him was enough to move the heart of the Lord Jesus. As soon as Jesus had seen him he said, "I must work." Have you never seen a man in London who has no particular oratory, and yet succeeds in obtaining alms on a large scale? I have seen him. He dresses like a labourer. He wears a tattered smock-frock, and he sits down in a corner where many pass by: his squatting-place is a little out of the rush of traffic, but near enough to secure attention from many passengers. He displays a spade much the worse for the use made of it by somebody else, and on it is written, "I am starving!" He looks gaunt and hungry; he is exceedingly well got up, and is as pale as chalk can make him. Oh, the quantity of halfpence that go into his old hat! How people pity him! He does not sing a mournful ditty; he does not speak a word; and yet many are moved by the fact that he looks as if it were true that he was starving. Now, my hearer, you need not be false in what you do if you set out your misery and sin before the Lord. To-night, when you reach home, kneel at your bedside, and say, "Lord Jesus, I cannot pray; but here I am. I am perishing, and I put myself within sight of thee. Instead of hearing my pleas, look at my sins. Instead of demanding arguments, look at my wickedness. Instead of oratory, which I have not, Lord, remember that I shall soon be in hell if thou dost not save me." I tell you, the bell will ring, and the great worker will feel that the time has come for him to labour; he will say in the words of my text, "I must work," and in you the works of God shall be made manifest. You shall be the workshop of Christ.

IV. One more head, and that is THE WORK-DAY. Our divine Master said, "I must work the works of him that sent me, *while it is day: the night cometh, when no man can work.*"

Now, listen. This is not meant about Christ the risen Saviour, but this refers to the Lord Jesus Christ as he was a man here on earth. There was a certain day in which he could bless men, and when that day was over he would be gone; there would be no Jesus Christ on earth to open blind men's eyes, or to heal the sick; he would be gone from among men, and be no more approachable as the healer of bodily disease. Our Lord as a man here on earth had a day. It was only a day—a short period, and not very long; he could not make it longer, for it was settled by the great Lord. The day of his sacrifice was appointed; he himself once said, "My hour is not yet come." But that hour did come. Our Lord occupied thirty years in getting ready for his life-work, and then in three years his warfare was accomplished. How much he crowded into those three years! Centuries of service could not equal the labour of that brief period. Brothers, some of us have had thirty years of work, but we have done very little, I am afraid; and what if we have only three years more? Let us feel the impulses of the coming eternity! Within a little while I shall no more look into the faces of the throng, they will remember me but as a name; therefore, I will preach as best I can while my powers remain, and my life is prolonged. Within a little while, my brother, you will not be able to go from door to door winning souls: the street will miss you and your tracts: the district will miss you and your regular visits. Do your work well, for your sun will soon set. These words of mine may be more prophetic to some present than we dream. I may be speaking to some who are nearing their last hour, and shall soon render in their account. Up brothers! Up sisters! Say, "We must work, for the night cometh, wherein no man can work." Life cannot be made longer if we wish to make it so: predestination will not lengthen out the thread when the hour has come to cut it off. Life will be short at the very longest, and, O how short with those who die young!

If you and I shall omit any part of our life-work, we can never make up the omission. I speak with solemn reverence of our divine Master, but, if he had not healed that blind man in the day wherein he lived on earth, he would have missed a part of the business upon which the Father sent him. I do not mean that as God, out of heaven, he might not have given the poor beggar sight, but that makes the case the more stern in its bearing upon us, since we have no such future to expect: if we do not serve men now, it will be out of our power to bless them from the skies. This narrative could never have appeared in the life of the Son of Man had he forgotten to be gracious to the blind man. His period of sojourn here below was the time for our Lord to work; if he had come back from heaven to heal the man, that would have been done in a second advent, and not in the first; and if even *he* omits anything from his first errand below, it cannot be put in again. When you and I have written a letter we add a postscript; when we have made a book we can write an appendix or insert something that we have left out. But to this life of yours and mine there can be no postscript. We must do our work now or never; and, if we do not now, even now, while our opportunity serves us, perform our service to our God, we can never do it. If you omitted anything yesterday, you cannot alter the fact of imperfect service on that day. If you are more zealous now it will be the work of to-day; but yesterday will still remain as incomplete as you left it. We must therefore be on the alert to do the work of him that sent us while it is called to-day.

To this conclusion I come, and here draw to a close—if our Lord Jesus Christ was so diligent to bless men when he was here, I feel certain that he is not less diligent to hear and heal them now in that spiritual sense in which he still works upon men.

Oh, that I knew how to lead you to seek my Lord and Master; for if you seek him he will be found of you as surely as you seek him. Christ has not lost the bowels of his compassion; he is not cold in heart or slack in hand. Go to him at once. I spoke just now to some of the chief of sinners, and I say to them again—Go to Jesus! Let me speak to some of you who are *not* the chief of sinners, you that have been hearers of the gospel and have only failed because you do not believe in Jesus. Go to him at once. *You* are backward, but he is not. He must still work, and still work while the gospel day lasts, for that gospel day will soon close. He is waiting and watching for you. Oh, come to him —come even now. "I do not know what it is to come," says one. Well, to come to Christ is simply to trust him. You are guilty: trust him to pardon you. "If I do that," says one, "may I then live as I did before?" No, that you cannot, for if a ship needed to be brought into harbour, and they took a pilot on board, he would say to the captain, "Captain, if you trust me, I will get you into harbour all right. There, let that sail be taken down." And they do not reef it. "Come," says he, "attend to the tiller, and steer as I bid you." But they refuse. "Well," says the pilot, "you said you trusted me." "Yes," says the captain, "and you said that if we trusted you, you would get us into port; but we have not got into port at all." "No," says the pilot, "you do not trust me, for if you trusted me you would do as I bid you." A true trust is obedient to the Lord's commands, and these forbid sin. If you trust Jesus, you must leave your sins, and take up your cross and follow him. Such trust shall surely have its reward : you shall be saved now and saved for ever.

God bless you, dear friends, for Christ's sake.

PORTION OF SCRIPTURE READ BEFORE SERMON—John viii. 59, and ix

---

HYMNS FROM "OUR OWN HYMN BOOK"—386, 607, 552.

THE TOP OF THE LADDER.

A Sermon

DELIVERED ON THURSDAY EVENING, OCTOBER 25TH, 1883, BY

C. H. SPURGEON,

AT THE METROPOLITAN TABERNACLE, NEWINGTON.

"And to know the love of Christ, which passeth knowledge, that ye might be filled with all the fulness of God."—Ephesians iii. 19.

THIS is a part of Paul's prayer for the Ephesian believers. It is the closing clause and consummation of it. It mentions the grandest boon for which he prayed. His prayer was like that ladder which Jacob saw, the top whereof did reach to heaven and God, and the apostle at the foot of it was not asleep, but looking up with eager eyes, and marking each rising round of light. Be it ours by sweet experience to ascend that staircase of light. May the Holy Ghost reveal it to us even now!

You must begin to read at the fourteenth verse. "For this cause I bow my knees unto the Father of our Lord Jesus Christ, of whom the whole family in heaven and earth is named, *that*"—this is one rung of the ladder. "That he would grant you, according to the riches of his glory, to be strengthened with might by his Spirit in the inner man; *that*"—here comes the second rung: one step helps you to reach the next; you are strengthened that you may rise higher and enjoy a further privilege. "That Christ may dwell in your hearts by faith; *that*"—this is the third rung. Oh, that the Holy Ghost may help you at once to take a firm footing upon it! "That ye, being rooted and grounded in love, may be able to comprehend with all saints what is the breadth, and length, and depth, and height; and to know the love of Christ, which passeth knowledge." Surely we are at the top of the ladder now, are we not? What a height! How glorious is the view! How solid the standing! How exhilarating the sense of communion with all saints and with the Lord of saints! Yet this is not the top of it. Here is another step—"*that* ye might be filled with all the fulness of God."

You see that the prayer begins with the gracious petition that we may be *strengthened*—"strengthened with might by his Spirit in the inner man, according to the riches of his glory;" the object being, that Christ may dwell in our hearts by faith. Before the Lord can dwell in us we must be strengthened—mentally and spiritually strengthened. To entertain the high and holy One—to receive into our soul the indwelling

No. 1,755.

Christ—it is necessary that the temple be strengthened, that there be more power put into every pillar and into every stone of the edifice. It is taken for granted that we have already been washed and cleansed, and so made fit for Christ to come and dwell within us. But we need also to be strengthened; for, unless we become stronger in all spiritual life, how is Christ to dwell in our hearts by faith? Unless we become stronger in love, and in all the graces of the Spirit, how, can we worthily entertain such a guest as the Lord Jesus? Ay, and we even need that our spiritual perception should be strengthened, that we may be able to know him when he does come and dwell in us. We need that our spirit should be elevated and lifted into a higher condition than as yet it has known, in order that we may be on a platform whereon we can have communion with Christ, and may, by a heavenly enlargement of mind and heart, be made able to the full to entertain the Lord of glory. We must be strengthened into stability of mind, that so Christ may dwell, abide, reside in our hearts by faith. Oh, brethren, everything has to be done for us; for, even when we are made clean enough for Christ to enter us, we are not strong enough. Even when the Lord has taken away the defilement, so that no longer " sin lieth at the door" to shut him out, yet even then we are too feeble to entertain so great a guest. We should be like Peter, who, when Christ came into his boat and filled it with fish, was too feeble to receive him, and therefore cried out in an agony of weakness, "Depart from me; for I am a sinful man, O Lord." "Oh," says one, "I should never say that." I do not know, brother. If the Lord were to favour you with such divine manifestations as he has given to the stronger saints, you might be overcome, and swoon with inward faintness, almost desiring that Christ would not draw so near to you. If the Lord should appear to you in his glory you would be afraid, and, like John in the Apocalypse, fall at his feet as dead. You need to be strengthened; for how else could you endure the vision of his splendour? the divine excitement of his infinite love? Paul, therefore, begins his requests for the Ephesians with a prayer for more strength for their inner man. Let us pray it to-night—"O Holy Spirit, strengthen my feeble mind, that I may be able to receive more of my Lord. Give me more capacity; give me a clearer perception; give me a better memory; give me an intenser affection; give me a larger faith." This is the first prayer—that you may be strengthened according to the riches of his glory, with might by his Spirit in the inner man. Be eager for this; plead now with all your hearts for me and for yourselves, that we may all be strengthened by the power of the Spirit of our God.

Now, having stood on the first step of the ladder, Paul goes on to pray that, when we are strengthened, we may be *inhabited:* that Christ may dwell in our hearts by faith. When the house is ready to receive him, and strong enough for such a wondrous inhabitant, may Jesus come, not to look about him as he did when he went into the temple—for we read that he looked round about him with indignation, and did not remain there,—but may he come on purpose to abide with us; not to tarry for a night and give us some transient visits of his love, sweet as that would be, but "that Christ may *dwell* in our hearts by faith." This will make you living temples for the indwelling Lord. Oh, but this is a great prayer; and when you are strengthened to receive so sacred a boon, may the Lord fulfil it to you till your communion with Christ shall be constant all the while you are awake, and when you wake in the night may you still be with him, being even now "for ever with the Lord." I pray that you may no longer envy the disciples in their walk to Emmaus, as though they were the most privileged of all mankind because they had one walk with Jesus; but may your fellowship be such that you entertain the Saviour day and night—going, may you take him where you go, and staying, find him where you stay. May you have his perpetual, unclouded presence with you, being strengthened up to that mark; for it is not every man that is capable of it. Oh, brethren, you must aspire to the power of grace at its full, being strengthened by the Spirit of God until Christ shall reside in your hearts by faith; that you may see him ever within you, having so clear a view of what Jesus is, and what he has done, that you may never again be vexed with doubts concerning him or his word. May you have such familiar intercourse with him that you may believe him implicitly, and never dream of distrusting him. As a child lies on its mother's bosom, so may you rest upon the love of Christ, leaning all your weight upon him. May you never have to inquire for your Well-beloved, but know that he abides within you, as surely as your heart remains in living energy within your body. Be not afraid to ask, and seek, and believe for this; the ladder is meant to be climbed; this experience is attainable: Christ may dwell in your hearts by faith. This second step of the ladder is worth reaching. Rise to it, ye struggling believers! The Lord bring us all to it by the Holy Ghost!

And when we climb thus far, what next? This third step is a broad one, and it has three parts to it. Its first part is *establishment*,—"That ye, being rooted and grounded in love." When you are strengthened, and when Jesus dwells in your heart, then you are no longer "carried about with every wind of doctrine," but you are rooted, like a cedar in Lebanon which receives but recks not of the stormy wind. You are no longer upset by doubts and fears, as a bowing wall is thrown over by a breeze; for you are grounded, like a well-built house, settled on its rocky foundation. Your wall has made its last settlement, and has settled down upon the eternal foundation which can never be removed, "Jesus Christ, the same yesterday, and to day, and for ever." No man attains to this rooted and grounded state unless Christ dwells in his heart. The indwelling is needful to the fixity of the house; but he that has Jesus dwelling in him laughs to scorn the whimsies and fancies which men call philosophies. He knows nothing about "advanced thought," for by the grace of God he has advanced as far as he wants to advance, since he has come to live in Christ and Christ has come to live in him. What is there beyond this as to firmness of basis and foundation? If there be anything beyond this, we do not know it, nor want to know it. We are perfectly content and satisfied to remain with the love of Christ abiding in our souls,—"that Christ may dwell in our hearts, that we may be rooted and grounded in love." For, oh! when the heart gets grounded in love—when it loves Christ and feels the love of Christ shed abroad in it by the Holy Ghost, it says, "Whither do ye invite me? To what fair havens could I sail? With what do you tempt me?

What can be sweeter under heaven or in heaven than that which I now enjoy, namely, the love of an indwelling Christ? Oh, evil sirens, you sing to me in vain! You might sooner tempt the angels in heaven to descend to hell than persuade my spirit to leave my Beloved who dwells in me and lives in me, and who has grounded and settled me in a deep sense of his eternal love."

Side by side with this very blessed establishment in the faith, for which I would bow my knee, as Paul did for the Ephesians, that you may all have it, comes a *comprehension* of divine love. How anxiously do I desire your firm settlement in the truth, for this is an age which needs rooted and grounded saints: this is a time when men need to be confirmed in the present truth and to hold it as with an iron hand. Side by side with that, however, we would have you receive this further blessing, namely, a comprehension of the love of Christ: "that ye may be able to comprehend with all saints what is the breadth, and length, and depth, and height;" that you may have no crude idea, but a clear and definite understanding of what the love of Christ is to you. As an arithmetician makes calculations and arrives at clear ideas, as a mechanic cubes a quantity and takes its length, and depth, and height, so may the Lord Jesus Christ's love be to you no more an airy dream, but a substantial fact, about which you know distinctly, being taught of the living God by the Holy Spirit. You know that Christ's love is an eternal love, without beginning; an everlasting love, without end; a love that knows no bound; a love that never lessens and cannot be increased; a love that burns freely in his heart towards you as an unworthy, undeserving sinner; a love which led him to live for you in human nature, and to die for you in his own body on the tree; a love which made him stand sponsor, surety, and substitute for you, and led him to bear your load of sin, and die while doing so, and bury that sin of yours in a sepulchre out of which it never shall rise. You know that it is a love which made him rise again, and mount the heavens, and sit at the right hand of God, still doing all for you,—living, that you may live; pleading, that you may be preserved; preparing heaven, that you may come there to dwell with him, and intending to come by and by that he may receive you to himself, that where he is, there you may be also. Oh, beloved, this is a delightful thing: first, to be strengthened, then to have Christ dwelling in you, and then to begin to know the measure of his unmeasurable love. This is to be taught of God, when you are able to speak of height, depth, length, breadth, and so see the Saviour's love to be a tangible, real, practical, efficient thing. How blessed to comprehend that divine love which, after all, is in-comprehensible! I know that some of you who have been lately con-verted think that you know all about it; but you do not; for I tell you freely that some of us who have now known the Lord for a third of a century must still confess that we have only coasted along the shore of this great world of love, while into the centre of the bright continent we have never yet been able to penetrate. I could introduce you to friends who have been fifty years in Christ, and though they hold a constant jubilee in the sense of his love, yet they will tell you that they are only scholars on the lowest form, beginning to spell out the alpha-bet of the grace of our Lord Jesus Christ. You do not know what lies before you, young saints; but press onward: ask the Lord to make you stronger, and you shall then entertain your Lord as a perpetual guest within your bosom, and shall come to know what fathers in the church have loved to learn, the heights and depths of love unsearchable. Be this our prayer at this moment—

"Come, dearest Lord, descend and dwell
By faith and love in every breast;
Then shall we know, and taste, and feel
The joys that cannot be express'd.

" Come fill our hearts with inward strength;
Make our enlargèd souls possess,
And learn the height, and breadth, and length,
Of thine unmeasurable grace."

Do not overlook the third part of this subject, which is "that you may know the love of Christ, which passeth knowledge,"—that you may have *acquaintance* with that love which can never be fully known. This is the subject upon which I would briefly descant, taking the whole verse as a step that leads to another step: "That ye may know the love of Christ, which passeth knowledge, *that*"—and now we come to the top step of all—"that ye might be filled with all the fulness of God."

Here are four things to talk about—*to know the love of Christ;* secondly, *to know it so as to be filled with all the fulness of God;* thirdly, *to be filled with the fulness of God;* and then, fourthly, *being full, what then?* Does not that mean that when we are full we shall overflow to the glory of him who filled us? God grant that we may! May the fulness of Jesus be glorified by our holy and useful outpourings!

I. First, then, TO KNOW THE LOVE OF CHRIST. Observe that Paul was not praying for people who did not know the love of Christ in the ordinary acceptation of the term. They did know it; they had heard all about it from himself; they had read about it in his epistles and in other gracious records. They knew the whole story of the love of Christ through apostolic teaching. Ay, and they knew it by faith, too. They had believed in the Lord Jesus Christ unto the salvation of their souls, so that in the first verse of this epistle he calls them "saints which are at Ephesus, and the faithful in Christ Jesus."

What does he mean by his prayer that they might know the love of Christ? He intended another kind of knowledge. I know very many people; that is to say, I have read about them; I have heard of them; I have seen them in the street, and they touch their hats to me, and I do the same to them; and thus I know them. This is a slender form of knowledge; yet I fear it is the kind of knowledge which most men have of Christ. They have seen him; they have looked to him, and, blessed be his name, there is life in a look, but they have gone no further. Even such a knowledge as that which comes by trembling faith is a knowledge that saves. But I will tell you the people I know best. They live with me in my own house: I see them every day, I am on the most familiar terms with them: this is the knowledge here intended. Read our text again. "That Christ may dwell in your hearts by faith," and then—"that you may know the love of Christ." Is not this the best way of knowing it? Jesus resides in your heart, which is the centre of *your* love, and then you know *his* love. He teaches you to love him, and, as you learn the sweet lesson, you begin to know how Jesus loves you. You come to know him by personal acquaintance, by having Christ dwelling in you so that you see him, hear him, feel his touch, and enjoy his blessed company. This kind of knowledge is the most precious of all knowledge, be the subject what it may.

You see the *modus* of this knowledge, the way in which it comes to us: it is a sure and efficient way, for by having Jesus to dwell in us, and by becoming rooted and grounded in love to him, we come to know him as we can never know him by being taught by our fellow men, or by all the reading or study in the world. This is the highest style of the science of Christ Crucified, for this comes of personal proof and experimental test, and therefore it is not to be taken from us, but is woven into our consciousness. We have been taught by certain modern philosophers that we do not *know* anything: I fancy our friends are not far off the mark if they only speak for themselves, but I demur to their representing *us*. They tell us that we only know that our senses have been operated upon, and perhaps we may know that certain things do thus operate, but we can hardly be sure of that. One of these philosophers kindly says that religion is a matter of belief, not of knowledge. This is clean in opposition to all the teaching of Scripture. Take your pencil and read through all the Epistles of John, and mark the word "know": it is repeated continually; in fact, it is the key-word of the Apostle's letter. He writes perpetually, "We know; we know; we know; we know." Truly, brethren, we *know* the love of Christ. When Jesus dwells in us, we do not merely believe in his love as a report, but we enjoy it as a fact: we have made its acquaintance; we have tasted, we have handled, we have experienced this heavenly boon. What a favour! To know the love of Christ! Do not forget that this only comes of Christ's dwelling in us, and of our being rooted and grounded in love to him.

"We cannot be certain of anything," says some one. Well, perhaps *you* cannot. But the man who has Christ dwelling in him says, "There is one thing I am certain of, and that is the love of Christ to me. I am assured of the loveliness of his character and the affection of his heart; I perceive that he himself is love: and I am equally clear, since he has come to live with me, that he loves *me*, for he would not have lived in my heart at all if he had not loved me. He would not cheer and encourage me; he would not rebuke and chasten me, as he does, if he did not love me. He gives me every proof of his love, and therefore I am sure of it. I will have no question raised; or if *you* raise it, you will kindly understand that I do not raise it; for I have come to this, that I know the love of Christ."

What a blessed knowledge this is! Talk they of science? No science can rival the science of Christ Crucified. Knowledge? No knowledge can compare with the knowledge of the love that passeth knowledge. How sweet it is to know love! Who wants a better subject to exercise his mind upon? And how precious is the love of Christ! The sweetest of all the sweets that life can yield—the source of love, the mirror of love, the model of love, the love which surpasses all love, as the knowledge of it surpasses all knowledge. Who would not be a scholar when the book he reads in is the heart of Christ? Who would not be a student when the science is Christ Crucified, the lesson-book Christ manifested, the tutor Christ glorified, and the prize Christ enthroned in the heart? Jesus is most dear from every point of view; but how charming is it to see him in the light of love, so as " to know the love of Christ"!

You see, then, *the way in which we come by our knowledge*, and *the certainty* there is in it, and *the sweetness* of the subject: I shall have to show you, as we go on, *the efficacy* of this knowledge; for when we know the love of Christ that passeth knowledge, it follows ere long that we come to be *filled* with all the fulness of God. Here is a sweet perfume brought into a man's house. For substance it seems to be a little thing: it can lie on his finger. Wait a few minutes, and it has actually filled the room. Every one exclaims, "What sweetness!" The fragrance perfumes all the chamber. They open the door: the delicious scent is in the passage, it has gone upstairs into every bedroom, till the fragrance is diffused through all the house, and if you open a window it invades the street and charms the passer-by. If the love of Christ is really known in the soul it is like a precious box of rarest aromatics; it diffuses itself till it fills our entire being. I do not wonder to find my text saying, "And to know the love of Christ, which passeth knowledge, that ye might be filled with all the fulness of God;" for the love of the Lord Jesus is the most filling thing in existence. In him dwelleth all the fulness of the Godhead bodily, and ye are complete in him, for of his fulness have all ye received, and grace for grace: how can we be otherwise than filled?

II. We must dwell a minute on that round of the ladder to which we have ascended—TO KNOW SO AS TO BE FILLED.

It is not every kind of knowledge that will fill a man. Many forms of knowledge make a man more empty than he was before. The knowledge of earthly luxuries tends to make a man hunger for them, and so a new vacuum is created in his mind. When he perceives that there is this or that delight to be had, then he becomes discontented till he gets it, and so he is emptier than he was before. Much of human knowledge is described by the Apostle thus, "Knowledge puffeth up; but love buildeth up." Sometimes the more men know the greater fools they become; for knowledge is not wisdom, though wisdom cannot be without knowledge. Knowledge in the hands of a fool is but a means of publishing his folly. Wisdom is the flower which grows out of knowledge; but all knowledge does not bear that flower: much of it is barren. Brethren, if you get a knowledge of Christ's love, it is a filling knowledge, for it contents the soul. When a man knows the love of Christ to him, every part of his being is satisfied. We are made up, as it were, of a number of horseleeches, every one of which cries, "Give. Give." Here is the heart craving for something to love. Oh, but when you love Christ, you have a heart's love that will satisfy you for all time! Where can such sweetness be? Your heart shall never go a-hungering again. His charms shall hold you fast. There is the intellect: what a horseleech it is! It is ever craving for more—more certainty, more novelty, more wonder; but when the intellect comes to know Christ it acknowledges that in him dwelleth all wisdom. To know the Eternal Son is to know the Father, and this is a knowledge which rests the understanding and fills up the mind. Imagination itself is content with Jesus. Hope cannot conceive anything more lovely; she gives up all attempts to paint a fairer than he; and she cries, "Yea, he is altogether lovely. This is my beloved, and this is my friend. O ye daughters of Jerusalem!" No power or passion that is vital to our manhood is discontented with the Lord Jesus Christ. Before conversion we gad abroad, and go to this house and to that to pick up scanty meals; but when Christ comes home to dwell with us we sup with him, and go no more out, since there is nowhere to be found anything that is as good as he, much less anything that can be better than he. When the love of Christ enters the heart, it is swiftly filled with a perfect satisfaction. A certain divine, not a thousand miles away, who has no very great love for the gospel, says that he can influence and enlighten most people except those who hold the views of a certain "notorious individual." That epithet I take to myself. He adds, "When once they receive his doctrinal teaching there is no stirring them an inch." Blessed be God for that. I scarcely hoped that the work was so well done, and I am glad of the worthy gentleman's certificate. So it is; when once you cast anchor in the port of Christ's love you wish for no more voyages. You will not change when you feel that it is well with your soul. You are convinced that there is no better article in the market than that which your souls have learned to feed upon, and so you are not inclined to go further and fare worse.

Again, when the soul comes to enjoy Christ it is filled in a most emphatic sense. It is not merely satisfied, but overjoyed. One said to me the other day, "I am sure that you have a contented heart." "Well," I replied, "if I were pinched with poverty you might talk of my contentment; but God blesses me so richly that I have passed beyond mere contentment, I have all things and abound. I feel as if I can bless God all day long." Christ's people are not merely safe and contented, they are filled; and well they may be, for there is enough in Christ for millions, and yet he is altogether ours. He has given himself to us as a glorious whole. A little patrimony may make a man contented, but what shall we say when our heritage is Christ himself? Contented? Why, our heart leaps as we survey our infinite portion.

> " In the heavenly Lamb thrice happy I am ;
> And my heart it doth dance at the sound of his name."

When you live in the full enjoyment of the Lord's presence and abide under a sense of his love, you feel more happy than tongue can tell. Your heart is too full to hold: it is like a vessel wanting vent; it possesses a joy unspeakable and full of glory.

Once more, when the love of Christ comes to work upon the soul, when it brings with it all its choice treasures, then the mind of the believer is filled with the fulness of God. What is it that the love of Christ gives to the objects of it? Let me ask another question. What is it which is worth having that it does *not* give? He gives us light for our darkness, eyes for our blindness, food for our hunger, cleansing for our defilement, garments for our nakedness, healing for our sickness. He gives us strength for our weakness, joy for our sorrow, comfort for our distress, deliverance for our peril, and triumph for our conflict. When Jesus comes to dwell in the heart, he brings with him such furniture, such provision, that our entire nature is equipped, furnished, provided for; in a word, "filled with all the fulness of God." Christ does not long dwell in an unfurnished house. Oh, you that have a poor, poverty-stricken religion of which you have to say, like the elder brother in the parable, "These many years do I serve thee, neither transgressed I at any time thy commandment: and yet thou never gavest me a kid, that I might make merry with my friends;" I beseech you, say so no more. Come, brother, alter that tune, and hear what the great Father says : "Son, thou art ever with me, and all that I have is thine." If Christ dwells in your heart, his Father is your Father, his God is your God, his heaven is your heaven ; ay, and his throne shall be your throne, for he will make you to sit where he sits at the right hand of God in glory. Oh, the blessedness of knowing the love of Christ ! It fills the spirit to the full.

III. In a sentence or two I will pass over the third point, namely, WHAT IT IS TO BE FILLED WITH ALL THE FULNESS OF GOD.

Does it not mean that self is banished; for if the fulness of God has filled you, where is room for self? Does it not mean that the soul is perfectly charmed with all that God does for it? "Filled with all the fulness of God." Does it not mean that every power of the entire nature is solaced and satisfied? Does it not mean that the whole man is occupied and inhabited by God—that the whole nature becomes permeated with grace, saturated with love, satisfied with favour, and full of the goodness of the Lord? I will not talk more of it at this time. I hope that you will know by experience what that fulness means, if you do not know it already. May the Holy Ghost give you this glad experience!

IV. I want to come to the practical point—that WHEREVER CHRIST DWELLS IN THE HEART BY FAITH WE RECEIVE THE FULNESS OF GOD INTO OUR SPIRIT, WITH THE DESIGN THAT WE MAY OVERFLOW.

Brothers, sisters, you know what it is to be empty, I dare say. Have you ever tried to pray when you are empty ? Yes, and the result is a very empty prayer. "Out of nothing comes nothing ; " and when there is no prayer in you, and you pray, why, it is no prayer at all. You try to praise, but if there is no praise in you, your attempted hallelujahs languish and expire. If true praise comes forth from you, it must first have been within you. But do you know what it is to pray when you are full of prayer? When the Lord has filled you with hungerings, and thirstings, and desires, and hopes, and expectations, what an overflowing of prayer is with you! When the season of prayer is over, and you go down to business, you cry, "Alas, I never knew a quarter of an hour fly so quickly as this has done! How refreshed I am! I made no effort to pray, but I poured out my soul like water before the Lord." Yes, because you have been filled with all the fulness of God, therefore you have prayed readily and with fulness. In singing, you have felt the same plenitude of devotion. Sometimes when you have been praising the Lord you have wished that you had all men's tongues in your mouth, and that you had all the songs of birds at your command, and all the music of the spheres. You have desired to make the stars your keyboard, to play upon them a glorious *Te Deum;* and yet you would not even then have praised your God as your heart desired. When you are full of praise, then you praise indeed. It is a blessed thing for our heart to get full towards God, for then we worship him with a full soul. It may be only full of regrets, and repentances, and desires; but yet if it be full, it is a blessed fulness. Even if you are only full of groans, and cries, and entreaties, it is well. When God dwells in you by the Holy Ghost as the Spirit of supplication and devotion, then you live towards God with vigorous life.

And, dear brethren, when you are all full of divine grace, you are filled for all the circumstances of life. You have lately buried a greatly-beloved one. The news came upon you on a sudden, but you were not afraid of evil tidings. Why? Because your heart was "fixed, trusting in the Lord." When the sad bereavement came it did not overwhelm you: at another time it might have done so, but the Lord was pleased so to fill you with his presence that you were quite prepared for the trouble. To-morrow morning if you go into the world filled with the fulness of God, afflictions may come in business: perhaps an extra heavy account will be sent in, and you will be perplexed as to how to meet it: but you will not mind it: 'you will be ready for the difficulty because the fulness of God will ballast you and save you from the rough winds. Perhaps to-morrow you will meet with a great success, and if you are not full of grace you will grow proud and lifted up; but if you are filled with all the fulness of God, if the Lord should make you as rich as Solomon you would not grow worldly. If you are filled with all the fulness of God you are as ready for prosperity as you are for adversity, and whatever happens to you in the future you will be prepared for it. If you are called upon to confess his name, if you are filled with all the fulness of God, courage will be yours; and if you are called to endure great suffering, patience will be ready, for the God of patience will grant you strength equal to your need. If a knotty problem poses you, and you are filled with God's wisdom, you will work it out. If you go forth filled with God, you are provided for every emergency. Come calamity or prosperity, whatever shape the temptation may assume, if the love of Christ has filled you with the fulness of God you are ready for it. See how prepared you will be to meet your brethren and benefit them. Suppose you should make one in a little gathering of believers, and they should ask you to speak a word, if you are full your speech will be worth hearing; but if you are empty, your communications will be empty also. Sometimes when we preach we are conscious of unfitness for the work because our soul is poverty-stricken. There cannot be much in our mouths if there is little in our hearts. Out of an empty sack you cannot shake a bushel of wheat, even if you shake it very hard. I have heard a brother pray a wearisome while, and I believe he was long because he had nothing to say. A horse can run many miles if he has nothing to carry. Long prayers often mean wind and emptiness. If you are full with a divine fulness, your lips scatter gems more precious than pearls and diamonds. Filled with all the fulness of God, your paths, like God's paths, drop fatness. Do you not know Christian men of that sort? They are millionaire Christians who make others rich. I know saints whom I rejoice to visit because I always learn from them. It is a privilege to be in the company of full saints, just as it is a misery to hear the clatter of empty professors. It is said that we English people feel delighted if we sit by the side of a lord: this I know, that if I get into the company of one of God's aristocracy, and have a quarter of an hour's talk with him, and a little prayer as well, I feel quite lifted up. My heart is glad within me when I see the grace of God abundant in a brother. I want you, brethren, to be full of sympathy, full of pity, full of mercy, full of wisdom; and when your brethren hear you speak they will be as men who have found running springs and filled up their vessels.

Lastly, if the love of Jesus Christ be in us so that we are filled with all the fulness of God, how ready we shall be to meet common folk that are not the Lord's people as yet! We shall have a word on wheels for all who cross our path. You find it difficult to get the right word at the right time when you are talking to seekers. Just so, brother: but may not that be because you are not full up to the brim? You are nearly empty, and it takes you a long time to turn your tub up and pour out the little drop which lurks at the bottom. If you were full up to the brim you would run over on all sides, and all around you there would be a holy moisture. If you are so full of spiritual life that you cannot help running over, you will by the Holy Spirit's power pour out the right expressions when they are needed, and thirsty souls will receive of the living water.

If we are quite full we may move about among ungodly men, and our presence will be a benediction to them. I read the other day of one who heard a man swear and tell a lie at the same time. He did not say anything; but the swearer was aware that the listener was aware of his falsehood. The reprover fixed his eye on the false-speaker, and was silent: that glance went to the other's heart, for it said more than a dozen hard names. What the reprover did not say had more power than what he might have said. Be zealous for the Lord, and he will tell you what to do, and guide you how to do it, if you are only full of his life.

"But I do not know how to speak," says one. Just so. You know that you have only a little living water at the bottom of your barrel, and you do not know how to get it out. "Oh, but I feel such a difficulty in speaking." If there is only a little in the tub, the difficulty is to get it out; but if you are full, that difficulty will vanish.

If the Lord has brought us to his fulness, it is a very high state to be in. Look at our blessed Master; wherever he was, and whatever happened, and wherever he went, he did the right thing there and then, and said the best thing that could be said, because the Holy Spirit rested upon him without measure. Oh, that the Holy Ghost would fill us also according to our capacity! If the water-carts go along the road in dusty weather with nothing in them, they will not lay the dust; and if you Christians go about the world empty, you will not lay the dust of sin which blinds and defiles society. If you go to a fountain and find no water flowing, that fountain mocks your thirst; it is worse than useless: therefore do not forget that if you ever become empty of grace, you mock those who look to you. Blessed be he of whom it is written, "Out of his belly shall flow rivers of living water." This spake Christ of the Spirit of God dwelling in men. God grant that you and I may understand his meaning!

If anybody is saying, " This is out of my line ; I have not come as far as this," I know it is so. I have not been talking to you. Yet I will not be altogether silent to you. Look to Jesus Christ at once, and you shall be saved. Trust him, trust him wholly. By faith you will begin to live. After you begin to live, you will be strengthened by the Spirit of the Lord. After you are strengthened Christ will dwell in your heart. After Christ has dwelt in your heart, you shall know the love that passeth knowledge; and after that you know the love that passeth knowledge, you shall be filled with all the fulness of God. Do not begin at the end, but take things according to God's order. A man who wishes to climb a ladder does not expect to put his foot upon the top round at the first step; he ascends by degrees. There is your first round—" Believe on the Lord Jesus Christ and thou shalt be saved." Take that first step at once. May the Lord help you ! Beginning with faith in Jesus, you shall persevere, and ascend till you reach the top of the ladder. The Lord be with you and in you to the full! Amen and Amen.

PORTION OF SCRIPTURE READ BEFORE SERMON—Ephesians iii.

HYMNS FROM "OUR OWN HYMN BOOK,"—769, 457, 463.

RENEWING STRENGTH.

A Sermon,

SUITABLE FOR THE CLOSE OF THE YEAR, DELIVERED BY

C. H. SPURGEON,

AT THE METROPOLITAN TABERNACLE, NEWINGTON.

"They that wait upon the Lord shall renew their strength."—Isaiah xl. 31.

HUMAN strength is of many kinds, but in any form it will spend itself in due time. God can lend to men immense *physical* force ; but though a man had the strength of a lion and an ox combined, he would one day fail. The force of flesh must fade like the grass to which it is likened. Samson sometimes becomes exhausted, and he is like to die of thirst, though he has slain a thousand men ; yea more, he must ultimately die and his mighty thews and tremendous muscles must yield to the worm and return to the dust of death. Since even granite and iron yield to constant wear and tear, assuredly man's frail body cannot long be a thing of strength.

> "Our days a transient period run,
> And change with every circling sun ;
> And while to lengthen'd years we trust,
> Before the moth we sink to dust."

Mental strength is a noble possession, but it also fails its owner, for at best it is a finite power. The wisest of men by-and-by feel the infirmities of age creeping upon them, and frequently present the sad spectacle of second childhood. Death pays no regard to science or eloquence. The fool dies, and as surely dies the senator, the philosopher, the divine. When you take up the skull of a sage, you find no weight of wisdom there, nor trace of all the curious movements of a potent brain. Knowledge, genius, imagination, prophetic fire, all depart ; even before death they often fail. Baffled by mysteries, balked by prejudice, blinded by pride, the man of great understanding may yet be driven to his wit's end.

So far as even *spiritual* strength is of the man, himself, so far as you can conceive of it apart from the immediate operation of the Holy Ghost, it also cannot be depended on. The most devout may grow lukewarm, the strongest believer may doubt, the most sanctified may backslide ; it is a heavenly strength, but so far as it is transfused into our humanity and becomes a part of ourselves, it also may wax weak, though, blessed be God, it can never utterly die.

No, 1,756.

Every form of human strength must of necessity spend itself, for the
world of which it forms a part decays, and by-and-by, like a worn-out
vesture, the heavens and the earth shall be rolled up and put away.
Some signs of age the creatures show already, but the time will come
when their strength shall utterly fail. The reason is that all strength
apart from God is derived strength, and is consequently measurable ; yea,
apart from God it is not strength at all, and consequently must come to
an end. The river runs on and the brook fails not, because they come
from fountains that are not affected by drought; but cisterns are dried
and reservoirs fail, because they have no springing well at the bottom of
them ; and if the pipes which supply them cease to flow, they are soon
left dry as a threshing-floor. Pools which are not self-supplied are always
liable to be exhausted as the water is drained from them. Let every
man know therefore that whatever his strength may be, of body, mind,
or spirit, if it be his own it will fail him one day. Let him see to it
therefore that he does not trust it ; especially that he does not trust it
with eternal hazards or rest upon it for his soul's safety, for which it
never can be equal. It will be a horrible thing to be leaning and to find
your staff fail you when you are on the edge of a measureless precipice.
It will be terrible to be building and to find your foundation washed
from under you, and all your handiwork carried away by the flood !
Yet so it must be if we are depending upon anything that comes of
ourselves. Our own righteousness, our own thoughts, our own religiousness, our own prayers, resolves, attainments, achievements,—everything
that is of ourselves must sooner or later prove themselves to be but
human, and over all things human it is best to write, " Vanity of
vanities, all is vanity." Mingled with all things human there are
portions of that all-dissolving acid which fall upon man's nature when
infinite justice said, " Dust thou art, and unto dust shalt thou return."

On the other hand, what a contrast there is as to divine strength !
That never fails. It seems almost a superfluity to say as much as that :
it abides in joyous fulness, never in the least diminished. With God
there are no years to make him decline with age, no labours to tax his
powers. With God our lives are but as the swing of the pendulum.
A thousand years in his sight are passed away as a watch in the night.
Millions of ages are nothing to him. He was God when as yet this sun,
and moon, and all these stars slept in his thought like unborn forests in
an acorn cup ; and he will be God when all this brief creation shall melt
back to nothing as a moment's foam dissolves into the wave that bore
it and is lost for aye. God changes not in any degree whatever : the
fountain of his almightiness still overflows. He made this world ; no
doubt he has made thousands more ; and has still an undiminished power
to create. All the worlds that we can see revolving in yonder sky are
perhaps as a single chamber in the mansion-house of creation : they
occupy an insignificant corner behind the door, compared to other and
vaster worlds that he has made. But the glorious Lord is just as ready
to make more : he is still the same for ever and for ever. In your dire
necessity you may draw largely upon him, but you cannot exhaust him.
You may bring your boundless wants and have them all supplied, but
you shall no more diminish his all-sufficiency than when an infant dips
his cup into the sea and leaves the sea brimming over upon ten thousand

leagues of shore. Oh, the glory of the strength of God ! I cannot speak of it. I will not contrast it with the strength of man. It would be to contrast everything with nothing, and infinity with non-existence.

What then ? These two things seem very far away—man with his faintness, his strength gradually drying up : God with his eternity and inexhaustible omnipotence. If we can bring these two together, if by an act of faith you that are human can be linked with the divine, what a wondrous thing will happen ! Then the sacred words of the text will be fulfilled and your strength will be renewed. Apt as it is to dry up, it will be renovated, freshened, filled up, increased, established. From the eternal deep that lieth under—that deep of which Moses said that it " coucheth beneath "—from that measureless fountain shall you draw strength which all eternity will not exhaust. You are weakness itself, but if you are united to the divine strength you shall be infinitely strong. The cipher is nothing, but with a unit before it it becomes ten. A man is nothing, but with God in him he makes hell tremble.

Now that is just my text, " They that wait upon the Lord shall renew their strength." If they are apart from God their strength will die out ; but when they are linked to God, and wait upon God·for everything, casting their nothingness upon his omnipotence, then shall they find their strength renewed. With God in him though the man were dead yet shall he live. Job says, "My bow was renewed in my hand." Grass cut down shall grow again when heaven's dew shall quicken it. The brook that was ready to dry up shall flow again when heaven remembers it and unseals its treasures. The skies that burned like brass shall be cooled with clouds again when the Lord thinks upon them. When the heart drinks life from the heart of God, and man is at one with his Maker, then all is well.

> " From God, the overflowing spring,
> Our souls shall drink a fresh supply ;
> While those who trust their native strength
> Shalt melt away and droop and die."

I have now to speak from my text, *first, upon how a true church may be described.* " They that wait upon the Lord." Secondly, upon *what such a church needs :* to renew its strength ; and, thirdly, *how such a church may renew its strength*, and that is by waiting upon the Lord. That which serves as a description *of* true believers serves also as a direction *to* true believers : They that wait upon the Lord are the men who may most hopefully be encouraged still to wait upon the Lord that their strength may be renewed.

I. First, then, here WE SEE HOW A TRUE CHURCH MAY BE DESCRIBED ; " They that wait upon the Lord."

A church such as a church ought to be, consists of men who *depend upon the Lord alone,* for waiting signifies dependence. Their hope is in God. They rest in God's righteousness as their righteousness, and they receive the great sacrifice provided by God to be their atonement and their acceptance. No man is really a Christian who finds his hope and confidence within himself ; he must be looking out of himself to God in Christ Jesus. It is absolutely essential that it should be so. He that is God's beloved is a believer in God ; that is to say, a truster in God, a waiter upon God. His one sole confidence is in God his Saviour. This being so with each individual, the whole church can sing,

> " Our spirits look to God alone,
> Our rock and refuge is his throne;
> In all our fears, in all our straits
> Our soul on his salvation waits."

If Christians are what they ought to be, they depend upon God alone in their church capacity. God's word is their only creed: they do not add to it anything whatever—no, not a sentence, a gloss, or a thought. They have greatly erred who look upon anything as the authoritative standard of faith but God's own word. I hear you say, "Do you not respect the Thirty-nine Articles?" However much or little I may respect them, it makes no difference to the fact that the church of God is not bound to any faith but that which God himself has revealed. " But the Westminster Assembly's Confession?" It must be treated in the same manner. That summary of doctrine is very admirable; but human creeds, as such, have nothing on earth to do with me. The point I have to do with is this, What does God say? What does his Word say? Within the covers of the Bible you find all theology. Nothing outside of this Book is binding on a Christian man as doctrine in the least degree whatever. The Bible and the Bible alone is the religion of Christians. "To the law and to the testimony: if they speak not according to this word, it is because there is no light in them." This word has life within it which rules in the souls of the Lord's elect. Blessed be the Spirit of God who dictated it; we yield implicit faith to all that he has revealed, and to nothing else. A true church of God will say, " We wait upon the Lord for teaching: this word of the Lord is to us our infallible source of doctrine, and that alone." Those who wait upon the Lord for their creed shall never need to give up their faith for something better, but they shall renew their strength.

Faithful to her Lord in doctrine, a true church also waits upon the Lord for grace, and has faith in the doctrines of grace as the testimony with which she is to work. What am I to teach to my people if I am a Christian minister? If a church is rightly constituted, it says to the pastor, "Teach you what God has taught. Preach Christ crucified. Preach not your own thoughts, nor notions of your own inventing, but what is revealed of God—preach you that, for it shall be the power of God unto salvation." I am always sorry when, in order to promote a revival, false doctrine is preached. I will preach no false doctrine if I know it—no, not to save the world. Of this I am assured that, if the truth will not save a man, a lie will not. If the bare unaltered truth of God will not break a man's heart, then it certainly will not break it when it is rounded and toned down and made to look pretty so as to suit the prevailing taste. No, a church that waits upon the Lord uses only the doctrine of Scripture as its battle-axe and weapons of war.

A church that is waiting upon the Lord always knows where its strength lies, namely, in its God. What is the power with which men are to be converted? Eloquence, say some. The church of God says, "Not so. Not by might, nor by power, but by the Spirit of the Lord." I solemnly believe that so much of human oratory as there is in a sermon, so much there is of the weakness of the flesh; for all the power must be of God working with the truth, through the Holy Ghost. Therefore we should use great plainness of speech and never speak for the sake of the language, but always for the sake of the truth we have to say, that God may bless it to the hearts of men. No man in this world was ever converted except by the Holy Spirit, and never will any man be truly converted by any other power. Bang your drum, brother, and blow your brass instrument if you like but neither cornet, flute, harp, sackbut, psaltery, dulcimer, nor any other kind of music, will ever save a soul. Deck your altar out as prettily as you like, and burn your most fragrant incense, but no soul ever finds heaven by the light of candles nor by the scent of censers. The gospel has salvation in it when the Holy Spirit works by it, but no other doctrine can save. The Spirit of the Lord alone must bless the truth, and he will bless the truth alone. This is the church's sole power with souls. Now, you Christian people that are trying to do good and glorify God, I pray you wait upon the Lord, and resolve that you will only go to God's work armed with God's truth and backed up by God's Spirit. Many in these days think that we want a great deal besides the Spirit of God, but they are in error. They think that the world is not to be converted and men saved in the old-fashioned way of preaching the Word of God with the Holy Ghost sent down from heaven; but let me assure you that it is to be converted in that way and in no other. Human agriculture is capable of daily improvement, but as the plans of the great Husbandman are perfect from the first, you may be sure that there will be no change in them. You may go through the world ranting and raving, or you may go arguing and discussing, but you cannot touch a dead heart to make it alive either by excitement or by philosophy. You cannot breathe into the nostrils of a dead soul the life eternal, though your winds should blow hot with fanaticism, or chill with rationalism. Spiritual life can only come in God's way, and it is God's way by the foolishness of preaching to save them that believe. From the gospel pulpit believing preachers work more miracles than your learned men will ever believe. God's word will not return unto him void; but man's word is void when it goes forth, and void it remains to the end of the chapter. The magicians and their enchantments cannot compare with the rod of Moses. One word of the Lord is stronger than all the rage of hell or the enmity of the world. We mean, whatever others do, to keep to "waiting upon the Lord," going to work in the Lord's way, and depending upon the Lord's power and upon that alone.

But waiting upon God means something more than dependence upon God; so I go a step farther: if we depend upon God *our expectation is from him.* We wait upon God as the birds in the nest wait upon the parent bird, expecting from her their food. Before she comes you hear their cries, and when she comes if you look into the nest you will see nothing but so many gaping mouths, all waiting, expecting to be filled by the mother-bird. Now, that is just what a church of God ought to be—a company of wide-opened mouths waiting to be filled by the Lord alone. "Open thy mouth wide, and I will fill it," says the Lord. Do you not think that some churches, and some Christians, with very small expectations, have scarcely learned to open their mouths at all? If the Lord were to convert a soul now and then, they would be pleased and express a grateful surprise; but do they expect to hear of hundreds added to the church at a time, or of thousands in a year brought to Christ? No, they think this may be done in some extraordinary instances in very large places, but they do not expect it in their gatherings. Oh, friends, let us expect more of God, and we shall receive more. Does he not always come up to our expectations? Does he not amaze us with the blessings of his goodness? Is he not able to do exceeding abundantly above all that we ask or even think? I find it such a blessing to have expecting people about me, for they make a flourishing church. Some brethren here at this time are men of great expectations, for even now while I am preaching they are planning whereabouts they will be in the aisle to talk with folk going out; they reckon that some will be converted by the word, and they are on the look-out to pick them up. These brethren are grieved and surprised if after a service they do not meet with one or two enquirers or convicted sinners, that they may join with them in tearful prayer. They are believers in the power of the gospel, and they act accordingly. When I fire the gun they are on the alert to pick up the birds, for they believe in the killing power of the Word. They could not be content with ineffectual preaching: they expect that the Word will be fruitful, and so they bring their basket to put the fruit in. Oh, if a church would but wait upon God in this sense of expecting great things from him, it should have them; for he will never allow his people to complain that he has been a wilderness to them. He will never raise their hopes to dash them to the ground. Is there any man alive who has believed in the Lord too largely, and expected too confidingly? Brother ministers, let us begin to expect more: not from *our* ministry because it is powerful, for it is nothing of the kind by itself; but from God's ministry through us, for if he speak by us why should not men yield to his voice though they will not yield to ours? If he be with us, can he not make us hammers that shall break the rocks in pieces? Can he not use even us to be as a fire to melt the iron hearts of men? So then a true church depends upon God and expects from God, and in this sense answers to the description—" They that wait upon the Lord."

To make up waiting, I think there is a third thing, and that is *patience* —to hold out, and wait the Lord's time and will. The three together— dependence, expectation, patience—make up waiting upon the Lord. This " patience " is to the uttermost desirable in a thousand matters, that we may endure affliction, persevere in holiness, continue in hope, and abide in our integrity. Patience is the long life of virtue, and sets on its head the crown of experience. It is no child's play to continue to suffer affliction with joyfulness, and to remain for years perfectly acqui- escent in the will of the Lord, let that will be what it may. It needs the eyes of faith to see God in the dark, to believe in his love when he is angry, and to rest in his promise when it tarries long. That little word WAIT is a word fit for a father in Christ, and cometh not out of the mouth of a babe in grace. Let us ask for grace to pronounce it aright.

> " Wait, my soul, upon the Lord,
> To his gracious promise flee,
> Laying hold upon his word,
> 'As thy day, thy strength shall be.'"

Some of my dear brethren in Christ are ardent followers of Christ, but they do not seem to have learned the meaning of that word "patience." They are working for Christ, and they are depending upon the Lord, and they are looking for results; but when they do not quite see them immediately, straightway they are offended and depressed. They are in such a hurry that they seem half inclined to cry "Why should I wait for the Lord any longer?" I daresay that you were much the same when you were children: you wanted everything there and then, and waiting was dismal work to you. We are all impatient as long as we are imperfect. It is the mark of the child that he is in a violent hurry where men are steady. Perhaps our father gave us some seed, and we hastened to sow it. We put in a little mustard and cress one morning, and then we thought that we would eat it for tea, but as we saw no sign of green we went and turned over the earth to see if the seed was sprouting. We were greatly surprised to find that it had not grown up green and ready to cut: we did not understand that the husbandman waiteth. We had a little apple tree, and we put it in the ground. The planting of that tree was a grand affair, and we reckoned upon many puddings being made out of the apples gathered from it next year. We were sadly surprised to see that the apples did not come. Yes, that is the spirit of children: their name is Passion, and not Patience; they live in the present hour, and have no power to extend themselves into days to come. The Lord sometimes sends us speedy results to our labours; it happens at times that the moment we speak conversions are wrought; but at other times it is not so—the truth works slowly and surely, and effects all the more precious results. We must wait for seed to grow, and for fruit to ripen. If we really wait upon the Lord we shall just keep on, resolved to abide in duty, determined to remain in prayer, undaunted in confidence, unmoved in expectation. We shall not fly into a passion with the Lord, and refuse to believe him any more, neither shall we run off to novelties, and fall into the fads and crazes of the day, to try this and to try that, because God's own way is a failure; but we shall say, I have done what God bade me. I have done it in dependence upon his Spirit, and I believe that good will come of it; and therefore I shall wait and watch. I shall be found moving when God moves; or sitting still when the Lord tarries; but I am sure that he will not fail the soul that waits upon him; all will be well; the blessing will come. What a sweet thing is the calm leisure of faith!—"He that believeth shall not make haste." Fret and worry, hurry and haste, are all slain by the hand of faith. God has plenty of time: nay, he fills eternity; and therefore he can bear with man's waywardness with much longsuffering. You and I are in feverish haste, but when we get to be linked with God we also can wait, even as God waiteth to be gracious, and hath patient compassion upon men.

That is a description of what a Christian ought to be, "waiting upon the Lord:" depending upon God, expecting from God, and patiently tarrying for God, till he shall give the desired blessing.

II. But now, secondly, we see WHAT THE LORD'S WAITING PEOPLE NEED. They need to *renew their strength.* Even those saints that wait upon God for everything, may grow faint, and require reviving

And that is, first, because *they are human.* As long as you and I are mortal we shall be mutable; as the world is full of changes, so are we. Some friends never seem to be either high or low in their feelings: their life has neither hills nor valleys in it, but is comparable to an unbroken plain: they traverse a perpetual level. It is not so with others of us: we are all Alps and Andes. These favoured pilgrims march steadily and evenly through the world, always at one pitch and pace; but others of us who mount up into the heavens in burning zeal and holy joy, go low, very low down, into the depths, till our soul sinketh because of sorrow. The best and bravest of the saints are poor creatures. Elijah on the top of Carmel, when he has brought fire from heaven, cries, " Take the prophets of Baal; let not one of them escape." Hear him, as he pleads with God, and unlocks the treasury of the rain. See him gird up his loins, and run before the chariot of Ahab. There is a man for you! If ever hero-worship might be tolerated, it is in the case of "this my lord Elijah." Look not too closely at the champion, for within twenty-four hours he is afraid of Jezebel; and soon he is whining, " O Lord, take away my life; for I am not better than my fathers." Do you blame him ? Do you fail to understand so sad a stoop from so great a height. Take heed of censuring a man so greatly approved of God as to be spared the pains of death. If you do as well as Elijah did, perhaps you may hear some nobodies blaming you in your hour of exhaustion; but as for me I cannot censure him, nor can any man that has ever enjoyed the heavenly delirium of high-strung zeal in the Master's service, and having been borne 'aloft on eagle's wings, at last falls upon the earth in absolute exhaustion. After high excitement there will come reaction. Creatures whose home is on the earth cannot always live upon the wing: they must feel faint at times; and hence the necessity of this blessed promise, "They that wait upon the Lord shall renew their strength." They will rise again: from their deepest depressions they will leap into supreme elevations: they shall dwell on the heights, they shall soar above the clouds. The very depths to which they dive are prophetic of the heights to which they will climb again. The Lord has said, " I will bring again from the depths of the sea."

They need renewing, also, because in addition to being human *they are imperfect*. The sin that dwells in us drags us down. However high we have ascended when we have walked in the light, still we have needed that the blood of Christ should cleanse us from all sin. Our natural corruption, and the imperfection and infirmity of our flesh are about us still, and these bring us down at times till we say with David, " I am this day weak, though anointed king. What a blessing it is that failing, flagging, fainting, falling spirits, by waiting upon the Lord, shall renew their strength! Even those who actually fall shall be recovered. "Though he fall, he shall not be utterly cast down: for the Lord upholdeth him with his hand." Though our sands run very low, God shall fill the glass again, and the believing man shall again rejoice in the Lord, and have confidence in the God of his salvation. Because we are human and imperfect, we cannot always be at our best: the sky is not always clear; the sea is not always at flood; the year is not always at summer; the sun is not always in the zenith; the moon is not always at her full; the tree is not always adorned with fruit; the vineyard does not always flow with wine; roses do not always blush, nor lilies always bloom. Creatures have their rises and their falls, and to us also there must be times when we need to renew our strength; and we shall renew it, for here the promise comes, "They that wait upon the Lord shall renew their strength."

Brethren, I will suppose that I am addressing some who have become weak and failing. You must renew your strength. It must be renewed, for otherwise *it will decline still further*, and this would be painful, dangerous, and dishonouring. The Lord would not have us utterly fail, nor fall prone upon the ground in the heavenly race; therefore, to those who have no might, he increaseth strength.

We must renew our strength, for *it is for our honour, comfort, and safety*. It is not to a Christian's credit that he should be weak. The glory of a man is his strength, and especially is his spiritual strength his honour. It is not for your comfort to be weak. When a man is feeble, he becomes a burden to himself; his sadness makes him stoop; he is feeble-minded, and ready to halt. "A wounded spirit who can bear?" It is not for your usefulness that you should be weak. What can you do for others when you yourself can hardly stand? It is not for your safety that you should be weak; for you will be liable to many attacks, and open to many injuries from sin, and extremely likely to be overcome by temptation. Blessed is that man who is "strong in the Lord, and in the power of his might." To him the joy of the Lord is his strength. The Lord Jehovah is his strength and his song; he also has become his salvation.

It is for God's glory, and for our own usefulness, that we should be strong; and if we fall into decline and weakness, pray do not let us stop there. Let us try to escape from a spiritual consumption. If I address believers, who lament that the whole church with which they are connected is getting weak, I charge them not to suffer it to be so with themselves. Brothers, shun a spiritual wasting away. A pining sickness is an awful disease for a church to die of. Do not linger in such a state. Up with you, and cry mightily unto the Lord, and you shall yet be restored; for it is written, "They that wait upon the Lord shall renew their strength."

At this time I should be very glad if this dear church, over which the Holy Ghost has made me an overseer, would have its strength renewed. Our ministry wants renewal that it may be fuller of power and grace. How weak it is if God be even a little withdrawn! Our Sunday school work requires constant renewal. Everything around us needs to be renewed, and revived, and refreshed; and just at this time I wish that it might be laid on the hearts of the members of the church to pray that we might renew our strength. Your minister grows old; not very old in natural age, it is true, but thirty years of continuous labour in preaching to so vast a congregation has taken much more out of his strength than almost any other form of service would have done; and therefore he needs to be invigorated again—physically, mentally, and spiritually. Many of you are in a like condition, and need that your strength be renewed like the eagle's. This can be done for us all by that great Master, in whose hand the residue of the Spirit abides. He can lay his hand on us, and say, "Be strong, Fear not." He can strengthen us to a degree of force far beyond our previous experience. The members of the church, and the officers of the church all desire, I know, that they should renew their strength just now : it is well that such a desire is on them.   May this desire for renewal become an insatiable craving with those of you who live near to God, and have power in prayer; then through your importunate intercessions the Lord may make good his promise, that this waiting congregation may renew its strength.   After thirty years unflagging prosperity we are as weak as ever apart from God, and need constant renewal of strength.   I see many reasons why it is imperative that we should have it at this present time.   Join, I pray you, in fervent prayer for it.

It is promised, and therefore, if we do not have it, it is our own fault. God's promises are our precepts.   What he promises to give, it is our duty to seek ; and if he promises that we shall renew our strength, why not let us have the promise fulfilled to our faith?   I wish that it might come to pass that my dear brethren and sisters in Christ here— men and women who are working for him, and are a little weary and faint—may be encouraged, cheered, refreshed, and led to say, " From this very time we will serve our Lord with all our youthful vigour, and with a great deal more.   We will labour in the service of the Lord our God with all our might, not slackening our right hand nor withholding the fulness of our strength, but giving our all to God."   O blessed Spirit, rouse thy children to renewed consecration, renewed zeal, renewed delight in holy service, renewed hope of victory !

III.   So I close with the third point, which is this—HOW ARE WE TO RENEW OUR STRENGTH ?   If we are God's people we must renew our strength *by continually waiting upon God.*

When a man wants his bodily strength renewed his purpose may be effected by eating a good meal.   He has grown empty through hunger, and there is nothing in him; he must be filled up with substantial nourishment, and then the human engine will generate fresh force. Oh, ye who are weak in spirit, come and feed upon Christ !   They that wait upon the Lord in that way, by feeding upon the body and blood of Christ, shall find him to be meat indeed, and drink indeed, and so they shall renew their strength.

Sometimes a man may renew his strength by taking a little rest.   He has grown weak through stern labour and long fatigue, and he must be quiet, and repose till he recovers.   Oh, ye weary, heavy-laden, where is there rest for you except in the Christ of God ?   Oh, come to God, and rest in him, and wait patiently for him !   Then shall your peace be as a river, and then shall your strength be restored right speedily.

We have known strength to be restored by a bath.   A weary one has plunged himself into the cool flood, and he has risen quite another man. Oh, for a baptism into the Spirit of God !   Oh, to plunge into the Godhead's deepest sea—to throw one's self into the might and majesty of God ; to swim in love, upborne by grace !

We have known men's strength renewed by breathing their native air. They have risen out of a hot and fœtid atmosphere into the cool breeze of the mountain side, and the bracing breeze has made them strong again.   Oh, to have the breath of the Spirit blowing upon us once again !   By him we were born, by him we were quickened, by him we have been revived from former faintness, and it is by breathing his divine life that we shall be filled with life again.   Oh, that at this moment we might each one feel the power of the Lord entering into us !

In a word, if a church wants reviving, if saints individually want reviving, they must wait upon God—first *in prayer*.　Oh, what a blessing a day's prayer might be !　If you cannot get as much as that, how much renewing may be gained in an hour's prayer !　When Archbishop Leighton used to go into his room, his servant said that he would remain there for two or three hours, having locked the door, and having nothing with him but his Bible and a candle.　Ay, then he came out to speak those gracious words which still linger in his works like the echoes of music.　His Bible and candle were the only earthly illumination that he needed, for prayer brought him light divine.　Get with God, brother ; be much with God.　I am sure that we, none of us, are enough alone with God ; but in prayer, laying hold upon the invisible, we shall win strength for service.

Add to that a *re-dedication* of ourselves to the Lord who bought us. This often helps us to renew our strength.　Go over again that blessed covenant which has made you one of the covenanted ones with God. You gave yourself years ago wholly up to your Lord, and you sometimes sing—

> " High heaven that heard that solemn vow,
> That vow renewed shall daily hear."

Let this day hear the renewal of it : let your covenant be solemnly rehearsed.　Consecrate yourself anew to God.

Then afresh realize your *entire dependence* upon God.　Put yourself into the Lord's hands absolutely.　Be like the sere leaf that is carried by the breath of the tempest.　When you have submitted yourself completely, and trusted entirely, setting both your strength and your weakness on one side, and giving yourself up for God to use you, oh, then you shall renew your strength.

Then go forward to *renewed action*.　In renewing your strength, ask the Lord that you may undertake fresh work, and that this work may be done to a nobler tune—that you may have more expectancy, more confidence, more faith, more God-reliance.　What things are done by men in common life with *self*-reliance !　But with *God*-reliance we work impossibilities, and miracles fly from us like sparks from the anvil of a smith.　When a man learns to work with God's strength and with that alone, he can do all things.　So would I stir my brothers up one by one, and then as a body, to work for God with renewed energy.

I have almost done.　I know that there are some here to whom this appears to have very slight reference.　Yet if you are an unconverted man, my dear friend, after all, this is a lesson for you ; for the pith of it all is that if ever you are to be saved you must get away from yourself into God, and your confidence must be in Christ the Son of God and not in your own strength.　One of my greatest delights is to see how our people die.　I have never for years visited the dying-bed of a single member of this church in which I have seen a shade of doubt, or the least suspicion as to their triumphant entrance into the kingdom.　I have been somewhat astonished to find it always so.　I just now sat by the bedside of one of our brethren who is melting away with consumption : and it was sad to see his wife lying by his side almost equally ill ; but when I spoke with him who was so soon to be with God, he said, "As for my faith, dear sir, it never wavers in the least degree. I have my times of depression of spirit, but I take no notice of that. You have told us not to look to feelings, but simply to trust in the infallible Word of a faithful God. Fifteen years ago, sir," said he, "one Thursday night I dropped into the Tabernacle to hear you preach, and, blessed be the day, I looked to Christ and found salvation. I have had plenty of ups and downs, but Jesus has never left me nor forsaken me, and I am not going to think that he will do so now. His word stands fast for ever. My strength is in my God." He added, "I am not resting upon man in any degree or measure, but wholly upon the faithful promise of God, and the precious blood of Christ." I wished that I could get into his place, and not come here to-night, but just slip off to heaven as he is doing. It makes one sure of the gospel when you see men dying so. It nerves me to come and tell it out again to men and women. The gospel which I preach to you is good to live upon, and good to die upon. If you will but trust my Lord you shall find it a blessed thing to depart out of this world, and be for ever with the Lord. Death shall lose every air of dread : every ghastly gloom shall be taken from it. It shall be but undressing to go to bed, that you may wake up in the morning in royal robes as a courtier of the King of kings. Only you must have done with yourself, and commit yourself to Christ. Say to-day in life what you will want to say when you come to die— "Father, into thy hand I commit my spirit." That is a gospel-prayer. If you are waiting upon the Lord in the sense of complete reliance upon the merit of Jesus, you shall in dying renew your strength, and leap out of your frail body into the presence and glory of God. In due time also you shall re-assume your body, but it shall be made like unto Christ's glorious body, and in its resurrection you shall emphatically renew your strength. Blessed be his name that he has taught many of us to wait upon the Lord! May he teach you all to do so, for Christ's sake. Amen.

PORTION OF SCRIPTURE READ BEFORE SERMON—Isaiah xl.

HYMNS FROM "OUR OWN HYMN BOOK"—676, 677, 957.